Psychology

The Search

for

Understanding

Psychology

The Search
for
Understanding

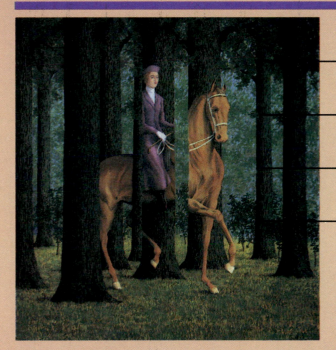

Janet A. Simons

Donald B. Irwin

Beverly A. Drinnin

West Publishing Company

St. Paul   New York   Los Angeles   San Francisco

Production Credits

Copyediting: Owana McLester-Greenfield and Rosalie
      Koskenmaki
Composition: Carlisle Graphics
Photo editor: Yvonne Alsip
Interior and cover designer: David J. Farr/Imagesmyth, Inc.
Technical illustrations: Asterisk Group
Anatomical illustrations: Mary Albury-Noyes and Mary Brozic/
      Medical & Legal Visuals, Inc.
Cartoon drawings: Jim Kiehne
Glossary preparation: Marilyn Irwin
Indexer: Deborah Smith
Cover: *The Blank Signature*; René Magritte; National Gallery
      of Art, Washington; Collection of Mr. and Mrs. Paul
      Mellon.

A Student Study Guide

A study guide has been developed to assist you in mastering the concepts presented in this text. It reinforces chapter material by presenting a programmed review of chapter material with review questions. The study guide is available from your local bookstore under the title *Study Guide to Accompany Psychology: The Search for Understanding*, prepared by Benjamin Wallace. If you cannot locate this book in the bookstore, ask your bookstore manager to order it for you.

COPYRIGHT © 1987 By WEST PUBLISHING COMPANY
50 W. Kellogg Boulevard
P.O. Box 64526
St. Paul, MN 55164-1003

Library of Congress Cataloging-in-Publication Data

Simons, Janet A.
  Psychology: the search for understanding.

  Bibliography: p.
  Includes index.
  1. Psychology.   I. Irwin, Donald B.   II. Drinnin,
Beverly A.   III. Title.
BF121.S525 1987   150   86-15657
ISBN 0–314–26213–X

Credits continued following index

Contents in Brief

Contents

Chapter Thirteen
Emotions and Stress 303

Chapter Fourteen
Personality: Type, Trait, and Psychodynamic Theories 325

Chapter Eighteen
Social Psychology: Attribution and Attraction 435

Chapter Nineteen
Social Psychology: Attitude Change and Social Influence 461

Preface

Psychology: The Search for Understanding is a collaborative effort of three veteran psychology instructors with a combined total of 41 years of experience teaching the introductory course. We began this project with the firm conviction that successful classroom teaching is a prime prerequisite for writing a textbook that assists students in mastering the basic concepts, terms, applications, and theories of psychology. We have experience (as students, instructors, or both) in public universities, private colleges, community colleges, extension campuses, and television instruction. Our students have ranged in age from 16 to past 60 and have come from a wide variety of economic backgrounds. From these varied experiences, we have learned what features, materials, and styles encourage the best learning across educational settings and student characteristics. Our collaborative effort has been further aided by the opportunities we have had to co-teach the introductory course with each other. Creating a semester-long dialogue about psychology has been a challenging instructional development technique and a stimulating experience for students. Our co-teaching experiences have enhanced our abilities to create a comprehensive, balanced, and accurate presentation of psychology that is, above all else, supportive of students' attempts to understand the complex, multi-faced discipline of psychology.

A Balance of Concepts, Process, and Application

This textbook is designed to present a full, rich picture of psychology and the work of psychologists. Throughout we have been guided by the objective of creating a balanced view of psychology. We balance contemporary, up-to-date topics and research results with historically significant events, classic research studies, and early theories that represent the roots of psychology. In striving to paint a comprehensive picture of psychology, we balance breadth with depth in our selection of topics and our discussions of research studies. We strive for a balance between concepts (the facts of psychology), process (the

methods of psychology), and application (the uses of psychology). Concepts are illustrated with everyday examples to which students can relate and with research findings that reveal how psychology works. The concepts and examples help students discover how useful psychology can be in their lives; the research coverage exposes students to the work of psychologists.

An Emphasis on Research—Classic and Contemporary

A major feature of this textbook is *The Research Process*. Twenty-three special research topics provide students with a detailed examination of psychological research. While one guideline to topic selection for these research features was student interest, we also deliberately chose a wide range of topics, a variety of research methodologies, and an assortment of studies from the classics to the most recent. This feature vividly illustrates the creativity of the research psychologist, the links between ideas, process, and theories, and the rigor of more than 100 years of scientific investigation in psychology. Research results and procedures are also an integral part of the remainder of the text's content.

Overall, a blend is achieved among the traditional research topics of psychology's heritage, contemporary topics, and exploration of possible future topics. Although the history of psychology is an important topic in Chapter 2, its presentation there is kept to a minimum in favor of integrating historical perspectives into specific chapter topics where students can perceive their relevance to the topics at hand. Some of the most recent content, issues, and applications are incorporated into *Exploring . . .* sections or in the *Relate* section at the end of each chapter. Other new topics are included directly in the text as natural progressions built upon more traditional topics, such as the imposter phenomenon as an outgrowth of need for achievement research. The Epilogue, *Psychology in the Future*, includes a speculative look at the future of the discipline.

xix

Clear, Understandable Prose

The balanced view of psychology presented in the text is complemented by a writing style that facilitates student comprehension of the material. Each chapter is the product of the mutual efforts of the three authors. Working together not only served to blend our individual ideas but also to merge our individual writing styles. To further assure that the level of writing, vocabulary, and sentence structure added to the clarity of our ideas, the entire manuscript was edited by an accomplished composition instructor. The result, we believe, is clear, understandable prose that makes challenging concepts and theories easier to grasp.

A Student Learning-Centered Approach

While a well-written, balanced, and accurate text is very important, we also believe that a text can be structured in ways that aid student learning. In fact, we believe student learning aids can be added without detracting from a book's content or appearance. To this end, we have incorporated the following features throughout the text.

To help students improve their study skills, the text's initial chapter cites research applications in areas such as learning, memory, and time management. Although the book can be used successfully without using this chapter, students who choose to read it will learn how to become more efficient, successful students. Specifically, students learn how to develop studying environments, how to manage their worries and stress, how to manage their time, and how to study for tests. Helpful memory strategies are presented at the beginning of the book rather than waiting until the memory chapter to introduce this highly useful information.

SQ5R Study Method

Also in the first chapter, the SQ5R study method is explained. SQ5R is an extension of Robinson's time-tested SQ3R method, in which students learn to survey, question, read, recite, and review. For several years we have encouraged our students to use this successful technique and two additional steps—write and relate. Students who use all seven steps state that the method helps them to learn more efficiently and effectively. Each chapter in the text is built upon the SQ5R format. Every chapter begins with an outline that provides a survey of the major topics in the chapter. *Focus Questions* help students pose questions and then search for answers as they read the chapter. Reading is also facilitated by a higher than average number of chapters (24 plus an epilogue and a statistics appendix), which results in shorter units of material to read. Recitation is encouraged by questions posed within the material and by the *Focus Question Answers*. The content material of each chapter ends with a *Relate* section that helps students to relate topics within the chapter to important issues, new research developments, or contemporary research problems. Students are encouraged to engage in further reading, relating, and writing in the *Things to Do, Things to Discuss,* and *Things to Read* sections. Review is provided in the chapter summary and list of key terms.

Quick Study Aids

Quick Study Aids (QSAs) are important student learning aids, interspersed within the chapters. QSAs are concise summaries or mnemonic memory strategies that actually show students how to learn complex concepts rather than simply testing to see if they have learned them. These sample QSAs serve as guides to encourage students to develop their own original QSAs for other concepts.

Things to Do, Things to Discuss, and Things to Read

The *Things to Do* and *Things to Discuss* suggestions may be utilized in several ways. The majority of the *Things to Do* can be completed in a short time with readily available materials. Some suggestions may be used as classroom exercises, while others might be used as experiential assignments or extra-credit opportunities. The *Things to Discuss* suggestions typically involve value judgments and encourage a wide range of responses. These discussion topics help students link the course content to other academic disciplines or to everyday aspects of their lives. The discussion topics may be used as journal assignments, small group projects, extra-credit assignments, or take-home examinations. A third section, *Things to Read,* provides suggestions for further reading about a chapter's topics. The selections include mostly recent titles with some important earlier works. These suggestions may be used for extra-credit book reviews and in-class presentations.

Vibrant, Full-Color Format

Careful consideration was given to each design feature in this text to assure that every element would enhance the student's ease of comprehending the material and facilitate mastery of the concepts and theories. The use of color throughout the text not only adds visual interest but also aids in organizing and clarifying the material. Just as concepts are supported by familiar examples that serve to make the material more relevant, the photos were chosen by the same criteria—they help students form vivid, easily remembered examples of important concepts.

A Wide Range of Supplements

The text is supported by a strong set of supplements. We wrote the *Instructor's Manual* with both beginning and experienced instructors in mind. For the beginning instructor, the *IM* is a handbook for developing an introductory course. The *IM* contains up-to-date, annotated media resources, teaching references, chapter objectives and summaries, mini-lecture topics and classroom demonstrations, and discussion topics. Experienced instructors will find the mini-lecture topics to be useful ways to update lecture notes and to include recent high-interest topics in their lectures.

The instructor's manual is accompanied by a colorful set of transparencies. The set of 128 graphics illustrate important concepts and principles from each chapter as well as many graphs and tables from the text. Additionally, the instructor's manual contains *Transparency Notes* that provide basic information about the illustrated concepts, principles, tables, or graphs and suggest ways to use the transparency in lectures and discussions.

The *Test Bank* consists of over 2,500 multiple-choice items. Items are categorized by type of item (factual, application, conceptual) and are indexed to the text pages. In addition, the test bank is available in computerized form. Diskettes are available for Apple and IBM PC and compatible microcomputers. This format permits easy editing, rearrangement, and addition of items to tailor the test banks to each instructor's individual needs.

Psychware, created by Robert S. Slotnick and the New York Institute of Technology, uses computer-assisted instruction to enhance students' understanding of basic principles and classic experiments in psychology. Ten programs cover topics in memory, conditioning and learning, cognitive development, and social behavior.

The program formats include experiments in which students serve as subjects, simulations, tutorials, and games. Included with this supplement are a *Faculty Guide* and a *Student Study Guide*.

For those students who want the support of a workbook, an excellent *Study Guide*, prepared by Ben Wallace of Cleveland State University, is available. The *Study Guide* provides opportunities for students to engage in a structured review of each chapter's objectives and to test their comprehension of the material before taking classroom exams.

Acknowledgments

From the onset, our writing of this text has been a collaborative activity, involving the efforts and support of many people—family, friends, colleagues, and many others whom we know only from a signature on a letter or a voice on the phone. To each person we express our appreciation for the help that has been given.

We are especially indebted to those who meticulously read parts or all of the drafts and final manuscript and provided us with detailed critiques that made important contributions to the final form and content of this book:

Valerie Aldrich, *Pan American University*
David Barkmeier, *Northeastern University*
Anne Bryan, *University of Minnesota-Duluth*
Judith Callan, *Marquette University*
William Ford, *Bucks County Community College*
Dee Graham, *University of Cincinnati*
Barbara Honhart, *Lansing Community College*
Michael Hughmanick, *West Valley College*
Stuart Karabenick, *Eastern Michigan University*
William Klipec, *Drake University*
Jan Larson, *The Menninger Foundation*
Ted Lewandowski, *Delaware County College*
Brad Lown, *State University of New York College, Buffalo*
Keith Schirmer, *Kellogg Community College*
Susan Shodahl, *San Bernardino Valley College*
Dominic Valentino, *University of Rhode Island*
Benjamin Wallace, *Cleveland State University*
Doug Wallen, *Mankato State University*
Charles Weichert, *San Antonio College*
John Whittle, *Northern Essex Community College*

We also want to express our appreciation for the expertise and warm support we have received from several key people in the production of this book. Paula Pickett provided the initial impetus that resulted in our signing a contract with West Publishing. Owana McLester-Greenfield provided invaluable assistance in polishing our prose. Diana Messersmith gave generously of her knowledge and time to assist in our library research. Yvonne Alsip skillfully guided the photo selection. David Farr created an exquisite design. Beth Wickum, production editor, masterminded a production schedule that included almost daily doses of reassurance for the harried authors. Nancy Crochiere deftly moved us from rough draft to final manuscript. We also want to thank the many unnamed people at West Publishing Company who contributed to the book's preparation, production, and promotion. Finally, we acknowledge and express our gratitude to Clark Baxter, our editor. For his sustaining faith in our abilities, his wisdom, his guidance, and his friendship, we are most grateful.

In closing, we want to acknowledge the contributions of those from whom we have learned much—our students and our own instructors. Therefore, we pay tribute to the students and professors at the colleges and universities where we have taught and learned:

The College of St. Francis
Des Moines Area Community College
Iowa State University
The University of Illinois
The University of Wisconsin Center System
Wittenberg University

Jan Simons
Don Irwin
Bev Drinnin

To my family, Betty, Harry, Bob, Peggy, Flo, Ben, and Michelle, for their years of support and influence. I especially appreciate their encouragement and their sacrifices while this book was being written.

To my teachers at Wittenberg University for igniting my interest in education, to the psychology faculty at Iowa State University for sharpening my knowledge about psychology, and to my students for their enthusiasm that helps me maintain my love of psychology and teaching.

—*Jan Simons*

To my parents, George & Lurene Irwin, for providing my education.

To my mentor, Dr. Ron Peters, for directing my education.

To my wife and son, Marilyn & Ben, for making my education worthwhile.

—*Don Irwin*

To my parents who instilled in me a love of learning and a belief in working hard to reach one's goals.

To my kids, Erin and Joel, for their understanding and tolerance during the writing process.

To my good friends who have been so supportive—especially to Lloyd and to Owana.

And to John who helped me through this project by doing more than his share of childrearing.

—*Bev Drinnin*

Psychology

The Search

for

Understanding

Focus Questions

1. To benefit the most from studying, should you schedule longer or shorter blocks of time for studying?

2. What are the advantages of using the SQ5R study strategy?

3. How can you use self-talk productively?

4. What features of each chapter are designed to help you study?

Chapter Outline

MANAGING TIME AND SPACE
Managing Your Study Time
Managing Your Study Space

STUDY STRATEGIES
SQ5R
Taking Notes
Taking Tests

SELF MANAGEMENT
Managing Test Anxiety
Managing Your Self-Talk

RELATE: Integration—Putting It All Together
Things to Do
Things to Discuss
Things to Read

REVIEW: Summary
Key Terms

Chapter 1

Applied Psychology and Student Success

All glory comes from daring to begin.
Eugene F. Ware

Welcome to psychology! The purpose of this chapter is to show you how to study more efficiently and, generally, how to manage your life more effectively. The advice presented in this chapter is taken from psychological investigations of studying and from related areas that have direct applications to the life of a student.

The management strategies presented here are fundamentals, but they require one important, active ingredient: YOU! These strategies will provide you with a plan. In turn, you must provide the proper attitude and motivation to make the plan work. You may be able to succeed without following these fundamentals, but you will not find out how much more you could have accomplished had you followed them. As the writer Somerset Maugham noted, "Only a mediocre person is always at his best."

Believing it's possible to improve your study skills is the first step toward achieving greater success as a stu-

1

dent. A positive attitude is important. Psychologists have shown that the beliefs people hold can have positive or negative consequences for their behavior (Ellis, 1984). A positive belief that you can improve your study skills sets the stage for improvement.

Equally important to greater success as a student is wanting to improve your skills. Motivation is a key to whether you succeed at anything you do. Getting out of life what you weren't willing to put into it is difficult.

A third step is practice. You must actively practice these fundamentals in order to experience their benefits. Reading about them is not enough; you must try them out and work with them. If you practice them, these study habits will become a part of your everyday behavior.

If you have been less than successful with your studying in the past, your lack of success may have been the result of ineffective study skills. Those ineffective skills became part of your ordinary ways of behaving through practice; in the same way, you can now learn more effective skills. Of course, changing habits is not easy. As Somerset Maugham observed, "The unfortunate thing about this world is that good habits are so much easier to give up than bad ones!" Yet bad habits can be broken and you can enhance your success as a student.

If you have been a successful student in the past, congratulations! However, you can still take advantage of the suggestions in this chapter to maintain and improve your good study habits. The techniques that follow will not only help you master this textbook and succeed in your psychology course but will also work for your other courses as well. Good luck on your journey toward success as a psychology student. This book is designed to help you every step of the way.

Managing Time and Space

Of course, you would never use any of the "excuses" from Exhibit 1.1, but most individuals, at some time or other, have wanted to excuse away mismanagement of time. Making the best use of your study time is central to developing successful study skills. Equally important is developing an effective study environment. Managing your study time and study space is discussed in the next two sections.

Managing Your Study Time

Time management has many facets. Scheduling time for the "have to's" and planning time for the "want to's," making sure that you do not miss appointments or dead-lines, and establishing where your time goes and where you want it to go are three of the more important aspects of time management. Most important, however, is gaining control of yourself, deciding what you want out of life, and enacting a plan to reach your goals.

You can start to control your time by becoming aware of how you now spend your time. One way is to keep a daily log, hour by hour, of your activities for one week. Your log will give you a fairly accurate accounting of how you usually spend your time.

EXHIBIT 1.1
"Reasons Why I Missed the Test"

Here are some frequently given reasons for missing an exam as well as "novel" approaches to try out on your instructor should you ever miss an exam. Adapted from Range, L.M., Morgan, M.A., and Leonberger, T., "Final impotence: reasons why I missed the exam," *Journal of Polymorphous Perversity*, 1984, *1*, 12-13.

I overslept.
I had to study.
I don't have enough money to buy the book, yet.
I thought if you had a C you didn't have to take this test.
My bike had a flat.
My grandmother (grandfather, aunt, etc.) died.
I lost my notes.
I thought I dropped this course.
I am going to drop this course.
I was in jail.
I'd rather take a make-up.
I forgot today was Tuesday.
My boyfriend (mother, father, aunt, dog) forgot to remind me.
I missed two classes, and I couldn't get the notes.
My dog chewed up my notes.
I didn't know we were having a test.
Tests are an artificial stratification of the learning process.
I ran out of Thorazine, and the voices told me to miss the exam.
It was the same time as my sex therapy.
I was in the middle of a peak experience.
My girlfriend asked me to make her a second cup of coffee.
There was no Dexedrine on the streets.
My adolescence got the best of me.
The naked city was getting to me.
I had to go to confession.
My mother is a paraplegic and I had to stay by the phone.
I just got married (divorced).
I woke up with a "personal illness."
I have agraphia and need to take the test orally.
I had to wait at home for the cable operator to install HBO.
It was my birthday (my mother's, my girlfriend's, my grandfather's).

For now, make a quick estimate of your time commitments by filling out the daily time inventory in Exhibit 1.2. The inventory is arranged in three categories because your daily schedule on Tuesdays and Thursdays may be different from your Monday-Wednesday-Friday and your Saturday-Sunday schedules. Were you fairly honest in your estimates? Did you have any time left, or did you run out of time before you began to study?

Perhaps after filling in your "actual" daily time inventory, you have decided to sleep less, cut down on the number of TV shows that you watch, and do less cleaning until the end of the semester so that you will have enough time to study. How much time do you need for studying? Obviously, some people need more, and others need less. Generally, you should plan on two hours of studying outside class for every hour that you attend class. In other words, if you are carrying twelve credit-hours this term, you should spend approximately twenty-four hours each week studying for those classes. As you can see, between attending classes and studying you have made a time commitment equivalent to a full-time job!

Now go back to Exhibit 1.2, and fill in how you would like to spend your time. Considering how you would ideally spend your time is the first step in enacting

a plan for effectively spending your time. Did you run out of time in your ideal day, too?

Perhaps you ran out of time because you haven't set priorities. Establishing priorities is not easy for most people. Interviews with new undergraduate students revealed that 40 percent did not have a regular study schedule (Main, 1980). When you have so much to do, setting priorities is difficult, but it should be done. Creating an ideal inventory will help. Doing so now at the beginning of the term will pay off at the end.

One way to establish your priorities is to spend more time on activities that have high payoffs (HIPOs) and spend less time on those that have low payoffs (LOPOs) (Rutherford, 1978). Attending class and studying are HIPOs for student success, while skipping class and watching TV are usually LOPOs for student success. A study (Lindgren, 1969) found that 85 percent of the students in the study with a B or higher grade average always or almost always attended class, while only 48 percent of the students with C or lower grade average did so. In contrast, 45 percent of the C or lower students were often absent from class compared to only 7 percent of the B or higher students. Therefore, if you wish to be a successful student, you must set attending class and

EXHIBIT 1.2
Daily Time Inventory

Activity	MWF			TT			SS		
	A	I	P	A	I	P	A	I	P
Sleep	—	—	—	—	—	—	—	—	—
Food preparation	—	—	—	—	—	—	—	—	—
Eating	—	—	—	—	—	—	—	—	—
Food clean-up	—	—	—	—	—	—	—	—	—
Household chores	—	—	—	—	—	—	—	—	—
Car care	—	—	—	—	—	—	—	—	—
Work for pay	—	—	—	—	—	—	—	—	—
Volunteer work	—	—	—	—	—	—	—	—	—
Time with family	—	—	—	—	—	—	—	—	—
Time with friends	—	—	—	—	—	—	—	—	—
Watching TV	—	—	—	—	—	—	—	—	—
Physical fitness	—	—	—	—	—	—	—	—	—
Class time	—	—	—	—	—	—	—	—	—
Studying	—	—	—	—	—	—	—	—	—
Other ___	—	—	—	—	—	—	—	—	—
___	—	—	—	—	—	—	—	—	—
___	—	—	—	—	—	—	—	—	—

Estimate how much time you actually spend each day on the following activities. Mark your estimates in the A (actual) column. Then decide how much time you would ideally like to spend on each activity. Mark these estimates in the I (ideal) column. Finally, decide on a practical compromise between your actual and ideal estimates. Mark these estimates in the P (practical) column.

studying as HIPOs.

Some HIPOs are urgent and have a deadline and, therefore, usually get done. An urgent HIPO is labeled a HIPO I. If you have ever stayed up late at night in order to avoid turning in a late assignment, you have experienced a HIPO I. Other high payoff activities do not have a sense of urgency to them and are labeled HIPO IIs. These activities are the easiest to put off but are nonetheless worthwhile to complete. For instance, going to the library today to start a project that is not due until mid-term is a HIPO II. However, if you put off starting the project long enough, this HIPO II will become a HIPO I.

Unlike the rewards for completing HIPO activities, the rewards for completing LOPO activities are small. Nonetheless, as a student, your life has many LOPOs: clearing off your desk, rewriting hastily written notes, browsing through the library, and rereading the directions to a class project, among others. Some LOPOs (LOPO IIIs)—keeping an organized study area, for instance—are necessary, routine tasks. Other LOPOs (LOPO IVs) are useless busywork. A common LOPO IV for you may be restudying something that you already know very well. Unfortunately, LOPO IV activities often get completed before more potentially rewarding projects are begun because they are mistaken for necessary and important tasks.

Recopying disorganized or sloppy classnotes is a useful HIPO II studying activity.

Quick Study Aid

HIPOs and LOPOs at a Glance

As you study this chart, create a visual image of your own personal examples of each type of payoff.

	HIPO I	HIPO II
HIGH PAYOFF ACTIVITIES	Urgent—High Priority	Non-urgent—High Priority
	Have deadlines to meet.	Often put aside unfinished.
	Be sure to finish these.	Plan more time for these.
	LOPO III	**LOPO IV**
LOW PAYOFF ACTIVITIES	Essential, Routine Task	Non-essential, Often Unnecessary
	Have flexible deadlines.	Often mistaken as important task.
	Work to be more efficient when doing these.	Eliminate completely or spend less time on these.

One of the problems most students encounter is that routine studying, which is rarely viewed as an urgent activity, is considered a LOPO; other activities appear to have higher immediate payoffs. However, studying is actually a HIPO II activity that should not be deferred. Although daily studying can be both difficult and time-consuming, it should not be put off. For greater student success, begin today to make routine studying a HIPO II that gets done.

Review for a few moments the activities that you included in the inventory of how you spend your time. How many of the activities qualify as HIPOs that are helping you reach your most valued goals? How many of your daily activities are LOPO IVs and really could be discarded?

Take time now to create a time schedule that is a realistic and practical compromise between your "actual" time inventory in Exhibit 1.2 and your "ideal." Using the estimates in the "practical" column, make a plan that you can live with, one that does include some leisure time. A recent book on college study skills suggests planning enough hours per week to meet the demands of your current course load while striking a flexible balance between classes and studying, work, and leisure time (Bradley, 1983). Schedule your best study times for your most difficult subjects. Take responsibility for following your schedule.

Here are several tips to keep in mind as you plan for your routine study time during the day.

— Become aware of your own **body rhythms**, those bodily cycles of changes in energy level and activity patterns. Plan your studying, as much as possible, for the times in the day when you are most alert and most productive.

— Big blocks of study time are generally inefficient since concentration is difficult to maintain for longer than an hour. If your study time occurs in large blocks, schedule regular breaks and take them. If concentration is a problem, begin by studying less more often.

Studying less may sound like odd advice, but the idea is to practice giving your full attention to the task for a short period of time, perhaps even as short as 5 minutes at the beginning. Set a goal of reading two pages (or whatever is a reasonable amount for you to read in the next five minutes). Force yourself, for those five minutes, to attend fully to your reading. If your mind starts to wander, immediately direct it back to the task. You can concentrate for five minutes! Then, after five minutes, check your progress. Take a mini-break, and review what you have just read. Next, set a new, slightly higher goal for yourself. As you master the skill of concentrating fully for short periods of time, gradually lengthen the time periods. Before long, with regular practice, you can be concentrating for half-hour or hour blocks of time.

Studying in small time blocks provides more opportunities for review and rehearsal of the information and provides more opportunities for consolidation of the information being learned between the study periods. As you may have already discovered, "cramming" all the information in at once just before an exam is a poor practice because it doesn't allow time to mentally sort out and consolidate the information.

— Practice is the key to making studying a familiar, patterned, rhythmic behavior.

— Setting time limits and sticking to them is important. Knowing when to stop is just as important as getting started. You need to stop before you lose your efficiency. Doing so will help you make each study period as productive as possible and will allow you to feel good about the time you spend studying. Stopping at appropriate times will also give you the chance to reward your good behavior.

— Concentrating fully for effective studying is hard work and tiring. Everyone needs some "down" time to relax, refresh, and reenergize.

THE PROCRASTINATOR'S WHINE

Just as these five tips can enhance your student success, procrastination can harm it. **Procrastination,** habitually putting off doing things, is a major problem for many students. For some, the desire to do their best creates blocks to getting started. Perfectionism causes them to worry excessively about failing and to put off getting started, thus avoiding possible failure. Obviously, telling someone to worry less about being perfect and more about simply accomplishing the task is good advice that is difficult to follow. Equally obvious advice, but much more practical, is simply to tell the person to GET STARTED! Read the first page. Write a first sentence. Do anything, but do something to get started.

Once started, try not to waste your time in excessive guilt over past procrastination and "wasted time." Everyone wastes time occasionally. In fact, wasting some time may be part of everyone's necessary "down" time. Learn to expect some backsliding, but avoid chronic time wasters:

— Do not waste time lamenting, "Things are beyond my control." If you don't take responsibility for controlling your time, who will?

— Don't fall into the trap of saying, "I'm too busy to study right now." Remember, studying is a high payoff activity, an important priority in your life.

— Don't let being a "slow starter" become a habit. Force yourself to get right to work. Divide and conquer! Divide your work into small tasks, and tackle one small task at a time.

— Resist the urge to daydream and engage in wishful thinking. When your mind wanders, practice bringing it back to the here and now. Try repeating the following sequence to yourself:

Where am I? Here.

What time is it? Now.

What is my goal? To finish my studying.

— Plan your study time for the fewest possible interruptions.

Now that you have some insights into how to gain control over your study time, consider the next topic, managing where you do your studying.

Managing Your Study Space

Your goal is to make studying a familiar, patterned, rhythmic behavior, a **habit.** Long before the term "psychologist" was coined, people had observed that humans (and other animals as well) are creatures of habit. Psychologists have noted, however, that whenever you do something in the same way, at the same time, and in the same place, not only does the behavior become habitual, but the **environmental cues** (stimulus cues) of that time and place serve to elicit the behavior from you. For example, the cues you get from your bedroom, your bed, and the time of day all help you become sleepy and fall asleep. If you have a regular, habitual bedtime, even when the cues of the bedroom and lying in bed are absent, the time of day will be enough to make you feel sleepy. As easily as environmental cues affect your sleep habits, they can affect your study habits. Therefore, in choosing where and when to study, make note of any existing habits associated with that time and place that will compete with your attempts to establish a study habit there.

Do you like to study while lying in bed? If you understand the idea of stimulus cues and competing habits presented in the previous paragraphs, you can see the problem with choosing your bed as a place to study. If you do try to study in bed, you may waste a lot of your study time nodding off to sleep!

Do you study at the kitchen table? There the environmental cues may cause your stomach to rumble and make you feel guilty about the dirty dishes in the sink! A desk in the den or in your room might appear to be ideal, but if you normally write letters, pay bills, and

Carefully choose the location at which you plan to study. If you study in bed, competing cues may make staying awake difficult.

talk on the phone in that location, you will probably find concentrating on your studying difficult.

Thus, if at all possible, choose a study area in which studying will be the only major activity that you routinely do there. If no place like that exists, then do your best to eliminate the competing cues. Remove the food from the table, and sit with your back to the sink. At night, darken the rest of the room to help mask the competing cues while you use a study lamp to focus your attention on your studies.

When you are on campus, try to choose a spot that will most likely be available each time you go there. Make a habit of going there at the same time each day. If you follow this advice, you will observe that many of the same people are there each time and that the traffic patterns, sights, and sounds are familiar to you. If you establish such a routine, you will experience another psychological phenomenon, **habituation.** In habituation, you no longer pay attention to stimuli that have become familiar and are relatively unchanging. Therefore, once the sights and sounds of your study space become familiar to you, you will experience fewer distractions as you study. On the other hand, if you study in a new spot each day, you will have a new set of sights and sounds with which to become accustomed. You will get less studying done. You will be working against studying as a routine habit.

Focus Question Answer

To benefit most from studying, should you schedule longer or shorter blocks of time for studying? Since studying is a high payoff activity (HIPO), how you manage your study time is important. Shorter blocks of time are more beneficial. If you study for shorter periods of time, but more frequently, the beginnings and endings of each session give you more opportunities to review and rehearse the material.

Study Strategies

Another aspect of effective studying involves analyzing your individual **learning style.** Learning style, or cognitive style, is the typical way in which you prefer to learn and think (Dunn & Dunn, 1978; Walter & Siebert, 1984). Learning style is highly individualized.

The statements presented in Exhibit 1.3 on the following page illustrate many of the factors that affect the ways in which you learn. You may prefer background music from your stereo or you may learn best when few, if any, background sounds are present. You may study best in informal settings, or you may need a hard chair and a flat surface in front of you in order to get much done. You may work best with others present, or you may study better when alone. Whatever your preferences are, do your best to arrange a study environment that takes your learning style into consideration. Remember that each person has his or her own individual learning style. Discover your style, and use that knowledge to improve your studying.

SQ5R

What is your favorite way to study? Do you read and reread the assigned chapters? Do you outline the textbook? Do you recopy or otherwise rework the notes that you take in class? Each of these strategies is a somewhat systematic approach to helping you learn the course material. However, the strategies have a common fault in that all require you to spend large of amounts of your precious study time doing LOPOs. When was the last time you were tested on your ability to make neat copies of classroom notes?

The payoff in most courses comes from being able to answer exam questions correctly, and to improve your skill at answering questions you must practice that skill. **Active recitation,** asking yourself questions about the material, is the surest way to know what facts you do and don't know before exam time rolls around.

Libraries provide quiet places for students to study. Find locations on campus where you can study effectively.

EXHIBIT 1.3
Factors Affecting Individual Learning Styles

Take time to determine your own preferences for each of these factors. Put a checkmark by the statements that are true of you.

1. Environmental Factors:

Light
_____ I like studying with lots of light.
_____ I study best when the lights are dim.

Sound
_____ I study best when it is quiet.
_____ I can block out noise when I work.

Temperature
_____ I concentrate best when I feel warm.
_____ I concentrate best when I feel cool.

Distractions
_____ I concentrate best with no distractions.
_____ I can ignore most distractions when studying.

Design
_____ When I study I like to sit on a soft chair or sofa.
_____ I study best at a table or desk.

2. Physical Factors:

Food intake
_____ I study better when I eat or drink while I study.
_____ I do not eat or drink while I study.

Time
_____ I study best early in the day.
_____ I study best late in the day.

Mobility
_____ I like to move about while studying.
_____ I rarely move about while studying.

3. Social Factors:

_____ I prefer to study alone.
_____ I study better when someone else is present.
_____ I remember more when I study with someone else.
_____ I like to study with a group of people.

4. Cognitive Factors:

Auditory vs. visual
_____ I remember best information I hear.
_____ I remember best information I read or see.

Internal vs. external
_____ I prefer to do things my own way.
_____ I like to be told what to do.

Left brain vs. right brain
_____ I prefer information presented in a logical, sequential way (left- brain).
_____ I remember the information better when the instructor uses unique, humorous, and sometimes weird examples (right-brain).

Global vs. analytic
_____ I prefer to "take it all in" and get the general idea.
_____ I like to analyze each individual segment.

Impulsive vs. reflective
_____ In class I quickly answer questions.
_____ I often pause to think before answering.

Adapted from Dunn, R., Dunn, K., & Price, G.E. 1975. *Learning style inventory.* Lawrence, KS: Price Systems.

Several systems incorporate active recitation as their main feature (e.g., Thomas and Robinson, 1972; Walter & Siebert, 1984). Basically, these systems are variations of SQ3R, an effective system designed by Dr. Francis Robinson over thirty-five years ago (Robinson, 1941). The acronym, SQ3R, stands for Survey, Question, Read, Recite, and Review. Two other valuable learning activities are writing and relating. The authors' updated version, **SQ5R**, includes these two additional steps.

SURVEY
QUESTION
READ
RECITE
WRITE
RELATE
REVIEW

Survey   Preparing to read a chapter in a textbook should be like preparing to go on a trip, for which most people decide on a destination, consult a roadmap and travel guide, and plan their journey. Begin your journey through a chapter in this text by surveying the major topics in the chapter outline. Scan the focus questions. Briefly look at each page, noting the number of key terms, the illustrations, and the other special features. Take time to read the chapter summary. Develop a sense of the important facts to gather from the chapter.

Question   This step is essential in decreasing the amount of time you spend actually reading the chapter and in increasing the amount of time you have available for actively processing the information. Practice the skill of turning textbook reading into the search for answers to important questions. Start by taking advantage of the focus questions at the beginning of the chapter. These questions are provided so you will already have some answers for which to search. Make the major topic headings into questions. For example, when you see SQ5R, ask yourself, "What does SQ5R stand for?" or "How do I use the SQ5R system?" When no major headings are given, ask general questions like, "What is the main topic of this paragraph?" and "Why is the topic important?" As you are formulating questions, do not neglect the figures and boxed materials. In time, as this ques-

Just as you look at a map to survey your choices of trails on a hiking trip, so too you should survey each chapter's content before you begin reading.

tioning step becomes easier for you, you will undoubtedly combine this step with the next one.

Read Actively read one section of the chapter at a time; that is, actively search for the answers to your questions. Do not concentrate on reading every word on every page. Instead, focus on locating the important points that are made in each section. The payoff is in locating and paying attention to important information, material most likely to appear on the exams.

Recite After you read, recite. Actively test your memory for what you have just read. After completing your search of the section, repeat the answers to your questions. If an answer escapes you, look for that information again. Look away from the page, and try to summarize in your own words what you have just read. Try to visualize each important term and give its definition. If you can not recall a term, quickly rehearse the information, and try again. Remember, recitation is a key step because you are practicing the very activity for which you will eventually be tested.

wRite Although this step was not included in Robinson's original system, you may choose to make it a part of both Read and Recite since writing is another way to actively involve yourself with the material you are studying and to help you highlight the major terms and concepts. Instead of underlining, use checkmarks and other symbols in the margins to help you quickly find the important points. You might use checkmarks ($\sqrt{}$) for important points, plus signs ($+$) for definitions, and question marks (?) for passages you do not understand. This system is much faster than underlining, and, in your review of the material, helps you locate key terms and their definitions. All too often, when students underline, they mark only those passages that make sense to them. Then when they review, they go over again the points they already understand and ignore the areas that they did not originally understand. So, if you must underline in your text, underline only those passages that need further study.

In addition to noting major terms and points, talk to your textbook. Write comments in the margins. Write your questions at the top and bottom of the page. Because physical actions such as writing while studying aid concentration and memory (Bradley, 1983), the act of writing may make attending to your thoughts easier. Writing may also pace the rate at which you study, giving you more time to consolidate the information.

For these reasons, writing the answers to your questions may help you remember more of the material. Writing is another way for you to make associations between what you already know and what you are learning. The more ways that you can interact with the information you want to learn, the better you will be able to remember the information. Include drawing as a part of writing, too. Draw pictures to help you tie ideas together. A picture can truly be worth a thousand words when you need to remember the information.

Relate The authors have added this step to Robinson's system to emphasize the importance of making connections between what you already know and what you are learning. Forming associations is the basis for long-term memory. **Integration,** understanding the material by interrelating it, is superior to rote memorization, but to accomplish integration you must take time to form the associations. The payoff is a better memory.

Try to find examples of the concepts from your own experiences. As part of relating to the information, see if you can apply it to your daily life. When you read about sensation and perception, use the ideas to help you understand your own perceptual experiences. When you study operant conditioning, apply the information to house-training your pet or toilet-training your child. Make the knowledge you learn truly yours by using it. In addition, look for similarities between concepts you learned in other courses and those you are now studying. Evaluate the ideas and divide them into those with which you agree and those with which you disagree. This step is your opportunity to integrate your knowledge. Make as many interconnections as you can; each one will make remembering easier.

Also use the Relate step to devise ways to help you remember the information. Jot down your memory tips for easier review, and exchange tips with other class members. Make special note of the ones that work well for you.

Review In this final step, repeat the techniques of Recite, wRite and Relate as often as necessary to assure yourself that you have mastered the information contained in the chapter. The basis for this step is overlearning with integration. To be effective, your review must be active. Say aloud the answers to the questions; study with a friend, and take turns quizzing each other. You might also try writing the answers on a sheet of paper or telling someone else about what you learned from the chapter.

Use review as a diagnostic step. In other words, pay attention to the areas that you have difficulty recalling. Then spend more time on those areas, and, if necessary, "actively" reread them.

Do not be satisfied with one good review. Frequent reviews give you practice in retrieving the information, which is the main skill that is required of you when taking tests. The essence of SQ5R is that you do not spend most of your study time trying to get the information into your head; instead, you spend most of your time practicing getting the information out of your head. Overlearning from frequent review produces less forgetting, one of the first facts established when psychologists began to study memory. The extra practice provides more opportunities to form associations with other information stored in memory.

Taking Notes

You can also use SQ5R to improve your note-taking during class. Anticipate your instructor's lecture by reviewing the assignment in the textbook and the notes that you took during the previous class. Ask yourself, "What topics are likely to be covered today?" "Where are we headed with this topic?" In other words, survey.

Listen actively to the lecture and class discussion. Keep mentally alert by asking yourself, "What is the main point the instructor is stressing?" "Is this a new term?" "What is its definition?" "Does this item sound like a good point for an exam question?" In other words, create questions to be answered in your notes.

Learn to "read" your instructors. Do they use set phrases, such as "a key point" or "pay particular attention to" to indicate the major topics and concepts in their lectures? Are the main points and important terms written on the chalkboard? Once you decode your instructor's style, recording the important facts from the lecture will be much easier.

Whenever possible recite actively in class. Participate! If you do not understand a point or if an example is unclear, ask the instructor to review the point or to expand upon the example given. Worry less about feeling foolish or asking a dumb question and more about making sure that you are not missing the information being presented. When the instructor asks a question, try to answer. You may not always want to be the one with your hand in the air, but at least try to answer the question in your head. When the class is asked to give examples, try. Your example may not always be the best one, but

your active participation will help you remember the ideas being presented.

Obviously, writing is the major feature of note-taking. The average lecturer speaks at a rate of 125-140 words per minute, while the average rate of note-taking is twenty-five words per minute (Bradley, 1983). Unless you are trained as a stenographer, taking down a verbatim record of what is said in class will be very difficult. Trying to record everything is like forcing yourself to read every word in the chapter; the effort is not necessary and is very inefficient. Using a tape recorder is equally inefficient since you have to spend another hour listening to the tape—a likely LOPO! Instead, take notes selectively. Be brief, and record only the essential words and important ideas.

Think of your notebook as a log in which you are going to make entries about the important points made in class. Leave a wide margin for adding later comments and notations, or skip several lines after each main point. Visualize your notes as the major topic headings in a chapter from your textbook. Include terms and their definitions, and be sure to make notes about graphs drawn on the board or transparencies shown on the overhead projector. Also, make notes about films or other media that are shown.

Use any "down" time during the class to your advantage. If the instructor stops to rewind the film, use the time to add to your notes and to mentally review the film. Use the time to ask a question about the film to help you remember what you just saw.

Relating and reviewing can be done during these "down" times as well. However, these two steps are best undertaken after the class period has ended. As soon as possible after class, survey your notes. Ask questions about what you have written; make additional notes, and rework the notes you have taken. Rewrite your notes only if rewriting is necessary to decipher what you have written.

Try to relate the lecture topics to the topics in the text. Jotting down textbook page numbers that correspond with the topic in your notes may be helpful. Check the definitions of terms in your notes with those in the text. As suggested earlier, do everything you can to make associations between the information in your notes and information you already know.

Finally, review your notes before each class, paying special attention to the notes from the previous class. Note any areas that you should ask your instructor about for further clarification. Review your notes at other times as well; practice retrieving the information.

Exploring . . .

Ten Tried and True Techniques for a Terrific Memory

These ten techniques, some of which have been in use for centuries, will help you improve your memory.

1. The Location Technique—Most students have attempted to use this technique when they have tried during a test to visualize the page in their notes on which the answer is located. To remember a series of items, first identify a series of locations, such as the rooms in your home, with which you are familiar. Form a vivid visual image of each of the items to be remembered, and associate that image with a piece of furniture in one of the rooms. The more vivid and exaggerated the association the better. To recall the information, mentally walk through your home, looking at the pieces of furniture. The location of each piece of furniture will serve as a retrieval cue to help you recall the vivid visual association and the information that you want.

2. The Link Technique—This technique works well for lists of items that must be remembered in a certain order. Begin by forming a vivid, exaggerated image linking the first and second items on the list. Then form a different, but equally absurd, image linking the second and the third items, and so on through the list. In this technique, as in the previous one, a mental picture can be worth a thousand words. The trick is to link the information together with easily recalled images. Try this technique with your next grocery list. Create a vivid image of a can of tomato soup inside a hamburger bun; then associate the bun with the next item on your list and so on until you have linked each item to the next.

3. The Peg Technique—Here is another technique for remembering lists or chains of information in order. Choose a peg word that is easily imaged and that rhymes with a corresponding number. The peg word will always stand for the same number and will be used to form an association with the information that you are memorizing. For example, common peg words for the numbers one through five are: one is a bun; two is a shoe; three is a tree; four is a door; and five is a hive. Begin by associating the first item on the list with the peg word, bun. Perhaps you will imagine the item in a gigantic hamburger bun. When, during a test, you must remember the first item on the list, think of a bun and mentally see the information in the bun.

4. The Sound-Alike Technique—Some words are difficult to form into vivid visual images. Therefore, this technique replaces the word with a sound-alike word or phrase; for example, Minnesota becomes "mini-soda." Try this technique with new terminology to help you remember the pronunciations. The neurotransmitter acetylcholine, for instance, may become "I see the colon."

Taking Tests

If you make a habit of SQ5R, you will become study-wise. If you wish to be a successful test-taker, you also must become **test-wise.** The following suggestions will help you improve your test-taking performance.

— Practice taking tests like those you will be given in class. Use tests in the study guide and old tests that the instructor may make available, or create your own. The key is practice.

— Practice mentally imagining the classroom, your study area, your notes, and the textbook. One study revealed that students who were tested in the same room in which they studied the material remembered significantly more of the information than students who were tested in a different room (Smith, 1979). Students tested in the different room but who first were asked to think about the room they had studied in remembered almost the same amount of information as those students tested in the original room.

— Familiarize yourself with the testing procedures. Know how much time you will have in which to take the test. Will you be penalized for wrong answers, or are you encouraged to make "educated" guesses? Will points be subtracted for misspellings and other grammatical errors? Will you need a special marking pencil? May you use

5. The Acronym Technique—An acronym is a word, actual or nonsensical, created by using the initial letters of the items to be remembered. "HOMES" is a common acronym used to remember the names of the five Great Lakes. The acronyms that you create for yourself should be easier to remember because of the extra effort you exert in making them.

6. The Acrostic Technique—An acrostic is an acronym expanded into sentence form. In an acrostic sentence, the initial letter of each word in the sentence stands for the first letter in each item that you want to remember. The sentence "Every Good Boy Does Fine" has been learned by untold numbers of beginning music students as a handy way to remember the notes associated with the lines on the treble clef staff. To learn Freud's five psychosexual stages (oral, anal, phallic, latent, genital), remember this sentence, "Ollie And Patricia Like Giraffes."

7. The Jingles Technique—"I before e, except after c" and "Thirty days has September" are classic rhyming examples of this technique, but the jingles do not always have to rhyme. You may remember how to set your clocks for daylight time by the jingle, "Spring forward, Fall back."

8. The 5 Ws Technique—The 5 Ws — who, what, why, when, and where—are essentials of the journalism profession. Use them to organize the information you are studying and later they will become memory pegs to help you recall the information. This technique is especially useful in preparing for essay exams.

9. The Rote Technique—Although rote memorization without accompanying understanding has been justifiably criticized as a poor learning technique, some material does require rote memorization. To use this technique, break the material into smaller units, practice active recitation (either orally or by writing), rehearse frequently, and be sure that you have overlearned the material.

10. The Flash Card Technique—All types of information can fit the flash card format, with questions on one side and their answers on the other or terms on one side with their definitions on the other. This technique can be combined easily with any of the previous methods. One advantage of the flash card approach is ease of reviewing. Once you learn an item thoroughly, you can remove it from the deck and concentrate on those items that are not well-learned.

Now, which technique are you going to use to remember these ten memory tips? Remember that in order for any of these techniques to work, you must practice using them. If you want to read more about memory, turn to Chapter 10, which focuses entirely on memory processes.

scratch paper or make notes on the test or answer sheet?

— Practice relaxation responses in order to overcome text anxiety and to remain calm during the test.

— Avoid panic. Do not rush.

— Scan the test. Look for questions that you can easily answer. Look for questions for which you have practiced the answers. Develop a feel for the test before you dive in.

— For any type of test, first answer the questions that you know. If you encounter difficulties with a question, move on to one that you can answer more easily.

— Concentrate on your own performance. Do not worry because others are finishing sooner than you. They may know less than you or have a different test-taking style.

— Allow time in which to go over your answers before you turn in your answer sheet.

— After the testing period, make notes about the test and the questions that were difficult for you. Take additional notes when you review the graded test. Review the notes when you prepare for a comprehensive final exam.

— Generally, prepare for all types of exams in the same way by using SQ5R. For multiple-choice and other objective tests, focus more on details, definitions, and specific facts. For essay questions, pay more attention to broad themes and the facts that support them.

— On objective tests in which blank answers count as wrong answers, answer every question, even if you must guess. On multiple-choice questions, improve the odds for guessing by first eliminating the obviously wrong alternatives.

— On essay and short-answer tests, pay attention to key words such as "discuss," "compare and contrast," "define," and "give examples." Do not merely give examples when the question asks for definitions.

— After the test is over and the scores are posted, go easy on yourself if your score is lower than you wanted. Wallowing in self-pity won't help you do better on the next exam. Put this test behind you, and concentrate on doing better on the next one. If you do well on an exam, take the time to compliment yourself.

Since test-taking is a skill that can be developed through practice, put yourself in training. Use SQ5R to focus your study time on active recitation, where you directly practice retrieving answers to questions.

Focus Question Answer

What are the advantages of using the SQ5R study strategy? SQ5R gives a plan of action for organizing your study time. Surveying the material helps you become oriented to the material, while questioning aids in identifying important topics and material. The approach to reading emphasized in SQ5R and the use of writing promote active involvement with the text. Active recitation, relating, and review help assure that the material is well-learned and readily available for later recall.

What strategies can you use to maximize test performance and minimize test anxiety?

 ## Self Management

An important aspect of developing good study habits is learning to effectively manage anxiety in your life. How you talk to yourself is also important in self-management.

Managing Test Anxiety

A student's life is an ever-changing array of courses, reading assignments, projects, reports, and exams. Not surprisingly, some students become victims of the pressures of student life. These pressures may result in paralyzing procrastination or attacks of panic as project deadlines and exam times near. Some students become physically ill.

How can you become a victor over these pressures rather than their victim? First, review the suggestions for improving your time management and your study habits. Good study habits that result in being well-prepared in advance of exams are one way to reduce the pressures of testing situations. If test anxiety—that tense, panicky feeling before and during the exam when you find remembering what you have learned almost impossible—is a major problem, you may want to seek some help from the counseling service at your college. The advice you receive may sound deceptively simple, but it can help you overcome the problem. You must want to change, believe that you can change, and practice changing.

Managing Your Self-Talk

A major technique for controlling test anxiety and a generally useful skill for dealing with the pressures of student life is managing your self-talk. Self-talk is the inner speech that people engage in with themselves, and it is usually very different from the speech they use with other people. While people are usually thoughtful, considerate, and rational in their conversations with others, they are often self-deprecating, berating, and irrational in their conversations with themselves.

Typical of self-talk is the habitual use of very specific shorthand put-downs. For example, when you have difficulty answering a test question, you may say to yourself, "YOU DUMMY!" This inner speech put-down is an automatic thought (Beck, 1976). The problem arises because you have made this statement to yourself so often that, no matter how irrational the thought is, you still believe it.

These shorthand phrases usually carry a lot of baggage with them. When you say, "YOU DUMMY!" you automatically "know" that a good student would know the

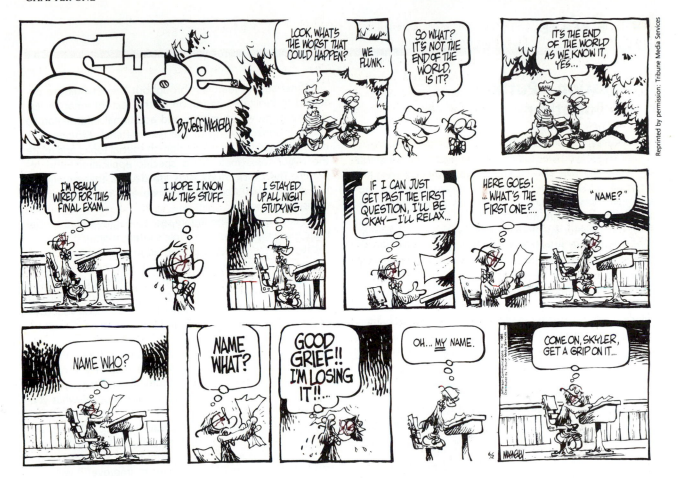

Reprinted by permission: Tribune Media Services

answer, that you are an awful student, that you ought to be a good student, that you should have studied more, that you are going to flunk, that your life is ruined, and so on. Such automatic thoughts are difficult to turn off once they have begun because they are so well learned.

However, you learned to use them and you can learn to not use them. You can learn to replace negative, depressing, irrational thoughts with more rational, positive thoughts (Ellis & Harper, 1975). Begin by becoming aware of your own specific automatic thoughts. Keeping a list of these thoughts may help you listen more sensitively to your mental conversations. Actively work at countering irrational thoughts with more rational ones. The next time you catch yourself saying, "I'll just die if I don't do well on this exam!" ask yourself if you will really die. What will actually happen if you do not do well on the exam? What can you do to prevent that from happening? Learn to recognize and reward yourself for what you do, rather than punishing yourself for what you did not do. The following specific positive thoughts may help you reduce test anxiety.

- "I don't have to be perfect."
- "I will do my best."
- "I am in control."
- "I can manage this situation."
- "It's only a test."
- "One step at a time."
- "It doesn't matter how others are doing."
- "I can relax."
- "The world will not end as the result of how I do on this exam."

Changing your habitual irrational thoughts may not be easy at first, but it is worth your effort. Good luck!

Focus Question Answer

How can you use self-talk productively? Avoid automatic negative thoughts. Actively work to make positive, rational statements. Use your inner self-talk to give yourself compliments and to help manage your test anxiety.

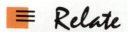
Relate

Integration—Putting It All Together

Integration is the process of increasing your understanding of the material you are studying by relating the new material to that which you already know and by interrelating the information that you are learning. This final section of Chapter 1 will show you how your textbook is designed to facilitate your efforts at integration.

In this chapter you have been introduced to a system, SQ5R, that is an effective way to study not only for this psychology course but for other courses as well. The SQ5R system provides the format for each chapter in this text. Each chapter begins with an *outline* of the chapter and ends with a *summary* and a listing of *key terms*. These features will allow you to **survey** easily the material in the chapter. Next to the chapter outline at the beginning of the chapter are *focus questions*. Each **question** focuses on a major topic or concept in the chapter and is designed to help you **read** actively by looking for the answer. Active reading is also promoted by dividing the major topics into smaller units and by asking further questions throughout the chapter.

In this chapter you were encouraged to **write** rather than underline in your textbooks. Using a system of notations, making comments in the margins, and writing questions and answers greatly facilitates the other three Rs in SQ5R—**recite**, **relate**, and **review**. You can easily recite actively by using each heading, key term, notation, comment, and question to prompt yourself to ask, "What is this?" "What do I know about it?" and "How does it relate to other things I know?"

Other special features throughout the chapter are designed to facilitate integration of the text information. *Exhibits* provide visual images and additional information to aid your understanding of the text material. *Exploring . . .* boxes add additional information on special topics and relate the major topic material to specific applications and research. The *Quick Study Aids* are devices that experience has shown help students integrate and remember information more easily.

In each chapter, the *Relate* section begins with a special topic that emphasizes that topic's integration with and application to the concepts presented in the chapter. For example, in this chapter you are seeing how the SQ5R system was applied to the design of this book. The special topic is followed by *Things to Do, Things to Discuss,* and *Things to Read*. These suggest further ways that you can, on your own or with other students, relate and integrate the information presented in the chapter.

Having originally used the summary and key terms to survey the chapter, after studying the chapter you can use them to review what you have studied. As always, you will want to make the review an active recitation of what you studied.

Throughout this chapter the importance of actively practicing the skills that are presented has been stressed. Without practice, no amount of positive attitude ("I know that I can improve!") or desire ("I really want to improve!") will help you obtain better study habits. Better study habits are worth the effort, and, as an added benefit, each time you practice, you get more of your studying done. To paraphrase a recent advertisement, "Improving your study habits may cost a little more, but you're worth it!"

Things to Do

This chapter may seem to you one very long "things to do" list. You are encouraged to work on those areas in which you feel the need to improve. Try the suggestions. Talk with other students to find out what strategies they use. Additionally, you may find these specific tasks useful.

1. If you do not have the opportunity during class, take time outside class to discuss the class with other students. Even though you may prefer to study alone, exchanging ideas, insights, study hints, and other useful information can be extremely beneficial. Do not think of your instructor and your textbook as the only sources of information in the course. Your fellow students have a wealth of information and ideas to share with you and, similarly, you with them.

2. For the first day of class give yourself an assignment to locate your instructor's office. Try creating a mental map to get you from where you live to the classroom and to the instructor's office. Visualize your instructor's name and face as part of the process.

3. Check out the library resources for psychology. Begin to read *Psychology Today,* a popular magazine that contains interesting articles about different areas in the discipline of psychology.

Things to Discuss

Think about these questions, and discuss them with other students and your instructor.

1. With the availability of so much information about learning how to learn and improving study skills, why are courses in effective studying rarely taught in elementary and secondary schools? Should learning how to learn be part of the elementary curriculum? Should courses in effective studying be offered in junior high and high school?

2. What are your reactions to this statement by Mark Twain: "We are only handicapped by what we think we can't do."

3. What do you envision as the "ideal" study environment, the one most conducive for effective studying? Does such a spot already exist? Could colleges feasibly construct "study" buildings incorporating the features of your "ideal" environment? What, if any, problems would have to be solved?

4. What are your reactions to this common student lament: "At least bad study habits are better than no study habits at all!" Do you agree? What would you say to a student who offers this statement as a rationale for not improving his or her study skills?

5. Considering what you presently know about study skills, what three pieces of advice about improving study skills do you think most important to give to someone?

6. Can you be too relaxed for an exam? What support exists for the answer you give? Does test anxiety serve any useful purpose? Support your answer.

Things to Read

Baddeley, A.D. 1982. *Your memory: A user's guide.* NY: Macmillan.

Carman, R.A. & Adams, R.W. 1984. *A student's guide for survival.* (2nd ed.). NY: Wiley.

Ellis, A. & Harper, R.A. 1975. *A new guide to rational living.* North Hollywood, CA: Wilshire Book Co.

Walter, T. & Siebert, A. 1984. *Student success: How to do better in college and still have time for your friends.* NY: Holt, Rinehart & Winston.

 ## Review

Summary

1. Time management consists of evaluating how you spend your time now, analyzing your priorities (HIPOs and LOPOs), setting up a schedule, and then following the schedule. Plan to study frequently for short periods of time, and study when you are most alert.

2. Managing your study space consists of choosing a study spot that has as few competing environmental cues and distractions as possible. Studying regularly in the same location will allow you to habituate to the remaining environmental cues. Consider your individual learning style when structuring your study environment.

3. SQ5R is a systematic method of studying that can help you use your time more efficiently and effectively. The steps are: Survey, Question, Read, Recite, wRite, Relate and Review.

4. Active listening, participating, and distinguishing between important and unimportant items in the lecture are effective strategies for note-taking.

5. The skills of relaxing, concentrating, and answering first those questions with which you are most familiar will help make you test-wise. Practicing for the specific kind of test beforehand will facilitate your performance.

6. Test anxiety can be overcome by being well prepared for tests, by using relaxation exercises to remain calm, and by being test-wise.

7. Changing your self-talk into more positive, rational thoughts is another way to reduce stress and its effects. If you recognize that negative automatic thoughts are a problem, you can begin to work actively to eliminate them and learn new ways of responding.

8. Better study habits do not happen overnight. They are the result of resolving to improve, followed by analysis of your needs, and continued practice over time. Although better study habits require considerable effort to create, they are worth that effort.

Key Terms

time management
HIPOs
LOPOs
body rhythms
procrastination
habit
environmental cues
habituation

learning style
active recitation
SQ5R
integration
test-wise
test anxiety
self-talk

Part One

Frameworks

Focus Questions

1. Should you trust common sense ideas about human behavior?

2. How can knowledge of psychology's past help you understand the field of psychology today?

3. How is psychology like watching a football game?

4. Which of the goals of psychology are directly relevant to your life?

5. How is science different from magic and religion?

Chapter Outline

WHAT IS PSYCHOLOGY?
Common Sense and Psychology
Pseudopsychologies

A BRIEF LOOK AT PSYCHOLOGY'S PAST
Structuralism
Functionalism
Behaviorism, Gestalt, and Psychoanalysis

CURRENT PERSPECTIVES IN PSYCHOLOGY
The Biological Perspective
The Behavioral Perspective
The Psychodynamic Perspective
The Cognitive Perspective
The Humanistic Perspective

THE GOALS AND WORK OF PSYCHOLOGISTS
The Goals of Psychology
Psychologists and Their Work
Bridges to Other Disciplines

RELATE: Three Ways of Knowing—Science, Magic, and Religion
Things to Do
Things to Discuss
Things to Read

REVIEW: Summary
Key Terms

Chapter 2

Perspectives of Psychology

The most beautiful thing we can experience is the mysterious. It is the source of all true art and science.

Albert Einstein

Students enroll in an introductory psychology course for a variety of reasons ranging from fulfilling a course requirement to pursuing personal interest in psychological issues to taking the first step toward a career in psychology. Whatever brings you to this course and this particular general psychology textbook, the authors hope that you will finish this class with your expectations met and exceeded. Psychology has much to offer you in terms of a scientific discipline, a framework for thinking about the world, and a way to modify behavior and lifestyles. Within this textbook, you will learn about the contents, processes, and applications of psychology.

Some of the ideas and topics that you will explore will be consistent with the ways in which you already think about the world because psychology has been welcomed into the everyday vocabulary, reading material, and activities of almost everyone. Vocabulary terms such as sibling rivalry, Type A behavior, bonding, erogenous zones, Freudian slips, and self-actualization have moved from the professional language of psychologists into the everyday conversations of non-psychologists.

In fact, psychology has pervaded the lifestyles of Americans and others. In the last decade, nearly half of the best-selling nonfiction books in the United States dealt with psychological topics (Zilbergeld, 1983). Psychological procedures such as behavior modification and transactional analysis have been widely adopted by school systems and industry. Today, many people receive counseling and guidance for their personal and career problems from the more than 280,000 professional counselors, 130,000 paraprofessional counselors, and 30,000 psychiatrists who work in the United States. More individuals in the United States work as psychological counselors than work in any one of the careers of librarian, firefighter, lawyer, police, dentist, pharmacist, or mail carrier (Zilbergeld, 1983). Many individuals have completed

psychology courses in high school or have enrolled in psychologically oriented workshops on diverse topics such as parenting, stress management, and death and dying.

Take a few minutes to answer the questions in Exhibit 2.1 and test your present knowledge about psychology.

You will probably feel "at home" with many of the topics that you study in this course. However, you may recognize basic differences between this course and your previous encounters with psychology. As a student in this course, you will be exposed to a wider range of topic areas, and you will look at these topics in a more scientific way than is typical in best-selling books, newspaper articles, or workshops. You will be asked to be more critical in interpreting theoretical ideas and research findings. You will also learn more about how psychologists do their research and counseling, and you will become a more informed and critical consumer of psychological services.

By the end of this introductory course, you will know more facts about psychology, but, more important, you

EXHIBIT 2.1
Test Your Knowledge About Psychology

Try the following quiz on psychological knowledge. Answer True or False for each of the following items. The answers will be given later in the chapter.

_____ 1. To change people's behavior toward members of ethnic minority groups, you must first change people's attitudes.
_____ 2. Memory can be likened to a storage chest in the brain into which material is deposited and from which the material can later be withdrawn. Occasionally, something gets lost from the "chest," and then you say you have forgotten.
_____ 3. Personality tests reveal your basic motives, including those of which you may be unaware.
_____ 4. Babies love their mothers because mothers fulfill their physiological needs for food, warmth, etc.
_____ 5. Blind persons can visualize in their minds how other people look by touching the people's faces.
_____ 6. The more highly motivated you are, the better you solve a complex problem.
_____ 7. The best way to ensure that a desired behavior will persist after training is completed is to reward the behavior every time it occurs throughout training.
_____ 8. A schizophrenic is someone with a split personality.
_____ 9. Blind people have unusually sensitive organs of touch.
_____ 10. Fortunately for babies, human beings have a strong maternal instinct.
_____ 11. Unlike humans, lower animals are motivated only by their bodily needs—hunger, thirst, sex, etc.
_____ 12. Psychiatrists are medical people who use psychoanalysis.
_____ 13. Children memorize much more easily than adults.
_____ 14. The ability of blind people to avoid obstacles is due to a special sense that develops in compensation for their absence of vision.
_____ 15. Boys and girls exhibit no behavioral differences until environmental influences begin to produce such differences.
_____ 16. Genius is closely akin to insanity.
_____ 17. The unstructured interview is the most valid method for assessing someone's personality.
_____ 18. While hypnotized, people can perform feats of physical strength that they could never do otherwise.
_____ 19. The more you memorize by rote (for example, poems), the better you will become at memorizing.
_____ 20. Children's IQ scores have very little relationship to how well they do in school.

Adapted from Table 1, p. 139, of Vaughan, E. D. 1977. Misconceptions about psychology among introductory psychology students. *Teaching of Psychology*, 4, 138-141.

will know how this knowledge was formulated, how it has been modified, and how psychologists continue to develop and shape new ideas. You will better understand the relationships between psychology and other discipline areas such as biology and philosophy. You will also become a better judge of what is sound, well-developed psychology and what is "pop psychology" or faddish psychology with little scientific backing. You will have the foundation for critically thinking about psychological findings.

What Is Psychology?

Psychology is often defined as the scientific study of the behaviors and mental processes of organisms. The Greek roots of psychology are *psyche,* which means "the human soul and mind," and *-ology,* which means "the study of"; literally, then, psychology means "the study of the human soul." Actually, however, psychologists are better at studying behavior than they are at understanding the human soul.

Psychology is a science. The first significant component in the definition of psychology is that psychology is *scientific.* Psychology is one of several organized bodies of knowledge that have been acquired with the use of the scientific methods of observation, description, control, and replication. Chapter 3 focuses on the scientific methodology of psychology.

Although psychology is scientific, it sometimes involves less precision than is desired by ideal standards. One reason for psychology's scientific shortcomings is that the science is relatively young, with its beginnings as a scientific discipline usually given as 1879. A second and more compelling reason for psychology's imprecision derives from the subjects of psychological research. When a chemist studies carbon atoms, the carbon atoms do not alter their course of activity because of self-consciousness or helpfulness, but when a psychologist studies the behavior of people, they may alter their behaviors for a number of different motives. Despite these obstacles, psychologists have acquired considerable scientific knowledge about humans' behavior and mental processes.

Psychology studies behaviors and mental processes. A second component of the definition of psychology is that *behaviors* are only part of what psychologists study. Behaviors are the actions and responses that organisms make. Psychologists often study overt behaviors because these behaviors are observable and measurable (i.e., the behaviors are publicly verifiable).

A third component of psychology's definition is that psychology involves the study of *mental processes.* Mental processes are covert, hidden processes—the activities of consciousness that are not observable by others. Psychologists studying the processes of cognition (thinking) and emotion may use a variety of techniques, from self-reports to advanced technology such as computerized axial tomography (CAT scans). Although some psychologists believe mental processes cannot be studied scientifically and therefore exclude the study of mental processes from their definition of psychology, the majority of psychologists believe that studying mental processes is an important aspect of psychology.

Psychology studies organisms. The final component of the definition of psychology is the word *organisms.* In addition to studying people, psychologists study many other species. Psychologists in a field called comparative psychology study animals in natural environments and in laboratories in order to understand the behavior of animals. By studying both people and animals, psychologists have discovered general principles of behavior; they have discovered, for instance, that rewards influence the learning and behavior of different species in similar ways.

Psychologists also study animals because some studies would be impossible or impractical to do with human beings. Unlike humans, laboratory rats can be bred to create identical genetic backgrounds so that hereditary and environmental factors can be studied under carefully controlled conditions. The lives of rats and chimpanzees can be controlled much more precisely than the lives of humans ever could be, and scientists can study the brains of animals in ways they could not ethically do with humans.

Although much valuable information has been acquired through animal studies, rats and chimpanzees are different from people, and psychologists must be careful to avoid anthropomorphism, the tendency to attribute human characteristics to animals. You may succumb to the anthropomorphic fallacy with your pets when you make statements such as "My dog Jesse knows he can get me angry by hiding my bedroom slippers" or "My cat Clyde acts like a spoiled brat." Although most pet owners remain anthropomorphic in their assumptions about their pets, psychologists seek to eliminate their tendencies to interpret the behavior and mental processes of animals in terms of human abilities. Psychologists must also eliminate the similar error of overgeneralizing from animal abilities to human behavior and mental processes.

An example of the anthropomorphic fallacy is interpreting this elephant's behavior as waving at its observers.

Common Sense and Psychology

Are you familiar with the proverbs in Exhibit 2.2? Can you think of an instance in which each is true? People sometimes believe that psychology is nothing more than common sense, because like the sayings in Exhibit 2.2 the results of psychological research also often appear to be obvious facts about human behavior. These common

EXHIBIT 2.2
Common Sense Proverbs

> It's never too late to learn.
> You can't teach an old dog new tricks.
> Opposites attract.
> Birds of a feather flock together.
> Two's company; three's a crowd.
> The more the merrier.
> Two heads are better than one.
> Too many cooks spoil the broth.

sense sayings make sense because they seem so obvious. However, when opposite statements both seem obvious, as in Exhibit 2.2, then knowing which advice to follow is difficult. Psychologists attempt to discover whether the behaviors that seem obvious are in fact true. They design experiments, for example, to explore when and why "opposites attract" and "birds of a feather flock together." The results of their studies appear to document the obvious because, after the fact, almost any behavior is easily seen as true of humans.

How many of the twenty items in Exhibit 2.1 did you answer as true? All twenty items are false. Yet each item was marked true by at least half of the introductory psychology students at the University of Pittsburgh in 1975–1976 (Vaughan, 1977). The first item was marked true by 92 percent of the respondents. Items 2–6 were marked true by more than 80 percent of the students. Items 7–10 were checked as true by more than 70 percent of the students, and items 11–15 were marked true by more than 60 percent of the respondents. To paraphrase the folk wisdom that common sense is not so common, the results of this study indicate common knowledge of psychology is not so common!

Psychologists in their research may appear to verify obvious truisms about human behavior because known outcomes seem more predictable. When presented with the results of a psychological study, the outcome appears more likely because the results are known. If people are asked to predict the outcome of an experiment, they are much less certain about what the results will be (Slovic & Fischhoff, 1977).

Common sense is not necessarily wrong. You will learn in Chapter 18 about social psychologists' research on what attracts people to one another. These studies indicate that both similarity (birds of a feather) and complementary needs (in a sense, opposites) are important factors in interpersonal attraction. But while common sense is not necessarily wrong, it fails to predict ahead of time which factors are important under what conditions. If your lover is going away on a trip, should you worry or be happy? Knowing that *out of sight is out of mind* and that *absence makes the heart grow fonder* is of little help. Once your lover returns, you will know which saying to apply, but not beforehand. In scientific psychology, research results provide a solid basis for understanding behavior before, not after, the fact.

Pseudopsychologies

"All that glitters is not gold," and all that seem like psychological findings are not scientific. The term **pseudopsychology** is used to describe superficial systems that appear to resemble psychology but fail to achieve scientific validity. The prefix *pseudo-* is Greek for "false." Yet, new pseudopsychologies pop up all the time to join the ranks of centuries-old ones such as astrology, graphology, numerology, palmistry, phrenology, and physiognomy. Apparently, pseudopsychologies are easier to create than to destroy.

Astrology Astrology is probably the best known of the traditional pseudopsychologies. Although astrology includes several well-developed systems based on the position of the planets and stars at the moment of a person's birth, psychologists have been unable to establish scientific evidence for any of the astrology systems. Critics of astrology question why centuries-old astrological systems have not been revised to fit more accurate, modern-day knowledge of planetary movements. Additionally, these critics wonder why the moment of birth is more important than any other moment of one's life (e.g., one's first birthday, the moment of conception).

Graphology Graphology is the study of personality through handwriting analysis. As one graphologist, Carlos Pedregal, describes the mechanism of graphology, "Writing is simply a set of printed gestures that originate at the subconscious level. The pen you choose to write with and how hard you press, the slant of your lines…, the shape of your letters and how they are grouped all combine to reveal facts about you that only a wife, husband or very close friend would know" (Gross, 1984, p. 90). Today some companies in this country and in Europe use handwriting analysis to gather information for career placement and advancement even though scientific studies of graphology fail to establish its accuracy in indicating personality.

Numerology In numerology, an individual's personality and destiny are thought to be determined by the letters in his or her name and the numbers of his or her birthdate. Numerologists may suggest that people change the spelling of their names to improve their destinies. On the advice of a numerologist, one superstar singer has been both Dionne Warwick and Dionne Warwicke during her career.

Palmistry Palmistry uses the lines and mounds in the hand to describe an individual's personality and to predict the person's future. One hand is used to determine the destiny with which the person came into this world, and the other hand is used to state what he or she is actually doing during this lifetime. Certain lines are supposed to indicate health, fortune, career, family, and length of life; differences in line length, shape, clarity, and markings determine specific predictions. In spite of palmistry's popularity, no scientific evidence to indicate that one's life is mirrored in one's hands has been found.

Phrenology and Physiognomy Phrenology and physiognomy were popular during the nineteenth century. Phrenology was based on the assumption that bumps on the head revealed personality characteristics, and physiognomy was based on the assumption that outward appearance was related to one's personality. When these pseudopsychologies were studied scientifically, both were found to lack validity.

Why Do Pseudopsychologies Persist? Why do pseudopsychologies remain popular in spite of their lack of support from the scientific community? Some of the reasons include:

1. Proponents of each pseudopsychology exaggerate the success of the approach. Some supporters claim to have scientific evidence that, in reality, is not scientific at all. For instance, books about biorhythms claim that business managers have been able to reduce accidents by informing employees about their "critical days." However, these studies do not meet all the criteria of scientific studies.

2. Usually the predictions of pseudopsychological strategies are quite flattering and most individuals like to believe positive statements about themselves. You might be more inclined to believe a palm reading that reveals a prosperous and long life and less inclined to accept the accuracy of a palm reading that reveals that your life will be miserable, luckless, and mercifully short. Most pseudopsychologies provide more positive than negative evaluations and therefore remain popular.

3. The descriptions developed through these strategies are so general that they are accurate to a degree. If your astrological horoscope for today says that "you should be careful during travel" and that "you can enjoy the company of good friends sometime after noon," the horoscope, which is widely applicable, seems to make good, if not astonishing, sense and is likely to come true.

4. Pseudopsychological analyses may serve as placebos; that is, they may be "fake" but still influence changes in behavior so that their predictions come true. If a numerologist convinces you that you will be much more successful in your business if you add an E to your last name, you may work longer, harder, and more efficiently than ever before because you are convinced that your efforts will finally pay off. Thereby, you may actually achieve great success.

5. Pseudopsychologies may appear to be highly accurate because of the **fallacy of positive instances,** in which individuals tend to remember confirmations of predictions but tend to forget disconfirmations. An example of the fallacy of positive instances is that you remember the "Aquarius traits" of someone you know was born on January 26th but fail to remember the "Leo traits" that this same individual exhibits.

6. Pseudopsychologies may be believed because they provide individuals with security. Life is sometimes unpredictable, and believing in pseudopsychologies allows individuals to believe they have more control over their destinies than they actually have. While a person could die in an automobile accident this afternoon, that person can feel more secure in knowing that his or her astrological chart predicts death from old age.

7. Finally, but perhaps most important, pseudopsychologies persist because they are fun and can be harmless hobbies. Many people read their daily horoscopes in the newspaper, but a much smaller portion of them actually base their lives upon astrological predictions. "What's your sign?" and "Have you ever had your palm read?" can be entertaining small-talk at social gatherings, but the answers usually do not determine people's future interactions with others.

Pop Psychology Pop psychology, popularized psychology loosely based on psychological facts, is a first cousin to pseudopsychology. Many of the psychological articles and quizzes found in magazines and many of the books in psychology sections of bookstores are pop psychology, suggesting that the authors of these materials have "gone a long way with a little bit of psychological knowledge." Some pop psychology is useful, while some is quite trivial or even misleading. For the most part, scientific research is needed to lend validity to many of the most popularized psychological ideas.

Although the public is currently flooded with pop psychology advice, pop psychology has been around for a long time. Popular advice experts in the nineteenth century included Sylvester Graham, who thought that longevity could be achieved by opening windows year-round, taking many cold baths, eating a vegetarian diet, and eating his own creation, graham crackers. His contemporary, Horace Fletcher, advocated "Fletcherism" or the belief that slow, thorough chewing of raw vegetables would promote the healing properties of the vegetables' cellulose (Zilbergeld, 1983).

In fairness, many of the criticisms of pseudopsychology and pop psychology can also be leveled against scientific psychology. Proponents of a particular theory or of a specific assessment tool may also overgeneralize their results, employ the fallacy of positive instances, and uncritically draw conclusions about their psychological concepts.

Focus Question Answer

Should you trust common sense ideas about human behavior? While many common sense ideas about behavior are wrong, other common sense notions have been supported by research studies. The major failing of common

Exploring . . .

Of Blood Types and Biorhythms

Pseudopsychologies gain acceptance because they seem, on the surface, to be plausible. Unfortunately, people sometimes accept a new way of determining personality or motivation without testing the strategy in scientific ways. Thus, while most individuals now see the nineteenth-century phrenology fad as a foolish craze because research has shown that phrenology does not accurately assess personality characteristics, some of these same individuals might unquestioningly accept any new system that is created and marketed. Two such popular modern systems are specifying personality characteristics on the basis of blood type and of biorhythms. The importance of blood types as an influence on personality traits seems unlikely, and at this time little scientific research has been done to assess its significance. Similarly, scientific research suggests that biorhythms do not significantly affect our daily lives (Brown, 1982).

Blood Types

In 1971 Toshitaka Nomi published *Good Combinations of Blood Types* that sold more than 700,000 copies in Japan. In his book, Toshitaka Nomi and his father Masahiko Nomi claim that blood types and personality reflect a real science because the theory is based on over 100,000 surveys. Other scientific evidence is scarce.

According to this pseudopsychology, individuals with type-O blood are aggressive, astute about power, and realistic; individuals with type-B blood are creative and individualistic; and individuals with type-AB blood are two-faced and moody, yet also pragmatic and people-loving. Persons with type-A blood are industrious, peace-loving, image-conscious, conscientious, and sticklers for details.

Nomi claims that his theory accounts for Japan's high-technology success, because 40 percent of the Japanese population has type-A blood, the ideal blood type for engineers and technicians. Nomi also emphasizes that while only 30 percent of the Japanese have type-O blood, most Japanese politicians, including 64 percent of the postwar prime ministers, do have that blood type.

In countering Nomi's theory, Takashi Fuke suggests that placing people into only four categories is of little value. Fuke proposes that if blood typing has any value, using the 240-plus types of blood groups might be more useful.

Despite the skepticism of Fuke and others, in the last two decades, more than forty books on personality and blood type have been published in Japan, and hundreds of magazine articles and TV spots have been done on the topic. While some Americans ask their dates "What's your (astrological) sign?" many Japanese ask their dates "What's your (blood) type?"

Biorhythms

Although the pseudopsychology of biorhythms was begun in 1906 by Hermann Swoboda, the popularity of biorhythms peaked in the 1960s and 1970s. Advocates of this pseudopsychology proposed that an individual's **biorhythms,** his or her cyclical pattern of physical, emotional, and intellectual ups and downs, could be used to make decisions about appropriate activities that would coincide with the person's particular potentials for that day (McConnell, 1978).

Biorhythms consist of three cycles—a physical cycle of twenty-three days, an emotional cycle of twenty-eight days, and an intellectual cycle of thirty-three days.

Because of the popularity of biorhythms—several books became top sellers, and computer programs for determining biorhythms are available—scientists have done numerous studies, a review of which (Wolcott et al., 1977) found no significant correlation between biorhythmic cycles and behavior. Although early supporters of biorhythms suggested that monitoring biorhythms was useful in avoiding accidents at work and during travel, carefully conducted scientific studies found no biorhythm significance for highway automobile accidents (Shaffer et al., 1978), mining accidents (Persinger et al., 1978), and airplane accidents (Kurucz & Khalil, 1977).

Although biorhythms seem to be a pseudopsychology, other types of rhythmicity in behavior have found more scientific support. The study of biological rhythms is called chronobiology.

sense is that an observation usually makes sense after the fact, not beforehand. You should be careful about uncritically accepting common sense ideas, pseudopsychologies, or "pop psychology" topics.

A Brief Look at Psychology's Past

One way to understand psychology is to understand its roots. Because a major foundation of psychology is philosophy, psychology history courses often begin with the Greek philosophers. Personality theories, which attempt to answer "What is the nature of humankind?" are still greatly influenced by philosophy.

Two philosophers who influenced the development of psychology are Rene Descartes and John Locke. Rene Descartes (1596–1650), a French philosopher, is best known for his statement, "I think, therefore I am." Descartes' philosophical position was that of interactive dualism, the belief that mind and body are different but interrelated. Descartes' belief that the mind influences the body and the body influences the mind is reflected today in the biological approach to psychology. Another seventeenth-century philosopher, John Locke (1632–1704), believed that mental processes are learned entirely through experience. **Empiricism**, with its emphasis on direct experience, currently influences scientific methodology and learning theories.

While Descartes and Locke influenced the philisophical basis of psychology, the scientific foundation of psychology can be seen in the work of the nineteenth-century physician Gustav Fechner (1801–1887), who worked out the relationship between the physical characteristics of a stimulus and the psychological experience of that stimulus. His contemporary, Herman von Helmholz (1821–1894), a German physiologist, studied reaction time, speed of nerve conduction, the workings of the eye, and the color vision process. The research of these two scientists contributed to the establishment, late in the nineteenth century, of psychology as a separate scientific discipline.

Structuralism

In 1879, German psychologist Wilhelm Wundt (1832–1920) established the first experimental psychological laboratory in Leipzig, Germany; this date marks the beginning of psychology as a science. Wundt's approach to psychology was that of **structuralism**, which focused on the structure or elements of the human mind. For struc-

turalists, the basic elements of experience were sensations—sights, sounds, and other sensory experiences. At his laboratory, Wundt studied many subjects by using physical measurements and introspective methods in topic areas that included reaction time, word associations, judgment, emotions, and attention. **Introspection**, the dominant method of study, involved the recording and analysis of experiences. A trained introspectionist in Wundt's lab carefully analyzed a sensation into its basic elements of size, shape, texture, color, and so on.

Structuralism was the dominant school of psychology in both Germany and the United States until 1920. Edwin Titchener (1867–1927) was the most notable American psychologist in the structuralist school. Titchener, a student of Wundt and a professor at Cornell University, was a rigorous introspectionist, spending hours in the laboratory carefully analyzing the elements of his own sensations.

Based on the work of Wundt, Titchener, and others, structuralism influenced the way in which mental processes are studied and led to the acceptance of subjective reports (personal accounts), which today are part of the psychological study of topics from hypnosis to problem-solving.

Functionalism

The most influential American psychologist of this early time period was William James (1842–1910), a Harvard psychologist whose view of psychology was that of **functionalism.** Unlike structuralism, functionalism emphasized a practical approach to psychology and the adaptability of people to their environments. These emphases led to the development of educational and industrial psychology.

Surprisingly, Titchener and James, who were responsible for producing two main branches of American psychology, did not meet until 1909, when Sigmund Freud lectured at Clark University. Their professional differences were many. James, who was more involved with practical applications of psychology than was Titchener, incorporated Charles Darwin's theory of evolution into psychology. James, but not Titchener, thought that psychic research was an appropriate part of psychology. The fundamental difference between these two important American psychologists has been described this way: James believed science and life should be blended together, and Titchener thought science should be isolated from life (Bjork, 1983).

The first psychologist, Wilhelm Wundt.

The first psychology lecture that William James heard was one he himself delivered.

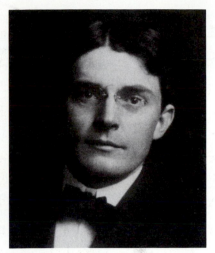

As a behaviorist, John B. Watson thought psychologists should study only observable, measurable behaviors.

Behaviorism, Gestalt, and Psychoanalysis

In the early 1900s John B. Watson (1878–1958), an American psychologist, began the **behaviorism** movement, and by 1920 behaviorism had replaced structuralism as the dominant movement in psychology. Psychologists in this movement rejected introspection, consciousness, and instincts and studied observable, measurable behavior. In many ways, this movement tried to make psychology as scientific as biology, physics, and chemistry. Watson's form of behaviorism currently influences psychologists who work with learning theory.

Another influential early American psychologist, German-born Max Wertheimer (1880–1943), believed that the whole of an experience is greater than the sum of its parts. This view, termed the **Gestalt** movement in psychology, continues to influence psychological ideas about perception, creativity, problem-solving, and therapy.

Possibly the most recognized name in psychology is Sigmund Freud (1856–1939), the founder of **psychoanalysis**. This movement in psychology evolved from Freud's insights and observations about the patients in his medical practice. Psychoanalysis emphasizes the influence of unconscious forces, impulses, and internal conflict on everyday behavior.

Focus Question Answer

How can knowledge of psychology's past help you understand the field of psychology today? The current perspectives in psychology that will be discussed in the next section are directly linked to previous ideas and movements in psychology and other related areas such as philosophy.

Current Perspectives in Psychology

Two fans, one with a seat near the fifty-yard line and the other near the goal line, are watching a college football game. Although they are watching the same two teams make the same plays, they are forming different impressions of the game and are reaching different conclusions about what they are observing. The fan who sits at the fifty-yard line and the fan who sits near one of the goal lines can describe different aspects of the game well. Which fan describes the game most accurately? Do you know more about the actual football game if you listen to one of the two fans describe the game in great detail or if you listen to some of the game's description from each of these two fans?

In some ways psychology is similar to the football game just mentioned, and psychologists sit in many sections of the stadium. All psychologists observe the behavior and mental processes of organisms, but their observations and conclusions are influenced by their views of the field. The current psychology stadium is divided into five main sections or perspectives, but the observations made within each section are often as diverse as the observations made across sections. In this course, you will wander around the entire stadium and catch a glimpse of psychology from each perspective. Psychologists tend to know the general view of all the perspectives but spend most of their time working with and learning in depth about only one or two of the perspectives.

The Biological Perspective

In the **biological perspective**, physiological psychologists study the relationships of biological systems, especially the brain and nervous system, to behavior and mental processes. In the last two decades, more growth in knowledge has occurred in physiological psychology than in any of the other perspectives.

A sampling of topics studied by this group of psychologists includes the effects of drugs on brain functioning, the actions of brain chemicals in schizophrenic individuals, the interactions between the left and right hemispheres of the brain, the effects of acupuncture on pain, the effects of stress on the anatomical development of the fetus, the role of the autonomic nervous system in stress reactions, and the biological determinants of obesity.

The biological perspective figures prominently in the material presented in the chapters on the biology of behavior (4), sensory processing (5), perceptual processing (6), states of consciousness (7), and therapy (23).

The Behavioral Perspective

The **behavioral perspective** focuses on overt behaviors, the process of learning, and the influences of the environment on an individual's behavior. Important since its establishment by Watson in 1913, behaviorism's influence peaked in the 1920s and became prominent again in the 1950s.

Behaviorally oriented psychologists study topics such as the effects of aversive stimuli on a smoker's behavior, rewards that make a laboratory rat run a maze most efficiently, reinforcements that improve grade school children's performance in math and reading, the effects of using token rewards on the behavioral management of prisoners, the treatment of phobias, the use of behavioral strategies in the treatment of eating disorders, and the use of painful stimuli to modify the behavior of child molesters.

The behavioral perspective has influenced all areas of psychology, and you will read about the influences of

behaviorism in nearly every chapter of this text, but especially in the chapters on learning (8 and 9), personality (15), and therapy (23).

The Psychodynamic Perspective

Inner forces such as drives, needs, emotions, purposes, and wishes are the focus of the psychodynamic perspective. This perspective emphasizes the "why" of behaviors and individual differences, and motivation and emotion are major areas of study. Historically, the **psychodynamic perspective** is based on Sigmund Freud's psychoanalytic theory of personality.

Topics studied by psychodynamic psychologists include the instinctive nestbuilding behaviors of weaver birds, the effects of unconscious motivation on everyday behaviors, the influence of childhood experiences on adult personality, the development of emotions in infants, the relationship between Rorschach Inkblot responses and goals in life, styles of parenting that contribute to the development of high achievement need, and the preferences of individuals who are high in sensation seeking.

The psychodynamic perspective is featured in the chapters on motivation (12), emotion and stress (13), personality (14), assessment (20), and therapy (23).

The Cognitive Perspective

The **cognitive perspective**, a growing perspective in contemporary psychology, focuses on the nature of cognitions, thoughts, beliefs, perceptions, problem-solving, and memory. Psychologists in the cognitive perspective try to study unobservable phenomenon in scientific ways. In addition to using subjective self-reports, cognitive psychologists currently use many technological advances such as biofeedback machines, PET scans, and CAT scans in their research studies.

Psychologists in this area study topics such as behaviors that enhance attitude change, ways in which intelligence strategies can be taught, effects of caffeine on memory, perceptual abilities of newborn infants, differences between highly creative and less creative individuals, and the capabilities of chimpanzees and gorillas to use language.

The cognitive perspective is highly evident in the chapters on memory (10), cognitive processing (11), social attitudes and behavior (19), assessment (20), and therapy (24).

The Humanistic Perspective

The **humanistic perspective** emphasizes the individual, or self, in psychology. Humanistic psychologists tend to focus on human concerns such as love, caring, intention, achievement, hatred, personal growth, and self-esteem. This area is influenced by the earlier philosophical movements of existentialism (analysis of existence) and phenomenology (analysis of experience). Emphasis is placed on individuals' capacities to make their own choices and to change if they so choose. The humanistic perspective has influenced a wide range of psychological topics such as Abraham Maslow's (1908–1970) concept of motivation and Carl Rogers' (1902–1987) client-centered psychotherapy.

Humanistic psychologists study topics such as the components of love, supportive conditions for self-actualization, conditions of therapy that enhance a client's personal growth, effects of warmth and contact on the personality development of monkeys, characteristics of married couples who remain satisfied after years of marriage, conditions optimal for raising preschool children, and strategies for decreasing human prejudice and bigotry.

The humanistic perspective is most evident in the chapters on personality (15), development (16 and 17), social psychology (18), and therapy (24).

Focus Question Answer

How is psychology like watching a football game? The biological, behavioral, psychodynamic, cognitive, and humanistic perspectives are similar to sitting in different places in a football stadium and viewing the game (psychology) differently from each location.

The Goals and Work of Psychologists

The Goals of Psychology

What do psychologists hope to accomplish? The goals of psychology are **description**, **explanation**, **prediction**, **control**, and **application**. These five goals form the basis of psychology as a discipline. In the next chapter, you will learn about the various research methodologies through which these goals are met.

Description   Objectivity and accuracy are needed to meet the first goal of description. Descriptions of behavior are based on external, observable features of a situation and are devoid of personal, subjective interpretations.

How would you conduct a descriptive study of the play habits of boys and girls in a preschool setting? You need to decide how often to observe what the children are doing, how to record the data (i.e., the information) objectively, which children to observe, and how long to make your observations. You might decide to record which toys the children are using at fifteen-minute intervals, which children are playing with "traditional boy toys" and which children are playing with "traditional girl toys." You need to define "boy toys" and "girl toys" before you begin your observations, and you need to know if the environment contains both boy and girl toys. A typical descriptive study of this sort finds that, by age three, most preschool boys play with "traditional boy toys" more often than three-year-old girls play with "traditional girl toys" (Bradbard & Endsley, 1983).

Explanation   The second goal of psychology is to explain or understand why a behavior occurs and to find an underlying process or relationship that accounts for the behavior. To do so, psychologists make inferences and speculate about inner states of organisms and significant aspects of the environment.

The differences in the play of three-year-old boys and girls might be inferred to be caused by biological sex differences, different assumptions by boys and girls about appropriate behavior for their gender, previous rewards and punishments given by parents or preschool teachers for toy choices, or peer group pressure to conform to sex roles.

Quick Study Aid

<hr>

An Acrostic for the Five Perspectives

When you have to remember several labels, prompt yourself with an acrostic, which uses the first letter of each term to form a sentence. The five current perspectives begin with the letters B, B, C, P, and H, letters that can be arranged into the following mnemonic sentence:

The **B. B. C. Produced Heidi.**

"B.B.C." stands for the biological, behavioral, and cognitive perspectives. "Produced" is associated with psychodynamic, and "Heidi" is helpful in recalling the humanistic perspective.

Psychologists study children at play to learn about gender differences in toy selection.

Prediction   The third goal of psychology is prediction. Psychologists want to know the likelihood that a particular event or relationship will occur in a given situation, and predictions are possible because behavior is somewhat consistent. In many areas psychologists are fairly accurate in predicting how most people will act in a situation; however, the ability to predict precise behavior for a particular person is not as well developed.

For example, if many observational studies and experiments indicate that most three-year-old boys play with "traditional boy toys" the majority of time, you can predict that your observations of boys in the preschool will find that boys play more frequently with these toys than with the "traditional girl toys." However, you cannot confidently predict which boys are most likely to deviate from the typical pattern and spend some time playing with dolls.

ACT and SAT college entrance exams, taken before a student enrolls in college, are another example of the use of prediction in psychology. Both these examinations are good predictors of college grades. On the whole, individuals who score high on one of these exams achieve higher grade point averages in college than those with lower scores. On the other hand, some individuals who score very high on college entrance exams flunk out of college, and other individuals who score below average on one of these exams graduate from college with honors. By considering more factors, such as achievement need, studying skills, and number of hours of studying, predictions might become more accurate, but psychologists are a long way from making the precise predictions made by chemists and physicists.

Control   The fourth goal of psychology is to control behavior. To achieve this goal, psychologists must understand a behavioral phenomenon well enough to be able to start the behavior, strengthen the behavior, weaken the behavior, and end the behavior. This goal requires knowing enough about the conditions that contribute to a behavior to create the necessary and sufficient conditions to cause the behavior to occur.

Attempting to control behavior may seem ominous and potentially evil. Yet while the ability to control behavior can be used in destructive, manipulative ways, it has equally as much potential for improving the quality of life. Far from being malevolent, the knowledge gained by pursuing this goal ultimately allows each individual to achieve a greater degree of control over his or her own behaviors.

To use again the example of the preschoolers' play with toys, suppose that research indicates that little boys would like to play with dolls, but social messages from parents and daycare personnel inhibit doll-playing behaviors and encourage playing with trucks. If parents and teachers would decide that little boys would benefit by playing with both trucks and dolls, psychologists could then suggest the types of communication and reinforcement that would encourage a broader play pattern in three-year-old boys.

Application   A fifth goal of psychology is its application to everyday situations to improve the quality of life. Many counseling and clinical psychologists work primarily with this goal of psychology in mind. Other psychologists have developed programs that have been adapted to industrial, home, and educational settings. Magazines such as the popular *Psychology Today* bring current psychological knowledge into the lives of Americans who are not professional psychologists.

Psychologists and Their Work

How many psychologists work in the United States, and what kinds of work do they do? A survey of the 50,000 members of the American Psychological Association, the major professional organization for psychologists, found psychologists in a variety of work settings, with the most common for Ph.D. psychologists being the university or college environment (38 percent), followed by hospitals and clinics (25 percent), and next by private practice (16 percent). Other work settings include government agencies, elementary and secondary schools, and business and industry (Stapp & Fulcher, 1983).

Areas of Specialization   Approximately 60 percent of Ph.D. psychologists list clinical or counseling psychology as their specialty. Another 10 percent of psychologists

label themselves developmental, social, or personality psychologists. Educational and school psychology and experimental psychology are the specialty areas of 9 percent of Ph.D. psychologists. Another 7 percent of psychologists are in industrial, organizational, or engineering psychology. Among psychologists with Master's degrees, the most common specialty area is also clinical and counseling psychology (Stapp & Fulcher, 1983).

The activities of psychologists include doing research, teaching, writing, consulting, and counseling.

Educational Backgrounds   If you wish to become a professional psychologist, you must go to graduate school and earn a Master's degree (M.S., M.A., or M.Ed.) in psychology. Most likely, you will go on to earn a doctoral degree (Ph.D., Psy.D., or Ed.D.), which is necessary for you to be qualified for many positions and to be licensed in many states. Other individuals who enjoy psychology may choose instead to become social workers or to earn degrees in a "hybrid" or interdisciplinary area such as human services.

Some individuals who major in psychology and hold undergraduate degrees (A.A., B.A., or B.S.) work as paraprofessionals. The term psychologist, when used correctly, refers only to individuals with advanced or graduate degrees in psychology.

Psychiatrists   Psychiatrists are not psychologists. Instead of going to graduate school, psychiatrists go to medical school. They are physicians (M.D.'s) who specialize in psychiatry and receive intensive training in the diagnosis and treatment of the physical causes of mental disorders. Of the mental health professionals, only psychiatrists can prescribe drugs to treat psychological difficulties. Psychiatrists receive varying amounts of training in psychology, depending on their specific medical school programs.

Psychoanalysts   **Psychoanalysts** are usually either psychologists or psychiatrists who have specialized in the theory and practice of Freudian psychoanalysis. Before treating others analytically, psychoanalysts usually undergo psychoanalysis themselves.

Bridges to Other Disciplines

Although psychology is a separate academic discipline, it is related to a number of other academic areas, the most significant being the other social sciences—sociology and anthropology. The major focus of psychology is the behavior of the individual; the major focus of sociology is the behavior of groups; the major focus of anthropology is the origin of cultures.

These three social sciences share similar methodologies and knowledge. For example, cross-cultural studies that reflect typical anthropological research are useful in determining the generalizability of psychological principles. Textbooks in psychology, sociology, and anthropology share some of the same examples and ideas. For instance, anthropologist Margaret Mead's work on sex roles in nonwestern cultures has been useful in generating research and theories in psychology. Similarly, sociological research on suicide has been helpful in developing psychological theories about who is likely to attempt suicide and why. Nonetheless, although the social sciences are closely related, each of these discipline areas uses terminology in slightly different ways and emphasizes different aspects of theory and methodology.

Psychology is also linked with academic areas outside the social sciences. As you read earlier in this chapter, one major foundation of psychology is philosophy. Descartes and Locke influenced psychological assumptions about the world; in a philosophy course today, the instructor might include the psychoanalytic theorists Sigmund Freud and Erich Fromm in one of the lectures.

Similarly, you can relate perceptual ideas to your art appreciation class, physiological psychology to your bi-

ology class, and social psychology to your marketing or political science class. One psychology teacher, Henry Gleitman (1984), suggests that a student could make the following intellectual linkage: "Consider John Locke and the idea that all knowledge comes through the senses, which is the starting point for a psychologist's concern with sensation and perception. I believe that students should know that John Locke was a spokesman of the English merchant class that had just rid itself of absolute monarchy and the last Stuart king. They should understand why Locke's opposition to built-in ideas can also be an argument against built-in ideas of the divine right of kings and ultimately against heredity privilege. If all human beings enter life with a *tabula rasa* (blank slate), then all distinctions between them must be entirely due to a difference in their environments. I want the students to see how this idea is incorporated in the *Declaration of Independence,* with its self-evident truth that 'all men are created equal': how it underlies the American belief that men and women are almost infinitely perfectable by proper changes in their environment, especially through education; and how it finds its modern expression in American behaviorism and its insistence on the paramount importance of learning and the near-limitless plasticity of animals and human beings." (Gleitman, 1984, pp. 424–425).

Not all the connections that can be made to other disciplines will be as complex and intellectual, but the more often you can relate the material in your psychology course to other courses and to your everyday experiences, the more easily you can remember and use this material.

Focus Question Answer

Which of the goals of psychology are directly relevant to your life? The goals of description, explanation, and prediction provide the substance that make the goals of control and application most relevant to everyday living. Because each goal is related to the others, the end result is a greater understanding of your behavior.

Three Ways of Knowing—Science, Magic, and Religion

Psychology is a science. In fact much of modern society is at least partially scientific in its approach to gaining knowledge about the world. In the past as well as today, two other approaches are used for knowing about the world—magic and religion. Because psychology is a science, most psychologists believe that magic and religion are less accurate ways to know about the world (Hayward, 1984). This section examines how the scientific approach to knowing about behaviors differs from magic and religion.

Science

Science as a way of knowing about the world emphasizes objective observation and active experimentation. Psychologists use scientific methods to obtain objective descriptions of behavior and to design experiments that test their explanations of behavior. This way of knowing goes beyond subjective personal experience to rely on objective, verifiable experiences. In this sense, psychology, like all sciences, is empirical. Because psychologists demand observable proof of their explanations of behavior, psychology may be viewed as an "I'll believe it when I see it" approach.

Because science is the dominating framework not only in psychology but in modern society, most people accept the current scientific assumptions about time, space, and cause-effect as representing truth. Yet these scientific assumptions have not always been considered obvious. "At other times, in other places, people have believed different things about the world they lived in. From their point of view, these beliefs were true because they too worked" (Hayward, 1984, p. 67).

Magic

Another way to know about the world is through **magic.** Unlike science, magic as a way of knowing about the world relies on personal subjective experience for knowledge. Knowledge in this approach comes from intuition, personal insight, and conjecture. Knowledge may also be received from those who presumably have achieved greater personal insight and from mysterious sources and unexplained powers. Ideas about magic have been prominent in history, and magical thinking is a part of all cultures today but is more prevalent among less technologically advanced societies. Examples of magical beliefs are listed in the accompanying table.

More than a way of thinking or a set of beliefs about the world, magic is the attempt to use rituals, spells, and

People who use the magic framework tend to agree with the following kinds of statements:

1. Some people can make me aware of them just by thinking about me.
2. Some numbers, such as 7 and 13, have special powers.
3. Personal belongings in my home can be moved even when no one is around.
4. Others can be harmed if I think bad thoughts about them.
5. I can sometimes sense when an invisible evil presence is around me.
6. Small rituals can be performed to ward off negative influences.
7. Energy can be gained or lost because of another's look or touch.

Adapted from Eckblad & Chapman, 1983.

medicines to exercise direct control over specific situations. People use magic to attempt to meet practical needs. Magical rituals and spells are used to try to influence the weather, personal health, or the success of agricultural crops. Tribal rain dances are an example of magical rituals. When a magical ritual seems to produce the desired results, the practitioner claims the ritual is successful; when failure occurs, the practitioner believes that the magician has failed but not the magic. Thus, the existence of magical effects cannot be verified because failures of magic do not count as disproof of the phenomenon. A parallel exists for those who believe in ESP (extrasensory perception). When ESP fails to be demonstrated, like the magician, the psychic is assumed to have failed, not ESP.

Although science and magic are both pragmatic in their approach to solving problems, magic is nonempirical and emphasizes belief and emotion, while science is empirical and emphasizes experience and reason. Magic represents a mystical route, and science represents a reasoning route to knowing about the world (Yinger, 1970).

Psychologists as scientists rarely express a belief in magic. Instead of relying on unexplained powers or conjecture, psychologists systematically investigate behavior. When an event apparently happens without reason, psychologists search for the reason. Those who believe in magic take such happenings as a sign of supernatural powers and seek no further explanations. Few psychologists believe in magic because magical phenomena defy explanation. Some people simply

As a discipline, psychology espouses a scientific world view. Religion and magic provide alternative views of the world.

dismiss those who believe in magic as superstitious; however, psychologists study magical beliefs and thinking to better understand and explain these interesting behaviors.

Religion

A third way to know about the world is through **religion.** Religion is based on faith, and knowledge comes from authorities, personal introspection and insight, and divine revelation. In magic the practitioner uses ritual and spells to intervene in the future, while in religion the practitioner uses ritual and prayers to ask God to intervene in the course of events (Yinger, 1970). In science, objective observations are used to verify knowledge, while religious proof comes from inner experience. As with magic, the approach of religion to knowledge defies independent verification. When what they want happens, religious persons say that God intervened; when intervention does not occur, religious persons say that God knew better than they did about what they needed.

Religion has been a prominent feature of past cultures and continues to be an important aspect of modern societies. Psychologists have dealt with religious issues in a va-

riety of ways. A number of prominent psychologists have studied and written about religious issues. In 1902, William James published his book, *Varieties of Religious Experience,* and in 1917 G. Stanley Hall published *Jesus, the Christ, in the Light of Psychology.* In addition to James and Hall, more recent psychologists such as Carl Jung, Gordon Allport, O. Hobart Mowrer, Abraham Maslow, Erich Fromm, Karl Menninger, and Rollo May have dealt with religious issues in their writings. Some psychologists incorporate a religious framework into their counseling practices. Division 36 of the American Psychological Association, a group of "psychologists interested in religious issues," is another way in which religious issues are a part of psychology. In contrast to these examples, a 1980 survey of thirty introductory psychology textbooks found no references to spiritual factors, and most of these books did not include religion or God in their subject indexes (Bergin, 1980).

Psychologists in their research studies have investigated a variety of religious issues such as mystical experiences, saintliness, prayer, glossolalia (speaking in tongues), religious dreams, meditation, religious persuasion, faith-healing, drug-stimulated religious experiences, religious influences in mental disorders, explanations of miracles, and the power of confession and forgiveness. As they do with magic, psychologists use the scientific approach to learn about individual differences between religious and non-religious individuals.

Most psychologists do not dismiss the ideas of magic and religion, but they prefer to gain their knowledge of behavior through applications of science. Beliefs and personal experiences are important to individual psychologists but collectively the discipline of psychology relies on objective observation and experimentation to reach its goals.

Things to Do

1. Obtain an issue of *Psychology Today* from your library or newsstand, and read one of the feature articles in the magazine. What was the main topic? What were the major points in the article? Could you relate the article's information to your own life or to other reading you have done? Did you agree with the author's position? What other kinds of information or examples do you wish had been included in the article?

2. Choose one of the books listed under *Things to Read.* Write a report summarizing the book's major points and your reactions to the book.

3. Learn about one of the important historical psychologists (e.g., Wilhelm Wundt, William James, Sigmund Freud, Carl Jung, Alfred Adler, Hermann von Helmholtz, Karen Horney, Anna Freud, Harry Harlow, Kurt

Lewin, Lewis Terman, Edwin Thorndike, Jean Piaget, Stanley Milgram, Fritz Perls, Ivan Pavlov, Gordon Allport) or a current, influential psychologist (e.g., Janet Spence, Roger Sperry, Judith Rodin, Erik Erikson, Carl Rogers, Carol Gilligan, Lawrence Kohlberg, Philip Zimbardo, Robert Zajonc, Elaine Walster, Robert Sternberg). Use the *Encyclopedia of Psychology,* general encyclopedias, articles in psychology journals, and books. Write a short report about the background of the psychologist you research.

4. Learn more about one of the pseudopsychologies (e.g., phrenology, palmistry, graphology, astrology), or develop your own pseudopsychology.

5. Ask a sociologist, psychologist, anthropologist, philosopher, and biologist to describe their views of the similarities and differences between their respective disciplines.

6. Make copies of the misconceptions quiz, and give them to other individuals to take. Which are the most common misconceptions?

7. Make a collection of newspaper and magazine clippings that relate to research and applied aspects of psychology. Which of the different perspectives in psychology are mentioned in the articles? What psychological topics are the main foci of popular concern?

Things to Discuss

1. Psychology is defined as the scientific study of the behaviors and mental processes of organisms. Do you think psychologists should study the behavior of plants? How would the study of plants be similar and dissimilar to the study of animals? If extraterrestrial beings exist, would psychologists study them, or would a new scientific discipline be needed?

2. What qualities differentiate human beings from other animals? If astronauts brought back beings from another planet, what do you think would be the criteria for deciding whether these creatures would be raised for food or given the rights and privileges of human beings?

3. How does psychology influence your life? List as many different ways as possible. Are most of these influences positive or negative?

4. Which of the five current perspectives seem most attractive to you at this time? Why?

5. How much of psychology is common sense? What evidence do you have to support your answer? Try supporting the opposite position.

6. What are the similarities and differences between psychology as a science and your personal religious beliefs? Do you believe that religion should attempt to prove itself scientifically? Do you believe that psychologists should study aspects of religion?

7. Why are pseudopsychologies and "pop psychologies" so popular? Do you believe that most people uncritically accept these ideas? Why? Of the pseudopsychologies, in which do you continue to believe? Why do you continue to believe in them?

Things to Read

Evans, R.I. 1976. *The making of psychology: Discussions with creative contributors.* NY: Knopf.

Guthrie, R.V. 1976. *Even the rat was white: A historical view of psychology.* NY: Harper & Row.

Hampden-Turner, C. 1981. *Maps of the mind.* NY: Macmillan.

Rubenstein, J. & Slife, B.D. 1982. *Taking sides: Clashing views on controversial psychological issues.* (2nd ed.). Guilford, CT: Duskin.

Watson, R.I. 1971. *The great psychologists* (3rd ed.). Philadelphia: Lippincott.

Review

Summary

1. Psychology is defined as the scientific study of behaviors and mental processes of organisms. Using scientific methodology, psychologists study both overt and covert behavioral processes in many different organisms.

2. Comparative psychologists study the behavior of various animal species in both their natural habitats and in the laboratory. Psychologists who work with animals must guard against anthropomorphism, the tendency to at-

38 FRAMEWORKS

PART ONE

tribute human characteristics to animals.

3. Pseudopsychologies are superficial systems that appear to resemble psychology but lack scientific validity. Astrology, biorhythms, blood typology, graphology, numerology, palmistry, phrenology, and physiognomy are examples of pseudopsychologies.

4. Pseudopsychologies persist for several reasons such as the overclaim of evidence, the overgeneralization of characteristics (especially positive characteristics), the fallacy of positive instances, and the fun of pseudopsychologies.

5. Philosophy is one of the major foundations of psychology. Psychology became a scientific discipline in 1879, when Wilhelm Wundt founded the first experimental psychology laboratory. The two earliest movements within psychology were structuralism and functionalism. Other important early movements included behaviorism, Gestalt, and psychoanalysis.

6. The five major current perspectives of psychology are biological, behavioral, psychodynamic, cognitive, and humanistic. Most psychologists are familiar with all five perspectives but focus their research and study within one or two of the perspectives.

7. The five goals of psychology are to describe, explain, predict, control, and apply.

8. Ph.D. psychologists work in a variety of settings, with the most common work environments being universities or colleges, hospitals or clinics, and private practice. The most common specialty area for psychologists is clinical or counseling psychology.

9. Psychologists receive training in graduate school programs, and psychiatrists receive training in medical school programs. Both psychologists and psychiatrists may become psychoanalysts.

10. Psychology has many historical and intellectual links to other academic disciplines such as sociology and anthropology are the social sciences.

11. Science, magic, and religion are three major modes for knowing and understanding the world. Science tries to understand the world by observing the seen world by the scientific method. Magic tries to use rituals to create changes in everyday situations. Religion involves beliefs and practices that deal with the ultimate conditions and meanings of existence.

Key Terms

psychology	psychodynamic perspective
comparative psychology	cognitive perspective
anthropomorphism	humanistic perspective
pseudopsychology	description
fallacy	explanation
of positive instances	prediction
empiricism	control
structuralism	application
functionalism	psychiatrists
behaviorism	psychoanalysts
Gestalt	science
psychoanalysis	magic
biological perspective	religion
behavioral perspective	

Focus Questions

1. How do your observations of people's behavior differ from observations made by psychologists?

2. With which of psychologists' methods of studying behavior are you most familiar?

3. What research problems would you encounter if you studied behavior in the same ways as psychologists study behavior?

4. If you were a subject in a research study, what ethical guidelines would you expect the psychologist to follow?

Chapter Outline

RESEARCH CONCEPTS
Objective Observation
Scientific Method—Hypothesis Testing
Theory and Law
Operational Definitions

RESEARCH METHODS
Naturalistic Observation
Case Studies
Correlational Method
Surveys and Sampling
Experimental Methods

RESEARCH PROBLEMS
Experimenter Bias
Subject Bias
Controlling Biases
Research and the Mass Media

RELATE: Research Ethics
Things to Do
Things to Discuss
Things to Read

REVIEW: Summary
Key Terms

Chapter 3

Research in Psychology

*We can be expected to look for truth
but not to find it.
Facts do not cease to exist because
they are ignored.*

Aldous Huxley

 Research Concepts

An introductory course in psychology includes the study of psychology's contents, research methods, and applications. This chapter examines the methods psychologists use as they study behavior.

Objective Observation

The research process in psychology begins with the everyday experience of observation. Psychologists observe the behavior of individuals in specific situations just as you might engage in "people watching" at shopping malls or airports. However, while you are free to conduct your observations of people in any manner you prefer and to speculate about the reasons for their behavior in any way you like, psychologists must follow specific guidelines for observing behavior.

41

One guideline psychologists follow is observing behavior objectively. **Objectivity** means that psychologists make observations without bias or subjectivity (personal point-of-view). While observing behavior, they attempt to set aside their own value systems and personal beliefs about the world. Making observations that are independent of the researcher's biases may be the most difficult aspect of psychological research.

Are you able to be an objective observer? Try to observe the behavior of others without going beyond what you actually observe; that is, leave out your personal assumptions and interpretations about the individuals you watch. Be certain to pay attention to all aspects of the behavior and the situation in which it occurs. Be certain also not to view the behavior of men differently than you view the behavior of women. Also, do not allow people's ages, races, clothing styles, heights, and weights to influence the way you interpret their behaviors. Are these requests impossible? Psychologists hope they are not impossible because they attempt to follow such criteria as part of objective observation.

Yet, like other people, psychologists may be unaware of how their personal beliefs are biasing their observations. Although psychologists try to be objective, they may not always succeed. Male researchers, for instance, tend to find more conformity and persuasibility in female subjects than do female researchers (Eagly & Carli, 1981). Because psychologists cannot totally remove subjectivity from their observations, they use careful research controls to minimize the effects of personal bias. In addition, research studies often are replicated (repeated) by other researchers to separate objective results from biased ones. If different researchers are able to obtain the same results when repeating the original experiment, then greater evidence exists for the objectivity of the original results.

Scientific Method—Hypothesis Testing

Objective observation is a major part of the **scientific method** used by psychologists to investigate questions about behavior. The scientific method is a process for identifying problems, formulating hypotheses, and conducting experiments to test hypotheses about behavior. From their own observations of people or from reading about other researchers' observations, psychologists identify a problem to investigate by using the scientific method. Often the problem is one involving the relationship between different variables (factors) affecting behavior. An experiment to investigate the relationship between the variables is designed; then, the results of the experiment are reported to other psychologists, who, on the basis of the new results, formulate new relationships to study. Thus the scientific method in psychology is an ongoing cycle of activities that leads to the discovery of new knowledge about behavior.

A second integral part of the scientific process is the **hypothesis**. A hypothesis is the researcher's tentative explanation of the relationship between the variables that he or she wants to study. The briefest definition of hypothesis is a "best educated guess." Hypotheses represent testable ideas about how the world operates. Through scientific research, hypotheses are either supported or, if unsupported, revised and tested again.

Since researchers may propose conflicting hypotheses on the same issue, research findings help determine which hypotheses are the most accurate explanations of behavior. An example of conflicting hypotheses is found in the current research on **schizoaffective disorder** (Meltzer, 1984). Persons with schizoaffective disorder display symptoms that are present in both schizophrenic patients (people who display disordered thinking and false perceptions) and in affective patients (people who display depression and manic behavior). Exhibit 3.1 reveals several of the conflicting hypotheses about schizoaffective disorder.

Researchers working with each of the hypotheses presented in Exhibit 3.1 can gather data or facts that will lead to greater understanding about schizoaffective disorder. During the fact-gathering process, some of the hypotheses will be eliminated or greatly modified because they will not be supported by the research findings. Other

EXHIBIT 3.1
Conflicting Hypotheses about Schizoaffective Disorder

1. An individual with schizoaffective symptoms has both schizophrenia and affective disorder.
2. An individual with schizoaffective symptoms has either schizophrenia or affective disorder.
3. An individual with schizoaffective symptoms has a variation of schizophrenia.
4. An individual with schizoaffective symptoms has a variation of affective disorder.
5. An individual with schizoaffective symptoms is in the middle of a continuum from "pure" schizophrenia to "pure" affective disorder.
6. An individual with schizoaffective symptoms has neither schizophrenia nor affective disorders, but suffers from a unique disorder.

Adapted from Meltzer, 1984. *Schizophrenia Bulletin, 10*, pp. 11–13.

hypotheses will be supported by data, and with enough support these specific statements about the relationships among the variables of schizoaffective disorder will appear less tentative and more conclusive as explanations of the disorder.

Theory and Law

Interrelated hypotheses that have been supported by research may be grouped together into a **theory**. A theory is a set of principles that organizes, explains, and predicts observed relationships among variables affecting behavior. Unlike individual hypotheses, theories imply a greater range of research support and a greater likelihood of truth, and they are therefore useful in explaining and predicting facts and in generating more research ideas. If a hypothesis is "an educated guess," then a theory is "a group of interrelated best guesses that have been supported by research."

Because theories represent tentative explanations, rival theories can co-exist in psychology. For instance, the psychoanalytic and behavioral interpretations of personality are quite different, yet both have received research support. Someday, however, psychologists may know enough about behavior and human nature so that only one theory of personality will exist. At that point, the one remaining theory will become a law of personality.

In science, a **law** is a theory that has been invariably supported by research while rival theories have failed to be supported. In physics, chemistry, and mathematics, many laws have been established. In psychology, on the other hand, few theories have been so consistently supported by research that they have become established as laws. In science, and especially in psychology, many more

hypotheses are tested than ever become part of a theory, and many more theories are formulated than ever become established as laws.

Sometimes psychologists create a different type of hypothesis to identify or explain unobservable, internal conditions that affect behavior. These explanations are called **hypothetical constructs** (intervening variables). Hypothetical constructs are inferences, concepts that explain internal connections between an environmental event and a person's behavioral response. Hypothetical constructs or intervening variables include intelligence, motivation, learning, and memory. Psychologists assume these hypothetical constructs intervene to mediate your behavioral responses. Yet you cannot point to them in yourself or in others; they are hypothetical. Many of the most interesting topics psychologists study—love, aggression, and creativity—are hypothetical constructs.

Operational Definitions

Hypotheses often require further definition before the relationships they represent can be investigated. The important terms in the hypothesis must be precisely defined so that others may know specifically what the researcher means when she or he uses those terms. These precise definitions are called **operational definitions**. In operational definitions, words are defined in terms of observable, measurable criteria. Operational definitions allow psychologists to compare their results, by enabling them to research the same phenomena.

Suppose that Dr. Noah Smokes and Dr. Nick O. Tine conduct separate studies on the effects of "heavy smoking" on verbal learning. If Dr. Smokes finds that "heavy smoking" has no effect and Dr. Tine observes that "heavy smokers" make three times as many errors in verbal learning tasks as nonsmokers make, which psychologist is correct? Is one psychologist's research inaccurate? Not necessarily.

The contradictory results could be explained by differences in each researcher's operational definition of "heavy smoker." If Dr. Smokes defines "heavy smokers" as those who smoke ten or more cigarettes each day while Dr. Tine defines "heavy smokers" as those who smoke at least two packs (or forty cigarettes) daily, the different outcomes of their experiments are not surprising. If Dr. Smokes and Dr. Tine report their research only in terms of "heavy smokers," they and others who read their research reports will be confused about the contradictory findings. However, in actual research studies the confusion would not exist because researchers like Dr. Smokes

---

Quick Study Aid

Brief Definitions of Hypothesis, Theory, and Law

Your retention of definitions will be better if you learn the briefest definitions possible. Use these brief definitions to remember the differences between hypothesis, theory, and law.

HYPOTHESIS—"best educated guess"
THEORY—"an interrelated group of hypotheses
                  supported by research"
LAW—"a theory invariably supported by research"

and Dr. Tine would include their operational definitions of "heavy smokers" in their research reports.

Some terms lend themselves to operational definition; others do not. Marriage is defined in terms of a legal license, but love is more difficult to put into observable, measurable terms. You probably have enough information to define operationally "an A student in psychology" (i.e., a 90% average on tests and projects), but you would have more difficulty defining in operational terms a good psychology student. Different students might create these operational definitions of "a good psychology student":

— Receives a B or an A for a course grade.

— Attends at least 80 percent of all class sessions.

— Spends at least six hours a week studying psychology.

— Asks at least two questions per week in class.

— Never falls asleep in class.

— Scores at the 70th percentile or higher on a standardized psychology test.

— Completes all assignments on time and writes adequately.

Although sometimes difficult to create, sound operational definitions help turn vague concepts into precise, measurable concepts.

Focus Question Answer

How do your observations of people's behavior differ from those made by psychologists? Psychologists strive for objective observations. They follow guidelines from the scientific method to assure that their observations will be independent of personal points-of-view and relatively free of bias. In your personal observations you do not need to follow such strict guidelines, nor do you need to create precise operational definitions of the terms you use.

  Research Methods

It is not only the observables and their relationships that may differ in each realm of experience, not only the definitions of space, time, state, and observer, but the very **methods of study** appropriate to each domain may differ. All methods are not suitable to all realms of experience, but each may be the only appropriate method for one or more (LeShan & Morganau, 1982, p. 146).

Psychologists have adapted many standard research methods to meet their specific research needs in studying behavior. As the authors of the quote observe, the methods developed by psychologists are suitable for psychology and are widely used in sociology and anthropology.

Naturalistic Observation

Naturalistic observation is a method for studying behavior in which a trained observer watches and records the behavior of subjects in their natural environments. The observer collects data without manipulating or changing the events that occur during the observation.

Consider the following fictitious study: Penelope did a naturalistic observation study at a banquet during an international conference of psychologists. Cherry pie was served for dessert, and Penelope noted how many diners began eating at the point of the pie and how many diners started elsewhere. Penelope also observed that nearly all the Americans turned their pie slices so the pie pointed toward themselves, and none of the other diners made this adjustment.

You could replicate this naturalistic observation by serving pie to some of your friends. Place a slice of pie in front of each person, making certain that the point of the pie faces away from the individual. When your guests begin eating, you will probably find that all the pie-eaters will first turn the points of the pie toward themselves. While your guests are eating, you will, of course, record their behaviors without manipulating or changing the elements of your naturalistic observation.

Have you observed behavior similar to that illustrated in the following example? Cary was watching people in the school cafeteria when he noticed that whenever Joe drank his cola, he looked into his glass. In contrast, Trudy looked over the top of her glass when she drank her cola. Cary observed eye-contact during drinking by other students in the room and noted that both looking-into and looking-over styles were common. Keeping a chart of these two drinking styles, he observed the behavior for males and females and discovered that the majority of males looked into their glasses while drinking, while the majority of females looked over their glasses. This description of differences in behavior between males and females is one of several sex differences discovered using naturalistic observation (Lindgren, 1969).

As the previous examples illustrate, naturalistic observation provides good descriptions of behavior, but this

EXHIBIT 3.2
Hypotheses about Behavior While Drinking

What would you speculate are the reasons that males are more likely than females to look into their glasses while drinking? Here are a few possibilities:

1. Men are clumsier and need to watch their beverages in order not to spill their drinks.

2. Women are more paranoid and scan the environment even while drinking so they can detect danger and potential enemies.

3. Males are more mathematically inclined and like to figure out when their glasses are half full, one-quarter full, and so forth.

4. Women are more socially oriented and look over their glasses to search for acquaintances with whom they can socialize.

5. Men are more paranoid about food and drink that is prepared for them, and they spend more time searching for bugs, crumbs, and other possible contaminants.

6. Drinking styles represent a genetically determined, biological sex difference.

method is unable to fulfill the other goals of psychology (explanation, prediction, control, and application). Cary discovered an interesting sex difference in drinking behavior, but from his observation alone he can not tell why the sex difference exists. However, Cary can speculate about the causes of the different drinking styles, and these speculations can then be translated into hypotheses that he can test by using other research methods such as experiments. Exhibit 3.2 lists possible hypotheses about why males are more likely than females to look into their glasses while drinking.

Naturalistic observation is often the beginning point for other research. After creating an objective description of behavior by using naturalistic observation, the researcher may brainstorm about possible causes for the observed behavior. The researcher then can decide which of the possibilities seems most likely and can develop a testable hypothesis.

On the other hand, good objective descriptions may be the only goal of a particular study. Jane van Lawick-Goodall (1971), who spent years studying chimpanzees in Tanzania, observed chimpanzee behaviors that could not have been seen in zoos or in laboratory experiments. Having observed a chimpanzee using a grass stem to invade a termite nest to catch termites, van Lawick-Goodall was the first scientist to confirm that chimpan-

zees use tools to gather food.

Like van Lawick-Goodall, anthropologists commonly use naturalistic observation to study other cultures because this method allows the scientist to gather data without changing the culture. Margaret Mead's (1935) early work with gender roles in nonwestern cultures of New Guinea illustrates how anthropologists use naturalistic observation. She observed several cultures in which the traditional American aggressive male and passive female roles were absent. Instead, Mead found that both males and females of the Arapesh culture were very aggressive and that women of the Tchambuli culture were more aggressive than men of that society.

An important aspect of good naturalistic observation is making certain that the subjects being observed are not affected by the presence of the researcher because people often change their behavior if they know they are being observed. One way to avoid this problem is to conceal the observer; for example, a researcher sometimes observes children playing at a daycare center by watching through a one-way mirror.

Another technique is for the observer to become a participant in the situation so that no one notices his or her presence. Imagine a researcher who is trying to determine the percentage of car drivers who make complete stops at stop signs. Would the researcher observe the same behavior while standing near the stop sign with clipboard in hand as he or she would while sitting on a bus stop bench, apparently working a crossword puzzle? The best procedure is for the observer to be unobtrusive so that the people being observed are less likely to deviate from their normal behavior. This procedure, however, and the use of hidden observers raise ethical questions about peoples' rights to privacy. Do psychologists violate subjects' rights to privacy by observing them without their prior knowledge or consent? To answer this question psychologists have devised a set of guidelines for the ethical treatment of subjects (APA, 1981). These ethical guidelines will be discussed later in this chapter.

In summary, the naturalistic observation method can provide rich, detailed descriptions of a wide range of behaviors in a variety of situations. This method helps create research topics and hypotheses and often can be used with topic areas unsuitable for experiments. However, naturalistic observation does entail disadvantages because the observer must be at "the right place at the right time," objective observation without modifying the behavior being observed is difficult to conduct, and the causes of the observed behavior cannot be discovered.

Case Studies

An intensive study of one subject is called a **case study** or the **clinical method**. This technique is used frequently to study the effects of therapy, the changes in behavior after injury or disease, or the personalities of individuals with atypical backgrounds. In Chapter 4 you will learn about "split-brain patients," individuals whose left and right hemispheres have been surgically separated to prevent severe damage from seizures. These patients have provided insight into the interactions between the left and right hemispheres of the brain, observations that could not have been obtained under other conditions. Similarly, people with war injuries, gunshot wounds, and brain tumors have provided case studies that have taught scientists much about the brain's functions. Case studies of individuals with mental disorders such as hypochondria, schizophrenia, multiple personality, and agoraphobia have provided psychologists with information about symptom patterns, possible causes of disorders, and the effects of various treatments.

As in naturalistic observation, objective observation is also important in case studies. Direct observation rather than third-person accounts assures greater accuracy. For years, anthropologists have received third-person descriptions of cannibalistic rituals and societies, yet no anthropologist has ever directly witnessed the cannibalism ritual. Recently, some anthropologists have suggested that cannibalism does not exist or, at least, is much rarer than previously thought. One researcher found nothing to confirm that "cannibalism was ever a customary part of any society, in any time or place" (Arens, 1979). As this example from anthropology illustrates, researchers need to be very cautious in their use of third-person accounts in case studies.

With both the clinical method and naturalistic observation, the representativeness of the subject is important. A single case study may not be representative of an entire group. Because one scientist observed one female praying mantis biting off a male's head after copulation, scientists believed for many years that this odd behavior always takes place after praying mantises mate. Recently, however, observations of greater numbers of mating praying mantises have shown that decapitation occurs in only a minority of cases. Thus, case studies, like naturalistic observations, can provide informative descriptions of behavior, but further research is often necessary to better understand the behavior.

The chief advantages of the clinical method are that psychologists can investigate unusual problems or events

and can gather intensive, in-depth information about single subjects. The main disadvantages of this method are that a case study may not be representative of a group and objectivity may be difficult to achieve.

Correlational Method

The **correlational method** is a research method used to establish relationships between two or more variables such as traits, events, or behaviors. Done in either natural environments or in laboratory situations, correlational studies have focused on the relationships between the amount of television viewing and the amount of aggressive behavior (as TV watching goes up, so does aggressive behavior), between hours of studying and scores on general psychology exams (more studying is associated with higher test scores), and between the number of weddings and suicides (both are most numerous in May–June).

In correlational studies, factors are examined for their co-relations, or links. Statistical procedures are used to find the associations among measured variables, and the resulting correlation coefficients can range from -1.00 to $+1.00$. A number close to zero indicates no relationship or a very weak relationship. As the coefficient approaches $+1.00$, a positive relationship exists, indicating that the two variables "vary" in the same direction—as one variable increases, the second variable also increases; as one variable decreases, the second variable also decreases. Graph A in Exhibit 3.3 illustrates the general direction of a positive correlation. A positive correlation exists for the relationship between studying and grades. Usually, the more you study, the better your grades will be.

EXHIBIT 3.3
Positive and Negative Correlations

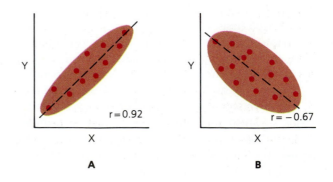

$r = 0.92$

$r = -0.67$

A

B

As the correlation coefficient approaches −1.00, a negative relationship exists, indicating that the two variables "vary" in opposite directions—as one variable increases, the other variable decreases. Graph B in Exhibit 3.3 illustrates the general direction of a negative correlation. A negative correlation exists for the relationship between amount of practice and golf scores. Typically, the more you play golf, the lower your golf score will be.

To summarize, + correlations indicate that both variables "move" in the same direction, while − correlations indicate that the variables "move" in opposite directions. The coefficient indicates the strength of the correlation, with numbers closer to 1 (+1 or −1) indicating stronger relationships. A correlation coefficient of −.67 is stronger than one of +.54. Correlation coefficients of +.43 and −.43 are equal in strength.

Correlation versus Causation   Strong correlation coefficients do not prove causation, even though they indicate a relationship. This frequent cause-and-effect error in reasoning can be attributed to the fact that most statistically analyzed variables might be explained by causation. A number of years ago George Snedecor, a statistician at Iowa State University, looked for examples to help students realize that even very strong correlation coefficients do not prove a cause-and-effect relationship between two variables. He looked for strong correlations that would not be readily interpreted as indicating cause and effect.

Snedecor found a correlation of over +.90 between the number of divorces per year and the number of bananas imported annually by the United States. Psychologists often think that a correlation over .30 is significant, and Snedecor found a nearly perfect correlation (+1.00) between bananas and divorces.

Consider which variable, bananas or divorces, could be the causative factor. Do you believe that eating bananas contributes to marital problems that lead to divorces? Do you believe that eating bananas can relieve some of the depression and anger people experience during divorce? Do you believe divorced individuals think that eating bananas will bring them good luck in their next relationships?

Even though you can predict very well in which year most divorces occurred if you know the number of bananas imported each year, the relationship between bananas and divorces probably is not a cause-and-effect relationship. In this example, the high correlation may be due to a third factor such as an increasing population over the years. A larger population each year would result in more people eating bananas and more people divorcing, even if the percentage of banana eaters and divorcing couples remained the same.

Many other highly correlated variables appear to be cause-and-effect relationships when they are not. IQ scores, for example, are correlated with the number of years of school completed, yet IQ alone does not get an individual through school—other factors such as effort, opportunity, internal motivation, and the expectations of others play a large role. Several years ago in Florida, a campaign to get politicians to outlaw cola sodas began because one man noticed that both the number of diagnosed cancer cases and the number of cola drinks being consumed were increasing. The man falsely assumed that drinking cola caused cancer.

Today, many individuals strongly believe that the full moon "causes" an increase in crime, aggression, mental illness, and bizarre behavior (Russell & Dua, 1983). Yet, on the basis of a review of thirty-seven studies on lunar cycles and behavior, two research psychologists discovered no evidence that the moon affects behavior

(Rotton & Kelly, 1985). According to this review, positive studies, such as one that concluded that more traffic accidents occur during full moons, were conducted in years when the full moons occurred on weekends, when many other factors related to weekend traffic patterns could be just as likely as the full moon to cause the increase in accidents.

As these illustrations indicate, correlational studies cannot be used to prove cause-and-effect relationships. Two variables may be linked together because one causes the other, because of their relationship to a third variable, or because of coincidence. Even when one variable appears to cause the second, the correlational method cannot confirm such a relationship. The relationship that Snedecor found between bananas and divorce is an excellent example of how very strong correlations can exist without a direct cause-and-effect relationship.

Do you believe that a full moon influences your behavior? Psychological research indicates that phases of the moon do not differentially influence human behavior.

Surveys and Sampling

Psychologists can use the **survey method** to measure many people on many variables. Using either written questionnaires or personal interviews, researchers ask about people's attitudes, beliefs, and behaviors. The Gallup, Roper, and Harris polls are three well-known examples of the survey method.

If every person in a group is surveyed, the researchers have surveyed the **population**. While a population could be everyone in a classroom, most populations are large groups of people. When the population is larger than several hundred people, surveying everyone in the group is usually not feasible. In these cases, researchers attempt to survey a **representative sample** of the population. To provide a representation of the total population, this sample must contain the same essential characteristics and proportions as the population. **Random sampling**, a procedure in which every individual in a population has an equal chance of being selected for the sample, is one way to create a representative sample.

How accurate are surveys? Some are quite accurate. Since 1954, the Gallup poll has erred by less than 2 percent in its predictions of the voting patterns of people in elections. Other surveys, however, have been quite inaccurate. In the 1936 presidential election, the magazine *Literary Digest* predicted that Franklin Roosevelt would be soundly defeated, yet he won by a landslide. The *Literary Digest* survey was conducted by telephone, and because of the Depression most people who owned telephones were economically well-off. Since people doing well economically were less likely to vote for Roosevelt than the average American, the sample was biased and produced inaccurate results. To obtain accurate survey results, researchers must have a representative sample. Do you think samples used by popular magazines such as *Ladies' Home Journal* or *Psychology Today* are representative of the general population of the United States?

In addition to securing a representative sample, researchers must also carefully word their questions so as not to bias the answers. The following questions are worded in ways that might influence the answers people give:

— "Should the federal government reduce military spending or should the country retain a strong defense against Communism?"

— "Which unacceptable sexual behaviors have you engaged in?"

— "Do you believe that women should be allowed to kill babies by abortion?"

These topics can be researched through surveys, but the wording of the survey questions should not influence the respondents' answers or inform them about which answers the researchers think are socially desirable.

Another problem with the survey method is the assumption that people remember how they behave and are aware of the motives behind their behaviors. Can you accurately reply to questions such as:

— "How many times a month do you date?"

— "How many lies do you tell in a week?"

— "When you were two, was your development normal for two-year-olds?"

— "How many times a day do you think about sex?"

— "What are your most central personality characteristics?"

— "How many hours do you study during a typical semester?"

People may want to be very accurate in their questionnaire responses and yet have to guess about some of the information. At other times, respondents may exaggerate the results or, because of self-consciousness, may distort or withhold true answers. Also, many people who participate in surveys try to give socially acceptable responses and be polite to the questioner. This **courtesy bias** is evident when potential voters give different responses about black and white candidates based on the racial background of the questioner (McKean, 1984).

Although the survey method is subject to flaws, carefully conducted surveys provide accurate data for making predictions about behavior. Like the methods of naturalistic observation and correlational studies, surveys also fulfill the goal of description. Also, like the pre-

ceding methods, surveys do not yield explanations of behavior.

Experimental Methods

Psychologists use the **experimental method** to provide explanations of behavior. In an experiment, the scientific method is used to establish the relationship between manipulated variables (called **independent variables**) and measured variables (called **dependent variables**), while other aspects (called **extraneous variables**) are controlled. Experiments ask the question, "Does the independent variable influence or affect the dependent variable?" This method is the only research method that provides information about causation.

Independent variables (IVs) are variables that the experimenter manipulates or varies in the experiment. The independent variable is the possible cause in the experiment. The dependent variables (DVs) are the

A farmer (experimenter) makes adjustments to his machinery; his adjustments (independent variable) affect the way his machinery operates (dependent variable).

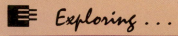

How to Read a Research Report

During this semester you may read a research report in one of the professional journals. Here are several tips for understanding research reports:

1. The title of the study sometimes helps you identify the independent and dependent variables. Many titles are in this format: "The effects of __IV__ on the __DV__." The title also identifies the subject matter of the study.

2. The abstract, which briefly summarizes the entire research study, provides a quick way for you to decide if the article is relevant to what you want to study. The abstract also helps you organize your reading of the report by summarizing the important information contained in the report.

3. The introduction gives the historical background of the research topic, provides a summary of relevant earlier research findings, offers theoretical explanations, and introduces the hypothesis of the present study.

4. The methods section contains a detailed description of how the study was conducted. The subjects used in the study are described, and the procedures of the study—the apparatus, directions to the subjects, and directions for conducting the experiment—are given. The methods section may mention assessment instruments or measuring devices used by the researchers.

5. The results section gives information about the data collected and the statistical procedures that were used. This section often includes charts, frequency tables, and bar graphs illustrating the results. Your mathematical and statistical background will determine how comfortable you are with the results section. You might want to pay attention to information about the level of significance as determined by statistical procedures. If the level of significance is given as p<.05, the results of the experiment would be found by chance fewer than five times out of a hundred. Similarly, if the level of significance is given as p<.01, the experimental results would be due to chance less than one time in one hundred.

6. The discussion section features the interpretation of results. In this section, the researchers present their personal assessments of the results. They may interpret their results from a particular theoretical perspective, or they may present alternative explanations for their data. The discussion section often includes comments about the limitations of the present research study and may suggest future research studies.

7. Finally, the references give bibliographic information about research studies reviewed and used by the authors. This section provides good sources of information if you want to learn more about the research topic.

---

measured outcome of the experiment; they are the effects of the independent variable.

Many everyday examples of independent and dependent variables exist. If you bake cookies, the oven temperature and baking time (IVs) influence the quality of the cookies (DV). If you plant tulips, the depth of the planting (IV) affects the height of the tulips and the size of the bloom (DVs). The number of hours you study (IV) affects your performance on an exam (DV). How much caffeinated coffee you drink (IV) affects how wide awake you feel during your eight o'clock class (DV). Try

Quick Study Aid

IVs and DVs

To remember the difference between an independent variable (IV) and a dependent variable (DV), picture a patient lying in a hospital bed with an IV in his arm. The patient's condition is DEPENDENT (DV) upon the IV (INDEPENDENT VARIABLE). The IV is the cause of the effects on the patient.

EXHIBIT 3.4
Independent and Dependent Variables

Can you identify the independent and dependent variables in these questions?

> **1. Does noise level affect subjects' ability to learn a list of nonsense syllables?**
>
> **2. Does alcohol consumption affect the number of errors on a maze learning task?**
>
> **3. Does playing video games influence brain wave patterns?**

ANSWERS:

> **1.** IV = noise level; DV = learning of nonsense syllables.
>
> **2.** IV = alcohol consumption; DV = maze learning errors.
>
> **3.** IV = playing video games; DV = brain wave patterns.

identifying the independent and dependent variables in Exhibit 3.4.

Extraneous variables are all the variables the experimenter wants to prevent from affecting the experiment. Extraneous variables need to be controlled or eliminated. If you are interested in whether your tulip bulbs grow better when planted four, six, or eight inches deep, you should make sure that all other conditions for the bulbs are equal. All bulbs should be planted in similar soil, at the same time of the year, and in locations with equal amounts of sunlight and rainfall. If variables other than the independent variable differ, the results of experiment may not be due to the independent variable.

Experiments involve both **experimental and control groups**. A control group provides a baseline against which the behavior of subjects in an experimental group is compared. In a simple experiment, the control group is not exposed to the independent variable while the experimental group is. Except for this difference in exposure, the control group and the experimental group are treated exactly alike.

Experiments use one or more control groups to provide comparison groups against which experimental group results can be measured. Without control groups, researchers cannot conclude whether the independent variable produced significant results.

A psychologist might begin an experimental study in the following way: "Hmmmm, I seem to learn more quickly after I drink caffeinated coffee." This observation becomes the hypothesis that "a moderate amount of caffeine improves memory." The psychologist then creates operational definitions for "a moderate amount of caffeine" (two ten-ounce cups of coffee) and "memory" (subject's performance on a test of a thirty-item word list studied for twelve minutes). Next, he or she chooses subjects and gives the experimental group the two cups of caffeinated coffee. The researcher uses two control groups; one group receives no beverage and one group receives two cups of decaffeinated coffee (see Exhibit 3.5). Next, the researcher tests the subjects on the word-list test. Finally, he or she analyzes the data to assess if the experimental group's performance on the memory task is significantly better than the performance of either control group.

In experimental studies, statistical procedures are used to decide if an independent variable produces a

EXHIBIT 3.5
Sample Study—Caffeine and Memory

Subjects Chosen Randomly from a Large Population

	CONTROL GROUP I	CONTROL GROUP II	EXPERIMENTAL GROUP
INDEPENDENT VARIABLE	GIVEN NO BEVERAGE	GIVEN 2 CUPS OF DECAFFEINATED COFFEE	GIVEN 2 CUPS OF CAFFEINATED COFFEE
	STUDY WORD LIST	STUDY WORD LIST	STUDY WORD LIST
DEPENDENT VARIABLE	PERFORMANCE ON WORD LIST TEST	PERFORMANCE ON WORD LIST TEST	PERFORMANCE ON WORD LIST TEST

Laboratory experiments may use either people or animals as subjects.

the horn. (Usually motorists wait longer before showing impatience with drivers of older cars.)

— A shoplifting incident is staged near males and females to determine which gender is more likely to report the incident to a store employee. (Females in groups are more likely to report the theft than individual females, but individual males are more likely to report the theft than males in groups. Family groups are most likely to report the shoplifting incident.)

— Persons dropped coins in elevators to see if other riders will help pick up the coins. (As the number of other elevator riders increases, assistance in picking up the dropped coins decreases.)

Unobtrusive Measurements **Unobtrusive measurements** are those that can be obtained without disturbing the subjects and without their awareness. Unobtrusive measurements can be made by studying the people's impact on the environment and by studying the artifacts they produce and discard (Webb et al., 1981). The following are a few creative examples of unobtrusive measurements.

— *Beer Consumption.* Researchers wanted to know the relationship between reported beer consumption and actual consumption of beer; therefore they measured re-

significant change in the dependent variable. Results are considered significant when differences between the experimental and control groups are unlikely to be the result of chance. The statistical procedures used by psychologists are described in the Appendix.

Laboratory and Field Experiments   Many psychological experiments are performed in laboratory settings where the researchers have maximum control over the variables in the experiment. The primary disadvantage of this approach is that the experimental situation may be artificial. Therefore, researchers often conduct **field experiments**, more realistic experiments in natural settings outside the laboratory. Although field experiments involve less control of important variables, they provide a more authentic environment for experimentation. The following are examples of field experiments:

— Drivers of old versus new cars remain stopped when a traffic light turns green; the dependent variable is the number of seconds until an impatient motorist honks

Try this field experiment. For several days, visit the library and sit at a table at which one person is already seated. During alternate trials, sit in the chair indicated by the red arrow or the blue arrow. Document the number of minutes until the person leaves the table. Studies indicate that the person will leave sooner when you sit in the chair with the red arrow than when you sit in the chair with the blue arrow. How would you explain these results?

ported beer consumption by conducting a house-to-house survey and measured actual beer consumption by counting beer cans in the garbage. Only 15 percent of the households reported beer consumption, yet 77 percent of the trash cans contained beer cans—in fact, in 54 percent of the households, trash cans contained at least eight beer cans (Rathje & Hughes, 1975).

— *Television's Effects on Reading.* One way to look at television's effects on reading is to look at library withdrawals. Researchers found that as the amount of reported television viewing increased, the checkout rate of fiction titles dropped, but the checkout rate of nonfiction titles remained the same (Webb et al., 1981).

— *Popularity of Museum Exhibits.* A Chicago museum estimated the popularity of various exhibits by comparing how often floor tiles around each exhibit needed to be replaced. Museum officials assumed that wear-and-tear of tiles correlated with the number of visitors to particular exhibits (Webb et al., 1981).

— *Mummy Studying.* Are you aware that scientists are facing a shortage of mummies to study? Once millions of mummies existed, but now only a few thousand remain. Since the fifteenth century, wrappings of mummies have been used to cure nausea, head wounds, and other ailments, and, until the 1970s, mummies could be pur-

chased for forty dollars an ounce in occult shops. Other mummies have been burned for locomotive fuel or had their linen wrappings recycled into paper. Many mummies have been sold as artifacts and relics or have been destroyed.

Why do scientists want to study mummies? The bones are examined for indications of diseases, injuries, abuse, diet changes, and medicines. Scientists can discover much about the lifestyles and behaviors of ancient peoples by studying mummy remains. For example, "mummy studiers" discovered by analyzing mummy remains that the modern antibiotic tetracycline was used by the Sudanese more than four thousand years ago (Webb et al., 1981).

Unobtrusive measurement, such as mummy study and examination of trash can contents, is a subtle, but difficult, way to study behavior. In the museum study, for example, extraneous variables could account for the wear-and-tear on the tiles. Floor tiles in a museum may wear more quickly near popular exhibits, but the tiles also will wear more quickly near water fountains, restrooms, and exits. Museum officials may conclude that a particular exhibit is popular because of the wear on the floor tile when the actual cause of the increased traffic is a nearby restroom. Yet, in spite of their limitations, unobtrusive measurements remain an ingenious way to study human behavior.

Psychologists study mummies to learn how people behaved in other times and places.

Exploring...

The Lost Letter Technique

The **lost-letter technique** has been used by psychologists since 1948, when it was developed to measure the honesty of people mailing lost letters that seemed to contain coins. The lost-letter technique involves "losing," in public places, stamped, unmailed letters addressed to individuals or committees representing specific attitudes. The differential rates of return for the letters reflect a measure of a community's attitudes toward the issue being studied. Typically, the letters are placed in shopping center stores or under windshield wipers of parked cars with an attached note reading "Found this next to your car."

Summary of Results

Group:	Number Returned:	Percent Returned:
1. Committee for the KKK	11	37
2. Committee for the NAACP	25	83
3. C. Simmons (Control)	26	87

Adapted from Table 1, Simmons & Zumpf, 1983, The lost letter technique revisited, *Journal of Applied Social Psychology, 13*, p. 513.

A recent lost-letter technique study (Simmons & Zumpf, 1983) done in Denver, Colorado, measured the return rate of letters addressed to the NAACP (a civil rights group), the KKK (a white supremacist group), and C. Simmons (the control group). Each group "lost" thirty letters, each letter was addressed to the same post office box number, and each letter contained the same message, which read:

> It has come to my attention that the film which was scheduled for our meeting may not be available. In case the film does not arrive, we should line up some speakers who are knowledgeable on the subject. There are only a few weeks left to work on this, so please be sure to get to all the meetings. Feel free to bring any guest who would be interested.
> (Simmons & Zumpf, 1983, p. 512).

As shown in the accompanying table, the letters addressed to the Committee for the KKK were returned less often than the letters addressed to the other two groups. The researchers interpreted the results as a rejection of the KKK (Simmons & Zumpf, 1983).

 ## Research Problems

Experimenter Bias

Although experimenters try to be objective in their research, they can inadvertently produce biased results. **Experimenter bias** can occur because of the way the experimenter gives directions to subjects or because of very subtle nonverbal gestures during the experiment. In one study of experimenter bias (Rosenthal, 1966), student research assistants were led to believe they were testing the abilities of "smart" and "dull" rats. The student researchers obtained better performances from the "smart" rats than the "dull" rats, although in fact the rats had been randomly assigned to the "smart" and "dull" groups. The students did not cheat; instead, un-

knowingly, the students handled the "smart" and "dull" rats differently.

Experimenters, like teachers with their students and parents with their offspring, may communicate their expectations to their subjects, who in turn behave according to the experimenter's expectations. This condition is known as **self-fulfilling prophecy.** The biasing effect of self-fulfilling prophecies was demonstrated in an experiment in which classroom teachers were told that, based on test results, they could expect some of their students to "bloom" during the school year (Rosenthal & Jacobson, 1968). Those students who were expected to "bloom" did, in fact, perform better, even though they had been randomly picked from among their classmates. As these examples show, researchers' expecta-

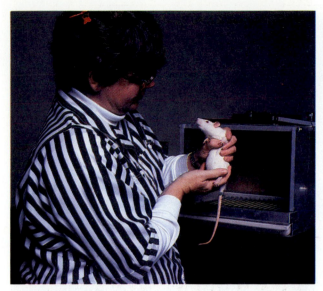

Experimenter bias can influence research results if it differentially influences the treatment of the subjects.

tions can unwittingly influence the behavior of their subjects, both human and animal, and produce biased results.

Subject Bias

One type of subject bias occurs because subjects try to please the experimenter and behave according to the experimenter's expectations rather than behave as they typically would. Some subjects behave in ways they think will look "normal" to the psychologist. Especially on sensitive topics such as political attitudes, sexual behaviors, and mental symptoms, subjects may not reveal all their beliefs and behaviors and may attempt to control the image they present to the experimenter.

A minority of subjects are "bad subjects" in that they set out to give false or misleading answers. Subjects may resent being part of a psychological study, and they may purposely sabotage the study by giving false responses. However, many more subjects are "good subjects" than "bad subjects." If you have the opportunity to participate in a research study, you will have first-hand experience with subject bias.

Controlling Biases

One way to control subject bias is to use placebos. A **placebo** is an inert substance or fake treatment used to make a control group more similar in appearance to the experimental group. In the hypothetical experiment on the effects of caffeine (Exhibit 3.5) , one of the control groups received a placebo of decaffeinated coffee. If the group receiving the decaffeinated coffee performed similarly to the other control group and below the experimental group, the researchers could conclude that the caffeine, not drinking a warm beverage, caused the memory improvement.

Although placebos have no medicinal effect, they sometimes have a psychological impact called the **placebo effect.** In a study of the placebo effect and pain (Beecher, 1959), 58 percent of 4,588 subjects given placebos reported relief from their headache symptoms. In the entire study, which included several different tests, about one-third of all the patients treated with placebos reported positive results. Placebo injections were even effective in controlling the pain of 43 percent of the cancer patients in the study as compared with 65 percent who experienced pain relief from morphine injections.

Both subject and experimenter bias can be controlled by using single- and double-blind techniques. In **single-blind studies,** the subjects are unaware of the experimental conditions in which they have been placed. This procedure reduces the effects of subject bias. In **double-blind studies**, the experimenter, as well as the subjects, does not know which group is the experimental or the control group. Under this condition both subject bias and experimenter bias can be controlled. In addition, the experimenter can use tape-recorded instructions to assure that the subjects not only hear the same instruction but hear them spoken in the same way. Through rigorous control procedures, researchers can minimize both experimenter and subject bias.

Research and the Mass Media

The results of psychological research are discussed daily in television news reports and interviews and are written about frequently in newspapers and magazines. How accurately does the popular press report on psychological research studies? The degree of accuracy varies tremendously, and as a wise consumer of psychology in the popular press, you need to be aware of typical reporting errors:

1. Sensational studies are reported more often than more ordinary findings. This tendency to report unusual findings may give readers a false impression of typical results from psychological research.

 *Exploring . . .*

The Golden Fleece Award

When is research valuable, and when is research a waste of time, effort, and money? Since 1975, Senator William Proxmire has awarded a monthly Golden Fleece Award to point out wasteful federal spending. Research grants from the National Science Foundation, National Institute for Mental Health, and other similar agencies have been frequent targets. Some of the studies that have received the Golden Fleece Award are studies in the social sciences.

— 1975—An $84,000 grant to find out why people fall in love.

— 1975—A $102,000 study of the effects of alcohol on aggressive behavior of sunfish, and a $90,000 study to determine whether young rats are more likely than adult rats to drink alcohol to reduce anxiety.

— 1976—A grant to study the aggression of drivers caught in traffic jams.

— 1977—A $27,000 study to determine why inmates want to escape from prison.

— 1977—A $2,500 study to discover why people are rude, cheat, and lie at tennis courts.

— 1978—Part of a $97,000 grant to study the behavior and social relationships in a Peruvian brothel.

— 1978—Use of federal tax dollars to exercise pregnant pigs on treadmills to relieve boredom and psychological stress.

— 1978—$219,592 to develop a curriculum package to teach college students how to watch television.

— 1979—Over $6,000 to determine if marijuana smoking has a bad effect on scuba divers.

— 1979—$90,000 over two years to study "Behavioral Determinants of Vegetarianism."

— 1980—A grant to study why bowlers, pedestrians, and hockey fans smile.

— 1982—A $40,000 study called "Food Preferences and Social Identity."

— 1984—A $465,000 study to identify the effects of orthodontia on psychosocial functioning.

— 1985—$160,000 study to determine whether someone can "hex" an opponent during a strength test by drawing an X on the opponent's chest.

After reading the list of award winners, you might vote to forbid any federal tax dollars for behavioral science research. Yet opponents of Proxmire's Golden Fleece Award argue that Proxmire misleads the public about what the chosen research studies actually involve. Frequently, the studies are taken out of the context of larger research studies, and Senator Proxmire does not attempt to inform the public about the possible relevancy of the studies.

For example, Proxmire's March 1975 award went to respected psychologist Ellen Berscheid for her National Science Foundation grants, totaling over $80,000, to study the psychological factors contributing to the country's growing divorce rate. Berscheid's serious research was called the "Federal Love Machine" in Proxmire's press release, in which the senator commented that "why people fall in love should be left to Elizabeth Barrett Browning."

Do not be misled. The studies chosen by Senator Proxmire represent a very small percentage of the millions of federal research dollars granted to social scientists each year. In the vast majority of these cases, the funds are used wisely. Reports of these latter studies appear daily in the media, and the results are relevant to people's lives. The Golden Fleece Awards tarnish the image of social science research that has studied the effects of divorce on children, the psychological risk factors in stress and heart disease, the effectiveness of treatments for drug and alcohol abuse, and countless other socially valuable topics.

2. Media reports of psychological studies often give only partial information. The report may fail to include information about the source of the study, the type of study, and the procedures used. Without complete information, readers cannot make independent conclusions about the quality of the research.

3. Correlational studies are often reported in ways that lead readers to believe the studies found cause-and-effect relationships when they did not.

4. Sometimes one person's opinion or one graphic case study is offered as proof for a conclusion. You need to be able to distinguish between experiments, correlational studies and surveys, case studies, and one researcher's "armchair" observations.

5. Some reports oversimplify studies or overgeneralize the results.

6. Many reports fail to distinguish adequately between observations and inferences.

To the mass media's credit, most major networks, newspapers, and magazines employ science reporters and editors who are skilled in presenting psychological and other scientific information to the public. The major difficulty they must overcome is condensing the original material into a much shorter presentation because essential elements of the experiment and important distinctions about the meaning of the results may be lost in the condensation. If you want to be certain of what the researcher discovered, you must read the original research report for yourself.

 *Relate*

Research Ethics

The following is the first paragraph to the Preamble in the *Ethical Principles of Psychologists,* published by the American Psychological Association (APA) in 1981. All members of the APA pledge to follow this code:

> Psychologists respect the dignity and worth of the individual and strive for the preservation and protection of fundamental human rights. They are committed to increasing knowledge of human behavior and of people's understanding of themselves and others and to the utilization of such knowledge for the promotion of human welfare. While pursuing these objectives, they make every effort to protect the welfare of those who seek their services and of the research participants that may be the object of study. They use their skills only for purposes consistent with these values and do not knowingly permit their misuse by others. While demanding for themselves freedom of inquiry and communication, psychologists accept the responsibility this freedom requires: competence, objectivity in the application of skills, and concern for the best interests of clients, colleagues, students, research participants and society. In the pursuit of these ideals, psychologists subscribe to principles in the following areas: (1) responsibility, (2) competence, (3) moral and legal standards, (4) public statements, (5) confidentiality, (6) welfare of the consumer, (7) professional relationships, (8) assessment techniques,

(9) research with human participants, and (10) care and use of animals.

The first paragraph of the Preamble to the *Ethical Principles of Psychology* describes the ethical goals of professional psychologists. These goals include concerns about general research ethics, human and animal subject rights, and the nature of psychology's goals and limitations.

Deception

Psychologists, especially social psychologists, have sometimes used *deception* in their research studies. Subjects are either directly misled through the directions given or through statements about the purpose of the research, or they are indirectly misled through the general appearance of the research. Deception can involve mislabeling psychological assessment instruments or using experimental *confederates,* people employed by the researcher who pretend to be "real" research subjects.

For example, in a classic study of conformity (Asch, 1955), subjects were asked to judge which of three lines matched a fourth one. All of the subjects in each group were confederates except one. The experimenter instructed the confederates to answer incorrectly to determine whether the "real" subject would conform (also answer incorrectly). Most subjects experienced some discomfort in the situation, and more than one-third of the subjects went against their own perceptions to agree with the answers given by the confederates.

Although most studies are done without deceiving subjects, some studies could not be accomplished without the use of deception. Proponents of allowing deception argue that the need to understand human behavior is more important than the temporary use of deception. They also suggest that most subjects would agree to be deceived during an experiment in order to participate in the experiment.

Ideally, psychologists would tell future subjects how deception will be used, get the subjects' permission, and then remove prior knowledge of deception and run the experiment. Since this procedure is impossible, the next best alternative is to use deception and then inform subjects about it after the experiment. At the very least, deception in psychological research should be kept at a minimum, and all subjects should be informed about the deception as soon as their role in the experiment is finished.

Invasion of Privacy

To keep subjects' research responses confidential, psychologists need to maintain effective security of written, taped, and videotaped materials that could reveal the identities of subjects. Special concerns about **invasion of privacy** arise in studies involving naturalistic observation, field experiments, and unobtrusive measures because these methods usually involve research designs in which subjects do not know they have participated in a psychological study.

Lasting Effects

Psychological research should minimize the distress felt by subjects. Because psychologists are unable to predict which studies will cause subjects discomfort or distress, eliminating all unpleasant experiences for subjects is probably impossible. A reasonable approach to this problem is to inform subjects before the experiment begins about the positive and negative effects of participating in the study so that the subjects may decide whether or not to participate in the study.

Rights of Human Subjects

Human subjects in psychological research have four basic rights: voluntary participation, confidentiality, informed consent, and debriefing. Psychologists should make every attempt to guarantee these human rights.

All psychology research should be conducted only with volunteers. Earlier practices of requiring introductory psychology students to participate in research studies or making prisoners participate in research studies are now considered unethical. Also, subjects' responses during the experiment should be kept anonymous and confidential and should not be used to determine employment or grades. Subjects always have the right to withdraw from the experiment at any time.

Subjects should give **informed consent** before they participate in a study. In other words, before subjects agree to participate, they should be informed of the basic characteristics of the study and the possible exposure to unpleasant stimuli. In addition, all subjects should be told that they have the right to withdraw their consent at any time during the study. Children and other individuals incapable of giving informed consent can be used as research subjects only with a parent's or guardian's consent. This protection of minors is so important that federal government regulations prohibit a researcher from going into high schools to ask students questions about sensitive topics such as drug use and sexual behaviors.

Finally, subjects are entitled to receive appropriate debriefing at the conclusion of their participation in the experiment. **Debriefing** means subjects are again told about the purpose of the study and are made aware of any deceptions used in the experiment. Researchers may also offer to inform subjects about the results of the study.

Animal Rights

The ethical guidelines for research with human subjects do not apply to animal subjects because animals do not volunteer to be research subjects, and advised consent is meaningless in the context of animal research.

The majority of psychologists carefully guard research animal rights, and the A.P.A. has adopted guidelines for the care and use of animals in research. Nonpsychologists also monitor the research being done with animals in various scientific disciplines, and the United States government has developed animal rights policies that must be adhered to in order to receive federal grants.

The housing and treatment of research animals is strictly regulated by governmental and professional agencies.

Ethical Concerns

Two ethical concerns about psychological research are: (1) Should psychology strive to be morally neutral? (2) Should psychologists (and others) not study some topics? On both issues, psychologists hold a wide range of beliefs (Steininger et al., 1984).

For example, while some psychologists emphasize that science must be neutral and objective, Abraham Maslow (1969) argued that psychology should not be morally neutral. Maslow said: "I am convinced that the value-free, value-neutral, value-avoiding model of science that we inherited from physics, chemistry, and astronomy, where it was necessary and desirable to keep the data clean...is quite unsuitable for the scientific study of life...where personal values, purposes and goals, intentions and plans are absolutely crucial for the understanding of any person and even for the classical goals of science, prediction, and control" (p. 725). While many psychologists agree with Maslow's position, many others disagree.

Another of the most fundamental ethical issues is whether restrictions on scientific research topics should be established. Do psychologists have a "right to know"? Some scientists believe that the more relevant issue is not whether scientists have a right to know but rather whether scientists have an "obligation to know." Psychologists generally believe that they should strive to replace speculation with fact. To be true to their goals, psychologists have an obligation to describe, explain, and make predictions about behavior so that knowledge may be applied to helping people achieve greater control of their lives.

Things to Do

1. On the same research topic, design a naturalistic observation study, a correlational study, a survey study, a laboratory experiment, a field experiment, and a study using unobtrusive measurements. What are the advantages and disadvantages of each of your research designs?

2. Read a research study in a psychology journal (e.g., *Journal of Personality and Social Psychology, Journal of Counseling Psychology, Journal of Abnormal Psychology, Journal of Developmental Psychology*), using the material from "How to Read a Research Report" as a guideline. In your written report, be sure to include the main points of the study and your personal reactions to the research findings.

3. With three other students, try to agree upon operational definitions for several terms such as "light sleeper," "good lover," or "good parent."

4. Find several newspaper articles featuring psychological research findings. Did the press cover the studies well? Are the explanations clear? Discuss your articles with others in your class to see if they evaluate the articles as you do.

5. Choose a current political or social concern, and design a study to obtain information about the issue (e.g., What are the effects of crowded prisons? How can schools help children learn? How does the threat of nuclear war affect children?).

6. Try one of the studies mentioned in the chapter, such as observing whether males and females tend to use different eye-contact strategies while drinking. Discuss your results in class, and compare them to the results obtained by your classmates.

7. Find two or more surveys in popular magazines such as *Ladies' Home Journal, Psychology Today,* and *Cosmopolitan.* How well-written are the questionnaire items? Do you think the results will contain a representative sample of the general public? Based on your sample surveys, do you think that surveys in popular magazines are accurate.

Things to Discuss

1. What research guidelines, in addition to those discussed in this chapter, would you establish to ensure ethical conduct in research?

2. As a subject in survey studies and experiments, would you be cooperative, mischievous, deceptive, or indifferent? In what kinds of research would you refuse to participate?

3. How do anthropologists, sociologists, and psychologists differ in their research strategies? How are they similar.

4. How might you test the saying "Too many cooks spoil the broth"? Identify the independent, dependent, and extraneous variables; operationally define your terms; identify the experimental and control groups. Can you generalize the results to other situations? Would you expect the same results with spaghetti?

5. Now that you have read about experimenter bias, do you notice similar biases from teachers, parents, employers, or friends?

6. Discuss the following quotations about science:
   a. "No amount of experimentation can ever prove me right; a single experiment can prove me wrong." Albert Einstein

b. "If I have been able to see farther than others, it was because I stood on the shoulders of giants." Sir Isaac Newton

c. "Truth in science can be defined as the working hypothesis best suited to open the way to the next better one." Konrad Lorenz

d. "Science is the refusal to believe on the basis of hope." C. P. Snow

e. "We have to live today by what truth we can get today and be ready tomorrow to call it falsehood." William James

7. Do psychologists have a responsibility to monitor the applications of psychology? Are psychologists obligated to make certain that psychological findings are used in ethical ways?

Things to Read

Barnes, J.A. 1979. *Who should know what?: Social science, privacy and ethics.* Cambridge, England: Cambridge University Press.

Brown, C. & Adams, W.R. 1968. *How to read the social sciences.* NY: Scott Foresman.

Gardner, M. 1975. *Fads and fallacies in the name of science.* Mineola, NY: Dover.

Hall, E. 1978. *Why we do what we do: A look at psychology.* Boston: Houghton Mifflin.

Kimble, C.A. 1978. *How to use (and misuse) statistics.* Englewood Cliffs, NJ: Prentice-Hall.

McCain, G. & Segal, E.M. 1969. *The game of science.* Monterey, CA: Brooks/Cole.

Review

Summary

1. Objective observation consists of observing behavior without allowing personal beliefs and values to interfere with what is perceived.

2. Research hypotheses are tentative explanations of the relationships between two or more variables. A group of interrelated hypotheses, supported by research, that predict and explain behavior form a theory. A theory that is invariably supported by research becomes a law.

3. Psychologists use operational definitions to define important concepts in terms of measurable, observable quantities. These definitions help psychologists communicate clearly their findings with other psychologists.

4. In the naturalistic observation method, trained observers watch and record behavior as it naturally occurs in the environment. Because of the importance of avoiding observer effects, naturalistic observation is done without intervening in the situation. Although this method provides rich descriptive information and often helps generate research ideas, the observed events may not be representative, and they may occur at inopportune times.

5. The case study or clinical method is an intensive study of a single case and is typically used to examine the effects of therapy and to study unusual behaviors and people. Disadvantages are: the case may not be representative, subjective interpretation is involved, and the situation may not be adequately controlled.

6. The correlational method examines the relationship between two or more variables by using statistical procedures. This method provides useful descriptions and predictions but cannot be used to determine a cause-and-effect relationship.

7. Through surveys, information can be collected from a large number of people. The quality of the questions and the representativeness of the subject sample are important in determining the value of a survey. Respondents may give socially desirable responses instead of accurate responses.

8. The experimental method is used to establish the relationship between the independent variable (which is manipulated by the experimenter) and the dependent variable (the subject's response) while other extraneous variables are held constant. The experimental process is the only research method that provides information about causation.

9. Experimental groups and control groups are treated exactly alike except with respect to the independent variable. The experimental and control groups receive different levels or conditions of the independent variable.

10. Psychologists have greatest control in laboratory experiments, but field experiments usually provide more natural settings for research.

11. Psychologists may use unobtrusive measures such as garbage and other remains of civilization to study behavior indirectly.

12. Typical research problems include experimenter bias, subject bias, and the placebo effect. Single-blind and double-blind experimental procedures are used to minimize research bias.

13. Popular press errors in reporting psychological findings include news coverage of sensational findings, partial information about how a study was conducted, and incorrect interpretations of the findings. Other common errors include using correlations to illustrate cause-and-effect, using a case study as proof of a general conclusion, and failing to distinguish between observations and inferences.

14. Psychologists pledge to follow ethical guidelines for research. Researchers should avoid deception, invasion of privacy, and undue harm to subjects. Human subjects have the right to be in studies voluntarily, to have their responses remain confidential, to give informed consent, and to be debriefed at the end of the study.

Key Terms

objectivity
scientific method
hypothesis
theory
law
hypothetical constructs
operational definition
naturalistic observation
case study
clinical method
correlational method
survey method
representative sample
random sampling
experimental method
independent variable (IV)
dependent variable (DV)
extraneous variable
experimental and control groups
field experiments
unobtrusive measurements
experimenter bias
self-fulfilling prophecy
subject-bias
placebo effects
single-blind studies
double-blind studies

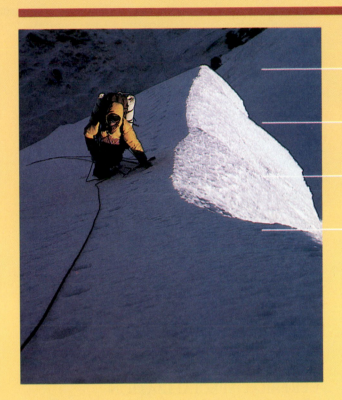

Part Two

The Mind-Body Connection

Focus Questions

1. What are the advantages of the newer brain research techniques?

2. In what ways do neurochemicals control your behavior?

3. How do your endocrine and autonomic systems work together to regulate your behavior?

4. Is any part of your central nervous system more important than other parts?

5. Which parts of your brain do you use when you speak?

6. Do you have one brain or two?

Chapter Outline

THE NERVOUS SYSTEM
The Major Divisions
Research Methods

THE NEURON AND NEURAL PROCESSING
The Neuron
Neural Transmission of Information
Synaptic Transmission
Neurotransmitters and Neuromodulators

THE ENDOCRINE AND AUTONOMIC SYSTEMS
Neuroendocrine System
Pituitary Gland
Adrenal Glands
Autonomic Nervous System

THE CENTRAL NERVOUS SYSTEM
Spinal Cord
Brainstem
Subcortical Structures
Cerebral Cortex

CEREBRAL SPECIALIZATION
Cortical Lobes
Language Specialization
The Research Process: The Split Brain

RELATE: Left Brain/Right Brain/Whole Brain
Things to Do
Things to Discuss
Things to Read

REVIEW: Summary
Key Terms

The Biology of Behavior

*The left side (of your brain) controls
the right side of your body and the
right controls the left half. . .
Therefore, left handers are the only
people in their right minds.*

Bill Lee

The Nervous System

Have you ever stopped to marvel at your ability to perform extremely complex activities with relative ease? Consider your actions in opening this book and reading these sentences. In one sense, you opened the book, found your place, and began reading "without thinking"; yet that sequence of actions required the coordination of many processes in your brain and elsewhere in your body. The act of reading is itself immensely complex. How are you able to engage in such complex activities with such ease?

Physiological psychologists (be sure to note the difference between *physio-* and *psycho-*) seek the answer to

65

this and other equally complex questions about the connections between biology and behavior. Their research contributes to understanding how people's brains direct the activities of their bodies, how people are able to perceive the world around them and store memories of those experiences, and how hunger, emotions, personality, and thought itself are regulated. Physiological psychologists argue that all behavior can be reduced to biological mechanisms, and the argument has some appeal. Surely, studying bodies directly is an easier task than speculating about and experimenting indirectly with complex behaviors.

The magnitude and complexity of the task of reducing behavior to its biological components become immediately apparent with the study of what Morton Hunt (1982) has termed "the universe within." The search through this microscopic universe for the biological mechanisms underlying human behavior leads inevitably to the nervous system, which is the major regulator of and communication link between all other organ systems of the body.

Neurosurgeon Joseph Bogen (1978) imagined this "universe within" of the brain as a walk-through museum. On a scale appropriate to a person walking along a neural pathway, the six-inch height of the brain would translate into a fifty-story building. The width of the museum would be slightly narrower than its length, and the building would encompass several city blocks. To complete the representation of the central nervous system, a broad boulevard leading up to the building could represent the spinal cord. This boulevard would be forty to fifty blocks long. The remainder of the nervous system could be included as a park crisscrossed with paths leading to and from the central nervous system. The entire museum complex would cover a land area larger than some cities.

The Major Divisions

Use Exhibit 4.1 to help you create a vivid visual image of the various divisions of the nervous system. The **central nervous system (CNS)** includes the **brain** and **spinal cord**, which are surrounded by the bones of the skull and the vertebrae of the spine. The protection the brain and spinal cord receive from their bony coverings is an indication of their central role in processing and organizing information and in regulating behavior.

The **peripheral nervous system (PNS)** refers to all the nervous system outside the CNS and consists of two branches, the **somatic nervous system** and the **auto-

nomic nervous system (ANS)**. Both PNS divisions carry information to the CNS along **afferent (sensory) nerves** and away from the CNS along **efferent (motor) nerves**. Incoming sensory information from sense receptors throughout the body is transferred to the CNS by the somatic branch. The CNS produces outgoing messages, which are carried by motor neurons to the skeletal muscles, resulting in reflexive or voluntary movement. In the autonomic branch of the PNS, the sensory nerves carry information from the heart, smooth muscles (such as the stomach), and glands to the CNS. The motor neurons, in turn, carry messages from the CNS to the heart, smooth muscles, and glands. The autonomic nervous system is further divided into two branches, the sympathetic and parasympathetic divisions. These divisions of the PNS are not isolated units; they carry information to and from many of the same structures and produce coordinated actions.

Research Methods

Progress in understanding coordinated activities of the nervous system directly parallels the development of new and more sophisticated techniques for studying the nervous system. The earliest techniques apparently focused on the brain for scientists have discovered human skulls with well-formed holes that appear to be the result of opening the skull to observe the brain. Researchers can only speculate about the intent of these prehistoric "surgeons," but ever since such crude attempts at neurosurgery, researchers have been devising special techniques to influence and record the activity of the brain and other parts of the nervous system.

Early research often involved studying the nervous systems of dead people. Later, researchers developed techniques to stain the neural tissue so they could see more easily the different neural structures. Other techniques used live subjects, generally animals, and involved destroying parts of the brain to observe how destruction of particular areas affected behavior. Eventually, scientists developed new methods that allowed more precise destruction of brain tissue. The ablation technique involved surgically removing a portion of brain tissue. Lesion techniques, in which localized areas of brain tissue were destroyed, were even more precise than ablation.

Fritsch and Hitzig (1870) were the first to use mild electrical stimulation to explore the surface structures of the brain. Horsley and Clarke (1908) devised an instrument that could locate precisely structures deep within the brain. Using their techniques, scientists were able

EXHIBIT 4.1
Bio-Behavior Funpark and Museum

EXHIBIT 4.2
A Pet Scan and an MRI Scan
Modern technology allows psychologists to observe brain processes with the aid of computers.

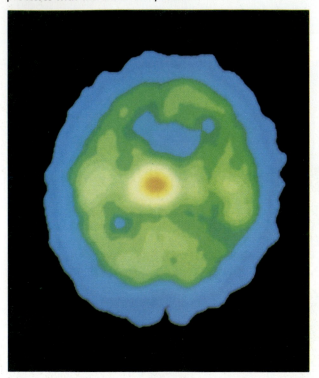

PET Scan

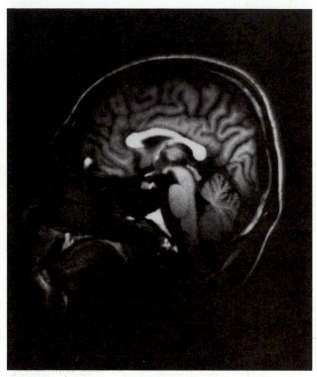

MRI Scan

[handwritten margin note: Berger described the human electroencephalogram]

to stimulate electrically and chemically areas beneath the cortex. Berger (1929) was the first to describe the human electroencephalogram (EEG). This technique allowed the study of the brain from the outside without doing neurosurgery or destroying brain structures in the process.

Today, several new techniques for recording activity in specific areas of the brain are providing even clearer descriptions of how the brain functions. Some of these techniques look at the structure of the brain. For instance, a **CAT (Computerized Axial Tomography) scanner** combines conventional X-ray techniques with computer-assisted imaging to produce an electronic picture of structures in different layers of the brain. **MRI** (magnetic resonance imaging) replaces X-rays with radio waves. A person is put into a strong magnetic field and radio frequencies are used to create magnetic resonance changes within the person's body. A computer is then used to analyze these changes and to create a picture. This technique can be made so sensitive that researchers are able to identify specific chemicals within the body (Shulman, 1983).

[handwritten margin note: CAT structure of the brain]

[handwritten margin note: MRI replaces X-rays with radio waves]

While CAT and MRI scanners can pinpoint structures in the brain, **PET (Positron Emission Tomography) scanners** can look at the function of brain structures (See Exhibit 4.2). The PET scan can look inside the brain of a living subject to observe the brain functioning. Subjects are given substances that emit positrons, atomic particles emitted by some radioactive substances. By using a radioactive sugar that emits positrons, the scanner can trace the brain's use of this sugar during different activities. Thus, when the subject looks at a stimulus, the PET scan shows greater activity in the visual areas of the brain.

[handwritten margin note: PET look at functions of brain structures]

The PET scan can be used with positron-emitting substances that act on neurotransmitter receptor sites in the brain. Using this approach, researchers have mapped the dopamine receptors in the brain of a live subject (Wagner et al., 1983). This technique allows researchers to observe, without harming it, a living brain that is actively processing, integrating, storing, and using information to regulate behavior.

Techniques such as the PET scan illustrate the great progress in physiological research methods from the days since prehistoric humans pounded holes in skulls. The modern techniques are not only producing fascinating discoveries about the nervous system but are also providing practical applications such as the diagnosis and treatment of nervous system disorders. The development of more sophisticated methods in the future holds the promise of even greater discoveries and applications.

Focus Question Answer

What are the advantages of the newer brain research techniques? Modern research techniques such as CAT and PET scans allow researchers to study both the structure and function of human brains in living subjects without damaging or destroying brain tissue.

The Neuron and Neural Processing

All the divisions, subdivisions, and individual nerves of the nervous system are composed of two basic types of cells, **neurons and glial cells (glia)**. Estimates of the total number of neurons and glial cells in the nervous system range from ten to 100 billion! The magnitude of this number is difficult to comprehend. If one million file cabinets were stored in the top ten floors of the "walk-through brain museum" with each cabinet containing 500 files, and if each file represented a single neuron, those 500 million files would represent a number smaller than the actual number of neurons in the one-inch outer layer of the human brain. In another comparison, the number of neurons in the brain is about the same as the number of stars in the Milky Way. If you are able to grasp these numbers, consider that estimates of the number of glial cells range from one for each neuron to ten for each neuron!

Well, enough of mind-boggling numbers. What do neurons and glia do? Glial (derived from the Greek term for "glue") cells form connective tissue that supports, protects, and binds together neurons. One type of glial cell forms **myelin**, a fatty substance that acts as insulation around parts of neurons. Marian Diamond, a neurophysiologist who studied a portion of Einstein's brain, found that it contained 73 percent more glial cells than the average human brain (Science, 1985). The significance of this fact is difficult to assess, since researchers are uncertain about the exact role of glial cells in neural functioning.

Although neurons are not as numerous as glia, they are more various. Over 200 different types have been

EXHIBIT 4.3
Neurons: The Basic Units of the Nervous System

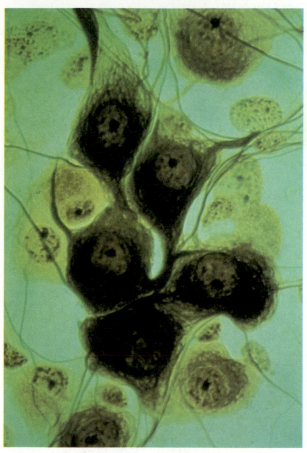

identified in the brain of mammals. Some neurons are shown in Exhibit 4.3.

The Neuron

Despite their differences in appearance, all neurons have in common three basic components (see Exhibit 4.4). Every neuron contains a **cell body (soma)**, which contains the nucleus of the cell. The information stored in the nucleus of the cell body provides the programs for managing the different cellular functions. One of the cellular functions is receiving and sending messages. This special function of neurons involves all the neuron's component parts.

Every neuron also has **dendrites**. Dendrites are the cell body's short, branching extensions that serve as the reception sites for incoming messages. Neurons rarely have only one dendrite; instead, most neurons have sev-

EXHIBIT 4.4
A Drawing of a "Typical" Neuron

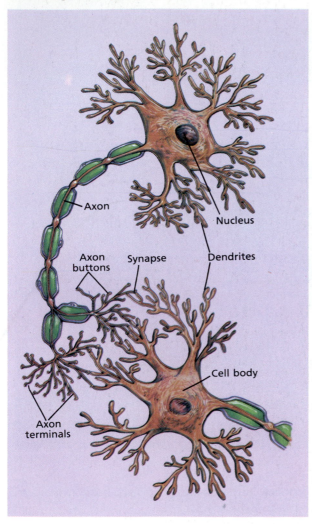

Axon

Nucleus

Axon buttons

Synapse

Dendrites

Cell body

Axon terminals

like structure called the **axon button**. Between the axon button and dendrite of the next neuron is a minute space called the **synapse** (See Exhibit 4.5).

The axons vary considerably in length. The axons of some spinal cord neurons are more than two feet long, while the axons of some brain neurons are microscopic. Yet all axons are designed to transmit information efficiently from one neuron to the next. The efficiency of some axons is improved by the insulation provided by a myelin sheath produced by glial cells. The myelin sheath is broken at regular intervals by nodes. The electrical message transmitted by the axon jumps from node to node, increasing the speed of conduction. Even with this special feature, messages in the nervous system do not travel as fast as jet airplanes, but some messages do travel faster than cars.

Neural Transmission of Information

In the nervous system, the transmission of messages is a complex electrochemical process with two distinct phases. The first phase is the conduction of the message within the neuron, and the second is the transmission of that information from one neuron to another. The two phases engage in an intricate interaction; in other words, what happens in the previous phase has a direct impact on the present phase. Both phases are easily influenced by other factors because each phase is the result of a delicate balance between chemical substances inside and outside the neuron and the exchange of these substances across the neuron's cell wall.

Neurons are able to store and produce energy much as the battery in a car does. The cell wall of the neuron

eral dendrites that branch and rebranch until they resemble the limbs of oak trees after they have dropped their leaves in the fall. So great is this microscopic branching that if the dendrites in the brain were laid end to end, they would stretch for several hundred thousand miles (Restak, 1984). This branching creates many receptor sites for receiving messages from other neurons. One neuron to a thousand or more neurons may send messages to the dendrites of a single neuron in the brain.

Finally, every neuron has a cell body extension that serves as the mechanism for sending messages on to other neurons. In most neurons, this extension is the **axon**. The branches at the end of the axon are called **axon terminals**. Each axon terminal ends in a swollen, bulb-

Quick Study Aid

Use Your Hand

Since no two neurons are exactly alike, do not spend time learning to draw the "typical" neuron in Exhibit 4.4. Instead, use your hand as a model. Let your four fingers represent the dendrites; let your thumb be the axon (i.e., *one* thumb, *one* axon); the palm of your hand, which represents the cell body, holds the fingers and thumb together and makes them functional. Wiggle your fingers, and remember that the dendrites are designed to receive messages. Wiggle your thumb, and remember that the axon is designed to send messages.

EXHIBIT 4.5
A Diagram of the Axon Terminals, Axon Buttons, and the Synapse

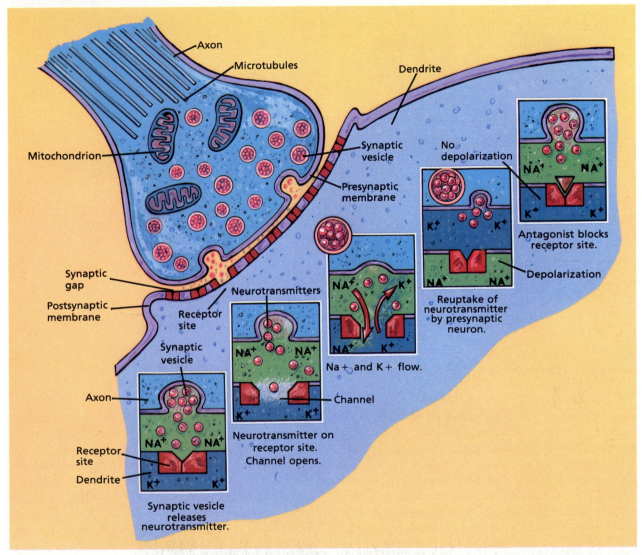

Source: Bloom, F. E., Lazerson, A., & Hofstadter, L. 1985. *Brain, mind, and behavior.*
NY: Freeman.

acts like the plate of a battery, storing more negative chemical ions (charged particles) on the inside of the cell wall and more positive ions on the outside of the membrane. This stored energy is called the neuron's **resting potential**. When the neuron conducts a message from its dendrites and along the axon, this stored potential energy is released and produces a current that flows through the neuron. When the energy is released, the neuron is said to have fired, and the neuron is no longer "at rest." The current flow produced when the neuron fires is the result of an active exchange of the positive and negative ions across the cell wall and is called the **action potential**.

The action potential is like the electrical energy produced from the battery when a driver starts a car. When the neuron fires, its stored energy is momentarily depleted, and the neuron loses its potential to produce action. Once the stored energy is depleted, the neuron must recharge (get the negative ions back on the inside and the positive ions back on the outside of the cell wall). During this time, the neuron is unable to send another message. The inability to conduct a message

EXHIBIT 4.6
The Neuron's Electrochemical Message

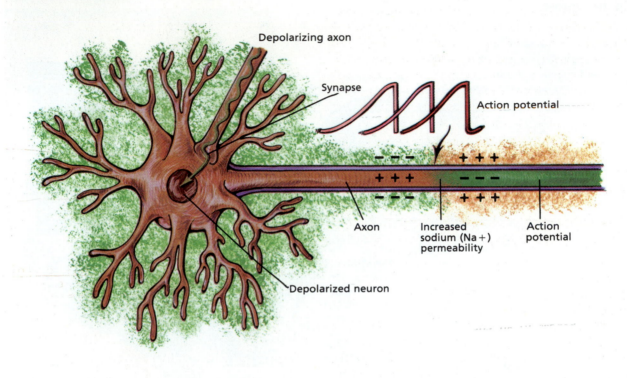

Source: Bloom, F. E., Lazerson, A., & Hofstadter, L. 1985. *Brain, mind, and behavior.* NY: Greeman.

during recharging is called **absolute refractory**. During the state of absolute refractory, the neuron is absolutely unresponsive to incoming messages from other neurons. During the recharging process, the neuron gradually becomes less unresponsive (**relative refractory**). At this point, a greater than normal incoming message is necessary to produce an action potential. While an hour or more may be required to recharge a "dead" battery, the neuron recharges in a fraction of a second. In fact, some neurons are capable of firing and recharging over a thousand times per second! Exhibit 4.6 depicts the sequence of electrochemical changes in the neuron—from resting potential, through the firing of the action potential, to the restoration of the resting potential.

The All or None Principle   Within the neuron, an **all or none principle** governs the firing of the action potential message within the neuron. Either the incoming messages from other neurons are sufficient to produce a full-strength action potential, or no message is conducted by the neuron. The chemical messages released from the axons of the sending neurons are summed together at the receptor sites on the dendrites of the receiving neu-

ron. If the sum of these messages is sufficient to change the neuron's cell membrane to its firing threshold, a full-strength action potential is created. Thus, the neuron operates as a binary system with two types of messages—all or none.

In this binary system, how are messages of graded strength possible? For example, how are you able to speak more loudly at some times than at other times or to detect that one light is brighter than another? Within the nervous system, messages with different strengths are created in two ways. The first way to send a stronger message occurs when neurons conducting the message send the message more frequently. This condition is analogous to knocking on a door when you want to come inside and knocking rapidly on the door when you want urgently to come inside. The second way to send a stronger message occurs when more neurons send the same message. To continue the analogy, sometimes when you want urgently to come inside, you knock on the door with both fists.

The Law of Forward Conduction   Within the nervous system, no matter how rapidly or how frequently neural messages are sent, the messages are always conducted in the same direction—from the dendrites, through the cell body, along the axon, to the dendrites of the next neuron. This feature of the nervous system is called the **law of forward conduction** and is responsible for the two separate pathways mentioned earlier, the sensory nerves and the motor nerves. Since information can move only forward from neuron to neuron, one set of neurons must bring messages to the CNS, and another set must carry information away from the CNS. Within the CNS, the law of forward conduction still applies. The same chain of neurons used to conduct a message from one part of the brain to another cannot be used to carry a return message. A different chain of neurons is necessary for the return message.

Synaptic Transmission

As the neural message is transmitted between neurons, the process changes. Within the neuron, the message is electrochemical in nature. When the action potential reaches the terminal buttons at the end of the axon, the message changes to an entirely chemical form. The chemical substance carries the message across the synapse from the terminals of the axon to the **receptor sites** (the receiving points) on the dendrites of the next neuron. The axon buttons, the synapse, and the dendrite's receptor sites form an intricately complex microscopic environment. The interplay of their constituent parts is similar to the complexities of a Beethoven symphony,

Dendrites branch from the soma in much the same way a tree branches.

Quick Study Aid

The Law of Forward Conduction

Building on the previous QSA, you can use both hands to help you remember the law of forward conduction. Touch the tips of your two thumbs together, and tell yourself that two axons cannot talk to one another. Touch the tips of your fingers of each hand together. Tell yourself that dendrites cannot talk to one another. Touch the tip of your thumb on one hand to the tip of one of the fingers on your other hand. Tell yourself "axons talk to dendrites, but dendrites never talk to axons." Either move the appropriate parts, or visualize: (1) A dendrite (finger on one hand) receiving a message; (2) The axon (thumb of the same hand) sending the message to a dendrite (finger of the other hand) and that axon (thumb of the other hand) sending the message forward.

in which the actions in one part of the orchestra are balanced by and influenced by the actions in other parts.

One section of the synaptic orchestra is comprised of the axon buttons. These bulb-like structures contain free-floating sacs called synaptic vesicles. When the action potential reaches the axon terminals, the entry of calcium ions $(Ca+)$ into the cell is increased. This action in turn brings the vesicles close to the synaptic surface, where they release their stored chemicals into the synapse. These chemicals are called **neurotransmitters**, and they are responsible for transporting the message across the synapse. A neurotransmitter acts like a key that fits locks at the receptor sites on the dendrites and soma of the receiving neuron. The neurotransmitters are the essential components in the synaptic transmission of information; they are the essential element that carries the message from the axon of a neuron across the synapse to the dendrites of another neuron.

Neurotransmitters and Neuromodulators

Neurotransmitters The nervous system is unequalled in its ability to process and regulate information, and the neurotransmitters are the information base of that system. Neurotransmitters are part of a precise circuitry in which specific chemical messages unlock chemically specific receptor sites. While at least thirty substances have been identified as possible neurotransmitters, these chemicals generally produce only two types of reactions at the receptor sites. Some neurotransmitters are classified as excitatory; when they are released, they create conditions that make the production of an action potential in the receiving neuron more likely. More of the neurotransmitters are classified as inhibitory; when released, these substances make the firing and sending of a message by the receiving neuron less likely. Neurons that release excitatory neurotransmitters are called excitatory neurons. Correspondingly, neurons that release

inhibitory neurotransmitters are called inhibitory neurons. While exceptions to this pattern exist, the excitatory/inhibitory classification is another indication of the essentially binary nature of the nervous system. Exhibit 4.7 lists some of the prominent neurotransmitters and their associated effects.

Neuromodulators Research conducted within the last fifteen years has identified a new set of chemical messengers in the brain. These messengers transmit and regulate information flow in the nervous system differently than do neurotransmitters. This new class of "informational substances" is actually a mixture of familiar body chemicals (hormones) given new functions and newly discovered substances (Cordes, 1985). These substances act to fine-tune the nervous system and, therefore, are called **neuromodulators**. More than fifty new neuromodulators have been discovered since 1971, with most

[Handwritten margin note: Excitatory create conditions that make production of an action potential in receiving neuron more likely]

[Handwritten note: inhibitory - these substances make the firing and sending of a message by receiving neuron less likely.]

EXHIBIT 4.7
Neurotransmitters

Neurotransmitters	Associated Effect
Acetylcholine	This transmitter is found at many synapses in both the central and peripheral nervous systems. Released at the neuromuscular junction, acetylcholine initiates muscle contractions. The brains of persons who die from Alzheimer's disease show a large decrease in the enzymes that synthesize acetylcholine, indicating that decreases in acetylcholine may be mediating some of the symptoms of Alzheimer's such as memory loss.
Dopamine	Dopamine is an inhibitory neurotransmitter concentrated in brain areas that control complex movement. Individuals who have Parkinson's disease, a neurological disorder characterized by muscular tremors and rigidity, suffer from a deficiency of dopamine. Treatment with L-dopa, a drug from which the body can produce dopamine, temporarily relieves the symptoms of Parkinson's disease.
Norepinephrine	Also recognized as the hormone noradrenalin, norepinephrine is primarily an inhibitory neurotransmitter produced in the brainstem. Depletion of norepinephrine is associated with sedation and depression. Increases in norepinephrine are associated with mood elevation.
Epinephrine	This transmitter is chemically the same as the hormone adrenalin. When released, epinephrine is excitatory and activates many of the same synapses activated by norepinephrine.
GABA	Gamma-amino butyric acid (GABA) is an inhibitory neurotransmitter involved in the control of movement. Without the effects of GABA, muscles begin to contract uncontrollably.
Serotonin	Serotonin affects sleep and mood. Drugs that deplete the serotonin and norepinephrine stored in neurons produce depression. Drugs that prevent their breakdown produce mood elevation.

of them having been discovered since 1980. Some neuromodulators are described in Exhibit 4.8.

The information coded in the neuromodulators functions like that of the information in the neurotransmitters; both are "keyed" to specific receptor sites. Uniquely, however, while neuromodulators function similarly to neurotransmitters, they are not usually produced or stored at sites next to their receptors. Instead, neuromodulators are produced at one site and are then transported throughout the body. Like honey bees in a field of flowers, the neuromodulators move about the body, pausing to land at those receptor sites that match their specific chemical structures.

The specific locations of neuromodulator receptor sites in the brain, in the spinal cord, and throughout the body suggest that the neuromodulators are a major link between the nervous system, the endocrine gland system, and the body's immune system. Within the central nervous system, these substances modify incoming sensory information, pain, emotion, mood, level of consciousness, sexual behavior, pleasure, respiration, appetite, and memory (Weber & Pert, 1984). Neuro-

modulators fine-tune neurons' receptiveness to specific neurotransmitters. Eventually, researchers may establish that neuromodulators are essential to overall health and that they play a role in regulating the spread of cancer cells (Cordes, 1985).

Endorphins Over 2,000 years ago the euphoric properties of opium were known to the Greeks and others, but not until the 1973 discovery of the brain's specific receptor sites for opiates (opium-like substances such as morphine) were the mechanisms for opium's actions in the nervous system identified (Pert & Snyder, 1973). The presence of opiate receptor sites suggested that the brain produces its own opiates. This hypothesis was confirmed in 1975 when researchers in Scotland, Sweden, and the United States discovered endogenous (from within the body) morphine-like substances in the brain (Snyder, 1977). The Scottish group called its morphine-like compounds **enkephalins**, meaning "of the head" (Hughes et al., 1975). The Swedish and American researchers chose the label **endorphins**, meaning "the mor-

EXHIBIT 4.8
Neuromodulators

Neuromodulators	Associated Effects
Beta-Endorphin	Beta-endorphin appears to modulate the body's responses to pain in much the same way morphine does. Acupuncture and placebos may produce their pain-relief effects by activating beta-endorphin.
Substance P	Unlike the endorphins, Substance P facilitates the processing of pain information. A drug that would block the action of this substance without causing other side-effects would be a very effective anesthetic.
Bradykinin	This substance is also thought to be important in the transmission of pain information. Injections of very small doses of bradykinin cause intense pain.
Vasopressin	Vasopressin is chemically the same as antidiuretic hormone (ADH) and is produced in the hypothalamus. As a neuromodulator, vasopressin has been linked to memory enhancement and learning. Vasopressin administered to healthy, depressed, and senile subjects significantly improved their memories and learning abilities (Weingartner et al., 1981).
Factor S	Factor S is involved in modulating sleep. This neuromodulator was isolated from the brain fluid of goats and sheep that were forced to stay awake. Injections of Factor S increases sleeping time in rabbits.
Dynorphin	One of the more recently discovered neuromodulators, dynorphin is powerful, as its name suggests. Dynorphin's effect on pain relief appears to be fifty times more powerful than beta-endorphin's and 200 times more potent than morphine's (Whitnall, Gainer, Cox & Molineaux, 1983).

EXHIBIT 4.9
The Endocrine Glands and Their Hormones

Tissue	Hormone	Target cells	Action
Pituitary, anterior lobe	Follicle-stimulating hormone Luteinizing hormone Thyrotropin Adrenocorticotropin Growth hormone Prolactin	Gonads Gonads Thyroid Adrenal cortex Liver All cells Breasts	Ovulation, spermatogenesis Ovarian/spermatic maturation Thyroxin secretion Corticosteroid secretion Somatomedin secretion Protein synthesis Growth and milk secretion
Pituitary, posterior lobe	Vasopressin Oxytocin	Kidney tubules Arterioles Uterus	Water retention Increase blood pressure Contraction
Gonads	Estrogen Testosterone	Many Many	Secondary sexual characteristics Muscle, breast growth
Thyroid	Thyroxin	Many	Increases metabolic rate
Parathyroid	Calcitonin	Bone	Calcium retention

Adrenal cortex	Corticosteroids
	
	Aldosterone
		Many
		
		Kidney
			Mobilization of energy fuels
			Sensitization of vascular
			  adrenergic receptors
			Inhibition of antibody formation
			  and inflammation
			Sodium retention

Adrenal medulla	Epinephrine Norepinephrine	Cardiovascular system, skin, muscle, liver, and others	Sympathetic activation
Pancreatic islets	Insulin Glucagon Somatostatin	Many Liver, muscle Islets	Increases glucose uptake Increases glucose levels Regulates insulin, glucagon secretion

Intestinal mucosa	Secretin
	Cholecystokinin
	Vasoactive, intestinal
	polypeptide
	Gastric, inhibitory peptide
	Somatostatin
		Exocrine pancreas
		Gall bladder
		Duodenum
		
		Duodenum
		Duodenum
			Digestive enzyme secretion
			Bile secretion
			Activates motility and secretion;
			  increases blood flow
			Inhibits motility and secretion
			Inhibits motility and intestinal
			  secretion

Source: Bloom, F. E., Lazerson, A., & Hofstadter, L. 1985. *Brain, mind, and behavior.*
NY: Freeman, p. 100.

phine within." Since that time, the term "endorphin" has come to be the generic term for naturally occurring opiate neuromodulators.

The endorphins are generally involved in the modification of pain and pleasure, level of consciousness, emotion, appetite, respiration, intestinal activity, blood pressure, and parts of the endocrine and immune systems. Endorphins are now widely used to explain such diverse effects as the success of acupuncture in relieving pain, increased pain tolerance during pregnancy, pain relief with placebos, "runner's high" resulting from regular vigorous exercise, and narcotic addiction. In the case of narcotic addiction, injecting narcotics into the addict's system signals the body to produce less of its morphine-like compounds. With less of its own naturally occurring endorphins present to rely upon, the body begins to call for more and more of the injected compound. When narcotic use stops, withdrawal symptoms occur because the body is left without the bulk of its natural pain-modifiers, the endorphins.

Focus Question Answer

In what ways do neurochemicals control your behavior? Neurotransmitters and neuromodulators have integral roles. All messages in the nervous system are carried from one neuron to the next by neurotransmitters. The neuromodulators help regulate important processes such as pain, pleasure, appetite, and emotion.

 ## The Endocrine and Autonomic Systems

Neuroendocrine System

The **endocrine system** is another chemically based regulatory system. The chemical regulators of the endocrine system are called **hormones**, from the Greek word meaning "messenger." Hormones are produced by glands, which release them into the bloodstream. Once in the bloodstream, the hormones affect specific target cells throughout the body. Exhibit 4.9 lists the endocrine glands, their hormones, the hormone target cell systems, and the effects of the hormones on those systems.

The endocrine glands are a diffuse system that has intimate connections with the nervous system. In fact, some identical substances work in both systems. Norepinephrine and vasopressin are examples of substances

that are both hormones secreted by endocrine glands and neurotransmitters or neuromodulators secreted by neurons. Traditionally, the endocrine system was considered a separate system, but due to its extensive interconnections with the nervous system the endocrine system is now more appropriately referred to as the **neuroendocrine system**.

Pituitary Gland

A key link between the two systems occurs in the **pituitary gland**. The pituitary has two major parts and is directly connected to the hypothalamus, a brain structure just above and behind the pituitary (see Exhibit 4.10).

The control mechanism by which this intricate system is regulated is **negative feedback**. In a negative feedback system, increases in one part of the system signal decreases in another part of the system. These decreases then signal decreases in the first part, followed then by increases in the second part. Thus, change in one part of the system brings about the opposite (negative) change in another part of the system.

The amounts of the thyroid stimulating hormone (thyrotropin) and thyroxine are maintained at very stable levels within the body by negative feedback. Thy-

EXHIBIT 4.10
The Hypothalamus/Pituitary Connection

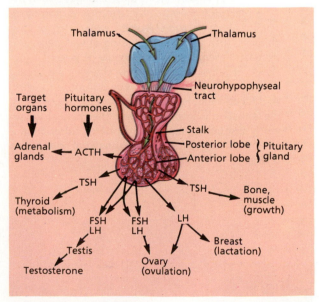

Adapted from Bloom et al., 1985.

Exploring . . .

Puzzling PMS

While men may remain somewhat oblivious to the day-to-day functioning of the endocrine systems, women have a recurring monthly marker, the menstrual period, to remind them that hormones are constantly at work within their systems. The continuing cycle of the female reproductive system provides a convenient backdrop against which women can recognize and judge other recurring events in their lives.

With the menstrual period as a marker, many women recognize emotional, physical, and behavioral changes the week or so before their periods begin. These changes can be grouped into four main categories:

1. Nervous tension, irritability, anxiety, mood swings.

2. Weight gain, swelling of limbs, breast tenderness, abdominal bloating.

3. Headache, craving for sweets, increased appetite, heart pounding, fatigue, dizziness/fainting.

4. Depression, forgetfulness, crying, confusion, insomnia.

As many as 70 percent of menstruating women are aware of at least one of these changes during the time preceding menstruation (Hopson & Rosenfeld, 1984). Although some women experience positive changes, such as a general feeling of well-being and increased energy, the vast majority of women experience negative changes. These changes are usually mild to moderate and not overly disruptive to women's functioning. However, as many as 10 percent of menstruating women, for whom the changes are severely disruptive month after month, suffer from a condition diagnosed as **premenstrual syndrome (PMS)**.

PMS is generally defined as the appearance of a variety of symptoms one to ten days before the beginning of the period, followed by the disappearance of those symptoms with the onset of the period. With the great variety of symptoms that are reported, finding a standard definition upon which all researchers and practitioners will agree is difficult. Katherina Dalton (1984), who coined the term premenstrual syndrome, defines PMS as "the presence of symptoms which recur regularly at the same phase of each menstrual cycle, followed by a symptom-free phase in each cycle." Dalton's definition places less emphasis on the particular symptoms and more emphasis on the timing of the particular symptoms a woman may experience.

Researchers reach even less agreement about cause than they do about definition. However, because of the close linkage between PMS and the menstrual cycle, disruption of the hormonal balance in the menstrual cycle is a likely cause. Some researchers believe that the hormonal imbalances are the result of nutritional deficiencies that make women who experience PMS more susceptible to stress (Hopson & Rosenfeld, 1984). These researchers believe deficiencies in the B vitamins and in magnesium bring about the imbalance.

Other researchers hypothesize that deficiencies in the pituitary hormone prolactin or low-blood sugar are possible explanations for PMS. One widely held view is that PMS is caused by low levels of the hormone progesterone (Dalton, 1984). A recent hypothesis suggests that PMS may be related to endorphin levels in the brain. PMS responds well to treatment with placebos which may increase production of endorphins in the brain. This hypothesis suggests that PMS results from the rise and then abrupt fall of endorphin levels during the week preceding the menstrual period. All these ideas remain as hypotheses without sufficient research support.

The incidence and severity of PMS correlate with several factors. Married women report more PMS symptoms, and the more children a woman has had the more severe the PMS symptoms are likely to be (Hopson & Rosenfeld, 1984). PMS symptoms increase with age, with women in their thirties being the most vulnerable. In addition, experiencing stress increases the severity of PMS, as does eating high levels of refined sugar and salt and not eating a nourishing diet. A lack of outdoor physical exercise also worsens PMS. Remember, however, that these correlations do not necessarily indicate causes of PMS.

Because of the lack of agreement about the causes of PMS, the lack of agreement about how to treat the condition is not surprising. Doctors prescribe a variety of drugs to treat individual PMS symptoms. For example, some doctors prescribe diuretics for bloating and an antidepressant for depression. Other doctors suggest stress management, elimination or reduction of salt and refined sugars in the diet, increased intake of B vitamins and magnesium (either through diet or supplements), and a regular outdoor exercise program. A controversial treatment involves giving large doses of progesterone to relieve the symptoms (Heneson, 1984). Successful management of PMS may involve a combination of these suggested treatments.

PMS is a puzzling neuroendocrine condition because the symptoms are not universal, the causes are unknown, and the treatments are varied. For women experiencing PMS, however, the symptoms are real, and the need for effective treatment is immediate.

rotropin from the pituitary affects target cells in the thyroid, causing more thyroxine to be synthesized and released. As thyroxine levels rise, the hypothalamus signals the pituitary to release less thyrotropin. As thyrotropin levels fall, the thyroid synthesizes and releases less thyroxine. Falling levels of thyroxine cause the hypothalamus to call for the release of more thyrotropin from the pituitary. Thus, slight fluctuations maintain each hormone at a constant, precise level.

Adrenal Glands

The adrenals, located on top of each kidney, are involved in another complex linkage in the neuroendocrine system. When a "threatening" physical or psychological stimulus occurs, the hypothalamus signals the pituitary to release large amounts of adrenocorticotropic hormone (ACTH). ACTH, circulating in the bloodstream, signals the adrenal glands to release epinephrine and norepinephrine into the bloodstream. The epinephrine directly affects the cardiovascular system. The norepinephrine causes the pituitary to release another hormone. This hormone also acts on the adrenal glands, causing the release of corticosteroids. The corticosteroids cause the liver to release its stored sugar, providing increased energy to fuel the body's reactions to the "threat." This complex sequence, which requires no longer than one or two seconds, is a major component in the set of responses regulated by the autonomic nervous system.

Autonomic Nervous System

The neurotransmitter, neuromodulator, and neuroendocrine effects discussed in the previous sections are given a unique twist in the autonomic nervous system (ANS). The ANS carries information to and from the heart, the glands, and the smooth muscles of the internal organs. What makes this portion of the nervous system unique is the coordinated regulation of behavior provided by two branches of the ANS, the sympathetic and parasympathetic. These two branches act in conjunction with the neuroendocrine system. Within each branch, the activities of widely separated organs and glands are coordinated. Generally, the two branches produce opposing effects in the same organs and glands (see Exhibit 4.11), but to view them as working against each other is a mistake. They work together to prepare the body to deal with and recuperate from stressful events.

EXHIBIT 4.11
Sympathetic and Parasympathetic Branches

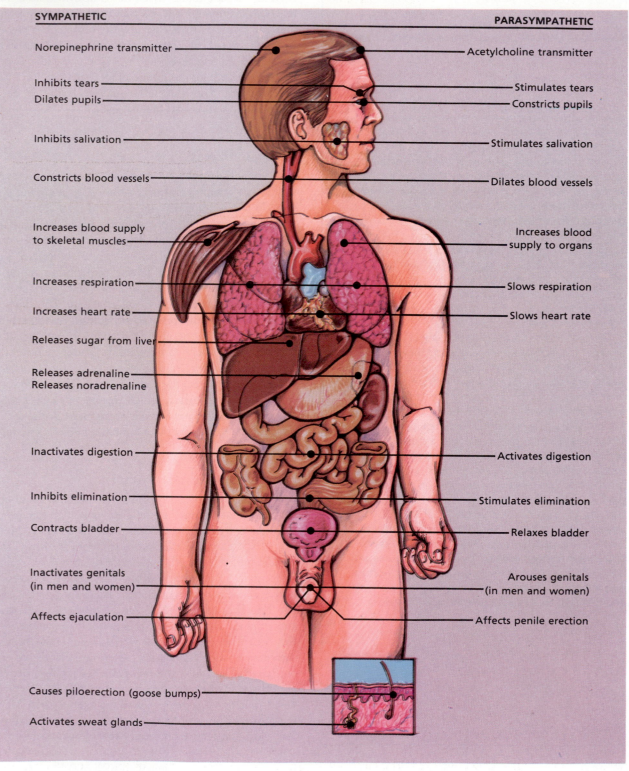

SYMPATHETIC

Norepinephrine transmitter

Inhibits tears
Dilates pupils

Inhibits salivation

Constricts blood vessels

Increases blood supply
to skeletal muscles

Increases respiration

Increases heart rate

Releases sugar from liver

Releases adrenaline
Releases noradrenaline

Inactivates digestion

Inhibits elimination

Contracts bladder

Inactivates genitals
(in men and women)

Affects ejaculation

Causes piloerection (goose bumps)

Activates sweat glands

PARASYMPATHETIC

Acetylcholine transmitter

Stimulates tears
Constricts pupils

Stimulates salivation

Dilates blood vessels

Increases blood
supply to organs

Slows respiration

Slows heart rate

Activates digestion

Stimulates elimination

Relaxes bladder

Arouses genitals
(in men and women)

Affects penile erection

The sympathetic branch prepares the body for emergency situations by activating the release of stored energy. This process is called the **fight or flight response**. The sympathetic branch mobilizes the body's energy to prepare for defense or for fleeing from a dangerous situation. Signals from the CNS cause the adrenal glands to release adrenaline, which in turn is primarily responsible for the coordinated effects.

The parasympathetic branch mediates a collection of effects designed to increase the body's energy reserves. While this function opposes that of the sympathetic branch, it represents a cooperative rather than an antagonistic function. One branch of the system provides quick energy, and the other branch assures that the depleted stored energy is replenished. When you become "excited," the sympathetic branch is most prominent. When you "calm down" after being excited, the parasympathetic branch is most prominent. Both these branches are intimately involved in your emotional responses and are integral parts of your reactions to stress (see Chapter 13).

Focus Question Answer

How do your endocrine and autonomic systems work together to regulate your behavior? The autonomic system signals the endocrine system's chemical messengers to produce coordinated actions such as preparing your body for defending against or fleeing from a threat. The central nervous system provides another connecting and coordinating link between the two systems.

The Central Nervous System

Paul MacLean (1978) has suggested that the CNS is composed of structures that evolved from earlier, simpler neural forms. According to MacLean, the spinal cord appeared first; the first brain then evolved from the spinal cord. In his *Triune Brain Theory*, MacLean suggests that we actually have "brains-within-brains." The first brain to appear, according to this evolutionary approach, was the reptilian brain. Today, structures that make up the reptilian portion of the brain are the brain stem, midbrain, reticular activating system, basal ganglia, and most of the hypothalamus (see Exhibit 4.12). The next brain to evolve was the paleomammalian (old mammalian), now comprising the limbic system. The last brain-within-a-brain to appear was the neomammalian brain, or the neocortex. Even this highly developed "thinking cap"

Quick Study Aid

The CNS

Use your arms and fists to make a handy reference model for the CNS. Make a fist with each hand by curling the fingers of each hand around their respective thumbs. Next, put your arms out in front of you with your wrists and forearms close together. Imagine that your forearms are fused together, and let them represent the spinal cord. On top of your imaginative spinal cord are your fused-together wrists, which now represent the brain stem. The actual size of your spinal cord and brain stem is proportionately much smaller than your forearms and wrists. However, the fists that represent your brain are approximately the same size as your actual brain. Your thumbs represent the bilateral structures of the hypothalamus, thalamus, basal ganglia, and the limbic system found in the center of the brain above the brain stem. Let your fingers represent the highly convoluted cerebral cortex. Of course, the fingers on the left hand represent the left cerebral hemisphere, and those on the right, the right cerebral hemisphere. Imagine several rubberbands drawing the middle two fingers of each hand together. These bands represent the corpus callosum, the major bridge of fibers between the two hemispheres.

You can use this handy model for one more memory aid. Let your little fingers represent the frontal lobes; your ring fingers represent the motor areas of the frontal lobes; your middle fingers represent the sensory areas of the parietal lobes; your index fingers represent the visual areas of the occipital lobes; and the backs of your hands represent the temporal lobes.

---

displays higher levels of specialization within the different lobes of the cerebral cortex and between the left and right hemispheres. While not everyone agrees with the Triune Theory, it does provide a useful way to group together the many varied structures within the CNS.

Spinal Cord

The spinal cord is far more complicated than the simple conduit from the PNS to the brain that it appears to be. Its central core of gray matter is made up of cell bodies of spinal cord neurons (see Exhibit 4.12). The outer layer of white matter is composed of bundles of myelin-coated axons, which leave the spinal cord at regular intervals. Thirty-one pairs of spinal nerves leave the

EXHIBIT 4.12
Components of the CNS

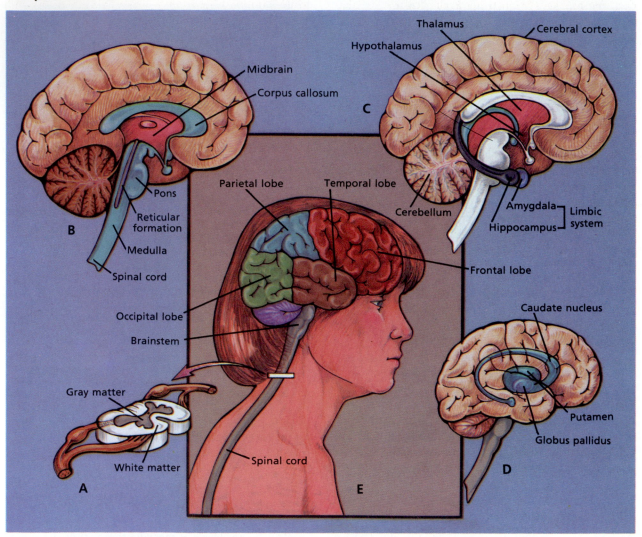

cord. They, along with the twelve cranial nerves that leave the brain directly, are the neural communication links between the brain and the rest of the body.

In addition to serving as a communication link, the spinal cord is responsible for the most basic behavior pattern, the **reflex arc**. The familiar knee-jerk response to being tapped just under the kneecap is a spinal cord reflex. Information carried by an afferent (sensory) neuron directly activates an efferent (motor) neuron in the spinal cord. The result is the muscle contraction that produces the knee jerk. Other reflexes are more complicated than this relatively simple reflex arc. "Flinching" when an object threatens to hit you in the face requires a greater number of neurons to produce the reflex.

Brainstem

As the spinal cord enters the skull, it widens slightly and becomes the **brainstem**. Technically, the brainstem consists of all the structures between the spinal cord and the cerebrum, except for the cerebellum (see Exhibit 4.12). These structures form a trunk on top of which are found the massive cerebral hemispheres. Typically, the brainstem is considered to be the structures from the spinal cord up to the midbrain.

Medulla   Approximately the first inch of the brainstem is the **medulla** (see Exhibit 4.12). Like each specialized area of the brain, the medulla has both shared and unique functions. It continues the function of communication conduit for incoming messages from the spinal cord and outgoing messages from higher brain centers. In addition, the medulla serves as the intake and outlet for ten of the cranial nerves (all but the optic and olfactory nerves). Within the medulla's inch of length, fibers bringing messages from the right side of the body cross over to the left side of the brainstem, and the reverse occurs for fibers carrying messages from the left side of the body. This crossing over of fibers also occurs for messages coming from the brain.

Centers within the medulla perform unique functions such as controlling blood pressure, heart rate, and spontaneous breathing. Sophisticated techniques developed for studying the brain have pinpointed at the sides of the medulla nuclei (concentrated areas of dendrites and cell bodies) that produce activity in the sympathetic branch of the ANS. This activity in the sympathetic branch, in turn, brings about an increase in blood pressure. Nuclei in the middle part of the medulla activate the parasympathetic branch, lowering the blood pressure. Any damage to the medulla is extremely life-threatening.

Pons   The medulla merges into the **pons** (see Exhibit 4.12). This area is the major link between the brainstem and the cerebellum ("pons" means "bridge"). The pons is situated at the crossroads of major pathways of motor information involving the higher brain center, the spinal cord, and the cerebellum. In addition to playing an important role in regulating several types of movement (including facial expression), the pons contains additional respiratory centers, relays auditory information from your ears, and controls salivation. The pons is an important sensory and motor area.

Midbrain   Sensory information from the eyes and ears goes to distinct locations in the next brainstem area, the **midbrain** (see Exhibit 4.12). All incoming sensory messages other than those for smell and some for sight must pass through the midbrain to get to the brain structures above this point. Similarly, all outgoing motor messages from above this point must pass through the midbrain.

Reticular Formation   Beginning in the lower portions of the brainstem and ending in the midbrain is a complex network of neurons running through the center of the brainstem; this network is called the **reticular formation** (see Exhibit 4.12). Part of this network is referred to as the **ascending reticular activating system (ARAS)** because it is responsible for alerting or activating other parts of the brain. The ARAS acts much like an alarm, causing you to focus your attention on certain stimuli while ignoring others. In a classic study, Moruzzi and Magoun (1949) positioned an electrode in the ARAS of an anesthetized cat. Mild electrical stimulation produced a pattern of arousal in EEG recordings from the cat's cerebral cortex. Later research confirmed the reticular formation is vital in maintaining normal sleeping/waking cycles. Stimulation of the ARAS will wake a sleeping animal, while destruction of the ARAS will produce a coma.

Cerebellum   Tucked under the back of the cerebral cortex and attached to the pons of the brainstem is the **cerebellum** ("little brain") (see Exhibit 4.12). The cerebellum resembles a "brain" in more than its outward appearance. The cerebellum's nearness to the major sensory and motor pathways of the CNS places it in an ideal position for influencing body tone and the coordination of movement. Pianists are able to position their hands above the appropriate keys and play intricate passages without "thinking" as a result of their well-functioning cerebellums. The cerebellum is especially important in fine motor control; without its influence, turning the next page in this book would become a jerky and disorganized process.

Subcortical Structures

One way to classify the parts of the CNS is to refer to the medulla and pons of the brainstem as the hindbrain. All CNS structures above the midbrain become part of the forebrain. Directly above the midbrain, but below the cerebral cortex, is a cluster of important subcortical structures (see Exhibit 4.12).

Thalamus   The paired structures of the **thalamus** are egg-shaped and are located directly above the brainstem (see Exhibit 4.12). The thalamus is best known for its role in integrating and relaying sensory information. All sensory information except smell passes through here on its way to various parts of the cerebral cortex. Also, areas of the thalamus are involved in integrating information from other brain sites before that information is passed on to the medulla and cerebellum. The thalamus is most easily visualized as a complex switchboard or relay station.

Hypothalamus   The **hypothalamus** (hypo means below) is situated below the thalamus (see Exhibit 4.12). Fortunately, this small, elongated structure nearly in the center of the head is very well protected because even the slightest damage to it is life-threatening. Within the hypothalamus are control centers for eating, metabolic activity, water balance, sexual behavior, body rhythm, and body temperature. The hypothalamus regulates water balance, which influences both thirst and blood pressure level. In addition, the hypothalamus is a key link between the brain, endocrine gland system, and the autonomic nervous system. Thus the hypothalamus, which comprises less than one percent of the brain volume, is not only at the center of the head, but it is also at the center of regulation for almost every basic body function.

Limbic System   The **limbic system** is composed of several closely interconnected structures within the paleocortex (old brain). These structures form an interface between the neocortex (new brain) and the brainstem (see Exhibit 4.12). They mediate information (particularly emotional information) passing to and from the cerebral hemispheres. When the paleocortex appeared in mammals, it represented a new level of integration within the brain. Animal species with less highly developed brains exhibited semi-automatic responses to their environment similar to reflexes; in humans, these responses are now controlled in the spinal cord and brainstem. The interconnections among the limbic system structures made possible greater variations in behavioral responses to sensory input. Responding became less all-or-none, fight or flight, and less standardized and repetitive. Humans are now capable of more specific and individualized responses to changes in their environment, such as displaying a wide range of emotions. The limbic system colors each experience with an emotional quality.

Amygdala   The limbic system is an interconnected circuit of neurons; it includes the amygdala, hippocampus, hypothalamus, parts of the thalamus, and other associated structures. The **amygdala** is an almond-shaped mass of cells positioned between the hippocampus and the hypothalamus (see Exhibit 4.12). Earlier research indicated that the amygdala may be a center for control of aggressive behavior. After surgical removal of the amygdala or electrical stimulation of the area, cats and monkeys exhibited a variety of changes in their aggressive behaviors. However, because of the complexity of the research findings from animals and humans, precise statements about the amygdala's role in aggression and other emotional behaviors are difficult to make.

Hippocampus   The **hippocampus** plays an important role in the formation of new memories (see Exhibit 4.12).

Removal of the hippocampus affects the formation of new memories; older memories, however, are unaffected. Thus the hippocampus functions in the process of consolidation, whereby new experiences become permanently stored in memory. Although people with damage to their hippocampal areas can perform newly learned tasks, they are perplexed because they cannot remember having learned to do the tasks.

Basal Ganglia   Located at the base of the cortex, the **basal ganglia** surround the structures of the limbic system (see Exhibit 4.12). Ganglia are collections of cell bodies of neurons. Along with the cerebellum, the basal ganglia assist in controlling movement. The basal ganglia receive information from the major sensory and motor areas of the cortex and are closely connected to the brainstem. From this position, they mediate the cortex's messages for voluntary movement; those movements are then fine-tuned by the cerebellum. When you spot a penny on the ground, the coordination provided by your basal ganglia begins the process of bending over and reaching down to pick up the coin.

Cerebral Cortex

The **cerebral cortex**, also called the neocortex, is the newest and most massive part of the highly evolved human brain. The wrinkled, convoluted surface of the cerebral cortex usually comes to mind when you visualize the brain (see Exhibit 4.12). Take a flat sheet of paper, and crinkle it up into a small ball. All the surface area of the paper is still contained within that much smaller ball. A similar process appears to have occurred in the development of the neocortex. If all the many folds in the cerebral cortex were smoothed out, the surface would cover more than six sheets of typing paper!

Another noticeable feature of the cerebral cortex is its two halves; these are termed the right and left **cerebral hemispheres**. To many people, each hemisphere looks like half a walnut meat. Just as the halves of a walnut are connected together, the cerebral hemispheres also are connected. The thick bridge of fibers connecting the two halves is the **corpus callosum**. The corpus callosum is the major communication link between the two hemispheres.

Focus Question Answer

Is any part of your central nervous system more important than the other parts? Each part of the central nervous system fulfills unique functions and operates in conjunction with the other areas; in this sense, each part is vital. You can, however, continue to live without the cerebral cortex, but you would exist in a coma. Therefore, the entire system must be intact for you to retain your fullest human capabilities.

Cerebral Specialization

The surface appearance of the cerebral cortex gives no indication of the several complex layers of neural cells that lie beneath the surface. The integrated action of these various cell layers and groupings is the source of the most complicated human abilities—language, memory, and thought itself. Although researchers have identified many highly specialized areas in the cortex, they are still unable to determine the specific functions of nearly 75 percent of the cortex.

In areas in which functions have been specified, the degree of specialization is remarkable (Geschwind, 1979). Some of the specialization is bilateral; in other words, it is found within the same areas of each hemisphere. Other areas of specialization have developed within only one of the hemispheres.

Cortical Lobes

The grooves and folds of the cerebral cortex serve as convenient landmarks for dividing the surface of each hemisphere into four lobes (see Exhibit 4.12). The **frontal**, **parietal**, **occipital**, and **temporal lobes** are named for the skull bones that cover them.

Each lobe processes information from the opposite side of the body. For example, areas in the right frontal lobe control movement on the left side of the body. Body sense information, such as pain messages, from the right side of the body is organized in the left parietal lobe. In vision, the arrangement is slightly more complex. Rather than processing information from the right eye, the left occipital lobe processes information for the right visual field, the area of vision to the right of the body's midline. Each eye sends information to both sides of the cerebral cortex.

Frontal Lobes   Messages beginning in the **motor cortex**, a portion of the frontal lobe, start the process of voluntary movement (see Exhibit 4.13). The mapping of this specialized area of the cortex began in the 1800s, when researchers discovered they could stimulate the surface of the brain with a mild electric current without

---

Quick Study Aid

Use Your Head

To help yourself remember the four lobes of the cerebral cortex, try using your head. Place the palm of one of your hands on your forehead while you think of the similarity between "front of head" and "frontal lobe." Now, move your hand to the top of your head while you think to yourself, "The parietal lobe is on top." Cup your hand over the back of your head while you think to yourself, "The occipital lobe is at the back." Next, put your fingertips on your temples while you think of the similarity between "temples" and "temporal."

To remember the specialized function of each lobe, try this. Think: "My *first move* was to the frontal lobe. The frontal lobe is for *voluntary movement*." "I can *feel* my hand over my parietal lobe. The parietal lobe is for *body senses*." "I have *eyes in the back of my head*. The occipital lobe is for vision." "My temporal lobes are above my *ears*. The temporal lobe is for *hearing*." Try these tips, and see if they work for you.

---

adversely affecting their patients. Subsequently, this technique has been used to probe carefully the entire cortical surface. Today neurosurgeons use the information gained from cortical mapping to distinguish between healthy and unhealthy tissue in patients with brain tumors.

Information about the frontal lobe's responses to electrical stimulation, as well as information gained through other research techniques, indicates that the frontal lobes are specialized for planning and executing purposeful behaviors. The frontal lobes, because of their close connections to the limbic system, also evaluate and make decisions about emotional information. For example, the frontal lobes decide whether a given situation is threatening or not.

Parietal Lobes   In the area of the parietal lobe known as the **somatosensory cortex**, the body senses of temperature, touch, pain, and body position are processed (see Exhibit 4.13). When this area is electrically stimulated, the person feels as if a particular body sense had been stimulated. A tingling sensation in a particular part of the body is commonly reported by subjects stimulated in this way.

Further processing of sensory information occurs in other areas of the parietal lobes. Damage to these areas

EXHIBIT 4.13
The Sensory-Motor Areas of the Cortex

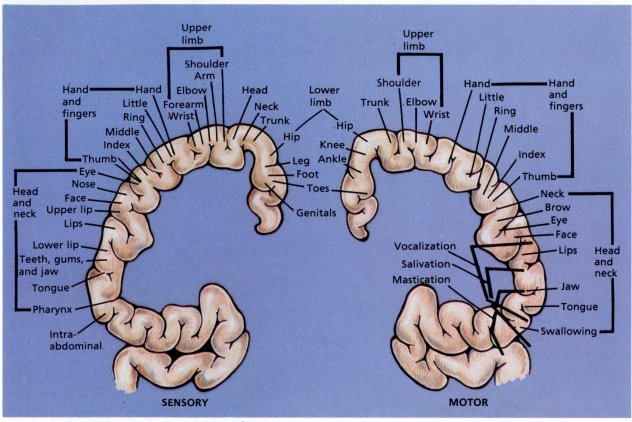

Adapted from: Penfield, W. & Rasmussen, T. 1950. *Cerebral Cortex of Man.* NY:
Macmillan. Renewed 1978 by Theodore Rasmussen.

results in agnosia or "not knowing." A person whose right parietal lobe was damaged showed no awareness of the left side of his body (Mountcastle, 1976). When asked to sketch a watch, the patient drew all the numbers on the right side and put no details on the left side of the drawing. Without the use of his right parietal lobe, the man seemed not to "know" about the external reality contained in the information coming from the left side of his body.

Occipital Lobes   The occipital lobes are also known as the **visual cortex**. Information from the eyes passes through the thalamus and goes to the back of the brain. The entire area of the occipital lobes integrates and analyzes visual information. Directly at the back of the occipital lobes are the primary receiving areas. Damage to these areas can result in blindness without any damage to the eyes; when only small portions are damaged, vision is lost in only small areas of the visual field. Surrounding the primary visual areas are the secondary areas. Damage

to the secondary areas produces a variety of visual agnosias ("not knowing"). For instance, individuals with damage to an area linked to recognition of faces can readily recognize familiar persons by the sounds of their voices but cannot recognize familiar faces (Benton, 1980). Thus, the occipital lobes are, in one sense, "eyes in the back of the head"!

Temporal Lobes   The temporal lobes, also known as the **auditory cortex**, are the central receiving areas for auditory information. While damage to the primary area in the auditory cortex results in hearing loss, stimulation of these areas produces perceptions of sounds. Changing the location of the stimulation changes the pitch and the loudness of the sound. During neurosurgery, while using electrical stimulation to map the temporal lobe, Wilder Penfield made a startling discovery (Penfield, 1957). His patient reported "hearing" auditory memories out of her past. Thus, the auditory cortex appears to be involved in more than forming auditory perceptions; it also plays a role in storing those perceptions once they are formed.

Association Cortex   The areas of the cortex for which specialized functions have not been identified are collectively referred to as **association cortex**. Lack of knowledge about the association cortex areas is due, in part, to limitations in the methods of studying the brain. However, as new methods are developed, advances in understanding the brain are made and each advance makes increasingly clear just how complex the brain is. The association cortex areas in each of the lobes have numerous interconnections, as well as important connections to subcortical and brainstem structures. The association cortex may be responsible for higher thought processes and creativity.

While uncertainty about the integration of information and activity among the four lobes of each hemisphere remains, the integration certainly does occur. Each area performs its special duties in coordination with the other areas in that hemisphere and in coordination with activities in the other hemisphere (Geschwind, 1979). Rarely, if ever, in a normally functioning brain does any one area function on its own, independent of the other areas. The brain is a fully integrated system.

Language Specialization

For reasons that are not clear, speech and language functions are localized in the left cerebral hemisphere for a majority of people. A definite connection with handedness exists. For over 95 percent of all right-handed persons, speech and language functions are localized in the left hemisphere, a fact that is consistent with the left hemisphere's control over the right side of the body. However, nearly 70 percent of all left-handers also have left-hemisphere control of language, suggesting that connections between language and writing are complex.

Awareness that, for most people, language is organized in the left hemisphere began in the early 1800s as physicians took note of their patients' speech abnormalities. Two great brain researchers, Paul Broca and Carl Wernicke, are credited with locating the specific language sites within the left hemisphere. Exhibit 4.14 shows the location of Broca's area in the frontal lobe and Wernicke's area in the temporal lobe. A tumor or damage in these areas produces two distinctly different types of **aphasia**, or language impairment.

In Broca's aphasia, an individual experiences difficulty in producing speech but does not experience impairment of language comprehension, reading, or writing.

The disability does not result from impairment of the muscles used in speaking because persons with Broca's aphasia are still able to sing. Also, the person is aware of the disability.

Individuals with Wernicke's aphasia are impaired in their ability to comprehend language and to read and write. Persons with this disability can speak fluently in terms of their rhythm, intonation, and use of grammar, but the content of their speech is often meaningless. In contrast to patients with Broca's aphasia, these patients appear unaware of their disability.

These aphasic impairments suggest a model for language organization. Wernicke's area appears to be responsible for the structure and meaning of speech. These foundation messages then pass to Broca's area, where they are translated into motor programs for speaking. These programs are then transferred to the adjacent motor cortex, where they produce the muscle contractions needed for speech.

EXHIBIT 4.14
Broca's and Wernicke's Areas in the Right Hemisphere

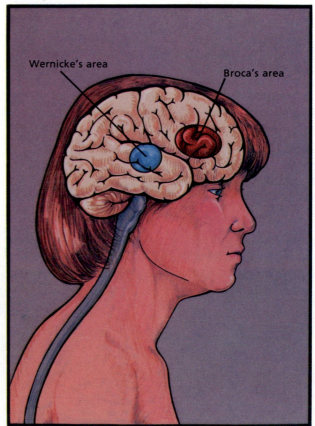

Wernicke's area

Broca's area

Adapted from: Bloom, F.E., Lazerson, A., & Hofstadter, L. 1985. *Brain, mind, and behavior.* NY: Freeman.

The Research Process: The Split Brain

Ironically, researchers often learn more about the brain's specialized functions when its normal, integrated functioning is disrupted by accident, disease, or experimental intervention. This observation has been particularly true in studying patients whose corpus callosum has been cut as a radical treatment for a severe form of epilepsy (Sperry, 1982). Cutting the major communication link between the two hemispheres prevents seizures beginning in one hemisphere from transferring to the other hemisphere. The treatment results in a so-called **split brain**. In the 1940s when this surgery was first performed, doctors observed no noticeable side effects in the patient's mental functioning. This finding was not unexpected, since the sensory systems provide information simultaneously to both hemispheres.

However, in the 1950s, Roger Sperry and his colleagues discovered that "split-brain" cats could learn something in one hemisphere while learning nothing in the other hemisphere. This finding led Sperry and his associate, Michael Gazzaniga, to look more closely at human split-brain patients. Their studies opened new vistas on the role of the left and right hemispheres in determining behavior. In 1981 Sperry received a Nobel Prize for his work in this area. Today, hemispheric specialization continues to be an area of intense study.

Results from Split-Brain Research   Under special testing procedures, the two hemispheres of split-brain patients reveal intriguing differences. If a person whose hemi-spheres have been disconnected is allowed to feel an object in his right hand without looking at it, he can describe it accurately since the information goes to the left hemisphere where language is organized (Gazzaniga, 1970). If the same procedure is followed with the left hand, the person's description is no more accurate than if he were guessing at what the object is. However, if the person is then shown a collection of objects containing the one he felt with the left hand, the individual is able to recognize it quickly and point to the correct item.

Special procedures, like those depicted in Exhibit 4.15, for using visual stimuli to test split-brain patients produce essentially the same results. The patient could talk about what she saw in her right visual field and processed in her left hemisphere. She could easily recognize and point to, but not talk about, what she saw in her left visual field and processed in her right hemisphere (Gazzaniga, 1970).

The initial interpretations of these results suggested that in most people the left hemisphere is specialized for language and speech, while the right hemisphere is skilled in processing spatial relationships. Later research indicated the left hemisphere processes information analytically and sequentially, in much the same way that language is analytical and sequential. The right hemisphere processes information holistically, as a whole unit, rather than as individual parts dealt with sequentially, one at a time.

These earlier ideas found wide acceptance and were

EXHIBIT 4.15
Tachistoscopic Presentation of
Visual Stimuli to Split-Brain Subjects

Adapted from Gazzaniga, M.S. 1970. *The bisected brain.* NY: Appleton Century-Crofts.

often augmented, without the accompanying critical research, to suggest that logic, reasoning, mathematical, and scientific skills are localized on the left side, while intuition, imagination, insight, and creativity were thought to be right hemispheric functions. In most cases, these distinctions represent over-extensions of subtle differences between the two hemispheres. Sophisticated research techniques now show just how subtle and complex hemispheric specialization is and how risky over-generalization of the research findings can be.

Research by Eran Zaidel (1975) demonstrated the specific language capabilities of the right hemisphere. Zaidel developed a special contact lens, the Z lens, that allows prolonged presentation of a stimulus with the certainty that only one hemisphere receives the information. Using this technique, Zaidel asserted that the right hemisphere could comprehend language, but that it was not capable of producing speech. According to Zaidel's research, the right hemisphere appears able to comprehend a vocabulary equivalent to that of an average ten-year-old's.

In summary, research has established that among split-brain patients the left hemisphere generally is responsible for language and speech and the right hemisphere has limited language capacity (Gazzaniga, 1983). However, even among split-brain patients, large individual differences in hemispheric specialization exist. Some split-brain patients do not display the expected language function differences between the left and right hemispheres (Myers, 1984). Therefore, researchers should be cautious about generalizing from these findings with split-brain patients to people whose corpus callosum remains intact.

Focus Question Answer

Which parts of your brain do you use when you speak? For the majority of people, areas in the temporal (Wernicke's area) and frontal (Broca's area) lobes of the left hemisphere are primarily responsible for speech. Wernicke's area provides the structure and meaning, while Broca's area translates the messages from Wernicke's area into motor programs.

Relate

Left Brain / Right Brain / Whole Brain

The immense, internal universe of your nervous system follows an organizational pattern of systems within systems. From a single neuron to the billions of neurons in the cerebral cortex, the pattern remains the same. The action potential within the neuron is a system within a system. As "systems," neurotransmitters, neuromodulators, and hormones are systems within systems. Another system within a system is the reflex arc. This organizational pattern is especially apparent in the cerebral cortex, where the systems are localized both in different lobes and in different hemispheres.

The separation and integration of functional systems within the cerebral hemispheres is termed **cerebral lateralization**, and it has intrigued researchers for a long time. In 1836 Marc Dax reported that autopsies of forty patients with speech disturbances revealed that all suffered from damage to the left hemisphere. Later, Broca and Wernicke discovered specific areas found only in the left hemisphere that were involved in language comprehension and speech. Recently, research with split-brain patients has provided additional knowledge of the major language and speech systems within the left hemisphere.

Results of these cerebral lateralization studies coincide with observations, both ancient and modern, of the differences between the right side of the body (controlled by the left hemisphere) and the left side of the body (controlled by the right hemisphere). In the ancient Chinese system of I Ching, two guiding principles—yin and yang—exist. Yin, the left side, is negative, dark, and feminine; yang, the right side, is positive, bright, and masculine. Modern researchers have distinguished between different types of problem-solving, another left/right hemisphere distinction.

The languages of various cultures make these same distinctions. The French word for left is *gauche,* which literally means "awkward." The English word *dexterous* means "skillful," while its root, *dexter,* denotes the right side of the body. The word that corresponds to dexter is *sinister,* which means "the left side of the body" and also means "evil."

Based on their experiences with handedness, most people believe that the left hemisphere is dominant over the right. Most people are right-handed; they write with their right hands, they tend to point with their right hands, and, generally, they can perform most skilled tasks better with their right hands. And the right preference pertains to more than the hand. People prefer using the right foot for kicking balls. Apparently, babies are born with this preference for the right. One study revealed that 65 percent of the newborns observed lay with their heads turned to the right (Michel, 1981).

What do these findings mean? Is the right hemisphere dominant at any time? Is the concept of dominance useful in explaining how the cerebral cortex functions? The answers to these questions have changed over the last two decades.

After more than a decade of studies with split-brain patients, the idea of left hemisphere dominance gave way to the idea of cortical lateralization, in which both hemispheres are viewed as making major, but separate, contributions to human functioning. As the intensive study of split-brain patients has clearly shown, in brains in which the corpus callosum has been cut, both hemispheres exhibit specialized functions. Dominance is not an issue because the hemispheres appear to function independently of each other.

Today, new techniques such as the PET scan provide the opportunity to observe directly living, intact brains as they process information, solve problems, and complete other tasks. Unlike the results from split-brain research, the results of these studies are creating a picture of an integrated, whole cerebral cortex. The particular area of cortex involved in a specific task now appears to be the result of a combination of specialized areas between and within each hemisphere and the particular thought process you are using at the moment. One study has found that the brain responds differently when presented with the same musical notes, but with different cognitive tasks (Phelps, Massiotta & Huang, 1982). For instance, if you are asked to decide if two notes are the same or different, your right hemisphere is activated. If you are asked to arrange the notes along a musical scale, your left hemisphere is activated. Results such as these indicate that the two hemispheres of the brain do have specialized functions that, in an intact brain, are activated in extraordinarily complex and flexible ways.

Can the complex integration of function ever be fully explained? Several people have tried, though their answers are somewhat speculative. Julian Jaynes (1976) believes that the two hemispheres work together cooperatively, with their functions shaped by the environment to which they are exposed. Jaynes believes that at earlier times, the two halves operated independently and that consciousness did not appear until written language was developed. If his specula-

tions are correct, what will the human brain be like in the future?

According to D. M. Tucker (1981), the cerebral hemispheres represent two functionally different information-processing subsystems. The system in the left hemisphere is viewed as a linear, sequential mode of processing that is involved with formulating, analyzing, and differentiating concepts. Tucker's theory meshes extremely well with the known language capabilities of the left hemisphere.

Further, Tucker believes that the right hemisphere organizes information by fusing sensory and cognitive elements into a global experience. The information is processed in a holistic manner as a unit, not sequentially as in the left hemisphere. As a result of its specialized information-processing properties for forming global impressions, the right hemisphere is specialized to facilitate arousal of emotional experience, according to Tucker. In other words, Tucker believes, suddenly feeling afraid in the presence of threatening stimuli is a function of the coordinated activity of the right hemisphere.

Some research results support his theory. Patients with damage to their right hemispheres miss more of the emotional content of verbal messages than do patients with damage to their left hemispheres. Do they also miss more of the emotional content of visual messages because the left side of the face appears to give more information about emotions than does the right side? In one study, full-face photographs were split down the middle, and composites of two left sides and two right sides were made. The left-side composites were rated as more emotional than the right-side composites (Sackheim et al., 1978).

Michael Gazzaniga (1985) argues for a modular organization model to explain the integrated functioning of the cortex. He believes that the entire cortex is composed of relatively independent, functioning modules that process information in parallel ways. Gazzaniga contends that these units often operate without conscious awareness. Because of this lack of awareness, people often do things without knowing why they do them. However, Gazzaniga maintains that a special "interpreter" module in the left hemisphere generates theories to explain everything a person does, whether or not the person consciously knows why he or she does it.

Gazzaniga's theory contains many challenging ideas and bears some similarities to Vernon Mountcastle's (1976) model of integrated brain functioning. Mountcastle believes that the cortex is organized into complex multicellular assemblies of approximately 100 neurons. He theorizes that these columns of neurons can be linked together to form information-processing modules. The grouping together of modules creates large functional units such as the motor cortex. The linkage of any module or subset of modules with other modules could change at any moment, depending on the information being received. Mountcastle believes that the processes are the same for everyone, but that the linkages are unique for each person. In this system, consciousness emerges as the activity of the whole system.

As diverse as these explanations are, they all contain a common feature. Each theory proposes, in some way, that the whole brain functions as a set of systems within systems. The theorists differ in their accounts of the number of systems, the location of the systems, and the linkage of the systems. You may have concluded that explaining the complexity of the cortex, or of the entire nervous system for that matter, as systems functioning within systems is inadequate and simplistic. Yet, for now, this model is the best one psychologists have been able to create.

At this point, the information you have learned about the biological foundations of behavior may seem perplexingly complex. You may also be aware that you have barely begun to understand the universe that lies within you. Each neuron may seem like a planet being influenced by other planets and by many other forces from within and from outside of its own galaxy. Your glimpse of this "universe within" may have brought the realization that this universe is as infinitely vast and mysterious as the universe that lies outside you.

Things to Do

1. Reaction time is the amount of time needed for the nervous system to receive the stimulus, process the information, and create a response. Try this trick with a reasonably smooth and flat dollar bill. Challenge your friend to catch the dollar bill when you drop it. Hold the length of the dollar vertically, and ask your friend to hold his or her thumb and index finger about an inch away on either side of Washington's head. When you release the dollar, your friend must try to catch it by snapping the thumb and finger together. The bill will fall away faster than your friend can react! However, do not bet the dollar bill on this outcome, because your friend may try to guess when you are going to release the bill and get lucky, or you may give an unintentional clue as to when you are going to release the dollar.

2. With another student in your class, take turns producing the knee-jerk reflex. Sit relaxed on a chair with one leg crossed over the other, so that your leg and foot move freely from the knee. Have the other person quickly tap just below the kneecap with the edge of his or her hand. Look away or close your eyes so that you do not anticipate the tap. Next try to produce the reflex while

tensing the muscles in your leg. Try to prevent the knee jerk by clasping your hands behind your head and pulling apart on them as hard as possible while being tapped beneath the kneecap. Compare and try to explain the results that you obtain under the different conditions.

3. To experience the differences in the amount of somatosensory representation in the cortex for different parts of the body, try this test. With your eyes closed, ask a friend to hold an undisclosed number of fingers against your back. Do this exercise several times, with your friend randomly varying the number of fingers used. How successful are you? Then, with your eyes still closed, have your friend hold varying numbers of fingers against your hand, while you try to identify the correct number. You should be more successful in judging the number of fingers held against your hand due to the hand's larger cortical area.

Things to Discuss

1. Imagine that you have the task of redesigning the nervous system. What systems and parts would you discard? What would you add?

2. After learning about the delicate neurochemical balance necessary for the nervous system to function normally, have your ideas about drug use (prescription, nonprescription, and recreational) changed? Discuss your views with your classmates.

3. From time to time, articles in the popular press claim that people use only 10 percent of their brain power. Based on what you have learned in this chapter, decide whether you agree with the statement.

4. One researcher has suggested that boys develop better spatial reasoning because they are more athletic than girls. In most sports, athletes must be aware of their own bodies in space and also aware of the spatial arrangement of the bodies of both teams' members. Playing team sports regularly may develop the brain structures also used in spatial reasoning. Apply what you know about brain specialization to evaluate this suggestion.

5. Neurosurgeons have developed the technology to transplant parts of brains and thereby to replace damaged or diseased areas. Many ethical issues are raised by this situation. One is the source of the donor tissue. With kidney and heart transplants, the donated organs of individuals who have been declared "brain dead" but who have been kept "alive" on life-support systems are used. To follow a similar procedure for brain transplants, neu-

rosurgeons would need to find a "live" brain from a "dead" body. Debate this issue with your classmates. Is using brain tissue from animals appropriate?

6. Currently the use of PET scans and MRI is limited to clinical settings and research. Do you think these techniques should be used with the general population? For example, should PET scans be given to help people decide which careers they want to pursue? In an attempt to detect abnormality, should police officers (or instructors, for that matter) be required to take PET scans before they are allowed to go on the job?

Things to Read

Bloom, F.E., Lazerson, A., & Hofstadter, L. 1985. *Brain, mind, and behavior*. NY: Freeman.

Hunt, M. 1982. *The universe within: A new science explores the human mind*. NY: Simon & Schuster.

Ornstein, R., Thompson, R., & Macaulay, D. 1984. *The amazing brain*. Boston: Houghton-Mifflin.

Restak, R.M. 1984. *The brain*. NY: Bantam Books.

Springer, S.P., & Deutsch, G. 1985. *Left brain, right brain* (2nd ed.). NY: Freeman.

Review

Summary

1. The two major divisions of the nervous system are the central nervous system (CNS), comprised of the brain and spinal cord, and the peripheral nervous system (PNS), which carries messages to and from the muscles, organs, and glands of the body. Messages are brought to the CNS by sensory or afferent neurons in the PNS. Messages are taken away from the CNS by motor or efferent neurons.

2. Understanding of the nervous system has advanced with the development of new research techniques. These techniques—the MRI, CAT, and PET scans—allow observation of the living brain without altering or damaging it.

3. Two basic types of cells in the nervous system are neurons and glial cells (glia). Neurons are designed for transmitting and processing information. The basic parts of a neuron are the cell body (soma), dendrites, and axon. Glial cells provide a support system for the neurons. Some glia produce myelin, an insulation for axons.

4. Within the neuron, an electrochemical process transfers information from the dendrites to the axon. The all or none principle indicates that neurons always fire at maximum strength. The fact that messages are always sent in one direction, from dendrites to axon to the dendrites of the next neuron, is known as the law of forward conduction.

5. Neurons communicate with one another across a minute gap, the synapse. Synaptic transmission of information involves the release of neurotransmitter substances from the axon of the sending neuron. These substances affect receptor sites on the dendrites of the receiving neuron.

6. Neuromodulators are chemical substances that modulate the effects of neurotransmitters and the activity of neurons. Endorphins are a class of neuromodulators that fine-tune the nervous system's reactions to pain and pleasure. The endorphins may be a major link between the body's immune system, the nervous system, and the endocrine system.

7. The endocrine system is a collection of glands that secrete hormones into the bloodstream. The endocrine system is closely tied to the nervous system through the hypothalamus and various neuromodulators. The pituitary and adrenal glands are also closely connected to the autonomic nervous system.

8. The sympathetic and the parasympathetic divisions of the autonomic nervous system work together to prepare the body to respond rapidly to stressful events and then to recuperate from them. The sympathetic branch readies us for fight or flight responses. The parasympathetic branch works to restore the energy expended by sympathetic action.

9. The reflex arc is a specialized system in the spinal cord for producing involuntary responses to stimuli. The spinal cord also serves as a conduit for information going to and from the brain.

10. Brainstem systems control many basic body functions. The medulla controls blood pressure, heart rate, and breathing, and the ascending reticular activating system regulates arousal, attention, and sleep. Information from the ears and some of the information from the eyes pass through specific areas of the midbrain.

11. The cerebellum coordinates body movement, especially fine motor control. The cerebellum is closely connected with the motor areas of the cortex, the basal ganglia, the brainstem, and the spinal cord.

12. The thalamus is a major sensory relay station, and the hypothalamus regulates many basic body functions and parts of the endocrine system. The hypothalamus and parts of the thalamus are components in the limbic system. The limbic system regulates emotional behavior, memory, and other processes.

13. The frontal lobes of the cerebral cortex control voluntary movement, planning, and judgment. The parietal lobes organize information from the body senses; the occipital lobes organize information about vision; and the temporal lobes organize auditory information. All four lobes have unspecified areas called the association cortex.

14. For most people, language and speech are organized in the left hemisphere, and visual and spatial relationships are organized in the right hemisphere. Epileptic patients with severed corpus callosums have provided a unique opportunity to study these specialized functions in a split brain.

15. Cerebral lateralization refers to the separation of specialized functions in the right and left hemispheres. However, these functions remain integrated in undamaged brains. Various models have been proposed to explain the integrated functioning of the whole brain.

Key Terms

central nervous system (CNS)
brain
spinal cord
peripheral nervous system (PNS)
somatic nervous system
autonomic nervous system (ANS)
afferent (sensory) neurons
efferent (motor) neurons
glial cells (glia)
myelin
cell body (soma)
dendrites
axon
synapse
all or none principle
law of forward conduction
neurotransmitters
neuromodulators
endocrine/neuroendocrine system

hormones
premenstrual syndrome (PMS)
fight or flight response
reflex arc
brainstem
ascending reticular activating system (ARAS)
cerebellum
thalamus
hypothalamus
limbic system
cerebral hemispheres
corpus callosum
frontal lobes
parietal lobes
occipital lobes
temporal lobes
split brain
cerebral lateralization

Focus Questions

1. How do your sense receptors gather information about the world?

2. Is grass really green?

3. How are you able to recognize the sounds of different musical instruments?

4. How are you able to distinguish between a caress and a pinch?

5. Will blind people someday be able to "see" with their skin?

Chapter Outline

THE BASICS OF SENSORY PROCESSING
Sensation and Perception
Transduction
Sensory Selectivity
Sensory Adaptation
The Research Process: Sensory Deprivation
Psychophysics

THE BASICS OF VISION
The Visual System
Light: The Physical Stimulus
Neural Processing of Visual Information
Color Vision

THE BASICS OF HEARING
The Auditory System
Sound: The Physical Stimulus
Neural Processing of Auditory Information

THE OTHER SENSES
Body and Skin Senses
Proprioception
Chemically Activated Senses

RELATE: Sensory Deficits—New Treatments for Old Problems
Things to Do
Things to Discuss
Things to Read

REVIEW: Summary
Key Terms

Chapter 5

Sensory
Processing

*We are walking in a cyclone of sounds
and smells and colors.*

Eben Given

 The Basics of Sensory Processing

Your senses introduce you to the world in which you
live. Your sensory processing systems enable you to gather
information about the world and to construct an awareness of reality. The complexity of these processes is recognized by authors Robert Rivlin and Karen Gravelle in
the following quote:

On the one hand, the senses are highly precise,
intricately programmed to provide an astonishingly
detailed report on the part of nature to which they are
sensitized. On the other hand, the senses sometimes
seem like an astonishing Rube Goldberg-like collection of
mechanical odds and ends that seem to have been
thrown together almost capriciously. We hear because
cells similar to shaving brushes push up against a
membrane in response to wavelike motions in the inner

95

ear. We taste because binder sites on the tongue attract molecules of foodstuffs like jigsaw puzzle pieces. We can tolerate enormous amounts of pain because a chemical secreted by the body prevents the sensation from being felt. (Rivlin & Gravelle, 1984, p.11)

In this chapter you will learn about the basic principles of sensation and the individual sensory processing systems. That you must use your senses to learn about sensory processing is one of the intriguing facets of this chapter.

Sensation and Perception

People are usually unfamiliar with the complex processes involved in creating their awareness of reality. **Sensation**, the process of converting physical energy into coded activity (messages) in the nervous system, is the initial phase in creating a psychological awareness of the physical world. **Perception**, the organization and interpretation of the information from the senses, is the final phase of the process. Sensation is the sensory input from which perception creates a meaningful experience.

The traditional practice of dividing into sensation and perception this process of forming a psychological view of reality has been challenged (most notably by J. J. Gibson, 1950, 1966, 1979). These divisions, however, provide a useful way of studying a very complex process. An example will help you realize why a distinction between sensation and perception is useful. Look at the drawing in Exhibit 5.1 for a few moments. This "reversing" cube can be seen in two different ways, but it cannot be seen both ways at the same time. The information your eyes sense remains the same, but the way your brain organizes the information changes. In this example, the process of sensation creates one input, but the process of perception creates two separate outputs.

Transduction

As the reversing cube example illustrates, your awareness of the world is not a direct process. When you look at the drawing of the cube, the light reflected into your eyes contains information about the drawing. However, the nervous system cannot yet use this information. In the eyes are special cells that are able to convert the information contained in light into a form the nervous system can use. This process of extracting information from the environment and converting that information into a form the nervous system can process is called **transduction**.

EXHIBIT 5.1
The Reversing Cube

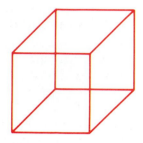

Look at this drawing for a few moments. Do you see a three-dimensional cube? Does the cube change perspectives?

Transduction is carried out by **sense receptors**, specialized cells in the skin, tongue, eyes, ears, nose, muscles, joints, and internal organs. The receptor cells trigger messages in the nervous system; these messages are transmitted to the brain. Since information arrives from so many sources, how are these sensory inputs kept separate in the nervous system? Why is information from the ears never confused with information from the eyes? To answer these questions, one early researcher proposed a law of specific nerve energies (Müller, 1838). Müller suggested that each receptor system generates its own particular neural energy in response to stimulation; messages from the ears, for example, are distinct from those from the eyes. Müller's theory has since been disproved and replaced with the knowledge that messages in the ner-

The ear's hair cells look like a series of brushes and complete the transformation of sound waves into neural impulses.

vous system are all coded in the same way. The code follows the all or none principle you learned about in Chapter 4.

Sensory Selectivity

Sensory receptors are highly selective; in other words, they respond to only those aspects of physical reality that fit their preset selection factors. For example, visual receptors respond to only a small portion of the light spectrum, and hearing receptors respond to only a certain range of sound waves. Responding to limited ranges of stimuli keeps the sensory systems from being overwhelmed. Nonetheless, even with a limited hearing range, you may encounter stimulus overload; when too many people talk to you at once, you may cover your ears with your hands to avoid the excessive information.

Further sensory selectivity occurs when certain relevant attributes of a situation are coded for processing and irrelevant information is ignored. The sense receptors transduce only selected features, or attributes, of the available information about the physical world.

Research on frog visual systems clearly shows this type of selectivity (Lettvin et al., 1959). A specially devised apparatus presented numerous visual patterns to the immobilized eye of a frog. Researchers recorded the neural impulses sent from the frog's eye to its brain. Amazingly, out of all the information available to the frog's eye, only four types of visual patterns are transduced into neural impulses and sent to the brain.

These four visual patterns contain information relevant to the safety and survival of the frog; the frog's visual receptors detect edges of objects, moving objects, dimming light, and movement of small, dark, roughly circular-shaped objects. Frogs react to edges, dimming light, and movement to avoid predators and danger, and they react to small, dark, roughly circular-shaped objects (flying bugs) to obtain food. Thus, frogs have visual receptors that selectively detect important environmental features.

Psychologists have also studied extensively the visual systems of cats and monkeys (Hubel and Wiesel, 1962, 1963, 1965, 1968) and have reported a similar arrangement of feature detectors, although cats' and monkeys' visual systems exhibit greater complexity and flexibility than those of frogs. On the other hand, researchers have obtained little evidence of the presence of feature detectors in humans; they presume, however, that responding to edges (the beginnings and endings of events and objects) is an element common to all visual systems.

Sensory Adaptation

Through a process called **sensory adaptation**, sensory systems respond more to changing stimulation (new events and objects) and less to unchanging stimulation. For instance, when you first step into a bathtub filled with hot water, the water feels very warm because of the great change in temperature. After a few minutes, you adapt to the unchanging water temperature, and the water no longer seems so warm. Receptors selectively respond to "edges" because stimulus change occurs there. This responsiveness to "edges" reduces the amount of information a sensory system must transduce to create a psychological awareness of reality.

Some background stimuli are so unchanging that the receptors cease to create neural messages. This aspect of sensory adaptation is most evident in smell and touch. Immediately after you walk into a greenhouse, you are very aware of the fragrances of the flowers. However, your smell receptors adapt very quickly to constant odors, and after a few minutes you no longer notice the fragrances. If someone else then enters the room, he or she may comment on the fragrances you no longer smell. Also due to the process of sensory adaptation, you may "lose contact" with the socks on your feet, the glasses on the bridge of your nose, and the ring on your finger. Your skin's receptors for touch and pressure undergo sensory adaptation to the constant pressure of your socks, glasses, or ring and no longer transduce that information.

Adaptation to smells occurs quickly. When you first step into a room filled with roses the fragrance seems overpowering, but after a few minutes you no longer notice the scent.

Selectivity Through Comparison Sensory systems also reduce and simplify their information load by responding comparatively, not absolutely, to stimulation. Instead of containing individual receptors to transduce each gradation of color, sound, or taste, sensory systems have receptors that convert the information from a stimulus to comparative terms. The following demonstration illustrates this feature.

Fill one pan with very hot water, one with very cold water, and a third with tepid water. Put one hand in the hot water and the other in the cold water. After two minutes, place both hands in the tepid water. The tepid water should feel cold to the hand that was in the hot water and warm to the hand that was in the cold water. Each hand adapted to the original water temperature, and neither hand transduced information about the absolute temperature of the tepid water. Instead, each hand converted the information about the tepid water to a comparison with the water in the first pan. The hot and cold stimuli produced different adaptation levels in each hand; the receptors in each hand coded different information about the tepid water.

The Research Process: Sensory Deprivation

Although many psychologists are interested in how people sense the myriad stimuli around them, other psychologists are more interested in what people experience when they are deprived of normal sensory stimulation. In the early 1950s researchers reported that **sensory deprivation** was generally an unpleasant experience (Heron, 1961). In one experiment (Bexton et al., 1954) subjects were paid twenty dollars a day to spend time in a small room and to have their sensory stimulation limited. Exhibit 5.2 depicts the arrangement of the room.

Except for brief periods during which the subjects were allowed to eat and use the toilet, they remained motionless on a bed. For visual stimulation, they wore translucent plastic visors that produced constant diffuse light. Auditory stimulation was limited to the constant hum of the air-conditioning equipment and further reduced by U-shaped pillows encircling their heads. To reduce skin sensations, subjects wore gloves and cotton-lined cardboard tubes over their arms. These conditions reduced greatly both the amount of sensory stimulation and amount of stimulus change.

This environment's effects on the subjects were most interesting. Within a few hours, subjects' performances on a variety of intellectual tasks declined. The subjects became bored and irritable, and they found doing noth-

EXHIBIT 5.2
Sensory Deprivation Room

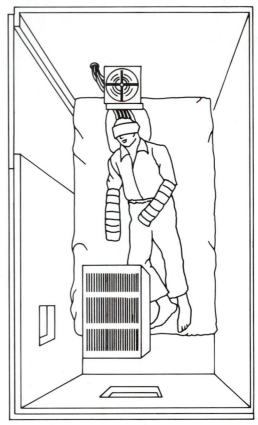

Adapted from the illustration by Eric Mose in ''The Pathology of Boredom'' by Woodburn Heron. *Scientific American*, January 1957.

ing for long periods difficult. Eventually, some subjects hallucinated geometric patterns and cartoon-like figures, such as a procession of eyeglasses walking down a street. Additionally, after experiencing sensory deprivation, subjects were more easily persuaded by arguments for the existence of ghosts (Zubek, 1969).

More than half the subjects asked to leave the room within forty-eight hours of beginning the sensory deprivation experiment. After leaving, some subjects experienced perceptual distortions such as straight lines appearing curved and stationary objects appearing to move. Almost all subjects said the experience was an unpleasant one.

Critics of the initial study maintain that the subjects felt discomfort not because sensory deprivation is unpleasant but because subjects were led to believe by the instructions they were given that the experience would be unpleasant. The results of a study in which subjects were told that sensory deprivation would aid meditation

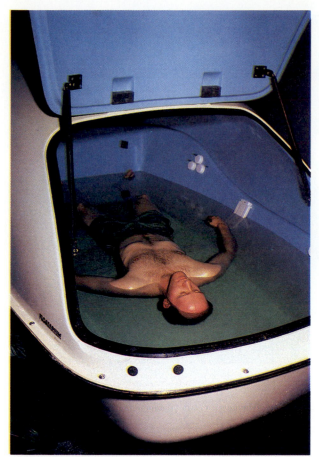

"Float tanks," tanks filled with a buoyant body-temperature solution and located in a darkened soundproof room, are an outgrowth of sensory deprivation research. Subjects commonly experience vivid mental images while floating in these tanks. Lilly (1972) reported experiencing fantastic out-of-body travel to other dimensions, which led him to conclude that reality is a creation of the mind. Available commercially in many parts of the country, float tanks are purported to promote relaxation. Some people, like Lilly, find the float tank experience a profound one; others become quickly bored. If you decide to experience sensory deprivation in a float tank, remember that your experience will result as much from your personal beliefs and expectations as from the sensory deprivation itself.

support this conclusion (Zuckermen, 1969). These subjects, who were exposed to the same conditions except for the instructions they were given, did not become irritable or hallucinate. Their performances on intellectual tasks improved rather than declined. Similarly, other researchers have reported that sensory deprivation sharpens subjects' abilities to see and hear, aids memorization, increases openness to new experiences, and helps people stop smoking (Suedfeld, 1975). A reasonable conclusion

from these research studies is that expectations about the effects of sensory deprivation determine, at least partially, subjects' responses to the experience.

Psychophysics

Psychophysics is the study of the change in psychological experience that results from change in a physical stimulus. The term psychophysics was coined because the early researchers in this area used physics as a model for studying sensation. These researchers, like the physicists they emulated, looked for laws of nature to describe the relationship between physical reality and psychological experience. Through their highly controlled laboratory experiments, the psychophysicists have established several basic principles of sensory processing.

Absolute Threshold   How dim a light can people detect? How much warmer must a room become before people notice the temperature change? Psychophysicists have provided answers to these questions by developing precise methods for determining thresholds of stimulation. An **absolute threshold** is the point at which people first become aware of the presence of a stimulus. Exhibit 5.3 lists the absolute thresholds of different sense systems.

To determine the absolute threshold for hearing, psychophysicists first present subjects with an inaudible tone. They increase the loudness of this tone in small, equal increments until subjects report hearing the tone. Then they present a series of tones, beginning with an audible tone. They decrease the loudness of this tone in small, equal decrements until subjects report no longer hearing

EXHIBIT 5.3
Absolute Thresholds

Sense	Detection threshold
Light	A candle flame seen at thirty miles on a dark clear night.
Sound	The tick of a watch under quiet conditions at twenty feet.
Taste	One teaspoon of sugar in two gallons of water.
Smell	One drop of perfume diffused into the entire volume of a three-room apartment.
Touch	The wing of a bee falling on your cheek from a distance of 1 cm.

From Galanter, 1962, p. 97.

Subliminal Perception

The attention given to the detection threshold led to the development of a related area of interest, **subliminal perception**. *Subliminal* refers to stimuli that are below the detection threshold. Researchers question if very weak stimuli, those below the conscious detection level, can unconsciously influence behavior.

To test this question, research in the 1950s attempted to show that moviegoers were influenced to buy popcorn when an advertisement was flashed on the screen too briefly for it to be consciously detected. Although these studies were poorly conducted and subject to many methodological flaws, they led to a public uproar about the presumed threat to individual freedom.

These initial studies by nonpsychologists prompted psychologists to study seriously this phenomenon. Evidence from several well-controlled studies in the 1970s supported subliminal perception (Corteen & Wood, 1972; von Wright et al., 1975), and many psychologists have concluded that subliminal perception does exist. Nonetheless, subliminal perception is so difficult to produce even under laboratory conditions that the effectiveness of subliminal advertising is unlikely. Although the public may still believe subliminal perception to be effective, advertisers have abandoned the use of subliminal advertising and now employ strong, attention-getting stimuli that are well above the detection threshold.

---

the tone. After many repetitions of this procedure, psychophysicists identify the absolute threshold as the point at which the probability of detecting the stimulus is equal to the probability of no longer detecting the stimulus; in other words, the absolute threshold is the point at which subjects detect a stimulus fifty percent of the time.

Although, theoretically and logically, a point exists below which stimulation cannot be sensed, psychophysicists have failed to find a single constant value. Because of this failure, the definition of absolute threshold is arbitrary, and the term **detection threshold** seems a more appropriate description of this situation in which the threshold is anything but absolute. Keep in mind the variability of absolute thresholds as you read the *Exploring . . .* section about subliminal perception.

Difference Threshold   The minimum amount of change in a physical stimulus necessary for its detection is called the **difference threshold** or, more commonly, the **just noticeable difference (j.n.d.)**. You might think that you would detect any change above the absolute threshold. However, if you reflect further, you will realize that while you can detect easily a very small difference in illumination in a dimly lit room, you need a much larger change in illumination to detect a j.n.d. in a brightly-lit room.

Ernst Weber (1834) realized that people experience the lighting of one candle in a dark room as a much greater increase in brightness than the lighting of one candle in a room in which one hundred candles already burn. He proposed that the j.n.d. is always the same proportion of the stimulus intensity, a formula now known as **Weber's law**. For example, the constant proportion for lifted weights is approximately 1/50. If you first lift 50 pounds, 50.5 will not seem noticeably heavier, but 51 pounds will seem *just* noticeably heavier. Similarly, 102 pounds is just noticeably heavier than 100 pounds. Several other examples of the application of Weber's law are found in Exhibit 5.4.

Psychophysical Scaling   Psychophysicists, in their quest for the psychological counterparts to the laws of physics, developed psychological scales for measuring sensation. One of the first attempts at **psychophysical scaling**, measuring the relationship between the physical intensity of a stimulus and the corresponding psychological experience of the intensity, was made by a German philosopher/physicist, Gustav Fechner (1860). Fechner seized upon Weber's law and the j.n.d. as an ideal unit measuring sensation; he regarded each j.n.d. as an equal unit of sensory experience. J.n.d.'s became the standard psychological unit of measurement for sensation, comparable to physical units such as inches and centimeters.

Fechner proposed that the psychological experience of stimulus intensity increases a constant amount with each j.n.d. in the physical intensity of the stimulus. In other words, Fechner maintained that each j.n.d. was psychologically equal. Fechner believed that he had succeeded in finding a relationship between sensory experience and physical reality. Nearly one hundred years elapsed before Weber's law was shown to be true only for the middle ranges of stimulus intensity and before Fechner's assumption that all j.n.d.'s are equal was questioned.

The **power law** established a mathematical relationship between psychological experience and stimulus intensity. Each sensory dimension has its own power function (Stevens, 1961; 1962). Exhibit 5.5 shows the scales for brightness and for pain from electric shock. The relationships between psychological experience and the stimulus intensities of brightness and pain are quite different; pain information is exaggerated psychologically, while brightness information is diminished. As these examples indicate, the individual sense systems selectively process information in accordance with the importance of different types of information.

Psychophysics and the Real World   At this point, you may be questioning the relevance of psychophysics to the real world. In an attempt to control relevant variables and to manipulate single stimuli in their experiments, psychophysicists have often created laboratory conditions that are far removed from everyday sensory processing. Despite these conditions, the results have

EXHIBIT 5.5
The Power Law

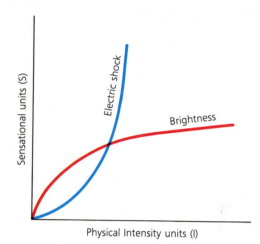

changed and improved people's lives. Stereo music components reflect the knowledge gained from auditory sensory processing experiments. Improvements in working conditions—light, sound, and other environmental factors—have resulted from other psychophysical studies. Even design improvements in jet plane cockpits are a direct outgrowth of early psychophysics research.

Focus Question Answer

How do your sense receptors gather information about the world? Your sense receptors selectively gather information from the environment and transduce it into forms that the nervous system can use. The absolute threshold and the difference threshold (j.n.d.) illustrate the amazing sensitivity of sensory systems.

The Basics of Vision

For humans, vision is the dominant sense. When visual information is available, humans rely on it above information obtained from the other senses. The common-sense saying "Seeing is believing" reflects this bias. Amazingly, the visual system processes 80 percent of all incoming sensory information. According to Neil McAleer, author of a recent book of amazing facts about the human body, even the visual technological feats of the NASA space program are dwarfed by comparison to the visual system's processing capabilities:

EXHIBIT 5.4
Values For Weber's Law for Various Senses in the Optimum Range of Sensitivity

Sense	Weber fraction
Deep pressure, from skin and subcutaneous tissue	1/77
Visual brightness	1/60
Lifted weights	1/52
Loudness of a 1000-Hz tone	1/12
Smell for rubber	1/11
Cutaneous pressure	1/7
Taste for saline solution	1/5

After Boring, Langfeld, & Weld, 1939.

[H]umankind has mounted robot eyes on a spacecraft and sent them to the far reaches of our solar system. *Vikings 1* and *2* took more than 50,000 images of the Martian surface from 1976 to 1980. During their planetary encounters *Voyagers 1* and *2* transmitted about 70,000 images of Saturn and Jupiter back to earth. The four encounters took place over a period of about 2 years, even though the actual rendezvous times were measured in days. In all, the image data from both spacecraft were made up of 387 billion bits and took hundreds of hours to transmit. Our eyes can transmit the same amount of data to the brain in just 6 3/4 minutes. (McAleer, 1985, p. 37)

The information-processing feats of the eyes are no more amazing than the totally automatic and unconscious way in which the processing occurs.

Humans, like many other animals, rely on vision for important survival functions. Vision is the primary sense you use to recognize food at a distance and to recognize threats to safety. You also use vision to recognize the changing features of the environment and to move about efficiently in the world. The aesthetic pleasure you obtain from viewing the scenic beauty of nature, the arts, and other members of the species derives from vision. Truly, vision is the most astounding sense!

The Visual System

The processing of visual information begins with the eye, a complex sensory organ with many parts (see Exhibit 5.6). The tough, white outer covering of the eye is called the **sclera**. The outward pressure of the fluid and structures within the sclera maintain the eye's characteristically ovoid shape. Attached to the sclera of each eye is a set of muscles that keep the eye within the skull's bony socket and produce movements that greatly expand the **visual field** (the area from which your eye receives information).

To determine your visual field, try staring straight ahead while keeping your eyes and head motionless. Note how far you can see to the left, right, top, and bottom of your visual field. Next, keeping your head motionless, rotate your eyes upward as far as you can, and notice how much more you can see. Continue to notice how much you can see as you rotate your eyes far to the left, downward, and then far to the right. Become aware of the pull of your eye muscles as your eyes focus on each position. These muscles produce over 200,000 coordinated eye movements every day—an average of two to three movements per second!

Light reflected from the visual field first passes through the transparent **cornea**, which bends the incoming rays of light and helps focus them. Because the cornea is deeply curved, it is three times more powerful in focusing light than is the lens. Light bent by the curvature of the cornea then passes through the **pupil**, an opening in the **iris**. The opaque iris, the colored part of the eye, is composed of two layers of muscles that control the size of the pupil and thus the amount of light entering the eye. One layer of muscles works to constrict, or decrease, the size of the pupil opening. This constriction occurs reflexively to bright light and acts as a protective mechanism for the sensitive receptor cells within the eye. Pupil constriction also occurs when you focus on close-up objects and when you sleep. The second layer of muscles dilates, or increases, the size of the pupil opening. Your pupils dilate under dim illumination; this dilation allows more light to enter. The pupils also dilate when you concentrate, experience pain or excitement, or experience positive emotional reactions.

Directly behind the pupil is the **lens**. The lens focuses the light by adjusting for distance and inverting and reversing the image on the **retina** at the back of the eye. The shape of the lens is controlled by a set of muscles that fine focus the image. These muscles bring distant objects into focus by making the lens thinner and near objects into focus by making the lens thicker. This process is called **accommodation** and is especially important when you look at objects close to you.

The lens does not always fine focus accurately. Nearsighted individuals have difficulty accommodating to distant objects, and farsighted individuals have difficulty accommodating to nearby objects. As you grow older, your lenses become more amber-tinted and opaque, lose their elasticity, and become thinner. Because of these changes, accommodating to close-up objects becomes more difficult, and you tend to become farsighted. Fortunately, eye glasses or contact lenses correct these problems caused by irregularities in the shape of the eye and the lens.

Another condition that prevents the lens from fine-focusing is cataracts. Cataracts are an extreme clouding and opacity of the lens; they obstruct the lens and eventually cause blindness. Luckily, modern technology has perfected techniques to replace damaged lenses with plastic lenses that restore vision. (For treatments of other vision deficits, see the *Relate* section.)

Retina   Literally and figuratively, the retina is the focal point of the visual system. A thin membrane about the

EXHIBIT 5.6
The Eye

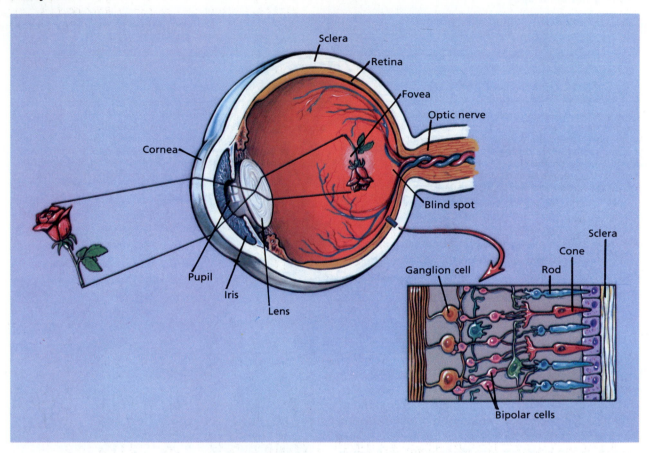

thickness of this page, it is draped against the curved back wall of the eye. Unlike a flat sheet or a projection screen, the retina extends forward from the wall and nearly reaches the muscles of the lens at the front of the eye. The resulting extensive surface area allows the retina to receive light from a wide range of angles.

The retina is composed of several interconnected layers of neural tissue and blood vessels. To gain a glimpse of the magnificence of the retina, follow these directions. Stand in front of a mirror, and shine a small penlight into one of your eyes. You see reflected in the mirror the retina's bright-red, outermost layer, which is composed of blood vessels. This reflection of light on the retina produces the red eyes that you sometimes see in photographs taken with electronic flash; the same effect causes the red eyes you see at night when a car's headlights shine directly into an animal's eyes.

The eyes' receptor cells, the **rods** and the **cones**, are in the innermost layer of the retina, facing the back wall

of the eye. The light must pass through the other retinal layers before reaching the rods and cones. The rods and cones absorb light energy and trigger messages in the nearby **bipolar cells**. From the bipolar cells, the messages go to **ganglion cells**. The axons of the ganglion cells form the **optic nerve**, which carries the messages to the brain.

Retinal Landmarks   Two retinal landmarks are the **fovea** and the **optic disk**. The fovea is situated in the center of the retina. When you look directly at an object, the image is focused directly on the fovea. An object that is three feet tall and fifty feet away will create a retinal image only slightly larger than the fovea. One million cones are packed into the pinhead-sized fovea, which allows humans to see fine detail.

The optic disk is the area of the retina in which ganglion cell axons come together to form the optic nerve. Because no receptor cells are within the optic

EXHIBIT 5.7
Locating the Blind Spot

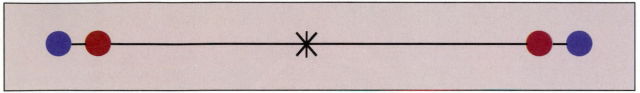

Close one eye while you stare at the X; move the book closer or farther away from your eye until you locate the spot where one of the dots disappears. Now open the eye you had closed while closing the other. Does one of the dots disappear on this side?

When the colored dots disappear, you realize they have not disappeared from the page. Without receptors in the optic disk, you are "blind" to the colored dots. Did you notice what happened to the black line when you positioned each dot in your blind spot? If the optic disk is truly a blind spot, why do you not see a gap in the black line? Although the answer is simple—the visual system fills in the gap—the process by which this occurs is not simple.

disk, this area is also called the **blind spot**. You can locate the blind spot in each eye by following the instructions in Exhibit 5.7. The blind spots are symmetrically positioned. However, when you look at an object with both eyes, you do not see two black holes in your visual field, because information that falls on the blind spot in your left eye does not land on the blind spot in your right eye and because processing that occurs in other parts of the visual system fills the gaps with appropriate information to eliminate the blind spots.

From the optic disks, the optic nerves from each eye carry messages to the **optic chiasma**. The optic chiasma is a crossover point at the base of the brain. At the optic chiasma, information from the inner half of each retina crosses over to the opposite side of the brain (see Exhibit 5.8), while information from the outer halves stays on the same side of the brain. In this way, information from the right half of the visual field eventually reaches the visual areas at the back of the left hemisphere, and information from the left half of the visual field goes to corresponding areas in the right hemisphere.

Rods and Cones   The rods and the cones are the first neural components in a chain of events that results in vision. These cells are responsible for selectively transducing the relevant properties of the light focused on the retina. Rods and cones are descriptively named. Under high magnification, rods look like cylindrically shaped, thin index fingers; cones look like plump thumbs. Each retina contains approximately 120 million rods and six million cones. The fovea is composed entirely of cones; from the fovea to the periphery of the retina are fewer and fewer cones. In contrast, rods are distributed in the

EXHIBIT 5.8
The Visual Field and Optic Pathways

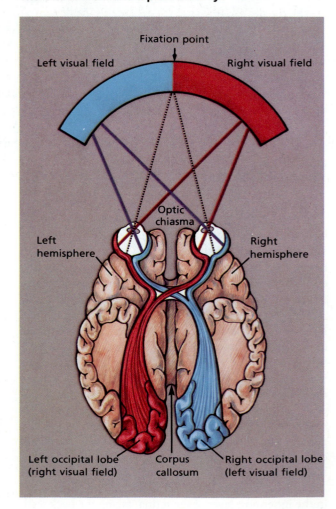

opposite manner; the greatest proportion is found in the periphery.

Rods and cones respond differently to light of varying intensities. Rods are sensitive to extremely low levels of light energy. This sensitivity makes possible the visual detection threshold mentioned earlier—seeing a candle flame thirty miles away on a clear night! The rods contain a light-sensitive chemical, **rhodopsin**. Light energy that strikes a rod is absorbed by the rhodopsin; this absorption generates a small electrical message. Under brightly lit conditions, however, the rhodopsin is broken down and absorbs very little light; at such times, rods are very insensitive to changes in light energy.

Cones function in essentially the same way as do rods, but with a different range of sensitivity. At low levels of illumination, cones are much less sensitive than rods. Cones, which are responsible for color perception and for fine detail detection, function best in daylight and bright artificial light; rods are used for night vision and for seeing in other dimly-lit conditions.

Dark and Light Adaptation   When your instructor turns off the lights to show a film, you will not be able to see very well immediately, but within a couple of minutes, your ability to see at this much lower level of illumination will improve. This adjustment of the sensitivity of rods and cones to lower illuminations is called **dark adaptation**.

In contrast, when you move from lower to higher levels of light, the rods and cones undergo **light adap-** tation. When your instructor turns on the lights after showing a film, you adapt to this higher level more quickly than you adapted to the darker conditions. Initially, when the light switch is flipped, your pupils constrict rapidly and you may squint your eyes to reduce the amount of light until the rods and cones adapt to this new level of light.

Light: The Physical Stimulus

As noted earlier, the rods and cones respond to only a limited portion of light energy, the **electromagnetic spectrum**. This continuum of physical energy also includes X-rays, ultraviolet light, infrared light, microwaves, radio waves, and TV waves (see Exhibit 5.9). Electromagnetic radiation is measured in units called **photons**.

Photons, which are emitted from a light source or reflected from the surface of an object, travel to the eyes along a wave-like path. The waves of light reaching the eyes can be measured on three physical dimensions: **wavelength**, **amplitude**, and **complexity**. People experience these three physical dimensions on the three corresponding psychological dimensions of **color (hue)**, **brightness**, and **saturation**.

Wavelength = Color (Hue)   The physical dimension of wavelength is coded in the visual system as information about color or hue. Any specific color you perceive results from the mixture of different wavelengths

EXHIBIT 5.9
The Electromagnetic Spectrum

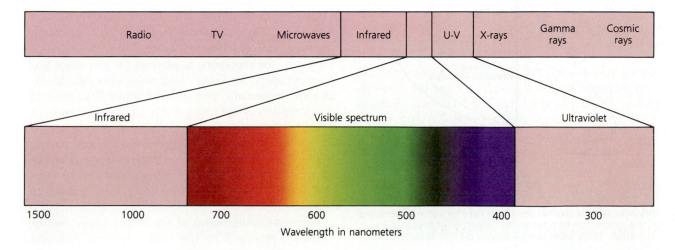

transmitted to the eyes. A pure color consists of light waves of a single wavelength (See Exhibit 5.10).

When equal amounts of all wavelengths are transmitted to the eyes, you see the color white; when no light waves are transmitted to the eyes, you see black. Technically, black, white, and the range of neutral grays are achromatic, without color. Actually, the entire world around you is without color, a fact people often "lose sight of." You see color because surfaces of objects reflect light of different wavelengths. Information processed from the different wavelengths produces the perception of color. Thus, color is the product of your visual sensory system.

EXHIBIT 5.10
The Color Spindle

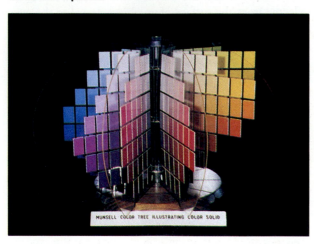

MUNSELL COLOR TREE ILLUSTRATING COLOR SOLID

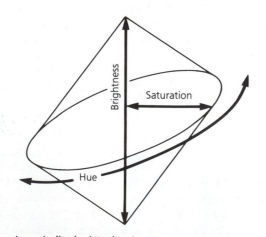

The color spindle depicts the three psychological dimensions of the perception of light waves: color, brightness, and saturation. Every color can be placed on this spindle.

Amplitude = Brightness   The psychological experience that corresponds to the amplitude of light waves is brightness. All colors have some degree of brightness; white contains the most brightness and black contains the least. Shades of gray vary in brightness as they range from nearly white shades to nearly black. Among colors of equal amplitude, those of longer wavelength (the reds) appear less bright than those of shorter wavelength (the blues).

Complexity = Saturation   The purest colors you experience are those produced by light waves of a single wavelength. When other wavelengths are mixed with the dominant wavelength, the wave form is more complex, and the color is less highly "saturated" with the dominant color. As the dominant wavelength becomes more diluted (less highly saturated), the color becomes more gray until zero saturation is reached, and you perceive a shade of neutral gray.

Neural Processing of Visual Information

The visual system can be described as an information selection and consolidation system. From the retina to the brain, the processing is selective for five major features of light: color (hue) , brightness, saturation (complexity), movement, and spatial features. The physical characteristics of light responsible for the perception of color, brightness, and saturation also are responsible for the perception of spatial properties and movement. You perceive size, shape, position, orientation, and movement as the result of a process that begins when light that varies in wavelength, amplitude, and complexity stimulates the retina.

The processing begins in the retina, where the information processed by 126 million receptor rods and cones is consolidated by a million or so ganglion cells. Despite the great consolidation, information from each region of the retina continues to be represented at each higher level of organization in the brain.

When the receptor cells of the retina are stimulated it affects the behavior of other cells at higher levels of the visual system. In the brain, cells at each level of processing use information that originated in receptor cells on the retina and that was consolidated by the previous levels (Hubel & Wiesel, 1979). By recording the electrical activity of single neurons, researchers have identified specific cells that, depending on their complexity, respond only to lines, or edges, or angles, or moving light, or length, or width, or other features.

At the first level of processing, detector cells respond to basic features such as bars, lines, and edges and the specific angles of these features in the receptor cells. At the next, more complex, level, the consolidated information from the feature detectors is analyzed for movement and changes in patterns of light intensity, or spatial frequency (DeValois & DeValois, 1980). At this level, spatial frequency detectors analyze the overall shape of a stimulus and the fine details in a stimulus pattern. Exhibit 5.11 illustrates this process of spatial frequency detection. At the highest levels, processing for pattern recognition occurs. Here, researchers think, the recognition of objects results from comparing incoming information with information stored in memory. Amazingly, this entire process happens in a split second and happens continuously throughout each moment of your waking day!

EXHIBIT 5.11
Spatial Frequency Detection

First look at this picture at close range; then, move farther away. At what point does a picture appear?

Visual Processing and the Real World A perplexing aspect of visual processing remains unresolved. The end product of sensory processing in the visual system is conscious awareness of the world. As detailed and successful as the studies of visual processing have been, no study has discovered how visual information is transformed into conscious experience. Although researchers understand quite well how the physical stimulus is processed and analyzed in the retina and the brain, they are still confronted with the eternal question, "How is it that we see?"

Color Vision

The mechanisms that produce the experience of an estimated seven million distinct hues have been studied for years by physicists, physiologists, and psychologists. All have confirmed the experience of color derives from wavelengths of light reaching the eyes; however, as in all sensory systems, the change from physical stimulus to neural impulse to perceptual experience is not direct. The cones are responsible for transducing information about wavelength. Three types of cones are found in the retina of humans (MacNichol, 1964). Each type of cone is sensitive to different ranges of wavelengths: one to red, one to green, and one to blue. Exhibit 5.12 shows the range of sensitivity for each type of cone. If cones are stimulated with light of a single wavelength, the color you experience will be one of the primary colors—red, green, or blue. You perceive longer wavelengths as red, shorter wavelengths as blue, and intermediate wavelengths as green.

Theories of Color Vision According to the Young-Helmholtz **trichromatic theory**, the experience of any specific color is dependent upon how much each type of cone is stimulated. When only red cones are stimulated, you experience red; when red and green cones are stimulated equally, you see yellow. Stimulating all three types of cones equally produces the visual sensation of white. The experience of black results from stimulating none of the cones.

In part, trichromatic theory was widely accepted in the past because it was consistent with what researchers knew about color blindness. **Color blindness** is the inability to distinguish between some or all colors. About 8 percent of males and 0.3 percent of females have some form of color blindness, but "blindness" is actually an inaccurate description of this condition; individuals who are totally color "blind" and see only shades of gray are extremely rare. The majority of color-blind people have

EXHIBIT 5.12
Range of Sensitivity for the Three Cone Types

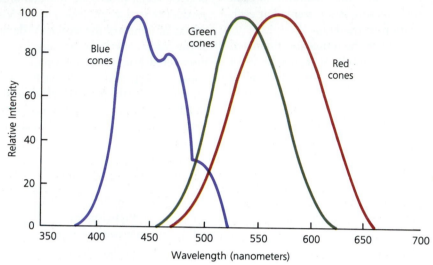

difficulty distinguishing between red and green. To see the effects of red-green deficiencies in one's color vision, look at Exhibit 5.13.

For decades, researchers were puzzled that color blindness is most often a deficiency in discriminating certain color pairs. They had observed red-green color blindness but had never encountered red-blue color blindness. Recently, research identifying specific genes linked to each type of cone has solved this puzzle (Na-

EXHIBIT 5.13
Example of the Effects of Red-Green Color Blindness

The photo on the right illustrates how a person with red-green color blindness sees the photo on the left.

then et al., 1986). These researchers found evidence that the genes responsible for red and green cones occur in tandem, but red-blue and blue-green genes do not often exist together. Thus, color-blind individuals are likely to be deficient in the red-green genes because they occur together; individuals are not likely to be missing both the non-adjacent red and blue genes or blue and green genes.

This new evidence, however, does not explain another interesting color phenomenon, **negative afterimages**. When your cones are stimulated for at least thirty seconds with a specific color of light and are then stimulated with white light, you see the complementary color. For example, if you first look at green and then look at white, you will see a red afterimage. Many computer operators experience "computer pink" negative afterimages after staring at green computer monitor images for several hours. Can you predict what color afterimages you would experience if the computer monitor screen were blue? To experience a negative afterimage, follow the instructions in Exhibit 5.14.

The trichromatic theory explains negative afterimages as fatigue in the receptors; for example, when you stare at a yellow stimulus, the red and green receptors become fatigued. When you then look at a white stimulus, the blue (unfatigued) receptors respond more than do the fatigued red and green receptors; thus, you experience blue, yellow's complementary color, as the negative afterimage.

EXHIBIT 5.14
Negative Afterimage

Stare at this figure for at least a minute and then look at a white sheet of paper. You should see the complementary colors when you look at the white surface.

Seeking to explain the color pairs observed in color blindness and the complementary nature of negative afterimages, Ewald Hering proposed an **opponent-process theory** of color vision (Hering, 1920). According to opponent-process theory, three underlying systems—red-green, blue-yellow, and dark-light function to process color information. In a theory consistent with information about color blindness and negative afterimages, Hering maintained that negative afterimages occur because receptors in each system can code only one of the opposing elements at a time. When green information is coded, red information cannot be coded. When a green stimulus stops, the system rebounds by coding red information.

Today, the trichromatic and opponent-process theories have been reconciled by combining them into a two-stage model of processing. In this model, the experience of color results from initial coding in a trichromatic system at the level of the receptors and further coding in an opponent-process system at other levels of the visual system (Hurvich, 1978). In the retina, three types of cones have been identified—red, green, and blue (MacNichol, 1964; Mollon, 1982)—and, in the thalamus, cells with opposing red-green and blue-yellow actions have been identified (DeValois et al., 1966). Thus, the two-stage model offers the best fit to the present data.

Focus Question Answer

Is grass really green? While philosophers may still debate this question, most psychologists would answer "no." You see green grass because cones in your retina process the physical characteristics of the light—wavelength, amplitude, and complexity—reflected from the blades of grass into the psychological characteristics of light—color, brightness, and saturation. In this sense, the green you see is really in your head.

 The Basics of Hearing

Audition (hearing) is no less remarkable than sight. The ears are extremely sensitive; if they were any more sensitive, you would be able to hear the blood flowing in the vessels of your ears. Further, the range of intensities people can hear is almost incomprehensible. The sound you hear when you stand close to a jet plane (well above the threshold for auditory pain) is 100 trillion times louder than the sound of a watch ticking twenty feet away (the auditory detection threshold). Exhibit 5.15 presents the loudness of several familiar sounds.

The Auditory System

The ear is divided into three sections—the outer ear, the middle ear, and the inner ear (see Exhibit 5.16). The **outer ear** consists of the **pinna** and the **auditory canal**. The pinna, the external, observable part of the

EXHIBIT 5.15
The Loudness of Familiar Sounds

Decibel Levels	
120	Where "sound" is experienced as pain. Amplification at many rock concerts.
100	Jet aircraft at 500 feet. Chain saw. A subway train.
80	Hearing loss occurs with prolonged exposure. Phone ringing. Noisy street traffic.
60	Quiet automobile. Normal level of conversation.
40	Quiet office.
20	Soft whisper.
0	The ticking of a watch at 20 feet under quiet conditions.

**EXHIBIT 5.16
The Ear**

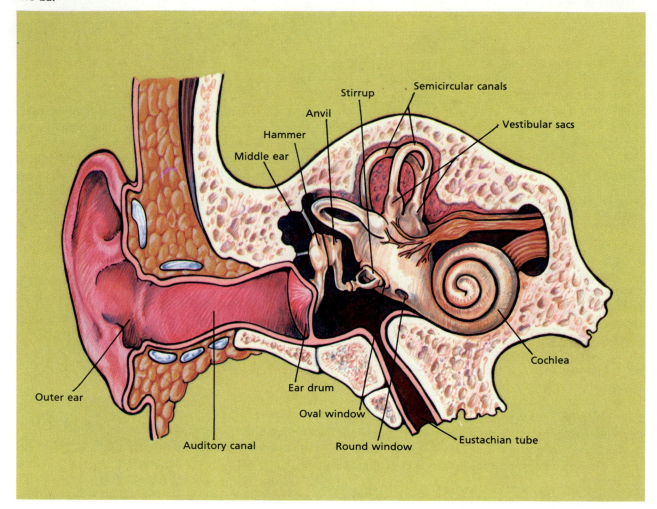

ear, collects and channels sound waves into the auditory canal.

The **eardrum (tympanic membrane)** separates the outer ear from the **middle ear**. When sound waves traveling down the auditory canal reach the eardrum, they cause the eardrum to vibrate. This process is similar to striking a drum; the skin on the opposite side of the drum vibrates. In both cases, the energy of the sound waves produces the vibrating movement. The eardrum, which is less than one-half inch in diameter and 1/250 inch thick, is ultrasensitive. At the threshold for hearing, the eardrum vibrates no more than two billionths of an inch!

The vibrations of the eardrum are transmitted to the bones in the middle ear—the **hammer (malleus), anvil**

(incus) and **stirrup (stapes)**. This chain of small bones (the smallest bones in the body) acts as an amplifier; it concentrates the sound vibrations on the **oval window** at the entrance to the inner ear. From the hammer at the eardrum to the stirrup at the oval window, the vibrations are amplified twenty-two times their original intensity. For this process to reflect accurately the sound waves in the outer ear, the air pressure must be equalized on both sides of the eardrum. The **eustachian tube**, a tube connecting the middle ear with the throat, equalizes the pressure and also permits drainage of fluid from the middle ear.

The sound vibrations in the middle ear are a transition from the sound waves in the air of the outer ear to the sound waves in the liquid of the coiled, snail-shaped, fluid-filled **inner ear (cochlea)**. The **basilar membrane** begins at the base of the cochlea and continues through the three coils to the tip of the cochlea. The basilar membrane is important because the auditory receptor cells, the **hair cells** of the **organ of Corti**, rest upon its surface.

Neural messages generated by the hair cells are then carried by the **auditory nerves** from the cochlea of each ear to the brainstem. Here, about 60 percent of the messages from each ear cross over to the opposite side of the brain, and the remaining 40 percent remain on the same side. The information continues on its ascending path, through the midbrain and then through the thalamus, on its way to the **auditory cortex** in the temporal lobes.

Sound: The Physical Stimulus

The physical stimuli for hearing are sound waves, which are created when vibrating objects transmit their energy into the surrounding air. Sound waves transmit the energy as small changes in air pressure. Like the concentric waves created by dropping a pebble into a pool of water, waves of sound radiate in all directions from their vibrating source. When sound waves reach the ear, their energy is eventually transduced into signals that are transmitted from the ear to the brain.

Sound waves, like light waves, can be described along three physical dimensions: wavelength (or frequency), amplitude, and complexity. Psychologically, you experience the physical characteristic of wavelength as **pitch**. Long wavelengths of low frequency produce low-pitched sounds. As the wavelength shortens and the frequency increases, the pitch you perceive rises.

The amplitude of sound waves is a measure of their intensity and translates into the psychological experience of **loudness**. Loudness is measured in units called **decibels (dBs)**. The detection threshold, the sound of a ticking watch at twenty feet, is zero dBs. Exposure to sounds louder than approximately 90 dBs can damage the auditory receptors, depending on how long you are exposed to such sounds.

Timbre is the psychological dimension that corresponds to the physical characteristic of complexity. You may already be familiar with timbre from listening to sounds produced by different musical instruments. You can distinguish between the sounds of a trumpet and a clarinet, even when the same tone is produced at the same intensity (loudness) on both instruments, because each instrument produces sound waves of different complexity. Through modern technology, electronic keyboards and synthesizers can reproduce so exactly the complex sound waves generated by different instruments that you may be unable to distinguish electronic sounds from those produced on traditional instruments.

Neural Processing of Auditory Information

Transduction occurs in the inner ear. The amplified pressure at the oval window generates in the cochlear fluid waves that reflect the frequency and amplitude of the sound waves in the outer ear. These waves, in turn, produce a traveling wave in the basilar membrane (Bekésy, 1960). (Shaking a rug or waving a streamer produces the same type of traveling wave.) The bulge of the traveling wave pushes the basilar membrane against the hair cells. Transduction takes place when this bending of the hair cells generates neural impulses. These neural messages are then carried from the ear to the brain by the auditory nerve. Each auditory neuron collects messages from a specific place on the basilar membrane. As the frequency of the wave changes, neural impulses are generated at different places along the membrane. The rate the hair cells generate neural impulses reflects the loudness of the sound (Zwislocki, 1981).

Transduction in the inner ear can also be set in motion by vibrations carried to the cochlea through bones other than those in the middle ear. For instance, when you speak, your jaw bones transmit vibrations to the cochlea; this process is called **bone conduction**. Normally, the sound of your voice that you hear is transmitted to the cochlea through both air conduction and bone conduction. Your tape-recorded voice sounds different to you because, in it, you hear only the air-conducted sounds of your voice. Others hear the tape-recorded air-conducted sounds as your voice.

Quick Study Aid

The Physical and Psychological Dimensions of Hearing

Physical Dimension		Psychological Dimension
Wavelength	=	Pitch
Amplitude	=	Loudness
Complexity	=	Timbre

WACs' PLANES LAND THEATRICALLY

(Planes are very loud; therefore, this QSA is for hearing.)

Coding for Loudness   Loudness is a function of the number and type of hair cells activated. **High threshold fibers**, one type of hair cell, fire only when they are bent by high frequency (high-pitched) sounds. Within the low- to mid-range of loudness, the number of firing hair cells determines how loud the sounds are. Very loud sounds are discriminated both by the number of hair cells and the number of high threshold fibers that fire. Sounds presented at an unchanging level of loudness seem to decrease in loudness over time. This perception of decreased loudness is an example of auditory sensory adaptation.

Coding for Pitch   Humans can discriminate pitches ranging from 20 to 20,000 Hz (Hz = Hertz, a unit of frequency equivalent to cycles per second). How are these pitches represented in the nervous system? Because humans can discriminate more than one pitch at a time, pitch theories must account for both simultaneous and successive pitch discrimination. Three major theories attempt to do so.

Place theory proposes that pitch is determined by which hair cells on the basilar membrane (their *place* on the membrane) are most affected by the sound. Research has established that *frequency* is represented by place on the membrane (Bekésy, 1961), but the idea that *pitch* is determined by place has not been proved. A second theory, **frequency theory,** states that pitch is determined by the firing rate in the auditory nerve. According to frequency theory, the auditory nerve functions like a telephone, faithfully reproducing the original stimulus frequencies. However, because neurons fire at a maximum rate of 1,000 times per second and humans can detect pitches up to 20,000 Hz (cycles per second), frequency theory cannot account for most of the human hearing range.

Volley theory proposes that pitch is a combination of the place of the hair cell displacement and the frequency at which the neurons fire. The volley principle says that a group of neurons firing at slightly different times produces a much higher firing rate than any one neuron produces. In other words, below 400 Hz, pitch is determined by firing rate alone (as in frequency theory); between 400 and 5,000 Hz, both place and rate combine to determine pitch, and, above 5,000 Hz, pitch is determined by the place of hair cell displacement on the basilar membrane (as in place theory). In summary, the combined ideas of place and frequency theories and the volley principle explain both fine pitch discrimination and the rapid response of the auditory system.

The Auditory Cortex   The auditory cortex processes incoming information much like the visual cortex does. Here, too, cortical cells are very specialized. Some cortical cells fire when a stimulus begins; some fire when a stimulus ends; and some fire when a stimulus changes. Still other cortical cells respond in more specialized ways, such as firing only to clicking sounds or to slight inflection changes in normal speech. Apparently not everyone processes auditory information in the same way. For example, only one in every 1,500 people has **perfect pitch**, the ability to identify any musical note. This capacity appears to be inborn, not the result of learning or of a highly developed memory (Klein et al., 1984).

Sound Localization   People use sound localization in conjunction with vision to locate a sound and judge its distance. The usefulness of this ability will be obvious to you if you think about your behavior when you hear brakes screeching as you cross a street. Detection of the direction of a sound usually requires **binaural information**—information from both ears. Sound localization results from differences between the times and the levels of loudness with which a sound reaches each ear. When sounds come from directly in front of, behind, or above you, they reach both ears at the same time. Under these conditions, you have difficulty localizing the source of the sound. If a sound is equidistant from both ears, you may turn or tilt your head to get the sound source closer to one ear, thus making sound localization easier.

In addition to the physical processes, experience and memory also contribute to detecting the distance of a sound. Typically, the first time you hear a sound, its loudness will not serve as a cue to distance because a sound must be familiar enough for you to know how loud that sound is at various distances. Having become familiar with a sound, your ability to judge its distance may improve, but generally people are less accurate in their judgments of the *distance* of sounds than they are in their judgments of the *direction* of sounds.

Focus Question Answer

How are you able to recognize the sounds of different musical instruments? You can distinguish between the sounds of different musical instruments because each instrument produces sound waves of different complexity. Processing in the auditory system converts the different complexities into the psychological dimension of timbre. Each instrument is associated with a specific timbre.

The Other Senses

Body and Skin Senses

Although vision and hearing have been studied most extensively, other senses also process important information about the body's external and internal environments. The **somesthetic senses** (body senses) are composed of receptors in the layers of the skin and in the internal organs. The internal receptors are responsible for experiences such as heartburn and nausea.

Receptor cells in the skin conduct messages for four basic **cutaneous senses** (**skin senses**): **touch** (pressure), **warmth**, **cold**, and **pain**. These receptors are unevenly distributed across the large surface area that makes the skin the largest sense organ. Each of the skin's numerous receptor cells transmits messages to a specific location in the somatosensory portion of the brain's parietal lobes.

Touch   Specialized touch receptors respond to slight movement (of a body hair), pressure (pressing steadily down on the skin), vibration (momentary touch or pressure), movement (movement while pressing down on the skin), and stroking movement (a touch that moves lightly across the skin).

Sensitivity to touch depends on the number of receptors in that area. Fingertips are especially sensitive because they contain nearly 50,000 receptors per square inch. In a fingertip, a single touch receptor responds to pressure of less than twenty milligrams—the weight of an average-sized fly! The tip of the tongue is the most sensitive area of the body; other sensitive areas are the lips and other areas of the face. The back and the soles of the feet are the least sensitive areas of the body.

As you may have noticed, the adaptability of the sense of touch is rapid. When a ring produces a constant pressure on your finger, you quickly adapt and lose awareness of the ring. The adaptability of touch is also demonstrated by the ease of learning through this sense. Learning to read Braille is a good example. The Braille alphabet is composed of patterns of small embossed dots; once Braille readers have learned to use the highly sensitive areas of their fingertips, they can read one hundred words or more per minute.

Temperature   Although specific types of touch receptors have been identified, specific types of temperature receptors have not. Instead, researchers have found warm and cold "spots." A hairless square centimeter of skin contains about six cold "spots" and two warm "spots." When a cold object stimulates a cold spot, you experi-

EXHIBIT 5.17
The Thermal Illusion

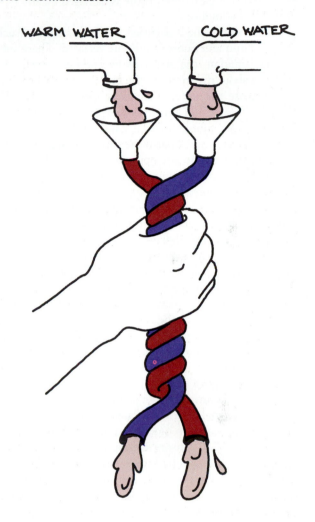

ence the sensation as cold, and, interestingly, when a warm object stimulates a cold spot, you also experience cold. A "hot" skin sensation seems to depend on stimulation of both warm and cold spots. The thermal illusion in Exhibit 5.17 is convincing evidence for this effect. The intertwined cool and warm tubes combine to create the experience of grasping a very hot object.

Pain   Researchers understand pain even less well than they understand touch and temperature. No specific physical stimulus exists for pain as it does for the other sensory systems. Eyes respond to light waves, ears respond to sound waves, and the skin responds to pressure, warmth, and cold. However, you feel pain if a light is too bright, a sound is too loud, a skin pressure is too great, or the temperature is too hot or too cold. Generally, you feel pain when tissue is damaged by any type of physical stimulus.

When skin tissue is damaged, certain substances (such as bradykinin and Substance P) are released. These substances stimulate the skin's nerve endings to transmit impulses about the injury to the brain. These substances also increase the nerve endings' sensitivity to stimulation. This increased sensitivity explains why you feel pain when an injured finger is barely touched.

Two specific nerve pathways carry pain signals to the spinal cord, across to the opposite side of the body, and on to the cerebral cortex. A set of "fast" nerve fibers carries information about sharp, pricking pain when the pain begins and ends quickly. A set of "slow" nerve fibers carries information about burning/searing pain or aching/throbbing pain. In other words, if you drop a hot iron on your big toe, almost instantly you will experience a sharp pain from the weight of the iron; these messages are carried by "fast fibers." Within a second or two, you will feel a throbbing pain from the blow and a burning pain from the heat of the iron; these pain messages are carried by "slow fibers."

A widely accepted theory of pain regulation is the **gate-control** theory (Melzack, 1973, 1980). According to this theory, the sensory pathways to the brain can handle only a limited amount of information at one time. Cells in the spinal cord act as "gates" that can be opened for sensory messages to proceed to the brain or closed to prevent too many sensory messages from reaching the brain. When the pain pathways are activated, the gates are opened to allow pain messages to reach the brain. But other sensory messages may compete with pain signals and cause the pain gates to close. Thus, rubbing an aching foot may relieve pain by sending competing sensory messages. The same principle is used to explain how listening to music while you have a cavity filled reduces pain.

Proprioception

The sense of **proprioception** provides information about the position of each body part in relation to the rest of the body and in relation to gravity. Through proprioception, you sense changes in the rate or direction of your body movements. Two distinct systems, the kinesthetic and vestibular systems, work together to provide proprioception information.

Kinesthesis   Through receptors in the joints, **kinesthesis** provides information about the relative positions of the parts of the body (Geldard, 1972). Other receptors

in the muscles and tendons respond to body movement. These receptors, along with visual receptors, give people the motor control necessary for coordinated movement. A temporary lack of kinesthetic sensation—attempting to walk when one foot is "asleep"—demonstrates kinesthesis' importance in coordinated movement.

Vestibular System   The **vestibular sense** combines information about the body's orientation with respect to gravity and changes in the rate and direction of body movement. The vestibular sense is commonly called the sense of balance. Its receptors are located in two structures associated with the inner ear: the **semicircular canals** and the **vestibular sacs** (see Exhibit 5.16).

The three fluid-filled semicircular canals are approximately perpendicular to each other, positioning that allows detection of head movement in any direction. The vestibular sacs are responsible for information about the head's (and the rest of the body's) orientation when the head is not moving. When you move your head,

The vestibular sense or sense of balance informs this child about the rate and direction of his body movement.

movement of the canal's fluid bends hair cells in the canals, thus sending impulses to the brain. Because the fluid in the canals continues to move after you have stopped, you may become dizzy and momentarily lose your balance if you move too quickly or spin yourself around as children like to do. When people consume too many alcoholic beverages, they become dizzy and unsteady while standing. The alcohol causes the fluid in the semicircular canals to become less dense; then, even though people move only slightly, the fluid moves around more than usual. Messages from the hair cells to the brain signal much greater movement (as when children spin around) than people are exhibiting, and they feel dizzy.

Chemically Activated Senses

Olfaction (smell) and **gustation** (taste) are two separate sensory systems that contribute greatly to the experience of the flavor of food. Many foods that taste similar (such as apples and potatoes) have very different flavors when their odors are combined with their tastes. Smell and taste often appear to be less important than vision or hearing, but each makes a unique contribution to your awareness of the world around you.

Smell The sense of smell plays an important role not only in eating but also in the detection of danger and in social interactions. Without your sense of smell you are much more likely to eat spoiled foods. You may also miss early warning signals about dangerous fires and gas leaks, since people usually smell the smoke before they see the fire. The billion-dollar toiletries industry attests to the importance of smells or lack of them in social interactions.

The physical stimuli for olfaction are chemical odor molecules floating in the air. The olfactory receptors are located in the **olfactory epithelium**, small patches of tissue in the upper half and roof of each nostril. Impulses from the olfactory epithelium travel without a synapse the short distance to the **olfactory bulbs** at the base of the brain. Smell is the only sense to be so directly wired into the brain, and this direct connection may be responsible for the fact that your olfactory memory is better than your visual memory.

The sense of smell depends on breathing to bring the odor molecules into the nostrils where the microhairs (cilia) of the receptor cells collect the molecules. Sniffing draws more odor molecules up to the receptor cells and increases the ability to sense different odors. At least two theories have been proposed to explain how odor molecules interact with the receptor cells to produce the sense of smell.

The **stereochemical theory** proposes that the receptor sites are of specific sizes and shapes that correspond to the sizes and shapes of the odor molecules that stimulate them (Amoore, 1965, 1970). According to this lock and key approach, you recognize different odors because specific odor molecule "keys" fit only specific receptor site "locks." Also, according to this theory, you recognize seven basic smells: ethereal, camphoraceous, musky, floral, minty, pungent, and putrid. The stereochemical theory is plausible but has not been conclusively supported by research findings.

A second theory, **chromatographic theory**, contends that you experience different smell qualities because odor molecules travel different distances in the nostrils and thus reach different portions of the olfactory epithelium (Mozell & Jagodowiez, 1973). To use the previous analogy, this theory is based on the location rather than the shape of the "lock." Each specific type of odor molecule is presumed to stimulate a specific place on the receptor surface.

These theories are similar in assuming that your awareness of smell results from odor molecules interacting with receptor cells in the olfactory epithelium. Research has yet to demonstrate how the receptor cells are able to transduce neural impulses from the odor molecules.

Despite the lack of strong research support for either theory, researchers have discovered many intriguing facts about the sense of smell. For instance, the human sense of smell is not as well developed as that of dogs; nonetheless, people can detect 1/400 billionth of a gram of methyl mercaptan in a liter of air (Methyl mercaptan is the substance mixed with natural gas to give the gas a detectable odor). Yet, as sensitive as the sense of smell is, some people have specific smell anosmia, or smell "blindness." Because of this condition, individuals with an otherwise good sense of smell cannot smell a certain odor. In one study, 47 percent of those observed could not detect the odor of urine, while 3 percent could not detect the odor of sweat (Amoore, 1967).

Additional interesting research has shown that siblings, parents, and spouses can recognize by smell with accuracy rates of 75 percent or better a T-shirt worn by their respective siblings, children, or mates. Also by smelling, most people are able to sort T-shirts worn by males from those worn by females. Generally, men are better at detecting odors than are women, but women are better at identifying and remembering smells (Cain, 1981).

Taste   The physical stimuli for gustatory sensations are food molecules dissolved in the saliva of the mouth. The receptor cells are grouped in a nested arrangement on the surface of the tongue, the roof of the mouth, and the throat, as shown in Exhibit 5.18. Several **taste receptor cells** are clustered together in a **taste bud**. About two hundred taste buds cluster together to form **papillae**, the surface bumps you see when you look at your tongue in a mirror.

The taste receptor cells surround a taste pore and contain several taste hairs that project out through the pore. These microhairs sense food molecules in the saliva and trigger a nerve impulse that then travels to the brain, where the information is combined with that from other receptors to create the experience of a specific taste.

Researchers generally accept four primary taste qualities (sweet, salty, sour, and bitter) as the basic taste sensations that combine to produce all the different tastes you experience. The individual taste cells respond to all four types of taste sensations but with different levels of sensitivity. When larger areas of the tongue are stimulated, however, you note specific areas of sensitivity. As shown in Exhibit 5.18, the tip of the tongue is most sensitive to sweet, the sides to sour, the back to bitter, and the entire tongue to salty. Research has also shown that the tongue more effectively senses sweet or salty,

while the rest of the mouth and the throat more effectively sense sour or bitter (Brown, 1975). Obviously, the taste process is quite complex.

The need for more research about the functioning of your taste system is apparent. However, knowledge about the process of tasting has progressed to the point that scientists can now explain many common taste experiences, such as the "toothpaste/orange juice effect." Have you ever experienced the most unpleasant taste that results from drinking orange juice immediately after brushing your teeth with toothpaste? Many toothpastes contain detergents to help dissolve food particles on the teeth. These same detergents also break down the fat-based cellular membranes of taste buds, temporarily interfering with your ability to taste the sugar in the juice. Other chemicals in the toothpaste also cause the ascorbic and citric acid in the orange juice to taste bitter and sour, thus increasing the unpleasantness of the taste (Rivlin & Gravelle, 1984).

Focus Question Answer

How are you able to distinguish between a touch and a caress? Different specialized receptors are responsible for generating messages about touches and caresses. Caresses do not stimulate "touch" receptors, and touches do not stimulate "caress" receptors.

EXHIBIT 5.18
Taste Sensitivities on the Tongue

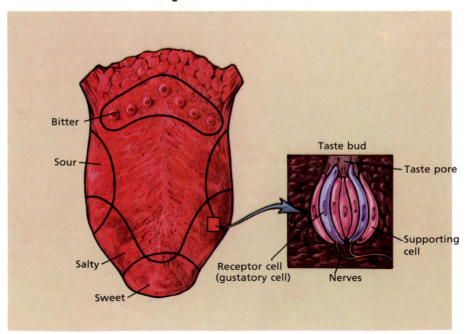

Relate

Sensory Deficits—New Treatments for Old Problems

Sensory deficits affect millions of people. In the United States, fully half the population will wear glasses at some time, and an estimated twenty million Americans currently suffer at least partial hearing loss. Some visual and auditory deficits result from the aging process, which also affects touch, taste, and smell. In addition to aging, common causes of visual deficits include: damage to the corneas, lenses, and other parts of the eye; misshapen eyeballs; diseases such as glaucoma and diabetes; and vitamin deficiencies. Hearing losses result from damage to the eardrum and bones of the middle ear (conductive deafness), damage to the receptors in the inner ear from prolonged exposure to loud sounds, and damage from diseases such as Meniere's (nerve deafness).

Vision

Sensory research and the associated technological developments have focused on vision, the dominant sense. Over the years, corrective lenses have been the most common treatment for nearsightedness, farsightedness, and astigmatism. Contact lenses, which are worn directly on the cornea, were a major improvement over eyeglasses because contacts brought the corrective artificial lenses much closer to the natural lenses. The latest innovation in corrective lenses is extended-wear contact lenses, which may be worn for several weeks without removal for cleaning, and contact lenses that reshape the eyeball.

A recently invented biofeedback device helps many nearsighted individuals improve their sight by training their eyes to focus at longer distances (Kariya, 1985); biofeedback devices measure body functions, such as blood pressure and muscle tension, thereby allowing a person to monitor and better control voluntarily those functions. Over a period of several months, patients learn to relax the muscles of the lenses, so the lenses can accommodate to more distant objects. However, this training does not always eliminate the need for corrective lenses and it does not correct for nearsightedness that results from elongated eyeballs, a condition that may be treated by corrective surgery.

Although biofeedback training is used to treat strabismus (crossed or wandering eyes), surgery is sometimes required to correct the eye muscle defect that causes the condition. If strabismus is uncorrected, it may be accompanied by amblyopia (lazy eye), in which the individual relies on the stronger eye and stops using the weaker eye. Uncorrected amblyopia leads to blindness in the weaker eye.

Glaucoma is an eye disease characterized by high intraocular pressure, hardening of the eyeball, and partial or complete loss of vision. Traditionally, ophthalmologists have treated it with drugs to relieve intraocular pressure and with surgery to remove scar tissue and obstructions. Now they use lasers to cut obstructing membranes, to vaporize scar tissue, and to open drainage pathways for fluid from the eye. For cataracts, doctors now use ultrasound to extract clouded lenses; then they implant artificial lenses in the eye. They may also use laser beams to clear clouded membranes that form after cataract surgery.

Of the major sensory deficits, blindness is the most difficult to treat. In the past, blind people have had to augment their other senses to compensate for lack of vision—touch tapping with a cane and relying on the vision of seeing-eye dogs. Both these approaches may eventually be replaced by newly developed ways for blind people to "see."

Computer technology has made possible a substitute visual system that allows blind people to "see" with their skin. In this high-tech system, visual images from a television camera are converted into vibrational patterns on the skin of the blind person's back. Light and dark images create different rates of vibration. After training with this device, a test group of blind subjects was able to identify objects such as coffee cups, stuffed animals, and telephones. The subjects learned best when they held and moved the cameras themselves. Although this technique is limited by the size of the apparatus and the relative insensitivity of the skin on the back, new advances may make feasible this visual aid for the blind.

In another intriguing area of research, an array of electrodes is implanted directly into the visual cortex of blind individuals. Direct electrical stimulation of the visual areas of the brain causes blind people to see patterns of glowing spots of light. Further advances in this research will undoubtedly occur as the field of robotics produces more information about how machines can be made to "see." If robot engineers can "teach" a robot to "see," they may be able to apply the computer technology to the plight of blind people. Today, regardless of the cause of a visual deficit, research and technology are providing ways for people to "see" or to see better.

Hearing

The first device people with hearing losses used was probably the hand cupped to the ear. Later inventions, like the ear horn, were simply extensions of the same principle of gathering more sound waves into the ear. Currently, modern hearing aids electronically amplify sounds. Unfortunately, increased amplification is an effective treatment only for conductive deafness. For people suffering from deafness due to deterioration from aging, hearing aids usually add to the confusion of sounds they hear.

The newest hearing aids are far from perfect, but they can selectively amplify those sounds the wearer has difficulty hearing. The newer models contain filters and directional microphones; these features remove much of the background noise and reproduce sounds with greater fidelity. Some hearing aids even transform sound frequencies that the individual cannot hear into frequencies the person can hear.

Like totally blind individuals, people who are totally deaf use their other senses to compensate. A common compensatory action is using the visual system to learn to read lips. A different approach is to train dogs to be the "ears" for deaf people just as they are the "eyes" for some blind people. Training a dog to respond to a variety of sounds—a ringing phone, a smoke alarm, an oven buzzer, an alarm clock, a crying baby—takes approximately six months.

While lip-reading and trained dogs can be used effectively to offset hearing deficiencies, many of the two million totally deaf individuals in the United States may soon benefit even further from two recent innovations. Now being tested are computerized eyeglasses, which will allow the wearer to "see" speech. The device consists of a pocket-sized microcomputer with a minimicrophone and eyeglasses with electronic lenses. The microphone picks up speech sounds, which the computer converts into symbols that are flashed on the special electronic lenses. The wearers learn to recognize these visual symbols of speech sounds. The glasses were designed for close-range, face-to-face conversations, but when deaf subjects combine the glasses with traditional lip reading, they become highly accurate in their speech recognition.

Electronic ear implants offer individuals with nerve deafness (deafness due to damage to the auditory nerve) the hope of hearing everyday sounds. The cochlear implant can mimic the mechanics of normal hearing. Thin platinum wires are implanted directly into the auditory nerve, bypassing the defective hair cells. The wires run from the cochlea to a minimicrophone and microcomputer (located outside the ear); these collect and analyze sound waves. Based on the frequencies of the sounds analyzed, the computer transmits small electric pulses to the auditory nerve, which then responds to these inputs as if they came from the hair cells. The first implants used only six wires; later implants contained more wires, thus improving the patient's ability to hear. Although implanting 25,000 wires to duplicate the number of hair cells in the inner ear is not feasible, reasonably good hearing can be obtained with a much smaller number of implants.

Each year produces new research findings about the sensory systems and new technological advances based on those findings. Improving the quality of life for people with sensory deficits serves as a great motivator for researchers in this area.

Things to Do

1. Try the following simple visual demonstrations. The physical stimulus for vision is electromagnetic radiation, but the receptors in the retina will respond to mechanical pressure. Close your eyes and push gently against the outer edge of your eye. What do you see? Is the spot colored? For the next demonstration, cut a ping pong ball in half. Lie down in a brightly-lit room and carefully place one half of the ping pong ball over each eye. Keep your eyes open, and remain quiet while you experience what happens when no patterned visual stimulation is presented to the eyes. This effect is called the ganzfeld phenomenon.

2. To construct prism glasses, tape two small prisms to the lenses of a pair of safety glasses. Wear these glasses, and try a simple activity like bouncing a ball. The longer you wear the glasses and the more active you are, the sooner you will adapt to the altered visual information. Once you have adapted to the glasses, you will find that you have to readjust to normal visual input when you take them off.

3. With your eyes closed and nostrils plugged, ask someone to help you sample room temperature milk, apple juice, grape juice, and several flavors of Kool-aid. Rinse your mouth with water between each drink. Which drink tasted most like it usually does? Could you correctly identify each drink? Follow a similar procedure with several foods, but mash them so they have the same texture.

4. Use blindfolds and earplugs to create visual and auditory deficits for several of your classmates. Instruct them to assist one another while they explore a room. Next, ask them to try moving about the room blindfolded with and without earplugs. In the absence of sight, does hearing improve your ability to navigate? If you know a blind person, ask him or her that question.

Things to Discuss

1. Many animals respond to different portions of the electromagnetic spectrum than those to which humans respond. How would human lives be different if people

responded to a wider range of stimulation, for example, if they were able to see ultraviolet rays? Would different visual capability help or hinder their survival?

2. In spite of strong evidence of the ineffectiveness of subliminal advertising, many people still believe it to be effective. Design an advertising campaign to "sell" the public on the ineffectiveness of subliminal advertising.

3. While humans are visually dominant, other animals, such as dogs, rely more heavily on their sense of smell. Imagine that another of your senses is more dominant than vision. What are the advantages of this arrangement? Does another sense become dominant if a person is blinded?

4. Americans buy deodorants to cover up or prevent natural body scents, and they buy perfumes and colognes to please and attract other people. What do you think would happen if people stopped using deodorants, perfumes, and colognes? Would people become more offensive or more attractive to each other?

5. People spray artificial scents on their bodies, artificially flavor their foods, and produce music on music synthesizers. Does the nose, the tongue, or the ear detect a difference between a natural and artificial stimulus? Does the increasing use of artificial sensory stimulation pose any dangers?

Things to Read

Frisby, J.P. 1980. *Seeing: Illusion, brain, and mind.* Oxford: Oxford University Press.

Gregory, R.L. 1978. *Eye and brain: The psychology of seeing* (3rd ed.). NY: McGraw-Hill.

Melzack, R. 1973. *The puzzle of pain.* NY: Basic Books.

Rivlin, R. & Gravelle, K. 1984. *Deciphering the senses: The expanding world of human perception.* NY: Simon & Schuster.

Sinclair, S. 1985. *How animals see: Other visions of our world.* NY: Facts on File.

Review

Summary

1. Sensation is the process of gathering information and converting it into neural impulses. The process of transforming physical energy into neural messages is called transduction. Perception is the process of organizing and interpreting these neural impulses.

2. Highly selective sense receptors respond to only certain features of a limited range of physical stimuli. Unchanging stimulation produces sensory adaptation, in which the receptors respond less or not at all.

3. Psychophysics studies the relationship between physical stimuli and psychological experience. The absolute threshold (or detection threshold) is the minimum amount of physical energy necessary to detect a sensation. The difference threshold is the minimum amount of energy change necessary to detect a just noticeable difference (j.n.d.) in the sensation.

4. The physical stimulus for vision, the dominant sense in humans, is electromagnetic radiation. The receptors (the rods and cones) are located in the retina. The fovea, located in the center of the retina, contains only cones. The periphery of the retina contains mostly rods. The optic disk (or blind spot) contains no receptors.

5. Cones function best under brightly-lit conditions and are responsible for detecting detail and color. The rods function best under dimly-lit conditions and account for most peripheral vision. Rods and cones adapt to different levels of light intensity. The receptors code information about the wavelength, amplitude, and complexity of light waves; the corresponding psychological experiences are color, brightness, and saturation.

6. The trichromatic theory explains color processing in the cones, and the opponent-process theory explains color processing at higher levels of the visual system. Negative afterimages and color blindness indicate the complex nature of color processing.

7. Receptor hair cells in the organ of Corti on the basilar membrane within the cochlea of the inner ear transduce the physical dimensions of sound waves (wavelength, amplitude, and complexity) into neural messages that are organized into the psychological dimensions of pitch, loudness, and timbre.

8. Place, frequency, and volley theories attempt to explain pitch discrimination. In volley theory, pitch is determined by the place on the basilar membrane in which

hair cells are stimulated and by the frequency of neural firing.

9. The somesthetic (body) and cutaneous (skin) senses provide information about touch, temperature, and pain from receptors in the skin and internal organs. Gate-control theory is a widely accepted theory of pain regulation.

10. The sense of proprioception provides information about body position and movement through the kinesthetic and vestibular senses.

11. The chemically activated senses of smell and taste interact in sensing the flavor of food. The stereochemical and chromatographic theories are two explanations of the transduction of odors by receptors in the nose. Taste receptors respond to each of the basic tastes—sweet, salty, bitter, and sour—with different sensitivities. Areas of the tongue are sensitive to different basic tastes.

12. New treatments for sensory deficits use computer technology to help blind people "see" with their skin. Cochlear implants mimic actual neural impulses to help people with nerve deafness to hear.

Key Terms

transduction
sense receptors
sensory adaptation
psychophysics
detection threshold
just noticeable difference (j.n.d.)
Weber's Law
psychophysical scaling
retina
rods
cones
fovea
blind spot
dark and light adaptation
wavelength
amplitude
complexity
color (hue)
brightness
saturation

trichromatic theory
color blindness
opponent-process theory
basilar membrane
hair cells
pitch
loudness
timbre
place theory
frequency theory
volley theory
somesthetic senses (body senses)
cutaneous senses (skin senses)
gate-control theory
proprioception
kinesthesis
vestibular sense
olfaction
gustation

Focus Questions

1. Do you see the world directly as it is, or do you see it indirectly as a result of higher-level processing?

2. Which Gestalt grouping principles explain your perception of the words in this question?

3. Can you perceive depth with only one eye?

4. Do you perceive the world accurately?

5. Do artists see the world differently than you do?

Chapter Outline

Chapter 6

Perceptual Processing

All our knowledge has its origins
in our perceptions.

Leonardo da Vinci

≡ Perceptual Frameworks

Perceptual processing is perplexing. For over one hundred years, psychologists have defined **perception** as the complex process in which the sensory messages are organized and interpreted. Most psychologists believe that sensations require organization and interpretation before an awareness of reality can emerge. Perception uses information from the sense receptors and information about past experiences from learning, memory, and other cognitive processes. Thus, perception is an indirect process, requiring the integration of many perceptual and nonperceptual elements. What, then, is so perplexing about perception?

Stop reading for a few moments, and focus on your ongoing awarenesss. Close your eyes, and open them. Did anything unusual happen? Presumably, your answer

123

is no. What did you notice? When you opened your eyes, did you notice a delay or a brief blank spot? You did not because conscious experience is immediate, direct, and ongoing. Your awareness does not stop when you close your eyes, even though you shut down one element in the perceptual system. Look around you. You see different objects with definite spatial relationships to one another, and you can accurately perceive their distances from you. Similarly, you hear different sounds, recognize them as familiar or unfamiliar, and perceive how far they are from you. Every other element of your awareness—touch, temperature, pain, and proprioception (sensing body movement or changes in position)—is also immediate, direct, and part of your ongoing experience. If you stand up, your perspective changes, but your perceptual world remains stable. Standing up does not cause the objects around you to change shape or the sounds to change pitch.

For everyone (even psychologists), perception is the immediate and direct experience of the world. You do not experience the textbook you are reading as an organized and interpreted neural happening in your head. You experience the book as a three-dimensional object with a specific size, shape, and weight, at a specific distance from you. Is the object, then, the stimuli reflected from the textbook, or is the object the organized and interpreted neural messages from the retina? These questions about reality and how people experience reality have intrigued both philosophers and scientists.

Consider the photo in Exhibit 6.1. It produces one sensation at the retina and two different perceptual perspectives at higher levels in the visual system. Does the fact that you perceive a two-dimensional photo as a three-dimensional object puzzle you? Are you equally puzzled to know that you perceive a three-dimensional window, which casts a two-dimensional image on the retina, as three-dimensional?

Perception researchers do not question that you perceive the properties of color, shape, texture, orientation, and distance independent of your viewing position. Neither do they question the motive for perceptual processing. The motive is to make sense of the world and to increase the chances of survival. The goal of perceptual processing is to attach meaning to objects and events sensed by the receptors. For example, you perceive the smell of freshly baked bread as something to eat, yet the neural messages from your nose are only part of the information your brain uses to "make sense" of the smell; other sense systems contribute information as well. Similarly, the experience of eating a slice of freshly baked

EXHIBIT 6.1
Ambiguous Figures

A: Look at the window in this photo. The combination of light and shadow create an illusion of a three dimensional "cube". Do you experience the "cube" reversing perspectives?

B: Which face did you perceive first—the young woman or the old woman? If you can see only one or the other of the faces, have someone help you find the second face.

bread does not consist of isolated perceptions of smell, taste, temperature, and texture. Instead, information from the separate sense systems converges in the brain and produces a meaningful perception of the event. That experience is also influenced by past experiences and present needs and expectations.

About these elements of perception, researchers agree. In other words, they agree on the end product of perceptual processing. They do not, however, agree about the process; the "What?" and "Why?" are not questioned, but the "How?" is soundly debated.

Theories of Perception

The heading for this section could read "Theories of Visual Perception." Because vision is the dominant sense, most researchers and theorists have focused on visual perception. As a contributor to the understanding of perceptual processing, psychologist Ralph Haber phrases the fundamental question of "How?" in the following way:

How do we perceive the layout of space? This is the granddaddy of big perceptual questions—ancient and modern. In its modern form, it has many components. How do we perceive the three-dimensionality of space so that objects are seen in their proper shapes and locations with respect to one another as well as to us? How do we perceive the intrinsic properties of visual space: the color, shape, texture, orientation, and distance of objects and surfaces around us, each independent of our momentary viewing position and distance from the scene? How do we integrate the continually changing visual results of our own movements as we locomote in space? How do we integrate the successive glances that arise as a result of our eye movements into a single panoramic view of the visual space around us? (Haber, 1985, p. 250-251)

Attempting to answer these questions, researchers have established two major perceptual theories. One approach, which was developed over one hundred years ago (Helmholtz, 1866), is called the **unconscious inference theory** because it assumes that perception of distance (in the absence of distance receptors in the retina) is based on unconscious inferences derived from other sources of information. According to this theory, an individual's receptor information serves as clues to what he or she senses. Then the individual constructs from these clues and from other non-sensory information a perception. The non-sensory sources of information include past experiences (memory) and assumptions (expectations) about the perceived object.

The philosophical root of unconscious inference theory is John Locke's idea of *tabula rasa*. Locke believed that newborn children's minds are like blank slates (*tabula rasa*), waiting to be inscribed with their experiences. The unconscious inferences used to organize perceptions come from memories inscribed on the tablets of the mind. American psychologist William James expressed Locke's view when he wrote that the world is, to the newborn, a "blooming, buzzing confusion" (James, 1890). Not until the newborn has acquired sufficient experience in the world can he or she form meaningful perceptions.

Modern proponents of the unconscious inference theory (Ittelson, 1960; Hochberg, 1978; Rock, 1984) contend that, because stimulus information from the retina is ambiguous, perception results indirectly from inferences. The window photo and the young woman/old woman figure in Exhibit 6.1 illustrate how ambiguous stimuli lead to the construction of different perceptions. Your perception of the cube changes as you reorganize the stimulus clues from the retina. The use of inferences is clearer when you look at the figure of the young woman/old woman. You organize the information from the retina in only one way but, depending on the unconscious inferences you make, the meaning you assign to the clues changes.

Criticisms of the unconscious inference theory focus on the research methods used to test it. Most researchers have chosen to study one retinal clue at a time under highly-controlled laboratory conditions (Brunswik, 1956). Critics maintain that the laboratory conditions are so far removed from the conditions of normal perceptual processing that the results say nothing about normal perception (Gibson, 1985). Normal perceptual processing involves an abundance of stimulus information, while most laboratory studies do not.

According to James J. Gibson, the primary critic of the unconscious inference theory, the abundant stimulus information is sufficient to provide for direct perception (Gibson, 1979). In his **ecological approach** to visual perception, Gibson argues that the perceiver continually interacts with the environment to produce a rich "optical flow" of information to the eyes. This information affords all that is needed to perceive directly the properties of visual space. Thus Gibson's theory, with its emphasis on the analysis of stimulus information, is sometimes called a **theory of direct perception**.

Gibson was strongly influenced by the early theoretical work in Gestalt psychology. As mentioned in Chapter 2, several German psychologists (Wertheimer, 1923; Koffka, 1935; Köhler, 1947) reacted against the view that perception results from merely adding together sensations. The Gestalt theorists maintain that a pattern of visual stimulation has properties that are greater than the sum of the individual parts of the pattern. The Gestalt psychologists also emphasize innate (unlearned) mechanisms of organization, an idea that fits well with the direct perception of stimuli stressed by Gibson.

Later in this chapter you will see how the ideas of Gibson and the Gestalt psychologists are used to explain the basic perceptual organization of stimulus information. As you will see, the direct perception position neglects the perceptual processing emphasized by the unconscious inference theorists, who in turn neglect the stimulus analysis stressed by Gibson (Haber, 1985). Neither theoretical position is totally adequate.

Although incomplete, both theories have contributed greatly to the understanding of perception. The direct perception researchers have investigated what stimulus information is available, while the unconscious inference theorists have explored how assumptions, prior knowledge, past experience, and processing strategies affect perceptual processing. No single theory of perception will be complete unless it merges the stimulus analysis approach of direct perception theory with the processing analysis approach of unconscious inference theory. No one has succeeded in merging these two theories.

Innate or Learned Process?

A major point of contention between these two theoretical positions is whether perceptual processing is innate (inborn) or learned. The direct perception theory emphasizes innate factors; the unconscious inference theory stresses the role of learning. Different areas of research provide support for both of these theoretical positions.

The role of learning in perceptual processing is weakly supported by studies of congenitally blind individuals (those blind since birth) whose vision was restored after they became adults (von Senden, 1960). Generally, researchers found that restoring visual capability does not immediately or successfully restore visual perceptual capabilities. Many of the patients had difficulty visually recognizing objects they could easily identify by touch. With effort, some patients developed object recognition, but others were so confused by their restored vision they reverted to dealing with the world as blind people. In contrast, for some patients the operation was highly successful, and they were able to see well shortly after sur-

gery. These exceptions weaken the case for learning as the sole basis for perception (Gregory, 1978).

Stronger evidence for the learning position comes from studies with animals. Kittens raised in a controlled visual environment in which they see only horizontal and vertical stripes appear to be "blind" to diagonal stripes, which they have never seen. One hypothesis is that the kittens do not see the diagonals because the specific receptors for detecting diagonal lines have become nonfunctional (Mitchell, 1980). Without appropriate stimulation, receptors for detecting specific features weaken and stop working.

Depriving kittens of other types of information will also alter their perceptions. In a now classic study, kittens were paired together in a special apparatus (Held & Hein, 1963). The apparatus, depicted in Exhibit 6.2, assured that both kittens would have nearly identical visual stimulation. One kitten was a passive viewer, while the other moved actively about in the test enclosure. Later, in a series of tests, the active kitten displayed normal perceptual abilities. The passive kitten, however, acted as if it were blind. It did not exhibit normal depth

EXHIBIT 6.2
Active and Passive Paired-Kitten Apparatus

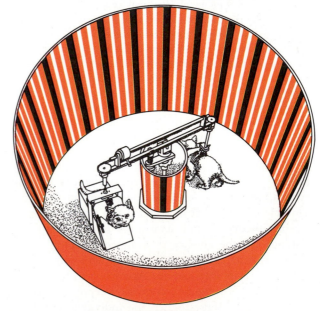

Adapted from an illustration by Eric Mose in "Plasticity in Sensory Motor Systems" by Richard Held. *Scientific American*, November 1965.

This apparatus assured that the kittens would have nearly identical visual stimulation but that only one kitten would have active movement. Without active interaction with its visual environment, the passive kitten failed to develop normal perceptual abilities.

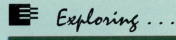

Exploring . . .

Studying Perception in the Newborn

Using the viewing box pictured here, Fantz (1961) recorded newborn babies' reactions to different visual stimuli. An infant can lie and look at different patterns while an observer records the length of time a pattern is reflected in the infant's cornea, a measure of the

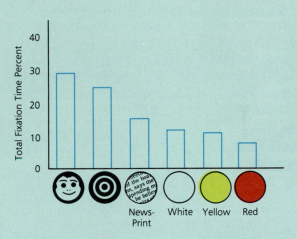

Adapted from an illustration by Alex Senenoick in "The Origin of Form Perception" by Robert L. Fantz. *Scientific American*, May 1961.

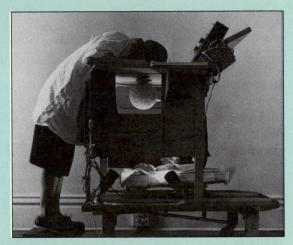

time the baby spends looking at the pattern. Fantz presented infants as young as ten hours old with two patterns at a time that varied in color, complexity, and familiarity; one pattern resembled a human face. He discovered that infants as young as ten hours to five days old look longer at patterns than at solid colors but that they look longest at the pattern resembling a human face.

perception and did not blink when an object was suddenly moved toward its eyes. Further, when the active kitten was held above a table and then lowered to the tabletop, it put out its paws to catch itself as it neared the table. In contrast, the passive kitten gave no indication that it perceived the table surface was getting closer; in fact, the researcher could lower the passive kitten until its head touched the tabletop. Deprived of appropriate proprioceptive experience, the passive kitten failed to acquire normal visual perception.

The results of the studies just mentioned clearly show that learning about the environment is necessary for the development of normal visual perception. The evidence from animal studies seems to support the learning view of perception. However, as you will see in the next

section, studies of newborn infants' perceptual capabilities support the innate position.

Perception in the Newborn

What can a newborn infant perceive? Before pioneering research in the 1950s and 1960s, the answer was "very little." Initially, American psychologists strongly supported the learning position and thus for many years did not adequately investigate the perceptual capabilities of newborns. Later, when researchers developed special testing procedures for newborns (Fantz, 1956), they suddenly discovered that many perceptual abilities once believed to be learned after birth are actually present at birth. The *Exploring . . .* section pictures the special apparatus used to investigate the perceptual abilities of newborns and the results of one study using this equipment.

At birth, infants show definite perceptual preferences. They prefer colored stimuli to black and white, curved lines to straight lines, and, most interestingly, drawings of human faces to other designs (Fantz, 1961; 1963; 1965). Additionally, infants as young as ten days old react defensively when objects move toward their faces. This reaction supports the position that depth perception is innate, not learned through experience (Bower et al., 1970).

Careful observation of newborns has shown that (1) they are more alert when inclined at an angle or held upright than when they are lying down, (2) they can turn their heads toward a light source, (3) they can follow a moving stimulus, and (4) they are best able to focus on objects less than a foot away (Behrman & Vaughn, 1983). Newborn babies are best able to see objects placed about 7.5 inches from their eyes. Interestingly, when you hold a baby in your arms and gaze down at it, the distance between your face and the baby's face is approximately 7.5 inches. This fact, coupled with the knowledge that newborns prefer viewing human faces to viewing other designs, leads to intriguing speculations about the purposes of these obviously innate capabilities. Does a baby's built-in preference for human faces help assure stronger bonding between the infant and its caregivers and thus increase its chances for survival?

Innate sensory abilities are not limited to the visual system. Research on taste and smell indicates that newborns prefer a sweet taste, can distinguish between at least four basic smells, and can reliably recognize their mothers' smell within six days after birth (MacFarlane, 1978). Infants also respond appropriately to what adults would label "painful stimuli." They react to pricking with a needle by attempting to withdraw and to circumcision with wakefulness and fussiness. Researchers of newborns' hearing find that shortly after birth infants turn or look toward the source of a sound, display rhythmic body movements while listening to human speech, prefer high-pitched sounds to lower-pitched ones, and prefer the sound of a human voice to other sounds (MacFarlane, 1978).

Evidence accumulated during the last three decades of research with newborns strongly supports the innate view of perceptual processing. However, the issue of innate versus learned bases for perception has not been resolved. Knowledge of the abilities present at birth and knowledge of the effects of perceptual experience encourage the investigation of the interplay between the two. The challenge of the next several decades will be to explore the precise interactions between innate and learned perceptual processing factors.

Several areas of perceptual processing reveal clearly this interaction between inborn perceptual capabilities and learning. Keep this relationship in mind as you read about stimulus organization, depth perception, motion perception, and perceptual constancies.

Focus Question Answer

Do you see the world as it is, or do you see it indirectly as the result of higher-level processing? The theory of direct perception contends that perceptual processing is innate and that the information from sensory receptors is sufficient to account for your perception of the world. The competing theory, unconscious inference theory, maintains that higher-level processes such as learning, thinking, and memory are necessary to explain the complexities of the perceptual process.

 Perceptual Organization

Gestalt psychologists have contributed greatly to an understanding of how sensations from our sense receptors are organized into a unified perception, or whole. (The German word *Gestalt* does not have a direct English equivalent, but it translates roughly as "form" or "figure" and is used to indicate a unified pattern or whole.) As you may recall, Gestalt psychologists believe that the whole is greater than the sum of its individual parts. They maintain that what you see when you look at a scene is a unified picture, not unrelated stimuli. The tendency at each level of perceptual organization is to perceive wholes rather than parts. To explain this aspect of perceptual organization, Gestalt psychologists formulated the **Law of Pragnanz**.

According to the Law of Pragnanz, the underlying principle of perceptual organization is that people will group stimuli into unified wholes whenever possible. In other words, whatever can be perceptually grouped together, will be grouped together. Gestalt psychologists also conclude that the **figure-ground relationship** (perceiving a figure against a background) is basic to organizing visual information. According to the Law of Pragnanz, stimuli that can be grouped together will form a unified whole as a figure against a background. Exhibit 6.3 shows an example of a visual stimulus with a reversible figure-ground relationship.

**EXHIBIT 6.3
Reversible Figure-Ground**

The Face-Vase Figure, can be seen as two facial profiles in red or a vase in white, depending on whether you perceptually organize the white area as the figure or the background.

The perceptual tendency to form "good" figures (the tendency to form the simplest, most regular figures) is so strong that you cannot avoid seeing in Exhibit 6.3 either a vase or two profiles, depending on which you see as the figure and which you see as the ground. The same tendency applies when you view the other ambiguous figures in this chapter. In fact, the tendency to form "good" figures is so strong that you may create a figure when none is actually present. Look at the drawing on the left in Exhibit 6.4. Notice the three incomplete black squares and the three sets of disconnected lines. Do you also see a solid white triangle of a slightly different color than the white background behind it? The triangle emerges in front of the lines and incomplete circles because the incomplete figures suggest that something is covering them. The alignment of the edges of the missing corners and the missing line segments also help organize the illusionary triangle (Rock, 1983).

In the drawing on the right in Exhibit 6.4, notice that you can see an illusionary figure even when the missing corners and lines are not aligned. You actually organize three figures in each drawing: the white figure in front of (or on top of) the black squares and the outline of the triangle with straight or curved sides. These drawings illustrate the interaction between innate and

**EXHIBIT 6.4
Illusionary Triangles with Subjective Contours**

Do you see a white triangle in each figure? The white triangles exist only in your head, the creation of your visual system.

Adapted from Coren, S., Porac, C., & Ward, L. M. 1984. *Sensation and perception* (2nd ed.). Orlando: Academic Press.

learned perceptual factors. Your tendency to organize the drawings into various figures is innate and compelling. However, your tendency to perceive the illusionary figure is neither innate nor direct. You depend on past experience to know that when a figure is only partially visible, another object is between that figure and you. When the suggestion of incomplete figures and alignment is absent, as in Exhibit 6.5, few naive observers see the illusionary triangle that you, as an experienced observer, can see (Rock, 1983). This difference between naive and experienced observers shows the role of learning factors in the interaction between innate and learned aspects in perceptual processing.

**EXHIBIT 6.5
Another Illusionary Triangle**

Naive observers rarely see the white triangle under these conditions, but because you have already seen the triangles in Exhibit 6.4, this white triangle with curved sides will also be apparent to you.

Rock, I. 1975. *An introduction to perception.* NY: Macmillan.

EXHIBIT 6.6
Examples of Gestalt Principles

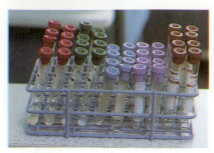

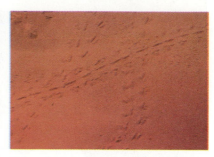

A: Similarity   **B**: Closure   **C**: Continuity

Gestalt Grouping Principles

In addition to the Law of Pragnanz, which yields the most basic perceptual relationship of figure-ground, the Gestalt psychologists developed other principles governing how stimuli are organized into whole figures. Examples of some of these principles are illustrated in Exhibit 6.6.

Closure.   Your perception of the white triangles in Exhibits 6.4 and 6.5 involves the Gestalt grouping principle of **closure**, the tendency to make complete, whole figures out of incomplete stimuli. You form a triangle with information about only its corner angles. Using other perceptual processes, you fill in the gaps and see a complete figure. Cartoonists rely extensively on the principle of closure and other Gestalt principles to increase what you see in what they have actually drawn. The *Exploring . . .* section examines cartoonists' use of these principles.

Proximity.   The principle of **proximity** is demonstrated by the grids of dots following this paragraph. This principle states that when all else is equal, stimuli that are close together (proximal) will be perceived as a unified whole. Thus, in grid A, in which the dots are equally close to one another, you perceive the grid as a square, with neither rows nor columns of dots predominating.

However, a simple change in the spacing of the dots so that some are closer together and others farther apart changes the perception; rows of dots emerge in grid B, while columns of dots emerge in grid C. The closer elements are grouped together into figures. Can you arrange the grid of dots so that you perceive diagonals instead of rows or columns?

Similarity.   An easy way to change the grid of dots into diagonal lines of dots is to color the appropriate dots (as in grid D). The spacing of the dots in grid D is the same as in grid A, but the similarity of the dots has changed. According to the principle of **similarity**, when all else is equal, the most similar stimuli will be grouped together. Common factors affecting grouping by similarity include similar size, shape, and orientation of elements.

Common Fate.   When stimuli share similarity of movement, the grouping principle of **common fate** is invoked. This principle states that elements moving in the same direction at the same rate will be grouped together. Wild animals often use common fate as a protective device. For example, by remaining absolutely motionless, the cottontail rabbit can often evade predators. The rabbit's coloration acts as camouflage to blur other cues for figure-ground. As long as the rabbit remains motionless, sharing a common fate with its background, it is difficult to see.

Continuity.   According to the principle of **continuity**, stimuli that suggest continuous patterns will be grouped together. Thus, in the figure following this paragraph the tendency is to see a wavy line cutting through a rectilinear line rather than two rows of geometric figures. In the same manner, the magician's trick of sawing a

A   B   C   D

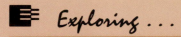 *Exploring . . .*

Cartoonists' Use of Gestalt Grouping Principles

Examine the *Dennis the Menace* cartoon. How many of the Gestalt grouping principles does the cartoonist use? Closure is used with several of the incompletely drawn butterflies. Perceiving Dennis' shirt relies on the proximity of the stripes; seeing the stripes relies on the principle of similarity. The principle of continuity causes you to see the electric lines passing behind Dennis. Distinct continuous edges help produce figural goodness (the principle of simplicity). The legs of Dennis' pants form an indistinct edge with the grass and, therefore, do not form a good figure.

The cartoonist in the following *B.C.* cartoon relies simply on the principles of continuity and common fate to create a humorous situation.

DENNIS THE MENACE

" BUTTERFLIES MAKE IT LOOK WINDY OUT EVEN WHEN IT ISN'T."

B.C.   **BY JOHNNY HART**

The statue against the blue sky exhibits characteristics of good figure-ground. Because of poor figure-ground contrast, the crab is camouflaged by its surroundings.

lady in half relies on the audience's perceptual tendency to see the lady's feet and ankles as continuous with her head and neck. The principle of continuity also contributes to your earlier perception of the illusionary white triangles in Exhibits 6.4 and 6.5.

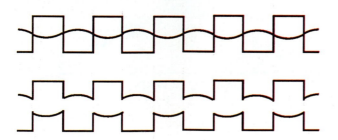

Simplicity. Gestalt psychologists call the patterns formed by the principle of continuity "good" continuation. The "goodness" results from the perceptual tendency to form the simplest figures and patterns. The principle of **simplicity** or **figural goodness** states that stimuli will be grouped into the simplest, most regular, and most symmetrical figures. Exhibit 6.7 demonstrates this principle by combining several shapes to create perceptions of new shapes. When the more complex shapes are combined, the elements are reorganized into "better," simpler, and more regular shapes.

The principle of simplicity carries through all the Gestalt grouping principles. Perceptual organizational processes form the best and simplest interpretations of sensory data. This economical approach to perceptual

organization fits well with the innate, direct perception theories. In fact, in the previously cited studies with restored vision, the figure-ground relationship was present even when other perceptual features were absent (von Senden, 1960). On the other hand, now that you have studied the figures used to illustrate the grouping principles, you should be able to look at them again and organize them in ways that run counter to the grouping principles. For example, your ability to see Exhibit 6.7's more complex shapes after they have been combined demonstrates the role of experience and your ability to change the inferences you use to form perceptions. Perceptual organization remains an interaction between innate and learned factors.

Focus Question Answer

Which Gestalt grouping principles explain your perception of the words in this question? You first organize the

EXHIBIT 6.7
Symmetry into Asymmetry

When the two symmetrical figures are combined, they form two asymmetrical figures with more complex shapes than the initial two shapes.

Quick Study Aid

Great Gestalt Grouping Principles

Cute	Cozy	Cats	Sleep	So	Peacefully
l	o	o	i	i	r
o	m	n	m	m	o
s	m	t	i	p	x
u	o	i	l	l	i
r	n	n	a	i	m
e		u	r	c	i
	F	i	i	i	t
	a	t	t	t	y
	t	y	y	y	
	e				

Use the first letters of the words in this sentence to help you recall the Gestalt Grouping Principles.

printed marks as figures against the background of the page. Then the closer proximity of some letters causes you to recognize different words. Finally the continuity of the words is broken by the question mark, allowing you to group the words together as a question.

Depth and Motion Perception

In your usual day-to-day perception of thē world, you not only organize the stimuli around you into meaningful patterns, but you also organize those patterns into their positions in the space around you. The perception of an object's distance from you is called **depth perception**. As indicated earlier, infants as young as ten days old show clear signs of depth perception; this finding demonstrates that with little or no learning newborns are able to perceive distance directly.

The Research Process: Depth Perception and the Visual Cliff

The innateness of depth perception has also been tested with an apparatus called the **visual cliff** (Gibson & Walk, 1960). As illustrated in Exhibit 6.8, the visual cliff consists of a glass-topped table divided in half. A "shallow" side is created by putting a checkerboard pattern directly under the glass, and a "deep" side is created by placing the checkerboard pattern on the floor. This apparatus has been used to test human infants of various ages and infants of many other species.

Studies with baby animals clearly support the existence of innate depth perception. The young animals avoid the deep side and resist efforts to push them over the simulated cliff. Even newborn chicks without prior visual experience avoid the deep side. Studies of humans indicate that six-month-old infants are more easily coaxed to crawl to their mothers across the shallow side than across the deep side. When infants as young as two months of age are placed on the deep side, they respond with a lower heart rate. In contrast, their heart rates show no change when they are placed on the shallow side (Campos et al., 1970). The heart rates indicates a differential reaction to the two conditions.

Visual cliff studies with human infants contain several problems, however. Typically, humans do not begin to crawl until about six months of age. By this age, babies have had considerable visual experience and many opportunities for perceptual learning. Additionally, the glass plate may result in conflicting information from the senses of vision and touch--the babies may "feel" solid ground and see a cliff. Because of these factors, interpreting the

EXHIBIT 6.8
The Visual Cliff

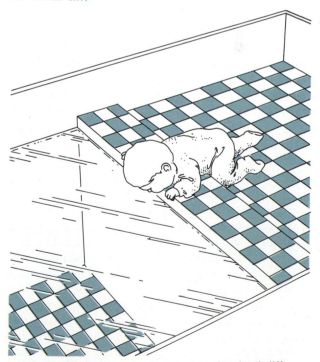

An infant's depth perception is tested on the visual cliff. Placed on the center board the child will crawl to his mother across the "shallow" side but not across the "deep" side.

visual cliff studies with humans is difficult. The infants' reluctance to crawl onto the deep side is evidence that they perceive depth, but at six months of age their reluctance does not indicate whether depth perception is innate. The change in heart rate indicates that the infants recognize a difference on the deep side, but the change does not necessarily indicate a recognition of depth. Therefore, the evidence from visual cliff studies with human infants is equivocal. However, the evidence from other animal species and from other lines of research with very young human infants (Bower et al., 1970) clearly indicates that depth perception is innate.

Binocular Cues to Depth

Cues to depth are of two basic types—monocular and binocular. Monocular cues are those that depend upon only one eye, whereas binocular cues depend upon both eyes. **Retinal disparity**, a binocular cue, occurs because your eyes, as a result of their different positions, receive slightly different views of the world. The disparity, or difference, between the two retinal images serves as a cue for depth when the two images are merged in the brain into a single perception. You can become more conscious of the unconcious operation of retinal disparity. Hold up your thumb in front of your face, about fifteen inches from your nose. Continue looking at your thumb and alternately open and close each eye several times. Your thumb will appear to move. The perceived movement results from each eye's different view of the thumb. Is the perceived movement greater when you hold your thumb closer to or farther away from your nose? What does this experience tell you about retinal disparity as a cue for depth perception?

You may have noticed that looking at your thumb directly in front of your nose is uncomfortable. The muscle tension required to focus both eyes on your thumb at such close range causes this discomfort. When you look at an object that is less than twenty five feet away, the muscles around your eyes work together, pulling each eye toward the other, causing the line of sight from each eye to converge on the object. The nearer the object is to you, the more the muscles must pull the eyes toward each other to achieve convergence. Looking at very close objects requires an uncomfortable amount of muscle tension. Thus, **convergence** is another binocular cue (requiring two eyes) to depth perception; more precisely, the feedback about muscular tension in the eye muscles serves as the cue. Convergence is most useful as a cue for distances under ten feet. Beyond a distance of twenty-

five feet, the eyes converge imperceptibly, if at all. Convergence is not innately determined because it requires learning the different amounts of muscular tension produced by looking at objects at different distances.

Monocular Cues to Depth

When you cover one of your eyes and look at the world, you remove the binocular cues for depth, but other depth cues are still available. Feedback from the muscles that control the shape of the lens in each eye provides a monocular cue to depth called **accommodation**. Accommodation helps you judge distances that are within four feet of your eyes. Beyond four feet accommodation adds little to your perception of depth.

The remaining monocular cues arise from one basic cue, **size-distance invariance**. In this cue, retinal images of nearby objects are large and full of detail, while retinal images of distant objects are small and lacking in detail. In the case of nearby objects, the image is spread over a greater area of the retina, allowing you to extract more information or detail from the image. With distant objects, the image is focused on a very small retinal area. Because the details of the object are compressed into an even smaller area, you are able to extract very little information from the image.

You experience compression of optical information when you view parallel lines like those shown in photo A in Exhibit 6.9. Cognitively, you know that the lines are parallel, or always equidistant from each other. Perceptually, with increasing distance, the retinal image of the lines becomes more compressed as you perceive the lines to be converging. This monocular cue is termed **linear perspective**.

Linear perspective is a compelling cue about depth and can be used in drawings to create illusions. The cylinders in Exhibit 6.10 appear to be graduated in size with the most distant cylinder being the largest. Actually, the cylinders are the same size. The use of linear perspective (converging lines) creates the perception of depth and contributes to the illusion. Surprisingly, artists did not begin to use linear perspective in their drawings and paintings until the fifteenth and sixteenth centuries. Paintings by Renaissance artists may have greater appeal than those of earlier artists partly because of the feeling of depth created by the use of linear perspective.

Photo B in Exhibit 6.9 demonstrates **texture gradient**. Details distinct in the foreground become less distinct with increasing distance and finally are blurred and indistinct on the horizon. Texture gradients are al-

EXHIBIT 6.9
Monocular Cues to Depth

How many monocular cues to depth can you recognize in these photos?

A: Linear Perspective

D: Height on a Plane & Interposition

B: Texture Gradient

C: Aerial Perspective

E: Shadowing

EXHIBIT 6.10
Gibson's Cylinders

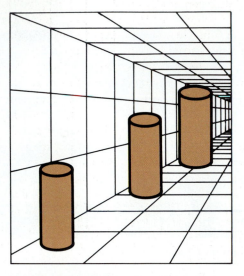

Are these cylinders different sizes? Measure them to find out. The three are actually the same size, but the artist's use of linear perspective makes them appear different.

James J. Gibson: *The perception of the visual world.* Copyright © 1950, renewed 1978 by Houghton Mifflin Company. Used by permission.

ways present. Whether you relax on a sandy beach, walk along a sidewalk, or stare at the carpeting in your classroom, you see nearer objects in greater detail and more distant objects in less detail.

Aerial perspective is a variation of texture gradient. You are able to judge the distance of objects projecting into the sky by the clarity with which you can see them. On a clear day, the air around you is just that—clear. However, as you gaze toward the horizon, the atmosphere appears more hazy. On a clear day, the images of dust and other minute particles in the air around you are not noticeable because they are so small and so widely dispersed on the retina. In contrast, information about dust and other particles in the distance is compressed on a much smaller area of the retina; thus, the sky at the horizon appears hazy. According to aerial perspective, since the nearby air appears clear and the distant atmosphere appears hazy, nearby objects projecting into the sky appear more brightly colored and sharper, and distant projecting objects appear more pastel and indistinct. Did you notice the effects of aerial perspective in photo C in Exhibit 6.9?

Two other monocular depth cues are **height on a plane** and **interposition**. Among objects in the same plane in photo D in Exhibit 6.9, those that are higher

on the plane appear more distant. Look at a nearby flat, horizontal surface, such as a tabletop or the floor. First look at the part of the surface nearest to you and then look across the surface to a more distant point. Did you notice that you raised your eyes to look at the greater distance? The cue of height on a plane is based on your tendency to look up to see more distant objects on the same plane. In a drawing, height on a plane can be combined with other depth cues to create the appearance of depth in the picture. Interposition, in which objects in the foreground overlap and block out portions of objects farther away, is one such clue. In photo D in Exhibit 6.9, the interposition of objects is an effective monocular cue for depth.

In **shadowing**, the distribution of light across a surface provides information about depth (Exhibit 6.9, photo E). The direction of the light source and the degree of shadow combine to indicate which part of a curved or a flat surface is closer. The addition of shadowing to a two-dimensional drawing increases the feeling of depth in the drawing.

From perceptual experience, you learn that objects that are the same size but at different distances produce different-sized images on the retina. **Relative size** is directly related to the size-distance invariance mentioned earlier. An object close to you creates a larger retinal image while the same object at a greater distance creates a smaller retinal image. From this information, you can judge the distance of objects of known size by how large they appear relative to each other. Artists add depth to their paintings by using relative size. For example, they draw trees in the background of a painting much smaller than trees in the foreground.

Another monocular cue based on the relationship of retinal images is **relative motion** or **motion parallax**. When you move your head, the images of nearby objects are moved a greater distance across the retina than are the images of objects farther away. To demonstrate this cue for yourself, cover one eye and point at an object on the wall across the room from you. Move your head in any direction. Which does your movement displace more—your pointing finger or the object on the wall? No matter how little or how much or in what direction you move your head, the movement will always displace your finger more than the object on the wall. Relative motion is an important depth cue because your eyes, head, and body are rarely motionless. Under normal conditions, you are usually producing a flow of moving retinal images that are a rich source of information about depth.

Depth perception is most accurate when you have both binocular and monocular cues to help you. When you look with both eyes, you have not only the monocular cues about the stimuli but also the binocular cues of retinal disparity and convergence. As the previous examples have illustrated, you can become aware of each cue individually, but normally you are not aware of the cues at all. Instead, you perceptually organize all the available cues to create the experience of depth. Much is known about the cues and how they are processed. On the other hand, little is known about how the perceptual processing transforms neurally coded information into an awareness that the three-dimensional world is "out there" and not "in here" in your brain.

Motion Perception

Motion perception has already been discussed in two ways. In Chapter 5, you read about the visual system's receptors, which detect movement. In this chapter, you have read about relative motion, a depth perception cue resulting from eye, head, or body movement. However, motion perception involves more than these two processes. For example, how are you able to detect whether the motion you perceive is an object moving or your eye moving?

Motion parallax—images of nearby objects move across the retina more quickly than images of distant objects—occurs whether you stand still while watching a moving object or move while watching a stationary object. The displacement or parallax occurs even when both you and the object move, if your rate of movement is different than the object's. For instance, if you stand by an open highway, you will notice that when a car appears in the distance, the car seems to move slowly at first. As the car comes closer, the retinal image that it produces not only becomes increasingly larger, but the image size changes at an increasingly faster rate. Thus the car appears to speed past you only to slow down as it recedes into the distance. Parallax or displacement of retinal images also occurs when you view stationary objects from the side window of a moving car. The pavement and roadside near the car appear to sweep by rapidly, while objects in the distance appear to move very little or to move slowly along with the car. When the road is rushing past you at 50 mph, why does a car passing you at 55 mph appear to move so slowly?

As the previous examples illustrate, you use higher perceptual processes to make sense of motion effects. Information about the movement of your body combines with information about movement of objects in your visual field to produce an appropriate perception of motion (Johansson et al., 1980).

Have you ever pulled into a parking space, stopped your car, and then quickly stepped on the brake again when you noticed your car moving forward? You may have been surprised and somewhat chagrined to realize that your car was not moving at all; instead, the car in the parking space next to you was backing out slowly. This illusion, called **induced motion**, occurred because your peripheral vision detected the movement of the car in the next space and organized that information as movement of your body. Induced motion can be created in the laboratory with a rotating drum room. Subjects sit stationary in the chair while the walls of the room spin, yet the perception that they are spinning is so compelling that subjects actually grab onto their chairs.

The **phi phenomenon**, the perception of **apparent motion** in stationary objects, also illustrates the existence of higher-level perceptual processes for motion. Movie marquees and advertising signs provide the most familiar examples of this phenomenon. When individual stationary lights are turned on and off in rapid succession, they produce the perception of a single moving light. The effect occurs whether you move your eyes or keep them stationary. Under controlled laboratory conditions, apparent motion can be created without activating the motion-detector cells in the retina (Rock & Ebenholtz, 1962). Thus, higher processing levels must be activated to produce this effect.

Another familiar type of apparent motion is **stroboscopic motion**, which occurs when you view a series

Everyday experiences, such as viewing the continuous motion of a water fall, may produce the illusion of induced motion.

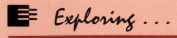

Exploring . . .

Perceptual Principles in the Other Senses

The text discussion centers on visual examples of the perceptual principles, but the same principles are at work in the other sensory systems as well. Before reading further, look back briefly at the Gestalt grouping principles. Do you recognize how these principles function in your other senses?

The figure-ground relationship is the most basic grouping principle. When you listen to music, the melody stands out as a figure against the background of the accompaniment. During a lecture, your instructor's voice becomes the figure set against the background of other sounds. When you lick an ice cream cone, sweetness becomes the figure that emerges from the background of other tastes in your mouth. When someone touches you on the shoulder, you organize the touch as the figure.

You are able to follow a friend's conversation in a noisy student lounge because you apply the principles of continuity and "good" continuation. Even if you do not hear everything your friend says, the principle of closure allows you to form complete words out of the incomplete sounds you hear. Sometimes closure is responsible for arguments that result when the speaker makes one statement and the listener hears another.

The principle of continuity also helps you feel a bug crawling up your leg. You organize the data from the sense of touch as one moving bug rather than a series of separate touches. Because of the principle of proximity, you group together the separate sensations from the bug's several feet. Similarly, the sensations produced when you shake hands are grouped together into a single, whole perception.

Can you apply the Gestalt principles to your sense of smell? The figure-ground principle should be easy to apply. Distinct odors are organized as figures against the background of other odors. But what principle applies when odors are mixed in foods like pizza? Does the principle of proximity apply to the aroma of pizza? Individual odors that are close together (coming from the same pizza) are grouped together and perceived as one aroma. With experience, you learn to recognize groupings of odors. Cinnamon and cloves have distinctive odors but when the two spices are mixed together they are usually perceived as one spice—pumpkin pie spice!

The Gestalt grouping principles are also evident in blind people's use of auditory cues for depth perception. As noted in Chapter 5, you use auditory cues to locate sounds and judge their distances. Just as sighted people depend upon monocular and binocular cues for depth perception, blind people depend upon monaural (one ear) and binaural (two ears) cues. Changes in loudness and timbre are important monaural cues, while temporal (time) differences and loudness changes are useful binaural cues.

of still pictures in rapid succession. This form of apparent motion is the basis for animated cartoons and all forms of motion pictures. You can experience the reverse of this effect by rapidly blinking your eyes while watching a moving object. The "picture" you see between blinks is like a single frame in motion picture film.

Focus Question Answer

Can you perceive depth with only one eye? You usually perceive depth by using both monocular (one eye) and binocular (two eyes) cues. If you attempt to judge distance using only one eye, you will not have retinal disparity and convergence to assist you. With only one eye you must rely on the monocular cues such as accommodation, linear perspective, texture gradient, aerial perspective, height on a plane, interposition, shadowing, relative size, and relative motion.

 ## Characteristics of Perception

This chapter began with a brief discussion of the "Why?" of perception; the Gestalt principles, depth cues, and motion cues address the question of "When?" or "Under what circumstances?" As stated earlier, the "How?" of perception is the debatable area. This section does not attempt to answer the question, but it does assume the answer is "higher processing levels." You cannot understand the characteristics of perception discussed in this section without assuming that learning influences perception.

Perceptual Constancies

When you first look down at the street from atop a tall building, the cars and people look like miniatures until you remember the distance from which you are viewing them. You then alter your perceptions and no longer see miniature cars and people; you see normal-sized cars and people viewed from a great distance. Recognizing familiar objects and events as stable and unchanging under widely varying stimulus conditions is known as **perceptual constancy**.

Psychologists who support the unconscious inference theory of perception maintain that infants need nearly two years of interaction with the environment to achieve a stable view of the world (Piaget, 1952). During the

Although these road graders produce images of different sizes on your retina, you perceive each grader as the same size.

first two years of life, children learn about size-distance invariance. Experience teaches them that changes in the size and shape of retinal images do not signal changes in the size and shape of objects; changing retinal images represent changes in the distance of the object and changes in the viewing angle. With experience, children learn to make adjustments for changing environmental conditions and for distortions due to the ever-changing retinal images.

— *Size constancy*. When you learn that a person or object remains the same size despite a variance in the size of the retinal image, you achieve size constancy. Research shows that almost all infants develop some size constancy by six months of age (Yonas et al., 1982).

— *Shape constancy*. If someone asks you to describe the shape of the clock on your classroom wall, you can probably safely answer, without even looking, that it is a circle. Yet when you look at a round clock, the retinal image is a circle only when you stand directly in front of it. From other viewing angles, the retinal image is a variation of an oval. Your ability to perceive the clock as round, regardless of your viewing angle, is known as shape constancy.

— *Brightness constancy*. You experience an object's brightness as unchanging even when the lighting changes. You interpret changes in brightness as changes in the level of illumination, not as changes in the brightness of the object. For instance, if you see a white cat and a gray cat in the same light, the white cat appears brighter, but a gray cat lying in the sunshine is brighter than a white cat lying in the shade. However, because of bright-

Quick Study Aid

Constance and Her Unchanging Dress

(The Perceptual Constancies)
Constance is unchanging; her dress is always the same SIZE, the same SHAPE, the same COLOR, and the same BRIGHTNESS!!

EXHIBIT 6.11
The Ames Distorted Room

Normal cues for size constancy are distorted in the Ames room. Like Alice in Wonderland people shrink and expand depending on their location in the room.

ness constancy, you adjust your perception and see the white cat as brighter.

— *Color constancy.* A gray cat looks gray whether it is lying in the sun or in deep shade. If you know an object's color, color constancy causes you to judge color variations as changes in illumination. Your visual system can make adjustments for the color distortions resulting from varying lighting conditions, but color photographic film cannot. Thus, color photographs often do not show colors as you experience them.

Senses other than vision are also characterized by perceptual constancies. You recognize a friend's voice even when it is distorted by a bad telephone connection. You also recognize the ringing of your telephone under various conditions. However, occasionally you are fooled

and run to answer the telephone only to discover that the ringing telephone is on a television show.

Other perceptual constancies can also create deceptions. Psychologist Adelbert Ames was particularly adept at creating perceptual deceptions. The Ames room illustrates a well-known perceptual deception that is often used at funhouses in amusement parks. The deceptions of the Ames room (shown in Exhibit 6.11) depend on both shape and size constancy. People appear to shrink and grow as they move along the back wall of the room. From the viewer's vantage point, the room appears rectangular; in reality, the back left corner is nearly twice as far from the viewer as the back right corner. The cues from the room are sufficient to evoke size and shape constancies based on experience with rooms. Even knowledge of the layout of the room is usually not enough to overcome the constancy effects. The tendency to see rooms as rectangular is so strong that seeing individuals change size is easier than seeing the room change shape.

Perceptual Illusions

The Ames perceptual demonstrations point out how context influences perception. In perception, context is often studied as **frame of reference**. Past experience provides a temporal (time) frame of reference from which to make perceptual judgments.

Studying perceptual illusions is a second way to study the effect of context, or frame of reference. In Exhibit 6.12, the Titchener illusion, which center circle is larger—the one surrounded by smaller circles or the one surrounded by larger circles? Even if you were aware of this illusion before reading about it, the effect of the surrounding circles is so powerful that the center circle

surrounded by smaller circles will undoubtedly still look larger to you. Did you measure the circles to assure yourself they are the same size? The illusions in Exhibit 6.12 are but a few of the more than two hundred geometrical illusions that have been catalogued (Gillam, 1980).

The Müller-Lyer illusion (Exhibit 6.12) is one of the most famous and certainly one of the most studied illusions. Line segment *b* looks shorter than line segment *a*, whether the lines are arranged horizontally or vertically. A widely accepted explanation of the Müller-Lyer illusion is based on the interaction between learned size constancy and the frame of reference created by the fins (Gregory, 1978). Without the fins, the length of the lines is easily judged. The fins create a frame of reference that provides linear perspective cues. Experience with many rectangular frames of reference, particularly rectangular rooms, contributes to this illusion. As is depicted in Exhibit 6.13, the Müller-Lyer lines suggest a two-

EXHIBIT 6.12
Visual Illusions

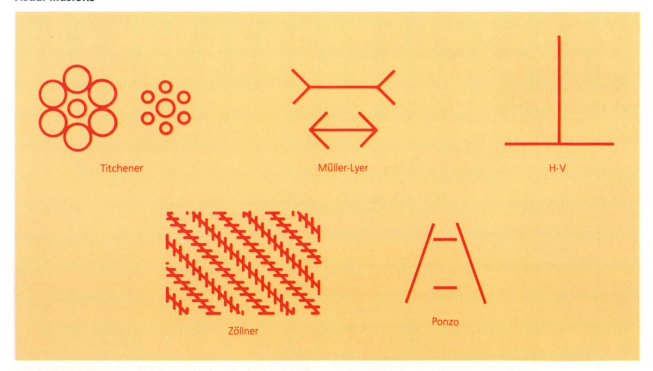

Titchener

Müller-Lyer

H-V

Zöllner

Ponzo

Here are some classic visual illusions. Even if you use a ruler, you may not be able to overcome these compelling illusions.
A. The two center circles are the same size in the Titchener illusion.
B. The two line segments in the Müller-Lyer illusion are the same length.

C. The two line segments are the same length in the horizontal-vertical (H-V) illusion.
D. The diagonal lines in the Zöllner illusion are parallel.
E. The two horizontal bars are the same length in the Ponzo illusion.

EXHIBIT 6.13
A Perspectives Explanation of the Müller-Lyer Illusion

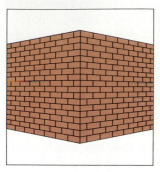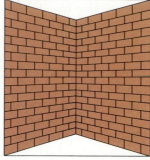

The perspectives explanation suggests that you interpret the arrow-like figures as three-dimensional representations of inside and outside corners.

dimensional representation of the near and far edges of a room or the inside and outside corners in a room. When the fins point in, they suggest a nearer edge or corner, and when the fins point out, they suggest a farther edge or corner.

Perceptually, you adjust the length of the line segments to fit your experience with the three-dimensional context suggested by the two-dimensional drawing. You perceptually lengthen line segment *a* while shortening line segment *b*. The result is dramatic. The fins cause you to misinterpret cues you normally use for maintaining size constancy.

A challenge to the misinterpretation of size constancy cues explanation has been made. When the fins are replaced with other shapes that do not create familiar frames of reference, as in Exhibit 6.14, the illusion persists (Rock, 1975). These results suggest the observer is not making the correct comparison. The observer appears to compare the two whole figures with one another, instead of just comparing the line segments. If the line segments and fins are physically separated or the observer is specifically instructed to pay attention just to the line segments, the illusionary effect is decreased (Coren & Girgus, 1972). Likewise, changing the length of the fins changes the magnitude of the illusion (Erlebacher & Sekuler, 1969). Thus, another interpretation of the Müller-Lyer illusion is that observers are confused by the fins and make incorrect comparisons.

Cross-cultural research supports the combination of experience and higher levels of processing interpretation of the Müller-Lyer illusion. Interestingly, individuals who live in environments with few rectangular shapes and

straight lines, such as members of the Zulu tribe in South Africa, do not experience the Müller-Lyer illusion (Deregowski, 1972; Gillam, 1980). This evidence indicates that the tendency to perceive the Müller-Lyer illusion is at least partially learned. An experiment was designed to test the role of higher processes in the perception of the Müller-Lyer illusion. A special apparatus flashed the line segments of the illusion into the left eye of a subject; at the same time, the fins were flashed onto the appropriate spots on the retina of the right eye. Subjects still experienced the illusion, which proves that the illusion does not take place in the retina but is the product of higher-level processing (Gillam, 1980).

Perceptual Set

Frames of reference also affect perceptual organization through **perceptual set**. Perceptual set refers to people's tendency to perceive what they expect to perceive or what makes sense to them. How often have you "seen" a dead animal along the road and as you came closer "discovered" it was a tire tread or a piece of trash? Your first perception of the object was based on your interpretation that an object lying along the road was likely to be a dead animal. Because of your expectations, the cues allowed you to organize the stimulus as a dead animal.

Your perceptual expectations are the product of your past experiences and your present attitudes, values, beliefs, and motivations. The role of motives and beliefs was dramatically demonstrated in a classic study with students from Dartmouth and Princeton (Hastorf and Cantril, 1954). Students from both colleges watched

EXHIBIT 6.14
Faulty Comparisons Explanation of the Müller-Lyer Illusion

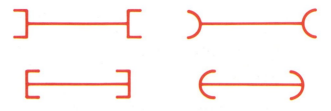

The faulty comparisons explanation suggests that you compare the whole figures, not just the line segments. Therefore, other types of fins that do not represent inside and outside corners also produce the illusion.

Reprinted with permission of Macmillan Publishing Co. from *An introduction to perception* by Irwin Rock, © 1975 by Irwin Rock.

PSI Phenomenon

Extrasensory perception (ESP) has been defined as the process of gathering information through senses other than sight, hearing, smell, taste, and touch. A more general term, *psi,* includes psychokinesis and four types of ESP. The scientific study of psi and similar phenomena is called *parapsychology.* The five psi phenomena parapsychologists most often explore are:

1) *Clairvoyance*—"second sight"; perceiving current events without visual or other basic senses.

2) *Precognition*—"seeing into the future"; perceiving events that will occur in the future.

3) *Retrocognition*—"seeing into the past"; perceiving past events without having used visual or other basic senses.

4) *Telepathy*—"reading minds"; knowing another's thoughts.

5) *Psychokinesis*—"demonstrating mind over matter"; changing or moving objects by force of will.

Although some psychologists classify psi phenomena as altered states of consciousness, the majority of psychologists believes that sufficient evidence to demonstrate the existence of such phenomena is lacking. A typical clairvoyance experiment uses Zener cards—a 25-card deck with cross, square, wavy lines, circle and star symbols. Subjects are asked to indicate which card they expect the experimenter to turn up next (which card they "see" next in the deck). Because subjects respond with one of only five alternatives, the chance of guessing correctly without "seeing" the card is one out of five, or 20%. Parapsychologists find a substantial lack of evidence in most clairvoyance experiments.

Critics of parapsychology cite the lack of experimental control in laboratory settings. For example, one explanation for correct guesses in several early clairvoyance studies is that the subjects could actually see the embossed designed through the cards. Similar flaws in research design have been found in tests of other psi phenomenon (e.g. subjects mumbling under their breath when trying to communicate telepathically). When researchers eliminate these methodological problems and attempt to replicate these studies, their results often fail to confirm earlier psi findings.

To be acceptable to scientists, ESP research needs to include four essential controls (Sargent & Eysenck,

1983):

1) Sensory cues must be eliminated.

2) ESP targets must be random. If an event is expected or can be logically predicted, the evidence for ESP is weak.

3) Results must be accurately and objectively recorded. Computer recording is one way to ensure accuracy and objectivity.

4) The results must be measured against chance levels (the possibility of an event occurring by chance).

For years, James Randi, a professional magician, has offered to duplicate—using illusion—any psi phenomenon reported by parapsychologists. Because magicians such as Randi have frequently disproven the claims of parasychologists and have revealed the fraud underlying many of their experiments, in 1984 the Parapsychological Association adopted the principle that researchers who suspect subjects of fraud should call in experienced conjurors (magicians) (Randi, 1984). Although Randi's ability to duplicate feats of telepathy or clairvoyance through "trickery" does *not* disprove the existence of psi phenomena, it does cast further doubt on the research.

Despite the lack of experimental evidence, many lay people believe in the validity of these unsubstantiated phenomena as firmly as they believe in astrology. A recent Gallup poll of American teenagers (ages 16 to 18) found that 51% of those surveyed believe in astrology, 62% believe in ESP, and 28% believe in Clairvoyance (Feder, 1985).

As you consider parapsychology and psi phenomena, keep in mind a basic principle of the scientific method (Chapter 3). The scientific method places the burden of proof on experimenters who propose a phenomenon's existence; contrary to this principle, many "believers" in ESP attempt to convince "nonbelievers" that a phenomenon's existence must be *disproved* or it is thereby confirmed. Remember also that belief is very different from evidence and that the scientific method of demands evidence. Whenever you hear or read of parapsychological findings, always compare the experimental group with the control group, search for experimenter bias, compare the results to those expected by chance, and search for alternate explanations.

 *Exploring . . .*

Eyewitness Testimony

Your knowledge of perceptual set and perceptual defense should cause you to question the reliability of eyewitness reports. People who subscribe to the saying "seeing is believing" may believe some highly inaccurate perceptions. Despite repeated efforts by psychologists to make the public aware of the inaccuracies of such reports, eyewitness testimony in criminal trials is often the evidence weighed most heavily by juries.

How accurate are eyewitnesses? In one study conducted on a college campus (Buckhout, 1974), a "crime" in which a college professor was attacked by an unknown assailant was staged. The mock attack was videotaped so eyewitness reports could be scored for accuracy. Of the 141 eyewitnesses questioned carefully about the "crime," only about 25 percent were accurate in their reports of the assailant's age, weight, height, etc. In a similar mock crime study (Buckhout, 1980), a film of a mugging was broadcast on a television news program. Immediately after the film, a lineup of six suspects in the mugging was shown. Viewers were asked to phone in and identify the assailant. Of the more than 2,000 people who phoned, 1,800 callers identified the wrong person. One-third of the callers thought the assailant was black or Hispanic when, in fact, the person was white. Apparently these callers expected the mugger to be black or Hispanic and they perceived him to be so.

Studies like these strongly demonstrate the inaccuracy of eyewitness testimony, and the second study points to the role of expectations in perception. This same researcher has uncovered actual criminal cases in which positive eyewitness identifications were proven wrong (Buckhout, 1974). In one case, two people were arrested for two separate crimes on the basis of eyewitness identification. Later, a third person confessed to having committed both crimes!

Slowly, police officers, lawyers, and judges are becoming convinced of the inaccuracy of eyewitness reports (Loftus & Monahan, 1980), but even greater efforts to convince jurists that eyewitness testimony is not conclusive evidence need to be made.

---

films of a football game between Dartmouth and Princeton. During the game, a popular Princeton player was injured by rough play. The Princeton students blamed the rough play on the Dartmouth team and believed that Dartmouth had committed twice as many penalties as Princeton. In contrast, the Dartmouth students believed the game was rough, but they blamed both sides equally. The Dartmouth students thought an equal number of penalties had been committed by both teams. The frames of reference of the Dartmouth students were obviously very different from those of the Princeton students.

Perceptual Defense

Can you be influenced by something you did not see? The question of whether perceptual set can cause you to *not* see something has intrigued psychologists for a number of years. This phenomenon, termed **perceptual defense**, is related to the question of subliminal perception. Perceptual defense studies question whether you can block out stimuli, particularly those that are threatening. The issue is complicated because before you can block out threatening stimuli, you must first recognize them as threatening. This processing must take place at an unconscious level.

An early perceptual defense study (McGinnies, 1949) tested college students' recognition of different categories of words. The word categories were emotionally laden words (e.g., rape, penis, bitch) and emotionally neutral words (e.g., rope, pencil, batch). Words were flashed very briefly on a screen. On each trial, the length of time a word appeared on the screen was increased until the subject could recognize the word well enough to tell the experimenter what it was. The concept of perceptual defense was supported; subjects took longer to recognize the emotionally laden words than to recognize the emotionally neutral words.

Other researchers quickly pointed out the methodological flaws in the so-called "dirty" word study (Howes

& Solomon, 1951). Two clear problems were (1) the lower familiarity of the "dirty" words because of their less frequent use and (2) the embarrassment the subjects felt when they said the words to the experimenter. However, when these objections and others were answered in later research, the phenomenon of perceptual defense was still supported (Erdelyi, 1974). Thus, perceptual defense appears to use frames of reference at an unconscious level of processing. In perceptual defense, you resist information that causes discomfort, embarrassment, or anxiety without being aware that you do so.

Perceptual Integration

This perception chapter emphasizes the perceptual processing of visual information. The emphasis is due partly to the greater amount of available research on visual perception and partly to the fact that humans are visually dominant. In **visual dominance**, visual information predominates over (is more likely to be relied on than) information from the other senses. Visual dominance explains why a ventriloquist is successful in getting you to hear words coming from a dummy's mouth. You see the dummy's mouth lip-synching while the sounds come from the ventriloquist's mouth. The visual information

dominates, and you perceive the sounds as coming from the dummy's mouth.

Although vision is dominant in humans, perceptual experience is based on the integration of information from all senses. In movie theaters with "state-of-the-art" sound systems that surround you with sound, your visual experience is enhanced. When information from two or more of the senses conflicts (as when you watch a ventriloquist's act), you may not be aware of the discrepancy; however, if you do become aware of it, the failure of integration can affect you dramatically. Consider your reaction when a movie soundtrack is out of synchrony with the screen action. You may find the situation so annoying that you prefer to leave the theater rather than attempt to integrate the "out of sync" soundtrack with the images on the screen.

Focus Question Answer

Do you perceive the world accurately? Some inaccuracies in perception result from perceptual constancies. Other inaccuracies are caused by illusions, perceptual set, perceptual defense, and visual dominance. Thus, the same characteristics that help people achieve a stable perception of world may also lead to inaccuracies like those occurring in eyewitness testimony.

 *Relate*

Art and Life

Throughout this chapter on perceptual processing, the various principles and concepts have been illustrated with artwork and photographs. The challenge has been to transfer onto the two-dimensional page representations of the processes used to perceive the three-dimensional world around you. All artists face this task when they attempt to create representations of their own perceptual experiences.

Visual artists who work on two-dimensional surfaces approach this task in a variety of ways. For example, some painters strive to create on canvas a realistic image of what they actually see. They want their artwork to be a faithful copy of the three-dimensional world they perceive. They achieve this realism in art by using the perceptual principles explained in this chapter.

Other visual artists seek to challenge their own perceptual processes and those of the people who view their artistic creations. These artists strive for new forms of expression

to represent what they see. In many ways, the Modern Art movement may seem the antithesis of Realism, but Modern Art achieves its effects by using the same perceptual principles Realism uses.

A third artistic approach is to create two-dimensional images that are not seen in the real three-dimensional world. Some artists strive to create realistic, impossible images that challenge the viewer in much the same way a Modern Art painting does; others work to create unrealistic, possible images that resemble the images of the Realists. The "surrealism" of this approach seeks to reveal the inner workings of the brain and the unconscious imagery of the "mind's eye." Like other artistic approaches, surrealism is grounded in the basic principles of perceptual processing.

Look closely at the rural scene painted by Grant Wood. Can you identify the various monocular (or, in this case, pictorial) cues to depth? Do you think Wood used effectively

Grant Wood, *The Birthplace of Herbert Hoover*

the cues to depth? Do you like this painting? What mood or feelings do you experience when you look at this picture? Do you think your feelings are aroused by the scene or by the way Wood chose to portray it? The answers to these types of questions form the basis for your appreciation of art. You may not consciously ask yourself such questions,

Pablo Picasso, *Tete*

but the answers determine if and why you like a painting. Your evaluations of the artist's technique and of the emotions the painting arouses contribute to your appreciation of art.

Look now at the Picasso painting. Ask yourself questions similar to those in the preceding paragraph. How does Picasso use the Gestalt grouping principles to create various figures and to focus your attention on different areas of the painting? Is the mood you experience while viewing this painting different from that which you experienced while

M. C. Escher, *Waterfall*

viewing the Wood painting? Can you account for the difference? In his search for new forms of expression, does Picasso challenge not only your view of art but also your view of the world?

Turn now to the Escher print. Escher's art differs from Picasso's. What you see directly challenges your perceptual processes. Escher employs the same basic perceptual principles used by Wood and Picasso, but he uses them to trick your perceptual system. When you restrict your frame of reference to a relatively small area of the print, you see what appears to be an authentic representation of a scene from life. However, when you enlarge your frame of reference, incongruities emerge and you see what appears to be both realistic and impossible. Does viewing this print evoke in you a mental state different from those created by the other two paintings?

These works reflect the artists' attempts to translate their perceptions into a visual image that others may see. Each translation reflects not only the artist's awareness of perceptual principles but also the artist's values, beliefs, and motivations—his perceptual set. Look at the painting reproduced on the cover of your textbook. What perceptual principles has the artist used. What do you think were the artist's motives in painting this picture?

Do artists see the world differently than you do? The answer is yes and no. Artists use the same perceptual processes that you use, and in this respect they see the world as you do. However, some exceptions exist. Van Gogh's use of curved lines may have been due to extreme astigmatism, and the blurred detail and dominant yellow cast in some of Monet's later paintings may have been caused by cataracts. These artists may literally have been painting what they saw.

Although artists like Van Gogh and Monet may have altered perceptual processes, a more likely explanation for your seeing the world differently than artists see it is that you do not share the same perceptual sets. Because of differences in past experiences, values, and motives, individual artists differ from each other in their perceptual sets and, thus, even they see the world differently from one another. No one sees anything exactly as someone else does. Differences in perception contribute to uniqueness. Each person is an artist who sees the world in his or her own way and creates his or her own pictures.

Things to Do

1. To demonstrate the difficulty of achieving perceptual accuracy, randomly pick a page of your textbook, and have everyone in your class count the words on that page. Did everyone get the same number? If not, how do you explain the inaccuracies? How could you accurately count the words on a page?

2. Here is a way to experience directly a changing retinal image. With your thumb and index finger, hold a pencil in a vertical position close to your face. Use the thumb and index finger of your other hand to measure the height of the pencil (put the index finger at the top of the pencil and the thumb at the bottom). Now keep your measuring hand close to your face, and move the pencil away to arm's length. Does the pencil, when compared to the frame of reference formed by your fingers, appear to shrink? Obviously, the pencil does not shrink and expand; the size of the retinal image changes.

3. To demonstrate the binocular depth cues of retinal disparity and convergence, try the following exercise. Place a paper clip on a tabletop about two and a half feet in front of you. Cover one eye with one hand. With your other hand, hold a second paper clip about six inches above the tabletop. Using just one eye, try to position the paper clip that you hold in your hand directly over the paper clip on the table so that when you drop the clip in your hand it will hit the one on the table. How accurate were you? Using both eyes, try the same task again. Were you surprised at the difference in your accuracy?

4. You may want to amaze your friends with this perceptual demonstration. The next time they are watching a spinning propeller, or any other rapidly rotating object, ask them to start humming. By humming higher or lower pitches until they reach the right frequency, they can make the spinning object (as they perceive it) seem to slow down, stop, or spin slowly in the opposite direction. The explanation of this perceptual oddity is not perceptual integration; the explanation involves the eyeball vibrations created by the humming sound. When you hum at the same pitch as the frequency of the rotating object, the resulting vibrations create a stroboscopic effect. Your vibrating eyes act like a strobe light and perceptually "freeze the action."

Things to Discuss

1. People rely on all their senses to obtain varied perceptual information about the world, and those with sensory disabilities compensate for the resulting loss of perceptual information. Imagine you have to give up one of your senses. Which sense would you choose? What would you do to compensate for that loss?

2. Many people have compared human vision and cameras. List the ways in which human vision is *not* like a camera. Which features of human vision resemble those of a camera? Are sophisticated video camera systems comparable to the human visual system? Will mechanical systems that duplicate the human visual system ever be invented?

3. When you watch a videotape, you watch an external event. When your visual system produces a picture, you watch an internal event. In each case, which part of you is watching the picture? How is that part related to the visual system? How could you investigate this experience?

4. Although subliminal advertising has been proven ineffective, a relatively new motion picture technique produces an experience that can be highly manipulative. The technique, called Showscan, involves photographing and projecting motion pictures at a faster than normal speed. The sixty frame per second rate is approximately the rate at which the eye transmits information to the brain. Subjects report the images are much more vivid and convincing than those from standard movies. Could this technique be used as an educational tool? Could Showscan be used effectively in advertising? Could Showscan become a brainwashing technique?

5. In the 1940s, a psychologist suggested that a mismatch between incoming information and anticipated information is the cause of fear. This suggestion makes fear a basic mechanism of perception. Does this idea fit your experience? What arouses fear within you? Could perceptual mismatch explain the fear of the unknown?

Things to Read

Coren, S. & Girgus, J.S. 1978. *Seeing is deceiving: The psychology of visual illusions.* Hillsdale, NJ: Erlbaum.

Fineman, M. 1981. *The inquisitive eye.* NY: Oxford University Press.

Haith, M.M. 1980. *Rules that babies look by: The organization of newborn visual activity.* Hillsdale, NJ: Erlbaum.

Loftus, E.F. 1979. *Eyewitness testimony.* Cambridge, MA: Academic Press.

Michaels, C.F. & Carello, C. 1981. *Direct perception.* Englewood Cliffs, NJ: Prentice-Hall.

Randi, J. 1980. *Flim Flam: The truth about unicorns, parapsychology, and other delusions.* NY: Lippincott & Crovell.

 ## Review

Summary

1. Perception is the complex process of organizing and interpreting sensations. Two theories—unconscious inference theory and the theory of direct perception—attempt to account for perceptual processing. Unconscious inference theory emphasizes the role of learning from past experience, and the theory of direct perception emphasizes the role of innate (inborn) factors.

2. Newborns, when tested with appropriate techniques, display many well-developed perceptual abilities; the findings of the past two decades suggest that several perceptual processes are innate, though these processes may be influenced by later experiences.

3. Gestalt psychologists believe that "the whole is more than the sum of its parts." The Law of Pragnanz (what *can* be grouped together, *will* be) is the basis for the figure-ground relationship and for the grouping principles of closure, proximity, similarity, common fate, continuity, and simplicity or figural goodness. These principles govern how stimuli are grouped together to form figures.

4. Depth perception relies on both binocular (two eyes) and monocular (one eye) cues. Retinal disparity, which is produced by the slightly different views the eyes receive, is a binocular cue to depth. The binocular depth cue of convergence (the degree to which the eyes turn inward) aids judgment of distances less than twenty-five feet. Many monocular cues to depth are based on size-distance invariance (the size of the retinal image is a function of the distance of the object). The monocular depth cues (linear perspective, texture gradients, aerial perspective, height on a plane, interposition, shadowing, and relative size) are also cues artists use to add depth to their two-dimensional drawings. Studies with the visual cliff apparatus and studies with very young infants indicate that depth perception is innate.

5. Relative motion (motion parallax) is both a monocular depth cue and a motion perception cue. Induced motion and apparent motion (phi phenomenon and stroboscopic motion) are common experiences of illusionary motion. The phi phenomenon is used to create moving arrows in advertising signs. Stroboscopic motion is used to produce motion pictures.

6. Perceptual constancies develop through learning and experience. Size, shape, brightness, and color constancies develop from an awareness that these properties of objects and events remain the same, regardless of viewing condition. An individual maintains a stable view of the world even though the retinal image changes constantly. Frames of reference play a role in perceptual constancies by allowing an individual to use the context of an object to form an estimate of the object's true size and shape.

7. Perceptual illusions occur when people misinterpret normal perceptual cues. In the Müller-Lyer illusion, people misinterpret linear perspective cues. When the fins that provide these cues are removed, the illusion disappears.

8. Perceptual set is the tendency for people to see what they expect to see. Because of perceptual defense, people may not see threatening or unpleasant stimuli. Both perceptual set and perceptual defense achieve their effects through internal frames of reference and higher-level perceptual processing.

9. In normal perception, information from all the senses is integrated into a coherent picture of the world. Because of visual dominance, information from other senses is adjusted to fit the information from the visual system. Perceptual integration failures are usually disconcerting experiences.

10. In art, as in life, the principles of perceptual processing are basic and essential. All artists, regardless of their approach, make use of perceptual principles to achieve desired effects.

Key Terms

unconscious inference theory
ecological approach
theory of direct perception
Law of Pragnanz
figure-ground relationship
closure
proximity
similarity
common fate
continuity
simplicity (figural goodness)
depth perception
visual cliff
retinal disparity
convergence
accommodation
size-distance invariance
linear perspective
texture gradients

aerial perspective
height on a plane
interposition
shadowing
relative size
relative motion (motion parallax)
induced motion
phi phenomenon (apparent motion)
stroboscopic motion
perceptual constancy
size constancy
shape constancy
brightness constancy
color constancy
frame of reference
perceptual set
perceptual defense
visual dominance

Focus Questions

1. How do psychologists define consciousness?

2. Are your sleeping hours spent in a uniformly relaxed state?

3. How might you benefit from hypnosis or meditation?

4. Upon which drugs that you might use could you become dependent?

5. How can you identify any sleep disorders you have?

Chapter Outline

CONSCIOUSNESS
Attention
Daydreams

SLEEP
Sleep Laboratories
Sleep Stages
Dream Theories
Sleep Needs
The Research Process: Sleep Deprivation

ALTERED STATES
Hypnosis
Meditation

DRUG-INDUCED ALTERED STATES
Alcohol
Other Central Nervous System Depressants
Central Nervous System Stimulants
Hallucinogens
Marijuana
Tobacco

RELATE: Sleep Disorders
Things to Do
Things to Discuss
Things to Read

REVIEW: Summary
Key Terms

States of
Consciousness

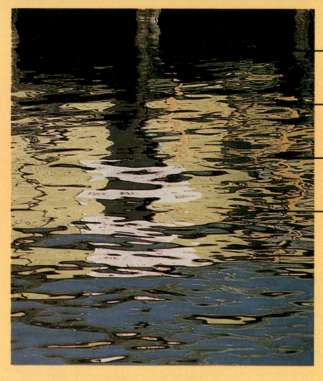

*Dreams are the touchstones
of our characters.*

Henry David Thoreau

 Consciousness

Thus far in this unit, the Mind-Body Connection, you have focused on the body—first on the nervous system and then on the sense receptor systems and perceptual processes. In this chapter, you will direct your attention to the mind.

The main ingredient of the *mind* part of the Mind-Body Connection is **consciousness**, an awareness of reality that includes awareness of your own existence, internal sensations, perceptions of external objects, emotions, dreams, thoughts, and memories. Creating a precise definition of consciousness that specifies how awareness occurs and upon which psychologists agree is very difficult. Most psychologists would agree with the description of consciousness used by psychologist Robert Ornstein in his book, *The Psychology of Consciousness:*

151

Ordinary consciousness is an exquisitely evolved personal construction, "designed" for the primary purpose of individual biological survival. Sense organs and the brain serve to select aspects of the environment most relevant for survival. Our ordinary consciousness is object-centered; it involves analysis, a separation of oneself from other objects and organisms. This selective, active, analytic construction enables us to achieve a relatively stable personal world in which we can differentiate objects and act upon them. (Ornstein, 1977, pp. 71-72)

Ornstein recognizes that consciousness varies; he writes of "ordinary consciousness." Furthermore, he suggests that ordinary consciousness is an active creation of your own making, a "personal construction."

Your personal construction of reality varies in two major ways. First, consciousness varies by degrees, or levels. Under ordinary conditions, you may consider only two levels of consciousness—conscious and unconscious. Psychologists, however, consider a continuum that ranges from comas at one endpoint through different levels of sleep and wakefulness to heightened levels of consciousness at the other endpoint. Heightened levels of consciousness include increased sensitivity to, or awareness of, the world around you and what one psychologist called peak experiences (Maslow, 1954). Another term, nonconscious, is not a synonym for unconscious; if you are nonconscious, you are unaware or are unable to be aware. Many bodily processes such as the functioning of the neurons in your spinal cord and the release of hormones into your bloodstream are never directly, consciously experienced; they are nonconscious.

Consciousness also varies by kinds, or states. Normal waking consciousness differs from altered states of consciousness. In this chapter, you will learn about altered states such as sleep, dream, hypnotic, meditative and drug-induced states. Particular attention is paid to psychoactive drugs because of their powerful mind-altering effects, their negative side-effects, and their potential for abuse.

Attention

A central process in consciousness is selective attention (attending to some sensations while ignoring others). Much more information is available to you than you can attend to at any one time. As a result, your sensory systems respond only to the stimuli that contain more information than others (those that are changing more than the others), and during perceptual processing you focus on (i.e., become aware or conscious of) only a limited number of these sensations. At any given moment, numerous sensory inputs vie for attention, and your awareness of ongoing events shifts as you selectively attend to different sensations. One model of selective attention (Broadbent, 1958) describes attention as a filter for sensory input. According to this model, you attend to only one channel of sensory input at a time. An example of this selective shift in attention, called the cocktail party effect, occurs when you are with a group of people engaged in numerous conversations. Your attention shifts from one conversation to another, but you are unable to attend to more than one conversation at a time. Numerous laboratory studies have investigated this selective attention phenomenon. As a result of dichotic listening studies, in which different information is sent to the two ears at the same time, Broadbent's model has been modified to include the ideas that nonconscious processing of sensory information does occur (Treisman, 1960) and that prior learning or knowledge, as well as the sensory input, guides the selection of information for attention (Neisser, 1967). Thus, your awareness of reality is constructed from conscious attention to selected sensory inputs and nonconscious processing of other sensory inputs and prior knowledge.

Daydreams

Among the various states of consciousness, daydreams occupy a position between the normal waking state and the drowsiness that precedes sleep. When people daydream, they shift the focus of their attention from the external to the internal world. Because daydreams cannot be identified by a unique physiological pattern, researchers must depend primarily on subjects' self-reports for information about daydreams. In these reports, a vast majority say they daydream (Singer, 1975), and they do so for a variety of reasons—to escape momentarily from boring, routine tasks or surroundings, to rehearse for future encounters, and to fantasize about unlikely occurrences.

Numerous daydream reports indicate differences in the type and content of peoples' daydreams. One study (Singer, 1978) identified three types: positive-vivid, characterized by a happy content and rich, elaborate detail; guilty-dysphoric, characterized by negativity, failure, and guilt; and mind-wandering-distractible, characterized by unpleasant content and undeveloped, disjointed ideas. Of these types, happy daydreams are the most common. Another study examined differences in the content of men's and women's daydreams; women daydream more about social interactions and relationships, and men daydream more about achievement, power, and acquisition of possessions (Singer, 1975). Daydreams, then, are a subset of the waking state of consciousness; in them, your attention wanders from the task at hand, and as you stare into space you cease to process sensory data from your surroundings and you focus on your internal images.

Focus Question Answer

How do psychologists define consciousness? Generally, consciousness includes an awareness of both external stimuli and internal mental processes. The term nonconscious describes processes of which you are not aware or cannot become aware. Researchers of altered states of consciousness study sleep, dreams, hypnosis, meditation, and drug use and abuse.

 Sleep

For centuries, people have speculated about sleep, a state in which many humans spend one-third of their lives. Aristotle believed that people become tired because eating, drinking, and physical exercise cause body matter to evaporate and fill up their heads. Then, while people sleep, the substances in their heads cool, descend into their bodies, and awaken them. Today, only the belief that sleep has a restorative function remains of Aristotle's hypothesis.

Another hypothesis—that a sleep-causing chemical circulates in the blood—was questioned in 1836, when Geoffrey Saint-Hilaire studied a pair of Siamese twins; their independent sleep/waking cycles suggested to him that a sleep-inducing blood substance did not exist (Evans, 1984). The search for a single such chemical continues to be unsuccessful, but currently much sleep research focuses on the role of different parts of the brain and different neurotransmitters in sleep and dream cycles.

Sleep Laboratories

Before the 1950s, people assumed that because they remembered so few of them dreams were rare events. Then, in the 1950s, the discovery of the connection between dreams and jerky eye movements beneath closed eyelids during sleep stimulated great interest in the area of sleep and dreams. During the late 1950s and the 1960s, sleep research boomed and by 1965 approximately two dozen sleep laboratories had been established in the United States (National Institute of Mental Health, 1965).

Although most contemporary sleep research relies on more complex physiological monitoring, the basic equipment of the sleep laboratories of the 1960s was similar to that used in today's sleep disorder clinics and hospital units. Currently, patients or subjects usually sleep in private bedrooms connected by an intercom system to a monitoring room. "Sleepers" arrive shortly before their bedtimes and are attached to several types of physiological monitors, including an electrocardiograph (an instrument used to diagnose heart disease), a myograph

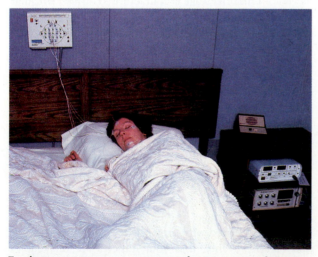

For diagnostic purposes, a patient spends one or two nights sleeping in a bedroom at a sleep laboratory. Electrodes attached to the face, skull and leg measure six or more biological functions,

including heart function, eye movements, leg muscle movements, and brain waves.

The Electroencephalograph (EEG)

The **electroencephalograph (EEG)** measures brain activity through a procedure that begins with pasting small pieces of conductive metal, or electrodes, onto the scalp. The electrodes pick up and transmit natural electrical brain changes; the device then amplifies and converts these changes to a graph on a continuous roll of paper. This graph provides a record of brain waves—up and down wave-like lines reflecting the positive and negative electrical changes in the various portions of the brain. Generally, the brain waves vary from slow, large, even electrical changes to fast, small, irregular changes.

As indicated in the graph, the EEG waves differ for wakefulness and each sleep state; this difference allows sleep researchers to plot the number of times each night a person cycles through the sleep stages and the length of time he or she spends in each stage. As you can see, a typical night's sleep for young adults includes five cycles, each somewhat different from the cycle before or after it. Adults spend approximately one and one-half to two hours per night in REM (dream) sleep in four or five increasingly longer blocks of time

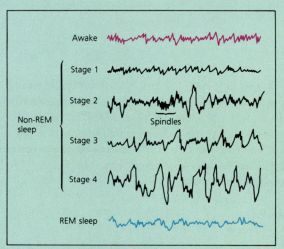

The brain activity of a young adult during a typical night's sleep. REM sleep increases until near waking.

(Melnechuk, 1983). Unless you are awakened during one of these REM periods, you will probably have only vague memories, if any, of your dreams.

(an instrument that records muscular contractions), and an electroencephalograph, or EEG (see the *Exploring . . .* section for an explanation of the EEG and the different types of brain waves it records). Through these devices and others, brain waves, eye movements, heart action, and leg muscle movements are monitored (many other physiological changes, such as carbon dioxide level and the chest's effort to breathe, may also be measured).

Sleep Stages

Drowsiness   Imagine you are lying comfortably in bed, feeling drowsy and relaxed. As you hover between waking and sleeping, you may experience **hypnogogic images.** You may hear voices or brief periods of music; you may see colors, lights, or geometric designs; or you may feel as if you are falling (Siegel, 1977). In this transitional stage, the EEG recording changes from rapid, irregular, waking state waves to slower, regular waves (alpha waves).

Stage 1   This brief stage is characterized by fast, irregular EEG waves. If someone calls your name, you are awakened easily and will probably say you were not asleep.

Stage 2   During this stage, your eyes may appear to be rolling slowly back and forth beneath your eyelids; this movement is not the same as the later rapid eye movements. The unique EEG of this stage shows quick bursts of waves, called **sleep spindles.** If you are awakened during this stage, you will probably feel as if you have been "lost in thought" instead of asleep.

Stage 3   In this stage, the EEG sleep spindles gradually become interspersed with large, slow waves (theta waves). You breathe evenly, and your muscles are relaxed. A louder noise is required to awaken you than when you were in Stage 2.

Stage 4   Now you have entered the deepest sleep stage; in it you rarely move, and you are oblivious to your surroundings. Sometimes termed delta sleep or slow wave sleep, this stage is characterized by slow, deep waves called delta waves. Sleepwalking, sleeptalking, night terrors (sudden, frightening awakenings—not bad dreams), and bedwetting are most likely to occur during this stage.

REM Sleep   About an hour after you fall asleep, you begin going through the stages in reverse order—from Stage 4 to Stage 3 to Stage 2. Approximately ninety minutes after you fall asleep, **rapid eye movements (REM)** signify you are dreaming; your eyes move jerkily beneath the lids as if you were watching a movie. The eye movement gives this stage its name. The other sleep stages are sometimes referred to as NREM stages, or non-rapid eye movement stages, because they lack this characteristic. The EEG pattern changes to rapid, irregular waves similar to those recorded when you are awake. Because of the wave similarity, the REM stage is sometimes referred to as **paradoxical** (an apparent contradiction) **sleep**.

The physiological changes that occur during REM sleep are enormous. Gone are the relaxed muscles and even breathing. Your body loses its muscle tone, your heart rate and respiration rate increase, males have erections, and females have vaginal engorgement (Kiester, 1980); the last two changes, which usually signal sexual excitement, occur during each REM sleep stage regardless of the dream content. Many people misunderstand the relationship between REM and dreams; they assume all dreams occur during REM sleep. In fact, although sleepers awakened during REM almost inevitably say they were dreaming, they may also report dreams when they are awakened during other sleep stages. REM dreams usually have an odd quality while dreams in other stages more closely resemble thinking or planning.

Dream Theories

Sigmund Freud, who published his dream theories at the beginning of the twentieth century, thought dreams represent wish fulfillments or conflicts of which you are not consciously aware. To him, dreams bridge the conscious and the unconscious and are filled with sexual symbols. Carl Jung, another well-known psychologist of the same time period, theorized that dreams serve a compensatory function; in other words, feelings or actions that you underemphasize during waking hours you overemphasize to the same degree in your dreams. Other dream theories

emphasize the influence of personality on dream content, the function of processing the past day's events, and the possibility of problem-solving during dreaming. Until recently, dream theorists assumed that dreams have a psychological function.

The most common explanation for REM has been that the brain produces images that the eyes scan as these images pass rapidly before the sleeper. However, a current explanation of dreaming, the **activation-synthesis hypothesis**, takes a very different approach. Now several dream researchers believe dreams represent the brain's attempt to explain why the eyes are "jiggling around" (Hobson, 1983). More specifically, these researchers believe that cells in the brainstem activate eye-movement neurons. Then, because no external images are coming in, the cortex must attempt to use stored memories to explain these movements. Although this theory differs significantly from previous theories, these theorists maintain at least one common belief: motivational states, memories, and personalities may influence what people dream (Hobson & McCarley, 1977).

Sleep Needs

Differences   Sleep patterns vary widely, and few people actually need or get the oft-cited eight hours of sleep. The amount of sleep people need decreases from infancy to old age, with infants averaging sixteen hours and people over fifty averaging only six hours of sleep per night (Hartmann et al., 1972). Additionally, as people age, the time to complete each sleep cycle increases. Children's sleep cycles are typically 50–60 minutes long, while adults' sleep cycles average 85–110 minutes (see

Babies spend much of their time sleeping, but the need for sleep decreases with age.

Exhibit 7.1). These wide variations indicate how individual sleep needs and patterns are.

Are people with very different sleep patterns different in other ways? One study discovered differences between long sleepers, those who average nearly nine hours per night, and short sleepers, those who average five-and-a-half hours per night (Hartmann, et al., 1972). Long sleepers take longer to get to sleep, get twice as much REM sleep, and recall more dreams. Their personality characteristics include anxiety, shyness, inhibition, and less aggression. In contrast, short sleepers often begin cutting back on sleep during adolescence, and they don't enjoy sleeping as much as do long sleepers. Short sleeper personality characteristics include ambition, energy, cheerfulness, conformity, assertiveness, and career-orientation.

Deprivation   Researchers have studied both REM sleep deprivation and total sleep deprivation. Although the-

orists cannot agree on the function of sleep or dreams, they do agree that both seem necessary. The amount of REM sleep people experience at various ages has been examined (see Exhibit 7.1). As you can see, newborns may spend 50 percent of their sleep time in REM sleep (Roffwarg et al., 1966). This percentage gradually declines; young adults spend about 20 percent of sleep time in REM sleep, and elderly people spend only about 15 percent in REM sleep (Maugh, 1982). If people are deprived of REM sleep, they compensate by experiencing longer than usual REM periods in their next sleep period. This phenomenon is termed **REM rebound**.

The Research Process: Sleep Deprivation

Decades of research have provided evidence of the effects of **sleep deprivation**. In a study undertaken in 1959, a 32-year-old disc jockey, Peter Tripp, remained awake

EXHIBIT 7.1
Patterns of Human Sleep Over a Lifetime

The graph shows changes with age in total amounts of daily sleep, both REM and non-REM, and percentage of REM sleep. Note that the amount of REM sleep decreases

considerably over the years, while non-REM diminishes less sharply.

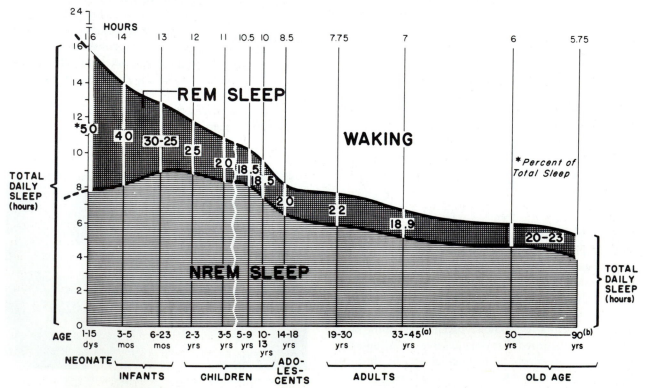

Roffwarg, H. P. 1966. Ontogenetic development of the human sleep-dream cycle, *Science*, April: 604–619.

(using stimulants) for 200 hours to benefit the March of Dimes. During that time, he was examined and tested by medical doctors and sleep researchers. After two days Tripp began experiencing visual illusions; he saw cobwebs in his shoes, a tweed suit turn into a suit of furry worms, and the inside of a dresser drawer catch fire. Simple daily tests of attention, memory, and mathematics researchers gave him became overwhelmingly difficult, and Tripp became frightened when he could not solve an algebra problem. After 170 hours, Peter was often unsure of his identity and feared the doctors were conspiring against him. At the end of 200 hours, he slept for thirteen hours and upon awakening found his symptoms had disappeared. Only one long-term effect was identified; he was mildly depressed for about three months after his sleep deprivation (NIMH, 1965).

Six years later, a seventeen-year-old high school student remained awake for 264 hours without using stimulants. Although his age seems to have moderated the effects, by the end of the fourth day, Randy Gardner became irritable and had difficulty concentrating or remembering. From approximately the ninth day on, he often left sentences unfinished and lapsed into reveries. His vision was blurred, and his right eye made involuntary sideways movements. After remaining awake for eleven days, Gardner slept fourteen hours and awoke cheerful and healthy. In contrast to Peter Tripp, Randy Gardner seemed not to experience any long-term effects (Johnson et al., 1965).

Sleep-deprived subjects often appear to be fully awake, but their EEG's often show momentary wave patterns resembling those seen in sleep. These two- to three-second sleep periods, characterized by bursts of slow waves, were observed as early as 1945 and have since been referred to as **microsleeps** (Liberson, 1945). The longer a person goes without sleep, the more frequent will be the microsleeps.

In summary, as sleep deprivation increases, you would become more susceptible to visual or tactile illusions, lapses of attention and concentration, and moments of microsleep. The urge to sleep would become progressively less resistible, and you might actually "sleep standing up."

Focus Question Answer

Are your sleeping hours spent in a uniformly relaxed state? No. If you are typical, you have four or five sleep cycles per night; in each cycle you go through increasingly deeper sleep stages—Stages 1, 2, 3, and 4. Each cycle is also characterized by REM or dream sleep, in which the EEG pattern resembles a waking EEG pattern.

 ## Altered States

Hypnosis

Misconceptions About Hypnosis   What are your images of hypnosis? You may imagine a hypnotist swinging a gold watch in front of a subject's eyes and saying, "You are very sleepy. Your eyelids are very heavy," whereupon the subject falls asleep involuntarily. You may remember seeing old movies in which evil-minded hypnotists put subjects into deep trances and instructed them to perform deeds against their wills. Alternately, if you have seen a hypnotist's nightclub performance, you may assume that hypnosis makes people act like roosters or strippers. Or you may imagine hypnosis is used to give people superhuman physical strength, tremendous memories or personalities. These images are misconceptions; hypnosis may help people change their behaviors or attitudes but it cannot be used to dominate people or to create new personalities.

Hypnosis was first publicized in Europe in the 1700s. Then, as now, people developed misconceptions about hypnosis. For example, in 1784, a committee that included Benjamin Franklin as one of its members declared that hypnosis, then called animal magnetism or mesmerism, was a fraud. Today only a minority of psychologists would agree with that position.

What Is Hypnosis?   The term **hypnosis** is derived from the Greek word "hypnos," which means sleep. This derivation helps maintain the false impression that hypnosis is similar to sleep; in fact, brain wave recordings during hypnotic trances show that hypnosis is more similar to a waking state than to a sleep state (Wester, 1984). The hypnotic state is often described as "a state of heightened awareness in which attention is focused intensely on the suggestions of the hypnotist" (Hilgard, 1974). Although most psychologists do not deny that hypnosis can affect people, many question whether the effects result from a distinct state of consciousness or from the power of suggestion.

One way to demonstrate that hypnosis is a separate state of consciousness would be to identify distinct physiological differences; these differences have not been found. Although subjects report feeling quite different than they do during normal waking states, the EEG (electroencephalograph) patterns are not different (Hilgard, 1974). Nonetheless, researchers cite evidence of relief from the pain of childbirth, dental procedures, phantom limbs, and headaches as evidence of the existence of a hypnotic state (Hilgard, 1974).

One researcher accounts for such effects by hypothesizing that suggestion is the only important aspect of hypnosis; he maintains that similar results can be achieved if a subject simply withholds critical attitudes, "thinks along with the instructions," and uses his or her imagination vividly (Barber, 1978). To test his hypothesis, researchers have duplicated studies that are cited as evidence of the hypnotic state. These studies tested the pain-relieving effects, the amnesia effects, and the posthypnotic suggestion effects among others. Generally, the effects attributed to hypnosis can be duplicated by nonhypnotic suggestion. You should not conclude from this evidence that hypnosis does not work, because it does; however, you may conclude, as many psychologists have, that the effects of hypnosis may be due to the power of suggestion and may be achieved in other ways as well. Further, the response to suggestion is not involuntary; a hypnotized subject can, at any time, stop paying attention to the hypnotist's suggestions. The hypnotized subject does not lose control; he or she voluntarily agrees to be open to suggestion (Confer & Ables, 1983; Conn, 1981).

Hypnotizability Researchers estimate that approximately 15 percent of the population would make excellent hypnosis subjects, 80 percent would be hypnotizable, and 5 percent could not be hypnotized (Cheek & LeCron, 1968). Two of the best predictors of whether hypnosis will succeed (whether the subject will follow the hypnotist's suggestions) are the subject's expectations that the hypnosis will work (Confer & Ables, 1983; Wadden & Anderton, 1982) and the subject's ability to imagine vividly while awake (Hilgard, 1974). A majority of people would evidence enough belief and imagination to be affected by suggestions given to them during hypnosis.

Hypnotherapy **Hypnotherapy** is the use of hypnosis in therapeutic settings. In addition to its use in pain-relief treatment, hypnosis is used to help people stop smoking, lose weight, and gain self-confidence. It is also used in the treatment of anxiety, stress, depression, and sexual dysfunctions (Wester, 1984). Psychologists disagree about using hypnosis to treat people with multiple personalities; some therapists maintain hypnosis can be used to make people consciously aware of their several person-

alities, and other therapists argue that hypnosis encourages the several personalities to continue rather than helping the person unify them (Confer & Ables, 1983; Kampman, 1976).

Meditation

Meditation is a general term for techniques by which people concentrate and focus their attention with the aim of producing a relaxed but alert waking state. Many people believe meditation reduces stress, improves attention and concentration, and provides its practitioners with extra energy. The two basic types of meditation are the trance type, in which the meditator attempts to shut out information from the senses and "turns inward," and the concentration type, in which the meditator attends fully to a thought or a sensation. If you practice the second type, you might focus your attention on your own breathing, a phrase, a word, or an object. Regardless of the specific technique, most meditators suggest you begin

Although meditation is not widely practiced in the United States, it has a long history in eastern countries.

Meditation Exercise

Find a quiet place, and assume a comfortable position; you may want to loosen your clothing. Before you try the following meditation exercise, spend a few minutes relaxing as much as possible. The amount of time you spend meditating can vary; many meditators suggest a minimum of twenty minutes at a time.

Gently close your eyes, and relax your muscles while you sit or lie comfortably. Are you breathing smoothly or hesitantly? Are your breaths shallow or deep? Now, breathe normally.

Notice if your inhalations and exhalations take the same amount of time. At what point does an inhalation turn into an exhalation? Does one flow from the other, or do you pause between them?

Now focus on the depth of your breathing. Attempt to make each breath deeper. Fill your lungs entirely, and notice how this feels. Each inhalation brings in more and more energy. Concentrate on your lungs filling with energy and spreading this energy to all parts of your body. With each exhalation, empty your lungs further than you did before. Can you make your lungs feel like deflated balloons? Imagine that each exhalation is sending your body tension gently out of your body. Imagine that the tension is flowing out your nose and out through your fingertips and toes.

Now attend to other aspects of breathing. Notice if you are drawing in more air through your left or your right nostril. Notice how the air warms as it travels within your body. Finally, notice the gentle rise and fall of your abdomen as you breathe.

Settle into a relaxed, regular breathing pattern. With each inhalation, say "in" silently and soothingly to yourself, and with each exhalation, say "out" slowly to yourself. Continue this relaxed, alert state for ten to twenty minutes.

by choosing a quiet place in which you can make yourself comfortable. The *Exploring . . .* section suggests a meditation technique you may wish to try.

As with hypnosis, the question of meditation as a separate state of consciousness arises. Transcendental Meditation (TM) has been studied experimentally, and early research results indicated that TM produces a decrease in bodily metabolism and a slowing of heart and respiration rates (Benson, 1976). In other studies, meditators have reported a reduction in overall tension (Carrington, 1977), less moodiness, less self-blame, and an increased sense of identity (Carrington, 1978). More recent research confirms the evidence of physiological changes but with one necessary addition. A control group of non-meditators who rested and relaxed each day as long as the experimental (TM) group meditated achieved the same reduction in physiological arousal (Holmes et al., 1983). Since most meditation research lacks such comparison to control groups, evidence for labeling it an altered state of consciousness is lacking. However, meditation may benefit you in much the same way as do other methods of relaxation.

Focus Question Answer

What benefits might you experience if you choose to be hypnotized or to meditate? If you expect hypnosis to work and you have a vivid imagination, then it will probably work for you; in other words, you will probably follow the hypnotist's suggestions. Applications of hypnosis include treatment of pain, help in quitting smoking, and help in losing weight. If you learn Transcendental Meditation procedures, you may induce positive changes, such as tension reduction and slower heart and respiration rates during meditation.

 ### Drug-Induced Altered States

People use a variety of drugs to intentionally alter their states of consciousness; drugs that alter mood or thought processes are **psychoactive**. Most people use at least one of the three most widely accepted, non-prescription psychoactive drugs—caffeine, alcohol, and tobacco.

In considering drugs and altered states of consciousness, two pairs of terms—use and abuse, legal and ille-

EXHIBIT 7.2
Psychoactive Drugs

Drug Category	Representative Drugs	Effects	Abuse	Dependence
CNS Depressants	Alcohol (ethanol)	incoordination, impairment of judgment, slurred speech	yes	yes
	Barbiturates and tranquilizers (Seconal, Nembutal, Phenobarbital)	mild euphoria, slurred speech, impaired judgment and concentration, sleep	yes	yes
	Opiods (opium, morphine, heroin, methadone)	euphoria, pain relief, reduced anxiety, drowsiness, incoordination	yes	yes
CNS Stimulants	Caffeine (coffee, tea, cola, chocolate)	lessened fatigue alertness, nervousness, insomnia, shakiness, upset stomach	?	?*
	Amphetamines (Benzedrine, Dexedrine, Methamphetamine)	increased heart rate and blood pressure, agitation, feelings of elation, talkativeness (controls narcolepsy)	yes	yes
	Cocaine (coca leaves)	excitement, increased confidence, increased stamina, uneven heart beat, possible seizures	yes	yes?**
Hallucinogens	LSD, mescaline, psilocybin, peyote	intensified perceptions, hallucinations, synesthesia, emotional changes	yes	no
Marijuana	pot, grass, tea	relaxation, increased heart rate and appetite, intensified perceptions, possible hallucinations	yes	yes
Others	PCP	euphoria, anxiety, mood changes, possibly violent behavior	yes	no
	Tobacco (nicotine)	calmness, sociability, long-term serious health problems	?***	yes?

*The APA (1980) lists neither a caffeine abuse disorder nor a caffeine dependence disorder; only a substance-induced intoxication disorder is cited.

** The issue of cocaine dependence is controversial. Although researchers do not agree about whether the withdrawal effects indicate physical dependence, many scientists have decided that cocaine is an addictive drug.

*** Even heavy tobacco use does not satisfy the criteria for substance abuse. The existence of physical dependence upon tobacco is still debated by some experts.

gal—often cause confusion. You may believe that using a legal substance never results in abuse or that using an illegal substance always results in abuse. On the contrary, people can use *or* abuse legal substances such as sleeping pills and tranquilizers, which have been prescribed by their physicians; people can also use *or* abuse illegal substances such as cocaine, marijuana, and heroin. The amount of the substance, the frequency and duration of its use, the situations in which it is used, and its interference in people's lives combine to determine the distinction between use (for recreational or medicinal purposes) and abuse.

Substance abuse results in an inability to abstain from a substance. Job and social functioning deteriorate; sometimes this deterioration results in the loss of a job, the loss of friends, or uncharacteristic aggression and its accompanying legal problems. **Substance dependence**, typically referred to as physical addiction, is indicated when a person experiences tolerance or withdrawal symptoms. People who develop a **tolerance** for a substance need increasing amounts in order to feel the same effects. If they are unable to obtain the substance and suddenly cease taking it, they experience **withdrawal** symptoms. Although these symptoms vary from substance to substance, they may include anxiety, restlessness, irritability, insomnia, and impaired concentration. Exhibit 7.2 lists drugs and their effects.

As you can see, most of the substances in Exhibit 7.2 fit neatly into four descriptive drug categories:

1. **Central nervous system depressants**—chemicals that slow the functions of the brain and spinal cord, resulting in sluggishness, incoordination, thickening of speech, and impairment of judgment. Sleep, coma, and even death may result from overdose.

2. **Central nervous system stimulants**—chemicals that speed up the functions of the brain and spinal cord, resulting in alertness, feelings of well-being, euphoria, exhilaration, and increased energy. Other symptoms include increased activity and aggressiveness.

3. **Hallucinogens**—chemicals whose effects are similar to hallucinations (false sensory perceptions). The effects include distortions of time and of visual, auditory, and skin sensations.

4. **Marijuana**—small doses of which have effects similar to those of amphetamines and large doses of which have effects similar to those of hallucinogens.

Quick Study Aid

Four Drug Categories

Drugs	Sometimes	Harm	Me
e	t	a	a
p	i	l	r
r	m	l	i
e	u	u	j
s	l	c	u
s	a	i	a
a	n	n	n
n	t	o	a
t	s	g	
s		e	
		n	
		s	

Alcohol

Alcohol is abused by more Americans than is any other drug (with the possible exception of caffeine). An estimated one in twenty people, or eleven to twelve million Americans, are dependent on alcohol (Pattison & Kaufman, 1982). People with alcohol problems are found in all social classes, in all occupations, in all age groups, and of all educational levels. People who begin drinking regularly as teenagers, particularly if they begin before age sixteen, increase their chances of later alcohol abuse (APA, 1980).

Effects   Alcohol is a central nervous system depressant and as such produces the physical and psychological effects described above. Chronic (frequent or of long duration) alcohol users develop one of several patterns: regular daily intake of large amounts, regular intake of large amounts on weekends only, and binges of heavy drinking. Many chronic users develop a tolerance for alcohol and need increasing quantities to achieve the same effects. People who experience "morning shakes" that are relieved by drinking alcohol are withdrawing from alcohol, a substance on which they have become dependent.

Why People Abuse Alcohol   Do drinkers become alcoholics because they inherit different physiological reactions to alcohol? Do they learn to be alcoholics? Or does alcoholism result from some combination of physiological and social factors? These questions reflect different views of the causes of alcoholism.

Many societies accept and approve of alchohol use at social and ceremonial functions.

Physiological or biological explanations of alcoholism follow two paths—genetic predisposition and physiological differences. Researchers who concentrate on genetics have found that children of alcoholics who are separated from their biological parents and raised by nonalcoholic parents still have an increased risk of alcoholism when compared with children of non-alcoholics (Schuckit et al., 1972). In other genetic studies, researchers have discovered that if one monozygotic twin (identical twin) is alcoholic, the chance the other twin will also become alcoholic is as high as 70 percent (Murray & Stabeneau, 1982). These studies and others indicate a biological factor in alcoholism.

Recent research on physiological differences between alcoholics and non-alcoholics has focused on brain wave patterns (Holden, 1985) and the liver's metabolism of alcohol. Other physiological researchers are investigating the role of neurochemicals such as endorphins and enkephalins in substance addiction. A major difficulty is determining whether physiological differences, if they are found, *explain* alcoholism or are a *result* of alcoholism.

In contrast to the physiological and biological explanations, learning theorists maintain that alcohol consumption behaviors are learned through rewards and imitation of others' behaviors. People may feel rewarded by the relaxation or slight euphoria that follows drinking or by the acceptance and admiration of their peers. Teenagers, or even younger children, may begin imitating their parents' alcohol consumption behaviors. As suggested in Exhibit 7.3, most children have ample opportunity to learn about psychoactive drugs at home. Although the precise interaction between the factors remains unclear, most experts agree that both biological and social learning factors contribute to alcoholism.

Other Central Nervous System Depressants

Barbiturates   **Barbiturates** are central nervous system depressants that are used medically to promote sleep and relaxation. First synthesized and made available during the early 1900s, they are safe and effective when used for relatively short periods at prescribed dosage levels. Small doses cause muscle relaxation and mild euphoria, but progressively larger doses cause slurred speech, unsteady gait, impaired judgment, and impaired concentration. Because barbiturates and alcohol are central nervous system depressants, ingesting a combination of these drugs exaggerates their effects and may cause death; this combination is one of the leading causes of accidental suicide in the United States.

Most barbiturate abusers fall into three categories: young males who use the drugs to get "high" or to combat

EXHIBIT 7.3
Learning Substance Use at Home?

Bill and Sue Jones and their children, twelve-year-old Terry and sixteen-year-old Mary, are a typical American family. In the morning, Bill and Sue hurriedly brew caffeinated coffee for themselves and heat hot chocolate (caffeine) for their children. Because Terry has been coughing, he took cough syrup (containing alcohol) throughout the night. He takes another dose before he goes to school. Bill's wisdom teeth were extracted several days ago, and he is in pain. He swallows two pain relievers that contain codeine; this medication was prescribed for him by his dentist. Sue has been under a great deal of stress since the family moved to a new locale and she changed jobs. Before she goes to work, she swallows a Valium tablet prescribed for her by her family physician. Three or four times per week Bill has a two-martini lunch with business clients. Both Bill and Sue have been trying but have been unable to stop smoking; they each smoke about a pack of cigarettes per day and more when they go to parties. Their daughter Mary does not smoke cigarettes but she sometimes smokes a joint (marijuana) with friends after school. Bill and Sue arrive home from work about 5:30 P.M. each day and spend a pleasant half hour having drinks and discussing the day. They frequently have wine with dinner, and Terry and Mary have colas (caffeine). Before bed, Bill and Sue have a nightcap (alcohol), and Bill sometimes takes a sleeping pill (sedative) to make sure he gets a "good night's sleep."

the effects of amphetamines; females thirty to sixty years old who begin taking barbiturates for insomnia and gradually use larger doses more often; and health-care professionals. The women in the second group rarely resort to buying their drugs on the streets; instead, they obtain from several physicians prescriptions that they fill at different pharmacies. People in the third group, doctors and nurses, have easy access and probably begin using barbiturates to reduce anxiety (APA, 1980; Liskow, 1982).

Chronic barbiturate users develop a tolerance and become dependent. If they withdraw abruptly, they may convulse or even die. Because of possibly severe withdrawal symptoms, heavy users should *not* be encouraged to withdraw "cold turkey" without medical supervision.

Opiods: Opium, Morphine, and Heroin Opium poppies are the source of the narcotic **opium** and its derivatives, **morphine** and **heroin**. The effects of these central nervous system depressants are euphoria, drowsiness, dreaminess, and, sometimes, lack of coordination. Heroin injections produce a "rush," a feeling of warmth and self-confidence and elimination of fears and worries. Regular use of opium, morphine, and heroin can result in physical dependence, which is characterized by increased tolerance and, when the drug is unavailable, withdrawal symptoms.

Physicians first separated morphine from raw opium in the early 1800s and administered morphine to Civil War soldiers for pain and dysentery. When many soldiers became addicted to it, scientists worked diligently to find a drug with morphine's pain-relieving properties but not its addicting potential. The result of this effort was heroin, which was used initially to treat morphine addiction; heroin was also substituted for morphine in over-the-counter remedies of the time. Unfortunately, heroin proved to be more potent and more addictive than morphine.

One treatment for heroin dependence is administering methadone, a synthetic narcotic much like heroin. Under careful supervision, addicts receive oral methadone doses to keep themselves heroin-free. Methadone treatment benefits addicts and society because addicts no longer need to obtain expensive, illegal heroin through

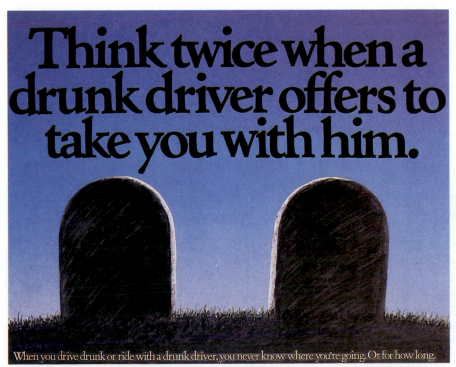

When you drive drunk or ride with a drunk driver, you never know where you're going. Or for how long.

Do you think the current efforts by the media to portray the negative effects of drugs will be effective in reducing drug use in our society?

criminal behavior, and they avoid the health risks associated with injecting impure street drugs. However, methadone is *not* a cure for heroin addiction; it is a substitute addiction.

The best way to eliminate heroin addiction would be to eliminate the drug from the market, and since the 1970s the U. S. government has helped fund attempts by several countries to decrease the availability of heroin; in these countries opium poppy farms have been converted to other crops. Unfortunately, and in spite of these attempts, worldwide production of heroin has increased more than 50 percent in the last five years (Taswell, 1985a). Presently, between 40 percent and 60 percent of the heroin that enters the U.S. comes from the Golden Crescent, the area comprising Iran, Afghanistan, and Pakistan (Jones, 1985).

Central Nervous System Stimulants

Caffeine   Coffee, tea, cola, chocolate, and cocoa—with these as its major sources, **caffeine** is surely the tastiest psychoactive substance. "Real" (not decaffeinated) coffee contains between 100 and 150 mg. of caffeine per cup, tea contains 50 to 75 mg. per cup, and colas and many other soft drinks contain 35 to 50 mg. (APA, 1980). Other readily available sources of caffeine are over-the-counter headache remedies, some cold tablets, and some diet pills. People who ingest as little as 250 mg. of caffeine can experience caffeine intoxication symptoms, which include nervousness, insomnia, increased urine production, upset stomach, and shakiness. Habitual users may have difficulty beginning a day without caffeine and, without it, they may experience headaches and irritability.

Amphetamines   Usually taken orally or intravenously, **amphetamines** cause psychological effects including agitation, feelings of elation and talkativeness; the physical symptoms include increased heart rate, elevated blood pressure, perspiration, and nausea. Amphetamine users often express suspiciousness of people around them, and they may behave violently. Chronic amphetamine use results in increasing tolerance; withdrawal symptoms of depression, fatigue, and nightmares may last for weeks after the person ceases ingesting amphetamines. The depression that accompanies withdrawal may be severe, and suicide is possible.

Cocaine   An estimated twenty million people in the U.S. have tried **cocaine**, and it is the drug of choice for

Although most people know coffee and tea contain caffeine, fewer people realize that colas and chocolates—often children's favorite snacks—also contain caffeine.

four to eight million people who are regular users (Stone et al., 1984). The Drug Enforcement Administration (DEA) estimates that Americans used between thirty-six and sixty-six tons of cocaine in 1981 and between sixty-four and eighty-four tons in 1984 (Lieber, 1986). Snorting, or inhaling, is the most common method of taking cocaine; this procedure may result in cracked and bleeding nasal membranes. Another method, injection, may cause artery deterioration and, if users share needles, susceptibility to hepatitis and AIDS increases. Freebasing is probably the most dangerous method of cocaine administration. In this procedure, a highly flammable solvent such as ether is used to produce a more concentrated substance; people then smoke this substance, which is very toxic and may trigger uneven heartbeat, respiratory paralysis, or grand mal seizures, any of which can be fatal.

An especially destructive form of cocaine, known as "crack" or "rock," is produced through a simple, inexpensive process. By mixing cocaine, baking soda, and water, dealers make a paste containing about 75 percent or more cocaine. The paste dries, hardens, and is cut into chips or "rocks," single doses of which sell for as little as ten to fifteen dollars (*Newsweek*, 1986). The low cost of producing crack, its low street price, and the ease of using it (usually by smoking it in a water pipe) make cocaine increasingly available to younger and younger users.

For several years, researchers have debated whether cocaine is addicting. The American Psychiatric Association (APA, 1980) does not list a cocaine dependence disorder because the association's definition of dependence requires demonstrated tolerance or physical withdrawal symptoms. Although chronic cocaine users who cease using it experience drug cravings, irritability, sluggishness, sleepiness, depression, and extreme hunger, many experts say these symptoms are psychological, not physical. If, instead of the APA's definition, addiction or dependence is defined as a loss of control over drug use, continued use despite negative consequences, and a cycle of use-recovery-relapse (Stone et al., 1984), then cocaine causes dependence.

Despite government efforts to halt the importation of cocaine into the U.S., the amount seized in South Florida alone increased from six tons in 1983 to twenty-five tons in 1985. Colombia, Peru, and Bolivia are the major cocaine-producing countries. The following estimates of annual cocaine income illustrate why many countries are reluctant to participate in coca plant eradication: Colombia—$2 billion; Peru—$1.5 billion; Bolivia—$1 billion; and Ecuador—$300 million. The incredible profit is illustrated by the difference between the $8,000 purchase price for a kilo of cocaine in Bogata, Colombia, and its sale on the streets in the U.S. for as much as $25 million (Kendall, 1985).

Hallucinogens

Sometimes called psychedelics or psychotomimetics, hallucinogens such as mescaline, psilocybin, and peyote intensify perception and may cause hallucinations (false perceptions), illusions (misinterpretations of real physical sensations), or synesthesias (e.g., seeing colors when you hear a loud sound). No evidence of the development of tolerance or dependence has been found in either laboratory settings or clinical observations. Although hallucinogen use rarely results in long-term abuse, even a single dose can be unnerving. People unprepared for the effects might find the unstable, unreal, changing sensations and perceptions very frightening. Among people who like the effects and abuse hallucinogens, the period of abuse is usually brief.

PCP **PCP**, or "angel dust", was developed as a tranquilizer but was rejected when it caused negative emotional reactions in one-sixth of the patients tested (Luisada, 1981). PCP can be swallowed, injected, smoked, or inhaled. The reactions to small doses usually last four to six hours and include euphoria, numbness, sweating, anxiety, and mood changes; other possible effects are hallucinations, suspiciousness, violent behavior, and suicide. The most dangerous problem with PCP is not its potential for dependence because no withdrawal effects have been identified; the danger is the unpredictability of individual reactions, specifically violent and suicidal behaviors.

Marijuana

Both marijuana and hashish come from the cannabis plant and can be smoked or taken orally. Common reactions to these drugs are relaxation, a sense of well-being, intensified perceptions, increased heart rate, and increased appetite. The biggest dangers to recreational users are legal penalties, automobile accidents resulting from slowed reaction time, and possible long-term physiological effects. Although an increased tolerance in chronic users has been substantiated, the existence of a withdrawal syndrome is controversial. A small number of marijuana users abuse the drug, but a more common pattern is recreational use that ceases after a time or ceases when it interferes with peoples' lives.

The U.S. Drug Enforcement Administration estimates the 1985 marijuana production in the U.S. at 1,700 metric tons. Government officials also estimate that marijuana is the most profitable crop in the United States next to corn. Probably because of the high profit potential, marijuana has surpassed pineapples as Hawaii's largest agricultural crop (Taswell, 1985b). If the availability of marijuana continues, its use is likely to remain widespread.

Tobacco

The battle lines between the smokers and nonsmokers have been drawn. Nonsmokers defend their right to clean air, and smokers defend their right to personal choice of behavior. In several states, smoking is now prohibited in most areas of public buildings; many hotels and motels offer "never smoked in" rooms or floors; airplanes have increasingly smaller smoking sections; and several life insurance companies offer discounts for nonsmokers. In some companies, workers vote on smoking policies. Long after most smokers and nonsmokers have acknowledged the dangers of smoking, the debate over individual rights continues.

In 1955, when research first revealed the health problems associated with tobacco smoking, 52 percent of American males and 24 percent of American females smoked (Seligman, 1985). Considerable change has occurred in the thirty years since. Bronchitis, emphysema, coronary artery disease, and a number of cancers are now *known* to be associated with smoking. Today, only 35

Exploring . . .

Designer Drugs

In underground laboratories, chemists create "designer drugs" by altering very slightly the chemical structure of already-illegal drugs (see below). Because the new chemical structure is not designated as illegal by the U.S. Drug Enforcement Agency (DEA), the manufacture, sale, and use of "designer drugs" is legal.

HOW UNDERGROUND CHEMISTS
STAY ONE STEP AHEAD OF THE LAW

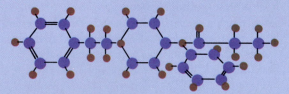

1. This is a molecule of fentanyl, a potent painkiller intended for use in hospitals. It was developed by Belgium's Janssen Pharmaceutica and introduced to the U.S. in 1968. Trade-named Sublimaze, the drug is 100 times as potent as morphine, but its effects last only 30 minutes. It is used in as many as 7 out of every 10 operations.

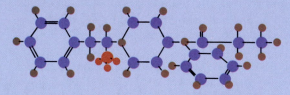

2. In 1979 a new synthetic drug—dubbed China White—showed up on the streets in California. It varied only slightly from the fentanyl molecule, but the small difference was enough to make it perfectly legal. The new formula was also twice as potent. In 1981 the Drug Enforcement Administration banned it after two deaths were reported.

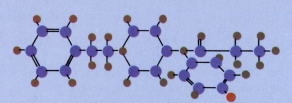

3. The underground chemists wasted no time. Before 1981 was over, they rolled out a new—and legal—version of fentanyl that differed by only one atom. Soon after, the DEA banned that as well. The chemists responded by churning out even more new variations with names such as Persian White, Mexican Brown, and Synthetic Heroin.

4. So far, the DEA has banned 10 designer versions of fentanyl. But the chemists are still at work. This latest derivative is 30 times more powerful than the original drug. The DEA outlawed it in March, but it is still appearing in the bloodstreams of overdose victims. And drug authorities are certain that it will not be the last deadly designer variation of Sublimaze.

Schulman, R. with Sabin, M. 1985. The losing war against "designer drugs," *Business Week*, June 24, 101–104. Reprinted from June 24, 1985 issue of *Business Week* by special permission, © 1985 by McGraw-Hill.

Designer heroin, which is potentially deadly, has been available in California since at least 1981 (U.S. News and World Report, 1985). In 1984 and 1985, several hospitalized heroin users who had overdosed on the "new" heroin became the subjects of extensive medical study. Their symptoms resembled those seen in late-stage Parkinson's disease victims—muscular rigidity, akinesia (an inability to initiate movements), inability to turn their heads, laborious or absent speech, and continuous swallowing and chewing. Untreated, the symptoms did not lessen or worsen, but when the patients took medications used to treat Parkinson's disease, they improved significantly.

Why experienced heroin users overdosed on designer heroin is answered by the variation in potency of several versions of one drug—fentanyl (see left). Although all variations of fentanyl resemble heroin, some are as much as 3,000 times as potent. Given this potency, you could hold in your hand what would become two hundred million doses after the drug is cut! As of June 1985, ninety-seven deaths had been attributed to overdoses of variations of fentanyl; another six deaths per month are expected (Schulman, 1985).

The prospects for "designer drugs" look profitable for outlaw chemists and frustrating for drug enforcement agencies. Until a specific chemical structure is banned, the agencies cannot take any legal action, and the banning of any questionable substance requires a minimum of thirty days, time enough for the drug designers to keep one step ahead of the law by moving their laboratories and changing the chemical structure of their drugs each time a version is put on the DEA's list. The prospect of enormous profits seems likely to keep these chemists in business.

percent of the men in the U.S. smoke, but nearly 30 percent of the women smoke (Seligman, 1985).

If you wish to stop smoking, have made unsuccessful attempts to stop, have an illness that is exacerbated by smoking, or experience withdrawal symptoms when you don't smoke, you are probably dependent on tobacco. Within two hours of the last cigarette, the heavy smoker will probably begin to experience irritability, anxiety, restlessness, headache, and gastrointestinal disturbances. These symptoms peak twenty-four hours after the last cigarette, but they may last as long as a week or more (APA, 1980). The need or desire for a cigarette can persist for months or even years.

For women, smoking entails two additional dangers. Women who smoke during pregnancy deliver babies who weigh significantly less than babies born to nonsmokers. When a woman smokes during pregnancy, her child is more likely to suffer from respiratory disorders, Sudden Infant Death Syndrome, and delays of three to five months in math and reading skills. The second danger concerns smoking and taking birth control pills; women who do both are more likely to have heart disease and circulatory problems than are women who engage in only one of these behaviors (Seligman, 1985).

Some health experts claim smoking is the number one cause of preventable death in the United States. If their claim is accurate, assisting people in their attempts to stop smoking helps prevent future health problems and death. Certainly, the Great American Smokeout day, which has been observed nationwide each fall since 1977, is an attempt to educate and support those who wish to quit smoking (for more "how to" information, see the *Relate* section in Chapter 8).

Focus Question Answer

On which drugs that you might use could you become dependent? The abuse of alcohol, barbiturates, opioids (opium, heroin, morphine), or amphetamines can result in an increasing tolerance for the substance; with any of these substances, withdrawal symptoms are indicative of physical dependence. Cocaine abuse produces a strong drug craving, but experts disagree on whether it causes dependence. Researchers have found an increasing tolerance to marijuana but disagree about the existence of withdrawal symptoms. Dependence on tobacco is characterized by withdrawal symptoms that, for heavy smokers, begin approximately two hours after the last cigarette.

 *Relate*

Sleep Disturbances and Disorders

Do you have difficulty sleeping at night? Do you awaken still feeling tired and needing more rest? Are you bothered by nightmares? Do you become sleepy during the day and take daytime naps? Do "yes" answers to these questions indicate that you have a sleep disorder? Not necessarily! Many college students experience sleep disturbances due to their lifestyles. Staying up late or all night to study for exams or to finish papers, early morning classes, anxiety about exams, late-night socializing, and nighttime jobs are part of many college students' regular routines. Regular, restful, undisturbed sleep is difficult to maintain under these conditions.

Many people report problems with sleeping. For approximately ten million people in the United States each year, the disturbance is severe enough to cause them to see physicians, who may reassure the patients and offer instruction for developing better sleep habits. For example, people suffering from disturbed sleep may consume a large amount of alcohol before going to bed, mistakenly believing the alcohol will help them sleep. While the alcohol may induce drowsiness and help the person fall asleep, when the effects of the alcohol diminish, the person may awaken. Also, persons reporting disturbed sleep may need to change their eating habits (paying specific attention to what they eat during the evening hours). Interestingly, the secret of the successful folk remedy of a warm glass of milk at bedtime has been discovered (Lindsley et al., 1983). Milk contains tryptophan, a protein substance that the body uses to produce the neurotransmitter, serotonin; serotonin is involved in producing sleep.

Other individuals may be advised to change their expectations regarding sleep. Expecting to fall asleep immediately every night and then to sleep continuously for eight hours may be unrealistic. Throughout the life cycle, the need for sleep varies; typically, as people age, they sleep for shorter lengths of time. Worrying that they do not fall asleep quickly may further delay sleep. These individuals often benefit from learning about normal sleep patterns and the possible variations in normal sleep.

Although many people may easily overcome disturbed sleep, others may experience recurring problems that may be diagnosed as one of several specific sleep disorders.

Insomnia

Insomnia, the inability to go to sleep, is the most frequently reported sleep disorder. Afflicted individuals most often have difficulty falling asleep, but their insomnia may also include frequent reawakening during the night or awakening too early in the morning without being able to go back to sleep. The causes of insomnia are many—irregular sleep habits, illness, poor diet, drug usage (prescription and non-prescription), and many other factors. Depression is a major cause of insomnia (Kales et al., 1976), and other emotional problems may include insomnia among their symptoms.

Many treatments to relieve insomnia have been tried, but most are only partially successful. Generally, treatment with drugs is ineffective. Because studies show that non-prescription drugs are no more effective than placebos (Webb & Bonnet, 1979), success with these remedies probably occurs only to the extent that users believe in them. Prescription sedatives, such as barbiturates, do relieve insomnia but not without side effects. Because of increasing tolerance to the drug's effects, people who use sedatives may increase their dosages and, as a result, risk lingering grogginess after awakening and the possibility of drug overdose. Also, sedatives cause disruption of the normal sleep cycle and prevent REM sleep. If an individual stops using the sedative, he or she may have nightmares and other sleep disturbances. To avoid these withdrawal effects, the individual may choose to continue using the drug. While no simple cures for insomnia exist, a combination of education about normal sleep cycles, changes in waking and sleeping routines, changes in sleeping conditions, and changes in diet appear to be most successful.

Narcolepsy

A sleep disorder far less frequent than insomnia is **narcolepsy**. Individuals with narcolepsy experience sudden, uncontrollable onsets of sleep during waking hours. This peculiar affliction causes them to fall asleep quickly for brief periods, often in the midst of a specific activity such as talking or walking. A narcoleptic's microsleep periods last from five to fifteen seconds and are most likely to occur when the person is highly anxious (Dement, 1976). The microsleep appears to be caused by the intrusion of REM sleep periods into waking periods. The rapid drop into REM sleep is accompanied by loss of muscle control and occasionally by hallucinations that may actually be the start of dreams (Dement & Baird, 1977). Because they lose muscle tone, narcoleptics often fall and must be careful to avoid hurting themselves and others when they suddenly go to sleep.

That narcolepsy is the result of a genetically caused defect was demonstrated with dogs (Guilleminault et al., 1976). Interbreeding of narcoleptic Doberman pinschers increased the number of narcoleptic offspring in each generation. The defect, an inherited inability to secrete dopamine (a neurotransmitter), affects the brain area that regulates REM sleep (Mefford et al., 1983). Stimulants such as amphetamines help stimulate the release of dopamine and therefore are partially helpful in treating narcolepsy.

Sleep Apnea

Another rare sleep disorder is **sleep apnea**, which causes individuals to stop breathing while asleep. Symptoms of this disorder include frequent cessation of breathing (from twenty seconds to two minutes at a time, hundreds of times each night), loud snoring, poor nighttime sleep (due to waking often to breathe), morning headaches, and daytime sleepiness (Guilleminault & Dement, 1978). When an individual with sleep apnea stops breathing, his need for oxygen builds until he wakes up enough to begin breathing again. The masculine pronoun is appropriate here because men are more likely than women to suffer from sleep apnea. The sex difference is linked to the male hormone testosterone. Researchers have discovered that lowering the level of testosterone in men with sleep apnea reduces the apnea; conversely, raising the testosterone levels increases their apnea (Sandblom et al., 1983).

The disorder is sometimes referred to as obstructive sleep apnea because snoring and cessation of breathing are more likely among individuals whose airways are obstructed. Many afflicted individuals are obese men with thick necks and men whose airways are obstructed by deformities or surgery (Cherniack, 1981). However, not all individuals who snore have sleep apnea. Snoring characteristic of sleep apnea is punctuated with short silences followed by loud snorts and gasps as the individuals begin breathing again. One treatment for severe sleep apnea involves inserting into the patient's throat a valve that can be opened at night to allow unobstructed breathing. Persons with milder symptoms may gain relief from sleeping with a pillow under their necks so their heads tilt backward, a position that more fully opens the airways.

Childhood Disturbances

Although insomnia, narcolepsy, and sleep apnea can occur in childhood, these disorders are typically associated with adults. In contrast, adults may experience the sleep disturbances of nightmares, night terrors, sleepwalking, and sleeptalking, but these phenomena are most prevalent during the childhood years (Anders et al., 1980). **Nightmares** are disturbing dreams that occur during the REM stage of sleep. Like other dreams, nightmares may be recalled vividly. In contrast to nightmares, **night terrors** are episodes of extreme panic during sleep, are not easily recalled, and occur during non-REM Stage 4 of the sleep cycle (Hartmann, 1981). In a night terror, the individual often awakens with a start

accompanied by feelings of extreme panic but is unable to pinpoint the source of the panic. The individual quickly falls asleep again and may not remember the episode in the morning. **Sleepwalking** and **sleeptalking** also occur during non-REM stages of sleep (Anders et al., 1980).

Nightmares, night terrors, sleepwalking, and sleeptalking are not immediate causes for concern. Many children do not experience these phenomena, and, among children who do, the episodes often disappear on their own. The disturbances associated with non-REM sleep stages (those other than nightmares) may be related to minor defects in the brain areas that control movement during sleep (Anders et al., 1980). A good course of action to follow is to provide reassurance and to eliminate potential hazards for those who sleepwalk. Contrary to popular opinion, individuals who sleeptalk rarely make sense and are extremely difficult to engage in conversation, and waking individuals during sleepwalking causes no damage. Under most circumstances, with each of these disturbances you need only to reassure the child until he or she falls asleep.

If, after reading this account of sleep disturbances and sleep disorders, you think that you or someone you know exhibits symptoms of one of the conditions, first be reassured that the severity of the symptoms varies widely and that mild cases may require no treatment. However, if your symptoms are severe, seeking medical attention is advisable. If you experience little difficulty in sleeping, as many people do, reading this section should cause you to appreciate your good fortune.

Things to Do

1. Contact local hospitals or physicians about the locations of nearby sleep laboratories. Inquire about the facilities, the physiological measurement devices they use, the most common sleep disorders among their subjects, and the most commonly prescribed treatments for each. Ascertain if treatment for sleep disorders is paid for by most insurance policies. Inquire about the charges for the sleep laboratory's services.

2. Contact a hypnotherapist and a stage hypnotist. Ask both the following questions and then compare their responses: What are the differences between a person's usual waking state and a hypnotic state? Is hypnosis an altered state of consciousness, or do the subjects voluntarily agree to pay attention to the hypnotist's suggestions? What applications of hypnosis do you recommend to people?

3. Compile a list of agencies and self-help groups that offer services for people who abuse various substances. You may wish to begin by inquiring about Alcoholics Anonymous, Narcotics Anonymous, Valium Users

Anonymous, the county or state mental health centers, and private agencies. Check with telephone hot lines about special groups for teenagers, women, veterans, and the families of abusers.

4. Call several alcohol inpatient and outpatient treatment centers in your area. Ask a representative of each program about the causes of alcohol abuse. Compare the answers from four or five agencies, and speculate about the differences in treatment approach based on beliefs about the cause of alcoholism.

Things to Discuss

1. Have you ever gone without sleep for more than forty-eight hours? How did you feel? How did sleep deprivation affect your intellectual and motor performance? How long did you sleep to "catch up"?

2. Would you volunteer as a subject for a stage hypnotist? Why? Why not? For which possible therapeutic reasons would you consent to hypnosis? Do you think it would be effective?

3. Do you or does anyone you know meditate regularly? What benefits does the meditator claim? Do you see any systematic differences between people who meditate and those who do not?

4. Do you believe that if children and teenagers could be convinced of the negative effects of substance abuse, fewer of them would experience drug problems? How would you handle the responsibility of imparting this information to school children? With what age children would you begin? What information would you provide?

5. Drug enforcement agencies have four tactics they can use to make a drug less available. First, if the drug is imported, agencies can attempt to prevent its cultivation in foreign lands. Second, they can attempt to prevent the drug's importation at the point of entry into the country. Third, they can attempt to arrest those who sell the drugs. Fourth, they can attempt to arrest and punish drug-users. Which of these ways is the government now using? Should the government devote more money and effort to different tactics?

6. Examine the effects of different drugs in relation to their legal standing. Should alcohol and tobacco, because they cause the greatest damage to the largest numbers of people, be illegal? Should marijuana possession be decriminalized?

Things to Read

Bowers, K.S. 1983. *Hypnosis for the seriously curious.* NY: Norton.

Coleman, R. 1986. *Wide Awake at 3 a.m.* NY: W. H. Freeman.

Dement, W.D. 1978. *Some must watch while some must sleep.* NY: Norton.

Dusek, D. & Girdano, D. A. 1980. *Drugs: A factual account* (3rd ed.). Reading, MA: Addison-Wesley.

Ray, O. 1983. *Drugs, society, and human behavior.* St. Louis: Mosby Co.

Stone, N., Fromme, M. & Kagan, D. 1984. *Cocaine: Seduction and solution.* NY: Clarkson N. Potter, Inc.

Weil, A. & Rosen, W. 1983. *Chocolate to Morphine.* Boston: Houghton Mifflin.

 ## Review

Summary

1. According to one definition, consciousness is a personal construction of reality. Psychologists recognize levels of consciousness ranging from comas to heightened awareness, and states of consciousness including meditation, hypnosis, sleep, dreams, and drug-induced states.

2. Through selective attention, you attend to only a limited number of the sensory stimuli present; the enormous amount of environmental information available to you makes this process necessary.

3. Virtually everyone daydreams, and usually the daydreams are pleasant. When you daydream, you selectively attend to internal mental processes and temporarily disregard external stimuli.

4. In sleep laboratories, subjects are attached to various monitors including EEG's, myographs, and EKG's. EEG's trace different brain waves for the following sleep stages: Stages 1, 2, 3, 4, and REM sleep.

5. REM sleep, sometimes called paradoxical sleep, is

characterized by dreams and by brain waves similar to those that occur in the waking state. Numerous physiological changes also occur. Traditional theories attribute a psychological meaning to dreams, while the activation-synthesis hypothesis contends that dreams are the brain's attempts to account for the eye movements. People deprived of REM sleep experience the REM rebound effect.

6. The necessary amount of sleep varies from person to person, but all people experience negative effects from total sleep deprivation. These effects include visual illusions, difficulty solving even simple problems, and problems with attention and concentration.

7. Physiological research has not identified hypnosis as a separate state, and psychologists disagree on whether hypnosis is an altered state or whether its effects are due to suggestion.

8. The goal of meditation is a relaxed, alert, waking state. Research evidence indicates that Transcendental Meditation, unlike hypnosis, has demonstrable physiological effects.

9. Caffeine, tobacco, and alcohol are the most commonly used psychoactive substances (drugs that alter mood or thought processes). Substance abuse is usually accompanied by social or job problems, and substance dependence (physical addiction) is characterized by increasing tolerance and by withdrawal symptoms that appear when a person stops taking the substance.

10. Central nervous system depressants (such as alcohol, opium, heroin, morphine, Valium, and barbiturates) slow the functions of the brain and spinal cord. Their effects include sluggishness, incoordination, slurred speech, and impaired judgment.

11. Central nervous system stimulants (such as caffeine, cocaine, and amphetamines) speed up the functions of the brain and spinal cord. Their effects include increased alertness, euphoria, exhilaration, and feelings of wellbeing.

12. Hallucinogens (such as LSD, mescaline, and psilocybin) affect visual, auditory, and temporal perceptions. Although people may abuse these drugs, dependence does not occur.

13. According to the American Psychiatric Association, tobacco produces physical dependence; this dependence produces withdrawal symptoms when a heavy smoker stops smoking. Another common drug, marijuana, may be abused by some users, but drug researchers disagree on whether people can become dependent (physically addicted) upon it.

Key Terms

consciousness
nonconscious
selective attention
cocktail party effect
dichotic listening
daydreams
electroencephalograph (EEG)
sleep spindles
rapid eye movement (REM)
paradoxical sleep
activation-synthesis hypothesis
REM rebound
sleep deprivation
microsleeps
hypnosis
hypnotherapy
meditation
psychoactive
substance abuse
substance dependence
tolerance
withdrawal
central nervous system depressants
central nervous system stimulants
hallucinogens
marijuana
barbiturates
opium
morphine
heroin
caffeine
amphetamines
cocaine
PCP
insomnia
narcolepsy
sleep apnea
night terrors

Part Three

Learning and Cognitive Processes

Focus Questions

1. How do you know when you have learned the definition of learning?

2. Can you unlearn a response once it has been classically conditioned?

3. Can you become conditioned to any stimulus?

4. How are your emotional reactions affected by classical conditioning?

5. What effects can classical conditioning have on your health?

Chapter Outline

THE NATURE OF LEARNING
What Is Learning?
Learning and the Behaviorists
Learning Paradigms

THE CLASSICAL CONDITIONING PARADIGM
Pavlov's Experiments
Acquisition and Extinction
Laboratory Studies
Everyday Examples

CLASSICAL CONDITIONING PERSPECTIVES
What Is Learned in Classical Conditioning?
The Research Process: The Role of Contingency in Classical Conditioning
The Limitations of Classical Conditioning

CLASSICAL CONDITIONING PHENOMENA
Generalization
Discrimination
Higher-Order Conditioning
Schizokinesis
Conditioned Emotional Responses

RELATE: Classical Conditioning and Health
Things to Do
Things to Discuss
Things to Read

REVIEW: Summary
Key Terms

Chapter 8

Learning and Classical Conditioning

The entire philosophy of life can be summed up in five words—"You get used to it."

Aldous Huxley

 The Nature of Learning

Although discussed as a separate topic in this chapter and Chapter 9, learning plays a role in almost every aspect of psychology. Your preferences for food and friends and your political views are influenced by learning. Your past successes as a student are the result of learning, and learning will continue to be a key psychological process in the remainder of your life. Thus the study of learning is an attempt to understand important, practical problems in your life. In Chapter 6, you discovered learning's role in perception. In future chapters, you will explore the impact of learning on motivated behaviors, emotions, personality, development, social behaviors, and the causes and treatment of mental illness.

175

What Is Learning?

How do you know when you have learned a concept such as perceptual constancy? When you read the concept for the first time, you probably do not think, "Now I have learned this idea." Instead, you probably have to read and think about perceptual constancies several times until you are certain that the idea will remain with you. You know that you have learned the concept when you can explain perceptual constancy in your own words, when you can correctly observe perceptual constancy in your everyday experiences, or when you can answer correctly a multiple-choice question about perceptual constancy.

You can be certain that you have learned when one of these observable changes in your behavior occurs; however, the actual learning is not directly observable. For this reason, learning is a hypothetical construct, or intervening variable. This point is confusing because everyone experiences the effects of learning and therefore believes that learning is not hypothetical but actual. Psychologists themselves also believe that learning exists, but their explanations of it are necessarily hypothetical because learning cannot be observed directly. They hypothesize that learning is the variable that intervenes between stimuli and responses and that links the stimuli and responses together.

Underlying the linking of stimuli and responses is the philosophical assumption of **associationism**. Associationism assumes that internal connections (learning) are most likely to occur when objects, behaviors, or experiences are close together in time or space. Accordingly, movie directors often play the same theme music each time a certain character appears on the screen. Thus, in the movie *Jaws*, foreboding theme music always accompanies the appearance of the shark; before long, the audience associates the music with the frightening shark. Once this association (learning) takes place, the audience can anticipate the appearance of the shark and become appropriately frightened each time the musical theme is played. Most psychologists agree that learning is an associative process.

Psychologists also generally agree that **learning** is a relatively permanent change in a person or animal as the result of experience, and that this change has the potential to change the person's or animal's behavior. This definition contains three key parts. First, learning is a relatively permanent change. The changes produced by learning may not last forever, but they are more lasting than transitory changes from processes such as fatigue or motivation. For example, once you have learned to play

Many people are now computer literate and use word processing programs at work or at home. This new skill is a relatively enduring change in behavior.

the piano, the change within you is established even though, your performance based on that learning may vary on certain days because you are tired or less interested in playing well.

Second, learning is the result of experience. This distinction separates learning from innate (inherited) factors that affect behavior. As you will see, learning can result from direct interactions with the environment, from observations of others' interactions, and even from reading a textbook as you are doing now. Reading skill is an example of the experience element of learning. You were not born with the ability to read; reading is a skill you acquired from experience. People can learn to read in many different ways, but you learned to read from your own specific set of experiences.

Finally, learning is an inner change that has the potential to change your behavior. The only way to be certain you have learned is to observe a change in your behavior. However, a change in behavior does not necessarily indicate learning. At the same time, no change in behavior does not necessarily indicate no learning because learning is just one of many factors that affect performance of behaviors. Your lack of performance could be caused by fatigue, a change in motivation, or emotion. For instance, if you learned how to read in school but refused to recite in front of a group, your lack of performance might cause your teacher to conclude that you had not learned to read when actually your non-reading behavior could be explained by your fear of performing in front of others. Because learning is an intervening variable, it is tested indirectly by measuring performance, or behavior. Although learning can occur without an immediate change in behavior, at some point you must observe a behavior change to know that learning has occurred.

Learning and the Behaviorists

Although most psychologists agree upon a general definition of learning, they do not agree completely on the nature of the associative process. One position, behaviorism, maintains that "learning represents an acquired tendency to respond in a particular way when confronted with a particular stimulus situation" (Logan, 1970, p. 6). Behaviorists contend that learning is represented by stimulus-response, or S-R, associations. Consider your behavior when driving a car and approaching a traffic light that changes to red. Do you apply the brakes because you have learned to make a braking response to the stimulus of a red traffic light (S-R associationism)? Behaviorists would interpret your behavior this way.

In contrast, cognitive psychologists believe that learning is represented by stimulus-stimulus, or S-S, associations. They recognize that thoughts and perceptions are changed through the learning process. Cognitive psychologists state that learning is "an acquired tendency to expect the occurrence of particular subsequent events whenever a particular stimulus situation occurs" (Logan, 1970, p. 6). The cognitive psychologists contend that when you approach a red light you apply the brakes because you have learned the meaning of a red light in this stimulus situation and you have learned what to expect if you fail to stop for a red traffic light (S-S associationism).

Learning Paradigms

The behaviorists and other learning theorists created several basic paradigms (models that illustrate the essential features of a process) to describe the common features of a variety of learning situations. The most basic forms of learning are called **conditioning**, and two conditioning paradigms are **respondent conditioning** and **operant conditioning** (Skinner, 1938). In respondent conditioning, you learn to respond to stimuli that reliably predict when other stimuli will occur; therefore, this paradigm is also called **signal learning**. Because respondent conditioning was the first paradigm to be studied extensively, it is now most often referred to as **classical conditioning**. Classical conditioning is the main focus of this chapter.

In operant conditioning, you learn to operate on your environment to obtain certain consequences. A term

that is used interchangeably with operant conditioning is **instrumental conditioning** (your response is instrumental in obtaining certain consequences). Operant conditioning is discussed in Chapter 9, and Chapters 10 and 11 on memory and cognitive processes explore other learning paradigms related to language acquisition and concept formation.

Focus Question Answer

How do you know when you have learned the definition of learning? While you can learn the definition without making an overt response, you must demonstrate a relatively permanent change in your behavior to be certain that learning has occurred. If today you can explain the definition to a friend, tomorrow apply the definition appropriately in a paper, and next week recognize the correct alternative in a multiple-choice question on a test, then you will have demonstrated that, as a result of experience, a relatively permanent change has occurred within you and the inner change has altered your behavior.

 The Classical Conditioning Paradigm

The classical conditioning paradigm was a serendipitous finding—the discovery of something valuable while looking for something else—by Ivan Pavlov (1849–1936). Pavlov, a Russian physiologist, was looking for innate factors that controlled gastric reflexes. He discovered,

Although Ivan Pavlov won a Nobel prize in 1904 for the role of salivation in the digestion of dogs, he is better known for his research on the process of classical conditioning.

EXHIBIT 8.1
Pavlov's Experimental Apparatus for Salivary Conditioning

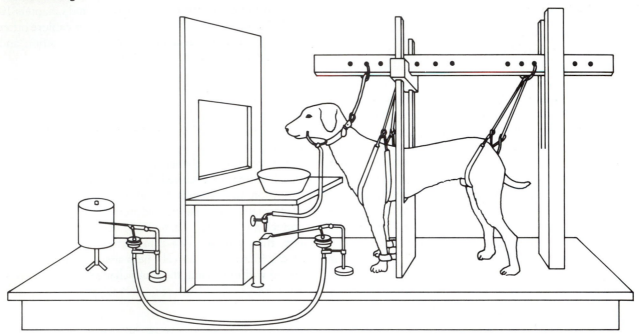

This figure illustrates the experimental setting for Pavlov's beginning research on the classical conditioning of the salivary response. A dog, fitted with a salivary tube, was held in a harness while sounds or lights were used as conditioned stimuli and meat powder in a dish was used to elicit the salivary reflex. The mechanical device recorded the timing and amount of saliva produced. The dog was conditioned when it salivated to the previously neutral tone or light.

Adapted from Yerkes and Morgulis, 1909.

for example, that food placed in a dog's stomach as well as in its mouth produces secretions of gastric juices in the dog's stomach and saliva in its mouth. Initially, he found the dogs' additional tendencies to salivate at the sight or smell of the food, or even at the sight of their food dishes, to be an annoying disruption of his carefully controlled studies. Then he realized he had happened upon an extremely important phenomenon—that reflexes occur not only to innate factors but to learned ones as well. After twenty years of studying digestive physiology, Pavlov turned his attention to this phenomenon of conditioned (learned) reflexes (Pavlov, 1906), but not before he was awarded a Nobel prize for his research on digestive physiology, one of the first Nobel Prizes given in medicine and the first awarded to a Russian.

Pavlov's Experiments

When Pavlov began to study what he called psychic secretions, he employed the same careful methodological approach that had marked his earlier studies of digestion. He arranged a set of precisely controlled conditions so he could observe how a neutral stimulus such as a food dish or the sound of his footsteps could become associated with an unlearned reflex, such as salivation. At the beginning of the experiment, each dog underwent minor surgery; a tube was implanted in a salivary gland duct so saliva flowing from the gland could be collected. A dog was held in a harness, and a mechanical device recorded the number of drops of saliva secreted from the salivary gland. Pavlov's experimental apparatus is illustrated in Exhibit 8.1.

In a typical experiment (Pavlov, 1927), the sounding of a tuning fork was followed immediately and automatically by the dropping of meat powder into the dog's food dish. Initially, only the meat powder elicited salivation—the tone did not. After several pairings of the tone and the meat powder, Pavlov tested the dog's response to the tone by presenting the tone without the

EXHIBIT 8.2
The Classical Conditioning Paradigm

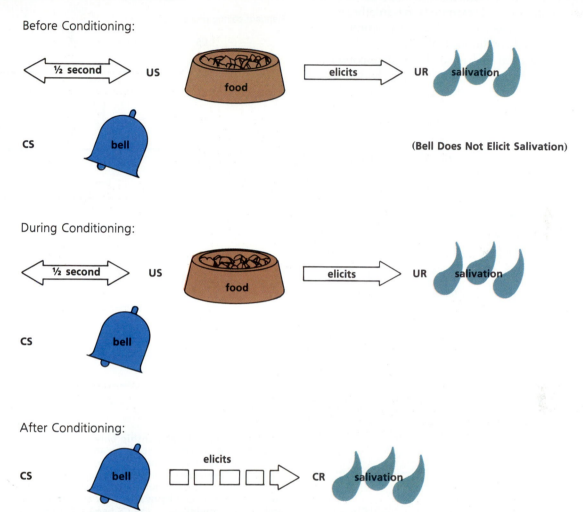

Before Conditioning:

½ second   US   food   elicits   UR   salivation

CS   bell   **(Bell Does Not Elicit Salivation)**

During Conditioning:

½ second   US   food   elicits   UR   salivation

CS   bell

After Conditioning:

CS   bell   elicits   CR   salivation

In this diagram, the solid line indicates that the relationship between the US (unconditioned stimulus) and the UR (unconditioned response) is innate and unlearned, while the dashed line indicates that the relationship between the CS (conditioned stimulus) and the CR (conditioned response) is learned. During the learning trials, the presentation of neutral CS is paired with the US, which elicits a response. The most effective interval between the CS and the US is one-half second. On test trials, the CS is presented without the US. If salivation occurs to only the CS, then conditioning has occurred.

meat powder. When the dog salivated to only the tone, conditioning was demonstrated. The essential elements of this experiment are included in the diagram of the classical conditioning paradigm in Exhibit 8.2.

Pavlov coined the terms that are still used today to describe the basic elements of conditioning. Because the relationship between the meat powder and the salivary response does not need to be learned, Pavlov labeled the meat powder an **unconditioned stimulus (US)**, and

he called the salivary response to the meat powder an **unconditioned response (UR)**. In other words, an unconditioned stimulus is any stimulus that produces an immediate, automatic reaction (an unconditioned response).

At the beginning of the conditioning trials, the tone is a neutral stimulus; it does not elicit the salivary response. However, after several pairings with the meat powder, the tone becomes a **conditioned stimulus (CS)** because it then elicits the salivary response. When the dog salivates to the conditioned stimulus, the response is called the **conditioned response (CR)**. In other words, the conditioned response is a learned reaction to the previously neutral conditioned stimulus.

The conditioned and unconditioned responses are easily confused because, in this example, both are salivary responses. However, the UR and CR are different responses. For example, the salivary response of Pavlov's dogs was greater when they salivated to meat powder than when they salivated to the tone. As you will see, many times the UR and CR differ not only quantitatively but also qualitatively.

Quick Study Aid

Keeping the Terminology Straight

The classical conditioning terminology is often confusing. Try these associations:

UNCONDITIONED IS UNLEARNED
US ———— UNLEARNED → UR
CONDITIONED IS LEARNED
CS ———— LEARNED → CR

As an additional aid, each time you encounter an example of classical conditioning, put the four basic elements into the paradigm diagrammed in Exhibit 8.2. Before long, you will have little difficulty keeping the terms straight!

In his initial experiments, Pavlov demonstrated how neutral events, such as tones and lights, could, with appropriate experiences, come to control behavior. These classic studies of basic learning laid the foundation for thousands of experiments that have investigated numerous features of classical conditioning. The results of these subsequent experiments have scarcely altered Pavlov's original findings; the classical conditioning paradigm remains unchanged.

Acquisition and Extinction

The process by which a conditioned stimulus comes to elicit a conditioned response is called **acquisition**, and an important element in that process is the timing of the CS-US pairing. In most conditioning studies, the presentation of the CS consistently precedes by a brief interval the presentation of the US. However, several

EXHIBIT 8.3
Temporal Relationships between the CS and US

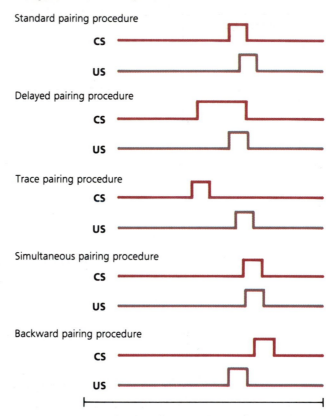

The temporal (time) relationship between the CS and the US affects the speed of acquisition and the strength of the resulting CR. In delayed conditioning, the CS begins before the US and overlaps with it; in simultaneous conditioning, the CS and the US begin and end together; in backward conditioning, the CS begins and ends after the US ends; and in trace conditioning, the CS begins and ends before the US begins.

temporal (time) relationships are possible (see Exhibit 8.3). The warning signals at a railroad crossing make a useful analogy for illustrating these CS-US pairings. The flashing lights stand for the CS, while the approaching train is analogous to the US.

The best conditioning is **delayed conditioning**, in which the CS begins before the US and ends at the beginning of the US, during the US, or after the US ends. Delayed conditioning is analogous to the normal situation in which warning signals begin to flash before a train is at the crossing and continue to flash while the train crosses. The warning signal analogy should make clear why delayed conditioning is best. Warning lights that did not begin to flash until the train was at the

EXHIBIT 8.4
Acquisition, Extinction, and Spontaneous Recovery

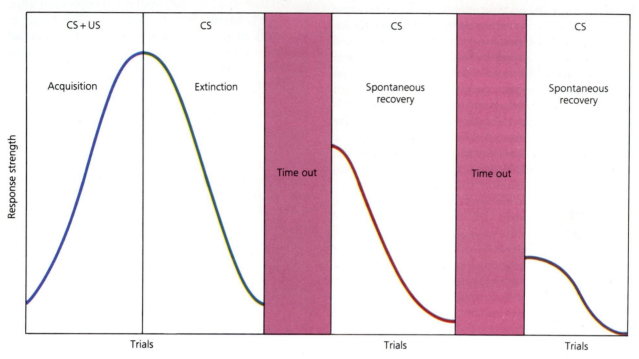

The curves represent changes in the strength of a salivary conditioned response during acquisition, extinction, and spontaneous recovery. The CR becomes stronger when the CS is paired with the US during acquisition; then, the strength of the CR decreases when the CS is presented alone during extinction, only to increase somewhat during spontaneous recovery after a rest period.

crossing (analogous to **simultaneous conditioning**) or, even worse, that did not flash until after the train had crossed (**backward conditioning**), would not warn you about the train. Another temporal relationship that is not as effective as delayed conditioning is **trace conditioning**, in which the CS begins and ends before the US begins. Trace conditioning is, however, more effective than either simultaneous or backward conditioning.

Generally, the best signal (CS) is one that begins enough in advance of the US to allow you to anticipate the appearance of the US but one that also overlaps with the US so that you correctly identify the CS as a signal for the US. In many conditioning experiments with animals and humans, the best CS-US interval is one-half second (Ross & Ross, 1971). Also, better conditioning (i.e., faster and stronger acquisition of the CR) occurs with more potent US's. For example, salivary conditioning is more rapid with larger amounts of food than with lesser amounts (Wagner et al., 1964). Generally, increasing the intensity of the US shortens the time needed for acquisition and produces a stronger CR.

After an organism has acquired a strong CR, the strength of the conditioned response can be weakened if the US is no longer presented. The process of presenting the CS without the US is called **extinction**. Pavlov studied extinction; after a dog had acquired a CR to a tone, Pavlov repeatedly presented the tone without the meat powder. Under these conditions, the dog salivated less and less and, finally, not at all. However, when the dog was allowed to rest for twenty minutes or longer, it once again salivated to the tone. Pavlov called this second occurrence **spontaneous recovery**.

Extinction and spontaneous recovery are interesting effects. The process of extinction provides a way for you to unlearn responses that are no longer useful. However, the presence of spontaneous recovery suggests that you do not simply unlearn the previously learned CR. Instead, new learning occurs; you learn to inhibit the CR associated with a specific CS. Stimuli (CS's) that are no longer effective signals gradually lose their ability to produce responses (CR's) because you learn to withhold the response. The changes in the strength of the CR during acquisition, extinction, and spontaneous recovery are graphed in Exhibit 8.4.

Laboratory Studies

Classical conditioning has been studied extensively in laboratory experiments that often appear to be of little relevance beyond the experiments themselves. Traditional laboratory studies have focused on conditioned responses such as salivation, pupil constriction, knee jerking, and eye blinking. You may recognize the usefulness of conditioned salivation in preparing your mouth for food but question the purpose served by understanding the conditioned eyeblink. Responses such as the eyeblink have been studied because they are reflexes like Pavlov's original salivary response and because they can be measured precisely to test hypotheses about classical conditioning.

The experimental set-up for eyeblink conditioning provides an opportunity to test your understanding of the components of classical conditioning. In eyeblink conditioning, subjects learn to blink when a light or tone is presented for a brief interval (Smith et al., 1969). Before you read on, try to answer these questions: How do researchers get subjects to blink to the light or the tone? What do researchers use for the US and the UR? What do they use for the CS? What is the difference between the UR and the CR?

Initially, in typical eyeblink conditioning experiments, the light or the tone is a neutral stimulus; it does not cause the subject to blink. However, a mild electric current to the eyelid will naturally cause a reflexive eyeblink. Therefore, researchers use the electric current to the subject's eyelid as an unconditioned stimulus (US) that elicits an unconditioned response (UR). The light or tone serves as the conditioned stimulus (CS). Pairing the CS and the US together leads to acquisition of a conditioned response (CR) of eyeblinking to the light or tone. Eyeblinking is both the UR and the CR. These responses differ in that the UR eyeblink is elicited by the US (electric current to the eyelid), while the CR eyeblink is elicited by the CS (the light or tone); also, the CR is not as strong as the UR. In the examples presented thus far, the CR and the UR appear to be similar, if not identical, responses. However, the relationship between the CR and the UR can be very complex, as is shown in the *Exploring . . .* section.

Contemporary classical conditioning researchers have expanded the range of responses and effects they study (Dickinson, 1980; Mackintosh, 1983). Researchers demonstrated classical conditioning of individual cells within the body when they paired passing an electrical current through a photoreceptor cell (the CS) with a bright light (the US) and conditioned the photoreceptor cell's nor-

mal response to light to occur to the presence of the current (Farley et al., 1983). Also, researchers have proven that classical conditioning will occur even when a subject is anesthetized. In one study (Weinberger et al., 1984), rats learned to fear a tone (the CS) that had been paired with a shock (the US); the conditioning occurred after the animals were anesthetized.

Other studies have centered on unconditioned stimuli that do not directly elicit reflexive responses. Byrne (1971) discovered, for example, that liking another person may result from classical conditioning. According to his findings, you tend to like people who agree with you. Agreement produces feelings of pleasure; thus, agreement can serve as a US that elicits feelings of pleasure, a UR. An agreeing person becomes a CS, which eventually produces feelings of pleasure, a CR. This example illustrates that some contemporary classical conditioning research is far removed from Pavlov's very mechanistic approach and differs greatly from the strictly traditional view that classical conditioning is based on reflexive responses.

Everyday Examples

Classical conditioning is much more than a laboratory phenomenon; it is a basic form of learning that permeates the daily existence of most living organisms. Even so,

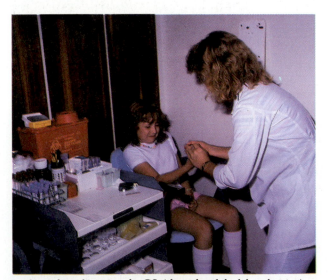

In classical conditioning, the CS (the sight of the lab technician) is repeatedly paired with the UCS (the finger prick). After several repetitions, the CS elicits a response (the CR) very similar to that elicited by the UCS—the UCR of pain and crying.

Exploring...

Complex Conditioning Relationships

Classical conditioning is a basic learning process. The CS serves as a signal that prepares you to respond to the US. Yet under certain circumstances, the CS elicits a response that is the opposite of the UR elicited by the US. For example, injecting a subject with insulin (the US) causes a reduction in blood suger (the UR). However, if a CS (such as a specific environmental cue) consistently precedes the injection, the conditioned response to this signal will be a rise in blood sugar (Flaherty et al., 1980; Siegal, 1975). The CS allows the subject's body to prepare for the response elicited by US by making a compensatory (counterbalancing) response to the signal. In other words, the CR (a rise in blood sugar) occurs to offset the UR (a decline in blood sugar).

In somewhat similar circumstances, drug users may unwittingly condition in themselves similar compensatory responses that can have drastic consequences (Siegal, 1975). Consider what happens when heroin addicts inject heroin, an opiate, into their bodies. The heroin acts upon the body, causing it to produce, along with other reactions, antiopiates that help the body defend itself against too much heroin or other opiates (Snyder, 1984). The heroin is a US, while the production of antiopiates is a UR. The situation in which the addict injects the heroin provides many potential CS's—the room, the furnishings in the room, the people present, the drug paraphernalia used. Sufficient pairings of these stimuli with the US (heroin in the body) may produce a CR (antiopiate production) before the heroin is ever injected.

The effects of this compensatory conditioned response are complex. Drug tolerance may be due, in part, to this type of conditioning (Siegal, 1977). For example, once conditioning has occurred, more antiopiates are present; thus, the addict needs to inject more heroin to obtain the same "rush" he or she experienced before conditioning. Also, the production of antiopiates caused by this conditioning may produce withdrawal symptoms that increase the user's craving for heroin. The most drastic outcome of this situation may be a drug overdose (Siegal et al., 1982). Drug overdose deaths from heroin occur more frequently in a new situation than in a familiar one. The absence of familiar cues (e.g., the CS's of the room or the people present) causes a much weaker compensatory antiopiate production (the CR), and without the CR of antiopiate production, the addict's body is not prepared for the normal amount of heroin. Thus, the addict unwittingly injects the same amount of heroin he or she injected before; unfortunately, that amount has become an overdose, and the addict may die from his or her reactions to the excessive amount. In this case, as research has shown, the normal learning function of classical conditioning becomes maladaptive.

clearcut everyday examples that fit the strict traditional laboratory definitions of classical conditioning are often difficult to identify. Certainly, when your mouth waters at the smell of steak cooking on your neighbor's grill or you feel more hungry at mealtimes than at other times during the day, you experience conditioned responses that directly parallel the kinds of responses conditioned in the laboratory.

Another everyday example of classical conditioning involves static electricity. Have you learned to be fearful of touching certain objects in your home during the wintertime, when static electricity is usually greater? The shock you receive is a US that elicits a UR of pain. The

CS may be the sight of the object as you are about to touch it or any other of a number of stimuli that consistently occur immediately before you experience the shock. After several pairings of the CS (the object) and the US (the shock), you become fearful when you see the object because you anticipate the pain of the shock. In a similar manner, children (and adults!) become fearful when they are about to receive an injection at the doctor's office because of previous pairings of the sight of the syringe (the CS) and the accompanying injection (the US). Many everyday examples of classical conditioning involve conditioning of emotional responses, a topic that will be discussed later in this chapter.

In some homes, while a person is showering, a drop in water pressure followed by a sharp rise in water temperature occurs whenever a cold water tap is opened elsewhere in the home. This situation creates another example of everyday classical conditioning. Can you apply the paradigm to this situation? What are the four essential components? The drop in water pressure is a signal (the CS) that consistently precedes a sharp rise in water temperature (the US). Jumping away when the temperature rises is the UR, while jumping away when the water pressure drops is the CR. If you stay in a motel in which similar conditions exist, the first time the water pressure drops, you will probably not react. However, you will quickly become conditioned to avoid the scalding water.

In many everyday occurrences, the conditions do not precisely fit the paradigm, yet the situations resemble classical conditioning. For example, pet owners are aware that their pets become conditioned to the sound of dry food hitting the dish, the sound of the dish being placed on the floor, or the smell of the food, stimuli associated with feeding. But what type of conditioning is involved when your cat comes running at the sight or sound of a can opener? What are the US, UR, CS, and CR in this situation? As it did with Pavlov's dogs, food in the cat's food dish may elicit reflexive salivation from the cat, but in a strict sense running toward food is not a reflexive behavior in cats, and neither are the behaviors of meowing, purring, and rubbing against your leg. However, in a less strict sense, seeing food can be considered a US and running toward the food, a UR. Under these looser conditions, a stimulus, such as the sight or sound of a can opener, can become a CS to which the cat learns to run if the stimulus consistently signals the appearance of catfood. In the next chapter, when classical and operant conditioning are compared, you will see that this example illustrates some of the shared features of classical and operant conditioning.

Focus Question Answer

Can you unlearn a response once it has been classically conditioned? Yes you can, in the sense that you can learn to stop making a conditioned response. This process is called extinction, and it involves presenting the CS without the US. However, as the phenomenon of spontaneous recovery demonstrates, you do not really undo the previous learning; instead, you learn to inhibit making the response to the CS because the CS no longer serves as an effective signal for the US.

 Classical Conditioning Perspectives

What Is Learned in Classical Conditioning?

Psychologists give two different answers to this question and the answers represent two different perspectives about the classical conditioning process. One perspective suggests that classical conditioning is based on **stimulus substitution**, or the CS taking the place of the US. This perspective derives from Pavlov's original observations. According to Pavlov (1928), when the CS and US are contiguous (are presented close together or overlapping in time) the animal or person links them together and eventually substitutes the CS for the US. Pavlov's views were actually a restatement of earlier philosophical ideas about associationism. **Contiguity** (being adjacent in time) is the important factor in the stimulus substitution account of classical conditioning. Theoretically, any stimulus that is contiguous with the US can become a CS, and in time substitute for the US, thereby producing a response similar to the UR. However, as you have already seen, certain CS's elicit conditioned responses that are very different from the responses elicited by US. An example is the previously discussed physiological reactions of addicts who routinely inject heroin in the same surroundings. These findings deny the stimulus substitution explanation of classical conditioning.

Advocates of a second perspective contend that a CS acquires informational value as a signal for a US (Rescorla, 1967). According to this viewpoint, learning in classical conditioning is based not on the contiguity of the CS-US but on the **contingency** of the US upon the CS. A contingency is established when the presence of one event is accompanied by the presence of a second event and when the absence of the first event is also accompanied by the absence of the second. In other words, because the occurrence of a US is contingent, or dependent, on the occurrence of a CS, a CS gains value from its ability to provide information about a US. The animal or person learns that a CS is a signal for a US. Under this contingency, the animal or person can then make a response (a CR) that prepares for a US and a UR. For example, in many households people learn that the drop in water pressure (CS) signals the inevitable change in water temperature (US). They can use this signal to make the CR of jumping back.

The Research Process: The Role of Contingency in Classical Conditioning

The contingency perspective has been supported by several important lines of research. First, researchers dem-

EXHIBIT 8.5
A Shuttle Box for Dogs

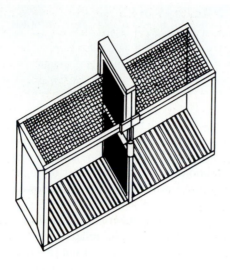

In the shuttle box, a current can be passed through the grid floor to provide a shock to the dog's feet. The dog can escape from or, under appropriate conditions, entirely avoid the shock by jumping over the partition. The drop gate is closed to confine the dog to one side of the box.

Adapted from Solomon & Wynne, 1953.

onstrated that conditioning will occur only if a US is contingent upon a CS (Rescorla, 1966; 1967). In one important study, dogs first learned to avoid shocks by jumping back and forth over a partition in a shuttle box (see Exhibit 8.5). During this initial training, the shocks occurred without any signals. The rate of jumping over the partition during this phase created a baseline against which the later conditioning of a CR could be compared.

Next, the dogs underwent a classical conditioning procedure in which different groups of dogs received different CS-US pairings. In each group, tones served as the CS, and shock served as the US. One group of dogs was exposed to random shocks and tones; the occurrence of the shocks was independent of the occurrence of the tones (no contingency). Occasionally, by accident, a tone would be paired with a shock, but the shock was equally likely to occur before, during, or after the tone. Thus the tone had no informational value as a signal for the US. With a second group of dogs, the tone was given informational value by making a shock more probable after a tone than at any other time (contingency). The dogs in the second group experienced the same number of CS-US pairings and the same number of total shocks as did the dogs in the first group; only the timing of the shock differed.

If contiguity is the basis for conditioning, then the two groups of dogs should have developed equally strong CR's of fear. However, if the contingency perspective is correct, then the two groups should have differed. Because of the CS's informational value, the dogs in the second group should have learned a CR of fear to the tone, while the dogs in the first group should not have been affected by the tone. These two alternatives were tested when the dogs were returned to the shuttle box. When their jumping rate stabilized, the dogs were exposed to the tone that served as the CS in the earlier conditioning. If a CR of fear had been conditioned to the tone, then the jumping rates of the second group of dogs should have increased because of the additional fear elicited by the tone.

The results supported the contingency alternative. When the tone was added, the dogs in the second group doubled their rate of jumping, while the dogs in the first group were unaffected (see Exhibit 8.6). Thus, this research established that contingency, not contiguity, accounts for the learning in classical conditioning.

In a second line of research (Seligman, 1968; Weiss, 1970), the contingency perspective was further sup-

EXHIBIT 8.6
Contingency versus Contiguity

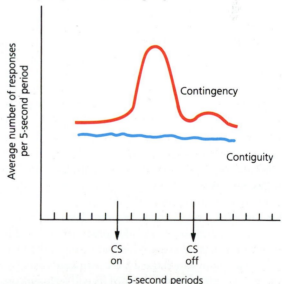

The graph shows the shuttle box jumping rates of dogs previously exposed to contingency conditioning and of dogs previously exposed to contiguity conditioning. The introduction of the tone is clearly marked by the dramatic increase in the jumping rates of dogs in the contingency conditioning. The performance of the dogs in the contiguity group was unaffected by the tone.

Rescorla, A. 1966. Predictability in number of pairings in Pavlovian fear conditioning. *Psychonomic Science, 4*, 383–384.

EXHIBIT 8.7
Experimental Design To Demonstrate Blocking

	Phase 1		Phase 2		Test Stimulus
Experimental Group	Sound CS	Shock US	Light/Sound CS	Shock US	Light
Control Group	(no treatment)		Light/Sound CS	Shock Us	Light

ported by investigating the effects of the absence of contingency. In a contingent relationship, not only does the presence of the CS have informational value, but the absence of the CS also has informational value. As the graph in Exhibit 8.6 indicates, the dogs became more fearful when the CS was present, but their fear was reduced when the CS was absent. When the US is contingent upon the CS, the absence of the CS is a signal that the US will not occur. In situations in which the US is electric shock, the absence of the CS is very valuable information.

In a noncontingent relationship, the presence or absence of the CS has no value as a signal. In noncontingent situations in which the US is electric shock, the lack of signals for either the presence or the absence of the US should produce continual fear. A condition of continual fear is associated with a number of negative physiological reactions, such as the development of stomach ulcers. In contrast, if, in contingent-shock situations, the presence and absence of the CS inform animals whether or not they should be fearful, then they should experience less fear than those in noncontingent-shock conditions. Indeed, this result was proven: rats exposed to noncontingent electric shock developed a much higher rate of stomach ulcers than did rats who received the same number of shocks, but for whom the shocks were preceded by a signal (Seligman, 1968; Weiss, 1970). Thus, according to this research, the effects of absence of contingency support the contingency perspective.

Finally, a third set of studies (Kamin, 1969) supported the contingency position and demonstrated two additional contingency effects—overshadowing and blocking. In situations in which the US is contingent upon two CS's that occur simultaneously, the CR will become conditioned to the CS to which the subject pays greater attention. This effect is called **overshadowing**. For example, when dogs conditioned to salivate to simultaneous CS's of a soft tone and a bright light were tested with either the tone or the light, only the bright light elicited a conditioned salivary response. Yet a control condition using just the soft tone as the CS demonstrated that the dogs could hear the tone and were capable of being conditioned to it. In a literal sense, then, the intensity of the bright light CS overshadowed the soft tone CS.

The overshadowing effect can be produced by prior experiences as well as by the relative intensity of the CS's. Once a contingency is established between the US and a specific CS, the addition of a second CS occurring simultaneously with the first will add no additional information about the US, and therefore no conditioning to the second CS will occur. This effect is called **blocking** (Kamin, 1969).

In a study designed to demonstrate blocking, one group of rats underwent prior conditioning experience in which the CS was sound and the US was electric shock (see Exhibit 8.7). This group of rats acquired a conditioned response of fear to the sound.

In a second phase of the experiment, this group underwent additional conditioning trials in which a second CS of light occurred simultaneously with the initial CS of sound. During this phase, a control group was also conditioned with the dual CS's of sound and light. When tested with just the light CS, the rats in the control group exhibited conditioned fear to the light, while the rats in the experimental group did not. Kamin concluded that, for the experimental group, the effects of the prior conditioning with the sound overshadowed the addition of the second CS and blocked any conditioning to the light. The rats in the control group became conditioned to the light because they lacked the prior experience with the sound CS and thus were not subject to blocking. These results show that the informational value of CS's can overshadow and block conditioning to other CS's that provide lesser amounts of or no additional information about the US.

These various lines of research clearly establish that CS-US contiguity is not sufficient to produce classical conditioning and, therefore, that stimulus substitution does not explain the learning that occurs in classical conditioning. These studies confirm that the necessary element of classical conditioning is CS-US contingency and that the informational value of the CS explains why conditioning occurs.

The Limitations of Classical Conditioning

Pavlov's studies demonstrated how animals and humans can acquire new behaviors beyond the rather limited repertoire of their innate reflexes. Pavlov believed that the conditioned response could explain all kinds of learning and that any stimulus contiguous with the US could become a CS (Pavlov, 1928). For many years, learning theorists believed that virtually any perceivable neutral stimulus could become a CS and that just about any response could be conditioned (Kimble, 1956). However, over the years this view of the generality of classical conditioning has been modified as a variety of research studies have identified limitations to animals' and humans' adaptability through classical conditioning (Kimble, 1981).

You have already read about the research that disproved Pavlov's ideas about stimulus contiguity and stimulus substitution and established that classical conditioning is limited to situations in which the US is contingent upon the CS. Additional research on **learned taste aversions** (classically conditioned avoidance of specific flavors) indicates that classical conditioning is limited in the types of stimuli and responses that can be conditioned (Garcia et al., 1956).

The research on learned taste aversions began in a manner similar to Pavlov's pioneering studies—serendipity played an important role. John Garcia was studying nuclear radiation's effects on laboratory animals when he observed that rats avoided drinking from the plastic water bottles in the radiation chambers but drank normal amounts of water from the glass bottles in their home cages. Like Pavlov before him, Garcia pursued this serendipitous finding. He considered various explanations for the effect and concluded that the rats were conditioned to avoid the plastic-flavored water in the chambers. In terms of the classical conditioning paradigm, the radiation to which the rats were exposed was a US that elicited nausea, the UR, in the rats. The plastic-flavored water became a CS with which the rats associated illness.

To investigate his hypothesis, Garcia and his colleagues designed a series of experiments in which illness was induced by irradiation or drugs after the rats had been exposed to a variety of flavors, sights, and sounds. In one study (Garcia & Koelling, 1966), one group of rats was given saccharin-flavored water to drink. Drinking the flavored water was sometimes followed by electric shock to the rats' feet and at other times by induced illness (from radiation poisoning or an injected drug). A second group of rats received the same US of foot shock or induced illness, but the CS was a combination of flashing lights and loud noises that were triggered by drinking from the water bottle containing plain water.

The intriguing results of this experiment indicated that certain combinations of stimuli and responses could be conditioned in rats, while other combinations could not. The first group of rats avoided the saccharin-flavored water when it was followed by induced illness but not when it was followed by foot shock. Conversely, the second group of rats avoided the "loud-flashing" water only when it was paired with the foot shock; no conditioning to the "loud-flashing" water and induced illness combination occurred. As these findings indicate, not every stimulus is a potential CS, and not every combination of stimulus and response can become associated through classical conditioning.

Garcia explained these results in terms of an evolutionary framework that assumes rats, other animals, and humans have built-in predispositions to learn adaptive survival behaviors for their particular environments. Avoiding flavors associated with previous illnesses has adaptive survival significance for rats who eat almost anything and therefore need to avoid substances that make them sick. Taste aversions can even be acquired before birth. Rats who were presented with an apple odor paired with lithium chloride during the fetal stage, would not nurse after birth on nipples brushed with apple juice (Smotherman, 1982). Garcia demonstrated that classical conditioning enables animals to adapt to their environments, but that specific environmental cues are potent CS's for certain responses. This research indicates that each species is predisposed to learn certain associations and not others (Kimble, 1981).

Focus Question Answer

Will you become conditioned to any stimulus? No. Pavlov and others reasoned that theoretically any perceivable neutral stimulus could function as a conditioned stimulus. However, research studies have shown that animals and humans are predisposed to become conditioned to some stimuli, while they will not become conditioned to certain other stimuli. Nonetheless, your great ability to adapt to your environment means that many stimuli are potential CS's to which you can become conditioned.

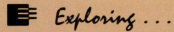

Learned Taste Aversions, Coyotes, and Cancer

The research on learned taste aversions, while contributing to theoretical discussions of classical conditioning, has also been applied to practical problems. Each year, sheep ranchers across the United States suffer losses from predators, especially from coyotes. Prevention measures have focused on destroying coyote populations to eliminate the threat, but this approach creates other problems by disrupting naturally occurring predator/prey cycles of which the coyote is a part. Garcia and several colleagues investigated learned taste aversions in coyotes and wolves and discovered that as few as one or two exposures to mutton tainted with lithium-chloride, an illness-inducing drug that produces severe nausea, were enough to condition an aversion to sheep (Gustavson et al., 1974). Presumably, the sight and smell of sheep as well as the taste of mutton became associated with illness because when coyotes with the conditioned aversion were placed in the presence of a lamb they often ran away and vomited. When these results were field tested by scattering lithium-tainted mutton over a sheep range, the number of predator attacks on lambs decreased greatly. Sheep ranchers now have an alternative way to control predator losses, a method that does not disrupt the predator/prey balance in nature.

Additional research on learned taste aversions in humans is being used to counteract loss of appetite associated with chemotherapy for cancer patients (Bernstein, 1978; Bernstein et al., 1982). One re-searcher studied cancer patients two years to sixteen years of age; she found that patients who ate a novel-tasting ice cream before receiving illness-inducing chemotherapy exhibited an aversion to the ice cream when they were tested four and one-half months later. In a second study, this researcher and several colleagues discovered that cancer patients also developed aversions to familiar foods eaten before receiving illness-inducing chemotherapy. However, if the patients ate both familiar and novel foods before the chemotherapy, they showed less aversion to the familiar foods and greater aversion to the novel foods (in this case unusual-tasting ice cream). Patients in a control group who ate very little before undergoing treatment exhibited the least amount of aversion to either familiar or novel food.

Taken together, these results suggest a pre-chemotherapy regimen. According to this research, cancer patients can best limit their taste aversions following chemotherapy by eating little or nothing for several hours before undergoing treatment. If patients eat anything during the several hours preceding chemotherapy, they should eat novel-tasting foods they will not encounter again after treatment. While this regimen has not been tested with a wide range of cancer patients receiving chemotherapy, if these observations are correct, the technique should limit patients' losses of appetite due to learned taste aversions.

 ## Classical Conditioning Phenomena

One of the remarkable features of Pavlov's studies of conditioning is that he so accurately described the phenomena of classical conditioning. Employing terminology still used today, Pavlov described and named the phenomena of stimulus generalization, discrimination, and higher-order conditioning. In this section, you will read about these phenomena and about schizokinesis and conditioned emotional responses.

Generalization

In the examples of classical conditioning presented thus far, the same CS situation was used to test for the presence of a conditioned response. In the everyday world outside the laboratory, you often encounter stimuli that are similar to but not the same as the CS. How do you react to these similar stimuli? For example, when you are in your neighbor's home, are you fearful of touching objects that are similar to objects that give you static electricity shocks in your own home? If you are fearful, you have experienced generalization of fearfulness to similar stimuli. **Generalization** is the process by which you react to similarities among stimuli.

This tendency for a conditioned response to be elicited by stimuli similar to the conditioned stimulus was called **stimulus generalization** by Pavlov. He included the term stimulus to emphasize that a general class of similar stimuli acquire the tendency to elicit the CR after the response to a specific CS has been conditioned. Dogs, which are conditioned to salivate to a tuning fork of a particular pitch (such as middle C), also salivate to tones higher or lower in pitch. However, the amount of salivation to similar tones is not as great as salivation to the original tone. Pavlov found that dogs trained to salivate to a tone would salivate not only to similar tones but also to bells and buzzers (Pavlov, 1927). In all cases, the amount of salivation was not as great as that produced by the original CS tone; however, the more similar the test stimulus was to the original CS, the greater was the amount of salivation (see Exhibit 8.8).

The phenomenon of generalization accounts for your ability to react to new situations that are similar to old ones. In a simple sense, generalization is a process that makes a little bit of learning go a long way. Without generalization, you would make a conditioned response

to only the exact CS that occurred when you were conditioned. You would have to learn anew each time you entered a different shower that a drop in water pressure is a signal for a possibly unpleasant experience. Thus, generalization is adaptive; it allows you to transfer to new, but similar, stimuli your learned responses to specific stimuli.

Discrimination

A process that complements generalization is **discrimination**, the process of learning to respond differently to similar stimuli. Although generalization extends the usefulness of your learning, you can overgeneralize and fail to react to important differences between stimuli. Cats and skunks are both small, furry animals, but their differences are more important than their similarities. You do not want to overgeneralize from cats to skunks. Discrimination is the process by which you learn to react to such differences.

Unlike generalization, which occurs without further learning, discrimination requires additional conditioning. Discrimination occurs as the result of a combination of acquisition and extinction. Pavlov demonstrated **stimulus discrimination** by first conditioning dogs to salivate to a particular tone (CS). In order for the dogs to learn to discriminate between the CS and similar-sounding tones, Pavlov had to extinguish their generalized responses to the similar-sounding tones. He did so in a series of trials by presenting dogs with the original CS tone always paired with meat powder (the US) and the similar tones never followed by meat powder. In this manner, the dogs' conditioned responses to the original CS underwent further acquisition, while at the same time their generalized responses to the similar tones underwent extinction. Discrimination training was complete when the dogs salivated to the original CS but not to the tones similar to the CS.

The greater the similarity between stimuli, the more difficult is learning to discriminate between them. Pavlov (1927) tested this principle by conditioning a dog to salivate at the sight of a circle projected onto a screen; meat powder served as the US stimulus. After establishing a salivary response to the CS of the circle, Pavlov began discrimination training by introducing a new stimulus, an ellipse (an elongated circle), which was never paired with the US of meat powder. After the dog learned to discriminate between the circle and the ellipse (it salivated to the circle, but not to the ellipse), Pavlov replaced the first ellipse with a more circular one. The dog learned to discriminate this second ellipse from the

EXHIBIT 8.8

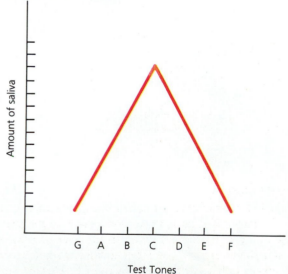

Test Tones

Tones that are more similar to the CS tone of middle C elicit more salivation. The more dissimilar to middle C the test tones are, the less salivation they elicit.

original circle. Pavlov continued in this manner, replacing each succeeding ellipse with a more circular one. The dog was able to learn these increasingly finer discriminations, but not without some interesting side effects. Pavlov noted that the dog's behavior in the conditioning apparatus changed dramatically. The formerly docile dog barked violently when it was taken into the experimental room and pawed and bit the apparatus. Pavlov concluded that the difficult task of making extremely fine discriminations had created in the dog "all the symptoms of a condition of acute neurosis" (Pavlov, 1927).

In summary, stimulus generalization allows you to respond to similarities between environmental stimuli, while stimulus discrimination allows you to respond differently to stimuli that have some features in common with other stimuli. You generalize first, and then, through additional experience, you learn which stimuli are functionally similar and which stimuli require different responses.

Schizokinesis

Certain conditioned responses are more complex than the relatively simple reflexive responses Pavlov studied. For example, a conditioned fear response is actually a complex combination of skeletal (muscular) and autonomic (glandular) reactions. The autonomic components of this complex response are acquired more easily and are more resistant to extinction. During extinction, the skeletal components of the conditioned fear response extinguish before the autonomic parts. This phenomenon is termed **schizokinesis** (Gantt, 1953; 1958). Thus, schizokinesis accounts for situations in which you formerly showed fear. Now, you appear calm on the outside, but you are still aroused internally. Because the muscular components are extinguished, your knees may no longer "knock" and your voice may no longer shake, but your palms may still sweat and your heart still pound.

A familiar example of schizokinesis is associated with dental work. You may be one of many people who have strong negative reactions to dental work. Even with improved equipment and procedures for blocking the pain,

Higher-Order Conditioning

Higher-order conditioning occurs when an established conditioned stimulus serves as the unconditioned stimulus in a new conditioning task. The original CS can substitute for the US in a new conditioning task because, during the original conditioning, it became a reliable signal for the US. For example, after dogs are conditioned to salivate to a tone, if the tone can then be paired with a new neutral stimulus, such as a light, the dogs will learn to salivate to the light (see Exhibit 8.9); they will, however, salivate somewhat less to the second-order CS of the light than they did to the original CS of the tone.

Theoretically, higher-order conditioning should be unlimited if the CR is sufficiently conditioned to each succeeding CS. In actuality, higher-order conditioning is limited by how many stimuli occur between the original CS-US pairing and the new CS. Also, the original US must be presented from time to time to maintain the higher-order conditioning. In animals, second-order conditioning is common, especially when the conditioned response is fear. Third-order conditioning (e.g., pairing touching the dog's leg with the second-order CS of the light) is difficult to establish because of the intermediate conditioned stimulus (the light) between the new CS (touching the dog's leg) and the original CS-US pairing (tone-meat powder).

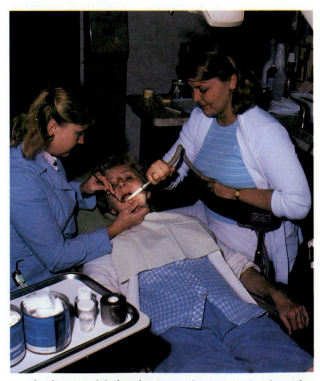

In schizokinesis, adult dental patients who appear relaxed may be having strong physiological responses to the situation.

EXHIBIT 8.9
The Higher-Order Conditioning Paradigm

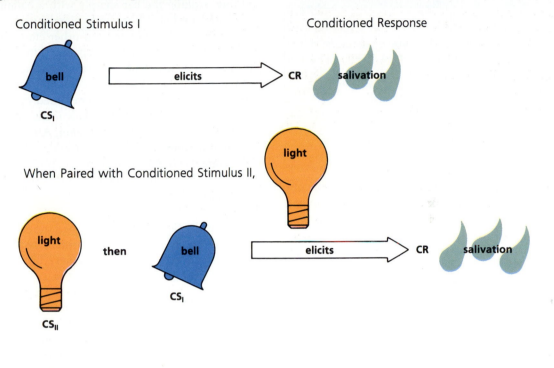

Conditioned Stimulus I

Conditioned Response

bell   CS_I   elicits   CR   salivation

When Paired with Conditioned Stimulus II,

light CS_{II}   then   bell CS_I   elicits   CR   salivation

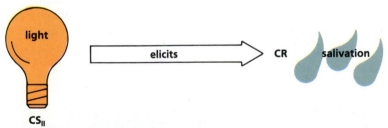

Eventually, with Enough Pairings:

light CS_{II}   elicits   CR   salivation

In the original, or first-order, conditioning, the tone is paired with the meat powder, which elicits salivation. A conditioned response of salivation to the tone is acquired. In second-order conditioning, a new neutral stimulus, a light, is paired with the tone. Eventually, the light elicits a conditioned response of salivation. In third-order conditioning, touching the dog's leg is paired with the light, resulting in a conditioned response of salivation to the touch.

drilling or scraping is unpleasant for many people. The drilling or scraping acts as an unconditioned stimulus that elicits muscular tension and autonomic arousal. The sight or the sound of the dentist's drill becomes a CS that elicits the same combination of reactions as the actual drilling. If you have acquired a conditioned fear of the dentist's drill, outwardly you may appear very calm as you recline in the dental chair, but inwardly you may be very excited. The reason for this split is schizokinesis.

Because you have repeatedly visited the dentist's office, many of your conditioned reactions, particularly the muscular components, have been extinguished. However, careful monitoring of your inner states may still reveal autonomic arousal, such as constriction of blood vessels and increases in blood pressure (Gantt, 1960). Concentrate on the phenomenon of schizokinesis during your next dental appointment and you may not notice the drill!

Conditioned Emotional Responses

Most people are aware from personal experience of **conditioned emotional responses**, the classical conditioning of positive and negative emotional reactions to previously neutral stimuli (Fantino, 1973). You may exhibit conditioned emotional responses to thunderstorms, tests, large dogs, spiders, or a wide range of objects or events because the particular object or event was present when you were previously frightened or emotionally aroused. Although laboratory experiments on conditioned emotional responses have investigated primarily the acquisition and generalization of negative emotional reactions such as fear and anxiety, conditioning of positive emotional reactions also occurs. For example, the smells of pine, bayberry candles, and roasted turkey may elicit a variety of pleasant emotions because you have associated these smells with pleasant holiday experiences. Similarly, the smell of pine may evoke the pleasant feelings you have associated with enjoyable vacations in the mountains, and the sight of seashells may bring back the relaxed feeling you experienced while vacationing at the seashore.

Negative conditioned emotions have been studied more frequently than positive conditioned emotions, in part because of Pavlov's use of electric shock as an unconditioned stimulus and because of Watson and Rayner's (1920) experiment with a subject known as "little Albert." Today, because of ethical considerations, this well-known experiment would not be undertaken. In a three-month period beginning when he was eight months old, Albert was classically conditioned to fear a white rat and other white, furry animals and objects. At the beginning of the experiment, Albert played fearlessly with a variety of objects including a white rat, a rabbit, a dog, a monkey, cotton, and a variety of masks. Watson and Rayner first conditioned Albert to become fearful and emotionally aroused at the sight of the white rat. They accomplished this conditioning by pairing the sight of the white rat (the CS) with a very loud noise (the US) created by holding a steel bar directly behind Albert and then striking the bar sharply with a hammer. The loud noise startled Albert and caused him to tremble and cry. Trembling, crying, and other emotional reactions were the unconditioned response. After only seven pairings of the white rat with the loud noise, Albert began to fear the rat, crying at the sight of it and fearfully withdrawing from it. His fear generalized to a rabbit, a dog, a fur coat, and a Santa Claus mask with a white beard, and, when tested a month later, Albert continued to exhibit a generalized fear of objects similar to the rat (i.e., white and/or furry). Watson and Rayner concluded that they had been successful in demonstrating the learning of a persistent, generalized conditioned emotional response.

Although psychologists questioned the ethics of conditioning fear in an otherwise normal, healthy child, they seized upon Watson and Rayner's findings as evidence that other emotional reactions such as phobias (irrational fears of objects or situations when no realistic threat is present) are the result of classical conditioning. However, the strong acceptance of Watson and Rayner's conclusions about stimulus generalization may have been misplaced. A recent reassessment of their experiment indicates that Albert's fear of the rabbit and the dog was not the result of stimulus generalization but of direct conditioning (Harris, 1979). Although neither the dog nor the rabbit was systematically paired with the loud noise (US), both were used as conditioned stimuli in

A phobia, such as an irrational fear of riding in elevators, may be a classically conditioned behavior.

several learning trials. Also, Albert was not as fearful of the animals and objects as was generally reported; at times he neither cried nor was fearful in their presence. Casting further doubt upon the generality of Watson and Rayner's research is the fact that other researchers (Jones, 1930; Bregman, 1934) were unsuccessful in their attempts to condition fear in children by using loud noise as the US. Nonetheless, in spite of reservations about Watson and Rayner's results, conditioned emotional responses remain an accepted part of classical conditioning phenomena.

Conditioned emotional responses can be learned through the process of **vicarious classical conditioning**, which occurs by merely observing conditioning in another person without directly experiencing the CS-US pairing. For example, in one experiment (Bandura & Rosenthal, 1966), subjects who observed another person receiving an electric shock (the US) paired with a light (the CS) exhibited an emotional response when they were tested with the light. They acquired a conditioned emotional response without directly experiencing the shock. Through vicarious classical conditioning, children may learn to react emotionally to certain situations because of their parents' emotional responses to those situations. A child may learn vicariously to fear swimming because he or she has observed a parent's fearful reactions to swimming.

Focus Question Answer

How are your emotional reactions affected by classical conditioning? Conditioned emotional responses are acquired in the same manner all classically conditioned responses are acquired. A neutral stimulus (CS) is paired with a situation (US) that causes emotional arousal (UR). Under certain conditions, only one pairing of the CS and the US is necessary for the CS to elicit a conditioned emotional response at a later time. The phenomenon of schizokinesis explains why, when certain conditioned emotional responses are evoked, you remain outwardly calm but are inwardly aroused.

 *Relate*

Classical Conditioning and Health

The classical conditioning paradigm has broad application in health-related learning. Several techniques—counterconditioning, systematic desensitization, and aversive conditioning—are based directly on classical conditioning procedures, but conditioning may affect recovery from certain illnesses without the intervention of these more formal techniques. Consider the experiences of a family known to the authors in which the son suffered from asthma attacks that were occasionally severe enough to require a trip to the hospital emergency room. At the hospital, the boy would receive an injection of epinephrine to relieve his symptoms. During one of the boy's attacks, the family was delayed for a few minutes in the hospital parking lot and, much to everyone's amazement, the boy's symptoms began to subside without his receiving the injection. Can you explain why? The injection was a US that relieved the symptoms and also caused the boy to relax (the UR); his relaxation contributed further to reducing the attack. Since entering the parking lot always preceded receiving the injection, the parking lot became a CS that caused the boy to relax (the CR) in anticipation of the shot. During the incident mentioned above, relaxing helped relieve the asthma symptoms. You may have experienced a similar conditioned response when you made a doctor's appointment after not feeling well for several days. In the past, making an appointment (CS) under the same conditions preceded the doctor's treatment (US), which led to your feeling better (UR). Therefore, in the most recent instance, simply making the appointment may have made you feel better (CR). You should note that these examples of conditioning have only limited usefulness for improving your health. You should seek appropriate medical care for asthma and other illnesses.

Although incidental classical conditioning is of limited usefulness, you can employ techniques such as counterconditioning to improve your health. **Counterconditioning** is a procedure for extinguishing one response while conditioning an incompatible response to the same CS (Jones, 1924). Conditioned emotional responses that are often difficult to extinguish can be modified with this technique. For example, little Albert's fear of white rats could have been modified by pairing the rat with a pleasant experience, such as receiving special attention or a special treat to eat. The sight of the rat would no longer be followed by a loud noise; instead, the rat would be paired with a pleasant event or object. The negative response of fear would be incompatible with the positive emotional reactions evoked by the pleasant experience. Therefore, the negative fear response would undergo extinction, while the positive, pleasant emotional responses would be strengthened. Gradually, the positive conditioned emotional response would replace the negative one.

Counterconditioning is easily self-administered. Consider how counterconditioning might be used with a person suffering from a mild case of insomnia (inability to sleep). Insomnia may result because a person enjoys staying awake. An individual may go to bed but continue a number of enjoyable activities such as watching television, eating snacks, talking on the telephone, or reading a book. Most of these activities are incompatible with falling asleep. Through conditioning, these activities may cause periods of insomnia because the person's bedroom becomes a CS for activities other than sleep. Through counterconditioning—removing the activities that are incompatible with sleeping and associating a pleasant routine with going to sleep—the bedroom can be reestablished as a conditioned stimulus for sleeping. If you have difficulty sleeping, you can easily follow this procedure. However, if your insomnia persists after you have tried this technique, seeing a physician for a physical examination and consultation would be advisable.

A specific type of counterconditioning used to treat phobias and related disorders is **systematic desensitization**, a form of therapy in which deep muscle relaxation is conditioned as the incompatible response (Wolpe, 1958; 1982). In the training procedure for systematic desensitization, patients first learn deep muscle relaxation and then are gradually exposed to situations in which they experience their phobias. The anxiety-provoking situations are presented in hierarchy, from least anxiety-provoking to most anxiety-provoking. Because relaxation is incompatible with anxiety, patients are gradually desensitized to the phobic situations.

Systematic desensitization has been used successfully to treat test anxiety (Sarason, 1978). Test anxiety is a condition with which virtually every college student is familiar, but certain students find the experience extremely debilitating. The tension and emotional arousal that test-anxious students suffer before and during exams affect their abilities to concentrate, to study effectively, and to remember information. A systematic desensitization program for test anxiety might proceed in the following manner: A counselor trains the test-anxious student to perform relaxation exercises, which the student practices daily at home. Next, working with the counselor, the student compiles a list of all the test aspects that cause him or her to become anxious; the student then ranks the various activities and situations from least anxiety-provoking to most anxiety-provoking. In a later counseling session, after the student becomes very relaxed, he or she is asked to imagine vividly for several seconds the least anxiety-provoking item on the test anxiety hierarchy. If the student starts to become tense, the exercise is stopped until he or she becomes more relaxed. Over several sessions, the student learns to stay relaxed even when imagining the most anxiety-provoking item on the list. At this point, the training moves from imagined situations to actual situations, again beginning with the least anxiety-provoking stimulus on the hierarchy. The sessions end when the student is able to control his or her anxiety reactions by remaining relaxed while taking tests. During the course of the training sessions, the student becomes desensitized gradually (i.e., the anxiety response to tests is extinguished), while counterconditioning of relaxation occurs.

In contrast to the gradual approach of desensitization, the techniques of **implosive therapy** and **flooding** attempt to extinguish phobic responses rapidly. In flooding, patients have to expose themselves to the situations they fear most. In some cases, patients must spend several hours in the actual situations. For example, persons afraid of riding in elevators might agree to ride up and down in elevators until they are no longer anxious. In implosive therapy, individuals may be asked only to imagine the fearful situations. This technique for the treatment of phobias attempts to create an inward explosion (an implosion) of anxiety. In all cases, these techniques are based on the extinction of conditioned responses. When the terrible events the patient has imagined do not occur in the actual anxiety-provoking situation, the conditioned anxiety responses are extinguished quickly.

While the technique of flooding is quite successful in treating phobias (Emmelkamp & Kuipers, 1979), it can be stressful for the patient. If you wanted to overcome a fear, would you rather use systematic desensitization or flooding? Most individuals choose desensitization training because it appears less threatening, it can be done gradually with little anxiety, and it teaches the valuable skill of relaxation.

Aversive conditioning differs from systematic desensitization by conditioning negative responses rather than positive ones. The idea is to eliminate unwanted behaviors, such as smoking or alcohol abuse, by conditioning negative reactions to the stimuli that are associated with the unwanted behaviors. For example, smokers who want to quit smoking may be helped by eliminating the pleasant associations with cigarettes and adding unpleasant associations. Aversive conditioning can be accomplished by pairing the act of smoking (an activity that the smoker may associate with relaxation) with an aversive US, such as mild electric shock. If each time they puffed on cigarettes smokers received mild electric shocks on their wrists, many would find quitting smoking easier to do. However, if this technique were used, discriminating between treatment sessions in which shocks are administered and other smoking situations would be easy, and smokers might discover that the treatment sesssion is the only effective CS for not smoking.

A more successful aversive technique for stopping smoking is satiation smoking. In this procedure, the smoker who wants to quit agrees to sit in a small, unventilated room and smoke continuously for one-half hour. Smoking in these conditions causes nausea, light-headedness, sore throat, congested lungs, and stinging eyes. After several sessions, these responses are conditioned to the stimuli of puffing on a cigarette, lighting and holding a cigarette, and taking a cigarette out of the pack; these formerly positive stimuli for smoking are changed into negative stimuli. Seeing, holding, lighting, and puffing cigarettes produce feelings of illness and therefore stopping smoking becomes easier.

Aversive conditioning has also been used with some success in treating alcoholism (Wiens & Menustik, 1983). One approach involves the use of a drug called antabuse (disulpriam) (Nathan, 1976; Weinberg, 1977). In the body, antabuse in combination with alcohol causes illness and vomiting. Repeatedly pairing the smell, taste, and consumption of alcohol with illness conditions strong feelings of nausea and revulsion to drinking alcohol. The unconditioned stimulus is antabuse in combination with alcohol, a combination that elicits the unconditioned response of illness and vomiting. The conditioned response is strong revulsion to the smell and taste of alcohol and to other stimuli associated with drinking. Although this form of treatment is somewhat successful, aversive conditioning is usually only part of a comprehensive alcohol treatment program (Mahoney & Arnkoff, 1978).

Techniques such as counterconditioning, systematic desensitization, and aversive conditioning—and their practical applications to everyday health problems and living situations—have led researchers a long distance from Pavlov's original experiments with salivating dogs. Nevertheless, modern techniques such as these have their roots in Pavlov's pioneering research and his classical conditioning paradigm.

Things to Do

1. To simulate a laboratory experiment in the acquisition of a classically conditioned eyeblink response, try the following exercise. You will need a drinking straw, pencil and paper, and a friend to assist you. Sit comfortably in a chair, and stare straight ahead; your assistant should sit to one side of you. Using the drinking straw, your assistant should direct a puff of air into the corner of your eye. The puff of air (the US) will cause you to blink your eyes (the UR). Your assistant should snap his or her fingers (the CS) immediately before blowing through the straw. Complete at least twenty acquisition trials before attempting a test trial, in which your assistant presents the CS without the US. The test trial should be unannounced; your assistant should avoid giving you any cues that a specific trial is a test trial (e.g., keep the straw in place, as if the finger snap will be followed by the puff of air). Your assistant should continue to intersperse test trials with trials in which the

CS and the US are paired. When you have made conditioned responses (blinked your eyes) on several test trials, try a different CS, such as a tap on your assistant's chair, to see if generalization occurs. Use the pencil and paper to record your responses and observations about the conditioning.

2. Keep a log for a day or longer, and record classical conditioning examples you encounter during the day. Fit each example into the classical conditioning paradigm, identifying the CS, the US, the UR, and the CR in each case.

3. Identify several situations in which you become fearful and examine them for conditioned emotional responses (be aware that fear in dangerous or threatening situations is a healthy response). Design a program based on extinction or systematic desensitization to eliminate an unwanted or inappropriate conditioned emotional response.

4. Read a research study in which classical conditioning was used to treat behavioral problems such as phobias, smoking, or alcoholism. Write a brief report about the study, including your personal reactions to the form of treatment used.

Things to Discuss

1. In what ways have you been classically conditioned in classroom situations? Can you recall both positive and negative examples of conditioning? Discuss with your classmates ways to eliminate the negative use of conditioning in schools.

2. To a degree, test anxiety is beneficial, because it increases motivation for studying and facilitates performance on exams. Should instructors deliberately make students anxious about taking tests as a way of improving students' scores? Can you pinpoint your specific level of anxiety that facilitates but does not hinder your performance on exams?

3. In what ways do parents classically condition their children, and in what ways do children classically condition their parents? Discuss your answers with several classmates. Do you believe that parents should be taught how to systematically condition their children? Should aversive conditioning techniques be included in that instruction?

4. Treatment programs that use aversive conditioning (such as electric shock and drugs that produce intense illness) to help people stop smoking or abusing alcohol are highly controversial. Discuss whether the advantages

of aversive conditioning offset the disadvantages.

5. An important restriction on aversive conditioning programs is voluntary, informed consent by the participants. Debate the pros and cons of requiring mandatory, involuntary commitment to aversive conditioning programs for persons convicted of offenses such as driving under the influence of alcohol.

6. In what ways do you become classically conditioned when you "fall in love"? Discuss the role of classical conditioning and conditioned emotional responses in romance. Are conditioned emotional responses part of the reason "breaking up is hard to do?"

Things to Read

Burgess, A. 1963. *A clockwork orange.* NY: Norton.

Catania, A.C. 1984. *Learning.* (2nd ed.). Englewood Cliffs, NJ: Prentice-Hall.

Huxley, A. 1932. *Brave new world.* NY: Harper.

Pavlov, I.P. 1927. *Conditioned reflexes.* London: Oxford University Press.

Skinner, B.F. 1974. *About behaviorism.* NY: Knopf.

Williams, R.L. & Long, J. D. 1982. *Toward a self-managed life style* (3rd ed.). Boston: Houghton Mifflin.

Review

Summary

1. Learning is a relatively permanent change in a person or animal, a change that results from experience and that has the potential to change the person's or animal's behavior. Learning is a hypothetical construct based on the assumption of associationism. Learning is the intervening process by which stimuli become associated with responses.

2. Behaviorism, a major perspective in psychology, emphasizes the importance of environmental events (stimuli) and a person's or animal's reactions (responses) to those events.

3. The most basic forms of learning are conditioning. Two models, or paradigms, of conditioning are respondent and operant conditioning. Classical conditioning is the term most often used for respondent conditioning, which is also known as signal learning. Operant conditioning is also referred to as instrumental conditioning.

4. Classical conditioning is the acquisition of a response (the CR) to a previously neutral stimulus (the CS) because the CS has become a reliable signal that a stimulus (the US) which elicits a reflex (the UR) is about to occur. In one of Pavlov's classic experiments, the CS was a tone, the US was meat powder, the UR was salivation to the meat powder, and the CR was salivation to the tone.

5. Acquistion of the conditioned response is the result of repeated pairings of the CS and the US. Optimal acquisition occurs with delayed conditioning, in which the CS begins just before the US to be an effective signal for it. The process of presenting the CS without the US is called extinction. The phenomenon of spontaneous recovery demonstrates that during extinction the original learning is not destroyed; instead, the animal or person learns to stop making the conditioned response.

6. Laboratory studies have investigated a variety of conditioning topics, such as comparisons of the CR and UR and the range of responses that can be conditioned. In some cases, contemporary researchers have broadened the scope of their studies to include unconditioned stimuli that do not directly elicit reflexive responses. Everyday examples of classical conditioning are numerous, but none is more obvious than your mouth watering at the smell of cooking food.

7. Learning in classical conditioning was originally believed to be the result of the CS substituting for the US. Later research demonstrated conclusively that the contingent relationship between the US and CS is responsible for conditioning. The CS is a signal that provides information about the occurrence of the US.

8. Classical conditioning is limited in its scope. Research studies on learned taste aversions have shown that animals and humans are predisposed to become conditioned to some stimuli, while they will not become conditioned to others.

9. Conditioning phenomena include: stimulus generalization, the tendency for a conditioned response to be elicited by stimuli similar to the conditioned stimulus;

stimulus discrimination, the process of learning to respond differently to similar stimuli; higher-order conditioning, the process by which an established CS serves as the US; schizokinesis, the tendency of muscular components of the CR to extinguish more quickly than the glandular components; and conditioned emotional responses, the conditioning of positive and negative emotional reactions to previously neutral stimuli.

10. Classical conditioning influences both people's health and their reactions to medical treatments. For example, phobias, acquired as conditioned emotional responses, can be treated successfully with the counterconditioning technique of systematic desensitization. Aversive conditioning can be used to condition negative associations to alcohol and cigarettes in people who want stop using these substances.

Key Terms

associationism
learning
respondent conditioning
operant conditioning
signal learning
classical conditioning
instrumental conditioning
unconditioned stimulus (US)
unconditioned response (UR)
conditioned stimulus (CS)
conditioned response (CR)
acquisition
extinction
spontaneous recovery

overshadowing
blocking
stimulus generalization
stimulus discrimination
higher-order conditioning
schizokinesis
conditioned emotional responses
vicarious classical conditioning
counterconditioning
systematic desensitization
implosive therapy
flooding
aversive conditioning

Focus Questions

1. Does the law of effect influence your study behavior?

2. How do positive and negative reinforcers shape your study behavior?

3. Which schedule of reinforcement will cause you to study most persistently?

4. Why do people become superstitious?

5. Is observational learning a uniquely human phenomenon, or can your pet dog learn from watching other dogs and you?

6. How does television influence your attitudes and behaviors?

Chapter Outline

THE OPERANT CONDITIONING PARADIGM
Thorndike and the Law of Effect
Watson and Behaviorism
Skinner and Operant Behavior

REINFORCEMENT AND PUNISHMENT
Positive and Negative Reinforcers
Primary and Conditioned Reinforcers
Intrinsic and Extrinsic Reinforcers
The Premack Principle
Positive and Negative Punishers
The Use of Punishment

ACQUISITION AND EXTINCTION
Shaping and Chaining
Stimulus Generalization and Discrimination
Factors Affecting Acquisition
Schedules of Reinforcement
Extinction
The Research Process: The Partial Reinforcement Effect

OPERANT CONDITIONING PERSPECTIVES
What Is Learned in Operant Conditioning?
Comparing Operant and Classical Conditioning
Limitations of Operant Conditioning

COGNITIVE PARADIGMS
Latent Learning and Expectancies
Observational Learning

RELATE: TV—Another Member of the Family
Things to Do
Things to Discuss
Things to Read

REVIEW: Summary
Key Terms

Operant Conditioning and Cognitive Paradigms

The unfortunate thing about this world is that good habits are so much easier to give up than bad ones.

W. Somerset Maugham

The Operant Conditioning Paradigm

If you know the answer to a question your instructor asks in class, do you hesitate, or do you confidently raise your hand? Many factors influence your behavior in this situation—your confidence that you know the answer, the specific instructor and class, and your past successes and failures in answering questions. In Chapter 8, you read how stimuli gain value as signals in the classical conditioning paradigm. In this chapter, you will explore the operant conditioning paradigm and you will learn how the consequences of your past behavior shape your future behavior.

At approximately the same time Pavlov was formulating the basic concepts of classical conditioning, American psychologists such as Edward Thorndike (1874–1949), John B. Watson (1878–1958), and B.F. Skinner

199

(1904–) were developing the concepts associated with the operant, or instrumental, conditioning paradigm. While Pavlov studied the effects of stimuli that reliably precede elicited responses, these psychologists explored the effects of stimuli that follow the voluntary behavior of people and animals. They wanted to explain, for example, based upon people's past experiences, why people act differently.

Thorndike and the Law of Effect

Thorndike

Thorndike (1911) was a pioneer in animal learning; he investigated learning in a variety of species including cats, monkeys, dogs, fish, and chickens. His best known experiments are studies performed with cats who tried to escape from cages called "puzzle boxes" (see Exhibit 9.1) by pulling strings, turning latches, and making other responses (Thorndike, 1898). The hungry cats received food when they escaped from the box. In these **trial-and-error learning** studies, Thorndike defined a trial as the subject's performance until the subject attained its goal. He found that the cats made fewer errors in later trials than in earlier trials. Because the animals escaped more quickly from the box on later trials, Thorndike concluded that the cats had learned because the stimuli of the box became associated with the actions that produced escape from the box. In other words, the cats' responses that were instrumental in obtaining food (in escaping) were strengthened. Thorndike's use of discrete trials became the model for one form of the operant conditioning paradigm, instrumental conditioning, in which the subject's responses during the trial are instrumental in obtaining a certain consequence.

Trial – until subject attained its goal

EXHIBIT 9.1
A Puzzle Box for Cats

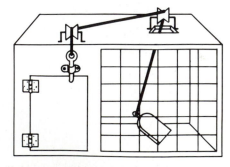

Using a similar box, Thorndike studied how cats learn to escape from the box to obtain food. Learning to unlatch the door is instrumental in the hungry cat obtaining food.

Thorndike emphasized that the cats' responses were strengthened because of the past consequences of similar actions. In the past, the effects of actions that unlatched the door were freedom and immediate access to food. Thorndike stated this relationship between the animal's responses and the consequences of its responses as the **law of effect**:

Of several responses made to the same situation, those which are accompanied or closely followed by satisfaction to the animal will, other things being equal, be more firmly connected with the situation, so that, when it [the situation] recurs, they [the responses] will be more likely to recur; those which are accompanied or closely followed by discomfort to the animal will, other things being equal, have their connections with that situation weakened, so that, when it [the situation] recurs, they [the responses] will be less likely to occur. (Thorndike, 1911, p.241)

In a simple sense, Thorndike's principle states that responses that produce pleasant consequences will be strengthened and responses that are not followed by pleasant consequences will be weakened.

Watson and Behaviorism

Although Thorndike began his experiments because he was searching for evidence of mental processes in animals, he created a fundamental principle of learning that refers only to stimuli and responses rather than to mental processes. The law of effect is very much in keeping with the ideas of the first person to call himself a behaviorist, John B. Watson. Watson was extremely outspoken in his belief that psychologists should study only overt (observable) responses, not unobservable mental processes. He wrote, "The time seems to have come when psychology must discard all references to consciousness" (Watson, 1913, p. 163).

Thorndike's description of learning in terms of connections between stimuli and responses appealed to Watson, and Watson's championing of this position did much to focus the study of learning on the role of external environmental factors. Watson believed so strongly that learning was dependent upon the external environment that he wrote, "Give me a dozen healthy infants, well-formed, and my own special world to bring them up in and I'll guarantee to take any one at random and train him to become any type of specialist I might select—doctor, lawyer, artist, merchant-chief, and yes, even beggar-man and thief, regardless of his talents, pen-

B.F. Skinner, noted for his research in operant conditioning, is the best-known American psychologist.

chants, tendencies, abilities, vocations, and race of his ancestors" (Watson, 1924, p. 82). Although contemporary psychologists are still influenced by Watson's viewpoint and writings, few are as extreme in their beliefs about the role of the environment.

Skinner and Operant Behavior

Thorndike and Watson laid the foundations for the work of B.F. Skinner, a radical behaviorist who believes that psychologists should study only observable behavior. Skinner has written, "The objection to inner states is not that they do not exist, but that they are not relevant in a functional analysis" (Skinner, 1953, p. 35). For Skinner the relevant aspect is the experimental analysis of behavior using the operant conditioning paradigm. Like his predecessors, Skinner, in his early work, applied his experimental analysis of behavior to the study of learning in animals (Skinner, 1938); however, he has gone far beyond the ideas of Thorndike and Watson in advocating that the principles of operant conditioning can and should be used for the general improvement of society. For example, in his novel *Walden Two* (Skinner, 1948b), Skinner describes how a utopia based upon operant conditioning could be developed.

In his experimental analysis of behavior, Skinner began by studying the responses of rats and pigeons that had effects upon their environments. He termed these responses **operant behavior**, responses that operate upon the subject's environment. Skinner contrived a very simple environment, an apparatus that soon become known

as a **Skinner box** (see Exhibit 9.2). In the relatively restricted environment of the Skinner box, a rat has only a limited number of ways in which it can operate on its environment. Skinner accepted Thorndike's law of effect but empirically defined satisfying consequences as any stimulus that reliably increases the frequency of the response that precedes it. Thus, Skinner devised a second form of the basic operant conditioning paradigm in which the subject is allowed to operate freely on its environment to obtain certain consequences. Like Thorndike's instrumental conditioning, Skinner's operant conditioning emphasizes the connection between the subject's responses and the consequences of those

EXHIBIT 9.2
Examples of Skinner Boxes for Rats

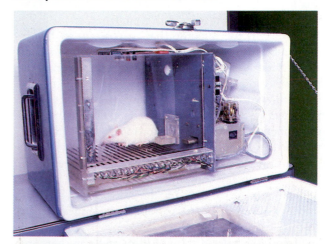

B.F. Skinner invented the Skinner box to study the operant behavior of rats. When the rat presses on the bar, a small amount of food drops into the food cup. The number of times the rat presses the bar is automatically recorded.

Operant behavior, responses that operate upon subjects environment

responses. However, Skinner's procedure removed the need for the discrete trials and allowed the experimenter to vary only the consequences that followed the subject's response.

Focus Question Answer

Does the law of effect influence your study behavior? Yes. When your studying is followed by satisfying consequences (high grades, less anxiety), you are likely to study more in the future. Similarly, when studying is not followed by pleasant consequences, then studying will be less likely in the future.

 ## Reinforcement and Punishment

The consequence of a subject's response in the Skinner box is either a **reinforcer**, any stimulus that strengthens the response that precedes it, or a **punisher**, any stimulus that weakens the response that precedes it. A hungry rat in a Skinner box is more likely to press the bar again when it receives a food pellet immediately after pressing the bar; a rat is less likely to press the bar again if pressing it is followed by foot shock. However, reinforcers and punishers are not stimuli associated only with laboratory experiments. If, after studying for your psychology exam, you earn an A on the test, the likelihood you will study for your next psychology exam will be strengthened. If, on the other hand, you earn an F on the exam, you will be less inclined to study for the next exam. For most students, receiving an A is a reinforcer while receiving an F is a punisher.

Two terms related to reinforcers and punishers are, obviously enough, reinforcement and punishment. **Reinforcement** is the process by which responses are made more likely because of their consequences, and **punishment** is the process by which responses are made less likely because of their consequences. Because Skinner defined these processes in terms of their effects on the future probability of responding, you must observe the effect of a given stimulus to determine if it is acting as a reinforcer or a punisher (Skinner, 1938). For example, is getting a B in a course a reinforcer or punisher? The only way to know is to observe the grade's effect on a student's subsequent performance. If the student studies more, then the B was reinforcing for studying. If the student studies less, the B was a punisher. A reinforcer or punisher cannot be defined independently of its effect on the behavior that precedes it.

Positive and Negative Reinforcers

As Thorndike stated, reinforcers strengthen responses in two ways—by providing satisfaction or by removing discomfort. A **positive reinforcer** is a stimulus whose occurrence increases the probability of the recurrence of a response that precedes it. Positive reinforcers are commonly referred to as rewards. In contrast to positive reinforcers, **negative reinforcers** are stimuli, such as electric shocks, whose removal increases the probability of the recurrence of a response that precedes it. Note that negative reinforcers are *not* the same as punishers. Both positive and negative reinforcers increase the probability that responses that precede them will recur. In contrast, punishers decrease the probability that responses that precede them will recur.

Positive reinforcers are relative to the person receiving them and to the situation in which they occur. Winning $100 in a lottery is not nearly as reinforcing to a person earning $100,000 a year as it is to a person earning $8,000 a year. Similarly, extra free time in the form of a longer recess may be very positively reinforcing to only some school-aged children. Thus, whether a stimulus acts as a positive reinforcement is determined by the context in which it occurs.

In contrast, negative reinforcement occurs when a response ends discomfort. The term *reinforcement* indicates that the response is strengthened, while the term *negative* refers to an unpleasant stimulus that causes discomfort and whose removal is reinforcing. In other words, negative reinforcement occurs when a person responds in order to escape from or avoid an event the person defines as bad. For example, if taking a pain reliever such as aspirin relieves your headache, your response of taking aspirin the next time you have a headache will be strengthened. Relief from your headache negatively reinforces taking aspirin for your headaches. Similarly, if you experience headaches frequently, you may eventually recognize certain situations in which you are likely to get headaches, and you may learn to take aspirin before you encounter these situations. If taking a pain reliever before you get a headache allows you to avoid the discomfort, then operant conditioning through the process of negative reinforcement has occurred, and you will be more likely in the future to take a pain reliever to avoid the possibility of a headache.

When the process of negative reinforcement is involved in people and animals learning to make responses to terminate or escape from an aversive (unpleasant) situation, the learning is called **escape learning. Avoid-**

ance learning, learning a response to prevent the occurrence of an aversive stimulus, is more complex. One explanation (Mowrer, 1947) suggests that both classical and operant conditioning are involved. According to this position, you become classically conditioned to fear headaches in certain situations, and your avoidance response of taking aspirins is negatively reinforced by the removal of the aversive stimulus (the fear of a headache or the expectation of pain). Your behavior of taking aspirin in certain situations before you have a headache is maintained by successful negative reinforcement and is self-perpetuating. As long as you take the aspirin and do not have headaches in those situations, you never have the opportunity to find out if you could have avoided a headache without taking the aspirin.

Can you think of other everyday examples of operant conditioning based on negative reinforcers? Do you know students who diligently finish their math assignments every night in order to avoid reprimands from their math instructors? Or do you know children who find that cleaning their rooms is the only way to stop their parents from constantly reminding them to keep their room in order? Although going to the dentist may involve a certain amount of discomfort, people endure the unpleasantness in order to escape from the pain of a toothache. In each of these examples, the rate of responding increases because people escape or avoid unpleasant stimuli.

Reinforcers establish and maintain specific behaviors through operant conditioning. Identifying the reinforc-

ers that operate in a given situation is often difficult because positive and negative reinforcers may both be present. For instance, not only did Thorndike's cats receive the positive reinforcer of food, but their latch-opening responses were also reinforced negatively when they escaped from the uncomfortable confinement of the puzzle box. A similar situation arises with students' study behaviors. Studying is reinforced positively when a student receives high marks on exams; in addition, the same study behaviors are reinforced negatively if the student avoids low marks on exams. Thus, in analyzing the reinforcers present in operant conditioning situations, you should note if a person's responses are followed by consequences that are satisfying to that individual or by consequences from which the person actively seeks to escape.

Primary and Conditioned Reinforcers

In addition to being classified as positive and negative, reinforcers are also divided into classes of innate and learned. **Primary reinforcers** (such as food, water, oxygen, and the absence of pain) are unlearned, innately reinforcing stimuli. Primary reinforcers are related to physiological needs and survival; for instance, food has more value as a reinforcing stimulus when you are hungry. Researchers who use food as a primary reinforcer in studies of operant conditioning deprive their subjects of food for several hours before the experiment so the subjects will be hungry.

Conditioned reinforcers (or secondary reinforcers) obtain their value through association with primary reinforcers. For example, for laboratory rats, the click of the mechanism when it drops food into the cup in the Skinner box can become a conditioned reinforcer. If bar-pressing is followed by the click of the mechanism, rats will continue to press the bar, although food is no longer given (Bugelski, 1938). For humans, money has been paired with a number of primary reinforcers and has become a potent conditioned reinforcer. In fact, money has been associated so often with so many primary reinforcers that, for most people, it has become a **generalized reinforcer**, a conditioned reinforcer that has value independent of its association with primary reinforcers.

Other examples of conditioned reinforcers are attention, smiles, giving approval, grades, promotions, and poker chips; each has the power to change people's behavior. In one study, subjects increased their use of plural nouns because the experimenter showed approval every

---

Quick Study Aid

Positive and Negative Reinforcers

To avoid confusion between positive and negative reinforcers and between negative reinforcers and punishment, remember that positive and negative reinforcers both increase the probability of a response, while punishment decreases the probability of a response.

REINFORCERS ———) INCREASES IN RESPONDING

Think of "positive" as receiving certain pleasant events; think of "negative" as escaping/avoiding or not getting certain unpleasant events. Therefore, simple definitions of these terms are:

POSITIVE REINFORCEMENT = GETTING "GOODS"
NEGATIVE REINFORCEMENT = NOT GETTING "BADS"

time a subject said a plural noun (Greenspoon, 1955). In the case of poker chips, even animals will work for tokens if they can exchange them for food (Wolfe, 1936). The use of tokens as conditioned reinforcers is discussed in the accompanying *Exploring . . .* section.

Intrinsic and Extrinsic Reinforcers

Reinforcers may also be classified as external events (**extrinsic reinforcers**) or internal events (**intrinsic reinforcers**). Extrinsic reinforcers are external stimuli such as money, approval from others, and grades; intrinsic reinforcers are internal stimuli such as pride, pleasure, and the reduction of anxiety.

Do extrinsic or intrinsic reinforcers provide greater satisfaction? The answer to this question may be different for every individual; however, an interesting study with children offered insights about the relationship between intrinsic and extrinsic reinforcers (Lepper et al., 1973). When young children who liked to draw (for whom drawing was intrinsically reinforcing) were given gold stars (extrinsic reinforcers) for drawing, they would no longer draw unless they were given gold stars. Drawing was altered from a behavior controlled by intrinsic reinforcers to one controlled by extrinsic reinforcers. In other words, the children focused more on the gold stars and less on the internal satisfaction they received from drawing. An analogous situation involves a person who chooses a career because he finds pleasure in the work but who eventually comes to see that he is working only for the money. Such a person may then switch careers because he does not like working only for money. The intrinsic reinforcer of work satisfaction was replaced by the extrinsic reinforcer of money.

On one hand, extrinsic reinforcers are useful in learning new behaviors. Receiving gold stars for practicing the piano may encourage a young child to keep practicing until playing the piano becomes enjoyable. On the other hand, extrinsic reinforcers may undermine behaviors already maintained by intrinsic reinforcers. Researchers offer the following suggestions for the effective use of extrinsic reinforcers (Greene & Lepper, 1974): Use extrinsic reinforcers for behaviors that currently have no intrinsic value to the individual; use small extrinsic reinforcers when needed; and gradually eliminate extrinsic reinforcers as a behavior becomes intrinsically reinforcing.

The Premack Principle

The effectiveness of reinforcers is relative to the person receiving them and to the situation in which they occur.

EXHIBIT 9.3
The Premack Principle
Rank these activities from most preferred (1) to least preferred (20). Higher ranked items can be used as reinforcements to increase the rate of lower ranked items.

_15_ Caring for pets		___ Doing aerobic exercises
_19_ Playing video games		___ Bowling
___ Doing laundry		___ Reading
___ Eating snacks		___ Doing dishes
___ Watching television		___ Swimming
___ Vacuuming		___ Writing an assignment
___ Studying		___ Going to the movies
___ Gardening		___ Cooking a meal
___ Listening to music		___ Washing a car
___ Making a bed		___ Taking a walk

Food is a potent primary reinforcer when you are hungry but not after you have just eaten a large meal. Earning a B on a test may be a positive reinforcer for a student who has earned only C's previously and a punisher for another student who has earned only A's. Psychologists studying the relativity of reinforcers have also discovered that the opportunity to engage in certain behaviors is intrinsically (internally) reinforcing and that the intrinsic value of different behaviors varies from person to person (Premack, 1965). For example, watching television may have high intrinsic value for one person, while another individual may not care to watch TV. Rank the behaviors in Exhibit 9.3 to discover some of your personal preferences.

Psychologist David Premack (1965) discovered that more highly preferred behaviors can be used to reinforce less highly preferred behaviors, a principle now known as **Premack's principle**. Premack demonstrated his principle with school children, pinball machines, and chocolate candy. Some of the children preferred playing pinball to eating chocolate, while the opposite was true for the other children. Premack made the opportunity to engage in the more-preferred behavior contingent on performing the less-preferred behavior. When children who preferred eating chocolate could earn the opportunity to do so by playing pinball, their rate of pinball playing increased. Similarly, when children who preferred playing pinball could earn the opportunity to do so by eating chocolate, their rate of eating chocolate increased. Recently, in an updated version of Premack's experiment, children's behaviors were changed by making the op-

Exploring . . .

Tokens as Conditioned Reinforcers

An interesting series of studies that illustrates why money is so powerful as a conditioned reinforcer was performed in the 1930s (Wolfe, 1936; Cowles, 1937). Chimpanzees were trained first to insert poker chips (analogous to money) into a "Chimp-O-Mat" vending machine that dispensed small amounts of grapes or raisins, a procedure that effectively paired the poker chips with food. After sufficient pairings with food, the poker chips became conditioned reinforcers that could be used to establish or maintain a variety of behaviors in the chimps.

In a typical experiment, after the tokens had become conditioned reinforcers, a chimp would have to work to obtain chips and then wait until later to exchange the tokens for food. For the chimpanzees, the tokens retained their reinforcing value for delays of an hour or more. The poker chips became conditioned reinforcers not because they continued to be directly associated with food but because they could be exchanged for food. Like money for humans, the chips became generalized reinforcers for the chimps. The animals would hoard the tokens, even when they could not be exchanged for food. In addition, the chimps would work as hard lifting a heavy weight in exchange for tokens as they would for obtaining food directly. They were able to discriminate between tokens that would operate the vending machine and those that would not; and, when given a choice, they would choose tokens that could be exchanged for two pieces of food rather than tokens that could be exchanged for only one piece of food (Wolfe, 1936).

This experiment is analogous to many people's work conditions. You may work for a week, two weeks. or a month before receiving your paycheck (tokens). Your paycheck, like the poker chips, has value because you can exchange it for primary reinforcers. You may save a certain portion of each paycheck and gain satisfaction from knowing that you have money in the bank. Although you may never spend the money in your savings account for primary reinforcers, ultimately the value of the money comes from its potential for obtaining primary reinforcers.

The laboratory research on the effectiveness of tokens as conditioned reinforcers has been applied to clinical and educational settings as well. For example, **token economies**, situations in which a token ex-

Chimpanzees can be taught to work for tokens that they can exchange for fruit in a "Chimp-O-Mat."

change system functions similarly to a monetary economy, have been established in hospital mental wards (Ayllon & Azrin, 1965). In a typical token economy, the tokens can be exchanged for desirable items such as snacks, opportunities to watch TV, and weekend passes. Patients earn the tokens by engaging in socially constructive behaviors such as dressing themselves, participating in activities, and interacting with others in socially acceptable ways. Although the token economy does not necessarily overcome the patients' problems, patients who were previously very dependent upon others for their care become more self-sufficient and more socially competent (Ayllon & Azrin, 1965). Token economies are also common in elementary classrooms, where tokens such as marbles may be earned for behaving in appropriate ways. The tokens may then be exchanged for special treats, extra recess time, and other desirable items. The tokens are usually earned easily, but they may also be taken away for inappropriate behavior. As these examples illustrate, what began as interesting laboratory studies of learning in chimpanzees has been helpful in improving human lives.

portunity to play video games contingent on behaving in appropriate ways (Buckalew & Buckalew, 1983).

For years, parents have applied the Premack principle without knowing its name. Did your parents ever say to you, "If you eat all your spinach, you may have dessert"? You can apply the Premack Principle to your own behavior, but be certain to arrange the contingency in the correct order. For example, if in Exhibit 9.3 you ranked listening to music first and studying sixteenth, you could increase your amount of studying by reinforcing yourself with listening to your favorite music for thirty minutes for every two hours you study.

Positive and Negative Punishers

In operant conditioning, punishment differs from reinforcement. With reinforcement, you actively seek the consequences of your responses—obtaining satisfaction and removing discomfort. With punishment, you do not actively seek the unavoidable, unpleasant consequences. Instead, you receive punishers (either self-administered or administered by others) after behaving in inappropriate or undesirable ways. Punishers suppress the recurrence of inappropriate behavior because you learn to avoid making responses that are followed by punishing consequences. Skinner (1953) has suggested that reinforcement and punishment involve the same operations used in opposite ways. Positive reinforcement is the addition of pleasant consequences after a response, and in a reverse way negative punishment is the withholding or removal of pleasant consequences following a response. Negative reinforcement is the removal of unpleasant consequences after a response; positive punishment is the addition of unpleasant consequences following a response. Therefore, **positive punishers** are stimuli such as spankings, verbal reprimands, and electric shocks, and **negative punishers** are stimuli such as removal of privileges, loss of money, and withdrawal of food; the occurrence of either type of stimuli decreases the probability that responses that precede them will recur (Logan & Wagner, 1965).

Parents often use punishment to suppress inappropriate behavior in their children. Perhaps as a child you received a spanking for playing in the street. The spanking was an effective positive punisher if it decreased the probability of your playing in the street again. When you were older, your parents may have withheld certain privileges, such as watching TV, dating, or use of a car, in an attempt to suppress inappropriate behavior. Again, these negative punishers were effective only if they de-

Quick Study Aid

Positive and Negative Punishers

Remember these phrases to distinguish between reinforcers and punishers and between positive and negative punishers:

REINFORCERS ———) INCREASES IN RESPONDING
PUNISHERS ———) DECREASES IN RESPONDING

POSITIVE PUNISHMENT = GETTING "BADS"
NEGATIVE PUNISHMENT = NOT GETTING "GOODS"

creased the probability of your engaging in the inappropriate behavior.

The Use of Punishment

Undoubtedly you can recall times when your parents' use of punishment was ineffective. To be most effective, punishers should be given consistently and immediately after each undesirable response (Schwartz, 1984). Spraying your pet cat with water from a squirt gun to stop it from clawing your furniture will produce the most effective conditioning if you are able to squirt the cat immediately every time it begins to claw. If the cat is only occasionally squirted for clawing or if the squirt is delivered after the cat has finished clawing, the cat's clawing behavior will be less effectively reduced.

In addition to not always being effective, punishment can also result in negative side effects (Newsom et al., 1983). First, punishment encourages escape and avoidance behavior. As a child, you may have run away from home to escape punishment. Or, having your hand slapped for taking cookies from the cookie jar without permission may have taught you to avoid the punishment by sneaking cookies when no one was around. In a similar manner, paying traffic fines for speeding may teach some adults to avoid the tickets by installing radar detectors in their cars.

Second, punishment, especially severe forms, causes generalized suppression of responses. For example, a student who is harshly reprimanded by a teacher for talking without permission may not only stop talking inappropriately in class but may also hesitate to talk at any time during the class. Third, if appropriate behavior is not reinforced while the inappropriate behavior is punished, other inappropriate behaviors may take the place of the behavior suppressed by punishment. For instance, a pet owner who has effectively punished her cat's clawing on the front of the sofa without reinforcing appropriate clawing on a clawing post may be chagrined to discover that the cat begins to claw the back of the sofa!

Fourth, delivering punishment often reinforces the person who does the punishing. For example, a parent who effectively suppresses a child's inappropriate behavior with a spanking removes the child's unpleasant behavior (a negative reinforcer) and at the same time receives the satisfaction of getting his or her way (a positive reinforcer). Under these conditions, persons being punished may also learn vicariously to use punishment to obtain similar reinforcers for themselves. Unfortunately, the punished person frequently learns aggressive actions, such as hitting and slapping. Thus, parents who use aggressive forms of punishment may inadvertently be teaching their children to act aggressively. Although punishment may be the most effective way to eliminate inappropriate behavior, most psychologists have followed Skinner's lead in emphasizing the use of reinforcers rather than punishers to change behavior (Skinner, 1953).

Focus Question Answer

How do positive and negative reinforcers shape your study behavior? You may study to obtain extrinsic positive reinforcers such as good grades and praise from your instructor and intrinsic positive reinforcers such as internal feelings of satisfaction and pleasure from learning. However, your study behavior may also be maintained by negative reinforcers such as avoiding poor grades and avoiding the anxiety that comes from being unprepared. Most of the positive reinforcers that maintain studying are conditioned, or learned, reinforcers. Reinforcing your study behavior with the opportunity to enjoy your favorite snack involves both a primary reinforcer and the Premack principle.

 Acquisition and Extinction

Acquiring new behaviors or maintaining old ones through operant conditioning follows the same procedures whether the conditioning occurs in a Skinner box or in your own home. Maintaining already-existing behaviors is generally easier than acquiring new ones because the behaviors already occur from time to time, affording an opportunity for reinforcement. Thus, maintaining existing study habits is easier than acquiring new ones because you already engage in those study behaviors from time to time. When the behavior you want to acquire occurs rarely or not at all, you have few, if any, opportunities for reinforcing the behavior.

Shaping and Chaining

Skinner encountered this problem when he attempted to train a rat to press a bar in a Skinner box to obtain a food pellet. Rats do not naturally engage in bar-pressing. Skinner shortened the time the rat needed to acquire the bar-pressing response by first reinforcing any response even remotely close to the desired response. At first, whenever the rat came close to the bar, it received a food pellet. When the rat was earning many pellets by staying close to the bar, Skinner withheld the reinforcer until the rat made a closer approximation (e.g., putting its head above the bar) to the bar-pressing response. Gradually, through reinforcing **successive approximations** to the desired response, Skinner trained the rat to press the bar. The process of reinforcing successive approximations to the desired response until the desired response is acquired is called **shaping**.

Shaping is used by animal trainers, teachers, and parents and can be used by anyone trying to acquire a new behavior. Some behaviors can be shaped within a few days or weeks, but others may take years. For instance, while you can quickly shape better study habits, Olympic ice skaters may require years of practice to shape their athletic skills. Operant conditioning and the process of shaping are illustrated in the toilet training procedures described in the accompanying *Exploring . . .* section.

Chaining   During acquisition of operant responses, several responses may be acquired in a specific sequence. This process of training a sequence of actions is called **chaining**. For example, a dolphin might be trained to perform a sequence of actions in which it first jumps high in the air, then jumps through a hoop, then pulls a dog on a raft, and finally tosses a ball through a hoop. The training of this sequence of behaviors is accomplished by first training the last response in the sequence and then working backwards. First, the dolphin learns to toss a ball through a hoop to obtain a fish to eat. Because of its association with the primary reinforcer of the fish, tossing the ball becomes a conditioned reinforcer that may then be used to reinforce learning to pull the raft. Next, pulling the raft becomes a conditioned reinforcer for jumping through a hoop (as well as a discriminative

Shaping Toilet Training Behaviors

Traditional toilet training often involves putting a toddler on a potty chair during likely urination or defecation times. When urination occurs, the parent praises or otherwise rewards the child and allows him or her to leave the potty. When the child takes too long or has "an accident," the parent may scold or sometimes spank the child.

Traditional techniques take much time and effort, create considerable parent-child conflict, result in anxiety for and tantrums by a frustrated child, and are accompanied by many "accidents." Even when the child is nearly successfully toilet trained, parents must still help the child get to the potty, clean up afterwards, and pull the child's pants up.

To eliminate these problems, behaviorists Nathan Azrin and Richard Foxx (1976) have developed for children who are at least twenty months old (with faster acquisition for children who are at least twenty-six months old) an operant conditioning technique in which the average child can be toilet trained in less than four hours. The psychologists call their training "toilet educating" because the children learn to perform all related toileting behaviors by themselves. The technique involves providing optimal learning conditions, shaping, using primary and conditioned reinforcers, and modeling.

The following tips are based on information contained in the book *Toilet Training in Less than a Day* (Azrin & Foxx, 1976):

— On the day toilet training is to be accomplished, provide an environment with minimal distractions. Other family members should be away on an outing, and the instructing parent should devote the day to the task at hand.

— To provide as many training opportunities as possible, have the child frequently drink beverages. The authors suggest that the child should consume at least eight ounces of liquid per hour.

— Offer small rewards when the child accomplishes correct steps in the procedures. The authors suggest using drinks, small candies, and, especially, salty treats such as potato chips and pretzels. The salty treats will encourage the child to consume more liquids.

— Initially, give praise for each step that the child follows. Later, reserve approval only for remaining dry and for using the potty correctly. Initially, frequently remind the child to check for dryness and see if he or she wants to use the potty. Later the child will use self-reminding.

— Before the toilet-training day, allow the child to observe parents and siblings engaged in toilet behaviors. On the toilet-training day, begin by having the child carry out all the toilet-training procedures with a doll that can wet. This step allows the child to benefit from observational learning and to clarify what the parent wants the child to do. The child can give the doll a drink, place it on the potty, make it urinate, give it praise and a small treat. With the doll, the child can also model inappropriate behavior such as pants-wetting.

— Have the child wear loose-fitting pants. Every few minutes ask the child to check to see if the pants are dry. If the pants are dry, give the child a treat.

— When the pants are wet, tell the child to change his or her own clothing. Avoid nagging and spanking.

— Begin with prompted potty trials that last until the child urinates or until ten minutes elapse. Throughout the day, gradually remove the prompting. Reinforce successful potty trials with praise, drinks, and treats. Teach the child to empty the potty and reinforce this action.

— Once the child is successful, switch the reinforcers from external to internal rewards, thereby allowing the child to feel "big," successful, competent, and independent.

Azrin and Foxx (1976) claim that their method reduces "accidents" by 90 percent at the end of the day and by 99 percent at the end of the week. Further, the authors maintain, some parents find that the child generalizes toilet-training to other aspects of daily life and increases self-feeding and self-dressing behaviors too.

Can toilet training really be accomplished in less than a day? Yes, if you pick the right day. If your child is not ready for toilet training, postpone the procedure for a few weeks, and make a renewed attempt at a later time. Even if training is not successful in less than a day, these procedures contain good advice. They are based on sound conditioning principles that emphasize positive reinforcement rather than punishment in helping a child acquire this important behavior.

Through the process of chaining, this duck was taught to perform a series of behaviors that resemble piano playing.

stimulus for tossing the ball). Finally, the dolphin learns to jump into the air. Each behavior serves as a conditioned reinforcer for the preceding response and a discriminative stimulus for the response which follows it. The chain of behaviors ends finally with the dolphin receiving the primary reinforcer of a fish to eat. The next time you see a trained animal at the circus or amusement park, remember that the trainer first conditioned the last response in the chain of behaviors involved in the trick.

Stimulus Generalization and Discrimination

In operant conditioning, **stimulus generalization** occurs when a response reinforced in the presence of a specific stimulus is also made to similar stimuli. For example, if pigeons are trained to peck a key in the presence of a red light, they will generalize their key pecking to similar situations involving red lights. The less similar the other red lights are to the original red light, the less likely the pigeons will be to peck the key. Stimulus generalization is prevalent outside the laboratory as well. Drivers reinforced for stopping in the presence of stop signs experience stimulus generalization when they apply the brakes whether the stop sign is newly erected and bright red or

old and faded. However, you may have noted that if the stop sign is old, faded, and bent, the tendency to come to a complete stop is weakened.

Stimulus discrimination occurs when a response reinforced in the presence of a specific stimulus is not reinforced in the presence of other stimuli. If pigeons are reinforced with food when they peck a key in the presence of a red light but do not receive food when they press a bar in the presence of a blue light, they will learn to discriminate and press the bar only when the red light is on. The red light becomes a discriminative stimulus for the availability of a reinforcer. You have undoubtedly learned many stimulus discriminations. For example, you probably do not insert coins into copy machines when the out-of-order sign is lit because you discriminate between functioning and nonfunctioning copy machines.

Factors Affecting Acquisition

Generally, acquisition of operant responses is faster when the reinforcer is larger (Wagner, 1961) and the delay between the desired response and the delivery of the reinforcer is shorter (Perin, 1943). The timing of the delivery of the reinforcer is especially important. For example, when rats learn to press a bar for a food reinforcer, even a few seconds' delay between the bar-press response and the delivery of the food greatly reduces the amount of learning, and delays of a minute or longer result in very little learning. In delay of reinforcement, responses the subject makes during the delay interval are critical. According to conditioning principles, a reinforcer will strengthen the response that immediately precedes the reinforcer. Thus, during the time of delay, if the subject makes responses incompatible with the response being trained, then the incompatible responses will be reinforced. For instance, if a rat stands on its hind legs to look out of the Skinner box during the delay interval, the rat will be reinforced for standing on its hind legs, a response that is incompatible with bar pressing. Learning of the desired response will be impaired because the subject learns incompatible responses.

Schedules of Reinforcement

A major factor affecting the acquisition of an operant response is the schedule of reinforcement, the schedule of when a reinforcer will be given for making a response. Acquisition occurs most quickly on a **continuous reinforcement** schedule, in which every response is followed by a reinforcer. On **partial reinforcement** (or intermittent) schedules, not every response is reinforced, and therefore the response is acquired more slowly. In the laboratory, conditions are easily arranged to provide continuous reinforcement. However, in the everyday world, partial reinforcement schedules are much more common than are continuous reinforcement schedules.

Many different schedules are possible, but all can be classified into two categories—those in which delivery of the reinforcer is based on the *number of responses* (ratio schedules) and those in which the schedule is based on the *time* between available reinforcers (interval schedules). Pay based on a piece rate (e.g., receiving a set amount of pay for every bushel of apples picked) is an example of a ratio schedule, while pay based on an hourly rate is equivalent to an interval schedule. In the first case, you determine the amount of money you will earn by the *number of responses* you make; in the second case, the amount of money you earn is a function of the amount of *time* you spend working.

Ratio and interval schedules can be either fixed or variable. On a **fixed ratio** (FR) schedule of reinforcement, the number of responses necessary to obtain a reinforcer is constant or fixed. For example, when you receive a candy bar each time you put coins in a vending machine, you operate under a fixed ratio of one response for one reinforcement (FR-1). An FR-1 is the same as continuous reinforcement—every correct response is reinforced. All other schedules are partial reinforcement schedules. In a Skinner box, a rat on an FR-6 schedule

EXHIBIT 9.4
Responding on a Fixed Ratio Schedule

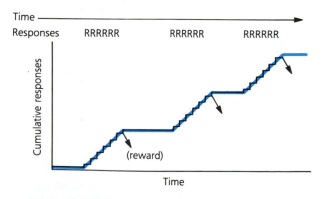

Fixed ratio schedules of reinforcement yield a characteristic response curve, in which the subject responds rapidly and steadily until it receives a reinforcement, at which time the subject pauses briefly.

Source: Adapted from Logan, F.A. 1970. *Fundamentals of learning and motivation.* Dubuque, IA: W.C. Brown. Figure 16, p. 87.

EXHIBIT 9.5
Responding on a Fixed Interval Schedule

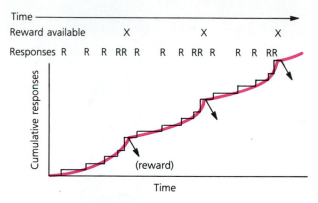

On a fixed interval schedule of reinforcement, reward is available after fixed intervals of time. The response curve shows a pause after receiving reinforcement and then an increasing frequency of responding as the time for the next reinforcement approaches. A continuous line drawn across the discrete steps made by each response yields a scalloped curve characteristic of responding on a fixed interval schedule.

Source: Adapted from Logan, F.A. 1970. *Fundamentals of learning and motivation.* Dubuque, IA: W.C. Brown. Figure 14, p. 85.

would have to press the bar six times before being given a food pellet. Under these conditions, rats learn to respond at a rapid but steady rate until they make the correct number of responses (see Exhibit 9.4).

The response rate on a **fixed interval** (FI) schedule, in which the amount of time before a response will produce a reinforcement is constant or fixed, is quite different from the rate on an FR schedule (see Exhibit 9.5). A typical fixed interval schedule for a pigeon in a Skinner might be an FI-15 seconds. If the pigeon could tell time, it would wait 15 seconds, peck the disk once, and receive its food. Can pigeons tell time? In a sense, yes; based on their performance in the Skinner box, pigeons are able to judge the passage of time. They do not respond immediately after being reinforced, but as the time at which food will again be available nears, their rate of responding increases. As is illustrated in Exhibit 9.5, the result is a cumulative response record with a characteristic scalloped effect. The scallop results from a slow rate of response at the start of the interval with an increasing rate of response throughout the interval and is distinctive of responding on a fixed interval schedule.

Unlike reinforcers in fixed schedules, reinforcers in variable schedules are available after unpredictable num-

EXHIBIT 9.6
Responding on a Variable Ratio Schedule

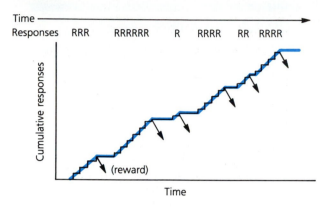

On a variable ratio schedule, the number of responses necessary to obtain a reinforcement varies unpredictably. The response curve for a variable ratio schedules produces the same high, steady rate of responding observed on a fixed ratio schedule, but the subject pauses for a shorter period of time after each reinforcement.

Source: Adapted from Logan, F.A. 1970. *Fundamentals of learning and motivation.* Dubuque, IA: W.C. Brown. Figure 17, p. 88.

bers of responses or intervals of time. On a **variable ratio** (VR) schedule, such as a VR 5-1, five bar presses may or may not produce a reinforcer for a rat in a Skinner box. Instead, one bar press might be followed by food and then the rat might press the bar seven times before receiving more food. On the average, however, the rat would receive a food reinforcer for every five bar presses. In other words, if you added together all the rat's bar presses and divided that number by all the rat's reinforcements, the ratio of bar presses to reinforcements would average five to one. Because the availability of reinforcement is unpredictable, the best response strategy on a variable ratio schedule is responding rapidly and steadily. However, as is illustrated in Exhibit 9.6, the subject often pauses after receiving the reinforcer but resumes responding more quickly than on a fixed ratio schedule. The classic example of a VR schedule is playing a slot machine; because payoffs occur after unpredictable numbers of responses, experienced players respond at a high, steady rate with only a brief pause after a payoff.

On a **variable interval** (VI) schedule, reinforcers are available after unpredictable amounts of time. A VI-20 schedule indicates that, on the average, a reinforcement is available every 20 seconds; however, another reinforcement may be available immediately after the previous one, or it may not be available until after a much longer interval. Dividing the total amount of elapsed

time between available reinforcements by the total reinforcements received will yield a value equal to the variable schedule. Responding on a VI schedule occurs at a relatively low but steady rate (see Exhibit 9.7). The rate is low because responding immediately after receiving a reinforcement is not always reinforced; the rate is steady because steadiness assures the subject of receiving every reinforcement soon after it becomes available. If you have ever taken a course in which the instructor gave "pop" quizzes at random times, you have directly experienced a variable interval schedule. The best strategy, when confronted with "pop" quizzes, is to study a little each day (a relatively low but steady rate of responding).

Extinction

In operant conditioning, extinction occurs when an operant behavior is no longer followed by a reinforcer. How quickly the response is extinguished depends upon which reinforcement schedule was used to establish and maintain the response. Continuously reinforced behaviors (FR-1) extinguish more quickly than do partially reinforced behaviors. Also, behaviors maintained on fixed schedules extinguish more rapidly than do behaviors reinforced on variable schedules. The reasons for these differences will be explored in the following section on the partial reinforcement effect.

EXHIBIT 9.7
Responding on a Variable Interval Schedule

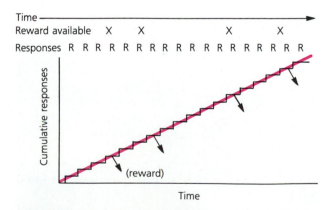

On a variable interval schedule, reinforcement is available after unpredictable intervals of time. As this graph indicates, the result is a low but constant rate of responding.

Source: Adapted from Logan, F.A. 1970. *Fundamentals of learning and motivation.* Dubuque, IA: W.C. Brown. Figure 15, p. 86.

Just as in classical conditioning, once an operant response has been extinguished, the response may reappear—an effect called spontaneous recovery. For example, a rat in which bar-pressing has been extinguished may begin pressing the bar again when returned to the Skinner box. In a similar manner, if you are accustomed to leaving a building by a specific exit but discover that the door is locked, you will stop trying to use that door. However, after a few weeks of using a different exit, you may once again try the former exit just to see if the door is unlocked.

The Research Process: The Partial Reinforcement Effect

Another interesting operant conditioning phenomenon is the **partial reinforcement effect (PRE)**, the greater resistance to extinction of responses established or main-

> ### Quick Study Aid
>
> ## Schedules of Reinforcement
>
> Use the following aids to remember important points about reinforcement schedules.
>
> **RATIO & RESPONSES**
>
> Both ratio and responses begin with R; ratio schedules are determined by number of responses necessary to obtain a reinforcer.
>
> **INTERVAL & INTERMISSIONS**
>
> Both intervals and intermissions are time periods; interval schedules are determined by the elapsed time or intermissions between available reinforcers.

While still fishing from a pier provides an example of a variable interval (VI) reinforcement schedule, fly casting provides an example of a variable ratio (VR) reinforcement schedule.

tained with partial reinforcement schedules. The PRE is of interest to psychologists for both theoretical and practical reasons. Theoretically, responses that are more consistently reinforced should be stronger, and the tendency of a response to persist during extinction should be a measure of its strength. The PRE directly contradicts this theoretical expectation—less consistently reinforced responses persist longer during extinction. Practically, to the extent that operant conditioning procedures can be used to modify the behavior of clients in therapy, shaping more effective behaviors that are resistant to extinction is of extreme importance.

In a typical research study demonstrating the PRE (Boren, 1961), six groups of rats were trained on different fixed ratio schedules (FR-1, FR-3, FR-6, FR-10, FR-15, and FR-21). Initially, all rats were deprived of food and all were trained to press the bar on an FR-1 schedule (continuous reinforcement). Then the control group remained on the FR-1 schedule while the other groups were shifted to their final schedules. Each group received 500 reinforcements on its final schedule before extinction began. Exhibit 9.8 shows the average number of responses made by each group during one hour of extinction. The more responses the rats made per reinforcement during acquisition, the more persistent bar pressing was during extinction. The less consistently bar pressing was reinforced during acquisition, the more resistant it was to extinction.

Essentially the same results were obtained in another study that used pigeons and variable ratio schedules (Hearst, 1961). Four pigeons were trained to peck a lighted response key. The apparatus could be pro-

the frequency of a response (salivation or key pecking) is increased or maintained by the presence of a reinforcing stimulus (meat powder or a food pellet), and in each case the subject's behavior comes under **stimulus control**. In classical conditioning, the conditioned stimulus controls the occurrence of the conditioned response. In operant conditioning, stimuli that signal the availability of a reinforcer (called **discriminative stimuli**) control the occurrence of operant responding.

For example, the sound made by an electric can opener can signal to a cat that if the cat runs to the kitchen, it will be fed. You may recall that the situation of a cat and a can opener was also used as an example that loosely fit the classical conditioning paradigm (the sound = the CS; running toward the food = the CR; sight of food = the US). Thus, the two paradigms share a common sequence of events. In classical conditioning, the sequence of events is CS —⟩ CR —⟩ US; in operant conditioning, the sequence is discriminative stimulus —⟩ conditioned operant response —⟩ reinforcing stimulus. The CS and discriminative stimulus exert stimulus control over the occurrence of a response; the response is followed by a stimulus, which reinforces the learning in the situation.

In both classical and operant conditioning, animals and people learn to respond to a stimulus (either a CS or discriminative stimulus) and learn what the consequence of that response will be (the occurrence of the US or reinforcing stimulus). The classical conditioning paradigm focuses on learning to make a response, while the operant conditioning paradigm focuses on learning the consequences of making a response. Yet both paradigms arise from a common sequence of events in which preceding stimuli signal making responses in anticipation of stimuli that will follow those responses.

Animals will most easily learn and retain tasks that reflect their natural abilities. Raccoons who have been taught to use plastic tokens to obtain food often revert to their natural instinct of washing food, and they begin washing the tokens. Hogs, which have strong rooting abilities, can be taught to locate truffles or to detect drugs and explosives.

Limitations of Operant Conditioning

Just as certain combinations of stimuli and responses can be classically conditioned and others cannot, limitations also exist for operant conditioning. Because of biological limitations, certain behaviors are impossible to establish with operant conditioning. Obviously, training a pigeon to bark for food is physically impossible. Beyond such obvious biological constraints, each species is predisposed to learn certain responses with ease and other responses with difficulty (Seligman, 1970). These predispositions exist on a continuum, specific to each species, which varies in the degree of **preparedness** (innate tendency to display specific behaviors) to make certain

responses. Raccoons, for example, exhibit high preparedness to use their paws to obtain food; among a variety of food-gathering behaviors, they instinctively hold food in their paws and wash the food before eating it. On the other hand, raccoons appear to be ill-prepared to use their noses to root food out of the ground. Hogs, however, innately root for food with their snouts but are ill-prepared to use their feet to manipulate it.

Many early behaviorists assumed that all responses possess equal potential for operant conditioning. However, the idea of varying degrees of preparedness contradicts the concept that any response can be conditioned by any reinforcer. The research of psychologists Keller and Marion Breland (1961, 1966), was especially important in establishing that responses compatible with responses the animal is instinctively prepared to make are easily conditioned, while incompatible responses are not. Working with thirty-eight different species—6,000 individual animals—the Brelands used operant conditioning techniques to train animals for entertainment purposes. For example, the Brelands trained a pig to carry a wooden coin in its mouth and to deposit the coin in a piggy bank; for doing this, the pig received food. Although the pig learned to perform the task, the animal eventually began to display behaviors more typical of the way pigs eat. The pig would drop the coin, push it with its snout, pick it up again, and toss it into the air. The Brelands called this return-to-species behavior when other behaviors are being reinforced **instinctive drift**. The pig drifted back to instinctive pig behaviors, even when doing so delayed receiving the food reinforcer.

The Brelands observed instinctive drift in other species with which they worked. For example, a raccoon trained to pick up a coin and drop it into a container eventually began to rub the coin against the sides of the container but would not drop it (Breland & Breland, 1961). In each case of instinctive drift, the animal reverted to behaviors for which it is instinctively prepared. Examples such as these from the Brelands' work demonstrate that the operant conditioning of responses is biologically constrained by the species' degree of preparedness to make a particular response.

Focus Question Answer

Why do people become superstitious? Superstitious behaviors are strengthened by the accidental occurrence of reinforcers (or punishers) after a specific response. If, after crossing your fingers for luck on an exam, you experience good luck by earning an A, you will be more likely to cross your fingers before the next exam, even though the amount of studying you did would be a better explanation for the grade you earned. Superstitious behaviors are often maintained not so much by the presence of good luck as by the absence of bad luck. If you knock on wood and nothing bad happens, knocking on wood is negatively reinforced by the absence of bad events.

▤ Cognitive Paradigms

The study of learning using classical and operant conditioning paradigms focuses on environmental stimuli and observable responses made by animals and people.

For many years, emphasis on external factors the behaviorists' obscured the work of cognitive psychologists, who study how a person's or animal's internal knowledge about the world influences what that person or animal learns. In this section you will read about several ways in which cognitive factors in learning have been investigated.

Latent Learning and Expectancies

A learning theorist who believed that learning is more than conditioning of stimulus-response connections was Edward C. Tolman (1886–1959). Tolman believed that when an animal or a person learns, the individual acquires understanding of the situation, knowledge that can be retained for future use (Tolman, 1932). This acquired knowledge (learning represented as thoughts or cognitions) is stored until the animal or person has a purpose for using the knowledge. Tolman and an associate, C.H. Honzik, demonstrated that rats that had been placed in a maze without food reinforcement retained knowledge of the maze (Tolman & Honzik, 1930). When these rats were given food at the end of the maze, their average number of errors quickly fell to match the errors made by a group of rats that had been reinforced in the maze throughout training (see Exhibit 9.10). The rats' performances did not reflect their knowledge until they had a purpose for reaching the goal box. The rats' knowledge was latent (present but not visible) until reinforcement began; therefore, this type of learning is called **latent learning**.

Tolman interpreted the results of his many studies with maze learning as evidence that animals form **cognitive maps**, mental representations of the environment (Tolman et al., 1946). He found that rats that had received food in the goal box of a maze would try a different path to the goal when the original path was blocked. Although they had never tried the new path before, the rats chose a route that brought them close to the goal box. Tolman concluded that the rats were goal-oriented, not response-oriented, and that they used their cognitive maps to move as closely as possible to the place at which they expected to find food. Tolman called the learned expectancies involved with cognitive maps **place learning**. Tolman proposed that subjects not only acquire expectancies (knowledge) about places but also about temporal relationships. Thus, Tolman believed that in classical and operant conditioning, animals and people actively acquire expectancies about places or the relationships of different events in time, rather than pas-

EXHIBIT 9.10
A Demonstration of Latent Learning

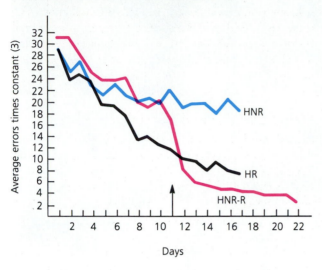

The maze performance of three groups of rats is plotted in this graph. Group HNR was hungry and received no reinforcement in the maze; these rats learned very slowly and continued to make many errors. Group HR was hungry and received food in the goal box of the maze; these subjects learned more rapidly than did Group HNR, and, after ten trials, made significantly fewer errors than Group HNR. Group HNR-R was hungry and received no food in the goal box during the first 10 trials, but received food on each trial thereafter. Group HNR-R's performance matched that of Group HNR as long as these rats received no food in the goal box; however, as soon as Group HNR-R received food in the goal box (on the eleventh trial), its performance quickly matched and surpassed that of Group HR. These results clearly demonstrate that Group HNR-R learned about the maze during the first ten trials but did not display that learning until after the eleventh trial, when food became available in the goal box.

Source: Tolman, E.C. & Honzik, C.H. 1930. Introduction and removal of reward, and maze performance in rats. *University of California Publications in Psychology, 4,* 257–275.

sively acquiring associations between stimuli and responses (Tolman, 1932).

Observational Learning

Tolman's research strongly indicated that animals and people can learn without being directly reinforced. The knowledge (cognitive expectancies, according to Tolman) you gain without direct reinforcement is acquired through observation of the world around you. **Observational learning**, also called **modeling** or **imitation**, occurs when you acquire skills and behaviors by observing and imitating others.

According to Albert Bandura (1977), a leading theorist and researcher in this area, neither direct performance of the behavior nor reinforcement is necessary for observational learning to occur. This type of learning forms the foundation for social learning theory as described in Chapter 15.

The basic features of observational learning are illustrated in a classic study by Bandura and his colleagues (Bandura et al., 1963). Four-year-olds were brought to a laboratory setting, where they observed one of three conditions of modeled aggression. In one condition, children observed real models (adult actors) hitting and kicking a large inflated doll; in a second condition, children saw the same actions on film; in a third condition, children saw a filmed cartoon character duplicate these actions. A fourth group of children was not exposed to any modeling of aggression. Observations of these children in a playroom setting showed that children from the three experimental conditions behaved more aggressively than children from the control group, but those who observed the real life model and the filmed model exhibited more aggressive behavior than did those who observed the cartoon character. None of the models or children were reinforced, and none of the children displayed aggressive behavior during the observation period. Yet their later performance in the playroom demonstrated clearly that they could imitate the specific aggressive actions that had been modeled earlier.

A second and similar study (Bandura, 1965) further clarifies the learning and performance distinction made by Tolman and social learning theorists such as Bandura. In this experiment, three groups of preschoolers watched films of aggressive models beating up on the inflated doll. However, in this study, one group of children watched an aggressive model who was rewarded with candy, pop, and praise; the second group watched an aggressive model who was punished with a scolding and a spanking for acting aggressively; and the third group watched a model who was neither reinforced nor punished for acting aggressively. Observing the model being punished effectively suppressed later imitation of the model's aggressive behavior by the children in the punished-model group; compared to the children's behavior in the other two groups, these children displayed fewer aggressive behaviors in the playroom. However, when all the children were offered rewards (stickers and fruit juice) for imitating the filmed model's behavior, all did so at relatively high levels and at similar rates. In other words, they all had learned from observation how to act aggressively, even the children who had seen the punished model.

Complex behaviors such as violin bow positioning, swimming strokes, and tennis swings are learned efficiently through the process of modeling.

Bandura effectively demonstrated that neither reinforcement nor an immediately observable response is necessary for learning to occur.

Peer models (such as colleagues, classmates, and best friends), expert models (such as parents, teachers, and professionals), and symbolic models (such as television characters and cartoon figures) are especially effective models. Even animals can learn from observing other members of their species and, in certain cases, from observing humans. Cats that frequently observed other cats obtaining food from a revolving turntable (a difficult task for a cat) quickly mastered the task compared to cats that had only infrequently observed other cats performing the task (Herbert & Harsh, 1944). In a study with a chimpanzee (Premack & Woodruff, 1978), the chimp, after viewing videotapes of human models, was able to choose the correct solutions to a series of problem-solving tasks.

From Tolman's (1922) beginning studies in the 1920s to the present (e.g., McAuley, 1985), research results clearly indicate the importance of cognitive forms of learning for both humans and animals. Cognitive processes play a central role in the lives of humans and provide the basis for the higher-order learning processes discussed in the next two chapters.

Focus Question Answer

Is observational learning a uniquely human phenomenon, or can your pet dog learn from watching other dogs and you? Experiments by Tolman and others demonstrated that animals are capable of learning by observing and of forming cognitive maps. Observational learning is not uniquely human but is widespread throughout the animal kingdom. Animals can learn by observing humans, and the reverse is also true. By observing birds, humans learned about many aspects of flight and eventually invented the airplane.

Relate

TV—Another Member of the Family

According to a recent Nielson survey (1985), nearly eighty-five million households contain a television set; in more than 90 percent of these households the TV is a color model. Over forty-eight million homes contain at least two television sets. People in an average household watch television more than seven hours each day and adults who watch TV spend more hours per week viewing television (an average of fifty-two hours) than working at their jobs (Nielson, 1985).

Obviously, many Americans spend more time with their TV sets than they spend with any family member. People turn on television to help themselves relax, learn, and enjoy a wide range of experiences; sometimes people turn on television just to end the silence in a home. The TV has become another member of the family, and like other members it plays many different roles—teacher, babysitter, entertainer, salesperson, and tour guide.

Clearly, television provides marvels beyond description, but it also creates concerns. For example, the National Institute for Mental Health has concluded that the consensus of research evidence indicates that viewing televised violence leads to more aggressive behavior in children and teenagers (NIMH, 1982). Television, for good or bad, provides influential models; it shapes attitudes and beliefs and modifies how individuals spend their time.

Because television viewers, especially young children, imitate the behaviors they observe being modeled on TV, television has the potential for changing viewers' behaviors in both positive and negative directions (Friedrich & Stein, 1973). TV characters can model positive, prosocial behaviors and negative aggressive behaviors; sex-roles can be portrayed in stereotyped or nonstereotyped ways. The selection of events to show on the news and to feature in entertainment shows affects the viewers' beliefs about the world. For example, children and adults who watch many hours of violent and aggressive TV shows tend to view the "real" world as more dangerous than it actually is (Berkowitz, 1984; Singer et al., 1984).

Initially, television may attract people's attention to a world situation—such as terrorist attacks, starvation in Ethiopia, or the plight of America's homeless—and may change their attitudes and compel them to act. But when television frequently shows certain behaviors or situations, viewers may become desensitized to these and similar situations. Children who often watch TV violence may choose to model the violence, but they may also become indifferent to witnessing violence (Berkowitz, 1984).

Psychologists have studied how television viewing affects behavior; following are a few of their recent findings:

— Four-year-olds who were frequent TV viewers displayed less self-restraint than did other four-year-olds. Six years later, the same subjects were found to be more aggressive, more restless, and more likely to believe in a frightening world than were other ten-year-old children (Singer et al., 1984).

— Tenth and eleventh graders who watch the most violent TV shows, ones in which characters brutally injure or kill each other, tend to play the more violent videogames. The amount of viewing of violent TV shows is also related to physical aggression level (Dominick, 1984).

— In a study of elementary school children in Finland and the United States, researchers found positive correlations between viewing TV violence and aggression (fighting, hitting, and kicking) for only boys in Finland but for both boys and girls in the United States. The aggressive children thought that violent TV shows portrayed reality; they identified with aggressive TV characters; and they had frequent aggressive fantasies (Huesman et al., 1984).

— A summary of televised violence studies concluded that laboratory studies provide consistent, but small, correlations between viewing television violence and aggressiveness, the deliberate intent to injure others. However, this researcher observed that few studies had been done to determine if viewing television violence in natural settings causes people to be aggressive (Freedman, 1984).

— Children looked at fifteen minutes of programming that varied in pacing (high or low) and format (high-continuity with successive scenes or low-continuity with a magazine format). They were then given a recall task of putting in order still photos of the program. Recall was superior with both high-continuity programs and with low-paced programs (Wright et al., 1984).

— Although television viewing increases with age (the elderly prefer informational over entertainment programming), the elderly are underrepresented and negatively stereotyped by television characters (Kubley, 1980).

— By viewing television, children do learn about good nutritional concepts, but the knowledge does not influence food preferences or consumption patterns (Peterson et al., 1984).

— Saturday morning television programs present an external view of the world. The characters are seldom in control of the events involving them and tend to rely on magic, other characters, and special devices instead of strength, thinking, effort, and realistic tools and devices (Bolick & Nowicki, 1984).

— Adults of various ages were shown news items at 9:30 A.M., 1:30 P.M., or 5:30 P.M. Immediate memory for news was best at 9:30 A.M. and worst at 5:30 P.M. As the day passed, recall of information about causes of events declined more than did concrete information about people and locations (Gunter et al., 1983).

From just this sampling of recent research results, television's pervasive effects are evident. The impact of viewing TV programs is still debated (Freedman, 1984), but one effect is certain—the amount of time spent watching TV is time not spent in other activities. This last effect may be most significant for the family unit and its individual members.

Things to Do

1. Read B.F. Skinner's novel, *Walden Two*, in which he describes how a society based on the principles of operant conditioning and reinforcement would function. Write a review of the book, focusing on your reactions to Skinner's ideas. Do you think that such a society could exist today? Then describe Skinner's utopia to several other people, and note their reactions.

2. Make a list of effective conditioned reinforcers in your life and determine why each became an important conditioned reinforcer for you.

3. Design a procedure using operant conditioning techniques to modify a personal behavior you would like to change. Perhaps you wish to stop smoking, to stop biting your nails, or to talk less and listen more during conversations. Will you use reinforcers, punishers, or both? Ask your friends to help you with your plan.

4. Make ten copies of the list of activities given in Exhibit 9.3 (Premack's principle) and ask friends to anonymously rank these activities. Compare your rankings with those of your friends. What are the most obvious similarities and differences? Combine your data with those from several other classmates. Compute the average ranking for each item, and share your results with your class.

5. For a week, keep a record of the time you spend studying different subjects. Pick one subject you believe you should study more and during the following week give yourself a reward for each study session you spend on that subject. Keep a record of the number of reinforcements you receive and the amount of time you study. Did your studying time on this subject increase? Did your overall study time increase, or did you study other subjects less?

6. Watch three hours of a major network's evening programming; record each instance of violence, aggression, and desirable (prosocial) behaviors depicted. On the same night of the week during subsequent weeks, make the same observations for the other two major networks. Compare your observations.

Things to Discuss

1. Do you believe that schools should use more operant conditioning techniques to modify students' behaviors? What are the advantages and disadvantages of regulating students' behaviors through operant conditioning?

2. What kinds of reinforcers and punishers did your parents typically use to modify and control your behavior? Compare your response with the responses of other students. In what ways have reinforcers and punishers used by parents changed over the past fifty years? What reinforcers and punishers have remained the same?

3. If operant conditioning is so effective in changing behavior, why is it not used more widely to modify people's behavior? Do people generally resist the idea of

using operant conditioning principles to shape a better society? Defend your answer.

4. When making career choices, many college students are swayed by the starting salary and earning potential of a given occupation. Which reinforcer is more important in your own career choice—the satisfaction you will receive from developing and using your abilities or the amount of money you will earn? Do you think greater career satisfaction will come from the first or second type of reinforcer?

5. Typically, many Americans who are registered to vote do not do so in local, state, and national elections. How could you use operant conditioning principles to get more people to vote in elections? Should you emphasize intrinsic or extrinsic reinforcers, or would punishment for nonvoting behavior be more effective than either kind of reinforcer? How would you incorporate the partial reinforcement effect into your plans?

6. Debate whether society would be less violent than it is if the violence depicted on TV were greatly curtailed

or eliminated. Create two sound arguments for both the pro and the con positions.

Things to Read

Axelrod, S. & Apsche, J. (eds.). 1983. *The effects of punishment on human behavior.* NY: Academic Press.

Miller, L.K. 1980. *Principles of everyday behavior analysis.* Monterey, CA: Brooks/Cole.

Skinner, B.F. 1948. *Walden two.* NY: Macmillan.

Skinner, B.F. 1971. *Beyond freedom and dignity.* NY: Knopf.

Skinner, B.F. 1974. *About behaviorism.* NY: Knopf.

Skinner, B.F. 1987. *Upon further reflection.* Englewood Cliffs, NJ: Prentice-Hall.

Williams, R.L. & Long, J.D. 1982. *Toward a self-managed lifestyle* (3rd ed.). Boston: Houghton Mifflin.

 ## Review

Summary

1. Thorndike studied how a cat's responses were instrumental in obtaining certain consequences. According to Thorndike's Law of Effect, responses followed by satisfying consequences are strengthened while responses followed by unpleasant consequences are weakened.

2. Watson thought that psychologists should study only overt responses rather than internal processes and consciousness. Skinner studied the predictable relationships between animals' and people's behaviors and the environmental events they experience.

3. Reinforcers increase the probability of responses that precede them while punishers decrease the probability of responses that precede them. Positive reinforcers are stimuli that an animal or person actively seeks to obtain while negative reinforcers are stimuli that an animal or person actively seeks to avoid or escape from. Primary reinforcers are unlearned, innately satisfying stimuli that are related to physiological needs and survival. Conditioned reinforcers are learned by their association with primary reinforcers.

4. According to the Premack principle, preferred behaviors can be used to reinforce (increase the rate of) less-preferred behaviors.

5. Positive punishers are aversive, unpleasant stimuli that an animal or person cannot avoid or escape from, while negative punishers represent the removal or absence of pleasant, desirable stimuli. To effectively suppress undesirable behavior, punishment should be given immediately and consistently. While punishment is an effective way to change behavior, its negative side effects cause learning theorists to emphasize reinforcement rather than punishment.

6. Shaping, the reinforcing of successively closer approximations to the desired response, allows faster acquisition of operant behaviors. In chaining, several operant behaviors are linked together through a process in which the last behavior in the chain serves as a conditioned reinforcer for the behavior that precedes it; each preceding behavior then becomes a conditioned reinforcer for the behavior preceding it.

7. Stimulus generalization and discrimination, extinction, and spontaneous recovery occur in both classical and operant conditioning.

8. Continuous reinforcement occurs when every correct response is reinforced, and partial reinforcement occurs when only some of the correct responses are reinforced. Faster acquisition occurs with continuous reinforcement, while more resistance to extinction occurs with partial reinforcement (the partial reinforcement effect—PRE).

9. In fixed and variable ratio schedules of reinforcement, reinforcers are received according to the number of responses made, but the number of responses is unpredictable with the variable schedule. In fixed and variable interval schedules, a reinforcer is available after a certain period of time has elapsed, but the amount of time is unpredictable on variable interval schedules.

10. Operant conditioning involves learning the contingency between the responses and the stimuli that follow them, while classical conditioning involves a contingency between the CS and the US. Classical and operant conditioning differ but also share several features. Like classical conditioning, operant conditioning is limited by certain biological constraints. Animals and people are prepared to acquire certain operant behaviors more easily than others and instinctively drift toward making those responses for which they are innately prepared.

11. Cognitive paradigms of learning focus on internal processes that affect learning. Tolman suggested that animals and people form cognitive maps and develop expectancies that represent cognitive learning. Bandura studied how individuals learn by observing models and imitating their behavior.

12. Television is an influential source of modeling. Although both positive and negative behaviors are modeled on TV, most of the research has focused on the effects of viewing televised violence and aggression. A general finding is that in children and adults higher levels of viewing of televised violence are associated with greater degrees of aggressiveness.

Key Terms

trial-and-error learning
law of effect
operant behavior
positive reinforcer
negative reinforcer
escape learning
avoidance learning
primary reinforcers
conditioned reinforcers
extrinsic reinforcer
intrinsic reinforcer
Premack's principle
positive punishers
negative punishers
shaping
stimulus generalization
stimulus discrimination
continuous reinforcement
partial reinforcement
fixed ratio (FR)
fixed interval (FI)
variable ratio (VR)
variable interval (VI)
partial reinforcement effect (PRE)
superstitious behavior
stimulus control
preparedness
instinctive drift
latent learning
observational learning
modeling

Focus Questions

1. In what ways is your memory like a computer?

2. When you remember an event from your past, how accurate is your memory?

3. What types of memory tasks are involved when you take essay and multiple-choice tests?

4. If you are angry when you study, will you score better if you also are angry when you take the exam?

5. When you forget information, can you distinguish between whether you did not store it in memory or you were unable to retrieve it from memory?

6. Which practical memory aids do you use routinely when you study?

Chapter Outline

MODELS OF MEMORY
Information-Processing Model
Storage and Transfer Model
Levels of Processing Model

TYPES OF MEMORY
Procedural, Episodic, and Semantic Memory
Reconstructive Memory

MEASURING MEMORY
Recall
Recognition
Relearning

MEMORY PROCESSING
Encoding Strategies
Organization in Storage
Retrieval Cues
The Research Process: The Tip-of-the-Tongue
    (TOT) Phenomenon
Biological Bases of Memory

THEORIES OF FORGETTING
Encoding Failures
Storage Failures
Retrieval Failures
Practical Memory

**RELATE: Practical Personal Memory
    Improvement**
Things to Do
Things to Discuss
Things to Read

REVIEW: Summary
Key Terms

Chapter 10

Memory

*Things ain't what they used to be
and probably never was.*

Will Rogers

What would you do if you suddenly lost your memory? Would you be able to answer questions on your exams? Would you recognize your friends? Would you recognize yourself when you looked in the mirror? Would you be able to ride a bike? Memory is the central hub around which revolve many other psychological processes; learning, perception, motivation, and thinking all use memory in some way. Because of its central role in other processes, memory was one of the first psychological processes to be studied systematically in psychological laboratories.

In Germany, over one hundred years ago, Hermann Ebbinghaus (1885) undertook the first recorded laboratory study of memory. Acting as his own subject, Ebbinghaus recorded the number of seconds he needed to memorize a list of **nonsense syllables**, meaningless three-letter syllables. He also measured how quickly he forgot

225

the list; after only one hour, he could remember only one-third of the list. However, Ebbinghaus observed that relearning the list took less time than did learning the list originally; the time savings indicated he had retained some memory of the list. With these studies, Ebbinghaus set the stage for the next one hundred years of laboratory research on memory.

Unfortunately, laboratory studies have rarely investigated aspects of memory that have the greatest practical application to everyday living. In fact, a leading researcher, Ulric Neisser (1982), noted that "If X is an interesting or socially significant aspect of memory, then psychologists have hardly ever studied X." Only recently have psychologists begun formal studies of forgetting familiar, meaningful information. Throughout this chapter, the intent is to integrate the concepts and principles of laboratory research with practical everyday applications.

 ## Models of Memory

Memory involves integrating your past experiences into your present and future life. To do so, you must store your past experiences for future use. Theorists have proposed many informal models of memory, most of which compare memory to a storehouse or receptacle. In one informal model, memory is likened to a junkbox in which your most recent past experiences lie on top of the heap and are most retrievable. Another model suggests memory is like a filing cabinet in which you file past experi-

Although retrieving information from memory has been compared to locating books in a library, the human memory is more complex than any library filing system.

ences in drawers and in folders within drawers. Yet another model compares memory to a library; this model emphasizes the memory's efficient system of classifying experiences and the many ways of retrieving these experiences.

Informal memory models have kept pace with advancing technology. Memory was likened first to a tape recorder and then to a video recorder, but computers have sparked even more interest as a memory model. Because computers are information processing devices created by humans, they reflect aspects of human memory and information processing. Although human memory is far more complex, computers supply a tangible model of the information processing in human memory.

Information-Processing Model

The **information-processing model** of memory identifies three phases that are common to all information-processing systems. The three phases are **encoding, storage**, and **retrieval**. Encoding involves coding information so it can be used by the system and organizing information for storage. Encoding occurs in three forms: **visual encoding** (coding an experience as a visual image), **auditory encoding** (coding an experience by sound), and **semantic encoding** (coding the experience by its meaning). Whether the system is a file cabinet, tape recorder, computer, or human memory, information must be encoded before further processing can occur. The second phase of the process involves storing the coded, organized information. This phase is commonly referred to as memory. In the third phase, information is retrieved from storage for further use. Retrieval is very important because failures in encoding or storage cannot be discovered until retrieval is attempted.

As the three forms of encoding suggest, you can code an experience in more than one way. Chapter 1 suggests the use of vivid visual imagery to help you remember the verbal material from your text. The success of this technique can be explained by the **dual coding theory** (Paivio, 1969), which proposes that if information is stored in two different ways, the probability of later recall is higher because retrieval of the information can occur in two ways. For example, information that you have both read in the text (visual encoding) and heard in class (auditory encoding) receives dual coding and should be easier to recall for a test. Many laboratory studies on dual coding support this very practical advice for improving your memory (Paivio, 1978).

One phenomenon associated with the encoding phase is **eidetic imagery**. After looking at a picture for less than

EXHIBIT 10.1
Storage and Transfer Model of Memory

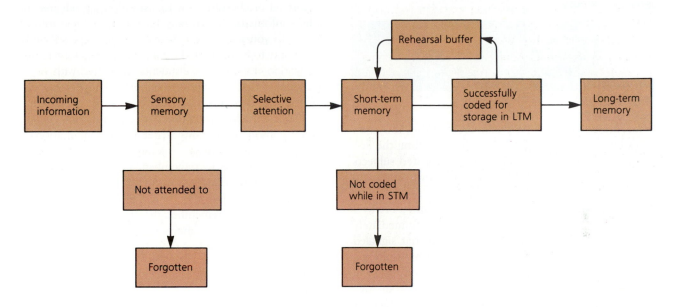

thirty seconds, some individuals are able to see the picture for up to four or five minutes after it has been removed from their view (Haber, 1980). This phenomenon is commonly called photographic memory, but the term is inaccurate; such individuals do not store photographs in their memory. Because they retain the visual image much longer than do other individuals, eidetic persons have a much longer time to encode information from the image. The remarkable memories of these eidetic individuals are directly attributable to their encoding abilities. Curiously, eidetic imagery occurs most frequently in children and rarely in adults.

Regardless of whether information has been coded visually, auditorily, or semantically, and whether it has been coded singly or dually, successful retrieval depends on locating and decoding the information stored in memory. If you store information encoded in only one way and then try to retrieve it in a different way, you are likely to have as much difficulty as you would if you were looking for information that was misfiled in a filing cabinet. For example, have you ever missed a test question because you searched your memory for information from the text when the question was over material presented in class? You may have incorrectly answered the question because you could not locate the information in memory.

Two major models (storage and transfer, levels of processing) attempt to explain the interaction between

the three phases of memory proposed by the information-processing model.

Storage and Transfer Model

The **storage and transfer model** of memory (Atkinson & Shiffrin, 1968) is a well-accepted view of the relationship between encoding, storage, and retrieval. This model describes three types of memory: sensory, short-term, and long-term. The major difference between the three types is the length of time the memory lasts. As you read the following descriptions, look at Exhibit 10.1, which illustrates the transfer of information between the three types of memory.

Sensory Memory **Sensory memory** registers moment to moment incoming information. If you do not pay immediate attention to a particular piece of information, you lose that information. Because information from all the senses registers in sensory memory, you can pay attention to only a small part of it; the rest is displaced by new incoming information and is irretrievably lost.

An ingenious set of experiments demonstrates the existence of sensory memory (Sperling, 1960). When people are given brief glimpses (1/20th of a second) of grids of letters or numbers like those in Exhibit 10.2, typically they can remember only four or five of the

EXHIBIT 10.2
Letter and Number Grids for Testing
Sensory Memory

```
I N C          9 3 8
A T O          6 7 0
P H Z          5 4 1
```

items. However, many people report that they saw more items but forgot them while they were recalling the first ones. Sperling devised a procedure that tested subjects on part of what they saw; they did not know beforehand which part they would have to recall.

In Sperling's experiment, subjects glimpsed briefly a letter grid like the one in Exhibit 10.2. Immediately following the glimpse, they heard a tone that signaled which row of the grid they were to recall. A high-pitched tone signaled the top row, a medium-pitched tone the middle row, and a low-pitched tone the bottom row. Sperling's subjects did well on this task because the tone helped them pay attention to particular rows of the grid and remember the letters before they were lost. In contrast, if Sperling delayed the tone by only one second, his subjects remembered very few of the letters.

Sperling demonstrated that sensory memory contains a moment to moment array of sensory information that is only partially available because of the brief time the information remains in sensory memory. Sperling's results indicate that at any one time you have more sensory information than you can possibly pay attention to. Yet before you lament the waste in this system, consider what life would be like if you remembered every sight, sound, and smell you experienced. One day of total recall would probably be enough to make you realize the advantages of the system you possess.

Short-Term Memory   If you pay attention to information in sensory memory, the information is transferred to **short-term memory (STM)**. Short-term memory holds the information you are currently using; it is your active, working memory. The label *short-term* well describes this memory. Probably someone has given you information over the telephone when you did not have a pencil and paper handy. If the caller asked if you needed to write down the information, you may have expressed confidence in your ability to remember, but later you may have been chagrined to discover you had forgotten it. Laboratory studies have confirmed that short-term mem-

ory is not as fleeting as sensory memory, but information in STM does fade quickly.

Instead of choosing not to write down a telephone caller's information, you may have repeated the information to yourself while you searched for a pencil and paper, only to be distracted for a moment and forget the information entirely. The distraction interfered with your attention to the information in short-term memory. To demonstrate the effect of interference on short-term memory, try the following task with a friend. First create several consonant trigrams (three-letter combinations, such as BJM, created from consonants). Give your friend one of the trigrams to remember, and instruct him or her to begin immediately counting backwards by threes from 2000. Stop your friend after fifteen seconds, and ask her or him to remember the trigram. Repeat this procedure with several different trigrams. If your friend remembers the trigram less than 10 percent of the time, you will have replicated an experiment that used the same procedure (Peterson & Peterson, 1959). The Petersons asked their subjects to count backwards to prevent them from rehearsing (consciously repeating) the trigram. After three seconds, subjects remembered the trigrams approximately 50 percent of the time, and after fifteen seconds, the subjects seldom remembered the trigrams. As these examples illustrate, short-term memory is, as its label says, short-term, and other information can easily interfere with information already contained there.

Probably you are also aware of another characteristic of short-term memory—its limited capacity. Miller (1956) observed that most people's capacity is between five and nine items, or bits of information; he described this limit as the "magical number seven plus or minus two." This capacity of "7 ± 2" is well documented in laboratory studies and everyday life. When you obtain a pre-recorded phone number from directory assistance, the number is delivered at a rate slightly faster than one digit per second. If the number falls within your area code, you probably ignore the first three bits of information and concentrate on the last seven digits of the number. If the three-digit prefix is also familiar to you, you may pay attention to only the last four digits. If the prefix is not familiar to you, paying attention to seven digits or seven bits of information is difficult but not unusually so. However, if you must remember the area code and seven digits, the task becomes difficult because ten digits exceeds most people's short-term memory capacity. The telephone companies acknowledge this difficulty and repeat numbers a second time.

A seven-digit phone number can be held comfortably in short-term memory, but interruptions during rehearsal may displace the number.

One way in which to deal with information exceeding the capacity of your short-term memory is **chunking**, or expanding the capacity by increasing the amount of information contained in each bit. Thus, by chunking a ten-digit phone number into a three-digit area code, a three-digit prefix and a four-digit suffix, you have only three bits to remember instead of ten. The seven bits of information to which you can attend in short-term memory can be chunks. Notice that the twelve syllables in the top line of Exhibit 10.3 are easy to remember because they are chunked together as three words, while the twelve unrelated syllables in the bottom line are very difficult to remember because they are not chunked together.

Long-term Memory   According to the storage and transfer model, if you want to remember information longer than while you are attending to it you must store it in **long-term memory (LTM)**. Researchers assume the capacity of long-term memory to be almost limitless and information, once stored in LTM, is not easily forgotten. Astounding memory feats have demonstrated this poten-

EXHIBIT 10.3
Chunking

CONVENTIONAL	HOSPITALIZED	PSYCHOLOGIST

HOS LOG ALI IST VEN PSY NAL TIO ZED CON PIT CHO

tial for unlimited, permanent storage (Neisser, 1982). One individual in the U.S.S.R. correctly remembered lists of fifty or more words or numbers after they had been presented to him only once; even more remarkably, with no forewarning, he correctly recalled the list more than fifteen years later (Luria, 1968). Such a remarkable memory is a mixed blessing, however; memorists often find they cannot escape their total recall, and their memories intrude on and disrupt their normal functioning.

To summarize, according to the storage and transfer model, information is first received in sensory memory. Information in sensory memory is immediately transferred to short-term memory, or it is forgotten within a fraction of a second. In short-term memory, which has a limited capacity, information is replaced by new information after twenty or thirty seconds if it is not actively rehearsed and transferred to long-term memory. Once information is encoded in long-term memory, it may remain available for retrieval as long as the person is alive. When information is retrieved from long-term memory, it returns to short-term memory. Examine again Exhibit 10.1, which illustrates this process.

Levels of Processing Model

Advocates of another model of memory, the **levels of processing model** (Craik & Lockhart, 1972), disagree with the storage and transfer model's emphasis on types of memory and storage. Instead, the levels of processing model stresses types of processing and encoding. This model describes one memory instead of three, and that memory is a function of the depth or level of processing the information receives. The greater the depth of processing, the better the memory of the information.

According to the levels of processing model, the features of the incoming information determine the level of processing. Any experience can be analyzed according to its superficial, or surface, features and its deeper meanings. Meanings, or semantic features, require a different level of processing than do surface sensory features. For example, noting whether, in the last paragraph, "levels of processing" was capitalized (a sensory feature) requires less processing than noting whether "levels of processing" and "depth of processing" mean the same thing. Because semantic features require more processing, they form longer lasting memories.

In an experiment to test the prediction that memory for meaning (semantically encoded information) is better than memory for surface sensory features (Craik & Tulving, 1975), sixty words were flashed briefly, one at a time, on a screen. Before each word was presented, the subjects were asked a specific yes/no question about the word. The questions were designed to control the subjects' level of processing. For example, the word *chair* might have been preceded by one of three questions: Is the word in capital letters? Does the word rhyme with bear? Is the word a piece of furniture? The first question requires encoding only the surface sensory features of the word, while the second question requires auditory encoding, which is a higher level of processing. The third question requires semantic encoding of the word, which is the deepest level of processing.

Later, the subjects were given a list of 180 words, including the sixty words they were shown previously. Their ability to recognize the words they had seen only briefly was as the model had predicted. The subjects recognized slightly more than 40 percent of the visually encoded words, 65 percent of the auditorially encoded words, and 90 percent of the semantically encoded words.

Practically, these results emphasize the encoding process. The evidence from this study and others clearly indicates that information processed beyond its surface features is easier to remember later. Therefore, as you study for this course and others, ask yourself questions that require semantic processing: "What is the meaning of this term? How is this concept related to the previous one? Is this an example of...?" The results of laboratory studies of both memory models (storage and transfer, levels of processing) apply directly to your everyday memory. Memory improvement suggestions based on these findings and others are reviewed in the *Relate* section of this chapter.

Focus Question Answer

In what ways is your memory like a computer? Both are involved in storing and retrieving information; they are information-processing systems. Your memory is far more complex than a computer, but computers can serve as models of human memory. Actually, since computers are created by humans, you might more appropriately ask, "How is a computer like my memory?"

 Types of Memory

As you have read, sensory memory is one of three memory types in the storage and transfer model. Researchers (Atkinson & Shriffin, 1971) have proposed that sensory memory can be broken down into separate types of mem-

ory for each sense: iconic (vision), echoic (hearing), haptic (touch), and so on. Of the various types of sensory memory, **iconic memory** and **echoic memory** have received the most attention. For a brief moment, iconic memory registers an exact visual image of what you have seen. Each brief visual image is immediately replaced by new, incoming visual information. Echoic memory, on the other hand, lasts as long as three or four seconds before it fades. This morning you may have noticed the slower disappearance of the auditory image if you continued to hear the buzzing of your alarm clock for a moment or two after you had turned off the alarm.

Procedural, Semantic, and Episodic Memory

Another system for dividing memory into types is based on memory tasks (Tulving, 1985). Because Tulving believes that memory is too complex to be dealt with as a single system, he proposes three major systems of memory: procedural, semantic, and episodic. **Procedural memory** (also called skill or action memory) is memory of how to perform certain skills or engage in certain actions, such as piano playing or bike riding. Because the "how to's" are stored as nonverbal actions in procedural memory, retrieval of this type of information occurs by engaging in the activity. For instance, if you have tried to tell someone how to ride a bike, you may have discovered that you had to go through the motions to talk about the skill.

Semantic memory stores facts; it is like a dictionary or encyclopedia and includes word meanings and usage;

Retrieval of procedural memories occurs when you engage in the specific motor skills or activities.

semantic memory also includes rules of language, formal logic, and inference. Concepts are stored in semantic memory without reference to personal experience or to time or place. When you are asked to cite the date of a major Civil War battle, you search for it in your semantic memory.

Where were you on Tuesday January 28, 1986, at 11:40 A.M. EST? When you recall information about your experiences within a specific context or time frame, you use **episodic memory**. (To find out what happened on this day, see the *Exploring . . .* section on flashbulb memory, a type of episodic memory.) Episodic memory is also referred to as autobiographical memory. While not every event in your life is stored in episodic memory, its content is sufficient to allow you to construct a fairly continuous personal history. Unlike semantic memory, in which the stored knowledge remains relatively stable, episodic memory requires frequent changes. Where did you put your car keys this morning? When did you last pay the paper carrier? Temporary events as well as more permanent ones must be continually encoded into episodic memory.

Reconstructive Memory

Updating information in episodic memory leads to another type of memory—**reconstructive memory**. From time to time, you retrieve information from episodic memory in order to reconstruct an event or time period. Can you reconstruct where you were so you can answer the question in the previous paragraph? How accurate is your memory? Even if you do not recall precisely where you were, you can probably reconstruct a reasonable guess from other knowledge. Were you in school in January, 1986? If so, what courses were you taking? What was your Tuesday morning schedule? By searching, you may be able to reconstruct a memory of that January morning even if you cannot remember it at all.

Now consider this possibility: At some time in the future, you are again asked where you were on that date. If you remember, are you recalling the original memory or the reconstructed one? The cognitive psychologist Jean Piaget, whose theories are discussed in Chapter 11, related an example of reconstructive memory from his life (Piaget, 1962). During his youth, Piaget clearly recalled an attempted kidnapping that occurred when he was two years old. He remembered that his nurse tried to stop the kidnapper, a crowd gathered, and, when a

police officer with a white baton arrived, the kidnapper ran away. He even reported recognizing the area of the Champs Elysées in Paris where the event took place. The only problem with Piaget's recollection is that the attempted kidnapping never occurred. When Piaget was fifteen, the nurse confessed to his parents that she had concocted the whole story. Between ages two and fifteen, Piaget had constructed a vivid memory of an incident that never occurred. Apparently, he had used information from others' stories to reconstruct an event and then to store that reconstruction as memory. How often have you done the same?

Piaget's reconstructed memory and laboratory studies reveal that the content of long-term memories can be changed (Loftus, 1980). For example, after viewing a film of an automobile accident, some subjects were asked how fast the car was going when it passed the barn. These subjects were much more likely to recall seeing the nonexistent barn than were subjects who were asked only how fast the car was going (Loftus, 1975). That leading questions and other after-the-fact information affect reconstructive memory has practical significance for eyewitness testimony (Loftus, 1979) because many of the problems with eyewitness testimony result from reconstructed memories replacing original or nonexistent memories. In a series of studies (Loftus & Palmer, 1974; Loftus & Loftus, 1975; Loftus et al., 1978; Loftus, 1980), the accuracy of eyewitness testimony was influenced by the length of time between the event and questioning the witness. The accuracy was also influenced by the way the witness was asked about the event and by events that happened after the event in question. However, modification of memory is limited and applies primarily to information about which people are unsure. Recollections are less likely to be altered if people have committed themselves (taken a public stand) or if they originally perceived the detail clearly (Loftus, 1980).

Focus Question Answer

When you remember an event from your past, how accurate is your memory? The accuracy can vary. If you originally perceived the event clearly, your memory may be highly accurate, and your reconstruction of the event is more accurate the more recently the event occurred. However, the accuracy may decline depending on how you are questioned about the event and on what other events happened after the event you are trying to recall.

Exploring...

Flashbulb Memories

Where were you on January 28, 1986, at 11:40 A.M.? If you do not remember where you were at exactly 11:40 A.M., chances are quite good that you do remember where you were and what you were doing at some point during the next two to four hours. One retrieval cue should trigger your memory—on that date the space shuttle *Challenger* exploded on its way into orbit, killing all seven on board.

With this cue, you probably experienced a **flashbulb memory**. A flashbulb memory results from the unexpectedness of the event that causes it, the short duration of the event, and the way in which the memory highlights personal elements occurring at the time of the event (Brown & Kulik, 1977). Several features of flashbulb memories stand out. Public events (such as the space shuttle explosion) and personal events (such as car accidents) share a dramatic feature—surprise. The unexpectedness of the event and its short duration combine to cause you to remember only part

of the experience. You can remember where you were and how you learned the news of the explosion, but you cannot recall everything that happened to you at that time. Some of the elements you remember may, on reflection, seem trivial; you may remember what you were wearing when you heard the news but forget with whom you discussed the tragedy.

Another important feature of this type of episodic memory is its autobiographical nature (Rubin, 1985). Your memory of public events is usually not about the news events themselves but about how you received the news. The personal nature of these memories has been explained as a useful way to store information to be easily recalled later (Brown & Kulik, 1977) and as a way in which people connect their personal histories to the larger history of their society (Neisser, 1982).

While important public events like plane crashes and assassinations can cause flashbulb memories, most

flashbulb memories are of events in people's personal lives. In one study, when college students were asked to discuss the three most vivid autobiographical memories of their lives, the memories reported most frequently were of injuries or accidents (Rubin & Kozen, 1985). These students were also asked about their memories for twenty events thought likely to evoke vivid recollections. The events and the percentage of students experiencing them as flashbulb memories were as follows:

EVENT	PERCENTAGE
1. A car accident you were in or witnessed	85
2. The night of your high school graduation	81
3. The night of your senior prom (if you went or did not)	78
4. An early romantic experience	77
5. A time you had to speak in front of an audience	72
6. Your first date—the moment you met him/her	57
7. The day President Reagan was shot in Washington	52
8. The night President Nixon resigned	41
9. The first time you flew in an airplane	40
10. Your seventeenth birthday	30
11. The day of the first space shuttle flight	24
12. The last time you ate a holiday dinner at home	23
13. Your first college class	21
14. The first time your parents left you alone	19
15. Your thirteenth birthday	12

Source: Printed with permission from *Psychology Today Magazine*. Copyright (c) 1985. American Psychological Association.

Do any of these events evoke flashbulb memories for you? Even if these incidents do not produce immediate clarity, you may have experienced **redintegration**. In redintegration, recalling one memory leads to the recollection of another and another. Only one cue is necessary to trigger an avalanche of associated memories. Flashbulb memories and redintegration show how durable some long-term memories can be.

 ## Measuring Memory

The primary way to learn about any memory process, whether that process is encoding, storage, or retrieval, is to measure how much information can be retrieved. Measuring retrieval involves several kinds of memory tasks that provide different amounts of cues to assist the retrieval.

Recall

Recall tasks ask you to retrieve information with only the cues in the questions to aid your search. Essay or short-answer exams are examples of recall tasks. Remembering a phone number or address without looking it up is also a recall task. Subjects in laboratory studies of memory are asked to recall information in the order it was presented (**serial recall**) or in any order they choose (**free recall**). Subjects asked to recall a list of words like the list in Exhibit 10.4, typically remember the first and last words on the list better than they remember words in the middle (see top graph, Exhibit 10.4). Better recall of the first words is called the **primacy effect**, and better recall of the last words, or the words seen most recently, is termed the **recency effect**. As illustrated in the lower graph in Exhibit 10.4, recall from long-term memory

EXHIBIT 10.4
Performance on Recall Tasks

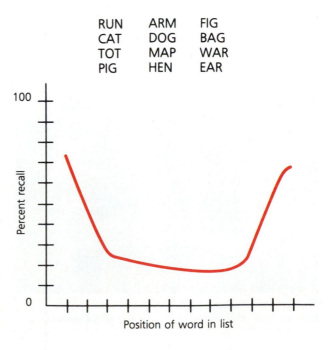

can explain the primacy effect while recall from short-term memory can account for the recency effect.

Recognition

Recognition tasks ask you to indicate if the presented information is stored in your memory. Recognizing a phone number as your friend's is usually easier than recalling the number without any cues. You may prefer multiple-choice exams to essay exams because the alternative answers help you recognize the correct answer. Such recognition tasks are more sensitive measures of memory (they indicate more completely what is retained in memory) than are recall tasks because even when subjects cannot recall material, they may recognize the correct material.

In one study, both recall and recognition tasks were used to test subjects' memories of their classmates' names and faces (Bahrick et al., 1975). The task may seem easy if you are a recent high school graduate, but the subjects' graduation dates ranged from three months ago to forty-seven years ago. As expected, after only three months, name *recall* was not as good as name or face *recognition*. Surprisingly, face *recognition* remained at approximately 90 percent up to thirty-four years after graduation. Name *recognition* did not decline from 90 percent until fifteen years after graduation. These findings present dramatic proof that some information remains in long-term memory a very long time.

Relearning

Recall that Ebbinghaus learned a list of nonsense syllables and then, after a period of time, relearned the list.

Their long-term memory for faces helped these old friends recognize each other at their thirty-year high school reunion.

This boy may forget the content of the books his father reads to him, but later he will be able to relearn the information more quickly than if he had never heard it.

His approach, called **relearning**, measures memory by the amount of **savings** in the time required to learn the list a second time. The assumption is that any savings results from memories retained from the first time. Tasks involving relearning are the most sensitive measures of memory but, because they are very time-consuming, they are seldom used in laboratory studies.

Outside the laboratory, however, examples of relearning are easy to find. If you once memorized a poem and then, over a period of time, forgot it, you may have found that learning the poem later was easier because you still retained some memory of it. The savings from relearning are particularly beneficial for students. Even though you have forgotten some material, studying for comprehensive final exams will be easier if you stored the information in your memory earlier in the term.

Focus Question Answer

What type of memory tasks are involved when you take essay and multiple-choice tests? Essay tests are recall tasks in which you must retrieve the information with

only the cues in the questions to aid your search. Multiple-choice tests are recognition tasks in which you must recognize if the information in the question is stored in your memory.

Memory Processing

As discussed earlier in this chapter, memories derive from encoding, storage, and retrieval. By focusing on each process separately, researchers have acquired considerable knowledge about how memories are formed, how forgetting occurs, and how memory can be improved.

Encoding Strategies

Rehearsal can be employed in the encoding process. Students often use **rote rehearsal**; they reread or repeat information again and again. As a memory strategy, rote rehearsal has received some research support. For example, when subjects were asked to recall words from a forty-eight-word list that had been presented to them only once at a rate of one word every 1.5 seconds, they remembered only 28 percent of the words on the list (Madigan, 1969). However, when some words were re-

peated twice during the presentation of the list, recall of the repeated words rose to 47 percent. These results imply that repetition leads to better recall through more opportunities for encoding.

Other studies suggest that active encoding strategies facilitate memories better than rote rehearsal does. One active encoding strategy, **elaborative rehearsal**, recodes material to be stored. **Recoding** is changing new information to a form that is easier to store; chunking is one example of recoding. Chunking involves rehearsing the larger chunks of material *and* rehearsing the code used to form the larger chunks. The additional asssociations formed in recoding make encoding and retrieval easier.

A second recoding strategy is reorganization of the material. An organizational scheme helps you establish associations between different parts of the information. For example, memorizing the bones of the body is much easier when the bones are organized into related groups. Recoding disorganized and unrelated information into a narrative story can also improve encoding and retrieval because the plot of the story links the unrelated bits of information (Bower & Clark, 1969). This recoding strategy increases the meaningfulness of the material, thereby making it easier to store and recall.

A final encoding strategy involves recoding verbal material. A combination of vivid visual images and concepts makes abstract concepts more concrete, dramatizes important meanings, organizes and relates the information, and stores the information in at least two ways (dual coding). The *Quick Study Aids* in this text make use of these three encoding strategies to help you improve memory for difficult and easily confused concepts.

Organization in Storage

Recoding material reduces and organizes it for more efficient storage in long-term memory. Once in storage, memories must be organized in ways that make them accessible for retrieval. Both semantic and episodic memories exhibit **clustering** during retrieval; in other words, related facts or ideas are recalled as a cluster. Imagine that you are asked to memorize a word list in which kinds of fruit, types of furniture, and articles of clothing appear in random order. When asked to recall this list, you will probably recall the kinds of fruit, the types of furniture, and the articles of clothing in separate clusters. You experience clustering in episodic memories when an appropriate context brings back a flood of memories about the same event. As these examples suggest, storing similar information together facilitates retrieval.

As the clustering effect illustrates, long-term memory storage is not a random system. Instead, you store memories in highly organized, interrelated networks, and you retrieve information through the appropriate networks (Anderson, 1983). To discover the organization of long-term memory storage, answer this question: What day of the week is today? If all memories were equally accessible to you, you could answer equally quickly on Wednesday, Sunday, or any other day. Yet subjects in one study took twice as long to answer on Wednesday as they did on Sunday, suggesting that the weekend network is more readily accessible than the weekday (Shanon, 1979). Weekdays also take longer to retrieve because you must search through a network of five weekdays compared to a network of only two weekend days. The closer to the weekend the weekday was, the more quickly subjects recalled it, thus suggesting that the networks are interconnected. Generally, stored memories are organized in related clusters of information, and connections between these clusters form interrelated networks of information. This organization in storage is evidenced by memory retrieval studies.

Retrieval Cues

Typically, students spend most of their study time trying to store information and most of their exam time trying to retrieve information. However, spending all your study time encoding does not assure that you will be able to retrieve information during exams. The SQ5R study strategy outlined in Chapter 1 emphasizes retrieval as much as encoding because in order to answer exam questions, you must be able to retrieve encoded material.

Retrieval is easier if appropriate internal and external cues are available when your memory is tested (Tulving, 1982). Exam questions are one type of external cue and answers are easier to retrieve if the information was originally stored as an answer to a question. This idea is known as **context-dependent memory** (Godden & Baddeley, 1975). To test this concept, say the months of the year as quickly as you can in alphabetical order. Since you stored the months in chronological order, retrieving them in a different order is difficult. Most people make several errors when they retrieve the months in alphabetical order, and they usually take more than a minute to complete the task. In contrast, most people can retrieve the months in chronological order in less than ten seconds. Having the same context for encoding and retrieval creates the strongest retrieval cues.

If you celebrate the holiday season in a similar manner each year, the setting may serve to bring back memories of previous holidays.

Ideally, you should take exams in the same context in which you studied for them. Research studies support this conclusion (Smith et al., 1978). In one exotic test of this concept, subjects had to remember a word list that was read to them while they were scuba diving ten feet under water or while they were on the beach. As the bar graph in Exhibit 10.5 shows, subjects' recall was best when they were tested in the same context in which they first heard the words (Godden & Baddeley, 1975).

A less exotic study of context-dependent memory investigated the effect of background music in a test (Smith, 1985). Three backgrounds were used: music, monotonous noise, and quiet. Recall for lists of words was better when the context remained the same. Interestingly, although both music and monotonous background noise produced context-dependent memory, a quiet background did not. When learning occurred in a quiet background, testing with quiet, music, or monotonous noise backgrounds caused no difference in performance. From a practical viewpoint, this study provides a reason for studying in quiet surroundings.

State-Dependent Retrieval   The importance of context as a retrieval cue is further supported by **state-dependent retrieval** (information that is retrievable only in the same psychological state in which it was originally stored). Research with alcohol and marijuana indicates that drug states cause state-dependent retrieval (Overton, 1972;

EXHIBIT 10.5
The Effects of Context on Memory

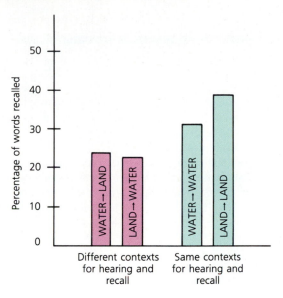

Different contexts resulted in a percent recall of just over 20 percent, while same contexts produced significantly higher recall percentages.

Source: Godden, D.R. & Baddeley, A.D. 1975. Context dependent memory in two natural environments: On land and underwater. *British Journal of Psychology, 66,* 325–331.

Eich et al., 1975). When they are sober, people cannot remember events that happened when they were drunk or high; however, when they become intoxicated again, they can remember the previously forgotten events (see the *Exploring . . .* section for more information about drugs' effects on memory).

Some researchers have shown that students in hypnotically induced happy or sad moods recall word lists better if they are in the same mood during recall as they were when they learned the word list (Bower, 1981). These findings suggest that emotional states can serve as retrieval cues. However, a recent study of 578 college students (Hasher et al., 1985) found that mild variations in mood (mildly depressed versus nondepressed) do not produce state-dependent retrieval. Although laboratory research supports state-dependent retrieval, its effects in everyday memory retrieval are not clear.

The Research Process: The Tip-of-the-Tongue (TOT) Phenomenon

Imagine you are playing a game of Psychological Trivia and are asked this question: What is Skinner's first name?

You either know the answer, or you do not, right? Actually, a third possibility exists. You may know that you know the answer but be unable to recall it at the moment. You may remember Skinner's initials and even the approximate length of his name and what it sounds like.

You probably have experienced this **tip-of-the-tongue phenomenon (TOT)** many times. This interesting retrieval failure is common in everyday and laboratory settings. In one study, college students were given the definitions of forty-nine uncommon English words and asked to name the words. The fifty-six students experienced TOT's a total of 360 times (Brown & McNeil, 1966).

The TOT phenomenon reveals an interesting aspect of memory—**metamemory**. Because of metamemory, you not only remember information, but you know if you know a specific piece of information. Metamemory checks whether specific information is stored in your memory, determines the amount of effort needed to find it, and decides which retrieval strategy to use.

Players in trivia games know almost immediately if they do or do not know the answer to the question; they know if the information is or is not stored. In the uncommon English words study, students used two common search strategies—searching for words by their meanings and by their sounds. They used the sound strategy most often and produced over two hundred sound-alike words. By using this strategy, students often guessed correctly the number of syllables, the initial letters, and prefixes and suffixes of the sought-after word.

In a similar study (Yarmey, 1973), fifty-three students were shown fifty photos of famous people and were asked the people's names. Students first tried to remember their professions and when they had last seen the people. If this strategy did not work, the subjects tried to recognize the first letters of the last names or the number of syllables in the name. Then they searched for similar-sounding names. Over six hundred TOT's were reported!

The next time you experience the tip-of-the-tongue phenomenon, try different search strategies. Eventually you may find a pathway that leads you to the answer.

Biological Bases of Memory

Thus far, all the memory processes and concepts presented in this chapter have been inferred from what people have or have not been able to remember. However, some researchers move from inferences to direct

Exploring . . .

Drugs and Memory

Drugs are part of the American lifestyle. People take drugs to speed themselves up (caffeine and amphetamines), to slow themselves down (sleeping pills and tranquilizers), and to alter their moods (alcohol and marijuana). How do these lifestyle drugs affect memory?

The first consideration is the amount of drug use; use and abuse of drugs are not the same. For example, researchers have found little evidence that moderate use of either alcohol or marijuana causes permanent physical damage to the brain (Loftus, 1980). Moderate drinking has little or no effect on short-term memory or on retrieval of old memories, but moderate drinking interferes with the transfer of new memories into long-term memory. Marijuana use seems to produce similar effects.

A primary factor in alcohol's effect on memory is the amount consumed on any given occasion. Consuming seven drinks on one occasion is far more disruptive to memory than having one drink every day for seven days. Similar dosage effects are found with caffeine, nicotine, and amphetamines; large doses disrupt memory (McGaugh, 1970).

Alcohol abuse clearly affects memory. Memory disturbance is one of the most common complaints of alcoholics who seek help, and two-thirds of chronic alcoholics experience blackouts, periods of time for which they have *no* memory. During blackout episodes, short- and long-term memories are not impaired, but the alcoholics are unable to form any new, long-term memories.

Memory loss during intoxication can be counteracted by giving people the drug zimelidine before they drink (Weingartner et al., 1983), and the effect of this drug suggests that other drugs that will improve or restore memory may be found. While some people see the search for memory-improvement drugs as symptomatic of a drug-dependent, pill-popping society, others recognize that such drugs may help people with memory loss due to strokes, brain damage, and a variety of brain disorders. Already, the neuromodulator vasopressin, which is used as a nasal spray, has produced improved memory formation and performance in depressed middle-aged women and senile elderly people. It has also minimized the memory loss of patients who have received electroconvulsive therapy (Weingartner et al., 1981).

The discovery of the memory-enhancing effects of vasopressin and other neuromodulators raises many issues (Rosenzweig, 1984). Should such drugs be controlled prescription drugs, available only for treatment of disease or brain damage? Or should these drugs be available so all people can learn efficiently?

---

investigation of the brain; they are searching for a physical basis for memory. Beginning in the 1920s, one psychologist studied rats' abilities to remember a maze after removal of different parts of their brains (Lashley, 1929). He systematically removed parts of the cerebral cortex in his search for the location of the memory of the maze. Regardless of which part of the cortex he removed, the rats still remembered how to run through the maze. After thirty years, Lashley gave up his search for the **engram**, or **memory trace**, the physical basis of memory. He concluded that memories are not stored in a specific spot in the brain (Lashley, 1950).

About the time Lashley ended his search for the engram, one of his students proposed the **cell assembly theory** to explain the physical basis of memory (Hebb, 1949). Hebb suggested that all psychological functions, including memory, exist as a result of activity in interconnected neural circuits called cell assemblies. He further theorized that activity in these neural circuits modifies the synapses between the individual neurons. Through the process of **consolidation**, memories that begin as reverberating electrical activity in neural circuits (short-term memories) are eventually stored as changes in the synapses of the cell assembly.

Subsequent research has supported many of Hebb's ideas. Disrupting the electrical activity of the brain with electroconvulsive shock (passing an electrical current, which activates many neurons and often causes seizures, through the brain) prevents the formation of long-term memories. Rats shocked immediately after a learning experience show no memory of the experience; the shock disrupts the electrical activity produced by the learning and prevents the formation of a long-term memory. However, if the shock is delayed for thirty seconds or more, rats exhibit memory of the learning experience (Duncan, 1949). Thus, in rats, the consolidation of memories from short- to long-term memory takes approximately thirty seconds. Clinical evidence from humans who have had epileptic seizures, strokes, or concussions also reveals lack of memory for events that immediately precede the disruptive event.

Another possible physical form of memory has been investigated with less success. In the 1960s, knowledge that the DNA molecule is the source of genetic memory focused attention on a similar protein molecule, RNA, as a possible source of experiential memory. Many studies reported that different kinds and amounts of experience resulted in changes in the kinds and amounts of RNA in the learner's brain (Hyden & Lange, 1970). Some of the most intriguing studies involved the chemical transfer of "memory proteins" between flatworms (Mc-Connell, 1962). In these studies, flatworms were trained to move toward a light. They were then fed to untrained flatworms, who subsequently learned the same responses in fewer training trials. However, later researchers have been unable to replicate these studies (Gaito, 1974).

The search for the physical basis of memory continues. Finding the engram holds the promise of solving many of the unknowns about behavior. If the physical basis for memory is established, both short- and long-term memory will be better understood. The discovery will also lead to a better understanding of how learning occurs and, possibly, to cures for a wide range of memory disorders.

Focus Question Answer

If you are angry when you study, will you score better if you also are angry when you take the exam? According to laboratory studies of state-dependent retrieval, the answer is yes. The results suggest that emotional states can serve as retrieval cues. Students who were in the same mood during recall as they were when they originally learned the material remembered better; however, this research has not been repeated with everyday classroom tests.

Theories of Forgetting

The topic of memory has two sides. You can focus on remembering, as this chapter has so far, or you can focus on forgetting. Forgetting can be due to failure to encode the experience, loss during storage, or inability to retrieve information from storage.

Encoding Failures

Perhaps you would expect many ordinary, everyday events to be in your memory because you have experienced them so many times. But if you have never paid close attention to such events, you may have failed to encode them as long-term memories. Researchers who tested people's ability to recall or recognize the correct arrangement of the features on the face of a penny (Nickerson & Adams, 1979) found that most people could not remember which way Lincoln's head faces or the correct wording of the inscriptions. Do you remember?

After all the pennies you have handled, this task should be easy. You should also be able to recall easily the exact location of the gauges (oil, water, lights) on your car's instrument panel. Yet you may never have encoded these everyday experiences in long-term memory. You may not have stored this information about pennies and your instrument panel because these features are not as important as other aspects (e.g., the size of a penny or the position of the needle on the gas gauge). If you encoded all the unnecessary features of each day's "mindless" automatic experiences, you would probably be overwhelmed by trivial memories.

Decay and Displacement Two early theories of forgetting are decay and displacement. **Decay theory** explains forgetting as a gradual loss of memory over time. Although psychologists no longer accept this theory as a complete explanation of memory, it does seem to explain sensory and short-term memory. Information is rapidly lost from sensory memory and information that is not actively rehearsed or recoded in short-term memory is lost within twenty to thirty seconds. *Decay* seems an appropriate way to describe this loss. However, the occurrence of flashbulb memories and recall of childhood events suggest that decay does not adequately explain forgetting long-term memories.

Displacement theory proposes that all memory has a limited capacity; forgetting occurs when memory becomes overcrowded and new memories displace older ones. Today, the displacement theory is considered only

Exploring . . .

Organic Memory Loss

Memory loss is a common symptom of brain damage resulting from strokes, diseases, injuries, exposure to toxins, and other traumas to the brain. Memory loss due to physical causes is termed organic amnesia. People who suffer from **retrograde amnesia**, a type of organic amnesia, lose memory of the past. Often their loss of memories from the recent past is greatest; they can recall more distant memories. People affected with **anterograde amnesia**, another type of organic amnesia, lose the ability to form new, lasting memories.

Stroke patients often exhibit both types of amnesia, but retrograde amnesia is usually more prominent. Their memory loss is greatest for events just prior to and during the strokes; their recall of older memories is better but not unaltered. Interestingly, as stroke patients recover, memories of earlier times return first and are followed by more recent memories.

A famous case study of an epileptic patient known as H.M. illustrates the effects of anterograde amnesia (Milner, 1972). H.M. suffered from such severe seizures that in 1953 doctors surgically removed a part of both temporal lobes. In doing so, they also removed or damaged most of his hippocampus. This operation successfully ended his seizures. However, after the operation, H.M. was unable to form any new, lasting memories. His mental abilities and his memories of events prior to the operation were unaffected, and his I.Q. score remained the same. Yet after more than thirty years, H.M. still cannot find his way around his new neighborhood, and often he can figure out his age only by subtracting his birth date from the current date.

People with **Korsakoff's syndrome**, another organic cause of memory loss, experience symptoms similar to H.M.'s. Korsakoff's syndrome is caused by chronic alcoholism and a thiamine (vitamin B_1) deficiency. This vitamin deficiency results from the inadequate diet that usually accompanies long-term alcohol abuse. People with Korsakoff's syndrome cannot form new memories (anterograde amnesia), and they suffer from some retrograde amnesia (Butters & Cermack, 1980).

Alzheimer's disease, a degenerative (irreversibly deteriorating) brain disease, is characterized by more extensive memory loss than that suffered by either H.M. or people with Korsakoff's syndrome. The symptoms of Alzheimer's include extreme loss of current and recent memory, emotional depression, disorientation (loss of one's sense of time, direction, or location), and hearing or seeing things that are not there.

While the disease can begin at any age, the likelihood of developing the disease increases with age. The usual onset is late middle age or later, and the onset of symptoms is often gradual. Because of the stereotype that forgetting is a sign of age, the early symptoms may go unnoticed; the accompanying depression may be attributed to other causes and treated in ways that mask the correct diagnosis. Alzheimer's can be diagnosed certainly only by surgically removing a tiny amount of the cortex. Examination of the tissue will reveal atrophy of the cerebral cortex and the hippocampus.

An estimated 1.2 million to 4 million Americans have Alzheimer's and an estimated 120,000 die of it each year (Wurtman, 1985). Although no effective treatment for Alzheimer's has yet been found, one radical approach is being investigated. Currently, researchers are experimenting with tissue implants in the brain, a treatment that has been tried with some success with Parkinson's disease, another degenerative brain disorder (Kolata, 1983). Research on Alzheimer's, Korsakoff's, strokes, and other organic causes of amnesia will continue. When these puzzles are solved, much more will be known about the memory process.

partially valid because the capacity of long-term memory is virtually limitless. However, since new information *does* displace older information in short-term memory, displacement theory is still used to explain losses from short-term memory.

Storage Failures

Other theories of forgetting focus on memory loss from long-term storage. Psychologists debate whether long-term memories are permanent (Anderson, 1980) or whether they may be lost over time (Loftus, 1980). A recent survey indicated that a majority of psychologists believe long-term memories are permanently stored (Loftus & Loftus, 1980). However, memories can be lost from storage in several ways.

Physical damage to the brain and other organic causes may produce forgetting. Traumatic injuries to the brain, strokes, brain disorders such as Alzheimer's disease, infectious neural diseases, and drug abuse can cause memory loss. The general term for this type of forgetting is **organic amnesia**. More information on memory loss due

EXHIBIT 10.6
Experimental Designs for Studying Interference

	Proactive Interference		
Experimental Group	Learn A	Learn B	Test B
Control Group	(rest)	Learn B	Test B
	Retroactive Interference		
Experimental Group	Learn A	Learn B	Test A
Control Group	Learn A	(rest)	Test A

to organic causes is found in the accompanying *Exploring . . .* section.

A different type of memory loss results from **interference** between new and old memories. You may forget because old memories interfere with a new memory (**proactive interference**) or because a new memory interferes with old memories (**retroactive interference**). For instance, when you move and need to remember your new address, you may write down an address that is a mixture of your old and new. This type of forgetting is proactive interference because memory for your previous address interferes with memory for your new one. When remembering the names of students from last semester's classes is difficult because of the new student names you have learned this semester, you are experiencing retroactive interference.

Proactive and retroactive interference are easy to demonstrate experimentally (Underwood, 1957). Exhibit 10.6 shows typical experimental designs for studying interferences, which have been used to explain the serial position effects mentioned earlier. Better memory for the first items on a list (the primacy effect) reflects the lack of proactive interference, while better memory for the last items on a list (the recency effect) shows the absence of retroactive interference. The middle of the list is most difficult to remember because it is both preceded and followed by other items and therefore subject to both proactive and retroactive interference.

Retrieval Failures

Have you ever misplaced your car keys? You know that they are not lost, but you do not know where to look for them. Misplacing your car keys is analogous to what happens in memory when you experience a retrieval

Quick Study Aid

Proactive and Retroactive Interference

Since the terms proactive and retroactive are easily confused, try these methods of keeping them straight. Bisect the words: *pro active* and *retro active*. Think of the prefixes as opposites—pro equals forward, and retro equals backward. Each is an active process. As shown in the illustration, remember old memories actively jumping forward to interfere with new memories; remember new memories actively jumping backward to interfere with old memories. Or you may notice that in PRoactive interference, the PRevious or PRior information interferes with the new information, while in REtroactive interference, the more REcent information causes the interference.

failure (in fact, forgetting where your car keys are *is* a retrieval failure; the memory is still there, but it is not accessible). Sometimes a single cue will get you on the right path to memory retrieval. For this reason, retrieval failures are also called **cue-dependent forgetting**. You should not be disappointed if your psychology instructor fails to recognize you as his or her student when you meet in a grocery store. Without the cues of the classroom, your instructor may recognize you but not remember you as his or her student.

The tip-of-the-tongue phenomenon is an example of cue-dependent forgetting, and TOT illustrates how important the right cue can be. Creating retrieval cues when new information is being encoded makes later retrieval of the information easier (Tulving, 1974). Mnemonics (memory improvement strategies) achieve their effect in this way. Storing information about the number of days in each month according to the poem "Thirty days have September . . ." creates retrieval cues that help you recall the correct information.

Another type of retrieval failure, **motivated forgetting**, is the active, purposeful failure to retrieve embarrassing, painful, or threatening memories. Freud thought this type of forgetting is a defense against anxiety, and he referred to it as **repression**. People repress information unflattering to or inconsistent with their view of themselves (Robbins, 1963). Repression also functions to protect and enhance feelings of self-esteem. For example, in one study, students who completed a study skills course bolstered their views of their improvement in study habits by remembering their previous study skill levels as lower than they actually were (Conway & Ross, 1984).

Practical Memory

Memory research has greatly increased psychologists' understanding of memory processes, but it has neglected many practical, everyday aspects of memory. Remembering to do specific tasks (**prospective memory**) is one area that has not been investigated extensively (Harris, 1984). From remembering to take out the garbage on Friday to remembering to let the dog out before bedtime, you must remember to do many activities in the future.

In a study of prospective memory and memory aids (Meacham & Leiman, 1975), students were given colored tags on key chains to remind themselves to do certain tasks on certain days. These external memory aids increased the likelihood they would remember to do the tasks on the appointed days. Both children and adults prefer external memory aids (rather than internal ones, such as making mental notes or using mental imagery) for prospective memory tasks (Kreutzer et al., 1975; Harris, 1980). The most effective cues involve activity, are specific reminders, and occur close to the time the remembering must occur (Harris, 1978).

Failures of prospective memory are called **absent-mindedness**. In these slips of action, people forget to do things. Although common, this type of forgetting can have tragic consequences in today's technological world and can easily result in airplane crashes or industrial accidents. Absent-mindedness is most likely to occur in highly familiar surroundings while you are performing routine, automatic tasks and while you are either preoccupied or distracted (Reason, 1984). The *Relate* section offers practical suggestions for improving your memory.

Focus Question Answer

When you forget information, can you distinguish between whether you did not store it in memory or you were unable to retrieve it from memory? Distinguishing between encoding and retrieval failures is often difficult. However, if you are able eventually to remember the information, you obviously did not fail to encode it. Retrieval failures are often due to not using the appropriate cues to gain access to the information.

Relate

Practical Personal Memory Improvement

Chapter 1 presents several techniques for improving your study habits and your memory. Foremost among these techniques is the *SQ5R* system. This system emphasizes *actively* processing information by organizing the material in meaningful ways and by practicing retrieval of the material.

Relate, the fourth R in the SQ5R system, is especially important in memory improvement. Relating improves encoding, storage, and retrieval. When you form relationships between what you are experiencing and what you have already experienced, you increase the meaningfulness of the material and make its storage in existing memory networks easier.

The most meaningful relationships you can form are those that have personal significance (Craik & Lockhart, 1972). You are more likely to remember information that refers to an event in your life (Bower et al., 1981) because personal experience provides the most meaningful network for associating material in memory; personal experiences also provide the easiest pathway from which to retrieve information. The context with which you are most familiar is yourself.

Psychology is easy to relate to your life because it is about you; the information in this text is directly relevant to your life. When information from certain subjects seems *not* to be about you and when you cannot easily relate information to your experience, ask yourself, "What do these ideas mean to me?" and "How can I use this information in my life?" Do not be troubled if the answers suggest the information is useless. The harder you try to relate information, even apparently useless information, to your personal experience, the easier remembering it will be.

To further aid your memory, make use of retrieval cues. Chapter 1 presents ten memory techniques (see box at right). Now, after studying Chapter 10, you should recognize that the first seven techniques are ways of creating distinctive, easily recalled retrieval cues. The *Quick Study Aids* scattered throughout the chapters make extensive use of these techniques. The key to the success of these mnemonic memory systems is their use of vivid imagery to create retrieval cues you can recall in a systematic order.

You will have to exert considerable effort to learn the techniques, and to achieve success you must use them regularly. But do not be skeptical about the usefulness of these systems. Their success has been demonstrated in both laboratory studies (Bower, 1973) and everyday life. In one study, college students who used mnemonics remembered 72 percent of the material, while students who used rote rehearsal

1. **The Location Technique.** Use vivid images to associate items to be remembered with locations in a room. Take a mental walk through the room to remember the items.
2. **The Link Technique.** Link together vivid images of items to be remembered. Create a story (narrative chaining) that links the items together.
3. **The Peg Technique.** Learn a series of peg words that rhyme with a number series (one is a bun, etc.). Form vivid images of items to be remembered with peg words.
4. **The Sound-Alike Technique.** Instead of forming vivid visual images, associate sound-alike words or phrases with the items to be remembered.
5. **The Acronym Technique.** Use the initial letters of items to be remembered to form words (HOMES to remember the five Great Lakes).
6. **The Acrostic Technique.** Form a sentence in which the initial letter of each word reminds you of an item to be remembered.
7. **The Jingles Technique.** Make up a rhyme such as "i before e except after c."
8. **The 5 W's Technique.** Learn five bits of information about the item to be remembered—Who, What, Why, When, and Where.
9. **The Rote Technique.** Use active recitation to rehearse material until it is overlearned.
10. **The Flash Card Technique.** Make flashcards to test your memory.

remembered only 28 percent of the material (Lorayne & Lucas, 1974). Professional memorists rely on these techniques for their astounding performances.

The last three techniques in Exhibit 10.7 improve memory by increasing the meaningful organization of the material (the 5 W's technique) or by increasing rehearsal time (rote memorization and flash cards). Increasing rehearsal time (recitation in the SQ5R system) encourages **overlearning**, in which you continue to study the material after you have committed it to memory. Overlearning is especially useful for material to which you have difficulty attaching meaning.

How you *schedule* your study time is also very important. Generally, **spaced practice**, studying regularly with time between study sessions, is more effective than **massed**

The most effective way to study for exams is spaced practice with intensive review.

practice, cramming or studying the material in a single session (Anderson, 1980). However, the strategy that produces the best classroom test performance is regular, spaced practice (studying) throughout the term, with massed practice (cramming) the night before the exam.

An important memory improvement study (Jenkins & Dallenbach, 1924) demonstrated that spacing of study periods reduces interference. Students who studied for a test immediately before going to bed did better on the test than students who studied and then remained awake during the interval before the test. Presumably, the students who slept after studying experienced less retroactive interference than did the students who remained awake. You can also limit the effects of interference by noting the primacy and recency effects. To increase the likelihood that you will remember important or difficult material, go over that material first or last in your study sessions.

Another useful memory technique is to use external as well as internal retrieval cues. Naturally, you will not be able to use notes when you take most of your exams, but writing notes to yourself is a helpful external cue for remembering to do activities (prospective memory). Make "to do" lists, and remember to look at them. Use alarm clocks and timers. Keep an appointment and assignment diary or calendar. If you need a reminder, change a feature of your daily routine. Instead of wearing string on your finger, wear a rubber band on your wrist. Make checking your external cues a part of your daily schedule.

Finally, practice the following pointers for remembering names and faces. Recall the previously mentioned study that demonstrated that people could remember the faces of their classmates for many years but could not as easily remember their classmates' names. People fail to remember names and faces usually because of encoding failures; as they are introduced, they do not listen carefully to people's names or look carefully at people's faces. Without paying attention,

you cannot hope to improve your memory for names and faces.

Begin by concentrating on people's names. Make sure that you hear their names correctly. Ask people to repeat their names if you cannot immediately repeat them to yourself. Rehearse the names frequently. When you meet several new people at once, write down their names as soon as you can. Second, concentrate on people's faces. Although staring may be impolite, you must look at people's faces if you are to associate them with their names. Merely following these two steps should be enough to improve your memory for names and faces. If you add a third step, forming vivid associations between people's faces and names, you will be amazed by your near-perfect memory.

All the suggestions in this section are successful techniques for improving your memory. One factor is common to all techniques, and it is necessary to assure your success in improving your memory. You must regularly practice and use the techniques; if you do not, your memory skills will decline to their former levels. You may protest that your busy schedule does not allow you time to practice these techniques, but consider this: People who think they do not have time to learn better memory systems are willing to accept the loss of time caused by their poor memory skills. Good luck improving your memory!

Things to Do

1. Read the descriptions of amazing memorists described in Ulric Neisser's book, *Memory Observed* (1982). Would you want such a good memory?

2. Test your episodic memory. Do you keep a diary or a daily log of your activities? (If you do not, find someone who does.) Have someone quiz you (or you quiz the other person) about events that are recorded in the diary. Ask two kinds of questions. Name the date, and ask the person to remember what he or she did on that day. Or, name an event or activity and ask the person to remember the date on which it occurred. Keep track of the strategies people use to retrieve memories from storage.

3. Pick several events that should produce flashbulb memories. Interview ten people about their memories of the events, and identify the similarities and differences in their remembrances. If other class members perform this activity, combine your observations and present them for class discussion.

4. Poll your classmates for their favorite external retrieval cues. Ask them to then assess their success in using each cue. Compile a list of the most successful and unique cues to share with your class.

5. Analyze your own study habits for examples of proactive and retroactive interference. Redesign your study procedures to eliminate as much interference as possible.

6. Try one of the memory systems listed in the *Relate* section. Keep a record of your progress as you learn the system. Note how successful you are in using the system and the likelihood you will continue to use it.

7. Analyze your past performance on essay and multiple-choice exams. Using the information in this chapter, devise a plan to improve your performance on each type of exam.

8. Interview elementary school students about their use of retrieval cues, mnemonic devices, and memory systems. Ask them to explain how they usually go about memorizing information for tests. Are they familiar with the ten techniques to improve memory?

Things to Discuss

1. When did you first receive formal instruction in memory improvement? Discuss your experiences with memory skill instruction. Should entire classes on memory improvement be taught? At what age should such instruction begin?

2. How accurate are your memories of early childhood? Do you, like Piaget, have memories of nonexistent events? Discuss with your parents your recollections of early childhood. How accurate are your parents' recollections of your early childhood?

3. Discuss with your classmates whether individual flashbulb memories for public events are more alike today than at earlier times in history because of worldwide media coverage of such events (e.g., the attempted assassinations of President Reagan and Pope John Paul II).

4. Which causes more forgetting—proactive or retroactive interference? Give as many reasons as possible in support of each type of interference.

5. Which of the two models of memory—storage and transfer or levels of processing—do you think best fits your experiences with memory? Cite examples to support your choice.

6. Which of the ten memory techniques in the *Relate* section have you used? Which ones do you prefer? Why?

7. Why is the alphabet song so widely used in America to teach young children the twenty-six letters of the alphabet? Does the song follow sound memory techniques? Can you devise a better way to teach young children the alphabet?

8. Relearning is the most sensitive way to measure what is retained in memory, followed by recognition tasks and then recall tasks. Yet relearning appears to be an impractical way to evaluate performance in schools. Is relearning practical for any type of evaluation? Should instructors be required to give only multiple-choice exams since recognition is a more sensitive measure of memory than recall?

Things to Read

Baddeley, A.D. 1982. *Memory: A user's guide.* NY: Macmillan.

Cermak, L.S. 1975. *Improving your memory.* NY: McGraw-Hill.

Loftus, E.F. 1979. *Eyewitness testimony.* Cambridge, MA: Harvard University Press.

Loftus, E.F. 1980. *Memory: Surprising new insights into how we remember and how we forget.* Reading, MA: Addison Wesley.

Neisser, U. (ed.) 1982. *Memory observed.* San Francisco: W. H. Freeman.

 ## Review

Summary

1. Memory plays a central role in many psychological processes. Ebbinghaus conducted the first laboratory studies of memory over one hundred years ago.

2. The information-processing model of memory is widely accepted. In this model memory processing proceeds through three phases: encoding, storage, and retrieval.

Information can be encoded visually, auditory, or semantically.

3. The storage and transfer model proposes three types of memory: sensory memory, short-term memory (STM), and long-term memory (LTM). Information in sensory memory is transferred to short-term memory, or it dis-

appears quickly. Information in STM must be actively processed by rehearsal, or it will be lost within twenty to thirty seconds. The capacity of STM is limited to approximately seven meaningful units, the size of which can be expanded by chunking. Active encoding transfers the information from STM into LTM, which has an almost limitless capacity. Information stored in LTM is relatively permanent but subject to ongoing revision.

4. In the levels of processing model, memory is a function of the degree of processing. More easily remembered information is thought to have received deeper levels of processing.

5. Procedural (memory of skills), semantic (memory of facts, meanings, and rules), and episodic (memory of personal history) comprise one system of classifying memories.

6. Reconstructive memory is the process in which long-term memories are revised and updated. It accounts for people's memories of events they never experienced.

7. As revealed by metamemory and the tip-of-the-tongue phenomenon, people know a great deal about what is stored in their memories, even when specific information cannot be recalled.

8. Recall, recognition, and relearning are three ways to measure memory. Recall involves reproducing stored information with few retrieval cues. In serial recall, information must be remembered in the order it was presented. In free recall, information may be recalled in any order. Recall produces both primacy and recency

effects. In recognition, the task is to identify information stored in memory. Relearning measures the amount of time saved in learning material for a second time.

9. Flashbulb memories are vivid personal memories formed at the time of an unexpected but significant event.

10. Active rehearsal is necessary to form long-term memories. Long-term memory is organized into clusters of related information, and the clusters are organized into larger networks. Retrieval cues are used to gain access to these networks. Context-dependent memory suggests that retrieval is best under conditions that duplicate those at the time the material was stored. State-dependent retrieval, a related concept, proposes that retrieval is best when a person is in the mood or state that he or she was in during storage of the experience.

11. The transfer of information from STM to LTM is called consolidation. Researchers unsuccessfully searched the brain for specific locations for memories.

12. Forgetting can occur because of encoding failures (decay and displacement), storage failures (physical damage and interference), and retrieval failures (cue-dependent forgetting and motivated forgetting). Interference effects can be proactive (old interfering with new) or retroactive (new interfering with old).

13. Internal and external retrieval cues can be used to aid prospective memory and limit absent-mindedness.

14. Most mnemonics, or memory systems, create retrieval cues to use both for storing and retrieving information.

Key Terms

information-processing model	recall	state-dependent retrieval
encoding	primacy effect	engram (memory trace)
storage	recency effect	cell assembly theory
retrieval	recognition	consolidation
dual coding theory	relearning	decay theory
eidetic memory	savings	displacement theory
storage and transfer model	rote rehearsal	organic amnesia
sensory memory	elaborative rehearsal	proactive interference
short-term memory (STM)	recoding	retroactive interference
long-term memory (LTM)	context-dependent memory	cue-dependent forgetting
levels of processing model	tip-of-the-tongue phenomenon (TOT)	motivated forgetting (repression)
reconstructive memory		prospective memory
flashbulb memory	metamemory	absent-mindedness

Focus Questions

1. In what ways do you think differently now than you did when you were eight years old?

2. Are you a logical person?

3. Which problem-solving strategy is best for you?

4. If you increase the size of your vocabulary, will you think better?

5. Can thinking be taught?

Chapter Outline

COGNITION: STRUCTURE AND PROCESS
Definitions of Thinking
Mental Structures
Theories of Cognitive Processing

REASONING AND LOGIC
Formal Reasoning
The Research Process: Investigating Natural
Reasoning Strategies

PROBLEM-SOLVING
The Problem-Solving Process
Types of Problems
Problem-Solving Strategies
Barriers to Problem-Solving

LANGUAGE AND THOUGHT
Characteristics of Language
The Whorfian Hypothesis
Thought, Language, and Metacognition

RELATE: Can Thinking Be Taught?
Things to Do
Things to Discuss
Things to Read

REVIEW: Summary
Key Terms

Chapter 11

Cognitive Processing

*Man's mind stretched to a new
idea never goes back to its
original dimensions.*

Oliver Wendell Holmes

 Cognition: Structure and Process

What exactly is thinking? Are you thinking when you
read this sentence? Are you thinking when you remember the quote by Oliver Wendell Holmes? Are you thinking when you make decisions, solve problems, and answer
questions? Are you thinking when you dream? These
questions suggest that thinking is a set of processes for
using information. But what about the structures that
underlie these processes? Are you thinking when you see
a picture in your "mind's eye"? Are you thinking when
you know or understand an idea? Does knowing that you
know an answer involve thinking? Thinking is a complex
activity that involves both structure and process. Thinking is the basis for your knowledge of the world and for
your actions based on that knowledge.

Definitions of Thinking

Cognition, a more formal term for thinking, refers to the ways in which you internally represent, process, and use information about the world. When you reason, judge, plan, decide, solve problems, remember, imagine, and speak, you engage in cognitive activity. A fundamental aspect of cognition is information processing—transforming, reducing, elaborating, storing, recovering, and using information (Neisser, 1967). **Cognitive psychology** is the study of these higher mental processes and structures. Cognitive psychology is part of an emerging interdisciplinary area called **cognitive science**, which emphasizes the understanding of mental representations (internal knowledge of the external world), analyses of thinking, and computer models of human thinking (Gardner, 1985).

A major difficulty in studying cognition is that mental representations and processes are private, internal events that each person experiences subjectively. As you may recall from Chapter 2, the first experimental psychologists used introspective methods in attempts to examine their own conscious awarenesses. However, such a subjective approach to studying thinking is flawed because many mental processes are not part of conscious awareness. Are you aware of how you recognize the words in this sentence? Are you aware of the processing involved when you respond to the following question: Does this sentence remind you of ice cream?

Because cognition is subjective, psychologists' objective methods cannot study it directly. They must infer cognition from behavioral observations, reaction time measurements, and direct recordings of the brain's neural activity. Often, when communication with subjects is difficult, as it is when studying infants and animals, researchers use behavioral observations to infer thinking. In a classic study, an ape named Sultan solved the problem of obtaining a banana that was beyond his reach outside his cage (Kohler, 1925). The necessary elements for solving the problem, a shorter stick and a longer stick, were within Sultan's view. Was Sultan thinking when he used the shorter stick to obtain the longer stick, which he then used to reach the banana? By answering yes, the researchers had to infer that Sultan's behavior was the result of internal cognitive processing.

The precision of reaction time measurement and the EEG recordings of neural activity may convince you that such methods of studying thinking are direct observations of it. However, these observations are indirect correlates of thinking; the act of thinking still must be inferred. Even when subjects are asked to say their thoughts aloud, the translation of thought into language requires that their thoughts must be inferred from their speech. This inferential basis has led cognitive psychologists to an abstract analysis of thinking. The analysis is abstract in the sense that it is not dependent on specific physiological mechanisms such as circuits of neurons. Certainly, biological information is helpful in understanding thinking, but thus far it has not been adequate for understanding thought processes.

Mental Structures

The abstract nature of cognitive analysis is most apparent in the suggested mental structures of thinking. In everyday speech, people talk about thoughts, ideas, and memories as actual entities, yet these entities are without ties to physical reality. The terms cognitive psychologists use are no less abstract—schemas, concepts, mental maps, and mental images. These terms refer to internal representations of knowledge, but they are not linked to any specific physiological structures.

Enactive, Iconic, and Symbolic Representation   Two major systems of mental structures have emerged from the research on cognition. One researcher suggests three types of representations of information as thought (Bruner et al., 1966). The first type, **enactive representation**, involves thinking in terms of physical actions. In the second type, **iconic representation**, thoughts are represented as concrete images. The most advanced form of processing, according to this view, is **symbolic representation** in which experience is translated into language and other abstract symbols.

How are enactive, iconic, and symbolic representation used in card games?

Try this exercise. Ask a friend who owns a car to describe the car to you. Watch carefully. After your friend makes a few initial statements about the car, does she or he look up or away? After a few minutes, ask the person to *tell* you where the ignition switch is located. What does your friend do now? Does the person *tell* you or *show* you the location of the ignition switch? A common response to these requests is to begin with a well-rehearsed set of words about the car ("It's a white, 1980 Chevy Citation that's starting to rust"), the person's symbolic representation of the car. Often, this initial response is followed by a slower set of responses as the person appears to be looking at an image of the car (the person's iconic representation) and translating features of the image into words. To the question about the ignition switch, most people use the appropriate hand to turn a nonexistent key in a nonexistent switch on a nonexistent steering column or dash (the person's enactive representation of the ignition switch). From your observations, would you infer that information is represented internally as symbols, images, and actions?

Declarative and Procedural Knowledge In a second system of mental structures, cognitive psychologists distinguish between two kinds of information to be represented internally—**declarative knowledge** and **procedural knowledge** (Best, 1986). Declarative knowledge is factual information that is easily described such as knowing your address and telephone number. Procedural knowledge is information that underlies skill performance. For example, reading and writing are skills that require procedural knowledge to perform. This knowledge is easier to *show* people than *tell* them. Procedural knowledge is "knowing how" rather than "knowing that." Reading these sentences is a cognitive process that involves both types of knowledge. You "know how" to read, and you "know that" each word has a definite meaning. You can easily declare the meaning of most of the words. However, you may find that telling someone the procedures you use for reading is difficult, although you can easily show the person how you read. Procedural knowledge is aligned with enactive representation, while declarative knowledge can exist as images or as symbols.

Imagery Images are clearly a part of most people's internal representations of information. In Chapter 1, the authors suggest visual imagery as a technique to improve your memory. Additionally, many famous scientists, writers, inventors, and artists (e.g., Einstein in developing his theory of relativity) claim that visual imagery enhances their creative thinking (Shepard, 1978). But do creative thinkers credit visual imagery for their success when, in fact, the success is due to other cognitive factors? Cognitive psychologists attempt to determine if imagery is a separate part of thinking or a by-product of other cognitive processes.

Beginning in the 1970s, several lines of research demonstrated support for mental imagery as a mode of thought separate from other cognitive processes (Kosslyn, 1983). In one study, subjects were asked to compare pairs of objects such as those shown in Exhibit 11.1

EXHIBIT 11.1
Stimuli for Mental Rotation Experiment

The above figures are samples of stimulus pairs in the Shepard and Metzler study of mental rotation. Pairs A and B differ in degree of rotation (the left figure in Pair A is rotated 80° from the position of the right figure). The left figure in Pair C cannot be matched by rotating the right figure.

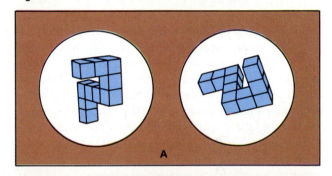

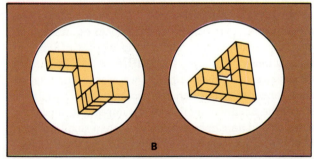

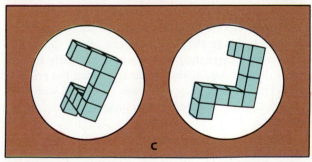

"Mental Rotation of Three-Dimensional Objects", Shepard, R. N. & Metzler, J. *Science*, Vol. 171, pp. 701–703, fig. 1, Feb. 19, 1971.

(Shepard & Metzler, 1971). They were to determine as quickly as possible whether the pairs are two views of the same object or views of two different objects. In the top and middle pairs, the objects are the same, but the objects on the right have been rotated to angles different from the angles of objects on the left. The subjects could determine that the objects are identical by mentally rotating one member of the pair until it matches the other. In the bottom pair, the objects are different from each other (no amount of rotation will get them to match). The researchers manipulated the degree of rotation between the pairs; then they measured the amount of time subjects took to say "same" or "different." Subjects who mentally rotated the images of the objects needed more time to say "same" or "different" to the pairs with greater rotation.

The results supported the researchers' predictions. The subjects took longer to respond to pairs with greater rotation, and the increase in time was proportional to the increase in rotation. The researchers maintained that the subjects were not just watching an image while other cognitive processes were at work. Instead, they said the mental rotation of the image was the cognitive process the subjects used to answer the question. Other researchers obtained similar results when they studied the mental rotation of letters of the alphabet (Cooper & Shepard, 1973). In these studies, subjects appeared to be inspecting a continuously changing mental image in the same way they visually inspect an actual object.

In a second line of research to determine that images are separate from other mental processes, researchers carefully explored the relationship of sizes of different mental images (Kosslyn, 1975, 1976, 1978). In the first of a series of studies, subjects were asked to imagine simultaneously two different-sized animals. The relative size of the simultaneous images was important. Imagining a rabbit and an elephant should create a small image of a rabbit, while imagining a rabbit and a fly should create a large image of a rabbit. Researchers reasoned that if subjects processed information by looking at the image, they should respond more quickly to questions about the large rabbit image than to questions about the small rabbit image (larger images are seen more clearly and in greater detail). Again, the results supported the predictions. The subjects' response times correlated with the size of the image inspected. Larger images produced faster responses.

The results of the other studies in this series also confirmed that processing information as images is a separate cognitive process. However, other researchers are not convinced by these studies and contend that the differences in processing time could be caused by other cognitive processes. For example, one group of researchers (Jonides, Kahn & Rozin, 1975) used congenitally blind individuals as the control group. Presumably, individuals who have been blind since birth cannot use visual imagery. Surprisingly, instructions to use mental imagery produced improved performance on a variety of tasks for both the sighted and blind subjects in the study. Determining what cognitive activities the blind individuals engaged in when they were asked to use mental imagery is difficult, but the results indicate that whatever they did was as effective for them as mental imagery was for the sighted individuals.

No one is critical of the results produced by either side of the mental imagery issue, but many question the interpretations of the results (Block, 1981). An experimental approach that can rule out one interpretation and support the other has not yet been devised. Yet from a practical viewpoint, mental imagery, regardless of the reasons for it, adds a rich dimension to thinking.

Cognitive Maps   Images are also used to create **cognitive maps**, which are mental representations of physical space. This idea was proposed by learning theorist E. C. Tolman (see Chapter 9), who suggested that animals, like humans, are capable of creating mental representations of the environments in which they live. Like other forms of imagery, cognitive maps have practical significance. You use your internal maps to locate your car in a parking lot and to give directions to people.

The ability to use cognitive maps improves with experience. Finding your way around a city that is new to you is difficult because you have not formed a mental map. After traveling in the city for a time, you may not bother to look at a map because, with experience, you have formed a cognitive map of the city. Active experience is important in forming internal maps. Preschool children who actively searched for a hidden object in an unfamiliar environment formed more accurate cognitive maps of the space than children who were passively led through the environment by an adult (Feldman & Acredolo, 1979). Although even young children use cognitive maps, the ability to do so improves with age (Siegel et al., 1979).

Try using your cognitive map to draw an actual map of your college campus. How accurate do you think your drawing is? When students at the University of Arizona were asked to do this (Saarinen, 1973), they sketched best the areas with which they were most familiar. For

EXHIBIT 11.2
Cognitive Map

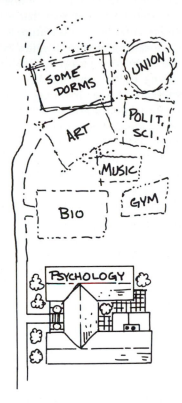

example, psychology majors were best at mapping the area near the psychology building and were less accurate at sketching other areas of the campus (see Exhibit 11.2). This study, like the study of preschoolers, supports the role of active experience in forming accurate cognitive maps.

Concepts and Concept Formation   **Concepts** are another way information is mentally represented. Concepts are mental categories of objects, events, people, and other living organisms. They represent a way of grouping together items and events that share common features. Some concepts are well-defined with specific features and definite boundaries; other concepts are ill-defined with ambiguous features and fuzzy boundaries. In some cases, the defining features of one concept overlap with the defining features of another concept. Laboratory studies suggest concepts are formed by identifying the common critical features (necessary characteristics) and deciding whether all or only some of those features must be present for an item to fit the concept (Bruner, Goodnow &

Austin, 1956). Everyday examples do not confirm this view of concept formation.

Outside the laboratory many concepts are ill-defined and appear to be formed by a different process (Rosch, 1978). Such concepts are not formed from a set of common features but are built around a representative example, or **prototype**. A prototype exhibits the typical features of a particular category. For example, a robin typifies many peoples' concept of *bird*. Robins are more easily recognized as birds than are geese and penguins. The prototype is usually the concept member that has the most features in common with other concept members and shares the fewest features with other concepts. Rank the list of fruits in Exhibit 11.3 from the one that is most typical to the one that is least typical of the concept category.

The list of fruits in Exhibit 11.3 is adapted from a list used in an actual study. Students in that study rated oranges and apples as the best examples of fruits and coconuts and avocados as the poorest examples (Rosch, 1975). Notice that although all the listed fruits bear a family resemblance, items rated as most typical within a category share the largest number of features with other members of the category (Rosch & Mervis, 1975).

The prototype denotes what is typical of category membership, while the **schema**, another mental structure, denotes what is essential about category membership. Although penguins exhibit very few of the features of the prototypical bird (the robin), penguins do possess the essential characteristics of birds. Therefore, penguins fit the schema of birds.

Schema, a more general term than prototype, represents a large mental structure that can be used to organize information. In this sense, schemas represent plans or procedures for classifying people, events, or objects

Although a robin or a sparrow is the prototype of the concept of bird, the concept is flexible enough to incorporate a penguin.

EXHIBIT 11.3
Ranking from Most to Least Typical Fruit

Are some of the fruits listed below better examples of fruit than others? Which one is the best example of a fruit? Use numbers one through twelve to rank the fruits from most to least typical. Rank number one the most typical and number twelve the least typical.

APPLE	—	GRAPEFRUIT	—
APRICOT	—	ORANGE	—
AVOCADO	—	PINEAPPLE	—
BANANA	—	RASPBERRY	—
COCONUT	—	STRAWBERRY	—
GRAPE	—	WATERMELON	—

From Rosch (1975).

(Neisser, 1976). For example, you have a schema for deciding which of your friends would enjoy watching a horror film with you, just as you have a schema for how to organize the information in this chapter. When the plans are about expected sequences of events and actions, the term **script** is used (Abelson, 1981). While schemas represent declarative knowledge, scripts represent procedural knowledge, such as how to play a piano or dance a ballet. Schemas and scripts represent the principal systems of plans for cognitive processing.

Theories of Cognitive Processing

The abstract analysis that produces the mental structures for thinking has also been applied to the process of thinking. The results are models that integrate the major information-processing systems of perception, learning, and memory. Most models of cognitive processing are based on earlier work in mathematics (Turing, 1936) and engineering (Shannon, 1938). This early work suggested that all information could be processed as a series of binary (two states—yes/no, on/off, true/false) decisions.

By the 1950s, these ideas emerged as the two distinct but closely connected fields of computers and cognitive psychology. Psychologists viewed computers as a way to simulate human thought (Simon & Newell, 1958), and cognitive processing was viewed as a flow of information through a system (Broadbent, 1958). Basic to both fields is the idea that information, when processed by humans or computers, is transformed from its initial state. Thus, concepts and images are transformations of the original input. This view is analogous to the manufacturing process in which raw materials are transformed into processed products.

Information processing theory is one of two major theories of cognitive processing. According to this theory, processing begins with raw data that is transformed into mental representations. This feature is often called "bottom up" processing because it relies on serial processing, or the completion of a series of steps. In information-processing theory, the individual elements of cognition (attending, perceiving, learning, and remembering) are organized into a series of sequential (in order) mental transformations that begin with sensory inputs (Dodd & White, 1980).

A second major theoretical approach to cognitive processing comes from the work of the Swiss psychologist Jean Piaget. In a career spanning sixty years, Piaget focused on the development of cognitive processes from infancy to adulthood (Piaget, 1952, 1970, & 1977). Like information processing theorists, Piaget believed that knowledge is constructed from the individual's interactions with his or her environment. However, Piaget's theory emphasizes "top down" processing. He proposed that the human system has built-in organizing factors,

Jean Piaget used the case study method to develop his theory of children's cognitive development. Other psychologists use the experimental method to test and refine his ideas.

mental operations, that process information from the environment and represent it as internal schemas.

Piaget proposed that an individual increases the number of his or her schemas through the process of **assimilation** and modifies them through the process of **accommodation**. When a person encounters new information, he or she attempts to incorporate the new experience into his or her existing knowledge. For example, babies who already know how to put their fingers in their mouths can use that knowledge to put new objects in their mouths. But if new experiences do not fit an existing schema, the schema is changed through the process of accommodation. Babies accommodate (change their internal schemas) when through experience they find that their existing knowledge of the world is inadequate. Toddlers develop a schema for things that fly in the air—the schema for "birdies." After further experience, they alter their schemas to include "planes," "butterflies," and other flying objects and organisms. Piaget believed that intellect is the ability to adapt to one's environment and that assimilation and accommodation

EXHIBIT 11.4
Piaget's Stages of Cognitive Development

Stage	Age	Characteristics
Sensorimotor	0–2	Experiencing world through senses and actions; achieving stable view of the world (object permanency)
Preoperational	2–7	Developing language and imagination but use of logic limited by egocentrism.
Concrete Operations	7–12	Increasing skill at thinking logically with concrete objects and events; mastering physical properties of matter (principles of conservation)
Formal Operations	12–16	Increasing skill at reasoning abstractly through the use of hypothetico-deductive reasoning

Quick Study Aid

Schematics for Assimilation and Accommodation

Use these images to distinguish between assimilation and accommodation. Visualize a round peg and a square hole. The round peg is the new experience, and the square hole is the existing schema. Assimilation—imagine squaring up the round peg so that it will fit into the existing square hole. Accommodation—imagine modifying the existing square hole so that the round peg will fit into it.

Or, use these two sentences:

ASSIMILATION MAKES THE NEW EXPERIENCE FIT THE OLD IDEA.

ACCOMMODATION MAKES THE OLD IDEA FIT THE NEW EXPERIENCE.

form the basis for human adaptive capabilities. Piaget proposed that the push to adapt comes from another internal process that he termed **equilibration**, the internal urge to keep knowledge in a balanced state. Concisely, Piaget maintained that people are motivated to make their new experiences fit their existing knowledge.

Piaget's major contribution to psychology was his ideas about developmental changes in cognitive processing. After carefully observing his own children and other children (see *Exploring . . . Piaget's Method—A Clinical Approach*), Piaget concluded that children pass through predictable, qualitatively different stages of mental operations as they develop into mature, logical, thinking adults. These stages, described in Exhibit 11.4, are controversial. Critics challenge the ages for Piaget's stages as well as the premise that all children go through the stages in the same manner (Selman, 1980). Despite these criticisms, Piaget's stages remain the most thoroughly researched descriptions of children's thinking.

In recent years Piaget's ideas have been reevaluated and revised (Modgil et al., 1983). Critics cite as important shortcomings in Piaget's theory his inattention to language's role in thinking (Siegal, 1978), his methodology (Donaldson, 1978), and his underestimation of children's cognitive achievements (Boden, 1979).

Piaget's Method— A Clinical Approach

Jean Piaget (1896-1980) had a remarkably long, productive, and influential career researching children's thinking. Trained as a biologist, he published his first research on mollusks when he was sixteen. Later, as a young adult, he helped give intelligence tests to children and became intrigued by the kinds of errors children made on test items. Piaget took a detour in his career as a biologist and studied the ways in which children acquire knowledge about the world and mentally represent that knowledge. Fortunately for the field of cognitive development, Piaget's career detour lasted a lifetime.

Due in part to his training as a marine biologist, Piaget based his theories about cognitive development on careful observations of children. Piaget studied how children come to reason and know about physical reality, but he did not use traditional laboratory experiments. Rather, Piaget relied on simple demonstrations and an adept use of clinical interviews to assess children's cognitive abilities.

The clinical method is the hallmark of Piaget's approach to studying children. Typically, in a conservation test (a test to determine if children recognize that certain physical properties of matter, such as the volume of liquid, do not change), he would work with one child at a time. Piaget would pose a simple task for the child; he would ask the child whether two lumps of clay were equal. He would then work with the child, adding or taking away clay from the lumps until the child said the two were equal. At that point, Piaget would roll one lump into a long "snake" or flatten it into a "pancake." He would then ask the child if the amounts of clay were still equal. Depending on the child's reply, Piaget would continue to question and listen intently to the child's answers, examining the answers for what they indicated about the child's reasoning.

After collecting volumes of observations, Piaget studied his notes and searched for commonalities that would allow him to generalize about children's thought processes. Piaget's efforts were enormous, and his insights were brilliant. Almost single-handedly, he created cognitive development as a field of psychology.

However, because Piaget's observations were based on loosely structured interviews, and because his clinical approach lacked the precise control measures of more traditional laboratory studies, other researchers

In the preoperational operational stage, young children use play to learn conservation of number, quantity, and volume.

criticize his method and his results. Criticisms of Piaget's methodology focus on the language demands (Siegal, 1978) and the task demands (Brown & Desforges, 1979). Critics contend that children who are given Piaget's conservation tasks may fail to understand or may misinterpret the tasks and the questions. The following study demonstrates their criticisms.

In a traditional test of conservation of number, children were asked to judge whether two rows of counters (beads on a metal rod) were equal in number (McGarrigle & Donaldson, 1975). The rows were equal in number, and the children said so. Then the experimenter purposely rearranged the counters in one row (the same number of counters) to make the row longer. Many children now reasoned that the longer row contained more counters and so failed to demonstrate conservation of number. The test was then repeated with the children who had failed to conserve number, but this time the row was "accidentally" lengthened by a "naughty teddy bear" as the child and the experimenter were playing. Under this condition, the lengthening of the line was an incidental happening to which the child's attention was not drawn. Most of the children, under this condition, were able to correctly judge that the two rows contained equal numbers of counters. The researchers concluded that the language and task demands of the traditional test defeated the children. Purposely changing the length of the row may have caused the children to misinterpret the task, and being asked a second time about the number counters may have caused the children to misunderstand the intent of the researcher's question. Thus, Piaget underestimated their abilities.

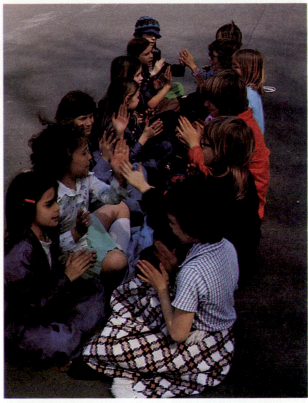

School-age children enjoy their ability to play games according to fixed rules.

From the reappraisal of Piaget's theory, a "neo-Piagetian" position has emerged (Pascual-Leone, 1980); it attempts to combine the two major theories of cognition—information-processing theory and Piaget's cognitive development theory. The neo-Piagetian position is based on an analysis of the information-processing strategies involved in Piaget's tasks. Many of Piaget's tasks required the use of several complex cognitive strategies, or plans for dealing with knowledge. This new position proposes that the number and complexity of children's cognitive strategies and the size of their "working" memories increase as they develop. Many mental plans become automatic with practice and experience. Thus, the neo-Piagetians have revised Piaget's original qualitative stage ideas to include quantitative increases in thinking strategies, memory, and automatic processing.

Focus Question Answer

In what ways do you think differently now than you did when you were eight years old? You now use more images and symbols in your thinking, you deal with more abstract ideas, and you reason hypothetically. You use cognitive maps and more complex plans, and you apply automatically more of your cognitive strategies.

> *Some people would rather die than think—in fact, they do.*
>
> **H. L. Mencken.**

Reasoning and Logic

In everyday usage, reasoning and thinking are interchangeable terms. However, in the study of thinking, **reasoning** refers to thinking for the purpose of making decisions, forming judgments, and solving problems. To complete these tasks, two general types of reasoning are used—deductive and inductive.

Deductive reasoning involves a "top down" approach. You begin with general ideas you believe to be true and derive specific conclusions from those general ideas. If you believe that all good students are prepared for class (a general assumption), and you know that you are not prepared for class, then you may reason (deduce) that you are not a good student. **Inductive reasoning** is a "bottom up" strategy; you reach general conclusions from a series of specific instances. If you observe that Joyce, Jim, and Bob, who are always prepared for class, always do well on exams, then you may generalize that if you are always prepared for class, you too will do well on exams. However, you may feel less certain about this second conclusion because someone who is well-prepared may still not do well on an exam. With inductive reasoning, you can never be completely sure that your conclusion is correct unless you have observed all the possible instances.

Logic is another term with both an informal and a formal meaning. Informally, logic refers to plausible inductive or deductive reasoning. When you refer to someone as a logical person, you usually mean you believe the person can give reasons to support conclusions and can make reasonable inferences from facts. In constrast, formal logic refers to the use of specific logical reasoning forms to construct valid arguments and to solve formal, logical problems.

Formal Reasoning

Have you taken a course in logic? A major part of logic courses is learning about **syllogisms**, which are formal deductive arguments. The basic syllogism form includes a major premise, a minor premise, and a deductive conclusion. Consider the following classic syllogism: (1) All men are mortal. (2) Socrates is a man. (3) Therefore, Socrates is mortal. If you accept the first two statements as true, then you must inevitably accept the conclusion as true. The relationship between the first two statements forms the basis for the truth of the deductive conclusion.

The rules of formal logic are not synonymous with the rules of thinking. Consider the results of a study in which educated and uneducated rural Mexicans were asked to respond to the following syllogism:

All the houses in Mexico City are large.
My friend has a house in Mexico City.
My friend's house is _____.

Both groups gave the correct response of "large" (Cole & Scribner, 1977). The educated group indicated that they knew the answer should be large because of the form of the argument; therefore, they used formal logic. The uneducated group did not; they based their answers on what they knew to be true of Mexico City, replying that they had heard about the large houses in Mexico City. The researcher found that as little as three years of education was all that was necessary to produce the shift from answers based on experience to answers based on logic. Formal logical reasoning appears to be a product of education and literacy.

Most people do not take courses in formal logic and are not familiar with its rules. Therefore, researchers study everyday reasoning in the laboratory by asking people to make estimates about events that could take place in their everyday lives.

The Research Process: Investigating Natural Reasoning Strategies

Much of what is known about everyday reasoning comes from studies done by the research team of Kahneman and Tversky. During nearly twenty years of collaboration, these researchers have used realistic examples to test people's use of heuristics in reasoning about everyday problems. A **heuristic** is a rule of thumb that provides a general guideline for reasoning; heuristics contrast with the specific rules used in formal logic.

One of Kahneman and Tversky's earlier studies demonstrates how heuristics can bias subjects' reasoning (Kahneman & Tversky, 1973). In this study, subjects were divided into two groups. The "engineer-high" group was told that a person had been picked at random from a sample of one hundred people. The group was further informed that thirty of the hundred people in the sample

were lawyers and seventy were engineers. The "engineer-low" group was told that the sample consisted of thirty engineers and seventy lawyers. Both groups were asked to estimate the odds that the person picked at random from the sample was an engineer. Both groups were accurate in their estimates, with the engineer-high group estimating about a 70 percent chance and the engineer-low group estimating about a 30 percent chance. Then the subjects were told that another person had been picked at random from the sample, and they were provided with the following description:

Jack is a 45-year-old man. He is married and has four children. He is generally conservative, careful, and ambitious. He shows no interest in political and social issues and spends most of his free time on his many hobbies, which include home carpentry, sailing, and mathematical puzzles. (Kahneman & Tversky, 1973)

The subjects were again asked to estimate the likelihood that the person was an engineer. Both groups estimated the chances that Jack was an engineer at greater than 90 percent. How would you explain these results? The estimated odds were greater (much greater in the engineer-low group) than the proportion of engineers in the sample. Kahneman and Tversky reasoned that the description of Jack was more representative of an engineer than of a lawyer. Because Jack was typical of engineers, the subjects in both groups disregarded the odds of selecting an engineer and concluded that Jack was an engineer. Particularly, the engineer-low group overlooked the low 30 percent odds of selecting an engineer from their sample. In this case, a heuristic caused the subjects to reason that Jack represented a prototype of engineers rather than to reason from the base rate of engineers in the sample. Kahneman and Tversky showed that heuristics are not only a strategy people use to simplify their everyday attempts at sound reasoning, but heuristics can also bias peoples' ability to reason soundly.

In a related study (Kahneman & Tversky, 1973), subjects were asked to estimate the proportion of words that begin with the letter K and the proportion of words in which K is the third letter. The rationale behind this task was that the greater ease with which subjects could think of words beginning with K would cause them to assume that words beginning with K were more common. In fact, words in which K is the third letter are three times as common as words beginning with K. The subjects' estimates were as the researchers had predicted, and once again, Kahneman and Tversky demonstrated that people use heuristic strategies in everyday reasoning and that the same strategy that facilitates reasoning can also bias it.

In their more recent work, Kahneman and Tversky (1984) have investigated how **framing**—the way in which a problem is presented—can bias an individual's reasoning about the problem. In a 1984 study, these researchers presented subjects with situations such as these:

Imagine that the U.S. is preparing for the outbreak of an unusual Asian disease, which is expected to kill 600 people. Two alternative programs to combat the disease have been proposed.

Subjects were then presented with two alternatives:

If Program A is adopted, 200 people will be saved. If Program B is adopted, there is 1/3 probability that 600 people will be saved and a 2/3 probability that no people will be saved.

Approximately 75 percent of the subjects picked program A, reasoning that the 2/3 probability that everyone might die was unfavorable odds compared to a sure bet that 200 people could be saved.

Interestingly, reframed but equivalent alternatives produced the opposite results with another group of subjects. These subjects were given the following two alternatives:

If Program A is adopted, 400 people will die. If Program B is adopted, there is a 1/3 probability that nobody will die, and a 2/3 probability that 600 people will die.

With this framing, approximately 75 percent of the subjects picked Program B, reasoning that the low probability of saving everyone was a better risk than the certainty that 400 people would die.

If this example does not seem real to you, consider if you are more likely to pay your electric bill promptly if the electric company: (1) gives you a discount for prompt payment, or (2) charges you a penalty equivalent to the amount of the discount for late payment. According to Kahneman's and Tversky's predictions, you will be more likely to avoid the penalty, even though you would pay the same amount in both cases.

Kahneman's and Tversky's research demonstrates that people rely on heuristics to make decisions and form judgments, and they do so somewhat uncritically. Although heuristics simplify everyday reasoning, they can produce biased and unsound reasoning in some situations.

Focus Question Answer

Are you a logical person? If you use sound formal logic and heuristics to guide your reasoning, you can probably answer yes. However, keep in mind that knowing *how* to use sound reasoning strategies does not guarantee that you will apply them effectively.

Chance favors the prepared mind.

L. Pasteur

 ## Problem-Solving

"Wanted: Practical problem solvers. Experience necessary. Wages commensurate with success in solving problems." Would you apply for this job? Your answer probably depends on your assessment of your problem-solving ability. Practical problem-solving ability is highly valued. In one study (Sternberg, 1982), when people from all walks of life, including experts on intelligence, were asked what behaviors they associate with intelligence, they listed practical problem-solving ability as one of the most important indicators. Certainly, the ability to solve problems has practical significance for everyone's life. In this section, you will learn about problem-solving as a cognitive process; you will also explore different problem-solving strategies and barriers to effective problem-solving.

The Problem-Solving Process

While a definition of problem-solving may hardly seem necessary, experts who study the problem-solving process define a problem as a situation in which you try to find the means to reach a goal (Chi & Glaser, 1985). The typical problem-solving sequence is familiar to most people. Generally, after you recognize you have a problem, you define the problem, plan a strategy for solving the problem, carry out your plan, and evaluate the effectiveness of your solution. Each step requires a series of cognitive actions. These general steps have been incorporated into most models of problem-solving.

The Gestalt psychologists were among the first to propose a fixed sequence of problem-solving steps (Wallas, 1926). These stages (also known as the steps in creative problem-solving) are:

1. **Preparation.** In the preparation stage, you recognize that you have a problem; you prepare to solve the problem by gathering useful information and by trying to

Unstructured play activities can encourage creativity and problem-solving.

understand the problem; you make initial attempts to solve the problem.

2.   **Incubation**. Incubation occurs when your initial attempts to solve the problem do not succeed and you set the problem aside. You no longer work consciously on the problem, but your unconscious processing may continue.

3.   **Illumination**. After a period of incubation, the solution to the problem often appears with a sudden burst of insight called the "aha experience."

4.   **Verification**. Sometimes your "blinding flashes of insight" during the illumination stage prove to be faulty solutions. Verification provides the necessary confirmation that your insight is indeed a workable solution.

Most research has centered on the incubation stage. In addition to the Gestaltists' proposal of unconscious processing, other researchers have suggested that your improvement in problem-solving ability after a period of incubation may be due to selective forgetting of faulty solutions so you can retrieve better solutions from memory (Simon, 1982). Another researcher (Anderson, 1981) suggests that incubation allows you to replace perceptions based on expectations with more useful perceptions.

Other problem-solving researchers (Newell & Simon, 1972) propose a different set of stages; these are based on the information-processing approach. In the first stage, you attend to the **task environment**; you examine the terms used to describe the problem or the components of the problem. In the second stage, you transform the task environment into a mental representation of the problem, the **problem space**. The problem space includes your perception of the goal, your present state in relation to the goal, and the possible strategies you may need in order to reach the goal and solve the problem. In the third stage, you construct from your problem space a **production system**, a plan or program for reaching the goal.

The Gestalt and information-processing approaches are similar. Both stress the importance of representing the problem correctly. Identifying the goal and its relation to your present condition is important during the preparation stage (or while representing the problem in the task environment). Also important is identifying the means available for reaching the goal and the restrictions governing your use of specific strategies. Consider the following classic problem-solving task:

The Dog, the Goat, and the Cabbages

A farmer has to cross a river in a boat big enough to carry only him and either his dog, his goat, or his cabbages. The cabbages will be eaten if they are left alone with the goat, and the goat will be eaten if it is left alone with the dog. How does the farmer take the dog, the goat, and the cabbages safely across?

Unless you already know the solution to this problem, you will probably spend time representing the problem in your problem space. You can do so by considering the various elements:

—   *The goal:* Transport the dog, goat, and cabbages safely across the river.

—   *The initial state:* The dog, goat, and cabbages are on the opposite side of the river.

—   *The means:* A boat that will hold only the farmer and either his dog, his goat, or his cabbages.

—   *The restrictions:* The goat cannot be left alone with the cabbages, and the dog cannot be left alone with the goat.

Representing the problem this way should help you realize that the goat is the key element—it cannot be left alone with either the dog or the cabbages. Have you discovered a workable solution? Compare your solution with the one at the end of the chapter summary.

Types of Problems

The way in which you represent a problem and the strategies you use will be determined partly by the type of problem. Some problems are well-defined, while others are ill-defined. **Well-defined problems** have clearly defined initial states and goals. "The Dog, the Goat, and the Cabbages" is a well-defined problem. **Ill-defined problems**, such as problems in which one of the parts is missing, may have vague initial states, unclear goals, or unclear strategies and restrictions. When faced with ill-defined problems, people often break the problem down into several well-defined subproblems (Voss et al., 1983).

One researcher divided all problems into three basic types (Greeno, 1978). The first type, **problems of inducing structure**, involves determining the relationship among elements of the problem. Analogy problems are representative of this type. Can you supply the missing terms in the following analogies?

Bird is to nest as _____ is to burrow.

Ocean is to _____ as _____ is to island.

_____ is to people as _____ is to national economy.

These analogy problems can be solved by first discovering the characteristics of the terms, then comparing the characteristics, and finally evaluating possible solutions (Pellegrino, 1985). You probably found the first analogy easiest to solve. When the number of features increases (the second analogy) or when the terms share few features (the third analogy), analogies become more difficult to solve. Possible solutions to the analogy problems appear at the end of the chapter summary.

The second problem type is **problems of transformation**. In these, the problem-solver must discover the sequence of operations that will transform the initial state into the goal. The Tower of Hanoi problem shown in Exhibit 11.5 is a well-known example of this type. The goal is to move the disks on peg 1 to peg 3 given that you may move only one disk at a time and that you may never place a larger disk on top of a smaller disk. The principle cognitive strategy you would use to solve this problem is **means-ends analysis** (Newell & Simon, 1972). With this strategy, you note the differences between the initial state and the goal state; then you attempt to reduce the differences between the two states. Did you recognize that the Tower of Hanoi and the Dog, the Goat, and the Cabbages problems are similar? Both solutions require you to use the strategy of means-ends analysis.

Problems of arrangement are the third type of problem in this system. Anagrams (scrambled words) are typical examples of problems of arrangement. In an anagram, you must rearrange the letters to form a word. Try unscrambling these anagrams.

EXHIBIT 11.5
The Tower of Hanoi Problem

Given state

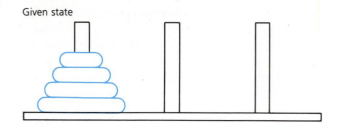

Goal state

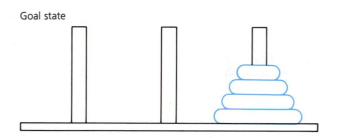

In this four-disk version of the Tower of Hanoi problem, a disk may be moved to another peg provided that it is not placed on top of a smaller disk. Only one disk may be moved at a time, and only the top disk on a stack may be moved. Can you move the stack of disks from the left peg to the right one without violating the instructions? The solution appears at the end of the chapter summary.

OLTO _____

ACTHE _____

SAHMR _____

ELVID _____

Are you aware of which cognitive strategy you used to discover the words? The approach used most often is called constructive search, in which a person systematically examines reasonable combinations of letters until he or she finds a word. Look again at the words you formed. Can you apply constructive search to rearrange the letters a second time and form four new words? The solutions to these anagrams appear at the end of the chapter summary.

Problem-Solving Strategies

The types of problems illustrated in the last section require different problem-solving strategies. While each type of problem has a principal strategy, the strategies overlap and are used in many different problem-solving situations. In this section, additional problem-solving strategies will be explored.

Trial-and-Error **Trial-and-error** strategies are relatively inefficient random searches for solutions. Problem-solvers resort to trial-and-error methods when other solutions are not readily apparent. However, even when more efficient systems are apparent, some people still rely on trial-and-error. In the game of Twenty Questions, many players persist in asking random, trial-and-error "Is it _____ ?" questions, even after they are shown a strategy that systematically narrows the possibilities (Irwin, 1986).

Algorithms When trial-and-error search becomes systematic rather than random, the strategy is called an **algorithm**. If you had difficulty constructing a word from one of the anagrams presented earlier, you may have methodically tested each possible combination of letters until you found a combination that created a word. (Five letters can be arranged 120 different ways.) By systematically searching all possible combinations, you would eventually discover a correct combination. Algorithms are strategies that guarantee correct solutions to problems. They are not always efficient, but they always result in a correct solution. Algorithms work best with well-defined problems with clearcut beginnings and goals. Some well-defined problems, however, are too broad or complex for the successful use of algorithms. Increasing a five-letter anagram by one letter increases the possible combinations to 720. An eight-letter anagram has over 40,000 possible combinations! A computer can produce those 40,000-plus combinations, but few people would want to search through the list.

Heuristics When solving problems as broad as eight-letter anagrams (or even five-letter ones), people usually use another strategy called a heuristic. Heuristics are rules of thumb based on knowledge and past experience with problem-solving. For example, you are aware that some letter combinations are more likely to occur than others. So in trying to unscramble an anagram, you use a heuristic when you try the more frequent letter combinations first. This approach shortens the search time, but it lacks an algorithm's certainty for finding a solution. The earlier discussion of everyday reasoning emphasized

Very young children use trial-and-error techniques to work jigsaw puzzles. As they grow older, they use more sophisticated problem-solving techniques.

Quick Study Aid

Remembering the Difference between Algorithms and Heuristics

Do you remember the fable of the tortoise and the hare? To remember the difference between algorithms and heuristics, think of algorithms as the tortoise and heuristics as the hare. Algorithms, like the tortoise, are slow but sure and will eventually finish the race. Heuristics, like the hare, are speedy and useful in the short-run but cannot always be counted on to produce results.

the importance of heuristics in organizing thinking and in creating biases.

Hypothetical Reasoning   Another problem-solving strategy is **hypothetical reasoning**. Using this approach you purposely make an assumption that was not part of the original task environment. To see how hypothetical reasoning can be used to add information, try solving the following problem about truthtellers and liars.

You are visiting a strange country with only two kinds of people—truthtellers and liars. Truthtellers *always* tell the truth and liars *always* lie. You hail the first two people you meet and ask, "Are you truthtellers or liars?" The first person mumbles something you can't hear. The second says, "He says he is a truthteller. He is a truthteller and so am I." Can you trust the directions these two may give you? (Hayes, 1981, p. 20)

You can use hypothesis testing on this problem. You do not know what the first person said, but you can hypothesize what he might have said. What if the first

person were a liar? What would he have mumbled? What if the first person were a truthteller? What would he have said? The key to solving this problem comes from hypothesizing about what each person might have mumbled. Did you conclude that both the liar and the truthteller would have mumbled the same thing—that he is a truthteller? With this new information, you can now conclude that the second person is a truthteller and that the first person is too. Thus, hypothetical reasoning and heuristics are related. A heuristic represents a hypothesis about the best strategy to use in solving a problem.

Barriers to Problem-Solving

Solving problems would be easier if you had only to pick the best strategy. Unfortunately, you may also have to overcome barriers to effective problem-solving. Sometimes you have to overcome barriers in the strategies themselves, as in the case of heuristics. As you have seen, heuristics are useful shortcuts, but they also create strong biases.

Another type of barrier and bias, **mental set**, develops from previous experience. Your previous successful experiences with solving certain problems create a mental set that predisposes you to try to solve similar problems in the same way. You may persist with previously

Do you have a mental set about what one can build from sand?

EXHIBIT 11.6
Luchin's Water Jar Problem

Problem	A	B	C	D
1	21	127	3	100
2	14	163	25	99
3	18	43	10	5
4	9	42	6	21
5	20	59	4	31
6	28	76	3	25

Using the quart quantities listed for each jar, how would you measure out the amount in column D? For example, in problem 1 you could fill jar B (127 quarts) and then fill jar A (21 quarts) once and jar C (3 quarts) twice from jar B (B − A − 2C = 100).

successful solutions even when easier solutions are evident. Exhibit 11.6 depicts a classic experiment that demonstrates the existence of mental set (Luchins, 1946).

Experience also plays a role in the problem-solving barrier of **functional fixity**. Many problems call for creative solutions in which you use old familiar objects in new ways. The more often you use an object for a specific function, the more difficulty you will have using that object in a novel way. Can you solve the problem of the strings described in Exhibit 11.7? Numerous solutions for this problem are possible. Most of the solutions involve either lengthening one of the strings or making a pendulum with one of the strings. What is available for lengthening the string? What can serve as a weight to make a pendulum?

Many items in Exhibit 11.7 could be used as a string extender or as a weight for a pendulum, but you may not have considered them because of their specific, fixed functions. For example, shoelaces and belts have fixed functions, but they can also serve as string extenders. Similarly, the wrench and magnet have very specific functions, but either could be used as a weight for a pendulum. Can you estimate how often you overlook obvious solutions because of functional fixity?

Focus Question Answer

When you have a problem to solve, which strategy is best? No one strategy is always best. However, systematic strategies are more effective than random trial-and-error searches. Depending on the type of problem, algorithms, heuristics, or hypothetical reasoning may be most effective. Remaining flexible is the key to choosing the best strategy and to overcoming problem-solving barriers.

EXHIBIT 11.7
The String Problem

Imagine that you are alone in this room. Your task is to tie the two strings together. The strings are close enough together to be knotted but far enough apart so that you cannot reach one string while holding on to the other. How will you tie the strings together?

Language and Thought

Can you think about an object for which you do not have a word? This question is central to an important cognitive issue—the role of language in thought. While you may have difficulty thinking about your answer to the question, you will certainly use language to communicate your thoughts about the answer. If you reflect for a moment on the mental structures discussed previously, you will realize that images are one way to think about an object for which you do not have a word. But how do you communicate those images to someone? You could use nonverbal communication—gestures, body movement, and posture. Or drawing a picture might be more effective than gesturing. Folk wisdom recognizes the importance of pictures by suggesting that a picture is worth a thousand words. With the proper skills, you might even communicate your thoughts through an artificial language such as a math equation, a computer program, or a musical score. However, most people do not bother with these forms of communication because communicating their thoughts is much easier when they use their native language.

Characteristics of Language

What makes language different from other forms of communication? Languages, either natural or artificial, share three properties. First, every language includes a set of basic symbols. In natural languages, the basic units are spoken sounds called **phonemes**. The English language has forty-six phonemes, which are represented in the written language by the twenty-six letters of the alphabet and certain letter combinations such as ch and sh. Second, each language has a system for assigning meaning to basic sound combinations. The basic unit of meaning in a language is called a **morpheme**; morphemes are combinations of phonemes to which meaning has been attached. Words, prefixes, and suffixes are examples of morphemes. Most other forms of communication have basic symbols with meaning attached to them.

However, languages have a third characteristic that sets them apart from other forms of communication. They have sets of rules, **syntax**, which are used to create an infinite number of meaningful word orders. The rules of syntax allow you to speak and write sentences that make sense to other people. These rules give human languages their unique position among the many forms of communication. But is language uniquely human? The *Exploring . . .* section examines this issue.

Your knowledge about the basic aspects of language usage is called **grammar**. Possession of this knowledge suggests that you can think about language at a cognitive processing level. A major theory about language, **transformational grammar** (Chomsky, 1957, 1983), proposes that language knowledge exists on two levels of cognitive processing. **Deep structure** refers to the level of abstract language rules that determine meaning. Processing at this level begins the ordering of words and meanings that you eventually speak. According to this theory, transformational rules are then used to process the deep structure into a **surface structure**, the actual order of the words in the sentence you produce. Chomsky used ambiguous sentences as evidence for his theory. The sentence "He enjoys flattering women" has one surface structure but two meanings (i.e., two deep structures): "He enjoys giving compliments to women" and "Women who flatter are enjoyable." Although the deep structures order the words and meanings differently, the transformation to the structure produces an ambiguous sentence. You are able to recognize the ambiguity because of the underlying deep structures.

Other features of transformational grammar include the idea that grammatical knowledge is based on **language universals**, innate predispositions found in all natural languages. Language universals can be thought of in two ways: first, as the features common to all languages and, second, as the rules for constructing language. This second feature leads back to the question of the relationship between language and thought. Are the rules for constructing language identical with the rules for all thought processes?

The Whorfian Hypothesis

In answering "yes" to the preceding question, linguist Benjamin Whorf argued that language determines the way you perceive and think about the world (Whorf, 1956). His viewpoint is called the **linguistic relativity hypothesis** or the **Whorfian hypothesis**. The basic idea is that the vocabulary and the structural rules of your native language limit you to thinking about the world within the confines of that language. If this idea is true, then cultural groups with different languages should think differently about the world. Whorf supported his hypothesis with observations from many language cultures. For example, he observed that Eskimos possess many different words for snow while other cultural groups for whom snow is not as important have only one or a few terms. Whorf maintained that the Eskimos' larger vo-

Language in Chimps and Gorillas

Is language a uniquely human characteristic? For years researchers have investigated the language capabilities of apes in an attempt to answer this question. In one of the first attempts to teach language to chimpanzees (Kellogg & Kellogg, 1933), a chimpanzee named Gua was raised with a human infant. The child learned to talk, but the chimp did not. Another attempt to teach a chimp named Viki to speak (Hayes, 1951) ended after she had learned to speak only four words in a three-year period.

Researchers who believed that chimps did not have the vocal apparatus to produce speech (Gardner & Gardner, 1969) taught ALS (American Sign Language, a system of hand gestures deaf people and others use to communicate) to another chimp. The chimp, Washoe, learned many signs and used them in her interactions with her signing human companions. Washoe even spontaneously combined signs to make new statements and requests. When she was given an infant chimp to raise, she taught the baby over fifty signs before it received any training from humans. However, despite her successes, Washoe failed to master syntax. She often changed the order of her signs without apparent reason. Washoe now lives in a primate colony and remains a focus of research (Fouts et al., 1984).

To further investigate chimps' language capabilities, other researchers have used plastic tokens for words (Premack, 1976) or special computer keyboard consoles (Rumbaugh, 1977). These projects and the studies with Washoe reveal that chimps can learn to use many different signs or symbols, that they can generalize the use of a sign from one situation to another, and that they can combine their "words" into larger units or statements. In addition, language training appears to improve chimps' ability to perform abstract reasoning tasks like analogies (Premack, 1983).

Does this evidence convince you that language is not uniquely human? In each of these cases, the chimp acquired only limited language capabilities, only with difficulty, and only after intense training. The training more closely resembled operant conditioning techniques used to teach complex behaviors to rats and pigeons than the way in which humans acquire language. Other relevant evidence comes from the study of a chimp named Nim Chimpsky (in honor of the linguist Noam Chomsky). After demonstrating Nim's apparent success with learning signs and creating

When Koko's pet kitten died, Koko used ASL to tell the trainers that she was very sad.

two-, three-, and four-sign combinations with a degree of syntactical order, Nim's trainer carefully analyzed videotapes of Nim's sign language production (Terrace, 1979). He discovered that Nim was reacting to prompts from his trainers and concluded that Nim's use of language consisted of merely imitating his trainers' signs. While imitation or subtle prompting may explain Nim's abilities, it is not a relevant criticism of the studies that used plastic tokens and computer keyboards.

Chimps clearly have the ability to learn some aspects of language, but no chimp has been able to use language as orderly, productively, and creatively as humans do (Aitchison, 1983). However, the research continues. A fascinating project with gorillas Koko and Michael has caught the attention of the general public (Patterson, 1981). For over a decade these gorillas have been coached in sign language. Koko signs to herself when she is alone and uses combinations of signs to express complex thoughts. Reportedly, she uses signs to joke, swear, and tell lies (Patterson, 1978). Koko received worldwide attention in January 1985 when newspapers published accounts of her reactions to the death of her pet kitten. When she was told about the kitten's death, Koko did not react immediately. After ten minutes, she began whimpering—a sound that gorillas make when they are sad. She signed "sleep cat" and "sad."

The continuing research with Koko, Washoe, and other apes may eventually produce the evidence necessary to answer the question posed earlier. Presently, most psychologists agree that a richly complex use of language remains an ability unique to humans.

cabulary for snow allows them to think differently about their world in which snow is an important part.

Whorf's ideas about linguistic relativity were tested in an experiment using color words (Berlin & Kay, 1969). On the basis of Whorf's ideas, individuals whose languages contain few color words should perceive colors differently than do individuals whose native languages have many color terms. However, the results of the color word study indicated that everyone sees colors in the same way regardless of their native language. Even among individuals whose language contains only two words for color, perceived color distinctions appear to be independent of the language they speak (Rosch, 1973). The Whorfian hypothesis suggests having many words for snow causes you to perceive snow differently. The results of these studies suggest that Whorf was wrong. From the findings of these studies you can infer that Eskimos have many terms for snow because snow is important to them and having observed the differences in snow, they created words to label the differences. Although the results from these studies do not support linguistic relativity, the Whorfian hypothesis is still widely used to explain differences in thinking among various cultures.

Quick Study Aid

Whorf Warps

To help you remember Benjamin Whorf's basic idea that language shapes the way you think, repeat this phrase: "WHORF WARPS." Form an image of language bending thought out of shape.

Thought, Language, and Metacognition

Cognitive psychologists are faced with an unanswerable question about the relationship between language and thought. Although the cross-cultural research on color naming suggests that thought controls language, everyday instances of language influencing thought are numerous. Descriptions and job titles are often changed so people think differently about the jobs (e.g., sanitation engineer, canine monitor, and flight attendant). Do you think differently when a car ad reads "pre-owned" rather than "used"? What images come to mind when you think of the words "nurse" and "orderly"? You might argue that these examples reflect rather than cause differences in thinking.

However, debating these distinctions may detract from more important aspects of the relationship between language and thought. Studying the similarities may be as useful as studying the differences. Both thinking and language production involve the integration of many separate processes. Neither activity occurs without the accompanying activities of attending, perceiving, learning, and remembering. Both thinking and language production involve conscious and unconscious processes, and both are monitored by a higher-order process termed **metacognition**.

Metacognition is your capacity to monitor your own thoughts. In metacognition, you analyze what you know and how well you know it. When you read an exam question, you are probably metacognitively aware if you know the answer. When you speak in class, you are probably simultaneously monitoring what you say and how well you say it. According to this approach, language and thought emerge as integrated processes monitored by metacognition.

Focus Question Answer

If you increase the size of your vocabulary, will you think better? From the linguistic relativity point of view, the answer is yes. From a practical perspective, the answer is also yes. Language and thought are integrated processes. Whether you believe that language shapes thinking or merely reflects what you think, improving your vocabulary increases the opportunities for language and thought to interact.

Relate

Can Thinking Be Taught?

The answer to this question depends largely upon your point of view. Traditionally, psychologists have believed that thinking is a fixed, unchangeable ability. In his cognitive-developmental theory, Piaget held that thinking is essentially a maturational process. He maintained that experience is necessary for thinking to develop, but the basic processes of assimilation and accommodation are innately determined. Recently, however, views about thinking have been revised. Many psychologists now maintain that thinking skills are not unchangeable but instead are very modifiable. A leading advocate of this view is Reuven Feuerstein, an Israeli clinical psychologist and a former student of Piaget.

Feuerstein maintains that the mind is moldable, like soft plastic (Feuerstein, 1980). He arrived at this conclusion when he worked with wayward, orphaned, and abandoned children who were immigrating to Israel at the time it became an independent nation. Many of these children were survivors of the Holocaust, and they were from diverse cultural backgrounds. On the basis of their scores on standard intelligence tests, some of these children were classified as mentally retarded. However, through his interactions with them, Feuerstein came to believe that many of them performed poorly on the tests because of cultural differences (they were disadvantaged by their different cultural backgrounds), while others did poorly because of cultural deprivation (they had failed to acquire basic, culturally transmitted knowledge about thinking such as the problem-solving process). Feuerstein preferred to label this second group "retarded performers" rather than "mentally retarded" (Feuerstein, 1979).

Feuerstein's answer to the question of whether thinking can be taught is an emphatic yes! He calls the ability to change your mental structures and contents **cognitive modifiability**. When you learn something, you modify the contents stored in cognitive structures. When you modify your thinking, you change the cognitive structures themselves. Feuerstein developed a test, the Learning Potential Assessment Device, that can be used to diagnose specific flaws in a person's thinking. On the basis of the diagnosis, Feuerstein developed tasks to modify an individual's thinking. These tasks form the basis of Feuerstein's **Instrumental Enrichment** program.

Instrumental Enrichment is based on a test-teach-test model. Individuals are diagnosed, taught with special tasks designed to meet their specific deficiencies, and retested to assess if they have removed the deficiency. The special tasks

involve **mediated learning experiences**, learning situations in which students work on specific tasks with active interaction with another person. The mediator (usually a parent, sibling, or teacher) actively guides the learner in appropriately responding to and learning from the tasks. Two typical enrichment tasks are described on page 269.

In contrast to the traditional cognitive view that maintains learning is the result of direct interaction with the environment without the intervention of another person, Feuerstein proposes that mediated learning experiences are more important for developing thinking skills because the mediator transmits to the learner basic cognitive knowledge such as how to regulate attention and to organize information. From Feuerstein's perspective, cognitive development is the result of combining individuals' direct experiences with the world and their mediated experiences with other people.

As a result of their lack of mediated learning experiences, culturally deprived individuals have a reduced capacity to modify their cognitive structures. This deprivation leads to flaws in thinking. Feuerstein believes that flaws in thinking are caused not by lack of interaction with the environment, but by lack of mediated instructions about the interactions. He believes that learning through direct interaction does not show the learner how to modify his or her cognitive structures but that mediated learning experiences do.

Through his work with children, Feuerstein identified many overlapping cognitive deficiencies. Do you recognize any of the following deficiencies in your own thinking?

— *Impulsiveness.* Individuals who display this characteristic tend to approach problem-solving tasks in a trial-and-error fashion. On multiple-choice exams, they often start looking for the answer before they understand the question. These individuals have failed to learn that deliberate behavior that follows a plan is a more useful strategy.

— *Inability to recognize problems.* Individuals with this impairment fail to recognize significant characteristics of problems. For example, many problems can be recognized by their inconsistencies and discrepancies such as the differences in the pan problem described on the following page. These individuals fail to pay attention to such differences.

— *Episodic grasp of reality.* Individuals with this problem have difficulty making connections between different events, perceiving relationships, and putting items in context. They

Examples of Instrumental Enrichment Problems

The object of these instructional exercises is to help students overcome various "cognitive deficiencies." Throughout, the teacher models, criticizes, praises, prompts, prods, and wheedles as necessary to help overcome flaws in the students' basic thinking skills. In the exercise on the left, the task is to trace broken lines so that some squares appear to be above others. Students who jump into the

task too quickly are apt to make mistakes; with help, they learn the value of controlling impulsivity. The exercise on the right, explaining how the full pot of water became empty, is designed to help students overcome the tendency to see related objects and events in isolation. The goal of the exercises is not to learn solutions to the problems but to master the thinking skills that can lead to solutions.

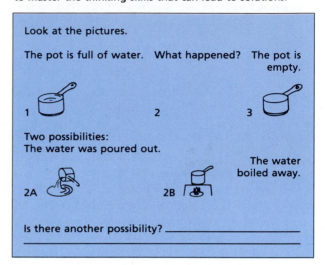

Darken the lines so that the smallest square will be underneath, and the largest square will be uppermost.

With a pencil, go over some of the lines so that the largest square will seem to be on the bottom, and the smallest square uppermost.

Darken the lines so that the center square will seem on top of the other two squares.

Look at the pictures.

The pot is full of water.   What happened?   The pot is empty.

1   2   3

Two possibilities:
The water was poured out.

The water boiled away.

2A   2B

Is there another possibility? _____
_____

From *Instrumental Enrichment: An Intervention Program* by Reuven Feuerstein. Copyright (c) 1980 by Scott, Foresman & Co. Reprinted by permission.

do not make a connection between the pan full of water and the empty pan in the above problem.

— *Failure to make comparisons.* Difficulties in making comparisons, such as how two objects are alike and how they are different, characterize people with this deficiency.

— *Inadequate spatial orientation.* This problem is demonstrated by individuals who have difficulty learning locations on maps. These people are aware of spatial relationships but fail to use them to orient themselves or to solve spatial problems.

— *General passiveness.* Individuals with this problem fail to recognize that they must take an active role in thinking and problem-solving. These individuals receive information passively and fail to actively generate any information. For example, when given a problem to work, these individuals do not attempt to work the problem.

Having examined these cognitive deficiencies, can you devise a plan using mediated learning experiences to modify faulty structures? The Instrumental Enrichment program is designed to provide structured mediated learning experiences that do so. Although it was originally designed for use with retarded performers, this program is now used with many kinds of older children and teenagers. In schools in

which the program is part of the school curriculum, teachers work with individuals or small groups in hourly sessions, three to five times a week. The entire program requires a two- to three-year period to deliver. This lengthy process reflects Feuerstein's goal of bringing about a permanent restructuring of the participants' skills.

How successful is Instrumental Enrichment in improving cognitive deficiencies? When the performance of Israeli children in a general enrichment program was compared with that of children in an Instrumental Enrichment program, the Instrumental Enrichment group showed significant improvement compared to the other "enriched" group (Feuerstein & Rand, 1977). Yet despite these promising results, Feuerstein's program needs to be tested by other researchers in different settings before it can be endorsed strongly.

In the meantime, you can take advantage of sensible suggestions derived from Feuerstein's years of study.

1. Arrange mediated learning experiences for yourself. Find a person who will work with you as your tutor.

2. Become an active learner.

3. Become aware of how you arrive at solutions while you attempt to solve problems.

4. Discard blind trial-and-error methods and use systematic approaches.

5. Look for the connections between events, analyze relationships, and put items into context.

6. Practice making comparisons.

7. Look for differences and discrepancies as well as similarities.

8. Practice using and making maps, both physical and cognitive.

Things to Do

1. Investigate the use of enactive, iconic, and symbolic representation among adults. Ask twenty people to give you directions to a location on campus. Observe closely how they give the directions. Notice whether they tell you (symbolic), create a map (iconic), or motion with their hands (enactive). After they have finished, ask them about their use of mental imagery while they were giving you the directions.

2. Attend a political debate, and analyze the participants' use of formal reasoning skills. Look for examples of deductive and inductive reasoning, sound arguments, and faulty reasoning.

3. Use one of the problem-solving sequences to solve a personal problem. Write down each step and your actions. Pay particular attention to representing the problem. Can you recognize any problem-solving barriers that might block your way to a solution? Be certain to evaluate your results. Was the systematic use of a problem-solving sequence effective for you?

4. Interview one or more bilingual individuals about their experiences and thoughts concerning language. Explore the advantages and disadvantages of growing up in a bilingual environment. Explore the relationship of bilingualism and thought. In which language do the bilingual people think and dream? Does the language in which they think and dream change? Do they know what causes them to shift from one language to the other?

5. Investigate your college's or university's courses in logic, formal reasoning, thinking, or cognition. Find out if your campus has a learning resource center that offers self-help programs for improving your thinking skills. Consider enrolling in a logic or thinking course or in a self-help thinking skills program.

Things to Discuss

1. Assimilation and accommodation are two of Piaget's most important concepts. Imagine a world in which people could only assimilate, never accommodate. How would people's thinking change? If you could use only one of these processes, which would you eliminate—assimilation or accommodation?

2. Based on your experiences and what you have learned from this chapter, would you advocate that people use more formal reasoning and less everyday reasoning? List the reasons, pro and con, for your position.

3. Think of a time when you solved a problem using trial-and-error. Based on the strategies presented in the text, what, if any, strategies would have been more effective? Is the trial-and-error strategy ever the most efficient way to solve a problem?

4. Dr. Dolittle is a character in a popular series of children's books. The good doctor can talk with animals. The research on language training with apes is attempting to do what children fantasize about when they read of Dr. Dolittle. In addition to a better understanding of the language process, how might people benefit from talking to animals? Assuming that animals could think of topics to talk about, how would life be different for them if they knew what other animals were thinking?

5. How should the teaching of thinking skills be incorporated into school curriculums? Should the basic skills of reading, writing, and computation be emphasized less, and thinking skills and cognitive strategies be emphasized more?

Things to Read

Desmond, A.J. 1979. *The ape's reflection.* NY: Dial Press/James Wade.

Gardner, H. 1985. *The mind's new science.* NY: Basic Books.

Hunt, M. 1982. *The universe within.* NY: Simon & Schuster.

Kahneman, D., Slovic, P., & Tversky, A. (Eds.) 1982. *Judgment under uncertainty.* NY: Cambridge University Press.

Patterson, F. & Linden, E. 1981. *The education of Koko.* NY: Holt, Rinehart & Winston.

Terrace, H.S. 1979. *Nim: A chimpanzee who learned sign language.* NY: Knopf.

Review

Summary

1. Cognition encompasses all the ways in which information is internally represented, processed, and used. Cognitive psychologists study thinking through abstract analysis and inference.

2. Three ways to represent information mentally are by actions, images, and symbols. Mental images have been studied extensively. Cognitive maps are internal representations of spatial relationships.

3. Concepts are mental categories of objects, events, and people. Naturally occurring concepts are built around a central prototype that exhibits the typical features of the category. Schemas denote what is essential about a category and are used to organize information.

4. According to information-processing theory, individual elements of cognition are organized into a sequential process. The sequence flows from the "bottom up," beginning with sensory input.

5. Jean Piaget studied the cognitive development of children. He proposed "top-down" processing, which uses assimilation and accommodation. Revisions of Piaget's ideas have combined his ideas about cognitive development with ideas from information-processing theory.

6. Reasoning generally refers to active, conscious thinking for the purpose of fulfilling a goal. Formal reasoning is used to analyze logically the soundness of arguments. Everyday reasoning strategies make use of heuristics as short-cuts in the reasoning process. Research has revealed that heuristics simplify everyday reasoning, but sometimes they produce biased, unsound reasoning.

7. To determine the best means for reaching a goal, problem-solving should follow a sequence of steps. Different types of problems and problem-solving strategies have been studied. Heuristics provide rules of thumb for searching for solutions, and algorithms produce sets of rules for testing every possible solution.

8. Thoughts can be communicated in a variety of ways, but most people use language. Languages are defined by three criteria: a set of basic symbols, a system for assigning meaning to the symbols, and a set of rules for ordering the meaningful symbols. Attempts to teach language to apes have been only minimally successful, but language research with apes still holds much promise.

9. Language and thought are closely intertwined. The linguistic relativity hypothesis, or Whorfian hypothesis, proposes that language shapes thought. Metacognitive processes continually monitor the integrated processes of language and thought.

10. The Instrumental Enrichment program designed by Feuerstein supports the idea that thinking skills can be taught through mediated learning experiences. Once cognitive deficiencies such as impulsiveness have been identified, mediated learning tasks can be devised to teach the missing skills.

Solution to the Dog, the Goat, and the Cabbages Problem The solution to this problem requires seven one-way crossings: 1. Take goat across; 2. return; 3. take dog across; 4. return with goat; 5. take cabbages across; 6. return; 7. take goat across.

Possible solutions to the analogy problem
Bird is to nest as *fox* is to burrow.
Ocean is to *continent* as *lake* is to island.
Blood is to people as *money* is to national economy.

Solution to the Tower of Hanoi Problem (Exhibit 11.5) This solution requires fifteen moves:
1. Move the smallest disk (disk 1) to the middle peg.
2. Move disk 2 to the third peg.
3. Move disk 1 to the third peg.
4. Move disk 3 to the middle peg.
5. Move disk 1 to the first peg.
6. Move disk 2 to the middle peg.
7. Move disk 1 to the middle peg.
8. Move disk 4 to the third peg.
9. Move disk 1 to the third peg.
10. Move disk 2 to the first peg.
11. Move disk 1 to the first peg.
12. Move disk 3 to the third peg.
13. Move disk 1 to the middle peg.
14. Move disk 2 to the third peg.
15. Move disk 1 to the third peg.

Solutions to anagram problems
tool, loot   marsh, harms
teach, cheat   lived devil

Key Terms

cognitive maps
concepts
prototype
schema
information-processing theory
assimilation
accommodation
deductive reasoning
inductive reasoning
syllogisms
heuristic
preparation
incubation
illumination
verification
problems of inducing structure
problems of transformation
problems of arrangement

trial-and-error
algorithm
hypothetical reasoning
mental set
functional fixity
phonemes
morphemes
syntax
grammar
transformational grammar
deep structure
surface structure
language universals
linguistic relativity (Whorfian) hypothesis
metacognition
cognitive modifiability
Instrumental Enrichment
mediated learning experiences

Part Four

Dispositional
Behaviors

Focus Questions

1. Does becoming "psyched up" for an exam help you score higher?

2. If you are overweight, do you judge how hungry you are by your hunger pangs or by the time of day?

3. How does your level of sensation-seeking influence your behaviors?

4. Can you increase your need for achievement level?

5. Do you think power is a positive or a negative force?

Chapter Outline

Chapter 12

Motivation

*Too much of a good thing
is wonderful!*

Mae West

Why? Why not? Have you ever responded to the first question, "Why?" with the second question, "Why not?" When psychologists ask "Why?" in regard to behavior, they seek answers about motivation. Although psychologists never completely agree on the meaning, **motivation** is generally considered to be an internal state that activates behavior and energizes, sustains, and directs that behavior toward a goal (Kleinginna & Kleinginna, 1981). For example, when you are hungry, food-seeking behavior is activated, and you look for food. However, at any given moment, you may experience several different motives. If you are on a diet, even though you are hungry, the behavior that is energized may not be food-seeking but food-avoidance behavior because your motive to lose weight is stronger than your hunger. For psychologists, motivation is a hypothetical construct, or intervening variable, an unseen process that must be

275

inferred from observable behavior. You cannot point to your hunger, but you can observe your hunger-motivated behaviors of food-seeking and eating.

Psychologists use several motivational terms—needs, drives, incentives, motives, and dispositions—to describe motivational factors. While these terms, along with less precise terms such as wants, wishes, and desires, may be used interchangeably in everyday language to refer to the activation of goal-directed behavior, each term has a distinct meaning. A **biological need** is defined as a physiological condition necessary for survival. In order to survive, you must eat food, drink fluids, breathe air, and eliminate wastes. While in a strict sense a need arises when a deficit exists in one of the physiological conditions necessary for survival, psychologists also use the term *need* somewhat loosely to indicate any internal state that motivates. For example, upon observing an animal exploring its environment, some psychologists would say the animal's behavior is motivated by a need to explore.

In distinguishing biological needs from **psychological drives**, internal states that impel an organism to act, psychologists use the term in both strict and loose senses. In a loose sense, need and drive are nearly synonymous because most biological needs produce psychological drives. For example, the biological need for food produces the psychological drive of hunger, a drive that causes an organism to seek food. However, in a strict sense, not every need gives rise to a drive, and not every drive is produced by a need. That your need for oxygen does not produce a drive that causes you to seek oxygen is evidenced by airplane pilots who are not aware of their lack of oxygen at high altitudes until they "black out."

Similarly, a biological need does not exist for the psychological drive that activates curiosity or exploratory behavior.

Drives refer to internal sources of motivation that push an organism to reduce the drive. Incentives, on the other hand, pull an organism toward a goal. An **incentive** is an organism's expectation of reward for making a certain response; the expectation is internal, but the source of that expectation lies in the external reward. Your study behavior may be motivated by the expectation of earning a good grade on an exam; however, the expectation, not the grade, is the incentive. Consider a food-deprived rat's performance in a straight alley like the one illustrated in Exhibit 12.1. The rat's hunger drive pushes the rat from the start box; the incentive of expecting food at the end of the alley (because of past experiences with finding food there) pulls the rat toward the goal box. Both drive and incentive are important in this situation. If the rat is not hungry, it will not be motivated to leave the start box; if the rat does not expect to find food in the goal box, even when hungry, it will not run to the end of the alley. Thus, although motivation is an internal state, it is the result of the interaction between internal and external forces.

Motive is the most general term used to designate an internal state that energizes behavior and directs it toward a goal. The category of motives contains needs, drives, and incentives. The distinctions among motivational terms may appear confusing because no precise rules for their usage exist. Psychologists use the strict definitions in designing motivational experiments and in their theoretical discussions, but many use the terms interchangeably at other times.

EXHIBIT 12.1
A Straight Alley Apparatus

A straight alley is a simple device for measuring the strength of responses. The apparatus can measure the speed of a hungry rat running from the start box to the goal box to obtain food and can also measure the rat's running speed (its response strength) in different segments of the alley.

Theories of Motivation

Because almost every question about behavior involves motivational concepts, psychologists have looked for factors that cut across all types of motivated behavior and have constructed theories to link those factors. Several theories of motivation will be discussed before specific types of motives are examined.

Instinct Theories

The first psychological theories of motivation emphasized the role of instincts. The term **instinct** is a general label for fixed, innate, goal-directed patterns of behavior that are typical of each member of the species; nest building in birds and the courtship behaviors of many species of animals are examples.

However, the term *instinct* eventually became less useful as a result of its being applied to numerous human behaviors that are neither universal nor unlearned. During the 1920s, psychologists tended to explain the motivation for human behavior in terms of instincts. For instance, William McDougall (1923), a noted psychologist of that period, proposed twelve basic human instincts; according to his theory, for instance, human social behavior was accounted for by a gregarious instinct, and a mother's love was explained by a parental care instinct. Other researchers proposed the existence of several thousand distinct instincts (Bernard, 1924). Psychologists gradually developed a penchant for calling any commonly observed behavior an instinct, a trend that led one observer to comment that humans must have an "instinct of a belief-in-instincts" (Ayres, 1921). This overly extensive use of instincts as explanatory concepts led psychologists to formulate more precise theories of motivation.

In the 1930s and 1940s, psychologists and especially **ethologists** (specialists engaged in the comparative study of animal and human behavior in natural environments) began to use the more precise term **species-specific behavior** rather than instinct (Tinbergen, 1951). Species-specific behavior refers to a universal, unlearned behavior within a species. A major component of species-specific behavior is the **fixed action pattern**, a concept denoting the immediate and unchanging motivated behaviors of all members of a species to certain releasing stimuli in the environment. For example, during the spring mating period for stickleback fish, when a female enters a male's territory, her presence is a releasing stimulus for a fixed action pattern in the male. Her presence triggers the

The seasonal migration of monarch butterflies is an instinctive behavior.

male's zigzag "dance"; in other words, her presence motivates the male to engage in certain courtship behaviors. His "dance" in turn signals a fixed action pattern in the female. Thus, the courtship continues in a series of unlearned behavior patterns characteristic of all mating stickleback fish.

Currently, many psychologists prefer the term **species-typical actions** to the terms instincts and species-specific behavior (Bindra, 1985). This term implies, especially as it applies to humans, that few behaviors are universal and fixed across a species and that many behaviors are the result of a complex interaction of internal states, environmental conditions, and past experiences. Also, a new field of study, **sociobiology**, is focusing once again on the inherited basis of social behavior in all species (Wilson, 1975). Sociobiologists believe that motivation is based on inherited genetic patterns that lead to behaviors that enhance the survival of the organism's genes (Kitchner, 1985). For example, sociobiologists propose that through the process of natural selection males of most species engage in reproductive behaviors more frequently and with more partners than do females because, in each previous generation, males who followed this pattern sired more offspring, assuring that more of their genes would survive. Thus, while sociobiologists have not returned full-circle to the idea of instincts, they have spiraled to a new understanding of heredity's role in motivation.

Drive Reduction Theory

In the 1930s and 1940s, with the decline of instincts as explanatory concepts and despite the rise of behaviorism with its emphasis on observable behavior, psychologists still found motivational concepts necessary. Psychologists knew, for instance, that hungry rats, having learned to press a bar to obtain a food reward, will gradually stop bar-pressing under two conditions—removing the food reward or allowing the rats to bar-press for food until they are no longer hungry. The change in performance in the first condition is explained by the learning process of extinction. However, the performance change under the second condition cannot be explained by learning because when the rats are again hungry, they resume bar-pressing. A motivational concept such as drive reduction is necessary to explain such temporary behavior variations that are not due to learning.

In 1943, psychologist Clark Hull introduced the concept of drive reduction as the basis for motivation. In his **drive reduction theory**, Hull proposed that biological needs resulting from specific bodily deficits (e.g. lack of food) produce drives, which are unpleasant states; in turn, these unpleasant states impel the organism to act to reduce the drive. Drive reduction is a satisfying experience for the organism, and therefore behaviors that result in drive reduction are reinforced so that the next time the organism experiences the drive, it is likely to repeat the same behaviors in order to reduce the drive. In this way, drive reduction becomes dependent upon **habits**, or previous learning. However, drive reduction also depends upon incentives (expectations about reward availability). An organism may know how to perform an action to reduce a drive but will not perform that habit because of lack of incentive (a lack of expectation that performance of the act in this situation will reduce the drive).

In addition, Hull (1943) suggested the concept of **generalized drive**, the idea that any source of drive can energize any behavior. According to the concept of generalized drive, a hungry rat that is also thirsty will run faster toward a goal box containing food than will a rat that is only hungry. The added drive activates a higher level of performance, even though the food does nothing to reduce the rat's thirst. Also, Hull distinguished between primary and secondary drives. **Primary drives** such as hunger, thirst, sex, and pain avoidance are unlearned, biologically based sources of motivation. All other motivation derives from **secondary drives**, external stimuli that acquire their motivational properties through association with primary drives. Once you have been bitten by an unfamiliar dog, just the sight of that dog will energize your behavior to run away or to prepare to defend yourself because the stimulus of the dog is associated with the pain you experienced previously.

For several years, drive reduction theory was very influential, partly because it provided an explanation for reinforcement. Whatever produced drive reduction was reinforcing. However, as its limitations became apparent, drive reduction theory became less influential. One line of research that was damaging to the theory demonstrated that animals, in the absence of biological needs, are strongly motivated to manipulate objects and to explore their environments (Berlyne, 1950; Harlow, 1953). Other researchers established that animals seek to increase, rather than reduce, stimuli associated with biological needs. For instance, hungry rats are motivated to drink a saccharine solution even though doing so does not reduce their hunger (Sheffield, 1950). Also, a male rat will continue to run to a goal box containing a sexually receptive female even though each time it does so, the increasingly sexually aroused male is removed from the box before ejaculation occurs (Sheffield et al., 1951). In both examples, the animals' motivated behaviors increase although their drives are not reduced. Because of these limitations, drive reduction theory is no longer considered a comprehensive theory of motivation; however, it remains a widely used explanation for motives based on biological needs.

Arousal Theory

An alternative to drive reduction theory is **arousal theory**, which explains, among other effects, why animals and people explore their environments and manipulate objects (they are motivated to raise their arousal levels). According to arousal theory (Hebb, 1955; Berlyne, 1967), the basis of motivation is the need to maintain an optimal level of arousal. Arousal refers to the overall level of physical activation within an organism, a combination of factors that includes muscle tension, heart rate, blood pressure, electrical activity in the brain, and other measurable physiological activity. The level of arousal varies from very low levels during deep sleep, through moderate to high levels during normal wakefulness, to very high levels during extreme excitement. Arousal is affected by motivation and other factors such as environmental stimuli, stimulus novelty, and drugs. Also, the optimum level of arousal varies between and within individuals. You may enjoy strolling in a park, while your friend enjoys running in a race. With experience, the same activities may lead to less arousal, causing a person to seek ex-

EXHIBIT 12.2
The Relationship between Arousal and Performance

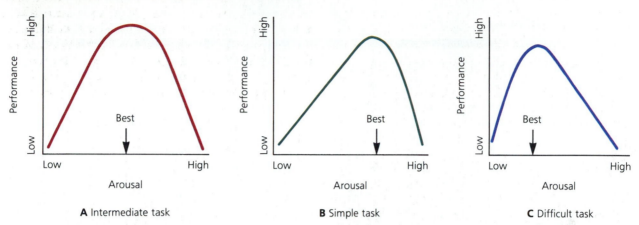

A Intermediate task   **B** Simple task   **C** Difficult task

A. Generally, intermediate levels of arousal produce the highest levels of performance.
B. and **C.** On simple tasks, the arousal level is higher for optimal performance while on more complex or difficult tasks lower levels of arousal produce the best performances.

periences that are more highly arousing (Zuckerman, 1979). For example, when you first acquired your driver's license, driving a car was probably very arousing; if you have now driven a car for many years, the activity may be arousing only occasionally.

The general relationship between an individual's performance (behavioral activation) and his or her arousal (physiological activation) is illustrated in *A* of Exhibit 12.2. Optimal performance occurs at intermediate levels of arousal. This relationship parallels an older mathematical function known as the **Yerkes-Dodson law** (Yerkes & Dodson, 1908). The Yerkes-Dodson law states that an optimum level of motivation exists for any task and that as task difficulty increases, the optimum level of motivation decreases (see *B* and *C* of Exhibit 12.2). For example, when athletes talk about "psyching" themselves for a game or when students refer to "getting psyched up for an exam," individuals in both groups are attempting to create their best level of arousal for the difficulty of the task they face. Both groups recognize that their performances will suffer if they are either over- or under-aroused. The basic ideas of the Yerkes-Dodson law are incorporated into arousal theory, but the term motivation has been replaced with arousal (of which, according to arousal theory, motivation is only one source). While exceptions to the Yerkes-Dodson law have been noted (Hochauser & Fowler, 1975), generally, as formulated in terms of arousal theory, optimum level of arousal varies as a function of task difficulty.

While experienced athletes often perform better in competitive meets than during practice, beginning athletes often perform better during practice. How does the Yerkes-Dobson law explain this difference?

Exploring . . .

Why Do People Act Aggressively?

The question posed in the title of this feature has intrigued psychologists for many years. Psychologists generally agree that to act aggressively is to behave in hostile or violent ways with the intent to harm others. However, psychologists do not agree upon motivational explanations for aggressive behaviors. Three theoretical viewpoints have been expressed—instinct (or inborn drive), the frustration-aggression hypothesis, and the social learning position.

Is Aggression Instinctual?

According to Konrad Lorenz, a Nobel Prize-winning ethologist, the basis for aggression in animals and humans is instinctual (Lorenz, 1966). This approach maintains that aggressive behavior is a naturally occurring, unlearned pattern of responses to specific environmental releasing stimuli. Lorenz believes that the aggressive instinct has been important for survival of species because of its role in the search for food and the protection of property and the young of a species. Although forms of aggressive behavior can be observed in most species, aggression, especially in humans, is not universal. The existence of great variations in the amount of aggressive behavior among humans and other animal species suggests that other factors also determine aggression.

Does Frustration Cause Aggression?

In 1939, a group of Yale University psychologists (Dollard et al., 1939) proposed that frustration, the blocking of efforts to attain a goal, leads to aggression. These researchers proposed that when people are frustrated, they will engage in physical or verbal aggression against the person or object thwarting them or against an uninvolved person who is nearby. However, evaluation of the frustration-aggression hypothesis indicates that aggression is not the inevitable outcome of frustration (Berkowitz, 1965). Although

frustration can lead to aggression, other outcomes (such as increased effort toward reaching the goal) may also occur. In fact, the reactions to frustration are highly individualized and vary greatly from situation to situation.

Is Aggressiveness Learned?

One explanation for the great variation in amount and kind of aggressive behavior displayed by humans is that aggression is a learned motive. Social learning theorists propose that humans learn to be aggressive because they are reinforced for their aggressive behavior and they are exposed to many humans who model aggressive behavior (Eron, 1980). Children begin the learning process at an early age when they observe other children and adults using aggression and obtaining their desired goals. A child who uses aggressive behavior to gain possession of a toy is reinforced by the opportunity to play with the desired toy. The social learning theory explanation of aggressive behavior is widely accepted among psychologists.

As these three theoretical positions suggest, aggressive behavior is motivated by a complex set of factors that may have innate origins but that are definitely influenced by learning and that may be induced, in part, by events such as frustration. Whatever set of factors is involved, aggressiveness is a highly stable characteristic of human behavior. According to one study conducted over a twenty-two year period (Huesmann et al., 1985), individuals who were rated as exhibiting high levels of aggression as eight-year-olds were found to exhibit high aggressiveness twenty-two years later at age thirty. The study also revealed a strong relationship between a subject's aggressiveness at age eight and the subject's child's aggressiveness when the child was eight years old. This study clearly shows that aggressive behavior, by whatever means the individual comes to exhibit it, is quite stable across time and generations.

EXHIBIT 12.3
Maslow's Hierarchy of Needs

SELF-ACTUALIZATION NEEDS
(realization of potential;
finding self-fulfillment)

ESTEEM NEEDS
(need to achieve, excel, gain
approval, and be competent)

BELONGING AND LOVE NEEDS
(need to affiliate, be accepted,
and exchange attention)

SAFETY NEEDS
(feelings of security and safety;
seeking pleasure; avoiding pain)

PHYSIOLOGICAL NEEDS
(needs of hunger, thirst, and sex)

Maslow, A.H. 1970. *Motivation and Personality*. (2nd ed.). NY: Harper & Row.

Metamotivational Theory

In an approach that differed from instinct, drive, or arousal theories, humanistic psychologist Abraham Maslow (1970) proposed a hierarchical classification of motives (see Exhibit 12.3). Maslow spoke of needs rather than motives and used the term more broadly than biological needs. At the base of Maslow's hierarchy are biological needs (such as hunger) and safety needs (such as the need to feel secure). Maslow believed that these most basic needs must be met before an individual will be motivated to strive to fulfill higher needs. Above the basic needs are psychological needs for belonging, love, and esteem. When these needs are met, an individual will then be able to seek to fulfill his or her potential and to find self-fulfillment.

This top level of Maslow's hierarchy, needs for **self-actualization**, represents one of his most significant contributions to motivational concepts. Self-actualization, the idea that people strive to fulfill their unique potentials, is a concept without distinct boundaries. According to Maslow, self-actualization is the full use of one's tal-

ent, capacities, and potentialities. Maslow classified the biological and psychological needs as **deficiency needs** because they involve striving to correct a physiological or psychological deficit. In contrast, he called needs for self-actualization **metamotives** (literally "beyond" motives) because they involve striving to grow beyond one's present condition toward a closer fulfillment of one's potential. Unlike the deficiency needs, which can be satisfied by removing a deficiency, needs for self-actualization are never completely fulfilled.

Although Maslow's ideas that certain motives take precedence over others and that humans strive to a higher level of being are appealing, Maslow's theory has been criticized for its lack of scientific rigor. In addition to the fuzziness of Maslow's concepts, his ordering of needs is not rigidly fixed. Prisoners and political activists engage in hunger strikes to make graphic statements or to call attention to societal issues. Even when satisfied, certain of Maslow's needs are no less compelling. Although you may be loved by many people, do you feel any less need for love? Despite these criticisms, Maslow's metamotivational theory has been widely applied in business and education (e.g., understanding and meeting workers' deficiency needs has been touted as a way to increase worker productivity), and part of the theory's appeal may lie in its emphasis on subjective feelings and its lack of objective rigor. Another fuzzy concept, unconscious motivation, is discussed in the accompanying *Exploring . . .* section.

Artistic expression is an attempt to fulfill Maslow's being needs.

Exploring . . .

Freud's Unconscious Motivation and Defense Mechanisms

Freud's contribution to the area of motivation was his proposal that the reasons people give themselves for behaving as they do are not the actual reasons for their behaviors. Freud (1915) suggested that people's actual motives are unconscious. According to Freud, **unconscious motivations** are the wishes, impulses, aims, and drives of which people are not aware. Furthermore, Freud maintained that many aspects of behavior are motivated from a desire to avoid anxiety. Through the unconscious use of **ego defense mechanisms**, individuals are motivated to reduce or avoid anxiety by distorting or denying aspects of reality. Although the existence of unconscious motivation is still hotly debated, almost everyone can recognize the behaviors described in Freud's defense mechanisms. Consider your own behavior and that of your friends as you read the following descriptions of defense mechanisms. How conscious are you of these unconscious motivators?

■ **Repression**—The fundamental defense mechanism, also called motivated forgetting, in which thoughts or events are kept from conscious awareness (e.g., forgetting an appointment with a person you dislike).

■ **Denial**—Protecting oneself from an unpleasant reality by refusing to perceive it (e.g., adamant denial that you are doing poorly in a course, even after receiving D's on the first three exams).

■ **Rationalization**—Forgetting the real reasons for your behavior and justifying your behavior through rational, but false, reasons (e.g., forgetting you performed poorly on an exam because you did not study and blaming the low grade on the wording of the test questions).

■ **Intellectualization**—Repressing the emotional aspects of a painful experience and talking about the experience in a formal, academic way (e.g., repressing your hurt feelings, while objectively analyzing the ten reasons for the break-up of your relationship).

■ **Compensation**—Dismissing a perceived weakness and excelling in another area (e.g., being too short to play basketball, so becoming an excellent wrestler).

■ **Regression**—Dropping one's mature behavior and acting in immature, childish ways (e.g., having a temper tantrum as an adult).

■ **Reaction Formation**—Repressing actual, dangerous impulses and expressing exaggerated behavior in the opposite direction (e.g., a father wanting to "kill his kids," but instead "smothering" them with love).

■ **Sublimation**—Repressing unacceptable impulses and engaging in constructive activities (e.g., repressing unacceptable sexual impulses and instead sculpturing nudes).

Focus Question Answer

Does becoming "psyched up" for an exam help you score higher? Yes, if you are able to recognize the conditions that produce your optimum level of arousal for test performance. Becoming too highly aroused (too "psyched up") can lead to poorer performance, as can lack of motivation. You can manage your arousal level by manipulating your level of drive motivation. You can reduce your fears by being overly prepared (drive reduction), and you can manipulate your level of incentive motivation by developing realistic expectations for the grades

(goals) you are likely to receive. If you are able to successfully "psych yourself up" for an exam, performing well on the test will help satisfy your needs for esteem.

 ## Primary Motives

Primary motives are the drives related to unlearned biological needs such as hunger, thirst, sex, waste elimination, oxygen, and pain avoidance. Due to a deficit or an anticipated deficit in a biological need, people act to satisfy the specific bodily need. This behavior requires adaptability and is influenced by learning because people must decide how to satisfy their biological needs according to what is available in the external environment.

A good example of this process is thirst. You experience thirst when you lose water from your body through perspiration, loss of urine, exhalation of water vapor from the lungs, or stresses from fever or illness. Your conscious awareness of thirst occurs as a result of a complex biological sequence, in which sensors trigger several coordinated physiological reactions when sufficient water loss occurs. Like other primary motives, thirst varies in strength and can be satisfied in many ways. How you choose to satisfy your thirst is influenced by the beverages that are available and by the amount of effort you must exert to obtain them. In your classroom building, the most efficient way to reduce your thirst may be to use a water fountain. In your home, you may be able to choose among a variety of satisfiers such as soda, milk, beer and water. Your choice will be influenced by how thirsty you are and by your previous experiences (from past experience you may know that you dislike the taste of beer, or you may already have drunk three cans of pop).

The process of satisfying sexual needs occurs somewhat differently. Although the sex drive, like thirst and other primary motives, is influenced and altered by learning and past experience, the sex drive is different because individuals enjoy increasing sexual arousal as well as reducing sexual tension. When you are hungry, you usually do not try to make yourself hungrier. However, with the sex drive, you are likely to seek higher sexual arousal before seeking to reduce the level of the drive. Also, the sex drive is the only primary motive in which activation of the drive occurs independently of the need.

Thirst is one of the primary motives because water is needed to maintain life.

With other primary motives, the drive becomes stronger until it is satisfied. With the sex drive, the reverse is true; abstinence from sexual behaviors is associated with a decrease in the level of sexual motivation (Masters & Johnson, 1970). Additionally, unlike the other primary motives, the sex drive is not necessary for individual survival but is necessary for species survival.

Research on each of the primary motives has provided interesting insights about the complex interactions between biological needs, psychological motives, and influences from the external environment. However, the extensive research on hunger has been most enlightening. The remainder of this section will be devoted to the topic of hunger.

Hunger

How do you know when you are hungry? The obvious answer may be "When I experience hunger pangs or my stomach growls." For many years, this response was the scientific answer as well. In an early study, a researcher swallowed a balloon, which was then inflated in his stomach. This procedure allowed for precise comparisons between the researcher's stomach contractions and his experience of hunger pangs (Cannon & Washburn, 1912). The subject's reported sensations of hunger pangs were highly correlated with his stomach contractions. Although contradicted later, this research concluded that hunger is due to nothing more than stomach contractions.

This conclusion was questioned when researchers began to investigate the causes of stomach contractions. Researchers discovered that people who have had their stomachs surgically removed still experience hunger and that animals still regulate their eating even when all the sensory nerves to the stomach have been severed. Obviously, then, hunger is caused by a factor other than stomach contractions. Other research suggested that hormonal, rather than neural, factors are responsible for hunger (Templeton & Quigley, 1930). When a hungry dog was given a transfusion of blood from a dog that had just eaten, the hungry dog's stomach contractions stopped. When the reverse transfusion was performed, blood from a hungry dog caused stomach contractions to develop in a dog that had just eaten. Originally, these effects were attributed to the level of glucose (sugar) in the blood. This hypothesis was, stated quite simply, that you become hungry when your blood sugar is low (Mayer, 1953).

The effects of low blood sugar can be studied by artificially lowering subjects' blood glucose levels. In one study, well-fed male subjects were injected with either saline solution or 2DG, a substance that inhibits glucose in the blood. With the passage of time, both groups experienced hunger, but the group that had been injected with 2DG experienced more hunger feelings than did the control group that received saline solution (Thompson & Harsha, 1977). These results support the relationship between blood sugar level and the experience of hunger. Another source of support comes from clinical and laboratory observations of diabetic individuals in which injections of insulin result in hunger. The insulin creates a state of low blood sugar, or **hypoglycemia**, which results in feelings of hunger and stomach contractions (Cofer & Appeley, 1964). Insulin's effect on hunger was thought to be the indirect result of lowering blood glucose levels until recently, when research in which high glucose levels were maintained while subjects received insulin injections established that increases in insulin directly cause sensations of hunger (Rodin, 1983).

Although insulin provides a hormonal trigger for hunger, other factors also determine the regulation of hunger and eating. The hypothalamus is an important brain center for regulating eating behaviors. Researchers experimenting with rats found that destroying an area of the hypothalamus, the ventromedial nucleus (VMH), results, among other effects, in extreme overeating, a condition called **hyperphagia**. The weight of the rats

eventually stabilizes, but at a new, obese level (Hetherington & Ranson, 1942). Also, rats with VMH lesions seem to become more sensitive to taste (Teitelbaum, 1957). Further research revealed that VMH lesions cause a decrease in the production of growth hormone and that this decrease leads to more insulin circulating in the bloodstream. The increased insulin level decreases the burning of fatty acids and encourages the deposit of fat (Struble & Steffens, 1975). Other studies found that when a rat's lateral hypothalamus (LH) is destroyed, the rat will stop eating and starve unless tube fed. After a period of tube-feeding, the rat will once again initiate its own feeding behavior (Anad & Brobeck, 1951; Teitelbaum & Stellar, 1954).

Research on hunger mechanisms in the hypothalamus led to the **dual hypothalamic theory of hunger**. According to this theory, the lateral hypothalamus and ventromedial hypothalamus control the initiating and ending of feeding (Stellar, 1954). In addition to the data from lesioned animals, support for this theory came from electrical and chemical stimulation studies in which stimulation of the LH caused a sated rat to begin eating, while stimulation of the VMH caused a hungry animal to stop eating (Miller, 1960; Grossman, 1960). Thus, the LH was considered a "feeding" center and the VMH a "satiety" center. In other words, destroying the LH

Hunger is the primary motive most studied by psychologists. Does biological need explain this eating behavior?

stops the urge to eat, while destroying the VMH causes the animal to be unable to stop eating.

The dual theory appeared plausible except that VMH-lesioned animals do not eat all the time and eventually stop overeating and the LH-lesioned animals start eating again after their body weight drops to a lower level. Other researchers interpreted these data to suggest that the hypothalamus might regulate hunger in another way by establishing a **set point** for body weight. The set point hypothesis proposes that each person has a set point for body weight; the set point is maintained by a homeostatic mechanism (Cabanac, 1971; Keesey & Powley, 1975). For example, rats whose body weights had been significantly reduced before destruction of the LH actually increased their eating after the surgery (Keesey & Powley, 1975).

If the set-point theory is true, certain people may be born with a tendency to be fat because they have high set points, and others may be born with a tendency to be skinny because they have low set points. Thus, each person's caloric needs are determined, in part, by his or her need to maintain a particular set point weight (Lukert, 1982). An overweight individual (a person with a high set point) who tries to lose weight by dieting must work against his or her body's homeostatic mechanism, which is designed to keep that individual's weight at a higher level. Similarly, an underweight individual trying to gain weight faces the same difficulty but in the opposite direction.

Unless you are a lucky person whose set point helps you maintain a physically aesthetic and healthy body weight, the concept of set point may be unwelcome news. However, current research is focusing on how individuals might be able to establish better set point levels for themselves. Researchers now believe that exercise can modify the set point. Vigorous exercise may lower the set point and help you maintain a lower body weight (Bennett & Gurrin, 1982).

Another physical factor in weight control and hunger is the number of fat cells within the body. The rule seems to be: "Fat cells can be created but not destroyed." When you lose weight, you make fat cells smaller, but you do not eliminate them (Lukert, 1982). If you lose twenty pounds, you have many tiny fat cells "waiting" to get back to their former size. Obese people, those 20 percent over their desirable weight, are estimated to have three times the number of fat cells of normal-weight persons (Bjorntorp, 1972). Other researchers are studying differences in types of fat cells. One type of fat, "brown fat," helps reduce the risk of weight gain by burning

excess calories through heat production. Interestingly, obese individuals have a lower percentage of brown fat (Rothwell & Stock, 1979), suggesting that they do not have the same weight control mechanisms as normal-weight individuals.

Several factors influencing hunger and eating are psychological and situational. Emotional stress can affect eating patterns. Generally, stress leads to overeating in both humans and in animals (Ruderman, 1985; Schachter et al., 1968). According to one hypothesis, overweight people do not learn during childhood to discriminate between hunger and emotions such as fear, anger, and anxiety. These individuals, even more than others, have a tendency to eat when upset (Bruch, 1961). Also, researchers have found that dieting people tend to eat more when they are anxious (Herman & Polivy, 1975).

In addition to stress, culture and family situations influence eating rituals and the significance of food. Important life events usually include food; birthdays and holidays are occasions for big meals and extra treats. However, just as eating can be socially stimulated, it can also be socially inhibited. People on diets eat less in the presence of an observer than they do when no observer is present (Herman et al., 1979). Thus, hunger motivation derives from internal bodily conditions and external factors.

The Research Process: Obesity and the Externality Hypothesis

When and how much you eat is influenced by internal cues such as hunger pangs and insulin level and external cues such as the taste of food, the time of day, and the social setting. The **externality hypothesis** proposes that obese people are more influenced by external cues than are normal-weight individuals. A study conducted by psychologist Stanley Schachter (1971c) illustrates research on the externality hypothesis. Schachter had normal-weight (NW) and overweight (OW) male college students skip a meal before participating in the study. All subjects were told that they were participating in a taste-testing experiment and that they were to eat the same food prior to the start of the experiment. To assure this consistency, subjects were told they would be fed at the psychology laboratory. Each subject was placed in a room by himself to eat a lunch of roast beef sandwiches. Subjects were given either one sandwich or three sandwiches, and each subject was told, "More sandwiches are in the refrigerator, so help yourself." The study was

EXHIBIT 12.4
Results of Schachter's "Taste-Testing Experiment"

	One Sandwich	Three Sandwiches
Normal Subjects	1.96	1.88
Obese Subjects	1.48	2.32

When the amount of visible food was greater, obese subjects consumed more sandwiches than did normal-weight individuals; however, when the amount of visible food was smaller, the obese subjects consumed fewer sandwiches than did normal-weight subjects.

Nisbett, R. E. 1968. Determinants of food intake in human obesity. *Science. 159*, 1254-1255.

arranged so that half the NW and half the OW subjects were given three sandwiches, and the other half of each weight group started out with only one sandwich.

Stop for a moment, and try to predict the results. How many sandwiches did hungry NW male college students eat if presented with one sandwich? If presented with three sandwiches? How many sandwiches did hungry OW male college students eat if presented with one sandwich? If presented with three sandwiches?

Of NW and OW subjects given one sandwich, the NW subjects ate more than the OW subjects. Does this result surprise you? As shown in Exhibit 12.4, the NW subjects averaged almost two sandwiches each, and the OW subjects ate an average of only one and one-half sandwiches. However, OW subjects presented with three sandwiches ate significantly more than NW subjects given three sandwiches. Under this condition, the OW subjects averaged two and one-third sandwiches, and the NW subjects averaged just under two sandwiches. The results are quite consistent with the externality hypothesis—NW subjects were influenced only a little by the visible stimuli of roast beef sandwiches; these subjects felt internally satisfied with approximately two sandwiches in both conditions. The OW subjects ate whatever they were given and only occasionally helped themselves to more in the refrigerator or left food on their plates.

Thus, the influence of environmental cues is significant for individuals with weight problems. Exhibit 12.5 summarizes research findings that support this conclusion. As one researcher observed, "The obese do not simply eat, they overeat once they are 'turned on' by potent stimuli" (Rodin, 1982, p. 50). However, certain researchers have suggested that the eating styles of obese and normal-weight persons differ only in small, inconsistent ways and that physiological factors play a larger role than psychological factors in determining eating behavior (Rodin, 1982; Stunkard et al., 1980). These researchers have attempted to link the externality hypothesis with the physiological factor of insulin production. They maintain, for example, that watching a steak being grilled increases insulin production in externally oriented obese individuals (Rodin, 1978). In a recent study, researchers preloaded individuals with either glucose or fructose (glucose, but not fructose, facilitates insulin production); two and one-half hours later, these subjects ate a buffet meal. Subjects with a glucose preload ate 500 calories more than did subjects with a fructose preload (Rodin, 1985).

In conclusion, you should note that people of all weights and shapes eat because of both internal and external cues. While persons more highly influenced by external cues do eat more when food is abundant, not all people influenced in this way become overweight. Other long-term regulatory biological mechanisms also play a role in determining who will become obese (Rodin, 1982).

Eating Disorders

How much should a female who is 5'5" weigh? If she weighs 135 pounds, you would probably say she is chubby. Yet 5'5" Marilyn Monroe weighed 135 pounds throughout her most popular Hollywood years. During the years of her career and earlier, what you might today term plumpness was considered attractive and desirable. Since the Fifties, however, thinness has become the American ideal. Unfortunately, many women have trouble reaching this ideal. Today's unrealistically thin beauty standards contribute to the popularity of diet books and diet clinics and to the high incidence of three eating disorders—anorexia, bulimia, and bulimarexia.

Anorexia nervosa is a fear of fatness that results in prolonged self-starvation and an accompanying weight loss of at least 25 percent of original body weight (Bemis, 1978). At least 85% of anorexics are females, usually teenagers. Unlike most obese people, anorexic individuals are highly successful dieters, but like their obese counterparts their condition can cause severe health problems and can become life-threatening.

Since a body composition of approximately 20 percent fat is needed to maintain menstruation, **amenor-**

EXHIBIT 12.5
Research on the Externality Hypothesis with Obese and Normal-Weight Subjects

One popular area of research in the 1960s and 1970s was the relative importance of internal and external cues on the eating behavior of persons of normal and excessive weight. Externality seems to play a role in weight problems, but the data do not fit as well for individuals who are more than 50 percent above ideal body weight (Leon, 1982; Rodin, 1981).

Many interesting investigations of the externality hypothesis have been made, and their results are highlighted in the following brief research summaries.

1. Normal-weight (NW) individuals bought less if they went grocery shopping immediately after a meal, but overweight (OW) individuals were more likely to buy more just after eating (Nisbett & Kanhouse, 1969).

2. NW subjects ate fewer crackers after eating sandwiches than they did when their stomachs were empty; OW subjects ate the same amount regardless of stomach fullness (Schachter, Goldman & Gordon, 1968).

3. OW persons ate more cashews when a dish of cashews was well-lit than when the nuts were dimly lit. Lighting was not a significant factor for the NW persons (Ross, 1974).

4. In a French restaurant, the waitress took more orders for desserts from OW individuals than from NW individuals if she carried an appetizing dessert with her while asking for dessert orders. When the waitress carried no dessert, all weight groups ordered the same amount of desserts (Herman, Olmsted, Polivy, 1983).

5. OW subjects ate more when bored than they did when interested in a situation (Rodin, 1982).

6. In one study, subjects were allowed to eat crackers. The clock in the experiment room was adjusted to run fast or slow to influence cognitions about how near dinnertime was. NW subjects decreased their eating with a fast clock in the room. OW subjects ate more with a fast clock than with a slow clock (Schachter & Gross, 1968). The clock's time served as an external cue to the OW subjects.

7. Schachter (1971c) asked NW and OW subjects to fill out a personality test. Shelled or unshelled almonds were available for all subjects to eat while filling out the

form. Half the NW subjects ate almonds whether shelled or unshelled. Nineteen of twenty OW subjects ate shelled almonds, but only one of twenty OW persons ate the almonds if they were unshelled. The study suggests that OW individuals are less likely to work hard for their food.

8. Similarly, another study (Schachter, 1971c) found that OW persons do not like to put out effort for their food. In Chinese and Japanese restaurants, five times as many NW westerners used chopsticks as did OW westerners—22.4 percent compared to 4.7 percent.

9. By having OW and NW groups drink milkshakes, Decke (in Schachter, 1971b) showed that OW individuals are more influenced by taste than are NW individuals. Regardless of taste, NW subjects drank approximately the same amount. OW individuals drank more of a good-tasting milkshake, but they drank little of the milkshake containing a bit of bitter-tasting quinine.

10. OW dieters who were told they had just consumed a high-calorie drink were more likely to binge than were NW people. On the other hand, OW nondieters who were given this information ate less than did NW people (Spencer & Fremouw, 1979).

11. OW Jewish college students were more likely to fast for religious observances than were NW Jewish students—83.3 percent to 68.8 percent. The more time the OW individuals spent in the synagogue (away from food cues), the less difficult was the fasting; this relationship between time in the synagogue and ease of fasting was not found for NW individuals (Schachter, 1971a).

rhea, the absence of menstruation, is a common symptom for female anorexics. Other physical complications of anorexia include hypothermia (low body temperature), electrolyte imbalance, hypotension (low blood pressure), severe fatigue, cardiac distress, and susceptibility to infectious diseases. The mortality rate of anorexic patients may be as high as 20 percent (Robbins, 1985). As you may remember, singer Karen Carpenter died of heart failure, a complication resulting from at least twelve years of problems with anorexia nervosa.

While each anorexic patient is unique, studies suggest some general behavior patterns of anorexics. Intense

fear of obesity entices the individual to severe fasting. She is likely to experience intense hunger pains but to deny them or to view the pangs as positive reinforcement of her dieting efforts. The anorexic may also become obsessed with exercising as a way to lose weight. The individual has a distorted body image that produces a situation in which she looks unhealthily skinny to others but fat to herself. In addition, the rate of anorexia is high among professions that require a strict body weight—dancing, modeling, and acting (Striegel-Moore et al., 1986).

The causes of anorexia are unclear. Hypotheses include a reaction to depression, a fear of adult responsibilities, a neurochemical imbalance, and a disturbed family structure (Bruch, 1980; Muuss, 1985). While research has failed to substantiate any of these ideas, treatment programs in which hospitalization to monitor the anorexic's food intake and to care for her health needs is combined with psychological counseling have been successful (Muuss, 1985). Too often, however, anorexics do not seek help and, once in a program, actively resist changing their eating patterns.

A second eating disorder, **bulimia**, involves an abnormal craving for or obsession with food and is accompanied by obsessive binge eating (Pope & Hudson, 1984). The general behavior pattern, which is often unconnected to feelings of hunger, involves diets and fasting, followed by binge eating. The most typical weight pattern is progressive weight gain with intermittent weight loss. Bulimics may be overweight, normal weight, or underweight, depending upon how much they diet between binges. Unlike anorexics, many bulimics are males. About 10 percent of the American population has been bulimic at some point; the percentage rises to 18 percent for females aged thirteen to thirty (Pope & Hudson, 1984).

Bulimics tend to believe strongly in physical attractiveness and the value of beauty. Bulimic women, for example, are more likely to agree with statements such as "attractiveness increases the likelihood of professional success" and "what is fat is bad, what is thin is beautiful, and what is beautiful is good" than are other women (Striegel-Mooere et al., 1986). Bulimic women also estimate lower body weights for their ideal body size than do nonbulimic women (Williamson et al., 1985).

Bulimia seems to be related to other psychological disorders, and three factors lead researchers to believe that depressive illness may be the underlying cause: first, a high percentage of bulimics suffer from a major affective disorder such as serious depression; second, many bulimic individuals have high rates of major affective disorders in their families; and, third, many bulimics respond favorably to antidepressants, which are used to treat affective disorders (Pope & Hudson, 1984). Other researchers have found that bulimics are more frequently subject to depression and anxiety than are obese or normal-weight nonbulimics (Williamson et al., 1985).

The third eating disorder is **bulimarexia**, a binge-purge cycle. Like bulimics, bulimarexics engage in binge eating. However, bulimarexics have the additional behavior of vomiting or using laxatives or diuretics to rid themselves of the food. Binges, usually done in private, average 4,800 calories consumed within an hour or two (Robbins, 1985). The binge is followed by anxiety and more bingeing, which is followed by guilt and then purging. This binge-purge ritual creates more guilt and a resolve to starve oneself; the resolution to fast leads to a hunger obsession, which results in further bingeing. Initially, the person may see the cycle as an ideal diet, but the diet leads to an inability to self-regulate the pattern—the bulimarexic may involuntarily vomit just by walking by a bathroom after eating. About half of bulimarexics eventually stop purging and engage only in bingeing.

Quick Study Aid

Eating Disorders

To remember the differences between the eating disorders, learn these simple definitions:

ANOREXIA-NON-EATING
BULIMIA-BINGEING ONLY
BULIMAREXIA-BINGEING AND PURGING

Counselors in eating disorder clinics report that over the years individuals often change from one eating disorder to another, suggesting that commonalities among the eating disorders exist (Robbins, 1985). Eating disorders may be similar to substance abuse disorders, and treatment programs that use a compulsive-addictive approach similar to that of Alcoholics Anonymous have been developed. Patients are educated about their destructive eating patterns and their difficulty in stopping these behaviors. In counseling, therapy focuses on the preoccupation with food, body size, and body image.

Focus Question Answer

If you are overweight, do you judge how hungry you are by your hunger pangs or by the time of day? According to the externality hypothesis, you pay less attention to your hunger pangs and more attention to the time of day. Other external factors such as the availability of food and the food's appearance and taste also affect overweight individuals' hunger motivation more than they affect the hunger motivation of normal-weight persons.

Stimulus Motives

A monkey will work to solve mechanical puzzles when its only reward is being able to look through a window into a new environment (Butler & Harlow, 1954). Satisfying curiosity and being allowed to explore a novel situation seem to be their own rewards for a monkey, and you have probably experienced the attraction and strength of curiosity and exploration drives in your life. Have you ever searched for presents days before your birthday or Christmas celebration and tried to figure out what the boxes contained? Have you ever read a page from your sister's secret diary? Have you ever skipped the middle of a mystery novel and read the last chapter to find out "whodunit"? Psychologists call the innate motives that help organisms investigate and know the environment **stimulus motives**. Stimulus motives such as curiosity, exploration, and manipulation serve multiple purposes, including adding to survival skills and increasing the variety of reinforcers in life.

Exploratory Behavior

Curiosity and exploration in children have been the subjects of much psychological research. All infants seem to have innate drives to learn about the world, but broad individual differences in the rate of **exploratory behavior** exist. Psychologists want to know what creates the individual differences in exploratory behaviors, how exploration strategies change as children grow older, and what factors in an environment can facilitate the amount of children's exploration.

Characteristics of Exploratory Behaviors According to simple definition, exploratory behaviors are responses to novel or discrepant stimuli (Henderson, 1984). Currently, researchers study four main characteristics of exploratory behaviors.

1. The need to explore is associated with a preference for visual complexity over less complexity (Nunnally & Lemond, 1973) and for auditory complexity over less complexity (Vandenberg, 1984). This preference for complexity has been measured by showing children twenty cards imprinted with four figures of varying complexity and asking the children to point to their preferred figure (Henderson, 1984) or by asking children to choose their favorite music from four choices of varying harmony complexity (Vandenberg, 1984).

2. The need to explore is associated with a preference for novelty and the unknown (Henderson & Moore, 1979). Several research studies have measured this preference by giving a child a toy and then offering the child the opportunity to exchange it for a different toy that is completely hidden behind a screen. Older children, especially girls, make more exchanges than do younger children (Henderson, 1984).

3. The need to explore is associated with breadth of examination (choosing to examine several objects briefly) and with depth of examination (choosing to examine a few objects for long periods of time). Researchers have used a variety of stimuli to measure breadth and depth of exploration. Obviously, the results of research studies focusing only on breadth differ from the results of studies focusing only on depth (Henderson & Moore, 1979). Some studies have used a box with many drawers containing small toys, and the researcher has measured the amount of time the child spends with each object, the total number of objects explored, and behaviors and verbal comments during play. Other studies have used puzzle boxes with switches and latches to manipulate, and researchers have noted what the child explores and manipulates and for how long (Henderson, 1984).

4. The need to explore is also associated, especially in younger children, with the use of social and informational question-asking strategies (Henderson & Moore, 1979; Vandenberg, 1984). Researchers have assessed this aspect of exploratory behavior with materials used to determine preference for breadth and depth of examination (Henderson, 1984).

Changes in Exploratory Behaviors with Age Although exploration of the environment begins with the newborn, the ways in which children explore the environment should change as perceptual, motor, and cognitive skills grow. To discover how exploratory behaviors develop and are modified, researchers have usually compared the performance of two or more age groups in exploring a novel situation. In one such study (Gunnar et al., 1984), researchers compared the exploratory behavior patterns of eighteen-month-old and thirty-month-old children as those patterns were influenced by the presence or absence of a playmate. At the beginning of the study, the young subjects had to leave their mothers' presence to explore the toys in the playroom. As you might predict, the older children left their mothers sooner (within approximately thirty seconds) than did the younger children (within approximately seventy-eight seconds). For both age groups, the presence of a playmate decreased the amount of time needed to leave the parent; the subjects averaged sixty seconds if alone and only thirty-six seconds if a playmate was present. However, the presence of a playmate had different effects on the exploratory behavior of the two groups while the children were in the playroom. The thirty-month-old children explored more in the presence of a playmate than they did when alone, but the eighteen-month-old children explored more when they were alone than they did in the presence of a playmate. The researchers suggested that these results might reflect a developmental change that occurs between the ages of two and three.

In another study (Vandenberg, 1984), children were given an opportunity to explore a wide range of toys. Older children, aged seven to nine, used a "sophisticated exploration" strategy in which they first looked at all the toy options and then chose which object to explore in detail. In contrast, the younger children, aged four to six, tended to play with the first object that captured their attention and failed to examine the entire array of objects. According to the researchers, the "sophisticated exploration" of older children may result because children in Piaget's concrete operations period are capable of more systematic thinking than are children in the preoperational period (see Chapter 11 for Piaget's theory).

In contrast to children who are two and one-half years old, children who are four and one-half years old accomplish more efficient, less redundant explorations of an environment. In one study, the children looked for an Oscar the Grouch toy in eight trash cans arranged in circle, semi-circle, or random patterns. The children's responses were measured for exhaustiveness (looking in each can) and redundancy (looking in some cans more than once). The younger preschoolers were more likely to explore in a nonexhaustive and redundant pattern (Wellman et al., 1984).

Recent studies (Bradbard & Endsley, 1983; Bradbard et al., 1986) have illustrated the effects of sex-role stereotypes on the exploratory behavior of children. Both preschool and elementary-school children ask fewer questions about and explore fewer objects that have been labeled for the opposite sex than when the same objects are labeled for their own sex. The effects of labeling on exploration increase with age, especially among boys. The result is that boys and girls learn different competencies because they attend to different materials based on gender appropriateness.

To summarize, children of all ages engage in exploratory behavior, but older children develop more use-

ful and efficient styles of exploring the world. Boys' and girls' exploratory behavior is affected by sex-typing of novel materials; both boys and girls do more exploring of and learning about materials they view as gender-appropriate.

Sensation-Seeking

Individuals who have a strong need to experience new events, adventures, and experiences are said to be high in **sensation-seeking**. You may be a sensation-seeker if you agree with several of the statements in Exhibit 12.6.

The characteristics of sensation-seekers include taking risks, enjoying daring sports (sky diving and mountain climbing), liking to gamble (especially when the stakes are high), experimenting with new experiences (meditating, driving race cars, and participating in encounter groups), and participating in psychology experiments involving hypnosis, sensory deprivation, and drug-taking (Clement & Jonah, 1984; Zuckerman, 1979). The relationship between sensation-seeking and drug usage is featured in the *Exploring . . .* section.

Many high sensation-seekers enjoy fast-paced and risky activities.

EXHIBIT 12.6
The Four Subscales of the Sensation-Seeking Scale (SSS)

The more the following statements describe you, the more you are a sensation-seeker. Except for the Experience Seeking Subscale, males agree with more items than do females. Agreement with items declines for individuals in their twenties and older.

I. THRILL AND ADVENTURE SEEKING
I often wish I could be a mountain climber.
I sometimes like to do things that are a little frightening.
I would like to take up the sport of water skiing.
I would like to try surfboard riding.
I would like to learn to fly an airplane.
I would like to try parachute jumping.
I would like to dive off the high board.
I would like to sail a long distance in a small but seaworthy sailing craft.
I think I would enjoy the sensations of skiing very fast down a high mountain slope.

II. EXPERIENCE SEEKING
I like some of the earthy body smells.
I like to explore a strange city or section of town myself, even if it means getting lost.
I have tried marijuana or would like to.
I would like to try some of the new drugs that produce hallucinations.
I like to try new foods that I have never tasted before.
I would like to meet some persons who are homosexual (men or women).
I often find beauty in the ''clashing'' colors and irregular forms of modern painting.
People should dress in individual ways even if the effects are sometimes strange.

III. DISINHIBITION
I like wild ''uninhibited'' parties.
I enjoy the company of real ''swingers.''
I often like to get high (drinking liquor or smoking marijuana).
I like to have new and exciting experiences and sensations even if they are a little unconventional or illegal.
I like to date members of the opposite sex who are physically exciting.
Keeping the drinks full is the key to a good party.
A person should have considerable sexual experience before marriage.
I could conceive of myself seeking pleasures around the world with the ''jet set.''
I enjoy watching many of the ''sexy'' scenes in movies.
I feel best after taking a couple of drinks.

IV. BOREDOM SUSCEPTIBILITY
I can't stand watching a movie that I've seen before.
I get bored seeing the same old faces.
When you can predict almost everything a person will do or say, he or she must be a bore.
I usually don't enjoy a movie or a play where I can predict what will happen in advance.
Looking at someone's home movies or travel slides bores me tremendously.
I prefer friends who are excitingly unpredictable.
I get very restless if I have to stay around home for any length of time.
The worst social sin is to be a bore.
I like people who are sharp and witty even if they sometimes insult others.
I have no patience with dull or boring persons.

From Zuckerman, Eysenck & Eysenck, 1978. Sensation seeking in England and America: Cross-cultural age and sex comparisons. *Journal of Consulting and Clinical Psychology, 46*, 139-149.

Sensation-Seeking and Drug Usage

Recently, several correlational studies (Carrol & Zuckerman, 1977; Galizo & Stein, 1983; Sutker et al., 1978) have explored the relationship between drug usage and the need to seek high levels of sensations. One study (Spotts & Shontz, 1984) matched users of cocaine, amphetamines, opiates, and barbiturates and nonusers and found that all four groups of drug users scored higher on Zuckerman's (1979) Sensation Seeking Scale (SSS) and subscales than did nonusers. When the drug users were analyzed as a single group, the Sensation Seeking Scale scores correlated positively with the number of drugs ever tried. In addition to correlating with SSS scores, the number of drugs tried also correlated positively with measures of extroversion, mania, and anti-social behavior. A second study (Satinder & Black, 1984) compared marijuana users and nonusers on the SSS and its subscales. Marijuana users scored higher than nonusers on all four subscales.

Not only do high sensation-seekers try more kinds of drugs, but they also rate the effects of drugs as stronger and more positive than do low sensation-seekers. Individuals who score high on the Disinhibition Subscale are especially likely to rate both stimulant and depressant drug effects as favorable (Kohn & Coulas, 1985).

The three studies just mentioned are correlational. Therefore, they can provide information about associations among various characteristics but they cannot confirm causal relationships among factors. These studies can only suggest that the need for change or stimulation increases the tendency to experience a variety of chemical substances and to like the effects of the drugs. None of the studies can indicate which individuals will choose to satisfy their sensation-seeking tendencies through drug experimentation and which sensation-seekers will choose other stimulating activities. However, the studies do suggest that once individuals make decisions to engage in drug experimentation, SSS scores could be useful in predicting which individuals will try a variety of drugs.

Sensation-seekers often daydream and are attracted to speculative ideas. They are good at expressing their emotions, are more open to new and unusual experiences and ideas, and enjoy travel and geographical moves (Blankstein et al., 1976; Jacobs & Kopperl, 1974). Sensation-seekers are also less anxious about physical harm, have greater tolerance for discomfort produced by painful stimuli, and have more tolerance for high-intensity stimuli. They even evaluate situations as less risky than do low sensation-seekers (Zuckerman, 1979).

High sensation-seekers often do well in areas of independent achievement but poorly in conventional achievement areas requiring persistence and hard work. Persons who agree with many statements on the Disinhibition subscale often receive low school grades, possibly because they are occupied with pursuing pleasures rather than studying (Zuckerman, 1979).

Most of the research on sensation-seeking involves correlational studies. The results provide a rich description of sensation-seeking behaviors and characteristics and also lead to speculation about what types of careers,

educational formats, and activities might be recommended to high and low sensation-seekers. However, researchers are just beginning experiments to determine if sensation-seeking tendencies are modifiable and if sensation-seeking level is largely the result of biology or learning.

One such study examined the effects of sensation-seeking levels on intimate relationships and concluded that a person's sensation-seeking tendencies change very little. In intimate relationships, people tend to choose and stay with persons with similar levels of sensation-seeking. People do not usually become more similar in sensation-seeking characteristics as a close relationship develops (Lesnik-Oberstein & Cohen, 1984).

Recent research also suggests that high sensation-seekers may have different brain chemistry than do low sensation-seekers, and the differences in preferred levels of sensations may be inherited (Zuckerman et al., 1980). Various studies have focused on the levels of monoamine oxidase, norepinephrine, and dopamine, all of which are substances central to physiological research on the mental disorders of depression and schizophrenia (Redmond et al., 1979; Schooler et al., 1978; Ballenger et al., 1983). Another study has revealed that individuals who score high on the disinhibition factor tend to have higher levels of gonadal hormones (Diatzman et al., 1978).

Focus Question Answer

How does your level of sensation-seeking influence your behaviors? Your level of sensation-seeking increases with increased preference for variety in life. Sensation-seekers differ in their choices of behaviors but, compared to others, when they try activities in a certain area, they experience a wider range of those activities. Usually, individuals like to be around other individuals with similar levels of sensation-seeking.

 ## Social Motives

While primary and stimulus motives are biological and help ensure survival, **social motives**, or secondary motives, are learned from interactions with people. When biologically based motives are reasonably satisfied, social motives are prominent in influencing a person's daily behaviors. Some social motives are listed in Exhibit 12.7, but an exhaustive list would be difficult to create because people can learn to strive for a great variety of goals. Individual differences can be attributed to people's pref-

EXHIBIT 12.7
Social Motives

ABASEMENT	Submitting passively.
ACHIEVEMENT	Accomplishing the difficult.
AFFILIATION	Valuing friendships.
AGGRESSION	Forcefully overcoming opposition.
AUTONOMY	Resisting influence.
CARE-GIVING	Liking to aid and protect others.
CHANGE	Wanting novelty and new places.
DEFERENCE	Supporting a superior.
EXHIBITION	Liking to make an impression.
LEISURE	Liking relaxation and amusement.
NURTURED	Liking to be protected and helped.
ORDER	Having things in their place.
POWER	Controlling one's environment.
REJECTION	Separating from others.
SELF-DEFENSE	Defending oneself
SENSUALITY	Seeking and enjoying the sensuous.
UNDERSTANDING	Asking and answering questions.

The need for achievement (nAch) is reflected in the desire to accomplish a difficult task.

erences in social motives and to their degree of persistence in reaching various social goals.

Psychologists wish to discover how social motives are learned and how they affect behavior and interpersonal relationships. The following section focuses on research findings about the need for achievement, the most extensively researched social motive. The *Relate* section features a second social motive, the need for power.

Need for Achievement

Need for achievement (nAch) involves the motivation for accomplishing a difficult task, competing to surpass others, and pursuing success and has been defined as "competition with a standard of excellence" (McClelland, 1984). Although researchers have measured nAch mostly in academic and vocational tasks, achievement need could be measured in any area of performance (Spence & Helmreich, 1983).

People can achieve through many behavioral styles. As shown in Exhibit 12.8, some individuals achieve directly by their own efforts, some individuals achieve through personal characteristics or through interactions with other people, and some individuals experience achievement indirectly through the efforts of others (Lipman-Bluman et al., 1983). Which of the achievement styles do you use most frequently?

Characteristics of Individuals with High Need for Achievement   How do individuals with high nAch compare with individuals with low nAch? Individuals with a high need for achievement are more internally motivated, ambitious, competitive, and independent in decision-making than are individuals with low nAch, and they can delay immediate rewards in order to work for larger, more important rewards in the future (Kukla, 1972). High need for achievement is associated with high work performance and definable work goals. A study of male scientists found a significant correlation between the number of published articles and citations in other articles and measures of achievement, need, autonomy,

originality, professional recognition, and commitment to work (Busse & Mansfield, 1984).

Characteristically, high need achievers take moderate risks—a position that allows both personal growth and successes. In contrast, low need achievers tend to choose easy, obtainable goals (the "no pain and no gain" approach) or nearly impossible, highly unlikely goals (the "it's not my fault" approach). One study involving

EXHIBIT 12.8
Achievement Styles

I. DIRECT STYLE. Individuals who tend to confront tasks directly and to achieve through their own efforts.
   A. INTRINSIC SUBSTYLE. Individuals who compare themselves to some standard of performance excellence.
      For example: A student who feels satisfied with B's and A's in college classes.
   B. COMPETITIVE SUBSTYLE. Individuals who express achievement through goals of doing better than others.
      For example: A student who feels satisfied if he or she earns a grade that is better than the grades earned by 90 percent of the students in the class.
   C. POWER SUBSTYLE. Individuals who are often in leadership positions. They control others to be able to accomplish achievement goals.
      For example: A student who organizes and leads a small study group for a class.

II. INSTRUMENTAL STYLE. Individuals who use themselves or others as a means to achievement goals.
   A. PERSONAL SUBSTYLE. Individuals who achieve through status, influence, reputation and personal characteristics.
      For example: A student who takes only those courses that will allow him or her to earn grades high enough to make the dean's list.
   B. SOCIAL SUBSTYLE. Individuals who use networking to achieve their goals.
      For example: A student who joins a fraternity or sorority because the organization can provide a lifelong set of social and career connections.
   C. RELIANT SUBSTYLE. Individuals who achieve by depending upon others for direction.
      For example: A student who continually checks with the instructor and classmates for information on how and what to study.

III. RELATIONAL STYLE. Individuals who achieve by contributing to the accomplishments of others.
   A. COLLABORATIVE SUBSTYLE. Individuals who achieve through group effort that includes the sharing of both responsibility and credit.
      For example: A student who prefers to work on group term papers and class projects and share a common grade.
   B. CONTRIBUTORY SUBSTYLE. Individuals who play a secondary role of helping others to achieve.
      For example: A student's spouse who financially supports and provides an environment that enables the student to be successful in his or her classes.
   C. VICARIOUS SUBSTYLE. Individuals who satisfy their own achievement needs by identifying with another's successes.
      For example: A student who feels pride and satisfaction when the college football team is victorious.

Adapted from Lipman-Blumen, J., Handley-Isakin, A., & Leavitt, H.J. 1983. Achieving styles in men and women: A model, an instrument, and some findings. In J.T. Spence (ed.). *Achievement and achievement motives: Psychological and sociological approaches.* San Francisco: W.H. Freeman.

children nine years old through eleven years old found that even at these early ages, this risk pattern has begun to develop; children who felt responsibility for their personal successes and failures tended to set intermediate, challenging goals (Meyer, 1968). Further, individuals with high need achievement not only choose more challenging tasks than do low need achievers, but they also choose, over a series of tasks, increasingly more difficult tasks and challenges (Kuhl & Blinkenship, 1979).

Interestingly, high need achievers work most diligently when they have been told that a task is difficult, and low need achievers work hardest when informed that a task is easy (Kukla, 1975). In other words, high need achievers are most motivated in situations that challenge and emphasize performance excellence.

Expectancy-Value Theory   According to the **expectancy-value theory** (Atkinson, 1974), five factors influence an individual's achievement need:

1. The first component is the *need to approach success,* or the hope for success, and is expressed in the positive striving toward a goal. An individual experiences this aspect when he or she works toward a job promotion, tries to improve a tennis serve, or is determined to master Chinese cooking.

2. The second factor is the *need to avoid failure,* or the fear of failure, and focuses on anxiety or the threat of possible failure. A person experiences this element when he or she studies anxiously for an exam in a course he or she is barely passing, stops taking piano lessons because improvement seems too difficult, or decides not to audition for a part in a play because the role will probably go to someone else.

3. The third component is *expectancy,* or one's estimated probability of success or failure with an achievement goal. Whether or not an individual thinks success is likely affects the amount of effort he or she is willing to exert. Thus, a student might not even start studying for a test if he or she believes failure is certain.

4. The fourth factor, the *incentive value* of success or failure, denotes the individuals' estimate of the accomplishment's worth. Individuals vary in the worth they place on employment, education, and status opportunities.

5. The last component is the tendency to seek external or *extrinsic rewards.* Need for achievement can be modified by the emphasis an individual places on rewards such as money, grades, awards, and praise.

Quick Study Aid

Remembering Expectancy-Value Theory

Think about the five factors of the expectancy-value theory in terms of your need to achieve in your psychology class:

1. The need for success is revealed when you study for an A.

2. The need to avoid failure is revealed when you study to avoid an F.

3. Expectancy is influenced by knowledge about grading curves, other students' abilities, and availability of study time.

4. Incentive involves the value you assign to psychological knowledge, good grades, and a college education in general.

5. Extrinsic rewards concern your desire for praise and good grades and your need to maintain a certain grade-point average in order to continue receiving a scholarship.

Fear of Success   A major modification of the expectancy-value theory was the addition of a sixth factor called the motive to avoid success, or **fear of success** (Horner, 1968). According to this factor, people may sabotage their own performances or avoid success because they expect that success will bring negative consequences. People may avoid success because they believe it will make extra demands upon them, require a tedious or stressful shift in self-concept, or make them feel uncomfortably different from their peers (Tresmer, 1977).

In the study (Horner, 1968) that first revealed the fear of success, each subject was asked to write a story about a medical student who finished at the top of the class at the end of first-term finals. Half the subjects were told that the top student was named John, and the rest of the subjects were told that the student was named Anne. The stories written about John were generally positive (e.g., he graduated near the top of his medical class, he went on to become a well-known surgeon). In contrast, many subjects wrote negative and unhappy stories about Anne (e.g., Anne quit medical school to become a nurse, Anne's classmates were angry at her high performance and severely physically hurt her). In examining the stories written by male and female subjects, the researcher discovered that 65 percent of the female subjects but only 10 percent of the male subjects wrote fear of success stories.

Because of these results, fear of success was originally thought to be a "women's problem"; researchers believed women would not compete against men on tasks that involved "masculine skills" because this competition might make women feel unfeminine and might be disapproved of by others. However, later research revealed that both men and women exhibit the need to avoid success, especially in unfamiliar situations. Rather than having a generalized fear of success motive, most individuals show fear of success in specific situations (Cook & Chandler, 1984). For example, you may do well in college but have some fear of success about making the Dean's list because then your family would expect you to get very high grades every semester.

Imposter Phenomenon

Some people who are driven to achieve seem to fear that their successes will be overturned and they will be revealed as frauds. These haunting fears have been labeled **the imposter phenomenon** (Harvey & Katz, 1985). The imposter phenomenon is caused by being a perfectionist and, therefore, never being able to meet one's own standards. Three main characteristics of people experiencing the imposter phenomenon are:

1. Believing they have fooled others into overestimating their abilities.
2. Minimizing abilities and intelligence and attributing well-earned successes to good luck, charm, good looks, or constant effort.
3. Constantly fearing being discovered to be fakes.

Imposter phenomenon is common among successful people—approximately 70 percent have experienced the imposter phenomenon during parts of their lives, and 40 percent are current sufferers (Harvey & Katz, 1985). One study found that 69 percent of practicing therapists have experienced the imposter phenomenon (e.g., "What qualifies *me* to try to help these people?") during their counseling sessions. College students performing at high levels are more susceptible to the imposter phenomenon than are students performing at average and below-average levels (Harvey & Katz, 1985).

Sometimes the imposter phenomenon develops because individuals attempt to live up to an above-average image of themselves held by family members or friends. The imposter phenomenon can also develop as a response to overhelpful and overprotective parents, an environment that can lead a person to doubt his or her abilities to be independent and competent (Harvey & Katz, 1985).

If you experience the imposter phenomenon, remind yourself that your feelings are personal perceptions and not necessarily objective reality. Try to accept compliments rather than to deny them and gradually learn to be flexible in your daily routines and more tolerant of personal errors (Harvey & Katz, 1985).

Focus Question Answer

Can you increase your need for achievement level? Yes, you can modify your nAch. First, you can evaluate yourself according to the five factors of the expectancy-value theory (hope for success, fear of failure, expectancy, incentive value, and extrinsic rewards) and work toward modifying these aspects to increase your need for achievement. Next, you can analyze your attitudes about fear of success and determine if you experience the imposter phenomenon. Remind yourself to take credit for the ability and effort behind your successes and not to take too much responsibility for failures. If your nAch level is already too high, tell yourself that breaks from work are important for your well-being, and then take those breaks.

The Need for Power

What are your attitudes about power? Do you consider power a positive force or a negative force? **Power,** derived from the Latin word *posse,* means "to be able," and Rollo May (1972) has defined power as "the ability to cause or prevent change." David McClelland (1975), pioneer of much psychology research on power, defined the need for power as the need to have an impact upon or control over others. In contrast to many Americans, both May and McClelland believe that power can be a positive force in society.

Rollo May (1972) believes that modern society is ambivalent and confused in its attitude toward power. May has written, "Power is widely coveted and rarely admitted." Perhaps this ambivalence comes from a belief that power is negative and innocence is a virtue. In reality, however, innocence is not always a positive force. Innocence can be misused to pretend that real problems do not exist, and it can be a euphemism for powerlessness, weakness, and helplessness, all undesirable characteristics. In addition, powerless individuals may explode into destructive forms of power such as violence, mental illness, and drug addiction. In other words, individuals need to express power or destructive, violent actions might result. To summarize May's position, power can be good when used properly.

Types of Power

Whether power is negative or positive depends upon the kind being expressed. Rollo May (1972) has proposed five types of power—two are negative, one can be either negative or positive, and two are positive.

1. Exploitative Power (used on another) Exploitative power, defined as using force on others, is the most destructive form of power. In exploitative power, the aggressor allows the victim no options in the exchange. Examples of exploitative power include making demands on a victim while holding a gun to his or her head or demanding that an employee engage in sexual behaviors or be fired.

2. Manipulative Power (used over another) A second negative power, manipulative power, pertains to individuals who are unequal in their power and resources. The person possessing more power influences the behavior of the other individual. Manipulative power is quite common in human interactions, including unfair interactions that sometimes occur between parent and child, teacher and student, therapist and client, and husband and wife.

3. Competitive Power (used against another) Competitive power can be negative or positive. In its negative form, one

A judge's power is enhanced by symbols of power such as American and state flags, state seals, judicial robes, and the height, size, and arrangement of furniture.

individual gets to advance because another person declines. In its positive form, competitive power is stimulating and constructive. Competitive power is represented by business exchanges, sibling rivalry, and football games.

4. Nutrient Power (used for another) In nutrient power, an individual is concerned with the welfare of another individual or individuals and uses his or her power to try to advance or comfort the other individual. Nutrient power exchanges are common between parent and child and intimate friends.

5. Integrative Power (used with another) Underlying this highest, most constructive form of power, which leads to growth and truth, is the concept "My power then abets my neighbor's power" (May, 1972, p. 109). In addition to the concern for others expressed in nutrient power, integrative power is performed with the other person instead of merely for the other person. For example, a student's challenging question may help a teacher present a more inspiring and creative lecture.

Developmental Stages of Power

As a contrast to May's five types of power, McClelland (1975) suggests four main power types, which develop in order; a person who has developed through all four stages is able to resort to any of the four stages. The first stage involves power through dependency and others' support. In this stage, a person derives power from being near sources of strength, such as friends, family, and employers. Individuals in this category often like work in which they serve a powerful person.

The second stage emphasizes autonomy and represents a shift from external to internal control. In this stage, individuals often emphasize having control over their own bodies and minds and therefore may enjoy body-building, dieting, yoga, and psychology. Stage-two individuals often collect possessions and view these possessions as extensions of themselves. Many psychologists advise people to act from this stage because of its emphasis on self-reliance.

The third stage emphasizes power through assertion and competition. Individuals in this stage like to influence others. A stage-three person who gives a gift to another person is likely to give the gift as a form of domination rather than as an act of sharing. As with Rollo May's competitive power, McClelland's competitive stage can be used in either positive or negative ways.

Stage-four individuals emphasize selfless service to an ideal such as togetherness, commitment, communion, or transcendence. These individuals satisfy power by subordinating personal goals to a higher authority. Type-four power individuals express themselves in fields such as politics, religion, science, and business. Note that McClelland's fourth stage reflects characteristics of May's nutrient and integrative power types.

Power Stress

Do you agree with McClelland and May that the ability to express power is important? Recent research suggests that inhibited NP (need for power) produces **power stress,** which entails several biological reactions. Inhibited NP creates chronic sympathetic activation resulting in high blood pressure, higher epinephrine levels, and an impaired immune system. Power stress is associated with more respiratory infections and more frequent and severe illnesses of many types (Fodor, 1985; McClelland, 1982). Thus, as May and McClelland have suggested, expression of power is necessary for an individual's physical health and mental well-being.

Power Research Tidbits

An assortment of need for power (NP) research findings includes:

▬ Males with high NP are more argumentative and more easily angered than are males with low NP (McClelland, 1982).

▬ Male emphasis on power is highest around midlife (Verloff et al., 1984).

▬ Throwing objects, taking off from work because one doesn't feel like going, and taking towels from a motel are all associated with NP of working-class males (Winter, 1973).

▬ NP of high school males predicts competitive sports participation in America but not in Germany (McClelland, 1975).

▬ For older adults, NP is significantly related to the number of credit cards they carry (Winter, 1973).

▬ High NP is associated with sleeping difficulties (McClelland, 1982).

▬ In intimate relationships, males often use power to have sex, but females use power more often to avoid sex (McCormick et al., 1984).

▬ High NP male college students own prestigious possessions, read flashy, status-oriented magazines, exploit sexual relationships, and like to gamble (Winter, 1973).

▬ High NP female college students lend valuable possessions more readily and frequently than other female college students; high NP male college students are less likely to lend valuable possessions than are other male college students (McClelland et al., 1972).

▬ Power can be achieved through wit and sarcasm (Nilsen, 1983).

▬ People in power positions give out less intimate information than do other people (Earle et al., 1983).

Things to Do

1. Use Exhibit 12.7, which lists social motives. Rank order these motives according to which are most important to you now; mark the most important motive 1; the second most important 2; and so on. Consider your rank-ordering of the motives. What does your ranking say about what you value? Do your day-to-day behaviors help you express and fulfill the most important motives? What could you do to help better meet your own needs? Now ask a significant person in your life to rank you on your social motives. Does this person perceive you in the same way you perceive yourself? Who more accurately ranked your motives—you or the other person? Why?

2. List your reasons for being a college student, and rank these reasons from most to least important. What are your motivations for being in school? What do you hope a college education will do for you? How do these motives influence which aspects of school you enjoy? How do they influence your study patterns? Your emotions while in school? How could college become a more satisfying experience?

3. Interview a therapist who deals with sexual dysfunctions, eating disorders, or relationship problems. Ask the therapist how client motivations influence the counseling process. Discover which techniques, if any, the therapist uses to modify motivational levels.

4. Look over Maslow's hierarchy of needs (Exhibit 12.3), and analyze your life according to Maslow's scheme. Which groups of needs are usually met, and which are not usually met? How do your fulfilled and unfulfilled needs affect your thoughts, emotions, and behaviors?

5. Design a program for modifying one of your motives, such as your need to achieve, your need for power, or your hunger drive.

6. Design a survey to assess how many students on your campus experience the fear of failure, fear of success, or the imposter phenomenon. What strategies do students use to cope with the accompanying unpleasant emotions?

Things to Discuss

1. Try to imagine life without ego defense mechanisms. How do you think life would be different? What are the advantages of a no-defense-mechanism life? What are the disadvantages? Which ego defense mechanisms would you miss most?

2. How would you respond to someone who said, "The only thing wrong with a fat person is lack of will power"? How might you combine research findings from the biological and psychosocial aspects of hunger to rebut the person's statement?

3. What are the advantages and disadvantages of being a high sensation-seeker? A low sensation-seeker? How could education, employment, and recreational facilities be designed to cater to the preferences of high sensation-seekers? Low sensation-seekers?

4. Do you think you are aware of the motivations that determine your behavior, or do you tend to believe that "real" motives are unconscious? Why do you believe as you do? What evidence from your personal experiences can you offer?

5. Relate an experience in which one of your primary motives took precedence over an important social motive

(e.g., wanting to study for a psychology exam to get a good grade but falling asleep; not going to a chemistry lab in order to have time to eat lunch). Can you relate an experience in which one of your social motives determined your behavior at the expense of a primary motive need?

6. Speculate about how much your family has influenced which motives are important to you. Did you model your parents' behaviors? Did you receive verbal messages about which motives were important? Which of your motives did they reinforce?

7. What social motives do you think are most common among Americans? What aspects of the national culture are influenced by these motives? Which social motives now play larger roles in individual lives than they did at the turn of the century?

Things to Read

Bennett, W. & Gurrin, J. 1982. *The dieter's dilemma.* NY: Basic Books.

Harvey, J.C. & Katz, C. 1985. *If I'm so successful, why do I feel like a fake? The imposter phenomenon.* NY: St. Martin's Press.

Maslow, A.H. 1970. *Motivation and personality* (2nd ed.). NY: Harper & Row.

McClelland, D.C. 1975. *Power: The inner experience.* NY: Irvington.

Pelletier, K.R. 1985. *Healthy people in unhealthy places.* NY: Delacorte.

Pope, H.G. & Hudson, J.I. 1984. *New hope for binge eaters: Advances in the understanding and treatment of bulimia.* NY: Harper & Row.

Schachter, S. & Rodin, J. 1980. *Obese humans and rats.* Hillsdale, NJ: Prentice-Hall.

Zuckerman, M. 1979. *Sensation-seeking: Beyond the optimal level of arousal.* Hillsdale, NJ: Erlbaum.

 ## Review

Summary

1. Motives are internal states that energize behavior and direct the organism toward goals. Motives can be needs, drives, or incentives.

2. According to instinct theories, all members of a species exhibit fixed, innate, goal-directed patterns of be-

havior called instincts. The current preferred term is species-typical actions, which acknowledges that behaviors are more flexible and less universal than the term instincts implies.

3. Drive reduction theory emphasized that biological

deficits create unpleasant tension called drives that individuals try to reduce.

4. Arousal theory suggests that sometimes organisms are motivated to raise rather than reduce arousal levels as all organisms try to maintain an optimal level of arousal. According to the Yerkes-Dodson law, as task difficulty increases, the optimum level of motivation decreases.

5. Maslow established a hierarchy of needs with deficiency needs (biological needs and safety needs), which aid survival, and metamotives (belonging, self-esteem, and self-actualization), which encourage personal growth.

6. Freud proposed that people's motivations are unconscious; that is, people are not fully aware of the reasons behind their behaviors. People use ego defense mechanisms to reduce or avoid anxiety by distorting or denying aspects of reality.

7. Hunger is one of the primary motives (unlearned biological needs). Hunger is influenced by physical factors such as hunger pangs, blood sugar level, and insulin production. Weight levels are partly determined by set point and number of fat cells. Hunger is influenced by psychological factors as well—social settings, emotions, and external cues. According to the externality hypothesis, more obese individuals than normal-weight individuals are influenced by external food cues.

8. Three eating disorders are anorexia nervosa (self-starvation), bulimia (bingeing), and bulimarexia (bingeing and purging). These eating disorders result from complex ideation taught by societal messages and family interactions.

9. Stimulus motives are innate drives to investigate and know the environment. The need to explore is the organism's response to novel or discrepant stimuli. As children grow older, they tend to use exhaustive and nonredundant searching of the environment and to briefly examine all options before choosing one object to examine in detail.

10. Individuals who are high sensation-seekers prefer adventures, thrills, risks, and new experiences.

11. Social motives are learned in interactions with other people. Social motives vary tremendously from individual to individual and play prominent roles in behavior. Persons with high need for achievement are usually moderate risk-takers, view themselves as ambitious and successful, and can delay present rewards for larger, future rewards.

12. According to the expectancy-value theory, need for achievement is comprised of five components: need for success, need to avoid failure, expectancy, incentive value, and extrinsic rewards. An additional factor is the fear of success, which causes individuals to sabotage their own successes because of perceived consequences of success.

13. Successful people who experience the imposter phenomenon believe they are going to be exposed as frauds. The imposter phenomenon is associated with perfectionistic standards and family backgrounds that were either too critical or too spoiling.

14. May proposes five types of power (exploitative, manipulative, competitive, nutrient, and integrative), while McClelland proposes four developmental stages of power (dependency, autonomy, competition, and commitment). Inability to express power needs may lead to power stress, which increases the risk of poor health.

Key Terms

biological need
psychological drives
incentive
motive
instinct
species-typical actions
sociobiology
drive reduction theory
arousal theory
Yerkes-Dodson law
self-actualization
deficiency needs
metamotives
unconscious motivations
ego defense mechanisms
primary motives
dual hypothalamic theory of hunger
set point
externality hypothesis
anorexia nervosa
bulimia
bulimarexia
stimulus motives
exploratory behavior
sensation-seeking
social motives
need for achievement
expectancy-value theory
fear of success
the imposter phenomenon
power

Focus Questions

1. What role does your brain play in your experience of emotion?

2. Do smiles have the same meaning throughout the world?

3. How does your personality type relate to stress and illness?

4. How can you tell when someone is lying?

Chapter Outline

EMOTIONS
Emotions and the Brain
Physiology of Emotion
Theories of Emotion
The Research Process: Epinephrine, Emotion and Cognition

EMOTIONAL EXPRESSION
Universal Expression of Emotion
Emotional Development
Nonverbal Communication of Emotion

STRESS
Defining Stress
Type A and Type B Personalities
Managing Stress
Relaxation as Stress Management

RELATE: Lies—Deception and Detection
Things to Do
Things to Discuss
Things to Read

Review: Summary
Key Terms

Chapter 13

Emotions and Stress

Emotion for the sake of emotion is the aim of art, and emotion for the sake of action is the aim of life.

Oscar Wilde

 Emotions

As you begin reading this chapter, take a minute to answer the following questions. Are you angry because you would rather be doing something else, determined to finish your assignment, or bored and sleepy because it's late in the day? Are you in a good mood or a bad mood? Has anyone ever said your temperament is like your mother's or father's? How did you feel the last time you took a test or asked your boss for a raise? Were your hands clammy? Did your knees shake? Was your stomach upset? Did your heart pound? What happened within your body? Emotion researchers attempt to answer questions like these.

To understand the research and theory within this topic, you must first learn the most commonly used terms. 303

Emotion is a term used differently by various experts but generally its definition includes subjective feelings, physiological arousal, and emotional expression. Although people often use the term as a synonym for **feelings**, experts confine their definition of feelings to the subjective experience (personal interpretation or labeling) of the physiological arousal. When you become physiologically aroused in certain situations, you say you feel angry; in other situations you say you feel happy. Longer lasting feelings are labeled **moods**; depressed moods, for instance, may last several hours or several days. In summary, emotion entails physiological changes that are accompanied by subjective feelings; when feelings persist, they become moods.

The inborn, biological, fairly permanent aspects of emotions are referred to as **temperament**. When people refer to someone's "nervous temperament," they usually mean the person typically displays the characteristic of nervousness, and the characteristic is not dependent on situational variables. Another frequently-used term is **affect**, the outward bodily and facial expression of emotion. You can often identify friends' moods by the affects, or the body language, they display. The five terms just presented are interrelated. You begin life with a general emotional reactivity level, your temperament; you experience feelings accompanied by physiological changes; you "get into" certain moods at times; and you express your emotionality to others through your affective responses.

Emotions and the Brain

Historically, the expression of emotion has often been linked to body parts other than the brain. Aristotle believed the brain was bloodless and the heart was the "seat of the soul." In the second century B.C., Galen believed that each of four humors was responsible for certain characteristics: phlegm caused sluggishness, black bile caused melancholia, yellow bile aroused the temper, and blood was responsible for vitality (Bloom, 1985). Today the idea that emotions originate in areas other than the brain has not completely disappeared; it can be seen in phrases such as "loving someone with all one's heart" and "What gall!" (gall is defined both as liver bile and as impudence or nerve).

Unlike Aristotle's or Galen's earlier, simplistic theories, current theories of emotion and emotional expression must consider many factors: genetics, culture, learning, context and physiology. Most basic to the discussion of emotion are the physiological factors—the role of different areas of the brain and the biochemical changes that accompany emotions.

Limbic system The **limbic system**, located over the brainstem and under the cortex, is important as a locus of the study of emotions (see Exhibit 13.1) . Experimental evidence indicates that within the limbic system the hypothalamus, amygdala, hippocampus, parts of the thalamus and other areas are involved in emotion. In the brainstem, the reticular formation serves as the alerting, or arousal, mechanism; the reticular formation filters incoming signals and passes on novel or persistent information. Only when you are aroused or alerted to new information can you begin to organize it and respond to it.

In 1937, anatomist James W. Papez proposed that several brain parts interact in emotional functioning. This idea contradicted an earlier theory that the thalamus was the primary center of emotion. Papez linked together the parts of the brain that are now called the limbic system in what he termed a "stream of feeling" (Papez, 1937). Years of studies have confirmed the important roles played by these brain parts.

Hippocampus Although the hippocampus's role in memory has been demonstrated, its role in emotion is not yet clear. Stored in the hippocampus are emotional memories, the emotional components of specific events; your recall of events brings with it the stored emotional component. Further, the hippocampus may be the limbic system site at which various anti-anxiety substances act. One researcher (Gray, 1977) measured the electrical activity of the hippocampal areas of "anxious" (fearful, frustrated) rats. Then he gave them anti-anxiety substances such as alcohol, barbiturates, and tranquilizers, and the electrical activity decreased. Could this result mean that greater electrical activity occurs in the hippocampal areas of anxious people? Do they unknowingly treat their emotional conditions when they use alcohol and barbiturates? These questions are highly speculative, and more research in this area is needed before researchers can draw conclusions about the hippocampus's role in emotions.

Amygdala Another part of the brain, the amygdala, also appears to play a role in emotion. When researchers removed the amygdala from a rhesus monkey that was dominant in its group, the monkey fell to the bottom of the social ladder (Rosvold et al., 1954). The researchers concluded this effect was due to the monkey's inability to make the appropriate social gestures, or outward

EXHIBIT 13.1
The Limbic System and Other Brain Structures
Involved with Emotions

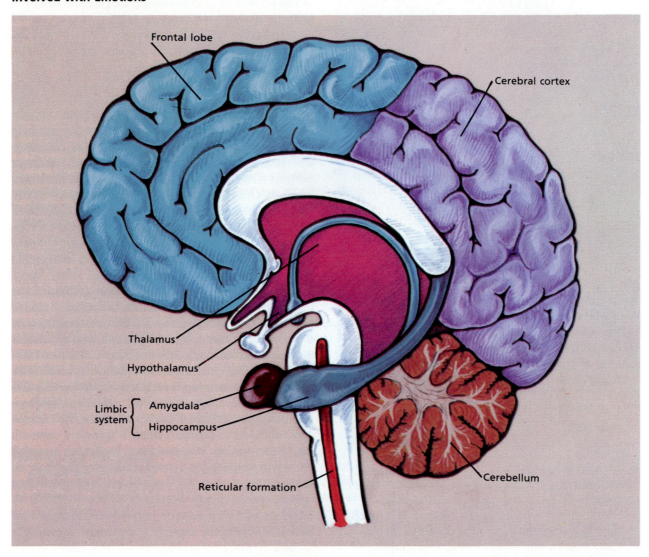

expressions of emotion, that the dominant monkey relies on to keep his position. Additionally, the story of Charles Whitman, the 1966 "Texas Tower" murderer, indicates that damage to the amygdala may affect human emotions. An autopsy revealed that Whitman suffered from a walnut-sized malignant tumor near his amygdala. In the following letter, written the day before his shooting spree, Whitman describes the frightening emotional changes that had taken place over the previous weeks:

I don't understand what it is that compels me to type this letter....I don't really understand myself these

days....I have been a victim of many unusual and irrational thoughts. These thoughts constantly recur, and it requires a tremendous effort to concentrate on useful and progressive tasks....After my death I wish that an autopsy would be performed on me to see if there is any visible physical disorder.....

It was after much thought that I decided to kill my wife, Kathy, tonight after I pick her up from work....I love her dearly, and she has been a fine wife to me as any man could hope to have. I cannot rationally pinpoint any specific reason for doing this....At this time though, the most prominent reason in my mind is that I truly do not consider this world worth living in, and am

An autopsy of Charles Whitman, the "Texas Tower" murderer who shot thirty-eight people, showed damage to his amygdala caused by a tumor.

prepared to die, and I do not want to leave her to suffer alone in it. I intend to kill her as painlessly as possible. (quoted in Johnson, 1972, p. 78)

The night Whitman wrote this letter, he shot his wife and mother. The next morning, he shot thirty-eight people, killing fourteen of them. How damage to the amygdala can create the emotional changes Whitman describes as well as its precise role in emotion is still unclear, but that the amygdala plays a role is certain.

Frontal lobes That the frontal lobes of the brain are also involved in emotion is confirmed by the effects of frontal lobotomies. From the 1930s through the 1950s, when frontal lobotomies were the most commonly practiced psychosurgery (Wetzel, 1984), over 100,000 such operations were performed in the United States (Heilman & Satz, 1983). In a summary of approximately fifty years of research on the effects of damage or lesioning of

the frontal lobes, investigators concluded that lobotomy patients demonstrate distinct alterations of emotional responses. These emotional changes are characterized by "a lack of sensitivity, more concrete thinking, more immediate reactions, a simpler and slower intellectual life, and impoverishment of imagination" (Heilman & Satz, 1983).

Physiology of Emotion

Sympathetic nervous system Although regions of the brain trigger emotional arousal, the sympathetic division of the autonomic nervous system induces the physiological changes that accompany emotion. The sympathetic nervous system mobilizes the "fight or flight response," which is characterized by elevated blood pressure, increased heart rate, reductions in processes such as digestion and elimination, and increased blood flow to the muscles. (A more complete description of the actions of the sympathetic nervous system is found in Chapter 4.)

Endocrine system The endocrine (hormone) system also plays a part in the "fight or flight" response. The hypothalamus signals the pituitary gland to increase secretion of the hormone ACTH (adrenocorticotropic hormone) in the bloodstream. This increase in ACTH promptly notifies the adrenal medulla to increase epinephrine and norepinephrine in the bloodstream. These endocrines help prepare various organs to deal with emergencies.

Despite the long and complex chains of responses that begin when you sense that a situation needs an immediate response or may pose a threat, the response time of the sympathetic nervous system is an almost unbelievable one to two seconds (Bloom, 1985). You will be thankful for this incredible speed the next time a child runs into the street in front of your car and you are able to brake quickly and avoid an accident.

Theories of Emotion

A review of the theories of emotion must begin with Charles Darwin's theory. In *The Expression of the Emotions in Man and Animals* (1872), he emphasized the contribution of evolutionary processes to facial and gestural expressions of emotion. Because he saw many human emotional expressions as remnants of attack or defense sequences, he hypothesized that as social animals evolved these expressions no longer signaled readiness for action but informed others of internal states and intentions. Darwin concluded that a few facial expressions of emotion are universal in human beings and, therefore, are genetically "wired in" behaviors of the human species.

James-Lange Theory In 1890, American psychologist William James published what became known as the **James-Lange theory**. James had combined his theory with that of Danish psychologist Carl G. Lange, who had published similar ideas in 1885. Basically, the James-Lange theory states that emotions result from the bodily changes that occur reflexively when a person is confronted by a situation. In other words, James assumed that the causes of emotion are internal and physiological and that an emotional experience follows this sequence (James, 1894): (1) a person's perception of an exciting fact or object; (2) a bodily expression such as weeping, striking out, or fleeing from the situation; and (3) experience of an emotion such as fear or anger. This theory contradicts the **common-sense theory** of emotion, wherein a person encounters a situation, experiences an emotion such as fear or anger, and then weeps, strikes out, or flees. (See Exhibit 13.2 for a summary of the James-Lange theory and other theories of emotion.)

Cannon-Bard Theory In 1929, physiologist Walter Cannon altered the James-Lange theory by asserting that the thalamus "caused" emotions. The **Cannon-Bard theory**, which was so labeled because Phillip Bard later modified Cannon's ideas, states that in situations that a person perceives to be emotion-arousing, the stimulus goes first to the thalamus. From the thalamus, signals are sent simultaneously to the cerebral cortex, which produces the emotion, and to the hypothalamus, which triggers the complex physiological changes (Cannon, 1929). In other words, the experience of an emotion and the physiological changes that accompany it occur at the same time.

Schachter and Singer's Cognitive Theory of Emotion More recently, Schachter and Singer (1962) proposed a two-component **cognitive theory of emotion**. The basic premise of their theory is that an emotional state involves both physiological arousal and a cognition (thought) about the emotion-arousing situation. According to this theory, emotional experience in everyday life occurs in the following sequence: (1) the emotion-arousing stimuli occur, (2) the person appraises the situation, and (3) the arousal and the attribution of the arousal to the stimulus situation occur simultaneously (Reisenzein, 1983). If, on the other hand, someone experiences unex-plained physiological arousal, he or she will seek an explanation for the arousal. If the person discovers a likely source of the physiological arousal, he or she will attribute the arousal to the source and label the emotion.

The Research Process: Epinephrine, Emotion, and Cognition

To test their theory, Schachter and Singer administered injections of epinephrine (also called adrenalin) to three groups of subjects. Subjects in the first group were told to expect the actual effects; subjects in the second group were told to expect numbness, itching, and a slight headache; and subjects in the third group were uninformed about the effects. (Actually, epinephrine causes physiological effects much like those felt in strong emotions such as anger or fear—heart rate and blood pressure increase, the face flushes, and hands tremble.) After the subjects had received their injections, they were asked to wait in a room with a person who supposedly had also received an injection (a confederate of the experimenter). On the instruction of the researchers, these confederates acted angry (they tore up their questionnaires and stormed out of the room) or euphoric (they threw paper airplanes and acted very happy). Schachter and Singer expected the subjects who experienced epinephrine's effects and had no explanation for them (the uninformed and the misinformed subjects) to be more influenced by the behavior of people around them. The researchers' expectations were fulfilled as measured by responses about the emotions they felt. The uninformed and misinformed subjects were more influenced by the confederates' behavior than were the accurately informed subjects. Finding themselves in a state of physiological arousal for which they had no cognitive explanation, they searched the environment for an explanation. Not only did they join the confederates in their displays of anger or euphoria, the subjects also reported feeling those emotions. However, a significant problem with the Schachter and Singer study was revealed when subjects who were injected with placebos were also influenced by the angry or euphoric confederates. Thus, the second component of the cognitive theory—that unexplained arousal may be experienced as different emotions according to cognitive circumstances—was brought into question. Only subjects who were physiologically aroused and searching for an explanation should have been so influenced. A recent reviewer of the evidence for the cognitive theory of emotion found very little support for this portion of the theory (Denzin, 1984). Interestingly, be-

EXHIBIT 13.2
Theories of Emotion

The following diagrams present a brief summary of the five theories of emotion discussed in this chapter.

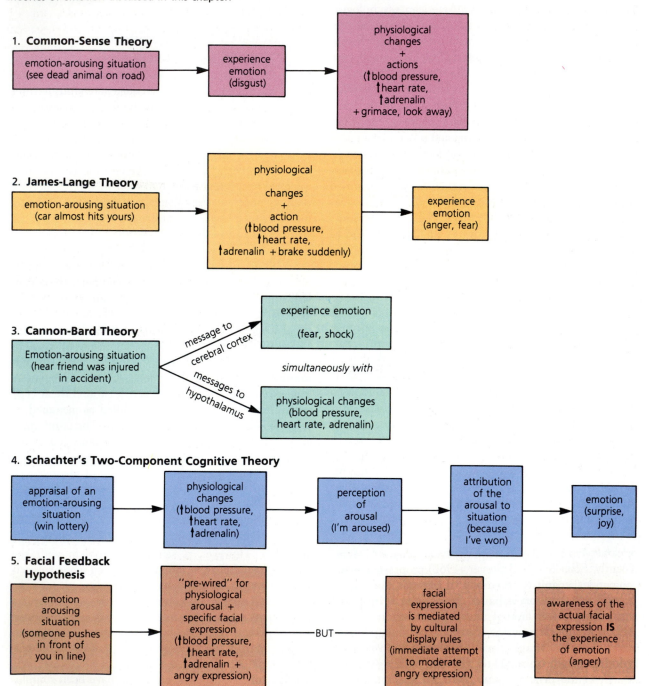

1. **Common-Sense Theory**

emotion-arousing situation (see dead animal on road) → experience emotion (disgust) → physiological changes + actions (↑blood pressure, ↑heart rate, ↑adrenalin +grimace, look away)

2. **James-Lange Theory**

emotion-arousing situation (car almost hits yours) → physiological changes + action (↑blood pressure, ↑heart rate, ↑adrenalin +brake suddenly) → experience emotion (anger, fear)

3. **Cannon-Bard Theory**

Emotion-arousing situation (hear friend was injured in accident)

message to cerebral cortex → experience emotion (fear, shock)

simultaneously with

messages to hypothalamus → physiological changes (blood pressure, heart rate, adrenalin)

4. **Schachter's Two-Component Cognitive Theory**

appraisal of an emotion-arousing situation (win lottery) → physiological changes (↑blood pressure, ↑heart rate, ↑adrenalin) → perception of arousal (I'm aroused) → attribution of the arousal to situation (because I've won) → emotion (surprise, joy)

5. **Facial Feedback Hypothesis**

emotion arousing situation (someone pushes in front of you in line) → "pre-wired" for physiological arousal + specific facial expression (↑blood pressure, ↑heart rate, ↑adrenalin + angry expression) — BUT — facial expression is mediated by cultural display rules (immediate attempt to moderate angry expression) → awareness of the actual facial expression **IS** the experience of emotion (anger)

[The diagram of Schachter's theory is adapted from Figure 1, page 241 of Reisenzein, R. 1983. The Schachter theory of emotion: Two decades later, *Psychological Bulletin, 94,* 239–264.]

cause of recent ethical considerations that prohibit the injection of epinephrine for experimental purposes, this specific experiment cannot be replicated.

The Facial Feedback Hypothesis Recently, theorists have proposed the **facial feedback hypothesis**, which rests on the idea that skeletal muscle activity associated with emotional expression plays a direct role in regulating the emotional processes. One proponent of the theory (Izard, 1977) stated: "Facial feedback plays its role in emotion activation in a rapid reflexive fashion, and awareness of facial activity or facial feedback is actually our awareness of the subjective experience of a specific emotion." However, **cultural display rules** (the rules that govern facial expression and that are followed by members of a social class, culture, or subculture) intervene between the innately determined facial display and the actual facial display. In studies to test the facial feedback hypothesis, when subjects were asked to arrange their facial muscles in fearful or happy emotional expressions, their physiological responses changed, but the subjects did not always report feeling the emotion they were portraying. Thus, one evaluator of facial feedback studies (Buck, 1984) concludes that even with increasing empirical support for some parts the hypothesis has neither been proven conclusively nor disproven.

Another current controversy in emotion research involves theorists who believe that cognitive appraisal of an emotional situation is important. The disagreement among these theorists concerns whether an emotional experience or state is *always* preceded by cognitive appraisal or whether some emotional experiences result from sufficiently intense physical stimuli. Members of one side of the controversy (Lazarus, 1982) maintain that emotional arousal cannot occur without prior cognitive appraisal. They argue that if people cannot observe or document the cognitive appraisal, it must therefore occur at an unconscious level. Opponents (Zajonc, 1984) maintain that sufficient experimental evidence shows that different brain parts are primarily responsible for cognition and emotion, and occasions exist when emotion may be experienced without prior cognitive appraisal. According to this position, emotional and cognitive systems usually function together but they can occur separately. The prior cognitive appraisal hypothesis definitely contradicts the facial feedback hypothesis; the opposing hypothesis does not.

Several recent theories have moved away from viewing emotions as purely physiological or psychological processes and have defined them as sociological processes. These theories propose that rules of emotional expression exist and that people learn to "manage" their emotions. These theories have added several dimensions to the study of emotion. They have brought emotion out of the unconscious into the conscious world, situated emotions in the social and cultural world, and suggested that interpretation, thought, cognition, and feeling are all involved in emotion (Denzin, 1984). Presently, emotion research is moving in two directions: it is further exploring internal and external changes associated with emotion and is investigating ways in which thoughts and interactions with others contribute to emotion.

Focus Question Answer

What role does your brain play in your experience of emotion? Your experience of emotion begins with the reticular formation in the brainstem; the reticular formation alerts or arouses the brain when stimuli are novel or persistent. Although researchers have not yet clearly identified the function of each, the parts of the limbic system—including the thalamus, hypothalamus, amygdala, and hippocampus—play a role in emotion. Your brain begins the process of emotional arousal, but it sends messages to the sympathetic nervous system to trigger the physiological changes associated with emotion.

 ## Emotional Expression

Universal Expression of Emotion

In 1872, Charles Darwin proposed that human facial expressions evolved because they helped the species survive. This proposal implies that basic facial expressions of emotion are universal to the human species. Studies conducted during the last two decades have at least partially confirmed Darwin's ideas.

One researcher, Sylvan Tomkins (1962, 1963), identified eight **primary affects** (emotions): happiness, sadness, anger, fear, disgust/contempt, surprise, interest, and shame. He maintained that each of these primary affects is based on a "pre-wired" (innate) physiological program in the central nervous system and that each is associated with a specific, universal facial display.

Another researcher (Plutchik, 1984) also identified eight primary emotions: joy, acceptance, fear, surprise, sadness, disgust, anger, and anticipation. Although this list of eight primary affects differs slightly from those identified by Tomkins, Plutchik's research lends further support to the hypothesis of primary emotions. This hy-

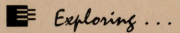

Research Tidbits about the Perception and Expression of Emotion

1. Perception of emotion seems to be more accurate when stimuli are presented so they first reach the right hemisphere (Heilman & Satz, 1983).

2. The expression of both positive and negative emotions is more intense on the left side of the face (Heilman & Satz, 1983).

3. Researchers have concluded that babies (average age, thirty-six hours) can discriminate happy, sad, and surprised expressions posed by a model, because the infants clearly imitated these expressions (Field et al., 1982).

4. Spontaneous expression of negative emotions is more inhibited by social learning than is spontaneous expression of positive emotions (Buck, 1984).

5. Considerable evidence suggests people decode the expressions of people known to them more accurately than they do the expressions of people unknown to them (Abramovich & Daly, 1979; Zuckerman & Prze-wuzman, 1979).

6. Females are better at sending and receiving nonverbal messages (Buck, 1976).

7. Emotional tears, such as those produced when you watch a sad movie, contain more protein than do tears induced by irritants (such as onions) (Frey, 1982).

8. In middle-class American culture, the following display rules (socially learned rules) hold (Ekman, 1972):
   a. Men are socialized to neutralize or mask fear and sadness.
   b. Women are socialized to neutralize or mask anger.
   c. Women are socialized to display more positive facial emotions.

---

pothesis has been supported by many cross-cultural studies (Ekman et al., 1972; Ekman & Friesen, 1975; Izard, 1977; Ekman, 1980), and the existence of a small number of primary emotions is now widely accepted.

Emotional Development

Given the universality of the expression of a few emotions, when does this expression develop in individuals? One researcher of infant emotion (Izard, 1982) has spent thousands of hours videotaping and then analyzing film of the faces of babies who had been subjected to a wide variety of situations, such as being given an ice cube to hold, having tape put on the backs of their hands, being given a favorite toy, being separated from and reunited with their mothers, having a balloon popped in front of their faces, and being given lemon rind and lime juice to taste. From his analysis of the videotapes, the researcher has identified the ages at which each of the primary emotions is first seen. That this order of development of emotion is the same for all his subjects suggests biological determination.

Children begin to express emotions at the ages listed in Exhibit 13.3, but when do they begin to "read" others' emotional expressions? In a 1971 study (Izard), over four hundred French and American children were shown photos of typical expressions of the primary emotions, and they were asked to produce appropriate labels for the photographed emotions. Only children who were at least nine years old averaged more than 50 percent correct. Four-year-old American children labeled correctly an average of only five or six of eighteen. This study suggests that accurate verbal labeling of emotional expressions does not occur until age nine or later.

A recent study of preschoolers attempted to determine whether children who have not yet acquired labels for particular emotions still perceive emotions as adults do (Russell & Bullock, 1985). The children were given twenty photographs and were asked to put into piles "the pictures of persons who feel most alike." The results revealed that four- and five-year-olds classify emotional expressions in much the same way adults do; for example, although four- and five-year-old children have not yet acquired the correct verbal labels, they see boredom and sleepiness as similar displays of emotion. That children display consistency in both their development of specific emotional expressions and in their ability to verbally label facial emotions implies a "pre-wiring" of the central nervous system.

Nonverbal Communication of Emotion

Kinesics, commonly called "body language," is the study of body movement, posture, gesture, and facial expression. Other ways of communicating nonverbally are the use of time, space, and touch (the *Exploring . . .* section examines the use of touch and how touches may be interpreted by others). These methods of nonverbal communication cannot accurately be labeled language because often the meanings are not clear beyond the verbal or situational context in which they are used. Nonetheless, they are clues to emotion. If you find a friend slouched down in a chair and staring into space, you may conclude she is tired or depressed. Where she is sitting, your knowledge of what has happened to her recently, and your knowledge of her usual posture give you clues about her mood. If, when she sees you, she smiles and points to a seat beside her, you will probably conclude that she welcomes your presence. Although

The expression of distress in response to pain is present from birth, but the emotional expression of sadness develops at three to four months of age.

EXHIBIT 13.3
Emotional Development

Expression of Fundamental Emotions	Approximate Time of Emergence
Interest	Present at birth
*Neonatal smile (a sort of half smile that appears spontaneously for no apparent reason)	
*Startle response	
*Distress (in response to pain)	
Disgust	
Social smile	4–6 weeks
Anger	3–4 months
Surprise	
Sadness	
Fear	5–7 months
Shame/Shyness/Self-awareness	6–8 months
Contempt	2nd year of life
Guilt	

*The neonatal smile, the startle response, and distress in response to pain are precursors of the social smile and the emotions of surprise and sadness, which appear later. Izard does not have evidence that they are related to inner feelings when they are seen in the first few weeks of life.

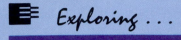

Exploring . . .

Touching

People touch not only intimates but acquaintances and strangers as well. Touch takes such forms as handshakes, pats, hugs, caresses, kisses, brushes, pinches, and strokes. The emotional reactions of recipients range from rage to happiness to indifference, depending on how, when, and where the recipients are touched. In American culture, women are more open than men about touching. Men may confine their touching of other men to ritual touching, such as shaking hands or clapping others on their shoulders. Men shake hands with each other more often than women do, and men often clap each other on the shoulder by way of congratulation. During sporting events (especially football games), men pat each other on the buttocks, as well as the shoulders and back. Outside sporting situations, the buttocks are a forbidden area of touch between adults who do not have an intimate relationship.

Non-vulnerable parts of your body (the hands, arms, and shoulders) may, under the right circumstances, be touched even by strangers and slight acquaintances without causing a negative reaction. In contrast, the face, top of the head, neck, torso, lower back, buttocks, pelvic area, legs, and feet are taboo touch areas for everyone except people with whom you are intimate (Kotulak, 1985). Of course, exceptions exist. When you try on shoes and the salesperson touches your feet, you are unlikely to be annoyed or upset. Obviously, too, by disrobing for a doctor's examination, you are giving him or her permission to touch you. Nonetheless, even though you have given permission, the doctor's touches may make you uncomfortable.

In an analysis of more than 3,000 individual touches, two researchers found that women touch approximately 50 percent more than men do; women average twelve touches a day, and men average eight (Kotulak, 1985). And how do these touches affect others? Students who were touched by a librarian gave higher evaluations to the library and to the librarian (Fisher et al., 1976). Psychiatric patients who were touched by their nurses increased their verbal interactions (Aguilerz, 1967). In one study, waitresses touched diners on the palm, the shoulder, or not at all; the "touched" diners left larger tips than did those who were not touched (Crusco & Wetzel, 1985), but in contrast to the findings in the library study, the big tippers did not evaluate the restaurant or the waitress more positively than did people who left smaller tips. Generally, touches on nonvulnerable parts of the body may positively affect the attitudes and behaviors of the recipients.

Although touching can be a positive experience, in the workplace touching is fraught with problems. Unwelcome touches may be interpreted as sexual harassment or as being sexually suggestive. Many babysitters, daycare workers, and teachers (especially males) have become wary of touching their charges. The recent flurry of sexual abuse charges against a handful of childcare workers has made people in many occupations fear their touches will be misinterpreted.

Because some kinds of touching are negative, schools and other social agencies offer training programs to children in an attempt to increase the reporting of child sexual abuse and the subsequent treatment of the victims. One of the central strategies in these programs is teaching children the difference between "good touches" and "bad touches."

When you touch others—children or adults—remember the following "rules." People usually dislike surprise touches, especially those that come from behind them. Touches for the purpose of moving people around are usually interpreted negatively unless you are obviously trying to help. Touching strangers is taboo unless the touch is part of an accepted function such as receiving change from cashiers, trying on clothes or shoes, or accidently brushing against people in crowded elevators. Generally, however, touching can be therapeutic and can positively alter others' opinions of you, so "Reach out and touch someone."

Nonverbal communication by this child and her grandfather clearly convey their delight with the story and with each other's company.

your "conversation" occurs without words, you interpret her emotions and her messages through her body movements, posture, gestures, and facial expressions.

Gestures are body, head, arm, hand, and face movements that express a person's ideas, opinions, or emotions. The three major categories of gestures are emblems, manipulators, and illustrators (Ekman et al., 1984). An **emblem** is a physical act that takes the place of words. People use emblems intentionally, and emblems have the same meaning for all members of an identified group. An example from American culture is nodding your head up and down to signify yes.

Manipulators are acts in which one part of the body rubs, picks, or grooms some other part of the body. These movements do not have specific meanings by themselves, but their increase often signifies nervousness (Ekman et al., 1984). Examples of manipulators are picking lint off your clothes, rubbing your hands together, and smoothing your hair.

Illustrators are physical acts that help explain the situation or the verbal content but by themselves have no meaning. Waving your arms, snapping your fingers, and pounding the table are illustrators. The same illustrator may be used with either positive or negative verbalizations and add different meanings to each (Ekman et al., 1984). For instance, pounding the table in the middle of a speech of praise for someone's accomplishments may be accompanied by the words, "Hear, hear!"

In this case, the pounding means you acknowledge and agree with the speaker. Pounding the table during an argument may emphasize that you will stand firmly on the issue and will not be persuaded to change your mind.

Proxemics is the study of how people use the space around them or how they place themselves in relation to others with whom they interact. Although learned cultural rules heavily influence how close you stand to another person, the distance is also influenced by your relationship with the other person. Edward T. Hall (1966), who is regarded as the father of proxemics, has identified four distance zones:

— *Intimate Distance:* 0-18 inches.
   At this distance, people feel comfortable with their lovers, their children or parents, and those whom they wish to comfort or protect. This distance involves considerable touch and little use of language.
— *Personal Distance:* 18 inches-4 feet.
   Usually, only family members and good friends are allowed into the close phase (18 inches-24 inches) of this noncontact distance. Other people are "kept at arm's length."
— *Social Distance:* 4 feet-12 feet.
   Most business and social discourse is conducted within this range. People at the closer distance (4-9 feet) are almost impossible to ignore. The farther distance (over 10 feet) is usually the minimum distance for ignoring people and continuing one's own tasks.
— *Public Distance:* 12 feet-25 + feet.
   This very formal distance includes the space usually accorded to important figures like heads of state. On a more familiar level, if instructors wish to establish a formal tone, they should arrange their classrooms to separate themselves from their students by twelve feet or more.

In most cultures, rules governing the use of space are well-established, and violations of those rules can cause a range of responses. Most friends feel uncomfortable in face-to-face situations if they come closer than four feet. A stranger who intrudes into your personal space feels very uncomfortable. And how do you feel when the stranger intrudes? A common example is people's discomfort in crowded elevators. The riders stand carefully and move little so they can avoid further intrusions; they usually keep eye contact to a minimum, and they stare at the space above the door as the floor numbers pass.

People's comfort at various distances from each other is determined by cultural rules and by their relationship.

Focus Question Answer

Do smiles have the same meaning throughout the world? From his research, Tomkins concluded that people display eight primary affects, facial expressions that convey the same meaning for all people. Happiness is one of the eight affects. Another researcher, who identified eight slightly different primary affects, identified joy as a universal emotion.

 ## Stress

Are you feeling overwhelmed? Do you apologize to friends for your irritability? Do you have difficulty sleeping? Do you often tell others, "I've been under a lot of stress lately"? Before reading more of this section, look through the Stress Exhaustion Symptoms listed in Exhibit 13.4, and check the symptoms you are experiencing now.

Defining Stress

The concept of stress is often associated with Hans Selye, who first applied the term to a collection of symptoms. As a medical student in Prague, Germany, in 1926, he observed that rats that were injected with noxious substances or injured and people who were ill or injured exhibited many of the same symptoms. Regardless of the type of insult to the body, the reaction was much the same. He called this set of similar symptoms the "syndrome of just being sick"; later he applied the term "stress" to this syndrome (Selye, 1978b).

Selye borrowed the term from physics and engineering, according to which stress occurs when a force encounters resistance, and that force deforms the material that resists it. Selye believed that the body's reactions, the way the body fights back when it is stressed, caused the symptoms he had observed. Based on his observations, Selye defined **stress** as "the nonspecific response of the body to any demand" (Selye, 1978b).

The **General Adaptation Syndrome (G.A.S.)** is Selye's label for the series of bodily changes generated by stress. The G.A.S. is triggered by unpleasant experiences (**distress**), pleasant experiences (**eustress**), prolonged exposure to heat or cold, and extreme fear or unhappiness (Selye, 1978b). Selye identified three stages in the body's response to stress:

EXHIBIT 13.4
Stress Exhaustion Symptoms

Check the symptoms of stress exhaustion you've noticed lately in yourself.

PHYSICAL
- __ appetite change
- __ headaches
- __ tension
- __ fatigue
- __ insomnia
- __ weight change
- __ colds
- __ muscle aches
- __ digestive upsets
- __ pounding heart
- __ accident prone
- __ teeth grinding
- __ rash
- __ restlessness
- __ foot-tapping
- __ finger-drumming
- __ increased alcohol, drug, tobacco use

EMOTIONAL
- __ anxiety
- __ frustration
- __ the "blues"
- __ mood swings
- __ bad temper
- __ nightmares
- __ crying spells
- __ irritability
- __ "no one cares"
- __ depression
- __ nervous laugh
- __ worrying
- __ easily discouraged
- __ little joy

RELATIONAL
- __ isolation
- __ intolerance
- __ resentment
- __ loneliness
- __ lashing out
- __ hiding
- __ clamming up
- __ lowered sex drive
- __ nagging
- __ distrust
- __ fewer contacts with friends
- __ lack of intimacy
- __ using people

MENTAL
- __ forgetfulness
- __ dull senses
- __ poor concentration
- __ low productivity
- __ negative attitude
- __ confusion
- __ lethargy
- __ whirling mind
- __ no new ideas
- __ boredom
- __ spacing out
- __ negative self-talk

SPIRITUAL
- __ emptiness
- __ loss of meaning
- __ doubt
- __ unforgiving
- __ martyrdom
- __ looking for magic
- __ loss of direction
- __ needing to "prove" self
- __ cynicism
- __ apathy

Reproduced from *Structured Exercises in Stress Management, Vol. 1.* Nancy Loving Tubesing and Donald A. Tubesing, Editors. Whole Person Press, Box 3151, Duluth MN 55803.

— Alarm Stage—A number of physical and psychological symptoms occur (see Exhibit 13.4). Bleeding stomach ulcers may cause enough pain to bring the changes to a person's attention. The adrenal cortex enlarges (more adrenalin is produced), and the thymus and lymph nodes shrink (the thymus and lymph nodes are responsible for the body's defense against infection).

— Resistance Stage—The organism functions despite the stress, and the changes associated with the alarm stage disappear. The organism resists until the stress stops or, if the stress is severe and prolonged, until the resistance is lost and exhaustion occurs.

— Exhaustion Stage—The changes that occurred in the alarm stage are repeated, but they are of greater severity. The end result, if the stress reaction does not cease, is death (Selye, 1978b).

The bodily changes that occur in the alarm stage are often associated with emotional arousal and a triggering of the sympathetic division of the autonomic nervous system. In earlier times, this "fight or flight" response was adaptive because people could meet more of the environmental threats by fighting or fleeing. In modern society, few of the circumstances that trigger this response (e.g. traffic jams, layoffs at work, flat tires, and midterm exams) can be met constructively by fighting an individual or by fleeing from the situation. People must confront the situations and therefore may experience increased blood pressure, heart rate, and adrenalin production many times each day. People who experience repeated sympathetic nervous system arousal have increased chances of illness.

Stress-related illnesses, which involve both physiological and psychological components, are called **psychosomatic illnesses**. Among the wide variety of illnesses judged to be psychosomatic are cardiovascular diseases, ulcers, asthma, migraine headaches, skin disorders, chronic back pain, and some cases of hypertension.

Numerous studies have demonstrated the connection between the activation of the sympathetic nervous system, impaired immune system functioning, and a variety of disease processes (Selye, 1978a). Since stress, including environmental threats to health and emotional arousal, is associated with disease, people need to be able to identify the stressors that are responsible for disease. Several theories attempt to identify these factors.

One theory (Holmes & Rahe, 1967) states that social stressors, changes in living patterns, are associated with later illness. The theory does *not* maintain that life changes cause illness, but that faulty adaptive responses to these changes increase a person's susceptibility to disease and bring about illness. More recent research (Holmes & Masuda, 1974) indicates that negative or undesirable life changes play a greater role in stress than do positive ones.

At least three categories of stressors contribute to your total stress load: chronic life stressors, everyday hassles, and catastrophic life events. Chronic life stressors, which usually last years, include unhappy marriages or family relationships, stressful occupations, crowded living and working conditions, and living in the modern world with its threats of violent crime, pollution, and war. Everyday hassles, short-term stressors several of which occur each day, include traffic jams and detours, sick babysitters, flat tires, broken appliances (or banking machines, heaven forbid!), and all the minor interruptions like ringing telephones. Catastrophic life events include serious injuries, loss of family members or property in natural disasters, wars, and victimization in violent crimes such as rape and assault.

Quick Study Aid

The General Adaptation Syndrome: Stages and Symptoms

```
G A S es     A R E      L E T H A L
e d y        l e x      e l e e n o
n a n        a s h      t e n a x w
e p d        r i a      h v s d i c
r t r        m s u      a a i a e o
a a o          t s      r t o c t n
l t m          a t      g e n h y c
  i e          n i      y d     e   e
  o            c o           BP, s   n
  n            e n                    t
                             p        r
                             u        a
                             l        t
                             s        i
                             e        o
                                      n
```

To remember the stages and symptoms of the General Adaptation Syndrome, remember the sentence in bold letters. The letters of the first word will remind you of the syndrome, the letters of the second word will remind you of the three stages of the syndrome, and the letters in the third word will remind you of the symptoms of the syndrome.

People's reactions to stressful situations vary considerably. Selye (1978b) believes a combination of genetic predisposition and society's expectations account for these differences, and he advocates that each person find his or her most efficient stress level. Whether physiological responses are genetically predetermined, are learned behaviors that occur in certain situations, or are a combination of both, people need to increase their awareness of their bodily reactions. These reactions help people meet challenges, and they warn people of too much energy expenditure and approaching illness.

Type A and Type B Personalities

Another approach links disease processes to stress through personality type and posits a "coronary personality" (Friedman & Rosenman, 1974; Glass, 1977). According to these researchers' classification, people with **Type A** personalities are aggressive, hostile, time-urgent, competitive, fast-paced, impatient, irritable, and work-involved. They tend to deny failure and fatigue, they put little energy into their interpersonal relationships, and they are prone to heart attacks. **Type B's**, on the other hand, tend to be calmer, less time-urgent, less aggressive, less prone to frustration, more organized, and more concerned with the quality rather than the quantity of the work they do (Friedman & Rosenman, 1974). Early critics of the Type A-Type B theory denied that personality traits determine the frequency of heart attacks; they suggested instead that Type A's acquire more of the bad habits associated with coronary disease (smoking, drinking, obesity, sedentary lifestyles) and the habits themselves account for the findings of a "coronary personality." To test the critics' hypothesis, researchers matched Type A's and Type B's according to their bad habits and their executive responsibilities at work. Results revealed Type A's still had significantly more heart attacks (Friedman & Rosenman, 1974).

However, more recent evidence again questions the predictability of coronary disease from Type A behavior alone. Several studies indicate that when Type A's and B's are matched on such variables as blood pressure, cholesterol level, and cigarette smoking, Type B's are as likely to be stricken with heart attacks as are Type A's. The specific personality Type A traits of hostility and cynicism are better predictors of heart disease than a person's overall level of Type A behavior (Tierney, 1985).

Differences in emotional expressiveness may also determine which Type A and Type B individuals will experience stress-related illnesses. The inability to express

People with Type B personalities are able to set aside their work and relax.

feelings verbally, **alexithymia**, is a quality found in patients with a variety of psychosomatic complaints (Flannery, 1977; Wolff, 1977). In a test of this idea, one researcher (Buck, 1981) found a positive correlation between the forehead EMG (a measure of the tenseness or movement of the muscles in the forehead) and the subject's stress rating; the correlation suggests that people who cannot admit their stress verbally are less facially expressive. Another researcher (Anderson, 1981) has suggested that impaired emotional expression may be a necessary, if not sufficient, factor preceding psychosomatic diseases such as heart disease, ulcers, and colitis.

In summary, stress is an ever-present part of life. Research clearly shows that an inability to adapt to the stress level in one's life and attitudes toward stressors contribute to psychosomatic illness. Certain personality traits also increase the likelihood of illness. As you read further, you will discover several valuable suggestions for controlling stress in your life.

Managing Stress

One approach to coping with stress has been applied specifically to "burnout". **Burnout** is a syndrome of emotional exhaustion that results from the constant emotional pressures associated with intense involvement with people over long periods of time (Pines & Aaronson, 1981). Workers experiencing burnout may treat the people they serve in a detached fashion. Because many of the expanding occupational areas are service-oriented, increasing numbers of people will be experiencing this syndrome.

Experts on burnout advise four major strategies for coping (Pines & Aaronson, 1981):

1. *Be aware of the problem.* Be aware that a problem exists and that burnout is usually a function of the situation, not the individual.

2. *Take responsibility for doing something about the problem.* Since *you* are experiencing the symptoms, *you* must take action rather than blame other people.

3. *Strive for clarity of thinking.* Distinguish between what cannot be changed, what is extremely difficult to change, and what can be changed. Distinguish between the "real" demands of a job and the demands you place on yourself.

4. *Develop tools for coping.* Change the situation or yourself, talk to others about your stress, and get involved in other activities (an indirect method of coping with stressful working conditions).

Another approach to coping with or controlling stress maintains that people benefit by knowing about aversive environmental events. According to **information control theories**, predictable aversive events cause less stress than do unpredictable aversive events. In one study (Katz & Wykes, 1985), eighty female volunteers were given six predictable electric shocks and six unpredictable electric shocks. The subjects reported less distress during the time periods before the predictable shocks than during the times before the unpredictable shocks, and they perceived the predictable shocks as less aversive. Their autonomic arousal was also less during the periods before the predictable shocks than during the period before the unpredictable shocks. Of the eighty women, 64 percent preferred the predictable to the unpredictable condition. Although researchers included in the tests measures of personality and anxiety, these elements did not account for the difference in the preference for the predictable shock condition.

This study indicates that knowledge of an upcoming stressful event, even when changing the situation is impossible, may lower a person's stress reactions. Therefore, people would be wise to gain as much information as possible about an upcoming aversive situation. If you are a new student on campus, you could locate the buildings in which your classes will be held. Or if you will be going to the hospital for a nonemergency treatment, you could drive to the hospital beforehand and locate the place of treatment, the office, or a patient room. Although not all the aversive or stressful events in your life are predictable, some of them are, and using the information control approach may help reduce your stress and your

autonomic responses (See Exhibit 13.5 for several general suggestions to help you reduce the effects of stress in your life.)

Relaxation as Stress Management

Most relaxation techniques involve a series of steps. First, you must realize that you are tense and that you can relieve that tension. Second, you need to choose from two basic styles of relaxation—passive and active. An active style, such as the well-known Jacobson relaxation tapes, instructs you to tense and relax each part of the body in a specific order. The passive style involves lying comfortably relaxed and becoming limp without com-

EXHIBIT 13.5
Stress Bandaids

The following suggestions can help you reduce the negative effects of too much stress in your life.

1. Exercise moderately.
2. Learn relaxation exercises.
3. Allow yourself leisure time.
4. Be more flexible.
5. Eliminate doing several activities or thinking about several topics at the same time.
6. Reduce hostility.
7. Maintain good friendships.
8. Engage in pleasurable activities.
9. Reduce negative self-talk.
10. Give up striving to do more and more work in less and less time.

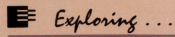

Relaxation by Sensory Awareness

Sit comfortably in a chair, and have someone read the following statements to you. You need not respond verbally to the items. Just listen to each statement, and let yourself react however you choose. No way is right or wrong. (Ask the reader to pause fifteen seconds between each item.)

1. Gently let your eyes close.
2. Allow yourself to sit heavily in your chair.
3. Can you imagine the space between your eyes?
4. Become aware of the distance between your ears.
5. Can you become aware of how close your breath comes to the back of your eyes every time you inhale?
6. Become aware of the space within your mouth.
7. Notice the position of your tongue within your mouth.
8. Can you feel your lips becoming soft?
9. Can you imagine a warm spring breeze against your cheek?
10. Can you imagine the sun radiating on the back of your neck?
11. Can you expand that warmth down your entire back?
12. Can you feel the weight of your arms pulling down your shoulders?
13. Can you become aware of one of your arms being more relaxed than the other?
14. Can you feel the space between your fingers?
15. Can you feel a warm breeze brush against your fingers?
16. Can you make your legs feel as limp as a rag doll?
17. Can you feel the floor beneath your feet?
18. Try to feel as if you are becoming a few inches taller by allowing yourself to stretch out through the bottom of your feet.
19. Can you imagine that your arms are growing?
20. As you inhale, pretend that the air is puffing you up like a balloon; as you exhale, feel like a balloon that is slowly losing its air.
21. Now picture your lungs as a bird's wings. As you slowly inhale, picture the wings rising gracefully. As you slowly exhale, imagine the wings lowering smoothly.
22. Can you feel yourself floating as if on a cloud?
23. Can you imagine that you are looking at something that is very far away?
24. Can you imagine in your mind's eye a beautiful object suspended a few feet in front of you?
25. Can you imagine that you hear a seashell at your ear?
26. Try to imagine your head sinking into a soft, fluffy pillow.
27. Check to see if you feel tension anywhere in your body. Send mental messages to those areas to eliminate the tension.
28. As you inhale, imagine your breath is sending energy to all areas of your body. As you exhale, imagine any tension is leaving your body through your fingertips and toes.
29. Can you allow yourself to sit where you are and enjoy your state of relaxation? (longer pause)
30. Can you allow your eyes to open? Open them now, and be wide awake and very comfortable.

Adapted from a tape by Janet A. Simons and Donald B. Irwin. Relaxation by sensory awareness. 1983. Developmental Educational Learning Institute. Des Moines, IA.

pleting any activities (Benson, 1976). (An example of the passive style is provided in the *Exploring . . .* section.) Each method of relaxation can be beneficial, and no method is right for everybody. Try several relaxation techniques to determine which best suits you.

One quick technique to relax and rid yourself of tension is "shaking." With your arms hanging loosely at your sides, shake your hands, then your arms and shoulders. Loosely shake each leg. This technique should help ease muscle tension and make you more relaxed, even if you have only a few minutes in which to do it (Sobel, 1976b).

Another technique is called **differential relaxation** (Sobel, 1976a). Using this technique, you can relax while you continue your daily routine, and through this method you may find your routine less taxing. Periodically during any activity, stop for a moment and try to identify muscle contractions or tensions that are not part of the activity you are performing. If you find any, relax those muscles. As you read this chapter, whether you are sitting or lying down, take note of tense muscles. Try to readjust your position and relax those muscles. You can use this relaxation technique almost anywhere, and no one will notice.

Another relaxation method many people enjoy is listening to tapes or records of sea sounds, forest sounds, or other nature sounds that have been specifically recorded for relaxation purposes. Even tapes of "anti-frantic" music have been written especially for this purpose.

Yet another relaxation alternative is **biofeedback**. In this method, a monitoring device provides you with knowledge about the variations in one of your biological responses. Through a combination of operant conditioning, knowledge of results, and classical conditioning, you learn to modify bodily functions usually classified as involuntary responses of the sympathetic nervous system.

This overview of several relaxation methods may help you choose a method that will benefit you. As a student, you experience stress both from the academic demands placed on you and from demands in other areas of your life. If you try one relaxation exercise and it doesn't seem to work, try another. Relax—your body will thank you.

Focus Question Answer

How does your personality type relate to stress and illness? More than a decade ago, researchers identified a Type A, or heart attack-prone, personality; you have a Type A personality if you are hostile, competitive, impatient, irritable, and time-urgent. More recent research has attempted to pinpoint the specific personality characteristics that make people illness- or heart attack-prone. Researchers have identified hostility, cynicism, and repressed emotional expression as contributors to illness.

Relate

Lies—Deception and Detection

During the last two decades, the use of the **polygraph**, or "lie detector," has greatly increased. About one million standard polygraph tests are being administered each year by private corporations, police departments, and federal agencies such as the Central Intelligence Agency and the Department of Defense (Ognibene, 1985). A congressional Office of Technology Assessment study of polygraphs found that 23,000 polygraph exams were conducted by the federal government in 1983; 90 percent of these were done by the Pentagon (Ognibene, 1985). Most of the remaining million-per-year polygraph tests are administered by private companies attempting to predict theft or to ferret out the thief once an incident has occurred. Since polygraphs now affect a million lives per year, their accuracy is a very important issue.

Usually, polygraph machines record three different functions. A cuff wrapped around the upper arm measures blood pressure, and one or two tubes tied around the torso measure respiration rate. A third function is the Galvanic Skin Response (GSR), which measures the electrodermal response (sweating) by placing electrodes on the fingers. Usually, the subject is first asked irrelevant, general information questions to establish a baseline rate of the physiological responses; then the "real" questioning begins.

The record of the person's physiological changes during questioning is examined for displacements from the baseline rate. The theoretical basis of the polygraph is that lying causes stress, which results in identifiable physiological changes the machine can detect. However, although height-

A polygraph or "lie-detector" machine measures physiological arousal. The large deflection in the above recording may be interpreted as evidence the person is lying.

ened physiological responses do indicate heightened emotion, the arousal may be due to emotions other than guilt and may result in inaccurate identifications of truthful and false statements. Therefore, the value of using polygraphs in both employment situations and criminal cases has been questioned. In its November 1983 report, the Office of Technology Assessment concluded that "while there is some evidence for the validity of polygraph testing as an adjunct to criminal investigations, there is very little research or scientific evidence to establish polygraph test validity in screening situations, whether they be pre-employment, pre-clearance, periodic or aperiodic, random or 'dragnet'" (Ognibene, 1985, p. 3C). Only a foolproof "lie detector" device would serve the many purposes for which polygraphs are now used.

Critics of the widespread use of the polygraph maintain that the device is not an accurate "lie detector" and that, in fact, various methods can be used to "fool" the polygraph. For instance, experimenters (Waid & Orne, 1982) have demonstrated that a low dose of an anti-anxiety tranquilizer reduces electrodermal response enough that the GSR cannot detect deception. Other researchers (Honts et al., 1985) reported training subjects to bite their tongues to produce pain and to press their toes against the floor to tense their muscles during the baseline recording. These subjects were able to produce higher physiological arousal when they responded to the general questions than when they lied about a staged crime in which they had participated. These subjects were able to "fool" two polygraph experts about half the time.

While most people may need to use such artificial techniques to "fool" the polygraph, certain individuals show little physiological response when they lie, and their lies therefore cannot be detected. A number of studies have shown that people who demonstrate sociopathic behaviors (people who do not distinguish between right and wrong and feel no guilt about destructive or antisocial behavior) and people who are very impulsive show lower electrodermal response, or lower GSRs, and are thus able to fool the polygraph (Hare & Craigen, 1974). A similar study used college students instead of identified sociopaths as its subjects and found that the deception of less highly socialized students (those who had not absorbed society's rules and felt little guilt when violating them) was more difficult to detect due to their low GSR responses. In contrast, highly socialized subjects (those who had absorbed society's rules and felt guilt when violating them) showed high GSR responses and were mistakenly classified as deceptive (Waid et al., 1979a, 1979b). Recent experiments such as these have raised two very important questions. First, how often are polygraphs unable to identify liars who can conceal their deception through drugs or low GSR responses? Second, how often do polygraphs misclassify innocent people because of high GSR responses due to a higher degree of socialization?

If polygraphs are not reliable "lie detectors," are people? According to Ekman (1985), the answer depends on who is lying, how well the liar is known to the detector, whether the lie is about something of consequence to the liar, and how much the liar and the detector have practiced their roles. Ekman found that most people can detect lies accurately only 50–60 percent of the time. However, he maintains that with several weeks of his training, people can raise their lie detection accuracy rates to 90 percent! Following is Ekman's summary of the best cues to look for when you try to detect lies (Ekman, 1985):

Signals of Deception

1. Tightening the lips—especially to hide anger.
2. Raising the voice—may be a clue to fear in an inexperienced liar.
3. Hesitation in answering—especially if the question should elicit an immediate response.
4. Looking away while talking.
5. Pausing between sentences—as if to think about an answer.
6. Microexpressions—flashes of expression before a more stable expression appears.
7. Lengthy facial expressions—those lasting five to ten seconds or more.
8. Smiles that don't use the muscles around the eyes.

Additional evidence suggests that lies told by women are detected more readily than those told by men, and that lies told to the opposite sex are detected more readily than those told to the same sex. Ingratiating lies are detected more successfully than lies told when a person is not trying to impress or gain something (De Pauls et al., 1985).

In summary, polygraph devices, or "lie detectors," are of questionable accuracy in detecting lies. The results may misclassify honest people as liars or may miss the lies of dishonest individuals. Neither are people very accurate lie detectors. As you can see, detecting others' lies or predicting when your lies will be go undetected is not an easy task!

Things to Do

1. Facially express Tomkins' eight primary emotions, one by one, to a friend. Ask your friend to guess which emotion you are portraying. If possible, do this exercise with people from other cultures, and ask them to guess which primary emotion you are expressing. Do your "research" results agree with Tomkins' and Ekman's?

2. Keep an Emotions Diary for one week, and answer the following questions:

— What events or situations make you feel anxious?

— What makes you fearful?

— What events or situations make you angry?

— What makes you feel joyful?

— What events or situations disgust you?

— What makes you feel guilty?

Which situations in your life do you associate with negative emotions? With positive emotions? Which aspects of your life could you change to alter your emotional responses?

3. While you are watching a fast-paced drama or a soap opera on television, test your skill at identifying emotions without the accompanying verbal cues. Arrange so a friend can hear the sound and you cannot (you could wear earphones with music to mask the sound). Tell your friend each time you identify an emotion portrayed by one of the actors. Ask your friend to give you feedback about your accuracy in "reading" the nonverbal emotional cues.

4. Choose a subject, and measure his or her heart rate. Have the person close his or her eyes and think of a terrifying situation. Did the heart rate increase? Choose another subject, measure the heart rate, and have him or her think of a calm and peaceful situation or imagine the relaxation he or she feels just before falling asleep. Did the heart rate decrease? If you have access to biofeedback equipment, try the same procedure while your subjects are connected to the biofeedback device.

Things to Discuss

1. Which theory of emotion best reflects your beliefs about how you experience emotion?

2. Discuss this statement: "To express emotions is a sign of weakness because one needs to be hard to survive in this world."

3. To what extent is an infant capable of showing emotional response? How would you interpret the smile of a six-week-old infant?

4. A fellow student tells you that academic courses affect him physically. He says that by the end of the semester he feels physically worn out and sometimes very ill. Based on the information in the stress section, explain his decline in physical health during the semester.

5. Cultural display rules indicate which emotional expressions are encouraged and which are discouraged within a culture. What cultural display rules have you learned? What were your parents' attitudes about the expression of emotions? How have cultural display rules and your parents' attitudes affected your display of emotions?

6. A friend who is scheduled to visit a foreign country does not speak the native language. However, she has confidence she can make others understand her messages by using only facial expressions and hand signals. Do you agree with her?

7. Which particular occupations do you perceive to be most stressful? Why? How might the physical effects of stress reveal themselves? How might workers in these fields cope with job-related stress?

8. Imagine you are a psychological consultant for a defense attorney and have been asked to make a case against the reliability of the polygraph. State your case.

Things to Read

Buck, R. 1984. *Nonverbal behavior and the communication of affect.* NY: Guilford.

Ekman, P. & Friesen, W. V. 1975. *Unmasking the face: A guide to recognizing emotions from facial clues.* Englewood Cliffs, NJ: Prentice-Hall.

Ekman, P. 1985. *Telling lies: Clues to deceit in the marketplace, politics, and marriage.* NY: W. W. Norton & Co.

Plutchik, R. 1980. *Emotion.* NY: Harper & Row.

Travis, C. 1982. *Anger: The misunderstood emotion.* NY: Simon & Schuster.

Woolfolk, R. & Richardson, F. 1978. *Stress, sanity, and survival.* NY: Signet.

Review

Summary

1. In the emotion process, signals are filtered by the reticular formation and are processed by various parts of the limbic system, including the thalamus, hypothalamus, amygdala, and hippocampus. The precise role of the frontal lobes and each part of the limbic system is not yet clear.

2. In emotion, the brain triggers the fight or flight response, or the arousal of the sympathetic nervous system. This response includes elevation of heart rate, blood pressure, and adrenalin in the bloodstream and increased blood flow to the muscles.

3. The major theories of emotion are the James-Lange theory, the common-sense theory, the Cannon-Bard theory, the two-component cognitive theory, and the facial feedback hypothesis. The theories differ on such issues as the role of cognitive factors and the order of occurrence of the perception of emotion and the physiological changes.

4. Primary affects are innate emotions that have universal expression and meaning in the human species. Studies of the development of emotions in infants and cross-cultural studies of universal emotions provide evidence of approximately eight primary affects.

5. Nonverbal communication includes kinesics (the study of body movement, posture, gesture, and facial expression) and proxemics (the study of the way people use the space around them).

6. Hans Selye defined stress as the body's nonspecific response to any demand. The General Adaptation Syndrome (G.A.S.) specifies the three stages of the stress reaction (alarm, resistance, and exhaustion) and the physiological and emotional characteristics of each.

7. Illness and disease may result from excessive and prolonged stress reactions. According to various hypotheses, psychosomatic illnesses result from: (1) poor adaptation to life changes, (2) Type A as opposed to Type B personality, (3) hostility, (4) impaired emotional functioning, or (5) a combination of these causes. People with Type A personalities are aggressive, hostile, competitive, time-urgent, impatient, and irritable. People with Type B personalities are less aggressive, less hostile, less time-urgent, and less prone to frustration.

8. Coping with stress is a function of genetic factors, learned coping styles, and knowledge of upcoming stressful events.

9. Various methods of relaxation, including the use of relaxation tapes, recordings of nature sounds, biofeedback, and differential relaxation, can be used to reduce stress and its accompanying physiological, emotional, and psychological symptoms.

10. Lie detection by machines or humans is subject to errors and ethical complications. Methods of "fooling" polygraph devices point to the the inaccuracy of the results. Although identified facial, vocal, and bodily movement cues assist in detecting lies, people are not very accurate at lie detection.

Key Terms

emotion
feelings
moods
temperament
affect
James-Lange theory
common-sense theory
Cannon-Bard theory
cognitive theory of emotion
facial feedback hypothesis
cultural display rules
primary affects
kinesics
proxemics
gestures
stress
General Adaptation Syndrome (G.A.S.)
distress
eustress
psychosomatic illness
Type A/Type B
alexithymia
coping
burnout
information control theories
polygraph

Focus Questions

1. Will your personality change during your adulthood?

2. Does your body shape determine your personality?

3. Can your personality be described in terms of traits?

4. How does your childhood influence your adult personality?

5. Is Freudian theory still relevant today?

Chapter Outline

WHAT IS PERSONALITY?
Defining Personality
Assumptions about Personality
The Research Process: The Stability of Personality during Adulthood

TYPE THEORIES
Sheldon's Constitutional Theory
Eysenck's Type Theory

TRAIT THEORIES
Allport's Trait Theory
Cattell's Factor Theory

PSYCHODYNAMIC THEORIES
Freud's Psychoanalytic Theory
Adler's Individual Psychology
Jung's Archetypal Theory

RELATE: Freudian Updates
Things to Do
Things to Discuss
Things to Read

REVIEW: Summary
Key Terms

Chapter 14

Personality: Type, Trait, and Psychodynamic Theories

*Ego creeps in on little cat feet
and fogs up the mind.*

Steve Shireman

 ## What Is Personality?

Defining Personality

What is **personality**? You might use the term personality as a synonymn for charm or social skill, but in psychology the term personality refers to the essential characteristics of a person. Personality has three major emphases: (1) personality is what is enduring and stable about an individual, (2) personality is the consistency that makes an individual predictable to others and gives a sense of an integrated self, and (3) personality is useful in explaining individual differences (Scroggs, 1985).

One of the most complete definitions of personality was written by Gordon Allport, a pioneer personality theorist, who said that personality is "the dynamic organization within the individual of those psychophysical

325

systems that determine his characteristic behavior and thought" (Allport, 1961, p. 28). Allport's definition emphasizes personality as an active mind-body interaction responsible for behaviors.

Assumptions About Personality

As you will see, personality theories differ because theorists differ in their assumptions about reality and human nature, as well as in their methods of studying personality issues (Scroggs, 1985). The assumptions you make about the world and human nature will influence which of the personality theories presented in Chapters 14 and 15 you prefer. Answer the following questions to determine your personal assumptions about reality and human nature. As you read about the various personality theories, try to figure out the theorists' positions on these same questions.

1. Do you assume you choose your own behaviors freely, or do you believe that your current behaviors have been determined by previous behaviors and events?

2. Does the past, the present, or the future play the most important role in your personality? Is your present personality primarily a product of experiences you have already had, or is your present personality more determined by your expectations about the future?

3. Do you believe that humans are basically good or basically bad? Does society help control a negative human nature, or does society corrupt a good human nature?

4. Do you assume people are logical beings or emotional beings? Are people characteristically rational or irrational in their lives?

5. Do you believe people act with purpose, or do you believe people make machine-like responses to their environment?

6. Do you assume you are like everybody else? Does your concept of human nature emphasize uniqueness or universality?

7. How much do you think your bodily processes and body shape influence personality? Do you view the body and mind as an interacting unit?

The Research Process: The Stability of Personality during Adulthood

Just as psychologists do not agree about the nature of personality, they also differ in their opinions of when and how much personality can change (Moss & Susman, 1980). Some psychologists believe that personality changes occur throughout adulthood but that more personality change is likely to occur during the early adult

Just as an artist never paints two eggs exactly alike, no two personalities are ever exactly alike.

years than during the late adult years (Bloom, 1964). This research process focuses on a new longitudinal study that explored the amount of personality stability during early and late adulthood (Finn, 1986). In a longitudinal study, data are collected in two or more time periods and are analyzed for the changes or processes that occur across the time periods.

Finn's (1986) study included two groups of male subjects who had taken the Minnesota Multiphasic Personality Inventory (MMPI), a well-known personality inventory, in 1947 and in 1977 as part of a longitudinal medical study. Group one consisted of seventy-eight subjects who were forty-three to fifty-three years old in 1947; group two consisted of ninety-six subjects who were seventeen to twenty-five years old in 1947. Thus, the comparison of 1947 and 1977 MMPI scores for group one provided an indication of personality stability from middle age to old age, and comparison of 1947 and 1977 scores for group two provided an indication of personality stability from early adult to middle adult years.

Since only 174 of 459 men who took the MMPI in 1947 retook the test in 1977, the researcher compared the 1947 MMPI profiles of "completers" and "noncompleters" of a 1977 test. This analysis revealed few differences in the profiles of "completers" and "noncompleters." The similarity of "completer" and "noncompleter" MMPI profiles for both age groups allowed the researcher to attribute experimental results to actual personality trait changes rather than to subject dropout factors.

Retest stability (the similarity between original and second test scores) was analyzed for seventeen factors by finding correlations between the 1947 and 1977 scores. Statistical procedures found significant differences (indicated by* in Exhibit 14.1) between group one and group two on eleven of the seventeen factors. Ten of the eleven significant findings supported Finn's hypothesis that less change in personality traits occurs in the older adult years. The exception was the characteristic of denying physical complaints, and this exception may be explained by the increase in actual physical illness in older adults compared to younger adults.

Exhibit 14.1 indicates how much the characteristics changed for each age group over the thirty-year period. For group one (older adults), several characteristics were

EXHIBIT 14.1
Differential Stability of Personality Characteristics over Thirty Years as Measured by Seventeen MMPI Factor Scales

Group 1: Middle to Old Age	Group 2: Young to Middle Adult
Low Stability:	Low Stability:
Denial of Physical Complaints*	Paranoia*
Depression	Depression*
Somatization	Somatization
Moderate Stability:	Moderate Stability:
Optimism vs. Pessimism	Optimism vs. Pessimism
Neurotic Anxiety	Restraint*
Social Extroversion	Neurotic Anxiety
Paranoia	Psychoticism*
Phobias	Cynicism*
High Stability:	Denial of Physical Complaints
Restraint	Social Extroversion
Psychoticism	Traditional Femininity*
Cynicism	Traditional Masculinity
Traditional Femininity	Phobias*
Delinquency	Family Attachment*
Traditional Masculinity	Intellectual Interests*
Family Attachment	High Stability:
Intellectual Interests	Delinquency
Religious Fundamentalism	Religious Fundamentalism*

*Indicates that the age group changed significantly more than did the other age group.

Adapted from Finn, S. E. 1986. Stability of personality self-ratings over 30 years: Evidence for an age/cohort interaction. *Journal of Personality and Social Psychology, 50*, p. 816.

highly stable (fairly consistent) over the thirty years, but for group two, only two characteristics were highly stable. Interestingly, delinquency and religious fundamentalism showed high stability for both age groups. The high stability suggests little change in behaviors and beliefs about both delinquency and religious fundamentalism throughout adulthood.

The characteristics of depression and somatization (e.g., fatigue, aches and pains) showed low stability for both age groups. Levels of depression and somatization in 1977 could not be predicted by scale scores in 1947. These characteristics are probably influenced more by current life events than by internal personality traits.

Some of the moderate stability traits from young adulthood to middle age become high stability traits from middle age to old age. That characteristics such as restraint, traditional femininity, family attachment, and intellectual interests were highly stable for only the older group suggests the tendency to become more sedentary and less adventurous with age (Finn, 1986).

Finn's study is important because it compares two fairly well-matched groups of male subjects over a thirty-year period. Still, results could be due to generational differences rather than to diminishing personality changes with increasing age. Finn also cautioned that his study illustrates increasing personality stability on self-report measures only, and he called for other longitudinal studies involving independent ratings of characteristics. While results of this study suggest that throughout the adult years personality becomes more stable, perhaps only people's beliefs about themselves become more consistent while their actual behaviors continue to change throughout their lives.

Focus Question Answer

Will your personality change during your adulthood? Although much similarity and consistency exist between your previous personality pattern and your current personality pattern, you can expect some personality changes during your adult years, especially your young adult years. Changes in personality characteristics may decrease significantly from middle adulthood on because you have found behavioral patterns that work for you and because redundancy of adult experiences can be dealt with efficiently by acting in similar ways. While significant personality changes may occur during and after middle adulthood, you may fail to perceive these changes.

 ## Type Theories

The two type theories described in this chapter are Sheldon's constitutional theory and Eysenck's type theory. **Type theories** describe people's personalities in terms of only a few discontinuous dimensions or categories.

Sheldon's Constitutional Theory

William Sheldon (1898–1970) grew up on a farm in Rhode Island, and his father's profession as an animal breeder influenced his belief that body type and personality are related; Sheldon saw the temperament and typical behaviors of animal species change as their body shapes were changed through breeding techniques. Sheldon's formal education included both medical school and graduate school in psychology.

Somatotypes   Sheldon (1942) measured the body shapes of many individuals and rated these individuals from one to seven on three dimensions, which represent Sheldon's three **somatotypes**, or basic body types. A person who is rated 4-4-4 is midpoint on all three dimensions. A person who is rated 7-1-1 (or 1-7-1 or 1-1-7) is extreme in one dimension. Most individuals are a mixture of components.

Individuals in one somatotype are called **endomorphs**, characterized as soft and round throughout the body; because they tend to overeat, their digestive tracts determine their appearances. Sheldon believed endomorphs' personalities emphasize relaxation, com-

The ideal body type for women continues to change; the endomorphic emphasis of the 1950's (Marilyn Monroe) was replaced by the ectomorphic ideal of the 1960's (Twiggy), only to be replaced by the mesomorphic emphasis exemplified by today's female athletes.

placency, love of physical comfort, love of food, slow reactions, sociability, and tolerance.

Persons in the second somatotype are labeled **mesomorphs**. Mesomorphs are muscular, firm, and relatively strong; their bodies are dominated by muscle, bone, and connective tissue. Sheldon described mesomorphic personalities as adventurous, assertive, energetic, risk-taking, aggressive, and competitive.

Ectomorphs, individuals in the third somatotype, have thin, flat, and fragile bodies. According to Sheldon, ectomorphs have the largest brain and central nervous system proportionately and are described as brainy, artistic, restrained, inhibited, and private.

Quick Study Aid

Sheldon's Somatotypes

Use the following tricks to remember the three somatotypes:

1. **END**OMORPHS HAVE BIG ENDS. Endomorphs are soft and round.
2. **M**ESOMORPHS AND MUSCLES START WITH M. Mesomorphs are hard and muscular.
3. E**CT**OMORPH CONTAINS THE SKINNY LETTER T. Ectomorphs are thin.

Sheldon believed somatotypes are constant and not particularly influenced by weight gain, weight loss, or nutritional factors. In his research, he found modest correlations between body type and personality, and he interpreted these correlations as support for his concept of physique-temperament associations.

Alternative Explanations   However, three other explanations might account for the appearance of a physique-temperament association (Engler, 1985). First, the relationship between physique and temperament may be caused by commonly accepted stereotypes to which individuals conform. An endomorph might act jolly because the individual has often heard "fat people are jolly." An ectomorph may decide to go to college after hearing numerous times "You look smart."

Second, rather than body type determining personality, the body type may influence the ability to succeed in activities. The muscular mesomorph could successfully adopt an aggressive, domineering style, but a fragile ec-

tomorphic individual who tried to be aggressive would probably be beaten up; therefore, a greater number of mesomorphs learn to act in dominant ways.

Third, environment may influence both physique and behavioral tendencies. An overprotective mother, by providing an abundance of nurturance and attention, may increase the chance of her child becoming overweight and encourage her child's love of physical comfort. Based on general appearance, more coaches might ask mesomorphic children to join their sports teams, on which these children then learn to be aggressive and competitive.

In other words, the relationship that exists between body shape and personality may or may not be a direct physique-temperament link. Today, most psychologists believe that Sheldon's theory is simplistic and that his ideas might better represent an index by which people judge each others' personalities rather than an actual causal relationship between body and personality.

Eysenck's Type Theory

Hans J. Eysenck (1916–) was born in Germany in 1916 and emigrated to England before World War II. During World War II, while working with military patients, he became intensely interested in the biological contribution to individual differences in personality. The author of over thirty books and six hundred articles, Eysenck is noted for taking controversial positions on psychological topics; he suggested, for example, that psychotherapy has little influence on people's behavior.

Personality Hierarchy   Eysenck (1967, 1970, 1982) believes personality is arranged in a hierarchy, as illustrated in Exhibit 14.2. Types are the top of a hierarchy; types are comprised of traits, traits are made up of habitual responses, and habitual responses are comprised of specific responses. According to Eysenck's hierarchy, a person who is an extrovert type is likely to have the trait of being sociable and may have a habitual response of being comical. The specific response is revealed in a single occurrence, such as telling jokes during psychology class. Eysenck's own research has centered on the type level of the hierarchy, since he believes identification of types provides the most information for making predictions about people's behaviors.

Types   Eysenck has proposed that the actual number of types is small and that personality is attributed primarily

EXHIBIT 14.2
Eysenck's Structural Model of the Personality, using the Extrovert Type

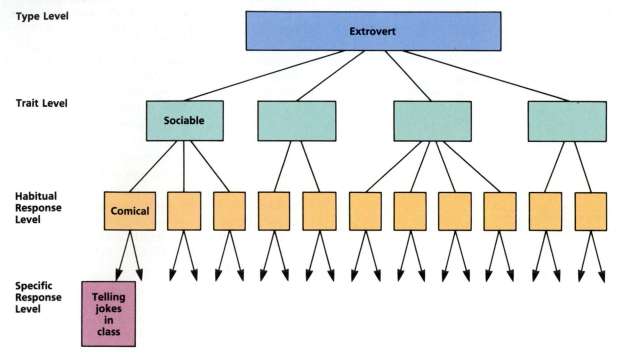

Type Level

Trait Level

Habitual Response Level

Specific Response Level

Extrovert

Sociable

Comical

Telling jokes in class

Adapted from Eysenck, H. J. 1953. *The structure of human personality*. London: Methuen & Co.

to two principal dimensions: **introversion-extroversion** and **stability-instability**. As shown in Exhibit 14.3, these two type dimensions can be used to cluster traits into four categories.

You are probably most familiar with the dimension of introversion-extroversion. Try to answer the questions in Exhibit 14.4 to evaluate your current knowledge about introversion-extroversion. Correct any misconceptions or lack of information.

Like Sheldon, Eysenck believes that biological processes heavily influence personality. In fact, Eysenck emphasizes heredity's role in determining the two types illustrated in Exhibit 14.3, and research studies illustrate that differences in autonomic nervous system reactivity and central nervous system excitation do exist for all the basic types (Young et al., 1980).

Focus Question Answer

Does your body shape determine your personality? Sheldon proposed that your body shape is associated with

your personality characterisitics. Your body shape may influence which activities you enjoy and how others perceive you. However, other psychologists, such as Eysenck, emphasize the role of biological processes on your personality rather than overall body shape. Many of the personality theorists who will be included in these two chapters believe that environment and learned factors play greater roles than body shape and biological processes.

 Trait Theories

Trait theories have in common the belief that personality is described by and behavior is controlled to a significant degree by relatively stable and enduring dispositions called **traits**. Traits display consistency and generality across situations. While type theories propose a few types, trait theories propose numerous traits. Two well-known trait theorists are Gordon Allport and Raymond B. Cattell.

EXHIBIT 14.3
Eysenck's Type Theory

The two type dimensions of introverted-extroverted and stable-unstable form four main personality styles.

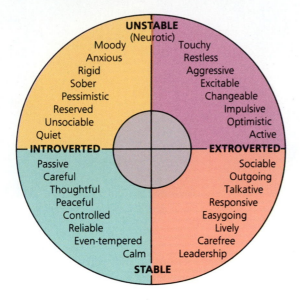

Adapted from Eysenck, H. J. & Eysenck, S. B. G. 1968. *Manual for the Eysenck personality inventory.* San Diego: Educational & Industrial Testing Service.

Allport's Trait Theory

Gordon Allport (1897–1967) received his Ph.D. from Harvard in only two years and wrote the first doctoral dissertation on the subject of personality traits. After studying abroad, he joined the faculty of Harvard, where he engaged in a variety of research projects and writing.

Theoretical Assumptions   At the beginning of this chapter, you read Allport's (1961) rather intricate definition of personality. Now you might appreciate his briefer version—personality is "what a person really is." Most of Allport's writings consist of an attempt to determine just what a person really is. He assumed that humans are different from animals. He believed that only people can engage in self-evaluation, are able to delay their actions, choose to live today in terms of future goals, and use language and culture. Allport criticized his contemporaries for studying white rats instead of studying people because he believed such study could produce only a psychology of white rats rather than add to the understanding of human behavior.

Allport also believed that studying abnormal personalities would not help psychologists understand healthy persons because apparent behavioral similarities may be

EXHIBIT 14.4
The Characteristics of Extroverts and Introverts Quiz

Extroversion and introversion are terms commonly used to describe people. Therefore, you may already know about some of the differences between extroverts and introverts. Read the following items compiled from research findings in the area. Then write E by the characteristics you think are more true of extroverts and I by the characteristics you think are more true of introverts.

1. They value exciting lives.
2. They value comfort.
3. They enjoy a variety of sexual activities.
4. They value wisdom.
5. They value obedience.
6. They need external stimulation.
7. They are good at judging amounts of time.
8. They speak rapidly.
9. They drive their cars with greater consistency in skill.
10. They quickly get drunk on alcohol.
11. They smoke cigarettes.
12. They have slow physiological habituation.
13. They are not easily influenced by sedatives.
14. They are shy.
15. They like loud parties.
16. They have high pain tolerance.
17. They display self-control.
18. They are book-oriented.
19. They enjoy practical jokes.
20. They usually plan ahead.
21. They salivate excessively if lemon juice is squirted in their mouths.
22. They are quickly classically conditioned to give an eye-blink response.
23. They have inhibited cortical processes.
24. They take risks.
25. They rate socially-oriented stories as emotional stories.
26. They are likely to continue making responses even if punished.
27. They have high physical arousal levels in the morning.
28. They are able to hold their breaths for long time periods.
29. They make up the majority of sociology and history majors.
30. They quickly learn to swim.

Answers To Extroverts-Introverts Quiz:

Items more characteristic of extroverts are: 1, 2, 3, 6, 8, 10, 11, 15, 16, 19, 23, 24, 25, 29, 30.
Items more characteristic of introverts are: 4, 5, 7, 9, 12, 13, 14, 17, 18, 20, 21, 22, 26, 27, 28.

Sources: Barnes et al., 1984; Collins & Cunningham, 1986; Corcoran, 1984; Eysenck, 1973; Feldstein & Sloan, 1984; Furnham, 1984; Pearce-McColl & Newman, 1986; Rim, 1984; Zakay et al., 1984.

caused by dissimilar characteristics. For example, both schizophrenic and mentally healthy individuals withdraw from reality; however, the schizophrenic withdraws because of an inability to confront the world, while the healthy adult withdraws from time to time for recreation that improves ability to confront the world (Allport, 1961).

Allport was also critical of psychologists who overemphasized the importance of the past. Allport believed people live today for tomorrow rather than as an automatic function of the past. Although psychologists may learn about people by delving into their past, people themselves are concerned primarily with the present and future.

Finally, Allport believed that an individual functions to meet biological survival and to express the self. A person first meets survival needs and then strives to build self-identity, self-esteem, material possessions, and interpersonal relationships. He also believed that motivation of behavior is conscious rather than unconscious.

Traits   Allport is most noted for his work in defining traits. He believed that traits are able to initiate and guide behavior, are arranged in a hierarchical fashion, and are independent of each other. Each person has unique traits—trait structures may reveal similarities, but any particular trait operates differently for each individual. Allport also differentiated between traits and habits, finding traits more generalized than habits. Cleanliness is a trait, but how you brush your teeth is a habit.

Allport believed traits are arranged in a hierarchical fashion so that more general traits take precedence over more specific traits and influence more situations. He developed three names for traits within an individual: cardinal, central, and secondary.

Cardinal traits, which are pervasive and dominate an individual's existence, are rare; few individuals have cardinal traits. Abraham Lincoln's honesty, and Albert Schweitzer's and Mother Teresa's humanitarianism are examples of cardinal traits because these traits have influenced most areas of their lives.

In contrast, everyone has **central traits**, the small number of traits that are highly characteristic of an individual. Central traits are the five to ten traits your closest friends could agree describe you. For example, your friends may say you are predominately creative, studious, considerate, ambitious, and caring. Central traits are the easiest part of a person's personality to infer because they operate in many situations.

Abraham Lincoln ("Honest Abe") may have exhibited the cardinal trait of honesty.

All other traits within an individual are called **secondary traits**. You have many secondary traits, but they influence fewer situations and fewer behaviors than do central traits. For example, your secondary traits could include being musical and liking the outdoors. Although secondary traits are less crucial to personality descriptions, they add color to the descriptions.

Cardinal, central, and secondary traits define the prominence of traits within an individual, but Allport was also interested in the traits that are prominent within many individuals within a culture. Allport appropriately called the traits exhibited by a majority of people in a society **common traits**. What common traits do you think are exhibited by people living in different regions of the United States? Many individuals believe that people in the Northeast tend to live fast-paced, ambitious lives and Midwesterners are more likely to lead slow, steady lives. Common traits in all regions of the United States might include materialism, optimism, and adaptability.

Cattell's Factor Theory

Raymond B. Cattell (1905–) was born in England into a family that set high work standards. His rigorous methodological approach might have been influenced by his father, an engineer. Cattell has said that the World War I years made him aware of the brevity of life, and after the war he quickly earned his B.S. college degree in chemistry and physics and a Ph.D. in psychology. In

Quick Study Aid

Allport's Traits

1. Remember that traits within an individual can be arranged in alphabetical order to reflect their importance: CArdinal, CEntral, and SEcondary.
2. Remember CARDINALS are rare in many parts of the United States, and few individuals possess CARDINAL TRAITS.
3. Remember that only common traits deal with traits across individuals. COMMON TRAITS are COMMON to many.

1937, he moved to the United States and gained a reputation as a prolific researcher and writer. He is noted for using factor analysis techniques, which reduce many traits into a small number of explanatory concepts, and for using these techniques to develop the **16PF personality questionnaire**, which measures the source traits that make up the main aspect of his theory (Cattell, 1984). Cattell has emphasized that the goal of psychology should be the ability to predict human behavior. Cattell wrote, "The personality of an individual is that which enables us to predict what he will do in a given situation" (Cattell, 1950, p. 2).

Surface and Source Traits   Unlike Allport, Cattell does not insist on individual uniqueness; instead, he emphasizes that basic traits are universal. With this assumption, Cattell (1950; 1979) began to study **surface traits**, which are traits that cluster together. For example, the surface trait of a depressed person might be made up of characteristics such as predicting undesirable outcomes, failing to join in group activities, and criticizing self and others. Cattell began with approximately 18,000 individual traits, which he eventually reduced to forty surface traits.

Cattell believes that these forty surface traits are produced by sixteen underlying traits called **source traits**. Cattell gave unique and unusual labels to many of these source traits (e.g., affecothymia, parmia, and ergic tension), but Exhibit 14.5 offers more common names.

Heredity vs. Environment   One of Cattell's goals has been to determine which traits are influenced primarily by heredity and which are influenced largely by environment. Cattell maintains that surface traits are a mixture of heredity and environment, but source traits are caused either by heredity or environment.

Cattell believes that general intelligence, ego strength (emotional stability), serious mindedness, superego strength (conscientiousness), and emotional sensitivity are largely determined by heredity. On the other hand, he believes that calmness, dominance, and relaxation levels are strongly influenced by past experiences.

Factor analysis, the research methodology Cattell developed and used in researching his theory, has both supporters and critics (Eysenck, 1984), but Cattell's theoretical structure and research strategies have generated more empirical research than have other personality theories (Wiggins, 1984).

The trait approach has contributed much to the area of personality assessment by self-reports and questionnaires, and this approach probably best reflects the way that people think about personality—personality consists of enduring characteristics called traits. However, as Walter Mischel, a prominent personality researcher, has written, "Although behavior patterns often may be stable, they usually are not highly generalized across situations" (Mischel, 1968, p. 282). In other words, traits do exhibit some temporal stability; people do show similar competencies, expectancies, values, and goals in measurements taken close in time (Mischel, 1973), but traits exhibit low cross-situational stability (Mischel, 1984).

Trait theories focus on between-person differences rather than on how people change when the situation changes. As a result, the strength of the trait approach is in classifying groups of people, and the weakness of the trait approach is in explaining the process of an individual's behavior (Mischel, 1985).

EXHIBIT 14.5
Adjectives Reflecting Cattell's Sixteen Source Trait Dimensions

outgoing-reserved	more intelligent-less intelligent
stable-emotional	dominant-submissive
carefree-serious	conscientious-expedient
bold-shy	tenderminded-toughminded
suspicious-trusting	imaginative-practical
shrewd-forthright	apprehensive-assured
controlled-casual	experimenting-traditional
tense-relaxed	self-sufficient-group-dependent

Adapted from Cattell, R. B. 1965. *The scientific analysis of personality*. Baltimore, MD: Penguin.

Focus Question Answer

Can your personality be described in terms of traits? Yes. In fact, you rely on good trait descriptions when you ask your instructor to write a letter of reference for you. The traits given in the letter can help potential employees decide whether you are more qualified than other individuals. However, neither the letter writer nor the potential employer would be able to make precise predictions about your behavior in a given situation because traits provide overall characteristics of personality but cannot make accurate predictions about behavior in a particular setting.

 Psychodynamic Theories

Psychodynamic theories view human behavior as originating from underlying forces that mold personality, shape attitudes, and contribute to emotional disorder. In some psychodynamic theories, these underlying forces are assumed to be unconscious. The psychodynamic theories emphasize tracing behavior to its origins, which are often assumed to be in childhood.

Freud's Psychoanalytic Theory

Sigmund Freud (1856–1939), the most important psychodynamic theorist, was born in Moravia, Germany, and moved to Vienna at age four. Freud was a good student who liked the humanities, but he chose science, from which he could make a better living. He went to medical school because medicine was one of the few professions that Jews in his culture were allowed to enter. After spending eight years doing neurophysical research, Freud began private practice in neurology and began to develop psychotherapy to help his many patients who suffered from psychologically caused problems rather than neurological problems.

Early in his practice, Freud used hypnosis to uncover the bases of his patients' problems, but he gradually developed his own counseling techniques. His central technique, **free association**, required the patient to say, without censorship, everything that came into consciousness. By observing his patients' free associations and by performing thorough self-analysis, Freud developed his complex personality theory, which he called psychoanalytic theory.

Unconscious Motivation   Fundamental to Freud's psychoanalytic theory is the idea of **unconscious motiva-** tion. Freud believed that most behaviors are unconsciously motivated, that people are usually unaware of their "true" motives and desires. He first became aware of the importance of the unconscious after he witnessed a posthypnotic suggestion demonstration in 1889 (Freud, 1940). He later observed the role of the unconscious in his own life and in his patients' lives. As a result of these experiences, Freud came to believe that, compared to the prominence of the unconscious, the conscious is only "the tip of the iceberg." Freud believed that uncon-

EXHIBIT 14.6
IN HIS OWN WORDS. Quotations from Freud's Writings

"...the ego stands for reason and good sense while the id stands for the untamed passions."
(1933)

"Nothing can be brought to an end in the unconscious; nothing is past or forgotten."
(1900)

"The question, 'What is the purpose of human life?' has been asked times without number; it has never received a satisfactory answer; perhaps it does not admit of such an answer."
(1930)

"To touch is the beginning of every act of possession, of every attempt to make use of a person or thing."
(1913)

"The command to love our neighbors as ourselves...is impossible to fulfill; such an enormous inflation of love can only lower its value and not remedy the evil."
(1930)

scious motivation explains a variety of behaviors, including neurotic symptoms (e.g., phobias, obsessions, and compulsions), everyday blunders, dream content, career choices, and personal preferences (Freud, 1900, 1901, 1910).

Freud believed everybody unconsciously uses **repression**, in which events and memories are pushed out of conscious awareness and into the unconscious. Repression occurs when you cannot recall crucial memories and important appointments. Generally, people repress more painful memories, such as a dentist's appointment, than pleasant memories. Although repression seems to allow individuals to deny and distort reality, the repressed instances do remain in the unconscious and can continue to influence behavior.

Unconscious motives also influence social institutions and culture. According to Freud, **sublimation** is the modification of unacceptable unconscious motives into socially acceptable activities. Arts, sciences, invention, religion, business, government, education, military, and sports all represent sublimated unconscious motives (Freud, 1913). Freud proposed, for example, that Leonardo da Vinci's interest in painting pictures of the Madonna was a sublimated expression of wanting intimacy with his own mother, from whom he had been separated at a young age (Freud, 1910).

Drives Freud believed that all behaviors are caused by *Trieb*, a German word that best translates as impulse or drive. He viewed these drives as pressures to act without conscious thought. Freud believed in three kinds of drives: self-preservation drives (e.g., hunger, thirst, and other physical needs), sexual drives (**libido**), and death drives (**thanatos**). Most of Freud's writings emphasize the role of the libido. In fact, the concept of the libido is so central that Freudian theory is often mistakenly considered to be pansexual. **Pansexualism** is the belief that sexual instincts motivate all of human behavior. However, Freud used the term "sexual" to denote anything that felt good or pleasurable. According to Freud's theory, eating gourmet meals, sunbathing, and enjoying a fireplace in winter would be "sexual" experiences. Freud used the term "sexual" as you might use the word "sensual."

The counterpart of libido, thanatos was not a major influence in Freud's theory until after World War I, which convinced him that some human behaviors are caused by a drive for destruction. War and fights are examples of the role of thanatos, but so are other activities that range from mild to extreme in risking death—riding roller coasters, playing football, mountain climbing, sky diving, and smoking cigarettes. Children playing "cops and robbers" are symbolically acting out thanatos.

Structures of Personality The three major structures of personality in Freud's psychoanalytic theory are: the id, the ego, and the superego. Drives are expressed through these three systems and their interactions with each other (Freud, 1923).

According to Freud, at a person's birth, all energy or drive is expressed through the **id** (Freud called this

"**A**nxiety makes repression and not, as we used to think, the other way around."
(1933)

"**N**o one who, like me, conjures up the most evil of those half-tamed demons that inhabit the human breast, and seeks to wrestle with them, can expect to come through the struggle unscathed."
(1905a)

"**...I** cannot escape the notion (though I hesitate to give it expression) that for women the level of what is ethically normal is different from what it is in me....We must not allow ourselves to be deflected from such conclusions by the denials of the feminists, who are anxious to force us to regard the two sexes equal in position and worth."
(1925)

"**I**t almost looks as if analysis were the third of those 'impossible' professions in which one can be sure beforehand of achieving unsatisfying results. The other two, which have been known much longer, are education and government."
(1937)

part of the personality *it*, but English translators used the Latin word *id*.) The id, which exists totally in the unconscious mind, operates by the **pleasure principle**; in other words, the id wants immediate gratification. The id's wishes and emotions are deeply self-centered and selfish.

Unfortunately, the id is hopelessly ineffectual in the external world. If someone or something does not assist the id in attaining immediate gratification, its only alternative is **primary process thought**, which consists of wish-fulfilling fantasies or dreams.

Id is the only personality structure that is present at birth, and for most newborns the id is sufficient because nurturing, devoted parents help gratify them. However, if id's needs are undergratified or overgratified, personalities become fixated, or permanently influenced. For example, giving an infant a pacifier might allow the baby to experience adequate sucking, a satisfying experience, but if the baby is always given a pacifier, the baby may be overgratified and overeat throughout his or her lifetime.

When an individual is an infant, the second personality structure develops from part of the id. This new part is called the **ego**, which means *I* in Latin. Ego comes into existence so that people can interact appropriately with the objective world. Ego is said to operate by the **reality principle**, with the goal of achieving gratification but being able to delay it. The ego, "the executive of the personality," serves as a mediator between the id and external reality. The ego of the personality recognizes, remembers, plans, and acts.

Note that the id and ego have the same goal—both want gratification. However, while the id wants the gratification *right now*, the ego is able to plan how to get gratification eventually. Freud called the ego, which is mostly conscious, the "faithful servant" of the id because the ego seeks pleasure wisely, considering both safety and practicality. According to Freud, the major task of personality development is building a strong ego.

When an individual is a toddler, the third and last personality structure begins to develop. The third structure is the **superego**, which is Latin for *above I*. Forming the moral arm of personality, the superego is harbored within the ego, and when superego and ego have the same goals, the two structures are hard to distinguish. However, when the superego goals are different from ego goals, psychological tension or conflict is produced. Therefore, Freud's model of personality has individuals typically operating in a state of psychological tension—most of which, fortunately, is kept out of awareness in the unconscious.

The superego becomes differentiated from the ego in order to have within the personality an abstract representation of the rules and regulations of society—a mental code of what is right and wrong. Therefore, the superego's goal is to be as good as it can and should be. Often the superego's goal does not match the gratification goals of the id and ego. While the ego may choose to postpone gratification, the superego often tries to block it permanently.

The superego is the part of your personality that tries to get you to be a perfect student. The superego gives you all sorts of messages: "You're wasting time—study!" "You could have been studying instead of watching that TV show." "Good, you are spending a little more time studying hard now." Meanwhile, your id tells you to forget that awful studying and go have fun. Picture the id saying "Gee, this is painfully boring stuff. Pack up those books. Let's party. Let's eat. Let's do anything but study." The ego, on the other hand, is likely to negotiate a "deal"— "How about studying for two hours and then going out for a while?" If you follow the messages of the ego or id, your superego may make you feel guilty.

The superego has two components, the conscience and the ego-ideal. The **conscience** consists of the moral messages learned from society, mostly from parents, and it can use guilt to punish and control behavior. For example, a child who takes a quarter from his mother's purse may feel guilty for breaking the moral messages he has learned about honesty. Many people experience guilt because their drives and society's goals are different. While personal instincts are selfish, societies aim for cooperation and order. For instance, during a gas shortage, society's goal is to fairly distribute the gas, but many individuals want to hoard all the gas they can get. Hopefully, a guilty conscience gets the majority of people to cooperate with gas rationing. The **ego-ideal** is the part of the superego that strives for perfection. The ego-ideal is the image a person creates of the best person he or she could be, that is, the "ideal ego." The ego-ideal tries to control behavior by rewarding the person with pride when he or she improves. Part of your ego-ideal might be to make the dean's list, and you would then feel good when you get an A on an examination.

The major functions of the superego are to (1) inhibit sexual and aggressive impulses of the id, (2) persuade the ego to substitute moralistic goals for realistic goals, and (3) strive for perfection (Scroggs, 1985). Although the superego opposes the goals of id and ego, the latter structures can influence the superego. For example, the corruption of the superego by the id occurs when, in a fit of righteous indignation, a person takes aggressive measures against those he or she considers wicked and sinful. A person who is opposed to all abortions because of a pro-life belief might act anti-life and actually endanger lives by bombing an abortion center.

Psychosexual Stages   Freud (1905b) believed that the adult personality is basically determined by the time individuals are six years old and that interaction with parents, especially with the mother, is the primary influence on personality. By age six, a person has passed through three of the five developmental stages called **psychosexual stages**. Each stage involves specific tasks of childhood development and focuses the libido on a specific area of the body.

Freud emphasized that in each psychosexual stage are specific tasks that need to be resolved, and how well these tasks are resolved determines their effects on a person's personality. When a developmental task is not resolved completely because of overgratification or undergratification, the result is **fixation** in the stage.

During each psychosexual stage, a different area of the body, called an **erogenous zone**, becomes the central location of pleasure. In the first stage, the mouth is the central location; in the second stage, the anus; in the third stage, the genitals. The corresponding psychosexual stages are called the oral stage, the anal stage, and the phallic stage. Experiences during each of the first three stages influence adult personality characteristics, as indicated in Exhibit 14.7. A fourth stage (from age six to twelve) is the latency stage, and the final stage is the genital stage.

The first psychosexual stage is the **oral stage**, which extends from birth to about one year of age. The eroge-

EXHIBIT 14.7
Adult Traits Acquired in the First Three Psychosexual Stages

Oral Traits (first year of life): optimism, pessimism, gullibility, suspiciousness, manipulativeness, envy, cockiness, abasement. Also, food preferences and oral habits such as drinking, smoking, and nail biting.

Anal Traits (from first year to third year): generosity, constrictedness, stubborness, acquiescence, orderliness, messiness, punctuality, precision, vagueness, persistence, and creativity.

Phallic Traits (from third year to sixth year): vanity, self-hatred, pride, humility, courage, bashfulness, gregariousness, stylishness, sexuality, sadness, gaiety, and chastity. Also, gender identity and sexual preference.

Source: based on information in S. R. Maddi, 1972. *Personality theories: A comparative analysis.* Homewood, IL: Dorsey Press, and B. Engler. 1985. *Personality theories: An introduction* (2nd ed.). Boston: Houghton Mifflin.

nous zone is the mouth region, and the two main sources of pleasure during the oral stage are sucking and biting. Fixations during the oral stage could show up in many adult personality styles. A gullible adult, Freud would say, was orally fixated and now "willing to swallow almost anything" he or she is told. A person who loves to learn also displays an oral characteristic. The person receives pleasure from oral incorporation and now takes in other substances, including "food for thought." Fixation in the latter part of the oral stage, when the child enjoyed biting, might develop into sarcasm, argumentativeness, or the love of debating issues.

Between the ages of one and three, the main focus of bodily pleasure shifts to the anal area. During the **anal stage**, the child deals with the emergence of aggressive impulses and the need to be independent of the parents. An important learning task is toilet training, which at times may be a struggle of wills between parent and child. Freud believed that a child seeks independence by controlling parents via toilet training. By "holding in" or "letting go" of bowel movements, the child is able to please or displease the parent.

Freud suggested that a strict and repressive parental approach could produce constipation in the child, resulting in "holding in," and that this result in toilet behaviors leads to an overall anal retentive personality, a personality characterized by obstinance, stinginess, and obsessive orderliness.

Quick Study Aid

Learning Freud's Terms

1. To remember Freud's three personality structures and their order of development, think PIES:
   Personality = **I**d + **E**go + **S**uperego.

2. To remember the psychosexual stages and their order, remember the silly sentence: OLLIE AND PHYLLIS LIKE GIRAFFES. The first letter of each word corresponds to the first letter of each stage, i.e., Ollie = Oral, And = Anal, Phyllis = Phallic, Like = Latency, and Giraffes = Genital.

According to Freud, adult cleanliness and orderliness styles are determined during the anal psychosexual stage.

According to Freud, some children gain their toilet training power through messiness; the resulting adult personalities feature disorderliness, cruelty, temper tantrums, aggressive language, and wanton destructiveness. Other children who were rewarded for producing bowel movements concluded that creating things was good and may develop artistic personalities.

The third psychosexual stage is the **phallic stage** and takes place from age three to six years. Freud assumed young children discover that touching their genitals is pleasurable. He also assumed children are told masturbation is bad and should not be done. Today, children receive a variety of messages about masturbation, but in Freud's Victorian era almost all children were reprimanded for engaging in "that terrible behavior." This negative attitude toward masturbation was due partly to the repressive attitudes toward sexuality and partly due to the medical belief that masturbation was bad for one's health. Until the 1930s, medical doctors believed that masturbation made one tired, mentally unbalanced, blind, and sick. Therefore, the children of Freud's era were given prohibitions about masturbation. For example, little boys were told, "Don't play with yourself, or it will fall off" and "If you don't stop touching yourself there, I'll have to cut it off."

Freud also believed that during the phallic stage, children fall in love with the opposite-sexed parent and try to resolve this dilemma by learning to identify with the same-sexed parent. Boys go through the Oedipus complex process, and girls go through the Electra complex process (Freud, 1905; Bettelheim, 1983; Blanck, 1984). In the **Oedipus complex**, young boys develop a libidinal, or sexual, attachment to their mothers. Freud maintained that this attachment is evidenced when a young boy wants to sleep with mother, wants to "marry Mommy when I get older," and likes to be around mother all the time. This libidinal attachment to mother establishes a rivalry with father. The boy may like dad going off on a business trip, may mentally plan ways to get father out of the house, and may compete with father to get mother's attention. At the same time, rivalry with father is disturbing. The boy fears that father's strength will defeat him, and that father will then punish him by cutting off his penis. Because the boy has been told he could lose his penis by masturbating, he concludes that the penis can also be lost by competing directly with father for mother's affections. The resulting **castration anxiety** leads the young boy to block his sexual love for his mother and identify with the strength of his father. This process resolves the Oedipal complex.

Resolution of the Oedipus complex results in the boy's identification with the male sex-role model. In contrast, Freud believed an unresolved Oedipus complex leads to a weak superego, feminine characteristics, over-identification with mothers, and male homosexuality. Some people today continue to hold Freudian ideas and mistakenly believe that male homosexuals come from families with dominant mothers and passive fathers.

Girls in the phallic stage need to resolve a different conflict. In the **Electra complex**, the young girl also starts out being in love with mother, who meets basic nurturing needs. At the same time, the three-year-old girl notices she lacks a penis and concludes that mother, out of jealousy, removed it. Feeling betrayed, the young girl blocks her love for mother and falls in love with father, who is endowed with a penis. The girl's feelings for father involve both love and **penis envy**. Because of penis envy, the girl hopes father will return her penis or give her a new one. When this event does not occur, the girl blocks her sexual feelings for father and, out of weakness, identifies with mother.

The Electra complex, unlike the Oedipus complex, cannot be fully resolved because the young girl is unable to get all she wishes; she does not get back the stolen penis. Therefore, Freud believed, every female needs to get married and give birth to a son, thereby coming as close as possible to producing a penis of her own. According to Freud, coming to terms with the Electra complex results in females who identify fully with the passive female gender role, and significantly unresolved Electra complexes result in weak superegos striving to gain superiority over men, masculine traits, and lesbianism.

Freud believed that the Oedipus or Electra complex continues to influence adult behavior. How can researchers determine whether or not these processes really occur and if they occur for all persons? Unfortunately, research attempts seem to trivialize Freudian theory. For example, in one experiment (Johnson, 1966), the researcher observed that more female than male college students failed to return No. 2 pencils used in standardized tests. Pencils, being longer than they are wide, were considered phallic symbols, and when more females kept the pencils, the researchers interpreted the behavior as evidence of penis envy!

Since Freud believed that by age six, a child's basic, future adult personality has been formed, he had less to say about the last two psychosexual stages. The **latency stage** occurs between the ages of six and twelve years. During this stage, the sex drive is forced underground, and children frequently sublimate or channel the libido into nonsexual activities. After age twelve, children enter the **genital stage**. In this stage, the main task is to redirect selfish gratification to gratification from genuine interaction with others. In the genital stage, personality style is influenced by the lingering effects of fixations, which are exhibited in adult sex roles, work style, and

people and object preferences.

Although few psychologists believe fully in Freud's psychosexual stages, most agree that he contributed greatly to modern psychology and cultural beliefs. Freud popularized the idea of unconscious motivation—the idea that people sometimes do things for reasons other than those they tell themselves. He was also the first theorist to emphasize the importance of childhood experiences in personality formation and the first professional to place importance on female and childhood sexualities. Freud was influential in developing the process in which therapists pay attention to what patients themselves say rather than simply prescribe to the patients. Finally, one of Freud's greatest contributions has been his influence on other theorists and therapists, among them Alfred Adler and Carl Jung.

Adler's Individual Psychology

Alfred Adler (1870–1937) was raised in Vienna. The second of six children of a successful merchant, his difficult, unhappy childhood included rickets, pneumonia, accidents, and the death of a sibling. For most of his

EXHIBIT 14.8
IN HIS OWN WORDS. Quotations from Adler's Writings

"To be human means to feel inferior." (1956)

"Inferiority feelings...are the cause of all improvements in the position of mankind." (1956)

"If ever we hear of a case of lying, we must look for a severe parent. A lie would have no sense unless the truth were felt as dangerous." (1931)

"No act of cruelty has ever been done which has not been based upon a secret weakness." (1956)

"It is easier to fight for principles than to live up to them." (1929)

"The truth is often a terrible weapon of aggression. It is possible to lie, and even to murder, with the truth." (1929a)

"The hardest things for human beings to do is to know themselves and change themselves." (1928)

"To live means to develop." (1964)

"You find what you planned to find." (1964)

school years, Adler was only an average student, but he later excelled and became a medical student at the University of Vienna, where he trained as an eye specialist. He had a general practice and later specialized in neurology and psychiatry.

Adler's ideas were always different from Freud's, and Adler was never Freud's student nor was he ever psychoanalyzed. Yet Adler and Freud benefited from an exchange of ideas that influenced the separate development of both their theories (Ansbacher, 1985). In 1902, Adler was invited to join Freud's weekly discussion group on psychoanalysis. When this group became the Vienna Psychoanalytic Society, Adler became the first president. However, by 1911 Adler and Freud differed so significantly in their approaches to psychoanalysis that the two ended their association; nearly one-third of the Vienna Psychoanalytic Society members left with Adler. Although both Adler and Freud practiced psychoanalysis in Vienna in the 1920s and early 1930s, they maintained separate pathways. Unlike Freud, Adler liked America

and visited the United States frequently. In the 1930s, to escape the Nazis, he moved to New York City where he had a private practice and taught medical psychology.

Social Purposefulness Adler (1927, 1929b, 1931, 1939) called his theory **individual psychology** to indicate the uniqueness of the individual and his or her responses to any situation. Adler believed that social factors are more important than the sex drive in shaping personality. He thought that people are motivated primarily by social interests and that basic life problems—work, friendship, and loving relationships—are social.

According to Adler, even activities that appear to be direct responses to physical stimulation may be heavily shaped by **social purposefulness**. For instance, when a young child falls and scrapes a knee, the child cries because of pain, but as the pain diminishes the tears end. Later, when the child has run home and found a parent, the child cries anew, as if in great pain. This second outburst of tears is for the parent's benefit, not because

 Exploring . . .

Sibling Rivalry

A recent study (Prochaska & Prochaska, 1985) explored children's views of the causes of and solutions to sibling rivalry. The subjects were fourth and fifth graders with an average age of nine and one-half years. The subjects reported nearly five fights a day, with the average fight time being eight minutes, followed by six minutes of bad feelings. However, the children reported that cooperation and fun with siblings was nearly twice as common as sibling fighting. The following exhibit summarizes what nine-year-olds believe to be causes of sibling fights and what they believe to be solutions to those fights.

Rank ordering of the top six causes and "cures" of sibling rivalry according to the views of fourth and fifth graders.

Top Reasons for Fighting	Top Solutions for Fighting
1. Being in a bad mood.	1. Getting a treat for being good.
2. Trying to get even.	2. Being disciplined (sent to room, scolded, or spanked).
3. Trying to protect room or toys.	3. Keep children busy with fun things.
4. Attempting to prove superiority over sibling.	4. Separating the children.
5. Being bored.	5. Giving each child equal things and attention.
6. Attempting to get parents' attention	6. Giving punching bags to each child.

Adapted from Prochaska, J. M. & Prochaska, J. O. 1985. Children's views of the causes and "cures" of sibling rivalry. *Child Welfare, 64,* 427-433.

of pain. The child cries to produce a social response from the parent.

Although Adler agreed with Freud that unconscious motivation exists, he placed much less importance on it. For Adler, the unconscious represented only memories for which people do not want to take responsibility. He believed the conscious content of the mind determines an individual's current behaviors. He also assumed that people are governed by goals and that rather than being driven by the past they live to attain future goals.

Striving for Superiority   Adler believed that all people are **striving for superiority** (Adler used the term *superiority* as other psychologists use the term *self-actualization*). The drive for superiority is a response to the universally experienced sense of inferiority, which develops out of relationships with others. People start out as inferior, helpless infants who must depend on superior, more competent parents; this helplessness in relationships with adults continues for years.

Overhearing unfavorable comparisons of oneself and others is another source of inferiority feelings, as is sibling rivalry. **Sibling rivalry** is the competition among siblings for the attention, affection, and approval of parents as well as the competition among siblings in sports, school, and other activities. On the whole, Adler felt that sibling rivalry is good because the resulting feelings of inferiority encourage competition and improvement, both of which in turn decrease the inferiority feelings. A recent study of sibling rivalry is featured in the *Exploring . . .* Section.

The feeling of inferiority is uncomfortable, and people try to overcome it. **Compensation** is the attempt to overcome imagined or real inferiorities and weaknesses. Usually, people choose to make up for a weakness in one ability by excelling in a different ability. For instance, a student who is poor in mathematics may work very hard to earn A's on English compositions. Or a person may strive to turn a weak personal characteristic into a personal strength; someone who sings poorly may decide to take voice lessons until he or she can sing quite well. Can you think of examples of compensation in your own life?

Overcompensation occurs when an individual either denies rather than accepts a real situation or makes an exaggerated effort to cover up a weakness. Two overcompensation patterns are **inferiority complex**, in which the individual feels highly inadequate, and **superiority complex**, in which the individual exaggerates self-importance to cover up an inferiority complex.

Family Atmosphere   According to the theory of individual psychology, a major influence on personality is the **family atmosphere**, which refers to the emotional relationships among family members. A good family atmosphere aids a child in actively and constructively striving for superiority; a poor family atmosphere prevents such striving. Adler thought, for example, that spoiling children is a harmful family style. Spoiled children who are excessively pampered and protected from frustrations are hindered from becoming independent and confident in their own abilities. Adler observed that spoiled children continue to expect others to meet their needs, usually fail to achieve their potentials, and have difficulty learning social feelings. Adults who were spoiled as children tend to dislike order and to express hostility to society's regulations. The family atmosphere sets the stage for how individuals will perceive the world. Another aspect of the family atmosphere, birth order, determines how individuals learn to interact in the world. Birth order is the topic of the *Exploring . . .* section.

Jung's Archetypal Theory

Another psychodynamic theorist is Carl Gustav Jung, who was born in Switzerland in 1875 and died in 1961. Eight of his uncles and his father were clergymembers. He described his father as weak and ineffectual and his mother as dominant and terribly inconsistent; his parents bickered frequently. Jung was the only surviving son of his

Carl Jung's personality theory reflects his wide-ranging interests in subjects including psychoanalytic theory, archeology, religion, parapsychology, mythology, and alchemy.

Birth Order Effects on Personality

What is your **birth order** place in your family? Are you the oldest child? The middle child? The youngest child? The only child? What aspects of your personality have been influenced by your place in your family constellation? Many psychologists have looked at birth order's impact on personality.

Adler (1927, 1929) emphasized that the family provides the child's earliest learning experience about his or her place in the world. The child generalizes from encounters within the family to other relationships outside the family. More recently, researchers have maintained that birth order effects are modified by many aspects such as age differences among siblings, gender differences among siblings, number of siblings, and special conditions, such as death or disability of a sibling or the late adoption of a child (Kidwell, 1981; Steelman & Powell, 1985). Birth order effects are usually stronger when all children within a family are of the same sex (Miller & Maruyama, 1976; Paulhus & Shaffer, 1981).

First-borns usually have the youngest, most anxious, most inexperienced, and most eager parents. First-borns do not have to vie with siblings for parents' attention. The abundance of attention they receive may make these children feel very special, and many first-borns retain a sense of specialness, capability, and self-esteem. However, because their inexperienced, anxious, beginning parents may also interfere more and demand more of them than of the other siblings, first-borns often feel inadequate when they do not live up to parental standards, are often more fearful and anxious as adults, and are often highly self-critical and cautious.

First-borns are born into an adult world. Striving to be like their parents, these children advance in verbal skills more quickly than do their siblings. In adulthood, first-borns test higher in verbal skills than do later-borns; they do not, however, exhibit a similar advantage in math tests (Forer & Stills, 1976).

The arrival of a second sibling can be traumatic for the first child, who is accustomed to all the parents'

attention, which suddenly goes to someone else. The first-born may feel "dethroned" and therefore make great efforts to get back on the throne. The oldest child may find that the way to regain the parents' approval and attention is by developing capability, responsibility, conformity, and achievement. As a result, adult first-borns measure higher in these traits than do later-born individuals. First-borns are especially good at academic achievements, leadership, and task-oriented occupations (Cicirelli, 1978; Zajonc, 1976).

In contrast, later-borns have always shared their parents with other siblings. Their parents tend to be less tense, older, more experienced, and more relaxed in the parent role. Later-borns may view older siblings as models, as superiors, as barriers, or as pacesetters. Often the second child develops skills different from those in which the oldest child excels in order to stand out. The second child may also exhibit a preference for the parent the oldest child does not turn to for advice and support (Forer & Stills, 1976).

Later-borns also tend to be less dependent on parents. They are more content than first-borns to move gradually from being a child to being an adult. Later-borns are often described as being less tense, more easy-going, more friendly, and more popular (Steelman & Powell, 1985; Zajonc, 1976). As first-borns use the advantages of strength, ability, and responsibility, later-borns overcome their competitive disadvantages by becoming a parent's favorite, by using less demanding tactics, by seeking parental protection, and by being good compromisers. From birth on, later-born children must interact with other children, and this fact makes many of them superior at people-oriented tasks (Steelman & Powell, 1985). Later-borns might also become good at social skills because as children they are overwhelmed by older siblings and good social skills help the later-borns survive and thrive (Miller & Maruyama, 1976).

The following are additional research findings about birth order effects:

— People tend to marry people of different birth order position, perhaps to regain earlier family relationships (Tolman, 1964).

— The impact of birth order on intellectual growth increases as individuals grow older (Zajonc et al., 1979).

— Oldest siblings receive more physical punishment (Palmer, 1966).

— When research subjects are asked not to talk to others about their participation in a psychology experiment, first-born subjects tell fewer persons than later-born subjects, suggesting that oldest siblings are better at keeping confidences (Wuebben, 1967).

— Oldest girls are more accurate in their perceptions of their own physical attributes than are later-born girls (Singer & Lamb, 1966).

— A large portion of obsessive-compulsive personalities are first-borns (Kayton & Borge, 1967).

— First-borns earn higher grades than later-borns in high school and college (Oberlander & Jenkin, 1967).

Although information on birth order effects is interesting, research on birth order is difficult to conduct and often suffers from a lack of precise definitions (e.g., division into only first-born and others versus division into first-, second-, and third-borns) and failure to look at factors such as spacing and gender differences (Ernst & Angst, 1983). Birth order research is made even more complicated by recent trends such as blended families, in which two groups of siblings from previous marriages are reared together. Yet most individuals believe their lives are shaped by the family position into which they are born. First-borns will probably continue to have more complete baby book records, and later-borns will probably continue to have an older brother or sister help them learn how to count and how to tie their shoes.

parents, and he described himself as a lonely and introverted child who relied heavily on fantasies, dreams, and visions, which he interpreted as the source of secret knowledge. He was convinced that his childhood home was haunted by ghosts and that his body contained two souls. Jung wanted to study archaeology but instead studied medicine because of a dream he once had (Jung, 1961).

Jung's seven-year professional and personal relationship with Freud ended in 1913 because of basic differences over the sex drive concept; Jung placed less emphasis on sexuality and more emphasis on spirituality than Freud. However, severing ties with Freud greatly affected Jung's emotional state, and he underwent a three-year period during which he was unable to read a scientific book. During this "dark period," he withdrew into himself and explored his fantasies and dreams. At the end of the three years, Jung emerged with his own creative personality theory called archetypal theory (Jung, 1961). Jung's archetypal theory (Jung, 1921, 1933, 1937, 1964) differs from most personality theories because Jung incorporates ideas from Eastern religions, mythology, and alchemy.

Psyche   Jung's term for the total personality is **psyche**. Psyche consists of three aspects—the ego, the personal unconscious, and the collective unconscious. The **ego** component of the personality is the individual's conscious perception of the self. Jung and Freud use the term ego in approximately the same way. Ego can think, feel, remember, and perceive, and it directs everyday functions of living. Ego is responsible for one's sense of identity and time continuity, but for Jung ego is *not* the center of the personality.

The **personal unconscious**, which consists of material that was once conscious but then was repressed or forgotten, is more important than the ego. Each personal unconscious is unique because no two persons have identical experiences and impressions. Jung believed that the personal unconscious often interacts with the conscious ego.

The experiential content of the personal unconscious is grouped into clusters of emotionally laden thoughts called **complexes**. Jung believed that complexes greatly influence a person's behavior. For instance, the mother complex is a cluster of all the individual's ideas and emotions about mothers. The content of the mother complex consists of impressions of how a person was mothered, images of mothering the person has seen personally or read about, and personal experiences of mothering. When a person is called upon to perform maternal behaviors, the mother complex influences these behaviors.

Jung further believed that every complex has a **constellating power**; the complex draws in new ideas and interprets the ideas. A complex can be conscious, partly conscious, or totally unconscious; it can even extend into the collective unconscious. A complex can grow and become powerful, possibly dominating the person. Jung thought that Adolf Hitler was dominated by a power complex.

The largest and most important component of the personality is the **collective unconscious**, which extends across persons and across generations. Jung believed that people are born with a psychological and spiritual "blueprint" built into the brain's structure. Therefore, the collective unconscious provides universal predispositions to interpret the world in the same way. Jung wrote, "Just as the human body represents a whole museum of organs, each with a long evolutionary period behind it, so we should expect to find that the mind is organized in a similar way. It can no more be a product without history than is the body in which it exists" (Jung, 1964, p. 67).

The collective unconscious is always unconscious, yet it penetrates the conscious through symbols, myths, dreams, art, ritual, literature, drama, alchemy, delusions, and hallucinations. Jung believed that on a general level the collective unconscious is directing the future course of humanity. The indestructible content form of the collective unconscious is **archetypes**, and they are the most influential part of the psyche. A list of archetypes can be generated by answering the question, "What must every human experience during life?" Exhibit 14.10 de-

EXHIBIT 14.9
IN HIS OWN WORDS. Quotations from Jung's Writings

"Your destiny is the result of the collaboration between the conscious and the unconscious." (1973)

"The unconscious is on no account an empty sack in which the refuse of consciousness is collected." (1973)

"The path to wholeness is made up of fateful detours and wrong turnings." (1961)

"Not perfection, but completeness is what is expected of you." (1973)

"...I had to make do with my own truth, not accept from others what I could not attain on my own." (1961)

"Nobody could rob me of the conviction that it was enjoined upon me to do what God wanted and not what I wanted." (1961)

"The decisive question for man is: Is he related to something infinite or not? That is the telling question of life." (1961)

"For a younger person it is almost a sin—and certainly a danger—to be too much occupied with himself; but for the aging person it is a duty and a necessity to give serious attention to himself." (1933a)

"In the last resort, every individual alone has to win his battle, nobody else can do it for him." (1973)

"Called or Not Called, God is Present." (carved on stone tablet over Jung's door)

EXHIBIT 14.10
Examples of Jungian Archetypes

The Self
The self archetype is the central archetype; it represents wholeness and unity of all parts of the personality. The self's representations in consciousness include *mandalas* (a variety of circular symbols) and the twelve signs of the Zodiac. Jung believed that this archetype is not consciously evident before middle age because people rarely achieve balance and self-actualization (living at one's full potential) in their lives before the age of forty.

Anima and Animus
Jung believed that one gender, male or female, is consciously manifested while the other gender is an unconscious component of the psyche. Anima is the female component of the male psyche, and animus is the male component of the female psyche. Jung thought that these archetypes enable people to understand the qualities of the opposite gender. Ideally, individuals learn from their conscious gender and their unconscious archetype; thus, they are able to overcome the duality of male and female and use both their masculine and feminine qualities.

Persona and Shadow
The persona and shadow represent two aspects of the self. The persona, or "mask," is the public self or social self and is the role prescribed by society. The persona is used to deceive others, but an individual who believes that his or her persona is the whole self commits self-deception. The other aspect of self is the shadow, an archetype of the darkest, deepest part of the psyche. The shadow is inherited from prehuman ancestors and contains every animal instinct. The shadow has a tendency to be immoral, aggressive, and passionate. The shadow archetype is represented symbolically by demons and devils, evil spirits and monsters.

Source: Adapted from *Man and his symbols*, by Carl G. Jung, et al. Copyright 1964. J. G. Ferguson Publishing Company.

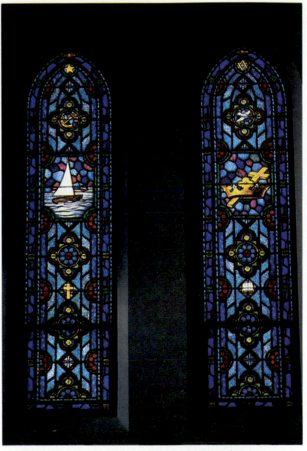

Jung believed that all religions are influenced by archetypes of the collective unconscious. The archetypes in these windows include stars, water, anchor, cross, crown, and mandalas.

scribes a few of Jung's archetypes. The *Exploring . . .* section features the dream interpretation systems of Freud and Jung.

Psychological Types   Jung believed that attitudes and thinking functions form eight psychological types, which are summarized in Exhibit 14.11. The two attitudes are introversion and extroversion. Introverts are drawn inward into the subjective world; extroverts focus on the

external, objective world. Whichever attitude is exhibited consciously, the opposite attitude is dominant in the unconscious. The ideal is to achieve a balance in the two attitudes. The four thinking functions consist of the two rational modes of thinking and feeling and the two irrational modes of sensing and intuiting. People should try to synthesize and balance the attitudes and thinking functions in order to become self-actualized, or fulfilled. Jung thought a person could not achieve this balace before he or she reached middle age.

Life Goals   According to Jung, the goal of life is to achieve harmony of the psyche, but psyche balance is extremely difficult to attain and must be actively sought. Harmony of the psyche requires a balance of the thinking, feeling, sensing, and intuiting ways of knowing the world, a balance between introversion and extroversion,

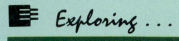

Exploring . . .

Freudian and Jungian Dream Interpretation

In many cultures throughout history, people have examined their dreams hoping to find solutions to problems and to find predictions about the future. Psychology offers several methods of dream interpretation; two of these are described in the following paragraphs.

Freudian Interpretation

According to Sigmund Freud (1900), dreams are the "royal road to the unconscious" because they reveal a person's unconscious mind. He believed that you dream about important unconscious conflicts that, if dreamed about directly, would traumatize you and make you unable to sleep. Therefore, so that you can sleep peacefully through the night you translate the conflicts into symbols and dream about the symbols instead. These symbols are expressed in two levels of dream content; the first level is manifest content, which is the dreamer's conscious perception of the dream, and the second level is latent content, which reveals the dream's hidden meaning.

To guide his dream interpretations, Freud listed over one hundred symbols for penises, nearly one hundred symbols for female genitalia, and over fifty symbols for sexual intercourse. To Freud, bananas, canoes, daggers, faucets, fountains, knives, spears, steeples, sticks, trees, umbrellas, and watering cans all signify dreams about penises. Similarly, boxes, cupboards, doors, gates, lakes, pockets, rooms, stoves, trunks, and vessels all represent dreams about vaginas. Freud also indicated that dreams about activities such as climbing, eating, floating, flying, riding, and seesawing are really dreams about sexual intercourse (Faraday, 1972).

At this point, you may think Freud believed all aspects of dreams are sexual symbols. Not so. To him, insects and other small animals often represented the subject's siblings, and figures of authority such as kings and queens represented parents (Garma, 1978). In his system of dream interpretation, Freud saw many dreams as expressions of conflicts and traumas that originated in early childhood.

Jungian Interpretation

Carl Jung's dream interpretation system places more emphasis on manifest content than on latent content. Jungian theory states that all aspects of people's natures are revealed in their dreams. In contrast to the fixed meaning of Freud's dream symbols, Jungian analysts emphasize the individual nature of dreams (Whitmont, 1978). These dream analysts may prefer to interpret a series of dreams rather than interpret each dream separately because the most important themes would recur (Faraday, 1972).

Jung believed dreams serve a compensatory function; in other words, whatever your consciousness underemphasizes, your dreams overemphasize in the same proportion. In doing so, your dreams serve as guides that help you become a more balanced person.

One facet of Jungian interpretation involves archetypal symbols, which are universal symbols such as Mother Earth, God, and Death. Although archetypal dreams are less common than compensatory dreams, archetypal dreams often seem very important to dreamers. In these dreams, archetypal symbols usually appear in contemporary form; for instance, a surgeon might represent Death (Whitcomb, 1978).

What would each of these theories suggest about a dream in which you are speeding along in a racecar? The Freudian approach would emphasize sexual content because of the movement and shape of the car. The Jungian approach would point out your risk-taking behavior in the dream and speculate that you are "playing it too safe" in your daily life.

If you are interested in recalling and interpreting your dreams, tell yourself before you go to sleep to remember your dreams. Keep a pad of paper beside your bed and immediately upon awakening jot down any dreams you can recall (Faraday, 1972).

EXHIBIT 14.11
Descriptions of Jung's Eight Psychological Types

Extroverts
1. Thinking extrovert—This individual likes to get facts, use reason, and think logically. He or she usually operates according to fixed rules and is a positive, dogmatic thinker. The thinking extrovert may be perceived as objective and cold because he or she tends to repress feelings.
2. Feeling extrovert—This individual is a sociable, talkative person who seeks harmony with the world. The feeling extrovert tends to repress thinking and be emotional, and he or she is respectful of authority and tradition.
3. Sensing extrovert—This type of person likes pleasure and is constantly seeking new sensory experience. The sensing extrovert appreciates good food, good art, and good times. This individual is socially adaptive and tends to repress intuition.
4. Intuiting extrovert—This impulsive, enthusiastic individual is guided by hunches rather than by facts. The intuiting extrovert is known to be very changeable and creative. This person also represses sensation.

Introverts
5. Thinking introvert—The thinking introvert is the subjective egghead who has an intense desire for privacy. This individual is socially inhibited, has poor practical judgment, and represses feelings.
6. Feeling introvert—This reserved, quiet, thoughtful, hypersensitive person can be childish and indifferent to others' feelings. The feeling introvert is quite loyal.
7. Sensing introvert—This person is artistic, passive, calm, and detached from other humans. The sensing introvert allows his or her life to be guided by whatever happens.
8. Intuiting introvert—This person is the odd, eccentric daydreamer. The intuiting introvert may be interested in mysticism or art, and his or her life is guided by inner experiences. Intuiting introverts believe that they are seldom understood by others.

Adapted from Jung, 1933b.

How is a dream about snakes interpreted? A Freudian analyst interprets snakes as symbols of male genitalia and a dream about snakes as an expression of sexual concern. A Jungian therapist views snakes as archetypal symbols of life's renewal and healing. Others interpret snakes as symbolizing temptation, treachery, and secret enemies.

velopment of different aspects of the personality. Although individuation is a difficult task, Jung believed it is a lower level of total personality development. The second, higher form of self-actualization is **transcendence**, a spiritual self-actualization. Transcendence involves a constant striving for unity, wholeness, and integration of the personality and the universe.

Focus Question Answer

How does your childhood influence your adult personality? Most psychologists believe that adult personality is influenced by childhood experiences. Freud emphasized childhood because he believed your basic adult personality was formed by the time you were six years old. Adler emphasized the child within his or her family, where family atmosphere and birth order influence basic perceptions and interaction styles. Of the psychodynamic theorists, Jung placed the least emphasis on childhood, since he believed that most significant personality development occurs in middle age.

and a balance between one's feminine and masculine characteristics.

Two types of self-actualization are needed to achieve complete harmony of the psyche. The first form of self-actualization is **individuation**, the fullest possible de-

 *Relate*

Freudian Updates

Freud has been dead approximately fifty years, and yet his theory lives on. Psychologists continually discuss Freud's ideas, test his theories in research experiments and case studies, and suggest new interpretations and modifications. This *Relate* section examines three ways in which some psychologists would like to update typical Freudian interpretations.

Feminists and Freud

Feminist therapists are male and female therapists who believe that counseling, psychology, and society should be nonsexist. Many feminist therapists and other psychologists believe psychoanalytic theory is inherently sexist, and some of Freud's assumptions cannot be altered to become nonsexist. Although some sections of his theory can be changed to treat men and women equally (such as changing *mother's* effects on the child to *parental* or *primary caregiver's* effects on the child), other sections cannot be modified because Freud believed in the biological inferiority of women. Freud wrote, ''Anatomy is destiny,'' and he wrote about women's *natural* feminine masochism (Hyde & Rosenberg, 1980). Many feminist psychologists object to Freud's relegating females to a lower position in life and his outright objection to the women's equal rights movement of the 1920s (Hyde & Rosenberg, 1980; Sherman, 1971).

Freud argued that since Electra complexes cannot be fully resolved, most women have immature superegos; therefore, compared to men, women do not develop their own values but adopt their parents' value systems and have only a weak sense of justice and social interest. Freud thought that men in their thirties are still youthful and open to change, but women in their thirties are rigid (Williams, 1977).

Yet, in spite of the sexist nature of his theory, Freud did pay more attention to women's concerns than did his contemporaries (Mitchell, 1974). Freud's psychoanalytic theory helped initiate the sexual revolution that, in turn, made parts of his own theory archaic.

Freud and Seduction Theory

In 1896, Freud presented at a medical meeting a paper in which he outlined his **seduction theory**—that hysterical neuroses are caused by premature sexual experiences. Based on the psychohistories of eighteen patients (six males and twelve females), he concluded that incest and other sexual abuse precede the development of some emotional disorders. His hypothesis was strongly rejected by his colleagues (Masson, 1984a).

By 1898, Freud had apparently revised his theory, for he wrote that patients with hysterical neuroses fantasize childhood sexual seductions rather than actually experience seduction by an adult. At the time, most psychologists believed that Freud had changed his beliefs due to self-analysis of his own childhood. Recently, however, Jeffrey Masson (1984a, 1984b) found in Freud's correspondence statements that suggest that Freud continued to believe privately that actual seduction, not fantasy, produces hysterical neuroses.

If Freud publicly backed away from his original position because of professional criticisms, it was one of the few times that he backed away from controversy. Most probably, Freud publicly changed his position to allow greater consistency within his psychoanalytic theory. Freud's daughter Anna wrote to Masson, ''Keeping the seduction theory would mean to abandon the Oedipus complex, and with it the whole importance of fantasy life, conscious or unconscious fantasy. In fact, I think there would have been no psychoanalysis afterwards'' (Travis, 1984, p. 48). One can only speculate that if Freud had maintained his original position, incest victims would have received help and attention throughout the twentieth century rather than in only the last few years.

Poorly Translated Freud

In *Freud and Man's Soul,* prominent psychoanalyst Bruno Bettelheim (1983) argues that Americans misunderstand much of Freud's psychoanalytic theory because Freudian concepts are poorly translated into English. Bettelheim first read and studied Freud's theory in German and then read Freud's theories in English.

Bettelheim believes German words were poorly translated and formal medical terms were sometimes substituted for Freud's more ordinary language. He maintains that some of Freud's emphases were left out or diminished in the translations.

The most basic mistranslation begins with the word *psychoanalysis.* Bettelheim believes that Freud carefully chose this word because it translates from the Greek as *soul analysis.* Freud viewed psychoanalysis as the spiritual journey of self-discovery and the emotional responding to the souls of others. The German versions of Freud's theory contain many references to the soul, but the word is not mentioned in English translations.

Trieb is another mistranslated word. *Trieb* means drive or impulse, yet the word was often translated as instinct.

Therefore, many books emphasize Freud's belief in the sex instinct when, more accurately, he believed in the sex drive.

To be correctly translated, the explanation accompanying the Oedipus complex should emphasize that the child's greatest wish is for the impossibility of carrying out his sexual love for his parent. Bettelheim suggests that Freud believed children accomplish this task unless their parents act seductively toward them. Most English translations of the Oedipus complex imply that the resolution of the conflict is entirely the child's responsibility.

Examples of the use of Greek and Latin terms instead of everyday language appear in the personality components of id, ego, and superego. Freud did not use these formal terms in German. He used the German word for *it* to refer to the id, the word for *I* to refer to the ego, and the word for *above-I* to refer to superego. English-speaking psychoanalysts seemed to prefer the formality of Latin.

Bettelheim believes that translators have made Freud sound more assertive and more certain than he meant to sound and have removed the humanistic and spiritual flavor from Freud's psychoanalytic writings.

Things to Do

1. Work with another student in the class. Take turns recalling earliest memories while the other person takes notes on what is recalled. After both of you have recalled memories, discuss your notes. How old were you in the earliest recalled memory? What connections and implications do you observe in the memories? What is the emotional tone of the recalled memories? Do these early memories relate to your present personality?

2. Use your imagination to engage the unconscious in dialogue with the ego. In these Jungian exercises, do not think in terms of verbal responses: A. Keep a collection of sketches or doodles and later try to interpret the common themes. B. Ask your unconscious a question. Then draw an image on paper with crayons or colored pens. Does the image answer your question? C. Create your own mandala, your symbol of the archetypal self.

3. Make a list of your parents' positive and negative characteristics as you perceive them now and another list as you perceived their characteristics while you were growing up. What are the similarities and differences between the lists? Why? Interpret your responses according to Freudian and Adlerian theory.

4. Go to a local art museum, or check out art books from the library. Explore the artwork for archetypal symbols.

5. Read one of Freud's famous case studies, such as Little

Hans, the Rat Man, the Wolf Man, or Anna O.

6. Find and read in a psychology journal a research article that tests a concept from one of the theories discussed in this chapter. What was researched in the study? Do the findings support the theoretical concept? Do you think the study is valid?

7. Explain to your best friends what central and secondary traits are. Then ask your friends to list your central and secondary traits. Compare the lists. Do your friends agree more about your central traits or about your secondary traits?

Things to Discuss

1. Which of the personality theories described in this chapter do you like best? Why does the theory appeal to you? Which of the theories do you like least? Why?

2. Freud has been dead approximately fifty years, but if he were living, how do you think he could update his theory or use modern events and beliefs to support his psychoanalytic theory?

3. How have your particular birth order position and family atmosphere affected your personality? How would you be different if your birth order position were different?

4. Is being an introvert or extrovert better? What are the advantages and disadvantages of each type? Support your position with examples. Do you think you inherit a tendency to be one or the other? Can an individual change significantly along the introversion-extroversion dimension? Do you view yourself as an introvert or as an extrovert? If you could change that aspect of yourself, would you? Why?

5. What are your assumptions about reality and human nature? Identify the assumptions of each of the major theorists in this chapter. With whom do you most agree?

6. What are the similarities between Freud and Adler? The differences? What are the similarities between Freud and Jung? The differences? What are the similarities and differences between Adler and Jung? Read the quotations of each of these psychologists. Whose sayings do you like best?

7. What are the common traits of Americans? Pick three other countries with which you are familiar (e.g., Japan, England, Germany), and list the common traits of individuals in these countries. What do you think creates the differences in the common traits? Do you think your descriptions are fairly accurate? What makes this task difficult?

Things to Read

Bettelheim, B. 1983. *Freud and Man's Soul.* NY: Knopf.

Hall, C. 1954. *A primer of Freudian psychology.* NY: New American Library.

Hall, C. 1973. *A primer of Jungian psychology.* NY: New American Library.

Jung, C.G. 1961. *Memories, dreams, reflections,* NY: Random House.

Scroggs, J.R. 1985. *Key ideas in personality theory.* St. Paul, MN: West.

Review

Summary

1. Personality consists of the essential, enduring characteristics of a person. Personality is useful in explaining individual differences and in helping predict what behaviors are likely to occur. Numerous personality theories exist because psychologists hold different assumptions about reality and human nature.

2. Type theories describe people's personalities according to a few dimensions. Sheldon's constitutional theory relates personality to the three body shapes of endomorph, mesomorph, and ectomorph. Eysenck's type theory features the dimensions of introversion-extroversion and stability-instability. Both theories emphasize that biology and heredity play significant roles in personality.

3. Traits are stable and enduring dispositions that determine behavior. Allport describes four kinds of traits: cardinal, central, secondary, and common. In Cattell's factor theory, traits are described as either surface traits or source traits. Allport emphasizes the uniqueness of one's traits, while Cattell emphasizes the universality of basic traits.

4. Research on traits has found temporal stability of traits, but the research has not found strong stability of traits across situations. The trait approaches are more useful for examining between-person differences than they are for explaining the personality process within a single person.

5. Freud's psychoanalytic theory emphasizes unconscious motivation. According to this theory, an individual's motives are expressed through the id, ego, and superego. The goal of id and ego is gratification; the goal of the superego is morality.

6. Freud believed that adult personalities are basically determined by the time people are six years old. Childhood development occurs in the psychosexual stages called oral, anal, phallic, latency, and genital. Freud thought that during the phallic stage, all boys experience the Oedipus complex, and girls experience the Electra complex. How well the processes are resolved has significant impact on adult personalities in the areas of sex roles, sexual preferences, and superego strength.

7. According to Adler's individual psychology, the basic drive is to strive for superiority by compensating for feelings of inferiority. Adler believed that family atmosphere, birth order, and sibling rivalry influence personality.

8. Jung divided the psyche into the ego, personal unconscious, and collective unconscious. Complexes of the personal unconscious often influence the conscious ego. The most important part of the personality is the collective unconscious, which extends across persons and generations. The content form of the collective unconscious is archetypes, such as the archetypes of the self, anima and animus, and persona and shadow.

9. Jung believed the goal of life is to achieve harmony of the psyche. Harmony is achieved through individuation and transcendence and by balancing attitudes and thinking functions.

10. Theories live beyond the theorist, and other persons contribute to the interpretation and understanding of a theory. Three modern considerations of Freud's psychoanalytic theory are the feminist reaction to psychoanalytic ideas, the discovery of Freud's belief in seduction theory, and Bettelheim's contention that Freud was poorly translated into English.

Key Terms

endomorphs
mesomorphs
ectomorphs
introversion
extroversion
cardinal traits
central traits
secondary traits
common traits
surface traits
source traits
unconscious motivation
libido
thanatos
pansexualism
id
ego
superego
pleasure principle
reality principle

conscience
ego ideal
psychosexual stages
fixation
Oedipus complex
Electra complex
social purposefulness
striving for superiority
sibling rivalry
compensation
overcompensation
family atmosphere
birth order
psyche
personal unconscious
complexes
collective unconscious
archetypes
feminist therapists
seduction theory

Focus Questions

1. Is your personality equivalent to your behavior?

2. Is your basic human nature positive, negative, or neutral?

3. What would living in the here-and-now be like?

4. How do your culture and era influence how you perceive yourself?

Chapter Outline

Chapter 15

Personality: Behavioristic, Humanistic, and Existential Theories

To love oneself is the beginning of a lifelong romance.

Oscar Wilde

In the previous chapter, you read about type, trait, and psychodynamic approaches to personality theories. In this chapter, you will read about behavioristic, humanistic, and existential approaches to understanding personality.

 Behavioristic Theories

Although the roots of behaviorism include the European experimentalists Ivan Pavlov (classical conditioning) and Hermann Ebbinghaus (memory), behaviorism itself represents a twentieth-century American movement. The behavioristic personality theorists developed their ideas in university research laboratories and later applied their ideas to counseling and personality assessment (Kendler, 1985).

353

Behaviorists focus on learning and the learning process and emphasize the environment's role in behavior. While radical behaviorists do not emphasize internal processes, other behaviorists do include in their theories internal, cognitive (thinking) processes, and all behaviorists place greater emphasis on the situation's role in determining behavior than do other personality theorists.

In what additional respects does behaviorism differ from other personality approaches? Behaviorism places less emphasis on heredity than do the type approaches. Although both behaviorism and trait approaches are mechanistic, trait approaches focus on internal processes and behavioristic approaches focus on external processes. Further, while both psychodynamic and behavioristic theories are analytical, psychodynamic theories place much more emphasis on internal processes. Humanistic approaches are more holistic and purposive than are behavioristic theories, which seldom study the organism as a whole being (Kendler, 1985).

Skinner's Radical Behaviorism

Burrhus Frederic Skinner (1904–) was born in Susquehanna, Pennsylvania. As a boy, Skinner was an inventive gadget-maker, and as a psychologist his skills led to inventions such as the Skinner experimental box (the first one was adapted from an ice chest), the "teaching machine" for programmed learning, and an improved baby crib, the "Air Crib."

Skinner was always a good student who loved books and writing stories and poems. He majored in English at college and was determined to become a writer. However, following college graduation, his writing career stalled and he eventually enrolled for his first psychology course in graduate school at Harvard, where he read the works of J. B. Watson and Ivan Pavlov and became an avid behaviorist. After receiving his doctoral degree in 1931, Skinner spent five years doing postdoctoral work at Harvard. In the late 1930s, while at the University of Minnesota, his writing on behavioral analysis firmly established his importance in the field of psychology. A decade later, he returned to Harvard University, where he still writes in retirement. His two best-known books are *Walden Two* (1948), about a commune organized according to behavioristic principles, and *Beyond Freedom and Dignity* (1971), a controversial work that reveals his deterministic philosophy.

In addition to contributing to personality theory, Skinner has influenced other areas of psychology, therapy, and society. His programmed learning and "teaching

EXHIBIT 15.1
IN HIS OWN WORDS. Quotations from Skinner's Writings

"I have no doubt of the eventual triumph of the position [behaviorism] . . . it will provide the most direct route to a successful science of man."
(1967)

"A prediction of what the average individual will do is often of little or no value in dealing with a particular individual."
(1953)

"There is no place in the scientific position for a self as a true originator or initiator of action."
(1974)

"I think the main objection to behaviorism is that people are in love with the mental apparatus."
(1967b)

"...a school system must be called a failure if it cannot induce students to learn except by threatening them for not learning."
(1958)

"If my theory survives twenty-five years, it will be amazing."
(1953).

machines" have influenced student workbooks and the design of computer software, and Skinner and other behaviorists had impact on the 1980 DSM-III classification of mental illness, which increased emphasis on behavioral definitions. In the 1950s, Skinner created the term behavior therapy, now one of the most popular types of psychotherapy. His work also influenced the growth of biofeedback techniques and behavioral medicine departments (Scroggs, 1985). Because of his prolific writing, innovative ideas, and diversity of interests, Skinner is one of the best known psychologists of all times. In 1970, his name was placed on a list of one of the one hundred most important people in the world (Guttman, 1970).

Personality Determined by Consequences   Central to Skinner's theory is his belief that an individual's current behavior is determined by the consequences of past behaviors. Since personal intentions do not cause behavior, a person who is honest, for example, is not honest because he or she wants to be honest but because in the past he or she has been reinforced for being honest.

Using pigeons and rats, Skinner has examined behaviors and reinforcements to discover the relationships that apply to all organisms, including humans. Refer to Chapter 9 to refresh your understanding of operant conditioning and reinforcement schedules, concepts that, according to Skinner, explain your behavior.

With only this brief introduction, you can understand why Skinner's theory is called **radical behaviorism**. Defining personality as merely a collection of behavior patterns and viewing creativity, freedom, and motivation as explanatory fictions (terms evoked whenever one cannot perceive the reinforcements that shape the behavior) comprise an extreme, radical position.

Quick Study Aid

Skinner's View of Personality

The essence of Skinner's radical behaviorism is:
PERSONALITY = BEHAVIOR

Skinner's theory is attractive to some theorists for four major reasons. First, the theory displays **parsimony**; in other words, the theory explains as much as possible in the simplest, briefest way. Second, radical behaviorism is a testable theory that can generate experimental study. Third, Skinner's theory is process-oriented and provides insight into how personality changes. Fourth, the theory has a wide range of applications in education, counseling, parenting, and industry. Yet in spite of these attractions, many psychologists believe Skinner is too extreme in minimizing the role of internal mental processes in determining personality. While Skinner emphasizes that the environment controls people's behaviors,

most psychologists would state that the environment influences rather than controls behaviors.

Bandura's Social Learning Theory

Albert Bandura (1925–) was born in the province of Alberta, Canada, to a family of wheat farmers. After undergraduate work at the University of British Columbia in Vancouver, Bandura received his doctoral degree in 1952 from the University of Iowa. Having completed a year's clinical internship in Kansas at the Wichita Guidance Center, he spent the rest of his psychology career at Stanford University. He has written several influential books, including *Principles of Behavior Modification* (1969) and *Social Learning Theory* (1977).

Bandura has done important pioneer work in the social learning of aggressive behavior and in the use of modeling techniques in behavior modification programs. In the 1970s, he called attention to the effects of television violence on children (see Chapter 9). Bandura's personality theory is called **social learning theory** because it attempts to explain personality as learned behavior within a social context.

Reciprocal Determinism   For Bandura (1977), behavior is the result of the interaction between an individual's inner cognitive process and environmental influences. Unlike Skinner, Bandura emphasizes the role of thinking and decision-making on behavior. According to Bandura's principle of **reciprocal determinism**, environmental stimuli, beliefs, and expectations influence behavior. In return, behavioral outcomes change the environment and influence beliefs and expectations. As illustrated in Exhibit 15.2, behavior, cognitions, and the environment are interlocking causes.

Bandura believes people think about what they are doing, and their cognitive capacities often determine the directions of their actions, first by deciding what environmental stimuli are perceived and then by deciding which factors to act upon. Thus, to take notes during a lecture you must first perceive which points are important to learn and then you must decide to include those points in your notes. People are also able to represent external events symbolically and to use these mental representations at a later time to guide their behaviors. For example, you may be shown a chemistry lab procedure during one class period and be required to remember how to use the procedure during the next lab period. Finally, as a result of earlier experience, people consider the **anticipated outcomes** of different kinds of

EXHIBIT 15.2
Reciprocal Determinism

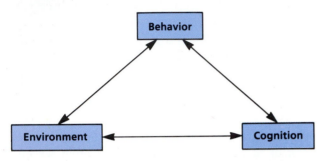

According to reciprocal determinism, behavior, cognitions, and the environment interact with each other and create changes. Thus, a behavior might change the environment, which then changes a cognition, which influences behavior.

Adapted from Bandura, A. 1978. The self-system in reciprocal determinism. *American Psychologist, 33,* 345.

behaviors. Anticipated outcomes regulate behavior to a large degree because they determine which behaviors are perceived as leading to rewards. If you used a study guide for your sociology course and found that the guide helped you study for your sociology tests, you might anticipate that you should buy a study guide for your psychology class as well.

Observational Learning or Modeling   A key idea in Bandura's social learning theory is **observational learning**, or **modeling**, according to which an individual acquires behavior patterns by watching someone else's behavior rather than by receiving reinforcements.

Bandura (1977) has identified four processes that govern observational learning, or modeling. The first process is attending to the modeled behavior. Research by Bandura and others indicates that attention is affected by more than mere exposure to the model. Individuals pay more attention to physically attractive models, nurturant models, high status models, and competent models. Advertisers often hire well-known athletes and actors to sell products because people are more likely to imitate these individuals than "ordinary folk."

The second process is remembering the modeled behavior. If encoding of an observed behavior into long-term memory is blocked, the behavior cannot be imitated. Imagery and verbal encoding help retain the model's behavior. You may have discovered that when you try to learn directions to a friend's house, you remember the route better if you form a mental map of the route

or if you carefully put the route into words such as "turn east at the second traffic light and then north at the gas station."

The third process involved in modeling concerns the motor reproduction processes. Behaviors can be modeled only if people have the ability to perform the behaviors. A four-year-old may watch his big sister ride a bicycle, understand the process involved, and yet be too young to ride the bicycle himself. In some cases, the modeled behavior may be tucked away into the memory and used to influence behavior at a later time. For instance, a young child may not be allowed to smoke her parents' cigarettes, yet by observing her parents' behavior she learns how to smoke cigarettes and, as a teenager, may make use of her past observational learning.

The fourth process affecting modeling is reinforcement and motivation. People may observe someone else's behavior and be capable of imitating it, but whether or not they actually imitate the behavior is determined by anticipated outcomes. Imitation occurs when an individual anticipates rewards and does not occur when he or she anticipates punishments. Therefore, according to observational learning, individuals acquire more behaviors than they actually perform, and they are more likely to imitate same-sex models, similar models, and especially models who are reinforced because these factors suggest that the same behaviors will be reinforced for them, too.

Bandura's social learning theory is a popular scientific and experimental approach to the study of personality

By observing models, children may learn behaviors even before they have the motor skills to perform them.

because it combines the importance of both internal variables and external variables by emphasizing reciprocal determinism and anticipated outcomes. The next behavioral approach to be examined places even stronger emphasis on cognitive determinants of personality.

Rotter's Cognitive Social Learning Theory

Julian Rotter (1916–) was born in Brooklyn, New York, to parents who were European immigrants. As an undergraduate, Rotter majored in chemistry; he then received graduate degrees in psychology from the University of Iowa and Indiana University. After serving as an army psychologist during World War II, Rotter joined the faculty of Ohio State University and, later, the University of Connecticut.

Rotter's cognitive social learning theory (Rotter, 1954; Rotter, 1982) is similar in many respects to Bandura's social learning theory. Both theories emphasize that past experiences influence current experiences and that current experiences can change attitudes and expectations for the future. Further, both theories emphasize that behavior is goal-directed, with people attempting to maximize rewards and minimize punishments. Finally, Bandura and Rotter consider the individual's inner workings an important part of the behavioral picture. However, Rotter employs different terms than does Bandura, and only Rotter presents basic predictive formulas for the likelihood of specific behaviors.

Behavior Potential According to Rotter, **behavior potential** (BP) is the probability that an individual will respond with a particular behavior when certain environmental conditions are present. The behavior potential of a situation is determined by two factors: expectancy and reinforcement value.

Expectancy is the person's subjective belief about the probable outcome of his or her behavior based on past experiences in similar situations. What is your expectancy of doing well on your next psychology test if you study hard for the test? Your answer depends on how well or poorly you did on earlier psychology tests and other college examinations.

One type of expectancies is called generalized expectancies (GE) because they are used in a wide range of situations. For example, you have a general idea of whether you believe you get reinforced if you work hard. This generalized expectancy is one factor determining how you expect to perform on a psychology test. A less

general expectation influencing your situation would be your perception of how well you are able to perform on tests; you may want to get an A in this psychology course but think you cannot, even if you study hard, because you have never earned an A in college. Expectancies can also be specific. Even if your college grade point average is low, you might expect to do well on your next psychology test if you have already done well on two previous psychology tests.

Some expectancies affect a variety of situations. One of the most generalized expectancies concerns whether you believe that getting reinforcements is dependent upon your behavior or whether you believe reinforcements are unconnected with your actions. Rotter referred to this generalized expectancy as internal-external **locus of control**. An individual with an **internal locus of control** believes that what he or she does is related to what he or she receives. If you have an internal locus of control, you probably believe that if you study hard you will do well on a test. In contrast, if you have an **external locus of control**, you probably believe that rewards are independent of behaviors and are controlled by forces external to yourself. As an externally oriented person, you might think studying is not as important as having good luck. Research on the internal-external locus of control concept is featured in Chapter 20.

Another factor important in determining behavior potential is **reinforcement value**, which refers to preferences for particular rewards. Each individual has characteristic preferences for reinforcements. Some individuals like to earn only A's in college, while others believe C's are good enough. People's preferences affect their behaviors in different situations. To predict a specific behavior, you need to know both a person's expectancy and reinforcement value.

Quick Study Aid

Rotter's Behavior Potential

You may find Rotter's theory useful and yet have trouble remembering his concepts. This shortcut abbreviation may help your recall.

To predict a specific behavior:

$$BP = E + RV$$

Potential for a specific behavior is determined by expectancy and reinforcement value.

Exploring . . .

The Nature of Maladjustment

Cognitive social learning theory can be used to describe the nature of maladjustment, or less than optimal reactions to situations (Katovsky, 1976). People's expectancies, minimal goals, and reinforcement values can lead them to behaviors that hinder their healthy personality growth.

People are maladjusted if they have high reinforcement value but low expectancy; a student who very much wants to make the Dean's list but does not believe she possesses the ability to get high grades would fall into this category. Another type of maladjustment occurs when an individual places high values on incompatible (or conflicting) reinforcements; a student who wants to make Dean's list but who also wants to party every night would experience this second type of maladjustment.

Maladjustment can also be created by inappropriate minimal goal levels. In one maladjustment situation, the individual sets inappropriately high minimal goal levels; an average student who sets A's as minimal goals is likely to experience failure and disappointment. In the other maladjustment situation, the individual sets very low minimal goals and appears to be unmotivated and bored; an intelligent student who wants to earn only C-'s is maladjusted in this way.

Rotter's social learning theory is useful in therapy in analyzing a person's problems and then in instructing the person to challenge his or her current ideas about expectancy, reinforcement value, and minimal goal.

Minimal Goal   Another term Rotter uses in his theory is **minimal goal**, which is the lowest level of potential reinforcement that would be satisfactory in a given situation. Minimal goal represents the dividing point between positive reinforcement and punishment. What is your minimal goal in terms of a grade for your psychology course? Would a D be a positive reinforcement? Would you consider a B punishment? Among the students in your psychology class, a wide range of minimal goal levels exists. Your minimal goals affect which behaviors you perform each day and how you and others describe your personality. The *Exploring . . .* section discusses how cognitive social learning theory can be used to explain maladjustment, and the research process section focuses on experiments generated from cognitive social learning theory.

The Research Process: Delay of Gratification

While the hypotheses of many personality theories are supported primarily by case studies and correlational studies, social learning theory and cognitive social learning theory are supported largely by experimental studies. One aspect, the role of expectancies in determining be-

havior, has encouraged much research about people's locus of control (see Chapter 20) and beliefs in delay of gratification. **Delay of gratification** refers to the ability to give up an immediate, small reward in favor of a larger, later reward. Research findings suggest that self-imposed postponements of rewards are more likely with individuals who have high expectations that the delayed rewards will actually occur.

All your past experiences with delayed gratification situations can influence your current decision-making about settling for an immediate reward or working toward an improved pay-off. However, you usually place most importance on the degree of success of delayed gratification in recent, similar settings. Recent delay of gratification experiences can affect your expectations about the likelihood of delayed rewards becoming reality. In one research study that supports these premises (Mahrer, 1956), the experimenter manipulated the delayed reward expectancies of second- and third-grade boys. For five days, each of the boys was told he would get a free balloon the following day for helping with a simple photograph-selection task. Boys in the high expectancy group received balloons on four of the five days, boys in the moderate expectancy group received balloons on two of

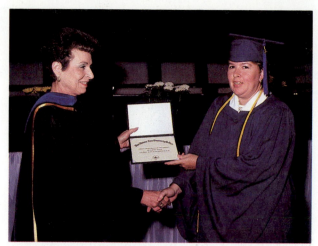

Some achievements require an ability to delay gratification for a long time.

the five days, and boys in the low expectancy group received no balloons during the five days.

Three days later, the same experimenter offered each boy a choice between a small airplane toy trinket immediately or a nicer, more desirable flying saucer toy the next day. Can you predict which toy the boys chose? Many of the boys in the high expectancy group chose the flying saucer toy, but boys in the low expectancy group were least likely to choose the flying saucer toy; because they had not received the promised balloons, they chose the certainty of the airplane trinket rather than the risk of waiting for the flying saucer toy. Can you recall times in your own life when you reacted in similar ways?

Mahrer's study included an additional variable that provides more information about the generalizability of expectancy modification. With half of the boys in each expectancy group, an experimenter other than the person who had promised the balloons offered the airplane or flying saucer choice. With a different experimenter, boys in all three expectancy groups were as likely to choose the flying saucer. The boys discriminated that the first experimenter's reliability in fulfilling delayed reward promises did not necessarily predict the reliability of the second experimenter.

Focus Question Answer

Is your personality equivalent to your behavior? Every personality theorist includes your behavior as part of your personality pattern, but only the radical behaviorists interpret your behavior as the equivalent of your person-

ality. Most psychologists include your thoughts, emotions, and motivations as aspects of your personality. Both Bandura and Rotter emphasize the role of thought and thinking processes on your behavior patterns.

 ## Humanistic Theories

Humanistic theories are approaches that focus on people's subjective experiences of the world, and these theories accept people's subjective experiences at face value rather than postulate forces such as unconscious processes.

Humanistic theories are holistic; they study the whole person rather than break the personality into small parts such as traits or instincts. As holistic theories, they focus on the concept of the self and on the mind-body unit as one interacting unit.

Humanistic theories also emphasize free will, asserting that individuals can freely decide and choose their own behaviors. The theories maintain that people are future-oriented, purposeful, and goal-directed, with emphasis on personal fulfillment (Scroggs, 1985). Humanistic psychology is controversial, and the *Exploring . . .* section discusses the causes of this controversy.

Maslow's Metamotivational Theory

Abraham Maslow (1908–1970) was born in Brooklyn, New York, to uneducated Russian Jewish immigrants. His was the only Jewish family in the neighborhood, and Maslow was shunned and taunted. He described himself

Before he became a humanist, Abraham Maslow had been trained in both psychoanalytic and behavioristic theories.

Exploring . . .

Humanism and the American Culture

Humanism arose out of perceived shortcomings in both psychoanalytic and behavioristic theories. Abraham Maslow, one of the most famous of humanistic psychologists, proposed humanism as a "third force" in psychology because he believed psychoanalytic theory was too pessimistic and behaviorism was too mechanistic to fully explain human nature. For Maslow, humanism was a reaction to the destruction of World War II—he wanted to believe that people's natures are positive rather than negative.

Humanism thrived in the post-war era, with its growing economy, expanded career and personal opportunities, and exposure to global ideas through travel and media. Technology helped take individuals from the drudgery of everyday chores into lives with increasing amounts of leisure time. America became a mobile society that believed in itself as the "land of opportunity"; realization of the American Dream was possible for anyone who tried hard enough. For the first time, the basic needs of most Americans were met, and many believed society should provide the right environment for people to fulfill themselves.

In the 1960s, humanism and society seemed compatible in many ways. Businesses developed worker-oriented environments and became more individualized, as evidenced by the retirement of the gray flannel suit as mandatory attire. Prison systems tried to reform and rehabilitate prisoners rather than merely mete out punishments. In schools, pupils were less likely to be treated in demeaning ways, less likely to be physically punished, and more likely to be placed in individualized educational programs. Most schools added to their curricula subjects intended to provide students with information that would help them lead better lives. Political movements emphasized desegregation, the Head Start Program, the Peace Corps, and equal rights.

Obviously, some individuals had fought for humane schools and work places, civil rights, and re-

Governmental programs during the 1960's were often based on the humanistic assumption of the basic "goodness" of people. Many programs attempted to fulfill the basic necessities of life so people could work toward fulfilling higher-order needs.

habilitation for criminals long before the popularity of humanistic psychology, but political movements such as "The Great Society" (during Lyndon Johnson's presidential era) grew simultaneously with the humanistic psychology movement.

Perhaps the humanistic assumption that human nature is basically good unless corrupted by society's mistakes added to people's resolve to fight governmental policies during the Vietnam War. However, the stress of this political period may have, in turn, increased the number of people who disagreed with humanistic philosophy. Americans who believe that citizens should follow governmental policy felt increasingly uncomfortable with the humanistic emphasis on individuals deciding their own goals. In recent years, as political conservatism has grown, humanism has become less popular.

Humanism is often attacked from a financial standpoint as well. These critics may believe in humanistic principles but believe even more strongly that America cannot afford the cost of putting humanistic principles into effect in business, government, and education. They may argue that teaching values, living skills, and aesthetic knowledge in the public schools takes too much time away from the basic reading, writing, mathematics, and science courses. They may believe that welfare programs help people meet their basic needs but at the same time take away people's initiative to improve their own lives. Such critics may consider rehabilitation programs for criminals worthwhile but not as important as providing safety for the rest of society. Some people who believe strongly that people would be good if they lived in supportive and positive environments have concluded that so many people have been so deeply frustrated for so long that correcting their problems would cost too much money, effort, and time.

In the future, humanistic principles may have greater or lesser impact on American life than they do today. What are the advantages and disadvantages of a humanistic philosophy influencing American society?

as a "shy and neurotic" child, and he retreated to books, libraries, and academic achievement. Maslow enrolled in law school after high school graduation, but he disliked law classes and dropped out after two weeks. He subsequently enrolled in a liberal arts college program and graduated from the University of Wisconsin.

Maslow first was behavioristic in perspective and then was influenced by Freudian and Gestalt psychology. Parenting and World War II led him to believe in both the complexity of human nature and the need for a positive psychology whose goal was peace and harmony. Out of his optimistic beliefs, humanism, the "third force" of psychology, was created (the first two forces are psychoanalyis and behaviorism). Maslow's popular hierarchy of needs was first published in 1941, and his prominence as a personality theorist began in 1954 with the publication of *Motivation and Personality* (revised 1970).

Human Nature   Maslow (1968) believed in the decency of human nature and in the universal tendency for growth. He emphasized that the biologically based inner nature of people is either neutral or good and that destructiveness, cruelty, and violence are not part of human nature but reactions against frustrations of not having basic needs met. The tendency to grow is illustrated in humanity's creativity and inventiveness as well as in the way children naturally enjoy learning new skills and abilities. Maslow suggested that psychotherapy is effective because of this tendency to positive growth.

Maslow believed that true human nature cannot be destroyed, but because human nature is delicate and weak it can be suppressed by cultural pressures, frustrating circumstances, and pain, all of which might lead to neurosis, illness, or immorality. However, even when one's nature has been suppressed and denied, the positive nature survives and waits for more supportive circumstances.

Maslow did discover value in frustration, pain, and tragedy; these experiences and conflicts provide opportunities for people to grow in self-knowledge, strength, and courage. When people hurt emotionally or physically, their basic natures make them attempt to alleviate suffering, thus moving them into renewals of self-respect and self-control (Maslow, 1968).

Personality Development   Maslow (1968) believed normal children choose to move toward positive growth because growth choices are satisfying, feel good, and bring pleasure. In contrast, their parents and other adults

EXHIBIT 15.3
IN HIS OWN WORDS. Quotations from Maslow's Writings

"Human nature is not nearly as bad as it has been thought to be."
(1968)

"To oversimplify the matter somewhat, it is as if Freud supplied to us the sick half of psychology and we must now fill it out with the healthy half."
(1968)

"Freud saw everything through brown-colored glasses."
(1968)

"The person who hasn't conquered, withstood, and overcome continues to feel doubtful that he could."
(1968)

"...every crime against one's own nature, every evil act, every one without exception records itself in our consciousness and makes us despise ourselves."
(1968)

"Though, in principle, self-actualization is easy, in practice it rarely happens."
(1968)

"There is a kind of a feedback between the Good Society and the Good Person. They need each other . . . ."
(1971)

"If you deliberately plan to be less than you are capable of being, then I warn you that you'll be deeply unhappy for the rest of your life."
(1971)

often try to get children to pick safety choices over growth choices. As shown in Exhibit 15.4, the children's growth choices enhance attractions but overlook inherent dangers. The adults' safety choices focus on danger at the expense of growth's attractiveness. Children usually learn to pick safety choices over growth choices in order to receive the approval of adults. At times during their lives, adults may need to relearn taking growth risks over safety in order to make changes in their personalities and life circumstances. People who over-rely on safety may feel as if they are living their lives according to the rules of others; only by taking risks can their personalities grow toward their potentials.

B-Needs In Chapter 12, you learned about Maslow's hierarchy of needs, which can be divided into D-needs

Children possess a natural inclination to explore the world, but they may learn to repress this need in order to maximize their security.

EXHIBIT 15.4
The Basic Human Dilemma of Safety and Growth

Each person contains two internal forces. One force clings to safety because fear makes the person perceive growth's dangers rather than its attractions. The other force moves toward psychological growth by enhancing the perception of the rewards of growth, building confidence, and minimizing the dangers involved in taking growth risks.

Adapted from Maslow, A. H. 1968. *Toward a psychology of being* (2nd ed.). NY: D. Van Nostrand Co., p. 47.

and B-needs. **D-needs**, or deficiency needs, are the motivations to reduce tension by meeting requirements for physiological survival and safety. D-needs are powerful determinants of behavior and must be satisfied before other needs can be considered. Thus, missionaries who are sent to poor countries often feed the people (meeting a D-need requirement) before they attempt to teach (meeting a B-need) because they are aware that very hungry people cannot be concerned with meeting spiritual needs.

B-needs, or being needs, are **metamotivations**, or growth tendencies. Metamotivational needs do not come from deficiencies but are "pushes" toward self-fulfillment. D-needs must be satisfied before individuals deal with B-needs, but individuals place more value on B-needs than on D-needs; for instance, earning an A on a composition paper is usually more satisfying than eating a cheeseburger. B-needs are opportunities for personality growth, creativity, and pride. According to Maslow, pursuing B-needs also leads to better mental health and greater uniqueness among people (Maslow, 1968).

People like to pursue B-needs and if the environment is sufficiently supportive they will continue to express themselves in new and positive ways. Maslow believed that people's basic nature makes them work toward fulfilling their highest potential; this tendency he called **self-actualization**. Self-actualization is an idealized goal that individuals spend a lifetime working toward rather than achieve at any one time.

Rogers' Self Theory

Carl Ransom Rogers (1902–1987) was the fourth of six children in a middle-class family in suburban Chicago. He considered careers in agriculture, history, and religion but while attending seminary classes he enrolled in psychology courses at Columbia University, receiving his doctoral degree in counseling psychology in 1931.

Rogers worked for the Society for the Prevention of Cruelty to Children in New York, taught, and wrote. Later he was associated with Ohio State University, the University of Chicago, and the University of Wisconsin. He developed a personality theory called **self theory** (Rogers, 1951) and a therapy called client-centered counseling (see Chapter 24).

Human Nature   Carl Rogers may have been the most optimistic of personality theorists. He assumed human nature is good and all people possess an **actualizing tendency**, a tendency to grow in positive ways once circumstances are supportive. Rogers emphasized that people are the best judges of what they should do with their lives and all have the capacity for self-improvement. Rogers' approach is reflected in his quoting (1961) of the ancient Chinese philosopher Lao-Tse, "If I keep from imposing on people, they become themselves."

Self   Rogers emphasized the **self**, or integrated person. The self results from an interaction of the organism and environment. This self is not a frozen entity but is always in process, changing minor aspects of itself so that the whole pattern of the self is altered.

Each person has an image of an **ideal self**, which represents the person one would most like to be (the term is equivalent to Freud's concept of ego ideal). As shown in Exhibit 15.6, **congruence** occurs when similarity exists between the real and ideal self, between

EXHIBIT 15.5
IN HIS OWN WORDS. Quotations from Rogers' Writings

> "...The basic nature of the human being, when functioning freely, is constructive and trustworthy."
> (1969)

> "We live by a perceptual 'map' which is never reality itself."
> (1951)

> "The good life is a process, not a state of being. It is a direction, not a destination."
> (1961)

> "...it is the client who knows what hurts, what directions to go, what problems are crucial, what experiences have been deeply buried."
> (1961)

> "In my relationships with persons I have found that it does not help, in the long run, to act as though I were something that I am not."
> (1961)

> "'Am I living in a way which is deeply satisfying to me, and which truly expresses me?' This I think is perhaps the most important question for the creative individual."
> (1961)

EXHIBIT 15.6
Congruence & Incongruence

CONGRUENT   INCONGRUENT

In a congruent individual, consistency between awareness and experience and between real self and ideal self exists. In an incongruent individual, major differences between awareness and experience exist and real and ideal self overlap only slightly.

experience, awareness, and expression of what one is and what one wants to be. **Incongruence** exists when the real and ideal selves are quite dissimilar and self-awareness and self-expression are inconsistent. Incongruences lead to psychological vulnerability and maladjustment. A person becomes dissatisfied, anxious, and depressed when the ideal self differs too much from the real self.

A significant difference between ideal and real selves may prevent an individual from trying to be more like the ideal self because failure seems certain. Instead, he or she may repress or deny aspects of the idealized self. Thus, a C-student may push out of awareness his or her desire to earn all A's and B's rather than experience the anxiety of not reaching a desired goal. On the other hand, when some similarity between ideal and real selves exists, the ideal self becomes an image toward which the person can strive. A college student whose ideal self earns all A's and B's may be more likely to work toward this goal if, during the previous semester, he or she earned all B's and one C than if he or she earned all C's and one D.

Rogers believed that all people would like to decrease incongruence and strive to be more like their ideal selves and that individuals achieve this goal if the environment supports their task. The goal of life is to become a fully functioning person by moving toward the image of the ideal self.

Fully Functioning Person   Rogers (1961) defined the **fully functioning person** as accomplishing the task of being

Mother Teresa's life seems to exemplify Rogers' suggestions for moving toward becoming a fully-functioning person.

one's true self. Conditions that help produce fully functioning persons are genuineness (congruence), empathic understanding, and unconditional positive regard (acceptance) from others. These conditions are the bases of the Rogerian client-centered counseling you will read about in Chapter 24.

To move toward becoming fully functioning persons, Rogers suggested, people must be willing to drop their masks or roles, give up self-concealment, and become more congruent. They must also stop fulfilling someone else's goals for their lives and learn how to please themselves, trust themselves, and make their own decisions in life. Not only should people not live their lives according to their family's and friends' prescriptions, but they should not automatically follow cultural expectations. They must trust themselves to know what to do with their own lives. Along with trusting themselves, people must accept others and the choices others make in their own lives (Rogers, 1961).

Focus Question Answer

Is your basic human nature positive, negative, or neutral? Just as you might disagree with other students' answers to this question, psychologists hold different positions. Your answer might influence which of the personality theories you prefer. Rogers and Maslow are typical of humanists, who believe that human nature is basically

positive. Freud's psychoanalytic theory is the most negative about human nature. Adler, a psychodynamic theorist, seems as positive as the humanists, while Jung takes a balanced approach that human nature is both good and bad. Typically, behaviorists such as Skinner, Bandura, and Rotter assume that human nature is neutral and whether people act positively or not depends on environmental forces. The existentialists, about whom you will read next, also take a neutral position but believe that you, rather than the environment, determine whether your nature is good or bad.

 ## Existential Theories

May's Existential Theory

Existentialism is a reaction against the idea of understanding humanness through only reason and thought; the position advocates adding emotional substance to human intellectual life. This approach emphasizes the freedom and responsibility of human lives and views life as a "process of becoming and emerging." In this section, you will learn about terms and concepts shared by all existential psychologists, including the popular contemporary existential psychologist Rollo May (1909–).

Rollo May was born in the Midwest into an anti-intellectual family, and May's career has been a reaction against that early attitude. During college, he edited a radical student magazine and studied art and philosophy, a background visible in all his writings. After graduation, he taught in Greece and also studied in Vienna under Alfred Adler. Back in America, because he found psychology simplistic, May enrolled in seminary classes to learn about important life issues that psychologists seemed to ignore—despair, suicide, purpose, and anxiety.

After serving briefly as a Congregational minister, he studied psychoanalysis and clinical psychology. His interest in existentialism mushroomed from his reading in existential philosophy when he spent three years in a sanatorium recuperating from tuberculosis. May emphasizes the importance of values within psychology and bridges the disciplines of philosophy and psychology.

Alienation   Central to May's existential theory is the concept of **alienation**, which occurs when people feel separated from an important part of existence and feel "cut off" from themselves, their roots, institutions, society, or God. May (1953) referred to alienation as emptiness or hollowness. Hollow people are indecisive, do not know their own desires and wants, and operate according to what they think they *should* want or what they think *others* want from them. Their alienation derives from a sense of powerlessness and produces loneliness. Alienated people usually feel lonely whenever they are physically alone, and being around people provides only a temporary sense of purpose in life.

Authenticity   May's term **authenticity** is equivalent to Maslow's self-actualization or Rogers's fully functioning person. According to May, authentic individuals have overcome alienation by accepting responsibility for their own lives and by taking risks beyond their typical natures and styles. To be authentic means to get out of typical "ruts" in life and try new experiences and challenges. You may have encountered college students who feel exhilarated and challenged by their decision to get their college degree and who may even say "I'm in college to find the real me."

In the process of becoming authentic, people must realize they are their own victims; decisions and circumstances they do not like are the results of their own shortcomings and faulty decision-making rather than actions that were "done" to them. Authentic people take full responsibility for both the good and the bad that occur in their lives. Interestingly, this recognition of personal responsibility is an important step in the recovery process of programs such as Alcoholics Anonymous.

In contrast, a person who avoids responsibility complains about the unfairness and cruelty of the circumstances into which he or she was born and places the responsibility for his or her life on **dasein**, the particular setting of one's life. Existentialists view dasein as a given with which people must work rather than use as an excuse. Avoiding, denying, or distorting dasein creates mental problems. In other words, people who blame their problems on poor parenting, poverty, being in the military, or having a learning disability are using their circumstances to excuse their own shortcomings and to avoid the work involved in improving their own lives.

Faulting dasein for one's life may lead to **anonymity**, the state of being anonymous or faceless. You experience anonymity when you have feelings of "being a nobody" or of "being only a face in the crowd." To avoid the unpleasantness of anonymity, people are driven to self-esteem, creativity, and finding meaning in life. Existentialists believe that anonymity can be countered by acts of **passion**, behaviors in which the person is completely involved emotionally. Passionate acts may involve artistic creations, involvement in political movements, participation in dance or theater, or achievements in a meaningful career. Regardless of the type of activity, implementing passion reduces neurotic symptoms. Unfortunately, the civilized, mechanized, modern world offers limited opportunities for passion, and some people

EXHIBIT 15.7
IN HIS OWN WORDS. Quotations from May's Writings

"A person's world cannot be comprehended by describing the environment, no matter how complex we make our description."
(1983)

"It is a startling fact that freedom has been considered, throughout human history, so precious that hundreds of thousands of human beings have willingly died for it."
(1981)

"The encounter with the being of another person has the power to shake one profoundly and may potentially be very anxiety-arousing. It may also be joy-creating."
(1983)

"Men and women devote themselves to making money when they cannot get gratification from making anything else."
(1981)

"Problems are the outward signs of unused inner possibilities."
(1981)

"Anxiety occurs because of a threat to the values a person identifies with his existence as a self."
(1967)

"What, then, shall we do? The only answer is: Be compassionate. The universality of evil makes human compassion necessary."
(1981)

decide that their only acts of passion are violent, destructive acts; for them, arguments and fights that involve anger and hatred may seem more passionate than constructive, healthy behaviors. Existentialists believe that every individual must search for constructive ways to act passionately because only constructive passion leads to a renewed self and an improved society.

Existential theories, then, emphasize commitment to behavior because ideas are useless unless they are acted upon. Acting equals taking responsibility and becomes an expression of passion and joy. The person who only reads about life is incomplete; the person who learns about life by experiencing a variety of life's events is fully, passionately alive. As a college student, studying, writing, and memorizing may be nonpassionate acts for you, and you may believe internships, field trips, and special, emotion-arousing speakers the more valuable aspects of your education. What can you do so more aspects of your college learning reflect passion and commitment?

Existentialists stress the importance of creating meaning in life, living passionately, and accepting the circumstances of one's existence.

Emotions and Personal Growth   Existentialists also believe that people are forced to confront two unsolvable, inescapable dilemmas in life: the limitations of the self and the certainty of death. Although people try to repress these dilemmas, eventually people must deal with them. In doing so, they experience **dread**, a long-lasting fear that can be defined as the fear of fear. Sometimes dread is so overwhelming that it leads to despair (the loss of all hope), which leads to depression and thoughts of suicide.

Fortunately, despair usually comes in waves and can be temporarily relieved by a person's becoming more dependent upon others or becoming closer in intimate relationships. A more satisfying and longer-lasting way to resolve feelings of despair is to make a commitment to living fully and passionately. If a person makes this choice, dread and despair lead to personal growth instead of depression. The person, aware of personal limitations, permits himself or herself to act even though the actions are imperfect; the person feels comfortable in expanding personal knowledge, even though knowledge about the self and the world must be imperfect. Because the person knows that death is a certainty and can occur at any moment, he or she decides to live each moment as completely and courageously as possible. As May (1953) has asked, "Does not the uncertainty of our time teach us the most important lesson of all—that the ultimate criteria are the honesty, integrity, courage, and love of a given moment of relatedness?" (p. 235).

The negative emotions of dread and despair are necessary to make a person "work through" the important questions of life's meaning, and, once a person has addressed these questions, he or she can make commitments to fulfill his or her dasein. This acceptance of one's unique and special life leads to joy, the most powerful human emotion. May has written, "Joy is the affect which comes when we use our powers. Joy, rather than happiness, is the goal of life, for joy is the emotion which accompanies our fulfilling our natures as human beings" (May, 1953, p. 84).

The alternative to joy is **existential anxiety**, an anxiety that results from perceiving that the self is distinct from the rest of the world and is therefore alone. Individuals experience anxiety when they are separated from their essential values, separation that leads to lack of security. Existential anxiety occurs when people get "stuck" between wanting-to-be and not-wanting-to-be (as if Hamlet had said, "To be and not to be") and creates barriers to creativity, passion, and intimacy. May (1977) believes that the competitive American culture increases anxiety because competitiveness isolates people from other human beings (increasing the essential loneliness involved with existential anxiety) and turns human beings into objects whose values depend solely on winning. People unsuccessfully try to fill this emptiness and lack of value with identity gained through possessions, drugs, or powerful, authoritarian political movements.

The Self and Freedom   Like other existentialists, May (1967) believes that each person creates his or her own self through experience and through relationships with other people. Part of the self is, of course, involved with preservation of one's own life, but a second part needs to relate and participate with other people. A third part of the self wants knowledge about the self and the world. The final part of the self wishes to transcend the immediate experience of life and find meaning and growth.

Because each aspect of creating the self entails risk, effort, and disappointment, people establish barriers against self-growth. May (1967) suggests that self-deception, misunderstanding experiences, and putting events out of conscious awareness prevents people from establishing true self-identities. These barriers are no longer needed when people take full responsibility for the tragedies or shortcomings in their lives. May (1953) suggests that the first step in breaking down barriers around the self is to rediscover feelings. Most people are out of touch with their feelings and need to increase awareness by simply asking themselves several times a day, "What am I feeling right now? What bodily sensations are occurring right now?"

May (1981) believes in both destiny and freedom. Destiny is a person's family, societal, and cultural background and his or her talents; destiny provides resources for living and also establishes limitations to life. Within the confines of one's ultimate destiny—death—are unlimited opportunities for freedom, choosing to pursue personal growth and to decide one's values. Although some people confuse freedom with rebellion or destruction, May envisions freedom as the positive capacity to mold the self and be open and ready to grow (May, 1953). People who are not ready for the responsibility of freedom often choose to abdicate freedom and conform to authority figures.

Perls' Gestalt Theory

Fritz Perls (1893–1970) had a colorful personality—he was the black sheep of his family, a drifter through Europe

and America, and, toward the end of his life, "psychology's guru." Despite a poor early educational record, Perls managed to graduate from medical school, specializing in psychiatry.

In 1926, he worked at the Institute for Brain-Injured Soldiers, where he gained an appreciation for people as whole, integrated beings. The following year, he went to Vienna for psychoanalytic training. In 1933, Perls fled Naziism, going first to Holland and then to South Africa. He returned briefly to Germany in 1936 to meet with Sigmund Freud and expected to be welcomed into Freud's

EXHIBIT 15.8
IN HIS OWN WORDS. Quotations from Perls' Writings

"A gestalt is an irreducible phenomenon. It is an essence that is there and that disappears if the whole is broken up into its components."
(1969b)

"Explanations don't help much in understanding."
(1969b)

"Most people take explaining as being identical with understanding. There is a great difference."
(1969a)

"Emotions are the very life of us."
(1973)

"I think there is a race going on between humanism and fascism, and I am very much in doubt as to the outcome of that race. . . . The humanist tends to live for self-actualization and to be alive. The fascist lives for exerting control and for making things out of people. I'm afraid the fascists are progressing more rapidly."
(Anderson, 1973)

circle of close friends; instead, Freud granted him only a four-minute interview. Perls's displeasure and disappointment with the meeting induced him to move away from psychoanalysis and to incorporate ideas from existentialism and Zen Buddhism into his theoretical framework (Anderson, 1973).

Perls wrote *Gestalt Therapy* in 1951 and founded the New York Institute for Gestalt Therapy in 1952. He first developed gestalt therapy and then addressed the issues of gestalt personality theory (Perls, 1973). Perls used the label *gestalt*, because he adapted the assumptions of gestalt psychologists' perception research (See Chapter 6) into personality areas (Henle, 1985). The gestalt personality theory combines features of existential theory, humanistic theory, and Zen Buddhism philosophy.

The Philosophical Approaches Perls (1970, 1973) believed in the existence of four basic philosophical approaches to understanding one's self and the world. The most common philosophy today is **science**, which Perls called "about-ism." According to Perls, the scientific approach attempts to remove emotional and genuine involvement with life, and its goal is interpretation. As a result, many individuals define themselves in terms of which aspects in their pasts determine their present personalities, but they fail to include emotions as a major element of their personalities.

A second philosophical approach is **religion**, which Perls labeled "should-ism." Perls believed "should-ism" is an overt or covert aspect of nearly all philosophies and religions. The religious approach is based on the experience of dissatisfaction and emphasizes self-improvement and unequal relationships in which someone has the power to tell another person how to live. This approach is useful in building awareness of values and ideals but often leaves people dissatisfied with their present life experiences.

Existentialism is the third approach. Existentialism, or "is-ism," involves an external attempt to achieve truth. Existentialists play "fitting games" by asking the question, "Does this concept fit reality?" The existential approach contributes much to Perls' theory because both existentialism and gestalt emphasize emotional awareness and expression, acting fully and passionately in life and the importance of constructing one's own selfhood. Yet, Perls believed that existentialists are too concerned with trying to answer the question "Why?"

He thought that the fourth, and most appropriate, philosophical approach was the **gestalt** ("how-ism"), which tries to understand human existence by asking

how instead of *why*. According to this approach, rather than attempt to discover the meaning of life or the reasons for one's existence, human beings should strive to live fully each moment. The process, or the *how*, of one's life is all that matters. In some ways, then, gestalt theory provides the existentialist with guidelines for practical daily processing of life. Perls believed that only by following the assumptions of his philosophical approach and theory would people live complete and full lives.

The Here-and-Now A primary assumption of gestalt theory (Perls et al., 1951; Perls, 1973) is that the only important aspect of time is the present, the **here-and-now**. The here-and-now equals true reality, and one's awareness should center on the present moment. Perls believed that healthy persons fully attend to immediate feelings and impulses and avoid both future expectations and past conditioning, thereby reducing both disappointments and anxieties. The concept of the here-and-now is similar to nonwestern personality philosophies, which influenced Perls theory; you can read about these philosophies in the *Exploring . . .* section.

Gestalt psychologists believe that focusing on the present also frees people from psychological enslavement by other people. In other words, relationships with other people should develop because of the joys and responsibilities of the relationships rather than because of obligations established in the past. The concept is summed up in Fritz Perls's *Gestalt Prayer* presented in Exhibit 15.9. Many people have embraced this verse as a liberating, humanizing plea for allowing people to live their own lives fully. Others interpret this verse as a selfish expression of the "Let me get mine, and you go find your own" philosophy of the "Me Decade." How do you interpret the Gestalt Prayer?

Quick Study Aid

Perls' Philosophical Approaches

To remember Perls' four philosophical approaches, rearrange the approaches and their brief definitions into the silly sentence:

ERGS IS HA.

ERGS are the four philosophical approaches—existentialism, religion, gestalt, and science; IS HA are the brief definitions in corresponding order "is-ism," "should-ism," "how-ism," and "about-ism".

Exploring...

Eastern Philosophies of Personality

Ideas about personality based on eastern religions and philosophies have different emphases than do western concepts of personality. Typically, eastern personality theories accentuate values, moral development, spiritual guidelines, living by "right patterns," and effort over results. Compared to the scientific nature of western personality theories, eastern views seem more magic- and religion-oriented. Because of these differences, only a few psychologists have integrated western and eastern ideas about human nature. Of the theorists you have read about in these two chapters on personality, Carl Jung and Fritz Perls have been most influenced by eastern philosophies.

Transcendence, or transpersonal experience, is a primary concept in eastern theories. According to transcendence, the individual is only a small unit of a much larger consciousness. A Hindu analogy is that a person is a wave, and the universe is the ocean. The wave represents the shape of the ocean for only a few moments of eternity; when the wave departs, all its elements remain as a part of the ocean (Frager & Fadiman, 1984). In other words, although your life is a short experience, your existence is always part of the universe. Embracing this point of view, most people in eastern religions place less importance on the individual ego than do western individuals.

Another influence of the concept of transcendence on western thought is found in Jung's idea of the collective unconscious. Jung believed that all individuals tap into the same source of human potential (as the wave is connected to the ocean). Like his eastern counterparts, Jung believed that individuals could learn to use this common source to enjoy richer, more creative and sharing lives.

A second primary eastern concept is **karma**, the deterministic belief that all actions have consequences. According to karma, every person is influenced by past actions, and present actions modify the future. Many westerners do not realize that karma can be positive as well as negative. The Hindu religion teaches that people can improve their karmas, thereby improving future circumstances, by becoming more positive in subconscious and conscious thoughts and by doing good acts. Similarities exist between karma and behaviorists' belief in actions leading to conse-

Eastern personality theories emphasize that each individual is a temporary representation of the entire universe.

quences and belief that expectancies influence behavioral choices. However, karma is presented as a more absolute and longer-term principle of life (since Hinduists believe in reincarnation, karma may influence future lives as well as one's present life).

Eastern philosophies of personality tend to be pragmatic in nature; that is, they provide guidelines for daily living. In yoga, for example, disciplined practice is developed to overcome the personal growth obstacles of ignorance, egoism, desire, aversion, and fear and to reach higher states of consciousness. Several varieties of yoga exist, with each variety building one area of discipline. In Hatha-Yoga, the body is purified and strengthened through postures, breathing and concentration exercises, and vegetarian diet. Karma-Yoga emphasizes action and serving others to overcome selfishness, laziness, and pride. Other forms of yoga teach discipline in devotion, knowledge, meditation, and mental control. While personality theories

EXHIBIT 15.9
The Gestalt Prayer

I do my thing, and you do your thing.
I am not in this world to live up to your expectations.
And you are not in this world to live up to mine.
You are you and I am I,
And if by chance we find each other, it's beautiful.
If not, it can't be helped.

Perls, F.S. 1969. *Gestalt therapy verbatin*. Lafayette, CA: The Real People Press.

(and the therapies developed from personality theories) do not demand a commitment as long-term as the practice of yoga, within psychology you can find advocates who suggest building skills in each of these areas to achieve personality growth.

The most direct eastern influence on gestalt theory is Zen Buddhism, which posits that the three characteristics of existence are impermanence, selfishness, and dissatisfaction, and the three obstacles to personal growth are greed, hatred, and delusion. Both Zen Buddhism and gestalt teach techniques that help individuals dismiss **maya** (illusion), accept reality, and decrease obstacles to growth. For example, both advocate living in the present, or here-and-now, because "the past is no more, and the future not yet," and both demand that followers give up resentments and regrets about past events. The techniques by which gestalt therapists teach their way of living will be discussed in Chapter 24; Zen Buddhists teach their way of living through the Four Noble Truths and the Noble Eight-Fold Path.

The Four Noble Truths are (1) Dissatisfaction exists; (2) Dissatisfaction is the result of desires or cravings; (3) Elimination of desires can eliminate suffering; (4) Living according to the Noble Eight-Fold Path can eliminate desires. The eight guidelines of the Noble Eight-Fold Path are right speech, right action, right livelihood, right effort, right mindfulness, right concentration, right thought, and right understanding (Suzuki, 1970). Again, many psychologists, especially those discussed in this chapter, advocate (in their own terminology) one or more aspects of these eight guidelines as a way to improve oneself.

What can you learn about personality if you study nonwestern philosophies? First, you can see which eastern ideas have already influenced western philosophies. Carl Rogers has adapted from Chinese philosophers the idea that each person can best decide what direction to take in life. Perls adopted the Zen Buddhism belief that living in the past or the future is an illusion. Second, if you read more about eastern philosophies, you will see a contrasting way to view the world. The west has a tendency to emphasis the individual, but the east views the individual as merely a temporary speck in the universal soul.

Psychological Growth   According to gestalt theory, psychologically healthy and mature individuals are self-supportive and self-regulating rather than dependent upon other people, the environment, or the past. People can grow psychologically by achieving closure or "finishing unfinished business," by making peace with old hurts and misgivings, by resolving issues, or by reaching compromises on issues. Closure involves forgiving negative feelings created by past events and relationships.

Perls (1973) suggested that closure is most difficult to reach in parent-child relationships, yet "finishing unfinished business" in this relationship is important for psychological growth. Each person has the task of relegating to the past the childlike, selfish, and dependent relationship with his or her parents and creating in the present a mature, equal relationship. Because of the nature of parent-child relationships, children feel guilt toward their parents (because parents do more for their children than their children can ever do for the parents), and children feel resentment toward their parents (because parents cannot meet all their children's needs and desires). Thus, adult offspring may harbor feelings of "owing parents" or "being owed by parents." According to Perls, to be psychologically healthy, individuals need to resolve "owing" relationships by realizing that between parents and children neither party "owes" the other. This realization leads to a sense of gratefulness toward parents and permits a complete and good relationship with them.

The process of psychological growth is a life-long process involving becoming in touch with all aspects of one's experience—actions, cognitions, and emotions. In the modern western world, most people have alienated their true feelings; much of the gestalt focus involves learning to express feelings.

Focus Question Answer

What would living in the here-and-now be like? You, like most people, spend much of your time planning for future events and some of your time reminiscing about the past. Sometimes your attention to the future or the past makes you unaware of the fullness of your experiences at the present moment. Stop right now, and focus on the totality of the moment. What are you perceiving through your senses and in your body? What are your thoughts? What are your feelings? What are you doing? Here and now, what is the integration of all the inputs of the moment?

 *Relate*

Zeitgeist and the Personality Theories

Zeitgeist means the spirit of the time—the moral and intellectual trend of any age or period. The personality theorists you have read about in Chapters 14 and 15 have been influenced by their zeitgeist, and the major theorists have also been able to influence the zeitgeist.

Sigmund Freud presents a good example of the impact of an era on a theorist. Today his theory seems to overemphasize sexuality, but people in the Victorian era in which he lived so repressed sexuality that sexual problems were more central to personality development. Also, during the Victorian era, the Protestant Work Ethic was very strong, and people were encouraged to postpone sexual behavior and marriage until age thirty and to spend the young adult years becoming productive and economically stable. This cultural attitude may be one reason Freud emphasized sublimation in his theory.

Another influence of the Victorian zeitgeist is revealed in Freud's use of energy and drive concepts in his theory. During the era in which Freud developed psychoanalysis, physics was considered the ideal, most advanced science. Other sciences tried to gain respectability by using terms resembling those employed in physics. Thus, concepts like libido and thanatos gained credibility because they were defined in terms of energy and drives.

Freud postulated only one main drive, the libido (or life drive), until the events of World War I. Influenced by the destruction and violence of the war, he then proposed the existence of thanatos or death drive. Perhaps if peace had lasted throughout his lifetime, Freud would have continued to propose only a life-affirming drive.

Once developed, Freud's theory was read and practiced by others. Psychoanalytic theory significantly influenced the ways in which people thought about themselves and other people. People incorporated Freud's ideas into their own beliefs about humanity (MacIntyre, 1985). Some ideas, such as unconscious motivation, existed before Freud, but the popularity of his theory brought the concept into zeitgeist. The ideas of Freud and his followers have been so incorporated into our moral and intellectual beliefs that many of their terms have become part of everyday language. People who have never taken a psychology course may chat about their erogenous zones, Freudian slips, subconscious ideas, sibling rivalry, introverted natures, birth order, superegos, and egos. Now that these terms are popular, conceptualizing what people are like without thinking in such terms is difficult.

Radical behaviorism was very popular during the 1920s and again during the 1960s. In both time periods, the zeitgeist was optimistic and youth-, change-, and progress-oriented. Behavior modification seemed to provide a good route for progress—change the environment, change the world! Learning theories provided the means for the unlimited improvement of humanity. Behaviorism also fit the zeitgeist of elevating empirical science above subjective experience. Many people in those decades believed that scientific research held the answers and they therefore perceived the world largely in scientific rather than religious terms.

Humanism evolved out of the destruction of World War II as psychologists and others searched for new beginnings and new faith in people. Humanism also was a counterresponse to the zeitgeist established by Freud's theory. Psychoanalytic theory emphasizes society's need to put controls on people; humanistic theory emphasizes people's need to grow beyond the restraints society places on them. Freudian theory emphasizes the past; humanism emphasizes the future. Psychoanalytic theory emphasizes the negative side of human nature, while humanism accentuates the positive side.

The emphasis on the biological aspects of personality seem to cycle in and out of favor in the zeitgeist of eras. Freud and type theorists place more emphasis on biology than do behaviorists and trait theorists. Currently, physiological aspects of behavior are a major trend. The biochemical and physiological emphasis in modern psychology is reinforced by the biotechnical developments of the last two decades.

Another aspect of the current zeitgeist is the emphasis

Circle the issues you think are most likely to influence events and the moral, intellectual, and emotional climate over the next decade.

Materialism	Equal rights	Spirituality
Educational opportunities	World peace	Animal rights
Global financial crisis	Violence	World hunger
Sexual permissiveness	Authoritarianism	Prejudice
Risk of nuclear war	Technology	Pollution
Religion in politics	Crime	Family size
Higher standard of living	Unemployment	A.I.D.S.
Two-career families	Terrorism	Atheism
Getting "back to basics"	Advances in science	Communism
Homosexual rights	Military spending	Illiteracy
Censorship	Patriotism	Farm crisis
Better health care	Homelessness	Fascism
Urban living	Crowding	Alien beings
More leisure time	Media influence	Divorce rate

on cognitive psychology. Developed in the 1960s in the work of Bandura and Rotter, cognitive psychology is now visible in the popularity of cognitive behaviorism, thinking strategies, and progress in intelligence testing (see Chapter 20). Perhaps the popularity of the computer has stimulated this trend.

What are the major trends in American culture today? How would you describe the zeitgeist? What changes in moral, intellectual, and emotional climate do you expect in the next decade? How might these changes influence psychological theory and research? Use the above list to indicate your personal beliefs about current cultural trends.

Based on your answers above, how might the zeitgeist influence psychology? Predict your answer here:

_____

_____

_____

_____

_____

Compare your predictions with those of other students in the class.

_____

Things to Do

1. Read a play or novel written by an existential philosopher (e.g., Jean-Paul Sartre's play *No Exit* or Albert Camus' novel *The Stranger*). How does the work reflect the existential concepts described in this chapter?

2. Try to spend one day focusing on the here-and-now as described in gestalt theory. What was your experience like? What difficulties did you encounter?

3. Make a list of the generalized expectancies and specific expectancies that most influence your behavior potential as a student.

4. Throughout a day, investigate the reasons for your behaviors. Do you do what you like, and do you like what you do? How aware are you of the choices you make throughout the day? (When you get up in the morning, do you really want to get up? Do you eat the breakfast you would like to eat or the one your culture tells you to eat?) How many of your activities do you freely choose to do?

5. According to the following traits, assess your real self and your ideal self. Rank yourself on a 1 to 5 scale with 1 = low, 2 = below average, 3 = medium, 4 = above average, and 5 = high. Assess your congruence level.

cheerful	persistent	responsible
restless	demanding	snobbish
honest	excitable	mature
brave	ambitious	calm
serious	friendly	artistic
humorous	intelligent	idealistic
understanding	warm	sensuous
opinionated	affectionate	selfish

Things to Discuss

1. What are the similarities and differences between Maslow's metamotivational theory and Rogers' self theory?

2. Which of the personality theories seem to be compatible with various political beliefs? Since all these theories have been developed by Europeans or Americans, what aspects of the theories reflect western assumptions about the world?

3. All the personality theorists discussed in Chapters 14 and 15 are males. Do you think their theoretical ideas describe both male and female personality? What concepts might be modified if postulated by female psychologists?

4. How would you modify public schools and colleges according to the concepts of behaviorism? Humanism? Existentialism?

5. The existentialists suggest that awareness of inevitable death provides motivation to live life more fully. Imagine that you had died and then were granted one more day on earth. How would you spend that day? Why? How similar is your imagined last day to your typical day now? Would increasing your awareness of life's brevity improve the way you spend your time?

6. Using the ideas you expressed in the *Relate* section, which of the personality theories do you think will still be popular at the start of the twenty-first century? Why?

7. An eclectic theorist selects and combines ideas from various theories. If you were an eclectic theorist, which ideas would you select from the various personality theories presented in Chapters 14 and 15? What assumptions influence your choices? Can you integrate your selections into a cohesive and compatible framework?

Things to Read

Maslow, A.H. 1968. *Toward a psychology of being* (2nd Ed.). NY: Van Nostrand.

May, R. 1983. *The discovery of being.* NY: Norton.

May, R. 1967. *Psychology and the human dilemma.* NY: Norton.

Perls, F.S. 1969. *In and out of the garbage pail.* Lafayette, CA: The Real People Press.

Rogers, C. 1980. *A way of being.* Boston: Hougton Mifflin.

May, R., Rogers, C., Maslow, A. et al. 1986. *Politics and innocence: A Humanistic debate.* NY: Norton.

Skinner, B.F. 1983. *A matter of consequences.* NY: Knopf.

Suzuki, S. 1970. *Zen mind, beginner's mind.* NY: Weatherhill.

 ## Review

Summary

1. Behavioristic personality theorists focus on the influence of learning and environment on personality. Radical behaviorists like B. F. Skinner do not consider internal aspects such as feelings, motives, and cognitions because internal aspects are not useful in predicting behavior.

2. Bandura's social learning theory emphasizes the role of reciprocal determinism and observational learning on personality. Bandura's theory is based on experimental research and has influenced the cognitive psychology movement.

3. Rotter's cognitive learning theory states that people can estimate the likelihood of a specific behavior by knowing an individual's expectancies and reinforcement values in a particular situation.

4. Humanistic theories emphasize subjective experiences, the self, and free will. These theories postulate behavior as goal-directed and purposeful.

5. Maslow's metamotivational theory assumes that human nature is neutral or good and should be encouraged rather than repressed. Supportive environments help individuals grow positively and progress toward their potentials.

6. Rogers's self theory starts with the assumption that human nature is good. People have an actualizing tendency, a tendency to grow in positive ways. People compare themselves with their ideal selves and experience dissatisfaction and anxiety when ideal selves and real selves are different. Congruence occurs when experience, awareness, and expression are consistent.

7. Existentialism emphasizes that people experience anonymity and alienation in their lives and instead need to become authentic. People need to deal with dread, despair, and anxiety and learn to experience joy, which results when people accept their lives and commit themselves to developing their creative selves.

8. Gestalt personality theory emphasizes living in the present moment and integrating all aspects of behavior, thoughts, and emotions.

9. All personality theorists are influenced by their zeitgeist, the spirit and outlook that are characteristic of an era.

Key Terms

radical behaviorism
parsimony
reciprocal determinism
anticipated outcomes
observational learning
behavior potential
expectancy
locus of control
reinforcement value
minimal goal
delay of gratification
D-needs
B-needs
metamotivations
self theory

actualizing tendency
ideal self
congruence
incongruence
fully functioning person
existentialism
alienation
authenticity
dasein
anonymity
existential anxiety
here-and-now
transcendence
karma
zeitgeist

Part Five

Interactive
Behaviors

Focus Questions

1. Has your development been an orderly or haphazard process?

2. What risks are involved with unplanned pregnancies?

3. What factors have influenced your identity as male or female?

4. Do you think about questions of morality just as someone of the opposite sex does?

5. Are parents who push their children to be superbabies harming them?

Chapter Outline

Chapter 16

Development: Infancy to Adolescence

*Life can only be understood
backwards, but must be lived
forwards.*

Sören Kierkegaard

 ## The Study of Human Development

These next two chapters will allow you to organize information about human behavior in a new way—along the dimension of the human lifespan. The study of human development focuses on the ongoing interaction of behavioral processes that result in developmental changes across time. You will read about important physical, cognitive, and psychosocial changes occurring at different stages in the lifespan. Each area of change is interactive; it acts upon the other areas and results in the cumulative change that is called development.

Developmental psychologists study these cumulative changes as they occur from conception to death. Lifespan human development studies look for similarities and dif-

379

ferences in human development and attempt to sort out the interactions of the major developmental forces of heredity and environment. Changes continue throughout the lifespan—both growth and decline. The inappropriateness of viewing childhood and adolescence as the primary growth periods and adulthood and old age as the primary decline periods should be readily apparent as you contemplate your own continued growth as an adult.

Developmental Perspectives

Over the years, several influential viewpoints have emerged in psychology. Developmental psychologists, like other psychologists, adopt a particular perspective because it reflects their own understanding of fundamental issues about human behavior as well as provides a useful framework for organizing their study of development.

These various frameworks focus attention on specific aspects of development and reflect philosophical differences about its nature.

The **biological perspective** emphasizes understanding human biology in order to understand development. From this perspective, development involves the interaction of biological mechanisms. If you can fully understand how the human body functions, you can fully explain human developmental processes. A primary focus within this framework is comparative studies between humans and other animals.

The **psychodynamic perspective** stresses that development is the result of inner forces of which you are not normally aware. Developmental psychologists adopting this point of view maintain that humans are born with an innate set of forces that shape and determine their later development. This framework generally focuses on personality development. Freud's psychoanalytic theory

Developmental psychologists may study cross-cultural child-rearing practices to determine the influences on individual differences.

is an important example of the psychodynamic perspective, and his stages of psychosexual development represent one of the first formal theories of development.

The **behavioral-learning perspective** emphasizes environmental factors in explaining development. While this position acknowledges the presence of hereditary factors, it views development as largely determined by environment. Hereditary factors provide a blueprint for development, but environment provides the actual materials. Developmental psychologists adopting this perspective focus on the role of learning and experience in shaping development.

Unlike the behavioral-learning perspective, which in its extreme form sees humans as passive responders to their environment, the **cognitive perspective** emphasizes the individual's active role in influencing his or her development. Generally, this position focuses on the development of thinking and related intellectual abilities. Cognitive development occurs as one attempts to make sense of the world. From the cognitive viewpoint, humans actively select and process information about the world and construct a meaningful internal representation of their knowledge.

The **humanistic-existential perspective** also stresses humans' active role in their own development, and developmental psychologists use this framework when they want to emphasize humans' potential to directly influence their ongoing development. Social and personality development are of primary interest from this perspective. An underlying belief is that people make conscious choices that directly affect how they develop. Development results from striving to fulfill the potential for growth that each person possesses. Existentially, a person's development means whatever that person chooses it to mean.

While many developmental psychologists prefer one of these perspectives, most probably employ a final approach, the **eclectic perspective.** This position draws upon the strengths of each position to develop a comprehensive picture of human development. The eclectic developmental psychologist does have definite preferences among the perspectives but also recognizes the value of viewing development from more than one perspective.

Developmental Issues

Woven throughout the perspectives just outlined are basic issues about the nature of human development. At the root of these issues is the controversy about the relative

Do you attribute these children's behaviors and characteristics to heredity or to environmental influences? This debate, the "nature-nurture" issue, is very controversial among developmental psychologists.

impact of heredity and environment. The **nature-nurture issue** is not a simple question of which factor—nature or nurture—is more important; research has shown that most development depends upon both heredity (nature) and the environment (nurture) and that both factors are inextricably intertwined from the moment of conception onward.

The nature-nurture issue is often translated into the related issue of **maturational factors versus learning.** The behavioral-learning perspective emphasizes the role of environmental experience and learning, while the biological perspective stresses the effects of maturational forces. Because maturation and learning, like heredity and environment, are intertwined in development, their relative contributions are difficult to determine. Maturational factors cannot be halted in developing individuals while environmental factors are studied, and studying maturational factors in the absence of learning influences is equally impossible.

A third issue involves the **activity versus passivity** of individuals in their own development. The biological, behavioral-learning, and psychodynamic perspectives tend to view individuals as passive participants. In contrast, the cognitive and humanistic-existential frameworks clearly believe that humans play a direct role in their own development and actively structure the nature of their experience.

A general resolution of these issues is not likely, just as unanimous acceptance of one developmental perspective is unlikely. These fundamental ideas about the nature of development shape the ways in which psychologists study and explain the similarities and differences in people's development.

Developmental Principles

Although many different perspectives and issues exist within developmental psychology, certain basic principles are recognized. These principles apply both to physical and to behavioral development and serve as the foundation for understanding the cumulative changes of development. No matter how haphazard or chaotic your own development may seem to you, human development does proceed from a set of governing principles that influence everyone's behavior similarly.

— **Orderliness** Developmental change is orderly. Two types of orderly change are quantitative and qualitative change. **Quantitative change** is a measurable change in the developing person's physical system or behavior. Growing taller and gaining weight are easily recognized quantitative changes, or changes in quantity or amount. Increases in vocabulary size, running speed, and number of friends are also quantitative changes. **Qualitative change** denotes a change in quality or kind. A baby who advances from not walking to walking undergoes a qualitative change, as does someone who changes from being single to being married.

— **Directionality** Physical and behavioral development is directional. The term **cephalocaudal** refers to development from the head downward. Physically, cephalocaudal development is readily apparent in the early prenatal development of the head region and in the advanced development of the head region in contrast to other parts of the body. Behaviorally, a baby can hold its head up before it can sit up, and the baby can sit up before he or she can stand up. The development of these behaviors exhibits a definite "head-to-tail" progression. The term **proximodistal** indicates a development from the middle of the body outward to the extremities. Proximodistal development is evidenced in the prenatal development of the organs in the middle of the body before the full development of arms and legs.

— **Differentiation** Qualitative changes occur along two dimensions. In development, physical systems and behaviors change from **simple to complex.** Simpler systems are replaced with more complex units. Infants begin with a relatively simple language system that differentiates into a much more complex system. Similarly, the systems also change from **general to specific.** Initially a baby's cries are generalized and nonspecific. With maturation and experience, the baby's cries differentiate into specific cries for hunger, discomfort, and other states.

— **Readiness** Physical development precedes behavioral development. The development of physical systems makes possible the development of new behaviors. The toddler cannot walk alone until his or her muscles, bones, and nervous system have matured sufficiently to accommodate the behavior of walking. The principle of readiness implies that the individual's level of physical development will signal when he or she is ready for new behavioral development.

— **Critical periods** At different times during development, the individual will be sensitive to different influences from the environment. For example, during the first three months of prenatal development, the developing fetus is particularly sensitive to negative environmental influences. Drugs, diseases, and X-rays, for example, can have devastating consequences for the developing individual during this early critical period. Critical periods may also exist for developing attachment between the baby and his or her caregivers and for developing perceptual abilities.

— **Individual differences** While the sequence of developmental changes is assumed to be approximately the same for everyone, the rate at which the changes occur is unique for each person. This fundamental tenet of human development can easily be seen in the physical changes of adolescence. Nearly everyone experiences the same sequence of changes accompanying sexual maturation, but a period of months or years can separate the occurrence of those changes in different individuals.

Focus Question Answer

Has your development been an orderly or haphazard process? Despite contradictory personal perceptions you may have, a principle of development is orderliness, which can be seen in the orderly sequence of physical development and in the directionality of growth. Orderliness is also apparent in differentiation, which always proceeds from simple to complex and from general to specific.

 The Beginnings of Development

Since each person's existence is due to the prior existence of his or her parents and each preceding generation of ancestors, studying the beginnings of development first involves examining patterns of genetic inheritance. Beyond the issues of heredity, the process of conception is chosen as an arbitrary beginning point for the study of human development.

Genetic Factors in Development

The biological blueprint for development is contained in genetic information stored in the nucleus of every cell in the body. The genetic information is contained in **DNA,** deoxyribonucleic acid, which forms the hundreds of thousands of genes collected together on the twenty-three pairs of chromosomes found in the nucleus of every cell. The only exceptions to this pattern are sperm and egg cells, which contain only half the number of chromosomes.

Heredity, the genetic transmission of information from one generation to the next, follows definite patterns of inheritance that stem from a pairing of information. Different bases are paired together to form the genetic code contained in the DNA molecule. Segments of the DNA molecule form the genetic units called **genes.** Genes exist in pairs called **alleles** in corresponding locations on pairs of **chromosomes.**

Alleles determine the particular characteristics of a physical trait. The alleles may represent either dominant or recessive traits. When both alleles in a gene pair are dominant or both are recessive the person is said to be **homozygous** for the trait. A **heterozygous** trait exists when one allele is dominant and the other allele in a gene pair is recessive. The particular allele configuration a person inherits is called the **genotype.** When at least one dominant allele is present in the genotype, the dominant trait will be expressed in the individual's **phenotype,** or actual physical make-up. Recessive traits appear in the phenotype only when the individual has a homozygous recessive genotype. Exhibit 16.1 depicts the common patterns of dominant and recessive patterns of inheritance.

A heterozygous individual carries information about a recessive trait in his or her genotypes but does not display the trait in his or her actual physical make-up, or phenotype. The labels dominant and recessive can be misleading. Do not think of dominant traits as good traits and recessive traits as bad. Dominance and recessiveness refer only to the pattern of genetic transmission, not to the quality or worth of the transmitted trait. Brown eye color is a dominant trait, while blue eye color is a recessive trait. Similarly, dominant does not necessarily refer to the more prevalent traits in a population. Having more than ten fingers or toes is a dominant trait, but

---

Quick Study Aid

Keeping the Prefixes Straight

To remember the differences between homo- and hetero- and also geno- and pheno-, try these hints:

HOMO (as in homozygous) means the same—The two O's are the same.

HETERO (as in heterozygous) means different—The E and the O are different.

GENO (as in genotype) refers to genetic appearance—**GENO = GENETIC**.

PHENO (as in phenotype) refers to physical appearance—**PHENO = PHYSICAL**.

---

most people are homozygous recessive for this trait and exhibit exactly ten fingers and ten toes.

The configuration for the pair of chromosomes that determines the sex of an individual is different for males and females. The configuration for females is an X-X pairing. For males, the configuration is an X-Y pairing. Genes on these so-called sex chromosomes follow a different pattern of genetic transmission called **sex-linked inheritance.** Color blindness is an example of a sex-linked trait. The genetic information for normal color vision is carried on the X chromosome (because the Y chromosome is shorter, the corresponding allele on the Y chromosome does not exist). The gene pool in the population contains many dominant genes for normal color vision and few recessive genes for color blindness. When a female is conceived, the odds are quite good that at least one of the alleles on the X-X chromosomes will be dominant for normal color vision. When a male is conceived, if the X chromosome contains a recessive gene for color blindness, the child will develop color blindness because the Y chromosome will not contain a dominant gene to counteract the recessive gene. The common pattern of transmission for this and other sex-linked traits is for the female to be a carrier of the trait but for the trait to be exhibited only in males. Exhibit 16.2 illustrates the sex-linked pattern of inheritance.

The patterns of genetic transmission described thus far apply to traits determined by a single pair of gene alleles. However, many inherited traits are influenced by several pairs of genes. When several pairs of genes are involved in the determination of the trait, the trait is called **polygenic.** Skin pigmentation is an example of a polygenic trait. One gene pair determines the presence

EXHIBIT 16.1
Patterns of Dominant and Recessive Inheritance

One affected parent has a single faulty gene (**D**) which *dominates* its normal counterpart (**n**).

Both parents, usually unaffected, carry a normal gene (**N**) which takes precedence over its faulty recessive counterpart (**r**).

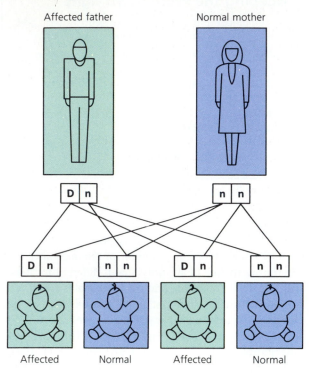

Each child's chances of inheriting either the **D** or the **n** from the affected parent are 50%.

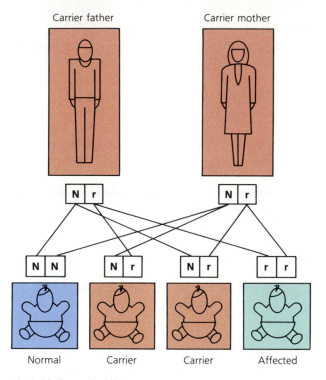

The odds for each child are:
1. a 25% risk of inheriting a "double dose" of **r** genes which may cause a serious birth defect.
2. A 25% chance of inheriting two **N**s, thus being unaffected.
3. A 50% chance of being a carrier as both parents are.

Dominant inheritance follows a pattern in which at least one parent must possess a dominant gene in his or her genotype before any of the parents' children will exhibit the dominant trait associated with that gene in their phenotypes. If both parents have at least one dominant gene for a particular trait, then the probability of any of their children exhibiting the trait is increased. If at least one parent has dominant genes on both alleles, the children will always exhibit the trait.

Recessive inheritance follows a pattern in which both parents must possess at least one recessive gene in order for any of their children to exhibit the recessive trait. Only when both parents have recessive genes on both alleles will all their children exhibit the trait.

Adapted from *Genetic counseling:* March of Dimes Birth Defects Foundation.

or absence of the skin pigment melanin, while several additional pairs determine the amount of melanin produced.

Conception

The moment of conception marks the uniting of a sperm from the father with an ovum (or egg) from the mother and the beginning of development for a new individual.

Conception is often described as a split-second event, but it is actually a process that can be described in terms of hours, days, and even years. At puberty, the hormonal balance in males and females changes. In both males and females, the new hormonal balance brings about the maturation of germ cells, ova in women and sperm in men. Through a special process called meiosis, the normal chromosomal make-up of cells (forty-six chromosomes arranged in twenty-three pairs) is reduced to

EXHIBIT 16.2
Sex-Linked Inheritance

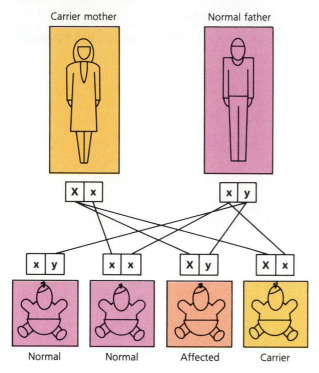

Carrier mother   Normal father

Normal   Normal   Affected   Carrier

The odds for each *male* child are 50/50:
1. 50% risk of inheriting the faulty **X** and the disorder.
2. 20% chance of inheriting normal **x** and **y** chromosomes.
For each *female* child, the odds are;
1. 50% risk of inheriting one faulty **X**, to be a carrier like mother.
2. 50% chance of inheriting no faulty gene.

Adapted from *Genetic counseling:* March of Dimes Birth Defects Foundation.

twenty-three single chromosomes in each germ cell. When the sperm and ovum unite during conception, a single cell, the **zygote** is formed; in the zygote, the twenty-three single chromosomes from each germ cell pair together to create the complete genetic information for the new individual.

Conception relies on so many factors that you might conclude it represents a miracle. Beginning with the achievement of sexual maturity at puberty and the production of viable sperm and ova, conception relies on the appropriate timing of several events. Approximately fourteen days before the start of the woman's menstrual period, ovulation occurs, and an ovum is released from the woman's ovaries. For conception to proceed normally, the egg must find its way into the fallopian tubes. Within twenty-four to forty-eight hours before or after

ovulation, the man, during intercourse, must deposit an ample number of sperm in the woman's vagina. Minimal fertility rates for sperm are approximately twenty million per ejaculate. Such large numbers are needed because sperm die very quickly. From the millions of sperm present initially, the actual number of sperm that reach the egg in the fallopian tube may be only 150 to 200. The genetic material from only one of these sperm will unite with the genetic material from the ovum to form the zygote.

The normal sequence for conception involves the release of one ovum and its subsequent fertilization by one sperm. Sometimes, more than one ovum is released during ovulation, and the opportunity for multiple births exists. When two ova are fertilized, two zygotes are formed, and the result is **dizygotic (fraternal) twins**. **Monozygotic (identical) twins** develop from a single zygote that splits into two individuals after fertilization. The number of multiple births in which several siblings are born at the same time has increased in recent years due to the use of drugs to stimulate ovulation in infertile women.

With so many factors involved, problems in conceiving a child should not come as a surprise. Rather, the opposite should be true; couples should be surprised when they encounter no difficulty in achieving conception. When infertility is a problem, many alternatives exist. The accompanying *Exploring . . .* section examines reproductive alternatives and societal problems created by their use.

Because of the current level of understanding of the reproductive process, knowledgeable couples can now carefully plan and actively choose when they will have children. By planning ahead, prospective parents have the opportunity to improve conditions for both the process of conception and for the subsequent prenatal development of their child.

Prenatal Development

Prenatal development can be divided into stages based on units of time or functional characteristics. The traditional view of a nine-month pregnancy calculates the beginning of the pregnancy from the onset of the woman's last menstruation. With greater numbers of planned pregnancies, however, the woman may know when ovulation actually occurred and can calculate the length of the pregnancy from the time of fertilization. Prenatal development is measured by weeks and months and larger units called trimesters, or three-month periods. Human

 *Exploring . . .*

Reproductive Alternatives: New Technologies and New Issues

Natural conception was the single method of reproduction until the last one hundred years of human existence. Infertile couples had two options—to remain childless or to adopt another person's child. Since the late 1800s and the advent of artificial insemination, new reproductive alternatives have become available to infertile couples. When the infertility is caused by the man's low sperm count, **AIH,** or **artificial insemination with the husband's sperm,** may be performed. The sperm from several ejaculations is concentrated, combined, and frozen until the appropriate time for insemination. **Artificial insemination by a donor (AID)** has been practiced in the United States since 1890. Couples seeking to conceive a child use AID when the man's infertility results from sterility or very poor-quality sperm or when the man has a disease that is transmitted genetically. Approximately 20,000 children are conceived through AID each year (Anderson, 1982).

In vitro fertilization involves removing an ovum from the ovary, fertilizing it with sperm in a petri dish, allowing the initial cell divisions to occur after fertilization, and then transplanting the embryo into a woman's uterus, thus creating a so-called test-tube baby. The first test-tube baby, born in England in 1978, resulted from an ovum and sperm taken from the baby's parents.

If a viable ovum cannot be obtained from the woman, the couple may choose to use **embryo transfer.** In this procedure, the man's sperm is used to artificially inseminate the donor ovum while the ovum is still in the donor's body. Five days later, the embryo is flushed from the donor's uterus and immediately transferred to the receiving woman's uterus (Bustillo et al., 1984). A variation of this technique involves freezing the embryo after conception until conditions are right for transfer to the recipient mother's uterus.

Couples in which infertility results from the woman's inability to maintain a pregnancy can raise children conceived with the man's sperm by using **surrogate motherhood**. In surrogate motherhood, the woman donating the ovum also carries and gives birth to the baby and then gives the child to the couple. Surrogate motherhood could be combined with any of the other techniques. Surrogate mothers could bear children conceived in vitro or carry transferred embryos. Both the ovum and the sperm could come from donors or from the couple seeking to have a child.

These new reproductive technologies have far-reaching implications and complications. A child today may have as many as five parents: the sperm donor, the egg donor, the surrogate who carries the child prenatally, and the parents who raise the child after his or her birth. Conception and pregnancy are no longer inseparably linked, and the separation of these processes as well as the added participation of one to three principal individuals (not counting the counselors, doctors, and technicians involved) raises serious ethical, legal, religious, and moral questions.

Consider the following complications presented by the use of these new methods:

■ When childless couples adopt children, the legal procedures are highly specified and closely regulated. However, the same degree of regulation does not exist for the new reproductive procedures that create conditions that parallel traditional adoption. As a result of new procedures, many children are raised by at least one of their biological parents. Must the non-biological parents adopt the children? How do non-biological parents differ from step-parents?

■ What rights do donors have? In one court challenge in 1983, a California man won weekly visitation rights to see a child conceived with his donated sperm (Andrews, 1984).

■ What rights should the children conceived by these techniques have? Should the children have the right to learn the identities of their biological parents? Should the children be told of the circumstances of their conception? With 20,000 AID births a year, the possibility is small but increasing that half-brothers and half-sisters could unwittingly marry and risk serious genetic complications for their offspring. Some doctors have already intervened to prevent marriages between children sharing the same donor (Andrews, 1984).

■ What consideration should be given to the psychological impact on the participants? Currently, counseling centers on the prospective parents and surrogate mothers. Other sperm and egg donors receive very little counseling.

■ Should the psychological conditions of donors and surrogate mothers be scrutinized as closely as are their physical conditions?

■ What should comprise selection criteria for donors, surrogate mothers, and recipient parents, and who should select? This particular issue is extremely complex and will be difficult to resolve.

■ Who, if anyone, should be liable if birth defects result from these procedures? Can AID children lay claim to their donor biological parents' estates?

■ The issue of paying someone for a surrogate pregnancy raises serious ethical and religious questions as well as legal problems. The new reproductive technologies emphasize the medical and scientific side of conception while, for the most part, they disregard the ethical and religious aspects of procreation.

■ Biological parenthood is now an option for many unmarried individuals. Will society be able to deal with large numbers of never-married parents and their children?

While the new technologies have brought the joys of parenthood to many infertile couples, the resolution of the accompanying complex social issues must keep pace with the expanding technology if the joys are to be kept from turning into nightmares.

prenatal development is normally complete about thirty-eight weeks after fertilization.

Those thirty-eight weeks are also divided into stages based on qualitative differences in the ongoing prenatal development. The **germinal stage** covers the period from conception to implantation of the developing cell mass into the mother's uterine wall. This stage is approximately two weeks in length, and cell division is a major characteristic. The developing embryo goes from a single cell, the zygote, to an ever-increasing mass of one hundred or more cells that differentiate into distinct tissue layers.

The next six weeks of prenatal development are termed the **embryonic stage**. A major characteristic of this stage is **organogenesis**, the process of developing the major organs and systems of the body. During organogenesis, three distinct layers of tissue that develop at the beginning of the stage differentiate into specific organ structures. From the outer layer of tissue, the **ectoderm**, develops the nervous system and sensory organs, the outer layer of skin and the skin's glands, and structures such as fingernails, toenails, and teeth. The muscular, skeletal, excretory, and circulatory systems and the sex organs develop from the **mesoderm**, or middle tissue layer. The **endoderm**, the inner layer, forms the respiratory and digestive systems, glands, and organs such as the liver.

During the embryonic stage, important support structures develop from other areas of the cell mass. The **amniotic sac** forms a protective membrane around the embryo. The sac is filled with **amniotic fluid**, which cushions the embryo from injury and helps maintain optimal temperature. The **placenta** forms from both maternal and embryonic tissues at the point at which implantation occurs. The placenta is a complex organ that allows the exchange of nutrients and waste products between the maternal and fetal systems, while also producing hormones needed to maintain the pregnancy. The **umbilical cord** connects the placenta with the developing baby. Blood vessels in the umbilical cord transport oxygen and nutrients from the maternal system to the baby and transport waste products from the baby to the mother. By the end of the embryonic period, the embryo is two million times larger than the single cell from which it originally developed (Harrison, 1978).

The **fetal stage** extends from approximately the end of the eighth week after conception until birth. The end of the embryonic stage and the beginning of the fetal stage is marked by the development of bone cells. The fetal stage involves both qualitative and quantitative

EXHIBIT 16.3
Prenatal Development

1 Month
During the first month, the embryo grows 10,000 times larger than the zygote. By the end of this period, it is ¼- to ½-inch in length. Blood is circulating through tiny veins and arteries as the heart beats 65 times per minute. The nervous system, digestive tract, and kidneys are forming. The umbilical cord transports nourishment-rich blood to the embryo in exchange for waste. Physical sex is not yet apparent.

2 Months
The embryo is about 1-inch long now and weighs only ⅟₁₃ of an ounce. The head with facial features developed is one-half the total body length. Hands and fingers are present as well as knees, ankles, and toes. The liver is producing blood cells, and the digestive tract is secreting juices to break down food the embryo receives. The kidneys are already removing waste products from the bloodstream. The skin of the embryo is so sensitive that it will react by flexing its trunk and moving its head and arms if its skin is stimulated.

3 Months
This begins the period of the fetus—the time when the immature organs and structures develop and the fetus prepares for birth. Fingernails and toenails have been added to the organism which now weighs an ounce and measures 3 inches in length. Also present are closed eyelids, vocal cords, and lips. The sex of the fetus is easily distinguished. The fetus may breathe in and/or swallow amniotic fluid and many urinate occasionally. Immature egg or sperm cells are beginning to form in the reproductive system. More reflex behaviors are appearing: The fetus will now squint if its eyelids are touched, make a fist if its palm is rubbed, suck if its lip is touched, and fan its toes if the sole of its foot is stroked.

4 Months
The mother may now be aware of movements by the fetus as it kicks and thumps in the uterus. This event is known as *quickening,* or feeling life. The fetus is now 8–10 inches in length and weighs about 6 ounces. The head is now one-fourth of the total body length, a proportion that will remain until birth.

5 Months
As the fetus grows larger, it becomes more active, and there is more force behind its movements. The fetus is now about 12 inches long and weighs between 12 and 16 ounces. Coarse hair may appear at the eyelids, eyebrows and scalp, and a soft downy hair called *lanugo* is formed that usually disappears before a full-term birth. The fetal heartbeat (along with other uterine and intestinal sounds) may be heard by placing an ear against the mother's abdomen. Although the fetus has a definite sleep-wake pattern and seems to prefer some positions in the uterus more than others, it would have little or no chance for survival on its own should birth occur at this point.

6 Months
The chances of surviving are a little better now, especially if the infant weighs at least 2 pounds. Most fetuses weigh about a pound and a half now and measure 14 inches in length. Fat is being deposited under the fetus' skin to give it a more rounded appearance; the eyes open and close, and the head can orient in all directions. Muscle strength has improved, and the child is capable of crying.

7 Months
Survival chances are good at this point since most fetuses weigh between 3 and 5 pounds. The greatest threat to survival is lung immaturity. Most reflex response patterns have been established: Crying, breathing, swallowing, and sucking are all apparent in the fetus' behavior. The lanugo may begin to disappear around this time.

8 Months
The 18–20-inch-long fetus is fast outgrowing its living quarters. Its movements are restricted because of the cramped conditions. The fetus now weighs between 5 and 7 pounds and continues to put on fat to help regulate temperature outside the womb.

9 Months
Growth rate slows considerably now as the baby readies for birth. Organ systems operate more efficiently; heart rate increases; the reddish color of the skin fades; and the skin is covered with a creamy substance called *vernix* designed to protect it. If the infant is born on or near its projected due date, it will have been in the womb for approximately 267 days, the amount of time necessary for humans to develop normally.

Adapted from: Papalia, D.E. & Olds, S.W. 1986. *Human development* (3rd ed.). NY: McGraw-Hill, pp. 58–61.

changes. Although the overall growth rate is somewhat slower than that of the embryonic stage, the fetus becomes large enough and active enough that the pregnant woman becomes very aware of the growth taking place within. The qualitative changes involve refinement of the organ systems developed in the embryonic stage and the addition of physical features such as hair and eyelashes. Exhibit 16.3 presents a month-by-month description of prenatal development.

Due to the rapid rate of development and, especially, to the presence of organogenesis, the germinal and embryonic stages represent a critical period in development. During this period, the developing embryo is particularly vulnerable to the presence of **teratogens**, environmental factors that affect prenatal development and cause birth defects. The specific effect of a teratogen depends upon the timing and duration of exposure (Hays, 1981). For example, the rubella virus is a potent teratogen, but its effects are much more devastating if the infection occurs during the critical period of the first eight weeks of prenatal development rather than during the last eight weeks. In unplanned pregnancies, the first eight weeks are especially critical because the woman may be unaware that she is pregnant and therefore may not take necessary precautions (such as abstention from or cautious use of drugs and avoidance of exposure to X-rays) to protect the embryo from potential teratogens.

Birth and the Newborn

One of the unsolved mysteries of human development is what signals the birth process to begin. Much is known about the events that occur during the three stages of the birth process, but the factor that determines that prenatal development is completed and that birth should begin remains unknown. The first stage of the birth process is **labor**, which involves contractions of the uterus and dilation of the cervix. The second stage, **delivery**, begins with the baby entering the birth canal, the woman's vagina, and ends with the birth of the baby. In the third stage, **afterbirth**, the umbilical cord, placenta, and fetal membranes are expelled from the uterus and the birth process is complete.

The **neonate**, or newborn baby, is immediately evaluated to assess its health status and the need for medical intervention. The **Apgar Scale** is a rapid and accurate method for evaluating the neonate (see Exhibit 16.4)

and is used in most hospitals. On a scale from 0 to 2, the baby is rated in five areas: color, heart rate, respiration, muscle tone, and reflex irritability. Ninety percent of all normal babies receive a combined score of seven or better, indicating that they are in good condition and require only routine medical supervision (Apgar & Beck, 1973).

High Apgar scores at one minute and five minutes after birth indicate that the baby is adjusting well to the transition from prenatal uterine environment to life on his or her own. High scores are a clear sign that the baby's respiratory system is bringing in oxygen and that the circulatory system is efficiently conveying oxygenated blood throughout the body. Other bodily systems, such as the digestive and excretory systems, must also begin to function on their own. Temperature regulation requires a longer transition time than do some of the other systems. Newborn babies lose body heat rapidly and must be kept warm until they become more efficient at regulating their own body temperatures.

At birth, the baby displays a number of innate reflex responses, such as sucking and rooting, which represent unlearned behaviors for obtaining food. The baby's sensory systems are well-developed, and the neonate is sensitive to touch all over the body. Hearing and vision function well. The newborn baby displays a clear preference for looking at a human face and for the sound of a human voice; the neonate will look in the direction of sounds he or she hears. The newborn reacts to strong

EXHIBIT 16.4
The Apgar Scale

Sign*	0	1	2
Appearance (Color)	blue, pale	body pink, extremities blue	entirely pink
Pulse (Heart rate)	absent	slow (below 100)	rapid (over 100)
Grimace (Reflex irritability)	no response	grimace	coughing, sneezing, crying
Activity (Muscle tone)	limp	weak, inactive	strong, active
Respiration (Breathing)	absent	irregular, slow	good, crying

*Each sign is rated in terms of absence or presence from 0 to 2; highest overall score is 10.

Adapted from Apgar, V. A. 1953. A proposal for a new method of evaluation of a newborn infant. *Anesthesia and Analgesia...Current Research, 32*, pp. 260-267. (International Anesthesia Research Society).

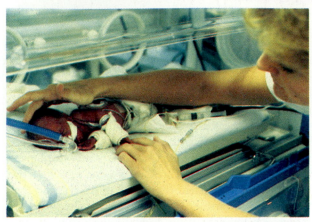

Premature infants often have Apgar scores lower than 7, and they may spend days or even weeks in incubators before they are able to go home.

odors, can reliably recognize his or her mother's odor by six days after birth, and can discriminate between different tastes, exhibiting a preference for sweet tastes. Pain sensitivity is present at birth. Additionally, infants display several distinct levels of sleep and wakefulness, ranging from quiet sleep, through quiet-alert wakefulness, to crying and fussiness. Infants are most responsive during the quiet-alert state.

Focus Question Answer

What risks are involved with unplanned pregnancies? Because the woman may be unaware she is pregnant, the greatest risk may be her failure to prepare for the pregnancy and to take precautions to avoid harming the developing baby. Avoiding potential teratogens in the form of drugs, virulent diseases, and environmental hazards such as X-rays is especially important during the critical period of the first trimester.

 ### The Infant, Toddler, and Preschool Years

The transition from the supportive intrauterine environment to independent existence lasts from two to four weeks after birth and is known as the **neonatal period**. This period is followed by the loosely defined stage of **infancy**, during which the baby moves from mostly reflexive behaviors to more purposeful behavior and greater mobility. When the baby begins to walk, the infant becomes a toddler. **Toddlerhood** emerges as an important stage for the child's expanding physical, cognitive, and

social development. The **preschool years**, from approximately three to five years of age, are marked by advancing mastery of physical, cognitive, and social skills.

Infancy and Toddlerhood

A major developmental task for the infant is becoming mobile. The principle of readiness is most evident in motor development. The well-defined sequence of behaviors that lead to walking directly follow development in the skeletal, muscular, and nervous systems (Lou, 1982). The child will not be ready to walk until development in these physical systems has reached an appropriate level. The period between birth and walking is filled with an impressive array of motor developments. The infant gains control of his or her head movements and masters sitting erect, rolling over, and crawling. The child learns to reach for, grasp, and release objects. Grasping on to furniture helps the child master standing erect, which eventually leads to the child's first tentative steps into toddlerhood.

The unification of motor actions and perception also occurs during this period, and the connection between the motor and sensory systems is nowhere more evident than when the infant in a highchair delights in repeatedly picking up toys and utensils from the tray and dropping them on the floor. The average eight-month-old infant, who has the eye-hand coordination necessary for reaching out and grasping, displays a definite purposefulness to his or her behavior (Hohlstein, 1982).

The repeated interactions of motor activity and perception also lead to the development of perceptual constancies. By actually grasping and manipulating objects, the infant learns that the size and shape of the objects remain constant despite changes in distance and viewing angle. The attainment of perceptual constancies stabilizes the world for the infant, creating opportunities for expanding cognitive development.

Cognitive development in infancy is described by Piaget's **sensorimotor stage** (see Chapter 11 for a discussion of Piaget's cognitive theory). The sensorimotor stage includes the developing purposefulness of the infant's motor behavior, the integration of information from the senses, the refinement of the ability to imitate, and the attainment of **object permanence**. Object permanence, the capacity to recognize that people and objects continue to exist even when the infant is not in sensory contact with them, may take as long as two years to become fully developed.

At two years of age, most toddlers are also well on their way to developing language. The average two-year-old has already produced prelinguistic sounds and his or her first word and may have spoken the first sentence. At this point, the child's speech is often telegraphic, conveying meaning but omitting many parts of speech. Generally, the child's ability to understand language precedes his or her ability to speak the language, and his or her early language follows grammatical rules that differ from those used by adults. Children develop language competency at widely varying rates, but the order in which they develop language is nearly constant (Brown, 1973).

Attachment

A major element of infancy is **attachment**, the development of an enduring bond between infant and caregivers. Attachment is a reciprocal relationship brought about by repeated interactions between the infant and his or her caregivers. The timing and duration of the interactions influence the quality of attachment. Certain researchers have emphasized the importance of immediate contact after birth between infant and parents (Klaus & Kennell, 1976), while others (Lamb, 1982; Myers, 1984a, 1984b) question whether early contact is critical for bonding to occur.

Freud proposed that pleasure derived from oral gratification during the oral stage is responsible for an infant attaching to his or her mother. Erik Erikson, who modified Freud's ideas by placing greater emphasis on social and cultural than on biological influences, emphasized that attachment develops from a balance between trust and mistrust resulting from infant-caregiver interactions. Healthy attachment comes from consistent care from the caregiver (the mother in Erikson's viewpoint) and leads to trust predominating over mistrust; however, enough mistrust remains to afford the child some self-protection. In essence, Freud's and Erikson's views pose the question, "Does attachment result from gratification from feeding or from the overall quality of the infant-caregiver interactions?"

An interesting answer to this question comes from the behavioral-learning perspective. In behavioral terms, the question becomes, "Do babies learn to love their caregivers because of specific food reinforcers or because of comfort reinforcers provided by the caregivers?" In a classic study (Harlow & Zimmerman, 1959), infant rhesus monkeys were separated from their mothers at birth and raised with two inanimate surrogate mother mon-

keys, cylinders of wire with wooden heads. One mother's wire body was covered with terrycloth (see Exhibit 16.5). Both the wire mother and the cloth mother could be fitted with baby bottles for feeding the infant monkeys. Some of the infants were fed from their wire mother and some from their cloth mother, but all infants had access to both mothers all the time.

Regardless of which mother fed them, the infant monkeys spent significantly more time clinging to their cloth mother. In other tests, when frightened by a "monster" (a toy robot), all infants ran directly to their cloth mothers and clung to them even when they had been fed by their wire mothers. The researchers concluded that **contact comfort**, the comfort provided by physical contact with a caregiver, is definitely more important than feeding in establishing attachment. The behavioral answer to the psychoanalytic question is that basic trust (developed from consistent caregiving) is more important than oral gratification in developing attachment.

The particular pattern of attachment that develops depends upon characteristics of the caregiver and the

**EXHIBIT 16.5
Surrogate Mother Monkeys**

Photo from Harry Harlow, University of Wisconsin Primate Laboratory.

infant. An infant characteristic affecting attachment is **temperament**, which refers to an individual's typical ways of responding to situations and people. Many children can be classified into one of three categories based on differences in temperament. In one study (Thomas & Chess, 1977), 40 percent of the children were classified as **easy** children who were cheerful, adapted easily to change, and exhibited regularity in sleeping and eating. Ten percent of the children were described as **difficult**. Difficult children were more excitable, less adaptable to change, and more irregular in biological functioning. **Slow-to-warm-up** children, represented by 15 percent of the sample, were not highly reactive in either a positive or a negative way and were slow to adapt to change but would, if given time, adapt, or warm up. Although not all children fit into one of the three categories and temperament is not necessarily consistent throughout childhood, these researchers concluded that the differences in temperament represented by these categories reflect inborn characteristics.

In addition, the caregivers also bring definite temperaments to their interactions with their children. Over time, parents learn to adjust their parenting to fit their children's response styles, and children learn to adjust their responses to fit their parents' ways of providing care.

Toilet Training

An important experience in the life of a toddler is **toilet training**. With the onset of toilet training, parents place on the child demands to control the biological functions of elimination. Not surprisingly, toilet training coincides with both Freud's and Erikson's second stages. Freud suggested that, in the anal stage, children's greatest pleasure comes from moving their bowels and that the way in which toilet training is accomplished determines the outcome of this stage. According to Erikson's second stage, called autonomy versus shame and doubt, healthy psychosocial development derives from children achieving a balance between acting on their own (autonomy) and recognizing those actions of which they are not yet capable (doubt). Parents contribute to the development of the child's autonomy by allowing the child some independence and self-control while retaining some control. Toilet training is a major activity in which children develop independence and self-control (autonomy).

Toilet training can be a major test of parenting skills. From Erikson's viewpoint, too little or too much parental control can make children fear losing self-control, feel ashamed at their inability to exert self-control, and doubt

their ability to act independently. In contrast, from the behavioral-learning viewpoint (Azrin & Foxx, 1981), toilet training is a matter of parents following a set of learning principles that emphasize modeling, imitation, and appropriate rewards and encouragement. These behavioral principles are explained more fully in an *Exploring . . .* section in Chapter 9.

From a practical point of view, toilet training is most easily accomplished when the child becomes maturationally ready to acquire the needed skills. Parental frustrations occur most often when training is begun before the child is physiologically capable of voluntary bowel and bladder control. Additionally, the child must be able to sense the need to use the toilet, be able to perform the other motor skills of toileting (walking to the bathroom, lowering the pants, sitting on the toilet, etc.), and possess sufficient language competency to understand the parents' instructions. Waiting until the child exhibits these skills should greatly facilitate toilet training.

Preschool Years

The world of the preschooler is one of expanding physical and mental competencies along with widening social interactions. Physically, preschoolers grow at a steady, but slower, rate compared to the rapid spurts in growth during infancy and toddlerhood. A noticeable change in body proportion occurs in the preschool years as preschoolers' trunks, arms, and legs lengthen and they lose their potbelly look. The preschoolers' expanding physical and mental competencies parallel the continuing development of their muscular, skeletal, and neural systems.

As children move into the preschool years, their expanding mental abilities include the capacity for **symbolic thought**. With symbolic thought, children move from understanding the world only through action to understanding the world through language, mental imagery, and memory as well (Elkind, 1981). In his **preoperational stage** of cognitive development (from approximately ages two to seven), Piaget described preschoolers' thought processes in terms of limitations. He believed that preschoolers are not yet capable of adult-like thought operations and therefore are *pre*-operational. Specifically, Piaget maintained that preschoolers' thought is marked by **egocentrism** (the inability to view the world from a reference point other than one's own), **irreversibility** (the inability to mentally reverse operations), and **centration** (the inability to focus on more than one aspect of a problem at a time). According to

Piaget, from maturation during the preschool years emerges the abilities to decenter, to reverse operations, and to see the world from others' points of view.

The preschoolers' increasing physical and mental capabilities influence their psychosocial development. Erikson described children in this period as facing a crisis of **initiative versus guilt**. Successful resolution of this crisis comes from striking a balance between initiative, which enables children to undertake new activities, and guilt, which causes children to examine the appropriateness of their actions. Too much emphasis on initiative may lead children to try to perform tasks beyond their abilities, while too much emphasis on guilt may inhibit children from trying new adventures. Parents can guide the development of a healthy balance between initiative and guilt by allowing children to do things on their own while also setting limits appropriate to the children's levels of abilities.

Part of the impetus for preschoolers' initiative is the process of **identification**. Identification as an aspect of personality development refers to children's adoption of the characteristics, behaviors, beliefs, and values of other individuals or groups. Preschoolers identify with their parents and adopt their behaviors and beliefs, but they also identify with siblings and other relatives, babysitters, and television characters. Through the identification process, a child defines and refines a core identity for himself or herself. An integral aspect of the identification process is awareness of gender. Much of the research on the identification process has focused on explaining the process of gender identification.

The Research Process: Theoretical Explanations of Gender Identification

Gender refers to the female and male sexes, but to what aspect of maleness and femaleness does the term refer? Does gender refer to the arrangement of your chromosomes (genetic gender)? Does it refer to the hormonal balance of androgens and estrogens in your body and the physical characteristics (genitalia) you possess (biological gender)? Does gender indicate your identification of yourself as female or male (core gender identity), or does it indicate your experience of being male or female and your subjective estimate of the degree of your own femaleness and maleness (gender identity)? What aspect of gender relates to **gender roles**, the specific set of culturally determined behaviors and characteristics deemed appropriate for you as a male or female? What aspect pertains to **masculinity/femininity**, the complex, poorly defined features of personality assigned to you on the basis of your gender? What is the relationship of all these

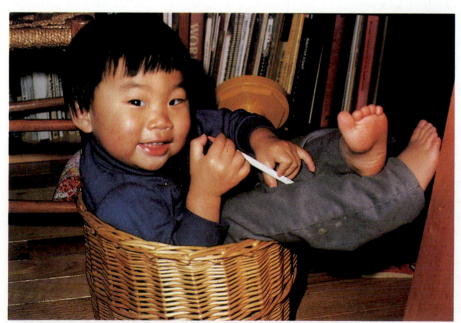

In their attempt to form an identity of their own, preschoolers try out various behaviors and characteristics.

factors to your **gender orientation**, your stable, subjective sense of affinity for one gender or the other, and your **gender preference**, the gender role you find most comfortable and desirable regardless of your core gender identity? With so many facets to the concept of gender, formulating theoretical explanations for gender identification, or **gender typing**, is a complex task. Following are several such explanations.

Psychoanalytic Theory   According to Freud, during the **phallic stage** at approximately age five or six, a child develops sexual feelings for the parent of the opposite sex, is unable to cope with those feelings, and therefore rejects those feelings by identifying with the parent of the same sex. As part of identifying with the same-sex parent, the child unconsciously adopts the parent's gender role—the characteristics, behaviors, and values exhibited by that parent.

However, Freud's views of identification are flawed because children develop a core gender identity much earlier in life (Kohlberg & Ullian, 1974). According to recent research, core gender identity is one of the first concepts that children acquire about themselves and is one of the few that remain unchanged throughout life. Since the concept of gender appears almost universally by age three genetic and biological factors appear to be involved.

Biogenetic Theory   From the biological perspective, gender identification is a function of genetic inheritance and biological maturation. According to this position, the production of testosterone, the primary male sex hormone, by genetic-gender male embryos masculinizes the brain and other body structures so that males (and, presumably, females with abnormally large amounts of testosterone) are predisposed at birth to a male gender identity that can be only partially modified by environmental influences (Money & Ehrhardt, 1972; Ehrhardt & Baker, 1974). In genetic-gender females, high levels of testosterone cause the development of masculinized external sex organs (Ehrhardt & Money, 1967). According to the biogenetic theory, gender roles evolve from biogenetic predispositions for males and females to behave differently.

Although these observations support the biogenetic position, evidence also suggests environmental factors. In a study of 113 individuals who were raised with an assigned gender different from their biophysical gender (Hampson, 1965), 90 percent exhibited a gender identity for the assigned gender. Such evidence indicates that gender identity is not innate.

Social Learning Theory   The behavioral-learning perspective emphasizes environmental influences upon gender identification. This view assumes that parents respond differently, depending on whether they perceive the gender of their child to be male or female. Social learning theory expands this view to include vicarious learning, or learning without the direct experience of the consequences, and observational learning in which children observe, imitate, and are reinforced or punished on the basis of the gender model they imitate.

To many people, the social learning approach makes more sense than either Freud's theory or the biogenetic approach; however, this position is equally difficult to prove. Critics claim that the initial assumption of parents' different treatment of boys and girls may be wrong (Maccoby & Jacklin, 1974). Although not everyone agrees with their interpretation of the data, Maccoby and Jacklin reviewed gender-typing studies and concluded that evidence does not support the premise that parents treat their sons and daughters differently.

Cognitive-Developmental Theory   The **cognitive-developmental theory** (Kohlberg, 1966) asserts that once children have identified themselves as female or male, they actively organize their knowledge of the world in light of the identity. According to this view, children's understanding of gender advances as their general cognitive development advances.

According to Kohlberg, children identify with and imitate same-sex parents and others of their same gender because they recognize that these individuals belong to the same category they do. The set of behaviors a child exhibits at any given age reflects his or her perceptions of what fits with being female or male. This set of behaviors changes as the individual's level of cognitive development advances and he or she reaches new levels of cognitive organization.

As is true of the other positions, the cognitive-developmental theory is not without weaknesses. Critics question why gender becomes the focal point for categorizing people when so many other possibilities exist (Bem, 1985). For example, in multiracial societies, the category of race would appear to be as useful and important as gender.

Gender Schema Theory   Explaining gender identification and the acquisition of gender roles may be better accomplished by combining elements from the theoretical positions. Bem's (1985) **gender schema theory** proposes combining ideas from the cognitive-developmental and social learning theories. Gender schema theory explains gender identification as a function of cognitive development and explains the acquisition of gender roles, the content of gender identity, as a function of social learning. According to Bem's theory, biogenetic factors provide the physical structures and the maturational plan for cognitive development.

Bem maintains, as did Kohlberg, that the concepts of femaleness and maleness are among the earliest schema (recall that schema are concepts created to make sense of the world) children form. Children form their core gender identities sometime during the first two to three years of their lives as a part of their ongoing cognitive development. Forming concepts of their maleness or femaleness provides children with a powerful tool for assimilating their experiences and, as they continue to develop, for accommodating their gender schema to fit their new and changing circumstances.

The cognitive side of gender schema theory emphasizes the individual's active role in choosing a gender role in light of that individual's core gender identity. The social learning side stresses that the available choices are a function of the models and reinforcements in the environment. Children begin early in their lives to learn what society expects regarding gender roles, and societal gender role expectations provide an external standard by which children compare their internal schema of gender identity. Children then evaluate those prescriptive roles in light of their own self concepts of gender. They adjust both their behaviors and their schema to remove discrepancies. Thus, gender schema theory synthesizes two major perspectives on development.

Focus Question Answer

What factors have influenced your identity as a male or female? Depending upon the theoretical interpretation you adopt, you could conclude that your gender identity was influenced by your resolution of conflicts in the phallic stage, by your biological inheritance and resulting hormonal structure, by your past learning experiences, or by cognitive processes that organize information about gender in alignment with your own self concept of gender. Gender schema theory maintains that your gender identity is a product of cognitive and social learning factors.

 The School-Age and Teenage Years

Most children enter kindergarten and begin their formal education around age five or six. Children between the ages of six and twelve are often referred to as **school-**

These children have entered the developmental stage where children begin spending more time with friends and less time with their families.

aged because they are in elementary school and because of the importance of the school experience in their lives. Although in one sense the teen years begin at thirteen, physical, cognitive, and social development are better guides than chronological age to the beginning of **adolescence**.

School-Aged Children

Physically, boys and girls begin school with similar growth patterns. By the end of this period when they are around 12, girls tend to be heavier and taller than boys because, on the average, they experience the prepubertal growth spurt earlier than boys. Typically, children double their weight and increase their height by one-third during this period. The health of school-aged children is generally good. One study found that 95 percent of school-aged children in the United States are in good or excellent health (U.S. Census Bureau, 1983).

Cognitively, at approximately age seven, children move into Piaget's stage of **concrete operations**. During this period, they acquire a new, reversible set of mental operations (Cowan, 1978). The operations are concrete in that they involve the mental manipulation of real, or concrete, objects and cannot yet be performed by using abstract symbols. However, this new level of cognitive organization allows school-aged children to take into account several aspects of a problem at once and to realize that a problem may have more than one solution. With these underlying skills, children can understand **conservation**, the principle that properties such as number, volume, and mass remain the same despite apparent transformations in the appearance of objects. Also, school-aged children acquire the ability to group objects by common attribute (classification) and to arrange objects by measurable dimensions (seriation).

A significant aspect of language development during this period is the appearance of a more sophisticated form of humor based on the understanding that the same word may have different meanings and that different words may sound alike. Is the following joke humorous to you? "How do you stop a bull from charging? Take away his credit card!"

Moral Development

The new cognitive abilities of school-aged children allow them to reason differently about moral questions of right and wrong. According to Piaget (1932), children pass through two stages of moral reasoning—the **morality of constraint** and the **morality of cooperation**. During the school-aged years, children move from the rigid moral concepts of constraint to the moral flexibility of cooperation. Piaget argued that moral development follows cognitive development.

Building on Piaget's concepts of morality, Kohlberg (1981, 1984) proposed a theory with six stages (see Exhibit 16.6). According to Kohlberg, moral reasoning guides moral behavior, and individuals progress through stages in a set sequence. Before age nine or ten, most children display **preconventional morality** and make moral judgements based on self-interest. As children move into the teenage years and the cognitive stage of formal operations, they develop **conventional morality** and seek approval by upholding society's standards. Kohlberg found that teenagers and many adults reason at the conventional level with a very rigid view of the standards. **Postconventional morality**, in which reasoning involves concerns for the welfare of society and for universal moral principles, usually does not develop until the late teens or later, if ever. Examples of each of these levels of reasoning are found in Exhibit 16.6.

Kohlberg's theory has provoked much criticism. Critics challenge his ideas about the invariant sequence of the stages and the inherent preference for postconventional morality. A cultural bias may also be present since studies in various cultures have revealed that postconventional morality is present only in western, industrialized societies (Edwards, 1982; Snarey, 1985). Also, Kohlberg's equating morality with justice may not be appropriate for nonwestern cultures.

Kohlberg's emphasis on justice and fairness has been criticized as a male perspective of morality (Gilligan, 1982). Gilligan contends that women's moral reasoning is based on a person-centered morality of responsibility and focuses on empathy and caring and that men's moral reasoning is a function of a justice-centered morality of rights. On Kohlberg's levels, women's concerns for social responsibility place them at the less advanced, conventional level of morality; a moral strength becomes a moral detriment when measured against male views of morality.

Gilligan proposes that as women's moral reasoning develops, they move through levels different from those of men. In Level 1, women are concerned with individual survival but move toward reasoning that shows concern for other people. At Level 2, women consider themselves responsible for the actions of others. As women move from Level 2 to Level 3, they seek to balance responsibility to others with responsibility to themselves. This transition is followed by Level 3—the morality of nonviolence—in which women establish a "moral equality" with others and become responsible for making moral decisions.

A final important concern about Kohlberg's theory is the linking of moral reasoning with moral behavior. Kohlberg's theory stresses moral reasoning as the major determinant of moral behavior. If Kohlberg's position is correct, then people should behave differently according to their levels of moral development, but researchers investigating this issue have found that people at the postconventional level of reasoning do not behave more morally than people at lower levels (Kupfersmid & Wonderly, 1980). These findings reaffirm classic research that investigated factors influencing cheating in children (Hartshorne & May, 1928-1930). In the earlier studies, children who cheated were just as likely to believe that cheating is wrong as were children who did not cheat. Furthermore, almost all the children cheated at some point, depending upon the characteristics of the situation (the pressure to do well and the likelihood of being observed). Therefore, critics of Kohlberg's ideas contend that moral behavior is the product of several factors, not just moral reasoning alone, and that acting morally rather than reasoning morally should be emphasized (Blasi, 1980).

Psychosocial Development Of School-Agers

For children ages six to twelve, school becomes the second most important influence on their lives (the number one influence is family). Children of this age spend pro-

EXHIBIT 16.6
Kohlberg's Stages of Moral Development

Level I: Preconventional (Ages 4 to 10 Years)

Emphasis in this level is on external control. The standards are those of others, and they are observed either to avoid punishment or to reap rewards.

Stage 1. Punishment and obedience orientation. "What will happen to me?" Children obey the rules of others to avoid punishment.

Stage 2. Instrumental purpose and exchange. "You scratch my back, I'll scratch yours." They conform to rules out of self-interest and consideration for what others can do for them in return.

Level II: Morality of Conventional Role Conformity (Ages 10 to 13)

Children now want to please other people. They still observe the standards of others, but they have internalized these standards to some extent. Now they want to be considered "good" by those persons whose opinions count. They are now able to take the roles of authority figures well enough to decide whether some action is "good" by their standards.

Stage 3. Maintaining mutual relations, approval of others, the golden rule. "Am I a good girl [boy]?" Children want to please and help others, can judge the intentions of others, and develop their own ideas of what a good person is.

Stage 4. Social system and conscience. "What if everybody did it?" People are concerned with doing their duty, showing respect for higher authority, and maintaining the social order.

Level III: Morality of Autonomous Moral Principles (Age 13, or Not Until Young Adulthood, or Never)

This level marks the attainment of true morality. For the first time, the individual acknowledges the possibility of conflict between two socially accepted standards, and tries to decide between them. The control of conduct is now internal, both in the standards observed and in the reasoning about right and wrong. Stages 5 and 6 may be alternate methods of the highest level of reasoning.

Stage 5. Morality of contract, of individual rights, and of democratically accepted law. People think in rational terms, valuing the will of the majority and the welfare of society. They generally see these values best supported by adherence to the law. While they recognize that there are times when there is a conflict between human need and the law, they believe that it is better for society in the long run if they obey the law.

Stage 6. Morality of universal ethical principles. People do what they as individuals think right, regardless of legal restrictions or the opinions of others. They act in accordance with internalized standards, knowing that they would condemn themselves if they did not.

From Kohlberg, L. 1973. Moral stages and moralization. The cognitive-developmental approach. In T. Lickona (ed.). *Moral development and behavior.* NY: Holt, Rinehart & Winston.

portionally more time with friends and classmates and less time with their families.

Theoretically, Freud viewed the elementary school years as an interlude in psychosexual development. He labeled this period **latency** to indicate the relative calm and stability of physical and sexual development. He believed that at this point the ego was developed well enough to control the unacceptable urges of the id and to allow cognitive development to become prominent.

In contrast, most neo-Freudians and non-Freudians view the years of middle childhood as a time of great energy and activity. Erikson maintained that these years involve the crisis of **industry versus inferiority.** School-agers are no longer content to play; they actively work to accomplish specific goals. At the same time, because their skills are not as great as those of adults, their industrious efforts may produce results that others deem inadequate and that fall short of their own expectations.

Failure, to whatever degree, leads to feelings of inferiority and helplessness. School-agers achieve a healthy resolution to this crisis by striking a balance between the desire for productivity and the inevitable feelings of inferiority.

In American society, two major outlets for schoolagers' industrious energies are schoolwork and competition. Successful efforts in both areas help create positive self-image and healthy self-esteem. However, problems can arise not only from feelings of inadequacy but also from too much emphasis on work. In the latter case, children can become absorbed in achieving technical competency and fail to develop healthy interpersonal relationships.

Adolescence

Adolescence is the period of transition from childhood to adulthood and is a phenomenon of the twentieth century. In the 1800s and before, the teenage years were not recognized as a special time of life. Instead, when children became old enough to perform adult labor, they were apprenticed to learn adult trades, or they immediately began to work like the adults they were considered to be. As western societies became increasingly industrialized and technologically advanced, the period of transition between childhood and adulthood lengthened, and the stage of adolescence emerged. Several forces linked together to produce this relatively new de-

velopmental stage. First, improved economic and nutritional conditions created better conditions for children's development. Consequently, children began to mature physically at earlier ages. At the same time, however, industrialization and technology led to the need for longer apprenticeships and more education before entering the workforce. Some people have argued that these latter outcomes were contrived to control entry into the workforce, but the effect was the same—to lengthen the period of transition from childhood to adulthood. As a result, the teen years have taken on a character of their own.

In many cultures, the transition to adulthood is very brief and occurs approximately the same time sexual maturity is achieved. The transition is often marked by dramatic rites of passage to celebrate the young person's initiation into adulthood. In industrialized societies with a lengthy stage of adolescence, the dramatic rituals have been replaced by a series of events that mark the teenager's gradual attainment of adult status. The accompanying *Exploring . . .* section describes some of the modern rites of passage in American society.

Teenagers

Adolescence begins with a period of rapid physical growth and developing sexual maturity called **pubescence**. On the average, pubescence begins for girls around age ten and for boys two years later at twelve. A variation of six to seven years is normal for rates of development in both boys and girls. With such wide variations, normal girls may begin showing signs of pubescence as early as age seven and normal boys as late as age sixteen. **Puberty** marks the end of pubescence and the point at which reproduction is first possible. Puberty occurs about two years after pubescence begins (on the average, at twelve for girls and fourteen for boys).

During adolescence, the primary sex organs enlarge and develop, and the appearance of secondary sex characteristics gives the teenagers more adult-like appearances. Physical appearance becomes a major concern, and many teenagers are dissatisfied with their appearances (Siegel, 1982), with greater dissatisfaction among girls than among boys of the same age. Early-maturing boys appear to have an advantage because they attain less childlike appearances sooner than their later-maturing counterparts (Jones, 1957; Siegel, 1982). Early-maturing boys also tend to be more poised, popular, and independent. Early maturation is not as advantageous for girls, however (Brooks-Gunn & Petersen, 1983).

Adolescence is often a time of turmoil, marked by physical, social, and psychological changes.

Exploring...

Modern American Rites of Passage

From the perspective of an American teenager, some nonindustrial societies' rites of passage into adulthood may seem not only dramatic but also barbaric. The rituals may include harsh tests of strength and endurance in which youths are subjected to circumcision, scarring of the body, tattooing, and other forms of physical mutilation. In other cultures, the rituals may have a more psychological impact and involve isolation and religious ceremonies. All these rites are relatively brief and end with a celebration of the newly-achieved adult status.

In American society, no single initiation rite exists. Instead, American teenagers experience many rites of passage that occur at different times during adolescence. Birthdays are obvious markers of progress toward adulthood and represent one type of American rite of passage. Your thirteenth birthday probably had more significance for you than did your twelfth. Other birthdays are significant because they grant you new rights and responsibilities. In many states, birthdays 14, 16, 18 and 21 are especially significant because those birthdays mark when you can apply for a learner's permit to drive a car, obtain a driver's license, become eligible to vote, and can legally buy alcoholic beverages.

Other American rites of passage retain the flavor of those from nonindustrial societies. Religious con-

firmation, such as the Jewish Bar Mitzvah, is one example of this type of rite. For certain individuals, enlisting in a branch of the Armed Forces may seem similar to the harsh initiation ceremonies described earlier.

With so many individual rites of passage, the beginning of adulthood in American society is unclear. Teenagers attain adult status in many ways. Physiological maturity is probably reached first and is usually recognized by the attainment of secondary sex characteristics that cause a person to look like an adult. Intellectual maturity is represented by the capacity for abstract thought and is recognized by society with such events as graduation from high school. Legal maturity is reached at several points with the granting of certain legal rights of adulthood. Sociological maturity occurs when a person becomes self-supporting and capable of supporting others. This type of maturity is evidenced in beginning a career, getting married, and having children. Nonetheless, all these adult statuses may be of little worth if the individual does not attain psychological maturity. With psychological maturity, an individual develops a stable identity, is able to form mature relationships, establishes a system of values, achieves independence from parents, and finally reaches the last rite of passage—recognition of his or her own adult status.

Early-maturing girls may feel conspicuous and, as a result, be less sociable and poised, more introverted and shy (Jones, 1957; Peskin, 1973). However, the teenage trials of early-maturing girls may have a silver lining since early maturing girls are better adjusted in adulthood than their later-maturing counterparts (Peskin, 1973).

Adolescence also marks movement into a new stage of cognitive development, **formal operations**. During this stage, teenagers develop the ability to think abstractly. They move from mental operations involving concrete manipulations to operations involving manipulation of abstract symbols. With **abstract thought** comes the ability to use **hypothetico-deductive reasoning** to explore cause and effect relationships. The use of logic

also advances, as does **metacognition**, the ability to reflect on one's own thought processes.

Teenagers spend a great amount of time thinking about themselves, a phenomenon termed **adolescent egocentrism** (Elkind, 1984). Because they think about themselves so much, teenagers have difficulty believing that others are not thinking about them as well, and, consequently, they create an **imaginary audience**. To teenagers, this observer, the imaginary audience, is as concerned about their thoughts and their behavior as they are. The effect of the imaginary audience is to make teenagers even more self-conscious about appearance.

A second aspect of adolescent egocentrism and another outgrowth of teenagers' cognitive development is the **personal fable**. The personal fable represents a form of self-centeredness in which teenagers become convinced that no one else has ever thought as they do; therefore, they are unique and not subject to the laws of probability and forces that govern the lives of ordinary people. Elkind has used the concept of the personal fable to explain adolescent risk-taking. The personal fable allows teenagers to think that because they are unique no harm will come to them: they will not get hooked on drugs, have car accidents, or become involved with pregnancies. As teenagers confront the world as it is and not as they would like it to be, they gradually lose their egocentrism. As they move through adolescence, most teenagers become less idealistic and more realistic in their self-appraisals.

Part of the teenager's egocentric thoughts involves a search for **identity**. In fact, Erikson proposed that the search for identity is the major psychosocial task of adolescence. In contrast, achieving mature adult sexuality is of prime importance in Freud's **genital stage** of adolescence. While the sexual urges of teenagers cannot be denied, Erikson's ideas currently receive more support and research interest than Freud's.

In Erikson's fifth stage, **identity versus role confusion**, teenagers confront the task of assessing the many possibilities and deciding who they will become. According to Erikson, career decisions are a significant element of the search for identity. (Erikson's own identity crisis involved a seven-year search for a career.) Role confusion is manifested by taking an excessively long time to reach adulthood, by regressing back to childishness, or by hastily committing oneself to a poorly con-

ceived course of action. Erikson contended that the teenager must resolve the identity crisis before he or she can achieve intimacy; however, according to Erikson, falling in love and becoming intimate with another can help the adolescent clarify his or her own identity.

Research on Erikson's ideas of identity formation has led to expanded views of identity and awareness of differences in male and female identity (Marcia, 1966, 1980). Marcia investigated the relationship between identity status and two elements of identity formation—crisis and commitment. Crisis refers to a time of conscious consideration of identity alternatives, while commitment involves adherence to a plan of action. Marcia developed four identity status categories based on the presence or absence of crisis or commitment, (see Exhibit 16.7). Individuals who have **identity achievement** have considered alternatives, have made choices, and are strongly committed to their choices. In the **foreclosure** status, individuals have made commitments without considering alternatives; they have accepted other people's plans for their lives rather than their own. People with **identity diffusion** may or may not have gone through crisis, but in either case they have avoided making commitments. Individuals in the **moratorium** category are in the process of considering alternatives and making decisions. They will be likely to make commitments and to achieve identities.

Gender differences in identity formation have been noted (Gilligan, 1983). Gilligan found a woman's identity is based more on her relationships with other people and less on her achievement of a separate identity. Other research supports this conclusion (Marcia, 1979). For

EXHIBIT 16.7
Marcia's Identity Status Categories

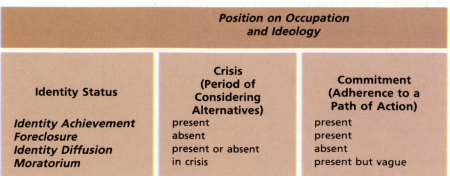

Identity Status	Position on Occupation and Ideology	
	Crisis (Period of Considering Alternatives)	Commitment (Adherence to a Path of Action)
Identity Achievement	present	present
Foreclosure	absent	present
Identity Diffusion	present or absent	absent
Moratorium	in crisis	present but vague

From Marcia, J. E. 1980. Identity in adolescence. In J. Adelson (ed.). *Handbook of adolescent psychology.* Reprinted by permission of John Wiley & Sons, Inc.

men, Marcia found the greatest similarity between men in the identity achievement and moratorium categories. For women, the greatest similarity is between women in identity achievement and foreclosure. Marcia concluded that maintaining a stable identity is so important for women that foreclosure, which allows women to achieve identity early in their lives, is as adaptive as struggling with crisis. Marcia also concluded, in contrast to Erikson's male-based pattern, that identity and intimacy develop simultaneously in women.

Focus Question Answer

Do you think about questions of morality just as someone of the opposite sex does? According to Gilligan, females' moral reasoning develops differently than males'. She contends that males' moral reasoning is justice-centered, while females' reasoning is based on person-centered responsibility with a focus on empathy and caring. Also, Gilligan maintains that Kohlberg's theory is a male perspective of morality and that the stages of moral reasoning development for females are different than those in Kohlberg's theory.

 *Relate*

Superbabies

American parents are pushing their children to learn more at an earlier age. Some parents begin intensively teaching their child in early infancy, while others start even earlier by reading aloud to the fetus during pregnancy. They exert their diligent efforts in the hope of producing a "superbaby"—a baby who achieves at a level more advanced than his or her age group. The concept of superbabies raises several important issues concerning early childhood education and parenting.

Fundamental to this issue is the continuing debate over the interaction of maturational (hereditary) and learned (environmental) factors. Parents who desire to advance their children's development are influenced by advocates of the nurture side of the nature-nurture controversy. Proponents of the nurture position propose that the normal interactions of heredity and environment may not represent optimal development, and that environmental opportunities should be emphasized.

The superbaby trend is influenced not only by the nature-nurture debate but by several other factors as well (Langway, 1983). The birth rate has declined. Parents are better educated and are having children at an older age. New knowledge about the neonate's abilities has increased expectations about what and when babies can learn. Animal studies indicating that enriched environments produce cognitive advantages suggest that the same could be true for humans. The success of compensatory education programs such as Head Start encourage similar programs for the nondisadvantaged. Also, the "crisis in education" reports create an atmosphere in which many parents feel that they must take responsibility for providing educational opportunities for their children. Finally, the increased availability of literature about infancy and the preschool years, along with the influence of programs such as television's *Sesame Street,* have em-

phasized to parents the importance of the first few years of life to a child's later development.

Parents who want to develop superbabies are themselves often competitive, successful, and economically well-off (Langway, 1983). They are usually older than average parents—often becoming first-time parents in their thirties—and tend to have only one or two children. These parents are from the "baby boom" generation and may be transferring the competitiveness of their peer group to their children.

Of course, not all new parents zealously adopt the parent-educator role, but for those who do, a wide range of infant education programs exists. Some programs can be learned at home from books. Other programs involve extensive training of the parent-educator. A third approach involves taking the infant to a class run by experts. Regardless of the approach, most of these programs emphasize cognitive development. However, certain programs are designed to work on the infant's physical abilities and coordination or to develop special abilities such as music. A few programs even stress providing enriched environments for fetuses and advocate, for instance, playing classical music during pregnancy.

One approach used in the cognitive programs is promoted by Glenn Doman, a long-time advocate of more formal education for infants (Doman, 1964). The Doman method, taught in one-week seminars at Doman's Better Baby Institute, teaches parents techniques for using flash cards with their infants three times a day. No research has been conducted on the program's effectiveness, but advocates cite case studies of toddlers who seem to know an unusual amount about topics such as art or geometry. Opponents, citing examples of preschoolers with flash card phobia, maintain that the new ABCs of babyhood are anxiety, betterment, and competition.

While the claims from the two sides of the issue are difficult to document, intense early learning is also criticized because the emphasis on cognitive abilities may impede the development of other skills. Social skill development is one area that may suffer as the result of intense early learning experiences.

Underlying critics' indictment of the singleness of purpose of the cognitive approach are the concerns that parents may be instilling in their children an inappropriate set of values toward learning and that these values will have negative consequences for children's later schooling and lives. Curiosity and intrinsic motivation to explore and learn are replaced with drill, exercise, and expectations for performance and achievement.

One critic believes that parents' intense educational efforts with infants and toddlers will not significantly influence the children's long-term cognitive development (Kagan, 1984). Kagan believes that the normal interactions between heredity and environment are sufficient for most children to grow in competence. Although admitting that environment is important, Kagan points to brain maturation as the principal determinant of the child's first few years of intellectual, moral, and emotional development. He notes that six months of brain maturation is necessary before infants are able to remember objects and ideas from the past. In summary, Kagan believes that children will grow in competence merely through contact with others and opportunities to explore things in their environment and suggests that maturational factors within the babies are as responsible or more responsible than parents' efforts. Thus, intense educational experiences before six months of age would appear to be futile, if not counterproductive.

If Kagan's views are correct, changes within the baby determine when an infant is ready for new or different cognitive experiences. Kagan and those who agree with his ideas believe that maturational factors determined by the baby's genetic program are the major influences on infant development. Accordingly, this maturational sequence can be modified very little by parents trying to program superbabies.

Because the interaction of nature and nurture has proven to be a most difficult problem for study, this issue may remain unresolved when today's babies are old enough to be grandparents. While psychologists continue to evaluate claim and counterclaim, parents will still harbor for their newborns great ambitions and expectations that will lead some to overzealous attempts to help their children fulfill those ambitions.

One approach (White, 1984) represents a reasonable compromise between the parents' needs to be involved with and do for their children and the children's needs to develop according to their own timetables. White's approach rec-

According to White, the role of a consultant is to provide children with the opportunity to explore the environment through the use of common objects.

ognizes the maturational competencies of infancy and the importance of appropriate environmental interactions to promote skill attainment and to foster further development. White trains parents to be consultants rather than teachers. The distinction between consultant and teacher is important. Rather than trying to teach specific content to the infant, the consultant checks to see that conditions allow the baby to learn in his or her own way.

The requirements to become one of White's consultant-parents are fairly simple. First, the parent must give the child ample opportunities to explore his or her physical environment. White believes that under this condition, as new competencies arise, the child will have the opportunity to develop them. Second, the parent must give the child ample opportunities to hear spoken language. More important than teaching the child to read at an early age is making certain the child has abundant exposure to spoken language. Third, the parent must give the child ample opportunity to develop social skills. This requirement may be the easiest of the three, in that it requires the parent simply to react to the child's needs with loving care.

These three conditions do not demand that the parent spend so many minutes each day in prescribed drills. Instead, they require that the parent oversee the day-to-day experiences of the child to assure that the child's maturational readiness is met with a rich and rewarding environment.

Things to Do

1. One of the most useful activities to do in conjunction with this chapter is to become a careful observer of the human development going on in your midst. Go to a shopping mall and notice the ages of people present. Look for similarities and differences among and between the various age groups. The opportunities for testing and applying your knowledge about human development are almost limitless in this situation.

2. For a more detailed observation of a particular age group, consider visiting a daycare center, preschool, or elementary/secondary school. Be certain to obtain permission to visit and observe in any of the suggested settings. Observing in one of these more structured settings will allow you the opportunity to compare many individuals of approximately the same age. Before making your observations, try to anticipate what you will see. Think of questions for which you want to find answers. Take good notes, which may be useful for other classes and projects.

3. Discuss with your parents and others who knew you as a child your early childhood development. If your parents kept a baby book for you, review the book's information about your early development. Make notes of any early characteristics that seem to have persisted throughout your later development.

4. Most adults have vivid memories of their teen years. How accurate are your memories of this time in your life? Interview a cross-section of young, middle-aged, and older adults about their memories of their teen years. What are the similarities and differences between the different generational experiences?

5. Try to remember your first date. Talk to friends about their early dating experiences. Talk with your parents and others in their age group about their memories of first dates. Talk with junior high school students about their first dating experiences. Which has changed more—dating from your parent's time to your time, or dating from your time to the present junior high scene?

Things to Discuss

1. This chapter focuses on a number of controversial issues regarding aspects of human development. A useful way to discuss these topics is to treat them as topics for formal debate. Make lists of pros and cons with strong support or sound reasoning behind them. Force yourself to take the side contrary to your personal beliefs, and debate the issue from that side as strongly as you can. On some of the issues, a formal debate may be the only way to assure a rational discussion of both the pros and the cons.

2. Think back over the various ages from infancy to the teen years. Make a case for the best and worst of those ages. Compare your responses with the responses of your classmates. How many of your classmates agreed with your choices? Did those who picked the same ages also choose the same reasons for picking those ages?

3. Would you divide the lifespan into the same stages as those described in the text? If you could alter the stages of the lifespan, would you change them from the way in which you experienced them? Would you eliminate some stages and lengthen others? Imagine that you had to explain human development to an alien from outer space. Would the stages of the lifespan be useful in your explanation?

4. Discuss with classmates the folklore of each person's childhood. Did everyone in the class learn to say, "Step on a crack and you'll break your mother's back"? What were your favorite indoor and outdoor games? What were your favorite riddles and jokes? What ghost stories did you tell one another on rainy nights? What perpetuates and perserves this folklore? From your discussions of the topic, can you trace any folklore changes that have occurred during your lifetime?

5. Discuss with your classmates the feasibility of a single national rite of passage for youth in the United States. What might that rite be? Would our society benefit from instituting a single rite of passage? What problems might it create? Which, if any, of the current rites of passage comes closest to being a national rite of passage?

Things to Read

Benson, P. & Williams, D. 1986. *Early adolescence: The quicksilver years*. San Francisco: Harper & Row.

Elkind, D. 1981. *The hurried child*. Reading, MA: Addison-Wesley.

Elkind, D. 1984. *All grown up and no place to go.* Reading, MA: Addison-Wesley.

Kagan, J. 1984. *The nature of the child.* NY: Basic Books.

Kohlberg, L. 1986. *The stages of ethical development from childhood through old age.* San Francisco:

Harper & Row.

Scarr, S. 1984. *Mother care/other care.* NY: Basic Books.

White, B.L. 1984. *The first three years of life: A guide to physical, emotional and intellectual growth* (rev. ed). Englewood Cliffs, NJ: Prentice-Hall.

 *Review*

Summary

1. Developmental psychologists study the cumulative physical, cognitive, and psychosocial changes that occur across the lifespan from conception to death. Their work is guided by several psychological perspectives. Most psychologists adopt an eclectic perspective that allows them to draw whatever is most useful from each of the frameworks.

2. Underlying the various developmental viewpoints are basic issues about the nature of human development. Psychologists continue to debate the merits of the different positions on these issues. However, they do not debate that human development is guided by a set of principles that influence everyone's behavior similarly.

3. Genetic factors provide the plan for development through the combination of information from the many genes contained on the twenty-three pairs of chromosomes found in the nucleus of every cell. The genetic transmission of this information from one generation to the next follows definite patterns of inheritance.

4. Conception, or fertilization, refers specifically to the uniting of a single sperm and ovum, but the process is influenced by many factors. The new reproductive technologies that aid infertile couples create complex issues for society.

5. Prenatal development is divided into three functional units: the germinal, embryonic, and fetal stages. Teratogens have their greatest negative effects during the critical periods of the germinal and embryonic stages.

6. The birth process consists of three overlapping stages: labor, delivery, and afterbirth. The Apgar Scale is one measure used to quickly assess the health and medical needs of newborns. At birth, the neonate possesses well-developed sensory systems and reflexes.

7. A major development task for infants is becoming mobile. Cognitively, infants are in Piaget's sensorimotor stage.

8. In their psychosocial development, infants and toddlers move through Erikson's stages of trust versus mistrust and autonomy versus doubt. Two major events during these periods are attachment to caregivers and toilet-training. Several theoretical positions provide insight about these processes.

9. Preschoolers experience a steady but slow rate of physical development. Piaget's preoperational stage describes preschoolers' cognitive development in terms of the limitations on adult-like thinking. According to Erikson, children in this stage face the psychosocial crisis of initiative versus guilt.

10. Gender identification is a major developmental issue with several theoretical explanations. Gender schema theory combines ideas about gender typing from the cognitive-developmental and social learning theories.

11. School becomes an important experience in children's lives between the ages of six and twelve. During the stage of concrete operations, school-agers develop the important mental operation of reversibility and master concepts of conservation. Kohlberg links moral development to cognitive development. Gilligan has proposed that moral development is different for men and women.

12. School-aged children experience an expanding social world and encounter the psychosocial crisis of industry versus inferiority. Healthy psychosocial development at this age involves balancing the desire for productivity with inevitable feelings of inferiority.

13. In industrialized societies, the period of transition from childhood to adulthood has lengthened and no longer involves a ritual for initiation into adult society. Adult status is accorded teenagers on the basis of a variety of physical, intellectual, legal, sociological, and psychological factors.

14. Attaining sexual maturity through the changes of pubescence and achieving cognitive maturity during the formal operation stage are important tasks of adolescence. The major psychosocial task for teenagers is resolving the crisis of identity versus role confusion.

Key Terms

biological perspective
psychodynamic perspective
behavioral-learning perspective
cognitive perspective
humanistic-existential perspective
eclectic perspective
nature-nurture issue
orderliness
quantitative change
qualitative change
directionality
differentiation
readiness
critical periods
individual differences
sex-linked inheritance
germinal stage
embryonic stage
fetal stage

teratogens
neonatal period
sensorimotor stage
attachment
preoperational stage
initiative versus guilt
gender
gender roles
gender typing
phallic stage
gender schema theory
concrete operations
conventional morality
industry versus inferiority
pubescence
formal operations
adolescent egocentrism
genital stage
identity versus role confusion

Focus Questions

1. Is your adult development affected more by your age or by the life events you experience during adulthood?

2. What are the pros and cons of remaining a single adult?

3. Will you live to be a hundred years old?

4. Will your sexual attitudes and behaviors change as you become older?

5. Should men and women have specific gender roles?

Chapter Outline

DEVELOPMENT IN ADULTHOOD
Continuity in Adult Development
Timing of Life Events

BECOMING ESTABLISHED IN THE ADULT WORLD
Lifestyles of Singles
Cohabitation
Choosing a Career

LIFE EVENTS IN ADULTHOOD
Marriage
Divorce
Parenthood
The Research Process: Aging
Death

ADULT SEXUALITY
The Sexual Response Cycle
Sexual Dysfunctions
Treatment of Sexual Dysfunctions

RELATE: Sex and Gender Differences
Things to Do
Things to Discuss
Things to Read

REVIEW: Summary
Key Terms

Chapter 17

Development: Adulthood

*I don't want to achieve immortality
through my work. I want to achieve it
through not dying.*

Woody Allen

Development in Adulthood

Are you the same person you were ten years ago? Answering this question is difficult because undoubtedly you have changed physically, mentally, and socially. But did you ever stop being the person you were ten years ago? The continuity of development across time allows you to be aware of both the changes and the stable features in your own development. Developmental psychologists look at both aspects—stability and change—as they study adult development.

Continuity in Adult Development

Unlike development during childhood and adolescence, with their growth spurts and shifts in cognitive skills,

407

development in adulthood appears more continuous and lacks clear-cut stages. Physical development reveals the gradual changes that occur across the adult years. Generally, physical abilities reach a peak early in adulthood. Muscular strength, sensory acuity, and reaction time are among the abilities that begin to decline gradually after the mid-twenties. Most middle-aged adults who remain in good health and exercise regularly become aware of gradual losses but find they can easily compensate for these changes, by wearing bifocal glasses, for instance. The magnitude of individual differences is great, with some older adults possessing greater physical prowess than some younger persons.

Another area of gradual change in adulthood is cognitive development. While many people assume that cognitive abilities follow the same path of decline as do physical abilities (peak in the twenties and decline thereafter), research results are mixed. One study (Schonfield & Robertson, 1966) found that ability to recall a previously learned list of words declined with the age of the subjects, while the ability to recognize the words remained stable across the subjects (ages twenty to sixty).

Differences also exist for fluid intelligence and crystallized intelligence (Cattell, 1965; Horn, 1970). **Fluid intelligence** involves the capacity to perceive relationships and to integrate that information cognitively. This type of intelligence is considered to be dependent upon brain development and independent of education and experience. By contrast, **crystallized intelligence** (specific, learned information) is determined by education and experience. Fluid intelligence begins to decline in the early adult years, but crystallized intelligence may continue to increase until the end of life. Cognitive development appears to be stable across the adult years because the declines in pure processing ability (fluid intelligence) are offset by the gains in processed information (crystallized intelligence). The wisdom that comes with age may be this ability to compensate for declines in one area of cognitive functioning with gains from another area (Schaie, 1977).

Unlike physical and cognitive development, psychosocial development in adulthood is marked by discontinuities. Several stage theories have been proposed to explain the observed changes in adult psychosocial development. One major issue is whether changes in adult psychosocial development represent a maturational plan similar for all adults, or whether the changes result from the timing of certain important events in adults' lives. Is adult development marked by ages and stages, or is it the result of the cumulative effects of a series of life events?

Erik Erikson, best known for his psychosocial stage theory, extended developmental psychology to a life-span approach.

These two positions on development in adulthood can be described by two models—the normative-crisis and the timing-of-events models (Papalia & Olds, 1986).

The **normative-crisis model** describes adult development as a function of age. The maturational plan of each age is accompanied by a specific crisis to be resolved. According to this model, individuals must resolve this sequence of age-related psychosocial crises for adult development to proceed smoothly. Failure to resolve the crisis of one age (e.g., intimacy versus isolation in early adulthood) will disrupt development at later ages. The psychosocial stage theories of Erikson (1963), Vaillant (1977), Gould (1978), and Levinson (1978) and the cognitive stage theory of Schaie (1977) are examples of the normative-crisis model (see Exhibit 17.1).

Timing of Life Events

Psychologist Bernice Neugarten (1980) has also proposed the terms life time, social time, and historical time to contrast the kinds of interactions that can occur between life events and a person's development. **Life time** corresponds to one's chronological age, or time since birth.

EXHIBIT 17.1
Stages in Adult Development

	ERIKSON	VAILLANT	GOULD	LEVINSON	SCHAIE	TIMING-OF-EVENTS MODEL
	ERIKSON: The three psychological crises of adulthood are a continuation of the sequence of five crises that occur in childhood and adolescence. Healthy resolution of each crisis involves dealing with the positive and negative outcomes so that the positive outcome is dominant.	**VAILLANT:** Vaillant's stages are based on data from a longitudinal study begun in 1938 with undergraduate males at Harvard University. He interviewed ninety-four men when they reached their early thirties (1950 and 1952) and again when they were in their late forties. The data support Erikson's stages, but Vaillant adds additional stages, *career consolidation* and *keeping the meaning versus rigidity.*	**GOULD:** These stages are based on information obtained from ratings of the content of psychiatric patient interviews and from questionnaire responses of a nonclinical group of subjects. Because of methodological flaws, you should use caution in interpreting Gould's data. However, Gould's stages clearly fit the normative-crisis model, and his study is the only major research project to study both men and women as adults.	**LEVINSON:** Levinson studied forty middle-aged men from various occupations. From his in-depth interviews, he concluded that the aim of adult psychological development is to build a *life structure.* As people shape their life structures, they move through stable stages followed by reappraisal during transition phases.	**SCHAIE:** According to this theory, adults continue to pass through stages of cognitive development. The social context influences not only what people think is important to know but also how they decide to use what they know. Children and adolescents are in an *acquisitive stage* where they learn skills and information.	**TIMING-OF-EVENTS MODEL.** Life events can be grouped by the normative ages at which they occur in a particular culture. Societal norms set individuals' expectations for when certain events should occur in their lives.
Early Adulthood (20–35)	**Intimacy versus Isolation.** Successful resolution of the identity crisis of adolescence allows the young adult to merge his or her identity with someone of the opposite sex. During this stage, young adults must work to balance the desire for intimacy with the desire to remain separate from others. Healthy development brings love, friendship, and closeness to others, while inability to develop a loving heterosexual relationship and friendships results in feelings of isolation.	**Establishment** (ages 20–30). This period involves becoming independent of parents, marrying and having children, and developing friendships. **Consolidation** (ages 25–35). During this stage, the men in Vaillant's sample compulsively and unreflectively devoted themselves to consolidating their careers and their families.	**Leaving Home** (ages 18–22). **Becoming Independent** (ages 22–28). **Questioning Self** (ages 29–35). **Sense of Urgency** (ages 35–43).	**Early Adult Transition** (ages 17–24). Form dream about how life will be. **Entering the Adult World** (ages 22–28). Build first life structure. **Age 30 Transition** (ages 28–33). Question past commitments and determine goals. **Settling Down** (ages 33–40). Build second life structure with focus on career and family. **Becoming One's Own Man (BOOM)** (mid- to late-30s). Become independent in career and leave tutelage of others.	**Achieving State** (late teens to early-30s). Emphasis is on how best to use knowledge to achieve potential and fulfill goals.	Leaving home; choosing a lifestyle (marriage, cohabitation, remaining single, parenthood); choosing an occupation.
Middle Adulthood (40–60)	**Generativity versus Stagnation.** Generativity involves establishing and caring for the next generation. A natural progression from the intimacy of early adulthood is becoming a parent and being concerned with childrearing during the middle adult years. Childless individuals can become generative by investing themselves in others' children, by helping lead youth activities, and by forming close relationships with children of friends and relatives. Stagnation results from failing to become actively involved in helping shape the next generation.	**Transition** (approximately age 40). Around age forty individuals begin to be less compulsive about their careers and more reflective about their goals. **Keeping the Meaning versus Rigidity** (ages 45–55). The movement begun in transition culminates when individuals relax about their careers, accept whatever progress they have made toward their goals, and reflect on the meaning of their lives while striving to avoid a rigid outlook on life.	**Settling Down** (ages 43–53). **Acceptance** (ages 53–60).	**Midlife Transition** (ages 40–45). Thoroughly reappraise all aspects of life, with possible moderate to severe midlife crisis. **Entering Middle Adulthood** (around age 45). Begin to build new life structure with new choices. **Age 50 Transition** (ages 50–55). Modify new life structure. **Culmination of Middle Adulthood** (ages 55–60). Build second middle-adult life structure.	**Responsible Stage** (late-30s to early-60s). Emphasis is on using knowledge to solve the real-life problems of those for whom the individual is responsible.	Raising a family, advancing in a career, participating in civic affairs.
Later Adulthood (60–75)	**Ego Integrity versus Despair.** Ego integrity comes from reviewing one's life in later adulthood and being satisfied with the results. When the individual has negatively resolved earlier crises, the life review will yield feelings of despair over the worth of the person's life.			**Later Adult Transition** (ages 60–65). Prepare for later adulthood. **Later Adulthood** (ages 65 onward).	**Reintegrative Stage** (later adulthood). Emphasis is on using knowledge for those tasks that are most meaningful to the person and that have a purpose.	Retirement, death of spouse and friends, one's own approaching death.

Neugarten has suggested that Americans are increasingly experiencing an *age-irrelevant* society in which chronological age reveals little about an adult's psychosocial development. Today, for example, people of all ages go to college, and many adults change occupations several times before retiring. **Social time** embodies the set of age expectations and age statuses within a society. Social time provides the measure against which adults decide whether their lifestyle choices are ahead of time, behind time, or on time. **Historical time** describes the effect of historical events on individuals' development. Historical occurrences such as wars, changing economic conditions, and changing societal values have different effects on people of different ages. For example, how the civil rights demonstrations in the late 1950s and early 60s have influenced you depends upon whether you were born during that time, were a teenager, or were a young, middle-aged, or older adult.

As Neugarten has shown with her concepts of social and historical time, a person's chronological age is often inadequate to describe the course of events in that person's life. The timing of lifestyle choices varies greatly among individuals. Another way to understand how sociohistorical context affects adult development is to examine the overlapping dimensions displayed in Exhibit 17.2. The divisions on each dimension represent a typical course of events across the lifespan of development. You can obtain a clearer picture of individual differences by placing on each dimension markers to correspond to events and phases in your own development, and then comparing your markers with those of other students in your class. If your class is typical of many today, you may be comparing information with a thirty-nine-year-old grandmother, a thirty-nine-year-old father of a toddler, and a nineteen-year-old with thirty-nine-year-old parents.

Another important distinction to be made about social time involves your own perception of the timeline of your development. Although your markers may differ considerably from the typical ones in Exhibit 17.2, your own sense of being "on time" or "out of synch" is influenced as much by your perceptions of the appropriateness of the timing of your life events as by society's norms for appropriate timing. This difference has been viewed as analogous to the difference in perspective between a biography and an autobiography of a person's life (Olney, 1980). The most detailed biography cannot reveal the inner awareness of what living a particular life is like. Both perspectives are needed to understand the complexities of adult development, but ultimately the meaning of a person's life is derived from the autobiographical approach.

According to the **timing-of-events model**, development is a function of when certain important events occur in a person's life. The occurrence of the events is judged not against a biological clock but against a social clock that represents society's expectations for when certain events should occur. When events occur as expected, the developmental process proceeds smoothly; when they do not, development is affected. According to this model, if you expect (and are expected by society) to marry for life in your twenties but are now in your thirties and have not married or have married and divorced, then your psychosocial development will be affected by the juxtaposition of age and events. Similarly, parents who have their first child in their mid-thirties find that their development in middle adulthood differs from the development of parents who had their first child in their early twenties. At thirty-five, the first set of parents will be coping with diapers and their thoughts about being parents of a preschooler, while the second set will be confronting their child's puberty and their thoughts about being parents of a teenager. The timing-of-events approach is a nonstage model that considers age only in relation to societal norms (see Exhibit 17.1).

To the extent that large numbers of adults experience the same life events at approximately the same time, the two models overlap in their descriptions of adult development. The normative-crisis model better explains the developmental similarities among large numbers of adults, and the timing-of-events model better explains individual differences among adults. Whenever an individual experiences life events in an order or time that differs from societal norms, the normative-crisis model will be less adequate in its explanation of that individual's development.

Each person's autobiography represents a fabric woven from the strands of the individual dimensions of his or her life. The complex fabric that results comes from a series of interrelated lifestyle choices across the various dimensions. The choices to go to college immediately after high school and then marry create a fabric very different from that created by deciding to marry and then go to college. From the autobiographical perspective, adult development appears to be less a regular, inevitable sequence of changes and more a series of decisions about what direction to follow regarding occupation, marriage, family, education, and economic independence.

Focus Question Answer

Is your adult development affected more by your age or by the life events you experience during adulthood? Ac-

EXHIBIT 17.2
Developmental Timelines

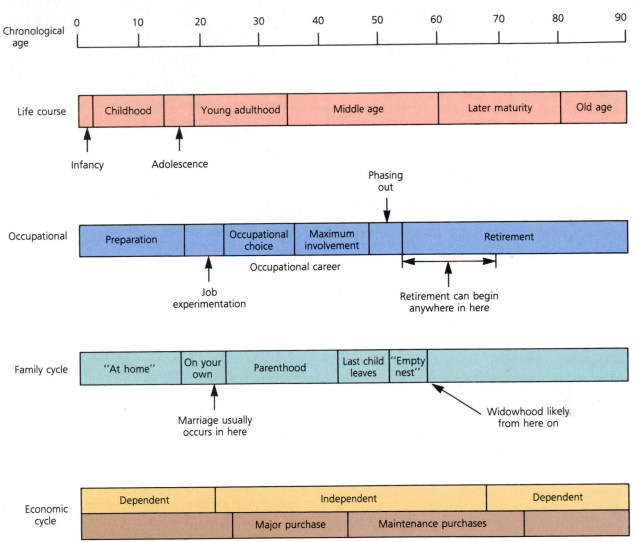

Atchley, R. C. 1975. The life course, age grading, and age-linked demands for decision making. In N. Datan & L. Ginsberg (eds.). *Life-span developmental psychology: Normative life crises.* NY: Academic Press.

cording to the normative-crisis model, your adult development is affected more by your age, with characteristic psychosocial crises to be resolved in early, middle, and late adulthood. On the other hand, the timing-of-events model suggests that the timing of certain events in your adult life is more important than age in determining your adult psychosocial development.

 Becoming Established in the Adult World

The transition from adolescence to adulthood involves breaking away from dependencies to a more independent existence. While some teenagers begin early to make all important decisions independently of their parents and others, many young people continue a semi-autonomous existence well into their twenties. Young adults who enter the military service or go on to college and other forms of career preparation often find that these institutions provide a bridge between leaving home and becoming established as adults. From the late 1950s onward, so many young people have followed this route into adulthood that a new stage—youth—has been proposed to describe the transition (Keniston, 1970).

The stage of **youth** applies to those individuals who have, in part, left their dependency upon their parents and have, in part, entered into adult life. Keniston suggests that youth have not yet fully committed themselves to adulthood because a major part of that commitment is entering into a career. Individuals in the youth stage make many lifestyle choices; they may decide to live alone or with others or to marry. They may even have made their occupational choices, but they are still preparing for those careers. When they finally enter their occupations, the economic independence they achieve will become a major marker of their adult status. Full adult status is usually reserved for individuals who not only make autonomous decisions but also have the economic independence to back up their decisions.

The transition from adolescence to adulthood, whether or not it involves a stage of youth, is not age-limited. Some individuals may move very quickly from economic dependency to self-sufficiency, while others may take eight or more years to reach the same point. The *Exploring . . .* section describes the stage of youth as a category that may be appropriate for people other than those who are leaving adolescence and entering adulthood.

Lifestyles of Singles

A major lifestyle choice in adulthood is marrying or remaining single. Thus phrased, singleness appears to be a homogeneous category. However, grouping all singles into one unit is a mistake because several different categories of nonmarried adults exist. Certain singles have never married, while others are single again after becoming divorced or experiencing the death of a spouse. Some single adults live with their parents; others live alone; and others share living quarters with other single adults. Although some individuals may choose to remain single, others may view their status as temporary, lasting only until they find suitable marriage partners. Despite certain stereotypes, most single adults are heterosexuals;

however, some single adults do have a homosexual gender orientation. Because of their diversity, single adults cannot be lumped within a single category.

The number of never-married young adults has increased dramatically since 1970. More than twice as many young adults are single today than were single in 1970. In 1983, among twenty-five- to twenty-nine-year-olds, nearly 30 percent of the women and 38 percent of men were never-married singles compared to 11 percent and 19 percent respectively in 1970 (U.S. Bureau of the Census, 1984). For thirty- to thirty-four-year-olds, the percentages also doubled from 1970, to 12 percent for women and 17 percent for men in 1983. Nearly one-half of all the households formed in the United States since 1980 consist of single adults living alone or with nonrelatives (U.S. Bureau of the Census, 1985). Such a substantial rise in the percentage of never-married young adults raises many questions about how this trend will affect society.

One way to begin studying the effects of this trend is to examine influences on the choice to remain unmarried. One study (Stein, 1976) interviewed a sample of sixty men and women. Their replies indicated that their choices not to marry were influenced by several positive advantages to remaining single and by several negative drawbacks to getting married. The positive advantages included autonomy, self-sufficiency, career opportunities, mobility, social and sexual freedom, and opportunities for change, for a variety of experiences, and for friendships. Negative aspects focused on the limitations of marriage—monogamy, lack of freedom for self-development and pursuit of personal goals, conformity to spouse's expectations, less mobility, and fewer opportunities for new experiences. The individuals in this sample based their decisions to remain single neither entirely on avoidance of marriage nor on attraction to the single lifestyle.

By their designated social status, never-married adults are set apart from other adults, yet many of the tasks and problems faced by never-married singles are also shared by married, widowed, and divorced adults. Finding jobs, advancing in careers, establishing homes, and maintaining friendships are just a few of adults' common concerns. Nonetheless, persons choosing to remain single encounter stereotypes that differ from those faced by adults in other categories. Common stereotypes include the belief that the individual's single lifestyle is not a choice but a matter of default resulting from the person's undesirability as marriage partner or inability to make

Youth—A Stage But Not an Age?

The stage of youth was originally proposed to encompass the transition into adulthood from the late teen years into the early twenties (Keniston, 1970). However, since college students of all ages share similar characteristics, the label of youth may apply not strictly to an age but rather to a stage that people may move in and out of at different times during their adult years.

In this respect, three characteristics of youth are especially interesting. Youth have been described as focused on occupational preparation, and this focus brings about a second paradoxical characteristic. While youths prepare for the future, they often defer some decisions and activities. They concentrate on fulfilling immediate short-term goals while postponing other goals until after their career preparation is over. Finally, because youth have completed the tasks of adolescence but have not fully assumed all responsibilities and commitments of adulthood, they must redefine their relationships with their parents and other important individuals in their lives.

College students and others training for specific occupations are certainly aware of the career focus in their lives. People always seem to ask, "When will you graduate?" or "Are you still in school?" As a college student, you may find these repetitive questions annoying. After all, you must finish your project by Monday, and you must study for the test on Friday. These short-term goals are more important than your more distant goal of graduating. You may be postponing marrying or moving to a new location until you finish your degree. Whether you entered college immediately after high school or are an older student, the immediate demands of your classes undoubtedly cause you to postpone some plans, at least until the end of the term.

Older students may be more sensitive than traditional younger students to the redefinition of roles involved with entering college. The older student is likely to have already established definite adult roles, and when he or she enters college, spouses, children, neighbors, and friends must adjust to the individual's new role as a college student. The older student often finds that family and friends question his or her choice and are threatened by the decision to go to college.

As these examples suggest, the characteristics of youth apply to college students of all ages. In fact, older students often report that they feel more youthful in their outlook as a result of attending college. Social forecasters have been predicting for several decades now that adults will retrain for one or more career changes during their working years. If their predictions are correct, youth may well be a stage that adults enter and leave several times during their adult years.

---

an emotional commitment. Others believe that never-married persons are single because they are sexually unattractive or because they are homosexual.

One hopes that these stereotypes will diminish as the increased numbers of individuals who choose to remain single influence society. Research has already disproven two additional stereotypical views of never-married singles—loneliness and sexual promiscuity. One study in which four hundred never-married, divorced, and remarried subjects were interviewed revealed that multiple sex partners and loneliness due to lack of companionship are more typical of divorced individuals than never-married singles (Cargan, 1981). Further studies should present an even clearer picture of today's never-married single lifestyle.

Cohabitation

An alternative to marrying or remaining single is **cohabitation**, the open living arrangement of an unmarried couple. Until recently, cohabitation was a relatively little used living arrangement. In 1970, according to the U.S. Bureau of the Census (1985), only 523,000 unmarried couples lived together. By 1984, the number had risen rapidly to 1,988,000 cohabiting couples; this number represents approximately one of every twenty-five couples who live together. In 1985, this sharply upward trend leveled off with an insignificant drop of 5,000 to 1,983,000 cohabiting couples (U.S. Bureau of the Census, 1985).

One likely explanation for the slight shrinkage in cohabitation is that, following the post-World War II baby boom, the number of young adults available for cohabitation is declining. The explanations for the incredible fifteen-year increase in cohabitation are more speculative. The increase has been attributed to the sexual revolution and its associated increase in premarital sexual experience, the relatively high divorce rate in the United States, young adults' greater fears of making commitments, economic conditions, the lengthening time period between sexual maturity and social maturity, and the decline of the basic family unit.

As a lifestyle choice, cohabitation offers the opportunity for learning about intimate relationships, for assessing ideas about marriage and a marriage partner, for developing a sexual relationship, and for increasing personal understanding and maturity. However, these opportunities also exist with other forms of dating and courtship, and research among married couples has indicated that cohabitation does not lead to better marriages (Jacques & Chason, 1979). Another study (Watson, 1983) found that during the first year of marriage couples who had not cohabited got along better than those who had, indicating that the "honeymoon" may already be over for cohabiting couples who marry.

Although unmarried, newly-cohabiting couples encounter some of the same problems newlyweds face, both newly-cohabiting and newly-married individuals must learn to balance their needs with those of their partners. They must achieve a balance between individual needs for independence and self-identity and collective demands of shared dependency and identity. They must learn to manage conflict within an intimate relationship and must also resolve the practical problems that arise when two people begin to share a household.

On the other hand, cohabiting couples do face problems not encountered by newlyweds. For example, marriage is a clearly defined status, while cohabitation is not. Husband, wife, and spouse are well-established terms for marriage partners; corresponding terms for cohabiting individuals have not been adopted into common usage. Furthermore, society overwhelmingly approves of marriage, but cohabitation receives greatly varying degrees of approval. Fear of parental disapproval may have been

one reason more than two-thirds of the cohabiting women in one study attempted to hide their living arrangements from their parents (Macklin, 1972).

Will the number of adults choosing cohabitation as a lifestyle remain stable, decline further, or resume its upward trend? Predicting the answer to this question is difficult. While the number of cohabiting couples in the United States is currently near its peak, the actual length of time most couples remain in this lifestyle is fairly short. Nearly two-thirds of cohabiting couples live together for less than two years before they marry or separate (Blumstein & Schartz, 1983). In attempting to assess cohabitation's impact on individual lives, one researcher has noted that most people are equally satisfied with either choice—cohabiting or traditional courtship before marriage (Watson, 1983). Among those dissatisfied with their premarital lifestyles, women are more likely to regret having chosen cohabitation, while men are more likely to regret not having chosen to cohabitate.

Choosing a Career

At the same time that young adults make lifestyle choices about marriage and parenthood, they also make decisions about their working lives. Most researchers agree that the process of occupation selection begins before the active choices of the early adult years. One theory of vocational choice (Ginsberg et al., 1951; Ginsberg, 1972) proposes that the process begins during a fantasy stage in childhood, when children imagine what they want to be without regard for reality or practicality. In the tentative stage of the teen years, more realistic decision-making takes place. Finally, in a realistic stage, young adults engage in extensive career exploration while narrowing their choices to specific careers and specific jobs within those careers.

Theories of vocational choice often emphasize how careers define individuals. For example, the **developmental self-concept theory** (Super, 1967; 1976) proposes that vocational choice begins in earnest during adolescence, when teens construct vocational self-concepts. This process begins with younger teens developing work ideas that coincide with their already existing self-concepts. Next, they specify careers by narrowing their choices. By the early twenties, most young adults begin to implement their vocational choices by completing their education and training and entering the workforce. According to Super, the process of vocational identity does not become stabilized until sometime between the ages of twenty-five and thirty-five, after which middle-aged adults seek to consolidate their careers and advance within them.

Another theory that looks at personality factors in vocational choice is Holland's **personality type theory** (Holland, 1985; Weinrach, 1984). Holland maintains that individuals select vocational environments that match their personality types. According to this viewpoint, people within the same occupation should have similar personalities, and job satisfaction should be related to the degree of match between personality and occupation. Holland has proposed six basic personality types and environments, which are briefly described in Exhibit 17.3. Note that Holland's theory suffers from a weakness characteristic of all personality type theories—his categories are too simplistic to describe the complex variations among individual personalities.

Each of these theories assumes that a person's career will follow an orderly progression from selection and entry, through adjustment and maintenance, to retirement. However, many people's work experiences do not follow an orderly sequence. Technological advances and changing economic conditions, locally and worldwide, have altered the occupational work cycles of many. Today, unemployment may be a recurring factor of many individuals' work cycles and a permanent feature of some.

As these theories suggest, the work adults perform is a major element of their self-concepts, and the definition of self through work has been a crucial issue in the social changes brought about by the greatly increased numbers of women working outside the home. The economic ramifications of comparable-worth legislation (equal pay for comparable work) are only part of the

EXHIBIT 17.3
Holland's Six Personality Types and Occupational Environments

Type	Personality Characteristics	Typical Occupations
Realistic	Physical, practical; prefers machines, tools, or animals; "masculine"	Machinists, truck-drivers, farmers, construction workers
Investigative	Theoretical, analytical, precise, methodical	Mathematicians, scientists, chemists, physicists, biologists
Artistic	Expressive, introspective, nonconforming, original	Artists, musicians, writers, decorators
Social	People-oriented, verbal; avoids machinery; "feminine"	Teachers, social workers, bartenders, funeral directors
Enterprising	Dominating, manipulative—especially for economic gain	Salespeople, politicians, lawyers, managers
Conventional	Structured; likes manipulating numbers and reproducing materials	Financial experts, file clerks, secretaries

Source: Holland, J. L. 1985. *Making vocational choices: A theory of vocational personalities & work environments,* 2nd ed, pp. 19–23. Adapted by permission of Prentice Hall, Inc., Englewood Cliffs, NJ.

Due to technological advances and other factors, the man operating this prototype industrial machinery may have to choose another career before he reaches retirement age.

adjustment society must make as women redefine who they are because of changes in the types of work they perform. Tasks for the future include understanding how to help women and men adjust to these changes, while technological advances continue to create both unemployment and new types of work for men and women.

Focus Question Answer

What are the pros and cons of remaining a single adult? The advantages include autonomy, self-sufficiency, career opportunities, mobility, social and sexual freedom, and opportunities for change, for a variety of experiences, and for friendships. The disadvantages include combating negative stereotypes of unmarried individuals and establishing life as a single in a society that favors couples and discriminates against single individuals.

   Life Events in Adulthood

In this section, you will read about several significant life events—marriage, divorce, parenthood, aging, death, and bereavement. You may not marry, divorce, or become a parent, but you certainly age, confront bereavement, and die. The occurrence and timing of these events in your life shape the pattern of development that is uniquely your own.

Marriage

Marriage is the only nearly universal lifestyle choice in American society. About 95 percent of American adults marry sometime during their adult years. Most marry during early adulthood, but the trend in recent years has been for young adults to marry at later ages. In 1985, the typical first-time bride and groom were 23.3 and 25.5 years old respectively (U.S. Bureau of the Census, 1985). These ages represent an increase of more than two years since 1970. While a two-year increase may seem insignificant, such a change has far-reaching implications for society. To begin with, fewer men and women are marrying in their teen years, and individuals who previously were married in their early twenties are now waiting until their mid-twenties to marry. One result of this change is a shortened time period for having children. This effect is compounded by couples waiting longer after marrying to have children. As a result, the birth rate has declined. In turn, fewer children will result in fewer demands on public services such as schools and, ultimately, fewer individuals entering the workforce in the future.

Although they are marrying at later ages, most adults do marry, and the United States' high marriage rate reflects the strong social pressures. Marriage receives society's blessings as the ideal way to achieve a stable, intimate relationship with assurances of an approved sexual outlet, an orderly process for rearing children, and lifelong companionship. An important measure of life satisfaction for adults is a happy, successful marriage (Campbell et al., 1975). The relatively high rate of divorce in the United States is accompanied by an even higher rate of remarriage for divorced individuals, presenting more evidence that the goal of a happy marriage is extremely important in American society.

Most people marry persons from social backgrounds similar to their own. Similar interests, values, religious views, traditions, and experiences increase the likelihood of achieving a happy, successful marriage. Yet whether individuals marry from within or outside their social groups, certain other elements are important prerequisites for successful marriage (Blood & Blood, 1978). These factors include emotional maturity and the capacity for love, both of which involve a realistic appraisal of one's ability for self-discipline, self-objectivity, and self-responsibility. Other important prerequisites are skill in communicating and in solving problems, flexibility in adapting to the other person and to change, commitment to the relationship, and willingness to exert effort toward solving common problems.

Social pressures have ensured that marriage continues to be the lifestyle choice of most Americans, despite the high divorce rates.

Marriages that last several decades are influenced by a cycle of typical stages but also reflect the influences of the timing-of-events model of development. Typically, the marriage cycle follows a pattern of a honeymoon and a beginning period of adjustment; these events are followed by child-rearing years, the empty nest when children leave home, and retirement years. This cycle is influenced by the individuals' ages at the time of marriage and by their decisions about having children and the number of children to have. If they decide to have children, the timing of the births of the children and their leaving home also may alter the marriage cycle.

Recently, however, the declining birth rate has changed the nature of the marriage cycle. Couples now spend an average of two years together before they have children, they have fewer children, and the life expectancy of each spouse has increased. The net result is fewer years of marriage devoted to childrearing and more years spent together without children. Since the early 1900s, approximately fourteen years of child-free living have been added to the marriage cycle (Glick, 1977).

Whatever the individual marriage cycle that a couple experiences, marriage is generally a healthy experience for both partners. Among the developed countries of the world, married individuals live longer than unmarried persons. Marriage appears to be particularly beneficial to men. Among men, married men have the lowest death rates, followed by never-married single men; widowed and divorced men have higher rates. Married individuals also report higher levels of happiness, measured by their feelings of life satisfaction and general well-being, than do never-married, widowed, or divorced individuals (Campbell et al., 1975). However, correlational data such as these do not imply that marriage causes people to be healthier and happier; rather, healthier and happier individuals may be more likely to marry and stay married. Longitudinal research with 4,000 married, separated, and divorced men supports the latter conclusion (Erbes & Hedderson, 1984). Divorced and separated men, compared with the men who stayed married, achieved lower scores on measures of psychological well-being long before they separated or divorced.

Divorce

Divorce is a lifestyle choice of many married adults. More than one million divorces are recorded in the United States each year, and until 1981, when a slight decline was noted, both the total number of divorces and the rate of divorce increased steadily. Today, divorce is common in all socioeconomic levels in the United States. However, certain factors are associated with higher rates of divorce: younger ages (teenagers) at the time of marriage, lower levels of education, lower levels of income, and premarital pregnancy. In one study, half the women who were pregnant before their marriages were separated or divorced from their husbands within five years of getting married (Sauber & Corrigan, 1970).

Of special concern is the impact of the high number of divorces on society and on the children of parents who divorce. The concepts of social and historical time are important in interpreting these effects. Social expectations regarding the appropriateness of divorce have changed considerably over the years and are reflected in fewer legal restrictions for divorce. The greater incidence of divorce has also lessened the social stigma experienced by divorcing families. Today, children of divorced parents attend school with many other children of divorced parents and are likely to have teachers who have been divorced; fifty years ago, a child of divorced parents may have been the only one in the classroom to have firsthand experience with divorce.

Although fewer religious, legal, and social obstacles to divorce exist and although conventional wisdom holds that staying together for the children is often not good for the children, the process of separation and divorce is complex and stressful for all involved. Most stressful appears to be the period before the decision to divorce (Santrock & Warshak, 1979; Albrecht, 1980). Divorced individuals, whether they initiate the divorces or are divorced by their spouses, experience grief similar to the grief of those who are widowed. The grieving process takes time and, as when a relationship is ended unexpectedly by death, a sudden and unexpected divorce is more likely to produce greater emotional problems and poorer adjustment to the situation (Spanier & Castro, 1979).

Divorce's effects on children depend upon a number of circumstances, including the number of children in the family and their ages at the time of divorce, the nature of the separation process, the financial circumstances of the family, and the degree of involvement and quality of the relationship with both parents following the divorce. While divorce is assumed to have a greater impact on younger children, even adult children are not immune from trauma. Fear, anger, depression, guilt, and despair are commonly experienced by children of all ages whose parents are divorcing. Common reactions also include physical symptoms such as headaches, stomachaches, vomiting, and disturbed sleep. Other stress reactions may involve lying, stealing, or, among teens, becoming very sexually active (Neal, 1983).

Children of divorcing parents encounter additional tasks beyond the normal challenges of psychosocial development. In a longitudinal divorce study including children aged three to eighteen at the time of the divorce (Wallerstein, 1983), Wallerstein has followed sixty California families over a period of years as they have adjusted to divorce. From his observations of these families' adjustment, he has suggested that the following six tasks are crucial for the healthy emotional development of children of divorce:

1. Acknowledging the reality of the marital rupture. In the presence of both parents, children need to be told about the divorce in words they can understand.

2. Disengaging from parental conflict and distress and resuming customary pursuits. Children should not be used as weapons or messengers in the conflict between the parents. The children's routines should be changed as little as possible as a result of the divorce.

3. Resolving the loss. Children should be allowed to grieve and should be encouraged to express the emotions they experience. They should be repeatedly assured of both parents' continuing love and concern.

4. Resolving anger and self-blame. Because of their egocentrism, preschoolers may be especially prone to blaming themselves for a divorce. All children need reassurance that they did not cause the divorce. They also need the opportunity to express their fears and anger; professional counseling or support groups may be useful.

5. Accepting the permanence of the divorce. Parents need to make clear the finality of the divorce so children do not engage in the unrealistic belief that they have the power to bring their parents together again.

6. Achieving realistic hope regarding relationships. Children must be reassured that although the relationship between their parents has ended both parents still desire to maintain loving relationships with them.

Remarriage Most children of divorcing parents will also have to adjust to their parents' remarriage to other individuals. Eventually, 80 percent of divorced individuals remarry, with most remarrying within two to three years. Today's trend is for people to marry at older ages and to divorce at younger ages (Glick & Norton, 1977). Accompanying this trend is a shorter time period between remarriage and redivorce. Although many remarriages also end in divorce (40 percent), 60 percent endure until one spouse dies. These current trends assure that many children will experience a new family unit, the **blended family**.

One estimate projects that in the 1990s, 25–30 percent of all children will be part of blended families at some point before their eighteenth birthdays (Glick, 1977). A blended family may be a simple structure in which the step-parent does not bring children from a previous marriage to the new marriage. Or, the blended family may be a more complex structure in which each partner brings children from a previous marriage, a situation wherein each spouse is both a step-parent and a biological parent. Certain blended families, such as those in which a divorcing step-parent receives custody of a nonbiological child and then remarries into a new blended family, beg for new words in our language since none exist to describe the complex relationships created.

Children have greater difficulty adjusting to the more complex blended families than to the simpler blended family structure (Hetherington et al., 1982). One study that compared the interactions in blended and intact families (Santrock et al., 1985) found the family atmosphere in intact families more positive, and in blended families relationships between children and biological parents more positive than relationships between children and their step-parents. Interestingly, the study revealed that in blended families with a stepfather, the biological mother performed most of the parenting duties, but in blended families with a stepmother, the biological father shared many more of the parenting responsibilities. Being a single father between the time of divorce and remarriage apparently helps such men gain skill and appreciation for parenting.

More research on blended and single-parent families' effects on the present and later lives of children is needed. Remember, however, that each family structure has many unique features that influence the adjustment of the family members in that unit. Positive and negative adjustments are found in intact families as well as in single-parent and blended families.

Parenthood

Today, more than ever, the decision to have children is truly an adult lifestyle choice. The ready availability of effective contraceptives has given couples the freedom to choose, and that freedom has altered a traditional reason for marrying—to have children. Nevertheless, despite the availability of choice, social pressures still strongly convey the message that "normal" people want to have children. The use of the term child*less*, rather than child*free,* to describe individuals who do not have children reflects this societal bias. Pressures to have children are so great that childless-by-choice couples are often viewed as selfish and self-indulgent, and many reproductive technologies have been developed to assist infertile couples (see Chapter 16). Of course, the presence of many unplanned pregnancies confirms that many couples do not actively choose parenthood as a lifestyle but become parents nonetheless.

A number of factors affect the decision to have or not to have children. Parenthood represents an irrevocable commitment, one with no trial period for reconsideration. Particularly, parenthood requires a long-term commitment of resources—time, energy, and money. The costs for raising a child from birth to age eighteen are now estimated at over $100,000, while no one can estimate the time and energy demanded during those first eighteen years. In one study of nearly two hundred couples with various family sizes, the two major reasons for having children were wanting to participate in the rearing of children and wanting the close relationship between parent and child (Campbell et al., 1982). The two major reasons for remaining childless were the financial costs and the couple's beliefs that a child would disrupt their educational and career goals.

Today, approximately 5–7 percent of American couples decide upon a childfree lifestyle (Veevers, 1980). Such couples tend to be above average in education and intelligence, to have good communication skills, and to have high marital satisfaction (Feldman, 1981). When compared to couples with children, childfree couples tend to base their relationships on equality of sex roles and to enjoy more activities together. Some people decide before they marry not to have children, with many making the decision while they are teenagers. However, the more common pattern, followed by two-thirds of childless couples, is perpetual postponement (Veevers, 1980). The decision to have children is first postponed in order to accomplish a specific goal such as finishing one's education. Then the decision is postponed for less specific reasons—"until we can better afford it" or "until we are more ready." In the third stage, the question is actively debated, but the decision is again postponed until a time when the couple believes their lives will be less disrupted. Finally, the couple accepts that by not deciding they have decided not to have children.

Parenting Styles Adults who do become parents soon realize that parenting demands many skills and continual adjustment as children grow and change. As people make the transition from nonparent to parent, they develop distinctive parenting styles. Earlier research (Baumrind,

Parenthood requires long-term emotional and financial committment; in return, parents expect to participate in a type of relationship unavailable with other adults.

1971) identified three major styles of parenting with respect to parental use of authority. **Authoritarian parenting** describes parents who are demanding and controlling and assert great power over their children. Such parents have demanding standards of conduct for their children and allow little give-and-take between child and parent. In contrast, **permissive parenting** characterizes parents who are undemanding and assert relatively little control over their children's behavior. **Authoritative parenting** represents the middle ground between the two extremes. Authoritative parents encourage independence within the reasonable limits they set. In these families occurs considerable verbal give-and-take between children and parents.

More recently, researchers have investigated these parenting styles along two dimensions: demanding/undemanding and accepting/rejecting (Maccoby & Martin, 1983). Using these two dimensions, researchers have concluded that the permissive parenting style involves two different forms. As shown in Exhibit 17.4, parents who practice **permissive-indulgent parenting** are highly involved with their children's lives but do little to control their children's behavior. In comparison, parents who follow the **permissive-indifferent parenting** style not only do not control their children's behavior but are also uninvolved with their children.

Each parenting style produces different effects. The demanding, controlling, rejecting, and punitive style of the authoritarian is associated with children who are anxious about social comparisons, who are ineffectual in social relationships, and who fail to show initiative.

EXHIBIT 17.4
Parenting Styles Classified on Two Dimensions

Authoritative	Child-Centered Accepting/Responsive Demanding/Controlling
Authoritarian	Parent-Centered Rejecting/Unresponsive Demanding/Controlling
Permissive-Indulgent	Child-Centered Accepting/Responsive Undemanding/Low Control
Permissive-Indifferent	Parent-Centered Rejecting/Unresponsive Undemanding/Low Control

Source: Maccoby, E. E. & Martin, J. A. 1983. Socialization in the context of the family: Parent-Child interaction. In P. E. Mussen (ed.). *Handbook of child psychology* (4th ed., vol. 4). Reprinted by permission of John Wiley & Sons, Inc.

Permissive-indulgent parenting is associated with impulsive children who are aggressive, dependent, and irresponsible. A major characteristic of children raised by permissive-indifferent parents is lack of self-control. Only the authoritative parenting style is associated with mostly positive outcomes. Children of authoritative parents exhibit the highest levels of social competency, self-reliance, and social responsibility.

You may have little difficulty classifying your own parents along these dimensions, but knowing what kind of parent you are or will be is much more difficult. Realizing that parents can learn more effective ways to deal with their children's behavior and that parents do change is comforting. Accompanying the choice to become a parent is the choice of the type of parent you would like to be.

The Research Process: Aging

The lifestyle of an adult occurs within the context of a physical body that matures and ages. At any point in adulthood, an individual can be described by his or her biological age, psychological age, and social age (Birren & Renner, 1980). **Biological age** is measured by life expectancy. Throughout adulthood, individuals' health habits, lifestyle choices, and disease factors affect life expectancy (see Exhibit 17.5). **Psychological age** is measured by capacity for adaptive behavior. Certain eighty-year-olds remain flexible in their outlooks and capable of adapting to the changes in their lives, while some individuals are "old" at thirty. Characterized by phrases such as "Act your age!" and "She acts like she's thirty!", **social age** is measured by the extent to which individuals conform to the expected social roles for any given age. While psychological and social factors definitely influence the aging process, most theories of aging focus on biological factors.

Several biological theories of aging have been proposed. Most acknowledge a genetically programmed limit to the lifespan, a limit based on research indicating that normal cells in the human body are capable of dividing only about fifty times (Hayflick, 1977). Hayflick estimates that the upper limit for longevity is 110 to 120 years. But if the **Hayflick limit** is correct, why do so many people die long before they approach the programmed limit?

A shortened lifespan is usually attributed to the accumulation of wear-and-tear on the body during the person's life. Lifestyle, health habits, and health risks interact with the genetic program to determine the actual lon-

EXHIBIT 17.5

Factors that Decrease Life Expectancy Expressed in Days Lost from Average Life Expectancy

The following health habits, lifestyle choices, diseases, and other factors reduce life expectancy. The reduction is indicated in the number of days lost from the nearly seventy-five-year average life expectancy for Americans today. The 3,500 days lost from being an unmarried male represent a 9.5 year loss from the average life expectancy.

Risk Factors	Days Lost
BEING AN UNMARRIED MALE	3,500
BEING MALE & SMOKING CIGARETTES	2,250
HEART DISEASE	2,100
BEING AN UNMARRIED FEMALE	1,600
BEING 30 PERCENT OVERWEIGHT	1,300
BEING A COAL MINER	1,100
CANCER	980
BEING 20 PERCENT OVERWEIGHT	900
BEING FEMALE & SMOKING CIGARETTES	800
BEING POOR	700
STROKE	520
HAVING A DANGEROUS JOB	300
INCREASING DAILY CALORIE INTAKE BY 100	210
DRIVING A MOTOR VEHICLE	207
ALCOHOL	130
WALKING DOWN THE STREET	37
DRINKING COFFEE	6
DRINKING DIET SODAS	2

Reprinted with permission from *Health Physics, 36,* Lee, I.S. & Cohen, B.L. A catalog of risks. © 1979, Pergamon Press.

gevity of that person. For example, you may have the genetic capacity to live to be 110, but if you are exposed for many years to a health hazard such as smoking, the hazard acts to limit the fulfillment of your genetic potential. Wear-and-tear on the body may damage certain cells, alter the genetic programs of others, and cause the body's immune system to malfunction. The capacity of the body's biological systems to recover from this stress—known as organ reserve—declines steadily after age thirty. At the same time, the mortality rate after age thirty doubles every eight years (Upton, 1977). Although a direct causal link between these processes has not been established, interest is currently focused on ways to maintain the body's organ reserve while fortifying the body against deterioration.

Exercise, diet, and other health habits have long been assumed to be important in counteracting the cumulative effects of aging. In one study of 7,000 persons aged twenty to seventy, observance of seven basic health habits was highly correlated with good health and also

with decreased rates of dying at any stage (Belloc & Breslow, 1972). In this study, the healthiest individuals, regardless of age, were people who maintained six to seven of the basic health habits listed in Exhibit 17.6. When compared over a five-year period to individuals who practiced three or fewer of the health habits, the healthy individuals always had lower death rates. During the five-year period, two-thirds of the oldest individuals with poor health habits died, while only one-third of the individuals the same age with good health habits died.

Among the seven health habits, regular moderate exercise has received special attention as a way to fortify the body against wear-and-tear and to maintain organ reserve. A longitudinal study of 17,000 Harvard University alumni (Paffenbarger et al., 1986), revealed that men who exercised moderately and regularly had mortality rates one-quarter to one-third lower than men who led more sedentary lives. The exercise was equivalent to five hours of brisk walking or four hours of jogging per week; more exercise was beneficial only to the point at which increased risk of injuries canceled out the benefits. This study found for men who exercised not only a reduced risk of death from heart disease but from all other diseases as well. Exercising men with high blood pressure had half the mortality rate of their less active counterparts. Smokers who exercised reduced deaths by approximately 30 percent. Although you must be cautious in applying these results to the general population because the sample contained mostly white men and no women, the results do encourage exercise as one way to increase life expectancy. Complete the questionnaire in the accompanying *Exploring . . .* section to estimate your own life expectancy.

Both physical and psychosocial factors are associated with definite patterns of aging. Eight basic patterns of aging grouped within four personality types are described in

EXHIBIT 17.6

Seven Basic Health Habits

1. EAT BREAKFAST
2. EAT REGULAR MEALS, AND AVOID SNACKS
3. MAINTAIN NORMAL BODY WEIGHT
4. DO NOT SMOKE
5. DRINK ALCOHOL MODERATELY OR NOT AT ALL
6. SLEEP REGULARLY 7-8 HOURS A NIGHT
7. EXERCISE MODERATELY AND REGULARLY

Source: Belloc, N. B. & Breslow, L. 1972. Relationship of physical health status and health practices. *Preventive Medicine, 1,* pp. 1171–1190.

How Long Will You Live?

The average life expectancy for someone born in the United States today is approximately 75 years. On the average, men live shorter lives, while women are expected to live longer than the average life expectancy. For men, the average life expectancy is 71 years and for women, nearly 78.5 years. To estimate your individual life expectancy, start with the number 75, and then add or subtract the years indicated in each item.

Average life expectancy 75

1. Initial Adjustments
   If you are a male, subtract 3 .... ____
      If you are a female, add 4 .... ____
      If you are between 30 and 40, add 2 .... ____
      If you are between 40 and 50, add 3 .... ____
      If you are between 50 and 70, add 4 .... ____
      If you are over 70, add 5 .... ____
2. Family History
      If any grandparent lived to 85, add 2 .... ____
      If 2 or more of your grandparents lived to 80, add 5 .... ____
      If all 4 grandparents lived to 80, add 6 .. ____
      If either parent died of a stroke or heart attack before age 50, subtract 4 ...... ____
      If any parent, brother, or sister under 50 has (or had) cancer or a heart condition or has had diabetes since childhood, subtract 3 .... ____
3. Marital Status
      If you live with a spouse or friend, add 5 ____
      If you live alone, for every 10 years alone since age 25, subtract 1 .... ____
4. Economic Status
      If your family income is over 50,000, subtract 2 .... ____
      If you have been poor for the greater part of your life, subtract 3 .... ____
5. Education
      If you have less than a high school diploma, subtract 2 .... ____
      If you have had 4 years of school beyond high school, add 1 .... ____
      If you have a graduate or professional degree, add 2 .... ____
6. Living Environment
      If you have lived most of your life in a rural area, add 2 .... ____
      If you have lived in an urban area, subtract 2 .... ____
7. Physical Condition
      If you are overweight by 50 pounds or more, subtract 8 .... ____
      If you are overweight by 30 to 50 pounds, subtract 4 .... ____
      If you are overweight by 10 to 30 pounds, subtract 2 .... ____
      For each inch your waist measurement exceeds your chest measurement, subtract 2 .... ____
8. Physical Exercise
      If you work behind a desk, subtract 3 ... ____
      If work requires regular, strenuous physical labor, add 3 .... ____
      If you exercise strenuously 5 times a week for at least 30 minutes, add 4 .... ____
      If you exercise strenuously 2 to 3 times a week, add 2 .... ____
9. Sleep
      If you regularly sleep more than 9 hours a day, subtract 4 .... ____
10. Smoking
       If you smoke 2 or more packs a day, subtract 8 .... ____
       If you smoke 1 to 2 packs a day, subtract 6 .... ____
       If you smoke one-half to 1 pack a day, subtract 3 .... ____
11. Alcohol Usage
       If you drink the equivalent of one and one-half ounces of liquor a day, subtract 1 ____
       If you drink more than 4 drinks a day, subtract 8 .... ____
12. Health Care
       If you are a man over 40 and have annual checkups, add 2 .... ____
       If you are a woman and see a gynecologist once a year, add 2 .... ____

Your Estimated Life Expectancy. .... ____

Source: Allen, R.F. & Linde, S. *Lifegain.* Morristown, N. J.: Human Resources Institute.

Exhibit 17.7 (Neugarten, Havighurst & Tobin, 1968). As you can see, the patterns of aging displayed by individuals with integrated (well-functioning) and armored-defended (achievement-oriented) personalities led to a higher degree of life satisfaction than the patterns exhibited by passive-dependent (strongly dependent and apathetic) and unintegrated (disorganized) individuals. As this research suggests, by choice or default, older adults vary greatly in the ways they live their lives. Older adults, like their younger counterparts, lead lives that are marked by their individual lifestyle choices. The lesson for younger adults from this research is that the older adults with the highest degree of life satisfaction were those individuals who remained actively involved in choosing the course of their lives.

Productivity, characterized by passing on skills and knowledge to other generations, can bring satisfaction to aging adults.

Dying

Two life events that increase in significance as a person ages are his or her own death and deaths of family members and friends. During the middle adult years, awareness of the increased likelihood of dying may trigger in certain individuals a so-called midlife crisis (Jung, 1968). Although the idea of a midlife crisis brought on, in part, by awareness of mortality may have achieved a significance beyond its research support (Farrell & Rosenberg, 1981), middle-aged adults do shift from thinking about how long they have lived to thinking about how long they will live before they die (Neugarten, 1967). The

awareness that fewer years remain than have passed may cause certain individuals to make major life changes and does produce, in most middle-aged adults, a reassessment of their lives and a rethinking of their attitudes about death.

In contrast, terminally ill people of any age are confronted with adjusting to their own deaths over much shorter time periods. After extensive interviews with terminally ill patients, Elisabeth Kübler-Ross (1969; 1974) proposed that dying patients progress through five stages

EXHIBIT 17.7
Personality Type in Relation to Activity and Life Satisfaction

Personality Type	Role Activity Type	Life Satisfaction
Integrated	Reorganized Focused Disengaged	High High High
Armored-defended	Holding on Constricted	High High to Medium
Passive-dependent	Succor-seeking Apathetic	Medium Medium to Low
Unintegrated	Disorganized	Low

Source: Neugarten, B. L., Havighurst, R. & Tobin, S. 1968. Personality and patterns of aging. In B. L. Neugarten (ed.). *Middle age and aging.* Chicago: University of Chicago Press, p. 174.

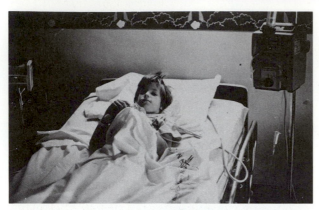

The family members of a terminally ill child may exhibit the emotions associated with Kübler-Ross' five stages as they attempt to adjust to the idea of death.

Although Kübler-Ross's ideas have been widely accepted among those who work with terminally ill individuals, other researchers have been unable to replicate her findings (Butler & Lewis, 1982). As an associated problem, Kübler-Ross's stages have been so widely disseminated and accepted they have become the standard, acceptable way to cope with impending death. A moment's reflection should allow you to realize that just as each person's life is unique, so is his or her dying unique (Kalish, 1981). Nonetheless, Kübler-Ross's ideas have been helpful in understanding how certain terminally ill individuals cope with imminent death, and they have provided a useful framework for considering how people adjust to other losses such as the loss resulting from divorce.

as they adjust to the awareness of dying. The five stages are: **denial**, "Not me"; **anger**, "Why me?"; **bargaining**, "Yes, me—but" (negotiating a better deal); **depression**, "Woe is me"; and **acceptance**, "It's all right with me."

Focus Question Answer

Will you live to be 100 years old? Hayflick estimates that the upper limit for longevity is 110 to 120 years. To live to be 100 requires that you inherit a potential

This Buddhist cemetery in Tokyo illustrates the cross-cultural differences in burial and cremation rituals.

for a long life and that you pursue a lifestyle that allows you to fulfill your genetic potential. Following seven basic health habits and, in particular, participating in regular moderate exercise are associated with longevity but are not guarantees that you will live to be 100 years old.

Adult Sexuality

Sexuality is an extremely complex concept in adult development. That humans are sexual beings permeates all other lifestyle choices in one manner or another. Each of the developmental perspectives presented in Chapter 16 reflects some dimension of sexuality. Biological factors control the physical aspect of sexual development and contribute directly to sexual functioning in adults. Psychodynamic factors are important influences on sexual feelings, sexual awareness, and sexual identity, as are cognitive factors from which understanding of one's sexuality is derived. Sexuality is one of the humanistic factors involved in the potential for growth and change. Sexuality encompasses far more than the physical aspects of sexual expression; its strands are interwoven into one's individual, interpersonal, and cultural being.

The physical aspects of sexuality follow a typical course of development for most adults. Young adults report the highest levels of sexual activity, and they are more sexually active today than they were several decades ago (Brecher et al., 1984). The high interest in sexual activity and the accompanying desire for intimacy create many sexual pressures. Marriage alleviates certain of the pressures, but it also creates new ones, because the couple must integrate sex with other aspects of living together.

In middle adulthood, very little biological change occurs in either men or women to affect their ability to function sexually, but sexual activity usually occurs less frequently. For middle-aged women, one major discontinuity of physical sexual development—**menopause**—does occur. Around age fifty, women's production of the hormone estrogen drops dramatically and causes the cessation of ovulation and menstruation. The most common physical symptoms, hot flashes and sweating, happen as the woman's body adjusts to a different hormonal balance, but the symptoms do not occur in all women. In contrast, men do not experience an abrupt shift in hormonal balance. While cyclical changes in hormonal balance do occur (Kimmel, 1974), most men experience only a gradual decline in fertility across the middle years of adulthood.

Older adults experience additional changes in the physical aspects of their sexuality; slower arousal and penile erection in men and decreased vaginal lubrication in women are examples. None of these physical changes prevents sexual activity, yet older adults are often stereotyped as lacking sex appeal and sexual capacity. Such societal stereotypes and other forms of ageism impose greater limits upon the sexuality of the elderly than do physical limitations or lack of a partner. Remaining sexually active and experiencing sexual satisfaction in the later years appear to be products of an earlier active, healthy sex life.

Across the adult lifespan, each lifestyle choice affects sexuality. Choosing to remain single creates different influences on sexuality and sexual expression than those created by choosing to marry. Parenthood changes many aspects of sexuality as does the decision to divorce. Even career advancement and occupational change affect sexuality. Whether the choices are expected or unexpected events, sexuality is affected nonetheless.

The lifestyle for certain adults includes a homosexual gender orientation. Their homosexuality is, in many respects, no different than the heterosexuality of the majority of the adult population. As a minority, however, homosexuals must deal with strong prejudices and stereotypes about their sexuality. In contrast to the prevailing stereotypes, gay men and lesbian women lead diverse lives and are not usually recognizable by appearance or occupational choice. Wide variations exist in the masculine and feminine behaviors of both heterosexual and homosexual men and women.

Research on the causes of homosexuality have focused on biological factors, on childhood development, and on learning. No firm support for any of the factors as causes has been found, perhaps because of the complexity of homosexuality. Despite stereotypes, homosexuals are not all alike, and the lack of support for any one factor may result because different types of homosexuality may originate in different ways.

Carefully designed studies have revealed that homosexuals are as well-adjusted as their heterosexual counterparts, and the American Psychiatric Association no longer views homosexuality as a mental illness. However, because of stereotypes and prejudices, homosexuals are assumed to follow a course of development different than that of heterosexuals. Little research evidence supports this conclusion, and to the extent that homosexuals do differ in their adult development, the differences are as likely to be caused by society's treatment of homosexuals as by the nature of homosexuality.

EXHIBIT 17.8
The Four Stages of the Human
Sexual Response Cycle

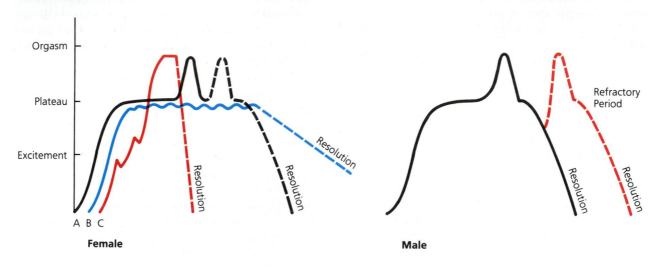

Masters and Johnson found three common variations for female sexual response: (A) multiple orgasm, (B) reaching plateau level without orgasm, and (C) one intense orgasm followed by rapid resolution. The typical male response pattern is the solid line; the dotted line indicates that some males experience a second orgasm and ejaculation following the refractory period.

Source: Masters, W. H. & Johnson, V. E. 1966. *Human sexual response.* Boston: Little, Brown.

The Sexual Response Cycle

Results of precise physiological recordings of subjects during intercourse indicate that the **human sexual response cycle** consists of four phases—excitement, plateau, orgasm, and resolution (Masters & Johnson, 1970). The first, or excitement, phase may last from a few min-

utes to several hours, depending upon intensity, continuance to effort, and situational circumstances (see Exhibit 17.8). The plateau phase is intense and brief. The shortest phase is the orgasmic phase, which lasts from three to ten seconds. In the resolution phase, the sexual system returns to a nonexcited state. A long excitement phase is related to a long resolution phase (Masters & Johnson, 1970). Exhibit 17.9 lists several common fallacies about the human sexual response.

The human sexual response cycle has also been described by a **triphasic model**, consisting of the desire phase, the excitement phase, and the orgasmic phase (Kaplan, 1979). Kaplan believes that 40 percent of all sexual problems may result from inhibitions in the desire phase. She also maintains that sexual dysfunctions of the excitement and orgasmic phases are easier to treat successfully than is inhibited sexual desire.

Sexual Dysfunctions

Sexual dysfunctions occur when sexual responses are impaired. In men, the main sexual dysfunctions are **impotence** (the inability to achieve or maintain an erection),

Quick Study Aid

Phases of the Human Sexual Response Cycle

Remember the phases of the sexual response cycle by using this acronym created from the first letters of each phase:

EXPLORE & DEO

EXPLORE stands for *e*xcitement, *pl*ateau, *o*rgasm, and *re*solution—Masters & Johnson
DEO stands for *d*esire, *e*xcitement, and *o*rgasm—Kaplan

EXHIBIT 17.9
Misconceptions About Sexual Behavior

Following are fallacies about the human sexual response.

1. Alcohol is a sexual stimulant.
2. Marijuana is an aphrodisiac.
3. Each person is programmed for a specific number of sexual experiences. When those experiences are depleted, sexual activity is over for that person.
4. Blacks have a greater sex drive than whites.
5. Sterilization reduces the sex drive of a woman or a man.
6. Menopause diminishes a woman's sex life.
7. A hysterectomy ends a woman's sex life and desirability.
8. Sexual ability and desire decreases rapidly after age forty.
9. Muscular men have the largest penises and make the best sexual partners.
10. Castration always destroys the sex drive.
11. A marriage is doomed if sexual adjustment is poor.
12. Sexual partners must try to achieve identical sexual response cycles and mutual orgasms.
13. Stopping or slowing down during intercourse can cause serious health problems.

Adapted from: *McCary's Human Sexuality*, Fourth Edition by James Leslie McCary, Ph.D., and Stephen P. McCary, Ph.D., c. 1982 by S. P. McCary and J. L. McCary. Used with permission of Wadsworth, Inc. Belmont, CA 94002.

premature ejaculation, ejaculatory incompetence (inability to ejaculate within the vagina), **retarded ejaculation,** and **painful intercourse**. In women, the principal dysfunctions are **anorgasmia** (inability to have an orgasm), **vaginismus** (involuntary vaginal muscle spasms in response to vaginal penetration), and **dyspareunia** (painful intercourse).

Among men, premature ejaculation is believed to be the most common sexual dysfunction, with 15–20 percent of American men having at least moderate difficulty with this problem (Masters & Johnson, 1985). Impotence is classified as either primary (never having been able to achieve and maintain an erection) or secondary (previously able to achieve and maintain an erection). However, since the inability to maintain an erection occurs at isolated times for nearly all men, a man is classified as having secondary impotence only if the problem occurs in at least 25 percent of his sexual encounters. The dysfunctions of ejaculatory incompetence, retarded ejaculation, and painful intercourse occur much less frequently than either premature ejaculation or impotence.

Among women, anorgasmia is the most frequently occurring sexual dysfunction. Many women are not or-

gasmic during every sexual episode, but they do not necessarily have a dysfunction. In fact, a woman is classified as having an orgasmic dysfunction only if her frequency of orgasm is so low that she experiences distress or dissatisfaction. The incidence of the other principal sexual dysfunctions in women is much lower than that of anorgasmia.

Several studies have estimated that only 10–20 percent of sexual dysfunctions are caused by organic (physical) factors (Kolodny et al., 1979; Kaplan et al., 1983). Diabetes and alcoholism are the two leading organic causes of impotence; other organic causes include infections, neurological diseases, and drugs. Many sexual dysfunctions are caused in part or entirely by psychosocial factors, which may be developmental (e.g., negative family attitudes toward sex or earlier traumatic sexual experiences), personal (e.g., anxiety, depression, or guilt), or interpersonal factors (e.g., poor communication skills or relationship conflicts).

Other sexual problems may arise but not necessarily lead to sexual dysfunction. **Inhibited sexual desire** may include either organic (e.g., hormone deficiencies) or psychosocial (e.g., prior sexual trauma) conditions. While inhibited sexual desire may be particularly distressing to men and women who experience it, their sexual functioning may not be impaired. Individuals with **sexual aversion**—a severe irrational fear of sexual contact—are capable of functioning sexually but are terrified of having a sexual encounter. Fortunately, over 90 percent of sexual aversion cases are successfully treated with appropriate sex therapy (Kolodny et al., 1979).

Treatment of Sexual Dysfunctions

Several approaches have been developed to help people experiencing sexual problems. Sex therapy as a treatment specialty was pioneered by the team of Masters and Johnson. The Masters and Johnson approach involves cotherapists working with couples during two weeks of daily therapy sessions, which include physical examinations, assessment of the problem, and training in techniques to solve the problem (Kolodny et al., 1979). A variation of the Masters and Johnson approach takes couples through thirty-four steps toward an ultimate goal of improved intimacy (Hartman & Fithian, 1979). Before 1970, sexual problems were most often treated by psychiatrists, many of whom followed a psychodynamic model. The aim of psychodynamic therapy is to uncover and resolve unconscious conflicts stemming from earlier psychological development. This approach may take years to conclude. In contrast, a more recent approach developed by Kaplan (1974; 1979) seeks to assist the client and his or her partner in achieving their sexual goals as quickly as possible. Kaplan's therapy blends techniques of several approaches. The Kaplan, Masters and Johnson, and Hartman and Fithian therapies all use behavior modification techniques to some extent.

As in other forms of therapy, the effectiveness of sex therapy is influenced by many elements and is difficult to assess. Success rates of 40–80 percent and higher have been reported (Kaplan, 1979; Nunes & Bandeira, 1980; Kolodny, 1981), but the success of the therapy depends upon the problem, the person, and the approach used by the therapist (Springer, 1981). Certain problems are more amenable to treatment than others; clients who are more motivated and have fewer other problems appear to receive the greatest benefit in the shortest time; and certain techniques work best for certain problems

(e.g., behavioral techniques for problems caused by faulty learning).

Focus Question Answer

Will your sexual attitudes and behaviors change as you become older? Although young adults are reported to have the highest levels of sexual activity, very few physical changes occur in either middle-aged men or women to affect their ability to function sexually. Older adults experience physical changes, such as slower arousal in men and decreased vaginal lubrication in women, but most of the changes in sexual behavior occur as a result of people's sexual attitudes. Their attitudes are strongly affected by society's expectations about the appropriateness of sexual activity as people age. Remaining sexually active and experiencing sexual satisfaction as you age appear to be the product of an earlier active, healthy sex life.

 Relate

Sex and Gender Differences— What Difference Does It Make?

In Chapters 16 and 17, you have studied how humans develop and change across the lifespan. Many strands of development weave in and out of the fabric of your life, and one strand prominent throughout your life is gender. From the time you are born, people around you stress the importance of gender. One study that investigated people's questions about new babies (Intons-Peterson & Reddel, 1984), found that 80 percent asked about the gender of the babies. "Is it a boy?" was asked more often than "Is it a girl?" as was "Is it a boy or a girl?" rather than "Is it a girl or a boy?" These questions set the stage for the continued emphasis, throughout the lifespan, on the differences between males and females.

These differences are the core of several fundamental issues of adult development. Traditionally, women and men have fulfilled different gender roles, role differences that were assumed to be based on inherent differences between men and women. More recently, this presumed link between role behaviors and biological characteristics has been seriously disputed. Important questions have been raised about the differences between women and men, about the origin of those differences, and about the value to individuals and to society in maintaining many of the differences.

The differences can be described along two dimensions—sex differences and gender differences. **Sex differences** are based on the biological differences between females and males. **Gender differences** denote psychosocial rather than biological characteristics. In Chapter 16, the terms gender identity, gender roles, and gender typing were used to refer to the nonbiological aspects of being female or male. These distinctions are important because very few sex differences have been found and because gender differences may be the result of strongly projected gender role stereotypes (Maccoby & Jacklin, 1974; Deaux, 1985).

In a landmark study, Maccoby and Jacklin (1974) carefully analyzed over 2,000 articles and books on sex differences in children for evidence of these differences. The researchers concluded that males and females are more alike than they are different, and they found insufficient evidence for a number of long-standing biases about sex differences. They discovered no evidence that girls are more social than boys and noted no difference in self-esteem throughout childhood and adolescence. Both sexes were equally skilled at simple repetitive tasks. Boys were no more analytical than girls, and girls were no more likely than boys to be persuaded by others and to imitate the behavior of others.

Traditional gender roles dictate that driving a tractor is "man's work," but a woman is quite capable of this task.

Having concluded their extensive research, Maccoby and Jacklin identified only four sex differences. Only the greater aggressiveness of boys was present in early childhood (and some psychologists believe this is a *biological* difference in *activity* level which then is *socialized* into a difference in *aggression* level); the other three differences did not develop until after age ten or eleven, at which time boys showed an advantage in mathematical and visual-spatial skills, while girls had greater verbal ability. More recently, the greater math ability of males has been challenged (Hyde, 1981) and reaffirmed (Benbow & Stanley, 1980), with the primary difference occurring in algebra ability (Becker, 1983). The spatial ability differences have been scrutinized with the same results. The male advantage occurs only on specific types of skills, such as the ability to mentally rotate an object. Importantly, training can significantly improve the math and spatial abilities of both women and men (Newcombe et al., 1983). Even the greater verbal ability of women has been shown to be a small sex difference (Benbow & Stanley, 1983).

With so few consistent sex differences between men and women, why do differences between the sexes remain so controversial? The answer lies partly in gender differences. Men have long been considered dominant, assertive, active, independent, and competitive, while women have been considered submissive, compliant, passive, dependent, and compassionate. These descriptions of gender differences represent gender role stereotypes that are incorporated into the concepts of masculinity and femininity. In stereotypical fashion, all individuals with a female gender identity are assumed to display the list of feminine traits, and individuals with a male gender identity are assumed to exhibit the masculine traits.

Gender typing describes the process and the degree to which an individual conforms to the gender role stereotypes for her or his gender. Since a person rarely, if ever, possesses all masculine traits and no feminine traits or vice versa, most individuals exhibit a mixture of femininity and masculinity. The **Bem Sex Role Inventory** (**BSRI**) (Bem, 1974) was devised to measure the extent to which people possess both masculine and feminine traits. Of thousands of people surveyed, Bem found that 50 percent were classified on the BSRI as traditionally masculine or feminine. Some individuals (15 percent) scored higher on the traits for the opposite gender, and the remaining 35 percent received high scores on both masculine and feminine traits, a condition termed **androgyny** (the word androgyny comes from the Greek roots for male, *andro,* and for female, *gyn.*)

Since androgyny is a broadly defined concept, researchers do not agree upon the nature of androgynous behavior. Some view masculine and feminine as co-existing but expressed by the person at different times, while others see the traits as fully integrated (Kaplan & Sedney, 1980). One study found that androgynous individuals have greater self-esteem, achievement motivation, and social competence than individuals who were strongly masculine or feminine or who have low scores in both areas (Spence & Helmreich, 1978). Research by Bem (1976) has shown that androgynous persons are more flexible in their behavior, tending to make decisions on the basis of the most effective course of action without regard to traditional gender roles. In contrast, masculine men and feminine women limit their actions to behaviors reflecting appropriate gender role stereotypes.

The existence of so few (and tenuous) sex differences suggests that observed differences between males and females are not innate but learned behaviors and raises the question of the value of gender roles. If Bem is correct, traditional masculine and feminine gender roles are restrictive, particularly for men.

Combining masculine and feminine traits has both advantages and disadvantages (Spence, 1984). An androgynous identity allows the effective use of feminine and masculine traits as needed. Research indicates that androgynous individuals have a dynamic, flexible approach to life as well as the most positive adjustment to life (Massad, 1981). However, another study found that masculine males show better overall adjustment (Jones et al., 1978). Masculine males are more creative and less introverted and feel more in control of their behavior, while androgynous males have more drinking problems. Another recent study of college students (Lee & Scheurer, 1983) revealed that, for men and women, the presence of masculine traits rather than androgyny is responsible for greater versatility and adaptability. The explanation for these mixed findings results from American society still offering greater rewards for masculine behavior.

The conflicting results from research on androgyny may stem from the different ages of the subjects studied or from sociohistorical changes across time. In the fifteen years since Bem began championing the concept of androgyny, American society has changed with some of the societal change occurring in gender roles. Men now spend more time on family work than they did twenty years ago (Pleck, 1981).

In 1986, for the first time, women held the majority of professional jobs in the United States (U.S. Bureau of Labor Statistics, 1986). Although men continue to dominate the fields of medicine, law, and engineering, women have made sufficient gains in those areas over the previous several years to comprise the overall majority in the fifty professional occupations surveyed by the Bureau of Labor. These changes in gender roles may signal a trend to greater androgyny; however, the research on androgynous roles is still contradictory (Taylor & Hall, 1982) and does not give a picture clear enough to determine that androgyny is preferable to masculinity and femininity. If society does move away from the independence of feminine and masculine patterns toward greater androgyny, the importance of gender as a psychological variable will decrease. Perhaps in the future, gender differences, like sex differences, will account for only a very small number of the differences between people.

Things to Do

1. As suggested in Chapter 16, an important activity is to observe the ongoing aspects of development in your midst. Carefully observe the adults around you. Are your observations biased by the perspective of your particular age? Talk with others in your age group and from other age groups about their experiences. What do younger people anticipate about being your age? How do your experiences compare with those of older adults when they were your age?

2. Many stereotypes exist for each stage of adulthood. With your classmates, make a list of those stereotypes. Investigate each stereotype to find the degree to which it accurately describes a particular stage of adulthood. Using the stereotypes, construct a true/false test, and give the quiz to adults of different ages. Compare responses from different age groups. Does the degree of belief in the stereotypes differ according to age groups?

3. Much of the research on stages of adult development has been conducted with men. Using Levinson's stages, interview several women of different ages about their experiences. Pool your responses with those of your classmates, and discuss your collective impressions of women's adult development. Do women and men follow the same path of adult development?

4. Interview several blended families about the positive and negative aspects of that living arrangement. Also, interview adults who are not part of blended families about their perceptions of the positive and negative aspects of blended families. Compare the responses of the two groups. Do people who are not in blended families have accurate perceptions of life in a blended family?

5. Locate three people who are at least one hundred years old. Interview them about their thoughts and feelings about living to one hundred. What do they consider to be the best and the worst aspects of living to this age? To what do they attribute their longevity?

Things to Discuss

1. Are college students considered adults? Debate this question by discussing Keniston's concept of youth as it applies to college students, by examining society's stereotypes of the college student, and by evaluating your experiences and your classmates' experiences as college students.

2. In the mid-80s, Barbie, the enduring doll for several generations, kept pace with social trends by becoming a Yuppie (a young, upwardly mobile professional), complete with an office environment and credit and business cards. Does Barbie's change indicate that society's views of women's gender roles have changed? What do children's toys reveal about adult development?

3. Some social scientists have suggested that today's higher rate of divorce and subsequent remarriage is associated with increased longevity. These researchers maintain that monogamy (marrying for life) worked well when the average life span was forty years but is less desirable since the average lifespan has nearly doubled. They propose that the practice of serial monogamy (being faithful to one person at a time during two or more marriages) is characteristic of today's longevity. Is marrying for life still the major expectation among adults? Do you think that serial monogamy is a workable idea?

4. With your classmates, discuss the impact of the "graying" of America. Become a social forecaster, and predict the changes in the next fifteen years as America becomes proportionately a nation of older adults.

5. Scientists have discovered neither the fountain of youth nor a way to stop the aging process. However, with plastic surgery and cosmetics, many of the visible signs of aging can be removed or camouflaged. Should people with gray hair dye their hair? Are facelifts worth the pain and expense? Discuss the double-standard for aging men and women and its implications about the underlying values of society.

Things to Read

Blythe, R. 1979. *The view in winter: Reflections on old age.* NY: Harcourt Brace Jovanovich.

Deaux, K. 1976. *The behavior of women and men.* Monterey, CA: Brooks/Cole.

Goodman, E. 1979. *Turning points.* NY: Fawcrest.

Kübler-Ross, E. 1975. *Death: The final stage of growth.* Englewood Cliffs, NJ: Prentice-Hall

Levinson, D. 1978. *The seasons of a man's life.* NY: Ballantine.

Pogrebin, L.B. 1984. *Family politics: Love & power on an intimate frontier.* NY: McGraw-Hill.

Rogers, C. 1972. *Becoming partners: Marriage and its alternatives.* NY: Harper & Row.

Secunda, V. 1984. *By youth possessed: The denial of age in America.* NY: Bobbs-Merrill.

Review

Summary

1. Development in adulthood follows a pattern of continuous, gradual change, with some functions (such as fluid intelligence) declining with age and others (such as crystallized intelligence) increasing across the adult years.

2. The pattern of adult psychosocial development has been described by the normative-crisis model, which proposes that age-related stages exist in adult development, and by the timing-of-events model, which holds that adult development is a function of when certain important life events occur for each individual.

3. The concepts of life time (developmental changes based on chronological age), social time (age expectations and statuses within a society), and historical time (the interaction between an individual's stage of development and historical events) describe differing perspectives on adult development.

4. The transition from adolescence to adulthood involves both leaving home (separating from dependency upon parents and family) and getting established (establishing a more independent existence for oneself). Keniston's concept of youth, which characterizes the developmental status of many college students, describes the halfway state of breaking former dependencies and establishing new independence. Several theories of vocational choice link personality factors with career decisions.

5. A major lifestyle choice for young adults centers on establishing intimate relationships with other people. Most people choose to establish intimacy through marriage, some choose to remain single, and some choose to cohabitate.

6. For married adults, divorce may become a major life-style decision. The divorce's effects on children depend upon many factors. Both positive and negative patterns of adjustment are found in the blended families that result from remarriage following divorce.

7. Becoming a parent represents an irrevocable lifestyle decision. Persons who become parents follow different styles of parenting, with authoritative parenting representing the most positive approach to rearing children.

8. Aging involves biological, psychological, and social factors. Theories of aging include the ideas of genetically programmed limits to the lifespan and the cumulative effects of wear-and-tear on the body. No one has been able to stop the effects of aging, but amount of exercise, type of diet, and other health factors can slow or accelerate the aging process. With aging comes the realization of the inevitability of dying. Kübler-Ross's five stages provide a framework for looking at how people adjust to the fact they are dying.

9. Sexuality is a pervasive aspect of adult development. While young adults report the highest levels of sexual activity, none of the normal physical effects of aging prevents middle-aged and older adults from engaging in sexual activity. The sexual response cycle is similar for men and women.

10. Men and women experience a variety of sexual dysfunctions. Individuals with impaired sexual responses may be treated successfully through several sex therapies.

11. Few sex differences, based on biological differences between females and males, have been found. Research findings indicate that both positive and negative factors are associated with being highly masculine, highly feminine, or androgynous (possessing both feminine and masculine characteristics).

Key Terms

fluid intelligence
crystallized intelligence
normative-crisis model
timing-of-events model
life time
social time
historical time
youth
cohabitation
developmental self-concept theory
personality type theory
blended family
authoritarian parenting
permissive parenting
authoritative parenting
Hayflick limit
denial

anger
bargaining
depression
acceptance
menopause
human sexual response cycle
triphasic model
impotence
premature ejaculation
anorgasmia
vaginismus
dyspareunia
inhibited sexual desire
sex differences
gender differences
Bem Sex Role Inventory
androgyny

Focus Questions

1. Do you judge your own behaviors in the same way you judge the behaviors of others?

2. How do stereotypes affect your feelings about people you meet?

3. What factors determine your attraction to others?

4. What characteristics should you look for in other people in order to have healthy relationships?

5. What values are important to you?

Chapter Outline

PERSON PERCEPTION
First Impression Formation
Attribution Process
Roles
The Research Process: Zimbardo's Stanford Prison Experiment
Perceptual Errors
The Just World Belief

STEREOTYPES AND PREJUDICE
Stereotypes
Prejudice
Reducing Prejudice

INTERPERSONAL ATTRACTION
Factors Influencing Attraction
Reinforcement-Affect Model
Exchange Theory
Balance Theory
Gain-Loss Theory

RELATIONSHIPS
Familiar Strangers
Self-Disclosure
Friendships
Love Relationships

RELATE: Whom to Fund—A Values Exploration
Things to Do
Things to Discuss
Things to Read

REVIEW: Summary
Key Terms

Chapter 18

Social Psychology: Attribution and Attraction

But humanity is never more sphinxlike than when it is expressing itself.
Rebecca West

Social psychology studies how social factors influence an individual's behaviors, thoughts, feelings, perceptions, and motives. Social psychologists examine people's behaviors in the presence, or the perceived presence, of others. Some of the topics they study you have already explored in this text—body language, aggression, touch, TV viewing influences, and eyewitness testimony. This chapter and the next focus on the social psychology areas of person perception and attribution, stereotypes, interpersonal attraction, attitudes and attitude change, and social influence. Since, in your day-to-day living, you seek explanations in these areas to help you understand your friendships, your values, and your behavior within groups, you are already an amateur social psychologist. As you read Chapters 18 and 19, see if you agree with research findings of professional social psychologists. 435

Person Perception

Person perception is the process of forming impressions about other persons. In forming these impressions, you place other individuals in meaningful categories based on both physical appearance (e.g., he is tall, she is slender, he is overweight) and on psychological factors (e.g., she is aggressive, she is friendly, he is ambitious).

Person perception processing makes everyday living a little easier. By perceiving others' behavior to have stable characteristics, you are able to use your impressions to explain other people's past behavior and to predict their future behavior. For example, if you have observed that some of your friends like to listen to country western music while other friends prefer rock music, you can easily determine which friends would want to accompany you to a rock concert.

First Impression Formation

You may have heard that "first impressions are lasting," and social psychology research supports this saying. A **first impression** is formed from initial knowledge you acquire about a person and often biases later information

you gain about the individual. Other people react just as strongly to the first impressions you make. You may remember, if you made a poor beginning with a teacher on the first day of elementary school, your struggle not to be thought of as the class troublemaker; on the other hand, if you were the "teacher's pet," you probably made such a good first impression that you were able to get away with many rule infractions.

Although you may have been unaware of the importance of first impressions as an elementary school student, you have certainly taken them into account in many subsequent situations. You dress up for a job interview to set the stage for your being seen as intelligent, competent, and sociable. When you first start dating someone, you display your very best behavior to impress the other person. As a college student, you use the first impression formation by submitting neatly typed term papers because you realize the paper's appearance influences an instructor's first impression of the paper's content.

After you have made a first impression, your personality traits will further influence how others react to you. However, not all personality traits have equal effects in

If you saw this lawyer representing a client in court, you would probably form very different first impressions than if you saw her after a successful hunting trip.

influencing the perceptions of others. For instance, in impression formation, the dimension of warm-cold has a more powerful effect than does the dimension of polite-blunt (Asch, 1946). The warm-cold influence was illustrated in a study in which psychology students were given short biographical descriptions of a guest lecturer. With one exception, all descriptions were identical; half referred to the lecturer as warm, and the other half referred to him as cold. Students who received the description containing the modifier *warm* participated more in the class discussion and rated the lecturer more positively than subjects who received the description that referred to the lecturer as *cold* (Kelley, 1950). As this study indicates, information you hear about an instructor before taking his or her class significantly influences how you interact with that instructor.

Research on impression formation has also found that negative traits tend to influence people more than positive traits. Perhaps because most people begin with positive impressions of people, negative information is particularly striking. People may also weigh negative information more heavily because they want to avoid negative, disagreeable people who create tension and unpleasantness in others' lives (Hamilton, 1980). Eight of the following ten most impression-modifying trait descriptions are negative: heartless, unscrupulous, unprincipled, immoral, cruel, horrid, nice, sincere, depraved, and corrupt (Feldman, 1966).

Attribution Process

Behavior makes more sense and becomes more meaningful when you think you understand what causes it. In the **attribution process,** people decide whether the cause of a behavior is within the person (trait) or outside the person (situational context). When a student does poorly on a test, the performance can be attributed to factors inside the person—low ability, lack of motivation, or lack of studying. However, the poor test performance can also be attributed to factors outside the person—a difficult test, a hard grading curve, or an unfair instructor.

Interestingly, according to the **fundamental attribution error** (Ross, 1977), people tend to underestimate the situation's influences and overestimate trait influences when judging other people's behavior. Thus, you are more likely to attribute another student's poor performance on an exam to internal factors such as inadequate studying or low ability. However, if your own performance is poor, you are more likely to attribute the

cause to situational factors such as a noisy room or an unfair test. This phenomenon occurs because you possess much more information about the situational factors surrounding your own behavior than those surrounding another person's behavior. Consistent with this explanation, one study found that the better an observer knew the other person, the more likely the observer was to attribute the other person's behavior to situational rather than personality factors (Nisbett & Ross, 1981). Thus, when you perceive your own behavior, you focus on the situation; when you perceive another's behavior, you focus on the person, and the situation is merely background.

According to **correspondent inference theory** (Jones & Davies, 1965), people make judgments about the causes of another's behavior by observing the behavior's impact on the environment. Isolatable, uncommon effects are most useful in making attributions about why a person has behaved in a certain way. For example, if you notice that someone enrolls in a psychology section with class discussions instead of a psychology section with formal lectures, you can infer that the individual likes classes that involve discussion. On the other hand, if a student signs up for a psychology section with class discussions instead of a calculus class with formal class lectures, you cannot determine that the student likes psychology more than calculus or discussion classes more than lecture classes.

Roles

A **role** is a set of behavioral expectations about people in a particular position based upon norms of people in that position. Some roles are explicitly defined; for instance, because of a written job description, a secretary would understand what the job of secretary entails. Other roles are defined by implicit assumptions; until the women's rights movement influenced businesses, for example, one implicit assumption about the secretary's role was that the secretary would make coffee for the boss.

Often, roles are convenient aspects of life. You do not wonder whether the postal worker, the firefighter, or the taxicab driver will bring you today's mail. When you are employed, you do not question that your boss is someone to whom you should listen and show respect. Without the existence of reliable roles, you would have to spend considerably more time determining the ground rules of every situation.

Roles also help you maneuver in new situations. Even on your first day in college, you knew what to do when

Although a secretary rarely has the assigned responsibility of pouring coffee for a boss or employer, others may assume this task is part of the secretarial role.

you attended class because you could infer the college student role from your student role in other settings such as high school. You had only to discover and make decisions regarding the new dimensions involved in being a college student rather than a high school student (for instance, your greater freedom in deciding whether or not to attend the day's classes and your greater responsibility for planning your studying). These decisions were probably difficult enough without having to start from scratch by asking yourself, "What is a student?"

The roles within a group or situation are often interrelated. For example, how you play the role of student is partly defined by how your teacher plays the role of teacher. Other co-related roles include husband-wife, coach-athlete, boss-employee, minister-church member, and parent-child. Sometimes people overdefine others by the roles in which they know them. You may think of the grocery clerk as only a clerk, when actually that person has many other roles (student, parent, and friend) that do not interact directly with the customer. Many teachers are amused that their students are surprised or even shocked to see them in a store—as if a teacher is only a teacher and is never released from the classroom.

People often project personality and behavior characteristics according to the roles others persistently assume. Yet even if those roles are randomly determined, others may see them as expressing people's personalities and abilities. In one study, the audience knew that the roles of questioner and answerer were randomly assigned, yet the audience reliably rated the questioner as more knowledgeable than the person who tried to answer the questions. The audience failed to take into account the

built-in advantage of the questioner role, a role that allowed a degree of control over the situation (Ross et al., 1977).

Roles can determine behavior more than you might realize. *The Research Process* describes a situation in which roles were much more important than personality characteristics in determining behavior. While the study may represent a case more extreme than typical, it reveals that behavior is significantly shaped by roles. Consider your own roles. When you are a college student in class do you act as you do when you are a son or daughter in your parent's home? Does your behavior change when you are at a party with your friends? If you are typical, you adapt to a wide range of roles, and doing so prevents you from becoming too dominated by any one role.

The Research Process:
Zimbardo's Stanford Prison Experiment

What would you be like if you spent two weeks as a prisoner? How would you be different if you were a prison guard? If you assumed these roles, would you behave as you do now? One of social psychology's classic studies explored the effects of roles within a prison by establishing a mock prison in the basement of the Stanford University Psychology Department (Zimbardo, 1975; Haney & Zimbardo, 1977).

Using a battery of psychological tests, Zimbardo and his colleagues carefully screened male college students and then randomly assigned these psychologically normal students the roles of guards and prisoners. The subjects agreed to participate in the study for two weeks.

Every mock prisoner wore a smock uniform with an I.D. number, a nylon stocking cap, and a symbolic chain around his ankle, an outfit that quickly thrust the subjects from the student role into the prisoner role by constantly reminding them that they were being punished and their identities did not matter. As the first step in the experiment, these subjects were picked up in a real police car, charged with a felony, and fingerprinted.

The guards wore khaki uniforms and silvered sunglasses and carried whistles and clubs. Their uniforms symbolized both anonymity and authority. The guards began the experiment by establishing the rules and procedures of the simulated prison.

The researchers found that both the prisoners and the guards assumed their roles very quickly. In their roles as guards, subjects were alert and suspicious and tended to emphasize discipline. Throughout the experiment, the guards doled out progressively harsher and more abusive punishment. Early in the experiment, punishments consisted of temporary loss of reading or talking privileges; later punishments included washing toilets by hand and long periods of time in solitary confinement. Approximately one-third of the guards were harsh and tyrannical, and the remaining guards did little to stop the bad guards.

During the experiment, the prisoners became increasingly apathetic, stressed, and depressed; some of them developed psychosomatic illnesses. Because of the guards' behavior and the prisoners' reactions, the experimenters decided to conclude the experiment on the sixth day rather than complete the full two weeks.

Zimbardo and his colleagues discovered that both the guard and prisoner subjects experienced **deindividuation,** loss of the sense of one's individuality. For the guards, the deindividuation or lowered self-awareness led to decreased amounts of fear and guilt about their aggressive and destructive behaviors. For the prisoners, deindividuation resulted in learned helplessness and powerlessness.

The subjects in Zimbardo's experiment had little trouble acting out their roles in predictable, stereotyped fashion. Do you think that the same process occurs in America's correctional institutions? Can parallels be drawn between the behavior of this study's guards and prisoners and the behavior of teacher and student, military officer and new recruit, or hospital nurse and admitted patient?

Zimbardo argues that his study and its Australian replication (Lovibond et al., 1979) strongly suggest that behavior is often more determined by the situational context than by the personalities of the actors in the situation. While some psychologists (Banuazizi & Movahedi, 1975; Thayer & Saarni, 1975) argue that the results could be explained in terms of **demand characteristics** (those features of the experiment that allow a subject to determine the purpose of the experiment and the expected features), most psychologists tend to agree with Zimbardo's conclusions.

Perceptual Errors

As the questioner-answerer experiment indicates, knowing someone's role can lead to misconceptions. In all areas of person perception and attribution processing, people do not always make the best use of information. They are subject to several perceptual errors. One perceptual error is the **actor-observer bias,** the overwhelming tendency to overestimate the role of the person and underestimate the role of the situation when attributing

someone else's behavior and to do the opposite when judging personal behavior (Jones & Nisbett, 1972). The other person is late for an appointment because he or she is typically tardy; however, you are late because you had to wait for several red lights and for a train to cross the road.

Quick Study Aid

The Actor-Observer Bias

Remember this principle by learning:
SELF & **S**ITUATION
(OTHER) **P**ERSON & **P**ERSONALITY

In addition, people tend to make **egocentric attributions,** or attributions based on their own behavior (Heider, 1958). Instead of thinking about what most people would do in a situation or relying on ideas from research findings, people interpret another's behavior according to how they themselves would behave or have behaved in that situation. Therefore, if you find your calculus III class entertaining and understandable and someone else considers the class boring and difficult, you might assume your position is typical and wonder what is wrong with the other person.

According to a third perceptual error—the **vividness effect**—people tend to be more influenced by vivid, concrete examples at the expense of available abstract, statistical, and logical information. For example, you might see a neighborhood child exhibit one loud and long temper tantrum and conclude that the child is ill-behaved even if individuals who know the child say that usually he or she is well-behaved. If you are a typical student, you may choose your instructors according to comments you hear from other students rather than sift through and evaluate your college's published student ratings of professors. The vividness effect also influences judgments about objects; for instance, many individuals purchase cars because of the recommendation of people who own those models rather than because of ratings in sources like *Consumer Reports*. In one experiment, subjects were more influenced by a panel of enthusiastic owners than by factual information sheets about a car (Nisbett et al., 1976).

A fourth perceptual error is **halo effect,** the tendency to judge a liked person favorably on most dimensions.

Do you make any logical perceptual errors when you look at this photo? Which traits do you assume go along with "poor" and "shabbily dressed"?

Because of the halo effect, teachers sometimes assume that individuals who have already displayed some positive characteristics must possess only positive characteristics. Another perceptual error is called **logical error,** according to which people assume that certain traits always go together. Kristen may assume that the traits of strength and assertiveness belong together and be surprised to meet Mark, a shy weightlifter. Susan may overlook the brilliance of Louise, a blonde female acquaintance, because Sue assumes that dumb and blonde go logically together. People who lose their jobs may find themselves the victims of logical perceptual error because some individuals unfairly connect the word unemployed with lazy.

An additional perceptual error is **leniency error,** the tendency to rate others favorably. On teachers' evaluations, students often mark instructors they did not particularly like as average, while the truly average instructor is likely to get above-average ratings. This tendency to be lenient in evaluations of others may explain why many

students become upset with themselves or the instructor when they receive C grades. Although a C grade represents a rating of adequate and average, students may interpret it as meaning something less. People do not like to view themselves as merely okay, and they are hesitant to perceive others that way.

People also operate according to the **error of central tendency;** they minimize the differences among individuals and lump people into a narrower range than actually exists. Thus, while a variety of people play sports, people may view "jocks" as more similar than they are. Similarly, people may think all mathematicians are introverted eggheads or all chess players are humorless stuffed shirts. The error of central tendency is more common when people are acquainted with only a few individuals within a category (Levine & Campbell, 1972). A person who is a Democrat probably believes Democrats are a diverse group because he or she knows many Democrats; in contrast, the person may believe all members of the Republican party are alike. As you can see, perceptual errors (summarized in Exhibit 18.1) help reinforce stereotypes.

The Just World Belief

A major element contributing to errors of person perception is people's tendency to perceive what they expect to see. The **just world belief** is one such expectation that influences behavior. The just world belief posits a causal relationship between what a person does and what happens to the person. You adhere to this concept if you assume that you will get what you deserve in your lifetime. To hold this belief, you must assume orderliness in the world, ability to control your own environment, and fairness in how the world operates (Lerner, 1980). The just world belief is found in many places—from the Bible's "As ye sow, so shall ye reap" to soap opera fans' thinking the wicked characters in their favorite programs should be punished.

A belief in a just world develops early in life. Piaget (1948) found that very young children believe in **immanent justice,** that bad behavior will automatically bring its own punishment. Many religions teach that sinners suffer while good people are rewarded—some people even see financial and personal successes in this lifetime as signs of eternal salvation (MacDonald, 1972). Similarly, schools and families teach that hard work and good values will pay off in good careers, many friends, respect, and wisdom. The just world belief may also be strengthened by observations that nice, friendly people tend to be happy and well-liked, and cruel, selfish people seem to be unhappy and alone.

You have probably noticed that the world does not always seem to be just—tragedies befall kind and hard-working individuals, and unworthy individuals often receive great rewards. Each year natural disasters such as earthquakes and hurricanes kill hundreds of people without regarding whether they deserve such fates. Why, then, does belief in a just world persist?

The just world belief continues because it helps people maintain a perception of the world's stability. The concept enables people to feel that life is predictable and also encourages good behavior and provides a way to tolerate bad times; after all, if you behave well, you will be rewarded eventually. This belief may also satisfy a need for happy endings. Perhaps most important, the belief helps people feel safer because it allows them to believe that bad events will not happen to them as long as they have done nothing to deserve bad events.

The just world belief is so strong that people may even alter reality to fit the concept. For example, people do not want to believe an innocent person can be a victim because they too could then become victims; therefore, they may find a way to blame the victim, find some reason for which he or she *deserves* to suffer. As a result, people may believe poor persons have done something to bring about their poverty, or they may believe crime victims are to blame for being victimized. In one study, subjects rated a young woman who became pregnant as a result of a rape by a stranger as much at fault as a woman who became pregnant due to contraceptive

negligence with her boyfriend (Stokols & Schopler, 1973). In another study, jurists with high belief in a just world gave harsher sentences to defendants and also found victims more culpable and deserving of being victims than did other jurists (Gerbasi et al., 1977).

In keeping with the just world belief, people assign heavier blame to a person as the consequences of a situation become more severe (Walster, 1966). People hold a driver more responsible for an accident in which someone is injured than one in which a car is dented. As a child, did you receive harsher punishment when your careless behavior knocked over an item or when it broke the item? As a student, do you criticize yourself more harshly for not studying for a test on which you earn a B+ or a test on which you receive a D−?

Another aspect of the just world belief is the assumption that it operates more in the lives of other individuals than in one's own life; the belief is translated into "people get what they deserve. Well, others, at least, get what they deserve." As you have read, in judging personal behavior, people pay more attention to the environment and often blame the circumstances of the situation rather than themselves. Nonetheless, they sometimes apply the just world effect to themselves, and consequently experience guilt about being mugged, raped, poor, or sick even when no strategies to avoid the misfortunes exist. For example, a study of twenty-nine individuals who were paraplegic or quadriplegic as a result of accidents revealed that most accident victims attribute more blame for their condition to themselves than objective analyses of the accident would attribute to the victims (Bulman & Wortman, 1977).

EXHIBIT 18.1
Perceptual Errors and Examples

Perceptual Error	Example
Actor-observer bias	"You fell because you are clumsy; I slipped because the floor was wet."
Egocentric attributions	"This psychology example is wrong because my family didn't do things this way."
Vividness effect	"They must have a bad marriage. I heard them arguing loudly a couple of months ago."
Halo effect	"No, he couldn't have cheated. I met him last week, and he seemed so nice."
Logical error	"Since he's a politician, he must be dishonest."
Leniency error	"There's no such thing as a bad boy."
Error of central tendency	"All junior high boys are so silly."

Focus Question Answer

Do you judge your own behaviors in the same way you judge the behaviors of others? No. Because you have different amounts of information available for your own behavior and another's behavior, you are likely to view your own behavior as largely determined by the situational context but view another's behavior as largely influenced by that person's personality.

Stereotypes and Prejudice

Stereotypes

The attribution process and the perceptual errors about which you have read contribute to overgeneralized impressions about members of a group. These impressions are called **stereotypes**, the characteristics that an individual believes are common to all members of a group or category (Hamilton, 1981). In some ways, stereotypes represent economy of thought and are useful when precise information about someone is not needed or wanted (Allport, 1954). You hold stereotypes about various groups and members of organizations such as the Boy Scouts, the Ku Klux Klan, and the Rotary Club. You also hold stereotypes about various professions, from college professors to police officers to florists. You may hold stereotypes toward members of various nationalities, races, or age groups. Although not all stereotypes are erroneous, they are extensions of your perception of roles and group norms and often result from perceptual errors since most

EXHIBIT 18.2
Who Stole the Money?

Alex

Barb

Cora

Daniel

Edwin

Fred

Georgia

Helen

Ten dollars and fifteen cents was stolen from Pamela Peabody's petty cash drawer. Each person pictured here had the opportunity to be alone in Peabody's office and knew where the money was kept. Which person do you think took the money? Who is the least likely suspect? Why? Ask other members of the class who they think took the money.

groups are not homogeneous (Allport, 1954). How do your stereotypes influence your responses to Exhibit 18.2, "Who Stole the Money?"

In part, stereotypes continue because, when people interact with others on the basis of stereotypes, individuals often respond on the basis of the stereotypes. A waiter in a Chinese restaurant might offer forks to black and caucasian customers but not to oriental customers because he or she assumes orientals would prefer chopsticks to forks. In turn, the oriental customers may become skilled at using the chopsticks even if they usually use forks. A **self-fulfilling prophecy** operates; that is, expectations about the person or situation help bring about the expected interaction.

People seem to selectively remember about an individual information consistent with the stereotypes they hold. Subjects who observed a twenty-minute videotape of a woman and man eating dinner and talking remembered different details of the videotape depending upon whether they were told the woman was a waitress or a librarian. Subjects who watched a librarian were more likely to remember she wore glasses than were subjects who watched a waitress (Cohen, 1977).

Stereotypes can be created, changed, and modified. Pepsi, for example, has created an image so favorable for "the Pepsi generation" that consumers want to join. Social movements spend part of their efforts creating more favorable stereotypes of their causes or members. In the 1960s, the phrase "black is beautiful" helped change both blacks' and whites' stereotypes about blacks.

Impressions and stereotypes can be formed about many aspects of identity and associations. The *Exploring . . .* section suggests that even your name can influence your behavior and others' interactions with you.

Prejudice

Stereotypes can have a large, unfair impact on people's lives. For example, some teachers hold negative stereotypes for the lower social classes. In a videotaped study, a child depicted in a lower-class environment was rated by teachers as less capable than the same child depicted in a middle-class environment (Darley & Gross, 1983). Research suggests that powerful negative stereotypes still affect women and racial minorities (Schonfield, 1982; Yarkin et al., 1982).

Stereotypes are cognitive overgeneralizations about a group, and emotionally charged negative stereotypes are called **prejudices. Ethnocentrism**, the belief that one's own group is superior to other groups, is a part of prejudice. Common prejudicial attitudes between blacks

EXHIBIT 18.3
Blacks' and Whites' Views of Themselves and Each Other

Blacks' view of:

Blacks: Intelligent, very religious, musical, sportsmanlike, loud, pleasure-loving, athletic, rhythmed, lazy, superstitious.

Whites: Deceitful, sly, intelligent, treacherous, dirty, industrious, lazy, cruel, selfish, nervous, conceited.

Whites' view of:

Blacks: Lazy, superstitious, ignorant, loud, musical, materialistic, poor, stupid, dirty, peace-loving, happy-go-lucky, very religious, feel inferior, pleasure-loving, militant, proud.

Whites: Industrious, intelligent, materialistic, ambitious, pleasure-loving, progressive, efficient, individualistic, neat, clean, mannerly.

Adapted from: Stephan, W. G. & Rosenfield, D. Racial and ethnic stereotypes. *In the eye of the beholder: Contemporary issues in stereotyping.* Arthur G. Miller, Ed. (Praeger Publishers, New York, a division of Greenwood Press, Inc, 1982), P. 100, copyright c. 1982 by Praeger Publishers. Used by permission of the publishers.

and whites in America are illustrated in Exhibit 18.3, which summarizes the races' stereotypes of their own and the other race. Yet many people with prejudices do not exhibit **discrimination**, behavior that reflects one's prejudicial attitudes. Researchers suggest that blacks and whites now act toward each other in less openly discriminatory ways. However, negative stereotypes are still common, and discrimination may alter small aspects of people's behaviors (Stephan & Rosenfield, 1982). In a study in which prejudiced and nonprejudiced white subjects evaluated fifty yearbook pictures, the dependent variable was the amount of time spent evaluating pictures of whites and pictures of blacks. Nonprejudiced subjects spent nearly the same amount of time evaluating pictures of blacks and whites, but prejudiced subjects spent significantly less time evaluating pictures of blacks than pictures of whites. The prejudiced subjects either actively avoided looking at the blacks or assumed the existence of less variation among the black faces (Sensenig et al., 1973).

Gordon Allport (1954) wrote, "Why do human beings slip so easily into ethnic prejudice? They do so because the two essential ingredients—erroneous generalization and hostility—are natural and common capacities of the human mind" (p. 17).

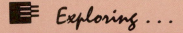

Exploring . . .

Name Popularity and Name Impressions

One of the first pieces of information people gather about someone is the person's name. If people receive business correspondence or a class list, for example, they may know and react to a name long before they ever interact with the actual person. Both psychology research and personal experiences suggest that not all names are treated equally. The frequency of first names is one of the most important factors in determining the impressions people form on the basis of names.

As you can see by comparing the most common names of 1925 and 1983 in the chart, popularity of names changes over the years. Because of these changes, you can sometimes guess the age of a person by name alone. Women named Mabel, Nellie, and Beatrice are likely to be older than women named Carol, Judith, and Sheila because Mabel, Nellie, and Beatrice were common names from 1900 to 1930 and the latter three names were most popular in the 1950s (Hargreaves et al., 1983).

Most changes in name popularity occur slowly, but movie and television stars, politicians, and news-makers can cause sudden increases or decreases in name popularity. Shirley Temple became a popular child star in 1934, and soon many more female babies were named Shirley. In the 1980s, television shows made the names Alexis, Fallon, Krystle (from TV's "Dynasty"), and Chase (of TV's "Falcon Crest") more popular (Dunkling & Gosling, 1983). After John Glenn's space flight in 1962, Glenn became a popular first name for boys. Although the name Adolf was popular in Germany before World War II, it became scarce in that country after the war (Hargreaves et al., 1983).

First names are generally liked more as they increase in familiarity. In a British study, the most liked names in the study (i.e., David, Peter, Richard, Clare,

Top ten names for boys and girls: 1925 and 1983

Boys 1925	Boys 1983 (white)	Boys 1983 (nonwhite)
1. Robert	Michael	Michael
2. John	Matthew	Christopher
3. William	Christopher	James
4. James	Brian	Brandon
5. Charles	David	Anthony
6. Richard	Adam	Robert
7. George	Andrew	Jason
8. Donald	Daniel	David
9. Joseph	Jason	William
10. Edward	Joshua	Brian

Girls 1925	Girls 1983 (white)	Girls 1983 (nonwhite)
1. Mary	Jennifer	Tiffany
2. Barbara	Sarah	Crystal
3. Dorothy	Jessica	Erica
4. Betty	Amanda	Ebony
5. Ruth	Nicole	Latoya
6. Margaret	Ashley	Candice
7. Helen	Megan	Jennifer
8. Elizabeth	Melissa	Brandi
9. Jean	Katherine	Nicole
10. Ann(e)	Stephanie	Danielle

Source: Dunkling, L. & Gosling, W. 1983. *The new American dictionary of first names.* NY: New American Library. With permission of Facts on File.

Elizabeth, and Sarah) had high familiarity ratings. The least liked names (i.e., Oswald, Balthasar, Clarence, Hilda, Ethel, and Gertrude) had low familiarity ratings (Colman et al., 1981). However, according to the

Popularity of the Name Susan in England.

Susan as name given per 10,000 girl births:

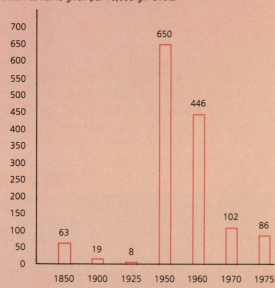

Source: Hargreaves, D. J., Colman, A. M. & Sluckin, W. 1983. *Human relations, 36,* 393-402.

preference-feedback hypothesis, as a first name begins to become overexposed due to its extreme popularity, fewer parents choose the name (Hargreaves et al., 1983). This phenomenon creates, over a period of years, a popularity cycle for first names, as illustrated for the name Susan in the bar graph.

Some psychologists suggest that your name can influence the way others interact with you as well as how you act. Your name produces the most favorable impressions if it is a fairly popular name. Unusual names have been associated with a number of characteristics, including:

— lower grade point averages (Joubert, 1983)

— higher numbers of mental adjustment problems (Hartman et al., 1968)

— increased numbers of academic failure (Ellis & Beechley, 1954)

— lower numbers in the professions (Willis et al., 1982),

— higher rate of inclusion in *Who's Who* and the Social Register (Zweigenhaft, 1977).

The research suggests that uncommon names create poor first impressions that may lead some individuals to have low opinions of themselves and to perform at low levels. On the other hand, the high rate of inclusion of unusual names in *Who's Who* and the *Social Register* suggests that individuals who overcome the negative first impressions created by their names actually achieve more than individuals given popular names.

Besides the cultural popularity of names, your own attitudes and feelings about names are influenced by individuals you have known in life. A special friend may endear a name to you forever, or you may never be able to stomach a name that was shared by the neighborhood bully. You may also react very differently to different forms of the same name (such as Kathy, Kathleen, and Katherine), and many individuals choose a name form that they believe projects the most favorable image.

What associations do you have for your own name? Have you noticed others' reactions to your name? Check with your friends to see if you agree on the best and worst names. Then ask people older and younger than yourself for their favorite and least favorite names. What preferences occur for each generation?

*Prejudices are what fools
use for reason.*

Voltaire

Reducing Prejudice

Teacher Jane Elliot deliberately created ethnocentrism and prejudice within her elementary school class by dividing her students into brown-eyed and blue-eyed groups, which were then treated differently. One of the groups was treated as superior and received more privileges. This group began to believe in its superiority and soon treated the out-group negatively by taunting and snubbing it. Later, Elliot reversed the desirability of eye colors and found that members of the once-superior group suddenly felt like outcasts. However, the new in-group, remembering the bad experience of being "out," was not as harsh in its treatment of the other group. Elliot's experiences and the results of a psychology experiment replicating her classroom exercise (Weiner & Wright, 1973) suggest that participating in such an exercise can reduce students' prejudices toward people unlike themselves.

Prejudice can also be reduced by overcoming stereotypes, a task that can be accomplished by increasing information about the variety of individuals within a group. People familiar with the customs of a culture tend to have fewer negative stereotypes and more positive attitudes toward members of that culture (Smith et al., 1980). Associating more frequently and as equals with members of a group discriminated against can reduce prejudice, as can working together on activities that require cooperation and interdependence. One technique, the **jigsaw classroom technique** (Aronson, 1984), encourages interdependence by giving each student only one part of the needed information so that students must learn to work together and share information in order to complete the assignment.

Focus Question Answer

How do stereotypes affect your feelings about people you meet? Stereotypes sometimes keep you from conceiving of alternative views of people and from acknowledging the whole range of individual differences. Yet stereotypes can provide quick impressions in situations in which you are not searching for precise information about individuals.

 Interpersonal Attraction

Think about one of your closest friends. Why is he or she your friend? How do you know that this person is

your friend? What elements were involved in forming a relationship with this individual? Are the same factors important reasons your friendship has continued? Do these same elements seem to determine all your friendships? Social psychologists study **interpersonal attraction** to determine the factors involved in attraction to other people. Social psychologists tend to see interpersonal attraction as an attitude toward another person.

Factors Influencing Attraction

Propinquity   Would you be interested in meeting a person who would be the perfect intimate friend for you? Terrific! Just one hitch—this person lives in Tokyo. Are you suddenly less interested? Psychologists have found that **propinquity**, or physical proximity, is important in determining interpersonal attraction. Physical nearness increases the chance of interacting with and getting to know another person. Researchers have discovered that the mere expectation you will get to interact with some-

Have you formed friendships with people who live very near you? How likely is it that you would have become friends if these people lived elsewhere?

one is enough to increase your liking of that individual (Darley & Berscheid, 1967).

Because of propinquity, people often become good friends with their neighbors. Four decades ago, psychologists studied the formation of friendships in a student housing complex (Festinger et al., 1950). They found that students formed more friendships with people who lived on the same floor on which they lived than with people who lived on the other twenty-one floors. On the same floor, students formed closer friendships with individuals living in the apartments nearest their own apartments. Next-door neighbors were four times more likely to interact socially than were people who lived at opposite ends of the hall. You may find this pattern matches your own experiences in a student dormitory or in your neighborhood. You may also notice that you become better friends with students who choose to sit in desks near yours.

Physical Attractiveness   Physical attractiveness is an especially important influence on interpersonal attraction in the early stages of a relationship. In dating situations, liking is influenced largely by the physical attractiveness level of the dating partner (Brislin & Lewis, 1968; Walster et al., 1966).

The **"beautiful is good" hypothesis** summarizes the physical attractiveness advantage (Dion et al., 1972). Attractive people are seen as more interesting, kind, exciting, sensitive, sexually responsive, and likely to have better futures than are less attractive individuals. Attractive persons obtain employment more easily (Dipoye et al., 1975) and, for most crimes, are given lighter sentences in criminal trials (Efran, 1974). Teachers tend to rate physically attractive children as more intelligent, as higher achievers in education, and as having parents who are more interested in what is happening in the schools (Clifford & Walster, 1973). Researchers have also discovered that people will exert more effort to please an attractive person than they will to please a less attractive person (Sigall et al., 1971).

The "beautiful is good" bias seems to occur across the lifespan. Attractive babies are rated more likeable, more intelligent, and better behaved than are less attractive babies (Stephan & Langlois, 1984). Attractive children are more favorably stereotyped than other children (Dion, 1973). When compared to less attractive elderly persons, the attractive elderly are perceived to possess more socially desirable personality characteristics, to have had more pleasant life experiences, and to have achieved greater occupational success (Johnson & Pittenger, 1984).

Do attractive people really behave better, achieve more, and lead better lives? Or do people just think they do? Psychologists have conducted studies to determine if the "beautiful is good" hypothesis reflects reality or if it represents a misconception. One study involving more than 1,300 students focused on the attractiveness ratings of high school yearbook pictures and socioeconomic and marital status fifteen years after high school graduation. Female attractiveness did not correlate with occupational status, educational level, or personal income, although female attractiveness did correlate with marriage to highly educated men with good incomes. Fifteen years after high school graduation, the least attractive males had achieved the highest levels of education as well as occupational status higher than that of the most attractive males (Udry & Eckland, 1984). This study suggests that the "beautiful is good" hypothesis affects perceptions of people's behaviors more than it affects people's actual behaviors.

Similarity   While propinquity may determine whether you meet someone to whom you could be attracted and physical appearance may influence the initial stages of a relationship, similarity plays a major role in long-term interpersonal attractiveness. Attitude similarity is positively related to attraction; in other words, as the proportion of similar attitudes increases, a person becomes more attracted to a stranger (Byrne & Nelson, 1965). People assume that someone with similar attitudes will like them, and people like someone who is like them (Backman & Secord, 1959).

Similar people are also reinforcing. People whose attitudes and values are similar usually agree in discussions, and agreement is very rewarding. Similar people also like to do the same activities; they see the same movies, play the same sports, and listen to the same music. Similarity reduces the time needed to make decisions and increases the number of pleasant activities that can be shared. No wonder, then, that people say "Birds of a feather flock together." The adage seems to be true.

Complementarity   On the other hand, you certainly have heard that "Opposites attract." In fact, oppositeness also seems to be a factor in interpersonal attraction. As you think about your friends and acquaintances, you may find you like some of them because they are very much like you and you like others because they are different from you. Research in this area suggests that opposites attract when the opposites help meet each other's needs. In other words, **complementarity of needs** or personalities can lead to or increase attraction. Thus, a great relationship might develop between a good talker and a good listener or between a dominant person and a more submissive person. Although similarity of values and interests is the best predictor of continuing relationships, complementarity is important in relationships that last longer than eighteen months (Kerchoff & Davis, 1962).

Competence **Competence**, or ability, also influences interpersonal attraction. Ability does not automatically lead to liking, but people prefer being around persons evaluated as competent. However, research findings suggest that an extremely competent person is more likeable if he or she makes an occasional blunder (such as spilling a bit of beverage or tripping over a shoelace) because the individual then seems to be more human; in contrast, a minor blunder will adversely affect an average person because such an act will make the individual seem less attractive in the eyes of others (Aronson et al., 1966).

Reinforcement-Affect Model

Interpersonal attractiveness is explained by four major theories: reinforcement-affect theory, exchange theory, balance theory, and gain-loss theory.

The **reinforcement-affect model** of attraction (Byrne & Clore, 1970) states that people learn to like individuals who are associated with events that arouse positive feelings. According to this theory, you may better like students who were members of a class in which you received an A than students who were members of a class in which you struggled to receive a C-. If you meet someone under crowded and extremely hot conditions, you will probably like that person less than if your meeting had occurred in less crowded and cooler conditions (Griffit & Veitch, 1971). You also like people more if they happened to be nearby when you received a reinforcer because you associate them with the pleasant feelings of the reward (Lott & Lott, 1974). Thus, the reinforcement-affect theory predicts that you could get others to be more attracted to you either by arranging to be with them in pleasant settings or arranging to be present when they receive reinforcements.

Exchange Theory

The **exchange theory** (Thibaut & Kelley, 1959) proposes that relationships are characterized by a concern for what one owes to others and for what one gets in return. Relationships are defined on the basis of a cost-reward ratio. Every relationship has its costs—aspects one has to tolerate in order to continue in the relationship. These

costs can be monetary, emotional, or behavioral (such as putting up with a roommate who squeezes the toothpaste tube in the middle). Every interaction with others also has its rewards—the aspects one likes about the other person and about being with that person.

According to the exchange theory, humans take a capitalistic view of relationships and decide on the basis of the profit produced whether to continue those relationships. In a **cost-reward analysis**, the individual is motivated to *maximize rewards* and to *minimize costs*. This approach may seem like a cold, calculating way to deal with relationships, but probably everyone has used it from time to time. Have you ever decided how much to spend on a birthday present by estimating how much the other person spent on yours?

Many individuals use exchange theory with Christmas card lists. They sit down in December and decide to whom they will send cards. When they come across the name of someone to whom they have sent holiday greetings for the last five years and from whom they have not received a card during the last three years, they calculate that have spent nearly a dollar in postage plus the costs of those cards without receiving anything in return. The costs are far greater than the rewards. Thus, bah humbug! Cross that individual off this year's tidings of great joy!

Another aspect of exchange theory is the **comparison level**, the level of reward one thinks is adequate in a relationship. The comparison level is influenced by past experiences with similar relationships. A relationship is gratifying if the cost-reward analysis yields an outcome that exceeds the comparison level. For instance, if your

To maximize rewards and minimize costs, you may remove from your holiday greetings list the names of people who no longer reply to your letters or cards.

EXHIBIT 18.4
Decision-Making According to Exchange Theory
The cost-reward analysis for a couple dating while
attending different colleges.

past experiences with dating partners have been extremely unsatisfactory, you may find that you enjoy being in a relationship with a mediocre person. Comparison level can also provide an explanation for why some individuals tolerate emotional and physical abuse in their relationships; they remember and evaluate on the basis of relationships that were worse.

Exchange theory also considers the **comparison level for alternatives**, or the lowest level of rewards one finds acceptable after considering the available relationships.

You might stay in a relationship that falls below your comparison level if, when you look at the people around you, you decide you currently have no better opportunities to move into. On the other hand, you might have a relationship with someone who meets your minimal comparison level but suddenly see that person less frequently because you spot the opportunity to develop an even more satisfying relationship with another.

As illustrated in Exhibit 18.4, couples who date in high school but who attend colleges geographically far apart sometimes stop seeing each other even though they still care about each other. Although their time together during vacations is rewarding and they enjoy the long-distance phone calls and cards, a cost-reward analysis shows that the phone bills, the Fridays and Saturdays without dates, and the loneliness are huge costs. The decision to discontinue the relationship may result from a comparison level of alternatives that indicates that several interesting potential dates at the same campus can offer the same rewards with fewer costs.

Balance Theory

A third interpersonal attractiveness theory is **balance theory** (Heider, 1958), which focuses on mental processes rather than on behavior. This theory assumes that people like their cognitions to be psychologically consistent, and when an inconsistent or unbalanced relationship among cognitions exists, negative psychological tension results. People then try to stabilize the relationship with the least possible effort. For example, an unbalanced state occurs when you like your friend but hate your friend's political views. You might create balance

by agreeing never to discuss politics with your friend. You might also resolve the conflict by making different friends who share your views and with whom you can discuss politics.

Giving up one or more friends in order to maintain a consistent psychological framework may seem drastic, but the situation does occur with some regularity. Individuals who have given up drugs may find that to maintain their new lifestyle they must stop seeing the friends with whom they used drugs and make a new circle of friends. Similarly, many individuals, after going through a divorce, find starting new friendships easier than remaining close to those friends who knew them as part of a couple.

Balance theory is consistent with the findings that similarity and complementarity of needs are involved in maintaining friendships since these two factors increase the amount of psychological consistency involved in a relationship. As illustrated in Exhibit 18.5, another conclusion that can be drawn from balance theory is that "People like their friends' friends and their enemies' enemies" (Aronson & Cope, 1968).

EXHIBIT 18.5
Balance Theory of Relationships

Balanced Relationships

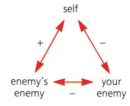
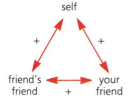
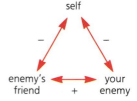

Unbalanced Relationships

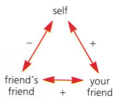

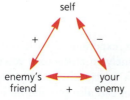

My enemy's enemy is my friend.

Use the phrase "My enemy's enemy is my friend" to illustrate the balanced and unbalanced relationship combinations.

Based on Aronson, E. & Cope, V. 1968. My enemy's enemy is my friend. *Journal of personality and social psychology, 8*, pp. 8-12.

Gain-Loss Theory

A fourth interpersonal attraction theory is **gain-loss theory** (Aronson & Linder, 1965). According to this theory, individuals like a person who becomes more positive toward them better than they like a person who has liked them all along; individuals are also hurt more if someone becomes more negative toward them over time than if the person has disliked them all along. One way to use this theory in a class with an instructor who likes questions and comments is to say little in the beginning of the semester and then to increase your participation and maintain high class participation for the rest of the semester. This increase in positive attitude toward class participation is often reciprocated by the instructor's positive attitude toward you. (Of course, this method is not the only way to acquire the instructor's positive response. You could also create the halo effect by revealing a positive, active approach during the first class.)

Quick Study Aid

The Gain-Loss Theory

You can remember the order of liking predicted by this theory by remembering:

GAIN > ALL POSITIVE > ALL NEGATIVE > LOSS

People may believe that someone's consistently positive evaluations indicate that the evaluator is simply a nice person rather than someone who is particularly attracted to them. On the other hand, a positive gain in evaluation leads people to believe that they personally had a positive impact on that individual; this conclusion makes them feel good, and people are most attracted to those who make them feel good. Similarly, people may interpret all negative evaluations of themselves as signs that the evaluator is a negative person, but a loss in evaluation leads people to conclude that they personally produced a negative impact in the situation; this conclusion makes them feel especially bad (Aronson & Linder, 1965). An alternative explanation is that negative evaluations in the beginning of an encounter arouse anxiety, which is reduced by the later positive statements; this anxiety reduction is a negative reinforcer that produces feelings of liking.

The *Exploring . . .* section explains how two of these interpersonal attraction theories interpret what happens in long-term relationships.

Focus Question Answer

What factors determine your attraction to others? Psychology researchers suggest that propinquity, physical attractiveness, similarity, complementarity, and competence influence whom you find attractive. Most important, however, are the cognitive processes (such as cost-reward analysis) you use in evaluating your relationships.

 Relationships

Familiar Strangers

You have many kinds of relationships with other people. The most frequent relationship is that of strangers. Strangers are all the people with whom you have brief, impersonal interactions such as passing on the street, eating in the same restaurant, and driving on the same highway. People do not pay much attention to the magnitude of the role that strangers play in their lives, but strangers can significantly affect how people act and feel. For example, research studies suggest that crowding intensifies feelings. Crowds make positive experiences seem even more positive and negative experiences seem more negative (Freedman, 1975). A big crowd at a football game may help you enjoy and celebrate your team's victory, but if your team loses that same crowd may add to your misery.

The category of **familiar strangers** is comprised of people you do not know but see often (Milgram, 1970). Urbanites who take a subway or train into work at the same time each day may recognize several passengers as being regular riders too. For years, the riders never exchange more than a nod or a "hello," yet they notice when a familiar stranger is absent or seems different than usual. Several people on your college campus may be familiar strangers; you recognize them and may even remember how they walk and dress, but you do not know their names and have never stopped to talk with them.

Self-Disclosure

Acquaintances comprise another group. People are usually more aware of individuals in this group than of strangers and familiar strangers because people have direct interaction with acquaintances. Acquaintances might exchange conversations about the weather, their kids, their classes, and their last operations, yet they do not reveal to each other the personal aspects of their lives.

People reserve the more intimate details about themselves for their friends; in other words, they usually self-

"How Can Love Survive?"

What do interpersonal attraction theories have to say about why relationships fail? Exchange theory and gain-loss theory offer two explanations for the break-up of relationships.

According to exchange theory, a new, intimate relationship is high on rewards and low on costs. American courting rituals include starting out on one's best behavior. One person asks the other out to a movie or restaurant; the other invites the person to a home-cooked meal or to a day of skiing. They freely exchange flowers, candy, and compliments. Each person shows great interest in what the other says and does. The new date laughs at stale or unfunny jokes, avoids rude remarks, and is patient when hearing redundant stories. The new date stifles yawns, belches, and grumpiness. No wonder people fall in love! Surely these conditions surpass the comparison level and make the new date look good in comparison to others.

After a time, however, the couple exchanges flowers and compliments less frequently, and when a gift is given, it's the "same old flowers" rather than a fresh, exciting experience. The rewards become fewer in number and smaller in effect. Over time, the couple goes less frequently to new restaurants, to bars, to dances, and to concerts. On the other hand, as the couple gets comfortable in the relationship, the persons belch, wheeze, hiccup, and snore in each other's presence. The costs rise; bad habits appear on a daily basis.

Soon, other alternatives in the environment look attractive. An exciting, new person may be ready to woo with "the works" that the current relationship no longer offers. At this point in many relationships, the end is beginning, and the people search for al-

ternative relationships—beginning a new round of cost-reward analysis.

According to gain-loss theory, because a new relationship is marked by impressing each other, the couple starts out with a series of positive evaluations of and behaviors toward each other (+ + + + +). Because this extremely positive approach is difficult to maintain over time, the couple soon sees an occasional negative experience, such as a quarrel or rude comment, slip into the relationship (+ + + + + − + + + − + + +). With time, fewer positive exchanges and a higher proportion of negative exchanges occur (+ + + + + − + + + + − + − + + + − − + + − − − +). This pattern represents a loss situation. Again, if other people in the environment are ready to provide many positive exchanges, the couple may decide to search for new partners.

After examining these two theories, you may wonder how any relationships become long-lasting. Some relationships endure because the persons learn to ignore negative remarks and other costs. People in other relationships find ways to turn the costs into rewards; for instance, the partners may discover greater reward in a comfortable evening at home than in going out on the town. Other individuals may work to maintain a relationship because they do not see better alternatives. Still other couples do not operate their relationships according to these theories but see their partnerships as **communal relationships**. In a communal relationship, a person is more concerned with the other person's welfare and meeting his or her needs than with getting an equal number of benefits from that individual (Mills & Clark, 1984).

---

disclose more freely with their friends. **Self-disclosure** occurs as persons in a relationship progress gradually from the superficial to the intimate by revealing more and more about themselves (Jourard, 1971). The two aspects of self-disclosure are breadth (the number of topics a person will disclose) and depth (how intimately the person discloses) (Altman & Taylor, 1973). Psychological health involves disclosing freely with friends and dis-

closing less intimately with casual acquaintances (Jourard, 1964). You can assess your usual self-disclosure style by using Exhibit 18.6.

Some studies of self-disclosure suggest that a norm of reciprocity usually exists—people tend to disclose approximately as much as others disclose to them. Persons who reveal less than they are told may be viewed as cold and less friendly, and people who tell much more than

EXHIBIT 18.6
Self-Disclosure Ladder

SELF
CLOSEST FRIENDS/INTIMATES
FRIENDS
ACQUAINTANCES
STRANGERS

On the intimacy ladder, indicate which items you would be willing to self-disclose to members on that rung by placing the number of the item within that space.
 1. Your junior high nickname
 2. Your weight
 3. Your worst physical feature
 4. Your sexual fantasies
 5. Your checking account balance
 6. Your religious beliefs and doubts
 7. Your alcohol and drug experiences
 8. Your hopes and plans for yourself ten years from now
 9. Your favorite actors
10. Your behavior in grade school
11. Your most embarrassing moment
12. Your biggest achievement
13. Your favorite relatives
14. Your college major
15. Your attitudes about death and dying

they are told may be considered maladjusted (Chaiken & Derlega, 1974). On the other hand, some people may choose not to disclose as much as the other person does because the other person's depth and breadth of disclosure may be interpreted as forcing self-disclosure. People prefer to feel free to choose their own levels of self-disclosure (Archer & Berg, 1978).

In a relationship, the amount of self-disclosure and the degree to which a person is liked are positively linked, but determining whether self-disclosure precedes liking or vice versa is difficult (Sigall, 1984). People prefer a person who will disclose intimacies to them but to few others (Taylor et al., 1969).

Whether measured by self-report surveys (Jourard, 1971; Komarovsky, 1964) or by disclosure levels in a laboratory setting (Gerdes et al., 1981), women disclose more than men. Even when men do disclose personal information, they usually do so to fewer persons (Komarovsky, 1976). Men's difficulty in self-disclosing may

account for their greater difficulty in coping with the death of a spouse (Stroebe & Stroebe, 1983) and with divorce (Weiss, 1976).

Friendships

How many friends do you have? How many of your friends do you consider close friends? Do you call one of these close friends your best friend? Are both males and females good friends? Is your best friend the same sex as you? Some people use the term friend to include those whom many people consider acquaintances. A survey of over 1,000 adults in California revealed that the respondents labeled approximately five-sixths of the people with whom they associated as friends (Fischer, 1982). However, most of the research on friendships focuses only on close friends.

According to recent research (Davis, 1985), 56 percent of the men surveyed and 44 percent of the women surveyed indicated that they have at least one close friend of the opposite sex. Twenty-seven percent of the subjects said that their best friend is of the opposite sex. Most characteristics of same-sex and opposite-sex friendships are identical, but same-sex friendships average higher levels of sharing, stability, and willingness to give to the other. Women's friendships tend to be more spontaneous and intimate than men's friendships (Caldwell & Peplau, 1982).

Friendship, or platonic love, has eight basic characteristics (Davis, 1985). Friends enjoy each other's company, accept rather than remake each other, have mutual trust, and respect the good judgment of each other. Friends also mutually assist each other, confide feelings and information, understand what is important to the other person, and are spontaneous in the friendship role.

Love Relationships

Love relationships include these eight characteristics and the additional characteristics associated with passion and caring (see Exhibit 18.7). Love relationships contain more ambivalence and more conflict than close friendships, and love relationships require more maintainance activities, such as trying to create solutions to problems. Love relationships are also more exclusive than friendships (Davis, 1985). For example, researchers found that people in close love relationships tend to have fewer friends, often disclose less to friends, and on the whole place less value on the opinions of their friends (Johnson & Leslie, 1982).

EXHIBIT 18.7
The Love Equation

LOVE =

FRIENDSHIP	+ PASSION	+ CARING
enjoyment	fascination	champion/
acceptance	sexual desire	advocate
trust	exclusiveness	giving the utmost
respect		
confiding		
understanding		
spontaneity		
mutual assistance		

Adapted from Davis, K. E. Near and dear: Friendship and love compared, *Psychology Today*, February 1985, p.24. Reprinted with permission from *Psychology Today Magazine*, Copyright (c), 1985. APA.

Although complete love relationships display all the characteristics of friendship plus passion and caring, other forms of love may omit one or two of these three clusters. Some individuals may be involved in passion relationships that do not include the qualities of close friendships or the aspects that make up a caring cluster. Other individuals may lovingly care for persons for whom they have not developed a friendship or passion (Davis, 1985).

Erich Fromm (1956) addressed the types of love in his classic book, *The Art of Loving*. The central aspects of what he called **productive love** are the four characteristics of care (feeling concern about the other), respect (accepting the person without changes), knowledge (liking to learn about the other person), and responsibility (responding to the needs of the other). Fromm believed that self-love, establishing these four aspects toward yourself, is a prerequisite for being able to genuinely love others. Brotherly or sisterly love is a reciprocal love of equals and contains the four aspects of productive love. Parental love also displays these four

Quick Study Aid

Productive Love

The characteristics of productive love can be remembered by using the aid:

CR-KR

which stands for care, respect, knowledge, and responsibility.

aspects but with an extra dose of caring; Fromm saw parental love as an unequal love—parents have unconditional productive love for their children, who may or may not return that love to the parent.

Fromm believed that healthy relationships display productive love aspects and encourage mutual respect and independence for each person. Unhealthy relationships are characterized by symbiotic or withdrawal-destructive characteristics. **Symbiotic relatedness** is a relationship in which one of the individuals loses or never attains independence. In **withdrawal-destructiveness**, distance, apathy, or aggression characterizes the relationship.

Maslow (1962) makes a similar distinction between healthy and unhealthy love relationships. **Being love** is a healthy state that involves two people who love one another by choice rather than need. **Deficiency love**, on the other hand, is a less productive love because it involves depending upon someone to meet one's needs and to decrease feelings of inferiority.

Psychologists have also divided love into passionate love and companionate love (Berscheid & Walster, 1978). **Passionate love** is characterized by absorption in another, intense physiological arousal, longing to see and be with the other, and the experience of ecstasy. Passionate love is fairly short-lived, lasting at most six to thirty months (Walster & Walster, 1978), and couples who base a relationship on passionate love tend to become disenchanted (McCary, 1978).

Companionate love, or conjugal love, is the affection one has for a person with whom one is sharing events and self. Companionate love includes trust, respect, appreciation, attachment, and loyalty. Companionate love is characteristic of the later stages of romantic relationships and plays the major role in long-lasting, satisfying marriages (Berscheid & Walster, 1978).

Having now examined several theories of love, you may wonder who falls in love faster—men or women? Do men or women cling longer to relationships? After a relationship ends, do men or women take longer to recover from a broken heart? Cultural stereotypes might lead you to answer, "Women, of course," but research findings suggest that the correct answer for each of the above questions is "Men" (Walster & Walster, 1978). One explanation that has been postulated to explain the difference is that traditional women date and marry men for financial security and socioeconomic status, while men date and marry for romance. Can you think of other possible explanations? How could you test your hypothesis? As American gender roles change, what changes would you expect in the romantic behavior of men and women?

Focus Question Answer

What characteristics should you look for in order to have healthy relationships? Fromm's characteristics of pro-

ductive love—care, respect, knowledge, and responsibility—form a strong foundation for good loving relationships. Another guideline is that love is a combination of friendship, passion, and caring.

 *Relate*

Whom to Fund—
A Values Exploration

Values make people do what they do; values influence people's decisions and guide their behaviors. Individuals acquire many of their values during childhood, and those values are subsequently affected by family, school, church, television, and peers.

Values clarification exercises such as "Whom to Fund" (Drinnin & Simons, 1981) help you understand your values and stereotypes. Increasing your awareness is the first step toward treating all persons as individuals.

Take a few minutes to complete the following activity, designed to help you explore your own values about public assistance programs. In this exercise, right and wrong answers do not exist. Base your decisions on what you think is best.

Whom to Fund?

Imagine for a few minutes that you are a state employee who evaluates clients' eligibility for public assistance funds. Your supervisor has just informed you that to minimize the role of federal government in regulating the distribution of the funds the current administration has terminated all present federal regulations and has ordered states to revise old rules and devise new regulations.

Until the state government has reformulated policies, case workers have been ordered to disperse funds as they see fit. You have been assigned ten applicants to evaluate for funding; you have funds to give to seven of the individuals. Keep in mind as you read the interview summaries that you are not bound by any government regulations. Also, be aware that no other source of federal financial aid is available. Set your own priorities for funding.

After reading all ten interviews, rank the applicants in order of your funding recommendations. Rank the individual who most deserves funding number 1; rank the individual you believe least deserves funding number 10. Applicants numbered 8, 9, and 10 will receive no public assistance.

Case 1: Beth Marks.

Beth is the mother of a nine-year-old daughter and a seven-year-old son. She is employed part-time as an exotic dancer

at the Pussycat Lounge. A neighbor has reported that Beth does not usually hire a babysitter for the children, even though her work hours are late in the evening, and that the children are usually not dressed properly. Beth asserts that her children are responsible, independent children who manage without the sitter she cannot afford. If she had more money, she says, her children would have nicer clothes. She cannot get money from either of the children's fathers because she does not know where they are. Beth wants public assistance so her children won't be left alone and so they will have their basic needs met.

Case 2: Ada Butler.

Ada is married to George, a man crippled and legally blinded from injuries he received while serving in the Army. George has an explosive temper that is sometimes directed toward Ada or one of the three children. George is not in a rehabilitation program and spends much of his time listening to his ham radio. Ada believes that George's disabilities are severe enough that she must stay home and take care of him and the children.

Case 3: Jane Dobbins.

Jane's husband, a business executive, left with his secretary nearly three years ago. Jane has not heard from him for nearly a year and does not know his current address. He has never sent any money for child support, and Jane believes he spends whatever money he earns on alcohol and gambling. Her savings are nearly depleted now, and many household items, such as the silver, have been sold. Jane believes that with public assistance she will be able to complete the last year and a half of her bachelor's degree and get a decent job to support Charles, 5; Missey, 6; David, 9; and Bunny, 11.

Case 4: Judy Young.

At age sixteen, Judy moved in with Bill, and her parents refused to have any contact with her because she was "living in sin." Judy has not been back to her home state to see

Beth Marks   Ada Butler   Jane Dobbins   Judy Young   Dorothy Portsmith

Dan Johnson   Georgia Bell   Sally Smith   Barbara Tyan   Mary Pilcher

The ten applicants.

her parents for two years, and she strongly believes they would not support her. Now, at eighteen, Judy is six-and-one-half months pregnant. When she discovered she was pregnant, she wanted to get married, but Bill abandoned her. He took most of their possessions with him; the radio, cassette tape player, and toaster were the most valuable items. Judy worked as a waitress until three weeks ago, when she was fired for being "too big and too slow." Judy has no relatives or friends to help her. She has no baby items and has not been seeing a doctor.

Case 5: Dorothy Portsmith.

Dorothy, a black woman, was married to Ralph for ten years; Ralph was in and out of the home for three subsequent years and, for the last two years, has not been around. He does not send child support and even during their marriage had a spotty employment record. The five children range from two-and-one-half years to eleven years. Dorothy occasionally babysits, but she believes she cannot find employment that will cover living expenses and daycare costs. She also thinks she should stay home to supervise her young children and keep them away from drugs and gangs.

Case 6: Dan Johnson.

Dan is a plumber's helper who takes home about $600 each month. From this amount he needs to pay rent, food, cloth-

ing, daycare costs for three children, and other expenses. His wife, Charlene, left with a boyfriend five months ago. The youngest child is ten months old, the twin girls are three years old, and the three other children are in elementary school. Dan wants to stay at home and raise his children. He says he thoroughly enjoys caring for his children and providing for their needs by giving them home-cooked meals and lots of love.

Case 7: Georgia Bell.

Georgia left her husband, Johnny, after he battered her for the second time, breaking her nose and chipping two teeth. She and the three children lived with her parents for a short while, but she was asked to make other arrangements because of her father's heart condition. Georgia and the children have moved in with her boyfriend, Mike. Although Mike likes Georgia's children, he doesn't want to support Johnny's offspring.

Case 8: Sally Smith.

Sally is seventy-eight years old and has been a widow for thirty years. Her two grown sons do not live near her. Sally is known to the social workers as an eccentric old lady likely to drink a six-pack of beer nearly every day. She often calls the office to voice her complaints. She has arthritis and various other symptomology. Her apartment is run-down, and the landlord is miserly with the heat. Sally's only income is a small social security check and $30 she receives each month from her younger son.

Case 9: Barbara Tyan.

During her interview, Barbara matter of factly handed you a list of the children's names—James Johnson, Willis Smith, and Sarah Franklin—along with their birthdates, social security numbers, and other pertinent information. She has just moved the family into the state and is living temporarily with her sister. A black activist, she was president of the Welfare Rights Organization in her former state and plans to be an activist in this state, too.

Case 10: Mary Pilcher.

Mary appeared very nervous during her interview. She has three children and is pregnant again. Her husband, Gary, has left her. For three months before she became pregnant and for the two-and-one-half months of her pregnancy, she has been heavily medicated for anxiety and depression. She desperately wants an abortion. She believes she is too nervous to hold down a job and needs assistance for her three children.

Now, take a few moments to rank the applicants. Use the following table for your rankings.

Ranking sheet
Rank order the ten applicants for funding.

Client	Rank
Case 1: Beth Marks	_____
Case 2: Ada Butler	_____
Case 3: Jane Dobbins	_____
Case 4: Judy Young	_____
Case 5: Dorothy Portsmith	_____
Case 6: Dan Johnson	_____
Case 7: Georgia Bell	_____
Case 8: Sally Smith	_____
Case 9: Barbara Tyan	_____
Case 10: Mary Pilcher	_____

1 = highest priority for funding.
10 = lowest priority for funding.

What factors were important in determining your rankings of the applicants? Did you pay particular attention to certain information? Did you ignore other information? Who do you think *most* deserves funding? Who do you think *least* deserves funding? Can you identify the values that govern your choices? What are those values?

Things to Do

1. Get together with four or five members of your class, and compare your individual rankings of the ten applicants in the "Whom to Fund" exercise. Then try to reach a consensus on which three applicants should not be funded. Write up your results and a summary of the discussion during the consensus-seeking process.

2. List a dozen different makes and models of cars (Corvette, Cadillac, Nova, Honda), and ask twenty students to choose from a list of adjectives (serious, ambitious, thrifty, thrill-seeking, reliable, dishonest, etc.), which adjective best describes someone who owns that kind of car. Your list of adjectives should be wide-ranging. Analyze your data to see if people are stereotyped by the cars they drive.

3. Get dressed up in your best clothes, and do a variety of activities in public—buy an item at a store, ride a public bus, tour a museum, check a book out of the library, ask a gas station attendant for directions, ride the swings at the public playground, etc. Then dress in your shabbiest clothes, and repeat your activities. Did people react to you in the same ways on both occasions? If not, how did their behavior toward you change? Did your feelings about yourself change?

4. Go to a card store, and examine the cards that are available to send to special persons in your life. What factors of interpersonal attraction do the cards emphasize?

5. With a couple of your classmates, try to observe social behavior in a public place. Good settings include restaurants, museums, crowded elevators, hospital waiting rooms, and grocery stores. Try to identify roles and group norms that shape behavior in that setting; for example, in a restaurant you could notice that people who sit down at a table that has not yet been cleared will not eat any of the food on the table—including wrapped food such as crackers.

6. Obtain a few photographs of male and female young adults who vary in attractiveness. Ask several students to examine the photographs and to judge the personalities and future careers of the people in the photos. Did you discover a "beautiful is good" bias?

Things to Discuss

1. How might some of the information you have learned in this chapter (e.g., actor-observer bias, just world belief, "beautiful is good bias," perceptual errors) influence you if you were a juror in a murder trial?

2. How does social psychology differ from other areas of psychology you have been studying?

3. How much do roles influence your behavior? Describe to other class members your behavior when you are in your student role, and indicate how your behavior differs when you are not in that role.

4. Discuss with others to what extent relationships are based on the exchange theory. Do you think living in a capitalistic society influences how much people use exchange theory in deciding which relationships are worth maintaining?

5. Support or rebut the following common-sense sayings with information you learned in this chapter:
   "Birds of a feather flock together."
   "Opposites attract."
   "Familiarity breeds contempt."
   "Beauty is only skin deep."
   "Men play at love in order to have sex; women play at sex in order to have love."
   "Absence makes the heart grow fonder."

6. What perceptual errors about students do teachers frequently make?

Things to Read

Allport, G. 1954. *The nature of prejudice.* Reading, MA: Addison-Wesley.

Aronson, E. 1984. *The social animal.* San Francisco: Freeman.

Fromm, E. 1956. *The art of loving.* NY: Harper & Row.

Kelley, H.H., et al. 1983. *Close relationships.* San Francisco: Freeman.

Mellen, S.L.W. 1981. *The evolution of love.* San Francisco: Freeman.

Norwood, R. 1985. *Women who love too much.* NY: St. Martins' Press.

Walster, E. & Walster, G.W. 1978. *A new look at love.* Reading, MA: Addison-Wesley.

 # Review

Summary

1. Usually, first impressions are more important than later impressions when one forms perceptions of individuals.

2. In attribution, people tend to overestimate the role of traits when evaluating the behavior of other persons and to overestimate the role of the situation when evaluating their own behavior.

3. Explicit and implicit roles are convenient aspects that permit knowledge about a situation's ground rules. Sometimes, however, people overdefine others according to others' roles, and sometimes roles overinfluence behavior. The Zimbardo Stanford prison experiment dramatically illustrated how roles affect behavior.

4. Several perceptual errors are common in person perception: actor-observer bias, egocentric attribution, vividness error, halo effect, logical error, leniency error, and error of central tendency.

5. A fairly common belief that influences attribution is the just world belief, which is the assumption that people get what they deserve during their lives. People may even alter reality to fit the just world belief.

6. A stereotype is a set of characteristics that an individual believes all members of a group possess. Powerful stereotypes affect attitudes and behaviors toward many groups. Stereotypes often lead to prejudices, emotionally charged negative stereotypes, and to ethnocentrism, the belief that one's own group is superior to other groups.

7. Prejudice can be reduced by increasing information about and contact with members of the stereotyped group and by performing tasks that require interdependence.

8. Propinquity, physical attractiveness, similarity, complementarity, and competence influence interpersonal attraction.

9. Interpersonal attractiveness occurs when (1) people are reinforcing to be around, (2) when people offer more rewards than costs, and (3) when interaction is psychologically consistent.

10. The most common relationship is with strangers; the interaction with familiar strangers is frequent but shallow.

11. Amount of self-disclosure is one factor that differentiates an acquaintance from a friend. Self-disclosure is usually reciprocal in topics and depth.

12. Love relationships entail the qualities of friendships plus passion and caring. Productive love involves care, respect, knowledge, and responsibility. Companionate love is more predictive of long-term, satisfying relationships than is passionate love.

13. Values clarification exercises allow individuals to explore their own values and attitudes.

Key Terms

social psychology
person perception
first impression
attribution process
fundamental attribution error
correspondent inference theory
role
deindividuation
demand characteristics
actor-observer bias
egocentric attributions
halo effect
logical error
leniency error
error of central tendency

just world belief
stereotypes
self-fulfilling prophecy
prejudice
ethnocentrism
"beautiful is good" hypothesis
reinforcement-affect model
exchange theory
balance theory
gain-loss theory
familiar strangers
self-disclosure
productive love
passionate love
companionate love

Focus Questions

1. Do your attitudes determine your behaviors?

2. How can you get people to like something they now dislike?

3. Why do your behaviors sometimes contradict your beliefs?

4. Are you a helpful person?

5. Can psychology influence your votes?

Chapter Outline

Chapter 19

Social Psychology: Attitude Change and Social Influence

*Think where man's glory
    most begins and ends,
And say my glory was
    I had such friends.*

William Butler Yeats

 Attitudes

What are attitudes? People talk about someone having a bad attitude, getting a new attitude, and holding political and social attitudes. **Attitudes** can be defined as relatively enduring organizations of beliefs, feelings, and behavioral tendencies toward events, objects, groups, or symbols (Himmelfarb & Eagley, 1974). Attitudes are used in many ways: to help organize and understand events, to provide the means to a goal, to allow people to display values, and to serve as ego defense mechanisms, which help people to deny or distort unacceptable impulses or situations (Pallak et al., 1984).

461

Measuring Attitudes

Psychologists use three major ways of assessing attitudes: self-report, physiological measures, and behavioral measures. Self-report measures include a variety of questionnaire and interview techniques. Self-reports can be flawed because subjects may try to give socially acceptable answers rather than reveal their real attitudes. Subjects may say, for example, that they favor racial equality or women's rights more than they actually do.

Some researchers have used physiological measures such as electrodermal response, heartbeat, and pupil dilation to indicate attitudes. Because physiological reactions can be measured without subjects' awareness and because subjects are usually not able to alter their responses, physiological methods do entail advantages. However, such measures can also be sensitive to variables other than attitudes; for instance, heartrate can be affected by task (e.g., problem-solving tasks increase heartrate, and vigilance tasks decrease heartrate), and skin resistance may change in the presence of novel stimuli. Also, while physiological measures can indicate the intensity of subjects' attitudes, the measures cannot indicate the direction of the attitudes. When facial expressions are used in attitude measurement, the opposite is true; facial expressions can indicate direction of attitude, but they are not good indicators of intensity (Pallak et al., 1984). Thus, physiological measurements of attitudes may also be subject to flaws.

Finally, attitudes can be measured by studying overt behavior, and some psychologists suggest using unobtrusive measures such as nonverbal behaviors, physical traces, and archival records (Webb et al., 1981). If a museum curator asks visitors, "Which is your favorite exhibit?" some visitors will answer with attempts to impress or please the curator. Therefore, the curator might better assess visitors' attitudes by using a number of unobtrusive measures; for instance, he or she might attempt to determine how closely visitors stand to various displays. In using visitor behavior to determine attitudes, however, the curator must be certain that he or she has chosen a representative problem and that the observed behavior does not occur for reasons other than the studied attitude. One visitor might stand near an exhibit because she likes the exhibit, while another visitor might stand near it because he is nearsighted.

Attitude Formation

Attitudes can be formed by several processes. Some attitudes are formed through classical, operant, or obser-

vational learning, while others develop in response to pressures for consistency and conformity (Pittman et al., 1984).

One determinant of attitudes is the **mere exposure effect** (Zajonc, 1968), according to which the more frequently people encounter an object or idea, the more favorably they evaluate the object or idea. Perhaps you have experienced this process with a popular song. The first time you heard the song, you may not have been particularly impressed. Yet, as radio stations continued to play the song, it "grew on you" until eventually you found yourself humming the tune. Consider how advertisers and political candidates also depend upon the mere exposure effect.

Attitudes and Behavior

Just as attitudes can affect behavior, behaviors can also modify attitudes. In one study, parents and students who participated in metropolitan school desegregation programs improved their attitudes toward desegregation, especially in the first year of participation (Parsons, 1984).

Overall, psychologists are not good at predicting behavior for any specific occasion on the basis of attitude alone, but they are fairly good at predicting from attitudes the total quantity of behavior. Thus, although psychologists cannot predict who will be in church on a particular Sunday, by assessing religious attitudes, they can fairly successfully predict who will be in church on most Sundays (Kahle & Berman, 1979).

Although people's behaviors are often influenced by their attitudes, behavior and attitudes can also be very different. A 1934 research study by LaPiere illustrated that attitudes do not always guide behaviors. With a Chinese couple, LaPiere visited 251 hotels and restaurants, and only one of the establishments refused service. Six months later, LaPiere sent to each of the establishments a questionnaire containing the question "Will you accept members of the Chinese race as guests in your establishment?" Ninety-two percent of the hotels and restaurants answered no.

Why did the questionnaire responses and the establishments' treatment of the Chinese couple differ? According to one explanation, acting upon some attitudes is difficult; responding prejudicially to a paper-and-pencil task is easier than actually being rude to people. According to another explanation, people feel more bias toward an entire group than they feel toward any specific couple. As a third possible explanation, owners and managers completed the attitudinal questionnaire, but desk clerks and waitresses performed the behavioral responses. This last explanation suggests that higher-level personnel exhibit more prejudices than do people in direct service to customers.

A more recent correlational study of attitudes and behavior was prompted by the cyanide-laced Extra-strength Tylenol capsules that killed seven people in Illinois in 1982. Researchers (Dershewitz & Levin, 1984) found that parents changed their attitudes about the safety of over-the-counter medications, but they did not change their use of these medications. As these results indicate, a change in attitude is not always sufficient to cause a change in behavior.

In fact, behavior sometimes has little to do with personal attitudes. Instead, individuals may act according to other people's wishes. Which high school students smoke marijuana is determined more by the number of friends who smoke than by the students' previous attitudes toward marijuana (Andrews & Kandel, 1979). Later in this chapter you will learn how conformity and obedience cause people to relinquish their own attitudes and act according to social pressures.

Additionally, behaviors do not always reflect attitudes because much behavior is "mindless," or automatic. **Mindlessness** refers to behavior that is habitual rather than responsive to actual environmental characteristics (Langer, 1978). Research findings suggest that when people are asked to do small favors, most respond only to the form of the request rather than to the substance of the request. In contrast, with large requests, people pay closer attention, and compliance rate is more heavily influenced by the reasons for the requests.

A study of persons who were using a copy machine and were asked to allow the experimenter to interrupt to make copies illustrated this tendency. In one condition, the experimenter asked to make only five copies; in the second condition, the experimenter asked to make twenty copies. The reason for the request also varied and consisted of "I need to make copies" or "I'm in a rush." As you can see in Exhibit 19.1, the reason given did not affect compliance with the small request of five copies, but it did affect compliance rate for the larger request of twenty copies (Langer et al., 1978).

Focus Question Answer

Do your attitudes determine your behaviors? Not always. Although a person's behaviors and attitudes are usually related, people sometimes do not act according to their attitudes. Acting upon certain attitudes may be difficult, and sometimes people act according to the wishes of other people. Often people act "mindlessly" and pay no attention to their attitudes.

Attitude Change

How can another person get you to change your mind? Your parents might like to modify your opinions, politicians want to influence your voting attitudes, and salesclerks would like to convince you their merchandise is excellent. Psychology suggests several strategies by which your views can be influenced and other strategies by which you can resist attempts to persuade.

Source, Message, and Context

Source   The source is the communicator of the persuasive message. Does the communicator's credibility affect the amount of opinion change? Consider your own ex-

EXHIBIT 19.1
Reactions to Copying Requests

	NO REASON	UNINFORMATIVE REASON (need to make copies)	INFORMATIVE REASON (in a rush)
SMALL FAVOR (5 copies)	.60	.93	.94
BIG FAVOR (20 copies)	.24	.24	.42

Source: Langer, E. J., Blank, A. & Chanowitz, B. 1978. The mindlessness of ostensibly thoughtful action: The role of "placebic" information in interpersonal interaction. *Journal of Personality and Social Psychology, 36*, 635-642.

perience. Does an authoritative or prestigious communicator affect you more than another person? Would a lecture given by a distinguished college professor influence you more than the same lecture presented by a graduate student? Are you more influenced by a television advertisement featuring a well-known personality or by the same advertisement featuring an unfamiliar person?

To determine answers to such questions, researchers asked subjects to read an article that varied in the expertness of the author. The author's expertness did not affect comprehension of the article, but expertness did influence the amount of opinion change. However, the effect of source credibility decreased with the passage of time. As shown in Exhibit 19.2, over a four-week period, more change occurred for the low credibility source, and less change occurred for the high credibility source. Thus, if you understand a communication, you can be persuaded by it, even if you initially dismiss the communication. According to the **sleeper effect**, over time the audience forgets the credibility of the source but remembers the message (Hovland & Weiss, 1951). This principle suggests, for example, that in a long jury trial, jurors will forget the questionable credibility of a witness, but the witness's testimony will affect the jury's verdict.

An effective way to influence amount of attitude change is to use an unexpected communicator (Wood

& Eagly, 1981). Individuals are more impressed by an ex-convict who argues for stricter law enforcement than by a district attorney presenting the same arguments. On the other hand, more attitude change results from a district attorney emphasizing the need for more lenient laws than from an ex-convict delivering the identical presentation. Individuals pay more attention and more readily accept someone's opinion if they do not expect the person to hold that position. How can political organizations and advertising companies take advantage of this effect?

Additionally, rapid speakers are rated as more credible, more trustworthy, and more persuasive than slow speakers. People who heard a taped message on "the danger of coffee drinking" at 190 words per minute instead of 110 words per minute rated the fast speaker as more knowledgeable, more intelligent, and more objective (Miller et al., 1976). Also, marketing researchers have found that people are more persuaded by commercials that are speeded up by 25 percent (MacLahlan, 1979).

Other speaker characteristics influencing persuasiveness are making eye contact with the audience, speaking without hesitation, and avoiding qualifying phrases such as "kinda," "I guess," "you know," and "well" (Hall, 1980). Research findings also indicate that good arguments are more persuasive when they originate from physically attractive people (Dion & Stein, 1978).

In addition to these elements of persuasiveness, listeners can be influenced by the degree of similarity with the communicator. On matters of personal values and taste, similar communicators are most persuasive. However, with factual matters, listeners are most influenced by a dissimilar communicator (Goethals & Nelson, 1973).

Message   The message is the content of the persuasion attempt. Which comprises the most effective message—presenting one side or both sides of an argument? Research indicates that one-sided arguments work best with audiences who already agree with the presenter's opinion and with audiences who know little about the issues. On the other hand, two-sided arguments are more effective with well-informed audiences or with audiences who initially disagree with the presenter's position (Hovland et al., 1949). Therefore, a Democrat speaking to Democrats can stick to the party position, as can a Republican talking to Republicans. However, if the audience is comprised of well-informed Independent voters, the speaker should present both sides of the argument (more convincingly emphasizing the speaker's own position, of course).

EXHIBIT 19.2
The Sleeper Effect

In concluding his or her message, should the communicator offer an explicit or implied conclusion? Explicit conclusions are most persuasive with complex issues and situations in which inferring the desired conclusion might be difficult. However, when the implied conclusion is obvious, it is more persuasive than an explicit conclusion because people do not like to be told what to think (Hovland & Mandell, 1952).

In a two-sided presentation, does the first or second speaker have the advantage? If a time interval separates the presentations, going second is advantageous. If opinion change is measured a considerable time after the presentations, going first is more effective (Miller & Campbell, 1959).

More attitude change occurs when a speaker uses vivid examples than when he or she presents general information. State lotteries depend upon people remembering the vivid examples of big winners rather than realizing that almost everyone loses. College students form more of their impressions of professors' abilities from a few vivid comments by friends than they do from published evaluations made by hundreds of students (Borgida & Nisbett, 1977). The **vividness effect** is illustrated by the large number of politicians who fill their speeches with anecdotes rather than facts. Politicians know that concrete examples capture attention and thus are more likely to influence attitudes.

Context   The context of the message, the situation and style in which persuasion is attempted, is also an important research variable. For example, people tend to be less critical of tape-recorded or videotaped messages than they are of written messages (Maier & Thurber, 1968). Therefore, the effectiveness of media format is best determined by the complexity of the message; complex messages should be in written form, and simple messages should have an audiovisual context (Chaiken & Eagly, 1976).

The following research tidbits illustrate the wide range of contextual factors that can influence persuasion:

— People who ate and drank while reading a message were more persuaded than those without refreshments (Janis et al., 1965).

— Subjects were more influenced by messages accompanied by folk music than by messages without music (Galizo & Hendrick , 1972).

— Subjects saw a slide of either a blue or beige pen while pleasant or unpleasant background music was played. Subjects who had heard pleasant music chose the pen color they had seen 79 percent of the time; subjects who had been exposed to unpleasant music chose the pen of the opposite color 70 percent of the time (Gorn, 1982).

— Fear-arousing messages can be effective if specific instructions are provided on how to avoid the danger (Janis & Feshbach, 1953; Rogers & Mewborn, 1976).

— Subjects were told to nod their heads either vertically or horizontally as they listened over headphone sets to an editorial. Subjects who moved their heads vertically later expressed more agreement with the editorial (Wells & Petty, 1980).

— Subjects were told they would be solving anagrams as an intelligence measure and then were left alone to work on the problems. Although most people value honesty, 71 percent of the subjects cheated on the task by working past the time limit. However, subjects who were made more self-conscious by working on the task in front of a mirror cheated only 7 percent of the time (Diener & Wallbom, 1976).

Quick Study Aid

Source—Message—Context

Use this abbreviated list to help you recall specific findings about the source, message, and context of attitude change.

SOURCE	MESSAGE	CONTEXT
expertness	one/two-sided	media format
unexpectedness	explicit/implicit	food and drink
speed of speaking	conclusions	music
speaking styles	order of presentation	fear
physical attractiveness	vivid/concrete examples	nodding
similarity		self-consciousness

Selling Strategies

Three popular techniques to persuade customers to buy are the foot-in-the door technique, the door-in-the-face technique and the low-ball procedure. The **foot-in-the-door technique** begins with getting a person to comply with a very small request. This compliant behavior increases the likelihood of compliance with a larger request at a later time. Would you be willing to put on your front lawn a large, unattractive sign saying "Drive carefully"? In one study, only 17 percent of the subjects agreed on first contact to place such a sign in their front yards. Other subjects were initially asked to sign a petition requiring state senators to work for safe driving legislation. A few weeks later, when these subjects were contacted by a different individual, 55 percent agreed to put the "Drive carefully" sign on their lawns (Freedman & Fraser, 1966). As a child, you used the foot-in-the-door technique when you asked to stay up "a little later" to see the end of a television program. If your parent agreed, you went on to ask for "just one more" TV show.

Interestingly, a technique contrasting with the foot-in-the-door method also works. With the **door-in-the-face technique**, the individual starts with a very large request and, after the request is refused, makes a smaller request. The high rate of compliance suggests that individuals respond to one compromise with another compromise (Cann et al., 1975). "Can I borrow fifty dollars?" "No way." "Well, can I borrow five?" "Yes, I guess so."

A third procedure is the **low-ball procedure**, in which an individual first gets a verbal commitment to honor a

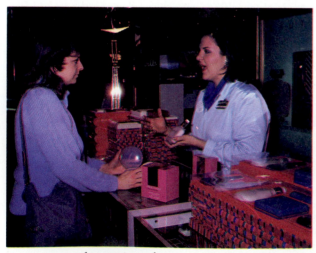

An *awareness of persuasion techniques is valuable to both salespeople and consumers.*

small request and then makes a larger request. The small task is never done, but the larger task is performed (Burger & Petty, 1981). The low-ball procedure is evidenced when a person asks you to help move a sofa on Saturday, and you consent to do so. On Saturday, the individual asks you to move a whole roomful of furniture. Your compliance is more likely than if you were asked initially to move all the furniture.

Cognitive Dissonance Theory

The *Exploring . . .* section presents the classic research study on cognitive dissonance theory, a theory that is quite simple yet has many applications. Cognitive dissonance theory helps explain why people can continue to believe a certain way when the facts do not fit the situation or are bolstered by only weak evidence (Lichtenberg, 1984).

The fundamental assumption of **cognitive dissonance theory** is that inconsistent cognitive elements are unpleasant. The theory suggests that people adjust their thinking (or sometimes their behavior) to reduce this mental tension. Since cognitive dissonance is greater when the cognitions involved are important to the individual, dissonance can be reduced by making one of the cognitions less important. Dissonance can also be reduced by changing a cognition or by adding a cognition (i.e., adding justification).

Smokers are aware that smoking can cause cancer and shorten their lifespans, and cognitive dissonance exists between the beliefs "I am a smoker" and "Smoking cigarettes will kill me." A smoker can reduce cognitive dissonance by adopting any of the following stances: (1) not thinking about smoking, (2) reasoning that he or she really doesn't want a long life, (3) reasoning that low tar and nicotine cigarettes reduce the risk, and (4) quitting smoking. Because people usually take the

Exploring...

Festinger and Carlsmith's Cognitive Dissonance Study

Leon Festinger developed his idea for cognitive dissonance theory after reading a report that after a 1934 earthquake in India rumors spread that worse disasters were imminent. Festinger reasoned that the rumors were "anxiety-justifying" and helped make the world consistent with feelings (Myers, 1983).

To test the concept of cognitive dissonance theory, Festinger and Carlsmith (1959) conducted a study in which all subjects turned wooden knobs on a pegboard over and over again for one hour. The control group's rating of the task ($-.45$) indicated that the task was not enjoyable.

The subjects not in the control group were placed in two experimental groups. Subjects in these two groups thought the experiment was over when the boring task had ended, but actually the real experiment still lay ahead. Each subject was informed that he or she had participated in a study on the effects of expectations on performance. Each subject was also told that the next subject was to participate in a different condition in which they expected the task to be interesting. Finally, each subject was told that the assistant who explains the experiment was unable to be present; the experimenter asked the subjects to assume the assistant's job. Subjects in one experimental group were paid one dollar each to convince the next subject that the task was interesting, and subjects in the other experimental group were paid twenty dollars apiece.

Convincing the next subject that the task was interesting was difficult because the subject was actually working for the experimenter. The pseudo-subject forced the subject-assistant to take several minutes to accomplish the task. If the subject-assistant said he had just participated in an experiment and had had a wonderful time, the pseudo-subject (or confederate) might respond, "Really? A friend of mine was in this experiment last week, and she said it was boring."

Before the real subjects left the laboratory, they completed a questionnaire on their reactions to the knob-turning experiment; the questionnaire was the dependent variable. One experimental group responded similarly to the control group (subjects did not like the task), but the other group indicated that the knob-turning task had been enjoyable (the ratings were $-.05$ and $+1.35$ respectively).

Who enjoyed turning the wooden pegs—subjects paid one dollar or subjects paid twenty dollars? You might assume that subjects who were paid more rated the task more favorably, but actually subjects who were paid only a dollar reported that they liked the task! Why? Festinger and Carlsmith believed those who were paid one dollar had insufficient justification for lying to the next subject. According to the researchers, the dollar subjects must have thought, "Gee, did I do a good job of convincing the next subject! Why? Well, the money couldn't have mattered because a dollar isn't much; I guess the task must have been okay." On the other hand, subjects who were paid twenty dollars might reason, "Why did I try so hard to convince that subject? Because anybody would have lied well for twenty dollars!" Both experimental groups acted in a way that reduced cognitive dissonance.

route requiring least work, the least likely option is to quit smoking.

Dissonance occurs after decisions are made. If a person has no choice regarding an inconsistent behavior, he or she will experience little or no dissonance, and little or no attitude change will occur. The person can merely reason, "I had no choice in this matter—it's not my inconsistency." On the other hand, when a person has freedom of choice, inconsistencies produce psychological tension.

Decisions that involve making choices among alternatives with both positive and negative qualities will create dissonance. The higher the proportion of negative qualities in the chosen alternative and the higher the proportion of positive qualities in the rejected option, the larger the amount of cognitive dissonance produced.

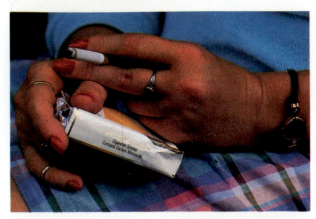

Through published research and the warning labels on cigarette packages, smokers have become aware of the health hazards of smoking, and they may experience cognitive dissonance.

One way to reduce the cognitive dissonance is to become selective in what you pay attention to after you have made a decision. Studies suggest that people have a tendency to avoid new, inconsistent information while experiencing cognitive dissonance. For instance, clinicians who had diagnosed a patient on the basis of personality tests tended to ignore contradictory information presented later (Mynatt et al., 1977). After making choices, people attempt to convince themselves that their choices were correct by selectively observing information that affirms their decisions.

How can you use cognitive dissonance theory in your life? If you are a parent wishing your child would keep a clean room, you might attempt the following technique. Try to determine the smallest amount of money for which your child will clean the room. When the child is done with the cleaning, he or she cannot conclude, " I did all that work because I was paid so much." Instead, the child will believe, "Since I was paid only a little and I still cleaned the room, I must not dislike cleaning that much." Internalization of cleanliness is more likely with this scenario than when parents bribe children with large rewards or threaten them with punishment.

Reactance Theory

Reactance is the unpleasant arousal that accompanies the perception that behavioral freedom has been eliminated. Reactance can occur even if the forced behavior is consistent with personal attitudes. In other words, when social pressure is blatant and the sense of freedom is lost, people often rebel. This phenomenon is called the "boomerang effect" (Brehm & Brehm, 1981).

You probably have had arguments that illustrate the boomerang effect. Perhaps your parents ordered you to do something you also thought you should do, but because they demanded you do it you did something else. Of course, your parents may have been clever enough to use "reverse psychology," telling you to do the opposite of what they wanted you to do, and when you rebelled, you ended up doing something of which they approved. Reverse psychology is illustrated in this overheard conversation between mothers of teenage daughters: "I don't know how you get Jenny to buy such nice clothes; my Wendy never listens to my shopping advice." "So, who listens? I figure out which clothes I can't stand and tell Jenny I like them best. That way, she never buys those far-out styles."

Actually having freedom to act is not as significant as perceiving that one has freedom to act in a situation. Thus, to get someone to change an attitude or behavior, you must create a situation in which the person has an illusion of freedom. For this reason, teachers often let students pick the day of an exam—"Would you prefer the test to be given on Tuesday or Thursday?"—because a choice provides a degree of behavioral freedom. Notice, however, that the main issue—"Should there be a test?"—is not a student decision. Parents also use the illusion of freedom. They do not ask their small children, "Do you want to go to bed tonight?" Instead, they provide an option, such as "Would you like your bedtime story before or after putting on your pajamas?" In any situation, the need for freedom and the ability to relinquish control vary according to past experiences. People are more likely to give up control without experiencing psychological reactance if they have just performed well on a task (Strube & Werner, 1984). Thus, if you have written an excellent term paper, you might be more likely to comply with your roommate's demand to do something right now than you would if you are struggling with your term paper. If you control one area of your life, you do not need as much control in another area.

The Overjustification Effect

Intrinsic motivation occurs when an activity is seen as an end in itself, when the activity is satisfying and rewarding for its own sake. **Extrinsic motivation** occurs when an activity is seen as a means to an end, when the activity is performed for an external consequence. The **overjustification effect** is the loss of interest that occurs when an individual shifts from an intrinsic to an extrinsic motivational orientation. If people are bribed or rewarded to perform an activity they already enjoy, the behavior is soon seen as externally controlled rather than intrinsically appealing. A person who is good at riding horses and who enjoys the activity may decide to enter riding competitions. However, after winning a couple of blue ribbons, the individual finds that *just* riding is not enough—only winning competitions is enjoyable.

One study revealed that children who expected to be rewarded for drawing pictures were less likely to draw in their free time than were children who did not expect to be rewarded (Lepper et al., 1973). In another study, subjects were asked to defend the position that students should have a say in course offerings. This view is popular among students, yet students who were paid $7.50 to defend the stance became less committed to the position than were students who defended the position for free (Benware & Deci, 1975). Being rewarded for something one already believes in can undermine the belief.

Do grades create overjustification in the classroom? Yes, sometimes. If grades are taken as symbols of competence, the grades do not decrease interest (Boggiano & Ruble, 1979). Praise may increase interest in learning if the verbal rewards are seen as informational, but praise will decrease interest if it is viewed as controlling (Deci, 1975). Teacher style determines how grades are used. Teachers who want control tend to produce extrinsic motivational orientations in their pupils; teachers who are informationally oriented tend to promote intrinsic orientations through the encouragement of self-control and feelings of confidence (Deci & Ryan, 1980).

Resisting Persuasive Appeals

Persuasion is not inherently good or bad. Good persuasion is labeled education, and bad persuasion is labeled propaganda (Myers, 1983). Because propaganda is widespread, you need to strengthen your abilities to resist such persuasion attempts, and you can use many strategies to do so.

Passive Techniques   Two fairly passive resistance strategies concern the way in which people distort the messages of a persuasive appeal. One distortion process is **assimilation**, in which listeners judge a speaker's position to be more similar to their own positions than it actually is. Assimilation minimizes pressure to change or adjust attitudes. The other distorting process is called **contrast**, which occurs when listeners judge a speaker's position to be more different from their own positions than it actually is. Contrast makes rejecting the speaker's mes-

sage easy. Both assimilation and contrast help people resist persuasion by allowing them to accept or reject the whole message without questioning their own stands.

Another process helpful in maintaining current beliefs is the **false consensus effect**, an egocentric bias that allows people to believe their attitudes are relatively more common and more appropriate than other positions (Mullen et al., 1985). By thinking their opinions are widely held, people feel less pressure to change attitudes and conform. For example, students were asked to wear an advertising "sandwich board" sign around campus. Students who agreed to wear the sign guessed that 62 percent of the students would agree to do the task; students who refused to wear the sign guessed that 67 percent of students would refuse to perform the task (Ross et al., 1977).

Active Techniques   An active technique to resist persuasion is to be forewarned about an attempt to sway attitudes (Myers, 1983). The saying "forewarned is forearmed" has some validity. The advantage is increased when individuals understand the various persuasion styles and the persuader's probable tactics because the listeners can adjust their own strategies accordingly (Kipnis & Schmidt, 1985). Exhibit 19.3 summarizes three persuasion styles and their advantages. Consistent with this model is the proposal that those with power and those without power use different persuasion techniques. The powerful use tactics of rationality, law, control, and discipline (i.e., the hard and rational strategies), while the weak use the tactics of justice, compassion, and relatedness (i.e., the soft strategy) (Steininger et al., 1984).

Commitment theory (Kiesler, 1971) proposes that attitudes become more resistant to persuasion attempts if people have publicly committed themselves to their current positions. Attitudes linked or bound to overt behaviors are more stable and less likely to be changed. Religions make use of this effect by having converts make public confirmations of their faith with practices such as baptism and confirmation. Commitment is also strengthened by engaging in behaviors that are multiple, important, unconstrained, and irrevocable.

Another form of active resistance is presented in **inoculation theory** (McGuire, 1964), according to which people defend their attitudes better if they have had practice defending them. McGuire makes effective use of an analogy between being inoculated with polio vaccine to resist polio and being exposed to a different position to resist persuasion. The injection of a weak polio virus allows the body to ward off a strong polio virus; similarly, by defending one's position against mild arguments, the mind is later able to ward off stronger arguments. A youngster who has been taught to defend his or her position of non-drug usage by being drilled with "And what are you going to say to a friend who offers you a joint?" will be better able to resist persuasion to use marijuana. Research has shown the inoculation technique to be effective in helping junior high school children resist persuasive appeals to smoke (Evans et al., 1981) and in helping elementary school children resist television advertising (Cohen, 1980). The following *Exploring . . .* section introduces you to some of the strategies advertisers use to persuade your buying habits.

Focus Question Answer

How can you get people to like something they now dislike? Although changing a person's attitude can be difficult, you can get someone to like something by using various techniques such as cognitive dissonance and overjustification. If you wanted to get a child to enjoy his or her chores and to like television less, you might pay the child a small amount of money to do the chores (using cognitive dissonance) and for two weeks reward the child with gold stars to watch television and then give no more gold stars for television viewing (using overjustification effect).

 ## Social Influence

Social influence occurs when individuals change their behaviors because of the behaviors or attitudes of others. Social psychologists study social influence in many areas, including social comparison, social facilitation, social loafing, conformity, obedience, leadership, and helping behavior.

EXHIBIT 19.3
Persuasion Styles

Strategy	General Description	Why Chosen	By Couples	By Managers
HARD (insistent)	Involves demanding, shouting, and asserting; may create loss of good will.	Influencer has the advantage. Anticipation of resistance. The behavior violates social or organizational norms.	Display anger and demand giving in. Make other feel stupid and worthless. Threaten to leave.	Order the person. Threaten poor performance evaluation. Get back-up from higher management.
SOFT (emotional)	Involves acting nicely and using flattery.	Infuencer is at a disadvantage. Anticipation of resistance. The goal is to benefit oneself.	Be warm and charming ahead of time. Ask nicely.	Act humbly. Tell the person she or he is competent enough to do the task.
RATIONAL (logical)	Involves logic and bargaining; demonstrates why compliance or compromise is the best solution.	Neither party has a power advantage. Resistance is not anticipated. The goal is to benefit both organization and self.	Offer to compromise. Discuss objectively.	Offer to exchange favors. Explain reasoning.

Adapted from Kipnis, D. & Schmidt, S. 1985. The language of persuasion. *Psychology Today*, April, 40-46. Reprinted with Permission from *Psychology Today Magazine*. Copyright (c) 1985. American Psychological Association.

 Exploring . . .

The Madison Avenue Touch

Advertising agencies seem to use psychological findings more than any other group, and you can witness ad agencies' use of attitude change strategies tens of thousands of times each year (Snyder & DeBono, 1985). In turn, psychologists study advertisements to determine their effects on people.

Advertisers use two major types of persuasion—the *soft-sell* approach and the *hard-sell* approach. In the soft-sell approach, the quality of the product is scarcely mentioned. The emphasis is on enhancing one's image, and product packaging takes priority over product characteristics (Fox, 1984). Examples of the soft-sell approach include the AT & T "Reach out and touch someone" ads and McDonald's "We do it all for you" ads.

The second approach is the hard-sell approach, which emphasizes qualities and functions of the product. These advertisements emphasize statistics, benefits, and comparisons with other products (Fox, 1984). Examples of the hard-sell approach include Total cereal ads and Weight Watchers ads, both of which emphasize nutritional and caloric contents of their products. Some advertisers use both strategies. Pepsi used soft-sell with its "Pepsi generation" campaign and hard-sell with its "Pepsi challenge" ads.

One group of studies (Snyder & DeBono, 1985) examined the appeal of soft-sell and hard-sell advertising on high and low self-monitoring individuals. High self-monitoring individuals try to adjust their personalities and behaviors to a situation. Low self-monitoring individuals do not mold their behaviors to the situation but guide behavior on the basis of internal information. The researchers made six advertisements for whiskey, cigarettes, and coffee; the two

advertisements for each product varied only in the written message given with each picture. One slogan was image-associated, and one slogan was product quality-oriented. As expected, high self-monitoring individuals favored the soft-sell ad, and low self-monitoring individuals favored the hard-sell ad. Following are additional research tidbits from psychological advertising studies:

— Using advertising displays, male models made more beer sales than did female models, and the attractiveness of the models was not a factor. However, attractive models sold more toilet paper, but the gender of the model did not have a significant effect (Caballero & Solomon, 1984).

— Subjects viewed a videotaped soccer game with 0, 4, or 9 beer commercials. Initial exposure to beer commercials increased consumption of beer, but continued exposure did not. Four or nine ads had no differential effect on total beer consumption (Kohn & Smart, 1984).

— Subjects completed stories about a man on a date in which the story formats varied only according to the young man's car and toothpaste brands. The subjects made sexier assumptions about the man who drove a Camaro and brushed with Ultra Brite than they made about the man who drove an Accord and used Crest (Baran & Blasko, 1984).

— With the passage of time, advertisements making humorous appeals were more persuasive than ads with serious appeals. Males were more susceptible than females to humorous persuasive appeals (Lammers et al., 1983).

Social Comparison Theory

Festinger's (1954) **social comparison theory** assumes people place importance on knowing the validity of personal beliefs by comparing their beliefs to physical reality and social reality. Physical reality is the world as known through the sense organs, and many people consider it to be the strongest test of belief validity. Social reality

is reality based on what other people, especially people whose beliefs are valued, say is true.

In the social comparison of abilities, Festinger (1954) believed that people want most to know how persons who are similar or slightly better than themselves perform. If you earn 41 out of 50 points on a psychology test, you may try to discover how your score compares to the scores of

You are most likely to compare your performance to that of people who are of similar or slightly higher ability. When playing pool, you are unlikely to use professional pool players as your comparison group.

others. If you ask your instructor if the test was easy or difficult, you learn very little if the instructor responds, "When I took it, I marked all the answers correctly" because you assume a psychology instructor would do better than you. Similarly, if your instructor adds, "and high school seniors averaged 32 on this test," again, you do not feel similar to the comparison group because you would expect to do better than high school seniors. You are most interested to know how other students in your class performed, especially those students you evaluate as having equal or higher ability.

Not only do people compare on the basis of those who are likely to perform in similar ways (Wheeler & Koestner, 1984), but people also compare their performances to other people who have similar characteristics such as gender (Miller, 1982). Social comparison process is used throughout the lifespan, and researchers have found that even preschool children initiate social comparison, especially with similar others (Chafel, 1984).

People also look to social reality to evaluate the appropriateness of their emotions. Schachter (1959) suggested that people try to affiliate and compare beliefs when they are in ambiguous settings. In one study, female college students in a high fear condition were greeted by "Dr. Gregor Zilstein," who informed them they were subjects in a study involving electrical shocks. The subjects observed wires and electrical equipment, a room labeled "Shock Room," and a sign that read "Danger! High Voltage! Authorized Personnel Only!" Subjects completed medical history forms and forms indicating

they would not sue the experimenter or college for any damage caused by the experiment. They were informed they would receive a series of strong electric shocks, but the shocks would cause "no permanent physical damage." In contrast, subjects in a low fear condition did not see the equipment, signs, or forms and were told they would experience only mild shocks that would produce a tickling sensation.

Subjects in both conditions were then allowed to choose to wait alone or with other participants in the experiment. A majority of the subjects in the high fear condition chose to wait with others, but only one-third of those in the low fear condition chose to wait with others. The results support the common-sense saying, "Misery loves company." A second study indicated that fearful subjects chose to wait with other fearful subjects but chose not to wait with subjects who were not also going to be shocked. Schachter subsequently modified the saying to "Misery loves miserable company."

More recently, the modified statement was further revised to "Misery sometimes seeks more miserable company." When people suffer misfortunes, they sometimes engage in **downward social comparison** by comparing themselves with others who are in even worse circumstances. One research study used subjects who were either happy or slightly depressed. These subjects could choose to be with a happy, neutral, or very unhappy person. More of the slightly depressed subjects than happy subjects chose to be with the very unhappy person (Bell, 1978). In fact, depressed subjects seem to make more use of social comparison information than do nondepressed subjects. The tendency to downward social comparison is best reflected in the phrase, "I thought I was bad off to have no shoes, until I met a person who had no feet."

Social Facilitation and Social Loafing Theories

Social Facilitation   Do you perform better when other people are around or when you are alone? Over fifty years ago, pioneer social psychologists found the answer to be "It depends." During a bicycle race, cyclists went faster when racing against another cyclist than when racing against the clock (Triplett, 1898). Being with others also accelerates performance on simple arithmetic tasks (Allport, 1920). Even ants increase their tunneling performance when in the presence of an ant audience (Chen, 1937). However, the presence of others is as-

Social facilitation theory predicts that a highly skilled pianist will play better in front of an audience than when she is alone, but a beginning piano student will make more errors in front of an audience than when she is alone.

sociated with slower learning of nonsense syllables (Pessin, 1933) and with slower maze-learning (Pessin & Husband, 1933).

The varying results were not explained until 1965, when Robert Zajonc formulated **social facilitation theory**. According to social facilitation theory, the presence of people increases arousal level. In turn, arousal enhances dominant responses and hinders less dominant responses. Therefore, on simple or well-practiced tasks people perform better in the presence of others, but on complex and novel tasks, people do better when alone. The social facilitation theory applies when competing with other people, when performing in the presence of an audience, or when working near a co-acting group (people doing something side-by-side but separately).

This theoretical explanation can be used to explain why beginning athletes make more careless errors in front of home crowds and why outstanding athletes are more likely to break records during Olympic meets than during practices. In a recent study, researchers (Michaels et al., 1982) found that good pool players improve their performances in the presence of an audience (percentage of made shots increases from 71 percent to 80 percent), but poor pool players decrease in accuracy when an audience is present (a drop from 36 percent to 25 percent).

Social Loafing People also affect individual performance when they work together. **Social loafing** is the tendency to exert less effort when efforts are pooled than when efforts are evaluated individually. Participants who thought they were one-person teams exerted tug-of-war

efforts 18 percent stronger than did those who thought three to six other persons were participating (Ingham et al., 1974). Another social loafing study instructed individuals to "clap as hard as you can" and found that six people clapping produced a sound less than three times as loud as one person clapping (Latane et al., 1979). More social loafing occurs among strangers than among friends (Williams, 1981). A recent analysis of forty-five social loafing studies found that social loafing occurs in a wide range of tasks, populations, and cultures (Williams & Jackson, 1986).

Recently, social facilitation theory and social loafing theory have been shown to be compatible, integrable theories (Jackson & Williams, 1985). Since working collectively reduces individual effort, working together also reduces arousal level. In line with social facilitation theory, lowered arousal level has a negative effect on simple tasks and a positive effect on difficult tasks. Therefore, social loafing results in worse performances on simple tasks and in better performances on difficult tasks.

If people are asked to clap as loudly as they can and their clapping is measured, each person will clap less loudly in a group than when he or she is alone.

Conformity and Obedience

Social Norms Have you ever felt pressure to go along with the crowd? Have you ever used the excuse, "Everybody else is doing it"? If so, you have experienced the power of social norms and conformity. **Social norms** are a group's or society's rules for acceptable and appropriate behavior. Social norms regulate how to act in a business organization, interact with an instructor, and behave in a restaurant. Some social norms differentiate appropriate behavior on the basis of gender, age, and status. Norms may interact with each other and contribute to subtle differences in people's behaviors. For example, more young female college professors than young male college professors allow students to address them by first name (Rubin, 1981). Many social norms seem to be arbitrary, yet they can have wide influence on behavior. In America, midwesterners tend to eat supper around five o'clock, but northeasterners are more likely to eat supper around seven o'clock, thus forming arbitrary norms around which lives are scheduled.

Sherif (1935, 1936) studied norm formation by looking at group effects on perceptual judgments about the **autokinetic effect**, apparent movement of a stationary pinpoint of light in a darkened room. Because the dark room takes away all reliable frames of reference, the eyes' natural saccadic movements cause the dot of light to seem to move around. You can experience this effect by going into a very dark room and watching the light entering through the keyhole; the spot of light will seem to move in various directions.

Sherif asked individuals to judge the distance they thought the pinpoint of light moved. He found that if he put subjects into small groups, over several subsequent trials their judgments of distance converged. Subjects created an average group norm based on their previous individual norms. A more recent study in this area (Sorrels & Kelley, 1984) revealed that subjects who participated alone reported more autokinetic movement than did subjects who believed they were participating with two subjects who reported no movement.

Conformity **Conformity** is the tendency to adopt the attitudes and behaviors of others due to group pressures. The classic conformity studies were conducted by Solomon Asch (1955, 1956), who used several **confederates** (accomplices of the experimenter who impersonate subjects) with each actual subject. Subjects and confederates were asked to make perceptual judgments about lengths of lines, choosing which of three lines matched a fourth

line. On the first two trials, the actual subject agreed with the other subjects. However, on the third and later trials, the confederates gave answers the subject realized were obviously wrong, and these wrong answers produced a conflict between physical and social reality. Did the subject trust his own evaluation of the lines and respond differently from the others, or did the subject disbelieve (or pretend to disbelieve) his own eyes and respond as the others did? Asch found that 37 percent of the subjects conformed consistently to the group's wrong answer, and three-quarters of the subjects conformed on at least one trial. Incidentally, a more recent replication of Asch's work (Perrin & Spencer, 1980) revealed lower rates of conformity, results the researchers attributed to changed attitudes on the value of conforming.

In another conformity study, military officers were asked to indicate whether a star or a circle was larger. The circle was one-third larger, yet 46 percent conformed to the star choice (Crutchfield, 1955). In a conformity study conducted at a liberal college, 58 percent of the subjects conformed and agreed with the statement "Free speech being a privilege rather than a right, it is proper for a society to suspend free speech when it feels itself threatened" (Krech et al., 1962).

Several factors influence the amount of conformity that occurs:

1. Ambiguity of stimuli. The task in the Asch experiments entailed low-level ambiguity and produced 37 percent conformity. A more ambiguous task of counting metronome clicks produced a 60 percent conformity rate (Shaw et al., 1957), and an even more ambiguous task of autokinetic movement had a conformity rate of 80 percent (Sherif & Sherif, 1946).

Stimulus ambiguity's effects on conformity are further illustrated by a recent study (Davis, 1984), in which 160 female college students were asked to rate the fashionableness of six women's suits in terms of present fashionableness and future fashionableness. More conformity occurred in the ratings of future fashionability, which is more ambiguous, than in the ratings of current fashionability.

2. Group size. The amount of conformity increases as group size increases up to five individuals (Asch, 1955; Gerard et al., 1968). One group of researchers recorded the number of passersby who looked upward when one or more persons stood on a busy sidewalk and gazed upward. The percentage who looked up increased as the number of confederates increased up to five, and then the percentages stabilized. When only one person was

*Conformity in dress, actions, and attitudes is usually quite
evident among high school cheerleaders and athletic teams.*

looking upward, approximately 40 percent of the passersby looked up; with two or three looking upward,
approximately 60 percent looked up; and with five looking upward, almost 80 percent of the passersby also looked
up (Milgram et al., 1969). Other research found more
conformity within a group when subjects are grouped
into several small groups than when they are placed into
a single large group (Wilder, 1977).

3. Unanimity. Asch (1951) found that when one confederate deviated from the other confederates, the subject's conformity rate dropped from 37 percent to under
10 percent. The greatest reduction by a single dissenter
occurs when the dissenter is the first in the group to
respond (Morris & Miller, 1975).

4. Cohesiveness. More conformity occurs when subjects
feel attracted to the group (Berkowitz, 1954), and when
future interactions are anticipated (Lewis et al., 1972).

5. Status. Subjects conform more to high-status indi-

viduals. More pedestrians will jaywalk after a well-dressed
individual jaywalks than after a poorly-dressed person
jaywalks (Lefkowitz et al., 1955). Similarly, a well-dressed
interviewer will persuade more people to participate in
a survey than will a poorly-dressed interviewer (Walker
et al., 1980).

6. Personality. Low self-confidence and low self-esteem
are associated with higher conformity rates (Santee &
Waslach, 1982). Highly self-conscious individuals conform more (Davis, 1984), as do individuals who are low
in assertiveness (Williams, 1984). Gender does not significantly affect the rate of conformity; a review of conformity studies indicated that in the oldest studies, females
were slightly more likely than males to conform, but in
the more recent studies, no gender difference occurs
(Eagly & Carli, 1981).

Why do people conform? People sometimes conform
because the group provides information that influences

their decisions; people also conform because they want to be accepted and not rejected (Deutsch & Gerard, 1955).

Three responses to social influence are possible (Kahn & Donnerstein, 1984): (1) Attitude change occurs if a person internalizes information into the belief system. (2) Compliance occurs if a person responds to the normative influence of the situation without changing beliefs. (3) Compromise occurs if the person attempts to establish new norms.

This third type of response, compromise, is often seen in group decision-making. In some studies, subjects first determine their individual solutions to given problems and then work in a group to achieve a single group position. Usually **group polarization**, in which the initial average position will be strengthened, occurs (Myers & Lamm, 1975).

Groupthink In contrast to group polarization is a dangerous type of conformity called **groupthink**, in which members of policy-making groups remain silent, thereby concealing individual doubts about a policy and creating an illusion of unanimity (Janis, 1972, 1982). Janis has suggested that the escalation of the Vietnam War, the Bay of Pigs crisis, and the attempted rescue of Iranian hostages are examples of groupthink.

Janis (1982) recommends several techniques to help avoid the pitfalls of groupthink:

1. Forewarn members of the policy-making group about problems created by groupthink.

2. Assign an impartial leader.

3. Give specific instructions that all doubts and differences in opinion should be expressed.

4. Assign a devil's advocate to argue against the majority's plan.

5. Reduce groupthink by working in small groups because each small group will produce different "perfect" plans.

6. Reevaluate the decisions of the first meeting during a second meeting.

7. Use outside experts, independent groups, or trusted associates as sounding boards.

The Research Process: Milgram's Obedience to Authority Studies

Would you administer shock to a fellow subject as part of a memory and learning experiment? In a series of studies he initiated in 1961, Stanley Milgram (1974) placed a wide range of subjects into that difficult situation. Subjects were put into a teacher role and told that the learner was to receive electric shocks for errors in a word-pair test. Subjects believed that the roles of teacher and learner had been randomly assigned; actually, the learner who seemed to get shocked was a confederate of the experimenter.

To administer the shocks, the subjects used an impressive-looking "shock machine" that displayed calibrations of 15-volt increments up to 450 volts. The shock levels were labeled "intense" at 255 volts, "danger" at 375 volts, and "XXX" at 435 volts. Subjects gave a 15-volt shock for the first error and increased the shock by one level for each subsequent error.

In addition to seeing the written warnings, the subject was able to overhear the reactions of the learner (these reactions were prerecorded to ensure that every subject's experience was identical). The learner's first indication of discomfort was a little grunt at 75 volts. At 120 volts, the learner shouted that the shocks were becoming painful, and at 135 volts, the learner emitted painful grunts. At 150 volts, the learner shouted, "Experimenter, get me out of here! I won't be in the experiment any more! I refuse to go on!" At 180 volts, the learner screamed, "I can't stand the pain!" At higher shock levels, additional comments about getting out of the experiment continued, with an agonizing scream at 270 volts. At 300 volts, the learner shouted that he would no longer provide answers to the memory test. A violent scream occurred at 315 volts, and the learner again emphasized that he was no longer a participant and would no longer provide answers. After 330 volts, no further verbal comments, screams, or answers occurred.

Psychiatrists estimated that only one in 1,000 subjects would go all the way to 450 volts; college students estimated that 3 percent of students would go to the 450-volt level. How many college students do you believe would continue to give shocks up to the 450-volt level? What is the highest level of shock you would give to the learner?

In one variation of the study using male college students, nearly two-thirds of the subjects continued to shock the learner up to the 450-volt level. Using the ad reproduced here (Exhibit 19.4), Milgram was able to use subjects with diverse careers and ages. Forty percent of his subjects were skilled and unskilled workers, 40 per-

EXHIBIT 19.4
Newspaper Announcement Used by Stanley Milgram to Recruit Subjects for His Obedience to Authority Studies

Public Announcement

WE WILL PAY YOU $4.00 FOR ONE HOUR OF YOUR TIME

Persons Needed for a Study of Memory

*We will pay five hundred New Haven men to help us complete a scientific study of memory and learning. The study is being done at Yale University.

*Each person who participates will be paid $4.00 (plus 50c carfare) for approximately 1 hour's time. We need you for only one hour: there are no further obligations. You may choose the time you would like to come (evenings, weekdays, or weekends).

*No special training, education, or experience is needed. We want:

Factory workers	Businessmen	Construction workers
City employees	Clerks	Salespeople
Laborers	Professional people	White-collar workers
Barbers	Telephone workers	Others

All persons must be between the ages of 20 and 50. High school and college students cannot be used.

*If you meet these qualifications, fill out the coupon below and mail it now to Professor Stanley Milgram, Department of Psychology, Yale University, New Haven. You will be notified later of the specific time and place of the study. We reserve the right to decline any application.

*You will be paid $4.00 (plus 50c carfare) as soon as you arrive at the laboratory.

TO:
PROF. STANLEY MILGRAM, DEPARTMENT OF PSYCHOLOGY, YALE UNIVERSITY, NEW HAVEN, CONN. I want to take part in this study of memory and learning. I am between the ages of 20 and 50. I will be paid $4.00 (plus 50c carfare) if I participate.

NAME (Please Print)..............................

ADDRESS..

TELEPHONE NO................ Best time to call you.......

AGE........OCCUPATION.................... SEX......
CAN YOU COME:

WEEKDAYS .... EVENINGS ......WEEKENDS.........

Source: *Obedience to Authority* by Stanley Milgram, copyright © 1974 by Stanley Milgram. Reprinted by permission of Harper & Row, Publishers, Inc.

cent were white-collar, sales, and business employees, and 20 percent were professionals. Twenty percent of the subjects were in their twenties, 40 percent were in their thirties, and 40 percent were in their forties. Again, 60 percent of the subjects proceeded to administer the highest shocks.

The amount of obedience was influenced by the situation. For example, when the learner was nearby, the subject was less likely to comply with the experimenter's orders to continue the shocks. On the other hand, when the subject-teacher did not actually administer the shock but performed some behavior that led to the learner being shocked, 90 percent proceeded to give the highest shock level.

Milgram concluded, "What is the limit of such obedience? At many points we attempted to establish a boundary. Cries from the victim were inserted; they were not good enough. The victim claimed heart trouble; subjects still shocked him on command. The victim pleaded to be let free, and his answers no longer registered on the signal box; subjects continued to shock him. At the outset we had not conceived that such drastic procedures would be needed to generate disobedience, and each step was added only as the ineffectiveness of the earlier techniques became clear. The final effort to establish a limit was the Touch-Proximity condition. But the very first subject in this condition subdued the victim on command, and proceeded to the highest shock level. A quarter of the subjects in this condition performed similarly" (Milgram, 1974, p. 188).

Milgram explained his results in terms of legitimate authority and agentic state. In **obedience**, someone or something is viewed as a legitimate authority, and the individual gives maximum receptivity to messages from that authority figure while becoming merely an agent, someone psychologically remote from his or her own beliefs. The obedient individual focuses on tasks that need to be done rather than on moral beliefs. The person accepts the authority figure's definitions of action and may turn to the authority for confirmation of self-worth. Often, the person distinguishes between the values of loyalty, duty and discipline, and personal values; in other words, the individual may state that the behavior is alien to his or her nature.

The results of the obedience to authority studies have been used to explain several world events. One of the first comparisons was between the experimental findings and the behavior of many Nazis in World War II. The obedient nature of the subjects was labeled the Eichmann

Phenomenon, after a Nazi bureaucrat who explained his sadistic behavior with "I was just following orders." Others have felt that My Lai during the Vietnam War and Watergate during the Nixon Administration involved similar aspects.

Can you think of other world events similar to these studies? Have you ever behaved like the subjects in Milgram's experiments? Does the obedience process help explain the effects of peer pressure?

Obedience vs. Conformity Although subjects in both conformity and obedience studies allow external sources to make their decisions, the subjects in Asch's conformity experiments conformed to a group, while the subjects in Milgram's obedience experiments obeyed an experimenter. Four major differences exist between conformity and obedience (Milgram, 1974):

1. Conformity occurs among individuals of equal status. Obedience occurs when one person decides another person is of higher status and has legitimate authority to prescribe behavior.
2. Conformity leads to sameness of behavior through imitation. Obedience involves compliance, i.e., the carrying out of an order rather than the imitation of an order.
3. The pressures to conform are implicit and involve spontaneous adoption. In obedience, the pressures to obey come from explicit commands.
4. Individuals tend to deny that conformity influences have occurred, but they use obedience as an explanation for their behaviors. Individuals who conform claim they are really autonomous; individuals who obey insist that the control of their behavior is not in their own hands.

Leadership

When individuals work together, leaders often emerge. When you think about different leaders to whom you have been accountable, you realize how they can influence group norms, amount of conformity, attitude change, and obedience. In what ways do personality traits and leadership styles affect group performance? What characteristics are typical of all leaders?

The traits common to most leaders comprise a rather short and obvious list. Leaders tend to be high on the crucial skills of intelligence, verbal ability, problem-solving skills, and experience. Leaders are good at interpersonal skills and are described as being responsible, cooperative, and popular. Usually, leaders have ambition

and desire for leadership, exhibited in the characteristics of initiative, persistence, and positive self-image (Shaw, 1983).

Leaders display one of three styles: autocratic, democratic, and laissez-faire (Lewin et al., 1939). An autocratic leader makes all decisions and assignments while avoiding participation in the group. A democratic leader encourages, assists, and participates in decision-making and other aspects of the group. A laissez-faire leader remains aloof, giving maximum freedom to group members.

Small groups of ten-year-old boys were exposed to each leadership style for six-week periods. The laissez-faire leadership produced less and poorer quality work. The autocratic leadership produced the highest level of work but also the most group hostility, scapegoating, dependency, and submissiveness. The democratic leadership created high work production and the highest level of originality. Nineteen of twenty boys in the study preferred the democratic leadership style (Lewin et al., 1939).

Leaders can also be divided into task-oriented leaders, who are good at influencing productivity, and socioemotional leaders, who are good at influencing interpersonal relationships. Since few people can fill both positions well, many groups have two leader specialists (Bales, 1958).

In the **contingency theory of leadership** (Fiedler, 1967), three conditions favor effective leadership. First, the leader is liked, respected, and viewed as a legitimate authority. Second, the group members know their roles and goals because the leader provides enough structure. Third, the leader has power to manipulate and distribute rewards and punishments.

Some people believe that men make better leaders than do women, but research on sex differences in leadership does not support this conclusion (Kahn & Nelson, 1984). Men and women perform almost equally in getting a group to work well (Stitt et al., 1983). In fact, many people prefer leaders who use a participatory style (i.e., asking the group for opinions) of leadership, and women are more likely to use this style than are men (Jago & Vroom, 1982).

Focus Question Answer

Why do your behaviors sometimes contradict your beliefs? While you often act upon your attitudes, you sometimes conform to someone else's attitudes. You might also choose to put your own attitudes aside and obey someone you view as a legitimate authority.

Of the various theories that attempt to explain helping behaviors,
which theory best accounts for the helpfulness of boy scouts?

 ## Helping Behaviors

Prosocial behaviors are a broad range of behaviors that
are positively valued by society. One category of prosocial
behaviors is **helping behaviors**, or intentional acts to
benefit another person. Social psychologists attempt to
determine the factors that influence people's willingness
to help in a situation.

The Helping Personality

A study of people who helped Jews escape Nazi Germany
and people who were Civil Rights workers in the 1960s
indicated that helpers are often marginal citizens who
lack association with social groups and who retain a close
identity with a highly moral parent (Rosenhan, 1970).
Some psychologists suggest that people-oriented individuals who are socially responsible, extroverted, and
sympathetic have higher rates of helping (Swinyard &

Ray, 1979). However, most researchers believe "the
helpful personality" does not exist and situational and
social influences play the major roles in deciding whether
a person offers help (Gergen et al., 1972).

Reinforcement and Modeling Theories

Reinforcement theory states that a decision to help is
based on consequences of helping in the past. People
are more likely to help others if they were reinforced for
previous helping and less likely to help others if past
attempts were punished. If you have lent class notes and
the borrower has thanked you, you are likely to lend
your notes again. However, if you have lent your class
notes to someone who did not return them for a week,
you are less likely in the future to lend your notes to any
student.

The concept of **reciprocal altruism** (Carnevale et
al., 1982) adds that people are likely to help when two

conditions are met: (1) the helper's costs are less than the helpee's benefits and (2) reciprocity is likely, either from the helped individual or from someone else. Thus, you might choose to share your class notes with another psychology student because your cost is low and because you anticipate that this student or another student will share notes with you in the future.

Modeling theory (Krebs, 1970) states that people can learn to be helpful by observing another person being helpful. Fifty percent more drivers stopped to help a woman fix a flat tire if they had previously witnessed someone who had stopped to help another malfunctioning car (Bryan & Test, 1967). Modeling of helping behavior can be done even through story characters. Second- and third-graders who heard stories about a generous character beng rewarded with angels' praise and a long, happy life exhibited more helping behaviors than did children who did not hear the stories (Franco, 1978).

Cognitive Model of Bystander Intervention

According to the **cognitive model of bystander intervention** (Latané & Darley, 1970), potential helpers ask themselves a series of questions and offer help if they can answer "yes" to all questions: (1) Is something unusual happening? (2) Is this situation an emergency? (3) Is my responsibility to help? (4) Can I decide what to do? (5) Should I act on my decision?

Ambiguous situations make answering "yes" to the first two questions more difficult, and victims receive less help when their situation is difficult to define. In contrast, victims who call out for help decrease the amount of ambiguity and actually receive more help (Clark & Wood, 1972).

An observer's sense of responsibility to help is influenced by several elements. Being empathic or in a good mood increases the rate of helping (Hoffman, 1981; Toi & Batson, 1982). Thus, individuals are more likely to offer help after hearing good news on a radio (Holloway et al., 1977) and when the weather is sunny (Cunningham, 1977). Negative emotions have mixed effects on helping behavior. Sadness, failure, and personal rejection tend to reduce helping, but guilt, shame, and sympathy often increase helping behavior (Rosenhan et al., 1981; Weyant, 1978).

Feelings of competence also increase the likelihood of taking responsibility to help. Individuals who were told they had a high tolerance for electric shocks were more likely to help someone who was receiving electric shocks (Midlarsky & Midlarsky, 1976), and persons who were told they were good at handling white rats were more likely to help an experimenter find white rats that had escaped in the laboratory (Schwartz & David, 1976).

The number of persons present also influences feelings of personal responsibility to help. In one study, subjects worked in a room as smoke poured through a wall vent for six minutes. When only one subject was in the room, the subject sought help 75 percent of the time; in contrast when three subjects were in the room, a subject went for help only 38 percent of the time (Latané & Darley, 1970). In another study (Latané & Rodin, 1969), subjects overheard a bookshelf crashing and a woman calling for help. Subjects who were alone helped 70 percent of the time; with two subjects, help was offered only 40 percent of the time.

Why does the presence of observers decrease the probability of a victim receiving help? According to the **diffusion of responsibility hypothesis** (Darley & Latané, 1968), as the number of people who witness an emergency increases, responsibility for action is shared or diffused throughout the group. As a result, each person feels less personally responsible for intervening. If you are the only witness to an emergency situation, you might reason, "Either I help, or no help is received." When two of you witness the situation, you might think, "I have only half the responsibility for taking action." With three observing an emergency situation, your responsibility drops to only one-third each, and so on. On the average, a victim will receive more help when fewer people are around to help.

Focus Question Answer

Are you a helpful person? While personality characteristics can influence your helpfulness, the main factors are situational. You are most likely to help when you can clearly define a situation as an emergency, when you are the only person who can help, and if you feel competent and well enough informed to help.

 *Relate*

Selling the Politician—A New Field for Psychology

Social scientists are playing larger and more diverse roles in political campaigns. From assessing potential voters' preferences to assessing campaign strategies, psychologists are adding to the folklore of ways to win elections. Few experts believe that the *right* campaign advertisement (the polispot) will win an election, but psychologists can help politicians hold on to current supporters, subdue the opposition, and avoid alienating undecided voters (Mendelsohn & O'Keefe, 1976).

Social scientists also conduct survey analyses of campaigns. One specialty area, **psephology**, attempts to predict votes by using voting intention, demographics, and attitude scale data (Ray, 1984). Watch election returns on television to observe psephologists' predictions based on voting booth exit interviews.

Media specialists and psychologists are continually developing theories about effective campaign techniques. Following is an assortment of research findings:

— The use of mass media in political campaigns is a primary cause of the decrease in partisan identification. As voters learn more about individual candidates through the media, they tend to vote for an individual rather than vote by party identification (Joslyn, 1981).

One persuasive strategy in polispots is to associate candidates with desirable concepts such as family and peace.

Television news programs are now the public's most trusted source of information about political campaigns (Oskamp, 1984). TV polispots have the greatest effects on poorly-informed voters and on people who do not listen to other sources of voting information (Atkin & Heald, 1976). Telephone contact appears to influence local and state elections rather than national elections (Oskamp, 1984).

One study looked at newspaper support in the 1968 presidential election and concluded that newspaper support of candidates can be influential in who wins the election. During this presidential campaign, 80 percent of American newspapers backed Richard Nixon over Hubert Humphrey. Readers of the pro-Nixon newspapers were 6 percent more likely to vote for Nixon than were readers of papers that supported Humphrey. Nixon won the popular vote by only 2 percent (Robinson, 1972).

Opinion polls measure public impressions of candidate popularity. Candidates like to be leading in the polls or to be seen as gaining in the polls since voters like to "get on the bandwagon" of the winner. People who believe that other voters agree with them become more publicly committed to their candidates and even engage in more political discussions (Glynn & McLeod, 1984).

Heavy press and advertising coverage allow the mere exposure effect to work in a candidate's favor (Diamond & Bates, 1984), and more favorable attitudes toward candidates positively correlate with amount of exposure to the candidate's television advertisements (Atkins, 1976).

Most strategists believe that a positive approach is safer than a negative approach. Attacking another candidate may be perceived as a reflection of a harsh, unpleasant trait of the candidate rather than as a criticism of the opponent. A negative campaign also provides free publicity to the opponent (Diamond & Bates, 1984).

Many politicians use the vividness effect, presenting striking examples and anecdotes rather than more general facts. As in other areas of attitude change, the vivid example is more influential than is more solid information.

Things to Do

1. Design a ten-item survey to measure attitudes on a specific topic. Ask your classmates to complete the questionnaire, and analyze the results. Was clearly wording the questions difficult? What research problems did you encounter, and how did you solve those problems?

2. Using television and magazine advertisements, classify ads as soft-sell or hard-sell approaches. What other attitude change strategies can you detect? How do TV and magazine ads differ in persuasion strategies?

3. Design an unobtrusive measurement study of student interest in your psychology class.

4. Take a common behavioral problem of children (such as temper tantrums, sibling fights, undone homework assignments, or untidy rooms) and design several psychological strategies by which parents could reduce the problem attitudes and behaviors.

5. Design a simple field experiment study on the topic of conformity, obedience, or helping behavior. If possible, conduct the experiment on campus, and analyze the results.

6. Break a social norm, and record your experience. Choose an activity that is not illegal or immoral; you might, for example, sing loudly in a public bus, eat in the school cafeteria without using utensils, face the back of a crowded elevator, or hold hands with a person of the same sex in a shopping mall. What did you feel like while breaking the norm? How did other people react to you?

7. Attend several group meetings. Analyze the leadership style of the person presiding over the meetings. How did his or her leadership style affect group members?

8. If a political campaign is currently being waged, consider that campaign. What attitudinal change and persuasive strategies are being used? Notice the pictures in the *Relate* section and in the current campaign. What psychological concepts are illustrated in the campaign pictures?

Things to Discuss

1. Make a list of things you have "grown to love" because of the mere exposure effect. Do exceptions to the mere exposure effect exist? Can "familiarity breed contempt"? What aspects of the mere exposure effect cause the difference?

2. How would the results of LaPiere's study of attitudes toward a Chinese couple differ if the study had been done in 1984 instead of 1934? Why?

3. Do you approve of using education-inoculation techniques to teach schoolchildren resistance to persuasive appeals? Have your group list specific topics and issues for which they would approve using education-inoculation techniques. What problems might develop from using the techniques?

4. Do you believe that Milgram's obedience to authority studies were ethical? Should psychologists be allowed to conduct studies such as Milgram's obedience to authority experiment or Zimbardo's Stanford Prison Experiment described in Chapter 18? Why or why not?

5. Applying some of the topics discussed in this chapter (e.g., reactance, conformity, social comparison), describe an adolescent's relationships with peers and parents.

6. What areas of social psychology could you incorporate into a campaign for student government office?

7. Of the concepts discussed in this chapter, which could be used by political strategists? How?

Things to Read

Derlega, V.J. & Grezelak, J. 1982. *Cooperation and helping behavior: Theories and research.* NY: Academic Press.

Eysenck, H.J. & Eysenck, M. 1983. *Mindwatching: Why People behave the way they do.* Garden City, NY: Anchor Press.

Janis, I.L. 1982. *Groupthink: Psychological studies of policy decisions and fiascoes* (2nd ed.). Boston: Houghton Mifflin.

Latane, B. & Darley, J.M. 1970. *The unresponsive bystander: Why doesn't he help?* NY: Appleton-Century-Crofts.

Lerner, M.J. 1980. *The belief in a just world: A fundamental delusion.* NY: Plenum Press.

Milgram, S. 1974. *Obedience to authority: An experimental view.* NY: Harper & Row.

Myers, D.G. 1980. *The inflated self.* NY: Seabury Press.

☰ Review

Summary

1. Attitudes are relatively enduring organizations of beliefs, feelings, and behavioral tendencies toward events and objects. Attitudes are assessed by self-report, physiological measures, and behavioral measures.

2. Attitudes influence behaviors, and behaviors also influence attitudes. Complying behaviors and mindless, automatic behaviors may not reflect personal attitudes.

3. Effectiveness of persuasion attempts is influenced by characteristics of the source, message, and context. The communicator has more immediate impact if viewed as an unexpected but trustworthy expert.

4. Three variations of selling techniques are the foot-in-the-door technique, the door-in-the-face technique, and the low-ball procedure. Although different, each has the goal of gaining compliance with a second request.

5. Cognitive dissonance theory assumes that inconsistent thoughts lead to attitudinal or behavioral change. After making decisions, people convince themselves that their decisions were good by selectively observing affirming information.

6. Reactance theory suggests that people like to believe they have freedom to choose their behaviors, and they rebel when they feel their freedom is taken away.

7. The overjustification effect occurs when people lose interest in an activity because of a shift from an intrinsic to an extrinsic motivational orientation.

8. Persuasive appeals can be resisted by assimilation, contrast, false consensus effect, commitment, and inoculation techniques.

9. According to social comparison theory, individuals compare their beliefs and abilities with those of people who are similar or slightly better because these comparisons offer the most useful information.

10. Social facilitation theory states that an audience improves performance of easy or well-rehearsed tasks and impairs performance of novel or complex tasks. When people work together, social loafing occurs, and each person exerts less individual effort.

11. Conformity is the tendency to adopt the attitudes and behaviors of others due to group pressures. Conformity is increased with ambiguous situations, unanimity, group cohesiveness, higher status of group members, and group size up to five individuals. Two other group decision-making processes are group polarization and groupthink.

12. Obedience occurs when people allow someone to become a legitimate authority. Milgram's studies found high rates of obedience.

13. Autocratic, democratic, and laissez-faire leaders produce differences in group behavior and attitude. Although leadership style preferences may differ, men and women seem to be equally good at leadership roles.

14. Situational factors are more important than personality in deciding when people choose to help. Past reinforcement patterns, expectations of reciprocity, modeling experiences, ambiguity in the situation, and number of bystanders all influence helping rates.

15. Social psychology concepts can be applied in many areas, including advertising and political campaigns.

Key Terms

attitudes
mere exposure effect
mindlessness
sleeper effect
foot-in-the-door technique
door-in-the-face technique
low-ball procedure
cognitive dissonance theory
reactance
overjustification effect
assimilation
contrast
false consensus effect
commitment theory
inoculation theory
social influence
social comparison theory
downward social comparison

social facilitation theory
social loafing
social norms
autokinetic effect
conformity
group polarization
groupthink
obedience
contingency theory of leadership
prosocial behaviors
helping behaviors
reinforcement theory
reciprocal altruism
modeling theory
cognitive model of bystander intervention
diffusion of responsibility hypothesis
psephology

Part Six

Assessment and Psychological Disturbance

Focus Questions

1. What are the characteristics of good assessment measures?

2. How can your personality be assessed?

3. What is your implicit definition of intelligence?

4. What would you experience if you took an intelligence test?

5. Are intelligence tests fair?

Chapter Outline

ASSESSMENT ISSUES
Normality and the Normal Curve
Reliability
Validity
Appropriate Use of Tests

PERSONALITY ASSESSMENT
Objective Tests
Projective Tests
Interviews and Situational Testing
The Research Process: Locus of Control

INTELLIGENCE THEORIES
Implicit and Explicit Theories
Factor Theories
Information-Processing Theories
Multiple Intelligences
Triarchic Theory

INTELLIGENCE ASSESSMENT
History of Intelligence Testing
The Stanford-Binet Intelligence Scale
The Wechsler Tests of Intelligence
Neuropsychological Testing
Intelligence Assessment Issues

RELATE: Intelligence Testing—The Black and White Issue
Things to Do
Things to Discuss
Things to Read

REVIEW: Summary
Key Terms

Chapter 20

Assessment: Personality and Intelligence

The test of a first-rate intelligence is the ability to hold two opposed ideas in the mind at the same time, and still retain the ability to function.

F. Scott Fitzgerald

Psychologists use questionnaires, projective tests, interviews, and situational testing to measure the personality, interests, intelligence, and aptitudes of individuals. In this chapter, you will read about general assessment issues and look at assessment of personality and intelligence.

 Assessment Issues

Normality and the Normal Curve

Norms are empirically established standards that allow psychologists to compare the scores of one individual with the scores of other individuals. As shown in Exhibit 20.1, measures of characteristics usually fall into a **nor-**

EXHIBIT 20.1
Depiction of a Normal Curve

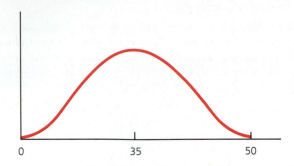

mal curve, a symmetrical, bell-shaped distribution with most scores clustered near the center.

If students in a college class are given a fifty-item examination and the average score is 35, more scores should lie between 30–40 than between 40–50 or below 30. Most measurements of characteristics, physical or behavioral, do fall into a normal curve.

Reliability

Reliability refers to the consistency of measurement. An assessment tool has test-retest reliability if successive measures produce the same (or nearly the same) scores. A yardstick is reliable if its length always measures thirty-six inches; an astrological system is reliable if Jan's birthdate always falls in the sign of Leo; a psychology course's exams are reliable if Kelsey tends to get Bs on all the tests. However, a bathroom scale that varies four pounds from one day to the next is unreliable.

Validity

Validity denotes that an assessment tool measures what it claims to measure. **Face validity** refers to first impressions of a test's validity; in other words, does the test appear to measure the right content? If your next psychology test consists only of ten algebra problems, the test lacks face validity.

Content validity is the assessment measure that represents the range of possible items. If you study diligently for a test on classical conditioning and operant learning, and the exam includes only questions about higher-order conditioning and schizokinesis, you might think that the test has poor content validity.

Criterion validity exists when test scores relate to actual performance. SAT and ACT scores display criterion validity because these college entrance examination scores correlate with actual college grades. On the other hand, most psychologists believe astrological horoscopes do not predict personality and life events; horoscopes lack criterion validity.

A test with validity is reliable; however, a reliable test may or may not be valid (Anastasi, 1982). If your psychology teacher gives five tests consisting of ten algebra problems each, the tests would be reliable but invalid. Students who know algebra would earn five fairly high scores, and those who have never had algebra would receive the lowest scores on every test. The consistency of scores means the tests are reliable, yet the test scores do not indicate what the students know about psychology; therefore, the tests lack validity.

Appropriate Use of Tests

Assessment measures should be used wisely and correctly. Proper interpretation includes knowing what the test can do and what the test cannot do. The test results need to be interpreted with appropriate norms; thus, a test normed on junior high students may be very inappropriate to use with college students. Further, in scoring a test, the clinical interpreter should be aware that a difference of a few points can significantly alter the meaning of the results. Much harm has been done by

---

Quick Study Aid

A Reliable and Valid Guide to Reliability and Validity

Point 1. Some students reverse the definitions of reliability and validity. To keep these terms straight, simply remember how you would use the terms in everyday situations.

"A reliable friend can always be counted on." (CONSISTENCY)

"A valid point is worth making." (SUBSTANTIAL, SOUND EVIDENCE)

Point 2. Valid tests are always reliable. Reliable tests are sometimes valid.

To remember that *reliability* is a prerequisite for *validity*, remember that R precedes V in the alphabet.

Personality test results are most valuable to clients when they are interpreted by psychologists.

taking test results either too casually or too seriously, by misunderstanding the meanings of various scores, by not understanding the limitations of test content, and by overestimating a test's capabilities. The test results also should be kept confidential between the clinician and the test-taker.

Measures of personality assessment are useful in clinical and research settings, but lay persons may too easily accept inventory results without considering a test's validity. Several years ago, a college instructor gave his students a personality inventory; later he gave every student the same vague, generalized personality description as the results of his or her personality inventory. The instructor discovered that 90 percent of his students rated the descriptions as being good or excellent descriptions of themselves. A recent replication found that even if students are given unflattering, bizarre personality descriptions as their test results, more than one in five students will rate the description as being good or excellent (Marks & Kammann, 1980).

Focus Question Answer

What are the characteristics of good assessment measures? Two of the most important characteristics of a good assessment test are reliability and validity. However, even more important than these qualities is the appropriate use of the assessment measures. To be an informed consumer of psychological testing, you should know what a test can and cannot do and should avoid being overinfluenced by test results.

   Personality Assessment

Objective Tests

Objective tests consist of a standard set of questions and are objectively scored. Objectively scored tests produce the same results regardless of the scorers. Objective questionnaires are either true-false or multiple-choice in format. The respondent's answers form scale scores that measure different aspects of personality, and these scale scores objectively determine a pattern of scores. The skilled psychologist then subjectively interprets this pattern of scores.

Objective tests can be scored in three major ways: norm-referencing, criterion-referencing, and ipsative scoring. Assume that you scored an 83 on a standardized psychology examination. In **norm-referencing,** your score of 83 would be compared to a norm group, and you might be told that you scored at the 79th percentile; of 100 test takers, only 21 achieved scores higher than yours. In **criterion-referencing,** your score would be related to absolute standards. You might be told that your pattern of answers indicates that you are similar to experimental psychologists and dissimilar to clinical psychologists. Finally, in **ipsative scoring,** your own scores would be compared to each other. In a test battery, your 83 in psychology might suggest that you do better in psychology than you do in math, chemistry, and geology but worse in psychology than you do in English and history.

The Minnesota Multiphasic Personality Inventory   Many personality assessment measures are objective tests, and in this chapter you will learn about the most common of these tests. The **Minnesota Multiphasic Personality Inventory (MMPI)** is the most thoroughly researched objective psychological test and the most frequently used personality assessment inventory. This 566-item instrument was constructed in 1939 at the University of Minnesota Hospitals and was published in 1943 (Hathaway & McKinley, 1940).

The respondent marks the items on the MMPI either true or false, and the average psychiatric patient requires 90 to 120 minutes to complete all items. The MMPI is an appropriate clinical assessment tool for patients who are at least sixteen years old and who have at least six years of formal education. Administering and scoring the MMPI are neither difficult nor time-consuming, but interpreting the results is very complex. Pictorially, the results of an MMPI test look like the example in Exhibit 20.2.

EXHIBIT 20.2
A Minnesota Multiphasic Personality Inventory Profile

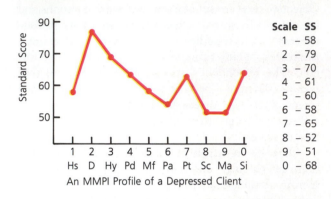

An MMPI Profile of a Depressed Client

Scale	SS
1	– 58
2	– 79
3	– 70
4	– 61
5	– 60
6	– 58
7	– 65
8	– 52
9	– 51
0	– 68

Since the eight clinical scales on the MMPI were based on the diagnostic system used by psychiatrists in the 1930s, only a few of the labels may be familiar to you. Today, these scales are usually referred to by number rather than by out-of-date psychiatric labels. Currently the MMPI is undergoing a major revision. The outdated terminology is being revised or deleted (e.g., references to streetcars and sleeping powders are being deleted) and items that are sexist or racist will be eliminated or revised. The new form should help in diagnosing modern concerns such as chemical dependency, eating disorders, and Type A personality. The revised form will feature separate norms for adolescents and adults.

Exhibit 20.3 provides a brief description of the personality aspects measured by each of the current MMPI

EXHIBIT 20.3
The Clinical Scales of the MMPI

Scale 1 **(HS) Hypochondriasis.** This thirty-three-item scale measures the person's concern with bodily functioning. People who score high on this scale have many somatic concerns and complaints.

Scale 2 **(D) Depression.** This sixty-item scale measures general dissatisfaction with life, poor morale, lack of hope, denial of happiness, and other aspects of depression. High scorers probably feel indecisive, hopeless, and perhaps suicidal; low scorers feel fairly comfortable with life.

Scale 3 **(Hy) Hysteria.** These sixty items measure both denial of emotional problems and specific somatic complaints. High scorers are often immature, egocentric, vain, and demanding. Low scorers may be conforming and suspicious.

Scale 4 **(Pd) Psychopathic Deviate.** Persons who score high on this fifty-item scale are impulsive, low in frustration tolerance, and immature, and they may act out sexually or angrily. Low scorers are very conventional, conforming, and moralistic.

Scale 5 **(Mf) Masculinity-Femininity.** This scale consists of items reflecting conventional masculine and feminine vocations, interests, and activity levels. The scale does not measure sexual preference, and many psychologists find this scale to be out of date.

Scale 6 **(Pa) Paranoia.** These forty items are designed to measure suspiciousness, delusions of persecution, sensitivity to criticism, basic mistrust of others, and the tendency to hold grudges. Many psychologists believe this scale is fairly weak.

Scale 7 **(Pt) Psychasthenia.** This scale contains forty-eight items that measure anxiety, dissatisfaction, rumination, and indecisiveness. High scorers on this scale tend to be moralistic, rigid, anxious, meticulous, and indecisive.

Scale 8 **(Sc) Schizophrenia.** The seventy-eight items on this scale measure unusual thought processes, peculiar perceptions, feelings of isolation, wish-fulfillment fantasies, and feelings of being different. Patients with schizophrenic symptoms usually score high on this scale, as do individuals who are lonely, isolated misunderstood fantasists.

Scale 9 **(Ma) Hypomania.** These forty-six items measure energy level. High scorers tend to be hyperactive, distractible, and expansive. Low scorers tend to be lethargic, apathetic, and fatigued.

Scale 10 **(Si) Social Introversion-Extroversion.** High scorers on this seventy-item scale are introverted, shy, withdrawn, and socially unskilled. Low scorers are confident, gregarious, and high in social skills.

Adapted from Newmark, C. S. 1985. The MMPI. In Newark, C. S. (ed.). *Major psychological assessment instruments*. Boston: Allyn & Bacon.

clinical scales. The standard profile also includes a Masculinity-Femininity scale and Social Introversion scale, as well as four validity scales, which are used to detect test-taking attitudes and distortions in test responses. Clinical researchers have developed more than 600 specialized scales to measure behavior and personality aspects such as repression, low back pain, prejudice, ego strength, dependency, overcontrolled hostility, and alcoholism (Newmark, 1985).

Interpretation of the MMPI profile involves looking at the interrelations of scales. To better understand the test-taker, clinicians attend to the two highest scales in his or her profile. Scales 4, 6, 8, and 9 are associated with lack of impulse control and excitement; scales 1, 2, 3, 5, 7, and 0 are associated with inhibition and control. When contradictory scales are elevated (e.g., 7–8 or 3–4), passive-aggressive behavior is likely (Newmark, 1985).

For example, Phil's profile of a two-point code type of 4–3 suggests that Phil tends to allow his anger to build until he explodes in rage. Phil is likely to handle conflict by blaming, dominating, and provoking others. Rather than work on his problems with handling stress and frustration, Phil tends to complain about others, use alcohol, and act violently from time to time. On the other hand, Cliff's 4–7 profile suggests that he has a cyclical pattern of acting out and then feeling guilty and remorseful for his actions. Because of Cliff's MMPI results, the psychiatrist suspects that Cliff abuses alcohol and other drugs and is sexually promiscuous. A third patient, Jill, has a profile in which her two-point code type is a 7–8. Jill is probably an excessive worrier who has trouble in situations in which she needs to be original or angry. Jill is likely to feel inferior, inadequate, insecure, and dependent upon others.

Projective Tests

Projective tests require test-takers to work with ambiguous stimuli such as pictures or inkblots. Underlying projective tests is the assumption that unstructured materials lead a test-taker to use his or her own life experiences and unconscious tendencies to organize and interpret the ambiguous stimuli. Supposedly, each person reveals internal emotions, ideas, and conflicts during projective tests. (You create your own projective test if you make objects or stories out of clouds or if you try to understand a child's crayon drawing of family members.) Two widely used clinical projective tests, the Rorschach Inkblot Test and the Thematic Apperception Test, are briefly described.

The game of finding pictures in the clouds is similar to the projective testing process.

EXHIBIT 20.4
An Inkblot Similar to Rorschach Inkblots

The Rorschach Inkblot Test   Hermann Rorschach published his famous inkblot pictures in 1921, and by 1925 the Rorschach cards had been brought to the United States, where psychologists developed five systems to interpret the cards. Recently, Exner has developed a comprehensive interpretation system for the Rorschach cards (Exner, 1974, 1978, 1982). The Rorschach Inkblot Test is currently the most widely used projective test (Erdberg, 1985).

The Rorschach cards consist of five black-white-and-gray cards and five cards containing color. The test-taker sees each card twice—once for a free association phase ("What might this be?") and once for an inquiry phase ("And where did you see that object?"). The highly trained interpreter examines many aspects of the responses. Since the average test-taker gives between two to five responses per card, a person who offers only one response per card might be viewed as depressed, resistant unimaginative, or perfectionistic. Location of objects on cards, perception of movement, content choices, and interpretation of color, shading, and texture in the inkblots are some of the elements involved in scoring (Erdberg, 1985).

Among psychologically healthy respondents, 32 percent of the responses involve the whole inkblot, 62 percent of the responses involve commonly used details, and only 6 percent of the responses involve uncommon details. For persons diagnosed as having schizophrenia, however, 22 percent of the responses involve uncommon details. Persons who respond frequently to the color por-

tions of the cards are more likely to be easily hypnotized and easily swayed by persuasion. Regarding content, respondents perceive a variety of objects, but on the average 40 percent of the responses involve animals, while 20 percent of the responses involve humans (Erdberg, 1985).

Exner (1974) believes that the Rorschach Inkblot Test displays both reliability and validity, but a review of many studies on the reliability and validity of the Rorschach suggests that only some psychologists find this projective test reliable and valid (Parker, 1983).

The Thematic Apperception Test   The **Thematic Apperception Test (TAT),** developed in the 1930s, requires test-takers to tell stories about twenty pictures (see Exhibit 20.5). Descriptions of five of the cards are given in Exhibit 20.6. The test-taker has clear directions to tell a story about each picture, and in scoring the TAT the clinician looks for recurring themes, conflicts, per-

EXHIBIT 20.5
A Picture Similar to TAT Cards

EXHIBIT 20.6
Descriptions of Five of the TAT Cards

- A young boy is contemplating a violin that rests on a table in front of him.
- A young pregnant woman stands in front of a rural farm scene that includes a muscular farmhand.
- A lean elderly man with clasped hands is standing among gravestones.
- A naked man is clinging to a rope he is climbing.
- A young boy sits in the doorway to a building.

sons, and settings. Which themes occur for particular cards and how frequently a theme occurs are important.

Although the TAT pictures are less ambiguous than the Rorschach Inkblots, the TAT's scoring procedures are more ambiguous than those of the Rorschach Test. Because of the ambiguity in scoring, **eisegesis** may be a particular problem with the TAT. Eisegesis is faulty interpretation that results because clinicians project their own interpretations and biases into the scoring process (Dana, 1985). With the TAT, psychologists listening to the same responses often reach different conclusions (Squyres, E. M. & Craddick, R. A. 1982).

Interviews and Situational Testing

Instead of objective and projective tests, interviews can be used to detect people's personalities. **Unstructured interviews** are informal conversations in which both the interviewer and interviewee determine the questions.

Interviewing is a commonly used evaluation technique for comparing several job applicants.

The unstructured interview allows much flexibility in content, but this type of interview also allows for vast differences among interviews, causing difficulties in comparisons among interviewees.

The **structured interview** involves asking each interviewee the same series of planned questions. In some employment settings, interviewers ask the same questions in the same order during each interview—a procedure that allows maximum fairness for interviewees.

Interviews also allow considerable data to be collected; information can be gleaned from verbal answers, body language, and interpersonal skills. However, interviewers are subject to stereotypes and preconceptions, and such reactions may affect the process and outcome of an interview.

In **situational testing,** behavior is rated by directly observing an individual in a simulated situation. Military war games and survival games fit into this category, as do "shooting practice situations" for police officers. In college, student teaching and practicums in employment situations are examples of situational testing. Two major concerns with situational testing are the expense and complexity of developing situational tests and concerns about choosing representative situations.

The Research Process: Locus of Control

Besides using personality tests in clinical assessment, psychologists use the tests in psychological research to understand individual differences. One prolific area of research began in the 1960s when Julian Rotter developed an inventory to measure internal-external locus of control. Since the 1960s, hundreds of research studies on locus of control have been conducted, and several additional locus of control questionnaires have been developed (Lefcourt 1976, 1981, 1983).

Locus of control is a generalized expectancy about the center of responsibility for the control of behavior. People with **internal locus of control** believe they control the destiny of their lives. They are convinced that skill, ability, and effort determine life experiences. In contrast, people with **external locus of control** believe their lives are determined by forces outside themselves—fate, chance, luck, or powerful others. Locus of control influences the way people view themselves and their opportunities.

College students with strong internal locus of control believe their grades are determined by their abilities and efforts. These students endorse the idea "The more I study, the better grades I get." They change their study

Individuals with an internal locus of control are more likely to choose carnival games based on skill, while individuals with an external locus of control prefer games based on chance.

to lower their behavioral goals.

— After experiencing task-failure, internals reevaluate future performances and lower their performance expectations; after failure, externals raise their performance expectations.

— Internals are better able to resist coercion.

— Internals are more likely to learn about their surroundings and to learn from their past experiences.

— Internals experience more anxiety and guilt with failures and use more repression to forget about disappointments.

— Internals find solving their own bouts of depression easier and are less prone to learned helplessness and serious depression.

— Internals experience more psychophysiological disorders.

— Internals are better at tolerating ambiguous situations.

— Internals are less willing to take risks.

— Internals are more willing to work on self-improvement and better themselves through remedial work.

— Internals derive greater benefits from social supports.

— Internals make better mental health recovery in the long-term adjustment to physical disability.

strategies as they discover inefficiencies, they raise their personal expectations after they succeed, and they worry when they feel they have no control over their assignments.

College students with strong external locus of control believe their grades are the results of good or bad luck, the teacher's mood, or God's will. These students agree with the statement "No matter how much I study, the teacher determines my grade. I just hope I'm lucky on this test." After they do well on a test, these students lower their expectations for future performance because they are certain their luck is bound to change, and for the same reason, after they fail a test, they are reasonably optimistic the next test will be better. External locus of control students are less likely to learn from past performances, and they have difficulty persisting in tasks.

Research studies on locus of control include experimental lab and field studies, and correlational-survey studies. Typically these studies measure locus of control beliefs and compare the most external individuals with the most internal individuals (most people are a mixture of beliefs). When compiled, the various research findings suggest the following characteristics are more typical of internals than of externals (Lefcourt 1976, 1981, 1983; Lefcourt et al., 1984; Schulz & Decker, 1985):

— Internals are more likely to work for achievements, to tolerate delays in reinforcement, and to plan for long-term goals.

— After experiencing task-success, internals are likely to raise their behavioral goals, but externals are likely

The development of internal-external locus of control is associated with family style and resources, cultural stability, and experience with effort-reward contingencies (Lefcourt, 1976). Many internal locus of control individuals have grown up in families that modeled typical internal beliefs. These families emphasized effort, education, responsibility, and thinking, and parents gave their children the reinforcements they had promised.

External locus of control is associated with lower socioeconomic status because poor people do have less control over their lives. Societies experiencing social unrest increase expectancies of being out-of-control, and individuals in such societies become more external in

Quick Study Aid

I-E Locus of Control

To distinguish between internal and external locus of control, remember: **the Internal locus of control is Inside, and the External locus of control is in the Environment.**

EXHIBIT 20.7
Mean Locus of Control Scores by Chronological Age Groups and Sex for Three Years

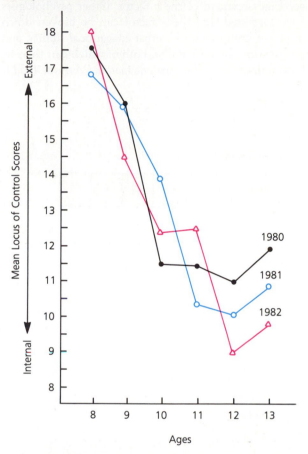

From Sherman, L. W. 1984. Development of children's perceptions of internal locus of control: A cross-sectional and longitudinal analysis. *Journal of Personality, 52,* 338-354.

orientation. During the Vietnam War era, for example, the average score on locus of control assessments moved toward the external orientation.

As children grow older, they gain many skills that give them more control over their environments. Fittingly, research has discovered that older boys and girls have significantly more internal scores than do younger children. These findings in a cross-sequential study (one that simultaneously uses longitudinal and cross-sectional strategies) are illustrated in Exhibit 20.7.

Many, but not all, psychologists believe that persons with internal locus of control orientations are psychologically healthier than those with external orientations. According to Lefcourt, who has analyzed many locus of

control studies, "There is good reason to believe, on the basis of the research reviewed, that an external control orientation and abnormal personal functioning are correlated" (Lefcourt, 1976, p. 7). Fortunately, locus of control orientation can be modified by therapy and by life experiences.

Focus Question Answer

How can your personality be assessed? Aspects of your personality can be assessed through hundreds of different objective or projective tests, interviews, and situational tests. Among the most well-known personality assessment instruments are the MMPI, the Rorschach Inkblot Test, and the TAT. Personality assessment is conducted for both clinical and research purposes.

Intelligence Theories

Implicit and Explicit Theories of Intelligence

Implicit theories of intelligence pertain to people's notions about intelligence. Psychology's intelligence experts tend to include three elements in their implicit ideas about intelligence—verbal intelligence, problem-solving skill, and practical intelligence. Although laypersons have similar concepts of intelligence, they place more emphasis on social skills and personal knowledge and less emphasis on motivation (Sternberg, 1985). Both psychologists and other adults believe that as children age intelligence is less perceptual-motor and more cognitive (Siegler & Richards, 1982).

Experts' implicit definitions of intelligence include the following:

— "The capacity to acquire capacity."—H. Woodrow
— "The ability to carry on abstract thinking."—L. M. Terman
— "The power of good responses from the point of view of truth or fact."—E. L. Thorndike
— "The capacity to learn or to profit by experience."—W. F. Dearborn.

Explicit theories of intelligence are based or tested on data collected from tasks of intelligence. Explicit theories tend to be factor theories that define a set of underlying abilities, cognitive theories that define the nature of intelligence in terms of information-processing, or combinations of these two types of theories (Sternberg, 1985).

Factor Theories

Spearman's g Factor Several decades ago, Spearman (1927) postulated that the set of intelligence abilities involves a hierarchical arrangement of factors. Spearman believed that a general factor, or **g factor,** affects all performances, and other factors, or **s factors,** influence more specific tasks. He believed that the g factor involves encoding, relations between items, and applications of inferred principles to new domains; analogy tasks are one good measurement of the g factor. Other psychologists have suggested that the g factor can be broken down into two group factors, verbal-educational ability and practical-mechanical ability, both of which can then be broken down into more specific factors (Vernon, 1971).

EXHIBIT 20.8
Factor Theories of Intelligence

1. Spearman

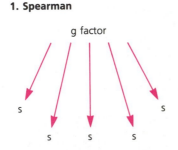

2. Thurstone

3. Guilford

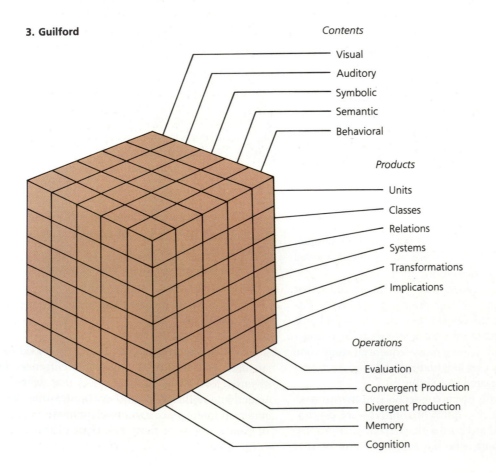

Thurstone's Primary Mental Abilities   Another early factor theory was proposed by Thurstone (1938). Unlike Spearman, Thurstone did not create a hierarchical arrangement of factors; instead, he proposed seven **primary mental abilities**—verbal comprehension, verbal fluency, number, spatial visualization, memory, reasoning, and perceptual speed.

Verbal comprehension can be measured by tasks involving vocabulary, synonyms and antonyms, and reading comprehension. Verbal fluency can be measured by tasks requiring a rapid production of work, such as generating as many words beginning with F as possible in one minute. Number tasks include working arithmetic word problems. Spatial visualization can be measured by tasks requiring the rotation or manipulation of geometric designs and symbols. The recall of sentences or paired-associates can be used to measure memory. Analogies and problem-solving tasks can be used to measure reasoning ability, and perceptual speed can be measured by a task such as crossing out e's in a long string of letters.

Guilford's 150 factors   A third type of factor approach is Guilford's (1982) cubic arrangement of factors. Guilford believes that every mental task involves operations, contents, and products. These three aspects form a $5 \times 5 \times 6$ cube for a total of 150 factors, and Guilford believes over one hundred factors have already been demonstrated. **Operations** include cognition, memory, divergent production, convergent production, and evaluation. **Contents** include visual, auditory, symbolic, semantic, and behavioral skills, and **products** include units, classes, relations, systems, transformations, and implications.

Quick Study Aid

Guilford's factors

Remember **COP**—to recall Contents, Operations, and Products.

Information-Processing Theories

Information-processing theories emphasize the cognitive nature of human intelligence. These theories attempt to explain intelligence by the cognitive processes that contribute to task performance. Many of the cognitive the-

ories focus on speed of mental processes. Beginning with Francis Galton in the nineteenth century, psychologists have tried to find a relationship between reaction time and intelligence. They explore the speed of the reasoning process in problem-solving, from initiation to response. This complex approach involves determining the performance components, the combination of the components, the representation of information, and the trade-offs made between speed and accuracy (Sternberg, 1985). Psychologists have discovered that, on complex reasoning tasks, highly intelligent people make correct responses in shorter time periods than other individuals (Jensen, 1982).

Cattell's fluid and crystallized intelligence   Raymond Cattell (1971) divided intelligence into fluid and crystallized abilities, which correlate but differ. **Fluid abilities** involve intelligence aspects related to maturation and physiological condition. The fluid abilities, which are more general and more innately determined, tend to improve during childhood and decrease during the older adult years. Fluid abilities relate to speed, flexibility, adaptation to new situations, and abstract reasoning. If you have good fluid intelligence, you are able to perceive relationships quickly and to solve a variety of problems.

Crystallized abilities are the intelligence aspects that are a function of experiences, learning, and culture. These abilities are comprised of acquired knowledge, general information, and accumulated experiences, and they are measured by vocabulary, logical reasoning, and mechanical knowledge. Crystallized intelligence tends to remain constant or to improve with age.

Multiple Intelligences

Some psychologists believe intelligence has been too narrowly defined into verbal, mathematical, and spatial abilities components, and Gardner (1983) adds four additional intellectual competencies: musical ability, bodily skills, social skills, and self-knowledge.

Besides providing experimental and psychometric support for these seven intellectual components, Gardner (1983) offers three additional reasons for proposing seven areas as basic intellectual components. First, each of these seven areas can be destroyed by specific brain damage. Second, **idiot savants** (mentally retarded individuals with one highly developed talent such as music or rapid calculation) and **prodigies** (persons who at a very early age show extraordinary talent in an area such as mathematics or music) exist for each of these seven components (read more about exceptional intelligence

Gardner suggests intelligence has several more factors than those tested by traditional intelligence tests. A skilled potter may score high on spatial intelligence.

in the *Exploring . . .* section). Third, each of these seven areas seems to involve unique cognitive skills.

Gardner (1983) also advocates the cultural relativity of intelligence, whereby intelligence is defined according to the abilities and skills important to a society. Thus, a culture existing across several islands might define intelligence as the ability to navigate by the stars (McKean, 1985). Currently, some psychologists believe the computer is redefining the concept of intellectual performance in the American society (Horn, 1979).

Triarchic Theory

Sternberg (1984, 1985) proposes a **triarchic theory** with three intelligence subtheories of context, components, and experience (depicted in Exhibit 20.9). Sternberg's theory of intelligence combines aspects of implicit, factor, and information-processing theories.

The contextual subtheory relates intelligence to an individual's external world; that is, intelligent behavior involves adapting to the present environment or selecting a better environment as well as shaping the environment to better fit the individual's needs, abilities, and values. Sternberg's theory emphasizes relevance and purposiveness in the real world.

The componential subtheory, which relates intelligence to an individual's internal world, defines the structures and mental mechanisms underlying intelligent behavior. The componential subtheory describes how intelligent behavior is generated—fluid and crystallized abilities, for example. Components of intelligence are elementary information processes involving metacomponents (planning, decision-making, monitoring, selecting), performance components (task execution), and knowledge-acquisition components.

The experiential subtheory relates intelligence to both the external and internal worlds in order to determine when behavior represents intelligence. Intelligence is best demonstrated when individuals solve relatively novel tasks and when individuals learn to automatize a performance strategy for a given task. People who are evaluated as highly intelligent or skilled in an area have been able to place many chunks of information and clusters of strategies into automation (Chi et al., 1982).

Following are several of Sternberg's (1985) ideas about intelligence:

— Evidence supports Spearman's concept of a general intelligence factor, Thurstone's primary mental abilities, Guilford's large number of intelligence factors, and Cattell's fluid and crystallized abilities.

— Vocabulary is one of the best measures of overall intelligence.

— The absolute value of intelligence in children increases with age because they acquire more sophisticated

EXHIBIT 20.9
Triarchic Theory of Intelligence

Componential Subtheory	Experiential Subtheory	Contextual Subtheory
metacomponents performance components knowledge-acquisition components	ability to deal with novelty ability to automatize processing	adaptation selection shaping

Adapted from Sternberg, R. J. 1985. *Beyond IQ: A triarchic theory of human intelligence.* Cambridge: Cambridge University Press. Copyrighted by and printed with the permission of Cambridge University Press.

Exceptional Intelligence

Intellectual giftedness

The psychometric (measurement) view of **intellectual giftedness** proposes that the gifted possess more latent mental abilities. The gifted have stronger abilities at verbal comprehension, reasoning, spatial visualization, and creativity. Information-processing psychologists emphasize not gifted individuals' greater amounts of mental skills but rather their better use of these abilities. The gifted might best be defined as having above-average insight and ability to deal with novelty (Sternberg & Davidson, 1983).

The gifted do better on standard IQ tests, are more efficient at dealing with novel tasks and situations, and have automatized, highly practiced performances. Gifted individuals are *analyzers* who can quickly tell which of their problem-solving skills are required in a situation; most gifted individuals are also *synthesizers* who are insightful and creative (Sternberg, 1985).

Intellectual retardation

Sternberg (1985) points out that **intellectual retardation,** significantly below-average intelligence, can consist of a varied combination of impaired components. Some retarded individuals have impaired metacomponent activation; in other words, they fail to know what to do with the knowledge they have. Intellectual retardation may also involve impaired feedback, inaccurate thinking components, impaired coordination, impaired automatization of cognitive strategies, inadequate knowledge base, inappropriate motivation, and structural limitations such as lowered memory capacity.

Most individuals who are mentally retarded (individuals with IQs of 70 or lower) have **familial retardation,** or retardation for which no known organic cause can be identified. Most cases of familial retardation involve mild retardation (IQ at least 50). Possible causes of the retardation include impoverished environment, inadequate medical care, poor nutrition, and deficient emotional support. Better early nutritional care, educational enrichment programs, and family training can improve the intellect of many of these retarded individuals.

About one-quarter of intellectual retardation has biological or organic causes such as genetic abnormalities, fetal damage, birth injuries, environmental toxins, and metabolic disorders. Examples of **organic retardation** include Down syndrome (caused by an extra chromosome), cretinism (caused by thyroid deficiency), phenylketonuria (caused by an enzyme deficiency needed to use the amino acid phenylalanine), microcephaly (caused by a recessive trait), and hydrocephaly (caused by accumulation of cerebrospinal fluid in the brain's ventricles). Phenylketonuria, hydrocephaly, and cretinism can be treated if detected early, but, when untreated, they are associated with severe and profound retardation (IQ of 35 or lower).

---

knowledge and more connections between knowledge and problem-solving strategies.

— Intelligence tests provide imperfect but fairly good predictions of academic achievement.

— People may perform at different ability levels on different intellectual functions.

— Intelligence is a necessary but not sufficient condition for creativity.

— Intelligent individuals often spend more time encoding because slow encoding seems to allow for more rapid, accurate later use.

— To a degree, intelligence can be trained by working with the metacomponents and performance-components.

— Intelligence can have different meanings in different cultures.

Focus Question Answer

What is your implicit definition of intelligence? If you define intelligence as many other people, your definition includes ideas about verbal ability, ability to solve problems, common sense, social skills, and personal knowledge. Has your implicit definition changed since your reading of intelligence theories?

 ## Intelligence Assessment

History of Intelligence Testing

One of the earliest approaches to intelligence testing was Gall's work with **phrenology,** the mistaken belief that the shape of one's skull indicates both mental capacity and personality characteristics. Similarly, Paul Broca pursued the misguided route that intelligence is positively related to actual brain size (Gould, 1981).

Francis Galton, a cousin of Charles Darwin, proposed in his 1884 book, *Hereditary Genius,* that intelligence is a fixed, inborn amount of mental capacity, and Galton tried to measure intelligence by measuring visual and auditory acuity and reaction time (Keating, 1984; Miller, 1984). Many American psychologists have also assumed that intelligence is inherited and constant in level.

Alfred Binet, a French psychologist, believed that intelligence is influenced by heredity, but, unlike Galton, Binet believed that intelligence can be modified through educational intervention (Keating, 1984). Along with Theodore Simon, Alfred Binet began in 1894 to measure children's abilities in various areas such as memory, attention, moral judgments, and verbal comprehension. By 1904, Binet and Simon were developing tests to distinguish bright from subaverage Parisian school children. The 1911 version of the Binet-Simon scale was used with French children three to fifteen years old. The average three-year-old child could point to facial features, repeat a six-syllable sentence, and name objects in a picture; the average fifteen-year-old adolescent could interpret facts, give three rhymes to a word within a minute, and repeat a twenty-six-syllable sentence (Miller, 1984).

In 1916, Lewis Terman at Stanford University translated Binet's work and established new American norms for Binet's scale. Like many of his contemporaries, Terman believed that because intelligence remains fairly constant throughout life, childhood scores on IQ tests could be used to predict adult intelligence (Miller, 1984).

Terman adapted Binet's method of determining IQ (**intelligence quotient**) to the formula IQ = $\frac{MA}{CA}$ x 100. In this formula, MA equals mental age, and CA equals chronological age. **Mental age** reflects the average capabilities of individuals at each age. An average IQ is 100 (actually a range from 90-110), and a person with an average IQ has an equal MA and CA. Therefore, if Lillian is five years old (CA) and has an IQ of approximately 100, Lillian's MA is five.

A person with an above average IQ has an MA larger than his or her CA because a highly intelligent individual is capable of correctly accomplishing tasks typical of older individuals. Diane is eight years old and can perform intellectual tasks typical of an average ten-year-old. Diane's IQ can be determined by the equation 10/8 x 100; her IQ is 125.

In contrast, a person of below average IQ has an MA smaller than his or her CA because this individual is less capable than the average person of the same chronological age. Although Jim is six years old, his mental ability is similar to that of the average four-year-old child. Jim's IQ is determined by the formula 4/6 x 100; Jim's IQ is only 67.

One of the earliest large-scale uses of intelligence testing was the United States Army's testing of World War I draftees, for which Robert Yerkes developed a written test called the Army Alpha and a pantomine version for illiterates, the Army Beta. Since that time, intelligence tests have been used in many forms for many purposes, with the heaviest usage for the purposes of selection rather than diagnosis (Scarr, 1981). Until recently, more emphasis has been placed on intelligence tests themselves than on learning and skill acquisition (Keating, 1984).

Out of this historical setting developed two major, current, individually administered intelligence tests—the Stanford-Binet test and the Wechsler scales. Exhibit 20.10 contains items typical of these tests and other standard intelligence tests.

The Stanford-Binet Intelligence Scale

Terman revised the Stanford-Binet test in 1937 and made further revisions in 1960 and 1972. The last two revisions involved modernizing some of the items and simplifying the scoring scheme. Due to changes in society, items became easier or harder than they had been in earlier years; since 1916, for example, the word *coal* has become less familiar while the word *Mars* has become much more familiar.

Today's **Stanford-Binet Intelligence Scale** consists of a series of subtests defined in terms of age level; in other words, items in a particular age-level subtest can be answered by the majority of children of that chronological age and older but by only a minority of younger children. For example, the average three-year-old child can copy

EXHIBIT 20.10
Examples of IQ Test Items

1. Insert the missing numbers:
   a. 2   5   8   11   _____.
   b. 7   10   9   12   11   _____.
   c. 8   12   16   20   _____   _____.
   d. 6   9   18   21   42   45   _____   _____.
   e. 4   9   17   35   _____   139.

2. Underline the odd-man-out.
   a. house   igloo   bungalow   office   hut.
   b. herring   whale   shark   barracuda   cod.
   c. lion   fox   giraffe   herring   dog.
   d. Jupiter   Apollo   Mars   Neptune   Mercury.
   e. dollop   clef   crab   condemn   albino   sink.

3. Underline which of these is not a famous poet:
   S T E A K   Y O R N B   C R E H U C A
   R A N I B A S   T H R O W D O W R S

4. Underline which of these is not a famous composer:
   Z O T R A M   S A T S U R S
   R E V I D   M A L E S O

5. Underline the odd-man-out:

6. Which of the five numbered figures fits into the vacant square?

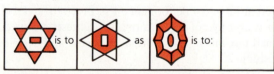

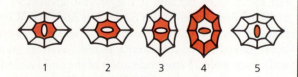

7. Underline the odd-man-out:

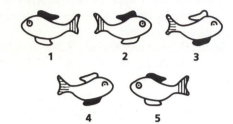

8. Underline the word which completes the sentence:

   Appetite is to food as concupiscense is to: _____.
   eating   sex   force   gluttony   drink

9. Which of the six numbered figures fits into the vacant square?

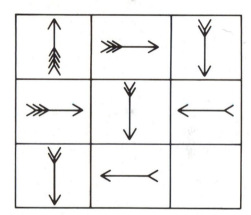

10. Which of the five numbered figures fits into the vacant square?

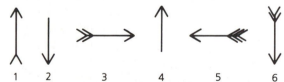

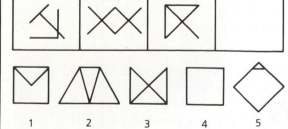

Source: Eysenck, H.J. 1962. *Know your own IQ*. NY: Penguin.

a drawing of a circle, but most two-year-old children cannot accomplish this task. Therefore, circle copying is in the three-year-old subtest. The kinds of questions asked at each age level vary, as do the types of skills tested. On the whole, the test items become more verbal as the test-taker grows older.

The Stanford-Binet Intelligence Scale provides only one score—an overall IQ score—without indicating the specific strengths and weaknesses of the test-taker. Although the test can be given to a preschool child, stability of IQ scores is better after the age of six. This intelligence scale works best with elementary school-aged children and is less valuable for college and adult populations.

The Stanford-Binet test should be given, scored, and interpreted by well-trained test examiners. The test often takes at least one hour for the test-taker to complete and a few hours for the professional to complete a written interpretation. The Stanford-Binet Intelligence Scale is considered reliable, even though an individual's retake test score may vary by ten points. The test also displays validity in predicting academic grades and success.

The Wechsler Tests of Intelligence

In 1939, David Wechsler published the Wechsler Bellevue Intelligence Scale. This scale became the Wechsler Adult Intelligence Scale (WAIS) in 1955 and was revised in 1981 (WAIS-R). The **WAIS-R**, used with individuals between the ages of sixteen and seventy-four, is the most commonly used clinical test in the United States (Lubin et al., 1984). The **WISC-R**, Wechsler Intelligence Scale for Children-Revised, can be used with children from six to seventeen years old, and the **WPPSI**, or Wechsler Preschool and Primary Scale of Intelligence, can be used with children from four to six-and-one-half years old.

Answers to Exhibit 20.10

1. a. 14.	3. SABRINA.
b. 14.	4. SALOME.
c. 24, 28.	5. 5.
d. 90, 93.	6. 2.
e. 69.	7. 2.
2. a. office.	8. SEX.
b. whale.	9. 4.
c. herring.	10. 4.
d. Apollo.	
e. sink.	

Children who practice tasks similar to those on intelligence tests may score higher than students who have not practiced such tasks.

The WISC-R The first Wechsler Intelligence Scale for Children was published in 1966, and a major revision was completed in 1974. Although the WISC-R can be used with all public school-aged children, limitations may exist for the lower and upper age limits. The average IQ score is 100, with fewer than 2 percent scoring 130 and above, and under 2 percent scoring 69 or below. Besides an overall IQ score, the WISC-R provides a verbal IQ and a performance IQ. Five of six verbal subtests and five of six performance subtests are used with each test-taker. The subtests are listed and described in Exhibit 20.11.

The WISC-R is the most widely used intelligence test for children because it has several advantages the Stanford-Binet Intelligence Scale does not. The WISC-R scales have more balance in verbal and performance items, provide more consistency in tasks over age groups and can provide a better indication of the child's relative strengths and weaknesses. The Stanford-Binet test is more appropriate when working with six- to eight-year-old children who have developmental delays or when working with profound or moderately mentally retarded individuals of all ages. In addition, the Stanford-Binet or WAIS-R should be used instead of the WISC-R when testing gifted adolescents (LaGrecia & Stringer, 1985).

The WAIS-R   The WAIS-R also involves five performance and five verbal subtests and results in a full IQ, verbal IQ, and performance IQ. With the exception of the Maze subtest, this scale has subtests similar to those of the WISC-R. Revisions made in 1981 include the substitution of gender-free language, the addition of minority individuals to the information and picture completion subtests, the revision of items, and the alternation of verbal and performance items to help maintain interest (House & Lewis, 1985).

The Wechsler Scales have reliability and validity levels similar to those of the Stanford-Binet Scales. In addition, the composition of the Wechsler subtests may allow the examiner to determine the test-taker's particular strengths and weaknesses and postulate concerns about brain damage. However, the Wechsler Scales, as well as the Stanford-Binet scales, are time-consuming and expensive because they must be administered and interpreted individually by well-trained examiners. Group intelligence tests are often administered because they are less expensive, more efficient and involve less training. Currently, psychologists can choose from approximately 200 IQ tests (Mohs, 1982).

Ideas about intelligence, thinking, and learning proposed by a variety of psychologists are currently being developed into intelligence tests. Ideas proposed by Jean Piaget (1950), featured in Chapter 11, have influenced the development of Feuerstein's (1979, 1980) Learning Potential Assessment Device (LPAD). This instrument not only attempts to measure the individual's current level of intellectual development but also explores the

EXHIBIT 20.11
WISC-R Subtests

Verbal Scales

1. *Information.* Scale contains thirty questions that test general knowledge. Scales are influenced by educational and cultural background.
2. *Similarities.* Test-taker indicates how seventeen pairs of words are alike. Subtest measures abstract thinking, logic, and verbal concepts.
3. *Arithmetic.* Eighteen math problems are orally solved. Problems measure numerical reasoning, computation, and concentration.
4. *Vocabulary.* Test-taker defines thirty-two words, measuring word knowledge and language.
5. *Comprehension.* Practical common sense and knowledge of norms are measured in seventeen questions.
6. *Digit Span.* Test-taker is read a series of digits that he or she repeats and another series of digits that he or she repeats in reverse order. Digit Span subtest measures short-term memory and attention span.

Performance Scales

1. *Picture Completion.* Test-taker identifies the missing parts in twenty-six drawings measuring long-term memory, visual alertness, and cognitive style.
2. *Picture Arrangement.* In this subtest, test-taker must rearrange pictures to tell twelve stories. The subtest measures nonverbal reasoning and sense of temporality.
3. *Block Design.* Test-taker translates eleven designs from a drawing into blocks. The subtest measures concept formation and visual-spatial organization.
4. *Object Assembly.* Test-taker performs four jigsaw tasks in which he or she puts together pieces to form familiar objects.
5. *Coding.* The coding subtest involves copying symbols, and measures both short-term memory and visual capabilities.
6. *Mazes.* Nine mazes are used to measure visual planning and foresight.

Adapted from LaGrecia, A. M. & Stringer, S. A. 1985. The Wechsler Intelligence Scale for Children—Revised. In Newmark, C. S. (ed.). *Major Psychological Assessment Instruments.* Boston: Allyn & Bacon.

process of the individual's thinking. LPAD results indicate a child's cognitive abilities and can also detect cognitive deficiencies such as impulsiveness, lack of planning, blurred perception, and failure to distinguish between essential and nonessential information. Four or five hours are needed to administer the LPAD's twelve subtests.

Gardner's and Sternberg's recent models of intelligence should influence intelligence tests of the future. In contrast to the standard Stanford-Binet and Wechsler Scales, new tests are likely to emphasize process over product and to work with the assumption that intelligence is modifiable rather than constant.

Neuropsychological Testing

A growing area of psychology, **clinical neuropsychology**, combines neurology and psychology, and another type of modern psychological assessment in neuropsychological testing. Neuropsychological tests are infrequently used for neurodiagnosis of brain damage because medical doctors better diagnose such injuries with the sophisticated technology of CAT scans, MRIs, and PET scans described earlier in Chapter 4. Instead, clinical neuropsychology is valuable in evaluating a neurologically impaired person's cognitive and behavioral strengths and weaknesses and in evaluating the rate of improvement or decline after brain injuries. After moderate and severe head injuries, patients typically have an eighteen-month recovery curve in which 85 percent of the cognitive and behavioral recovery occurs. Frequent neuropsychological testing during this year-and-one-half period allows plotting of the rate of improvement. A neuropsychological test battery may also indicate possible referrals for medical neurological examinations (Barth & Macciochi, 1985).

Many neuropsychological tests have been developed, and one of the most popular is the **Halstead-Reitan Neuropsychological Test Battery** (HRB). Halstead began work on this test battery in the 1930s, and the current format retains five of his original tests. Reitan revised and added other diagnostic tests (Barth & Macciochi, 1985). The HRB allows trained examiners to determine level and pattern of performance, differences in right-left abilities, and specific symptoms of neuropathology.

The HRB includes the following tests as well as the administration of an MMPI and a WAIS-R. Some clinical neuropsychologists add to the HRB other tests such as the Strength of Grip Test and achievement tests.

1. *Halstead Category Test.* Two hundred and eight slides of geometric figures are divided into seven subsets containing from eight to forty slides. Subjects are asked to determine the underlying principle of each subset. This particular test measures problem-solving, abstract learning, concept formation, and judgment.

2. *Seashore Rhythm Test.* Subjects listen to thirty fast-paced pairs of rhythmic beats with similar tone and volume and determine whether the pairs are identical or different. The test measures auditory perception and speed of processing.

3. *Speech-Sounds Perception Test.* This slow-paced test presents sixty nonsense words with an "ee sound" in a taped presentation. Subjects then choose which of four printed words has been said (e.g., the subjects may hear "weej" and then must select the word from weech, yeech, weej, yeej). This test requires attention, concentration, verbal and auditory perception, and language processing.

4. *Tactual Performance Test (TPT).* Blindfolded subjects are given a wooden board with spaces for geometric shapes. First using the dominant hand, the test-taker places the shapes into the board for three trials. The test-taker repeats the task with his or her nondominant hand and finally with both hands. Last, the blindfold is removed, and the subject draws the board and the geometric shapes. Scoring involves time needed to complete the trials and accuracy of the drawings. The TPT measures right-left differences in motor, tactile, and kinesthetic skills and requires spatial abilities and memory.

5. *Finger Oscillation Test.* For five consecutive ten-second trials with each index finger, subjects tap a lever that mechanically counts the number of finger taps. The test provides a measure of right-left differences in motor speed and skills.

6. *Trail Making Test.* Subjects must draw lines connecting appropriately numbered and lettered circles, using the skills of visual scanning, verbal and numerical processing, and sequencing skills.

7. *Halstead-Wepman Aphasia Screening.* In this test, subjects follow over thirty simple commands so a variety of aptitudes, including receptive and expressive language, mental manipulation, and writing names of pictured objects, can be measured.

8. *Sensory-Perceptual Examination.* Tactile, auditory, and visual abilities are tapped by tasks that require the test-taker to identify which finger or hand is being touched, which ear is receiving a low-level sound, and into which perceptual field an object is entering. (Barth & Macciochi, 1985).

Intelligence Assessment Issues

What Can IQ Tests Do?   IQ tests do a fairly good job of predicting academic grades and occupational status. IQ test scores correlate with academic success because tasks involved in IQ tests are similar to the kinds of tasks assigned in school. IQ scores also correlate with occupational status because in American culture academic success is usually a prerequisite to occupational status. However, within an occupation, IQ scores are not able to tell which workers will be most successful and which will be less successful.

Who's Smarter—Men or Women?   This question has probably been asked throughout the history of humankind. In the nineteenth century, Paul Broca claimed that men are smarter than women because men have larger and heavier brains. A counterposition stated that women are smarter than men because women's central nervous systems make up a larger proportion of total body weight (Gould, 1981).

Today researchers are interested in a variety of gender differences, including possible brain differences (see Chapter 4) and behavioral differences (see Chapter 16), but the question of which gender scores higher on IQ tests is easy to answer—males and females have equal IQs. In fact, items on the Stanford-Binet and Wechsler tests were carefully chosen to be fair to both genders. However, IQ tests are frequently criticized for being biased in other ways. The *Relate* section of this chapter focuses on the issue of racial bias in intelligence tests.

Are You Born Smart? Or Do You Get Smart?   Psychologists have yet to determine how much of IQ is inherited and how much is influenced by environment. Until the 1930s, most psychologists believed that intelligence is an innate potential that cannot be modified. Some psychologists, notably Arthur Jensen (1969, 1980), hold this position today, and Hans Eysenck (1981) es-

A genetic factor in general intelligence is suggested by findings that identical twins have more similar test scores than do non-identical twins.

timates that intelligence is nearly 80 percent hereditary.

Today, however, most psychologists assume that heredity is not the sole determinant of IQ. Monozygotic (identical) twins average a six-point difference in IQ scores, while dizygotic (fraternal) twins average a ten-point difference. Nontwin siblings tend to display a fourteen-point difference between IQ scores (Plomin & DeFries, 1980). Additional research findings indicate that the IQs of adopted children fall between the scores of the biological parents and the adoptive parents (Bouchard & McGue, 1981).

As a result of such findings, most psychologists view intelligence as an interaction between heredity and environment and believe that intelligence can be modified to a degree. Feuerstein believes that, rather than measuring IQ, psychologists need to measure learning modifiability, which is "the capacity to change, to grasp, to adapt better to the world" (Mohs, 1982, p. 24).

When IQ scores change, psychologists have difficulty deciding if the changes are due primarily to environmental or genetic influences. Every Stanford-Binet and Wechsler standardization sample from 1932 to 1978 created a higher standardized norm than for the previous sample. In this forty-six-year period, the mean IQ of Americans increased nearly fourteen points (Flynn, 1984). Why has the IQ of Americans been rising? If you attribute the increase to genetics, you must consider that forty-six years is a short time period in which to produce such significant genetic changes.

How Does IQ Change with Age? Which saying do you think is truer? "You can't teach an old dog new tricks" or "You aren't getting older; you're getting better." **Longitudinal studies**, in which a group of people is studied over a period of time, can help psychologists understand how intelligence changes with aging. Longitudinal studies provide information about intra-individual change as well as inferences about inter-individual variability (Schaie, 1983b).

In 1919, in the first reported long-term study of adult intelligence, Iowa State University tested 363 freshmen with the Army Alpha Test. In 1950, 127 of these subjects were retested; in 1961, more data were collected from 96 of the subjects. This longitudinal research looked at verbal, numerical, and relations factors. In the 1950 data, verbal scores had increased significantly, relations scores had increased somewhat, and numerical scores had decreased slightly. In 1961, only the numerical scores showed a significant decrease (Cunningham & Owens, 1983).

Another longitudinal study followed until 1973 the intellectual development of twins who had first been studied by Kallman and Sander in 1946. The results showed that cognitive functioning on a nonspeeded test remained steady until at least age seventy-five. Female subjects in this study outscored male subjects (Jarvik & Bank, 1983).

A third study, the Seattle longitudinal study, collected data from 1956 until 1977 using Thurstone's Primary Mental Abilities. The study's results are summarized in Exhibit 20.12. In the Seattle study, the researchers

EXHIBIT 20.12
Longitudinal Estimates of Age Changes in Intelligence for Men and Women in the Seattle Longitudinal Study

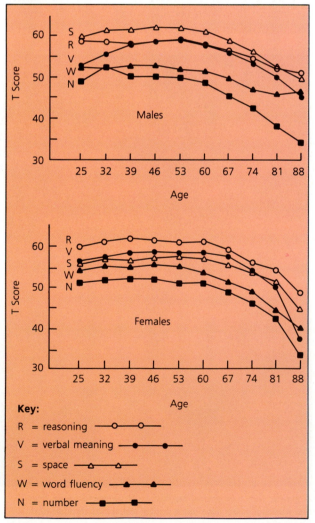

From Schaie, K. W. (ed.) 1983. *Longitudinal studies of adult psychological development.* NY: Guilford. p. 105, fig. 4.6.

Exploring . . .

The Redden-Simons Rap Test (1986)

DIRECTIONS: Choose the most appropriate answer, and write the letter on the space by the question.

_____ 1. Don't play the dozens.
a. Don't gamble.
b. Don't talk about others' family members.
c. Don't try to stay up 'round the clock.
d. Don't date too many people at once.

_____ 2. She's a mary jane girl.
a. She smokes marijuana.
b. She's someone's pet project.
c. She has a pimp.
d. All of the above.

_____ 3. I copped a Jones.
a. I made an alibi to the cops.
b. I'm trying to keep up with my neighbors.
c. I developed a heroin addiction.
d. I killed a policeman.

_____ 4. I got some new kicks.
a. I just got some good drugs.
b. I've just been in a fight.
c. I've got some good gossip for you.
d. I've got some new shoes.

_____ 5. Let me throw down on this plate.
a. Let me check the quality of this marijuana.
b. Let me snort some coke.
c. Let me finish eating.
d. Let me steal this car.

_____ 6. He left to cop a button.
a. He's in the bathroom.
b. He left to buy twenty dollars of coke.
c. He left to go change his clothes.
d. He's in the bedroom with his woman.

_____ 7. She's buff.
a. She's got a cute rear end.
b. She's overweight.
c. She's wearing leather.
d. She's got polished manners.

_____ 8. She's a hershey.
a. She loves chocolate candies.
b. She dates only black men.
c. She's a transsexual.
d. She's a very sweet person.

_____ 9. He bumped me.
a. He tried to start a fight.
b. He sold me bad drugs.
c. He missed my vein and injected dope into my muscle.
d. He took me on a date but brought somebody else home.

_____ 10. He got juked.
a. He got stabbed.
b. He got ripped off for drugs.
c. He partied all night.
d. He died of bad drugs.

_____ 11. Got a rig?
a. Do you have a car?
b. Do you have a needle?
c. Do you have an idea?
d. Do you have a game plan?

_____ 12. Boost it.
a. Up the ante.
b. Support your friends.
c. Increase one's drug tolerance.
d. Play with a needle after registering.

_____ 13. Dog food.
a. Heroin.
b. Cocaine.
c. Downers.
d. Amphetamines.

_____ 14. Dogs.
a. Drugs.
b. Feet.
c. Leftovers.
d. Tired-looking eyes.

_____ 15. Nice whites.
a. An insult toward white people.
b. Good cocaine supply.
c. Clean sheets.
d. Good teeth.

_____ 16. Speedball.
a. Amphetamines.
b. Cocaine and heroin combination.
c. LSD with amphetamines.
d. Amphetamines and alcohol.

continued

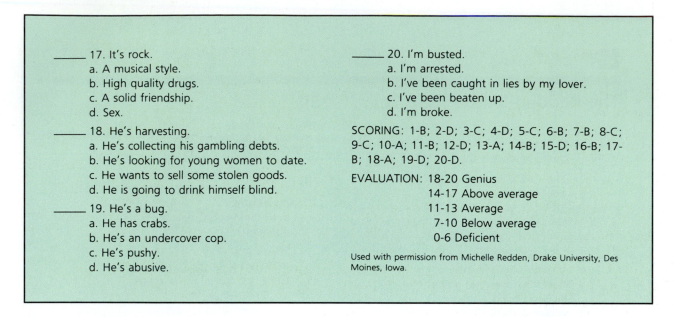

_____ 17. It's rock.
    a. A musical style.
    b. High quality drugs.
    c. A solid friendship.
    d. Sex.

_____ 18. He's harvesting.
    a. He's collecting his gambling debts.
    b. He's looking for young women to date.
    c. He wants to sell some stolen goods.
    d. He is going to drink himself blind.

_____ 19. He's a bug.
    a. He has crabs.
    b. He's an undercover cop.
    c. He's pushy.
    d. He's abusive.

_____ 20. I'm busted.
    a. I'm arrested.
    b. I've been caught in lies by my lover.
    c. I've been beaten up.
    d. I'm broke.

SCORING: 1-B; 2-D; 3-C; 4-D; 5-C; 6-B; 7-B; 8-C; 9-C; 10-A; 11-B; 12-D; 13-A; 14-B; 15-D; 16-B; 17-B; 18-A; 19-D; 20-D.

EVALUATION: 18-20 Genius
                14-17 Above average
                11-13 Average
                 7-10 Below average
                 0-6 Deficient

Used with permission from Michelle Redden, Drake University, Des Moines, Iowa.

found that IQ remains basically stable through the forties with only small changes in the late fifties. A little decline occurs during the seventies with substantial decline in the eighties. Researchers found that fluid abilities decline earlier and crystallized abilities exhibit sharp declines only in advanced old age (Schaie, 1983a). As these three studies indicate, the answer to the previous question is yes, you can teach an old dog new tricks; however, learning new tricks may take a little longer, and some kinds of tricks are easier to learn.

Are IQ Tests Fair? Many psychologists believe intelligence tests are fair only to individuals who have been exposed to mainstream America because these tests are based on middle-class knowledge, customs, experience, and education. If your own background is mainstream America, you may not perceive the cultural biases of standardized tests, but taking the test in the _Exploring_ . . . section, the Redden-Simons Rap Test (1986), may sharpen your perceptions. This test reverses the usual test biases, and lower-income "street people" especially do better on it than do middle-class individuals. How did you do? If the Redden-Simons Rap Test were used to determine IQ scores, would you consider the test fair? Why or why not?

Chances are, you would not like this test to be used as an intelligence test. However, taking this test may have made you more aware that typical intelligence tests are unfair to some groups of people.

One proposed solution is to develop **culture-fair tests**, tests that do not disadvantage subgroups of the culture. However, development of culture-fair tests is difficult, and present attempts are only somewhat successful. Most culture-fair tests minimize vocabulary and use items such as geometric manipulations and progressive matrices (i.e., determining which figure comes next in a series of four). Still, some researchers believe that nonverbal tests may be more culturally biased than verbal tests (Jensen, 1985). The _Relate_ section looks at a major aspect of this issue—the use of intelligence tests with black Americans.

Focus Question Answer

What would you experience if you took an intelligence test? Depending upon the particular test, you would probably work with verbal, mathematical, and spatial orientation items. The test could be individually or group administered. Ideally, the items would represent content you are likely to have encountered in everyday living; whether this criterion were met would depend upon how well the items were chosen and how typical your background is. What else would you experience? Well, probably some curiosity and some anxiety.

 *Relate*

Intelligence Testing—The Black and White Issue

Black Americans score an average of 85 on standardized IQ tests—about 15 points below the average for white Americans. Many psychologists attribute this difference in scores to cultural disadvantages such as poor nutrition, fewer educational resources and opportunities, financial concerns, and inadequate medical care. Other psychologists suggest that poorer test performance by blacks indicates that standardized intelligence tests are designed to be fair to individuals with middle-class backgrounds but can be unfair to individuals with different backgrounds. Some black Americans may not have been exposed to customs and information that make up intelligence test items. Language usage and vocabulary of black and white Americans may differ. You experienced this kind of language bias when you took the Redden-Simons Rap Test (1986).

In 1969, Arthur Jensen wrote an article for the *Harvard Educational Review* in which he stated that black Americans are genetically inferior to whites in intelligence. In the 1970s, Jensen divided intelligence into Level I intelligence, which consists of short-term memory and rote learning abilities, and Level II intelligence, which consists of reasoning, abstraction, and problem-solving. Jensen claimed that the larger black-white differences occur with Level II (Jensen, 1985).

By the 1980s, Jensen (1985) was proposing that the differences in black and white IQ scores reflect racial differences in g factor. The implications of this position are evident in Jensen's own words: "g discriminates more accurately than any other factor between average persons and persons diagnosed as mentally retarded by independent, nontest criteria, and between average persons and those who are recognized as intellectually gifted on the basis of their accomplishments."

Jensen (1980) claims current IQ tests are not biased because they do not over- or under-predict the job or educational performances of one group (e.g., race, sex, socioeconomic level, ethnicity) compared to another group. Poor people and racial minorities with a certain IQ score do about the same as do middle-class whites with that IQ score when compared in academic performance and on other tasks (Cole, 1981).

Other researchers strongly disagree with Jensen's research and conclusions, and several findings contradict Jensen's belief that racial differences in IQ are mostly genetically determined. One study (Scarr & Weinberg, 1976) compared IQ scores of white and black children who were adopted by white families. In these families, adopted black children av-

Average IQ of White Families with Adopted Black Children

Family members	Average IQ
Adoptive mothers	118
Adoptive fathers	121
Their biological children	117
Adopted white children	111
Adopted black children	106

Scarr, S. & Weinberg, R. A. 1976. IQ test performance of black children adopted by white families. *American Psychologist, 31,* 726-739.

eraged an IQ score of 106, or 6 points above the average IQ score of white Americans. The data of this study, which is summarized in the table above provide strong support for the position that intelligence is strongly influenced by environmental circumstances.

In another study (Scarr & Carter-Saltzman, 1982; Scarr et al., 1977), researchers proposed that if genetics is the important factor in intelligence, and if a racial difference in IQ exists, a relationship between the degree of white ancestry and the intellectual skills of black Americans should exist. The researchers tested 362 black children, aged ten to sixteen, with the Raven Progressive Matrices, a vocabulary test, and three other tests. Degree of white ancestry was determined by analyzing subjects' blood samples for fourteen blood factors. Based on blood sample analysis, the researchers estimated percentage of European ancestry for each subject.

The researchers found nonsignificant correlations from .15 to −.12 between degree of white ancestry and intelligence scores and concluded that genetic differences are not largely responsible for differences in IQ scores between the two races.

One possible explanation for the black-white differences in IQ scores comes from Robert Zajonc's work on family size (Zajonc, 1986). According to Zajonc, large families provide poorer intellectual climates for children because of the undesirable ratio of adults to children; as a result, children with many siblings have lower IQ averages. According to Zajonc's **confluence theory**, intellectual development of a family member is influenced by the contributions of all family members, and adults have more verbal skills to contribute than do siblings. Zajonc states, "The pool of words surrounding the only child at age 5 is different from the pool surrounding the second-born child of the same age who has a 7-year-old sibling. As families get larger, children's intellectual development suffers, and the effect is accentuated by birth order—the more older siblings a person has, the lower his or her intellectual level because of the decrease within the family intellectual environment'' (Hall, 1986, p. 48). The fact that in America black families tend to be larger than white families may help explain the IQ differences of blacks and whites.

Things to Do

1. Ask a counselor to let you take an objective personality inventory, such as the Minnesota Multiphasic Personality Inventory (MMPI), Edwards Personal Preference Schedule (EPPS), or Myers-Briggs Type Indicator. Have the counselor explain the results to you. How well does the inventory describe your personality?

2. Make copies of the general personality description found in Forer's 1949 article, "The Fallibility of Personal Validation: A Classroom Demonstration of Gullibility" (Journal of Abnormal and Social Psychology, 44, 118-123). Design a twelve-item questionnaire that appears to be a personality test. Give your personality test to ten students, and then give each student the Forer personality description as his or her test results. How many students believed that the test adequately measured their personalities?

3. Ask an astrologer about the reliability and validity of horoscopes, and then ask a social scientist the same questions. How could you scientifically study the reliability and validity of horoscopes?

4. Design a research study on locus of control. What is your hypothesis? Your independent variable? Your dependent variable?

5. Give several people the Redden & Simons Rap Test (1986) and get their reactions to the fairness of the test. Do these individuals believe that this test would be a valid measure of intelligence? Why?

6. Read about creative arts therapy or talk with a creative arts therapist. How do creative arts therapists use drawings and poetry in personality assessment?

7. Ask a personnel officer what kinds of personality assessment instruments are used with employees and potential employees. How is the decision about an instrument's appropriateness for the employment situation made?

Things to Discuss

1. What are the advantages and disadvantages of internal locus of control? Of external locus of control? What strategies could you employ to modify someone's locus of control?

2. What guidelines would you establish for the use of personality inventories and intelligence tests in educational settings? In employment settings? In legal settings?

3. What is your implicit definition of intelligence? Why? Which of the explicit theories in the chapter do you prefer? Why?

4. In what ways are assessment assumptions and tools influenced by culture and politics?

5. Research findings suggest that the Japanese have a higher average IQ score (111) than do Americans (100). In fact, approximately 10 percent of Japan's population scores higher than 130 on IQ tests, but only 2 percent of Americans score this high (Mohs, 1982). What possible reasons explain the difference in Japanese and American scores?

Things to Read

Aero, R. & Weiner, E. 1981. The mind test. NY: Morrow.

Bloom, B.S. 1985. Developing Talent in young people. NY: Ballantine.

Eysenck, H.J. & Kamin, L. 1981. The intelligence controversy. NY: Wiley.

Feldman, R.D. 1982. Whatever happened to the quiz kids? Perils and profits of growing up gifted. Chicago: Chicago Review Press.

Gardner, H. 1983. Frames of mind: The theory of multiple intelligences. N.Y.: Basic Books.

Gould, S.J. 1981. The mismeasure of man. NY: Norton.

Review

Summary

1. Most personality and physical characteristics fall into a normal curve, with most individuals' scores clustered around the average amount of the characteristics.

2. A good assessment measure exhibits reliability, which refers to consistency of measurement, and validity, which denotes the instrument's measurement of what it is intended to measure. Face validity, content validity, and criterion validity are three important types of test validity. A valid test is a reliable test; a reliable test may or may not be valid.

3. Questionnaires that are objective tests are objectively scored and produce the same results, regardless of the scorers. The Minnesota Multiphasic Personality Inventory is the most widely used objective personality questionnaire.

4. Projective tests consist of ambiguous stimuli to which the test-taker projects his or her own personality characteristics. The two most commonly used projective tests are the Rorschach Inkblot Test and the Thematic Apperception Test. Some clinicians think projective tests are useful, reliable, and valid. Others believe the tests are susceptible to eigenesis, or the projection of the clinician's values onto the test-taker's answers.

5. Interviews and situational testing can also assess behavior and personality. Interviews may be structured or unstructured.

6. Individuals have general expectations about the locus of control in their lives. Individuals with internal locus of control believe their destinies are largely shaped by skill, ability, and effort. Individuals with external locus of control believe their destinies are shaped primarily by fate, luck, chance, and powerful others.

7. Laypeople and psychologists have implicit, or everyday, notions about intelligence. Implicit theories of intelligence emphasize verbal intelligence, spatial and numerical skills, social and intrapersonal knowledge, and motivation.

8. Spearman's g factor, Thurstone's primary mental abilities, and Guilford's 150 factorial model are early intelligence concepts that still influence current research and theory on intelligence. Another historical approach to intelligence, information-processing, often emphasized rate of processing of problem-solving strategies and knowledge.

9. Cattell divided intelligence into fluid and crystallized intelligence. Fluid abilities refer to problem-solving strategies, and crystallized abilities comprise knowledge and facts. With age, fluid abilities seem to decline slowly, while crystallized abilities tend to hold steady or increase.

10. Two current models of intelligence are presented by Gardner and Sternberg. Gardner emphasizes multiple intelligence and maintains that basic IQ tests measure only three of seven basic frames of intelligence. Sternberg's triarchic theory breaks intelligence into contextual, componential, and experiential aspects. Both theories imply that intelligence is modifiable.

11. IQ testing began with the work of Binet and Simon at the beginning of the twentieth century. Currently, the Wechsler Intelligence tests and the Stanford-Binet tests are the most well-known and widely used IQ tests.

12. Neuropsychological testing allows clinicians to assess the extent of impaired abilities due to brain injury and to chart the rate of improvement over the months following brain injury.

13. Intelligence seems to change with age, and sound longitudinal studies suggest higher IQ scores for older adults than earlier cross-sectional studies suggested.

14. Psychologists debate the fairness of intelligence tests to some portions of the population. Ideally, culture-fair tests should be developed.

15. For twenty years, a controversial topic in psychological assessment has been the IQ differences between blacks and whites. A small number of psychologists suggest the 15-point difference is due to genetic inferiority or differences in the g factor; most believe the differences result from test bias or environmental differences.

Key Terms

norms
normal curve
reliability
validity
objective tests
norm-referencing
criterion-referencing
ipsative scoring
Minnesota Multiphasic Personality Inventory
    (MMPI)
projective tests
Rorschach Inkblot Test
Thematic Apperception Test (TAT)
eisegesis
unstructured interviews
structured interviews
situational testing
internal locus of control
external locus of control
implicit theories
explicit theories
g factor

s factors
primary mental abilities
operations
contents
products
fluid abilities
crystallized abilities
idiot savants
prodigies
intellectual giftedness
intellectual retardation
triarchic theory
phrenology
mental age (MA)
Stanford-Binet Intelligence Scale
WAIS-R, WISC-R, and WPPSI
clinical neuropsychology
Halstead-Reitan Neuropsychological Test Battery
    (HRB)
longitudinal studies
culture-fair tests
confluence theory

Focus Questions

1. Which behaviors are labeled abnormal?

2. Are your anxieties normal, or are they symptoms of an anxiety disorder?

3. In addition to anxiety, what symptoms might indicate you are suffering from a psychological disorder?

4. What conditions associated with the Vietnam War led to the development of post-traumatic stress disorder in numerous Vietnam era veterans?

Chapter Outline

Chapter 21

Psychological
Disorders

Much Madness is Divinest sense—
To a discerning Eye—
Much sense—the starkest Madness

Emily Dickinson

≡ Abnormal Behavior

What is abnormal behavior? The answer to this question depends upon how the evaluator of behavior defines abnormality. People usually evaluate behavior according to the behavioral rules, spoken or unspoken, they see as applicable to a particular situation. How would a person running nude down a street be evaluated? If you were a police officer, you probably would evaluate the behavior as an illegal act. If you were a minister, you might evaluate the behavior as an immoral act. If you were a mental health professional, you might interpret running in the nude as a symptom of a disorder. Finally, if you were a college student in a fraternity and knew the person was behaving in this manner as part of an initiation ritual, you would probably consider the behavior a harmless

515

prank at worst, and you might even admire the person's daring. Thus, the same behaviors are viewed differently depending upon the situation and upon the person doing the evaluating.

Definitions of Abnormal Behavior

Abnormal behavior can be defined according to several models. The **statistical model** of abnormal behavior equates mental health with *normal* or *average* behavior. Abnormal behavior is any behavior that does not conform to the average. A characteristic (e.g., height, or weight) can be graphed according to its frequency, and those individuals who exhibit more or less than an average amount of the characteristic (those who are much taller or much shorter, much heavier or much lighter) are statistically abnormal (see Exhibit 21.1).

One of the problems with the statistical model of abnormal behavior is that a behavior, such as abuse within the family, may be statistically normal but not desirable. For example, every year an estimated 17,000,000 children are kicked, punched, and bitten by their parents (Thompson et al., 1985). This statistic indicates that these forms of abuse are not statistically abnormal, but most people would agree that such behavior is not desirable. An additional problem with the statistical model is that, although a label of statistical abnormality does not by itself imply that a characteristic or behavior (such as fathers receiving child custody in divorce cases) is undesirable or wrong, many people interpret statistical abnormality negatively.

The **ideal state model** constructs criteria for an *ideal* state of mental health. When compared to an ideal,

Although being a mother and being confined to a wheelchair is statistically abnormal, this fact tells you little about how this woman functions in her role as a mother.

many or most people would be found lacking in some areas. For instance, does a dedicated, productive artist working in isolation exhibit abnormal behavior because he or she does not demonstrate the ability to interact well with others? According to both the statistical model and the ideal state model, the answer would be yes, but is the artist's behavior undesirable?

The **personal distress model** proposes a different way of defining abnormal behavior. This model defines abnormal behavior on the basis of negative and uncomfortable emotional states. Yet, personal distress may be an indication of problems, or it may be a normal reaction to certain crisis situations. Further, some severely mentally ill persons may experience little or no distress or awareness of their inability to function appropriately. Therefore, including personal distress as a necessary criterion for abnormal behavior leads to the inclusion of people who are not usually labeled abnormal and the exclusion of others who are generally considered abnormal.

The **cultural or situational model** of abnormal behavior proposes that behaviors are not inherently normal or abnormal but are judged so within the context of the culture or situation in which they occur. According to this view, behaviors that are considered abnormal in one culture or situation may be considered normal, or even desirable, in another. For instance, if you were sitting on a park bench on an 80° F. summer day and you saw a man dressed in rubber boots, a heavy winter coat, and a stocking cap, you would probably consider his behavior abnormal, but if you were sitting on a bench waiting for a bus on a 20° F. winter day, you would consider his

EXHIBIT 21.1
A Normal Curve

Frequency of Occurrence

40%

30%

20%

10%

Shortest ⟵——————⟶ Tallest

Heights of Canadian Women

Do you find this woman's ankle tattoo attractive? Abnormal? Strange? Your answer probably depends on what you learned to consider appropriate or normal.

behavior normal. According to the cultural or situational model, the behavior itself does not determine its normality; the appropriateness of the behavior to the culture or situation does.

The **medical model** of abnormal behavior uses physical illness as an analogy for psychological/mental illness. The process of looking at abnormal behavior then follows this pattern: diagnosis (usually involving labeling) of the causes of the problem; treatment to arrest or cure the problem; and establishing a prediction of the course of the problem (predicting the likelihood of recovery or degeneration). Although the medical model dominates the mental health care delivery system, many professionals criticize the assumption that single, or even multiple, causes of abnormal behavior can be identified. Others criticize this model for another reason. When people are physically ill, most assume both the causes and treatments are outside their control. Similarly, if people think they are mentally *ill,* they will feel more helpless and less able and willing to take responsibility for changing their behaviors.

Of the models of abnormal behavior described, no model is without flaws in its application. However, no model is without usefulness in contributing to the total picture of abnormal behavior. The influence of the medical model is especially evident in commonly used diagnostic systems.

Diagnosis

Diagnosis is the classification or labeling of a disease or disorder. This term has traditionally been used to refer to physical ailments, but its use has been extended to

emotional or psychological disorders. Possibly the most practical question that can be asked about a diagnostic system is whether its use entails more benefits than drawbacks. Ideally, a diagnostic system would help a clinician (therapist) identify important information about a problem or disorder and organize that information so as to enable him or her to choose the most effective treatment and to formulate the most accurate **prognosis** (course of the disorder). Unfortunately, the ideal is rarely realized.

The benefits of a diagnostic system are dependent upon its inter-rater reliability (amount of agreement on diagnosis among raters) and its validity (degree to which the system measures what it says it measures). With a reliable diagnostic system, the same patient would receive the same diagnosis from several different diagnosticians. However, with the currently used systems, diagnostic reliability has been shown to vary between countries, between geographical areas within a country, between different settings (a busy outpatient facility versus a research center), and between diagnostic categories (Schumer, 1983). Generally, high diagnostic reliability is difficult to achieve.

Diagnostic validity is a measure of how closely the description of a particular category, encompassing both the symptoms that are included and those that are excluded, resembles the actual nature of the disorder. Validity is more difficult to measure than is reliability. This difficulty is seen in the research on schizoaffective disorder, which may be a separate disorder, a subtype of schizophrenia, or a subtype of the affective disorders (Meltzer, 1984). (Chapter 22 provides more information on schizoaffective disorder.) Identifying which of these formulations is most valid is very important in determining which treatments are most effective and in determining an accurate prognosis.

A more general problem with diagnostic systems—the negative effect of labeling—is acknowledged by many psychologists and psychiatrists. Labels are often negative, and they may be used to justify actions against certain individuals. The effects of a label may last far longer than the effects of the disorder (the *Exploring . . .* section examines the effects of labeling).

Despite the problems associated with diagnostic systems, these systems are functional in several ways. They serve as practical ways to organize and categorize the vast amount of information available in the domain of abnormal behavior, and they are a useful shorthand for communications between mental health professionals. The *DSM III* (*Diagnostic and Statistical Manual of Mental Disorders,* third edition) is the most widely used diag-

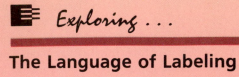

Exploring...

The Language of Labeling

Labeling theory is the term applied to the study of the labeling process. The goals of research in the area are to understand why people apply labels, the process of applying labels, and the effects of labels on the labeler, on the labeled person, and on the interactions between them. *How* people think about certain individuals is reflected in the language they use to describe the individuals, but is the opposite also true? Does the way in which people describe certain individuals influence the way in which people think

Words, Words, Words

Immediately below is a long list of words that people use to refer to "abnormal" behavior, followed by a much smaller list of words that refer to "normal" behavior. Can you add to these lists? Why is the first list so much longer than the second?

Words that Refer to "Abnormal" Behavior

mentally ill	emotionally ill
crazy	off one's rocker
sick	freaked out
insane	batty
mad	cracked
abnormal	running amuck
deranged	being tetched
demented	going haywire
deviant	gaga
aberrant	spooky
disordered	spacey
pathological	*meshugah*
psychopathic	maniacal
loco	off the wall
screwball	*non compos mentis*
bats in the belfry	unbalanced
wacky	has personality problems
out of one's skull	monomaniacal
mad as a hatter	schizy
not having all one's	stark-mad
marbles	loony
off one's nut	nut
flipped out	crackpot
flaky	freak
psychotic	kooky
neurotic	goofball
psychoneurotic	a screw loose
manic	going berserk
eccentric	becoming unhinged
odd	buggy
weird	psycho
bizarre	dotty
queer	irrational
lunatic	spaced out
mentally diseased	taking leave of one's
unstable	senses
nutty as a fruitcake	

Words that Refer to "Normal" Behavior

sane, sanity	*compos mentis*
reasoning	in possession of one's
balanced	senses
emotionally healthy	well adjusted
mentally healthy	normal
in possession of one's	soberhead
faculties	in one's right mind
soundminded	all there
rational	have it all together
stable	being all together
emotionally mature	

From *Abnormal Psychology* by Florence Schumer. Copyright © 1983 by D. C. Heath and Company. Reprinted by permission of the publisher.

of the individuals? The Whorfian hypothesis states that people's views of the world are formed, at least in part, by the language they learn and use to describe the world. If the hypothesis is true, the language people use to describe normal and abnormal behaviors influences people's views of these behaviors. Read through the list of synonyms for normal and abnormal behavior, and notice the harsh, negative quality of the synonyms for abnormal behavior.

For several decades, Thomas Szasz, a noted psychiatrist, has been an outspoken critic of diagnosis and, more generally, the labeling process. He has objected to labeling interpersonal, social, or communication problems as mental illness or disease. According to Szasz, behavior that offends or seems very strange to friends, relatives, or society is generally what brings people to the attention of medical or legal authorities; authorities then use the power of language to justify their treatment of these individuals. The following excerpts from *The Theology of Medicine: The Political-Philosophical Foundations of Medical Ethics* (1977)* clarify Szasz's position:

> . . . Language, the oldest but still the most reliable guide to a people's true sentiments, starkly reveals the intimate connection between illness and dignity. In English, we use the same word to describe an expired passport, an indefensible argument, an illegitimate legal document, and a person disabled by disease. We call each of them invalid. To be an invalid, then, is to be an invalidated person, a human being stamped not valid by the invisible but invincible hand of popular opinion. While invalidism carries with it the heaviest burden of indignity, some of the stigma adheres to virtually all illness, to virtually any participation in the role of patient (p. 19).

> How are involuntary psychiatric interventions—and the many other medical violations of individual freedom—justified and made possible? By calling people *patients,* imprisonment *hospitalization,* and torture *therapy;* and by

*Copyright Thomas Szasz, reprinted by permission.

calling uncomplaining individuals *sufferers,* medical and mental-health personnel who infringe on their liberty and dignity *therapists,* and the things the latter do to the former *treatments.* This is why such terms as *mental health* and the *right to treatment* now so effectively conceal that psychiatry is involuntary servitude (p. xix).

Carl Rogers, the originator of client-centered therapy, has also long opposed the diagnostic emphasis that has been part of traditional psychiatry and psychotherapy. Unlike Szasz, whose ideas are often considered radical or at least controversial, Carl Rogers is clearly in the mainstream of current psychological thinking. His view of the effect of diagnostic labeling is clear in the following excerpt from his 1961 book, *On Becoming a Person.*

> . . . Can I meet this other individual as a person who is in the process of *becoming,* or will I be bound by his past and by my past? If, in my encounter with him, I am dealing with him as an immature child, an ignorant student, a neurotic personality, or a psychopath, each of these concepts of mine limits what he can be in a relationship . . . If I accept the other person as something fixed, already diagnosed and classified, already shaped by his past, then I am doing my part to confirm this limited hypothesis. If I accept him as a process of becoming, then I am doing what I can to confirm or make real his potentialities (p. 55).

What conclusions can be reached about the effects of language on the labelers, on those who are labeled, and on the interactions between them? Should psychiatrists and psychologists cease attaching diagnostic labels to their patients? While some psychologists and psychiatrists advocate this position, most mental health professionals believe that discontinuing the diagnostic process is unrealistic. Although Szasz believes that the purpose of labeling is to give chosen people the power to impose rules of behavior on other people, most therapists acknowledge both the benefits as well as the problems with labeling systems.

nostic system in the United States. Understanding the terminology in the DSM III is very important if you wish to communicate with mental health professionals, who use terms such as depression and anxiety in ways that overlap with everyday definitions but are often more specific. The information provided in Chapters 21 and 22 will help you learn part of the language used by mental health professionals.

The DSM III

The DSM III (1980) was developed by the American Psychiatric Association over a period of years (1974-1980) in conjunction with another diagnostic system used by the World Health Organization, The International Classification of Diseases (ICD-9). The categories of mental disorders in these two systems overlap somewhat; however, while the ICD-9 includes both physical and mental disorders, the DSM III includes only mental disorders. The DSM II (the second edition) was the most widely used system in the United States from its publication in 1968 until the publication of the DSM III in 1980. The DSM III includes more information and more specific and detailed criteria for diagnosing each disorder than did the DSM II. In contrast to the DSM II, which lists 145 categories, the DSM III lists 230 categories of mental illness. Exhibit 21.2 contains a list of only the major categories of the DSM III.

EXHIBIT 21.2
General Diagnostic Categories in the DSM III:
Axes I and II

Axis I
Disorders Usually First Evident in Infancy, Childhood, or Adolescence
  Mental retardation
  Attention deficit disorder
  Conduct disorder
  Anxiety disorders of childhood or adolescence
  Other disorders of infancy, childhood, or adolescence
  Eating disorders
  Stereotyped movement disorders
  Other disorders with physical manifestations
  Pervasive developmental disorders
Organic Mental Disorders
  Dementias arising in the senium and presenium
  Substance-induced
Substance Use Disorders
Schizophrenic Disorders
Paranoid Disorders
Psychotic Disorders Not Elsewhere Classified
Affective Disorders
Anxiety Disorders
Somatoform Disorders
Dissociative Disorders (or Hysterical Neuroses, Dissociative Type)
Psychosexual Disorders
Factitious Disorders
Disorders of Impulse Control
Adjustment Disorders

Axis II

In Children (Primarily)	*In Adults (Primarily)*	
Specific Developmental Disorders	Personality Disorders	
Developmental reading disorder	Paranoid	Borderline
Developmental arithmetic disorder	Schizoid	Avoidant
Developmental language disorder	Schizotypal	Dependent
Developmental articulation disorder	Histrionic	Compulsive
Mixed specific developmental disorder	Narcissistic	Passive-aggressive
Atypical specific developmental disorder	Antisocial	Atypical, mixed, or other personality disorder

American Psychiatric Association Diagnostic and Statistical Manual of Mental Disorders, Third Edition. Washington, D. C., copyright APA 1980. Used with permission.

One of the criticisms of earlier diagnostic systems was the failure to take into consideration life situations that could influence diagnosis, treatment, and prognosis. In response to this criticism, the DSM III advises the use of five axes; Axes I and II include the specific mental disorders listed in Exhibit 21.2. A mental health professional may list one or more disorders on each of these two axes. For instance, a psychologist could list a diagnosis of major depression on Axis I and a diagnosis of compulsive personality disorder on Axis II.

Axis III is used to specify physical illnesses or conditions (such as hypertension, diabetes, or paraplegia) that are present in the individual and possibly relevant to the therapy. Axis IV is used to rate the psychosocial stressors (such as job loss, marital separation, or death of a family member) that contributed to the person's current symptoms. The rating scale is a seven-point scale ranging from "none" to "catastrophic." Information about psychosocial stressors is particularly important for predicting the prognosis of a disorder. In general, the more severe the psychosocial stressors preceding the symptoms, the better the prognosis.

Axis V is used to record the highest level of functioning displayed by the individual during the previous year. Social relations, occupational functioning, and the use of leisure time are taken into consideration. For many people, the goal of treatment will be a return to the highest level of functioning achieved during the year preceding the symptoms. Even when psychosocial stressors are severe (i.e., death of a family member or injuries resulting in the loss of a job), if an adequate level of functioning existed previously, the person is likely to return to that level of functioning when the symptoms subside.

The DSM III, including its multiaxial system and its vocabulary, provides a structure for viewing the various manifestations of abnormal behavior. Information on each disorder includes: central symptoms, usual age of onset, usual course or outcome of the disorder, impairment of functioning, complications, predisposing factors, prevalence rates, sex ratio, and familial pattern. Although the information in the DSM III is very complete and complex, the information presented in Chapters 21 and 22 is, by necessity, much briefer and less complete. The information in these chapters will consist primarily of descriptions of the disorders and the accompanying symptoms. In addition, the theories of etiology (cause or origin of a disorder) will be presented for several disorders.

Neuroses and Psychoses

Neuroses and psychoses are two psychological terms that people often use in everyday language. Although many people use the terms almost interchangeably to mean "craziness" or mental illness, mental health professionals use the terms more specifically to refer to two different types of disorders. Although the DSM II categorized several disorders as *neuroses*, the DSM III is organized differently and does not use this term. Despite the absence of formal definitions of neuroses and psychoses within the DSM III, mental health professionals continue to use the terms.

Neuroses refers to disorders in which the symptoms (e.g., anxiety, panic) are distressing and unacceptable to the person who has them. An individual with a neurosis does not have problems discerning reality, nor is the individual likely to violate social norms. The symptoms are long-term and not tied to specific events, and a person with neurotic symptoms is usually not hospitalized. Chapter 21 includes information about disorders that were previously labeled neuroses, as well as information concerning other disorders.

In contrast, **psychoses** refers to disorders in which individuals may be unable to correctly evaluate their perceptions of the world around them; they may confuse what is real and what is not. The symptoms of psychoses include hallucinations, delusions, incoherent speech, and loss of contact with reality. These symptoms are frightening to the persons experiencing them and to people around them. People diagnosed as psychotic are more likely to be hospitalized than are those diagnosed as neurotic. Chapter 22 provides information about disorders that fit the definition of psychoses and about other disorders as well.

The Research Process: The Incidence of DSM III Disorders in the United States

In 1978, NIMH (National Institute of Mental Health) researchers began planning for the most comprehensive survey of mental disorders ever conducted in the United States. They made decisions about an appropriate population to survey, the size of the sample, the interviewing instrument to use, the data analysis to be done, and, finally, the cost of these procedures. While previous studies of mental disorders had concentrated on either community residents or people who had received treatment for mental illnesses, the NIMH researchers sought "to identify both treated and untreated prevalence rates of both the severe mental disorders . . . as well as the less severe disorders . . ." (Regier et al., 1984a, p. 938).

One of the researchers' first steps was the development of a diagnostic instrument that could be used reliably by mental health professionals and lay interviewers alike. The resulting Diagnostic Interview Schedule (DIS) "assesses the presence, duration, and severity of individual symptoms" through a set of interview questions. Then a computer program organizes the symptoms into groups and provides a DSM III based diagnosis (Regier et al., 1984a).

When this longitudinal study is complete, nearly 20,000 people from five sites (Baltimore, Maryland; New Haven, Connecticut; St. Louis, Missouri; Los Angeles, California; and Durham, North Carolina) will have been interviewed at least twice, one year apart. The researchers hope to answer the following questions: What is the six-month prevalence rate of specific psychiatric disorders? What is the lifetime prevalence of specific psychiatric disorders? Which individuals with mental illnesses use health and mental health services? How often? What are the prevalence rates of specific psychiatric disorders in various age groups? How do prevalence rates for males and females differ?

The results reported in October 1984 reflect the information gathered at three of the five sites (Baltimore, St. Louis, and New Haven) during the first interviews with nearly 10,000 respondents. The information contained in Exhibit 21.3 is an estimate of the prevalance of mental disorders in the United States based on the data from these three sites.

Because of the large sample and the completeness of the survey, the results are considered to be the most accurate representation of mental illness rates to date. Several of the major findings are summarized below:

1. Until this study, depression was considered the most common mental disorder in the United States. The survey suggests that anxiety/somatoform disorders (13.1 million) are more common than depression and the other mood disorders combined (9.4 million). More surprisingly, in a six-month period, more people experience phobic disorders (11.1 million) than experience an affective (mood) disorder (9.4 million) (Myers et al., 1984).

2. Previous studies indicated that more women than men suffer from mental illnesses. Although more women suffer from phobias and depression, more men experience problems with alcohol abuse, drug dependence, and an-

EXHIBIT 21.3
The Estimated Six-Month Prevalence of DSM III Disorders among Americans Age Eighteen and Older

Disorder	Estimated % of Americans	Estimated # of Americans
Any Disorder	18.7%	29.4 million
Anxiety/Somatoform Disorders	8.3%	13.1 million
Phobia	7.0%	11.1 million
Panic	0.8%	1.2 million
Obsessive Compulsive	1.5%	2.4 million
Somatization	0.1%	.1 million
Antisocial Personality	0.9%	1.4 million
Affective Disorders	6.0%	9.4 million
Manic Episode	0.7%	1.0 million
Major Depressive Episode	3.1%	4.9 million
Dysthymia	3.2%	5.1 million
Schizophrenic/Schizophreniform	1.0%	1.5 million
Substance Use Disorders	6.4%	10.0 million
Alcohol Abuse/Dependence	5.0%	7.9 million
Drug Abuse/Dependence	2.0%	3.1 million
Cognitive Impairment (Severe)	1.0%	1.6 million

The estimates listed above are projections made by NIMH based on the data they collected at three sites and on the 1980 Census. NIMH believes these projections are the best estimates available at this time of national rates of mental disorders. Adapted from Tables 1–7 distributed at a press briefing by NIMH in October 1984. For more information, see the *Archives of General Psychiatry*, October 1984, *41*, 931-989.

tisocial behavior. When the rates for all disorders are taken into account, men and women are equally troubled (Freedman, 1984).

3. Fewer than one-fifth of those with a current diagnosis of one of the mental disorders had received treatment in the past six months. Those who did receive treatment were more likely to have visited a general physician than a mental health specialist (Regier, 1984b).

4. Between 29 percent and 38 percent of those interviewed had experienced at least one psychiatric problem during their lifetimes (Robins et al., 1984).

5. For both men and women, the incidence of psychiatric problems dropped by about 50 percent after the age of forty-five. The lowest rate of emotional disturbance was found in persons over sixty-five (Robins et al., 1984).

6. College graduates have far fewer mental disorders than do non-college graduates (Robins et al., 1984).

Confirmation of these findings, as well as new information on selected subgroups of people over sixty-five and Mexican Americans, awaits the completion of the interview process, the data analysis, and the publication of the results.

Focus Question Answer

Which behaviors are labeled abnormal? The answer to this question depends on how abnormality is defined. Each of five models—statistical, ideal state, personal distress, cultural or situational, and medical—reflects a different view of abnormality. The medical model predominantly determines which behaviors are viewed as abnormal and diagnosed as symptoms of psychological disorders.

▤ Anxiety Disorders

Anxiety is defined as "apprehension, tension, or uneasiness that stems from the anticipation of danger" (DSM III). Anxiety is the central characteristic of the group of disorders that includes the phobic disorders, anxiety states, and post-traumatic stress disorder.

Phobic Disorders (Phobic Neuroses)

Phobias are irrational fears of objects, situations, or activities resulting in a great desire to avoid the feared stimulus. Phobic individuals realize their fears are unreasonable, yet they are unable to overcome them. The distinction between common fears (such as fears of snakes,

EXHIBIT 21.4
Some Common Fears and Phobias and Their Uncommon Names

Heights	Acrophobia
Open Spaces	Agoraphobia
Cats	Ailurophobia
Thunder	Asterophobia
Lightning	Ceraunophobia
Enclosed Spaces	Claustrophobia
Dogs	Cynophobia
Horses	Equinophobia
Dirt, Germs, Contamination	Mysophobia
Snakes	Ophidiophobia
Darkness	Nyctophobia
Running Water	Potamophobia
Fire	Pyrophobia
Stage Fright	Topophobia
Animals	Zoophobia

From *Panic: Facing Fears, Phobias, and Anxiety* by S. Agras. NY: W. H. Freeman and Company. Copyright © 1985.

dogs, or storms) and phobic disorders is the degree to which the fear interferes with the person's life. For instance, you may dislike crowded elevators and become anxious when you must ride in an elevator, but a phobic disordered individual would avoid the situation completely, even if the avoidance meant not applying for or taking a job that requires riding elevators.

The three types of phobias are: simple phobias (single phobias, such as fears of dogs, spiders, high places), social phobias (fears of situations in which others might scrutinize the person), and **agoraphobia** (fear of going to public places or fear of being left alone). Exhibit 21.4 contains a list of common fears and phobias and their formal names.

The following examples are typical of the types of phobias:

— *Simple Phobia (dogs)*. Sarah is twenty-three years old, lives in a small town, and walks to work every day. She had carefully planned her route to work to avoid all houses where dogs might be in the yards, but recently on her way to work, a dog barked at her unexpectedly from only a few feet away. She arrived at work a few minutes later, breathing heavily, heart pounding, sweating, and trembling all over. Sarah realizes her fear of dogs is unreasonable, but she cannot talk herself out of it. She has experienced this fear of dogs since she was twelve, and with careful planning has been able to avoid situations in which dogs might be present. Sarah has no other symptoms and has not sought treatment.

Fears of storms and lightning are common, but if your fear is irrational, causes you great anxiety, and causes you to drastically alter your behavior, you have a phobic disorder.

■ *Social Phobia (urinating in public restrooms).* Bill, a college student, makes sure he urinates before driving off to class each day. By limiting his intake of liquids, he can usually wait to use the bathroom until he returns home in the afternoon. Several times in the past, he has stood at urinals in public restrooms and been unable to urinate. Bill fears embarrassment and humiliation if he should be unable to urinate in front of others, and he therefore avoids the situation. On the rare occasions Bill cannot avoid using public restrooms, he goes into a stall and waits until everyone has left before attempting to urinate.

■ *Agoraphobia.* Susan finally decided to seek therapy when her daughter was eight years old. For several years, Susan had been semi-housebound. She felt safe from her fears only in her home and in her car if she was driving. Susan's husband tolerated her reclusive behavior, but he missed their evenings out at restaurants or movie theaters. Susan's daughter had been doing most of Susan's shopping for several years. During the years she was semi-housebound, Susan was often depressed and anxious.

During several periods, she used alcohol, antianxiety drugs, or sleeping pills to calm herself enough to overcome her fears. These chemicals caused other problems, but they did not relieve her intense fear of going places outside her home. One day at a shopping center, Susan sent her daughter into a shoe store with a charge card and instructions to charge several pair of shoes and bring them to the car. Suddenly, Susan realized how dependent she was upon her small child and decided to seek therapy. Through behavior modification techniques, she very gradually began to attempt going places she had not been to in years. With each new location she visited, her fears surfaced, but her world expanded.

People with simple or social phobias that do not interfere greatly with their daily lives rarely seek treatment. Agoraphobics, on the other hand, often seek therapeutic help because the avoidance accompanying agoraphobia can gradually restrict a person to his or her home or even, in rare cases, to one room. Many cases of agoraphobia begin with a series of panic attacks, but panic attacks can occur in individuals who have no other symptoms.

Exploring . . .

Panic Disorder

Picture yourself completing your grocery shopping and heading toward the checkout counter when suddenly you feel terrified. You feel as if you are dying, going crazy, or losing control. Your heart races; you shake all over; you suffer chest pains, breathe with difficulty, and experience a weird sense of unreality. The terror washes over you in waves. These symptoms last several minutes. You have just had a **panic attack**.

Panic attacks are unlike the anxieties and fears experienced by people with simple or social phobias. Panic attacks are unpredictable; they do not occur in similar places each time, nor do they occur in places the person fears. Surprisingly, one-fifth of all panic attacks occur during the night and awaken the sufferer. A typical attack lasts approximately twenty minutes; during this time, the individual's heart rate increases by approximately forty beats per minute, but, contrary to many sufferers' beliefs, the beat does not become irregular (Agras, 1985). Individuals who suffer numerous panic attacks in various public locations may develop fears of going to public places and hence become agoraphobic. Except for severe cases or those in which panic attacks are accompanied by agoraphobia, panic disorder is rarely incapacitating, and it seems to be common (DSM III). In one study of 186 presumably normal young adults, 34.4 percent of the subjects reported one or more panic attacks during the previous year (Norton et al., 1985). The panic symptoms these subjects listed as most severe were heart pounding, trembling, and sweating.

The following statements reflect the research that has attempted to locate links between panic attacks and other disorders:

1. Approximately two-thirds of the individuals with panic disorder also show symptoms of depression (Pines, 1984).
2. Studies of identical twins show a 40 percent risk

to the second twin if one twin suffers from panic attacks; in fraternal twins, the risk is only 5 percent (Pines, 1984).
3. EEG sleep recordings of patients with panic disorder indicate difficulty falling asleep, many nocturnal awakenings, and increased movements. This finding is consistent with findings of other researchers who have discovered chronic physiological arousal in panic disorder patients (Uhde, 1984).
4. The agoraphobia-panic attack syndrome "runs in families" (Agras, 1985).
5. "Children of parents suffering both depression and agoraphobia had twice the risk of experiencing a major depression as children of parents with only depression" (p. 38, Agras, 1985).

These findings and others led researchers to formulate a biological model for explaining panic disorders (Carr & Sheehan, 1984). According to this model, neuroendocrines acting upon a specific location in the brainstem trigger panic attacks. Thomas Udhe, a panic attack researcher at the National Institute of Mental Health, believes that at least 80 percent of the sufferers can expect their symptoms to improve or be cured if they take medication. The cure rate may be even higher if therapy accompanies the medication (Horstman, 1986). In spite of those who posit a biological basis for panic disorders, many psychologists continue to attribute this disorder to traumas and anxieties in childhood or to traumas in adulthood.

Although treatment success is now possible, an interesting question remains. Since the usual anxiety symptoms (physiological changes brought on by the sympathetic nervous system) are most successfully relieved by valium-like (antianxiety) drugs, why is anxiety in the form of panic attacks most successfully treated with antidepressants? Further research is needed to explore the possible biological basis for this disorder and its relationships to other psychological disorders.

Anxiety States (Anxiety Neuroses)

Included in this group of disorders are panic disorder, generalized anxiety disorder, obsessive-compulsive disorder, and post-traumatic stress disorder. Approximately 13.1 million people in the United States suffer from one of the anxiety state disorders or one of the phobias— that is, an astonishing 8.3 percent of the population or one in every twelve persons (see Exhibit 21.3).

The following paragraphs describe types of anxiety states:

— *Generalized Anxiety Disorder.* Individuals diagnosed as having a generalized anxiety disorder show symptoms of what is referred to in everyday language as "nervousness." These people are often shaky, jittery, restless, and unable to relax, and they worry and fear future misfortunes. In addition, these individuals may experience physiological arousal: elevated pulse and respiration, upset stomach, dry mouth, clammy hands, and pounding heart. Many people experience these symptoms for short periods of time preceding or following major events in their lives, but the generalized anxiety disorder diagnosis is not used if the symptoms are a result of a psychosocial stressor or if the symptoms last only several days or a couple of weeks.

— *Obsessive-Compulsive Disorder* (Obsessive-Compulsive Neurosis). Individuals with obsessive-compulsive disorder experience **obsessions** (ideas or images that repeatedly seem to take over thoughts) and/or **compulsions** (senseless behaviors that are performed repeatedly). Initially, at least, the person usually attempts to ignore the thoughts or to resist performing the behaviors.

Examples of obsessions include thoughts of violence against family members and thoughts of being contaminated by germs. Howard Hughes, a reclusive multimillionaire, suffered from both obsessions and compulsions. He was obsessed by a fear of contamination by other people. To avoid contamination, he placed a Kleenex on his hand before he touched another person. He also insisted that his employees perform many elaborate cleansing rituals to assure his safety from their touch and germs (Time, 1976).

Bathing in a repetitive, stereotyped manner is an example of a compulsion. People with bathing compulsions may feel they *have to* complete an entire ritual without error before they can dress. Such a ritual may involve first washing the elbows six times in a clockwise, circular fashion, next washing the arms eight times from

Washing one's hands repeatedly in a ritualistic manner is an example of a compulsion.

hand to shoulder, then washing the torso in six-inch concentric circles, etc. As you can see from these examples, obsessions and compulsions can interfere considerably with a person's social life, work, and interpersonal relationships.

— *Post-Traumatic Stress Disorder (PTSD).* What do rape victims, survivors of World War II death camps, and survivors of airplane crashes and earthquakes have in common? A small number of the people in each group suffer from **post-traumatic stress disorder** (**PTSD**). The symptoms may appear shortly after the triggering event and last less than six months, or they may not appear until years later. Although triggering events may be either contrived (e.g., war) or natural (e.g., flood), they are usually more psychologically traumatic than a typical negative life event such as a death in the family or a car accident.

Symptomatic of post-traumatic stress disorder are repeated recollections of the event. Psychic numbing, another symptom, involves a "dulling of emotional feeling, especially a lessened ability to experience intimacy and tenderness" (DSM III). An individual with this disorder may also complain of anxiety. Additional symptoms include sleep disturbances, nightmares in which the event is relived, depression, and an inability to concentrate.

Another symptom common to survivors of disastrous events or circumstances is guilt. Sometimes termed "survivor's guilt," it may be evidenced in rape victims' statements of "If only I'd done this . . ." or "If I'd fought harder . . . ." Guilt in the form of self-blame may serve a function for rape victims; if they can believe that changing their behaviors would have allowed them to avoid being raped, they can take action. If they see themselves as victims of fate, if they do not believe they could have taken action to avoid or alter the situation, they feel helpless.

People who live through tornadoes, floods, or airplane crashes may feel guilty about surviving when others did not. They may ask, "Why me? What did I do to deserve to live?" Survivors of World War II death camps and certain wartime situations may feel guilty about surviving when others did not or about the actions they took to increase their chances of survival. For example, some death camp survivors violated their moral codes to get enough food to survive. Similarly, some Vietnam veterans experience guilt over not rescuing buddies when doing so would surely have meant their own deaths, or over shooting civilians suspected of carrying grenades. The *Relate* section of Chapter 21 examines PTSD among Vietnam veterans.

Focus Question Answer

Are your anxieties normal, or are they symptoms of an anxiety disorder? The degree to which anxieties interfere with your life is central to the distinction between normal anxiety and anxiety disorders; however, the line between them is not precise. For instance, the line between common fears and phobias is not clear. If you become anxious when you drive across bridges but you continue to cross bridges when necessary, your fear interferes little with your life. If, as a salesperson, you drive many miles out of your way to avoid driving across bridges and you are often late for your appointments, this fear interferes with your life and is a phobia disorder. Similarly, the line between nervousness and generalized anxiety disorder remains unclear.

 ## Other Disorders

Dissociative Disorders

To dissociate means "to separate from," and **dissociative disorders** are a separation from normal consciousness or identity. Included in this category are amnesia, fugue, and multiple personality. **Psychogenic amnesia** is "a sudden inability to recall important personal information" (DSM III). This disorder is most likely to occur in war situations and natural disasters, although it can occur in other situations that an individual believes to be intolerable. Amnesia usually begins suddenly and terminates suddenly.

Another disorder most common in wartime and natural disasters is **fugue**. Following a severely stressful situation, an individual may travel to another location, assume another identity, and be unable to recall his or her former identity. As with amnesia, recovery is often sudden, and fugue rarely recurs. Although frequently seen in soap operas, fugue is in reality rarely diagnosed.

Multiple personality refers to the existence of two or more distinct personalities within one individual. These personalities may be quite different from each other, and stressful events may trigger the transition from the dominance of one personality to another.

During the past several decades, case studies of multiple personality have appeared in books and movies and on television. Although this disorder may have existed for thousands of years, only about two hundred written case reports existed as of 1980; all these dated from the seventeenth century on (Bliss, 1980). The best-known examples of multiple personality in the United States are Eve and Sybil. Told by her therapist, Eve's story reached the public in a book and a movie in 1957; both were titled *The Three Faces of Eve*. Chris Sizemore, the "real" Eve, has since written her own story, *I'm Eve* (1979). Sybil's story was told by her therapist in the book *Sybil* (1973), and Sybil's name became widely recognized following the television movie. Primarily through these two books and movies, the public became aware of multiple personality, despite its rarity.

The DSM III (1980) lists the following features of multiple personality:

1. Within the individual exist two or more distinctly different personalities, each of which has its own behavior patterns and social relationships.
2. An original, or primary, personality and several subpersonalities may be identified. The primary personality

usually has no knowledge of the other personalities.

3. The subpersonalities are almost always very different from the primary personality, and "they" may report being a different sex, a different race, a younger age, or of different parentage.

4. The several personalities may report "losing time"— having no memory for specific times or events.

Individual psychiatrists and psychologists differ greatly on how they view multiple personality. Orne, a prominent expert on hypnosis, believes therapists may be "creating" cases of multiple personality through suggestion (Rogo, 1985). This expert and five other consultants were asked to examine Kenneth Bianchi, who was accused in the Los Angeles Hillside Strangler case (during the fall and winter of 1977 and 1978, the bodies of ten women who had been raped and then strangled were found on various hillsides of Los Angeles County). Orne testified that Bianchi was malingering (faking the disorder) and diagnosed him as an antisocial personality. Ralph Allison, a forensic psychiatrist with ten years of experience identifying and treating multiple personalities, first diagnosed Bianchi as a case of multiple personality and testified to this effect at Bianchi's trial (Allison, 1984). Allison had used the results of hypnosis sessions, IQ tests, handwriting samples, and art creations to argue for a diagnosis of multiple personality. Kenneth (Bianchi's major personality) claimed to have been amnesic to the many murders described and committed by Steve, a subpersonality (Watkins, 1984). In late 1979, Bianchi was sentenced to two consecutive life terms in Washington and six concurrent life terms in California. In 1981, when Allison reexamined old information and considered new evidence, he concluded that his first diagnosis had been incorrect (Allison, 1984).

Some researchers speculate that specific childhood traumas, such as near drowning, a sibling's or parent's death, head injury, or sexual traumas, bring on the first breaks into different personalities (Confer & Ables, 1983). Others suggest that a disturbed family may be a prerequisite for multiple personality. The pathology (disturbance) could involve strong conflicts between parents, sibling rivalry encouraged by the parents, or the death of a favorite parent before the individual is six years old (Confer & Ables, 1983). Yet another explanation is that the young child, usually a girl, begins creating alternate personalities between the ages of four and six in response to intolerable situations such as incest. Although the child does not recognize the process at the time, she creates the personalities through self-

hypnosis and the accompanying amnesia. If she has an alternate personality, she can relegate her unpleasant or forbidden emotional experiences to another, and then she will no longer recall or have to deal with the frightening experience (Confer & Ables, 1983). Alternates or subpersonalities are often responsible for coping with stressful experiences, usually those involving great anger, suicidal actions, or sexual behaviors, the expression of which is forbidden to the individual. The *Exploring . . .* section presents a case study of Rene, a woman diagnosed with multiple personality disorder.

Somatoform Disorders

Somatoform means "taking bodily form," and in **somatoform disorders** psychological conflicts take bodily form. All disorders in this category have the same essential feature of physical symptoms that have no apparent organic explanation. In malingering (feigning physical illness), the reported physical symptoms are under voluntary control; in somatoform disorders, the symptoms are *not*

Hypochondriacs, who are preoccupied with their physical symptoms, may have medicine chests that look like this one.

 *Exploring . . .*

A Case Study of Multiple Personality

A twenty-seven-year-old married woman, Rene had green eyes and auburn hair. She was neat, shy, guilt-ridden, self-effacing, dependent, depressed, sexually repressed, and scared. During therapy sessions, the following information about her family and childhood surfaced.

— Rene's mother attempted suicide when Rene was five; Rene's mother's sister died in a suicide attempt, and Rene's mother's brother was frequently in state mental hospitals.

— Rene's father had a history of alcohol abuse, and one of her brothers drank heavily. Rene's other brother received a psychiatric discharge from the Army.

— Rene's mother beat her, burned her with cigarettes, and held her head under water when she washed Rene's hair.

— Rene witnessed both of her parents having extramarital sexual liaisons.

— Rene's mother gave Rene paregoric and sometimes locked her in the wardrobe when a lover came to the house.

— Rene's mother made sexual advances to both Rene and her brother.

— Rene's grandfather, whom she loved, died when she was five.

— Rene was raped by her father when she was eleven, the same year her parents divorced.

In therapy, Rene spoke about the beginnings of her alternate personalities. She said, "I considered running away. I knew at four years old I was going to be brought back. I ran away several times and I was always brought back. I knew I had to find a way out so the imaginary people started but then they became very real, very real until they were" (p. 70, Confer & Ables, 1983). Here, then, are the alternate personalities that emerged.

— Jeane, whose purpose was to deal with anger and fear, was nineteen years old, wore blue jeans and a T-shirt, had a strong voice, and was a rebellious, spunky, pot-smoking teenager. She was assertive and had a brave facade.

— Stella, whose purpose was to avoid physical abuse, was eighteen years old, seductive and impulsive. To avoid abuse, Stella was placative, flattering, and conciliatory toward Rene's mother and provocative and appealing to Rene's father.

— Bobby, whose purpose was to be aggressive enough to withstand assaults, was twenty years old. He threatened to kill Rene's husband and her parents. His function was to express "black anger."

— Sissy Girl, a four-year-old who played a minor role, was the personality whose head was held under water and who was burned with cigarettes. When she appeared, she sucked her thumb and curled up in a fetal position.

— Mary, whose purpose was to deal with guilt and sadness, was soft-spoken and had the capacity to forgive.

From a case study presented in Confer, W.N. & Ables, B.S. 1983. *Multiple personality: Etiology, diagnosis and treatment.* NY: Human Sciences Press.

---

under voluntary control. The following descriptions illustrate the variety and possible severity of physical symptoms that can be displayed with no disease process present.

— *Hypochondriasis.* In contrast to malingerers, **hypochondriacs** do not fake their illnesses; they unrealistically interpret normal aches and pains as symptoms of more serious illness. Their fears often result in "doctor shopping" and requests for excessive diagnostic procedures, and they often become angry with their doctors, whom they believe do not take them seriously enough or give them enough care.

— *Conversion disorder.* The identifying feature of conversion disorders is the loss of (or change in) physical functioning when no organic damage can be found; examples are paralysis, blindness, and false pregnancy. For instance, a pianist about to make his debut might suddenly find that one of his hands is paralyzed and indeed may show no reaction if someone sticks his "paralyzed" hand with a pin. **Conversion disorder** was more common several decades ago; today it is rare. Its rarity is attributed by some psychologists to people's greater knowledge of how the human body functions; for instance, people may be less likely to experience blindness due to a conversion disorder when they are aware of the many causes of blindness and the physical tests that can detect the causes.

— *Psychogenic pain disorder.* Individuals with **psychogenic pain disorder** experience great pain even though they have no diseases or injuries that account for the pain. They often consult numerous doctors, use painkillers excessively, and assume the role of an invalid.

Quick Study Aid

Somatoform Disorders

Somatoform—Taking bodily form (soma = body).

1. **Hypochondriasis**—Think of "hypos" (injections). Overestimate illness and the need for medical treatment.
2. **Conversion Disorder**—Conversion of psychological stress to physiological malfunctioning.
3. **Psychogenic Pain Disorder**—Pain of psychological origin. No known disease or physical abnormality (psycho = psychological; genic = origin).

Personality Disorders

Personality disorders are characterized by maladaptive, enduring personality traits that are first seen in adolescence or earlier and that last throughout the person's lifetime. These traits are not developed as the result of a specific incident, nor is their expression limited to specific circumstances. For many of the personality disorders (see Exhibit 21.2), the dominant personality trait is clear from the label. For instance, the dominant personality trait of compulsive personality disorder is compulsiveness; similarly, the dominant traits of paranoid, narcissistic, avoidant, and dependent personality disorders are indicated by their labels. Often, the person with a personality disorder is unhappy with his or her behavior and attitude but may seem unable to change, even when he or she tries.

The personality disorder of most obvious concern to society is **antisocial personality disorder**. Individuals with

this disorder, which occurs in males three times as often as in females, display a "history of continuous and chronic antisocial behavior in which the rights of others are violated" (DSM III). People later diagnosed as antisocial personalities often engaged in lying, cheating, stealing, and truancy in childhood. Frequently, before age fifteen, the individual will have been arrested for delinquency, been suspended from school, run away from home several times, chronically violated school and home rules, and initiated fights (DSM III). Adults with this disorder have difficulty remaining employed and maintaining long-term relationships, and they may frequently get into fights. Another noticeable characteristic is impulsive decision-making without consideration of the long-term consequences.

One researcher who reviewed the studies relating childhood and adult antisocial behaviors concluded that children with high rates of antisocial behavior tend to persist in this behavior; in other words, once a high level of such behavior has been established, youths tend to maintain that level rather than drop to lower levels. As children who display antisocial behavior become older (from age six to sixteen), they tend to engage in fewer overtly antisocial acts (fights and disobedience) and more covertly antisocial acts (thefts and use of alcohol and drugs) (Loeber, 1982).

Because behaviors typical of antisocial personality disorder begin so early in life, researchers have looked for genetic links. In this process, the age-old issue of the inheritability of criminality is being reexamined. In the 1960s, the trend was to attribute behavior and personality to environmental factors. In the 1980s, a great emphasis has been placed on biochemical and genetic causes. In a 1985 book, two Harvard professors, Wilson and Herrenstein, maintain that criminals differ from nonoffenders in IQ, body type, personality, and impulsivity (Leo, 1985). With the increasing sophistication of this research, perhaps new answers to an old question will emerge.

Disorders of Impulse Control

Although other disorders such as antisocial personality may involve impulsive behavior, impulsivity is the main symptom of this category of disorders. Included in the **disorders of impulse control** are pathological gambling, kleptomania, pyromania, intermittent explosive disorder, and isolated explosive disorder (DSM III, 1980). Contact with the legal system is one of the major complications stemming from these disorders.

Exploring . . .

A Case of Pathological Gambling

A forty-eight-year-old attorney was interviewed while he was being detained awaiting trial. He had been arrested for taking funds from his firm, which he stated he had fully intended to return after he had a "big win" at gambling. He appeared deeply humiliated and remorseful about his behavior, although he had a previous history of near-arrests for defrauding his company of funds. His father had provided funds to extricate him from these past financial difficulties, but refused to assist him this time. The patient had to resign his job under pressure from the firm. This seemed to distress him greatly since he had worked diligently and effectively at his job, although he had been spending more and more time away from work in order to pursue gambling.

He had gambled on horse racing for many years. He had been losing heavily recently, had resorted to illegal borrowing, and was now being pressured for payment. He stated that he embezzled the money to pay off these illegal debts because the threats of "loan sharks" were frightening him so that he could not concentrate or sleep. He admitted to problems with his friends and wife since he had borrowed from them. They were now alienated and giving him little emotional support. His wife had decided to leave him and live with her parents.

During the interview the patient was tense and restless, at times having to stand up and pace. He

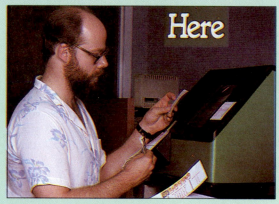

Although many people gamble sometimes or in some places, pathological gamblers are people who continue to gamble despite problems with their jobs, their families, and the law.

said he was having a flare-up of a duodenal ulcer. He was somewhat tearful throughout the interview, and said that although he realized his problems stemmed from his gambling, he still had a strong urge to gamble.

This case study is number 57 from Spitzer, R. L., Slodol, A. E., Gibbon, M., & Williams, J. B. W. 1981. *DSM-III case book.* Washington, DC: American Psychiatric Association. Used with permission.

A similar pattern is seen in all these disorders: a build-up of tension before the behavior, a failure to resist the urge to complete the behavior, and a release of tension or even an experience of pleasure following the behavior. In **pathological gambling** people gamble chronically despite the associated problems with their jobs, marriages, families, and financial situations. Although they may embezzle money or lie to borrow money from friends or relatives, they do intend to repay it. The *Exploring . . .* section contains a case study of a typical compulsive gambler.

Kleptomania involves the impulsive theft of items that are not of immediate use and for which the indi-

viduals usually have enough money to pay. The major problem associated with kleptomania is the possibility of arrest for shoplifting, but very few cases of shoplifting are due to kleptomania. Theft due to kleptomania can be distinguished from ordinary shoplifting in several ways. First, most shoplifting cases involve the theft of objects for personal use or for resale for monetary gain. Further, thefts not due to kleptomania are often carefully planned ahead of time, show no evidence of a failure to resist an impulse, and may involve several people.

In another disorder of impulse control, **pyromania**, a person does not resist his or her impulse to set fires. A person with this rare disorder, which is more common in males than in females, may be recognized because he "hangs around" fires or sets off fire alarms. A very small percentage of arsonists behave in a way that fits the description of an impulse disorder. David Berkowitz, the "Son of Sam" serial murderer, reportedly set more than 2,000 fires and made 337 false alarms in New York City from 1974 through 1977 (Wooden, 1985). Pyromania was only one of several diagnoses assigned to Berkowitz.

Both intermittent and isolated **explosive disorder** involve the loss of control of aggressive impulsives, a loss that frequently results in serious damage to property or physical injury to another person. Individuals so diagnosed often describe their outbursts of aggressive behavior as "spells" or "fits." The behavior between or before episodes does not indicate unusual aggressiveness or impulsivity. Acquaintances or co-workers are often taken by surprise when the individual explodes in a manner they have not seen before and that is out of proportion to the situation.

One case study (DSM III, 1980) involves a forty-four-year-old man with no history of either outbursts of aggressive behavior or hospitalization for mental illness. One day, he unexpectedly attacked a co-worker and beat him to death with an axe. Witnesses said they had observed no previous problems between the two men, who had worked together for fifteen years.

Focus Question Answer

In addition to anxiety, what symptoms might indicate you are suffering from a psychological disorder? The symptoms indicative of the dissociative disorders include amnesia for specific periods of time, inability to recall one's identity, and the display of several personalities that are very different from each other. Indicative of personality disorders are maladaptive, long-lasting personality traits. The major symptom of the impulse disorders is an inability to resist an impulse and a release of tension following the completion of the behavior. Symptoms of other disorders are discussed in Chapter 22.

 *Relate*

Delayed Post-Traumatic Stress Disorder Among Vietnam Vets

How the Vietnam War Was Different

The Vietnam War differed from preceding wars in its psychological casualty rate. During World War II, 23 percent of the evacuations were for psychiatric reasons; in Korea, that rate dropped to 6 percent. In what came as a surprise even to the psychologists and psychiatrists serving in Vietnam, the psychological breakdown of combatants was only twelve per one thousand or 1.2 percent (Bourne, 1970). Few soldiers broke down during their tour of duty, but the number who have experienced psychological symptoms since then is surprising (Goodwin, 1981). Already 200,000 veterans of this most recent war have sought help through the government for PTSD symptoms. Of the 2.8 million Americans who served in Vietnam, one million saw combat duty. Some psychiatrists estimate that as many as 500,000 of these soldiers will eventually request therapy (Langone, 1985).

The high rate of delayed stress reaction among Vietnam veterans has led to research comparing the Vietnam War with other wars. Discussed below are a few of the differences that have been identified.

1. A tour of duty in Vietnam lasted twelve months (thirteen months for Marines); the going-home date was figured for each individual, and whole units were never rotated together. Such individual, prescheduled going-home dates destroyed the *esprit de corps* of the fighting units in Vietnam, but they did help some marginal soldiers cope well enough to go home before serious symptoms emerged (Goodwin, 1981). By contrast, in World War II, whole units went off to war together, fought and sometimes died together, and came home together.

2. Since the average age of the U.S. combat soldier in Vietnam was under twenty, as compared to twenty-six in World War II (Wilson, 1979), Vietnam was the first U.S. war in which the majority of the combat soldiers were teenagers. These young soldiers had not clearly sorted out who they were before their lives were interrupted by the war's traumatic events. When the soldiers returned, many of them felt much older than their age peers who had not been in Vietnam. Many felt they had lost time they could never regain and had had experiences that had changed them permanently.

This memorial, dedicated in 1982 to the veterans of the Vietnam War, provided delayed recognition to these veterans for their service to their country.

3. The trip home for soldiers from Vietnam was sometimes accomplished in an astounding thirty-six hours, and most traveled from rice paddy to the family living room in less than one week (Goodwin, 1981). This quick transition left little time to process the experience and prepare for the adjustment of rejoining society. In contrast, soldiers returning from World War II often came via a ship that took days and sometimes weeks before landing in the United States. Once in the United States, the soldiers boarded troop trains that slowly crossed the country. One by one, these soldiers said goodbye to comrades. While World War II veterans have held reunions and exchanged stories ever since the war ended, rarely have Vietnam veterans attempted to contact those they knew in Vietnam.

4. Soldiers who served in Vietnam returned home to screaming anti-war crowds that called them "baby killers." Peers of those who fought in Vietnam demonstrated against the war; families were often just thankful their soldiers had survived. Because of the country's mixed feelings about the war, Vietnam veterans were usually encouraged to "get on with life," find a job, and act as if nothing had happened. The Vietnam war did not end in victory, nor did it have an official end. The return home for soldiers who served in World War II was very different; veterans found a grateful country, welcoming wives and families, and ticker tape parades to celebrate their victory and their courage.

5. The fighting in Vietnam was unlike that of any other war. In Europe in World War II, the soldiers fought for a piece of ground and claimed it as theirs; in Vietnam, an area could be taken during the day, lost during the night, and retaken again and again. Civilians were not a dangerous part of previous wars; in Vietnam, by contrast, women, children, and old people could be the "enemy," and no one could be trusted. In previous wars, the combatants usually wore uniforms; in Vietnam, the soldiers often could not distinguish between their enemies (the North Vietnamese army), their friends (the South Vietnamese army), and civilians.

Symptoms of Delayed Post-Traumatic Stress Disorder

The symptoms of PTSD among Vietnam veterans are often more severe and may be expressed differently than symptoms experienced by individuals exposed to other traumatic events. The depression felt by the veterans is sometimes accompanied by substance abuse since, in Vietnam, they often learned to numb themselves or dull the pain and anxiety with drugs or alcohol. Veterans with PTSD often remain isolated and fantasize about living "off the land" in the wilderness. A few have made their fantasies into reality; others maintain their isolation by changing jobs and moving frequently. Some of these former soldiers sleep with weapons near them or with their glasses on; they seem unable to leave behind the fears of being taken by surprise by the enemy. Additionally, many feel irritable and full of rage that can explode into violent behavior against those closest to them. Feeling unable to control their anger, some Vietnam veterans with these symptoms question their sanity and walk out of the lives of their families. Wives and other family members of veterans describe a coldness and uncaring quality they sense in the former soldiers. In explanation, some veterans say they had to block out their emotions in order to survive in Vietnam and now are unable to experience those emotions again. A few veterans with this disorder experience "flashbacks" and relive incidents from the past. Flashbacks are often triggered by sounds, smells, or other cues that remind the veterans of Vietnam. These cues may be helicopter sounds, hot, muggy days, or backfiring cars that sound like faraway explosions. All the symptoms they describe may be the result of exposure to very traumatic circumstances at a particularly vulnerable age.

THOUGHTS BY A YOUNG VETERAN

The years others knew as youth, I spent learning the meaning of Death.

The times others spent learning to love, I passed hoping to live through endless nights.

The moments others remember as laughs in classrooms, I remember as terror in the jungle.

The instants of pleasure taken for granted by others, I remember as forgotten hopes—long ago crushed by the reality of war.

The unfulfilled dreams of others are yet to be thought by me since I am in search of my elusive youth, looking for years lost in combat, which are no more—and will never be.

From p. 72 of *Post-traumatic Stress Disorders of the Vietnam Veteran*, ed. by Tom Williams, Psy. D., published by the Disabled American Veterans, 1981.

Help Is Available

The DAV (Disabled American Veterans) provides help through the Vietnam Veterans Outreach Program, and the VA (Veterans Administration) provides help through Operation Outreach (the Vet Center program). Veterans who experience PTSD symptoms are usually encouraged to participate in group therapy with other Vietnam veterans. Group therapy sessions are scheduled at locations other than large office buildings, mental health centers, or VA hospitals and are led by psychotherapists who may also be Vietnam veterans.

Veterans who experience PTSD symptoms often display poor social skills. Through homework assignments, such as joining social groups or socializing with co-workers, and through socializing with and supporting each other, group therapy members can improve their social skills. Physical activities such as jogging or lifting weights may help reduce anxiety symptoms and depression. For sleep disturbances, one experienced group leader (Williams, 1980) recommends a warm bath and a snack at bedtime. He advises veterans who lie awake longer than thirty minutes after retiring or who awaken from nightmares to get up and read or watch television until they are tired. For those who continue to have difficulty sleeping, Williams recommends leaving a light on and sleeping on the floor or a couch.

Partners or wives of veterans with PTSD may benefit greatly from groups for partners of Vietnam veterans. In these groups, partners learn the typical characteristics displayed by the veterans, the reactions of other veterans' partners, and new methods for dealing with the stress in their lives.

Therapy for veterans suffering from PTSD symptoms may involve individual, group, or family sessions, and medications such as Valium may be prescribed. In therapy, veterans improve quickly, but the improvement may not be permanent; nightmares, hyperalertness, and depression may recur. When such symptoms occur in veterans who have participated in group therapy, the veterans will be better able to cope (Wil-liams, 1980). For these veterans, drop-in therapy groups satisfy the need for occasional support from people who understand what they have been through.

Things to Do

1. Arrange an appointment with a nurse or physician in the campus student health center or a counselor at the student counseling center. Question this person regarding the most common psychological problems among the students on your campus.

2. Survey several business owners or managers about their attitudes toward psychological disorders. Because businesspeople are responsible for formulating the policies for hiring personnel and may exert considerable influence in the community, their attitudes are of great importance. The following are questions you could ask in your survey:

a. What causes psychological problems?

b. If a person has been diagnosed as having a psychological disorder, will he or she always be somewhat unstable?

c. If an individual is qualified for a job, how does past psychiatric hospitalization influence your decision to hire this individual?

d. Are people who are receiving outpatient therapy for psychological problems trustworthy?

e. Do you hire people who tell you they have psychological problems or are receiving therapy?

3. Read a biography or autobiography of a person diagnosed as having multiple personalities. *The Three Faces of Eve* by Thigpen and Cleckly, *I'm Eve* by Sizemore, *Sybil* by Schreiber, and *The Minds of Billy Milligan* by Keyes may be the easiest to locate. Ask a librarian to help you locate others.

4. Arrange with your local Vets Center/Vietnam Era to speak with a physician or therapist who deals with Vietnam veterans or nurses suffering from PTSD. Ask this professional to list or describe the symptoms of PTSD. How does this list or description compare with the text description?

Things to Discuss

1. The text includes five models or ways of defining abnormal behavior. Which most closely resembles the way you define abnormality? Cite an example of abnormal behavior as you define it.

2. Do you believe the size and the complexity of the vocabulary used by psychologists and psychiatrists are necessary? Or do they use the vocabulary to maintain an aura of knowledge and magical healing power?

3. Does your experience with people coincide with the results of the NIMH study? Do you know more people who suffer from anxiety than from depression? Do more women than men you know suffer from phobias and depression? Do more men than women you know have problems with alcohol abuse, drug dependence, and anti-social behavior?

4. Discuss with your classmates some of your fears. Are these rational fears or phobias? Do your fears interfere in your life enough for you to consider therapy?

5. Do you consider yourself superior to a person with a psychological disorder? Do you have friends who have sought therapy for psychological disorders? Do you con-sider these friends to be more or less stable and trust-worthy than other friends?

Things to Read

Agras, S. 1985. *Panic: Facing fears, phobias, and anxiety.* NY: W.H. Freeman.

Barlow, D.H. 1985. *Clinical handbook of psychological disorders.* NY: Guilford Press.

Keyes, D. 1981. *The minds of Billy Milligan.* NY: Random House.

Laing, R.D. 1985. *Wisdom, madness and folly.* NY: McGraw-Hill.

Schreiber, F.R. 1973. *Sybil.* Chicago: H. Regenery.

Seidenberg, R. & DeCrow, K. 1983. *Women who marry houses.* NY: McGraw-Hill.

Szasz, T. 1977. *The theology of medicine.* NY: Harper Colophon.

Walker, L.E. 1980. *The battered woman.* NY: Harper & Row.

Review

Summary

1. Five models that illustrate the many ways of defining abnormal behavior are the statistical model, the ideal state model, the personal distress model, the cultural or situational model, and the medical model.

2. The influence of the medical model is evident in the *Diagnostic and Statistical Manual of Mental Disorders, Third Edition* (1980). This manual is the most widely used diagnostic system in the U.S. and includes the termi-nology used by most psychologists and psychiatrists.

3. Anxiety disorders are characterized by apprehension, tension, and uneasiness. Included are the phobic dis-orders, post-traumatic stress disorder, panic disorder, generalized anxiety disorder, and obsessive-compulsive disorder.

4. The characteristic symptom of dissociative disorders is a separation from normal consciousness or identity. This group of disorders includes amnesia, fugue, and multiple personality.

5. The central feature of somatoform disorders is physical symptoms with no organic cause. The category includes hypochondriasis, conversion disorder, and psychogenic pain disorder.

6. Personality disorders are characterized by maladap-tive, enduring personality traits that begin in adoles-cence or earlier. Antisocial personality disorder involves delinquent behavior in childhood and adolescence and, in adulthood, involves a poor work record, felony arrests, and aggressive behavior.

7. Disorders of impulse control—pathological gambling, kleptomania, pyromania, and the explosive disorders—involve a pattern of tension build-up, a failure to resist completing the behavior, and a release of tension fol-lowing the behavior.

8. Delayed post-traumatic stress disorder involves stress symptoms, chronic or delayed, experienced as a reaction to an unusually psychologically traumatic event (war, rape, natural disaster, etc.). The symptoms include in-trusive recollections, nightmares, depression, anxiety, and aggressive behavior.

9. The symptoms of and information about psycholog-ical disorders are often complex and cannot be ade-quately summarized in a few phrases; reread the sections in the text when the summary statement does not stim-ulate your memory.

Key Terms

statistical model
ideal state model
personal distress model
cultural or situational model
medical model
diagnosis
prognosis
DSM III
neuroses
psychoses
anxiety
phobias
agoraphobia
panic attack
obsessions
compulsions

post-traumatic stress disorder (PTSD)
psychogenic amnesia
fugue
multiple personality
somatoform disorders
hypochondriasis
conversion disorder
psychogenic pain disorder
personality disorders
antisocial personality disorder
disorders of impulse control
pathological gambling
kleptomania
pyromania
explosive disorder

Focus Questions

1. What distinguishes normal mood changes from mood swings characteristic of the affective disorders?

2. What symptoms might you experience if you suffered from schizophrenia?

3. Which theories attempt to explain why an individual becomes schizophrenic?

4. How can a family help a schizophrenic family member?

Chapter Outline

Chapter 22

Mental Illness

O' darkness!
O' in vain!
O' I am very sick and sorrowful.
Walt Whitman

What is being "crazy" like? What is "madness" or "possession"? Generally, until the late 1800s, religious definitions of mental illness prevailed. Mental illness was defined as possession by evil spirits or the devil, and the treatments included beatings and drownings, confinement in straightjackets and dungeons, and isolation in asylums. What characteristics of mental illness so frighten and alarm societies that such drastic measures are taken? Chapter 22 discusses the symptoms of what are sometimes termed the severe mental disorders—the affective (mood), paranoid, and schizophrenic disorders. Of these, the paranoid and schizophrenic disorders and part of the affective disorders are **psychoses**, mental disorders whose shared symptom is a difficulty in determining what is real. The remaining affective disorders are characterized

539

**EXHIBIT 22.1
Madness: A Poet's Perspective**

> ### Much Madness Is Divinest Sense
> **Emily Dickinson**
>
> Much Madness is Divinest sense—
> To a discerning Eye—
> Much Sense—the starkest Madness—
> 'Tis the Majority
> In this, as All, prevails—
> Assent, and you are sane—
> Demur—you're straightway dangerous—
> And handled with a Chain—

by mood disturbances but not by difficulties determining reality; the nonpsychotic affective disorders are the first topic in this chapter.

Affective Disorders

Dysthymic and Cyclothymic Disorders

The major characteristic of dysthymic and cyclothymic disorders is a mood disturbance lasting at least two years. During this time, people may display short periods (a couple of months, at most) of normal mood. People diagnosed with either of the disorders exhibit no difficulty distinguishing what is real from what is not; in other words, they are not psychotic.

Dysthymic disorder The prefix *dys-* means "diseased" or "bad," and dysthymic disorder consists of a long-term "bad" or depressive mood. Usually, the depressive mood comes on gradually and is not preceded by a specific traumatic event. Individuals with dysthymic disorder experience feelings of sadness, lose interest in their surroundings, and lose their pleasure in living. Generally, this type of depression begins in early adulthood.

Cyclothymic disorder The prefix *cyclo-* means a "cycle" or "up and down fluctuation"; cyclical or up and down mood swings characterize this disorder. The down, or depressive, phase resembles dysthymic disorder; in other words, people feel pessimistic about the future, cry, withdraw socially, feel fatigued, and often suffer sleep dis-

turbances (DSM III). During the up, or manic, phase, people experience the reverse symptoms; they overestimate their accomplishments, need less sleep, possess more energy, act inappropriately friendly and chatty, and may spend money recklessly or make foolish business investments (DSM III).

The mood changes that most people display periodically do not fit the definitions discussed above. For most people, mood swings follow stressful events in their lives and last for periods much shorter than two years. If you do not get a promotion you really wanted or quarrel seriously with a friend or spouse, or if your possessions are damaged by a natural disaster, you may experience depression. If you are accepted to the college of your choice, become engaged, or win at the racetrack, you may experience great elation. As you react to other events in your life, you may become anxious, depressed, or withdrawn or experience a mixture of these symptoms. Such mood disturbances may interfere temporarily with your ability to function as you had previously functioned, but within weeks or months you will probably return to your former functioning level. The term used for these temporary, event-induced mood disturbances is **adjustment disorders**; the term itself implies that people are going through a period of adjustment, and although they are currently having difficulties, they will soon return to their former functioning levels. The following section discusses mood changes that are more extreme and are more likely to disrupt a person's life.

Most people experience periods of depression that last for several hours, days, or weeks. Compared to their peers, young college students experience a high level of depression.

Major Affective Disorders

Although most people's moods range from elation to depression, a small number of people experience prolonged extreme moods. These prolonged extremes of mood—either manic episodes or major depressive episodes—are termed **major affective disorders**; they can disrupt a person's life, career, family, and social patterns. In a six-month period, approximately 3 percent of the U.S. population, or 4.3 million American adults, suffer from a severe affective disorder (Myers et al., 1984). About one out of every four Americans will experience a severe affective disturbance some time in their lives (Lobel & Hirschfeld, 1984).

Manic Episodes   Have you ever felt so restless you could not sit down or sleep your usual amount, so talkative you had to find someone to listen, or so full of ideas you couldn't keep your mind on one subject? Then you have experienced, at least for a short time, the symptoms of mania. **Mania** is diagnosed when the symptoms described above persist for more than one week and are accompanied by inflated self-esteem, distractibility, and involvement in activities that are likely to entail negative consequences (DSM III). Manic individuals may exhibit difficulties with their perceptions of reality; these psychotic symptoms include delusions (false beliefs) and hallucinations (false perceptions).

Manic individuals may call their friends at all hours and be unaware of their intrusiveness and the inconvenience they cause. They may give advice freely and at length on subjects about which they have no expertise. They may start new businesses on the spur of the moment or paint or compose what they are certain will be masterpieces. One midwestern woman, for example, purchased a greenhouse and had it moved to her home, began a macrame business, and purchased several cockatoos for breeding purposes—all during one manic episode. She paid little attention to her inability to afford these ventures and spoke confidently of her business acumen and her certainty of success. During her **manic episodes**, the woman rarely consulted her husband about her expenditures, and financial and legal difficulties often arose.

Depressive Episodes   **Depressive episodes** are characterized by feelings of sadness, worthlessness, and guilt or by loss of interest or pleasure in all or almost all of that which formerly gave joy. (An inability to experience pleasure or joy is termed **anhedonia**.) Other symptoms of depression include changes in appetite and sleep patterns, feelings of fatigue regardless of how much one has slept, and inability to think clearly or to make decisions. Many depressed people think frequently about death, and they may attempt suicide. The *Exploring* . . . section provides information about suicide rates, warning signs, and ways in which you can help someone who has expressed suicidal thoughts.

Bipolar Disorder and Major Depression

Four distinct diagnoses are included in the severe mood disorders. A person who experiences one or more manic episodes is diagnosed as having a **bipolar disorder**, manic (even though he or she has never experienced a depressive episode). A person who experiences one or more depressive episodes but has never had a manic episode is diagnosed as having a **major depression**. A person who is currently depressed but has had at least one previous manic episode is diagnosed bipolar disorder, depressed. Finally, if a person exhibits both manic and depressive symptoms at the same time or in rapidly alternating periods, the diagnosis is bipolar disorder, mixed. The common term for bipolar disorder is manic-depression.

George Frederick Handel, the great eighteenth century composer who wrote The Messiah, *suffered from manic-depression.*

Exploring . . .

Suicide Information

Have you ever thought of committing suicide? If so, you are not alone. Most people occasionally have thoughts like: "The struggle isn't worth it any more"; "Everything seems hopeless"; "Everyone would be better off without me"; "There is no other way out of this dilemma." Each year in the United States, 200,000 people attempt suicide, and at least 25,000 are "successful" (Wetzel, 1984). This statistic indicates that five million living Americans have attempted suicide (Ornstein, 1985).

Although suicide attempts are usually associated with depression, psychotic individuals are also at risk because they may respond to hallucinations or delusions directing them to kill themselves. Suicide is attempted by people of all ages; victims are as young as five years of age and as old as eighty-five or more. The following list summarizes the known facts about suicide in the United States (Wetzel, 1984):

— 12 percent of all suicide attempts are made by adolescents.

— Suicide is the number two cause of death among teenagers.

— The highest suicide rate is among white elderly males over sixty-five (at highest risk are white males over eighty-five).

— Among the middle-aged and elderly, the suicide rate for whites is three times that for blacks.

— The higher an individual is on the social ladder, the greater the risk of suicide.

— Women are five times as likely as men to attempt suicide.

— Three times more men than women commit suicide.

— Men select more lethal methods (hanging, jumping, drowning, guns) than women (pills, gas, poison, cutting veins).

— One-fourth of all suicides are associated with alcohol abuse.

— Suicide is the seventh most common cause of death.

— A person hospitalized for depression sometime during his or her life is thirty times more likely to

San Francisco's Golden Gate Bridge, from which numerous people attempt suicide each year, has a telephone in the middle; from it suicidal people can call for help.

commit suicide than a nondepressed person (Sargent & Swearingen, 1983).

Warning Signs

No behavior or warning sign is displayed by all people who attempt suicide; however, several signs are commonly exhibited by suicidal people. First, many people indicate verbally that they want to die or are unable to bear living any more, or they refer to how others will feel after their deaths. A second warning sign is self-injurious acts, even if the acts do not seem serious at the time. Other warning signs include giving away possessions, setting one's affairs in order, or suddenly making a will; these behaviors may indicate the person has decided to act. Situations that may precede suicide attempts include injuries that impair a person's ability to function as he or she previously did, surgeries that mutilate the person, or notification the person has cancer or another seriously debilitating illness.

What Can a Friend Do?

Listen. Listening with empathy means trying to step into another person's shoes and see the world through his or her eyes; empathic listening also includes temporarily withholding judgment and advice. Saying "Chin up" or "Things aren't as bad as they seem" is

The first episode in the course of a bipolar disorder is typically experienced between the ages of twenty-five and thirty (Perris, 1982), and 20 percent of first episodes occur before the age of twenty (Jefferson, 1982). The initial episode of a bipolar disorder is often a manic episode, and most people suffer several recurrences of both manic and depressive episodes (Consensus Development Panel on Mood Disorders, 1985). Although people diagnosed as bipolar disorder (as opposed to major depression) experience shorter episodes of mood disturbance, they have a higher mortality rate from suicide and other causes (Perris, 1982).

inappropriate when a friend or family member has expressed suicidal thoughts. You should respond to statements or actions like those described above as possible indicators of suicidal intent.

A common myth states that asking people if they have thought about suicide will give them ideas they did not already have. Since no support for this myth exists, you may wish to ask the person directly about suicidal thoughts and intentions. The seriousness of people's intentions *may* be reflected by whether or not they have acquired the means necessary to attempt suicide. If you listen with empathy after you ask about suicidal intentions, your concern and your willingness to discuss an otherwise taboo subject may act as deterrents; the person may feel a renewed closeness to another human being.

One short-term way to deal with a suicidal person is to elicit a promise that he or she will abstain from any personal harm for a specified time period. This approach can serve two purposes. First, many people are unwilling, even when they are desperately depressed and considering suicide, to break their promises. Second, this approach delays a suicidal action; since the situation may change or the depression may lift, this delay could save the person's life. Even of those who have unsuccessfully attempted suicide once, only 10 percent kill themselves at a later time (Wekstein, 1979).

Finally, providing information about crisis or suicide telephone counseling, mental health centers, or therapists may be helpful. If you follow these guidelines and the person still attempts or completes suicide, you will have helped as best you could. If a friend or family member has attempted or committed suicide, you may find the following excerpt helpful:

Remember, whoever you may be—professional helper, friend, or lover—we cannot *solve* the problems of others, nor can we make decisions for them. We can only respect and care for them, offering ourselves as a calm, stable fellow traveller who reaches out to their own core of stability. Given this much, they will do the rest, usually (though not always) choosing life (Wetzel, 1984, p. 310).

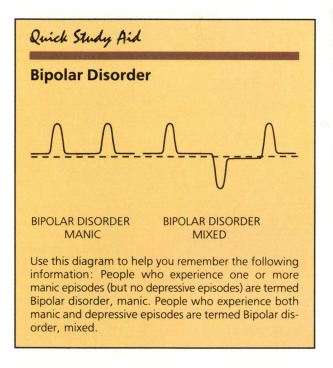

Quick Study Aid

Bipolar Disorder

BIPOLAR DISORDER
MANIC

BIPOLAR DISORDER
MIXED

Use this diagram to help you remember the following information: People who experience one or more manic episodes (but no depressive episodes) are termed Bipolar disorder, manic. People who experience both manic and depressive episodes are termed Bipolar disorder, mixed.

The first episodes for individuals suffering from major depression typically occur between the ages of forty and forty-five (Perris, 1982), and at least twice as many women as men suffer from major depression. A person's risk of recurrent episodes of major depression after he or she has suffered one episode is estimated at approximately 60 percent (Coryell & Winokur, 1982).

Some individuals suffering from major depression or from bipolar disorders have episodes of affective disturbances separated by periods of normal mood and functioning; these normal moods may last many years. Others suffer from clusters of episodes of affective disturbance, and still others experience an increased frequency of episodes as they grow older (DSM III).

Severe affective disturbances are well-documented, both historically and cross-culturally, among the rich and the poor, the educated and uneducated, and people in all professions (see Exhibit 22.2 on depression among literary figures). Treatments for the affective disorders (including psychotherapy and medications) are discussed in Chapters 23 and 24. Most mental health practitioners now acknowledge that antidepressant medications and lithium (used primarily to treat bipolar disorder) can substantially reduce both the frequency and the severity of manic and depressive episodes.

Etiology of the Affective Disorders

Psychodynamic, cognitive, and other theories about the origin or cause of psychological problems seem to readily explain normal or less severe mood changes. In contrast, the research on the major affective disorders indicates a genetic inheritability factor. Although children of people with bipolar disorders experience no higher incidence of nonaffective psychological disorders, they definitely experience a higher incidence of affective disorders. However, their mood swings may be much less severe than those characteristic of bipolar disorders (Klein et al.,

EXHIBIT 22.2
Depression among Literary Figures

Thomas Wolfe (1900-1938), an American novelist, said, "We who dwell in the heart of solitude are always the victims of self-doubt."

"....all of the joy and singing of the day goes out like an extinguished candle, hope seems to me lost forever, and every trust that I have ever found and known seems false." (*God's Lonely Man.*)

Virginia Wolfe (1882-1941), an English novelist, suffered severe depression on and off until she finally killed herself by walking into a river with stones in her pockets. She believed that her severe depression was essential to her work.

Franz Kafka (1883-1924), an Austrian novelist, suffered depression for months on end. His sense of helplessness guided his work, which is suffused with gloominess and futility.

John Keats (1795-1821), an English poet, wrote:
"Darkling I listen; and, for many a time I have been half in love with easeful death." (*Ode to a Nightingale*)

Johann Wolfgang von Goethe (1749-1832), a German poet and dramatist, declared at the end of his life that his life had been "nothing but pain and burden, and I can affirm that during the whole of my seventy-five years, I have not had four weeks of genuine well-being. It is but the perpetual rolling of a rock that must be raised up again forever."

Leo Tolstoy (1828-1910), a Russian novelist (author of *War and Peace*) and philosopher, wrote, "I felt that something had broken within me on which my life had always rested, that I had nothing left to hold on to, and that morally my life had stopped. . . . I did not know what I wanted. I was afraid of life; I was driven to leave it; and in spite of that I still hoped for something from it." (*My Confession.*)

Dorothy Parker (1893-1967), an American writer, wrote: "Razors pain you, Rivers are damp, Acids stain you, And drugs cause cramp. Guns aren't lawful, Nooses give, Gas smells awful, You might as well live." (*Résumé*)

Tennessee Williams (1912-1983), an American dramatist, wrote the following after his play, *Glass Menagerie*, became a success: "I was unaware of how much vital energy had gone into this struggle until the struggle was removed. I was out on a level plateau with my arms still thrashing and my lungs still grabbing at air that no longer resisted. This was security at last. I sat down and looked about me and was suddenly depressed."

"I was walking around dead in my shoes, and I knew it but there was no one I knew or trusted sufficiently, at that time, to take him aside and tell him what was the matter." ("On a Streetcar Named Success, "*The New York Times,* November 30, 1947)

Herman Hesse (1877-1962), a German novelist, wrote, "Every occasion when a mask was torn off, an ideal broken, was preceded by this hateful vacancy and stillness, this deathly constriction and loneliness and unrelatedness, this waste and empty hell of lovelesssness and despair." (*Steppenwolf*)

1985). The research concerning the inheritability of major depressive disorder, although less clear than the research on bipolar disorder, also indicates a genetic factor.

Another hypothesis about the etiology of affective disorders involves the brain substances, the neurotransmitters. The following hypotheses regarding the two most frequently implicated neurotransmitters, norepinephrine and serotonin, are supported by research: (1) norepinephrine depletion causes depression; (2) serotonin depletion causes depression; (3) depletion of both norepinephrine and serotonin causes depression; (4) norepinephrine depletion with normal levels of serotonin causes depression; and (5) serotonin depletion with normal levels of norepinephrine causes depression (Wetzel, 1984). In spite of such support, research findings are inconsistent, and no single neurotransmitter theory adequately accounts for the causation of the affective disorders. The most recent evidence emphasizes the interactions between different processes.

A further indicator of physiological differences between severely depressed and normal people has been found. When dexamethasone (synthetic cortisone) is administered to subjects from both groups, nondepressed individuals react by suppressing the secretion of cortisol (an adrenal secretion), and depressed individuals react by increasing their cortisol level after a brief suppression of it. Researchers have developed the dexamethasone suppression test (the DST) in the hope of being able to predict depression or suicidal behavior, but because other illnesses, including a family history of bipolar disorder, increases the rate of positive results the test cannot yet be used to identify depression. Further research may increase the usefulness of the DST's application.

Current research on the affective disorders has concentrated on identifying genetic and biochemical factors. This research has been applied to the development of medications to control the symptoms and reduce the length and severity of manic and depressive episodes. Despite the obvious value of this research, genetic and biochemical factors cannot, by themselves, explain or predict which individuals will suffer from an affective disorder. Life events, levels of stress, coping skills, and other factors also contribute to an individual's risk factor.

Focus Question Answer

What distinguishes normal mood changes from mood swings characteristic of the affective disorders? The two major distinctions are the length and the severity of the mood change. Most people experience mood changes that last days or even weeks, but the symptoms are not severe enough so they interfere markedly with people's ability to function. Another criterion is the presence of an event preceding the mood change; mood changes that are severe, lengthy, and not preceded by significant life events are more characteristic of affective disorders.

The Schizophrenias

Schizophrenia is most accurately described as a group of disorders with a few shared features as well as distinguishing features for each subtype. Schizophrenic disorders typically begin in late adolescence or early adulthood and are equally common among females and males. In three-fourths of the cases, the onset of symptoms occurs between the ages of sixteen and twenty-five; development of the schizophrenic disorders after the age of thirty is uncommon. Paranoid schizophrenia, in which the onset is usually later, provides the exception to this rule (Torrey, 1983).

A therapist diagnoses schizophrenia only if the individual has experienced symptoms of the disorder for at least six months. The course of the schizophrenias consists of an acute phase followed by a residual phase, in which the individual returns, at least partially, to his or her former functioning level. The number of acute episodes, the amount of recovery to previous functioning levels, and the number of times a person is hospitalized depend upon the person's life stressors, social environment, compliance with medication routines, and other factors.

Symptoms of Schizophrenia

Rarely will one person experience all (or even most) of the following symptoms. In an individual, several specific symptoms may be almost continuously present, while other symptoms may rarely or never be present. Because each person is unique, symptom patterns vary widely.

During the period preceding the first active phase and during the residual phase(s), sufferers may be withdrawn and socially isolated. Family members or friends may observe an odd emotional quality (either inappropriate emotional reactions or little emotional reaction), peculiar behaviors (such as talking to themselves), and odd ideas or speech patterns. Individuals with schizophrenia may exhibit decreased interest in personal hygiene and grooming and decreased ability to effectively handle their studies or their work environments.

Recent studies indicate that poor community and interpersonal functioning often precede the development of schizophrenic disorders (Wallace, 1984). Inadequate social and problem-solving skills and less supportive social networks may cause people to experience greater stress from life events. This additional stress, combined with a vulnerability to schizophrenia and poor coping skills, may then trigger a schizophrenic episode (Lukoff et al., 1984).

One symptom of the active phase of schizophrenia is **illusions**, alterations of the senses causing real external events to be misperceived. An example of an illusion is perceiving the sound of the wind as thousands of people clapping.

Another symptom of schizophrenia is feeling overwhelmed by numerous thoughts or chains of thought at the same time. A response consistent with one of the chains of thought may seem inappropriate or nonsensical to an observer (see Exhibit 22.3 for a poetic description of this symptom). Often, people with schizophrenia have particular difficulty sorting out messages when the incoming messages are complex and arrive simultaneously on different sensory channels.

Delusions, another symptom of the active phase of schizophrenia, are false beliefs about the external world, beliefs that an individual firmly maintains despite an absence of supporting evidence (Exhibit 22.4 provides a first-person account of delusions). Five types of delusions are defined below:

— *Delusions of persecution.* The individual believes he is being persecuted or conspired against by a person or

EXHIBIT 22.3
Schizophrenia: A Thought Disorder

I Felt a Cleaving in My Mind
Emily Dickinson

I felt a Cleaving in my Mind—
*   As if my Brain had split—*
I tried to match it—Seam by Seam—
*   But could not make them fit.*

The thought behind, I strove to join
*   Unto the thought before—*
But Sequence ravelled out of Sound
*   Like Balls—upon a Floor.*

EXHIBIT 22.4
Delusions: A Personal Account

David began to suspect and then perceive that a federal agency was observing him. From a moment of insight explaining many peculiar, recent events in his life, he knew that he had been accused of treason for slandering Americans during his psychotherapy. Specifically, he had told his psychiatrist that Americans were debasing him "like Nazis." Wondering whether the Federal Bureau of Investigation was observing him, David decided to employ his telepathic powers to find out. An agent at a local agency told him there was no investigation. David read the agent's mind, however, and determined that the Central Intelligence Agency was conducting an investigation. [The author described his emotions and thoughts in the third person "to convey a sense of my psychological distance from the experience".]

SOURCE: Zelt, D. 1981. First person account: The Messiah Quest. *Schizophrenia Bulletin, 7,* 527-532.

group (e. g., he is being followed by FBI agents).

— *Delusions of grandeur.* The individual believes she is a very important person (e. g., she is a savior or a queen).

— *Somatic delusions.* The individual believes his body functioning is changed (e. g., he has no stomach, or his body is rotting).

— *Delusions of being controlled.* The individual believes she is under the control of an outside agent (e. g., she is controlled by radio waves from Russia).

— *Delusions of reference.* The individual believes stimuli in the environment have a particular significance for him (e. g., commercials on television are giving him personal messages).

Hallucinations, yet another symptom of schizophrenia, are sensory perceptions in the absence of external stimulation; they may be associated with any of the sense organs. Auditory (hearing) hallucinations are most common, but people have also described visual (sight), gustatory (taste), olfactory (smell), and tactile (touch) hallucinations. Many hallucinations are negative; for example, people may hear accusatory voices, smell foul odors, or taste unpleasant flavors in the foods they eat.

A person suffering from schizophrenia often experiences an altered sense of self, a feeling of unreality or hollowness or a questioning of his or her identity. Some schizophrenics become fearful of absorbing others or being absorbed into others; this fear, sometimes referred to as a loss of ego boundaries, results in a person losing a sense of separateness and losing awareness of where he or she ends and another person begins.

Affect, the moment-to-moment expression of emotion, is often altered by schizophrenia. Affect may be *blunted* (a lessened range and intensity of emotional expression), *flattened* (a lack of expressed emotion), or *inappropriate* to the situation (laughing upon being told sad news). Many psychological disturbances are characterized by changed affect, and this symptom, if not accompanied by several others, is never enough evidence to diagnose schizophrenia.

Another change, behavior change, may include a reduction in spontaneous movement and repeated, apparently purposeless movements. In addition to the symptoms described above, people with schizophrenia often speak illogically or incoherently. They may switch from one unrelated subject to another, without realizing they make little sense to listeners.

These symptoms, then, characterize the schizophrenias (Exhibit 22.5 presents a very personal account of the experience). Remember that no single symptom is present in all cases. More important, remember that if people who have been diagnosed as schizophrenic are not in an active phase and have regained an adequate functioning level, the disorder may not be apparent to observers.

Types of Schizophrenia

The **disorganized type** of schizophrenia is distinguished by incoherent speech, by social impairment, and often by silly affect. Individuals with disorganized schizophrenia may display odd behaviors (such as grimaces), and they may giggle or snicker to themselves almost continuously.

The **catatonic type** of schizophrenia is characterized by very excited behavior, stuporous behavior, or an alternation of the two states. During excited phases, catatonic schizophrenics may yell or sing and exhibit greatly increased motor activity, and they may pose a threat to their caretakers. During quiet phases, they sit staring

EXHIBIT 22.5
Symptoms of Schizophrenia: A Personal Account

But I'm still searching, questioning—looking inside now rather than on the library shelves—just wanting to feel a little comfortable. I know all the negatives: Schizophrenia is painful, and it is craziness when I hear voices, when I believe that people are following me, wanting to snatch my very soul. I am frightened too when every whisper, every laugh is about me; when newspapers suddenly contain curses, four-letter words shouting at me; when sparkles of light are demon eyes. Schizophrenia is frustrating when I can't hold onto thoughts; when conversation is projected on my mind but won't come out of my mouth; when I can't write sentences but only senseless rhymes; when my eyes and ears drown in a flood of sights and sounds...and on and on, always more.....

SOURCE: McGrath, M. E. 1984. First person account: Where did I go? *Schizophrenia Bulletin, 10*, 638-640.

and unblinking as if they are in a stupor. Also during the quiet phase, these sufferers may assume odd postures from which they resist outside attempts to reposition them.

People diagnosed as having **paranoid type** schizophrenia suffer less social impairment than do people with other types of schizophrenia. The identifying characteristics are delusions of grandeur and persecution or delusional jealousy. People who display delusional jealousy may repeatedly accuse their spouses of unfaithfulness, despite a lack of any supporting evidence.

Undifferentiated type schizophrenia is a catch-all diagnosis for people who display obvious psychotic symptoms but do not fit the descriptions of the previous diagnoses. A final type of schizophrenia, **residual type**, refers to clients who have been previously diagnosed as schizophrenic but are currently experiencing no psychotic symptoms. As you can see, the schizophrenias share several common symptoms and, in addition, are characterized by specific symptom patterns.

Schizoaffective Disorder

A decades-old debate continues to rage over the existence of **schizoaffective disorder** which, in the past, was included with the schizophrenias. This diagnosis refers to individuals whose symptoms are a mixture of schizophrenic symptoms and affective (mood) disorder symptoms. According to some clinicians, schizoaffective disorder should not be a separate diagnostic category because, they maintain, it is a variation of the affective disorders. Genetic studies support this theory by showing a larger contribution to the transmission of the disorder

---

Quick Study Aid

Symptoms of Schizophrenia

Hallucinations = False Perceptions
Illusions = Misperceptions
Delusions = False Beliefs

Use these brief definitions to help you remember the definitions of three of the major symptoms of schizophrenia.

from the affective disorders than from the schizophrenic disorders (Abrams, 1984). Other experts view the psychoses as a continuum with schizophrenia at one end, the affective disorders at the other end, and schizoaffective disorder midway between the two. Long-term outcome studies indicate that schizoaffective individuals fare better than those diagnosed as schizophrenic, but they fare significantly worse than individuals with affective disorders (Tsuang & Simpson, 1984).

This issue, like many others in the study of mental illness, has several sides, and research can be cited to support all positions. Regardless of the continuing debate, the schizoaffective diagnosis will continue to be used, and some individuals will continue to show this puzzling mixture of symptoms.

Prognosis in Schizophrenia

Prognosis refers to the probable course or outcome of a disorder or the probability the sufferer will recover. Numerous variables affect the prognosis of an individual who has been diagnosed as schizophrenic. No single variable by itself predicts prognosis, but, taken together, the following variables are predictive (Torrey, 1983):

1. Good prognosis—if the individual exhibited normal social interactions and school success before the onset of symptoms.
2. Good prognosis—if the family has no history of schizophrenia. The greater the number of close relatives with schizophrenia, the poorer the prognosis.
3. Poor prognosis—if the onset of symptoms occurred when the individual was young (the onset of schizophrenia symptoms usually occurs between ages sixteen and twenty-five).
4. Good prognosis—if the onset of symptoms was sudden. If onset was gradual and occurred over a period of months or years, the prognosis is poor.
5. Good prognosis—if the onset of symptoms was immediately preceded by a major life event or crisis.
6. Good prognosis—if the individual suffers from catatonic or paranoid symptoms or if depression and other emotions are present.
7. Poor prognosis—if the individual has flattened affect or an absence of expressed emotion.

Although an individual's symptoms and his or her history prior to the onset of schizophrenia symptoms can be used to predict that individual's prognosis, these factors do not predict the general prognosis for people diagnosed as schizophrenic. Based on an examination of twenty-five studies of long-term outcomes, one researcher found what is sometimes called "the rule of thirds." Approximately one-third of the patients hospitalized and diagnosed as schizophrenic will have recovered completely ten years later. Approximately one-third will have improved but not recovered completely, and the final third will probably remain unimproved ten years later (Torrey, 1983). The *Exploring . . .* section examines the course of the illnesses of four identical quadruplets, all of whom have been diagnosed as schizophrenic.

Because of the rapid development of new drugs for the treatment of psychoses, "the rule of thirds" may be overly negative. Before the 1950s, a person who developed psychotic symptoms was likely to spend twenty, forty, or even sixty years in a hospital. Now, except for a small minority of the most severe cases, most people with schizophrenia will be hospitalized only when their symptoms become severe, and they will spend most of their lives outside hospitals.

Focus Question Answer

What symptoms might you experience if you suffered from schizophrenia? During an active phase of schizophrenia, you might experience illusions, delusions, and overwhelming numbers of thoughts, as well as changes in your moods, thoughts, perceptions, and behaviors. During a residual phase, you would not experience these symptoms. Some schizophrenic individuals, whose symptoms come and go, are able to function well for large portions of their lives.

 ## The Etiology of Schizophrenia

Varying degrees of support exist for theories about the **etiology** (cause or origin) of schizophrenia. The theories can be divided into three types: genetic, experiential, and physical (physiological or biochemical). To date, no single theory successfully explains why particular individuals become schizophrenic and why some schizophrenic individuals suffer from a more severe or chronic course of the illness than others.

Genetic Theories

At the turn of the century, many physicians who treated schizophrenia considered it a brain disorder rather than a psychological disorder. For example, in his early works, Freud wrote that he did not think schizophrenia could be treated by psychoanalysis. Later, in 1938, Franz Kallman published a study titled *The Genetics of Schizophrenia.* Although he couldn't prove a genetic predisposition for schizophrenia, his results indicated his belief in a genetic cause.

The Research Process below summarizes research findings about the familial transmission of schizophrenia. At this point, the support for a hereditary predisposition to schizophrenia seems undeniable. Individuals with family histories of schizophrenia possibly inherit greater or lesser degrees of susceptibility, and stress, illness, poor nutrition, and life crises then combine with their susceptibility and lead to the development of the disorder.

The Research Process:
Genetics and Schizophrenia

The genetic research on schizophrenia has taken many forms, one of which is **family pedigree** studies. In this type of genetic study, the incidence of schizophrenia is traced through several generations of the same family. In a second type of genetic study, **risk studies**, investigators survey the blood relatives of schizophrenic individuals and compare the incidence results to those of a matched group of nonschizophrenic individuals. For example, in one study, researchers surveyed the families of eighty-four chronic schizophrenics. The rate of chronic schizophrenia in the blood relatives of chronic schizophrenics was 7.1 percent, while the rate of chronic schizophrenia in the relatives of the control group was

This eighteenth century illustration, from The Rake's Progress *by William Hogarth, shows the interior of Bedlam, a public madhouse that housed London's mentally ill beginning in 1676.*

For at least one hundred years, the hospital was a popular resort for London sightseers who paid a small fee to see the lunatics.

Exploring . . .

The Genain Quadruplets

The Genain quadruplets first came to the attention of the National Institute of Mental Health when they were twenty-four years old. To protect their privacy, they were given aliases that represent the initials of the institute (NIMH); they became known as Nora (birth weight 4 lbs. 8 oz.), Iris (birth weight 3 lbs. 5 oz.), Myra (birth weight 4 lbs. 4 oz.), and Hester (birth weight 3 lbs.). Because all the identical quadruplets have been diagnosed as schizophrenic, they have provided a rare opportunity to study the genetic and environmental causes of schizophrenia; the chance that a person would be both schizophrenic and a surviving quadruplet is one in one-and-one-half billion births.

An examination of both parents' family histories for psychiatric disorders has provided information about possible genetic factors. Although Mrs. Genain's side of the family seems to have been mentally healthy, Mr. Genain's mother suffered a "nervous breakdown" in her teens, and her recovery took three years. Mr. Genain was the youngest of his mother's nine children. Following her later pregnancies, she became angry and depressed and threatened to kill her husband and herself. Mr. Genain's oldest brother was described as a slow learner who never did learn a trade. The second-to-youngest son was described as "strange" by his family; their descriptions indicate he hallucinated, cried often, and wandered about aimlessly. Another of Mr. Genain's brothers drank heavily and became irrational when he was angry.

The staff researchers at NIMH found Mr. Genain himself to be suspicious, irritable, and withdrawn. Mrs. Genain was overprotective of her daughters and in her mind had paired them off as a set of "good" twins (Myra and Nora) and a set of "bad" twins (Hester and Iris).

When the quadruplets were children, they were not allowed to have friends visit them, to visit other children's homes, or to participate in social activities. When Hester and Iris were eleven, Mrs. Genain became frustrated with her many attempts to stop them from masturbating and, on medical advice, had both circumcised (a flap of skin was removed from the

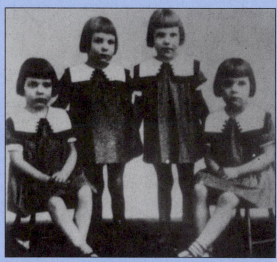

The Genain quadruplets, shown here as children, have been diagnosed as schizophrenic, and were examined at the National Institute of Mental Health in 1963 when they were 24 years old, and again in 1984.

clitoris). To keep the girls from pulling out their stitches, Mrs. Genain tied their hands to the bedposts for thirty days.

During her high school years, Hester had spells of tongue-clicking, sighing, and vomiting. She was destructive, irritable, and depressed, and she dropped out of high school. The other three quadruplets completed high school. After high school both Nora and Myra held jobs, but, even when they were in their twenties, Mr. Genain insisted on having lunch with them, picking them up from work each day, and opening their mail. He became angry and threatened them if they tried to establish social lives for themselves. Several times during their childhood and early adulthood, he barged into social events and took his girls home.

In 1963, when the quadruplets were twenty-four years old, they were first examined by NIMH. Myra was married and living with her husband; Nora had a part-time job and was living with her mother. Both

Hester and Iris were hospitalized. When the quadruplets were fifty years old, NIMH researchers again tested them extensively. By the second examination (1984), both Hester and Iris had been hospitalized more than fifteen years. Myra had attended business college after her first NIMH visit, had worked as a secretary, had married, and had had children. Nora had been employed for at least seven of the twenty-some years since her first NIMH visit.

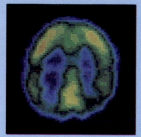

Normal

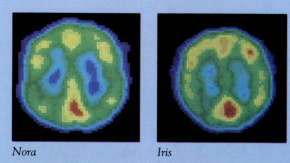

Nora   Iris

Myra   Hester

A PET scan of a normal brain shows areas of high energy use in the frontal lobes, seen at the top of the PET scans. The Genain quadruplets' PET scans, however, all show energy use at the bottom of the scans, possibly indicating hallucinations.

One portion of the 1984 examination of the quadruplets consisted of biomedical tests. Because researchers have found brain shrinkage in some people with schizophrenia, a CAT (Computerized Axial Tomography) brain scan was done on all four subjects. The results showed no shrinkage in their brains. A second biomedical test, a brain wave test to determine the amount of alpha rhythm activity in different parts of the brain, was also conducted. Alpha waves appear when subjects relax and let their minds wander and cease when subjects open their eyes or pay attention to a stimulus. All four quadruplets showed less alpha wave activity than do normal subjects. Because hallucinations may reduce or eliminate alpha wave activity and because three of the four quadruplets described having had hallucinations on other occasions, hallucinations were suggested as a way to account for the alpha wave test results.

An additional biomedical test, a positron emission tomography (PET) scan, was obtained for each woman. To obtain PET scans, researchers inject radioactive sugars into subjects' brains. Then, while subjects lie resting quietly in a dark room with their eyes closed, the scans are obtained. Normally, the PET scan reflects highest energy use in the frontal lobes, but each of the four sisters showed high energy use in her brain's visual regions at the back of the head. Again, as in the alpha wave measurement, hallucinations during the scanning period were suggested as an explanation for the results.

Studies of the Genain quadruplets have added significantly to researchers' knowledge of schizophrenia. Because the four individuals are identical quadruplets and therefore have nearly identical genes, the differences among them must be due primarily to environmental causes or to interactions between heredity and environment.

SOURCES: Buchsbaum, M. S. 1984. The Genain quadruplets. *Psychology Today*, 18 no. 8, 46-51; Bernheim, K. F. & Lewine, R. R. J. 1979. *Schizophrenia: Symptoms, causes, treatments*. New York: W. W. Norton.

only 0.6 percent (Baron et al., 1985).

A third type of study, **twin studies**, provides an excellent test of the genetic influence of an identified disorder because identical (monozygotic) twins have nearly identical genetic information. Twin studies indicate that if one identical twin develops schizophrenia, the other twin has a 50 percent chance of developing it, too. (Falloon et al., 1984) Obviously, factors other than genes are at work here; otherwise, both identical twins would always suffer from the disorder, or both would always escape schizophrenia. Could the environment or stress be responsible for the discrepancy? Is schizophrenic behavior learned from a schizophrenic parent?

Adopted-twin studies attempt to answer these questions. In these studies, researchers follow twin offspring born to a schizophrenic parent and adopted out shortly after birth. In the late 1960s, several researchers chose Denmark as the ideal location in which to conduct this type of study. Denmark keeps records of each citizen from birth until death, and the records include admissions to psychiatric hospitals and diagnoses. The Denmark studies indicated that although the adoptive relatives of the twins showed no higher incidence of schizophrenia than did the general population, the biological relatives of the adoptees showed a 10 percent incidence of schizophrenia (Restak, 1984). One group of researchers reached the following conclusion: "Thus, it has been concluded from these adoption studies that the genetic predisposition to schizophrenia is relatively unaffected by the family environment in which a child is raised. But a disturbed family environment may contribute to the severity of the disorder—a highly relevant finding for the clinician" (Falloon, 1984, p. 26).

Studies of the genetic inheritability of schizophrenia point out the need for isolating the environmental factors that protect some individuals or reduce the severity of their disorder despite their increased familial risk (the *Relate* section provides information on how families can help schizophrenic family members).

Experiential Theories

As a group, experiential theories attempt to explain the etiology of schizophrenia in terms of life experiences. The **schizophrenogenic mother** theory attributes schizophrenia in adults to being reared by a schizophrenogenic (schizophrenia-causing) mother, a mother who was unable to properly cuddle and fondle her child and who could not provide the support and security the child needed during the first few years of life.

The **double-bind theory** emphasizes the communication between the mother and the child and within the family as a whole. According to this theory, a preschizophrenic child is in a "damned if you do and damned if you don't" position. For example, a child may be verbally criticized for not showing more affection toward the parent; then when the child does show greater affection that affection is rejected or punished.

Other researchers have clearly demonstrated that the families of schizophrenics often display distorted role structures, marital discord, and difficulties in problem-solving communication strategies. Although these family characteristics are similar to those found in families with a chronically physically ill member and are therefore not exclusively characteristic of families of schizophrenics, the problems do make more difficult the therapy with a schizophrenic person who resides at home (Falloon et al., 1984). Treatment programs specifically developed to treat these family difficulties have been developed (see the *Relate* section).

Identification with and, later, acting like a schizophrenic individual is another theory of the causation of schizophrenia. However, identifying with a schizophrenic mother should not be confused with the theory of a schizophrenogenic mother.

R. D. Laing and other experiential theorists view schizophrenia as an experience, not an illness. They propose that schizophrenia is a growth process and a way for a person to grow, develop, and learn about himself or herself and nature. Still other theorists see schizophrenia as a growth stage, much like adolescence, that most individuals "grow out of."

Within the framework of looking at schizophrenia as caused by life experiences, some sociologists and social psychiatrists have examined culture and socioeconomic status as possible causes. Most research in this area supports the following conclusion: the lower the socioeconomic status of one's parents, the greater are one's chances of being impaired by a psychiatric illness. However, this finding lumps all psychiatric illness together and does not specifically address the issue of social causes of schizophrenia.

Psychologists who have tried to reconcile the genetic theories with the experiential theories have concluded that a genetic predisposition must be present before a person can develop schizophrenia. Nevertheless, most people with a demonstrable genetic predisposition to schizophrenia (see Exhibit 22.6) do not become schizophrenic; therefore, life experience influences such as stress, traumatic events, and family and socioeconomic

EXHIBIT 22.6
Families and Schizophrenia

A One parent had schizophrenia: 10% Risk

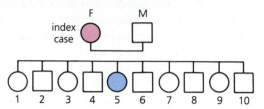

B One sibling or non-identical twin had schizophrenia: 10% Risk

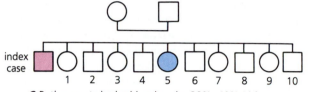

C Both parents had schizophrenia: 20%–40% Risk

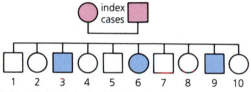

D Identical twin had schizophrenia: 50% Risk

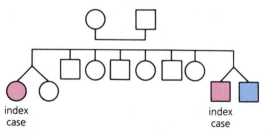

■ Indicates index case of definite schizophrenia,
■ Indicates vulnerable family member at risk to develop schizophrenia.

This chart summarizes the extensive research into the genetic influence on the risk of schizophrenia. According to the chart, if one of your parents has a diagnosis of schizophrenia, you have a 10 percent chance of developing schizophrenia but a 90 percent chance of *not* developing it. If both of your parents have a diagnosis of schizophrenia, you have a 60-80 percent chance of *not* developing the disorder. Remember, this chart indicates only the risk factors; many variables help determine the actual occurrence of schizophrenia in an individual.

Adapted from Falloon, I. R. H., McGill, C. W., & Boyd, L. B. 1984. *Family care of schizophrenia: A problem-solving approach to the treatment of mental illness*. NY: Guilford Press, p. 28.

factors may be important in determining the actual development of symptoms.

Physiological and Biochemical Theories

To investigate the physiological and biochemical causes of schizophrenia, researchers must distinguish between factors that *cause* symptoms of schizophrenia and factors that *accompany* schizophrenia or are *caused by* schizophrenia. Instead of being a single disease with a single cause, schizophrenia is probably a collection of disorders with many causes and a variety of accompanying physiological or biochemical differences.

Schizophrenia-like symptoms are seen in people with severe Vitamin B_6 deficiencies, late-stage syphilis, and some inflammations of the brain. A small number of those diagnosed as schizophrenic may have altered immune systems and, for these people, steroids may be more helpful than antipsychotic medications (Larson, 1984). Some psychologists speculate that the development of schizophrenic symptoms results from a viral infection, which may occur prenatally. A small subgroup of schizophrenics experience flare-ups of their symptoms when they consume gluten, a component of cereal grains. A gluten-free diet would benefit these schizophrenics (Restak, 1984).

Technology has made possible the measurement of brain differences between nonschizophrenics and people diagnosed as schizophrenic. EEG (Electroencephalographs) research indicates that schizophrenics may have less alpha rhythm activity than nonschizophrenics, CAT brain scans show brain shrinkage in *some* people diagnosed as schizophrenic, and PET scans measure which portions of the brain are most active during specific conditions (the results of these measures of the Genain quadruplets are contained in an *Exploring . . .* section). Such measurements show that some individuals diagnosed as schizophrenic have measurable brain differences as compared to nonschizophrenics. However, the results do *not* indicate if the differences caused, preceded, or resulted from schizophrenia.

The discovery in the 1950s that a class of medications, now known as antipsychotics or neuroleptics, reduces many symptoms of schizophrenia led to the **dopamine hypothesis**. This hypothesis attempts to explain how neurotransmitters in the brains of schizophrenics differ from those in nonschizophrenics and how the medications reduce symptoms. Neuroleptics, or antipsychotics, seem to work by blocking or binding-up the dopamine receptors, thereby reducing the dopamine uptake. When people with schizophrenia are given large amounts of neuroleptics (which reduce the dopamine), Parkinson-like symptoms result. From these two pieces of information, researchers have concluded that Parkinson's disease is in some sense the biochemical opposite of schizophrenia; in Parkinson's disease, dopamine production is reduced by a loss of dopamine-producing cells, while in schizophrenia an excess of dopamine is reduced with the neuroleptic medications. These findings and others suggest that schizophrenia is accompanied by an excess of dopamine transmission between the neurons in the brain. Currently, conclusive evidence about the precise brain site at which the excess dopamine is produced has not been found.

Research into the etiology, prognosis, biochemical treatments, and psychotherapies for schizophrenia continues. Despite many gaps in knowledge, most researchers believe the future for schizophrenic individuals is more optimistic than it has ever been.

Research Problems

Research on the more severe mental disorders has been difficult for several reasons. Many symptoms displayed by individuals who were hospitalized before the 1950s are probably the result of living for many years in a state hospital system, where alienation, isolation, inadequate nutrition, and poor physical hygiene were common. Old textbooks even listed poor gum health and a high rate of tuberculosis as symptomatic of schizophrenia (Mendel, 1976). In other words, researchers who examine the long-term course of schizophrenia may be recording symptoms caused by institutionalization rather than by the mental illness.

Another research problem is the low reliability (consistency) of diagnosis from one professional to another. Because of low diagnostic reliability, psychologists who study patients or clients with a particular diagnosis may not be studying a homogeneous group; in other words, patients or clients with the same diagnosis may not demonstrate the same symptoms. An additional diagnostic problem is that a number of professionals, believing that labeling has been misused to discriminate socially, economically, and politically against the mentally ill, have refused to diagnose or have even intentionally misdiagnosed (Mendel, 1976). If the undiagnosed or misdiagnosed patients or clients then become subjects in a study, the results are of questionable value.

Further, clinicians who diagnose and treat mentally ill individuals are usually middle-class and often have limited knowledge of the subcultures of American society. Unless they familiarize themselves with the normal behavior of people from these subcultures, the clinicians tend to see many lower class behaviors as **psychopathological**, stemming from a mental illness, rather than as culturally learned. This cultural diagnostic bias may partially explain the higher percentage of individuals from the lower socioeconomic classes who are diagnosed with serious mental illnesses.

One interesting problem in research is that since antipsychotic medications became available in the 1950s, few, if any, studies have been able to investigate the course of serious mental illnesses in subjects who have not been medicated. Because antipsychotic medications clearly reduce the symptoms of schizophrenia for some individuals, schizophrenics who have never been medicated are now almost nonexistent.

In spite of these research problems, studies on schizophrenia and the major affective disorders are being published at such a phenomenal rate that the accepted ideas are constantly being revised. This state of constant change is good news for those who suffer from serious mental illnesses because as a clearer picture of the disorders develops, new biological and psychological treatments become available.

Focus Question Answer

Which theories attempt to explain why an individual becomes schizophrenic? Three major types of theories have postulated the etiology of schizophrenia—genetic, experiential, and physiological or biochemical theories. Genetic theories are supported by family studies that reflect a definite inheritability factor. Experiential theories rely on the mother's influence, the family's influence, and cultural or socioeconomic factors to explain the etiology of schizophrenia. Physiological and biochemical theories are supported by evidence from new technological instruments that measure differences between the brain functions of schizophrenics and nonschizophrenics.

 *Relate*

A Schizophrenic in the Family

One out of every one hundred people develops schizophrenia during his or her lifetime. Because schizophrenia develops most frequently during late adolescence or early adulthood, while the person is still living at home, schizophrenia becomes a family problem. Families often ask, "What should we do?"

The question of where the person will reside may arise even before the family seeks outside help, and the question will certainly arise after a person has been hospitalized. Should the family member return home to live with the family? Can he or she live independently? Is a halfway house or a supervised living arrangement appropriate?

Therapists disagree about an adult schizophrenic family member living at home. One expert says (Torrey, 1983, p. 155), "As a general rule I believe that most persons with schizophrenia do better living somewhere other than at home." However, regardless of therapists' opinions, in reality at least 25 percent of schizophrenics discharged from hospitals return to live with their families (Talbott, 1978). Furthermore, approximately 95 percent of the young adult chronic schizophrenics — individuals who have never been hospitalized and who abuse medications, overuse emergency rooms, and avoid professionals—live at home (Larson, 1984). The question, then, is how can their families help them?

The following suggestions provide general guidelines for interacting with a schizophrenic family member living at home. Because people with schizophrenia vary considerably, the suggestions should be used as a starting point only and should be altered to fit the situation.

Relating to Schizophrenic Family Members

1. Communicate briefly, concisely, and unambiguously.

2. When you respond to the family member's delusions, don't use sarcasm or humor, and don't try to talk him or her out of the delusions. Encourage the person to express his or her delusions only in private.

3. Expect the person to be emotionally aloof at times. He or she may wish to be around conversations and people but be unable to participate.

4. Provide a place in the house to which the person can withdraw and be alone.

5. Minimize noise and the number and scale of social events in the house.

6. Help the person establish a predictable and simple daily routine.

7. Help the person find leisure activities he or she enjoys. Try activities with low sensory input or single sensory channel input.

8. Develop a quiet, calm, confident attitude*.

High and Low Expressed Emotion

Recent research to determine the family's effects on a previously hospitalized person with schizophrenia has often involved a concept called **expressed emotion**. A relatively lengthy explanation of this term is necessary because the term measures more than the emotional expressiveness of a family.

High expressed emotion (High-EE) is a label assigned to a family that displays the following characteristics: (1) frequent critical comments involving resentment, disapproval, dislike, or guilt induction; (2) hostility expressed in the form of personal criticism rather than criticism of behavior; and (3) marked emotional overinvolvement. Families express emotional overinvolvement through overprotective attitudes toward the person and by frequent intrusions into situations in which the family's help is neither sought nor desired. Emotional overinvolvement is also characterized by constant worrying over small matters concerning the household. High-EE relatives believe that much of the schizophrenic's bizarre behavior is deliberate and that the person could control the behaviors if he or she wanted to do so (Falloon et al., 1984).

Low expressed emotion (Low-EE) is defined as the absence of High-EE characteristics within a family. Low-EE families generally believe the family member with schizophrenia has an illness and cannot control his or her behavior.

Family Style and Relapse Rate

An individual who experiences thinking disturbances, delusions, and hallucinations is often hospitalized, but with good supportive therapy and drug therapy, 75-80 percent of these patients experience almost total remission of their symptoms (Falloon et al., 1984). At this point, then, many discharged persons who have been diagnosed as schizophrenic come home to live with their families. The task for the former patients, their families, and their therapists is to keep these patients from relapsing.

---

*Adapted from "How to Behave Toward a Schizophrenic" (pp. 160–166) *Surviving Schizophrenia: A Family Manual* by E. Fuller Torrey, M.D. Copyright © 1983 by E. Fuller Torrey. Reprinted by permission of Harper & Row Publishers, Inc.

Relapse rate is defined as the percentage of patients who relapse (reexperience their symptoms and return to the hospital) within a given time period. Although a few studies have chosen longer time periods, most studies have specified periods of six, nine, or twelve months. Generally, in these studies, families are interviewed and, based on the interview information, labeled either High-EE or Low-EE. Then, at the end of the chosen time period, the relapse rate of High- and Low-EE groups is compared.

From their studies, Falloon et al. (1984) concluded that EE is the best *single* predictor of relapse (compliance with the medication routine was also very important). In one EE study, 58 percent of the patients who returned to homes in which one or more family members was rated as High-EE relapsed; among patients living in Low-EE households, only 16 percent relapsed during the same time period (Falloon et al., 1984). Several studies confirm that patients who live with High-EE relatives relapse *significantly* more often than do those who live with Low-EE relatives.

These findings led some mental health professionals to change their approach to families of schizophrenics. In a study of family therapy of schizophrenia, one group of researchers found that relatives of the patients in the control group (no family therapy) rarely knew the patient's diagnosis and were uninformed about the management of schizophrenia (Berkowitz et al., 1984). As result of these findings, new family therapies for schizophrenia emphasize the role of relatives as members of the treatment team. This approach provides an enormous contrast to the earlier approach of withholding information and blaming the family, an approach that was common until recently and that, unfortunately, can still be found.

Family therapies for schizophrenia, despite their differences in theoretical positions, agree on the following features of the role of the therapist:

1. The therapist joins with the family and the patient in a team effort.
2. The therapist educates the family about the illness, its symptoms, and its effects on family behavior and on the person with schizophrenia.
3. The therapist trains the family in improving communication patterns (Low-EE vs. High EE) and in recognizing the signs of relapse.
4. The therapist changes the therapy structure to include relatives as co-therapists and caretakers.
5. The therapist conducts multiple family meetings for the purpose of establishing a support group and social contacts for the relatives (McFarlane et al., 1984).

After a comparison of the effectiveness of different individual therapies with family therapies, one researcher concluded: "... the evidence from at least half a dozen studies would indicate that no further research on the intensive individual psychotherapy of schizophrenia based on psychodynamic or interpersonal principles is warranted." (McFarlane et al., 1984 p. 611). Obviously, he considers family therapy a distinct improvement over individual therapy.

Undeniably, many schizophrenic individuals live with their families, which are often uninformed about the schizophrenic's diagnoses, symptoms, and medications, and about ways of coping with the stress of living with a mentally ill person. Many families express gratitude for the information provided by the family therapists and for acknowledgment of their roles as part of the treatment team. The benefits to the family combined with significantly lower relapse rates make family therapy of schizophrenia a very positive and effective alternative to individual psychotherapy for schizophrenics who live with their families.

Things to Do

1. Ascertain what support groups for individuals (or their families) with diagnoses of bipolar disorder, depression, or schizophrenia are available in your area. Mental health centers, hospitals, psychiatrists, and social service agencies are sources from which to acquire this information.

2. Obtain an older textbook, preferably one published before 1960, and read the sections on the topics included in this chapter. Compare the information on etiology, prognosis, and treatment. How have the changes in etiology, prognosis, and treatment altered the lives of individuals diagnosed as schizophrenic, depressive, or bipolar disorder?

3. To make the symptoms and the lives of people with these disorders more real to you, read a book about individuals diagnosed as mentally ill. Here are a few suggestions:

   a. *Will There Ever Be a Morning?* by Frances Farmer. A first person account of mental illness and treatment during the forties and fifties.

   b. *Is There No Place on Earth for Me?* by S. Sheehan. The story of a woman diagnosed as having chronic schizophrenia and the therapies she received between the time of her diagnosis as a teenager and her middle thirties.

   c. *The Bell Jar* by Sylvia Plath. A novel that parallels the life of the author in many respects—descriptive of the symptoms of severe depression and suicidal ideas.

4. Interview an employee of an inpatient psychiatric unit and an employee of a half-way house (or group home). Compare their answers to a series of questions. Following are a few suggestions:

What are the diagnoses of the people with whom you work?

What are patients with schizophrenia like?

What do you believe causes schizophrenia?

What do you believe causes depression?

Are the individuals with whom you work capable of leading normal lives?

Things to Discuss

1. Think of a time you experienced each of the following:
inappropriate affect
auditory hallucinations
delusions of persecution
flattened affect
visual hallucinations
To what did you attribute these experiences? Share your experiences with your classmates. How frequently do these behaviors and feelings occur?

2. How does your behavior change when you are depressed? Do you spend more time or less time with other people? Do your eating and sleeping habits change? Does your activity level change? How do other people act when they are depressed?

3. Peter Pan advised, "Think lovely thoughts, and up you'll go." Does thinking positively work for you? Does

thinking negative thoughts make you depressed?

4. How would you react if one of your family members was diagnosed as schizophrenic? In what ways would your family life be altered if such a schizophrenic family member lived at home?

5. Do you experience mood swings? How extreme and how frequent are the swings?

6. Most people have suicidal thoughts at one time or another. Have you had such thoughts? Under what circumstances?

Things to Read

Bernheim, K.F., Lewine, R.R.J., & Beale, C.T. 1982. *The caring family: Living with chronic mental illness.* NY: Random House.

Hazleton, L. 1984. *The right to feel bad.* NY: Ballantine Books.

Lester, G. & Lester, D. 1976. *Suicide: The gamble with death.* Englewood Cliffs, NJ: Prentice-Hall.

Torrey, E.F. 1983. *Surviving schizophrenia: A family manual.* NY: Harper & Row.

Vine, P. 1982. *Families in pain: Children, siblings, spouses and parents of the mentally ill speak out.* NY: Pantheon.

Wilson, L. 1968. *This stranger, my son.* NY: Putnam.

 ## Review

Summary

1. Psychoses are characterized by an inability to distinguish reality. The various subtypes of schizophrenia and the major affective disorders are considered psychotic disorders.

2. Dysthymic disorder and cyclothymic disorder are characterized by mood swings lasting two years or more and an absence of psychotic symptoms.

3. The major affective disorders include the bipolar disorders and major depression. Individuals with a major depressive disorder experience single or recurrent episodes of depression, while people with bipolar disorders experience both manic and depressive episodes.

4. An increased risk of suicide is indicated for people with a major affective disorder or schizophrenia. Several

behavioral signs may predict suicidal intent. Friends and family members can help prevent suicide by listening, by eliciting personal commitments, and by referring the suicidal person to skilled professionals.

5. Research indicates a genetic predisposition to the affective disorders, and various biochemical differences between "normal" people and individuals with the affective disorders have been found.

6. Symptoms common to the schizophrenias include social withdrawal, emotional changes, delusions, hallucinations, illusions, and an altered sense of self.

7. The subtypes of schizophrenia include the disorganized type, the catatonic type, the paranoid type, and the undifferentiated type, each of which has specific iden-

tifying symptoms.

8. Schizoaffective disorder, characterized by symptoms of both schizophrenia and the affective disorders, is not yet clearly identified as a type of schizophrenia, a variation of the affective disorders, a combination of both types of disorders, or a separate disorder.

9. The prognosis of a schizophrenic can be predicted by examining the person's symptoms and history. A sudden onset of symptoms preceded by a life crisis and good adjustment prior to the onset of symptoms are positive predictors. A family history of schizophrenia, an absence of emotion, and a young age at onset are negative predictors.

10. Although family studies support a genetic predisposition to schizophrenia, other factors such as stress, traumatic events, and socioeconomic level influence the development and severity of the disorder.

11. Experiential theories attribute the cause of schizophrenia to the mother, family interactions, and family communication patterns. Changing a family's interactions can positively influence the family and the relapse rate for a schizophrenic living with his or her family.

12. Dominant among the physiological and biochemical theories of schizophrenia is the dopamine hypothesis, which posits that excess dopamine at the synapse is responsible for the symptoms of schizophrenia.

13. Upon discharge, many people who have been hospitalized and diagnosed as schizophrenic return to their family's home. Family therapy provides information about schizophrenia to the family and teaches the family Low-EE behaviors; Low-EE (as opposed to High-EE) families are associated with much lower relapse rates of schizophrenic clients.

Key Terms

psychoses
major affective disorders
manic episodes
depressive episodes
bipolar disorder
major depression
schizophrenia
illusions
delusions
hallucinations
affect
disorganized type
catatonic type

paranoid type
undifferentiated type
residual type
schizoaffective disorder
prognosis
etiology
schizophrenogenic mother
double-bind theory
identification
dopamine hypothesis
psychopathological
high expressed emotion (High-EE)
low expressed emotion (Low-EE)

Part Seven

Therapeutic Models

Focus Questions

1. What information will help you with various therapy decisions?

2. Are ECT, psychosurgery, and drugs effective forms of therapy?

3. How is individual (Adlerian) therapy similar to and different from psychoanalytic therapy?

4. Which psychological disorders do behavior therapy techniques treat most successfully?

5. How could the homeless deinstitutionalized mentally ill affect you?

Chapter Outline

THERAPY
Self-Help
Therapy Decisions
Therapy Issues

BIOMEDICAL THERAPIES
Historical Therapies
Modern Therapies
The Research Process: Treatment for the
    Seriously Mentally Ill

PSYCHODYNAMIC THERAPIES
Psychoanalytic Therapy
Individual (Adlerian) Therapy

BEHAVIOR THERAPIES
Techniques Based on Operant Conditioning
Techniques Based on Social Learning
Techniques Based on Classical Conditioning
Evaluation

RELATE: Deinstitutionalization
Things to Do
Things to Discuss
Things to Read

REVIEW: Summary
Key Terms

Chapter 23

Therapy: Biological, Psychodynamic, and Behavioral Models

*People don't change. They only stand
more clearly revealed.*

Charles Olsen

 Therapy

To provide therapy is to provide treatment for an illness or a disability. **Psychotherapy** is psychological therapy (or treatment) for a mental or emotional illness. Providers of psychotherapy include psychologists, psychiatrists, psychoanalysts (Chapter 2 specifies the required training and education for each specialty), and a variety of counselors and therapists. Other individuals who may function as therapists are family members, friends, physicians, teachers, and ministers, priests, and rabbis. This list is certainly not all-inclusive; anyone who listens and provides support and understanding may temporarily function as a therapist.

Chapters 21 and 22 describe various psychological disorders, and Chapters 23 and 24 describe many types

561

of therapy, both psychological and nonpsychological, used to treat these disorders. Chapter 23 first examines several issues about therapy and therapists and then explains biomedical, psychoanalytic, and behavioral therapies. Chapter 24 focuses on humanistic-existential and cognitive therapies and briefly describes additional therapies.

Self-Help

For people who believe they need help, self-help strategies (strategies that do not involve professional therapists) may be sufficient or may be the first step in a series of steps that culminates in the decision to see a particular therapist for a specific type of therapy. Although the usefulness of self-help strategies varies from person to person, the usefulness is influenced by the following factors: type of problem, immediacy of need, insurance coverage or amount of disposable income, availability of other therapies, reading skills, level of insight, self-image, and knowledge of and preference for specific approaches to a problem.

Self-help strategies include reading books, writing to newspaper "therapists" like Ann Landers or Dr. Ruth Westheimer, calling radio or television "therapists" for advice, calling telephone counseling lines, calling specific "hot lines" (e.g., suicide, drug, runaway, or teen pregnancy emergency telephone counseling), and joining self-help support groups. During the past ten to fifteen years, demands for self-therapy through books has led to a new genre of books. Early self-help authors such as Albert Ellis (*A New Guide to Rational Living*) and Wayne Dyer (*Your Erroneous Zones, Pulling Your Own Strings*) have been joined by hundreds of other authors who promise cures for depression, loneliness, boredom, shyness, and other problems. These books are an economical, convenient, private way to obtain information and to simulate therapeutic experiences. The major problem with such books seems to be the deceptive advertising and unvalidated claims found on book jackets (Fisher, 1984); these claims often promise far more than the usual reader will gain from the books.

Advice from newspaper, radio, or television "therapists" may be quite good, but an individual who needs help will have difficulty providing specific situational information in a letter or in the few minutes allotted by a media host. Without enough information, a "therapist" may unintentionally give inappropriate advice. An additional concern is media therapists' qualifications, which range from years of therapy and teaching experience to a complete lack of psychological training. For instance,

This large display of self-help and "pop psych" books in a typical bookstore illustrates the accessibility of such information and the popularity of these books.

one New York radio call-in show that provides teenagers with advice about "love problems" features a twenty-three-year-old high school dropout as the "therapist". Although he flaunts his lack of credentials and seems surprised people take his show seriously, several listeners have taken his show seriously enough to complain to the Federal Communications Commission (Gaitskill, 1986). This radio "therapist" is not typical, but he does illustrate the problem people face when they attempt to acquire credible information from media therapists.

Telephone counseling is often geared specifically to crisis intervention (e.g., suicide and drug hot lines) or to serving those who cannot or will not come to a therapy center. The clients include teenagers who lack transportation, runaways who fear disclosure, and people who have neither the money nor the inclination to speak face-to-face with a therapist. Although the training for telephone counselors is usually supervised by professional therapists, the primary goal of telephone counseling is rarely long-term counseling. Instead, the goal is to temporarily resolve a crisis, to provide information to the caller, or to provide a referral to an appropriate social service agency or therapist.

The last self-help strategy examined here is support groups. Members of a support group usually have in common a particular problem or situation; members range from parents of learning disabled children, spouses and families of chemical abusers, and women who have had mastectomies to families with a schizophrenic member, rape victims, and ex-mental patients. The services or intentions of these groups are extremely diverse—lobbying for rights for a specific group, providing information to those involved and to members of the community, providing social and psychological support for members through regular meetings, and acting as liaisons or advocates in medical or legal matters. While members may gain valuable help from support groups, some groups may be unhelpful or provide inaccurate information. You should verify the reputation and helpfulness of a group before you join it. More generally, remember that expertise and psychological training may be lacking in self-help sources.

Therapy Decisions

One of the most basic decisions to be made when a person needs help is whether this help should involve changing the person or the situation. The choice often depends upon society's definition of the problem and society's perception of its cause. If bizarre behaviors are attributed to poverty, a lack of social services, or a lack of knowledge about how to behave, then changing the person's situation will be the logical choice. In contrast, if bizarre behaviors are attributed to personality disturbances, learned behavior, biological sources, or any other cause within the individual, then the person will be the logical target of change. Chapters 23 and 24 describe therapies that reflect an effort to change the individual rather than the situation. As you will see, family therapy is an exception; the goal of family therapy is family change and, hence, a change in the person's situation, but most family therapists make no attempt to change the larger situation—the society.

The decision to include the client's family in therapy is determined by a number of factors including the client's competence to make decisions, the therapist's beliefs about the causes and the treatments of mental illness, and the willingness of the family to participate. Whatever the cause of mental illness, the family can be detrimental to an individual's progress, or the family can be instrumental in helping an individual recover (see the *Relate* section of Chapter 22).

Another therapy decision concerns the benefits and appropriateness of individual and group therapies. Therapy groups, as referred to in this text, differ from support groups. A therapy group is usually conducted by a therapist with specific training in group therapy, and the group meetings are likely to be held at the therapist's office or a mental health center. In group therapy, confidentiality may be a problem; despite promising the group not to disclose personal information outside the group, some members may do so. Nonetheless, group therapies have much to recommend them—exposure to and feedback from others with similar problems, opportunities to try out new skills in an accepting atmosphere, and therapy for less cost than individual therapy. A well-trained group therapy leader will assure a warm, safe atmosphere and will protect an individual from other members who become too abusive or confrontive.

Everyone is a possible consumer of mental health services and as such can benefit from information about therapy claims, choices, and outcomes. The *Exploring . . .* section provides information that rebuts several common therapy myths.

Therapy Issues

Ethical issues in therapy abound. Just as doctors, lawyers, and teachers are faced with certain moral and ethical dilemmas, so too are therapists. The major topics of ethical concern include engaging in sexual relationships with clients, imposing one's values on clients, breaking confidentiality, marketing one's services, and hospitalizing clients against their will. Since each of these topics has been repeatedly and extensively examined in the media, only a brief overview of a few issues is presented here.

Therapeutic relationships are, by their nature, unequal in power and in control (Dujovne, 1983). Therapists hold the expertise, they charge for their services, they choose to see or not see a client, they schedule the sessions on their turf, and they often verbally control the content of the therapy sessions. Any time one person has more power or control in a relationship, the opportunity for exploitation and manipulation arises. In addition, because therapists are human, they may grow to love or wish to have sex with particular clients. A conservative estimate indicates that 5 percent of practicing therapists have engaged in intercourse with their clients (Holroyd and Brodsky, 1977). The belief among therapists, that sexual relationships with clients are unethical and possibly damaging to the clients is not universal, but the belief is widely held. Sexual relationships with clients are prohibited by the ethical codes of behavior of therapy professionals, the large majority of whom have adopted these codes. Therapists who engage in sexual behaviors with their clients risk malpractice suits or other

Exploring...

Therapy Myths

In *The Shrinking of America: Myths of Psychological Change* (1983), clinical psychologist Bernie Zilbergeld, Ph.D., identifies common beliefs that make Americans large-scale consumers of the several hundred types of available therapy. According to Zilbergeld, Americans believe that life is best understood in psychological terms, that events have hidden messages only experts can decipher, that all people can benefit from psychological help, and that therapists know what people need better than people themselves do. From these beliefs stem eight widely held misconceptions, or myths, about therapy:

Myth No. 1: There is one best therapy.

Although many therapists believe their particular therapeutic approach is superior to all others, research evidence does not support any one approach as treatment for all problems. For many common problems for which people seek psychotherapy, the well-known approaches produce similar results. Individual, group, and couples therapy formats show the same or similar outcomes. Exceptions include the greater effectiveness of behavior therapy for phobias and sexual problems and the greater effectiveness of couples therapy for relationship problems.

Myth No. 2: Counseling is equally effective for all problems.

Although psychotherapy is recommended for almost all problems, it is *not* equally effective for "whatever ails you." Simple (single) phobias, low self-esteem, sexual problems of premature ejaculation in males and lack of orgasm in females, and certain marital problems are often successfully treated in psychotherapy. Depressions, especially severe ones, and the schizophrenias are probably best treated through biomedical interventions. Psychotherapy has poor success rates with people who demonstrate addictive behaviors or deviant sexual behaviors.

Myth No. 3: Behavior change is therapy's most common outcome.

Clients often feel better about themselves and feel good about their therapy even when no behavior change can be documented. The development of self-understanding and an increased ability to cope are also important outcomes of psychotherapy. The value of these outcomes may be underestimated and the value and effects of behavior change overestimated.

Myth No. 4: Great changes are the rule.

"Cures" or dramatic changes are the exception rather than the rule; modest changes in behavior and coping

---

legal actions as well as loss of their professional licenses (Knapp, 1980).

The issue of confidentiality is quite complex, and therapists must consider what is best for the client, what and when information is legally protected, what is best for society, and what loyalty is owed to the employing agency. The law may mandate a therapist's disclosure of a client's confidences when a child has been abused, when a client's mental health is in question in a civil legal action, and when a malpractice suit has been filed against the therapist. A therapist may choose to disclose so-called confidential information when the client has

threatened suicide, is in need of hospitalization, is a danger to others, or has threatened to commit a crime dangerous to society or to other persons (Corey et al., 1984).

Therapists must also answer several difficult questions about clients' rights when therapists consider the issue of involuntary hospitalization: How dangerous is the client? Does he or she intend to commit suicide? At what point do society's rights outweigh the rights of the individual? Do the mentally ill have the same rights as other citizens? Probably the most honest and straightforward way a therapist can approach the issue of in-are more common. If dramatic success stories were typical, therapists themselves, who are trained in methods of personal change, would be free of the problems experienced by their clients, yet research evidence does not indicate that therapists are freer than others from anxiety, depression, and bad habits.

Myth No. 5: The longer the therapy, the better the results.

In studies of therapy outcomes, therapies as short as twenty-five sessions or less have been compared with those lasting one, two, three, or five or more years. Although the research reveals no relationship between length of therapy and results, some therapists and some laypersons continue to believe that more is better. Therapists may cling to this myth because if they do not succeed with a client within a certain time they wish to continue the therapy until they do.

Myth No. 6: Therapy changes are permanent or at least long-lasting.

The evidence for permanent change is mixed, but the relapse rates for some problems range from 50–90 percent. Psychotherapy for addictive behaviors is especially characterized by high relapse rates.

Myth No. 7: At worst, counseling is harmless.

Many studies support the idea that therapy is quite capable of producing harm. Studies of group therapy clients indicate that a small percentage of the group members are worse off after treatment than before treatment and that the results can be traced to the therapy. Even during individual therapy, some clients become psychotic, commit suicide, or become so mentally ill they need hospitalization. Probably, some of these problems result from the therapy while the rest would have occurred regardless of therapy.

Myth No. 8: A single uninterrupted course of therapy is the rule for most clients.

In the past, this statement reflected reality, but it no longer does. Many clients now seek therapy intermittently from the same therapist or from several different ones. Clients may seek additional therapy because the first course was unsatisfactory or ineffective in solving the identified problem, because new problems arise, or because they desire more growth. Whatever the reason, years of continuous or intermittent therapy have become the rule for some clients.

Adapted from Zilbergeld, B. 1983. *The shrinking of America: Myths of psychological change*. Boston: Little, Brown.

voluntary hospitalization is to inform the client at the beginning of therapy of the circumstances under which confidentiality will not be upheld and the circumstances under which the therapist might initiate the legal process of hospitalizing the client against his or her will.

Marketing therapy services, in and of itself, raises ethical questions regardless of who imposes restrictions—therapists, professional organizations, or the legal system. Marketing is an ethical issue because therapists can mislead or take advantage of people who need help; advertising a therapy without exaggerating or overly enthusiastically promising results is difficult. Difficult, too,

is a therapist's decision regarding disclosure of his or her values within a therapy session. For instance, if a female client tells her therapist that she wishes to attend college and then get a job but that her husband has seriously discouraged her attempts at independence, the therapist's values quickly become relevant; the therapist must decide either to disclose or conceal his or her beliefs about men's and women's roles. Because of the many decisions and ethical issues involved in a therapy relationship, choosing the right therapist is very important. The *Exploring . . .* section contains questions you may wish to ask a therapist before you make a choice.

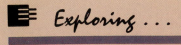

Exploring . . .

Choosing a Therapist

You may wish to ask a prospective therapist the following questions. Although many therapists or their secretaries will answer these questions over the telephone, some therapists may invite you to a short session specifically to discuss therapy arrangements. Therapists often do not charge or charge very little for an inquiry session.

If you decide to ask the following questions, remember that therapists *cannot* with certainty predict client behavior or the outcome of therapy. Therefore, their answers to the last three questions may include phrases such as "It depends on the client" or "It depends on the circumstances." If you feel comfortable with the therapist and think a helping relationship could evolve, you may want to consider him or her. If you have an immediate negative reaction, see another therapist.

1. What are your credentials?
2. May I speak with your colleagues or former clients about your expertise?

3. What are your fees? Do you have a sliding fee scale? Will my insurance pay for my therapy? What arrangements can I make for paying my fees?
4. Will I participate in individual, family, or group therapy?
5. Under what circumstances would you disclose information I have told you?
6. What is your view of men's and women's roles in society and in families?
7. What is your opinion on the role of biomedical therapies such as medication and electroconvulsive therapy (ECT)?
8. How many therapy sessions do you estimate will be required?
9. Under what conditions would you hospitalize a client against his/her will?
10. How many sessions with no progress do you allow before referring a client to another therapist?

Focus Question Answer

What information will help you with various therapy decisions? The availability and cost of different types of therapies, the credentials of various therapists, your insurance coverage for mental health care, and your preference for individual, family, or group therapy will influence your therapy decisions. In addition, therapists' stands on specific therapy issues may help you choose a particular therapist.

 ## Biomedical Therapies

Underlying the modern biomedical therapies is the theoretical framework of biological, neurological, or neurochemical causes of mental illness. Included in the biomedical therapies are electroconvulsive therapy (ECT), psychosurgery, and pharmacological treatments (drugs).

Historical Therapies

Direct physical interventions for treating emotional and physical problems were used as long ago as 10,000 years. **Trepanation (or trephination)** was used in ancient societies to allow the evil spirits or demons causing the madness to escape from the possessed person's head. This procedure, which was usually performed by a shaman or medicine man, consisted of drilling a small circular hole in the skull. Other methods of eliminating evil spirits included attempts to please or placate the gods through various rituals.

For treating people with "frenzies," Hippocrates (460–355 B.C.) prescribed one of the first recorded humane treatments—sending the patients to the country. Other humane treatments the ancient Greeks prescribed for emotional problems included recreational activity, walking, gymnastics, and custodial care. Less humane physical therapies administered during the same period included chaining violent persons, beating them, and prescribing medicinal potions for them.

From approximately the fifth to the fourteenth century A.D., mental illness was viewed as a sign that the body was a battleground on which God and the devil were struggling. Physical treatments during this time attempted to make the body unfit for habitation by the devil. Generally, increasingly harmful procedures were tried—insults, incantations, blood-letting, immersion in scalding water, and forced vomiting. During the fifteenth through the seventeenth centuries, mental illness and witchcraft were often synonymous. The above treatments, as well as burning at the stake and drowning, were used to chase out the devil. Reform and eventually a gradual movement away from physical treatments came in the late 1700s and early 1800s.

Modern Therapies

Electroconvulsive Therapy First developed in the late 1930s, **electroconvulsive therapy (ECT)** is now used primarily in the treatment of severe depression. The typical ECT method is to attach electrodes to both temples and to pass through the temples an electric current of 70 to 130 volts for 0.1 to 0.5 seconds (Kalinowsky, 1980). However, because of the weeks (or sometimes months) of memory loss caused by ECT, some practitioners advocate stimulating only the nondominant brain hemisphere instead of stimulating both brain hemispheres, as described above. In one analysis of the research on ECT, a group of practitioners concluded "There is substantial agreement that unilateral nondominant ECT causes fewer verbal memory deficits." The group also concluded that studies contrasting the effectiveness of stimulating one hemisphere versus stimulating two hemispheres do not clearly favor one method over the other (Janicak et al., 1985). The value of ECT in proportion to its reported side effects is hotly debated, and the positions vary from suggestions to ban its use to reports of high rates of effectiveness and low rates of complications.

A group convened by the National Institutes of Health (NIH) to study ECT estimated that between 30,000 and 100,000 patients in the United States are treated annually with ECT. In the past, complications such as fractured vertebrae, circulation problems, and skin burns were not uncommon, but the use of sedatives, muscle relaxants, short-acting anesthetics, and less electricity has currently reduced the complication rate to approximately one per 1,400 patients treated. The NIH group concluded that memory loss is the most serious of the

therapy's side effects and that ECT is demonstrably effective for only "a narrow range of severe psychiatric disorders in a limited number of diagnostic categories"—specifically, severe depressions lacking a triggering event and characterized by delusions and acute mania (Consensus Development Conference on Electroconvulsive Therapy, 1985).

Psychosurgery **Psychosurgery** denotes surgery on neural pathways with the intention of changing emotion or behavior. In 1935, Portugese physician Egas Moniz began experimenting with a surgery he called a leucotomy (elsewhere called a lobotomy). In this surgery, Moniz severed the pathways between the frontal lobes and the thalamus of the human brain. This surgery was gradually replaced by the transorbital lobotomy, in which a physician introduced an instrument through the eye sockets above the eye and then severed the central nerve tracts (Freeman & Watts, 1950).

Moniz originally proposed his surgery as a treatment for schizophrenia, but variations of his surgery were used most often with patients who did not respond to any other kind of treatment and with violent and extremely emotional patients. From its advent in 1936 as a form of therapy until its decline in the 1950s, lobotomies were performed on an estimated 40,000 or more people in the United States alone (Kalinowsky, 1975). Currently, several hundred psychosurgery procedures are performed yearly in the United States, but unlike early lobotomies, these surgeries require very precise methods; small areas of the brain are destroyed through surgery, implantation of electrodes, laser beams, or the direct application of chemicals into brain tissue (Schumer, 1983).

The research on psychosurgery does not clearly indicate how these procedures ameliorate emotion or behavior or even if they do result in emotional or behavioral change. As is the case with psychosurgery, an ethical dilemma exists when a treatment has irreversible effects that cannot be predicted or explained.

Pharmacological Therapies Since the 1950s, more and more **pharmacological interventions** (drugs that affect the body, behavior, or emotion) have been possible. In addition to cardiovascular drugs, antibiotics, pain medications, arthritis drugs, birth control pills, hormones, and drugs for ulcers, drugs to make people feel calmer, go to sleep, stay awake, reduce hallucinations, be less anxious, or be less depressed are available. Physicians write more than 129.3 million prescriptions for tranquilizers (drugs that reduce anxiety) and antidepressants

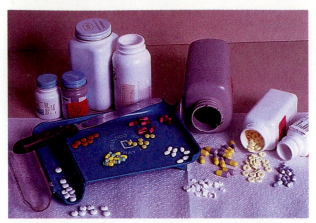

Chemotherapy, one of the biomedical treatments for mental illness, is especially appropriate for people suffering from schizophrenia or severe affective disorders.

(drugs that lessen depression) per year (Farrell, 1985). If the yearly prescriptions for these two types of drugs were divided equally among all members of the U.S. population, every man, woman, and child would get a little over one-half of a prescription of the drugs.

Drugs that are prescribed for the treatment and control of emotions, mood, and psychotic symptoms are called **psychotropic drugs**. As better psychotropic drugs for treatment of the severely mentally ill became available in the 1950s and 1960s, fewer patients spent long periods of time, or even lifetimes, in mental institutions (Exhibit 23.1 contains a first-person account of treatments in mental institutions before the advent of psychotropic drugs). Although drugs have been overused in institutions to quiet patients and make them easier to care for by fewer staff members, drugs have also made more normal lives possible for millions of people. Unfortunately, people have often placed too much faith in drug therapy, and thousands of patients who needed supportive therapy in addition to drugs were released from institutions during the 1960s, 1970s, and 1980s. The process of deinstitutionalization and its effects, both positive and negative, are described in the *Relate* section of this chapter.

Psychotropic drugs sometimes result in rapid improvement that, itself, can produce new psychological symptoms. One researcher reports the case of a forty-two-year-old woman who had lived with depression for fifteen years. Given both psychotherapy and antidepressants, she improved so rapidly her social interactions were disrupted. Apparently the subject's social contacts found her abrupt changes difficult to adapt to and opposed the treatment (Sporty & Plon, 1984). Ideally, the

physician should inform the patient about the length of time before the drug is expected to work and the changes in mood or emotions the patient should expect.

Antianxiety Drugs **Antianxiety drugs**, sometimes termed the minor tranquilizers, are prescribed rather routinely by physicians for persons experiencing anxiety, tension, restlessness, insomnia, and irritability. Librium, Valium, Tranxene, Miltown, Serax, and Equanil are trade names of common antianxiety drugs, which typically produce relaxation, less anxiety, and slight sleepiness. If these drugs are prescribed for a patient who is both anxious and depressed, however, greater depression may result.

Antianxiety drugs, which are CNS (Central Nervous System) depressants, are associated with overdoses, particularly when the drugs are combined with alcohol. Physicians and pharmacists should be certain to mention to patients that these drugs should not be taken with alcohol because the combined effect is greater than a simple addition of the effects of both. In addition, when people take antianxiety drugs in moderate or large doses over a period of time and then discontinue using them, withdrawal symptoms—anxiety, tremors, shakes, even hallucinations or convulsions—may result. Because of the tolerance effect (the need for an increased dose to get the same effect) and the withdrawal effects, antianxiety drugs should be used under close medical supervision, in crisis situations, and for relatively short time periods.

Antipsychotic or Neuroleptic Drugs Variously called **antipsychotics**, **neuroleptics**, or major tranquilizers, these drugs reduce delusions, bizarre behavior, severe anxiety, and agitation. Although neuroleptics are generally prescribed only to people who demonstrate psychotic behavior (primarily schizophrenics), they may be given in small doses to nonpsychotic hospital patients to treat nausea. The trade names of common antipsychotics are Thorazine (in the past, the most frequently used neuroleptic), Prolixin (a long-lasting injectable neuroleptic), Compazine, Stelazine, Mellarill, Haldol, Navane, Loxitane, and Moban. Available since the mid-1950s, these chemicals have had a dramatic effect on the treatment of the seriously mentally ill.

When patients first begin taking these chemicals, they may experience sleepiness, dry mouth, slight constipation, and nasal stuffiness. If the side effects are uncomfortable or persistent, the physician can prescribe a different neuroleptic; an individual may experience fewer side effects from one drug than from another. A serious

EXHIBIT 23.1
Institutional Treatment before Psychotropic Drugs

In mental institutions before the mid-1950s, when antipsychotic, antianxiety, and antidepressant medications became available, physical treatments were used almost exclusively. The most common treatments were restraints, ice water treatments, insulin-induced seizures, electroconvulsive therapy, and lobotomies. The following excerpts detail the institutional experiences of Frances Farmer, a popular, talented, beautiful movie star of the 1930s. In total, Farmer spent eight years in a mental institution, five of those years between the spring of 1945 and the spring of 1950. Her autobiography begins:

For eight years I was an inmate in a state asylum for the insane. During those years I passed through such unbearable terror that I deteriorated into a wild, frightened creature intent only on survival.

And I survived.

I was raped by orderlies, gnawed on by rats, and poisoned by tainted food.

And I survived.

I was chained in padded cells, strapped into strait-jackets, and half drowned in ice baths.

And I survived.

The asylum itself was a steel trap, and I was not released from its jaws alive and victorious. I crawled out mutilated, whimpering and terribly alone.

And I did survive.

The three thousand and forty days I spent as an inmate inflicted wounds to my spirit that could never heal. They remain, raw-edged and festering, for I learned there is no victory in survival—only grief (p. 9).

In another excerpt, Farmer describes one of the wards on which she lived:

Three days after my consultation with Dr. Conway, two orderlies fastened a belt, with built-in handcuffs, around my waist and manacled my wrists. Leg irons with about a foot of chain circled my ankles.

I offered no resistance.

Taking short, hopping steps I was led through a large door, and as I heard it clang noisily behind me, I knew that I had pressured my way into a nightmare. My new leaf had been too late in turning.

I looked down the long line of beds filled with naked women twisting, jerking, groaning, screaming, while others ran up and down the aisle repeatedly ignoring anything that got in their way. Some gibbered to themselves in animated conversation. Those tied in chairs shook their heads as if trying to clear their minds of cobwebs. Others drifted aimlessly through the ward, carrying mops or rags.

The ward bristled with attendants. This was the area of shock. Electric shock. Insulin shock. Hydrotherapy. Experimental medication. Women who had not been able to adjust were brought here for treatment. And I was petrified (p. 196).

Later in the book, Frances Farmer describes a series of hydrotherapy treatments:

Before I could organize myself, the trustee had taken down three canvas straps from a hook on the wall and had looped one around my chest, pinning my arms against my sides until my breath was cut short. The second was buckled around my thighs, and the third around my ankles.

She left the room as I tottered to keep my balance. I tried to hop after her but tumbled headlong. My chin cracked against the floor and I felt a sharp pain as my teeth sliced my lower lip. I lay there screaming, flopping, trying to maneuver myself into a sitting position, but, tied as I was, I was able to do little more than rock back and forth on my stomach.

The trustee returned with a student nurse and another attendant, who pulled me to my feet and stood behind me while the nurse checked my bindings, easing the one around my chest. I was still screaming and gabbling, spitting blood from my mouth, but the wound was ignored. They picked me up, one by the ankles, the other by the shoulders and dropped me into the empty tub, bruising my spine.

They pulled the heavy canvas sheet up to my neck, and while one tightened the neck drawstring, the other took a long dirty rope and looped it under the lip of the tub, gathering the canvas into the lasso. She tugged and pulled while the other one stretched the sheet across the tub. The rope was wound around and around until it made a tight band that kept the canvas secure.

The first crash of icy water hit my ankles and slipped rapidly up my legs. I began to shake from the shock of it, screaming and thrashing my body under the sheet, but the more I struggled, the more I realized that I was helplessly restricted in a frozen hell.

I began to gnaw on my lip, flinching from the pain of my teeth digging into the wound but praying that it would take my mind off the freezing water that burned my body like acid....

Hydro was a violent and crushing method of shock treatment, even though it was intended to relax the patient. What it really did was assault the body and horrify the mind until both withered with exhaustion.

I lay there in the glacier grip until my mind had gone blank. I felt it slipping from me, but I tried to keep it active by thinking of addresses, phone numbers, nursery rhymes. I counted forward and backward. I became confused. I recited the alphabet, but everything was jumbled. I struggled, and screamed, and froze. Then, like the incoherent woman calling for Arnold, I slid out of awareness and tumbled into a gibbering, scrambled maze.

I do not remember the other two women being taken from the tubs. And when they finally came for me, I was past audible speech or functional movement. I remember being lifted onto a cart, and then the straps fell off. The cap was pulled from my head, and my ears were unplugged. Somewhere, I heard a voice, but it was like a resounding echo.

"My God," it said. "She's nearly chewed off her lip. She'll have to be gagged next time." (pp. 198-200).

possible adverse effect of large doses (or lesser doses over a long period) of these chemicals is **tardive dyskinesia**, an involuntary movement disorder with symptoms similar to those of Parkinson's disease (involuntary muscle actions such as face twitching and gait, motor, and posture disturbances). Adverse side effects must be weighed against a neuroleptic's positive effects, and patients who experience positive changes from neuroleptics may be willing to tolerate the side effects.

Antidepressants   **Antidepressants** function exactly as the name implies—they elevate mood and thereby reduce depression. They are more effective with severe depressions unrelated to stressful events than they are with situationally triggered depressions such as grief reactions. Two major groups of antidepressants—Tricyclics and MAO inhibitors—cause different side effects. MAO inhibitors may interact with such foods as aged cheeses, chocolate, and chicken liver and cause dangerously high blood pressure. Because of this interaction, Tricyclics are prescribed more frequently than MAO inhibitors. Unlike the antipsychotic drugs, whose effects are often noticeable within hours, antidepressants take one to three weeks to benefit a patient.

Lithium   First developed by Cade in Australia in 1949, **lithium** was accepted in 1970 by the Food and Drug Administration for clinical use in the United States. One of the oldest of the modern psychotropic drugs, lithium remains one of the most effective (Murray, 1985). However, patients receiving lithium must have regular blood tests to monitor the lithium level within the blood because the drug is usually effective only within a relatively narrow blood level range; too much is toxic or even fatal while too little is ineffective. The dosage necessary to achieve the same blood level varies widely from person to person.

More specifically, lithium is lithium carbonate—a natural salt—which is most effectively used to treat manic states (see Chapter 22). Generally, lithium has fewer side effects than other psychotropic medications when it is properly administered and when blood levels are checked. As one review of the lithium studies has indicated, a further advantage of the drug is its demonstrated ability to reduce recurrences of the symptoms of bipolar disorder (Murray, 1985). Another review of lithium studies has found that preventive treatment with lithium or antidepressants "can substantially prevent recurrent episodes of unipolar depression" (Consensus Development Panel on Mood Disorders, 1985).

Today, new chemical structures, as well as combinations and alterations of already-known chemical structures, are resulting in numerous new psychotropic drugs. The general direction within chemical research is toward drugs with fewer side effects, less potential for interaction with alcohol, less potential for abuse, and greater specificity for treating mental illness. Several new drugs that simultaneously treat anxiety and depression are being tested. Therapy in the future will probably continue to include the use of psychotropic drugs to alter people's moods and emotions.

Other Biomedical Therapies   Two other biomedical treatments are large doses of vitamins and kidney dialysis (a blood-filtering treatment for malfunctioning kidneys). Although both therapies have been used primarily to treat schizophrenics, research has not demonstrated the effectiveness of the treatments. Vitamin therapies probably do not alter the symptoms of mental illness *unless* the person has been suffering from a vitamin deficiency. Similarly, kidney dialysis probably alters psychotic symptoms only if those symptoms result from abnormally functioning kidneys.

Biomedical therapies (ECT, psychosurgery, and psychotropic drugs), even the most effective, are usually prescribed in combination with psychotherapy. The following sections describe psychodynamic and behavioral therapies, which are used alone or in conjunction with biomedical therapies in the treatment of psychological disorders.

The Research Process: Treatment for the Seriously Mentally Ill

Before the 1950s advent of neuroleptic drugs, nonpsychological treatments for serious mental illness were standard. Hospitalization, sometimes for life, was common. Now, approximately thirty-five years after the first neuroleptic drug was approved for use and approximately twenty-five years after the plan to have community mental health centers replace institutional care was approved, what is the quality of the care available to the seriously mentally ill? In a recent study (1986) published by the Public Citizen Health Research Group, E. Fuller Torrey and Signey M. Wolfe attempt to answer this question.

The Subjects   For the purpose of the study, the "seriously mentally ill" were defined as people with schizophrenia, bipolar disorder, schizoaffective disorder, paranoid dis-

EXHIBIT 23.2
Where the Seriously Mentally Ill Live

26,000 are in jail

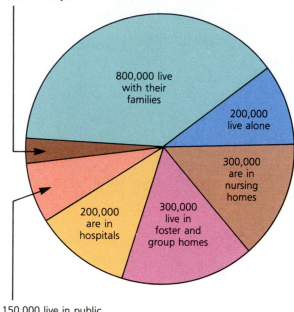

800,000 live with their families

200,000 live alone

300,000 are in nursing homes

200,000 are in hospitals

300,000 live in foster and group homes

150,000 live in public shelters or on the streets

order, and several other less common psychotic disorders. Of the estimated two million seriously mentally ill people in the United States, most suffer from schizophrenia or bipolar disorder.

After defining the term and estimating the number of seriously mentally ill, the next question is, "Where do they live?" According to information gathered from census data, government estimates, National Institute of Mental Health estimates, and numerous other studies, the seriously mentally ill live in the locations indicated in Exhibit 23.2. As you can see, more seriously mentally ill people live in nursing homes than in psychiatric (mental) hospitals, and almost as many live in public shelters and on the streets as live in hospitals. The largest group—1,000,000 (or half the estimated total)—lives with their families or by themselves.

Information Sources   Each of the fifty states as well as the District of Columbia was rated on a five-point scale for inpatient care and for outpatient (community) care of the seriously mentally ill. Each state was then ranked according to its combined scores. The information used to rate the states was obtained from twelve different sources. Among these sources were federal or state hos-

pital licensing evaluations, internal state surveys, NIMH investigations and Department of Justice investigations; the researchers obtained information from these sources through the Freedom of Information laws. Other sources of information included interviews with experts (many of whom had served on mental health-care evaluation teams), surveys of family consumer groups, and surveys of expatient groups.

Results   The following statements summarize the researchers' results.

1. The researchers found no statistical correlation between the quality of care for the seriously mentally ill and the state's per capita (per person) mental health expenditure. The top three states in mental health expenditures are: (1) the District of Columbia ($176.17), which ranks 43rd in its care; (2) New York ($74.06), which ranks 26th in its care; and (3) Delaware ($51.33), which ranks 48th in its care. In contrast, the three states ranked highest for quality of mental health care—Wisconsin, Rhode Island, and Colorado—spend $20.32, $31.54, and $24.88 respectively (p. 33).

2. The researchers found no statistical correlation between quality of care for the seriously mentally ill and per capita numbers of either psychiatrists or psychologists. Since most of these professionals are in private practice, they rarely treat the seriously mentally ill (p. 38).

3. The average combined inpatient and outpatient ratings of states within the four geographical areas vary. The average is highest (6.33) for states in the northeast, second (5.5) for states in the midwest, third (4.85) for states in the west, and lowest (4.35) for states in the south (p. 45).

4. Leadership in state mental health agencies is "probably the single most important factor in determining the quality of state services for the seriously mentally ill" (p. 46). Leadership by the governor or state legislators is also very important.

5. Well-organized, strong consumer groups that represent the seriously mentally ill are very important. In states in which such consumer groups (some are expatient groups) are strong, the quality of services is much more likely to improve (p. 47).

Exhibit 23.3 shows the combined ratings (of a total of 10 points) of each state; the five categories are:

EXHIBIT 23.3
Combined Ratings for Inpatient and Outpatient Care for the Seriously Mentally Ill by States

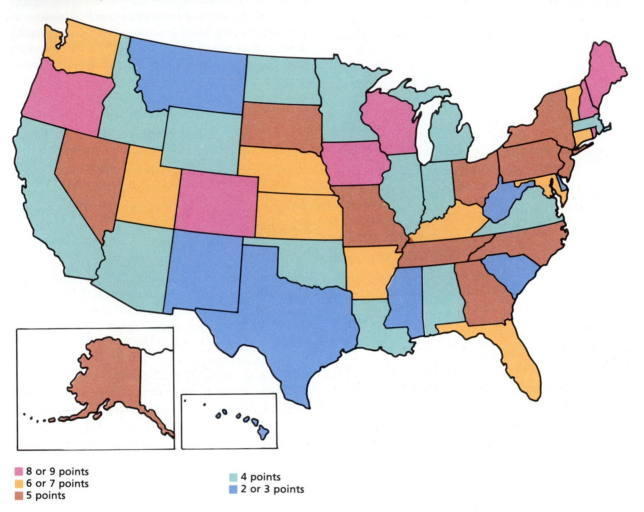

- 8 or 9 points
- 6 or 7 points
- 5 points
- 4 points
- 2 or 3 points

— States receiving ratings of 8 or 9 points
— States receiving ratings of 6 or 7 points
— States receiving ratings of 5 points
— States receiving ratings of 4 points
— States receiving ratings of 2 or 3 points

Focus Question Answer

Are ECT, psychosurgery, and drugs effective forms of therapy? ECT is most appropriately used with and most effective in the treatment of severe depression; its major adverse side effect is memory loss. Although lobot-

omies were popular during the 1940s and 1950s, very few and only very precise psychosurgeries are currently performed. Psychotropic drugs, when appropriately prescribed, are effective for treating a wide range of psychological disorders but are most helpful to people with schizophrenia and the major affective disorders.

 Psychodynamic Therapies

Psychodynamic therapists, whether followers of Freud, Adler, Jung, or others, share the following beliefs (Price & Lynn, 1986):

1. Much of human behavior is motivated by unconscious needs and conflicts.

2. Abnormal behaviors that appear irrational do not occur by chance; they have causes and are meaningful.

3. The client's present difficulties are rooted in childhood experience. Therefore, a thorough knowledge of the client's life history is essential to treatment.

4. The client's relationship with the therapist is an essential aspect of therapy.

5. Emotional expression and the opportunity to reexperience emotionally significant past events are important aspects of therapy.

6. When the client achieves intellectual and emotional insight into previously unconscious material, the causes and the significance of symptoms become apparent, and the symptoms may disappear.

In the following sections, two types of psychodynamic therapies are described—Freud's psychoanalytic therapy and Adler's individual therapy.

Psychoanalytic Therapy

As you will remember from Chapter 14, the underlying theory of psychoanalysis involves the concepts of id, ego, and superego; the five stages of personality growth; and the unconscious and conscious. The goal of psychoanalysis is to make conscious material from the unconscious and to reintegrate into the personality previously repressed material. Since, in Freud's view, therapy cannot possibly eliminate all personality defects, the goal of analysis is a state of homeostasis, or equilibrium, for the client.

Sigmund Freud (1856-1939), the originator of psychoanalytic theory and therapy, first screened his patients to determine which were suitable candidates for psychoanalysis. According to Freud's criteria, suitable candidates were less than fifty years old, reasonably intelligent, not massively depressed, confused, or psychotic, without deep-seated character defects, and willing and able to undertake the costly, demanding process. Freud insisted that clients devote one hour six days each week to analysis, which he estimated could take from

Sigmund Freud (1856–1939) originated psychoanalysis, a type of therapy in which the goal is to bring material from the unconscious to conscious awareness.

six months to well over one year. Currently, the American Psychoanalytic Association recommends that clients participate in at least four analytic sessions each week, and analyses last two to five years or more (Abeles, 1979).

Techniques   Five of the major techniques used in psychoanalysis are free association, analysis of transference, analysis of resistance, interpretation, and dream analysis. **Free association** is the "rule" of psychoanalysis; throughout therapy, the client is encouraged to reveal anything that comes to mind, even if the thoughts seem unimportant, unpleasant, or silly. Free association is the vehicle for uncovering material that is then analyzed and interpreted.

Analysis of transference is the process in which the therapist analyzes the client's disclosures for evidence of repressed feelings toward people who were significant in the patient's early life. Analysts assume a client will express toward his or her therapist feelings similar to those the client expressed toward his or her mother, father, sibling, or spouse in the past.

Analysis of resistance results from the analyst's recognition and interpretation of the client's resistance. Clients may express resistance through tardiness, refusal to express their feelings freely and candidly, or denial of the analyst's interpretation of the client's disclosure.

Freud called dreams the "royal road to the unconscious," and modern analysts assume that dream content is the conscious expression of unconscious reactions to events. In **dream analysis**, the "real" meaning of the dream is derived not from the dream's actual content but from an interpretation of the symbols appearing in the dream (Chapter 14 describes Freudian dream interpretation).

Finally, analysts employ the **interpretive process** throughout the sessions; this process is central to the role of the psychoanalyst. Generally, psychoanalysts limit their interventions to identifying and explaining to the client the source of unconscious conflicts and interpreting the material presented during therapy.

Evaluation   Although psychoanalytic terminology has become a permanent part of everyday life, psychoanalysis is usually limited to clients with relatively high incomes because of its long-term nature and, therefore, high cost. Yet, in spite of its length and cost psychoanalysis may be ineffective; little objective research validates the effectiveness of the therapy. Most studies of psychoanalysis have relied on clinical observations, in which the analyst

Quick Study Aid

Psychoanalytic Therapy Techniques

To remember the five psychoanalytic techniques, remember "Freud is AFRAID."

Freud is **A**— Analysis of resistance
          FR—Free association
          A— Analysis of transference
          I— Interpretation
          D— Dream analysis

provides all the information, provides the analysis, interprets the data, and evaluates the results. Clearly, subjectivity may have influenced the outcomes of these studies.

Individual (Adlerian) Therapy

In 1902, Alfred Adler (1870-1937), a practicing general physician, began attending with Freud weekly meetings of a group that later became the International Psychoanalytic Association. Adler was the first president of this association in 1910, but by 1911 he had left the association and broken permanently with Freud (Rychlak, 1981). After coining the term **individual psychology** to describe his theory, Adler went on to practice therapy in ways that were ahead of his time; he was the first to publicly practice group and family therapy. In addition, his real concern for equality for women set him apart from other therapists of his era (Dinkmeyer et al., 1979).

Adlerian therapy views the individual as an indivisible whole, one who has the freedom to choose a direction in life. According to this position, the individual in need of therapy has grown up in a disturbed family environment and has acquired inaccurate perceptions of self and the world. As a result, he or she has adapted a particular maladaptive style of life. The goal of therapy is mental health, and Adler used social interest (the willingness to cooperate with others for the common good) as his criterion for mental health (Ansbacher & Ansbacher, 1956).

The four stages of Adlerian therapy are: (1) establishing an empathic relationship between the counselor and client; (2) helping the client understand the beliefs and feelings, motives and goals that determine his or her lifestyle; (3) helping the client develop insight into his or her mistaken goals and self-defeating behaviors; and

(4) helping the client consider alternatives to the problem behavior or situation and make a commitment to change (Shilling, 1984, p. 57). Adlerian therapy has been referred to as a psychoeducational process because its goal is both instructional and psychological.

Techniques   Although Adlerian therapists use a large variety of techniques, only a sampling of those used in each stage are described in this text. The initial stage of a therapy relationship involves attentive listening, communicating an understanding of the client's meanings and feelings, tentative interpretation of nonverbal behavior, acceptance of silence, and development of an implicit or explicit contract (Dinkmeyer et al., 1979). The goals of the first stage are the development of a trusting relationship and the gathering of information about the client's behaviors and ideas.

The purposes of the second phase of therapy are to understand the client's lifestyle and to determine how it affects the individual's functioning. The therapist probes about the client's social relationships, long-term and short-term goals, and family constellation (relationships between members of the family in which the client grew up). Paraphrasing the client's words, confronting the client about behaviors or beliefs, and formulating tentative interpretations characterize the therapy process (Shilling, 1984).

The final phase of therapy emphasizes problem-solving and decision-making skills. Together, the client and therapist examine goals and alternative behaviors; the client makes decisions, commits himself or herself to change, and acts to meet the goals.

Individual therapists function in many settings including private practice, schools, jails, and community mental health programs. They practice individual, marriage, family, and group therapy. Adlerians have been therapy innovators in such areas as multiple therapy (one client with several therapists) and marriage counseling involving the entire family, and Adler himself developed the first child guidance clinic. Adlerian therapy is considered a short-term therapy, especially when compared to psychoanalysis; therapists expect observable evidence of positive change within three months or less (Mosak & Dreikurs, 1973).

Evaluation   As is true of psychoanalysis, few research studies validate individual psychotherapy; few Adlerians have studied the therapy's effectiveness through methods other than clinical observation. However, two major advantages of Adlerian, or individual, therapy are its

education of clients in skills that will continue to benefit them after therapy and the variety of settings and forms in which the techniques can be applied. Because of these characteristics, individual therapy is widely available to a broad range of clients.

Focus Question Answer

How is individual (Adlerian) therapy similar to and different from psychoanalytic therapy? Both types of therapists elicit information about a client's family and its early influence on the client. Both types of therapists gather information, make interpretations, and convey those interpretations to the client, thus helping the client gain insight into his or her behavior. Psychoanalytic therapy is long-term, whereas individual therapy is short-term. Psychoanalysts assume insight will lead to changes in the client; individual therapists educate clients in decision-making and problem-solving skills.

Behavior Therapies

Unlike psychoanalysis or individual therapy, behavior therapy has no single person associated with its development. Although originating at the outset of the twentieth century, behavior therapy developed primarily during the 1950s and 1960s. Behavior therapists believe maladaptive behaviors are learned behaviors that are unsatisfactory to the individual or bring the individual into conflict with the environment. In accordance with this belief, behavior therapists ask three initial questions (Shilling, 1984, p. 132):

1. What behavior is maladaptive and with what frequency does it occur?
2. What aspects of the situation or environment support and maintain the symptom?
3. What situational or environmental events are amenable to manipulation?

Behavior therapists have long acknowledged the necessity of expressing warmth, empathy, and nonjudgmental acceptance to establish and maintain a therapeutic relationship. Only if a client senses the therapist's positive attitude and feels respected will he or she cooperate in a manner necessary for treatment to be effective. Each client is approached with the same attitudes and theory about behavior, but the therapy strategies chosen for each client are very specific to the behavior the *client* wishes to change.

All behavior therapies are based on one of three learning methodologies—classical conditioning, operant conditioning, or social learning. (See Chapters 8, 9, and 15. Beck's cognitive behaviorism, based on these learning principles and on cognitive psychology, is discussed in Chapter 24.) A behavior therapist assumes responsibility for choosing the most appropriate therapy technique and for applying the technique to the problem the therapist and client have mutually agreed upon. Each technique is most effective when applied to specific types of problems and when practiced by an experienced therapist trained in behavior therapies.

Techniques Based on Operant Conditioning

Self-control or self-management programs are often carried out with clients who want to lose weight, gain weight, quit smoking, or reduce or quit drinking or taking drugs. In these programs, goals are mutually agreed upon by the client and the therapist, who then helps the client arrange his or her environment or social relationships so they will reinforce desirable behaviors and extinguish or punish undesirable behaviors. The baseline behavior (frequency or amount of the behavior present before initiation of the program) is measured, the goal is chosen, charts are kept, progress is continually evaluated, and the techniques are altered if success is not forthcoming. Although these methods were developed only decades ago, excerpts from Benjamin Franklin's autobiography indicate that he used similar procedures over a century before their formal development (see Exhibit 23.4).

Token economies are behavior modification programs often used in institutional settings to reward ap-

This teacher uses a "fifty marbles system" that resembles both self-management programs and token economies. Each time the teacher "catches" the class behaving well, she deposits a marble in the jar; when the students earn fifty marbles they are treated to a special activity such as baking cookies in the school's kitchen or eating pancakes made especially for them by the school's principal.

EXHIBIT 23.4
Benjamin Franklin's Self-Management Program

The following excerpts are from Chapter 6 of the *Autobiography of Benjamin Franklin* (1771/1965). As you read Franklin's account of his attempts to change his behavior, compare his process and techniques to those of current behavior therapy. How was Benjamin Franklin able to conceive of and use behavior therapy techniques so many years before their formal development?

It was about this time I conceived the bold and arduous project of arriving at moral perfection. I wished to live without committing any fault at any time, and to conquer all that either natural inclination, custom, or company might lead me into. As I knew, or thought I knew, what was right and wrong, I did not see why I might not always do the one and avoid the other. But I soon found I had undertaken a task of more difficulty than I had imagined. While my attention was taken up, and employed in guarding against one fault, I was often surprised by another; habit took the advantage of inattention; inclination was sometimes too strong for reason. I concluded, at length, that the mere speculative conviction that it was in our interest to be completely virtuous, was not sufficient to prevent our slipping; and that the contrary habits must be broken, and good ones acquired and established, before we can have any dependence on a steady, uniform rectitude of conduct. For this purpose I therefore tried the following method.

Benjamin Franklin identified thirteen virtues he wished to work on: temperance, silence, order, resolution, frugality, industry, sincerity, justice, moderation, cleanliness, tranquility, chastity, and humility.

I made a little book, in which I allotted a page for each of the virtues. I ruled each page with red ink, so as to have seven columns, one for each day of the week, marking each column with a letter for the day. I crossed these columns with thirteen red lines, marking the beginning of each line with the first letter of one of the virtues, on which line, and in its proper column, I might mark, by a little black spot every fault I found upon examination to have been committed respecting that virtue upon that day.

TEMPERANCE
Eat not to dullness; drink not to elevation.

	Sun.	M.	T.	W.	Th.	F.	S.
Tem.							
Sil.	•	•		•		•	
Ord.	•	•			•	•	•
Res.		•				•	
Fru.		•				•	
Ind.			•				
Sinc.							
Jus.							
Mod.							
Clea.							
Tran.							
Chas.							
Hum.							

I determined to give a week's strict attention to each of the virtues successively. Thus, in the first week, my great guard was to avoid every least offense against Temperance, leaving the other virtues to their ordinary chance, only marking every evening the faults of the day. Thus, if in the first week I could keep my first line, marked T, clear of spots, I supposed the habit of that virtue so much strengthened, and its opposite weakened, that I might venture extending my attention to include the next, and for the following week keep both lines clear of spots. Proceeding thus to the last, I could get through a course complete in thirteen weeks, and four courses in a year. And like him who, having a garden to weed, does not attempt to eradicate all the bad herbs at once, which would exceed his reach and his strength, but works on one of the beds at a time, and having accomplished the first, proceeds to a second, so I should have, I hoped, the encouraging pleasure of seeing on my pages the progress made in virtue, by clearing successively my lines of their spots, till in the end, by a number of courses, I should be happy in viewing a clean look, after a thirteen weeks' daily examination.

propriate behaviors. For each of a number of desirable behaviors, an assigned number of tokens (poker chips or other small items) is awarded to the client. At the end of a set time period, patients can exchange their tokens for reinforcers such as special privileges, trips, cigarettes, stationery, candy, or books. Unfortunately, the behavior change does not generalize well to other environments.

The solution to this difficulty lies in fading out the reinforcers to establish a habitual behavior before the patient transfers to another environment or in persuading others in the new environment to continue the reinforcement system. Exhibit 23.5 illustrates how token economies can be used to reinforce and increase socially desirable behaviors.

EXHIBIT 23.5
A Sample Token Economy

Patients in institutions may be placed on token economies. Usually, supervisors list on a chart various socially acceptable behaviors and the number of tokens the client will receive for each completed behavior.

1. Dressing before coming to the breakfast table..............5 tokens
2. Combing your hair before coming to the breakfast table...........2 tokens
3. Making your bed before 11 A.M .... 4 tokens
4. Spending a minimum of four hours each day out of your room.......8 tokens
5. Engaging in a formally conducted social activity each day.......6 tokens
6. Engaging a staff person in conversation for three minutes..........4 tokens
7. Going for a walk with a staff person...........................5 tokens

The chart can specify several desirable behaviors, and the number of tokens for each should reflect the difficulty and importance of the behavior for that individual. The reinforcers to be purchased should also reflect the individual's wants; if the patient enjoys watching sporting events on television, walking into town with a staff member, placing long distance calls to family members, or eating pizza on Friday nights, these privileges can serve as reinforcers. The client should be able to exchange tokens for reinforcers on a pre-set hourly, daily, or weekly schedule that he or she has been informed of ahead of time.

Shaping, which consists of reinforcing closer and closer approximations to the desired goal, may be used in conjunction with self-management programs or token economies. In many cases, if a therapist or the client waited until the complete, perfected behavior occurred, no reinforcement would take place. For example, if a client attempts to stop smoking or to decrease it to a specific level, reinforcement should initially be given for any decrease in smoking. Gradually, the criterion for reinforcement should be made stricter.

Techniques Based on Social Learning

Modeling is based on social learning or vicarious learning through observing the behavior of others. A behavior therapist may use modeling to help a client learn appropriate behaviors for certain social settings, better problem-solving skills, or better parenting skills. In addition, a therapist may model a lack of fear toward the object of a client's phobia as part of a program for treating phobias.

Techniques Based on Classical Conditioning

Behavior therapy techniques based on classical conditioning (see Chapter 8) include systematic desensitization, aversive conditioning, flooding, and implosion. In classical conditioning, any stimulus that immediately precedes an unconditioned stimulus will come to elicit the same unconditioned response if the stimuli are paired often enough. In **aversive conditioning**, an unwanted habit or behavior is repeatedly paired with a stimulus that elicits a negative reaction, usually pain or nausea. For instance, in a treatment to stop smoking, a smoker may be given cigarettes to which a substance causing nausea has been added. The previously pleasurable or neutral acts of taking a cigarette out of the pack, striking a match, lighting the cigarette, and inhaling become associated with nausea.

In aversive therapy, a wide range of aversive stimuli have been used—electric shock, chemicals that cause

Biofeedback machines of several types measure physiological functions (e.g., GSR or digital temperature) and provide information to the user. Biofeedback may be used to teach relaxation to anxious clients or to teach relaxation as the first step in systematic desensitization.

nausea, insults, and images of nauseating or anxiety-provoking scenes. Thus arise ethical questions about the use of aversive stimuli, especially if clients are incarcerated or unconsenting persons. Further, aversive therapy may elicit anger, fearfulness, and anxiety from clients. Because evidence suggests that aversive conditioning is only moderately effective, a behavior therapist would rarely use it except with consenting clients who had been fully informed of the procedure.

The application of **systematic desensitization** to the treatment of phobias is described in the *Relate* section of Chapter 8. In systematic desensitization, the client is first taught to relax. A commonly used exercise for achieving relaxation is the Jacobsen (1929) technique, in which the client is first taught to discriminate between muscle tension and relaxation and is then taught to relax when told to do so. Following the relaxation training, the client and therapist construct an anxiety hierarchy of the client's fears, ranking them in ascending order from least to most anxiety-provoking (see Exhibit 23.6). Finally, the therapist instructs the client to imagine the

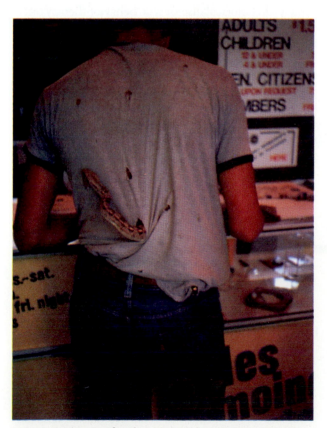

Phobias may be treated with systematic desensitization, flooding, implosion, or having a client observe a model who is unafraid.

EXHIBIT 23.6
An Example of an Anxiety Hierarchy
Wolpe (1958) described the anxiety hierarchy of a patient as follows:

A. Fear of hostility

1. Devaluating remarks by husband
2. Devaluating remarks by friends
3. Sarcasm from husband or friends
4. Nagging
5. Addressing a group
6. Being at a social gathering of more than four people (the more the worse)
7. Applying for a job
8. Being excluded from a group activity
9. Anybody with a patronizing attitude

B. Fear of death and its accoutrements

1. First husband in his coffin
2. At a burial
3. Seeing a burial assemblage from afar
4. Obituary notice of a young person dying of a heart attack
5. Driving past a cemetery
6. Seeing a funeral (the nearer the worse)
7. Passing a funeral home
8. Obituary notice of an old person (worse if died of heart disease)
9. Inside a hospital
10. Seeing a hospital
11. Seeing an ambulance

C. Fear of symptoms (despite knowing them to be insignificant)

1. Extra systoles (rhythmic heart contractions)
2. Shooting pains in chest and abdomen
3. Pains in left shoulder and back
4. Pain on top of head
5. Buzzing in ears
6. Tremor of hands
7. Numbness or pain in fingertips
8. Dyspnea after exertion (labored breathing)
9. Pain in left hand (old injury)

From Wolpe, J. 1958. *Psychotherapy by reciprocal inhibition.* Stanford: Stanford University Press.

lowest item on the anxiety hierarchy and to relax while imagining it; this procedure is repeated through the increasingly anxiety-provoking items of the hierarchy until the client can remain calm and relaxed while imagining the most anxiety-provoking stimulus. Although systematic desensitization was originally applied only to phobias, it is now used to treat a wide range of problems including fears of social interactions, enclosed spaces, open spaces, animals, disease, and death, as well as nightmares, stuttering, anorexia nervosa, excessively frequent urination, depression, anxiety, seizures, and compulsive, ritualistic behaviors of various kinds (Kazdin & Wilcoxon, 1976).

Successful treatment of irrational fears does not necessarily require the client to move successively through a desensitization hierarchy. In two other phobia treatments, **flooding** and **implosion**, the client is placed immediately at the highest level of the anxiety hierarchy. The flooding approach involves *direct and prolonged exposure* to the stimulus at the top of the hierarchy; implosion involves *imagining* the same stimlulus. The use of implosion therapy is described in the *Relate* section of Chapter 8.

Quick Study Aid

Therapy Techniques Based on Classical Conditioning

To remember the four therapy techniques based on classical conditioning (implosion, systematic desensitization, flooding, and aversion), remember the following sentence:

The tornadoes that caused the trailers to IMPLODE and the SYSTEMATIC FLOODING were AVERSIVE to the trailer park residents.

Evaluation

Behavior therapy is apparently effective for treating a diversity of behaviors, but how it works is not yet entirely clear (Yates, 1975). The advantages include involving clients in specifying their problem behaviors, supplying clients with information about their role in the process, and providing clients with reinforcement information that may be valuable to them in the future. Behavior therapies offer hope for behavior change to people who are usually unable to benefit from nonbiomedical therapies—the long-term institutionalized mentally ill, young children, and very retarded individuals. Criticisms of behavior therapies focus on the specificity of the problem or behavior that is treated; the goal is to alter a habit or behavior, not, more generally, to improve the client's functioning. Nonetheless, acceptance of behavioral techniques is now widespread, and many other types of therapists use them as an addition to their own therapy styles.

Focus Question Answer

Which psychological disorders do behavior therapy techniques treat most successfully? While the overall effectiveness of behavior techniques is difficult to determine, each technique is most successful for treating specific types of disorders. For example, systematic desensitization, flooding, and implosion are most effective in treating phobias and other irrational fears. Token economies successfully increase socially acceptable behaviors in institutional settings, and aversive techniques are best applied to unwanted habits or behaviors.

 *Relate*

Deinstitutionalization and the Homeless Mentally Ill

Deinstitutionalization refers to the enormous reduction in the numbers of patients residing in large mental institutions. The population at state and county mental hospitals fell from a high of 559,000 in 1955 to less than one-fourth of that number in 1980 (Bassuk, 1984). When considering the subject of deinstitutionalization, three major questions arise: What caused this movement? What forms of treatment replaced institutional care? How many mentally ill people are homeless?

How Deinstitutionalization Began

A combination of factors triggered the emptying of large mental institutions. First, psychotropic drugs (particularly neuroleptics) began to be widely available in the mid-1950s; these drugs reduced patients' symptoms to the extent that thousands of the mentally ill could live outside hospitals. Second, these drugs seemed particularly desirable in the 1960s because of the then-popular notion that mental hos-

pitals were "snake pits" that intensified mental illness in residents. Many experts, believing that mental illnesses were caused by one's family or by society, felt treatment in the community was more appropriate than institutionalization. This preference for community care was influenced by a third factor, the enormous and growing demand for mental health care and the overwhelming cost of this care. Many people assumed that mental health care could be provided more cheaply in a community setting. Finally, the 1960s were characterized by the civil rights movement, many of whose ideas came to be applied not just to racial minorities but also to the mentally ill.

The movement toward community care got under way in 1963, when Congress passed and President Kennedy signed the Community Mental Health Centers Act. The first step in deinstitutionalization had begun; the graph at right shows the dramatic reduction that has occurred since the Community Mental Health Center Act was passed. The second step, provision of alternative mental health care for the mentally ill, has not been adequately carried out. Fewer than half the community mental health centers needed to serve the entire population have been built, and of the centers that are in place, many do not coordinate their efforts with those of the area institutions that discharge patients (Bassuk, 1984). Too few group homes and halfway homes adds to the lack of adequate care for patients who have been discharged from hospitals.

Where Did the Hospitalized Mentally Ill Go?

Many communities do not have the social supports, the appropriate housing (group homes or halfway houses or other semi-supervised living units), the job training programs, or the connections with the mental institutions to supervise a patient's transition from hospital to independent living. Unable to manage entirely on their own, many patients may be hospitalized over and over for short time periods; this process is referred to as the "revolving door"

phenomenon. Discharged mental patients often find housing in single-room-occupancies (SRO's), most of which are located in large cities. Unfortunately, this source of inexpensive housing has been shrinking as cities eliminate rundown hotels to make room for new condominiums as part of urban development projects. If this trend continues, more and more of the very poor and the mentally ill will be living on the streets.

In addition to the previously hospitalized patients who are discharged to SRO's or to their families, some go to nursing homes. Currently, inpatient mental health care is often provided by facilities without a mental health care label. More chronic mental patients may reside in and more mental health dollars go to nursing homes than to any other single mental health setting (Kiesler, 1982a). Although according to Medicaid regulations no more than 50 percent of a nursing home's patients may have a primary mental diagnosis (i.e., no more than 50 percent of the patients may be admitted with mental disorders rather than physical disorders), nursing homes in at least four states have been charged with violating this rule (APA Monitor, 1982). Just as nursing homes may be providing the bulk of long-term care for the seriously mentally ill, general hospitals without psychiatric units may be providing more instances of brief inpatient care than are those settings labeled mental health-care providers (Kiesler, 1982b). Little research has been done on these "new" mental health-care facilities and their effectiveness in terms of cost and treatment.

The Homeless

Although experts agree that the number of people living on the streets is growing, they cannot agree on a figure. The National Coalition for the Homeless put the figure at 2.5 million for 1983, an increase of 500,000 over its estimate for the year before. Governmental agencies have estimated

Numbers of Hospitalized Mentally Ill during This Century

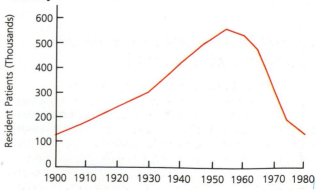

Adapted from an illustration in "The Homelessness Problem" by Ellen L. Bassuk. *Scientific American*, July 1984.

that about one-third to one-half million Americans are homeless (Bassuk, 1984). Estimates for 1985 range from 350,000 to three million, but regardless of number, more people are homeless today than at any time since the Great Depression.

How many of the homeless are mentally ill? Dr. Irwin Perr of the Rutgers Medical School in New Jersey states: "A composite of studies indicates that 35% [of America's homeless] have schizophrenia and 10% (have) significant clinical depression. . . . some 25% to 50% have alcohol- and drug-abuse problems" (Time, 1985). In a recent NIMH-funded survey of the homeless in Ohio, 27 percent said they had sought treatment for drinking problems, and 18 percent said they had been in state mental hospitals (Alter et al., 1985). The discrepancy between the number of people who say they have been in mental hospitals (18 percent in the Ohio study) and the findings that a higher percentage are mentally ill (many experts estimate about 40 percent) is accounted for by deinstitutionalization. Not only were thousands of people released from institutions, but fewer people who would have been hospitalized were ever admitted. Of an estimated two million seriously mentally ill people in the United States, approximately 150,000 or 13 percent of them now live in public shelters or on the streets (Torrey & Wolfe, 1986).

How are the homeless, a high percentage of whom are mentally ill, treated? In an attempt to save lives, several cities have passed new laws requiring police to round up people from the streets and take them to shelters any night the temperature falls below a certain level. However, this treatment may not be as humane as it seems; these homeless people may be victims of violence or theft within the shelters, and they may be forced to leave the shelters early in the morning. In Greenwich Village in 1984, barbed wire was placed over hot-air grates to keep the homeless from sleeping on them. In San Diego, a shelter for the homeless was destroyed by arson (Time, 1985). In Santa Barbara, grocers pour bleach over their discarded food to discourage hungry vagrants from eating the garbage (Time, 1986).

What is the solution? Politicians have proposed that support for assistance (shelters, food, and clothing) for the homeless will have to come from private sector donations, yet the private sector seems unwilling to provide such support. A recent study reveals that corporate philanthropy devoted to buying art has risen, but contributions for human services programs have decreased substantially (Alter et al., 1985).

Why, in spite of its initial bright prospects, has the community health movement failed, and can this failure be remedied? A critic of the community mental health center movement gives the following answer.

The community mental health movement failed primarily because the federal and state governments never allocated the money needed to fulfill its promise. American society is currently trying to solve the problem cheaply, giving the mentally ill homeless at best emergency refuge and at worst no refuge at all. The question raised by the increasing number of homeless people is a very basic one: Are Americans willing to consign a broad class of disabled people to a life of degradation, or will they make the commitment to give such people the care they need? In a civilized society the answer should be clear. (Bassuk, 1984)

Things to Do

1. Locate the local branches of several professional organizations of social workers, clinical psychologists, psychiatrists, and sex therapists. Obtain and compare copies of their ethical codes of behavior.

2. Ask a variety of people to answer true or false to the eight myths in the Exploring . . . section. Ask the respondents to state their reasons for believing the myths to which they answer true. Do your results confirm Zilbergeld's notion that these misconceptions are widely believed?

3. Write down your opinions about psychotropic drugs, ECT, and involuntary hospitalization as well as your expectations for a therapist. Discuss your preferences with a friend or family member. Then if you ever need mental health care and are unable to make decisions, at least one person will know your views.

4. Examine your local newpaper and telephone book for advertisements for different therapies and therapists. What results from therapy do the ads promise or imply?

5. Find out if your community has a telephone number you can dial to obtain information about community services. Call your local mental health center, and inquire about its services. Ask about cost of the services and about the center's funding sources.

6. Your community may not have a large inpatient mental health facility, but local hospitals may have psychiatric units for those diagnosed as mentally ill. Visit an inpatient facility (you may have to schedule an appointment), and ask which therapies are most often used there. Ask what proportion of the inpatients are receiving psychotropic medications. Note: The patients' rights to privacy may prohibit a visit to patient areas of a hospital.

Things to Discuss

1. Imagine you are a therapist in a mental health center. What would you do in the following situations?

a. A fifteen-year-old, referred by the school system for nonattendance, has spoken at length about disagreements with his parents and their use of physical punishment. Now he tells you he plans to leave for another state without telling his parents.

b. Following a 5 o'clock appointment, an attractive client who is separated from his/her spouse inquires about going out for dinner together to discuss other problems. You find this client sexually attractive and your interests quite compatible.

c. An elderly man has disclosed his feelings of uselessness and the emptiness of his life now that his wife is dead. He feels "it is not worth going on" and he has indicated that suicide is preferable to his present life. You know he has a lethal quantity of pain pills in his possession.

2. What should the United States do about the homeless mentally ill? As you formulate your answer, consider the civil rights of individuals, the rights of communities, the role of private philanthropy, the role of the state and federal governments, and cost effectiveness.

3. Under what conditions would you consent to ECT for yourself? A family member? A stranger?

4. Have you taken or would you take psychotropic drugs to alter your moods and emotions? Under what conditions?

5. What advice would you give a friend or family member about choosing a therapist?

6. What uses of behavior modification techniques have you observed in institutions such as schools, workplaces, prisons, or mental institutions? What ethical questions should be considered when these techniques are applied to captive audiences?

Things to Read

Bandura, A. 1969. *Principles of behavior modification.* NY: Holt, Rinehart & Winston.

Goleman, D. & Speeth, K.R., (eds.) 1982. *The essential psychotherapies.* NY: New American Library.

Sacks, O. 1985. *The man who mistook his wife for a hat and other clinical tales.* NY: Summit Books.

Valenstein, E.S. 1985. *Great and desperate cures: The rise and decline of psychosurgery and other radical treatments for mental illness.* NY: Basic Books.

Wander, P.H. & Klein, D.F. 1981. *Mind, mood, and medicine.* NY: Farrar Straus Giroux.

Review

Summary

1. Psychotherapy (treatment for a mental or emotional illness) is provided by professionals such as psychiatrists, psychologists, and counselors or by nonprofessionals such as religious leaders, friends, teachers, or family members.

2. Self-help strategies that may be useful to people are reading books, consulting media "therapists," calling telephone crisis lines, and joining support groups.

3. Therapy decisions confronting the client or the therapist are: individual, family, or group therapy; involuntary hospitalization; use of biomedical therapies; exceptions to confidentiality; sexual behavior between therapist and client; length of therapy; fees for therapy. Many therapy decisions involve ethical issues.

4. Historically, physical therapies were used almost exclusively to treat mental illness. Modern biomedical therapies include electroconvulsive therapy, psychosurgery, and pharmacological interventions.

5. Psychotropic drugs are prescribed for the treatment and control of mood, emotion, and psychotic symptoms. Antianxiety drugs, neuroleptic (antipsychotic) drugs, antidepressant drugs, and lithium are the major types of psychotropic drugs. Tardive dyskinesia is an involuntary movement disorder associated with large doses and/or long-term use of the neuroleptic drugs.

6. Five of the major techniques used in psychoanalytic therapy are free association, analysis of transference, analysis of resistance, dream analysis and the interpretive process. Psychoanalysis involves approximately four sessions per week and is long-term therapy.

7. First developed by Alfred Adler, individual therapy

is generally short-term therapy, is practiced in a variety of settings, and encompasses a large number of techniques. Some of the most frequently used techniques are attentive listening, tentative interpretation, acceptance of silence, paraphrasing, and teaching problem-solving and decision-making skills.

8. Based on classical, operant, or social learning, behavior therapy techniques are most effective when applied to specific types of problems. Self-control or self-management, token economies, and shaping are based on operant conditioning; modeling is based on social learning; and aversive conditioning, systematic desensitization, flooding, and implosion are based on classical conditioning.

9. Despite being criticized for their specificity, behavioral techniques are used by many types of therapists with populations not suitable for other types of therapy.

10. The deinstitutionalization movement began in the 1960s and led to a greater than 75 percent decrease in the population of inpatients at mental institutions between 1955 and 1980. Today, approximately 150,000 seriously mentally ill people live in public shelters or on the streets. Too few community mental health services and alternative living arrangements are available.

Key Terms

psychotherapy
trepanation (trephination)
electroconvulsive therapy (ECT)
psychosurgery
pharmacological interventions
psychotropic drugs
antianxiety drugs
neuroleptics (antipsychotics)
tardive dyskinesia
antidepressants
lithium
free association
analysis of transference

analysis of resistance
dream analysis
interpretive process
individual psychology
self-control (self-management)
token economies
shaping
modeling
aversive conditioning
systematic desensitization
flooding
implosion
deinstitutionalization

Focus Questions

1. Are you responsible for choosing behaviors that give your life meaning?

2. Can changing the way you think about the world and your behavior affect your mental health?

3. Should you join a growth group, or should you join a therapy group?

4. How do current therapy ideas differ from those of ten, twenty, or thirty years ago?

Chapter Outline

HUMANISTIC-EXISTENTIAL THERAPIES
Frankl's Logotherapy
Rogers' Client-Centered Therapy
Perls' Gestalt Therapy

COGNITIVE THERAPIES
Ellis' Rational-Emotive Therapy
Beck's Cognitive Therapy

OTHER WELL-KNOWN THERAPIES
Glasser's Reality Therapy
Berne's Transactional Analysis
The Research Process: Effective Therapy for
    Depression
Groups, Groups, and More Groups

RELATE: Three Decades of Therapy
Things to Do
Things to Discuss
Things to Read

REVIEW: Summary
Key Terms

Chapter 24

Humanistic-Existential, Cognitive, and Other Therapy Models

No one can make you feel inferior without your consent.

Eleanor Roosevelt

What is the purpose of therapy? Is its purpose to change behavior (as behavior therapists emphasize) or to undertake in-depth analysis of the personality (as psychoanalysts emphasize)? To some psychotherapists, the purpose of therapy is to answer the questions, "Who am I? Why do I exist?" To other psychotherapists, the purpose is to eliminate irrational beliefs; still other therapists emphasize cognitive processes.

You may wonder how and when such diverse ideas about therapy developed and which therapy is best or most effective. In this chapter, you will read descriptions and evaluations of several major types of therapy. The *Relate* section examines the therapy trends of the last three decades.

587

Humanistic-Existential Therapies

Unlike the traditional Freudian theorists, who believe people are driven by negative instincts and desires that need to be controlled, the humanists believe people are basically good and have an innate tendency toward self-actualization. They believe the function of a therapist is to provide a safe environment in which the growth potential of the client can be released.

Existentialist therapies trace their roots to philosophical concerns about what being human means and how each individual experiences his or her existence. Existentialist therapies are characterized by an attitude or world view rather than by an accepted set of techniques.

In the following discussions of Rogers' client-centered therapy and Frankl's logotherapy, you may notice similar views of the therapist's role and of the relationship between client and therapist. This similarity between the existential concepts and client-centered therapy has been growing (Patterson, 1986), and many therapies are now most accurately labeled humanistic-existential. Gestalt therapy, as described and practiced by Fritz Perls, is among the most widely practiced and accepted of the humanistic-existential therapies (Kaplan & Sadock, 1985).

Frankl's Logotherapy

Victor Frankl (1905-), born in Vienna, was trained as a psychiatrist with a psychoanalytic orientation. He first wrote about existential analysis and **logotherapy** in 1938, but his theoretical conceptions and therapy methods were refined and tested by his experiences during World War II. Frankl spent from 1942 to 1945 in German concentration camps; his mother, father, brother, and wife died in the camps or gas chambers. During his imprisonment, Frankl became convinced the environment does not make a person behave in specific ways; rather, the environment's effect on a person depends upon the attitude the person brings to the situation. Reflecting upon his prison camp experiences, Frankl (1965) wrote, ". . . we saw how, faced with the identical situation, one man degenerated while another attained virtual saintliness."

In his writings, Frankl emphasizes the uniqueness of each human being and the finite quality of life. He maintains that, rather than decreasing the meaning of life, an examination of the finiteness of your existence and the certainty of your death gives added meaning to the hours and days of your life. If life were not finite, you could attach little meaning to how you spend your time because time would go on forever.

According to Frankl, the three distinctly human qualities are spirituality, freedom, and responsibility. Spirituality, as Frankl uses the term, does not have a religious connotation; it refers instead to the uniquely human part of a person—the spirit, the philosophy, or the mind. Freedom, as Frankl defines it, is freedom *from* instincts, heredity, and the environment and freedom *to* make decisions. With the freedom to make decisions comes the responsibility for those decisions. The questions clients discuss in therapy often focus on issues such as why they exist, what they want from life, and the meanings of their lives (see Exhibit 24.1).

Techniques   Many existential psychotherapists use primarily psychoanalytic techniques, while others differ little from client-centered therapists. Frankl, in his book *The Doctor and the Soul: From Psychotherapy to Logotherapy* (1965), describes only two techniques. Throughout his writings and those of other existential therapists, you will find an emphasis on the relationship between the therapist and client and a negative attitude toward specifying techniques. The therapist-client relationship does not emphasize diagnosis of mental illness; it emphasizes the therapist's role in helping the client experience freedom, responsibility, and the capacity to change his or her life by making different choices. The client is not an object to be analyzed but an "existential partner."

Paradoxical intention is a logotherapy technique most appropriately used with clients with obsessive-compulsive and phobic conditions or with clients who are fearful and anxious about situations and who therefore withdraw from or avoid them. A fear of fainting and collapsing

Humanist therapists believe their function is to provide a warm, safe, supportive atmosphere in which their clients can grow toward self-actualization.

can be treated by instructing the client to try to faint and collapse and by instructing the client to repeat this attempt each time he or she feels the fear. According to Frankl, the patient will be unable to faint and collapse and will probably see the humor in trying to do so (Frankl, 1965). Frankl emphasizes the role of humor in paradoxical intention and in dereflection.

Dereflection is a technique used primarily to divert attention from the self. Frankl (1965) cites the treatment of a nineteen-year-old man whose speech disturbance had developed when he was six years old: "We attempted to make one thing clear to him: that he would have to give up any ambition of becoming a good orator. We further explained that to the degree to which he became resigned to being a poor speaker, he would, as a matter of fact, improve his speech. For then he would pay less attention to the *how* and more to the *what* of his speech" (pp. 206–207). In other words, once a person accepts a problem and its implications, the person ceases think-

ing and worrying about that behavior. According to Frankl, the behavior then improves on its own.

Evaluation   One of the criticisms of logotherapy and, indeed, of existential therapies in general is the lack of a systematic statement of the practice of therapy. Other often-cited criticisms are the use of numerous abstract concepts and the lack of research about the effectiveness of the approach. Although Frankl (1965) specifies how logotherapy can be used in conjunction with biological treatments for treating clients with schizophrenia and other psychotic disorders, logotherapy is most appropriate for clients with anxiety disorders and less appropriate for clients who are psychotic. Also, because of the philosophical nature of the discussions that are likely to occur during therapy, clients who are introspective and whose verbal, intellectual, and social abilities are relatively high may benefit greatly from this therapy. However, clients who function at lower intellectual levels or who are

EXHIBIT 24.1
Existential Questions

Existential philosophers are often stereotyped as believing that life has no meaning. Nothing could be further from Victor Frankl's ideas. To him, people give their lives meaning through the choices they make and the attitudes they bring to work, suffering, love, life, and death. The following questions reflect the issues many people examine when they try to find meaning in their lives.

1. What does personal freedom mean to you? Do you believe you are the person you are largely as a result of your choices?

2. Are you able to accept and exercise your own freedom and make significant decisions by yourself? Do you attempt to escape from freedom and responsibility? Are you inclined to give up your autonomy for the security of being taken care of by others?

3. Do you agree that every person is fundamentally alone? In what ways have you attempted to ameliorate your experience of aloneness?

4. What is your experience with anxiety? Does your anxiety result from the consideration that you must choose for yourself, the realization that you are alone, the fact that you will die, or the realization that you must create your own meaning and purpose in life? How do you deal with anxiety in your own life?

5. What do you value most? What would your life be like without these items? What gives your life meaning and a sense of purpose?

6. Do you believe that, unless you take death seriously, life has little meaning?

7. Have you experienced an "existential vacuum"? Is your life without substance, depth, and meaning at times? What is the experience of emptiness like for you, and how do you cope with it?

8. Do you believe that anxiety is a motivational force toward growth and that personal growth and change usually entail anxiety?

Adapted from *Theory and practice of counseling and psychotherapy*, 3rd Edition, by G. Corey. Copyright (c) 1986, 1982, 1977 by Wadsworth, Inc. Reprinted by permission of Brooks/Cole Publishing Company, Monterey, CA 93940.

dealing with hunger, poverty, or the lack of other basic survival needs are unlikely to be interested in discussions of the meaning of life and of self-actualization (Corey, 1977).

Logotherapy's contributions include addressing philosophical questions that trouble many people, not only those diagnosed as mentally ill. Therapists' attitude toward clients is refreshingly nondehumanizing; it conveys great respect and optimism accompanied by an emphasis on individual choice and responsibility. Finally, the attitude toward death as something that gives life meaning rather than as an end to be feared is a positive contribution.

Rogers' Client-Centered Therapy

The personal history of Carl R. Rogers, the originator of **client-centered therapy**, is summarized in Chapter 15. From his early interest in medieval history, philosophy and religion to his continuing reevaluation of his theory and its applications at well past eighty years of age, Rogers himself is a fascinating subject. In contrast to many of the existential therapists, Rogers has, from the initial proposals of his ideas in the early 1940s to the present, considered his ideas tentative, and he has welcomed research that would clarify his ideas or prompt him to alter them. Reflective of this spirit of willingness to be guided by new ideas, Rogers' approach to therapy and theory has gone through four stages.

The first stage, the nondirective stage, encompassed the decade of the 1940s and was characterized by an

Carl R. Rogers, (right), best known as the originator of client-centered therapy, was a leader of the group counseling movement and of humanistic education.

emphasis on attentive listening, acceptance of the client, and clarification of the client's verbalizations. In 1951, Rogers published the book *Client-Centered Therapy*, which reflected the major idea of the second stage—rejecting the concept of the dependent patient in favor of the responsible client. In this second stage, techniques received less emphasis, the therapist reflected back to the client both the message's content and feeling, and the therapist was seen as providing a supportive environment in which the client could choose to change. The experiential stage, which began in the late 1950s, incorporated even more existential ideas; the following passage written by Rogers in 1961 illustrates this point:

To the therapist, it [the process of therapy] is a new venture in relating. He feels, "Here is this other person, my client. I'm a little afraid of him, afraid of the depths in him as I am a little afraid of the depths of myself. Yet as he speaks, I begin to feel a respect for him, to feel my kinship to him. I sense how frightening his world is for him, how tightly he tries to hold it in place. I would like to sense his feelings, and I would like him to know that I stand with him in his tight, constricted little world, and that I can look upon it unafraid. Perhaps I can make it a safer world for him. I would like my feelings in this relationship with him to be as clear and transparent as possible, so that they are a discernible reality for him, to which he can return again. I would like to go with him on the fearful journey into himself, into the buried fear, and hate, and love which he has never been able to let flow in him. I recognize that this is a very human and unpredictable journey for me, as well as for him, and that I may, without even knowing my fear, shrink away within myself from some of the feelings he discovers. To this extent I know I will be limited in my ability to help him. I realize that at times his own fears may make him perceive me as uncaring, as rejecting, as an intruder, as one who does not understand. I want fully to accept these feelings in him, and yet I hope also that my own real feelings will show through so clearly that in time he cannot fail to perceive them. Most of all I want him to encounter in me a real person. I do not need to be uneasy as to whether my own feelings are "therapeutic." What I am and what I feel are good enough to be a basis for therapy, if I can transparently be what I am and what I feel in relationship to him. Then perhaps he can be what he is, openly and without fear. (Rogers, 1961b)

In the fourth stage, the person-centered stage, Rogers shifted his attention from individual and group therapies to broader applications of his theory. He began applying his ideas to education, industry, and society (Shilling, 1984).

Despite a shift in emphasis during the third and fourth stages, Rogers' therapy is still generally referred to as client-centered therapy. The basic goal of the therapeutic process is for the client to move toward self-actualization. To accomplish this task, the person must have: (1) an openness to experience; (2) a trust in himself or herself; (3) an internal locus of control (a looking to the self for answers and evaluation of the self); and (4) an acceptance that growth is a continuing process (Rogers, 1961a).

Techniques Labeling certain behaviors as client-centered therapy techniques and discussing those techniques seems to contradict the spirit of Rogers' therapy. As Rogers developed this theory, techniques received less and less emphasis. Although the client-centered stage focused on establishing a therapeutic climate in which the client has the opportunity to engage in self-exploration and to experience his or her full range of feelings, specific therapist behaviors are seen only as vehicles for communicating respect for the client. The client is viewed as basically good, striving toward self-actualization, and responsible for his or her own behavior.

The three central characteristics a therapist should convey to a client are:

1. **Acceptance (unconditional positive regard)**—a liking of or warmth for the client, a warmth that carries no judgment or evaluation.

2. **Congruence**—a realness or genuineness, the opposite of which is playing a role.

3. **Empathy (understanding)**—a sense of the client's world as if the therapist sees it from the client's viewpoint. In his later writings, Rogers gave empathy the highest priority of the three characteristics (Rogers, 1975).

Although they may not be techniques in the sense that dream analysis is a psychoanalytic technique, active (or attentive) listening and reflection (or paraphrasing) are the central elements of client-centered therapy. **Attentive listening** involves paying close attention to what the client says and communicating that attentiveness to the client through the nonverbal cues of body position, eye contact, and tone of voice. **Reflection or mirroring** consists of reflecting back to the client the content and feelings of the message and a nonjudgmental attitude of acceptance.

Quick Study Aid

Rogers—The ACE Therapist

To remember Rogers' three therapist characteristics, remember that Rogers is an ACE therapist.

A - Acceptance
C - Congruence
E - Empathy

Evaluation Probably the most frequently cited criticism of Rogers' client-centered therapy is its seemingly unrealistic belief in an innate goodness and growth potential in all human beings. Another criticism pertains to the vagueness of the definitions of terms, a vagueness that disturbs people who insist on operational definitions. One of the major strengths of this approach is the emphasis on research and on changing the theory of therapy when new information is found. Certainly, the strong belief in individuals' ability to change in a growth-oriented direction is another strength. Although this therapy is described in this chapter in terms of its use in individual therapy, client-centered therapy has been used with couples and groups, in weekly sessions or marathon sessions. In addition, Rogers was at the center of the group-counseling movement and is one of the fathers of the basic encounter group (Rogers, 1970). The client-centered ideas have also been applied to humanistic education (Rogers, 1969), industry, and international relations.

While Rogers (1957) has hypothesized that the therapy conditions he describes are the "necessary and sufficient conditions" for therapeutic change, many other therapists, particularly the cognitive therapists, have questioned Rogers' assumption (Ellis, 1959). Frustrating to some therapists is the limiting of the therapist's role to nondirective techniques; in client-centered therapy, directive techniques such as questioning, probing, interpreting, analyzing, informing, and teaching are virtually absent. Perhaps because of its limitations, client-centered therapy has evolved in several directions; one direction is toward absorbing more existential ideas and the other direction is toward a more cognitive orientation.

Perls' Gestalt Therapy

More than most therapies, **Gestalt therapy** is very closely tied to the personality of its founder, Fritz Perls (1893–

Gestalt therapy, originated by Fritz Perls, relies on a variety of techniques to help clients resolve unfinished business from the past so they can function better in the here-and-now.

1970), who described himself as a physician, a psychoanalyst, a scholar, a pilot, and a "dirty old man" (Perls, 1969). In intensive workshops, which essentially consisted of individual therapy in front of a group, Perls was charismatic, self-assured, and often provocative and dramatic. Two leading proponents of Gestalt therapy observed that, "When the master works, it is hard to discriminate between what is his *style* and what is the theory which supports his style" (Polster & Polster, 1973, p. 286).

Perls considered Gestalt therapy one of the existential therapies; Gestalt therapy combines both existentialist concerns about how people experience their present existence and Gestalt psychology concerns about how people perceive themselves and the world. Gestalt therapy assumes that individuals can deal with their life problems, that people use the past to escape responsibility and to blame others, and that clients will become "unified and whole" if they resolve unfinished business (leftover feelings from the past that interfere with present functioning).

As with client-centered therapy, the goal of Gestalt therapy is to help clients live fuller lives and move toward self-actualization. To achieve this goal, clients must *experience* feelings in the "here-and-now," not talk *about* feelings. The emphasis on responsibility is apparent in the goal of helping clients determine how they are preventing themselves from feeling and experiencing; therapy is not seen as a problem-solving process but as a process in which clients gain greater ability to solve their own problems.

Techniques Gestalt therapy is practiced with individuals, with groups, or with individuals within groups. In the latter variation, one member of a group volunteers to be on the "**hot seat**." Through a variety of techniques, the therapist focuses his or her attention almost exclusively on this client; involvement by the other group members is rarely elicited at this stage. Therapists, as well as clients, are expected to express feelings that occur in the "here-and-now." Therapists and clients are urged toward "full personal expression" and toward a wide variety of authentic responses including shouting, crying, suggesting, admonishing, and talking about themselves (Kempler, 1973).

In contrast to client-centered therapy and logotherapy with their dearth of techniques, Gestalt therapy relies upon so many techniques that people may see it as gimmicky. Ten of the most often used Gestalt techniques are briefly summarized in Exhibit 24.2. As in client-centered therapy and logotherapy, the personal interaction between the therapist and the client is seen as the central part of the therapeutic process; the techniques are viewed only as tools to be used to help clients gain greater awareness of feelings and body messages.

Evaluation Research on the effectiveness of Gestalt therapy and its techniques is sparse. In a study of seventeen therapy groups with nine different theoretical approaches (two of the groups were Gestalt groups), one Gestalt group was rated as highly successful and one was rated as least beneficial of the seventeen. Closer examination of the therapy sessions revealed that differences among all groups were largely dependent upon the personality characteristics of the leaders, rather than on the theoretical orientations they espoused (Lieberman et al., 1973). Although observers were impressed with the striking changes that took place during Perls' workshop demonstrations, little evidence in the form of follow-up studies supports the lasting effects of the changes. Although Perls believed himself to be the best therapist for the treatment of neurosis in the United States (Perls, 1969), he has only testimonials to support his belief.

An advantage of Gestalt therapy is its application to a variety of settings; however, caution should be exercised in the choice of clients. Shepherd (1970) warns against the use of confrontive techniques or reenactments of emotional experiences with clients who are psychotic. As to the appropriate clientele for Gestalt therapy, she comments: "In general, Gestalt therapy is most effective with overly socialized, restrained, constricted individuals—often described as neurotic, phobic, perfectionistic, ineffective, depressed, etc. — whose functioning is limited or inconsistent, primarily due to their internal restrictions, and whose enjoyment of living is minimal. Most efforts of Gestalt therapy are therefore directed toward persons with these characteristics" (pp. 234–235).

Criticisms of Gestalt therapy focus on the lack of a solid theory, the perception of the techniques as gimmicky, and the anti-cognitive or anti-intellectual nature of Perls' writings. On the positive side, gestalt therapy offers a unique basic combination of existential and humanistic ideas accompanied by attention to the concept of the *whole* person in the environment. The inclusion of dream work, attention to nonverbal behavior, and emphasis on responsibility and self-actualization pull together ideas from several other therapies. In addition, many therapists and clients find the active, confrontive nature of gestalt therapy quite appealing.

EXHIBIT 24.2
A Selection of Gestalt Techniques

The "games" of Gestalt therapy have been collected by Levitsky and Perls (1970) and are presented here as they were summarized by Patterson (1986). Notice the apparent contradiction between the emphasis on individual responsibility and independence and the connotation of the word *patient; patient* denotes one who is under treatment by an expert.

1. *Games of Dialogue.* The patient assumes the roles of aspects of the split personality and carries on a dialogue between those aspects. These parts include the topdog (superego or should) versus the underdog (passive resistant), aggressive versus passive, nice guy versus scoundrel, masculine versus feminine, and so forth.

2. *Making the Rounds.* The patient extends a general statement or a theme (for example, "I can't stand anyone in this room") to each person individually, with additions pertinent to each.

3. *"I Take Responsibility."* The patient is asked to follow each statement about himself or herself or about his or her feelings with "... and I take responsibility for it."

4. *"I Have a Secret."* Each person thinks of a personal secret involving guilt or shame and, without sharing the secret, imagines how others would react to it.

5. *Playing the Projection.* When a patient expresses a projection, he or she is asked to play the role of the person involved in the projection to discover the conflict in this area.

6. *Reversals.* The patient is asked to play a role opposite to his or her overt or expressed behavior (for example, to be aggressive rather than passive) and to recognize and make contact with the submerged or latent aspect of himself or herself.

7. *The Rhythm of Contact and Withdrawal.* The natural inclination toward withdrawal is recognized and accepted, and the patient is permitted to experience the security of withdrawing temporarily.

8. *Rehearsal.* Since much of thinking is rehearsal in preparation for playing a social role, group members share rehearsals with one another.

9. *Exaggeration.* Exaggeration is also a repetition game. When the patient makes an important statement in a casual way, indicating that he or she does not recognize the statement's importance, the patient is required to repeat the statement again and again with increasing loudness and emphasis.

10. *May I Feed You a Sentence?* The therapist creates a sentence he or she believes to represent something significant for the client and instructs the client to repeat the sentence over and over. The client determines the appropriateness of the therapist's interpretive sentence.

Adapted from Patterson, C. H. 1986. *Theories of counseling and psychotherapy.* NY: Harper & Row, pp. 365–366.

Focus Question Answer

Are you responsible for choosing behaviors that give your life meaning? According to existential therapists, your choices about how to spend your time give meaning to your life. The realization that your life is finite and the awareness of your responsibility for choosing how to spend your limited time give your life meaning and also cause the anxiety you feel.

 ## Cognitive Therapies

In contrast to the existential-humanistic therapies, which emphasize individual emotional reactions, cognitive therapies emphasize logic and reasoning. Cognitive therapies assume that changing people's irrational beliefs or illogical thinking can change their attitudes and behaviors and thereby help them better solve problems. Two representative cognitive therapies are discussed here—Albert Ellis' rational-emotive therapy and Aaron Beck's cognitive therapy. Both Ellis and Beck were trained in psychoanalysis, became dissatisfied with it, and subsequently began to experiment with more active, directive therapy techniques.

Ellis' Rational-Emotive Therapy

Ellis (1913-) first developed rational psychotherapy in the 1950s, and it has been called **rational-emotive therapy (RET)** since 1962. Underlying RET is the assumption that emotions do not cause disturbed thinking—disturbed thinking causes negative emotions. To Ellis, therapy includes establishing a relationship in which the therapist is nonjudgmental, accepting, warm, and respectful toward the client. However, in contrast to Rogers, Ellis believes the relationship is of secondary importance in therapy; it is not absolutely necessary nor is it usually sufficient to help the client. Further, because nondirective therapies are too time-consuming, Ellis advocates a directive, teaching style (Ellis, 1975).

Techniques   Ellis believes clients must first realize, either on their own or through the therapist's teaching, that the cause of emotional disturbance is irrational beliefs, that these negative emotions continue because clients keep repeating the irrational beliefs to themselves, and that improvement can come only through the hard work of challenging those irrational beliefs. Clients are instructed to examine their statements and beliefs; they are taught to identify the **activating events** that, the

clients often say, cause their negative feelings. Ellis, however, denies that events *cause* emotions; he maintains that the combination of the event and the **irrational beliefs** that are part of the client's **belief system** lead to the **consequences**, or **negative emotional experiences**. The purpose of therapy, then, is **disputing irrational beliefs** and replacing them with logical, rational ones (Ellis, 1977). Exhibit 24.3 contains eleven statements that Ellis lists as the most common irrational beliefs.

Homework assignments, as well as other behavioral methods such as desensitization, operant conditioning, and assertion training, are incorporated into RET therapy sessions (Ellis, 1974). RET is practiced in both individual and group settings and in a combination of the two. The length of therapy varies because teaching clients the basics of RET may take as little as one to ten sessions or as long as several years (Ellis, 1973).

EXHIBIT 24.3
Irrational Beliefs

According to Ellis, the following irrational and superstitious beliefs are almost universally held in American society. Belief in these *false* ideas and continual self-indoctrination with them lead to neurosis and other emotional disturbance (Ellis, 1962).

1. A person must be loved or approved by virtually everyone in the community.
2. A person must be perfectly competent, adequate, and achieving in order to be considered worthwhile.
3. Some people are bad, wicked, or villainous and therefore should be blamed and punished.
4. When events are not as a person wants them to be, catastrophe results.
5. Because unhappiness is caused by outside circumstances, a person has no control over it.
6. Dangerous or fearsome things are causes for great concern, and a person should continually dwell upon their possibility.
7. Avoiding certain difficulties and self-responsibilities is easier than facing them.
8. A person should be dependent upon others and should have someone stronger on whom to rely.
9. Past experiences and events are the determinants of present behavior; the influence of the past cannot be eradicated.
10. A person should be quite upset over other people's problems and disturbances.
11. Every problem has a right or perfect solution; that solution must be found, or the results will be catastrophic.

Adapted from Ellis, A. 1962. *Reason and emotion in psychotherapy*. Secaucus, NJ: Citadel Press. p. 61. Published by arrangement with Lyle Stuart.

Quick Study Aid

Rational-Emotive Therapy (RET)

To remember Ellis' rational-emotive therapy system, remember **A B C D**:

A (Activating Event or experience)
+
B (Belief System—how the individual perceives or interprets A)
=
C (Consequences or emotional disturbance)
D (Disputing Irrational Beliefs in the Belief System—what the client is taught in therapy)

Evaluation The reverse of the criticism of gestalt therapy is appropriate here; while gestalt therapy emphasizes only emotions and is anti-cognitive, RET goes to the other extreme and emphasizes logic and reason almost to the exclusion of emotion. Ellis's active instruction in challenging irrational beliefs and instruction in RET theory sometimes seem more akin to persuasion techniques than to therapy. As with other "talk" therapies, RET is probably least effective or even ineffective with clients who are schizophrenic and more effective with verbal, educated clients (Ellis & Greiger, 1977).

Beck's Cognitive Therapy

Aaron T. Beck (1921-) has studied neurology, psychiatry, and traditional psychoanalysis. Like Ellis, he became disappointed in psychoanalysis and, after careful study and practice of behavior therapy, rejected it as well. He went on to develop **cognitive therapy**, which, as he defines it, "consists of all the approaches that alleviate psychological distress through the medium of correcting false conceptions and self-signals" (Beck, 1976, p. 214).

According to Beck, maladaptive **automatic thoughts** arise involuntarily in an individual; they do not result from logic and reasoning. The goal of cognitive therapy is to challenge the validity of these automatic thoughts and to replace these misconceptions and misinterpretations with logical and reasonable ideas (Patterson, 1986). Beck views therapy as a process in which an accepting, warm, empathic, nonauthoritarian therapist collaborates with a client to solve specific problems; through this process, the client acquires problem-solving skills he or she can apply in other situations. Beck's

approach is different from rational-emotive therapy in that Ellis assumes an emotionally disturbed person subscribes to one or more of the common irrational beliefs; Beck, on the other hand, first asks the client for evidence that substantiates a statement before he assumes the statement is illogical.

Techniques Because cognitive therapy is based on the commonsense idea that people's thoughts and statements about themselves are important and that emotional disorders are characterized by distorted thinking, a cognitive therapist uses techniques that reduce distorted thinking. Although Beck is not specific about the therapist's use of his techniques, the basic steps of the process are to help the client recognize maladaptive thoughts, identify the maladaptive thoughts that occur during an experience, distance himself or herself from the maladaptive thoughts, and test the thoughts for verifying evidence. Finally, the therapist assists the client in replacing his or her unrealistic rules, such as "I should always be at my best."

Evaluation Both the criticisms and the positive evaluations that have been applied to Ellis' RET are appropriate here. Although Beck (as compared to Ellis) seems to subscribe less to the view of therapist as expert and more to that of therapist as helpful gentle collaborator, both therapists emphasize logic and reason and downplay the role of emotion.

In 1983, a review of forty-eight studies was designed to determine the efficacy of cognitive behavior therapy in general. In this review, cognitive behavior therapies were defined as "those treatments in which at least one component of the therapy specifically focused on the patient's maladaptive beliefs" (Miller & Berman, 1983, p. 42). Both Ellis's rational-emotive therapy and Beck's cognitive therapy fit this definition. The last two sentences of the review's report provide a clear summary and a direction for further study:

Yet, despite clear evidence that cognitive behavior therapies are more effective than no treatment, there is little evidence that they are more effective than other widely practiced psychotherapies. If proponents of cognitive behavior therapies wish to advocate this treatment over others, they will need to demonstrate convincingly either that it is superior to other psychotherapies or that it is the treatment of choice for specific disorders (Miller & Berman, 1983, p. 50).

School counselors may use puppets to describe situations to children, who are then asked to talk about how the characters would feel and behave in the situations. This method allows students to discuss feelings, behaviors, and solutions to problems that they may otherwise be reluctant to discuss.

Focus Question Answer

Can changing the way you think about the world and your behavior affect your mental health? According to cognitive therapists, irrational or illogical thoughts lead to disturbed emotional responses. In accord with this belief, they see the goal of therapy as eliminating or changing these thoughts. Logical, rational thoughts, according to the cognitive therapists, lead to greater mental health.

 Other Well-Known Therapies

Glasser's Reality Therapy

In 1957, William Glasser (1925–) formulated **reality therapy** in response to the ineffectiveness he felt when dealing with juvenile delinquent girls in a residential setting. As a psychiatrist with a master's degree in clin-ical psychology, he disliked the lack of therapy, the low discharge rate, and the high recidivism (repeater) rate at the facility. After successfully using reality therapy with the juvenile delinquent girls, Glasser employed his new therapy with patients in a Veterans Administration hospital. He recounted his therapy concepts and experiences in *Reality Therapy: A New Approach to Psychiatry* (1965).

Glasser believes all people have one single basic need—the need for identity. In addition to positing this basic principle, Glasser uses at least eight characteristics to define reality therapy (Corey, 1977):

1. Reality therapy equates mental illness with irresponsible behavior and mental health with responsible behavior.

2. Reality therapy emphasizes present behavior rather than feelings or attitudes.

3. In the focus on the present, reality therapy discourages recounting the past or one's miseries; rather, the therapy stresses the client's successes, positive qualities, and potentials.

4. Reality therapy emphasizes the importance of the client placing value judgments on his or her behavior and determining if this behavior is contributing to success or failure in his or her life.

5. Reality therapy rejects the process of transference in favor of a warm, genuine therapist-client relationship to help the client fulfill his or her present needs.

6. Reality therapy rejects examination of the unconscious in favor of examination of the client's present life and behaviors. The therapy does not view insight as essential to producing change.

7. Reality therapy eliminates punishment. Glasser expects the therapist to give praise when clients act in "responsible ways" and to show disapproval when they act irresponsibly.

8. Teaching responsibility, with an emphasis on morals, standards, value judgments, and right and wrong behavior, is a core concept of reality therapy.

Techniques Glasser describes few specific therapeutic techniques, but he recommends an involved sensitive therapist who encourages self-disclosure from the client, encourages the client to maintain a friendly, optimistic demeanor, obtains a commitment from the client to carry out behavioral plans, and accepts no excuses if the client fails to complete the plans (Glasser & Zunin, 1973).

Appropriate to a wide range of clients, reality therapy encourages optimism and responsibility for one's behavior.

Evaluation Reality therapy is practiced in a variety of settings including individual therapy, group therapy, and marital therapy, and it seems well-suited to short-term crisis-intervention. Glasser's ideas have been applied outside therapy, most notably to school systems. In his book, *Schools Without Failure* (1969), he proposes a program to eliminate failure; he emphasizes thinking instead of rote memory work, introduces relevance into the curriculum, substitutes discipline for punishment, creates motivation and involvement, helps students develop responsible behavior, and establishes ways of involving parents and community members in the school.

The emphasis on assuming responsibility, evaluating one's present behavior in terms of its success or failure, and committing oneself to a plan of action are real strengths of this therapy approach (the *Exploring . . .* section examines an Eastern therapy—Morita therapy— that is characterized by very similar ideas). However, critics question whether the role of a therapist should include rewarding behavior he or she values as responsible and showing disapproval of behavior he or she labels irresponsible. A much stronger criticism can be made of Glasser's view of psychotic symptoms and psychoses as irresponsible behavior. Glasser fails to account for the very responsible behavior of many mentally ill persons before the onset of their symptoms. He also fails to acknowledge the schizophrenia research, which indicates probable neurochemical differences.

Does Control Theory Differ from Reality Therapy? In his 1984 book, *Control Theory*, Glasser states that behavior consists of what we do, what we think, and what we feel; as a corollary to this assumption, he proposes that, regardless of how we feel, we have control over what we do. In this most recent work, Glasser expresses a very anti-deterministic or anti-behavioristic view that was far less obvious in his previous writings; in *Control Theory*, he states: ". . . we are not controlled by external events, difficult as they may be. We are motivated completely by forces inside ourselves. . . (p. xiii). . . . As I explained in the first chapter, any theory that contends that our behavior is a response to outside events or stimuli is wrong" (p. 39).

Currently, Glasser also places greater emphasis on the biological sources of behavior. He states, "We are at our core biologic beings: that we satisfy some of our genetic instructions psychologically rather than physically makes neither the instructions less urgent nor the source less biologic" (p. 9). Glasser believes the following four psychological needs are encoded in our genes:

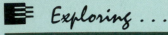 Exploring . . .

Morita Therapy: "The Japanese Way to Building a Better Life"

A contemporary of Freud, Shoma Morita was a psychiatrist, physician, and department head at a top medical university in Tokyo. He observed that some of the suffering he saw did not stem from medical problems but from "misunderstandings about life." From his knowledge and experience, Morita developed a system of therapy based on the ideas of Zen Buddhism. His therapy was first seriously practiced in the United States after World War II, and research evidence about its effectiveness began to appear in the 1970s. By 1980, a program was developed to train and certify practitioners of Morita guidance and, as of 1984, ten trainees had completed their training at two institutes in Los Angeles and one on Maui, Hawaii (Reynolds, 1984).

Morita therapy does not posit as a goal insight into the childhood causes of one's present suffering, and it discourages discussions about feelings and their origins. Evident throughout Moritist writings is an emphasis on behavioral commitment. Discussions, understandings, and even decisions to act are not enough; only behavior counts. The following excerpt expresses succinctly the Moritist relationship between feelings, behavior, and control.

The doing is what is important, not the result. From the Moritist point of view, no act is merely instrumental. Every act is an end in itself. The

In Morita therapy, A Japanese therapy based on the Zen Buddhist idea of purposeful living, the therapist may assign meditation, Zen koans, or writing one's own obituary.

quality of our attention in action is crucial. . . . With every fully attended activity I am working not only on the project at hand but on myself as well. Behavior is what counts. Not emotion. Not even the results of behavior. What I do is the only thing in life that I can control. No one can guarantee a life of good feelings. No one can guarantee that our efforts will bring the results that we hope for. We must be clear on what is controllable (Reynolds, 1984, p.18).

the need to belong—to love, share, and cooperate; the need for power; the need for freedom; and the need for fun. His continuing theme is the ability of people to take control of their lives.

In *Control Theory*, Glasser expresses disapproval of hospitalization unless a person is dangerous and disapproval of medications, except for very brief periods. In this book, Glasser denies mental illness and explains the behaviors that are so labeled as creative behaviors the person uses to gain control of his or her life. Many psychiatrists and psychologists question the validity of this position.

The answer to the question posed at the beginning of this section seems to be yes, differences between reality therapy and control theory do exist. In his most recent book, Glasser places greater emphasis on biological sources of needs and his **control theory** has an anti-behaviorist stance despite including what seems to be positive reinforcement. In addition to making these changes, Glasser also alters the language he uses to describe symptoms; he changes many nouns to verbs, e.g., headaching instead of having a headache, anxieting instead of being anxious, and phobicking instead of having a phobia. As these language alterations imply, Glasser assumes the

The three fundamental principles of the Moritist method are to accept your feelings as they are (rather than use energy and attention trying to analyze them), know your purpose, and do what needs to be done. Morita therapists may assign meditation as a way of learning to still the mind and allow attention to be focused on the reality of the moment. Zen *koans* (puzzles with solutions that must be arrived at by more than rational thought) are sometimes used in the practice of Morita therapy in the United States to teach the student the Moritist approach to living. Therapists may also ask students to write obituaries or eulogies to help them examine their long-term purposes. This assignment does not emphasize thinking about death; rather, the task helps the student order his or her life before death.

Many of the writings of Western psychological theorists reflect similarities to Moritist ideas, the existential writers probably having most in common with Morita. Perls' writings indicate he stayed briefly in a **Morita therapy** hospital in Japan, and the influence is evident in his occasional inclusions of a Zen story or passage in his writing and therapy.

The idea of distinguishing what people can control is central to Glasser's control theory, while another Morita excerpt reflects a similarity to Ellis' rational-emotive theory: "Let me repeat, neurotic people are

not ill; they have bad habits of thinking and acting that result in unnecessary suffering for them and for others" (p. 13).

In Morita guidance, clients or patients are thought of as students who need "re-education and practical training in living effectively" (p. 13). The therapist is thought of as a teacher who uses lectures, readings, conversations, and exercises to teach a student to deal with discomfort and suffering. The similarity to the existentialist idea of responsibility is evident in the Moritist therapist's attribution of any change in the student's life to the student's efforts. The therapist is only the teacher; the student is responsible for the learning.

In the United States, psychoanalytic, behavioral, and existentialist techniques and Rogerian-like unconditional acceptance of the client may be combined with this therapy based on the Zen Buddhist idea of purposeful living. The following instruction was written by David K. Reynolds, the leading teacher of Moritist therapy in the U. S.:

So don't seek anxiety-free living; don't strive for constant bliss. Choose rather to continue your struggle. Resolve to react forcefully to the challenges of reality. Hold to your goals. Fight your fight. And live with purpose (Reynolds, 1984, p. 53).

individual is responsible for and can control his or her symptoms.

Berne's Transactional Analysis

Eric Berne (1910–1970) was a psychiatrist who for twenty years received periodic psychoanalytic training from such notables as Erik Erikson. The rejection of Berne's application for membership in the San Francisco Psychoanalytic Institute in 1956 may have been caused, at least partly, by his espousal of group therapy methods and his insistence on an active role in therapy, both of which

are rejected within traditional psychoanalysis (Steiner, 1974). Berne was a prolific writer, and two of his books, *Games People Play* (1964) and *What Do You Say After You Say Hello?* (published posthumously in 1972), became best sellers.

In Berne's theory of **transactional analysis (TA)**, personality is divided into three **ego states**—the Parent, the Adult, and the Child. The Parent represents the actual messages, whether nurturing or critical, people received from their parents; "shoulds" and "oughts" are the property of the Parent ego state. Spontaneity, creativity, and expression of feelings characterize the Child ego state. A processor of information, the Adult ego state unemotionally and nonjudgmentally deals with external reality.

According to Berne's theory, humans have a need to be touched, both physically and emotionally; he labeled this need a hunger for **strokes**. Psychological health depends upon getting enough positive strokes—words, touches, or expressions of affection or appreciation. Positive strokes make people feel they are "OK," and negative strokes—abuse, humiliation, ridicule, and criticism—make people feel they are "not OK." Feelings about themselves and others that people acquire during their early years result in what Berne labeled four **life positions** (Berne, 1964):

— I'm OK, You're OK—psychologically healthy position.

— I'm OK, You're Not OK—blaming others.

— I'm Not OK, You're OK—depression, powerlessness, withdrawal.

— I'm Not OK, You're Not OK —loss of hope and interest in life.

In their interactions with others, people send out from one of their ego states messages directed to a particular ego state of the receiver. Receivers then reply from one of their ego states, addressing the message to a particular ego state of the original sender. This process is labeled a **transaction**. Transactions may be complementary—the sender gets the predicted response from a specific ego state of the other person—or crossed—the sender gets an unexpected response from an ego state that was not addressed.

Techniques   Berne stressed that showing concern for the patient, practicing good observation skills, and indivi-

dualizing therapy take precedence over techniques. He wrote, "It is, unfortunately, difficult to offer more than a few general suggestions as to how to deal with people who are by definition the epitome of individuality" (Berne, 1961). Berne, for the most part, left to his followers the task of elaborating upon his few techniques. Berne did, however, specify some initial steps. First, after the therapist has informed the client of the services the therapist can offer, the therapist and client should create a contractual agreement. In this contract, the client should state the goals of therapy, and the therapist should agree to those goals. As progress is made or conditions change, the contract should be amended or expanded. The method for beginning therapy is to very directly teach the client the essentials of the theory and the concepts and terminology accompanying it (Berne, 1961). Following this instruction, the client and therapist, in an individual or group therapy setting, can begin analyzing the client's ego states and the transactions. Although Berne emphasized the simplicity of his theory, the glossary of approximately one hundred words in *What Do You Say After You Say Hello?* belies his assertion.

Evaluation   Berne's emphasis on the simplicity of his ideas has had several outcomes: (1) Both lay and professional people have misperceptions about Berne's complex theory. (2) Transactional analysis has not been taken seriously by some professionals, possibly due to its popularity. (3) Because of these misperceptions and TA's use by minimally trained therapists, transactional analysis has been misused by controlling and manipulative practitioners (Patterson, 1986). A positive aspect of TA is the contract or agreement between client and therapist; this agreement immediately establishes the direction of the therapy. The contract and teaching the client the theory and the terminology make possible the client's full participation in his or her own analysis.

Research comparing TA's effectiveness to other group or individual therapies has not been forthcoming. Just as the initial success of gestalt therapy may have resulted from Perls' personality and involvement with his clients, so too the success of TA may have been due to Berne and not to his techniques. In practice, therapists often combine parts of TA with other therapies; common combinations include psychoanalytic techniques, Gestalt techniques, and psychodrama (Patterson, 1986). More research and comparison of outcomes of various "insight" or "talk" therapies is badly needed. *The Research Process* examines one recent study that compared biomedical and cognitive treatments of depression.

Quick Study Aid

An Analysis of Transactions—Berne

To remember Berne's three ego states, remember the PAC person.

A PAC person is composed of three ego states:

PAC = **P** arent
A dult
C hild

The Research Process: Effective Therapy for Depression

Most studies of therapy effectiveness have compared one type of therapy to no therapy; the no-therapy (control) group has usually been comprised of people on an agency's waiting list. Various studies have examined the effectiveness of different therapies conducted by differently trained individual therapists treating a wide variety of clients suffering from a range of diagnoses. Systematic comparison of two or more treatments of clients with the same diagnoses have been rare.

In 1977, the National Institute of Mental Health (NIMH) began planning the Treatment of Depression Collaborative Research Program (TDCRP), the first large-scale psychotherapy research program to be conducted at more than one site. The planners chose clients suffering from major depressive disorders as the subjects for the study. Generally, the outpatient treatment for depression consists of antidepressant drugs, psychotherapy, or a combination of the two. The TDCRP was formulated to compare the effectiveness of two types of brief psychotherapy, a commonly prescribed antidepressant, and a placebo (Elkin et al., 1985).

Research Design   The study included four treatment groups (cognitive behavior therapy, interpersonal psychotherapy, antidepressant plus clinical management, and placebo plus clinical management) of twenty patients each at three different sites. During the two years that preceded the official beginning of the study, the therapists were trained to conduct therapy sessions in very similar fashion; videotapes of therapy sessions conducted by the participating therapists were compared to assure uniformity in therapy approaches.

Beck's cognitive behavior therapy (CB) is based on the theory that depression results from distorted thinking and clients' unrealistic views of themselves and the world. CB therapists help clients think more realistically about their psychological problems and thereby reduce their symptoms. Interpersonal psychotherapy (IPT) is based on the theory that depression results from interpersonal problems and poor social functioning. IPT focuses on mastery of social roles and adaptation to interpersonal situations; IPT therapists assume that if interpersonal relationships improve, improvements in other areas will follow.

The antidepressant treatment group received imipramine and clinical management (CM) sessions in which a physician assessed the client's status, provided a generally supportive atmosphere, and managed the client's

Exercise or other physical activities may be part of some group approaches. People who suffer from chronic pain may exercise, learn relaxation techniques, obtain new information, and use biofeedback training.

medication level. The placebo group received a placebo (fake pill) and CM; these clients were also assessed and supported. Supposedly their medication level was also managed. All the clients were assessed for depressive symptoms before therapy began and at four, eight, twelve, and sixteen weeks (all therapies lasted approximately sixteen weeks). Follow-up evaluations were planned at six, twelve, and eighteen months. The study ended in late 1986, and many statistical comparisons are still being done (Elkin et al., 1985).

Results   Of the 239 clients who entered treatment, 162, or 68 percent, completed fifteen weeks of treatment; according to a rating scale of depression, 44% of the clients were "severely depressed" at the beginning of the study. The following statements summarize the study's initial findings as they were presented at the American Psychiatric Association Annual Meeting on May 13, 1986:

1. All the treatment conditions resulted in a reduction of depressive symptoms, but fewer of the clients in the placebo group than in the other three groups showed full recovery.

2. Although the antidepressant (imipramine) clients showed a more rapid reduction of their depressive symptoms, the psychotherapy clients caught up by the end of therapy.

3. Clients who were severely depressed did not do well

in the placebo plus clinical management treatment condition, but no significant difference was found between the effectiveness of the four treatment conditions for less severely depressed clients.

4. Interestingly, only the Interpersonal Psychotherapy (IPT) was significantly more effective than placebos for the severely depressed clients.

In summary, severely depressed patients should be treated with therapy more active than the supportive treatment received by clients in the clinical management (CM) condition. For less severely depressed clients, a variety of therapies, including minimal support and encouragement, may be effective. Further analysis of the results will provide information about which clients will be most likely to benefit from specific types of therapies and which therapies will better prevent the recurrence of depressive symptoms.

Groups, Groups, and More Groups

This chapter begins with discussions of therapies that are primarily individual, proceeds through therapies used in both individual and group settings, and ends with techniques used *only* in group settings. In Exhibit 24.4, the description of group therapy distinguishes it from other group techniques. Group therapy resembles individual therapy in that both are conducted by professional therapists in formal settings, and the clients are people with identifiable psychological problems. In contrast, support groups like Reach for Recovery (for women who have had mastectomies) and growth-oriented groups like encounter or sensitivity groups are aimed at "normal" people who have similar characteristics or needs.

Married couples, family members, residents of institutions, workers at particular companies, and students—all can be and have been the target of one or more group techniques. Generally, the advantages of group techniques, both therapeutic and growth-oriented, involve exchanging information, learning from others, and improving one's social skills. Exhibit 24.4 presents brief descriptions of the purposes and techniques of a variety of groups. In choosing therapy, whether you prefer individual or group, be certain you respect and have confidence in the therapist and are motivated to work to change.

Alcoholics Anonymous (AA) groups provide support for alcoholics who have chosen sobriety; the regular, frequent *meetings and close contact between group members make AA one of the most successful approaches to treatment for alcoholism.*

EXHIBIT 24.4
A Potpourri of Groups

Type	Purpose	Description	Techniques
Group Therapy.	To help individuals change or modify disordered behavior so they can function more appropriately.	Usually conducted by one or more therapists (psychiatrists, psychologists, etc.) in an institutional setting (clinic, hospital, or private facility).	Generally meet one to two hours per session for six or more months. Leadership is dependent upon the theory and training of the therapist.
Personal Growth Groups—may include encounter, sensitivity, human awareness, human potential, and T-groups.	To emphasize personal growth in normal, often middle-class individuals.	Usually take place in unstructured, informal settings; led by lay or professional democratic leaders who stress participation and self-disclosure.	Varied techniques may include confrontation, trying new behaviors, sensory awareness, and other activities.
Marathon Groups—a generic term usually indicating the length of time rather than the type of therapy.	To increase self-awareness and self-understanding; to break down defenses and encourage openness.	Usually meet fifteen to twenty hours or may meet all weekend with short breaks. Often, these are encounter or sensitivity groups.	Depending upon the specific leader technique, uses the same techniques as those used in personal growth groups.
Special Groups—e.g., Alcoholics Anonymous, Parents Anonymous, Synanon, Weight Watchers.	To exchange information; to provide a supportive environment with others who have the same problem.	Usually have regular, frequent meetings supplemented by other supportive contact. Usually begun and conducted by lay persons.	Depending upon the group and leader, includes confronting, encouraging responsibility, exchanging information, etc.
Psychodrama (associated with Jacob Moreno).	To permit individuals to gain insight into their motivation and needs; to help individuals express feelings.	May take place on a stage. The therapist is "play director," and participants act out their feelings. Other participants may play the roles of parts of the self, family members, etc.	Uses role reversal, mirroring, (exact imitation of) a person's behavior; all techniques emphasize dramatic portrayal of emotions.

Focus Question Answer

Should you join a growth group, or should you join a therapy group? You may join a growth group to broaden you life or gain new understandings, and you may join a support group with others who are experiencing similar life circumstances. In contrast, you would join a therapy group only if a psychotherapist recommended it. The advantages to group participants are learning from other people whose lives are similar and increasing one's social skills. The benefits you gain from a group experience will be determined by the leadership qualities of the psychotherapist or lay leader and by your motivation to learn and change.

 *Relate*

Three Decades of Therapy

The following three charts list many of the major contributors to the theory and practice of therapy in the United States during the decades of the fifties, sixties, and seventies. It does not include all the contributors of each era, nor does it include all the major publications of the people listed.

Trends

The Early Years

During the twenties and thirties, while psychoanalysis flourished in Europe, behavioral psychology was just beginning to grow in the United States. The forties marked an important change in therapy in the United States. Due in part to World War II, the demand for psychotherapy greatly in-

creased and, for the first time, clinical psychologists began to be allowed to practice therapy. Prior to the forties, clinical psychologists had been permitted to do only diagnostic testing; psychotherapy had been almost exclusively the province of psychiatrists and psychoanalysts (who were usually also psychiatrists).

The Fifties

During this decade occurred two major developments in the theory and practice of therapy—Rogers's book on nondirective, or client-centered, therapy and several publications by behavioral therapists. Although the behavioral therapists continued practicing therapy and publishing their ideas, be-

Therapy of the Fifties, Sixties, and Seventies

The Fifties		
Person	*Therapy*	*Major publications*
John Dollard (psychologist) & Neal Miller (psychologist and psychoanalytically trained)	combination of Reinforcement Theory and Psychoanalytic Therapy	1950—*Personality and Psychotherapy: An Analysis in Terms of Learning, Thinking and Culture.*
Joseph Wolpe (psychiatrist)	Behavior Therapy	1958—*Psychotherapy by Reciprocal Inhibition* 1966—*Behavior Therapy Techniques: A Guide to the Treatment of Neuroses* (other books in 1960s and 1970s)
Carl Rogers (psychologist, exposed to psychoanalytic thought)	Client-Centered (humanistic therapy) (see also *The Seventies*)	1951—*Client-Centered Therapy* 1961—*On Becoming a Person*
Fritz Perls (psychiatrist, trained in psychoanalysis)	Gestalt Therapy (existentialist therapy)	1947—*The Beginning of Gestalt Therapy* 1951—*Gestalt Therapy: Excitement and Growth in Personality* (with Hefferline & Goodman)
Albert Ellis (psychologist and psychoanalytically trained)	Rational-Emotive Therapy (RET)	1962—*Reason and Emotion in Psychotherapy*

haviorism did not achieve widespread popularity until the sixties. The fifties were the era of client-centered therapy. The growing need for mental health services and the resentment toward the cost and time involved in psychoanalytic therapies enhanced the popularity of Rogers' humanistic therapy.

The Sixties

The attraction of behaviorism's scientific approach and its emphasis on techniques and technicians reflected the spirit of the time. In behavioral therapy, the therapist is seen as an expert who evaluates the situation, arranges different environmental contingencies, and quickly eliminates the client's symptoms. By the late sixties and the early seventies, behavior modification techniques had achieved widespread support among professionals and the public. Criticisms about behavioral therapy's misuse and its reputed unfeeling nature did not prevail until the mid-seventies.

The Seventies

The decreasing emphasis on behavioral psychology and the growth of cognitive psychology were the central develop-ments of the seventies. Cognitive psychologists had been publishing their ideas during the sixties, but behaviorism was *the* therapy of the decade. During the seventies, however, public criticism of using behavioral techniques in institutional settings such as schools increased, and public acceptance of cognitive therapies, which had existed since Ellis published his rational therapy ideas in the mid-fifties, increased. The seventies also produced a proliferation of new therapies or therapeutic intervention techniques (but not new theories). One article written in the mid-seventies refers to 130 sub-schools of psychotherapy (Parloff, 1976).

Now and in the Future

Patterson (1986) believes that despite these numerous divergences the therapies can be divided into two major categories or approaches to therapy. He labels the first a technological approach (epitomized by behavioral therapies) and the second a humanistic approach (client-centered therapy and the existential therapies). He speculates that the existential therapies never achieved professional prominence or public popularity due to the lack of specific therapy procedures and competition with the "scientific" cognitive therapies.

The Sixties

Person	Therapy	Major publications
Victor Frankl (neurologist, psychiatrist)	Logotherapy (existentialist therapy)	1959—(in German, 1946) *From Death Camp to Existentialism* 1966—*Man's Search for Meaning.* 1965—(in German, 1946) *The Doctor and the Soul*
Rollo May	Existential-Humanistic Therapy	1961—*Existential Psychology* 1967—*Psychology and the Human Dilemma* 1969—*Love and Will*
Eric Berne (psychiatrist, trained in psychoanalysis)	Transactional Analysis	1961—*Transactional Analysis in Psychotherapy* 1964—*Games People Play: The Psychology of Human Relationships*
William Glasser (psychiatrist, trained in psychoanalysis)	Reality Therapy	1961—*Mental Health or Mental Illness* 1965—*Reality Therapy* 1969—*Schools Without Failure* (1984—*Control Theory*

Patterson (1986) identifies two trends of the eighties: (1) "a trend (backward) toward the more directive, controlling, authoritarian, or 'therapist-knows-best' approaches of the past" (p. 539); and (2) "the apparent trend toward eclecticism" (p. 542). Glasser's control theory seems to typify the first trend. In describing the new eclectic therapies, Patterson states, "It is a classic example of the blind men defining an elephant, with one describing its trunk; another, its tail; yet another, its leg; and so on. The various approaches have little in common. We have yet to see a truly **eclectic** system of psychotherapy, which would integrate the valid elements of the major theories and practices" (p. 542).

Things to Do

1. Answer the existential questions in Exhibit 24.1. Is your philosophy of life similar to that of the existentialists?

2. Rational-emotive therapy (RET) maintains that people have many "do's," "ought's" and "should's" in their lives. Identify ten to which you subscribe. (You should succeed at everything. You ought to be tough. You should do what is right. You should be perfect. You should always work to your full potential. You ought to do what is expected of you.)

3. Aaron Beck calls self-talk "automatic thoughts" because the thoughts are swift, packaged in as few words as possible, and unquestionably accepted as fact. These thoughts are often too blaming, too rigid, or downright erroneous. Identify several situations in which you experience negative emotional reactions. Examine and test the validity of your thoughts about these situations.

4. Make a list of several types of group therapy, and ask a psychologist, a psychiatrist, a psychology teacher, and a social worker for their opinions of the therapies. Ask each respondent to specify the most appropriate clients for each therapy.

5. Arrange an interview with a psychotherapist who works at a local mental health center. The following list of questions may help you structure your interview.

The Seventies

Person	Therapy	Major publications
Fritz Perls (psychiatrist, trained in psychoanalysis)	Gestalt Therapy (existentialist therapy)	1969—*Gestalt Therapy Verbatim* 1969—*In and Out of the Garbage* 1973—*The Gestalt Approach and Eyewitness to Therapy* 1975—*Legacy from Fritz*
Donald Meichenbaum (psychologist)	Cognitive-Behavior Modification	1974—*Cognitive-Behavior Modification* 1977—*Cognitive-Behavior Modification—an Integrative Approach* 1985—*Stress-Inoculation Training*
Aaron Beck (psychiatrist, trained in psychoanalysis)	Cognitive Therapy	1976—*Cognitive Therapy and the Emotional Disorders* 1979—*Cognitive Therapy of Depression* (with Rush, Shaw, and Emery)
Carl Rogers (psychologist, exposed to psychoanalytic thought)	Client-Centered (humanistic therapy)	1969—*Freedom to Learn* 1970—*On Encounter Groups* 1972—*Becoming Partners—Marriage and Its Alternatives*

a. Do you see your patients on an individual or group basis?

b. Which types of therapy do you find most valuable? Which are used most often by other therapists here?

c. Which therapy techniques do you find particularly effective?

d. How often are drugs prescribed for clients? Are drugs used in conjunction with other therapies?

Things to Discuss

1. Would you want your therapist to give you his or her opinions? Advice? Suggestions about activities in which to engage? Would you want your therapist to make judgments about the irrationality of your beliefs?

2. Do you think gestalt therapy, with its emphasis on experiencing moment-by-moment feelings, underemphasizes the importance of cognition? Do you believe RET, with its emphasis on rational thinking, gives enough attention to emotions and feelings?

3. Existentialists, as well as other therapists, may view therapy as a process of teaching a client a philosophy of life. Is this therapy goal appropriate? If so, does the goal assume the therapist has the *correct* or *better* philosophy of life?

4. Glasser believes a therapist should praise the client who acts responsibly and show disapproval of the client who acts irresponsibly. Does this approach encourage the client to adopt the therapist's values so the client can be liked and accepted? Is this approach appropriate? Do all therapists make value judgments about their clients' behaviors, thoughts, and feelings?

5. Review the therapies, and determine the relative emphasis within each therapy on changing behavior versus gaining insight. Which emphasis has greater appeal for you?

6. Morita therapy, with its underpinning of Zen Buddhist philosophy, may conflict with some of the prevailing cultural attitudes in the United States. Identify the similarities and the differences between Morita therapy and American cultural attitudes.

7. The prevailing therapeutic models changed during the fifties, sixties, and seventies. Which model do you favor most? If eclecticism is the "wave of the future," which ideas from different schools of therapy do you hope will contribute most significantly to eclecticism?

Things to Read

Beck, A. 1976. *Cognitive therapy and the emotional disorders.* NY: International Universities Press.

Berne, E. 1964. *Games people play: The psychology of human relationships.* NY: Grove Press.

Dean, A. 1986. *Night light.* NY: Harper/Hazelden Books.

Ellis, A. & Harper, R. 1975. *A new guide to rational living.* Rev. ed. Hollywood: Wilshire Books.

Frankl, V. 1963. *Man's search for meaning.* Boston: Beacon Press.

Glasser, W. 1984. *Control theory: A new explanation of how we control our lives.* NY: Harper & Row.

Harris, A.B. & Harris, T.A. 1985. *Staying OK.* NY: Harper & Row.

Polster, E. & Polster, M. 1973. *Gestalt therapy integrated.* NY: Brunner/Mazel.

 # Review

Summary

1. The existential-humanistic therapies combine ideas of both schools of therapy; the therapies are characterized by belief in an innate growth potential, belief in the value of the therapist-client relationship, emphasis on choice and responsibility, and the search for meaning in life.

2. Frankl's logotherapy specifies only two techniques—paradoxical intention and dereflection—and these techniques can be used most effectively to treat clients with anxiety disorders.

3. Client-centered therapists are nondirective; according to Rogers, the "necessary and sufficient" condition of positive therapeutic outcome is a therapist-client relationship in which the therapist is accepting, congruent, and empathic.

4. A "here-and-now" orientation, a reliance on the expression of feelings and emotions, and an abundance of techniques characterize Perls's gestalt therapy, which is usually practiced in group settings.

5. Ellis's rational-emotive therapy and Beck's cognitive therapy are representative of the cognitive therapies, which emphasize logical thinking. Ellis advocates a directive, teaching approach in which he instructs the client in the art of identifying and disputing irrational beliefs. Beck works in collaboration with clients to identify automatic thoughts and to test their validity.

6. A Japanese Zen Buddhist-based therapy, Morita therapy, exhibits clear similarities to the existentialist therapies, which Morita's writings predate. Morita therapy emphasizes accepting feelings, knowing one's purposes, and, most important, doing what needs to be done.

7. Glasser's reality therapy advocates teaching values and responsible behavior through a warm, genuine therapist-client relationship and conditional acceptance of client behaviors. The focus is on present behavior, the client's evaluation of its success or failure, and commitments to change behavior.

8. Berne's Transactional Analysis therapy conceptualizes personality as consisting of three ego states—the Parent, the Adult, and the Child. The "OKness" of a person is based on early experiences. A TA therapist teaches clients to analyze their ego states and transactions so as to improve the clients' functioning in interpersonal interactions.

9. A variety of therapy, personal growth, and support groups are available. These groups may differ in duration, setting, purpose (therapy, growth, support), and techniques used by professional or lay group leaders.

10. The fifties were the era of client-centered therapy; the sixties were characterized by an enormous popularity of behavior therapy; in the seventies, the popularity of traditional behaviorism decreased, while the popularity of the cognitive therapies increased. The trend in the eighties is toward eclecticism.

Key Terms

logotherapy
paradoxical intention
dereflection
client-centered therapy
acceptance (unconditional positive regard)
congruence
empathy (understanding)
attentive listening
reflection or mirroring
Gestalt therapy
"hot seat"
rational-emotive therapy (RET)
activating events
irrational beliefs
belief system
consequences (negative emotional experiences)
disputing irrational beliefs
cognitive therapy
automatic thoughts
reality therapy
control theory
Morita therapy
transactional analysis (TA)
ego states
strokes
life positions
transaction
eclectic

Psychology in the Future

Summing up, it is clear the future holds great opportunities. It also holds pitfalls. The trick will be to avoid the pitfalls, seize the opportunities, and get back home by six o'clock.

Woody Allen

 ## A Changing Psychology in a Changing World

One hundred years ago life was more predictable than it is today because change occurred more slowly. If they wished, people were able to choose fairly stable, predictable lives in which they followed in their parents' footsteps and expected their children to be able to follow in theirs. If people wanted to make major changes in their lives, they could migrate to new geographical locations and live pioneer existences. Just a little more than a century ago, people could gradually become accustomed to new inventions, new ideas, and new lifestyles.

609

Consider how much life on the farm has changed since this was a typical country scene.

Today's world is vastly different. Now all people must deal with radical life changes because each year brings massive alterations that thrust individuals from one lifestyle into new, as yet unknown, lifestyles. If previous generations were geographical pioneers, this generation and future generations are time pioneers, or as the late anthropologist Margaret Mead said, "immigrants in time" (Barr, 1986).

Not all people feel comfortable with change, and even those who enjoy it may find its current dizzy pace exhausting and confusing instead of invigorating. Yet no aspect of life today provides a haven from change. Change affects today's family, industry, information, and environment as rapidly and strongly as it affects individual lives.

One hundred years—1800 to 1900—were required to double the existing knowledge of 1800. The information pool next doubled in half that time—1900 to 1950. Subsequently, the doubling of knowledge occurred in only one decade—1950 to 1960. Today, the information pool doubles in only a few years (Barr, 1986).

One result of this immense influx in information is that much of the knowledge you have already acquired is, or soon will be, obsolete, insufficient, inaccurate, or even harmful. You (and all people) will need to constantly update the knowledge and skills by which you survive and prosper in the world. An educational diploma used to last a lifetime; today, education must be viewed as a continuing process.

Change in scientific knowledge is especially evident. Over 90 percent of all scientists who have ever lived are current, active scientists (Barr, 1986). The scientific discipline of psychology celebrated its centennial in 1979, and in the few ensuing years psychological information has mushroomed. When William James published his noted textbook *Principles of Psychology* in 1890, he was able to include virtually every major concept known to psychologists. Today, any introductory psychology textbook requires revisions as soon as the book is published. Such progress is wonderful because it promises better solutions to current problems, but it also can leave "heads spinning" and make people wish for earlier times when stability was more prominent than change. Nonetheless, massive, rapid changes will surely continue, and you should be prepared to make the most of such a world.

Predicting Psychology's Future

By creating images of what the future might hold, individuals can determine the priorities of the present and develop plans and dreams for making the future better. Of course, predictions about the future are quite speculative, and more often than not wrong, as you can see from Exhibit E.1 and as William James himself has proven. In 1909, when James predicted that no one would bother to discover the thousandth decimal of *pi*, he failed to anticipate the computer. The thousandth decimal of *pi* is 9. Recently, in only thirty hours, a computer determined the first 16,777,216 places after the decimal (Gardner, 1985). What lies ahead for psychology? Here are a few guesses about its future directions:

— Psychotropic drugs will continue to play a large role in treating mental illnesses such as schizophrenia and affective disorders, but new drugs will be more specific in nature and have fewer disabling side effects.

— The relationship between biology and psychology will continue to grow. One offspring area, sociobiology, will become more specific and less speculative in its proposals. Sociobiologists will continue to gather evidence from the work of anthropologists.

— More specialized treatment centers will be developed to work with concerns such as pain control and relief,

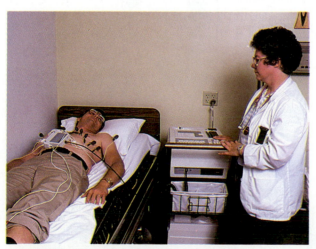

Because of the increasing emphasis on biological causes of behavior, psychology and medicine will increasingly be paired in the treatment of various disorders.

EXHIBIT E.1
Predicting the Future

Predictions about the future are speculative, and, more often than not, wrong, as these examples of faulty forecasting illustrate.

"There is no likelihood man can ever tap the power of the atom."
ROBERT MILLIKAN, Nobel Prize in Physics, 1923.

"Sensible and responsible women do not want to vote."
GROVER CLEVELAND, 1905.

"Everything that can be invented has been invented."
CHARLES H. DUELL, Director of U.S. Patent Office, 1899.

"The abolishment of pain in surgery is a chimera . . . 'Knife' and 'pain' are two words in surgery that must forever be associated in the consciousness of the patient."
DR. ALFRED VELPEAU, 1939.

"The bomb will never go off, and I speak as an expert in explosives."
ADMIRAL WILLIAM D. LEAHY, 1945.

"My figures coincide in fixing 1950 as the year when the world must go to smash."
HENRY ADAMS, 1903.

"If we take the world of geometrical relations, the thousandth decimal of *pi* sleeps there, though no one may ever try to compute it."
WILLIAM JAMES, 1909.

sleep disorders, and eating disorders. These treatment centers will be sites of important research studies.

— Concerns with prison conditions and rehabilitation programs will lead to innovative programs. In one type of program, computerized, lightweight "anklet re-straints" will allow nonviolent prisoners to be sentenced to their own homes and monitored from a different location.

— Brain tissue transplants and genetic engineering will provide cures or remissions for some organic disorders, but unfortunately ethical concerns in these areas will not be dealt with until after problematic situations have already occurred.

— Advancement will be made in technology to correct sensory deficits and to help paraplegics walk.

— New research concerns and treatment programs for the elderly will be developed because of the needs of an aging America. Jobs will develop in preretirement counseling, leisure programs for the elderly, and retirement home management.

— The "scratch 'n sniff" phenomenon now popular for children's stickers and perfume advertisements will expand into other consumer areas and will be used for creating moods by aromas, using pheromes to influence humans and animals, and adding smells to movies.

— More knowledge about the biological and psychological contributions to obesity and anorexia will lead to better treatments, including use of chemical interventions to mislead the brain's set point. Research results will lead to connections between eating disorders and chemical dependency disorders.

— Psychology will place less emphasis on S-R theory, or radical behaviorism. At the same time, behavioral techniques will continue to expand in educational, therapeutic, and industrial settings.

— Government and industry will increase their use of lie detection, drug testing, and personality assessment at the expense of individual rights. The degree of resulting harm will depend upon regulation of the testing industry. See the accompanying editorial cartoon for a contemporary comment on this issue.

■ Developmental psychologists will do more research on the family and, especially, extended and blended families. More individuals will use counseling to work out arrangements with former spouses and new step-relatives.

■ Creative methods of dealing with infertility will be refined. Counseling specialists will deal with the psychological aspects of technological pregnancies.

■ Medications will be developed to slow down or perhaps stop the progress of Alzheimer's disease.

■ Psychological assessment tools and procedures will be refined to determine which individuals should receive organ and tissue transplants.

■ Computer simulation will replace live animals in many research studies.

■ School curricula will emphasize direct teaching of thinking strategies.

■ Newer IQ tests based on triarchic theory or developmental theories will gradually become more popular than the standard Wechsler and Stanford-Binet tests.

■ Psychologists will become more involved in the peace movement, both as concerned citizens and as experts in attitude change. One editorial cartoonist's view of where the world is headed on this issue is depicted at the bottom of the page.

■ Dream machines that can trigger, influence, and record the dreams of sleepers will be developed.

■ Psychologists will help the zoo movement of preserving species by designing appropriate environments.

■ Part of the population will become more androgynous, and the other part will push more strongly for a return to gender typing with traditional male and female roles.

■ The computer's role in psychological research and counseling will increase. In counseling, computers will be especially productive for intake interviews, career assessment, and personality assessment.

■ Researchers will specify which areas of the brain malfunction during schizophrenia and some affective disorders.

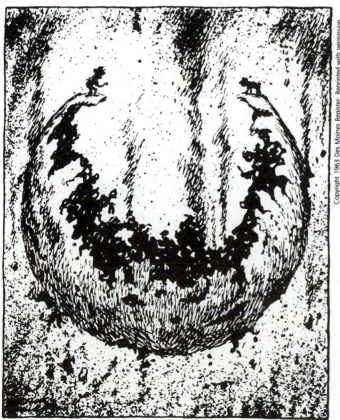

Copyright 1963 Des Moines Register. Reprinted with permission.

"I said — we sure settled that dispute didn't we?"

— Counseling sessions and workshops will continue to offer many stress management and time management programs as people continue to deal with massive amounts of societal change.

— More former mental patients will organize and manage community-based apartments and programs for mental patients, and they will hire only professionals who care about patients and know about current treatments. Self-help groups of individual patients and their families will have increased influence on professionals and politicians.

— Psychologists will explore ways to prevent violence—through childrearing practices, the legal system, and counseling programs. Victims of violence and recovering batterers will receive most help in self-help groups.

 ### Your Predictions

By thinking about psychology's previous accomplishments, psychology's present emphases, and other academic disciplines, try to predict psychology's development in the future. Before doing so, consider the views on the future presented in Exhibit E.2.

1. Start with yourself.
   a. What aspects of this book and your psychology course were most meaningful for you?
   b. Which psychology topics do you expect to use the most in your personal life?
   c. What topics do you wish psychologists would explore or do further research in because doing so would improve the quality of your life?

2. Current psychology.
   a. Which topics presented in this book do you think will expand in importance? Why?
   b. Which topics do you think will be less important in the future? Why?
   c. Which topics are most important for the quality of life in the future? Why?
   d. Create for each chapter one prediction for a discovery (or, at least, exploration) in the coming years.

3. Other academic disciplines.
   a. Think about several (a minimum of five) additional academic disciplines (e.g., anthropology, art, biology, business, chemistry, drama, economics, English, foreign languages, geography, geology, history, journalism, math, music, political science, sociology). For each of the other academic disciplines, list at least one way in which that particular area might influence psychology (e.g., fine arts combined with psycholog-

EXHIBIT E.2
Views on the Future

"When all else is lost, the future still remains."
BOVEE

"I never think of the future. It comes soon enough."
ALBERT EINSTEIN

"There was a wise man in the East whose constant prayer was that he might see today with the eyes of tomorrow."
ALFRED MERCIER

"No one can walk backward into the future."
JOSEPH HERGESHEIMER.

"I want to do away with everything behind man, so that there is nothing to see when he looks back. I want to take him by the scruff of his neck and turn his face toward the future."
LEONID ANDREYEV

"I believe the future is only the past again, entered through another gate."
PINERO

"The weal or woe of the future will be decided neither by the attacks of wild animals nor the natural catastrophies nor by the danger of world-wide epidemics, but simply by the psychic changes in man."
CARL GUSTAV JUNG

"Things are more like they are now than they have ever been before."
DWIGHT D. EISENHOWER

ical counseling becomes creative arts therapy; archaeologists who study mummies may learn about physical abuse patterns that can be compared to current psychological studies on family violence).

b. List at least one way in which psychological research and findings can be used by each of the other academic disciplines (e.g., use of Maslow's hierarchy of needs within business).

4. Global concerns.

a. Make a list of several current global concerns (e.g., famine, earthquakes, inflation, pollution, arms control, distribution of wealth, spiritual growth).

b. How does psychology influence these concerns?

c. How could psychology influence these world concerns?

d. How could psychologists conduct research on the various world concerns?

5. And in the future . . .

a. Of the predictions offered earlier, mark the five you think are most likely to come true.

b. Create your own list of predictions about psychology's future. Dream big!

Things to Do

1. Compare psychology textbooks published during each decade since the 1950s. What topics appear in only the most recent textbooks? What topics have declined in emphasis over the years? What topics are emphasized throughout the years? Did you detect significant modification in recurring topics or concepts?

2. Compare a current copy of a psychology journal with a decade-old issue of the same journal. What research topics are featured in each issue? Is current research conducted differently than previous research was conducted? How do the political and social climates of the times affect the popularity of research topics?

3. Visit a large local bookstore, and peruse the titles and topics of psychology books. What topics are popular? What kinds of books appear to be most helpful? Try to think of a topic that could result in a popular book.

4. Compare your predictions with those of your classmates. Are the predictions similar? Dissimilar? Why? Which predictions seem most interesting to you? Why?

Things to Discuss

1. New ethical concerns will undoubtedly accompany the psychological research and applications resulting from technological progress. Create a list of these concerns, and make recommendations for ethical guidelines.

2. What do you think a psychology career will be like in the future? Describe a typical day in the life of a psychologist of the twenty-first century.

3. What information you have learned in this psychology course will be most useful to you during your lifetime?

4. What childrearing practices would best prepare the next generation to deal with rapid change?

Things to Read

Fisher, J.D., Bell, P.A., & Baum, A. 1984. *Environmental psychology* (2nd ed.). NY: Holt, Rinehart & Winston.

Fromm, E. 1976. *To have or to be.* NY: Harper & Row.

Geller, E.S., Winett, R.A., & Everett, P.B. 1982. *Preserving the environment.* NY: Pergamon.

Horowitz, I.A. & Willging, T.E. 1984. *The psychology of law.* Boston: Little, Brown.

Kozol, J. 1985. *Illiterate America.* Garden City, NY: Anchor Press/Doubleday.

Marks, J. 1979. *The search for the "Manchurian Candidate": The CIA and mind control.* NY: New York Times Book.

Focus Questions

1. How do descriptive statistics help you organize data?

2. How do inferential statistics help you analyze data?

3. How are statistics commonly misused?

Appendix Outline

DESCRIPTIVE STATISTICS
Frequency Distributions
Measures of Central Tendency
Measures of Variability
Transformed Scores
Normal Curves

INFERENTIAL STATISTICS
Populations and Samples
Inference and Probability
Statistical Tests
Statistical Significance

RELATE: Abuse and Misuse of Statistics
Things to Do
Things to Discuss
Things to Read

REVIEW: Summary
Key Terms

Statistics: Organizing and Analyzing Data

There are three kinds of lies: lies, damned lies, and statistics.
Benjamin Disraeli

 Statistics: Organizing and Analyzing Data

Throughout this book you have read about the results of studies conducted by psychologists in their attempts to understand behavior. In each study psychologists collected *data* (observations) about certain aspects of behavior and interpreted the significance of their observations. In Chapter 3 you read about the major ways in which psychologists design studies to systematically collect useful data about behavior. Data can be collected in naturalistic observation studies, correlational studies, case studies, and experiments. Each method of data collection follows its own set of procedures, but all methods result in a collection of observations that must be organized and analyzed.

Statistical methods provide uniform mathematical procedures for organizing, analyzing, and evaluating the data collected by psychologists. The purpose of this appendix is to introduce you to the basic concepts and procedures involved in statistical methods used by psychologists. If you pursue an interest in psychology as an undergraduate major, you will probably be required to take at least one course in basic statistical methods. If your interest in psychology continues to develop and you attend graduate school, you will probably take several statistics courses. Regardless of whether you continue to take courses in psychology, a basic knowledge of statistics is a valuable asset in understanding the myriad of research results reported in the popular media today.

 Descriptive Statistics

Psychologists use descriptive statistics to make sense of the observations they collect while conducting research studies. **Descriptive statistics** are used to quantify, organize, and summarize large amounts of data so that the prominent features of the data can be easily grasped.

Consider the data from a hypothetical experiment presented in Exhibit A.1. In this experiment two groups of 15 subjects each were asked to rate 20 sentences.

Subjects in Group I were asked to rate each sentence on how easy or how difficult it was to imagine as a vivid visual image, while subjects in Group II rated each sentence on how easy or how difficult it was to pronounce. After rating the sentences, subjects answered questions about them. The number of correct answers indicates the amount of incidental learning that occurred while the subjects were rating the sentences; however, the data as displayed in Exhibit A.1 are difficult to comprehend. Descriptive statistics can be used to organize the data and to summarize its major characteristics so that any differences between the two groups can be seen more easily.

Frequency Distributions

Data can be organized to make them more meaningful by arranging them in a frequency distribution. In a **frequency distribution,** the data are arranged to show the number of times (the frequency) each score occurs. By examining the frequency distributions in Exhibit A.2, you can quickly determine that three of the visual imagery subjects obtained scores of 15. With only 15 subjects in a group, a frequency distribution may appear to offer little advantage over visually scanning the data. However, many experiments have 100 or more subjects

EXHIBIT A.1
Recall Scores for Incidental Learning Experiment

Group I: Visual Imagery	Number of Correct Responses	Group II: Pronunciation	Number of Correct Responses
SUBJECT 1	20	SUBJECT 1	6
SUBJECT 2	12	SUBJECT 2	9
SUBJECT 3	15	SUBJECT 3	15
SUBJECT 4	16	SUBJECT 4	10
SUBJECT 5	18	SUBJECT 5	8
SUBJECT 6	13	SUBJECT 6	11
SUBJECT 7	7	SUBJECT 7	10
SUBJECT 8	20	SUBJECT 8	7
SUBJECT 9	19	SUBJECT 9	8
SUBJECT 10	20	SUBJECT 10	10
SUBJECT 11	15	SUBJECT 11	9
SUBJECT 12	17	SUBJECT 12	12
SUBJECT 13	15	SUBJECT 13	9
SUBJECT 14	18	SUBJECT 14	10
SUBJECT 15	14	SUBJECT 15	8

per group, a situation in which visual scanning is both inefficient and error-prone.

The arrangement of subjects' responses can be further clarified by graphing the information in the frequency distribution. A **histogram,** a bar graph of a frequency distribution, allows you to easily see the distribution of scores in a set of data. The data for the incidental learning experiment are displayed as histograms in Exhibit A.3. The same data are plotted as points connected by straight lines in the **frequency polygons** in Exhibit A.4. In either the frequency polygons or the histograms, you can see at a glance that the visual imagery group generally had higher scores than the pronunciation group. Graphs of frequency distributions also allow researchers to quickly assess two other features of sets of data—central tendency and variability.

Measures of Central Tendency

Central tendency refers to describing a set of data by a single typical, average, or "middle" score. Three mea-

sures of central tendency are the mean, the median, and the mode.

The Mean   The **mean** is the arithmetic average, obtained by adding together all the scores in the distribution and dividing by the number of scores in the distribution. The sum of the 15 visual imagery scores is 240; 240 divided by 15 is 16; 16 is the mean for that set of scores. Similarly, the mean for the pronunciation group is 9.5. The calculation of this descriptive statistic, the mean, allows you to more clearly see the higher overall average performance of the visual imagery group compared to the pronunciation group. An advantage of the mean as a measure of central tendency is that it is a descriptive statistic that is influenced by every score in the distribution. The mean is the balance point in the distribution where the weight of the scores above that point exactly balances the weight of the scores below that point. However, because of the mean's sensitivity to extreme scores, when a distribution contains a few extremely high or extremely low scores, the mean may not accurately reflect the typical response in a distribution.

EXHIBIT A.2
Frequency Distribution of Correct Responses of Visual Imagery and Pronunciation Subjects

Visual Imagery		Pronunciation	
Number of Correct Responses	*Number of Subjects (Frequency)*	*Number of Correct Responses*	*Number of Subjects (Frequency)*
20	2	20	0
19	2	19	0
18	2	18	0
17	1	17	0
16	1	16	0
15	3	15	1
14	1	14	0
13	1	13	0
12	1	12	1
11	0	11	1
10	0	10	4
9	0	9	3
8	0	8	3
7	1	7	1
6	0	6	1
5	0	5	0
4	0	4	0
3	0	3	0
2	0	2	0
1	0	1	0
0	0	0	0

The Median   The **median** is calculated by finding the midpoint of a set of scores. For example, in the visual imagery group, 16 is the score exactly in the middle of the distribution (with 7 scores above and 7 scores below that point). The median is often easily calculated by arranging the scores from highest to lowest and counting in to the middlemost score, but the median requires more precise calculations when the middlemost score is a value shared by several data points, as occurs in the pronun-

ciation group. Unlike the mean, the median is not influenced by the size of extreme scores.

The Mode   The **mode** is the most frequently occurring score in a distribution and is therefore easily obtained from a frequency distribution. The mode for the visual imagery group is 15 and for the pronunciation group, 10. While the mode is easily calculated, it shares none

EXHIBIT A.3
Histograms of Hypothetical Data

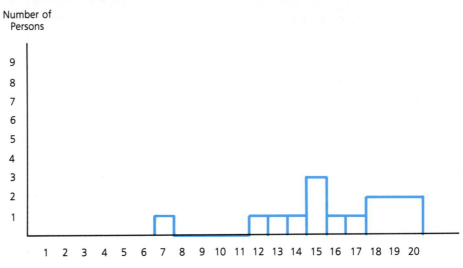

Recall Scores (Visual Imagery)

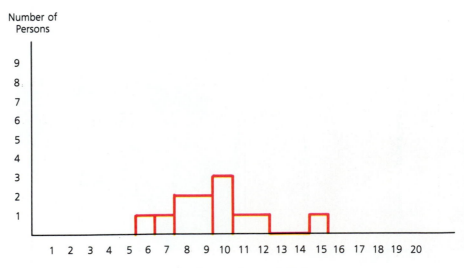

Recall Scores (Pronunciation)

of the advantages of either the mean or the median and is seldom used in other statistical calculations.

Measures of Variability

The mean and median as measures of central tendency indicate the center of a distribution of scores, while **variability** indicates the dispersion of the scores around that center. When every score in a distribution is the same, no variability exists. When just one score is different from all the rest, variability exists in the distribution. The more the scores differ from one another, the greater the degree of variability. Variability is typically measured in three ways—by the range, the variance, and the standard deviation.

The Range The **range,** the difference between the highest and the lowest scores in a distribution, is the simplest measure of how widely dispersed a set of scores is. For the incidental learning experiment, the range is 13 for the visual imagery group and 9 for the pronunciation group. The range is rarely used as a measure of variability since it is so easily affected by an extreme score. The range indicates how much the highest and lowest scores vary from one another, but it does not indicate how much the remaining scores in the distribution vary from each other.

The Variance The **variance** is a measure of variability that indicates how much every score in the distribution

EXHIBIT A.4
Combined Frequency Polygons for Hypothetical Data

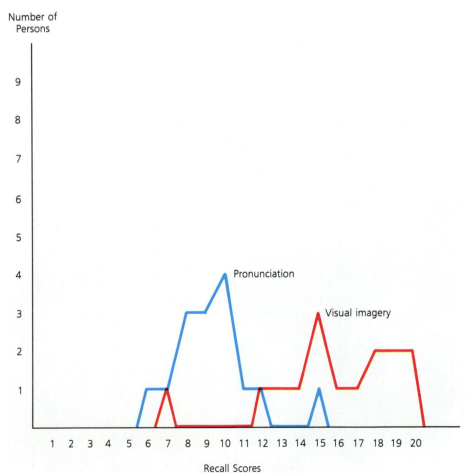

varies from every other score. The variance is calculated by determining the average of the squared deviations of every score from the mean. In simple steps, the deviation of each score from the mean is obtained by subtracting the mean from each score; the value obtained for each score is squared; and the average is obtained by adding together all the squared deviations and dividing by the number of scores in the distribution. Because the variance expressed in squared units is an abstraction, the square root of the variance, the standard deviation, is the most commonly used concrete measure of variability.

The Standard Deviation The **standard deviation** is the square root of the variance and has several statistical properties which make it the most useful measure of variability. Calculations of standard deviations for the incidental learning experiment are shown in Exhibit A.5. The formula used in Exhibit A.5:

$$s = \sqrt{\frac{\Sigma(x-\bar{x})^2}{N}}$$

is one of several equivalent formulae that may be used to calculate the standard deviation. As you can see from the calculations in Exhibit A.5, the variability of scores is greater for the visual imagery group than for the pronunciation group.

Transformed Scores

For comparison purposes, transforming data to standard units is often useful. Transformations involve adding, subtracting, multiplying, or dividing each score by a constant number. Commonly used transformed scores are percentiles and standard scores.

A **percentile** indicates the percentage of subjects who scored at or below a certain score. In the incidental learning experiment example, one way to see if a score of 12 in the visual imagery group indicates a comparable level of achievement to a 12 in the pronunciation group is to transform the original data to percentiles. In the visual imagery group, two of the 15 subjects scored at or below 12. Dividing 2 by 15 and multiplying by 100 equals 13 percent. In the visual imagery group, the subject who earned a score of 12 is at the 13th percentile and did as well or better than 13 percent of the other subjects in that group. In the pronunciation group, 13 of the 15 subjects had scores at or below 12. The subject in the

EXHIBIT A.5
Computation of Standard Deviations

Group I: Visual Imagery					Group II: Pronunciation				
Subject	Score	Mean	$(x-\bar{x})$	$(x-\bar{x})^2$	Subject	Score	Mean	$(x-\bar{x})$	$(x-\bar{x})^2$
1	20	16	4	16	1	6	9.5	−3.5	12.25
2	12	16	−4	16	2	9	9.5	−0.5	.25
3	15	16	−1	1	3	15	9.5	5.5	30.25
4	16	16	0	0	4	10	9.5	0.5	.25
5	18	16	2	4	5	8	9.5	−0.5	.25
6	13	16	−3	9	6	11	9.5	1.5	2.25
7	7	16	−9	81	7	10	9.5	0.5	.25
8	20	16	4	16	8	7	9.5	−2.5	6.25
9	19	16	3	9	9	8	9.5	−1.5	2.25
10	20	16	4	16	10	10	9.5	0.5	.25
11	15	16	−1	1	11	9	9.5	−0.5	.25
12	17	16	1	1	12	12	9.5	2.5	6.25
13	15	16	−1	1	13	9	9.5	−0.5	.25
14	18	16	2	4	14	10	9.5	0.5	.25
15	14	16	−2	4	15	8	9.5	−1.5	2.25
	240		0	172		142		0	65.75

$$S_I = \sqrt{\frac{172}{15}} = 3.51$$

$$S_{II} = \sqrt{\frac{65.75}{15}} = 2.17$$

pronunciation group who had a score of 12 is at the 87th percentile (13/15 × 100 = 87). Clearly, the subject in the pronunciation group with a 12 performed at a much higher level with respect to the others in the pronunciation group than did the subject in the other group with a score of 12 with respect to that group.

The constants used to transform scores to percentiles are the number of subjects and 100. The transformation constants in one type of standard score, the **Z score,** are the group's mean and standard deviation. When the group mean is subtracted from each score and that value is divided by the group standard deviation, the resulting distribution of transformed scores will have a mean of 0 and standard deviation of 1. Thus, this transformation creates a standard distribution in which the units of measurement are standard deviation units and for which comparisons between different sets of data are easier to make.

The negative numbers created by transforming data to Z scores can be avoided by using another standard score transformation, the T score. A **T score** is obtained by multiplying a Z score by 10 and adding 50. For example, a Z score of 1.5 transforms to a T score of 65. Thus, the T score transformation eliminates negative numbers by creating a standard distribution with a mean of 50 and a standard deviation of 10.

Normal Curves

Many characteristics of humans are determined by a large number of factors, each of which has only a small influence by itself (e.g., height, intelligence, and verbal ability). Because the number of factors is large and the influence of each factor is relatively unpredictable, the occurrence of these characteristics within the population approximates the mathematical distribution of events due to chance. The distribution of chance events can be determined by a mathematical formula and, when graphed as a probability distribution, has a characteristic bell-shaped curve known as the **normal curve.** The concept of "normal" applies to the shape or form of a distribution. As the normal curve in Exhibit A.6 illustrates, the measurement of events or characteristics that are normally distributed results in measurements that cluster around the center of the distribution and decrease towards the tails, or extremes, of the distribution. Thus, as was pointed out in Chapter 20, most people are of average intelligence. As you move in either direction from the mean for intelligence, you find fewer people at each level. Two or more distributions may be bell-shaped but have different means and standard deviations. Therefore, many normal curves exist, all having similar bell shapes and certain properties in common.

EXHIBIT A.6
The Normal Curve

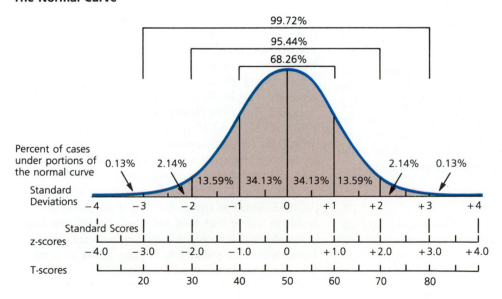

One of the common properties among normal curves is the fixed relationship with the standard deviation. The standard deviation marks off a specific proportion of scores on either side of the mean. These specific proportions are indicated as percentages in Exhibit A.6. Because these proportions are constant, for any set of normally distributed data approximately 68 percent of the scores will always fall within one standard deviation either side of the mean. Also, because Z scores are measured in standard deviation units, Z scores mark the same specific areas under the normal curve. The invariant nature of this relationship becomes very useful when researchers analyze their experimental results to determine how often events are likely to happen by chance.

Focus Question Answer

How do descriptive statistics help you organize data? Descriptive statistics allow you to summarize a large set of data by creating frequency distributions and calculating the central tendency of and the variability within the distribution. With just two descriptive statistics, such as the mean and the standard deviation, you can summarize the important aspects of a set of data.

 Inferential Statistics

Descriptive statistics, by themselves, are usually not sufficient to allow psychologists to determine whether the differences they observe between the performances of the experimental and control group subjects are caused by the independent variables in their experiments. In addition, psychologists want to assess whether the results they obtain in individual experiments are generally true for all people. For example, in the incidental learning experiment, are the observed differences between the two groups due to the different rating methods used by each group? How probable are the results for people in general? Answers to these types of questions are provided by **inferential statistics.** Psychologists and other researchers use inferential statistics to analyze and evaluate the results of their experiments and to determine what conclusions, or inferences, can be made from their studies.

Populations and Samples

Inferential statistics are used to make judgments about a population based on observations from a sample of that population. In statistics, a **population** is an entire set of observations, while a **sample** is a partial set of obser-

vations from a population. Researchers are careful to define the populations and samples with which they are working, because a population in one analysis may be a sample in another. All the students enrolled in classes at your school represent both the student population at your school and a sample of all the students enrolled in colleges and universities. Likewise, all the students enrolled in psychology classes at your school constitute your school's psychology student population and are a sample of the students enrolled at your college or university.

Psychologists rely on inferences from samples because observing entire populations is usually impractical. However, generalizations from samples may not be reliable for several reasons. First, a sample may not be representative of the population. Students in an introductory psychology class are more likely to be a representative sample of the students at your school than students in an advanced personality theories course (A broader cross-section of students are likely to enroll in the introductory course than in the advanced course). Second, smaller samples are less reliable than larger samples. As the sample size increases, the data collected from the sample more reliably reflect how the entire population would react. This fact is related to a third condition in which the reliability of inferences from samples is influenced by the degree of variability in the population. The more homogeneous the population is, the smaller the sample size that is needed to provide reliable inferences.

Inference and Probability

Inferential statistics are based upon mathematical probability. In a simple sense, inferential statistics are used to assess the probability that the sample observations are true of the entire population or to assess the likelihood that the independent variable caused the observed differences in the dependent variable. The first case is similar to asking whether or not a coin (the sample) that produces nine heads in a row is from a population of unbiased coins. The chance of getting a head on a single toss of a coin is 50-50 ($p = .5$), while multiplying the probability of each separate event together yields the probability of getting a series of heads in a row. Therefore, the probability of nine heads in a row is $.5 \times .5 \times .5 \times .5 \times .5 \times .5 \times .5 \times .5 \times .5$, which equals .001953. Based on this probability, if you predicted nine heads in a row and then saw them occur, you might conclude that the outcome (the coin or the toss) was biased since the probability of nine heads in a row is very small under unbiased conditions.

In the second case—inferring that the independent variable is the causal factor—the task is to determine the probability that the data from two different groups of subjects come from the same population and that the differences between them are due only to chance. For example, the differences in recall between the two groups in the incidental learning experiment appear to be fairly large, but if both are samples from a population in which large variations in recall exist, then the observed differences could be due to chance. Both kinds of inferences are based on statistical probabilities. Calculations of these statistical probabilities form the basis for inferential statistical tests.

Statistical Tests

Statistical tests are used to assess the probability that the independent variable or chance factors are responsible for the observed differences in sets of data. Mathematically, the process is straightforward. The researcher collects data about a specific experimental hypothesis, calculates descriptive statistics to summarize the data, chooses an appropriate statistical test, performs mathematical calculations using the descriptive statistics, compares the calculated values for the statistical test with a table of comparison values, and draws a conclusion based upon the comparison of the calculated and tabled values.

While the mathematical process is straightforward, the statistical tests are based upon an indirect process. The psychologist's experimental hypothesis usually states that the independent variable will have a certain specifiable effect. However, inferential statistical tests are based on testing the condition that the independent variable has no effect, a condition called the **null hypothesis.** For example, in the incidental learning experiment, the experimenter is interested in which method of rating the sentences will produce greater amounts of incidental learning as measured by the ability to recall information about the sentences. The null hypothesis for this experiment is that no difference actually exists between the two samples of scores and that any observed differences are actually due to chance. If the researcher is able to reject the null hypothesis, then support is indirectly given to the **alternative hypothesis,** that the observed differences are due to the independent variable.

Another way of expressing this rationale for statistical tests is to say that the null hypothesis states that the observations from the two groups actually represent scores from the same population which differ only because of errors due to sampling. In this way the alternative hypothesis states that the two sets of observations actually represent samples from two different populations (e.g., one population exists for performances using the visual imagery method, while another population exists for performances using the pronunciation method). An important assumption of this approach is that rejecting the null hypothesis does not prove the alternative hypothesis conclusively; the chance always exists, however small, that the two samples came from the same population because the decision to reject the null hypothesis is based upon a probability. Thus, evidence in support of the alternative hypothesis is always gained indirectly by assessing the probability that the null hypothesis is wrong.

Statistical Significance

The results of an experiment become statistically significant when the probability that the null hypothesis is true is quite small. **Statistical significance** means that the observed differences are very likely due to the effects of the independent variable and are not very likely due to the chance effects of sampling within and between groups. By convention, statisticians have agreed that whenever the probability that the null hypothesis is true is less than or equal to .05 (i.e., 5 times out of 100 such results would be due to chance), then the null hypothesis can be rejected in favor of the alternative hypothesis.

The .05 standard defines a level of confidence which all researchers can refer to in making a decision about whether or not to reject the null hypothesis. If researchers want to be more confident that they are correct in rejecting the null hypothesis, they can adopt a more stringent standard such as .01. At the .01 level, the probability is less than or equal to one chance in 100 that the data would occur if the null hypothesis were true. Because statistical tests allow fairly precise calculations of the confidence level, researchers usually report the results of the test and the degree of statistical significance in terms of the highest level of confidence achieved such as $p < .01$ or $p < .001$. Thus, for the hypothetical incidental learning experiment, the conclusion from a statistical test (the t-test for the difference between two means) is that the results are statistically significant at $p < .0001$. Only 1 time in a 10,000 would the observed data occur from chance. Therefore, the null hypothesis is rejected and the data are interpreted as supporting the alternative hypothesis that the independent variable produced the observed effects.

The results of experiments may be statistically significant but lack significance in another sense. This second meaning of significance refers to the relevance of the results. For example, a researcher might discover that significantly more males than females look into their glasses when drinking. While this observation may be highly significant statistically, its statistical significance indicates nothing about its relevance to understanding the differences between women and men. Such observations may be relatively unimportant in understanding male/female differences. Statistical significance simply means the observations are not likely to be due to chance.

Focus Question Answer

How do inferential statistics help you analyze data? Inferential statistical tests provide a mathematical basis for deciding whether the sample data are due to the effects of the independent variable or to chance. The process is indirect, allowing conclusions to be made about the effects of independent variable by first assessing the probability that the observed differences are due to chance. If the probability is small that chance factors caused the observed effects, the experimenter can conclude that the observed effects are due to the independent variable.

 Relate

Abuse and Misuse of Statistics

An important aspect of understanding statistical concepts is becoming a wise consumer of statistical information. Daily, you are confronted with a barrage of statistics. One headline proclaims that the crime rate is significantly lower, while another article notes a 5 percent increase in reported crimes. An advertiser claims that a new study finds that Brand X toothpaste gets teeth significantly whiter than the competing brands or that Brand X contains significantly more of an active ingredient than the competing brands. The frequent use of statistics to bolster arguments and to make reports more factual inevitably leads to some misuse and occasional abuse of statistics. As noted in an old saying, "Figures don't lie but liars do figure!" The goal for the educated consumer of statistics is to be able to recognize the misuses and outright abuses of statistics and statistical reasoning.

Many abuses of statistics exist. Abuse of statistical information occurs when individuals intentionally set out to use false information. Unfortunately, certain individuals do not hold the truth in high regard and use false statements to support their arguments and claims. The most effective defense against this tactic is to check carefully the sources for the individual's statistics and to demand that the person explain how the numbers were obtained.

Other forms of abuse such as using small or unrepresentative samples are more subtle. The testimonial of one person is often used as evidence that everyone will react in the same way. How convinced are you that because one person believes his or her clothes are brighter after using Brand X detergent that your clothes will also appear brighter? You should be skeptical of claims based on very small samples or single cases. Careful selection of biased subjects creates an unrepresentative sample and biased results. Pay attention to how often advertisers announce that subjects for their tests are randomly chosen from a broad cross-section of consumers. If you do, you will observe that the number is exceedingly small. Wise consumers should always find out how large the sample was and how the subjects were selected.

Unfortunately, abuses of statistical information are so numerous that books have been written about the subject (see *Things to Read*). Equally deplorable, though, are the frequent, unintentional misuses of statistics. Misuse of statistics occurs when individuals unintentionally misapply statistical procedures. Without careful attention to the selection of unbiased samples and to the appropriate selection of descriptive statistics and statistical tests, misuses of statistics can occur. Guarding against this misuse of statistics requires educated users of statistical techniques as well as educated consumers. The time may have arrived for statistical thinking to become a "new" literacy to augment the basic skills of reading, writing, and arithmetic. This need was anticipated by the historian H. G. Wells when he wrote, "Statistical thinking will one day be as necessary for efficient citizenship as the ability to read and write."

Although statistical literacy may help curb the abuses and misuses of statistics, another obstacle remains for consumers of statistics. What do you do when knowledgeable users of statistics disagree about the appropriate statistics to use? As a case in point, a news report contrasted the crime statistics reported by the Bureau of Justice Statistics' annual *National Crime Survey* and by the FBI's annual *Uniform Crime Report* (Knight-Ridder News Service, 1986). The Bureau of Justice Statistics reported that the crime rate for 1985 was the lowest rate in 13 years. However, the FBI's crime report stated that reported crimes rose 5 percent in 1985.

The two groups use different approaches for gathering their respective data. The Bureau of Justice Statistics conducts interviews twice a year with more than 100,000 people about their personal contact with crime. From these interviews, the Bureau estimates the total number of crimes committed nationwide in a year. On the other hand, the FBI compiles the number of reported crimes from nearly 16,000 law enforcement agencies. The FBI's figures for 1985 indicate that about 12.5 million crimes were reported to the police, while the Bureau of Justice Statistics estimated that 34.9 million crimes were committed during the same period. Neither approach is a clear misuse of statistics; yet which approach provides a clearer picture of crime in the United States for 1985? The FBI statistics are based on the numbers of reported crimes but does not include unreported crimes. The Bureau of Justice Statistics includes unreported crimes as well as reported ones but estimates the occurrence of both from sample data.

While a philosophical question could be raised about whether a crime is a crime if it is not reported, the problem here is to understand the different statistical information. Because both groups are knowledgeable about the appropriate use of statistics, if you must choose between the two reports, you can make an informed choice since both groups openly report the statistical methods they use to obtain their data. Even in this situation, the best practice for a wise user of statistics is to become knowledgeable about statistics yourself.

Things to Do

1. Obtain a daily newspaper or a weekly news magazine and mark every use of statistics in both articles and advertisements. Make a frequency distribution of the number of times each type of descriptive statistic is used. Take particular note of the misuse or abuse of statistical information. Compare your findings with those of other students in your class.

2. To gain firsthand experience with the effects of sampling, gather 50 bottle caps and mark each cap with a number from one to 50. Put the caps in a container and draw out a sample of 5 caps from the population of 50 bottle caps. The mean of all the numbers from one to 50 is 25. Add the five numbers you withdrew from the container and divide the sum by 5 to obtain the sample mean. How close is your sample mean to the population mean of 25? Replace the caps, mix the 50 caps, and withdraw another sample of 5 caps. Calculate the sample mean and compare it to the population mean. Follow this procedure a total of 10 times. Ten samples should

be enough to give you some understanding of sampling error. Add together the ten sample means and divide by 10. Is this mean of the sample means a better estimate of the population mean? Try withdrawing larger samples. What effect does sample size have on estimating the population mean from a sample mean?

3. Carefully analyze the use of statistics by advertisers in both the print and electronic medias. Find examples of accurate use and abuse of statistics. In your abuse examples, what did the advertiser do or not do that caused you to conclude that the advertiser was abusing statistical information? Which type of advertising do you think is more successful?

Things to Discuss

1. A statistician with his head in the oven and his feet in the refrigerator was heard to remark, "On the average, the temperature is just right!" Discuss whether or not you believe that descriptive statistics, such as the mean, that condense data to a single representative number, create an unrepresentative picture.

2. Are inferential statistics needed less today than in earlier times? With computers and modern electronic technology, data can be more easily collected from every member of large populations. In what situations are samples and inferential statistics important tools for learning about the characteristics of populations?

3. Which approach do you think is more practical and effective in combating the abuse of statistical information: stricter controls on advertisers' use of statistics or greater education of consumers about the uses and abuses of statistics? Should statistical literacy become one of the "new" literacies along with computer literacy?

4. One controversial use of inferential statistics has been the use by media networks of exit poll samples of voting patterns to predict the outcomes of elections. Debate whether this use of inferential statistics should be banned.

Things To Read

Huff, D. 1954. *How to lie with statistics.* NY: Norton.
Kimble, G. 1978. *How to use (and mis-use) statistics.* Englewood Cliffs, NJ: Spectrum Books.
Pagano, R.L. 1981. *Understanding statistics in the behavioral sciences.* St. Paul, MN: West Publishing Company.
Shaughnessy, J.J. & Zechmeister, E.B. 1985. *Research methods in psychology.* NY: Knopf.

 *Review*

Summary

1. Statistical methods provide uniform mathematical procedures for organizing and analyzing the data collected by psychologists.

2. Descriptive statistics are used to organize and summarize large collections of data. Two types of descriptive statistics are measures of central tendency and measures of variability.

3. Three measures of central tendency are the mean (the arithmetic average), the median (the middlemost score), and the mode (the most frequently occurring score). Because the mean reflects the influence of every score in the distribution, it is the preferred measure, except when the size of a few extreme scores distort the picture of central tendency it presents.

4. Three measures of variability are the range (the difference between the highest and lowest scores), the variance (the average of the squared deviations of each score from the mean), and the standard deviation (the square root of the variance). The standard deviation is the preferred measure of variability because it reflects the influence of every score in the distribution and is expressed in regular rather than squared units.

5. Transformed scores such as percentiles, Z scores, and T scores make comparisons between different sets of data easier.

6. The distribution of chance events has a characteristic bell-shaped curve known as the normal curve. The fixed relationship between the normal curve and the standard deviation creates specific proportions of normally-distributed scores on either side of the mean. This property is useful in calculating the frequency of events that happen by chance.

7. Inferential statistics are used to assess the probability that sample observations are true of a population or to assess the likelihood that the independent variable caused the observed differences in the dependent variable.

8. Inferential statistical tests provide a mathematical basis for deciding whether the sample data are due to the effects of chance (the null hypothesis) or to the effects of the independent variable (the alternative hypothesis). If the probability is small (less than 5 percent) that chance factors caused the observed effects, then the experimenter rejects the null hypothesis and concludes that the observed effects are due to the independent variable.

9. Statistical significance means that the observed effects are not likely to be due to chance. Statistical significance does not assure the relevance or usefulness of the results.

10. The abuse of statistical information occurs when individuals intentionally set out to use false information, to mislead, or to misrepresent in an attempt to bolster their arguments or claims. The misuse of statistics occurs when individuals unintentionally misapply statistical procedures. Gaining a basic understanding of statistical reasoning and procedures is one way to counteract the abuses and misuses of statistics.

Key Terms

descriptive statistics
frequency distribution
histogram
frequency polygon
central tendency
mean
median
mode
variability
range
variance
standard deviation
percentile
Z Score
T Score
normal curve
inferential statistics
population
sample
null hypothesis
alternative hypothesis
statistical significance

Glossary

Absent-mindedness   A failure of prospective memory.

Absolute refractory   The inability of neurons to conduct a message during recharging.

Absolute threshold   The arbitrary point at which people first become aware of the presence of a stimulus fifty percent of the time.

Abstract thought   Thought involving manipulation of symbols.

Acceptance   The fifth and final stage of a terminally-ill individual's adjustment to dying.

Acceptance (unconditional positive regard)   A liking or a warmth for the client that carries no judgement or evaluation.

Accommodation   1. The changing of the lens by a set of muscles to fine focus the image. 2. A monocular cue to depth based on feedback from the lens muscles as they change the shape of the lens to focus on nearby objects. 3. The idea proposed by Jean Piaget that says when a person encounters new information there is an attempt to modify it to fit existing knowledge.

Acquaintance   A person whom one is more aware of than strangers and with whom one has direct interactions.

Acquisition   The process by which a conditioned stimulus comes to elicit a conditioned response or a response is learned during operant conditioning.

Action potential   The current flow produced when the neuron fires as a result of an active exchange of the positive and negative ions across the cell wall.

Activating events   According to Ellis, the perceived cause of negative emotions.

Activation-synthesis hypothesis   The belief that dreams represent the brain's attempt to explain movement of the eyes.

Active recitation   A self-questioning skill used as an aid to learning.

Activity versus passivity   A controversial issue of human development in which the biological, behavior-learning, and psychodynamic perspectives tend to view individuals as passive participants, while the cognitive and humanistic-existential frameworks believe that humans play a direct role in their own development.

Actor-observer bias   The overwhelming tendency to overestimate the role of the person and underestimate the role of the situation in the attribution of another's behavior but to do the opposite when judging personal behavior.

Actualizing tendency   The tendency to grow in positive ways once circumstances are supportive.

Adjustment disorders   Temporary, event-induced mood disturbances.

Anhedonia   The inability to experience joy or pleasure.

Adolescence   The period of transition from childhood to adulthood.

Adolescent egocentrism   The tendency of teenagers to spend great amounts of time thinking about themselves.

Adopted-twin studies   Studies of twins adopted after birth and reared in different environments to study the influence of heredity and environment.

Aerial perspective   The monocular depth cue in which nearby objects projecting into the sky are seen distinctly while the details of such objects become less distinct and more hazy with increasing distance.

Affect   The moment-to-moment expression of emotion.

Afferent (sensory) nerves   The nerves in the peripheral nervous system that carry information to the central nervous system.

Afterbirth   The third stage of birth in which the umbilical cord, placenta, and fetal membranes are expelled from the uterus.

Agoraphobia   An irrational fear of being alone or in public places such that fear and avoidance dominate the person's life.

Aha-experience   The reaction occurring when an individual experiences insight during the problem solving process.

AID (Artificial insemination by a donor)   A reproductive alternative in which sperm from a donor are used when the woman is fertile but the man is infertile.

AIH (Artificial insemination with the husband's sperm)   A process whereby sperm from several ejaculations is concentrated, combined, and frozen until the appropriate time for insemination.

Alexithymia   The inability to verbally express feeling, found in individuals with psychosomatic complaints.

Algorithms   A strategy of problem-solving in which a trial-and-error search becomes systematic rather than random.

Alleles   Pairs of genes found in the chromosomes that determine the particular characteristics of a physical trait.

629

or none principle The principle that states that either the message being sent to a neuron from other neurons is sufficient to produce a full-strength action potential, or no message is conducted by the neuron.

Alternative hypotheses Proposed effects of the independent variable.

Alzheimer's disease A disease causing an organic loss of memory including extreme loss of current and recent memory.

Amenorrhea The absence of menstruation that is a common symptom of female anorexics.

Amniotic fluid The fluid inside the amniotic sac that cushions the embryo from injury and helps maintain optimal temperature.

Amniotic sac A protective membrane around the embryo filled with amniotic fluid.

Amphetamines Stimulants that cause psychological effects such as agitation, feelings of elation, and talkativeness, and physical symptoms such as increased heart rate, elevated blood pressure, perspiration, and nausea.

Amplitude The physical dimension of light that corresponds to the perception of brightness.

Amygdala An almond-shaped brain structure located between the hippocampus and the hypothalamus that plays a role in emotional behavior.

Anal stage The second psychosexual stage that includes ages one to three.

Analysis of resistance The therapist's acknowledgement and interpretation of the client's resistance as shown by the client's tardiness, denial, and reluctance to express feelings.

Analysis of transference The process in which the therapist analyzes the client's disclosures for evidence of repressed feelings towards people who were significant in the client's early life.

Androgyny A condition in which individuals possess both highly masculine and feminine traits.

Anger The second stage of a terminally ill individual's adjustment to dying.

Anonymity The state of being anonymous or faceless.

Anorexia nervosa A fear of gaining weight that results in prolonged self-starvation and an accompanying weight loss of at least 25 percent of original body weight.

Anorgasmia A sexual dysfunction in women involving the inability to have an orgasm.

Anterograde amnesia A type of organic amnesia that causes the loss of the ability to form new, lasting memories.

Anthropomorphism The tendency to attribute human characteristics to animals.

Antianxiety drugs Minor tranquilizers prescribed for anxiety, tension, restlessness, insomnia, and irritability.

Anticipated outcomes The regulation of behavior in which certain behaviors are perceived as leading to rewards.

Antidepressants Drugs that elevate mood and reduce depression.

Antipsychotics (neuroleptics) Major tranquilizers used to reduce delusion, bizarre behavior, severe anxiety, and agitation.

Antisocial personality disorder A disorder characterized by the individual having a "history of continuous and chronic antisocial behavior in which the rights of others are violated." (DSM III)

Anvil (incus) One of a chain of small bones that act as an amplifier in the middle ear.

Anxiety "Apprehension, tension, or uneasiness that stems from the anticipation of danger." (DSM III)

Apgar scale A rapid and accurate method for evaluating the health status of neonates.

Aphasia Language impairment involving the inability to speak caused by a tumor or injury to speech centers in the brain.

Application The goal of psychology to apply psychological knowledge to everyday situations to improve the quality of life.

Archetypes The indestructible content form of the collective unconscious.

Arousal theory A theory that states that the basis of motivation is the need to maintain an optimum level of physical activation within the organism.

Ascending reticular activation system (ARAS) The part of the reticular formation responsible for alerting or activating other parts of the brain.

Assimilation 1. The idea proposed by Piaget that says when individuals encounter new information they attempt to fit the information into existing schemas. 2. A distortion process in which a speaker's position is judged to be more similar to the listener's own position that it actually is.

Association cortex The areas of the cortex of the brain for which specialized functions have not been identified.

Associationism The assumption that learning is most likely to occur when objects, behaviors, or experiences are close together in time or space.

Attachment The development of an enduring bond between infant and caregivers.

Attentive listening Paying close attention to what the client says and communicating that attentiveness to the client.

Attitude A relatively enduring organization of beliefs, feelings, and behavioral tendencies toward events, objects, groups, or symbols.

Attribution process   The process in which people decide whether the cause of a behavior is within the person or outside the person.

Audition (hearing)   The ability to hear.

Auditory canal   The part of the outer ear that carries sounds from the pinna to the eardrum.

Auditory cortex (temporal lobe)   A section of the cerebral cortex of the brain that is the central receiving area for auditory information.

Auditory encoding   Coding an experience by sound.

Auditory nerves   The collection of nerve fibers carrying information from each ear to the brain.

Authenticity   The idea that authentic individuals have overcome alienation by accepting responsibility for their own lives and by taking risks beyond their typical natures and styles.

Authoritarian parenting   A parenting style in which parents are demanding and controlling and assert great power over their children.

Authoritative parenting   The parenting style in which parents encourage independence in the children within reasonable limits.

Autokinetic effect   The apparent movement of a stationary pinpoint of light in a darkened room.

Automatic thoughts   According to Beck, the involuntary maladaptive thoughts that do not result from logic or reason.

Autonomic nervous system   A division of the peripheral nervous system that carries messages to and from glands and smooth muscles.

Aversive conditioning   The conditioning of negative responses rather than positive ones to stimuli that are associated with unwanted behavior.

Avoidance learning   Learning a response to prevent the occurrence of an aversive stimulus.

Axon   The part of a neuron that serves as the mechanism for sending messages on to other neurons.

Axon button   A swollen, bulb-like structure at the end of the axon terminal where neurotransmitters are stored.

Axon terminals   The branches at the end of the axon.

Backward conditioning   The ineffective technique in which the conditioned stimulus begins after the unconditioned stimulus.

Balance theory   A theory focusing on the achievement of consistent cognitions in relationships.

Barbiturates   Depressants to the central nervous system that are prescribed for sleep and relaxation.

Bargaining   The third stage of a terminally-ill individual's adjustment to dying.

Basal ganglia   The structures in the brain located at the base of the cortex that assist in controlling movement.

Basilar membrane   A specialized membrane in the inner ear whose movements in response to mechanical sound vibrations bend the hair cells that generate neural messages about sound.

"Beautiful is good" hypotheses   The idea that physical attractiveness is advantageous in interpersonal attraction.

Behavioral perspective   The study of overt behaviors, the process of learning, and the influences of the environment on an individual's behavior.

Behavioral-learning perspective   The developmental viewpoint that emphasizes environmental factors in explaining development.

Behaviorism   A major viewpoint in psychology that emphasizes that objective observation of behavior is the only proper procedure for psychological study.

Behavior potential   According to Rotter, the probability that an individual will respond with a particular behavior when certain environmental conditions are present.

Being love   A healthy state in which two people love each other by choice rather than need.

Belief system   A client's set of beliefs that, according to Ellis, may contain irrational beliefs.

Bem Sex Role Inventory (BSRI)   A questionnaire devised to measure the extent to which people possess both masculine and feminine traits.

Binaural information   The sound information obtained from both ears.

B-needs (being needs)   The motivation toward self-fulfillment, better mental health, and greater uniqueness among people.

Biofeedback   The use of a monitoring device, such as an electromyograph, to inform an individual about changes occurring in his or her internal physiological systems.

Biological age   One's life expectancy.

Biological need   A physiological condition necessary for survival.

Biological perspective   1. The study of the relationships of biological systems, especially the brain and nervous system, to behavior and mental process. 2. The developmental viewpoint that places human development in an evolutionary framework and emphasizes understanding human biology in order to understand development.

Biorhythms   An individual's cyclical pattern of physical, emotional, and intellectual ups and downs.

Bipolar cells   The specialized cells in the retina that process visual information before it is sent to the brain via the optic nerves.

Bipolar disorder   A disorder characterized by one or more manic and depressive episodes.

Birth order   An individual's age ranking among siblings.

Blind spot (optic disk)   The area of the retina in which ganglion cell axons come together to form the optic nerve and that has no receptor cells.

Blocking   The condition in which once a contingency is established between the unconditioned stimulus and a specific conditioned stimulus, the addition of a second conditioned stimulus will not add additional information and no conditioning to the second CS will occur.

Body rhythms   The bodily cycles of changes in energy level and activity patterns.

Bone conduction   The transmission of sound vibrations through the bones of the skull to the inner ear.

Brainstem   The part of the brain beginning where the spinal cord enters the skull that regulates basic bodily senses and functions.

Brightness   The psychological perception of the amplitude of light.

Brightness constancy   The learned perceptual characteristics that an object's brightness is unchanging even when the lighting changes.

Bulimarexia   An eating disorder characterized by a binge-purge cycle.

Bulimia   An abnormal craving for food and accompanied by obsessive binge eating.

Burnout   A syndrome of emotional exhaustion that results from the constant emotional pressures associated with intense involvement with people over long periods of time.

Caffeine   A stimulant found in common foods as coffee, tea, chocolate, and many soft drinks.

Cannon-Bard theory   A theory of emotion that states that in situations that a person perceives to be emotion-arousing, the thalamus simultaneously signals physiological arousal and cognitive awareness.

Cardinal traits   The traits that dominate and influence most areas of a person's life.

Case study (clinical method)   An intensive study of one subject.

Castration anxiety   A boy's fear of losing his genitals because of his desire to take his father's place with his mother.

CAT (Computerized Axial Tomography) scanner   A device that combines X-ray techniques with computer-assisted imaging to produce an electronic picture of structures in different layers of the brain.

Catatonic type of schizophrenia   The display of excited behavior and stuporous behavior, or an alternation of the two.

Cell body (soma)   The part of a neuron that contains the nucleus of the cell.

Central Nervous System (CNS)   The part of the nervous system that includes the brain and spinal cord.

Central nervous system depressants   Chemicals that slow the functioning of the neurons in the brain and spinal cord.

Central nervous system stimulants   Chemicals that speed up the functions of the neurons in the brain and spinal cord.

Central tendency   A description of the typical, average, or middle score of a distribution.

Central traits   A small number of traits that are basic characteristics of an individual.

Centration   The inability to focus on more than one aspect of a problem at a time.

Cephalocaudal   Development from the head downward.

Cerebellum   The part of the brain under the back of the cerebral cortex and attached to the pons that regulates fine motor control.

Cerebral cortex (neocortex)   The most massive outer layers of the human brain where perception and higher mental processes occur.

Cerebral hemispheres   The left and right cerebral hemispheres that make up the two halves of the cerebral cortex of the human brain.

Cerebral lateralization   The separation and integration of functional systems within the cerebral hemispheres of the brain.

Chaining   The operant conditioning procedure used to train a sequence of actions in which the last response in the chain is trained first.

Chromatographic theory   A theory that proposes that different smell qualities are experienced because odor molecules travel different distances in the nostrils and reach different portions of the olfactory epithelium.

Chromosomes   Found in the nucleus of cells in 23 pairs, they carry a genetic blueprint.

Chunking   A way to deal with information exceeding the capacity of short-term memory that groups together information so that more is contained in each bit.

Clairvoyance   The perception of current events without visual or other basic senses.

Classical conditioning   The learning that results from a signal (CS) that reliably predicts the occurrence of a second stimulus (US).

Client-centered therapy   A therapeutic approach originated by Carl Rogers in which the client is given a supportive environment in which to work through his or her own problems.

Clinical method (case study)   An intensive study of one subject.

Clinical neuropsychology   A combination of neurological and psychological assessment techniques that are used to evaluate a neurologically-impaired individual's cognitive and behavioral abilities, and such an individual's rate of improvement or decline after brain injury.

Closure   A perceptual grouping principle in which the tendency is to make complete, whole figure out of incomplete stimuli.

Clustering   The efficient storage in long term memory that groups together related facts or ideas.

Cocaine   A stimulant derived from the coca plant.

Cocktail party effect   The selective shift in attention that results from being in a group engaged in numerous conversations.

Cognition   A formal term for thinking that refers to the way information about the world is represented, processed, and used.

Cognitive-developmental theory   Kohlberg's theory that states that once children have identified themselves as female or male, they actively organize their knowledge of the world in light of that identity.

Cognitive dissonance theory   The theory that inconsistent cognitive elements are unpleasant and that people will adjust their thinking to reduce the resulting mental tension.

Cognitive maps   Mental representations of physical space.

Cognitive model of bystander intervention   A model that suggests that potential helpers first ask themselves if some unusual emergency is occurring requiring their response in which they can decide what to do and whether to help.

Cognitive modifiability   Feuerstein's idea that mental structures and contents can be changed as new things are learned.

Cognitive perspective   1. The study in contemporary psychology that focuses on the nature of cognitions, thoughts, beliefs, perceptions, problem-solving, and memory. 2. The developmental viewpoint that emphasizes the individual's active role in influencing his or her development.

Cognitive psychology   The study of higher mental processes and structures such as information processing.

Cognitive theory of emotion   The idea that an emotional state involves both physiological arousal and thoughts about the emotion-arousing situation.

Cognitive therapy   A therapy developed by Beck, consisting of approaches aimed at correcting false conceptions and self-signals.

Cohabitation   The open living arrangement of an unmarried couple.

Cold   A sensation experienced when a stimulus colder than the skin is applied to an area of the skin containing receptors for cold.

Collective unconscious   The belief by Jung that people are born with a psychological and spiritual "blueprint" built into the brain's structure.

Color (hue)   The psychological perception of the wavelength of light.

Color blindness   The inability to distinguish between some or all colors.

Color constancy   The learned perceptual characteristic that an object's color remains unchanged even under changes in illumination.

Commitment theory   A theory that proposes that attitudes become more resistant to persuasion attempts if people have publicly committed themselves to their current positions.

Common fate   The perceptual grouping principle that states that elements moving in the same direction at the same rate will be grouped together.

Common-sense theory   A theory of emotion that states that a person encounters a situation, experiences an emotion, and then reacts.

Common traits   The traits exhibited by a majority of people in a society.

Communal relationships   A relationship in which each person is more concerned with the other person's welfare and needs than with obtaining an equal number of benefits from the relationship.

Companionate love   Love characterized by affection for and sharing with another person.

Comparative psychology   The study of animals in natural environments and in laboratories in order to better understand the behavior of animals and humans.

Comparison level   The level of reward a person thinks is adequate in a relationship.

Comparison level for alternatives   The lowest level of rewards one finds acceptable after considering the available relationships.

Compensation   An attempt to overcome imagined or real inferiorities or weaknesses.

Complementarity of needs   The idea that people with opposing characteristics are attracted to each other when the opposing characteristics help meet the other person's needs.

Competence   A factor influencing interpersonal attraction in which people are attracted to a person considered to be competent.

Complexes   Clusters of emotionally laden thoughts that Jung believed influence a person's behavior.

Complexity   The physical dimension of light that corresponds to the perception of saturation.

Compulsions   Senseless behaviors that are performed repeatedly.

Concepts A way to mentally represent information by grouping together items and events that share common features.

Concrete operations A stage of cognitive development during which children at about age seven acquire a new, reversible set of mental operations based on the mental manipulation of real objects.

Conditioned emotional responses The classical conditioning of positive and negative emotional reactions to previously neutral stimuli.

Conditioned (secondary) reinforcers Stimuli that obtain their reinforcing value through their association with primary reinforcers.

Conditioned response (CR) A learned reaction to a previously neutral conditioned stimulus.

Conditioned stimulus (CS) A neutral stimulus that after acquisition elicits a conditioned response.

Conditioning The most basic form of learning.

Cones Receptor cells in the innermost layer of the retina that are responsible for transducing information about color and fine detail.

Confederates Accomplices of the experimenter who impersonate subjects.

Confluence theory Zajonc's theory that the intellectual development of an individual is influenced by the contributions of all family members.

Congruence 1. A state of consistency between the real and ideal self, between experience, awareness, and expression of what one is and what one wants to be. 2. A therapist characteristic in which the therapist exhibits genuineness without playing a role.

Consciousness An awareness of reality that includes a person's awareness of his or her own existence, internal sensations, perceptions of external objects, emotions, dreams, thoughts, and memories.

Conscience Moral messages learned from society that control behavior by guilt.

Consequences (negative emotional experiences) According to Ellis, the outcomes of irrational beliefs.

Conservation The principle that properties such as number, volume, and mass remain the same despite apparent changes in appearance.

Consolidation The transfer of information from short-term to long-term memory.

Constellating power A belief held by Jung that every complex draws on new ideas and interprets the ideas.

Contact comfort The comfort provided by physical contact with a caregiver.

Contents In Guilford's theory of intelligence, the aspects of intelligence including visual, auditory, symbolic, semantic, and behavioral skills.

Content validity The degree to which a test includes a representative range of items.

Contiguity In classical conditioning, the idea that learning occurs from the contiguous pairing of the conditioned and unconditioned stimuli.

Contingency A condition in which the presence of one event is accompanied by the presence of a second event, and when the absence of the first event is also accompanied by the absence of the second.

Contingency theory of leadership The theory that leadership is contingent on respect for the leader, known roles and goals for group members, and the leader having the power to distribute rewards and punishments.

Continuity The perceptual grouping principle in which stimuli that suggest continuous patterns will be grouped together.

Continuous reinforcement A situation in which every desired response is followed by a reinforcer.

Contrast A distortion process in which a speaker's position is judged to be more different from the listener's own position than it actually is.

Control The goal of psychology to understand a behavioral phenomenon well enough to be able to start the behavior, strengthen the behavior, weaken the behavior, and end the behavior.

Control group Subjects in an experiment that are not exposed to the independent variable.

Control theory A later formulation by William Glasser that places greater emphasis on biological sources of needs and on an anti-behaviorist stance than did his earlier reality therapy.

Conventional morality The second level of moral development according to Kohlberg.

Convergence A binocular cue to depth based on the feedback from muscle tension created by the eyes as they converge while focusing on near objects.

Conversion disorder A disorder characterized by the loss of (or change in) physical functioning without organic causes.

Cornea The transparent shell of the eye that bends the incoming rays of light and helps focus them.

Corpus callosum A thick set of fibers between the cerebral hemispheres of the brain that is the major communication link between the two hemispheres.

Correlational method A research method used to establish relationships between two or more variables such as traits, events, or behaviors.

Correspondent inference theory A theory that proposes that people make judgments about the causes of another's behavior by observing the impact of the behavior on the environment.

Cost-reward analysis An analysis in which positive outcomes (profits) lead to continuation of a relationship, while negative outcomes (losses) lead to the end of the relationship. The motivation in this analysis is to maximize rewards and minimize costs.

Counterconditioning The procedure for extinguishing one response while conditioning an incompatible response to the same conditioned stimulus.

Courtesy bias Socially acceptable answers given by respondents in a survey.

Criterion validity The degree to which test scores relate to other performance measures.

Critical periods The principle of development that states that at different times the individual will be more sensitive to influences from the environment.

Crystallized abilities Intellectual factors related to experience, learning and culture.

Crystallized intelligence Specific, learned information acquired through education and experience.

Cue-dependent forgetting A failure of memory retrieval due to the lack of a single cue needed for remembering.

Cultural display rules The rules that govern facial expression and that are followed by members of a social class, culture, or subculture.

Culture-fair tests Tests that do not disadvantage subgroups within a culture.

Cultural (situational) model The model of abnormal behavior that proposes that behaviors are not inherently normal or abnormal but are judged so within the context of the culture or situation in which they occur.

Cutaneous senses Receptors in the skin that are sensitive to touch, warmth, cold, and pain.

Dark adaptation The adjustment of the sensitivity of the rods and cones to lower illuminations.

Daydreams The shift in focus of attention from the external to the internal world.

Debriefing A condition in which subjects are told at the conclusion of an experiment the purpose of the study and are made aware of any deceptions used.

Decay theory A theory that explains forgetting as a gradual loss of memory over time.

Decibels (dbs) Units of loudness.

Declarative knowledge Factual information that is easily described.

Deductive reasoning A type of reasoning beginning with general ideas believed to be true and deriving specific conclusions from those general ideas.

Deep structure A level of transformational grammar that refers to the level of abstract language rules that determine meaning.

Deficiency love A relationship that involves depending upon someone to meet one's needs and to decrease feelings of inferiority.

Deficiency needs (D-needs) Motivations to reduce tension by meeting requirements for physiological survival and safety.

Deindividuation The loss of the sense of one's individuality.

Deinstitutionalization The movement away from institutionalizing mentally ill individuals in large mental institutions towards caring for these individuals in community-based treatment centers.

Delayed conditioning Conditioning in which the conditioned stimulus begins before the unconditioned stimulus and ends at the beginning, during, or after the unconditioned stimulus.

Delay of gratification The ability to give up an immediate, small reward in favor of a later, larger reward.

Delivery The second stage of birth where the fetus travels through the birth canal and is born.

Delusions False beliefs about the external world that an individual maintains despite an absence of supporting evidence.

Demand characteristics The features of an experiment that allow a subject to determine the purpose of an experiment.

Dendrites The parts of a neuron that serve as the receptor sites for incoming messages.

Denial The first stage of a terminally-ill individual's adjustment to dying, marked by denial that one's death will occur sooner than expected.

Dependent variables The measured variables in an experiment that may change as a function of the independent variable.

Depression The third stage of a terminally-ill individual's adjustment to dying.

Depressive episodes Periods of feelings of sadness, worthlessness, guilt, and loss of interest in previously pleasurable things.

Depth perception The perception of an object's distance from you by use of monocular and binocular cues.

Dereflection A logotherapy technique used to divert attention from the self.

Description The goal of psychologists to be objective and accurate in observing behavior.

Descriptive statistics Procedures used to quantify, organize, and summarize large amounts of data so that the prominent features of the data can be easily grasped.

Detection threshold   A more appropriate term for describing the absolute threshold, since no constant value for the absolute threshold exists.

Developmental psychologist   A scientist who studies human development and changes in human behavior from conception to death.

Developmental self-concept theory   A theory that emphasizes how career and vocational choices coincide with the teen's or young adult's developing self-concept.

Diagnosis   The classification or labeling of a disease or disorder.

Dichotic listening   The sending of different information to the two ears at the same time.

Difference threshold (just noticeable difference, j.n.d.)   The minimal amount of change in a physical stimulus that a subject can detect.

Differential relaxation   A technique to relax during one's daily routine that may make the daily routine less stressful.

Differentiation   The principle of development that states that qualitative changes occur along the dimensions of simple to complex and general to specific.

Difficult infant   An infant temperament in which an infant is classified as excitable, less adaptable to change, and more irregular in biological function.

Diffusion of responsibility hypothesis   The idea that as the number of people who witness an emergency increases, responsibility for action is shared or diffused throughout the group, with the result that each person feels less responsible for helping.

Directionality   The principle of development that states that physical and behavioral development occurs along two directions—cephalocaudal and proximodistal.

Discrimination   1. The process by which one learns to respond differently to similar stimuli. 2. Behavior that reflects one's prejudicial attitudes.

Discriminative stimulus   In operant conditioning, a stimulus that signals the availability of a reinforcer.

Disorders of impulse control   A disorder characterized by impulsiveness and lack of control; disorders include pathological gambling, kleptomania, pyromania, and explosive disorders.

Disorganized type of schizophrenia   A disorder characterized by display of odd behaviors, incoherent speech, and, often, a silly affect.

Displacement theory   A theory that proposes that all memory has a limited capacity and that forgetting occurs when memory becomes crowded and new memories displace old ones.

Disputing irrational beliefs   The purpose of rational-emotive therapy; the goal of RET is to replace irrational beliefs with rational ones.

Dissociative disorders   Disorders characterized by a separation from normal consciousness or identity.

Dizygotic (fraternal) twins   Twins resulting from the fertilization of two ova by two separate sperm and resulting in the formation of two zygotes.

Door-in-the-face technique   The selling technique in which refusing to comply to a very large request leads to compliance with a smaller request.

Dopamine hypothesis   An explanation of how the neurotransmitter dopamine in the brains of schizophrenics differs from that in non-schizophrenics' brains.

Double-bind theory   A theory that emphasizes conflicting communications between mother and child and within the family as a whole.

Downward social comparison   The effect that occurs when people suffer misfortunes and sometimes compare themselves with others who are in even worse circumstances.

DNA (Deoxyribonucleic acid)   A complex protein molecule in the form of a double-helix chain in which genetic information is transmitted and stored.

Double-blind studies   An experimental condition in which neither the experimenter nor the subjects know in which treatment condition (the experimental or control group) a subject is.

Dread   The long-lasting fear that can be typified as the fear of fear.

Dream analysis   A Freudian technique for interpreting the symbolic meaning of dreams.

Drive reduction theory   A theory that proposes that biological needs resulting from specific bodily deficits produce drives that impel the organism to act to reduce the drives.

Dual coding theory   The idea that if information is stored in two different ways the probability of later recall is higher because retrieval of the information can occur in two ways.

Dual hypothalamic theory of hunger   A theory that states that nuclei in the lateral hypothalamus and the ventromedial hypothalamus control the initiation and end of feeding.

Dyspareunia   The term for painful intercourse experienced by women.

Eardrum (tympanic membrane)   A membrane that separates the outer ear from the middle ear and vibrates as sound waves strike it.

Easy infant   An infant temperament classified as cheerful, easily adaptable to change, and exhibiting regularity in eating and sleeping.

Echoic memory   A type of memory in which the sensory image is remembered for three or four seconds before it fades.

Eclectic perspective   The viewpoint that draws upon the strengths of all perspectives for a comprehensive picture of human development.

Ecological approach   The position advocated by J. J. Gibson that the stimulus environment affords all the information necessary for forming perceptions (see *theory of direct perception*).

Ectoderm   The outer layer of tissue in a developing embryo that develops into the nervous system, sensory organs, outer layer of skin, skin glands, and structures such as fingernails, toenails, and teeth.

Ectomorph   One of Sheldon's somatotypes in which individuals are characterized as having thin, flat, and fragile bodies with a personality that is described as brainy, artistic, restrained, inhibited, and private.

Efferent (motor) neurons   The neurons in the peripheral nervous system that carry information away from the central nervous system.

Ego   A structure of personality in psychoanalytic theory that comes into existence so that a person can interact with the objective world and which acts as a mediator between the id and external reality.

Egocentric attributions   People's tendencies to make attributions based on their own behavior.

Egocentrism   The inability to view the world from a reference point other than oneself.

Ego ideal   A structure of the ego that strives for perfection.

Ego states   As defined by Berne, the parent, the adult, and the child voices within each person.

Eidetic imagery   A phenomenon associated with the encoding phase in which some individuals are able to see a picture for as long as four or five minutes after it has been removed.

Eisegesis   The faulty interpretations that result when clinicians project their own interpretations and biases into the scoring of personality and other assessment devices.

Ejaculatory incompetence   A sexual dysfunction involving inability to ejaculate within the vagina.

Elaborative rehearsal   A memory strategy in which information is recorded for storage.

Electra complex   The Freudian explanation of sex-typing in females in which a girl starts out being in love with her mother but later feels betrayed by her mother because of her lack of a penis.

Electroconvulsive therapy (ECT)   A treatment for severe depression that involves passing an electric current through the temples of the head.

Electroencephalograph (EEG)   A device that measures the activity of the neurons in the brain by the use of recording electrodes.

Electromagnetic spectrum   The range of electromagnetic radiation that includes visible light waves as well as ultraviolet light, infrared light, radio waves, and microwaves.

Embryo transfer   A reproductive technique in which sperm are used to artificially inseminate a donor ovum while the ovum is still in the donor's body. After five days the fertilized ovum is removed from the donor and transferred to a recipient's uterus.

Embryonic stage   The period from two weeks to eight weeks in prenatal development when organs systems are being formed.

Emotion   A term referring to a set of complex reactions to a stimulus involving subjective feelings, physiological arousal, and behavioral expressions of the emotion.

Empathy (understanding)   A therapist characteristic in which a therapist has a sense of the client's world as if from the client's viewpoint.

Empiricism   The belief that all knowledge is learned through experience.

Enactive representation   One type of cognitive representation that involves thinking in terms of physical actions.

Endocrine system   A chemically based regulatory system involving the release of hormones from the endocrine glands in the body.

Endoderm   Inner layer of tissue in the developing embryo that forms the respiratory and digestive systems, glands, and other organs.

Endomorph   One of Sheldon's somatotypes in which individuals are characterized as having soft, round bodies with a personality that emphasizes relaxation, complacency, love of food and physical comfort, slow reactions, sociability, and tolerance.

Encoding   The first phase of the information-processing model that involves coding information so that it can be used by the system and stored in the system.

Endorphins   The endogenous morphine-like substances produced in the central nervous system (see *enkephalins*).

Engram (memory trace)   The idea that memory is stored in structures in the brain.

Enkephalins   Another name for endorphins (see *endorphins*).

Environmental cues (stimulus cues)   Environmental stimuli that elicit specific behaviors.

Episodic memory   A type of memory involved in recalling information about experiences within a specific context or time frame.

Equilibration   Piaget's term for the internal process that motivates people to keep their cognitive information in a balanced state.

Erogenous zone   An area of the body that is a central location of pleasure during psychosexual development.

Error of central tendency   The tendency to minimize differences among people when forming perceptions of people.

Escape learning   Learning to make responses to terminate or escape from an aversive (unpleasant) situation.

Ethnocentrism The belief that one's own group is superior to other groups.

Ethologists Specialists engaged in the comparative study of animal and human behavior in natural environments.

Etiology The cause or origin of a behavior or a disorder.

Eustachian tube A tube connecting the middle ear with the throat that functions to equalize the pressure on either side of the eardrum and permits drainage of fluid from the middle ear.

Exchange theory A theory that proposes that relationships are characterized by a concern for what one owes to others and for what one gets in return.

Existential anxiety Anxiety that results from the perception that the self is distinct from the rest of the world and is therefore alone.

Existentialism The reaction against the idea of understanding humanness only through reason and thought; advocates adding emotional substance to human intellectual life.

Expectancy The person's subjective belief about the probable outcome of a behavior, based on past experiences in similar situations.

Expectancy value theory A theory that proposes that five factors influence an individual's level of achievement.

Experimental group Subjects in an experiment that are exposed to a treatment condition to which a control group of subjects is not exposed.

Experimental method A method used by scientists to establish the relationship between manipulated (independent) variables and measured (dependent) variables while other variables are controlled.

Experimenter bias The bias in an experiment resulting from the way the experimenter gives directions to subjects or from nonverbal gestures during the experiment.

Explanation The goal of psychologists to understand why a behavior occurs and to find an underlying process or relationship that accounts for the behavior.

Explicit theories Theories of intelligence based on data collected from performing intellectual tasks.

Exploratory behavior Behavior motivated by innate drives to learn about the world.

Expressed emotion The degree to which a schizophrenic's family expresses negative emotions about the schizophrenic's condition.

Externality hypothesis A hypothesis that proposes that obese people are more influenced by external hunger cues than are normal-weight individuals.

External locus of control The belief that rewards are independent of behaviors and are controlled by forces external to an individual.

Extinction The condition occurring when the conditioned stimulus is presented without the unconditioned stimulus, or when a response is not reinforced.

Extraneous variables Other factors besides the manipulated (independent) variable that may influence the outcome of an experiment.

Extrinsic motivation The motivation that arises when an activity is performed for an external consequence or is seen as a means to an end.

Extrinsic reinforcer An external stimulus that serves as a reinforcer.

Face validity The degree to which a test appears, on the face of it, to measure what it claims to measure.

Facial feedback hypothesis The idea that skeletal muscle activity associated with emotional expression plays a direct role in regulating the experience of emotion.

Fallacy of positive instances Situations in which individuals tend to remember confirmations of predictions but tend to forget disconfirmations.

False consensus effect An egocentric bias that allows people to believe their attitudes are relatively more common and more appropriate than other people's attitudes.

Familial retardation Mental retardation for which no known organic cause can be identified.

Familiar strangers People one does not know but sees often.

Family atmosphere The emotional relationships among family members.

Family pedigree A genetic study in which a characteristic is traced through several generations of the same family.

Fear of success The idea that some people may avoid success because they expect achieving success would bring negative consequences.

Feelings The subjective experiences associated with physiological arousal.

Fetal stage The period during prenatal development from about eight weeks after conception to birth.

Figure-ground relationship The basic perceptual organizing principle of grouping stimuli as a figure against a background.

Field experiments Experiments conducted in natural settings outside the laboratory.

Fight or flight response A process brought about in the sympathetic division of the autonomic nervous system that prepares the body for emergency situations.

First impression   The impression formed from the initial knowledge one acquires about a person that often biases later acquired information.

Fixation   The result of non-resolution of a developmental task of a psychosexual stage as the result of overgratification or undergratification.

Fixed action pattern   A concept denoting the immediate and unchanging motivated behaviors of all members of a species to certain releasing stimuli in the environment.

Fixed Interval (FI) schedule   A reinforcement schedule in which the amount of time before a response will obtain a reinforcer is constant or fixed.

Fixed ratio (FR) schedule   A reinforcement schedule in which the number of responses necessary to obtain a reinforcer is constant or fixed.

Flashbulb memory   A type of memory that results from the unexpectedness and short duration of a striking event that causes one to remember personal experiences associated with the event.

Flooding   An attempt to extinguish a phobia through concentrated exposure to the anxiety producing situation.

Fluid abilities   The intellectual factors related to perceiving relationships quickly and solving problems (see fluid intelligence).

Fluid intelligence   The capacity to perceive relationships and to integrate that information cognitively.

Foot-in-the-door technique   The selling technique in which first getting a person to comply with a very small request leads to the person later complying with a much larger request.

Foreclosure   Marcia's identity status in which an individual has made identity choices without considering alternatives.

Formal operations   Piaget's fourth stage of cognitive development in which abstract thought develops.

Fovea   The center of the retina that contains only cones and allows perception of fine detail.

Frame of reference   The context in which perceptions occur, including past experiences as well as the present situation.

Framing   The way in which a problem-solving task is presented.

Free association   A psychoanalytic technique in which a patient can say without censorship anything that comes into his or her consciousness.

Free recall   A recall technique in which information can be recalled in any order.

Frequency distribution   Data arranged to show the number of times (frequency) each score occurs.

Frequency polygon   A frequency distribution plotted as a line graph.

Frequency theory   A theory that proposes that pitch is determined by the firing rate of auditory receptor cells.

Friendship   A relationship involving enjoyment of each other's company, mutual trust, and respect for the good judgment of the other person.

Frontal lobe   The portion of the cerebral cortex in the forepart of each hemisphere that is specialized for planning and executing purposeful behaviors.

Fugue   A dissociative disorder characterized by the affected individual traveling to a different location, assuming another identity, and being unable to recall his or her former identity.

Fully functioning person   A person accomplishing the task of being one's true self.

Functional fixity   A barrier to problem solving in which the more often one uses an object for a specific function, the more difficult it is to use the object in a novel way.

Functionalism   The viewpoint that stresses a practical approach to psychology and the adaptability of people to their environments.

Fundamental attribution error   The tendency to underestimate the situation's influence and overestimate trait influences when judging the cause of other people's behavior.

Gain-loss theory   An interpersonal attraction theory based on an individual's greater attraction to those people who become more positive in their evaluations of them and being less attracted to those people who become more negative in their evaluations.

Ganglion cells   The neural cells in the retina that integrate information from the rods and cones.

Gate control theory   A pain perception theory that proposes that due to the limited amounts of information sensory pathways to the brain can handle at one time, pain information will not be transmitted to the brain when the pathways are carrying other information.

Gender   The sex of an individual.

Gender differences   The psychosocial (not biological) differences between males and females.

Gender orientation   The stable, subjective sense of affinity for one gender or the other.

Gender preference   The gender one finds most desirable as a sexual partner regardless of an individual's core gender identity.

Gender roles   The specific set of culturally determined behaviors and characteristics deemed appropriate for a male or female.

Gender schema theory Bem's theory that explains gender identification as a function of cognitive development and explains the acquisition of gender roles as a function of social learning.

Gender typing The process by which a person identifies his or her gender.

Generalized anxiety disorder A disorder characterized by nervousness, restlessness, and inability to relax while preoccupied with worry and fear.

Generalized reinforcer A conditioned reinforcer, such as money, that has value independent of its association with primary reinforcers.

Genes The genetic units of heredity composed of DNA.

Genotype The particular allele configuration a person inherits.

General adaptation syndrome (G.A.S.) Selye's description of the series of bodily changes generated by reactions to stress.

General to specific The developmental principle that states that systems change from general, nonspecific systems to particular, more complex systems.

Generalization The process by which one makes conditioned responses to stimuli that are similar to the conditioned stimulus.

Generalized drive The idea that any source of drive can energize behavior.

Genital stage Freud's fifth psychosexual stage during which teenagers achieve mature adult sexuality.

Germinal stage The period in prenatal development from conception to implantation, approximately two weeks in length.

Gestalt A German word for *form* or *whole*, denoting in psychology the belief that the whole of an experience is greater than the sum of its parts.

Gestalt therapy A form of therapy closely tied to the personality of its founder, Fritz Perls, combining existential concerns about how people experience their present existence with Gestalt concerns about how people perceive themselves and the world.

Gestures The movements of body, face, or extremities that express a person's ideas, opinions, or emotions.

g Factor Spearman's concept of a general factor of intelligence that affects all performances.

Glial cells (glia) The cells in the nervous system that form connective tissue that support, protect, and bind together neurons.

Grammar The rules that govern basic aspects of language usage.

Group polarization In group decision-making, the strengthening of the group's initial average position.

Groupthink A type of conformity in which members of policy-making groups remain silent, thereby concealing individual doubts about a policy and creating an illusion of unanimity.

Gustation (taste) The sense of taste stimulated by food molecules dissolved in the saliva of the mouth.

Habit A familiar, patterned, rhythmic behavior.

Habituation A condition in which attention is no longer paid to stimuli that have become familiar and are relatively unchanging.

Hair cells The receptors cells embedded in the Organ of Corti, responsible for transducing mechanical sound vibrations into neural auditory messages.

Hallucinations Sensory perceptions in the absence of appropriate external stimulation.

Hallucinogens Chemicals that cause false sensory perceptions.

Halo effect The tendency to judge a liked person favorably on most dimensions.

Halstead-Reitan Neuropsychological Test Battery (HRB) A neuropsychological test that allows trained examiners to determine an individual's level and pattern of performance, differences in right-left abilities, and specific symptoms of neuropathology.

Hammer (malleus) One of a chain of small bones that act as an amplifier in the middle ear.

Hayflick limit An estimate that states that the upper limit for longevity is 110 to 120 years.

Height on a plane The monocular cue to depth based on the tendency to look up to see more distant objects.

Helping behaviors A category of prosocial behaviors involving intentional acts to benefit another person.

Heroin An addictive narcotic derived from opium that affects the central nervous system.

Heterozygous The condition when one allele in a gene pair is dominant and the other is recessive for a specific trait.

Heuristic A rule that provides a general guideline for reasoning.

Higher-order conditioning The type of conditioning that occurs when an established conditioned stimulus serves as the unconditioned stimulus in a new conditioning task.

High expressed emotion (High EE) A label for families of schizophrenics who display critical negative emotions, hostility, and emotional overinvolvement in their family interactions.

High threshold fibers One type of hair cells that fire only when they are bent by high frequency sound vibrations.

Hippocampus A structure in the brain that is important in the formation of new memories.

HIPO High payoff activities such as studying for the next exam.

Histogram A bar graph of a frequency distribution that graphically displays the distribution of set of data.

Historical time The effect of historical events on individual's development.

Homozygous The condition when both alleles in a gene pair are dominant, or both are recessive for a specific trait.

Hormones The chemical regulators of the endocrine system produced by the endocrine glands.

"Hot seat" A Gestalt therapy technique in which the therapist in a group therapy session focuses his or her attention almost exclusively on one client.

Humanistic-existentialist perspective The developmental viewpoint that stresses humans' active roles in their own development.

Humanistic perspective The position in psychology that emphasizes the individual or self and human concerns of love, caring, and self-esteem.

Human sexual response cycle The four-stage cycle of excitement, plateau, orgasm, and resolution experienced by men and women during sexual arousal.

Hyperphagia A condition of extreme overeating resulting from damage to areas of the hypothalamus and limbic system.

Hypnogogic images An experience of colors, lights, geometric designs, or the feeling of falling during the transitional stage between waking and sleeping.

Hypnosis A state of heightened awareness in which attention is focused intensely on the suggestions of the hypnotist.

Hypnotherapy The use of hypnosis in therapeutic settings.

Hypochondriasis A disorder characterized by excessive concern about one's health and unrealistic interpretations of normal symptoms as symptoms of more serious illness.

Hypoglycemia A state of low blood sugar within individuals that results in feelings of hunger and stomach contractions.

Hypothalamus The part of the brain located below the thalamus near the center of the head involved in the regulation of basic body functions such as hunger, thirst, and the neuroendocrine system.

Hypothesis The researcher's tentative explanation of the relationship between variables to be studied.

Hypothetical constructs (intervening variables) Concepts that explain internal connections between an environmental event and a person's behavioral response.

Hypothetical reasoning A strategy of problem-solving in which an assumption is purposely made that was not part of the original task environment.

Hypothetico-deductive reasoning Logical thinking based on if/then, cause and effect relationships.

Iconic memory An initial form of memory that registers for a brief moment an exact image of what one has experienced.

Iconic representation One type of cognitive representation where thoughts are represented by images.

Id A structure of personality in psychoanalytic theory that exists totally in the unconscious mind and is the source of motivation.

Ideal self The image that represents the person one would most like to be.

Ideal state model The model of abnormal behavior that defines abnormality as deviation from a set of criteria for an ideal state of mental health.

Identification 1. The adoption by children of the characteristics, behaviors, beliefs, and values of other individuals and groups. 2. A theory that schizophrenia in some persons is caused simply by identifying with or acting like a schizophrenic person.

Identity One's sense of who one is.

Identity achievement Marcia's identity status in which the individual has considered alternatives and has committed to a choice.

Identity diffusion Marcia's identity status in which the individual has avoided making a commitment.

Identity versus role confusion Erikson's fifth stage in which teenagers achieve a stable identity by fusing various roles together.

Idiot savant A mentally retarded individual with one highly developed talent such as music or rapid calculation.

Ill-defined problems Problems with vague initial states, unclear goals, or unclear strategies and restrictions.

Illumination The third step in the problem-solving process in which the solution often appears in a sudden burst of insight.

Illusions Perceptual events in which external stimuli are misperceived.

Illustrators Physical acts that help explain a situation or verbal content but by themselves have no meaning.

Imaginary audience Teenagers' beliefs that others are as concerned about them as they are.

Immanent justice The belief that bad behavior will automatically bring its own punishment.

Implicit theories   The theories of intelligence based on people's everyday notions about intelligence.

Implosive therapy   A technique used to treat phobias that attempts to create an inward explosion of anxiety to extinguish the anxiety responses.

Imposter phenomenon   The fear of people driven to achieve that their successes will reverse and show them to be frauds.

Impotence   The inability to achieve and maintain an erection.

Incentive   An organism's expectation of reward for making a specific response; the expectation is internal, but the source of the expectation lies in the external reward.

Incongruence   The condition when a discrepancy between the real and ideal selves exists and self-awareness and self-expression are inconsistent.

Incubation   The second step of the problem-solving process in which one sets aside the problem when first attempts to solve it fail while unconsciously continuing to search for a solution.

Independent variables   The manipulated variables in an experiment that the experimenter is interested in studying.

Individualization   The first form of self-actualization that is the fullest possible development of different aspects of the personality.

Individual differences   The principle of development that states that the sequences of developmental changes is assumed to be approximately the same for everyone but that the rate at which the changes occur is unique for each person.

Individual psychology   1. The view that the individual is an indivisible whole with freedom to choose a direction in life. 2. Adler's theory that emphasizes the uniqueness of the individual and his or her responses to any situation.

Induced motion   An illusion of movement produced by a moving background against a stationary object.

Inductive reasoning   A type of reasoning that reaches general conclusions from a series of specific instances.

Industry versus inferiority   Erikson's fourth stage that occurs in the middle childhood years when children are no longer content to play and work to accomplish specific goals, but whose efforts often fall short of their expectations.

Infancy   A period after the neonatal period in which the baby moves from mostly reflexive behaviors to more purposeful behaviors and greater mobility.

Inferential statistics   The statistical procedures used to analyze the results of experiments and to determine what conclusions, or inferences, can be made.

Inferiority complex   An overcompensation pattern in which the individual feels highly inadequate.

Information control theories   The idea that predictable aversive events cause less stress than do unpredictable aversive events.

Information-processing model   A model of memory involving encoding, storage, and retrieval of memories.

Information processing theory   A theory that proposes that initial processing begins with raw data that is then transformed into mental representations.

Informed consent   The experimental condition in which subjects are informed of the basic characteristics and possible exposure to unpleasant stimuli before they participate in an experiment.

Inhibited sexual desire   A sexual problem arising from either organic or psychosocial conditions but not necessarily resulting in sexual dysfunction.

Initiative versus guilt   Erikson's third stage, in which a child needs to seek a balance between the ability to undertake new activities and the examination of the appropriateness of his or her actions.

Inner ear (cochlea)   The coiled, snail-like structure that contains the specialized components necessary for transducing mechanical sound vibrations into coded neural messages about sound.

Inoculation theory   A theory that proposes that people defend their attitudes better if they have had practice defending them.

Insomnia   A sleep disorder in which an individual experiences an inability to fall asleep.

Instinctive drift   A return to species specific behaviors when other behaviors are being reinforced.

Instrumental enrichment program   A program developed by Feuerstein, based on a test-teach-test model as a way to improve an individual's intellectual performance.

Instrumental learning (operant conditioning)   Learning responses that are instrumental in obtaining reinforcers; learning to operate on the environment to obtain certain consequences.

Integration   Understanding material by interrelating it through making connections between what is already known and what is being learned.

Intellectual giftedness   A condition in which an individual is assumed to possess more mental ability than most other people.

Intellectual retardation   A condition in which an individual possesses significantly below-average mental ability.

Intelligence quotient (IQ)   An indicator of intelligence originally defined as the ratio of mental age (MA) to chronological age (CA) multiplied by 100; $IQ = MA/CA \times 100$.

Interference   A memory loss resulting from the mixing of new and old memories.

Internal locus of control   A generalized expectancy that the location of responsibility for control is internal (within the person).

Interpersonal attraction   The study of factors that attract people to one another.

Interposition   The monocular cue to depth in which objects in the foreground overlap and block out portions of objects farther away.

Interpretative process   The central psychoanalytic process of analyzing and explaining the client's unconscious conflicts.

Intervening variables (hypothetical constructs)   Concepts that explain internal connections between an environmental event and a person's behavioral responses.

Intrinsic motivation   Any activity that is satisfying and rewarding for its own sake.

Intrinsic reinforcer   An internal stimulus, such as pride or pleasure, that serves as a reinforcer.

Introspection   A subjective method for observing, recording, and analyzing personal sensory experience.

Introversion-extroversion   One of the dimensions in the personality type theory proposed by Hans Eysenck.

Invasion of privacy   The ethical issue concerning the need to keep subjects' research responses confidential and to limit unnecessary invasions of subjects' private lives.

In vitro fertilization   The process of removing an ovum from the mother, fertilizing it in a petri dish with sperm from the father, allowing initial cell divisions to occur, and then transplanting the embryo to the mother's uterus.

Ipsative scoring   A scoring procedure in which the test-taker's scores on a battery of tests are compared to each other.

Iris   The colored part of the eye composed of two layers of muscles that control the size of the pupil and therefore the amount of light entering the eye.

Irrational beliefs   According to Ellis, the true cause of negative emotions.

Irreversibility   The inability to mentally reverse operations.

James-Lange Theory   A theory of emotion that states that emotions result from the bodily changes that occur reflexively when a person is confronted by a situation.

Jigsaw classroom technique   The encouragement of interdependence by giving each student only part of needed information so students must share information in order to complete an assignment.

Just noticeable difference (j.n.d.) or difference threshold   The minimal amount of change in physical stimulus necessary to detect a change in the stimulus.

Just world belief   The belief in a causal relationship between what a person does and what happens to the person.

Karma   The deterministic belief that all actions have consequences.

Kinesics (body language)   The study of body movement, posture, gesture, and facial expression.

Kinesthesis   The information provided about the relative positions of the parts of the body.

Kleptomania   The impulsive theft of items that are not of immediate use and for which the individual usually has enough money to pay.

Korsakoff's syndrome   An organic loss of memory associated with chronic alcoholism and thiamine deficiency.

Labor   The first stage of birth that involves contractions of the uterus and dilation of the cervix.

Language universals   The innate predispositions found in all natural languages that are the basis of grammatical knowledge.

Latency stage   The fourth psychosexual stage that occurs between the ages of six and twelve.

Latent learning   The learning of responses without active performance of the response.

Law   A theory that has been invariably supported by research while rival theories have failed to be supported.

Law of effect   Thorndike's principle that states that responses that produce pleasant consequences will be strengthened and responses not followed by pleasant consequences will be weakened.

Law of forward conduction   The process whereby messages are always conducted in the same direction within the nervous system— from the dendrites through the cell body, along the axon, to the dendrites of the next neuron.

Law of Pragnanz   The underlying principle of perception that stimuli are grouped into unified wholes whenever possible.

Learned taste aversions   Classically conditioned avoidance of specific tastes.

Learning   The relatively permanent changes in a person or animal as the result of experience with the potential to change the person's or animal's behavior.

Learning style (cognitive style)   Typical way in which one prefers to learn and think.

Leniency error   The tendency to rate others favorably.

Lens   The part of the eye directly behind the pupil, which focuses the light by adjusting for distance and inverting and reversing the image on the retina.

Levels of processing model   A model of memory that stresses types of processing and encoding and that memory is a function of the depth of processing the information received.

Libido   One of Freud's three kinds of drives that cause people to act without conscious thought.

Life position   The four conditions in transactional analysis beginning with I'm O.K., You're O.K.

Lifetime   The time since one's birth.

Light adaptation   The adjustment of the sensitivity of the rods and cones of the eyes to higher levels of light.

Limbic system   The interconnected structures in the brain that form an interface between the neocortex and the brainstem and mediate information to and from the cerebral hemispheres.

Linear perspective   A monocular cue to depth represented by the converging of parallel lines with increasing distance.

Linguistic relativity hypothesis (Whorfian hypothesis) The idea that the vocabulary and structural rules of one's native language limit thinking about the world within the confines of that language.

Lithium   A psychotropic medication used to treat anxiety and depression.

Locus of control   A generalized expectancy about the location (internal or external) of the responsibility for the control of behavior.

Logic   Plausible inductive or deductive reasoning, as well as the use of specific logical reasoning forms to construct valid arguments and to solve formal logical problems.

Logical error   The erroneous tendency to assume that certain traits always go together, such as friendliness and honesty.

Logotherapy   A form of existential therapy developed by Victor Frankel, based on finding the meaning of one's life.

Longitudinal studies   Research conducted with a group of people who are studied over a period of time.

Long-term memory   A type of memory that is almost limitless in capacity and in which information once stored is not easily forgotten.

LOPO   Low pay-off activities such as recopying legible notes.

Lost-letter technique   An unobtrusive measurement technique in which letters addressed to individuals or committees representing particular attitudes are "lost" in public places. The differential rates of return for the letters reflect a measure of a community's attitudes.

Love relationships   Relationships in which the characteristics of friendship, caring, and passion are present.

Low-ball technique   The selling technique in which obtaining a verbal commitment to honor a small request leads to compliance with a larger request.

Low expressed emotion (low EE)   The absence of high EE characteristics in a schizophrenic's family and the acceptance of schizophrenia as an illness (see *high expressed emotion (high EE)*.

Magic   A way of knowing about the world that relies on personal subjective experience for knowledge.

Major affective disorders   Prolonged extremes of mood that may be disruptive to a person's life.

Major depression   A disorder characterized by one or more depressive episodes.

Mania (manic episodes)   Periods of restlessness accompanied by inflated self-esteem, distractibility, and involvement in activities that persist over time.

Manipulators   Acts in which one part of the body rubs, picks, or grooms some other part of the body.

Marijuana   A substance containing a psychoactive chemical that facilitates functions of the brain and spinal cord, and in large doses can cause hallucinations.

Masculinity/femininity   Complex, poorly defined features of personality based on gender.

Massed practice   Studying material in a single session.

Maturational factors versus learning   A controversial issue of human development in which the behavioral-learning perspective emphasizes the role of environmental experience and learning, while the biological perspective stresses the effects of maturational forces.

Mean   The arithmetic average calculated by adding together all the scores and dividing the sum by the number of scores in the distribution.

Means-ends analysis   A strategy of problem solving that notes the differences between the initial state and the goal state and then attempts to reduce the difference between them.

Median   The midpoint of a set of scores.

Mediated learning experience   A model that involves special tasks in learning situations where a student actively interacts with another person who guides the learner to appropriate responses.

Medical model   The model of abnormal behavior that uses physical illness as an analogy for psychological/mental illness.

Meditation   A technique to concentrate and focus attention in order to produce a relaxed but alert waking state.

Medulla   A specialized area of the brain that comprises approximately the first inch of the brainstem.

Memory trace (engram)   The idea that memory is stored in a specific spot in the brain.

Menopause   The time around age 50 when women's production of estrogen drops dramatically and causes the cessation of ovulation and menstruation.

Mental age   The average intellectual capabilities of individuals at each age.

Mental operations   Idea proposed by Piaget that states that the human system has built-in organizing factors that process information from the environment and represent it as internal schemas.

Mental set   A barrier to problem-solving where previous experiences with solving certain problems predisposes one to try solving similar problems in the same way.

Mere exposure effect   The effect that the more frequently people encounter an object or idea, the more favorably they evaluate the object or idea.

Mesoderm   The middle tissue layer in a developing embryo that develops into the muscular, skeletal, excretory, and circulatory systems and sex organs.

Mesomorph   One of Sheldon's somatotypes in which individuals are characterized as having muscular, firm, and relatively strong bodies with a personality that is described as adventurous, assertive, energetic, risk taking, aggressive, and competitive.

Metamemory   The knowledge one has about his or her memory; the knowledge that a particular piece of information is known and how to retrieve it from memory.

Metamotives   The term used by Maslow to describe the striving to grow beyond one's present condition toward a closer fulfillment of one's potential.

Microsleeps   Short periods of sleep lasting 2–3 seconds, often observed in persons who are sleep-deprived.

Midbrain   A specialized area of the brain located at the top of the brainstem, that receives sensory information from the eyes and ears.

Middle ear   A section of the ear containing the hammer, anvil, and stirrup bones.

Mindlessness   Behavior that is habitual rather than responsive to actual environmental characteristics.

Minimal goal   The lowest level of potential reinforcement that would be satisfactory in a given situation.

Minnesota Multiphasic Personality Inventory (MMPI)   A thoroughly researched objective psychological test and the most frequently used personality assessment inventory, consisting of 566 true/false statements.

Mode   The most frequently occurring score in a distribution.

Modeling (imitation observational learning)   The observational learning of skills and behaviors by observing and imitating others: the idea that an individual acquires behavior patterns by watching someone else's behavior rather than by receiving reinforcements.

Monozygotic (identical) twins   Twins resulting from one zygote splitting into two individuals after fertilization.

Modeling theory   The theory that people can learn to be helpful by observing another person being helpful.

Morality of constraint   The first stage of Piaget's theory of moral development.

Morality of cooperation   The second stage of Piaget's theory of moral development.

Moratorium   Marcia's identity status in which the individual is in the process of considering alternatives and making decisions.

Morita therapy   A therapy developed in Japan by Shoma Morita based on the ideas of Zen Buddhism.

Morpheme   The basic unit of meaning in a language that may be a phoneme or combinations of phonemes to which meaning has been attached.

Morphine   A narcotic derived from opium that affects the central nervous system and has been used medically since the 1800s to relieve pain.

Motor cortex   A portion of the frontal lobe of the brain that starts the process of voluntary movement.

Motivated forgetting   Memory retrieval failure that is an active, purposeful failure to retrieve embarrassing, painful, or threatening memories.

Motivation   An internal state that activates behavior and energizes, sustains, and directs that behavior toward a goal.

Motive   A general term used to designate an internal state that energizes behavior and directs it toward a goal.

MRI (magnetic resonance imaging)   A device that uses a powerful magnet and radio waves to detect small resonant changes in the cells in the body. A computer analyzes these changes and creates a picture.

Multiple personality   A dissociative disorder characterized by the existence of two more distinct personalities within one individual.

Myelin   A fatty substance that acts as insulation around parts of neurons.

Narcolepsy   A sleep disorder in which sudden, uncontrollable onsets of sleep during waking hours occurs.

Naturalistic observation   A method for studying behavior in which an observer watches and objectively records the behavior of subjects in their natural environments.

Nature-nurture issue A controversial issue of human development involving the relative impact of heredity and environment.

Need for achievement The motivation for accomplishing a difficult task, competing, and pursuing success.

Negative afterimages The afterimage of a complementary color when the cones are first saturated with a specific color of light and then stimulated with white light.

Normative crisis model A description of adult development in which each age is accompanied by a specific crisis to be resolved.

Negative feedback The control mechanism for the neuroendocrine system in which increases in one part of the system signal decreases in another part of the system.

Negative punisher A stimulus whose withdrawal causes a decrease in the probability of the recurrence of the response that precedes it.

Negative reinforcer A stimulus whose removal increases the probability of the recurrence of the response that precedes it.

Neonatal period The transitional period from the intrauterine environment to independent existence lasting from two to four weeks after birth.

Neonate The term used to describe a newborn baby.

Neuroendocrine system A term that refers to the extensive interconnections between the nervous system and the endocrine system.

Neuromodulators A newly-discovered class of chemicals that act to fine-tune the nervous system.

Neuron A single cell, the basic unit of the nervous system designed to receive and send messages.

Neuroses Disorders in which the symptoms are distressing and unacceptable to the person who has them.

Neurotransmitters The chemicals that when released carry a nerve impulse across the synaptic gap between two neurons.

Nightmare A disturbing dream that occurs during the REM stage of sleep.

Night terrors Episodes of extreme panic during sleep that are not remembered, occurring during non-REM, stage 4 of the sleep cycle.

Nonsense syllables Meaningless three-letter syllables.

Normal curve The bell-shaped distribution of chance events and of many human characteristics that are determined by a large number of factors, each of which has only a small influence by itself.

Norm-referencing The situation in which a test-taker's score is compared to a norm group.

Null hypothesis The condition tested by inferential procedures that the independent variable has no effect.

Obedience The situation in which an individual gives maximum receptivity to messages from an authority figure while becoming merely an agent of the authority figure.

Objective tests A test in which each item can be scored in only one way, assuring that two or more scorers will obtain the same results.

Objectivity The method whereby observations are made without bias or the influence of personal points of view.

Object permanence The capacity of an infant to recognize that people and objects continue to exist even when the infant is not in sensory contact with them.

Observational learning Responses learned through observation of others without direct reinforcement of the responses.

Observational learning (modeling) The idea that an individual acquires behavior patterns by watching someone else's behavior rather than by receiving reinforcements.

Obsessions Ideas or images that repeatedly seem to take over one's thoughts.

Obsessive-compulsive disorder A disorder characterized by repetitive thoughts and repetitive behaviors.

Occipital lobe (visual cortex) A section of the cerebral cortex at the back of the brain that integrates and analyzes visual information.

Oedipus complex In Freudian theory, a young boy's sexual attachment to his mother.

Olfaction (smell) The sense of smell stimulated by chemical odor molecules floating in the air.

Olfactory bulbs The structures located at the base of the brain to which smell impulses travel from the olfactory epithelium.

Olfactory epithelium The small patches of tissue in the upper half and roof of each nostril containing the sense receptors for smell.

Operant behavior Responses that have an effect (operate) on the environment.

Operant conditioning (instrumental learning) The process of learning to operate on the environment to obtain certain consequences.

Operational definitions Defining terms by stating the operations one must follow to observe what is meant by the term; a precise objective way to define terms.

Operations In Guilford's theory of intelligence, the aspects of intelligence involving cognition, memory, divergent production, convergent production, and evaluation.

Opium Narcotic made from opium poppies that is a depressant to the central nervous system.

Opponent process theory An explanation of color pairs observed in color blindness and negative afterimages that states that three opposing systems—red-green, blue-yellow, and dark-light function to process color information.

Optic chiasma The crossover point in the optic nerves at the base of the brain where information from the different portions of the right and left visual fields crosses over to the other side of the brain.

Optic disk (blind spot) The area of the retina in which ganglion cell axons come together to form the optic nerve that has no receptor cells.

Optic nerve The nerve that carries messages from the eye to the brain.

Oral stage The first psychosexual stage that extends from birth to about one year of age.

Orderliness The principle of development that states that developmental change is orderly.

Organ of Corti The specialized organ in the inner ear in which the receptor cells for hearing are embedded.

Organic amnesia A general term for forgetting caused by damage to the brain and other organic causes.

Organic retardation Mental retardation for which known organic or biological causes exist.

Organogenesis The process of developing the major organ systems of the body during the embryonic stage of prenatal development.

Outer ear The section of the ear consisting of the pinna and the auditory canal.

Oval window The structure located at the entrance to the inner ear that collects the concentrated sound vibrations from the middle ear.

Overcompensation The denial rather than the acceptance of a real situation and the exaggerated effort to cover up a weakness.

Overjustification effect The loss of interest that occurs when an individual shifts from an intrinsic to an extrinsic motivation orientation.

Overlearning Continuing to study material after it has been learned to a minimum criterion.

Overshadowing The effect that occurs when the unconditioned stimulus is contingent upon two conditioned stimuli that occur simultaneously, the conditioned response will become conditioned to the conditioned stimulus to which the subject pays greater attention.

Pain An unpleasant, noxious sensation due to stimulation of free nerve endings or damage to nerve tissue.

Painful intercourse A treatable sexual dysfunction.

Panic attack Unpredictable, overwhelming, terrifying attacks of anxiety.

Pansexualism The belief that sexual instincts motivate all human behavior.

Papillae The clusters of taste buds on the tongue.

Paradoxical intention A logotherapy technique in which the client is asked to do the thing he or she fears.

Paradoxical sleep A term that refers to the rapid eye movement stage of sleep, called paradoxical because of the similarity of EEG wave patterns in this stage of sleep to those of a person who is awake.

Paranoid type of schizophrenia A type of schizophrenia characterized by the display of delusions of persecution and grandeur or delusions of jealousy.

Parietal lobe A section at the top of the cerebral cortex that is specialized for processing sensory information.

Parsimony The simplest, briefest way to explain an experimental effect.

Partial reinforcement A situation in which the desired response is not reinforced every time it is produced.

Partial reinforcement effect (PRE) The greater resistance to extinction of responses established or maintained with partial reinforcement schedules.

Passionate love A relationship characterized by absorption in another person, intense physiological arousal, longing, and ecstasy.

Pathological gambling An impulse disorder associated with compulsive, chronic gambling.

PCP (angel dust) An hallucinogen that was originally developed as a tranquilizer but was found to create negative emotional reactions in many people.

Penis envy In Freudian psychoanalytic theory, the desire of females to possess penises.

Percentile A transformed score that indicates the percentage of subjects who scored at or below a certain score.

Perception The complex process in which sensory messages are organized and interpreted.

Perceptual constancy The recognition of familiar objects and events as stable and unchanging under widely varying stimulus conditions.

Perceptual defense The unconscious use of frames of reference to resist information that causes discomfort, embarrassment, or anxiety.

Perceptual set The frame of reference in perception resulting from past experiences; the tendency to perceive what a person expects to see.

Perfect pitch The ability to correctly identify any musical note.

Peripheral nervous system   All of the nervous system outside of the central nervous system, consisting of the somatic nervous system and the autonomic nervous system.

Permissive-indifferent parenting   Parents who are uninvolved in their children's lives and who do not control their children's behavior.

Permissive-indulgent parenting   Parents who are highly involved in their children's lives but who do little to control their children's behavior.

Permissive parenting   A parenting style in which parents are undemanding and assert relatively little control over their children's behavior.

Personal distress model   The model of abnormal behavior that equates abnormal behavior with negative and uncomfortable emotional states.

Personal fable   A form of self-centeredness in which teenagers become convinced that they are unique and not subject to the same effects as other people.

Personality   The characteristics of a person that are stable and enduring, that make an individual predictable to others, and that are useful in explaining individual differences.

Personality disorders   Disorders characterized by maladaptive, enduring personality traits appearing in adolescence or earlier.

Personality type theory   A theory that maintains that individuals select careers that match their personality types.

Personal unconscious   Material that was once conscious but was later repressed or forgotten.

Person perception   The process of forming impressions about other people.

PET (positron emission tomography) scanners   Devices that use computers to generate images of radioactive emissions from cells in the brain from which the function of brain structures can be investigated.

Phallic stage   Freud's third stage of psychosexual development that takes place from ages three to six.

Pharmacological interventions   The prescribing of drugs that affect the body, behavior, or emotions.

Phenotype   An individual's actual physical make-up based on his or her genotype.

Phi phenomenon (apparent motion)   The perception of movement in stationary objects such as the lights on movie marquees in which the rapid turning on and off of individual lights in succession is perceived as a single moving light.

Phobias   Irrational fears of objects, situations, or activities that result in a great desire to avoid the feared stimulus.

Phonemes   Sounds that are the basic units of spoken language.

Photons   The measurement units for electromagnetic radiation.

Phrenology   The mistaken belief that the shape of one's skull indicates mental capacity and personality characteristics.

Physiological psychologists   Psychologists who study connections between biology and behavior.

Pinna   The part of the outer ear that is the external, observable part of the ear.

Pituitary gland   A gland found at the base of the brain that is a key link between the nervous system and the endocrine system.

Placebo   An inert substance or fake treatment given to make a control group similar in appearance to the experimental group.

Placebo effect   The psychological impact of receiving a placebo in an experiment.

Place learning   An acquired expectancy about places associated with cognitive maps.

Placenta   The complex organ that allows exchange of nutrients and waste products between the maternal and fetal systems.

Place theory   A theory that proposes that pitch is determined by which hair cells on the basilar membrane are most affected by the sound vibrations.

Polygenic   The condition in which several pairs of genes are involved in the determination of a trait.

Polygraph (lie detector)   A device that measures physiological reactions such as the galvanic skin response and the change in heart and respiration rate, used in lie detection.

Pons   A specialized area of the brainstem that is a major link between the brainstem and the cerebellum.

Population   An entire set of observations; every person in a group.

Positive punisher   A stimulus that causes a decrease in the probability of the recurrence of the response that precedes it.

Positive reinforcer   A stimulus whose occurrence increases the probability of the recurrence of a response that precedes it.

Postconventional morality   The third level of moral development in Kohlberg's theory.

Post-traumatic stress disorder (PTSD)   Emotional or other disturbances whose symptoms appear some time after an individual has experienced a traumatic event.

Power   The ability to cause or prevent change.

Power law   A mathematical relationship between psychological experience and stimulus intensity.

Power stress   Severe biological reactions created by inhibited need for power.

Precognition The perception of events that will occur in the future.

Preconventional morality The first level of moral development in Kohlberg's theory.

Prediction The goal of psychologists to know the likelihood that a particular event or relationship will occur in a given situation.

Preference feedback hypothesis The idea that as a first name becomes overexposed due to its extreme popularity, fewer parents choose the name for their children.

Prejudice Emotionally charged negative stereotypes.

Premack principle The principle that more highly preferred behaviors can be used to reinforce less highly preferred behaviors.

Premature ejaculation A common sexual dysfunction among men.

Premenstrual syndrome (PMS) Negative changes occurring in some women just ahead of their monthly menstrual periods.

Preoperational stage Piaget's second stage of cognitive development describing preschoolers' as not being capable of adult understanding.

Preparation The first step of the problem-solving process in which one recognizes the problem and prepares to solve it by gathering information and trying to understand the problem.

Preparedness The innate tendency of each species to display specific behaviors.

Preschool years The period of development from about three to five years of age.

Primary affects The idea that basic emotions such as happiness, sadness, anger, and fear are innate to the central nervous system and that each is associated with a specific facial display.

Primacy effect The ability to recall the first words in a word list better than the remaining words on the list.

Primary drives Drives that are unlearned biologically based sources of motivation such as hunger, thirst, sex, and pain avoidance.

Primary mental abilities Thurstone's theory that intelligence consists of seven primary abilities.

Primary process thought A structure of the id that allows wish-fulfilling fantasies and dreams.

Primary reinforcers Unlearned, innately reinforcing stimuli.

Proactive interference Memory loss as the result of old memories interfering with new memories.

Problem of arrangement The third type of problem outlined by Greeno where the elements must be rearranged to form a reasonable new arrangement.

Problems of inducing structure The first type of problem outlined by Greeno that involves determining the relationship among elements of the problem.

Problems of transformation The second type of problem outlined by Greeno in which the problem solver must discover the sequence of operations that will transform the initial state into the goal.

Problem space The second step in problem-solving based on the information-processing approach in which the task environment is transformed into a mental representation of the problem.

Procedural knowledge The information that underlies skill performance.

Procedural memory The remembrance of how to perform certain skills or how to engage in certain actions.

Procrastination The habit of putting off doing what one should do.

Prodigies Persons who show extraordinary talent in an area such as music or mathematics at a very early age.

Production system The third step in problem-solving based on the information-processing approach where from the problem space a plan for reaching the goal is constructed.

Productive love A type of love characterized by care, respect, knowledge, and responsibility.

Products In Guilford's theory of intelligence, the aspects of intelligence involving units, classes, relations, systems, transformations, and implications.

Prognosis The probable course or outcome of a disorder or the probability the patient will recover.

Projective tests Tests that use ambiguous stimuli with the assumption that unstructured materials lead a test-taker to use (project) his or her own life experiences and unconscious tendencies in interpreting the ambiguous stimuli.

Propinquity The factor of physical proximity that influences interpersonal attraction.

Proprioception The receptor system that provides information about the position of each body part in relation to the rest of the body and in relation to gravity.

Prosocial behaviors The broad range of behaviors that are positively valued by society.

Prospective memory The remembrance of how to do specific tasks.

Prototype A mental structure that is an exhibit of the typical features of a particular category.

Proxemics The study of how people use the space around them or how they place themselves in relation to others with whom they interact.

Proximodistal Development from the middle of the body outward to the extremities.

Proximity The perceptual grouping principle in which, when all else is equal, stimuli that are close together (proximal) will be perceived as a unified whole.

Psephology The study of vote predictions based on voting intention, demographics, and attitude scale data.

Pseudopsychology A description of superficial systems that appear to resemble psychology but fail to achieve scientific validity.

Psyche Jung's term for the total personality.

Psychiatrists Physicians who specialize in psychiatry and receive intensive training in the diagnosis and treatment of the physical causes of mental disorders.

Psychoactive drugs Drugs that alter mood or thought processes.

Psychoanalysis A type of therapy begun by Freud that emphasizes the influence of unconscious forces, impulses, and internal conflict on the client's behavior.

Psychoanalyst Psychologists or psychiatrists who specialize in the theory and practice of Freudian psychoanalysis.

Psychodynamic perspective The developmental viewpoint that stresses that development is the result of inner forces of which one is not normally aware.

Psychogenic amnesia A sudden inability to recall important personal information without organic causes.

Psychogenic pain disorder A disorder characterized by the experience of great pain without disease or injuries to account for the pain.

Psychokinesis The process of changing or moving objects by force of will.

Psychological age One's capacity for adaptive behavior.

Psychological drives The internal states that impel an organism to act.

Psychology The scientific study of the behaviors and mental processes of organisms.

Psychopathological behaviors Disorders stemming from mental illness rather than cultural learning.

Psychophysical scaling A measure of the relationship between the physical characteristics of a stimulus and the corresponding psychological experience of those characteristics.

Psychophysics The study of the change in psychological experience that results from change in a physical stimulus.

Psychosexual stages The developmental stages of personality set forth by Freud.

Psychoses Disorders in which individuals may be unable to correctly evaluate their perceptions of the world around them.

Psychosomatic illness Stress-related illnesses that involve both physiological and psychological components.

Psychosurgery Surgery on the nervous system with the intention of changing emotions or behavior.

Psychotropic drugs Drugs prescribed for the treatment and control of emotions, mood, and psychotic symptoms.

Puberty The end of pubescence and the point at which reproduction is first possible.

Pubescence The period of rapid physical growth and developing sexual maturity.

Pupil The opening in the iris of the eye through which light bent by the curvature of the cornea passes.

Qualitative change A change in the quality or kind of development.

Quantitative change A change in the amount of development within a physical system or behavior.

Radical behaviorism A form of behaviorism associated with B. F. Skinner that states that an individual's current behavior is determined entirely by the consequences of his or her past behaviors.

Random sampling A procedure in which every individual in a population has an equal chance of being selected for the sample.

Range A measure of variability calculated by subtracting the lowest score from the highest score in a distribution.

Rapid eye movements (REM) The quick, jerky movements of the eyes during sleep that indicate that dreaming is occurring.

Rational emotive therapy (RET) A form of psychotherapy developed by Ellis in which the underlying assumption is that disturbed thinking causes negative emotions.

Reactance The unpleasant arousal that accompanies the perception that behavioral freedom has been eliminated.

Readiness The principle of development that states that physical development always precedes behavioral development.

Reality principle A structure of the ego that has the goal of achieving gratification but is able to delay it.

Reality therapy A therapy developed by Glasser based on focusing on responsible behavior in the present situation without punishment.

Reasoning Thinking with the purpose of making decisions, forming judgements, and solving problems.

Recall The retrieval of information from memory with only the cues of the problem to aid the search.

Recency effect The ability to recall the last words in a word list better than those nearer the beginning.

Receptor sites The receiving points on the dendrites of the postsynaptic neuron that are the targets of the neurotransmitters.

Reciprocal altruism The idea that people are likely to help when the costs of helping are less than the benefits and that reciprocity is likely from the helped person or from someone else.

Reciprocal determinism A principle that states that environmental stimuli, beliefs, and expectations influence behavior while behavioral outcomes change the environment and influence beliefs and expectations.

Recoding The memory strategy in which new information is changed to a form that is easier to store.

Recognition One way of measuring memory in which one only identifies information previously learned.

Reconstructive memory A type of memory using episodic memory to reconstruct an event or time period.

Redintegration The type of memory retrieval in which the recollection of one memory leads to the recollection of other associated memories.

Reflection (mirroring) A client-centered therapy technique consisting of reflecting back to the client the content and feelings that he or she expresses.

Reflex arc The most basic behavior pattern mediated by the spinal cord.

Reinforcement-affect model of attraction The idea that people are attracted to individuals who are associated with events that arouse positive feelings.

Reinforcement theory The explanation that present behavior is the result of the past consequences an individual has experienced.

Reinforcement value A factor in determining behavior potential that refers to preferences for particular rewards.

Relapse rate The percentage of patients who reexperience their symptoms and return to the hospital within a given period of time.

Relative motion (motion parallax) The monocular depth cue whereby, when a person moves his or her head, the images of nearby objects are moved a greater distance across the retina than are the images of objects farther away.

Relative refractory The period of gradually greater responsiveness during the recharging process in the neuron.

Relative size The monocular depth cue whereby the relative size of known objects is used to judge distance.

Relearning A technique for measuring memory by learning again previously learned but forgotten material.

Reliability The consistency with which a test or other assessment device measures.

Religion A way of knowing about the world based on faith and knowledge that comes from authorities, personal introspection and insight, and divine revelation.

REM rebound The condition in which persons deprived of REM sleep experience longer than usual REM sleep in the next sleep period.

Representative sample A small group taken from the whole population that contains the same essential characteristics and proportions as the population from which it was drawn.

Repression A purposeful failure to retrieve memories as a defense against anxiety.

Residual type schizophrenia A type of schizophrenia in which individuals have been diagnosed as schizophrenic but who currently have no psychotic symptoms.

Respondent conditioning (classical conditioning) Learning to respond to stimuli that reliably predict when other stimuli will occur (signal learning).

Resting potential The stored energy within a neuron.

Retarded ejaculation A sexual dysfunction in which ejaculation is greatly delayed.

Reticular formation A network of neurons running through the brainstem and involved in attention and activating the cortex.

Retina A thin membrane at the back of the eye where images are focused containing the visual receptor cells, the rods, and the cones.

Retinal disparity A binocular depth cue based on the difference (disparity) between the two retinal images.

Retrieval The third phase of the information-processing model that involves getting information from storage for further use.

Retroactive interference Memory loss caused by new memories interfering with the retrieval of old memories.

Retrocognition The perception of past events without having used vision or the other senses.

Retrograde amnesia A type of organic amnesia in which loss of memory of the past is gradually recovered.

Rhodopsin A light sensitive chemical present in the rods that is involved in the transduction of light energy into neural energy.

Risk studies Genetic studies of schizophrenia in which the blood relatives of schizophrenics are surveyed and the incidence of schizophrenia is compared to that of relatives of non-schizophrenics.

Rods Receptors in the innermost layer of the retina that are most sensitive to low levels of light energy.

Rorschach Inkblot Test A widely used projective test in which test-takers give their reactions to symmetrical inkblots.

Role A set of behavioral expectations about people in particular positions based on norms for those positions.

Rote rehearsal A memory strategy in which information is reread or repeated again and again.

Sample A partial set of observations.

Saturation The psychological perception of the degree of color purity in a light wave.

Savings The difference between the amount of time needed to relearn information and the amount of time needed to initially learn it.

Schema A mental structure that denotes what is essential about category membership.

Schizoaffective disorder A disorder whose symptoms are a mixture of schizophrenic symptoms and affective disorder symptoms.

Schizokinesis A condition in which the skeletal components of a conditioned fear response extinguish before the autonomic parts.

Schizophrenogenic mother theory The theory that attributes schizophrenia in adults to being reared by mothers unable to cuddle and support their children in their first years.

School-aged A period of development from ages six to twelve characterized by the importance of the school experience.

Science A way of knowing about the world that emphasizes objective observation and active experimentation.

Scientific method A process for identifying problems, formulating hypotheses, and conducting experiments to test hypotheses about behavior.

Sclera The white, tough outer covering of the eye.

Script A plan for the cognitive processing of expected sequences of events and actions.

Secondary drives External stimuli that acquire their motivational properties through association with primary drives.

Secondary traits Traits that influence fewer situations or behaviors than central traits.

Seduction theory The belief by Freud that hysterical neuroses are caused by premature sexual experience.

Selective attention The process of attending to some sensations while ignoring others.

Self-actualization Maslow's idea that people strive to fulfill their unique potential.

Self-control (self-management) program A program where goals are agreed upon by the client and the therapist, and the therapist helps the client to arrange the environment to reinforce desirable behaviors and to extinguish undesirable ones.

Self-disclosure The revelation of details about one's life and self.

Self-fulfilling prophesy The situation in which expectations about a person or situation help bring about the expected outcome.

Self-preservation A Freudian term for the basic motive to insure continuation of an individual's life.

Self-talk The inner speech that people engage in with themselves.

Self theory A personality theory proposed by Rogers that emphasizes the self, or integrated person.

Semantic encoding The coding of an experience by its meaning.

Semantic memory A type of memory that stores facts, rules of language, formal logic, and inferences.

Semicircular canals Fluid-filled canals attached to the inner ear that detect head movement in any direction.

Sensation-seeking The strong need to experience new events, adventures, and experiences.

Sense organs Specialized cells in the skin, tongue, eyes, ears, nose, muscles, joints, and internal organs that carry out transduction.

Sensorimotor stage Piaget's first stage of cognitive development that includes, among other things, the attainment of object permanence.

Sensory adaptation The process by which sense receptors respond more to changing stimulation and less to unchanging stimulation.

Sensory memory A type of memory that registers moment-to-moment incoming information.

Sensory deprivation A research process in which subjects are deprived of normal sensory stimulation.

Serial recall The remembrance of information in the order it was presented.

Set point A hypothesis proposing that each person has a set body weight that is maintained by homeostatic mechanisms.

Sex differences The biological differences between females and males.

Sex-linked inheritance A genetic inheritance pattern linked to the X and Y sex chromosomes.

Sexual aversion A severe, irrational fear of sexual contact.

s Factors Spearman's concept of specific factors of intelligence that affect more specific tasks than the g factor.

Shadowing The monocular depth cue based on the distribution of light across a surface.

Shape constancy The learned perceptual characteristic that a person or object remains the same shape despite changes in the shape of the retinal image.

Shaping The reinforcing of successive approximations until a desired response is learned.

Short-term memory (STM) A type of memory that holds the information currently being used; the active, working memory.

Sibling rivalry The competition between siblings for the affections and approval of their parents.

Signal learning (classical conditioning) Learning to respond to stimuli that reliably predict when other stimuli will occur.

Similarity The perceptual grouping principle that states that when all else is equal the most similar stimuli will be grouped together.

Simple to complex The developmental principle that states that physical systems and behaviors change from simpler systems to more complex ones.

Simplicity (figural goodness) The perceptual grouping principle that states that stimuli will be grouped into the simplest, most regular, and most symmetrical shapes.

Simultaneous conditioning The condition that occurs when the conditioned stimulus begins at the same time as the unconditioned stimulus.

Single-blind studies Experimental conditions in which the subjects are unaware of the experimental conditions in which they have been placed.

Situational testing A form of assessment in which the interviewee's behavior is observed while the individual performs in a simulated situation.

16 PF personality questionnaire A personality assessment questionnaire that measures the source traits that make up the main aspects of Cattell's theory of personality.

Size constancy The learned perceptual characteristic that a person or object remains the same size despite changes in the size of the retinal image.

Size-distance invariance The monocular cue to depth in which retinal images of nearby objects are large and full of detail while retinal images of distant objects are small and lacking in detail.

Skinner box An apparatus that provides a simple environment for testing operant behavior.

Sleep apnea A sleep disorder in which individuals stop breathing while asleep.

Sleep deprivation The condition of remaining awake for longer than normal periods of time.

Sleeper effect The effect that, over time, an audience will forget the credibility of the source but will remember the message.

Sleep spindles The quick bursts of electrical activity in the brain as shown on EEGs during stage 2 of sleep.

Sleeptalking A sleep disturbance that occurs during non-REM stages of sleep.

Sleepwalking A sleep disturbance that occurs during non-REM stages of sleep.

Slow-to-warm-up infant An infant temperament that is not highly reactive in either a positive or a negative way but is slow to adapt to change.

Social age The extent to which one conforms to the expected social roles for any given age.

Social comparison theory Festinger's theory that assumes people place importance on knowing the validity of personal beliefs by comparing their beliefs to physical and social reality.

Social facilitation theory Zajonc's theory that the presence of people increases arousal level, which in turn enhances dominant responses and hinders less dominant responses.

Social influence The effect that occurs when individuals change their behaviors because of the behaviors or attitudes of others.

Social learning theory Bandura's theory that attempts to explain personality as a learned behavior within a social context.

Social loafing The tendency to exert less effort when efforts are pooled than when efforts are evaluated individually.

Social motives Secondary motives that are learned from interactions with other people.

Social norms A group's or society's rules for acceptable and appropriate behavior.

Social psychology The study of how social factors influence an individual's behaviors, thoughts, feelings, perception, and motives.

Social purposefulness The condition in which activities that appear to be direct responses to physical stimulation may be shaped by the need to produce social responses.

Social time The set of age expectations and age statuses within a society.

Sociobiology A field of study focusing on the inherited basis of social behavior in all species.

Somatic nervous system A division of the peripheral nervous system that carries messages to and from the skin and skeletal muscles.

Somatoform disorders Disorders in which psychological conflicts are converted into physical forms.

Somatosensory cortex A portion of the parietal lobe in which the body senses of temperature, touch, and pain are processed.

Somatotypes Measures of the body shapes of individuals suggested by Sheldon to explain personality.

Somesthetic senses Senses of the body composed of receptors in the layers of the skin and in the internal organs.

Spaced practice Studying regularly with time between study sessions.

Species-typical actions Behaviors that are common within a species.

Split brain The result of cutting the corpus callosum as is sometimes done as a radical treatment for severe epilepsy.

Spontaneous recovery The recurrence, after a lapse of time, of a previously extinguished classically-conditioned response.

SQ5R A study system that uses seven learning activities: survey, question, read, recite, write, relate, and review.

Stability-instability One of the dimensions in the personality type theory proposed by Hans Eysenck.

Standard deviation The square root of the variance; the most useful measure of variability.

Stanford-Binet Intelligence Scale An individual intelligence test that consists of a series of subtests defined in terms of age level.

State-dependent retrieval Memory retrieval dependent on the same psychological state in which it was originally stored.

Statistical model The model of abnormal behavior that equates mental health with normal or average behavior.

Statistical significance The condition in which the observed differences in an experiment are not very likely due to chance and are very likely due to the effects of the independent variable.

Stereochemical theory The theory that proposes that the receptor sites for smell are of specific sizes and shapes that correspond to the sizes and shapes of the odor molecules that stimulate them.

Stereotypes The characteristics an individual believes are common to all members of a group or category.

Stimulus control The situation in operant and classical conditioning in which a stimulus controls the occurrence of a conditioned response or signals the availability of a reinforcer.

Stimulus discrimination The situation that results when a response reinforced in the presence of a specific stimulus is not reinforced in the presence of other stimuli.

Simulus generalization The tendency for a conditioned response to be elicited by stimuli similar to the conditioned stimulus, or when a response reinforced in the presence of a specific stimulus is also made in the presence of similar stimuli.

Stimulus motives Innate motives that help organisms investigate and learn about the environment.

Stimulus substitution In classical conditioning, the event that occurs when the conditioned stimulus takes the place of the unconditioned stimulus.

Stirrup (stapes) One of a chain of small bones in the middle ear that act as an amplifier.

Storage Commonly referred to as memory; a second phase of the information-processing model involving storing coded, organized information.

Storage and transfer model A view of memory that describes three types of memory: sensory, short-term, and long-term.

Stress Any physiological or psychological change that imposes a demand for adjustment upon an individual.

Striving for superiority A response to the universal sense of inferiority that develops out of relationships with others.

Stroboscopic motion A type of apparent motion that occurs when a series of still pictures is viewed in rapid succession.

Strokes According to Berne, the human need to be touched both physically and emotionally.

Structuralism The viewpoint that perceptions are the sum of the basic elements of experience.

Structured interview A form of personality assessment that involves asking the interviewee a preplanned set of questions.

Sublimation A psychoanalytic idea that unacceptable unconscious motives are modified into socially acceptable activities.

Subliminal perception The idea that stimuli that are below the detection threshold may unconsciously influence behavior.

Substance abuse An inability to abstain from the use of a substance.

Substance dependence A physical addiction shown by a tolerance towards a substance or withdrawal symptoms.

Successive approximations In the training of an operant response, the giving of a reinforcer for closer and closer approximations to the desired response.

Superego A structure of personality in psychoanalytic theory that forms the moral arm of personality and is harbored within the ego.

Superiority complex An overcompensation pattern in which the individual exaggerates self-importance to cover up an inferiority complex.

Superstitious behavior Behavior strengthened by the accidental occurrence of a reinforcer following a response.

Surface structure A level of transformational grammar that is the actual order of the words in a sentence that is produced.

Surface traits Traits of personality that cluster together.

Surrogate motherhood A reproductive alternative in which a woman, the surrogate mother, donates the ovum and also carries and gives birth to the child before giving the child to an infertile couple.

Surrogate mother monkeys Wire or cloth covered cylinders with wooden heads made to substitute for real monkey mothers.

Survey method A research method used to measure many people on many variables with the use of questionnaires or personal interviews.

Syllogisms Formal deductive arguments.

Symbiotic relatedness A relationship in which one of the individuals loses or never attains independence.

Symbolic representation The most advanced type of cognitive representation in which experiences are translated into language and other abstract symbols.

Symbolic thought The idea that children in the preschool years move from understanding the world only through action and images to understanding it through language and other symbol systems.

Synapse The minute space between the axon button and the dendrite of the next neuron.

Syntax The rules of a language that are used to create an infinite number of meaningful word orders.

Systematic desensitization A type of counterconditioning in which relaxation is conditioned as the incompatible response for the treatment of phobias and related disorders.

Tardive dyskinesia An involuntary movement disorder with symptoms like Parkinson's disease caused by large doses of antipsychotic drugs.

Task environment The first step in problem-solving based on the information-processing approach in which the terms used to describe the problem are examined.

Taste bud A sensory receptor on the tongue containing the receptor cells for gustation (taste).

Taste receptor cells The cells located in taste pores within the taste buds on the tongue responsible for transducing information about taste.

Telepathy "Reading minds"; knowing another's thoughts.

Temperament The inborn, biological, permanent aspects of an individual's emotional reactions.

Temporal lobe (auditory cortex) A portion of the cerebral cortex at the side of the brain that is the central receiving area for auditory information.

Teratogens Environmental factors that affect prenatal development and cause birth defects.

Test anxiety A panicky, tense feeling caused by the pressures of a test situation.

Test-wise Possessing the skills needed to perform well on tests.

Texture gradient The monocular depth cue in which nearby details are distinct and become less distinct with increasing distance.

Thalamus The part of the brain located directly above the brainstem that integrates and relays sensory information to the cerebral cortex.

Thanatos (death drive) One of Freud's three kinds of drives that cause people to act without conscious thought.

Thematic Apperception Test (TAT) A projective test that requires test-takers to tell stories about 20 ambiguous pictures.

Theory Interrelated hypotheses that have been supported by research.

Theory of direct perception The theory that perceptions are formed directly from the information provided by the stimulus environment (see *ecological approach*).

Timbre The psychological dimension that corresponds to the physical characteristic of complexity.

Time management Controlling the use of time by determining what one must do and what one wants to do, and establishing where time goes and where one wants it to go.

Timing-of-events model A description of adult development in which development is a function of when certain important events occur in a person's life.

Tip-of-the-tongue (TOT) phenomenon The experience of attempting to retrieve from memory information that can nearly but not completely be recalled.

Toddlerhood The period when a baby begins to walk, marked by expanding physical, cognitive and social development.

Toilet training The process of learning to control the biological functions of elimination.

Token economy A method of behavior modification in which participants earn tokens that can be exchanged for other reinforcers; often used in institutional settings to reward appropriate behavior.

Tolerance In substance dependency, the need for increasing amounts of a substance in order to experience the same effects.

Touch The sense created by specialized receptors in the skin that respond to movement, vibration, and pressure.

Trace conditioning   The situation that occurs when the conditioned stimulus begins and ends before the unconditioned stimulus begins.

Traits   The relatively stable and enduring characteristics that can describe personality and control behavior.

Transaction   A message from one ego state to another.

Transactional analysis   A therapy developed by Berne based on three ego states: the parent, adult, and child.

Transcendence   1. A second higher form of self-actualization that is a spiritual self-actualization; 2. The idea that the individual is only a small unit of a much larger consciousness.

Transduction   The process of extracting information from the environment and converting it into a form the nervous system can process.

Transformation grammar   A theory that proposes that language knowledge exists on two levels of cognitive processing.

Trepanation (trephination)   A procedure performed by a shaman, consisting of drilling a small circular hole in the skull to eliminate evil spirits.

Trial and error   A strategy of problem-solving that is a relatively inefficient random search for a solution.

Trial and error learning studies   Thorndike's initial studies on learning in animals from which he formulated his ideas about instrumental conditioning.

Triarchic theory   Sternberg's theory that intelligence consists of context (an individual's external world), components (an individual's internal world), and experience (an individual's relation to both the internal and external worlds).

Trichromatic theory   The theory that states that the experience of any specific color is dependent upon how much each type of cone is stimulated.

Trieb   A German word used by Freud that translates as *impulse* or *drive*.

Triphasic model   A description of the human sexual response cycle in terms of three phases: desire, excitement, and orgasm.

T score   A transformed score obtained by multiplying a Z score by 10 and adding 50.

Twin studies   Studies using identical twins to assess the relative influences of heredity and environment.

Type A personality   A classification for people with aggressive, time-urgent personalities, associated with increased risk of heart attacks.

Type B personality   A classification for people with calm, less time-urgent personalities.

Type theories   Personality theories that describe people's personalities in terms of only a few discontinuous dimensions or categories.

Umbilical cord   The structure that connects the placenta with the developing fetus and transports oxygen, nutrients, and waste products to and from the maternal system.

Unconditioned response (UR)   An immediate, automatic reaction to an unconditioned stimulus.

Unconditioned stimulus (US)   Any stimulus that produces an immediate, automatic reaction (an unconditioned response).

Unconscious inference theory   The theory that perceptions are based on unconscious inferences derived from sources of information other than the sense receptors.

Unconscious motivation   A psychoanalytic idea that states that people are usually unaware of their true motives and desires.

Undifferentiated type of schizophrenia   A type of schizophrenia in which individuals display a variety of obvious psychotic symptoms.

Unobtrusive measurements   Measurements obtained without disturbing the subjects and without their awareness.

Unstructured interview   A form of personality assessment involving informal observations in which the interviewer and interviewee determine the questions.

Vaginismus   Involuntary vaginal muscle spasms in response to vaginal penetration.

Validity   The degree to which an assessment device measures what it claims to measure.

Variability   The dispersion of data in a distribution.

Variable interval (VI) schedule   A reinforcement schedule in which reinforcers are available after unpredictable amounts of time.

Variable ratio (VR) schedule   A reinforcement schedule in which the number of responses necessary to obtain a reinforcer is unpredictable.

Variance   A measure of variability that indicates how much every score in a distribution varies from every other score.

Verification   The fourth step in the problem-solving process in which the necessary confirmation is provided that a workable solution has been found.

Vestibular sacs   Structures that contain the receptors responsible for sensing information about head and body orientation when the head is not moving.

Vestibular sense   The sensory system responsible for combining information about the body's orientation with respect to gravity and changes in the rate and direction of the body's movement.

Vicarious classical conditioning Conditioning that takes place by observing conditioning in another person without directly experiencing the CS-US pairing.

Visual cliff An apparatus used to test the depth perception capabilities of infant animals and humans.

Visual cortex (occipital lobe) A section of the cerebral cortex at the back of the brain that integrates and analyzes visual information.

Visual dominance The condition in which visual information predominates over information from the other senses.

Visual encoding The coding of an experience by visual images.

Visual field The area from which each eye receives information.

Vividness effect The tendency of people to be influenced by vivid, concrete examples at the expense of available abstract, statistical, or logical information.

Volley theory A theory of pitch encoding based on successive groups of neurons firing to match the rate of incoming sound vibrations.

WAIS-R The Wechsler Adult Intelligence Scale-Revised; an individual intelligence test involving both verbal and performance measures for use with individuals from age 16 to 64.

Warmth A sensation experienced when a stimulus warmer than the skin is applied to an area of the skin containing receptors for warmth.

Wavelength The physical dimension of light that corresponds to the perception of color.

Weber's law The law described by Weber that the just noticeable difference is always a constant proportion of the stimulus intensity.

Well-defined problems Problems with clearly defined initial states and goals.

Whorfian hypothesis (linguistic relativity hypothesis) The idea that the vocabulary and structural rules of one's native language limit one's thinking about the world to the confines of that language.

WISC-R The Wechsler Intelligence Scale for Children-Revised; an individual intelligence test involving both verbal and performance measures for use with children age 6 to 17.

Withdrawal-destructiveness A relationship characterized by distance, apathy, or aggression.

Withdrawal In substance dependence, symptoms associated with suddenly ceasing to use the substance.

WPPSI The Wechsler Preschool and Primary Scale of Intelligence; an individual intelligence test for use with children from age 4 to 6½.

Yerkes-Dodson law A law that states that an optimum level of motivation exists for the optimal performance of any task and that as task difficulty increases, the optimum level of motivation decreases.

Youth A developmental stage proposed by Keniston in which individuals have completed the tasks of adolescence but have not yet fully committed themselves to adulthood.

Zeitgeist The spirit of the times; the moral and intellectual trend of any age or period.

Z score A score transformed by subtracting the mean and dividing by the standard deviation.

Zygote A single cell formed when the sperm and ovum unite during conception.

References

Chapter 1

Baddeley, A.D. 1982. *Your memory: A user's guide.* NY: Macmillan.

Beck, A.T. 1976. *Cognitive therapy and the emotional disorders.* NY: International Universities Press.

Bradley, A. 1983. *Take note of college study skills.* Glenview, IL: Scott Foresman.

Carman, R.A. & Adams, R.W. 1984. *A student's guide for survival* (2nd ed.). NY: Wiley.

Dunn, R. & Dunn, K. 1978. *Teaching students through their learning styles: A practical approach.* Reston, VA: Reston.

Dunn, R., Dunn, K., & Price, G.E. 1975. *Learning style inventory.* Lawrence, KS: Price Systems.

Ellis, A. 1984. Rational-emotive therapy. In R.J. Corsini (Ed.). *Current psychotherapies* (3rd ed.). Itasca, IL: Peacock.

Ellis, A. & Harper, R.A. 1975. *A new guide to rational living.* North Hollywood, CA: Wilshire Book.

Lindgren, H.C. 1969. *The psychology of college success.* NY: Wiley.

Main, A. 1980. *Encouraging effective learning.* Edinburgh: Scottish Academic Press.

Range, L.M., Morgan, M.A., & Leonberger, T. 1984. Final impotence: Reasons why I missed the exam. *Journal of Polymorphous Perversity, 1,* 12–13.

Robinson, F.P. 1941. *Effective behavior.* NY: Harper & Row.

Rutherford, R.D. 1978. *Administrative time power.* Austin, TX: Learning Concepts.

Smith, S.M. 1979. Remembering in and out of context. *Journal of Experimental Psychology: Human Learning and Memory, 5,* 460–471.

Thomas, E.L. & Robinson, H.A. 1972. *Improving memory in every class: A sourcebook for teachers.* Boston: Allyn & Bacon.

Walter, T. & Siebert, A. 1984. *Student success: How to do better in college and still have time for your friends.* NY: Holt, Rinehart & Winston.

Chapter 2

Bergin, A.E. 1980. Psychotherapy and religious values. *Journal of Consulting and Clinical Psychology, 48,* 98.

Bjork, D.W. 1983. *The compromised scientist: William James in the development of American Psychology.* NY: Columbia University Press.

Bradbard, H.R. & Endsley, R.C. 1983. The effects of sex-typed labeling on preschool children's information-seeking and retention. *Sex Roles, 9,* 247–260.

Brown, F.M. 1982. Rhythmicity as the emerging variable for psychology. In F.M. Brown & R.C. Graeber (Eds.). *Rhythmic aspects of behavior.* Hillsdale, NJ: Erlbaum.

Eckblad, M. & Chapman, L.J. 1983. Magic ideation as an indicator of schizotypy. *Journal of Counseling and Clinical Psychology, 51,* 216–217.

Evans, R.I. 1976. *The making of psychology: Discussions with creative contributors.* NY: Knopf.

Gleitman, H. 1984. Introducing psychology. *American Psychologist, 39,* 421–427.

Gross, L. 1984. How write you are. *Ladies' Home Journal, 101,* 88–91.

Guthrie, R.V. 1976. *Even the rat was white: A historical view of psychology.* NY: Harper & Row.

Hampden-Turner, C. 1981. *Maps of the mind.* NY: Macmillan.

Hayward, J.W. 1984. *Perceiving ordinary magic: Science & intuitive wisdom.* Boulder: New Science Library.

Kurucz, C.N. & Khalil, T.M. 1977. Probability models for analyzing the effects of biorhythms on accident occurrence. *Journal of Safety Research, 9,* 150–158.

McConnell, J.V. 1978. Biorhythms: A report and analysis. *Journal of Biological Psychology, 20,* 13–24.

Nomi, T. 1971. *Good combinations of blood types.* Cited in *People,* 1985 (April 29), 23, 89.

Persinger, M.A., Cooke, W.J., & Janes, J.T. 1978. No evidence for relationship between biorhythms and industrial accidents. *Perceptual Motor Skills, 46,* 423–426.

Rubenstein, J. & Slife, B.D. 1982. *Taking sides: Clashing views on controversial psychological issues* (2nd ed.). Guilford, CT: Duskin.

Shaffer, J.W., Schmidt, C.W., Zlotowitz, H.T., & Fisher, R.S. 1978. Biorhythms and highway crashes. *Archives of General Psychiatry, 35,* 41–46.

Slovic, P. & Fischhoff, B. 1977. On the psychology of experimental surprises. *Journal of Experimental Psychology: Human Perception and Performance, 3,* 544–551.

Stapp, J. & Fulcher, R. 1983. The employment of APA members: 1982. *American Psychologist, 38,* 1298–1320.

Vaughan, E.D. 1977. Misconceptions about psychology among introductory psychology students. *Teaching of Psychology, 4,* 138–141.

Watson, R.I. 1971. *The great psychologists* (3rd ed.). Philadelphia: Lippincott.

Wolcott, J.H., McMeekin, R.R., Burgin, R.E., & Yanowitch, R.W. 1977. Correlation of general aviation accidents with the biorhythm theory. *Human Factors, 19,* 283–293.

Yinger, J.M. 1970. *The scientific study of religion.* London: Macmillan.

Zilbergeld, B. 1983. *The shrinking of America: Myths of psychological change.* Boston: Little, Brown.

Chapter 3

American Psychological Association. 1981. *Ethical Principles of Psychologists.* Washington: American Psychological Association.

Arens, W. 1979. *The man-eating myth.* NY: Oxford University Press.

Asch, S.E. 1955. Opinions and social pressure. *Scientific American, 193,* 31–35.

Barnes, J.A. 1979. *Who should know what?: Social science, privacy and ethics.* Cambridge, England: Cambridge University Press.

Beecher, H.K. 1959. Generalization from pain of various types and diverse origins. *Science, 130,* 267–268.

Brown, C. & Adams, W.R. 1968. *How to read the social sciences.* NY: Scott Foresman.

Eagly, A.H. & Carli, L.L. 1981. Sex of researchers and sex-typed communications as determinants of sex differences in influenceability: A meta-analysis of social influence studies. *Psychological Bulletin, 90,* 1–20.

Gardner, M. 1975. *Fads and fallacies in the name of science.* Mineola, NY: Dover.

Hall, E. 1978. *Why we do what we do: A look at psychology.* Boston: Houghton Mifflin.

Kimble, C.A. 1978. *How to use (and misuse) statistics.* Englewood Cliffs, NJ: Prentice-Hall.

LeShan, L. & Morganau, H. 1982. *Einstein's space and Van Gogh's sky: Physical reality and beyond.* NY: Macmillan.

Lindgren, H.C. 1969. *An introduction to social psychology.* NY: Wiley.

Maslow, A.H. 1969. Toward a humanistic biology. *American Psychologist, 24,* 724–735.

McCain, G. & Segal, E.M. 1969. *The game of science.* Monterey, CA: Brooks/Cole.

McKean, K. 1984. The fine art of reading voters' minds. *Discover, 5,* 66–69.

Mead, M. 1935. *Sex and temperament in primitive societies.* NY: Morrow.

Meltzer, H.Y. 1984. Schizoaffective disorder: Is news of its nonexistence premature? Editor's introduction. *Schizophrenia Bulletin, 10,* 11–13.

Rathje, W.L. & Hughes, W.W. 1975. The garbage project as a nonreactive approach: Garbage in . . . Garbage out! In H.W. Sinaiko & L.A. Broedling (Eds.). *Perspectives on attitude assessment: Surveys and their alternatives.* Washington: Smithsonian Institution.

Rosenthal, R. 1966. *Experimenter effects in behavioral research.* NY: Appleton-Century-Crofts.

Rosenthal, R. & Jacobson, L.F. 1968. Teacher expectations for the disadvantaged. *Scientific American, 218,* 19–23.

Rotton, J. & Kelly, I. 1985. Much ado about the full moon: A meta-analysis of lunar-lunacy research. *Psychological Bulletin, 97,* 286–306.

Russell, G.W. & Dua, M. 1983. Lunar influences on human aggression. *Social Behavior and Personality, 11,* 41–44.

Simmons, C.H. & Zumpf, C. 1983. The lost letter technique revisited. *Journal of Applied Social Psychology, 13,* 510–514.

Steininger, M., Newell, J.D., & Garcia, L.T. 1984. *Ethical issues in psychology.* Homewood, IL: Dorsey Press & Dow-Jones-Irwin Dorsey Professional Books.

van Lawick-Goodall, J. 1971. *In the shadow of man.* NY: Houghton Mifflin.

Webb, W.J., Campbell, D.T., Schwartz, R.D., Sechrest, L., & Grove, J.B. 1981. *Nonreactive measures in the social sciences.* Boston: Houghton Mifflin.

Chapter 4

Benton, A.L. 1980. The neuropsychology of facial recognition. *American Psychologist, 35,* 176–186.

Berger, H. 1929. Uber das elektrenkephalgramm des menschen. *Arch. Psychiat. Nervenkr., 87,* 527–570.

Bloom, F.E., Lazerson, A., & Hofstadter, L. 1985. *Brain, mind, and behavior.* NY: Freeman.

Bogen, J. 1978. The giant walk-through brain. *Human Nature, 1,* 40–47.

Cordes, C. 1985. Neuropeptides: Chemical cruise steers emotions. *APA Monitor, 16,* 18.

Dalton, K. 1984. *The premenstrual syndrome and progesterone therapy* (2nd ed.). Chicago: Yearbook Medical Publishers.

Fritsch, G. & Hitzig, E. 1870. Ueber die elektrische Erregbarkeit des Grosshirns. *Arch. Anat. Physiol. Wiss. Med., 37,* 300–332.

Gazzaniga, M.S. 1970. *The bisected brain.* NY: Appleton-Century-Crofts.

Gazzaniga, M.S. 1983. Right hemisphere language following brain bisection: A 20-year perspective. *American Psychologist, 38,* 525–537.

Gazzaniga, M.S. 1985. *The social brain: Discovering the networks of the mind.* NY: Basic Books.

Geschwind, N. 1979. Specializations of the human brain. *Scientific American, 241,* 158–168.

Heneson, N. 1984. The selling of PMS. *Science 84, 5,* 67–71.

Hopson, J. & Rosenfeld, A. 1984. PMS: Puzzling monthly symptoms. *Psychology Today, 18,* 30–35.

Horsley, V. & Clarke, R.H. 1908. The structure and functions of the cerebellum examined by a new method. *Brain, 31,* 45–124.

Hughes, J., Smith, T.W., Kosterlitz, H.W., Fothergill, L.A., Morgan, B.A., & Morris, H.R. 1975. Identification of two related penta-peptides from the brain with potent opiate against activity. *Nature, 258,* 577–579.

Hunt, M. 1982. *The universe within: A new science explores the human mind.* NY: Simon & Schuster.

Jaynes, J. 1976. *The origins of consciousness in the breakdown of the bicameral mind.* Boston: Houghton Mifflin.

MacLean, P. 1978. The triune brain. *American Scientist, 66,* 101–113.

Michel, G.F. 1981. Right-handedness: A consequence of infant supine head-orientation preference. *Science, 212,* 685–687.

Moruzzi, G. & Magoun, H.W. 1949. Brain stem reticular formation and activation of the EEG. *Electroencephalog. Clin. Neurophysiol., 1,* 455–473.

Mountcastle, V.B. 1976. The world around us: Neural command functions for selective attention. *Neurosciences Research Program Bulletin, 14* (Suppl.), 1–47.

Myers, J.J. 1984. Right hemisphere language: Science or fiction? *American Psychologist, 39,* 315–320.

Ornstein, R., Thompson, R., & Macauley, D. 1984. *The amazing brain.* Boston: Houghton Mifflin.

Penfield, W. 1957 (April 27). Brain's record of past: A continuous movie film. *Science News Letter,* 265.

Penfield, W. & Rasmussen, T. 1950. *The cerebral cortex of man.* NY: Macmillan.

Pert, C.B. & Snyder, S. 1973. Opiate receptor demonstration in nervous tissue. *Science, 179,* 1011–1014.

Phelps, M.E., Mazziotta, J.C., & Huang, S.C. 1982. Study of cerebral function with positron computed tomography. *Journal of Cerebral Blood Flow and Metabolism, 2,* 113–162.

Restak, R.M. 1984. *The brain.* NY: Bantam Books.

Sackheim, H.A., Gur, R.C., & Saucy, M.C. 1978. Emotions are expressed more intensely on the left side of the face. *Science, 202,* 434–436.

Science. 1985. Inside Einstein's brain. *Science 85, 6,* 6.

Shulman, R.G. 1983. NMR spectroscopy of living cells. *Scientific American, 248,* 86–93.

Snyder, S. 1977. Opiate receptors and internal opiates. *Scientific American, 236,* 752–760.

Sperry, R. 1982. Some effects of disconnecting the cerebral hemispheres. *Science, 217,* 1223–1226, 1250.

Springer, S.P. & Deutsch, G. 1985. *Left brain, right brain,* (2nd ed.). NY: Freeman.

Tucker, D.M. 1981. Lateral brain function, emotion, and conceptualization. *Psychological Bulletin, 89,* 19–46.

Wagner, H.N., Bruns, H.D., Dannals, R.F., Wong, D.F., Langstrom, B., Duelfer, T., Frost, J.J., Ravert, H.T., Links, J.M., Rosenbloom, S.B., Lukas, S.E., Kramer, A.V., & Kuhar, M.J. 1983. Imaging dopamine receptors in the human brain by positron tomography. *Science, 221,* 1264–1266.

Weber, R.J. & Pert, C.B. 1984. Opiatergic modulation of the immune system. In E. Muller & A. Genazzani (Eds.). *Central and peripheral endorphins: Basic and clinical aspects.* NY: Raven.

Weingartner, H., Gold, P., Bullenger, J.C., Smallberg, S.A., Summers, R., Rubinow, D.R., Post, R.M., & Goodwin, F.K. 1981. Effects of vasopressin on human memory functions. *Science, 211,* 601–603.

Whitnall, M.H., Gainer, H., Cox, B.M., & Molineaux, C.J. 1983. Dynorphin-A-(1–8) is contained within vasopressin neurosecretory vesicles in rat pituitary. *Science, 222,* 1137–1139.

Zaidel, E. 1975. A technique for presenting lateralized visual input with prolonged exposure. *Vision Research, 15,* 283–289.

Chapter 5

Amoore, J.E. 1965. Psychophysics of odor. *Cold Springs Harbor Symposia in Quantitative Biology, 30,* 623–637.

Amoore, J.E. 1967. Specific anosmia: A clue to the olfactory code. *Nature, 214,* 1095–1098.

Amoore, J.E. 1970. *Molecular basis of odor.* Springfield, IL: Charles C. Thomas.

Bekesy, G. von. 1960. *Experiments in hearing.* NY: McGraw-Hill.

Bekesy, G. von. 1961. Concerning the fundamental component of periodic pulse patterns and modulated vibrations observed in the cochlear model with nerve supply. *Accoustical Society of America, 33,* 888–896.

Bexton, W.H., Heron, W., & Scott, T.H. 1954. Effects of decreased variation in the sensory environment. *Canadian Journal of Psychology, 8,* 70–76.

Boring, E.G., Langfeld, H.S., & Weld, H.P. 1939. *Introduction to psychology.* NY: Wiley.

Brown, T.S. 1975. Olfaction and taste. In B. Scharf & G.S. Reynolds (Eds.). *Experimental sensory psychology.* Glenview, IL: Scott Foresman.

Cain, W.S. 1981. Educating your nose. *Psychology Today, 15,* 49–56.

Corteen, R.S. & Wood, B. 1972. Autonomic responses to shock-associated words in an unattended channel. *Journal of Experimental Psychology, 94,* 308–313.

DeValois, R.L., Abromov, I., & Jacobs, G.H. 1966. Analysis of response patterns of LGN cells. *Journal of the Optical Society of America, 56,* 966–977.

DeValois, R.L. & DeValois, K.K. 1980. Spatial vision. *Annual Review of Psychology, 31,* 309–341.

Fechner, G. 1966. *Elements of psychophysics* (D.H. Howes, & E.G. Boring, Eds.; H.E. Adler, Trans.). NY: Holt, Rinehart & Winston. (First German edition, 1860.)

Frisby, J.P. 1980. *Seeing: Illusion, brain, and mind.* Oxford: Oxford University Press.

Galanter, E. 1962. Contemporary psychophysics. In R. Brown, E. Galanter, E.H. Hess, & G. Mandler. *New directions in psychology.* NY: Holt, Rinehart & Winston.

Geldard, F.A. 1972. *The human senses.* NY: Wiley.

Gibson, J.J. 1950. *The perception of the visual world.* Boston: Houghton Mifflin.

Gibson, J.J. 1966. *The senses considered as perceptual systems.* Boston: Houghton Mifflin.

Gibson, J.J. 1979. *The ecological approach to visual perception.* Boston: Houghton Mifflin.

Gregory, R.L. 1978. *Eye and brain: The psychology of seeing* (3rd ed.). NY: McGraw-Hill.

Hering, E. 1920. *Grundzuge der Lehr vs. Lichtsinn.* Berlin: Springer-Verlag.

Heron, W. 1957. The pathology of boredom. *Scientific American, 196,* 52–56.

Hubel, D.H. & Wiesel, T.N. 1962. Receptive fields, binocular interaction and functional architecture in the cat's visual cortex. *Journal of Physiology (London), 160,* 106–154.

Hubel, D.H. & Wiesel, T.N. 1963. Shape and arrangement of columns in cat's striate cortex. *Journal of Physiology (London), 165,* 559–568.

Hubel, D.H. & Wiesel, T.N. 1965. Receptive fields and functional architecture in two nonstriate visual areas (18 and 19) of the cat. *Journal of Neurophysiology, 28,* 229–289.

Hubel, D.H. & Wiesel, T.N. 1968. Receptive fields and functional architecture of monkey striate cortex. *Journal of Physiology (London), 195,* 215–243.

Hubel, D.H. & Wiesel, T.N. 1979. Brain mechanisms of vision. *Scientific American, 241,* 150–162.

Hurvich, L.M. 1978. Two decades of opponent process. In F.W. Bilmeyer & G. Wyszecki (Eds.). *Color 77.* Bristol, England: Adam Hilger.

Kariya, S. 1985. Mending myopia. *Omni, 8,* 32.

Klein, M., Coles, M.G.H., & Donchin, E. 1984. People with absolute pitch process tones without producing a P300. *Science, 223,* 1306–1309.

Lettvin, J.Y., Maturana, H.R., McCulloch, S.W., & Pitts, W.H. 1959. What the frog's eye tells the frog's brain. *Proceedings of the Institute of Radio Engineers, 47,* 140–151.

Lilly, J.C. 1972. *The center of the cyclone.* NY: Julian Press.

MacNichol, E.F. 1964. Three pigment color vision. *Scientific American, 211,* 48–64.

McAleer, N. 1985. *The body almanac.* Garden City, NY: Doubleday.

Melzack, R. 1973. *The puzzle of pain.* NY: Basic Books.

Melzack, R. 1980. Psychological aspects of pain. In J.J. Bonica (Ed.). *Pain.* NY: Raven.

Mollen, J.D. 1982. Color vision. *Annual Review of Psychology, 33,* 41–85.

Mozell, M.M. & Jagodowiez, M. 1973. Chromatographic separation of odorants by the nose: retention times measured across in vivo olfactory mucosa. *Science, 181,* 1247–1249.

Muller, J. 1838. *Handbuch der Physiologie des Menschen fur Vorlesungen* (Vol. II). Coblenz.

Nathan, J., Thomas, D., Hogness, D.S. 1986. Molecular genetics of human color vision: The genes encoding blue, green, and red pigments. *Science, 232,* 193–202.

Rivlin, R. & Gravelle, K. 1984. *Deciphering the senses: The expanding world of human perception.* NY: Simon & Schuster.

Sinclair, S. 1985. *How animals see: Other visions of our world.* NY: Facts On File.

Stevens, S.S. 1961. The psychophysics of sensory functions. In W.A. Rosenblith (Ed.). *Sensory communication.* Cambridge, MA: MIT Press.

Stevens, S.S. 1962. The surprising duplicity of sensory metrics. *American Psychologist, 17,* 29–39.

Suedfeld, P. 1975. The benefits of boredom: Sensory deprivation reconsidered. *American Scientist, 63,* 60–69.

von Wright, J.M., Anderson, K., & Stenman, U. 1975. Generalization of conditioned GSRs in dichotic listening. In P.M.A. Rabbitt, & S. Dornic (Eds.). *Attention and performance V.* NY: Academic Press.

Weber, E.G. 1949. *Theory of hearing.* NY: Wiley.

Weber, E.H. 1834. *De pulsu, resorptione, auditu et tactu: Annotationes anatomical et physiological.* Leipzig: Koehler.

Zubek, J.P. 1969. Sensory and perceptual-motor processes. In J.P. Zubek (Ed.). *Sensory deprivation: Fifteen years of research.* NY: Appleton-Century-Crofts.

Zuckerman, M. 1969. Variables affecting deprivation results and hallucinations, reported sensations, and images. In J.P. Zubek (Ed.). *Sensory deprivation: Fifteen years of research.* NY: Appleton-Century-Crofts.

Zwislocki, J.J. 1981. Sound analysis in the ear: A history of discoveries. *American Scientist, 69,* 184–192.

Chapter 6

Behrman, R. & Vaughn, V. 1983. *Nelson textbook of pediatrics.* Philadelphia: Saunders.

Bower, T.G.R., Broughton, J.M., & Moore, M.K. 1970. Infant responses to approaching objects: An indicator of response to distal variables. *Perception and Psychophysics, 9,* 193–196.

Brunswik, E. 1956. *Perception and the representative design of psychological experiments.* Berkeley: University of California Press.

Buckhout, R. 1974. Eyewitness testimony. *Scientific American, 231,* 23–31.

Buckhout, R. 1980. Nearly 2,000 witnesses can be wrong. *Bulletin of the Psychonomic Society, 16,* 307–310.

Campos, J.J., Langer, A., & Krowitz, A. 1970. Cardiac responses on the visual cliff in prelocomotor human infants. *Science, 170,* 196–197.

Coren, S. & Girgus, J.S. 1972. Differentiation and decrement in the Mueller-Lyer illusion. *Perception & Psychophysics, 12,* 446–470.

Coren, S., Porac, C., & Ward, L.M. 1984. *Sensation and perception* (2nd ed.). Orlando: Academic Press.

Deregowski, J.B. 1972. Pictorial perception and culture. *Scientific American, 227,* 82–88.

Erdelyi, M.H. 1974. A new look at the new look: Perceptual defense and vigilance. *Psychological Review, 81,* 1–25.

Erlebacher, A. & Sekuler, R. 1969. Explanation of the Muller-Lyer Illusion: Confusion Theory Examined. *Journal of Experimental Psychology, 80,* 462–467.

Fantz, R.L. 1956. A method for studying early visual development. *Perceptual and Motor Skills, 6,* 13–15.

Fantz, R.L. 1961. The origin of form perception. *Scientific American, 204,* 66–72.

Fantz, R.L. 1963. Pattern vision in newborn infants. *Science, 140,* 296–297.

Fantz, R.L. 1965. Visual perception from birth as shown by pattern selectivity. In H.E. Whipple (Ed.). New issues in infant development. *Annals of the New York Academy of Science, 118,* 793–814.

Feder, K.L. 1985. Spooks, spirits, and college students. *Humanist, 6,* 17–19, 32.

Fineman, M. 1981. *The inquisitive eye.* NY: Oxford University Press.

Gibson, E.J. & Walk, R.D. 1960. The "visual cliff." *Scientific American, 202,* 64–71.

Gibson, J.J. 1979. *The ecological approach to visual perception.* Boston: Houghton Mifflin.

Gibson, J.J. 1985. Conclusions from a century of research on sense perception. In S. Koch and D.E. Leary (Eds.). *A century of psychology as science.* NY: McGraw-Hill.

Gillam, B. 1980. Geometrical illusions. *Scientific American, 242,* 102–111.

Gregory, R.L. 1978. *Eye and brain: The psychology of seeing* (3rd ed.). NY: McGraw-Hill.

Haber, R. 1985. Perception: A one-hundred year perspective. In S. Koch and D.E. Leary (Eds.) *A century of psychology as science.* NY: McGraw-Hill.

Haith, M.M. 1980. *Rules that babies look by: The organization of newborn visual activity.* Hillsdale, NJ: Erlbaum.

Hastorf, A. & Cantril, H. 1954. They saw a game: A case study. *Journal of Abnormal and Social Psychology, 49,* 129–134.

Held, R. & Hein, A. 1963. Movement produced stimulation in the development of visually guided behavior. *Journal of Comparative and Physiological Psychology, 56,* 872–876.

Helmholtz, H. 1962. *Treatise on physiological optics* (Vol. 3.), (J.P. Southall, Ed. and Trans.). NY: Dover Press. (First German edition, 1866).

Hochberg, J. 1978. *Perception* (2nd ed.). Englewood Cliffs, NJ: Prentice-Hall.

Howes, D.H. & Solomon, R.L. 1951. Visual duration threshold as a function of word probability. *Journal of Experimental Psychology, 41,* 401–410.

Ittelson, W.H. 1960. *Visual space perception.* NY: Springer.

James, W. 1890. *Principles of psychology.* NY: Holt.

Johansson, G., von Hofsten, C., & Jansson, G. 1980. Event perception. *Annual Review of Psychology, 31,* 27–63.

Koffka, K. 1935. *Principles of Gestalt psychology.* NY: Harcourt Brace.

Kohler, W. 1947. *Gestalt psychology.* NY: Liveright.

Loftus, E.F. 1979. *Eyewitness testimony.* Cambridge, MA: Academic Press.

Loftus, E.F. & Monahan, J. 1980. Trial by data: Psychological research as legal evidence. *American Psychologist, 35,* 270–283.

MacFarlane, A. 1978. What a baby knows. *Human Nature, 1,* 74–81.

McGinnies, E. 1949. Emotionality and perceptual defense. *Psychological Review, 56,* 244–251.

Michaels, C.F. & Carello, C. 1981. *Direct perception.* Englewood Cliffs, NJ: Prentice-Hall.

Mitchell, D.E. 1980. The influence of early visual experience on visual perception. In C.S. Harris (Ed.). *Visual coding and adaptability.* Hillsdale, NJ: Erlbaum.

Piaget, J. 1952. *The origins of intelligence in children.* NY: International University Press.

Randi, J. 1980. *The truth about unicorns, parapsychology, and other delusions.* NY: Lippincott & Crovell.

Randi, J. 1984. Parapsychology: A doubtful premise. *Humanist, 5,* 23–27, 42.

Rock, I. 1975. *An introduction to perception.* NY: Macmillan.

Rock, I. 1983. *The logic of perception.* Cambridge, MA: MIT Press.

Rock, I. 1984. *Perception.* NY: Scientific American Books.

Rock, I. & Ebenholtz, S. 1962. Stroboscopic movement based on change of phenomenal rather than retinal location. *American Journal of Psychology, 75,* 193–207.

Sargent, C. & Eysenck, H.J. 1983. *Know your own PSI-Q.* NY: World Almanac Publications.

von Senden, M. 1960. *Space and sight,* (P. Heath, Trans.). NY: Free Press.

Wertheimer, M. 1923. Untersuchungen zur lehre von der gestalt, II. *Psychologische Forschung, 4,* 301–350.

Yonas, A., Pettersen, L., & Granrud, C.E. 1982. Infants' sensitivity to familiar size as information for distance. *Child Development, 53,* 1285–1290.

Chapter 7

American Psychiatric Association. 1980. *Diagnostic and statistical manual of mental disorders.* Washington: American Psychiatric Association.

Anders, T., Caraskadon, M., & Dement, W.C. 1980. Sleep and sleepiness in children and adolescents. In I. Litt (Ed.). *Adolescent medicine. Pediatric Clinics of North America, 27,* 29–44.

Barber, T.X. 1978. "Hypnosis", suggestions, and psychosomatic phenomena: A new look from the standpoint of recent experimental studies. In J.L. Fosshage & P. Olsen (Eds.). *Healing: Implications for psychotherapy* (Vol. 2). NY: Human Sciences Press.

Benson, H. 1976. Your innate asset for combating stress. In J. White, & J. Fadiman (Eds.). *Relax: how you can feel better, reduce stress, and overcome tension.* NY: Confucian Press.

Bowers, K.S. 1983. *Hypnosis for the seriously curious.* NY: Norton.

Broadbent, D.E. 1958. *Perception and communication.* London: Pergamon Press.

Carrington, P. 1977. *Freedom in meditation.* NY: Anchor-Doubleday.

Carrington, P. 1978. The use of meditation in psychotherapy. In A.A. Sugarman & R.E. Tarter (Eds.). *Expanding dimensions of consciousness.* NY: Springer.

Cheek, P. & LeCron, L. 1968. *Clinical hypnotherapy.* NY: Grune & Stratton.

Cherniak, N.S. 1981. Respiratory disrythmias during sleep. *New England Journal of Medicine, 305,* 325–330.

Coleman, R. 1986. *Wide awake at 3 A.M.* NY: Freeman.

Confer, W.N. & Ables, B.S. 1983. *Multiple personality: Etiology, diagnosis, and treatment.* NY: Human Services Press.

Conn, J.H. 1981. The myth of coercion through hypnosis. *International Journal of Clinical and Experimental Hypnosis, 29,* 95–100.

Dement, W.C. 1976. *Some must watch while some must sleep.* NY: Norton.

Dement, W.C. & Baird, W.P. 1977. *Narcolepsy: Care and treatment.* Stanford, CA: American Narcolepsy Association.

Dusek, D. & Girdano, D.A. 1980. *Drugs: A factual account* (3rd ed.). Reading, MA: Addison-Wesley.

Evans, C. 1984. *Landscapes of the night: How and why we dream.* NY: Viking Press.

Guilleminault, E., Passouant, P., & Dement, W.C. 1976. *Narcolepsy.* NY: Spectrum.

Guilleminault, E. & Dement, W.C. (Eds.). 1978. *The sleep apnea syndrome.* NY: Alan R. Liss.

Hartmann, E. 1981. The strangest sleep disorder. *Psychology Today, 15,* 14–18.

Hartmann, E., Baekeland, F., & Zwilling, G. 1972. Psychological differences between long and short sleepers. *Archives of General Psychiatry, 26,* 463–468.

Hilgard, E.R. 1974. Hypnosis is no mirage. *Psychology Today, 8,* 120–128.

Hobson, J.A. 1983. Sleep mechanisms and pathophysiology: Some clinical implications of the reciprocal interaction hypothesis of sleep cycle control. *Psychosomatic Medicine, 45,* 123–139.

Hobson, J.A. & McCarley, R.W. 1977. The brain as a dream state generator: An activation-synthesis hypothesis of the dream process. *American Journal of Psychiatry, 134,* 1335–1348.

Holden, C. 1985. Genes, personality, and alcoholism. *Psychology Today, 19,* 38–44.

Holmes, D.S., Solomon, S., Cappo, B.M., & Greenberg, J.L. 1983. Effects of transcendental meditation versus resting on physiological and subjective arousal. *Journal of Personality and Social Psychology, 44,* 1244–1252.

Johnson, L.C., Slye, E.S., & Dement, W. 1965. EEG and autonomic activity during and after prolonged sleep deprivation. *Psychosomatic Medicine, 27,* 415–423.

Jones, A.K. 1985. The prospects for Pakistan's opium farmers—relief or oppression? *Cultural Survival Quarterly, 9,* 16–19.

Kales, A., Caldwell, A.B., Preston, T.A., Healey, S., & Kales, J.D. 1976. Personality patterns in insomnia: Theoretical implications. *Archives of General Psychiatry, 33,* 1128–1134.

Kampman, R. 1976. Hypnotically induced multiple personality: An experimental study. *The International Journal of Clinical and Experimental Hypnosis, 24,* 215–227.

Kendall, S. 1985. South American cocaine production. *Cultural Survival Quarterly, 9,* 10–11.

Kiester, E., Jr. 1980. Images of the night. *Science 80, 1,* 36–43.

Liberson, W.T. 1945. Problem of sleep and mental disease. *Digest of Neurology & Psychiatry* (vol. 13). Hartford, CN: The Institute of Living.

Lieber, J. 1986. Coping with cocaine. *Atlantic Monthly, 257,* 39–48.

Lindsley, J.G., Hartmann, E.L., & Mitchell, W. 1983. Selectivity in response to L-tryptophan among insomniac subjects: A preliminary report. *Sleep, 6,* 247–256.

Liskow, B. 1982. Substance induced and substance use disorders: Barbiturates and similarly acting sedative hypnotics. In J.H. Greist, J.W. Jefferson, & R.L. Spitzer (Eds.). *Treatment of mental disorders.* NY: Oxford University Press.

Luisada, P. 1981. Phencyclidine. In J. Lowinson, & P. Ruiz (Eds.), *Substance abuse.* Baltimore: Williams & Wilkins, 209.

Maslow, A.H. 1954. *Motivation and personality.* NY: Harper & Row.

Maugh, T.H. 1982. Sleep-promoting factor isolated. *Science, 216,* 1400.

Mefford, I.N., Baker, T.L., Boehme, R., Foutz, A.S., Ciaranello, R.D., Barchas, J.D., & Dement, W.C. 1983. Narcolepsy: Biogenic amine deficits in an animal model. *Science, 220,* 629–632.

Melnechuk, T. 1983. The dream machine. *Psychology Today, 17,* 22–34.

Murray, R. & Stabeneau, J. 1982. Genetic factors in alcoholism predisposition. In E. Pattison, & E. Kaufman (Eds.). *Encyclopedic handbook of alcoholism.* NY: Gardner Press.

National Institute of Mental Health (NIMH). 1965. *Research on sleep and dreams.* Rockville, MD: NIMH.

Neisser, U. 1967. *Cognitive psychology.* NY: Appleton-Century-Crofts.

Newsweek. 1986. Kids and cocaine. *Newsweek,* March 17, 58–65.

Ornstein, R.S. 1977. *The psychology of consciousness* (2nd ed.). NY: Harcourt Brace Jovanovich.

Pattison, E. & Kaufman, E. (Eds.). 1982. *Encyclopedic handbook of alcoholism.* NY: Gardner Press.

Ray, O. 1983. *Drugs, society, and human behavior.* St. Louis: Mosby.

Roffwarg, H.P., Muzio, J.N., & Dement, W.C. 1966. Ontogenetic development of the human sleep-dream cycle, *Science, 152,* 604–619.

Sandblom, R.E., Matsumoto, A.M., Schoene, R.B., Lee, K.A., Giblin, E.C., Bremner, W.J., & Pierson, D.J. 1983. Sleep apnea induced by testosterone administration. *New England Journal of Medicine, 308,* 508–510.

Schuckit, M., Goodwin, D., & Winokur, G. 1972. A study of alcoholism in half-siblings. *American Journal of Psychiatry, 128,* 1132.

Schulman, R. & Sabin, M. 1985. The losing war against 'designer drugs'. *Business Week,* June 24, 101–104.

Siegel, R.K. 1977. Hallucinations. *Scientific American, 237,* 132–139.

Seligman, J. 1985. Women smokers: The risk factor. *Newsweek,* November 25, 76–78.

Singer, J.L. 1975. Navigating the stream of consciousness: Research in daydreaming and related inner experience. *American Psychologist, 30,* 727–739.

Singer, J.L. 1978. Experimental studies of daydreaming and the stream of thought. In K.S. Pope & J.L. Singer (Eds.). *The stream of consciousness: Scientific investigations into the flow of human experience.* NY: Plenum.

Stone, N., Fromme, M., & Kagan, D. 1984. *Cocaine: Seduction and Solution.* NY: Potter.

Taswell, R. 1985. Heroin—an overview. *Cultural Survival Quarterly, 9,* 6–8.

Taswell, R. 1985. Marijuana/Hashish. *Cultural Survival Quarterly, 9,* 7–9.

Treisman, A.M. 1960. Contextual cues in selective listening. *Quarterly Journal of Experimental Psychology, 12,* 242–248.

U.S. News & World Report. 1985. "Designer drugs"—murder by molecule. *U.S. News & World Report,* Aug. 5, 14.

Wadden, T.A. & Anderton, C.H. 1982. The clinical use of hypnosis. *Psychological Bulletin, 91,* 215–243.

Webb, W. & Bonnet, M.H. 1979. Sleep and dreams. In M.E. Meyer (Ed.). *Foundations of contemporary psychology.* NY: Oxford University Press.

Weil, A. & Rosen, W. 1983. *Chocolate to morphine: Understanding mind-active drugs.* Boston: Houghton Mifflin.

Wester, W.C. II & Smith, A.H. (Eds.). 1984. *Clinical hypnosis: A multidisciplinary approach.* Philadelphia: Lippincott.

Chapter 8

Bandura, A. 1977. *Social learning theory.* Englewood Cliffs, NJ: Prentice-Hall.

Bandura, A. & Rosenthal, T.L. 1966. Vicarious classical conditioning as a function of arousal level. *Journal of Personality and Social Psychology, 3,* 54–62.

Bernstein, I. 1978. Learned taste aversion in children receiving chemotherapy. *Science, 200,* 1302–1303.

Bernstein, I.L., Webster, M.M., & Bernstein, I.D. 1982. Food aversion in children receiving chemotherapy for cancer. *Cancer, 50,* 2961–2963.

Bregman, E.O. 1934. An attempt to modify the emotional attitudes of infants by the conditioned response technique. *Journal of Genetic Psychology, 45,* 169–198.

Burgess, A. 1961. *A clockwork orange.* NY: Norton.

Byrne, D. 1971. *The attraction paradigm.* NY: Academic Press.

Catania, A.C. 1984. *Learning* (2nd ed.). Englewood Cliffs, NJ: Prentice-Hall.

Dickinson, A. 1980. *Contemporary animal learning theory.* Cambridge: Cambridge University Press.

Emmaelkamp, P. & Kuipers, A. 1979. Agoraphobia: A follow-up study four years after treatment. *British Journal of Psychiatry, 134,* 352–355.

Fantino, E.J. 1973. Emotion. In J.A. Nevin (Ed.). *The study of behavior.* Glenview, IL: Scott Foresman.

Farley, J., Richards, W.G., Ling, L.J., Liman, E., & Alkon, D.L. 1983. Membrane changes in a single photoreceptor cause associative learning in Hermissenda. *Science, 221,* 1201–1202.

Flaherty, C.F., Uzwiak, A.J., Levine, J., Smith, M., Hall, P., & Schuler, R. 1980. Apparent hyperglycemic and hypoglycemic conditional responses with exogenous insulin as the unconditioned stimulus. *Animal Learning and Behavior, 8,* 382–386.

Gantt, W.H. 1953. Principles of nervous breakdown: Schizokinesis and autokinesis. *Annals of New York Academy of Science, 56,* 143–163.

Gantt, W.H. 1958. *Physiological bases of psychiatry.* Springfield, IL: Charles C. Thomas.

Gantt, W.H. 1960. Cardiovascular component of the conditional reflex to pain, food, and other stimuli. *Physiological Review, 40,* 266–291.

Garcia, J., Kimeldorf, D.J., Hunt, E.L., & Davies, B.P. 1956. Food and water consumption of rats during exposure to gamma radiation. *Radiation Research, 4,* 33–41.

Garcia, J. & Koelling, R.A. 1966. Relation of cue to consequence in avoidance learning. *Psychonomic Science, 4,* 123–124.

Gustavson, C.R., Garcia, J., Hawkins, W.G., & Rusiniak, K.W. 1974. Coyote predation control by aversive conditioning. *Science, 184,* 581–583.

Harris, B. 1979. Whatever happened to little Albert? *American Psychologist, 34,* 151–160.

Hebb, D.E. 1980. *Essay on mind.* Hillsdale, NJ: Erlbaum.

Huxley, A. 1932. *Brave new world.* NY: Harper.

Jones, H.E. 1930. The retention of conditioned emotional reactions in infancy. *Journal of Genetic Psychology, 37,* 485–497.

Jones, M.C. 1924. The elimination of children's fear. *Journal of Experimental Psychology, 7,* 383–390.

Kamin, L.J. 1969. Predictability, surprise, attention and conditioning. In B.A. Campbell & R.M. Church (Eds.). *Punishment and aversive behavior.* NY: Appleton-Century-Crofts.

Kimble, G.A. 1956. *Principles of general psychology.* NY: Ronald Press.

Kimble, G.A. 1981. Biological and cognitive constraints on learning. In L.T. Benjamin, Jr. (Ed.). *The G. Stanley Hall Lecture Series* (Vol. 1). Washington: American Psychological Association.

Logan, F.A. 1970. *Fundamentals of learning and motivation.* Dubuque, IA: Brown.

Mackintosh, N.J. 1983. *Conditioning and associative learning.* NY: Oxford University Press.

Mahoney, M.J. & Arnkoff, D.B. 1978. Cognitive and self-control therapies. In S.L. Garfield & A.E. Bergin (Eds.), *Handbook of psychotherapy and behavior change* (2nd ed.). NY: Wiley.

Nathan, P.E. 1976. In H. Leitenberg (Ed.). *Handbook of behavior modification and behavior therapy.* Englewood Cliffs, NJ: Prentice-Hall.

Pavlov, I.P. 1906. The scientific investigation of the psychical faculties or processes in the higher animals. *Science, 24,* 613–619.

Pavlov, I.P. 1927. *Conditioned reflexes* (G.V. Anrep, Trans.). London: Oxford University Press.

Pavlov, I.P. 1928. *Lectures on conditioned reflexes: Twenty-five years of objective study of higher nervous activity (behavior of animals)* (Vol. 1; W.H. Gantt, Trans.). NY: International Publishers.

Rescorla, R.A. 1966. Predictability and number of pairings in Pavlovian fear conditioning. *Psychonomic Science, 4,* 383–384.

Rescorla, R.A. 1967. Pavlovian conditioning and its proper control procedures. *Psychological Review, 74,* 71–80.

Ross, S.M. & Ross, L.E. 1971. Comparison of trace and delay classical eyelid conditioning as a function of interstimulus interval. *Journal of Experimental Psychology, 91,* 165–167.

Sarason, I.G. (Ed.). 1978. *Test anxiety: Theory, research, and applications.* Hillsdale, NJ: Erlbaum.

Seligman, M.E.P. 1968. Chronic fear produced by unpredictable electric shock. *Journal of Comparative and Physiological Psychology, 66,* 402–411.

Siegal, S. 1975. Evidence from rats that morphine tolerance is a learned response. *Journal of Comparative and Physiological Psychology, 89,* 498–506.

Siegal, S.H. 1977. Morphine tolerance acquisition as an association process. *Journal of Experimental Psychology: Animal Behavior Processes, 3,* 1–13.

Siegal, S., Hinson, R.E., Krank, M.D., & McCully, J. 1982. Heroin "overdose" death: Contribution of drug-associated environmental causes. *Science, 216,* 436–437.

Skinner, B.F. 1938. *The behavior of organisms: An experimental analysis.* NY: Appleton-Century-Crofts.

Skinner, B.F. 1974. *About behaviorism.* NY: Knopf.

Smith, M.C., Coleman, S.R., & Gormesano, I. 1969. Classical conditioning of the rabbit's nictitating membrane response at backward, simultaneous and forward CS-US intervals. *Journal of Comparative and Physiological Psychology, 69,* 226–231.

Snyder, S.H. 1984. Drug and neurotransmitter receptors in the brain. *Science, 224,* 22–31.

Smotherson, W.P. 1982. Odor aversion learning by the rat fetus. *Physiology and Behavior, 29,* 769–771.

Solomon, R.L. & Wynne, L.C. 1953. Traumatic avoidance learning: Acquisition in normal dogs. *Psychological Monographs, 67,* (Whole No. 354).

Tolman, E.C. 1932. *Purposive behavior in animals and man.* NY: Appleton-Century-Crofts.

Wagner, A.R., Siegal, S., Thomas, E., & Ellison, G.D. 1964. Reinforcement history and the extinction of a conditioned salivary response. *Journal of Comparative and Physiological Psychology, 58,* 354–358.

Watson, J.B. 1913. Psychology as the behaviorist views it. *Psychological Review, 20,* 158–177.

Watson, J.B. & Rayner, R. 1920. Conditioned emotional reactions. *Journal of Experimental Psychology, 3,* 1–14.

Weinberg, J.R. 1977. Counseling the person with alcohol problems. In N.J. Estes & M.E. Heinman (Eds.). *Alcoholism: Development, consequences and intervention.* St. Louis: Mosby.

Weinberger, N.M., Gold, P.E., & Sternberg, D.B. 1984. Epinephrine enables Pavlovian fear conditioning under anesthesia. *Science, 223,* 605–607.

Weiss, J.M. 1970. Somatic effects of predictable and unpredictable shock. *Psychosomatic Medicine, 32,* 397–408.

Wiens, A.N. & Menustik, C.E. 1983. Treatment outcome and patient characteristics in an aversion therapy program for alcoholism. *American Psychologist, 38,* 1089–1096.

Williams, R.L. & Long, J.D. 1982. *Toward a self-managed life style* (3rd ed.). Boston: Houghton Mifflin.

Wolpe, J. 1958. *Psychotherapy by reciprocal inhibition.* Stanford, CA: Stanford University Press.

Wolpe, J. 1982. *The practice of behavior therapy.* NY: Pergamon.

Yerkes, R.M. & Morgulis, S. 1909. The method of Pavlov in animal psychology. *Psychological Bulletin, 6,* 257–273.

Chapter 9

Amsel, A. 1962. Frustrative nonreward in partial reinforcement and discrimination learning: Some recent history and theoretical extension. *Psychological Review, 69,* 306–328.

Axelrod, S. & Apsche, J. (Eds.). 1983. *The effects of punishment on human behavior.* NY: Academic Press.

Ayllon, T. & Azrin, N.H. 1965. The measurement and reinforcement of behavior of psychotics, *Journal of the Experimental Analysis of Behavior, 8,* 357–383.

Azrin, N.H. & Foxx, R.M. 1976. *Toilet training in less than a day.* NY: Pocket Books.

Azrin, N.H. & Holz, W.C. 1966. Punishment. In W.K. Honig (Ed.), *Operant behavior.* NY: Appleton-Century-Crofts.

Bandura, A. 1965. Vicarious processes: A case of no-trial learning. In L. Berkowitz (Ed.). *Advances in experimental social psychology* (Vol. 2). NY: Academic Press.

Bandura, A. 1977. *Social learning theory.* Englewood Cliffs, NJ: Prentice-Hall.

Bandura, A., Ross, D., & Ross, S. 1963. Imitation of film-mediated aggressive models. *Journal of Abnormal and Social Psychology, 66,* 3–11.

Berkowitz, L. 1984. Some effects of thought on anti- and prosocial influences of media events: A cognitive-neoassociation analysis. *Psychological Bulletin, 95,* 410–427.

Bolick, T. & Nowicki, S., Jr. 1984. The incidence of external locus of control in televised cartoon characters. *The Journal of Genetic Psychology, 144,* 99–104.

Boren, J.J. 1961. Resistance to extinction as a function of the fixed ratio. *Journal of Experimental Psychology, 61,* 304–308.

Breland, K. & Breland, M. 1961. The misbehavior of organisms. *American Psychologist, 16,* 661–664.

Breland, K. & Breland, M. 1966. *Animal behavior.* NY: Macmillan.

Buckalew, L.W. & Buckalew, P.B. 1983. Behavioral management of exceptional children using video games as reward. *Perceptual Motor Skills, 56,* 580.

Bugelski, R. 1938. Extinction with and without sub-goal reinforcement. *Journal of Comparative Psychology, 26,* 121–134.

Cowles, J.T. 1937. Food-tokens as incentive for learning by chimpanzees. *Comparative Psychology Monographs, 14* (No. 5).

Dominick, J.R. 1984. Videogames, television violence, and aggression in teenagers. *Journal of Communication, 34,* 136–147.

Freedman, J.L. 1984. Effect of television violence on aggressiveness. *Psychological Bulletin, 96,* 227–246.

Friedrich, L. & Stein, A. 1973. Aggressive and prosocial television programs and the natural behavior of preschool children. *Monographs of the Society for Research in Child Development, 38* (4, Serial No. 151).

Greene, D. & Lepper, M.R. 1974. How to turn play into work. *Psychology Today, 8,* 49.

Greenspoon, J. 1955. The reinforcing effect of two spoken sounds on the frequency of two responses. *American Journal of Physiology, 68,* 409–416.

Gunter, B., Jarrett, J., & Furnham, A. 1983. Time of day effects on immediate memory for television news. *Human Learning: Journal of Practical Research & Applications, 2,* 261–267.

Hearst, E. 1961. Resistance-to-extinction functions in the single organism. *Journal of the Experimental Analysis of Behavior, 4,* 133–144.

Herbert, M.J. & Harsh, C.M. 1944. Observational learning by cats. *Journal of Comparative and Physiological Psychology, 37,* 81–95.

Huesman, L.R., Lagerspetz, K., & Eron, L.D. 1984. Intervening variables in the TV violence-aggression relation: Evidence from two countries. *Developmental Psychology, 20,* 746–775.

Kubley, R.W. 1980. Television and aging: Past, present, and future. *Gerontologist, 20,* 16–35.

Lepper, M.R., Greene, D., & Nisbett, R.E. 1973. Undermining children's intrinsic interest with extrinsic reward: A test of the "overjustification" hypothesis. *Journal of Personality and Social Psychology, 28,* 129–137.

Logan, F.A. 1970. *Fundamentals of learning and motivation.* Dubuque, IA: Brown.

Logan, F.A. & Wagner, A.R. 1965. *Reward and punishment.* Boston: Allyn and Bacon.

McAuley, E. 1985. Modeling and self-efficacy: A test of Bandura's model. *Journal of Sport Psychology, 7,* 283–295.

Miller, L.K. 1980. *Principles of everyday behavior analysis.* Monterey, CA: Brooks/Cole.

Miller, N.E. 1969. Learning of visceral and glandular responses. *Science, 163,* 434–445.

Mowrer, O.H. 1947. On the dual nature of learning—a reinterpretation of "conditioning" and "problem solving." *Harvard Educational Review, 17,* 102–148.

National Institute of Mental Health (NIMH). 1982. *Television and behavior: Ten years of scientific progress and implications for the eighties* (Vols. 1 & 2). Washington: U.S. Government Printing Office.

Nevin, J.A. 1973. The maintenance of behavior. In J.A. Nevin & G.S. Reynolds (Eds.). *The study of behavior.* Glenview, IL: Scott Foresman.

Newsom, C., Favell, J.E., & Rincover, A. 1983. Side effects of punishment. In S. Axelrod & J. Apsche (Eds.). *The effects of punishment on behavior.* NY: Academic Press.

Nielson, A.C. 1985. *Nielson television index: National audience demographic report* (30th ed.). Northbrook, IL: A.C. Nielsen.

Perin, C.T. 1943. A quantitative investigation of the delay-of-reinforcement gradient. *Journal of Experimental Psychology, 32*, 38–51.

Peterson, P.E., Jeffrey, B., Bridgwater, C.A., & Dawson, B. 1984. How pronutrition television programming affects children's dietary habits. *Developmental Psychology, 20*, 55–63.

Premack, D. 1965. Reinforcement theory. In M.R. Jones, (Ed.). *Nebraska symposium on motivation.* Lincoln: University of Nebraska Press.

Premack, D. & Woodruff, G. 1978. Does the chimpanzee have a theory of mind? *The Behavioral and Brain Sciences, 4*, 515–526.

Schwartz, B. 1984. *Psychology of learning and behavior* (2nd ed.). NY: Norton.

Seligman, M.E.P. 1970. On the generality of the laws of learning. *Psychological Review, 77*, 406–418.

Singer, J.L., Singer, D.G., & Rapaczynski, W.S. 1984. Family patterns and television viewing as predictors of children's beliefs and aggression. *Journal of Communication, 34*, 73–89.

Skinner, B.F. 1938. *The behavior of organisms.* NY: Appleton-Century-Crofts.

Skinner, B.F. 1948(a). "Superstition" in the pigeon. *Journal of Experimental Psychology, 38*, 168–172.

Skinner, B.F. 1948(b). *Walden two.* NY: Macmillan.

Skinner, B.F. 1950. Are theories of learning necessary? *Psychological Review, 57*, 193–216.

Skinner, B.F. 1953. *Science and human behavior.* NY: Macmillan.

Skinner, B.F. 1971. *Beyond freedom and dignity.* NY: Knopf.

Skinner, B.F. 1974. *About behaviorism.* NY: Knopf.

Skinner, B.F. 1987. *Upon further reflection.* Englewood Cliffs, NJ: Prentice-Hall.

Thorndike, E.L. 1898. Animal intelligence: An experimental study of the associative processes in animals. *Psychological Review Monograph Supplement, 2* (Whole No. 8).

Thorndike, E.L. 1911. *Animal intelligence.* NY: Macmillan.

Tolman, E.C. 1922. A new formula for behaviorism. *Psychological Review, 29*, 44–53.

Tolman, E.C. 1932. *Purposive behavior in animals and man.* NY: Appleton-Century-Crofts.

Tolman, E.C., & Honzik, C.H. 1930. Introduction and removal of reward and maze performance in rats. *University of California Publications in Psychology, 4*, 257–275.

Tolman, E.C., Ritchie, B.F., & Kalish, D. 1946. Studies in spatial learning. I. Orientation and the short-cut. *Journal of Experimental Psychology, 36*, 13–24.

Wagner, A.R. 1961. Effects of amount and percentage of reinforcement and number of acquisition trial on conditioning and extinction. *Journal of Experimental Psychology, 62*, 234–242.

Watson, J.B. 1913. Psychology as the behaviorist views it. *Psychological Review, 20*, 158–177.

Watson, J.B. 1924. *Behaviorism.* NY: People's Institute.

Williams, R.L. & Long, J.D. 1982. *Toward a self-managed lifestyle* (3rd ed.). Boston: Houghton Mifflin.

Wolfe, J.B. 1936. Effectiveness of token-rewards for chimpanzees. *Comparative Psychology Monographs, 12* (No. 60), 1–72.

Wright, J.C., Huston, A.C., Ross, R.P., Calvert, S.L., Rolandelli, D., Weeks, L.A., Ralissi, P., & Potts, R. 1984. Pace and continuity of television programs: Effects on children's attention and comprehension. *Developmental Psychology, 20*, 653–666.

Chapter 10

Anderson, J.R. 1980. *Cognitive psychology and its implications.* NY: Freeman.

Anderson, J.R. 1983. Retrieval of information from long-term memory. *Science, 220*, 25–30.

Atkinson, R.C. & Shriffin, R.M. 1968. Human memory: A proposed system and its control processes. In K.W. Spence & J.T. Spence (Eds.). *The psychology of learning and motivation: Advances in research and theory* (Vol. 2). NY: Academic Press.

Atkinson, R.C. & Shriffin, R.M. 1971. The control of short-term memory. *Scientific American, 224*, 83–89.

Baddeley, A.D. 1982. *Memory: A user's guide.* NY: Macmillan.

Bahrick, H.P., Bahrick, P.O., & Wittlinger, R.P. 1975. Fifty years of memory for names and faces: A cross-sectional approach. *Journal of Experimental Psychology, 104*, 54–75.

Bower, G.H. 1973. How to . . . uh . . . remember. *Psychology Today, 7*, 63–70.

Bower, G.H. 1981. Mood and memory. *Psychology Today, 15*, 60–69.

Bower, G.H. & Clark, M.C. 1969. Narrative stories as mediators for serial learning. *Psychonomic Science, 14*, 181–182.

Bower, G.H., Gilligan, S.G., & Monteiro, K.P. 1981. Selectivity of learning caused by affective states. *Journal of Experimental Psychology: General, 110*, 451–473.

Brown, R. & Kulik, J. 1977. Flashbulb memories. *Cognition, 5*, 73–99.

Brown, R.W. & McNeil, D. 1966. The "tip-of-the-tongue" phenomenon. *Journal of Verbal Learning and Verbal Behavior, 5*, 325–337.

Butters, N. & Cermak, L.S. 1980. *Alcoholic Korsakoff's syndrome.* NY: Academic Press.

Cermak, L.S. 1975. *Improving your memory.* NY: McGraw-Hill.

Conway, M. & Ross, M. 1984. Getting what you want by revising what you had. *Journal of Personality and Social Psychology, 47*, 738–748.

Craik, F.I.M. & Lockhart, R.S. 1972. Levels of processing: A framework for memory research. *Journal of Verbal Learning and Verbal Behavior, 11*, 671–684.

Craik, F.I.M. & Tulving, E. 1975. Depth of processing and the retention of words in episodic memory. *Journal of Experimental Psychology: General, 104*, 268–294.

Duncan, C.P. 1949. The retroactive effect of electroshock on learning. *Journal of Comparative and Physiological Psychology, 42*, 32–44.

Ebbinghaus, H. 1913. *Memory: A contribution to experimental psychology.* H.A. Ruger & C.E. Bussenius (Trans.). NY: Columbia University Press (Originally published, 1885).

Eich, J.E., Weingartner, H., Stillman, R.C., & Gillin, J.C. 1975. State dependent accessibility of retrieval cues in the retention of a categorized list. *Journal of Verbal Learning and Verbal Behavior, 14*, 408–417.

Gaito, J.A. 1974. A biochemical approach to learning and memory: Fourteen years later. In G. Newton & A.H. Riesen (Eds.). *Advances in psychobiology* (vol. 2). NY: Wiley.

Godden, D.R. & Baddeley, A.D. 1975. Context-dependent memory in two natural environments: On land and underwater. *British Journal of Psychology, 66*, 325–331.

Haber, R.N. 1980. Eidetic images are not just imaginary. *Psychology Today, 14*, 72–82.

Harris, J.E. 1978. External memory aids. In M.M. Gruneberg, P.E. Morris, & R.N. Sykes (Eds.). *Practical aspects of memory.* NY: Academic Press.

Harris, J.E. 1980. Memory aids people use: Two interview studies. *Memory and Cognition, 8*, 31–38.

Harris, J.E. 1984. Remembering to do things: A forgotten topic. In J.E. Harris & P.E. Morris (Eds.). *Everyday memory, actions and absent-mindedness.* NY: Academic Press.

Hasher, L., Rose, K.C., Zacks, R.T., Sanft, H., & Doren, B. 1985. Mood, recall, and selectivity effects in normal college students. *Journal of Experimental Psychology: General, 114*, 104–118.

Hebb, D.O. 1949. *The organization of behavior: A neuropsychological theory.* NY: Wiley.

Hyden, H. & Lange, P.W. 1970. Brain cell protein synthesis specifically related to learning. *Proceedings of the National Academy of Sciences, 65*, 898–904.

Jenkins, J.G. & Dallenbach, K.M. 1924. Oblivescence during sleep and waking. *American Journal of Psychology, 35*, 605–612.

Kolata, G. 1983. Brain grafting shows promise. *Science, 221*, 1209–1210.

Kreutzer, M.A., Leonard, C., & Flavell, J.H. 1975. An interview study of children's knowledge about memory. *Monographs of the Society for Research in Child Development, 40* (1, Serial No. 159).

Lashley, K.S. 1929. *Brain mechanisms and intelligence.* Chicago: University of Chicago Press.

Lashley, K.S. 1950. In search of the engram. *Symposia of the Society of Experimental Biology, 4*, 454–482.

Loftus, E.F. 1975. Spreading activation within semantic categories: Comments on Rosch's "Cognitive representations of semantic categories." *Journal of Experimental Psychology, 104*, 234–240.

Loftus, E.F. 1979. *Eyewitness testimony*. Cambridge, MA: Harvard University Press.

Loftus, E.F. 1980. *Memory: Surprising new insights into how we remember and why we forget*. Reading, MA: Addison-Wesley.

Loftus, E.F. & Loftus, G.R. 1980. On the permanence of stored information in the human brain. *American Psychologist, 35,* 409–420.

Loftus, E.F., Miller, D.G., & Burns, H.J. 1980. Semantic integration of verbal information into a visual memory. *Journal of Experimental Psychology, 4,* 19–31.

Loftus, E.F. & Palmer, J.C. 1974. Reconstruction of automobile destruction: An example of the interaction between language and memory. *Journal of Verbal Learning and Verbal Behavior, 13,* 585–589.

Loftus, G.R. & Loftus, E.F. 1975. *Human memory: The processing of information*. NY: Halsted Press.

Lorayne, H., & Lucas, J. 1974. *The memory book*. NY: Ballentine Books.

Luria, A.R. 1968. *The mind of a mnemonist*. Lynn Solotaroff (Trans.). NY: Basic Books.

Madigan, S.A. 1969. Intraserial repetition and coding processes in free recall. *Journal of Verbal Learning and Verbal Behavior, 8,* 828–835.

McConnell, J.V. 1962. Memory transfer through cannibalism in planarians. *Journal of Neuropsychiatry, 3,* monograph supp. 1.

McGaugh, J.L. 1970. Time-dependent processes in memory storage. In J.L. McGaugh & M.J. Hertz (Eds.). *Controversial issues in consolidation of the memory trace*. NY: Atherton.

Meacham, J.A. & Leiman, B. 1975. Remembering to perform future actions. Paper presented at the meeting of the American Psychological Association, Chicago, September. In U. Neisser (Ed.). 1982. *Memory observed*. San Francisco: Freeman.

Miller, G.A. 1956. The magical number seven, plus or minus two: Some limits on our capacity to process information. *Psychological Review, 63,* 81–97.

Milner, B. 1972. Disorders of learning and memory after temporal lobe lesions in man. *Clinical Neurosurgery, 19,* 421–446.

Neisser, U. 1982. Memory: What are the important questions? In U. Neisser (Ed.). *Memory observed*. San Francisco: Freeman.

Nickerson, R.S., & Adams, M.J. 1979. Long-term memory for a common object. *Cognitive Psychology, 11,* 287–307.

Overton, D.A. 1972. State-dependent learning produced by alcohol and its relevance to alcoholism. In B. Kissin & H. Begleiter (Eds.). *Physiology and behavior* (Vol. 2). NY: Plenum.

Paivio, A. 1969. Mental imagery in associative learning and memory. *Psychological Review, 76,* 241–263.

Paivio, A. 1978. Dual coding: Theoretical issues and empirical evidence. In J.M. Scandura & C.J. Brainerd (Eds.). *Structural process models of human behavior*. Leiden: Nordhoff.

Peterson, L.R. & Peterson, M.J. 1959. Short-term retention of individual verbal items. *Journal of Experimental Psychology, 58,* 193–198.

Piaget, J. 1962. *Play, dreams, and imitation in childhood*. NY: Norton.

Reason, J. 1984. Absent-mindedness and cognitive control. In J.E. Harris & P.E. Morris (Eds.). *Everyday memory, actions and absent-mindedness*. NY: Academic Press.

Robbins, L.C. 1963. The accuracy of parental recall of aspects of child development and of childrearing practices. *Journal of Abnormal and Social Psychology, 66,* 261–270.

Rosenzweig, M.R. 1984. Experience, memory, and the brain. *American Psychologist, 39,* 365–376.

Rubin, D.C. 1985. The subtle deceiver: Recalling our past. *Psychology Today, 19,* 38–46.

Rubin, D.C. & Kozen, M. 1985. Cited in D.C. Rubin, 1985. The subtle deceiver: Recalling our past. *Psychology Today, 19,* 38–46.

Shanon, B. 1979. Yesterday, today, and tomorrow. *Acta Psychologica, 43,* 469–476.

Smith, S.M. 1985. Background music and context-dependent memory. *American Journal of Psychology, 98,* 591–603.

Smith, S.M., Glenberg, A.M., & Bjork, R.A. 1978. Environmental context and human memory. *Memory and Cognition, 6,* 342–355.

Sperling, G. 1960. The information available in brief visual presentations. *Psychological Monographs, 74,* 1–29.

Tulving, E. 1974. Cue-dependent forgetting. *American Scientist, 62,* 74–82.

Tulving, E. 1982. *Elements of episodic memory*. NY: Oxford University Press.

Tulving, E. 1985. How many memory systems are there? *American Psychologist, 40,* 385–398.

Underwood, B.J. 1957. Interference and forgetting. *Psychological Review, 64,* 49–60.

Weingartner, H., Gold, P., Ballenger, J.C., Smallberg, S.A., Summers, R., Rubinow, D.R., Post, R.M., & Goodwin, F.K. 1981. Effects of vasopressin on human memory functions. *Science, 211,* 601–603.

Weingartner, H., Rudorfer, M.V., Bachsbaum, M.S., & Linnoila, M. 1983. Effects of serotonin on memory impairments produced by ethanol. *Science, 221,* 472–473.

Wurtman, R.J. 1985. Alzheimer's disease. *Scientific American, 252,* 62–74.

Yarmey, A.D. 1973. I recognize your face but I can't remember your name: Further evidence on the tip-of-the-tongue phenomenon. *Memory and Cognition, 1,* 287–290.

Chapter 11

Abelson, R.P. 1981. Psychological status of the script concept. *American Psychologist, 36,* 715–729.

Aitchison, J. 1983. *The articulate mammal: An introduction to psycholinguistics* (2nd ed.). NY: Universe.

Anderson, J.R. (Ed.). 1981. *Cognitive skills and their acquisition*. Hillsdale, NJ: Erlbaum.

Berlin, B. & Kay, P. 1969. *Basic color terms: Their universality and evolution*. Berkeley: University of California Press.

Best, J.B. 1986. *Cognitive psychology*. St. Paul, MN: West.

Block, N. (Ed.). 1981. *Imagery*. Cambridge, MA: MIT Press.

Boden, M. 1979. *Piaget*. Glasgow: Fontana.

Broadbent, D.E. 1958. *Perception and communication*. London: Pergamon.

Brown, G. & Desforges, C. 1979. *Piaget's theory: A psychological critique*. Boston: Routledge & Kegan Paul.

Bruner, J.S., Goodnow, J., & Austin, G.A. 1956. *A study of thinking*. NY: Wiley.

Bruner, J.S., Olver, R.R., & Greenfield, P. 1966. *Studies in cognitive growth*. NY: Wiley.

Chi, M.T.H. & Glaser, R. 1985. Problem-solving ability. In R.J. Sternberg (Ed.). *Human abilities: An information processing approach*. NY: Freeman.

Chomsky, N. 1957. *Syntactic structures*. The Hague: Mouton.

Chomsky, N. 1983. On the representation of form and function. In J. Mehler, E.C.T. Walker, & M. Garrett (Eds.). *Perspectives on mental representation*. Hillsdale, NJ: Erlbaum.

Cole, M. & Scribner, S. 1977. Cross-cultural studies of memory and cognition. In R.V. Vail, Jr. & J.W. Hagen (Eds.). *Perspectives on the development of memory and recognition*. Hillsdale, NJ: Erlbaum.

Cooper, L.A. & Shepard, R.N. 1973. Chronometric studies of the rotation of mental images. In W.G. Chase (Ed.). *Visual information processing*. NY: Academic Press.

Desmond, A.J. 1979. *The ape's reflection*. NY: Dial Press/James Wade.

Dodd, D.H. & White, R.M., Jr. 1980. *Cognition: Mental structures and processes*. Boston: Allyn & Bacon.

Donalson, M. 1978. *Children's minds*. Glasgow: Collins.

Feldman, A. & Acredolo, L.P. 1979. The effect of active versus passive exploration on memory for spatial localization in children. *Child Development, 50,* 689–704.

Feuerstein, R. 1979. *The dynamic assessment of retarded performers*. Baltimore: University Park Press.

Feuerstein, R. 1980. *Instrumental enrichment*. Baltimore: University Park Press.

Feuerstein, R. & Rand, Y. 1977. *Studies in cognitive modifiability. Instrumental enrichment: Redevelopment of cognitive functions of retarded early adolescents*. Jerusalem: Hadassah-Wizo-Canada Research Institute.

Fouts, R.S., Fouts, D.H., & Schoenfeld, D.J. 1984. Sign language conversational interaction between chimpanzees. *Sign Language Studies, 42,* 1–12.

Gardner, H. 1985. *The mind's new science*. NY: Basic Books.

Gardner, R.A. & Gardner, B.I. 1969. Teaching sign language to a chimpanzee. *Science, 165,* 664–672.

Greeno, J.G. 1978. Natures of problem-solving abilities. In W.K. Estes (Ed.). *Handbook of learning and cognitive processes* (Vol. 5). Hillsdale, NJ: Erlbaum.

Hayes, C. 1951. *The ape in our house.* NY: Harper & Row.

Hayes, J.R. 1981. *The complete problem solver.* Philadelphia: Franklin Institute Press.

Hunt, M. 1982. *The universe within.* NY: Simon & Schuster.

Irwin, D.B. 1986 (February). Classroom observations.

Jonides, J., Kahn, R., & Rozin, P. 1975. Imagery instructions improve memory in blind subjects. *Bulletin of the Psychonomic Society, 5,* 424–426.

Kahneman, D., Slovic, P., & Tversky, A. (Eds.). 1982. *Judgement under uncertainty.* NY: Cambridge University Press.

Kahneman, D. & Tversky, A. 1973. On the psychology of prediction. *Psychological Review, 80,* 237–251.

Kahneman, D. & Tversky, A. 1984. Choices, values, and frames. *American Psychologist, 39,* 341–350.

Kellogg, W.N. & Kellogg, L.A. 1933. *The ape and the child.* NY: McGraw-Hill.

Kohler, W. 1925. *The mentality of apes.* NY: Harcourt, Brace, & World.

Kosslyn, S.M. 1975. Information representation in visual images. *Cognitive Psychology, 7,* 341–370.

Kosslyn, S.M. 1976. Using imagery to retrieve semantic information: A developmental study. *Child Development, 47,* 433–444.

Kosslyn, S.M. 1978. Measuring the visual angle of the mind's eye. *Cognitive Psychology, 10,* 356–389.

Kosslyn, S.M. 1983. *Ghosts in the mind's machine.* NY: Norton.

Luchins, A.S. 1946. Classroom experiments on mental set. *American Journal of Psychology, 59,* 295–298.

McGarrigle, J. & Donaldson, M. 1975. Conservation accidents. *Cognition, 3,* 341–380.

Modgil, S., Modgil, C., & Brown, G. 1983. *Jean Piaget: An interdisciplinary critique.* Boston: Routledge & Kegan Paul.

Neisser, U. 1967. *Cognitive psychology.* NY: Appleton-Century-Crofts.

Neisser, U. 1976. *Cognition and reality: Principles and implications of cognitive psychology.* San Francisco: Freeman.

Newell, A. & Simon, H.A. 1972. *Human problem solving.* Englewood Cliffs, NJ: Prentice-Hall.

Pascual-Leone, J. 1980. Constructive problems for constructive theories: The current relevance of Piaget's work and a critique of information-processing simulation psychology. In R.H. Kluwe & Y.H. Spada (Eds.). *Developmental models of thinking.* NY: Academic Press.

Patterson, F. 1978. Conversations with a gorilla. *National Geographic, 154,* 438–465.

Patterson, F. & Linden, E. 1981. *The education of Koko.* NY: Holt, Rinehart & Winston.

Pellegrino, J.W. 1985. Inductive reasoning ability. In R.J. Sternberg (Ed.). *Human abilities: An information processing approach.* San Francisco: Freeman.

Piaget, J. 1952. *The origins of intelligence in children.* M. Cook (Trans.). NY: International Universities Press.

Piaget, J. 1970. Piaget's theory. In P.H. Mussen (Ed.). *Carmichael's manual of child psychology* (3rd ed.). NY: Wiley.

Piaget, J. 1977. *The development of thought: Equilibrium of cognitive structures.* NY: Viking.

Premack, D. 1976. *Intelligence in ape and man.* Hillsdale, NJ: Erlbaum.

Premack, D. 1983. The codes of man and beasts. *The Behavioral and Brain Sciences, 6,* 125–167.

Rosch, E.H. 1973. On the internal structure of perceptual and semantic categories. In T.E. Moore (Ed.). *Cognitive development and the acquisition of language.* NY: Academic Press.

Rosch, E.H. 1975. Cognitive representations of semantic categories. *Journal of Experimental Psychology: General, 104,* 192–233.

Rosch, E.H. 1978. Principles of categorization. In E.H. Rosch & B.B. Lloyd (Eds.). *Cognition and categorization.* Hillsdale, NJ: Erlbaum.

Rosch, E.H. & Mervis, C.B. 1975. Family resemblances: Studies in the internal structure of categories. *Cognitive Psychology, 7,* 573–605.

Rumbaugh, D. (Ed.). 1977. *Language learning by a chimpanzee: The Lana project.* NY: Academic Press.

Saarinen, T.F. 1973. The use of projective technique in geographic research. In W.H. Ittelson (Ed.). *Environment and cognition.* NY: Seminar Press.

Selman, R.L. 1980. *The growth of interpersonal understanding: Developmental and clinical analyses.* NY: Academic Press.

Shannon, C.E. 1938. A symbolic analysis of relay and switching circuits. Master's thesis, Massachusetts Institute of Technology; published in *Transactions of the American Institute of Electrical Engineers, 57,* 1–11.

Shepard, R.N. 1978. The mental image. *American Psychologist, 33,* 125–137.

Shepard, R.N. & Metzler, J. 1971. Mental rotation of three-dimensional objects. *Science, 171,* 701–703.

Siegal, A.W., Allen, G.W., & Kirasic, K.C. 1979. Children's ability to make bidirectional distance comparisons: The advantage of thinking ahead. *Developmental Psychology, 15,* 656–665.

Siegal, L.S. 1978. The relationship of language and thought in the preoperational child: A reconsideration of non-verbal alternatives to Piagetian tasks. In S. Siegal & C. Brainerd (Eds.). *Alternatives to Piaget.* NY: Academic Press.

Simon, H.A. 1982. In M. Hunt. *The universe within.* NY: Simon & Schuster.

Simon, H.A. & Newell, A. 1958. Simulation of cognitive processes: A report on the Summer Research Training Institute, 1958. In Social Science Research Council. *Items, 12,* 37–40.

Sternberg, R.J. 1982. Who's intelligent? *Psychology Today, 16,* 30–39.

Terrace, H.S. 1979. *Nim: A chimpanzee who learned sign language.* NY: Knopf.

Terrace, H.S. 1979. How Nim Chimpsky changed my mind. *Psychology Today, 13,* 65–76.

Turing, A.M. 1936. On computable numbers, with an application to the Entscheidungs-problem. *Proceedings of the London Mathematical Society,* Series 2, *42,* 230–265.

Voss, J.F., Tyler, S.W., & Yengo, L.A. 1983. Individual differences in the solving of social science problems. In R.F. Dillon & R.R. Schmeck (Eds.). *Individual differences in cognition.* NY: Academic Press.

Wallas, G. 1926. *The art of thought.* NY: Harcourt Brace Jovanovich.

Whorf, B.L. 1956. Science and linguistics. In J.B. Carroll (Ed.). *Language, thought, and reality: Selected writings of Benjamin Lee Whorf.* Cambridge, MA: MIT Press.

Chapter 12

Anand, B.K. & Brobeck, J.R. 1951. Localization of a "feeding center" in the hypothalamus of the rat. *Proceedings of the Society for Experimental Biological Medicine, 77,* 323–324.

Atkinson, J.W. 1974. The mainspring of achievement oriented activity. In J.W. Atkinson & J.O. Raynor (Eds.). *Motivation and Achievement.* Washington: Winston.

Ayres, C.E. 1921. Instinct and capacity: I. The instinct of belief-in-instincts. *Journal of Philosophy, 18,* 561–566.

Ballenger, J.C. et al. 1983. Biochemical correlates of personality traits in normals: An exploratory study. *Personality and Individual Differences, 4,* 615–625.

Bemis, K.M. 1978. Current approaches to etiology and treatment of anorexia nervosa. *Psychological Bulletin, 85,* 593–617.

Bennett, W. & Gurin, J. 1982. *The dieter's dilemma.* NY: Basic Books.

Berkowitz, L. 1965. The concept of aggressive drive: Some additional considerations. In L. Berkowitz (Ed.). *Advances in experimental social psychology* (Vol. 2). NY: Academic Press.

Berlyne, D.E. 1950. Novelty and curiosity as determinants of exploratory behavior. *British Journal of Psychology, 41,* 68–80.

Berlyne, D.E. 1967. Reinforcement and arousal. In D. Levine (Ed.). *Nebraska Symposium on Motivation.* Lincoln: University of Nebraska Press.

Bernard, L.L. 1924. *Instinct.* NY: Holt, Rinehart & Winston.

Bindra, D. 1985. Motivation, the brain, and psychological theory. In Koch, S. & D.E. Leary (Eds.). *A century of psychology as science.* NY: McGraw-Hill.

Bjorntorp, P. 1972. Disturbances in the regulation of food intake. *Advances in Psychosomatic Medicine, 7,* 116–147.

Blankstein, K.R., Darte, E., & Donaldson, P. 1976. A further correlation of sensation seeking: Achieving tendency. *Perceptual and Motor Skills, 42,* 1251–1255.

Bradbard, M.R. & Endsley, R.C. 1983. The effects of sex-typed labeling on preschool children's information seeking and retention. *Sex Roles, 9,* 247–260.

Bradbard, M.R., Martin, C.L., Endsley, R.C. & Halverson, C.F. 1986. Influence of sex stereotypes on children's exploration and memory: A competence versus performance distinction. *Developmental Psychology, 22,* 481–486.

Bruch, H. 1961. Transformation of oral impulses in eating disorders: A conceptual approach. *Psychiatry Quarterly, 35,* 458–481.

Bruch, H. 1980. *The golden cage: The enigma of anorexia nervosa.* NY: Random House.

Busse, T.V. & Mansfield, R.S. 1984. Selected personality traits and achievement in male scientists. *Journal of Psychology, 116,* 117–131.

Butler, R. & Harlow, H.F. 1954. Persistence of visual exploration in monkeys. *Journal of Comparative Physiological Psychology, 47,* 258–263.

Cabanac, M. 1971. Physiological role of pleasure. *Science, 173,* 1103–1107.

Cannon, W.B. & Washburn, A.L. 1912. An explanation of hunger. *American Journal of Physiology, 29,* 441–454.

Carroll, E.N. & Zuckerman, M. 1977. Psychopathology and sensation seeking in "downers", "speeders", and "trippers": A study of the relationships between personality and drug choice. *International Journal of the Addiction, 12,* 591–601.

Clement, R. & Jonah, A. 1984. Field dependence, sensation seeking, and driving behavior. *Personality & Individual Differences, 5,* 87–93.

Cofer, C.N. & Appley, M.H. 1964. *Motivation: Theory and research.* NY: Wiley.

Cook, E.A. & Chandler, T.A. 1984. Is fear of success a motive? An attempt to answer criticisms. *Adolescence, 19,* 667–674.

Daitzman, R.J., Zuckerman, M., Sammelwitz, T., & Ganjam, V. 1978. Sensation seeking and gonadal hormones. *Journal of Biosocial Science, 10,* 401–408.

Dollard, J., Doob, L.W., Miller, N.E., Mowrer, O.H., & Sears, R.R. 1939. *Frustration and aggression.* New Haven: Yale University Press.

Earle, W.B., Giuliano, T., & Archer, R.L. 1983. Lonely at the top: The effect of power on information flow in the dyad. *Personality and Social Psychology Bulletin, 9,* 629–637.

Eron, L.D. 1980. Prescription for reduction of aggression. *American Psychologist, 35,* 244–252.

Fodor, E. 1985. The poser motive, group conflict and physiological arousal. *Journal of Personality and Social Psychology, 49,* 1408–1415.

Freud, S. 1915. Instincts and their vicissitudes. In S. Freud. *The collected papers.* NY: Collier.

Galizio, M. & Stein, F.S. 1983. Sensation seeking and drug choice. *International Journal of Addictions, 18,* 1039–1048.

Grossman, S.P. 1960. Eating and drinking elicited by direct adrenergic and cholinergic stimulation of hypothalamus. *Science, 132,* 301–302.

Gunnar, M.R., Snior, K., & Hartup, W.W. 1984. Peer presence and the exploratory behavior of eighteen- and thirty-month-old children. *Child Development, 55,* 1103–1107.

Harlow, H.F. 1953. Mice, monkeys, men, and motives. *Psychological Review, 6,* 23–32.

Harvey, J.C. & Katz, C. 1985. *If I'm so successful, why do I feel like a fake? The Imposter Phenomenon.* NY: St. Martin's Press.

Hebb, D. 1955. Drive and CNS. *Psychological Review, 62,* 243–253.

Henderson, B. 1984. Parents and exploration: The effect of context on individual differences in exploratory behavior. *Child Development, 55,* 1237–1245.

Henderson, B. & Moore, S. 1979. Measuring exploratory behavior in young children: A factor-analytic study. *Developmental Psychology, 15,* 113–119.

Herman, C.P., Olmsted, M.P., & Polivy, J. 1983. Obesity, externality, and susceptibility to social influence: An integrated analysis. *Journal of Personality and Social Psychology, 45,* 926–934.

Herman, C.P. & Polivy, J. 1975. Anxiety, restraint, and eating behavior. *Journal of Abnormal Psychology, 84,* 666–672.

Herman, C.P., Polivy, J., & Silver, R. 1979. Effects of an observer on eating behavior: The induction of "sensible" eating. *Journal of Personality, 47,* 85–99.

Hetherington, A.W. & Ranson, S.W. 1942. Hypothalamic lesions and adiposity in the rat. *Anatomical Record, 78,* 149–172.

Horner, M. 1968. Sex differences in achievement motivation and performance in competitive and non-competitive situations. Unpublished dissertation, University of Michigan.

Hochhauser, M. & Fowler, H. 1975. Cue effects of drive and reward as a function of discrimination difficulty: Evidence against the Yerkes-Dobson law. *Journal of Experimental Psychology: Animal Behavior Processes, 1,* 261–269.

Huesman, L.R., Eron, L.D., Lefkowitz, M.M., & Walder, L.O. 1985. Stability of aggression overtime and generations. *Developmental Psychology, 20,* 1120–1134.

Hull, C.L. 1943. *Principles of behavior.* NY: Appleton-Century.

Jacobs, K.W. & Kopperl, J.S. 1974. Psychological correlates of the mobility decision. *Bulletin of the Psychonomic Society, 3,* 330–332.

Keesey, R.E. & Powley, T.L. 1975. Hypothalamic regulation of body weight. *American Scientist, 63,* 558–565.

Kitchner, P. 1985. *Vaulting ambition: Sociobiology and the quest for human nature.* Cambridge, MA: MIT Press.

Kleinginna, P.R., Jr. & Kleinginna, A.M. 1981. A categorized list of emotion definitions, with suggestions for a consensual definition. *Motivation and Emotion, 5,* 355.

Kohn, P.M. & Coulas, J.T. 1985. Sensation seeking, augmenting-reducing, and the perceived and preferred effects of drugs. *Journal of Personality and Social Psychology, 48,* 99–106.

Kuhl, J. & Blankenship, V. 1979. The dynamic theory of achievement motivation: From episodic to dynamic thinking. *Psychological Review, 86,* 141–151.

Kukla, A. 1972. Attributional determinants of achievement-related behavior. *Journal of Personality and Social Psychology, 21,* 166–174.

Kukla, A. 1975. Preferences among impossibly difficult and trivially easy tasks: A revision of Atkinson's theory of choice. *Journal of Personality and Social Psychology, 32,* 338–345.

Lesnik-Oberstein, M. & Cohen, L. 1984. Cognitive style, sensation seeking, and assortative mating. *Journal of Personality and Social Psychology, 46,* 112–117.

Lipman-Blumen, J., Handley-Isaken, A., & Leavitt, H.J. 1983. Achieving styles in men and women: A model, an instrument, and some findings. In Spence, J.T. (Ed.). *Achievement and achievement motives: Psychological and sociological approaches.* San Francisco: Freeman.

Lorenz, K. 1966. *On aggression.* London: Methuen.

Lukert, B. 1982. Biology of obesity. In B.B. Wolman (Ed.). *Psychological aspects of obesity: A Handbook.* NY: Van Nostrand Reinhold.

Maslow, A.H. 1970. *Motivation and personality* (2nd ed.). NY: Harper & Row.

Masters, W.H. & Johnson, V.E. 1970. *Human sexual inadequacy.* Boston: Little, Brown.

May, R. 1972. *Power and innocence: A search for the sources of violence.* NY: Norton.

Mayer, J. 1953. Glucostatic mechanism of regulation of food intake. *New England Journal of Medicine, 249,* 13–16.

McClelland, D.C. 1975. *Power: The inner experience.* NY: Irvington.

McClelland, D.C. 1982. The need for power, sympathetic activation, and illness. *Motivation and Emotion, 6,* 31–39.

McClelland, D.C. 1984. *Achievement motivation.* NY: Free Press.

McClelland, D.C., Davis, W.N., Kalin, R., & Wanner, E. 1972. *The drinking man.* NY: Free Press.

McCormick, N.B., Brannigan, G.G., & LaPlante, M.N. 1984. Social desirability in the bedroom: Role of approval motivation in sexual relationships. *Sex Roles, 11,* 303–314.

McDougall, W. 1923. *An outline of psychology.* London: Methuen.

Meyer, W.U. 1968. In H. Heckhausen. Achievement motive research. *Nebraska Symposium on Motivation.* Lincoln: University of Nebraska Press.

Miller, N.E. 1960. Motivational effects of brain stimulation and drugs. *Federation Proceedings, 19,* 846–853.

Muuss, R.E. 1985. Adolescent eating disorder: Anorexia nervosa. *Adolescence, 79,* 525–536.

Nilsen, A.P. 1983. WIT: An alternative to force. *Etc., 40,* 445–450.

Nisbett, R.E. 1968. Taste, deprivation and weight determinants of eating behavior. *Journal of Personality and Social Psychology, 10,* 107–116.

Nisbet, R.E. & Kanouse, D. 1969. Obesity, food deprivation and supermarket shopping behavior. *Journal of Personality and Social Psychology, 12,* 289–294.

Nunnally, J.C. & Lemond, L.C. 1973. Exploratory behaviors in human development. *Advances in Child Development and Behavior, 8,* 59–109.

Pelletier, K.R. 1985. *Healthy people in unhealthy places.* NY: Delacorte.

Pope, H.G. & Hudson, J.I. 1984. *New hope for binge eaters: Advances in the understanding and treatment of bulimia.* NY: Harper & Row.

Redmond, D.E., Jr., Murphy, D.L., & Baulu, J. 1979. Platelet monoamine oxidase activity correlates with social affiliative and agonistic behaviors in normal rhesus monkeys. *Psychosomatic Medicine, 41,* 87–100.

Robbins, S. 1985. Lecture on anorexia, bulimia, and bulimarexia. April, Iowa Lutheran Hospital, Des Moines, IA.

Rodin, J. 1978. On social psychology and obesity research: A final note. *Personality and Social Psychology Bulletin, 4,* 185–186.

Rodin, J. 1982. Obesity: Why the losing battle? In B.B. Wolman (Ed.), *Psychological Aspects of Obesity: A Handbook.* NY: Van Nostrand Reinhold.

Rodin, J. 1983. Obesity: An update. Invited address, American Psychological Association, Anaheim, CA.

Rodin, J. 1985. Insulin levels, hunger, and food intake: An example of feedback loops in body weight reduction. *Health Psychology, 4,* 1–24.

Ross, L. 1974. Effects of manipulating the salience of food upon consumption by obese and normal eaters. In S. Schachter & J. Rodin (Eds.). *Obese humans and rats.* Hillsdale, NJ: Erlbaum/Halsted.

Rothwell, N.J. & Stock, M.J. 1979. Regulation of energy balance in two models of reversible obesity in the rat. *Journal of Comparative and Physiological Psychology, 93,* 1024–1034.

Ruderman, A.J. 1985. Dysphoric mood and overeating: A test of restraint theory's disinhibition hypothesis. *Journal of Abnormal Psychology, 94,* 78–85.

Satinder, K.P. & Black, A. 1984. Cannabis use and sensation-seeking orientation. *Journal of Psychology, 116,* 101–105.

Schachter, S. 1971a. Eat, eat. *Psychology Today, 5,* 45–47, 78–79.

Schachter, S. 1971b. *Emotion, obesity, and crime.* NY: Academic Press.

Schachter, S. 1971c. Some extraordinary facts about obese humans and rats. *American Psychologist, 26,* 129–144.

Schachter, S., Goldman, R., & Gordon, A. 1968. The effects of fear, food deprivation, and obesity on eating. *Journal of Personality and Social Psychology, 10,* 91–97.

Schachter, S. & Gross, L.P. 1968. Manipulated time and eating behavior. *Journal of Personality and Social Psychology, 10,* 98–106.

Schachter, S. & Rodin, J. 1980. *Obese humans and rats.* Hillsdale, NJ: Prentice-Hall.

Schooler, C., Zahn, T.P., Murphy, D.L., & Buchsbaum, M.S. 1978. Psychological correlates of monoamine oxidase in normals. *Journal of Nervous and Mental Diseases, 166,* 177–186.

Sheffield, F.D. & Roby, T.B. 1950. Reward value of a non-nutritive sweet taste. *Journal of Comparative and Physiological Psychology, 43,* 471–481.

Sheffield, F.D., Wulff, J.J., & Becker, R. 1951. Reward value of copulation without sex drive reduction. *Journal of Comparative and Physiological Psychology, 44,* 3–8.

Spencer, J.A. & Fremouw, W.J. 1979. Binge eating as a function of restraint and weight classification. *Journal of Abnormal Psychology, 88,* 262–267.

Spence, J.T. & Helmreich, R.L. 1983. Achievement-related motives and behaviors. In J.T. Spence (Ed.). *Achievement and achievement motives: Psychological and sociological approaches.* San Francisco: Freeman.

Spotts, J.V. & Shontz, F.C. 1984. Correlates of sensation seeking by heavy, chronic drug users. *Perceptual & Motor Skills, 58,* 427–435.

Stellar, E. 1954. The physiology of motivation. *Psychological Review, 61,* 5–22.

Striegel-Moore, R.H., Silberstein, L.R. & Rodin, J. 1986. Toward an understanding of risk factors for bulimia. *American Psychologist, 41,* 246–263.

Struble, J.H. & Steffens, A.B. 1975. Rapid insulin release after ingestion of a meal in the unanesthetized rat. *American Journal of Physiology, 229,* 1019–1022.

Stunkard, A., Coll, M., Lundquist, S., & Meyers, A. 1980. Obesity and eating style. *Archives of General Psychiatry, 37,* 1127–1129.

Sutker, P.B., Archer, R.P. & Allain, A.N. 1978. Drug abuse patterns, personality characteristics, and relationship with sex, race, and sensation-seeking. *Journal of Consulting and Counseling Psychology, 46,* 1374–1378.

Teitelbaum, P. 1957. Random and food-directed activity in hyperphagic and normal rats. *Journal of Comparative and Physiological Psychology, 50,* 486–490.

Teitelbaum, P. & Stellar, E. 1954. Recovery from the failure to eat, produced by hypothalamic lesions. *Science, 120,* 894–895.

Templeton, R.D. & Quigley, J.P. 1930. The action of insulin on the motility of the gastrointestinal tract. *American Journal of Physiology, 91,* 467–474.

Thompson, D.A. & Harsha, D.W. 1977. Hunger in humans induced by 2-Deoxy-D-Glucose: Glucoprivic control of taste preference and food intake. *Science, 198,* 1065–1068.

Tinbergen, N. 1969. *The study of instinct.* NY: Oxford University Press. (Originally published in 1951).

Tresemer, D.W. 1977. *Fear of success: An intriguing set of question.* NY: Plenum Press.

Vandenberg, B. 1984. Developmental features of exploration. *Developmental Psychology, 20,* 3–8.

Verloff, J., Reuman, D., & Feld, S. 1984. Motives in American men and women across the adult life span. *Developmental Psychology, 20,* 1112–1158.

Wellman, H.M., Somerville, S.C., Revelle, G.L., Haake, R.J. & Sophian, C. 1984. The development of comprehensive search skills. *Child Development, 55,* 472–481.

Williamson, D.A., Kelley, M.L., Davis, C.J., Ruggiero, L., & Blovin, D.C. 1985. Psychopathology of eating disorders: A controlled comparison of bulimic, obese, and normal subjects. *Journal of Consulting and Clinical Psychology, 53,* 161–166.

Wilson, E.O. 1975. *Sociobiology: The new synthesis.* Cambridge, MA: Harvard University Press.

Winter, D.G. 1973. *The power motive.* NY: Free Press.

Yerkes, R.M. & Dodson, J.D. 1908. The relation of strength of stimulus to rapidity of habit formation. *Journal of Comparative Neurology and Psychology, 18,* 459–482.

Zuckerman, M. 1979. *Sensation seeking: Beyond the optimal level of arousal.* Hillsdale, NJ: Erlbaum.

Zuckerman, M., Buchsbaum, M.S., & Murphy, D.L. 1980. Sensation-seeking and its biological correlates. *Psychological Bulletin, 88,* 187–214.

Zuckerman, M., Eysenck, S., & Eysenck, H.J. 1978. Sensation seeking in England and America: Cross-cultural age and sex comparisons. *Journal of Consulting and Clinical Psychology, 46,* 139–149.

Chapter 13

Abramovich, R. & Daly, E.M. 1979. Inferring the attributes of a situation from the facial expressions of peers. *Child Development, 50,* 586–589.

Aguilera, D.C. 1967. Relationship between physical contact and verbal interaction between nurses and patients. *Journal of Psychiatric Nursing, 5,* 5–21.

Anderson, C.D. 1981. Expression of affect and physiological response in psychosomatic patients. *Journal of Psychosomatic Research, 25,* 143–149.

Benson, H. 1976. Your innate asset for combating stress. In J. White & J. Fadiman (Eds.). *Relax: How you can feel better, reduce stress, and overcome tension.* NY: Confucian Press.

Bloom, F.E., Lazerson, A., & Hofstadter, L. 1985. *Brain, mind, and behavior.* NY: Freeman.

Buck, R. 1976. *Human motivation and emotion.* NY: Wiley.

Buck, R. 1981. Sex differences in psychophysiological responding and subjective experience: A comment. *Psychophysiology, 18,* 349–350.

Buck, R. 1984. *The communication of emotion.* NY: Guilford.

Cannon, W.B. 1929. *Bodily changes in pain, hunger, fear, and rage: An account of recent researches into the function of emotional excitement* (2nd ed.). NY: D. Appleton.

Crusco, A.H. & Wetzel, C.G. 1984. The Midas touch: The effects of interpersonal touch on restaurant tipping. *Personality and Social Psychology Bulletin, 10,* 512–517.

Darwin, C. 1955. *The expression of the emotions in man and animals.* NY: Philosophical Library. (Originally published 1872.)

De Paulo, B.M., Stone, J.I., & Lassiter, G.D. 1985. Telling ingratiating lies: Effects of target sex and target attractiveness on verbal and nonverbal success. *Journal of Personality and Social Psychology, 48,* 1191–1203.

Denzin, N.K. 1984. *On understanding emotion.* San Francisco: Jossey-Bass.

Ekman, P. 1972. Universal and cultural differences in facial expressions of emotion. In J. Cole (Ed.). *Nebraska Symposium on Motivation.* Lincoln, NE: University of Nebraska Press.

Ekman, P., Friesen, W.V., & Ellsworth, P. 1972. *Emotion in the human face.* NY: Pergamon.

Ekman, P. & Friesen, W.V. 1975. *Unmasking the face.* Englewood Cliffs, NJ: Prentice-Hall.

Ekman, P. 1980. Biological and cultural contributions to body and facial movement in the expression of emotion. In A. Rorty (Ed.), *Explaining Emotions.* Berkeley: University of California Press.

Ekman, P., Friesen, W.V., & Bear, J. 1984. The international language of gestures. *Psychology Today, 18,* 64–69.

Ekman, P. 1985. *Telling lies: Clues to deceit in marketplace, politics, and marriage.* NY: Norton.

Field, T., Woodson, R., Greenberg, R., & Cohen, D. 1982. Discrimination and imitation of facial expressions in neonates. *Science, 218,* 179–181.

Fisher, J.D., Rytting, M., & Heslin, R. 1976. Hands touching hands: Affective and evaluative effects of an interpersonal touch. *Sociometry, 39,* 416–421.

Flannery, J.G. 1977. Alexithymia: I. The communication of physical symptoms. *Psychotherapy and Psychosomatics, 28,* 133.

Frey, W.H., II, DeSota-Johnson, D., & McCall, J.T. 1981. Effect of stimulus on the chemical composition of human tears. *American Journal of Ophthalmology, 92,* 559–567.

Friedman, M. & Rosenman, R.H. 1974. *Type A behavior and your heart.* NY: Knopf.

Glass, D.C. 1977. *Behavior patterns, stress, and coronary disease.* Hillsdale, NJ: Erlbaum.

Gray, J.A. 1977. Drug effects on fear and frustration: Possible limbic site of action of minor tranquilizers. In L.L. Iversen, S.D. Iversen, & S.H. Snyder (Eds.). *Handbook of Psychopharmacology* (Vol. 8), 433–529. NY: Plenum.

Hall, E.T. 1966. *The hidden dimension.* Garden City, NY: Doubleday.

Hare, R.D. & Craigen, D. 1974. Psychopathy and physiological activity in a mixed-motive game situation. *Psychophysiology, 11,* 197–206.

Heilman, K.M. & Satz, P. 1983. *Neuropsychology of human emotion.* NY: Guilford.

Holmes, T. & Masuda, M. 1974. Life changes and illness susceptibility. In B.S. Dohrenwend & B.P. Dohrenwend (Eds.). *Stressful life events: Their nature and effects.* NY: Wiley.

Holmes, T.H. & Rahe, R.H. 1967. The social readjustment rating scale. *Journal of Psychosomatic Research, 11,* 213–218.

Honts, C.R., Hodes, R.L., & Raskin, D.C. 1985. Effects of physical countermeasures on the physiological detection of deception. *Journal of Applied Psychology, 70,* 177–187.

Izard, C.E. 1971. *The face of emotion.* NY: Appleton-Century-Crofts.

Izard, C.E. 1977. *Human emotions.* NY: Plenum.

Izard, C.E. (Ed.). 1982. *Measuring emotions in infants and children.* NY: Cambridge University Press.

James, W. 1894. The physical basis of emotion. *Psychological Review, 1,* 516–529.

Johnson, R.N. 1972. *Aggression in man and animals.* Philadelphia: Saunders.

Katz, R. & Wykes, T. 1985. The psychological difference between temporally predictable and unpredictable stressful events: Evidence for information control theories. *Journal of Personality and Social Psychology, 48,* 781–790.

Kotulak, R. 1985. The language that has no words. *Des Moines Register,* June 11.

Lazarus, R.S. 1982. Thoughts on the relations between emotion and cognition. *American Psychologist, 37,* 1019–1024.

Ognibene, P.J. 1985. Unfair and dangerous to rely on lie detector. *Des Moines Register,* February 10, 1C and 3C.

Papez, J.W. 1937. A proposed mechanism of emotion. *Archives of Neurology and Psychiatry, 38,* 725–744.

Pines, A.M., Aaronson, E., & Kafry, D. 1981. *Burnout: From tedium to personal growth.* NY: Macmillan.

Pluchik, R. 1984. Emotions: A general psychoevolutionary theory. In K. Scherer & P. Ekman (Eds.). *Approaches to emotion.* Hillsdale, NJ: Lawrence Erlbaum.

Reisenzein, R. 1983. The Schachter theory of emotion: Two decades later. *Psychological Bulletin, 94,* 239–264.

Rosvold, H.E., Mirsh, A.F., & Pribram, K.H. 1954. Influence in amygdalectomy on social behavior in monkeys. *Journal of Comparative and Physiological Psychology, 47,* 173–178.

Russell, J.A. & Bullock, M. 1985. Multidimensional scaling of emotional facial expressions: Similarity from preschoolers to adults. *Journal of Personality and Social Psychology, 48,* 1290–1298.

Schachter, S. & Singer, J.E. 1962. Cognitive, social, and physiological determinants of emotional state. *Psychological Review, 69,* 379–399.

Selye, H. 1978a. *The stress of life.* NY: McGraw-Hill.

Selye, H. 1978b. They all looked sick to me. *Human Nature, 1,* 58–63.

Simons, J.A. & Irwin, D.B. 1983. Relaxation by sensory awareness (Cassette Recording). Des Moines, IA: Developmental Educational Learning Institute.

Sobel, S.S. 1976a. Differential Relaxation. In J. White, & J. Fadiman (Eds.). *Relax: How you can feel better, reduce stress, and overcome tension.* NY: Confucian.

Sobei, S.S. 1976b. Shaking. In J. White & James Fadiman (Eds.). *Relax: How you can feel better, reduce stress, and overcome tension.* NY: Confucian.

Tierney, J. 1985. Type A's maybe now you can relax. *Science, 6,* 12.

Tomkins, S. 1962. *Affect, imagery, and consciousness: The positive affects* (Vol. 1). NY: Springer.

Tomkins, S. 1963. *Affect, imagery, and consciousness: The negative affects* (Vol. 2). NY: Springer.

Travis, C. 1982. *Anger: The misunderstood emotion.* NY: Simon & Schuster.

Tubesing, N.L. & Tubesing, D.A. (Eds.). 1983. *Structured exercises in stress management* (Vol. 1). Duluth, MN: Whole Person Press.

Waid, W.M., Orne, M.T., & Wilson, S.K. 1979a. Effects of level of socialization on electrodermal detection of deception. *Psychophysiology, 16,* 15–22.

Waid, W.M., Orne, M.T., & Wilson, S.K. 1979b. Socialization, awareness, and the electrodermal response to deception and self-disclosure. *Journal of Abnormal Psychology, 88,* 663–666.

Waid, W.M. & Orne, M.T. 1982. The physiological detection of deception. *American Scientist, 70,* 402–409.

Wetzel, J. 1984. *Clinical handbook of depression.* NY: Gardner.

Wolff, H.H. 1977. The concept of alexithymia and the future of psychosomatic research. *Psychotherapy and Psychosomatics, 28,* 376.

Woolfolk, R. & Richardson, F. 1978. *Stress, sanity, and survival.* NY: Signet.

Zajonc, R.B. 1984. On the primacy of affect. *American Psychologist, 39,* 117–123.

Zuckerman, M. & Przewuzman, S. 1979. Decoding and encoding facial expressions in preschool-age children. *Environmental Psychology and Nonverbal Behavior, 3,* 147–163.

Chapter 14

Adler, A. 1927. *The practice and theory of individual psychology.* NY: Harcourt, Brace & World.

Adler, A. 1928. *Understanding human nature.* London: Allen & Unwin.

Adler, A. 1929a. *Problems of neurosis.* London: Kegan Paul.

Adler, A. 1929b. *The science of living.* NY: Greenberg.

Adler, A. 1931. *What life should mean to you.* Boston: Little, Brown.

Adler, A. 1939. *Social interest.* NY: Putnam.

Adler, A. 1956. In H.L. Ansbacher & R. Ansbacher (Eds.). *The individual psychology of Alfred Adler: A systematic presentation in selections from his writing.* NY: Harper & Row.

Adler, A. 1964. In H.L. Ansbacher & R. Ansbacher (Eds.). *Superiority and social interest: A collection of later writings.* NY: Viking.

Allport, G.W. 1961. *Pattern and growth in personality.* NY: Holt, Rinehart & Winston.

Ansbacher, H.L. 1985. The significance of Alfred Adler for the concept of narcissism. *American Journal of Psychiatry, 142,* 203–207.

Barnes, G.E., Malamuth, N.M. & Check, J.V. 1984. Personality and sexuality. *Personality & Individual Differences, 5,* 159–172.

Bettelheim, B. 1983. *Freud and man's soul.* NY: Alfred A. Knopf.

Blanck, G. 1984. The complete oedipus complex. *International Journal of Psycho-Analysis, 65,* 331–339.

Bloom, B.S. 1964. *Stability and change in human characteristics.* NY: Wiley.

Cattell, R.B. 1950. *Personality, a systematic theoretical and factual study.* NY: McGraw-Hill.

Cattell, R.B. 1965. *The scientific analysis of personality.* Baltimore, MD: Penguin.

Cattell, R.B. 1979. *Personality and learning theory: Vol. 1. The structure of personality and its environment.* NY: Springer.

Cattell, R.B. 1984. The voyage of a laboratory, 1928–1984. *Multivariate Behavioral Research, 19,* 121–174.

Cicirelli, V.G. 1978. The relationship of sibling structure to intellectual abilities and achievement. *Review of Educational Research, 48,* 365–379.

Collins, J.E. & Cunningham, M.R. 1986. Induced and preexisting mood states: An interactive influence on the behavior of extraverts and introverts. Midwest Psychological Association.

Corcoran, D.W.J. 1964. The relation between introversion and salivation. *American Journal of Psychology, 77,* 298–300.

Engler, B. 1985. *Personality theories: An introduction* (2nd ed.). Boston: Houghton Mifflin.

Ernst, E., & Angst, J. 1983. *Birth order: Its influence on personality.* Berlin: Springer-Velag.

Eysenck, H.J. 1953. *The structure of human personality.* NY: Wiley.

Eysenck, H.J. 1967. *The biological basis of personality.* Springfield, Ill: Charles C. Thomas.

Eysenck, H.J. 1970. *The structure of human personality* (3rd ed.). London: Methuen.

Eysenck, H.J. 1973. *Eysenck on extraversion.* NY: Wiley.

Eysenck, H.J. 1982. *Personality, genetics, and behavior.* NY: Springer-Verlag.

Eysenck, H.J. 1984. Cattell and the theory of personality. *Multivariate Behavioral Research, 19,* 323–336.

Eysenck, H.J. & Eysenck, S.B.G. 1968. *Manual for the Eysenck Personality Inventory.* San Diego: Educational & Industrial Testing Service.

Faraday, A. 1972. *Dream power.* NY: Coward.

Feldstein, S. & Sloan, B. 1984. Actual and stereotyped speech tempos of extraverts and introverts. *Journal of Personality, 52,* 188–204.

Finn, S.E. 1986. Stability of personality self-ratings over 30 years: Evidence for an age/cohort interaction. *Journal of Personality and Social Psychology, 50,* 813–818.

Forer, L.K. & Still, H. 1976. *The birth order factor: How your personality is influenced by your place in the family.* NY: McKay.

Freud, S. 1900. The interpretation of dreams. In J. Strachey (Ed. & Trans.). *The standard edition of the complete psychological works of Sigmund Freud* (Vol. 4 & 5). London: Hogarth Press.

Freud, S. 1901. The psychopathology of everyday life. In J. Strachey (Ed. & Trans.). *The standard edition of the complete psychological works of Sigmund Freud* (Vol. 6). London: Hogarth Press.

Freud, S. 1905a. Fragment of an analysis of a case of hysteria. In J. Strachey (Ed. & Trans.). *The standard edition of the complete psychological works of Sigmund Freud* (Vol. 8). London: Hogarth Press.

Freud, S. 1905b. Three essays on the theory of sexuality. In J. Strachey (Ed. & Trans.). *The standard edition of the complete psychological works of Sigmund Freud* (Vol. 7). London: Hogarth Press.

Freud, S. 1910. Leonardo Da Vinci and a memory of his childhood. In J. Strachey (Ed. & Trans.). *The standard edition of the complete psychological works of Sigmund Freud* (Vol. 11). London: Hogarth Press.

Freud, S. 1913. Totem and Taboo. In J. Strachey. (Ed. & Trans.). *The standard edition of the complete psychological works of Sigmund Freud* (Vol. 13). London: Hogarth Press.

Freud, S. 1923. *Introductory lectures on psycho-analysis.* J. Riviera (Trans.). London: Allen & Unwin.

Freud, S. 1925. Some psychical consequences of the anatomical distinction between the sexes. In J. Strachey (Ed. & Trans.). *The standard edition of the complete psychological works of Sigmund Freud* (Vol. 22). London: Hogarth Press.

Freud, S. 1930. Civilization and its discontents. In J. Strachey (Ed. & Trans.). *The standard edition of the complete psychological works of Sigmund Freud.* London: Hogarth Press.

Freud, S. 1933. New introductory lectures on psycho-analysis. In J. Strachey (Ed. & Trans.). *The standard edition of the complete psychological works of Sigmund Freud.* London: Hogarth Press.

Freud, S. 1937. Analysis terminable and interminable. In J. Strachey. (Ed. & Trans.). *The standard edition of the complete psychological works of Sigmund Freud.* London: Hogarth Press.

Freud, S. 1940. Some elementary lessons in psycho-analysis. In J. Strachey. (Ed. & Trans.). *The standard edition of the complete psychological works of Sigmund Freud* (vol. 23). London: Hogarth Press.

Furnham, S. 1984. Personality and values. *Personality & Individual Differences, 5,* 483–485.

Garma, A. 1978. *The psychoanalysis of dreams.* Northvale, NJ: Aronson.

Hall, C.S. 1954. *A primer of Freudian psychology.* NY: New American Library.

Hall, C.S. & Norby, V.J. 1973. *A primer of Jungian psychology.* NY: New American Library.

Hyde, J.S. & Rosenberg, B.G. 1980. *Half the human experience: The psychology of women* (2nd ed.). Lexington, MA: Heath.

Johnson, G.B. 1966. Penis envy or pencil needing? *Psychological Reports, 19,* 758.

Jung, C.G. 1933a. *Modern man in search of a soul.* NY: Harcourt, Brace.

Jung, C.G. 1933b. *Psychological types.* NY: Harcourt Brace.

Jung, C.G. 1961. *Memories, dreams, and reflections.* NY: Random House.

Jung, C.G. 1964. *Man and his symbols.* NY: Doubleday.

Jung, C.G. 1973. In G. Alder (Ed.). *Letters.* Princeton, NJ: Princeton University Press.

Kayton, L. & Borge, G.F. 1967. Birth order and the obsessive-compulsive character. *Archives of General Psychiatry, 17,* 751–754.

Kidwell, J.S. 1981. Number of siblings, sibling spacing, sex and birth order: Their effects on perceived parent-adolescent relationships. *Journal of Marriage and the Family, 43,* 50–64.

Maddi, S.R. 1972. *Personality theories: A comparative analysis.* Homewood, IL: Dorsey.

Masson, J.M. 1984a. *The assault on truth: Freud's suppression of the seduction theory.* NY: Farrar, Straus & Giroux.

Masson, J.M. 1984b. Freud and the seduction theory. *The Atlantic Monthly,* February, 33–60.

Miller, N. & Maruyama, G. 1976. Ordinal position and peer popularity. *Journal of Personality and Social Psychology, 33,* 123–131.

Mischel, W. 1968. *Personality and assessment.* NY: Wiley.

Mischel, W. 1973. Toward a cognitive social learning reconceptualization of personality. *Psychological Review, 80,* 252–283.

Mischel, W. 1984. Convergences and challenges in the search for consistency. *American Psychologist, 39,* 351–364.

Mischel, W. 1985. Looking for personality. In S. Koch & D.E. Leary (Ed.). *A century of psychology as science.* NY: McGraw-Hill.

Mitchell, J. 1974. *Psychoanalysis and feminism.* NY: Pantheon.

Moss, H.A. & Susman, E.J. 1980. Constancy and change in personality development. In O.G. Brim & J. Kagan (Eds.). *Constancy and change in human development.* Cambridge, MA: Harvard University Press.

Oberlander, M. & Jenkin, N. 1967. Birth order and academic achievement. *Journal of Individual Psychology, 23,* 103–109.

Palmer, R.D. 1966. Birth order and identification. *Journal of Consulting Psychology, 30,* 129–135.

Paulhus, D. & Shaffer, D.R. 1981. Sex differences in the impact of number of older and number of younger siblings on scholastic aptitude. *Social Psychology Quarterly, 44,* 363–368.

Pearce-McCall, D. & Newman, J.P. 1986. Expectation of success following noncontingent punishment in introverts and extraverts. *Journal of Personality and Social Psychology, 50,* 439–446.

Prochaska, J.M. & Prochaska, J.O. 1985. Children's views of the causes and "cures" of sibling rivalry. *Child Welfare, 64,* 427–433.

Rim, Y. 1984. Importance of values according to personality, intelligence and sex. *Personality & Individual Differences, 5,* 237–239.

Scroggs, J.R. 1985. *Key ideas in personality theory.* St. Paul, MN: West.

Sheldon, W.H. 1970. *The varieties of temperament: A psychology of constitutional differences.* NY: Harper. (First printed 1942)

Sherman, J.A. 1971. *On the psychology of women: A survey of empirical studies.* Springfield, IL: Charles C. Thomas.

Singer, J.E. & Lamb, P.F. 1966. Social concern, body size and birth order. *Journal of Social Psychology, 68,* 143–151.

Steelman, L. & Powell, B. 1985. The social and academic consequences of birth order: Real, artifactual, or both? *Journal of Marriage and the Family,* 117–124.

Tolman, W. 1964. Choices of marriage partners by men coming from monosexual sibling configurations. *British Journal of Medical Psychology, 37,* 43–46.

Travis, C. 1984. Assault on Freud. *Discover, 5,* 45–51.

Whitmont, E.C. 1978. Jungian approach. In J.L. Fosshage & C.A. Loew (Eds.). *Dream interpretation: A comparative study.* NY: SP Medical & Scientific Books.

Wiggins, J.S. 1984. Cattell's system from the perspective of mainstream personality theory. *Multivariate Behavioral Research, 19,* 176–190.

Williams, J.H. 1977. *Psychology of women: Behavior in a biosocial context.* NY: Norton.

Wuebben, P.L. 1967. Honesty of subjects and birth order. *Journal of Personality and Social Psychology, 5,* 350–352.

Young, P.A., Eaves, L.J. & Eysenck, H.J. 1980. Intergenerational stability and change in the causes of variation in personality. *Personality & Individual Differences, 1,* 35–55.

Zajonc, R.B. 1976. Family configuration and intelligence. *Science, 192,* 227–236.

Zajonc, R.B., Markus, H., & Markus, G. 1979. The birth order puzzle. *Journal of Personality and Social Psychology, 37,* 1325–1341.

Zakay, D., Lomranz, J., & Kaziniz, M. 1984. Extraversion-introversion and time perception. *Personality & Individual Differences, 5,* 237–239.

Chapter 15

Anderson, W. 1973. Fritz Perls revisited. *Human Behavior, 2,* 16–23.

Bandura, A. 1969. *Principles of behavior modification.* NY: Holt, Rinehart & Winston.

Bandura, A. 1977. *Social learning theory.* Englewood Cliffs, NJ: Prentice-Hall.

Bandura, A. 1978. The self system in reciprocal determinism. *American Psychologist, 33,* 345.

Frager, R. & Fadiman, J. 1984. *Personality and personal growth* (2nd ed.). NY: Harper & Row.

Guttman, N. 1977. On Skinner and Hull: A reminiscence and projection. *American Psychologist, 32,* 321–328.

Henle, M. 1985. Rediscovering Gestalt psychology. In S. Koch & D.E. Leary (Eds.). *A century of psychology as science.* NY: McGraw-Hill.

Katovsky, W. 1976. Social-learning theory analyses of maladjusted behavior. In W. Katkovsky & L. Gorlow, (Eds.). *The psychology of maladjustment: Current concepts and applications* (3rd ed.). NY: McGraw-Hill.

Kendler, H.H. 1985. Behaviorism and psychology. In S. Koch & D.E. Leary (Eds.). *A century of psychology as science.* NY: McGraw-Hill.

MacIntyre, A. 1985. How psychology makes itself true—or false. In S. Koch & D.E. Leary (Eds.). *A century of psychology as science.* NY: McGraw-Hill.

Mahrer, A.R. 1956. The role of expectancy in delayed reinforcement. *Journal of Experimental Psychology, 52,* 101–106.

Maslow, A. 1968. *Toward a psychology of being* (2nd ed.). NY: Van Nostrand.

Maslow, A. 1970. *Motivation and personality* (rev. ed.). NY: Harper & Row.

Maslow, A. 1971. *The farther reaches of human nature.* NY: Van Nostrand.

May, R. 1953. *Man's search for himself.* NY: Norton.

May, R. 1967. *Psychology and the human dilemma.* NY: Van Nostrand Reinhold.

May, R. 1977. *The meaning of anxiety.* NY: Norton.

May, R. 1981. *Freedom and destiny.* NY: Norton.

May, R. 1983. *The discovery of being.* NY: Norton.

May, R., Rogers, C., Maslow, A. et al. 1986. *Politics and innocence: A humanistic debate.* NY: Norton.

Perls, F.S. 1969a. *Gestalt therapy verbatim.* Lafayette, CA: Real People Press.

Perls, F.S. 1969b. *In and out of the garbage pail.* Lafayette, CA: Real People Press.

Perls, F.S. 1970. Four lectures. In J. Fagan & I.L. Shephard (Eds.). *Gestalt therapy now.* NY: Science & Behavior Books.

Perls, F.S. 1973. *The Gestalt approach: Eyewitness to therapy.* Ben Lomond, CA: Science & Behavior Books.

Perls, F.S., Hefferline, R.F. & Goodman, P. 1951. *Gestalt therapy.* NY: Dell.

Rogers, C.R. 1951. *Client-centered therapy: Its current practice, implications and the theory.* Boston: Houghton Mifflin.

Rogers, C.R. 1961. *On becoming a person: A therapist's view of psychotherapy.* Boston: Houghton Mifflin.

Rogers, C.R. 1969. *Freedom to learn.* Columbus, OH: Merrill.

Rogers, C.R. 1980. *A way of being.* Boston: Houghton Mifflin.

Rotter, J.B. 1954. *Social learning and clinical psychology.* Englewood Cliffs, NJ: Prentice-Hall.

Rotter, J.B. 1982. *The development and application of social learning theory: Selected papers.* NY: Praeger.

Scroggs, J.R. 1985. *Key ideas in personality theory.* St. Paul, MN: West.

Skinner, B.F. 1948. *Walden two.* NY: Macmillan.

Skinner, B.F. 1953. *Science and human behavior.* NY: Macmillan.

Skinner, B.F. 1958. Teaching machine. *Science, 128,* 969–977.

Skinner, B.F. 1967a. Autobiography. In E.G. Boring & G. Lindzey (Eds.). *History of psychology in autobiography* (Vol. 5). NY: Appleton-Century-Crofts.

Skinner, B.F. 1967b. An interview with Mr. Behaviorist: B.F. Skinner. *Psychology Today, 1,* 20–25, 68–71.

Skinner, B.F. 1971. *Beyond freedom and dignity.* NY: Knopf.

Skinner, B.F. 1974. *About behaviorism.* NY: Knopf.

Skinner, B.F. 1983. *A matter of consequences.* NY: Knopf.

Suzuki, S. 1970. *Zen mind, beginner's mind.* NY: Weatherhill.

Chapter 16

Anderson, J.K. 1982. *Genetic engineering.* Grand Rapids, MI: Zondervan.

Andrews, L.B. 1984. *New conceptions.* NY: St. Martin's Press.

Apgar, V. 1953. A proposal for a new method of evaluation of a newborn infant. *Anesthesia and Analgesia . . . Current Research, 32,* 260–267.

Apgar, V. & Beck, J. 1973. *Is my baby all right?* NY: Trident.

Azrin, N.H. & Foxx, R. 1981. *Toilet training in less than a day* (2nd ed.). NY: Pocket Books.

Bem, S.L. 1985. Androgeny and gender schema theory: A conceptual and empirical integration. *Nebraska Symposium on Motivation, 32,* 179–226.

Benson, P. & Williams, D. 1986. *Early adolescence: The quicksilver years.* San Francisco: Harper & Row.

Blasi, A. 1980. Bridging moral cognition and moral action: A critical review of the literature. *Psychological Bulletin, 88,* 1–45.

Bloom, B.S. 1985. *Developing talent in young people.* NY: Ballentine.

Brooks-Gunn, J. & Petersen, A.C. 1983. *Girls at puberty: Biological and psychosocial perspectives.* NY: Plenum Press.

Brown, R. 1973. *A first language: The early stages.* Cambridge, MA: Harvard University Press.

Bustillo, M., Buster, J.E., Cohen, S.W., Hamilton, F., Thorneycroft, I.H., Simon, J.A., Rodi, I.A., Boyers, S., Marshall, J.R., Louw, J.A., Seed, R., and Seed, R. 1984. Delivery of a healthy infant following nonsurgical ovum transfer. *Journal of the American Medical Association, 251,* 889.

Cowan, P.A. 1978. *Piaget with feeling: Cognitive, social and emotional dimensions.* NY: Holt, Rinehart, & Winston.

Doman, G. 1964. *How to teach your child to read.* NY: Random House.

Edwards, C.P. 1982. Moral development in comparative cultural perspective. In D.A. Wagner & H.W. Stevenson (Eds.). *Cultural perspectives on child development.* San Francisco: Freeman.

Ehrhardt, A. & Baker, S.W. 1974. Fetal androgens, human central nervous system differentiation, and behavior sex differences. In R.C. Friedman, R.M. Richart, & R.L. Vande Wiele (Eds.). *Sex differences in behavior.* NY: Wiley.

Ehrhardt, A. & Money, J. 1967. Progestin induced hermaphroditism: I.Q. and psychosocial identity. *Journal of Sexual Research, 3,* 83–100.

Elkind, D. 1981. *The hurried child.* Reading, MA: Addison-Wesley.

Elkind, D. 1984. *All grown up and no place to go.* Reading, MA: Addison-Wesley.

Gilligan, C. 1982. *In a different voice: Psychological theory and women's development.* Cambridge, MA: Harvard University Press.

Hampson, J.L. 1965. Determinants of psychosexual orientation. In F.A. Beach (Ed.). *Sex and Behavior.* NY: Wiley.

Harlow, H.F. & Zimmerman, R.R. 1959. Affectional responses in the infant monkey. *Science, 130,* 431–432.

Harrison, R.G. 1978. *Clinical embryology.* NY: Academic Press.

Hartshorne, H., & May, M.A. 1928–1930. *Moral studies in the nature of character: Vol. 1. Studies in deceit; Vol. 2. Studies in self control; Vol. 3. Studies in the organization of character.* NY: Macmillan.

Hays, D.P. 1981. Teratogenesis: A review of the basic principles with a discussion of selected agents: Part III. *Drug Intell. Clinical Pharm., 15,* 639–640.

Hohlstein, R.R. 1982. The development of prehension in normal infants. *American Journal of Occupational Therapy, 36,* 170–176.

Jones, M.C. 1957. The late careers of boys who were early—or late—maturing. *Child Development, 28,* 115–128.

Kagan, J. 1984. *The nature of the child.* NY: Basic Books.

Klaus, M.H. & Kennell, J.H. 1976. *Maternal-infant bonding.* St. Louis: Mosby.

Kohlberg, L. 1966. A cognitive-developmental analysis of children's sex-role concepts and attitudes. In E.E. Maccoby (Ed.). *The development of sex differences.* Stanford, CA: Stanford University Press.

Kohlberg, L. 1976. Moral stages and moralization. The cognitive-developmental approach. In T. Lickona (Ed.). *Moral development and behavior.* NY: Holt, Rinehart & Winston.

Kohlberg, L. 1981. *The philosophy of moral development: Essays on moral development* (Vol. I). San Francisco: Harper & Row.

Kohlberg, L. 1984. *The philosophy of moral development: Essays on moral development* (Vol. II). San Francisco: Harper & Row.

Kohlberg, L. 1986. *The stages of ethical development from childhood through old age.* San Francisco: Harper & Row.

Kohlberg, L. & Ullian, D.Z. 1974. Stages in the development of psychosexual concepts and attitudes. In R.C. Friedman, R.M. Richart, & R.L. Vande Wiele (Eds.). *Sex differences in behavior.* NY: Wiley.

Kupfersmid, J. & Wonderly, D. 1980. Moral maturity and behavior: Failure to find a link. *Journal of Youth and Adolescence, 9,* 249–261.

Lamb, M.E. 1982. Second thoughts on first touch. *Psychology Today, 16,* 9–11.

Langway, L. 1983. Bringing up superbaby. *Newsweek,* March 28, 62–68.

Lou, H.O.C. 1982. *Developmental neurology.* NY: Raven.

Maccoby, E.E. & Jacklin, C.N. 1974. *The psychology of sex differences.* Stanford, CA: Stanford University Press.

March of Dimes. 1984. *Genetic counseling.* White Plains, NY: March of Dimes Birth Defects Foundation.

Marcia, J.E. 1966. Development and validation of ego identity status. *Journal of Personality and Social Psychology, 3,* 551–558.

Marcia, J.E. 1979 (June). Identity status in late adolescence: Description and some clinical implications. Address given at a symposium on identity development at Rijksuniversitat Groningen, The Netherlands.

Marcia, J.E. 1980. Identity in adolescence. In J. Adelson (Ed.). *Handbook of adolescent psychology.* NY: Wiley.

Money, J. & Ehrhardt, A. 1972. *Man & woman, boy & girl.* Baltimore: Johns Hopkins.

Myers, B.J. 1984a. Mother-infant bonding: The status of the critical period hypothesis. *Developmental Review, 4,* 240–274.

Myers, B.J. 1984b. Mother-infant bonding: Rejoiner to Kennel and Klaus. *Developmental Review, 4,* 283–288.

Nilsson, L. 1977. *A child is born.* NY: Dell Publishing.

Papalia, D. & Olds, S.W. 1986. *Human Development* (3rd ed.). NY: McGraw-Hill.

Peskin, H. 1973. Influence of the developmental schedule of puberty on learning and ego functioning. *Journal of Youth and Adolescence, 2,* 273–290.

Piaget, J. 1932. *The moral judgement of the child.* NY: Harcourt, Brace & World.

Scarr, S. 1984. *Mother care/other care.* NY: Basic Books.

Siegel, O. 1982. Personality development in adolescence. In B.B. Wolman (Ed.). *Handbook of developmental psychology.* Englewood Cliffs, NJ: Prentice-Hall.

Snarey, J.R. 1985. Cross-cultural universality of social-moral development: A critical review of Kohlbergian research. *Psychological Bulletin, 97,* 202–233.

Thomas, A. & Chess, S. 1977. *Temperament and development.* NY: Brunner/Mazel.

U.S. Bureau of the Census. 1983. *Statistical abstract of the United States: 1983* (103rd ed.). Washington: U.S. Bureau of the Census.

White, B.L. 1984. *The first three years of life: A guide to physical, emotional & intellectual growth* (rev. ed.). Englewood Cliffs, NJ: Prentice-Hall.

Chapter 17

Albrecht, S.L. 1980. Reactions and adjustments to divorce: Differences in experiences of males and females. *Family Relations, 29,* 59–68.

Allan, R.F. & Linde, S. 1981. *Lifegain.* Morristown, NJ: Human Resources Institute.

Atchley, R.C. 1975. The life course, age grading, and age-linked demands for decision making. In N. Datan & L. Ginsberg (Eds.). *Life-span developmental psychology: Normative life crises.* NY: Academic Press.

Baumrind, D. 1971. Current patterns of parental authority. *Developmental Psychology Monographs, 4,* (1, Pt. 2).

Becker, B.J. 1983. *Item characteristics and sex differences on the SAT-M for mathematically able youths.* Presented at the annual meeting of the American Educational Research Association, Montreal.

Belloc, N.B. & Breslow, L. 1972. Relationship of physical health status and health practices. *Preventive Medicine, 1,* 409–421.

Bem, S.L. 1974. The measurement of psychological androgyny. *Journal of Consulting and Clinical Psychology, 42,* 155–162.

Bem, S.L. 1976. Probing the promise of androgyny. In A.G. Kaplan & J.P. Bean (Eds.). *Beyond sex-role stereotypes: Readings toward a psychology of androgyny.* Boston: Little, Brown.

Benbow, C.P. & Stanley, J.C. 1980. Sex differences in mathematical ability: Fact or artifact? *Science, 210,* 1262–1264.

Benbow, C.P. & Stanley, J.C. 1983. Sex differences in mathematical reasoning ability: More facts. *Science, 222,* 1029–1031.

Birren, J.E. & Renner, J. 1980. Concepts and issues of mental health and aging. In J.E. Birren & R.B. Sloane (Eds.). *Handbook of mental health and aging.* Englewood Cliffs, NJ: Prentice-Hall.

Blood, B. & Blood, M. 1978. *Marriage* (3rd ed.). NY: Free Press.

Blumstein, P. & Schwartz, P. 1983. *American couples: Money, work, sex.* NY: Morrow.

Blythe, R. 1979. *The view in winter: Reflections on old age.* NY: Harcourt Brace Javonovich.

Brecher, E.M. & the Editors of Consumers Reports Books. 1984. *Love, sex, and aging: A Consumers Union Report.* Boston: Little, Brown.

Butler, R.N. & Lewis, M.I. 1982. *Aging and mental health* (2nd ed.). St. Louis: C.V. Mosby.

Campbell, A., Converse, P.E., & Rogers, W.L. 1975. *The quality of American life: Perceptions, evaluations, and satisfactions.* NY: Russell Sage.

Campbell, F.L., Townes, B.D., & Beach, L.R. 1982. Motivational bases of childbearing decisions. In G.L. Fox (Ed.). *The childbearing decision: Fertility, attitudes, and behavior.* Beverly Hills, CA: Sage.

Cargan, L. 1981. Singles: An examination of two stereotypes. *Family Relations, 30,* 377–385.

Cattell, R.B. 1965. *The scientific analysis of personality.* Baltimore: Penguin Books.

Deaux, K. 1976. *The behavior of women and men.* Monterey, CA: Brooks/Cole.

Deaux, K. 1985. Sex and gender. *Annual Review of Psychology, 36,* 49–81.

Erbes, J.T. & Hedderson, J.J.C. 1984. A longitudinal examination of the separation/divorce process. *Journal of Marriage and the Family, 46,* 937–941.

Erikson, E.H. 1963. *Childhood and society.* NY: Norton.

Farrell, M.P. & Rosenberg, S.D. 1981. *Men at midlife.* Boston: Auburn House.

Feldman, H. 1981. A comparison of intentional parents and intentionally childless couples. *Journal of Marriage and the Family, 43,* 593–600.

Ginzberg, E. 1972. Toward a theory of occupational choice: A restatement. *Vocational Guidance Quarterly, 20,* 169–176.

Ginzberg, E., Ginzberg, S.W., Axelrad, S., & Herman, J.L. 1951. *Occupational choice: An approach to a general theory.* NY: Columbia University.

Glick, P.C. 1977. Updating the life cycle of the family. *Journal of Marriage and the Family, 39,* 5–13.

Glick, P.C. & Norton, A.J. 1977. Marrying, divorcing and living together in the U.S. today. *Population Bulletin, 32,* 2–38.

Goodman, E. 1979. *Turning point.* NY: Fawcrest.

Gould, R.L. 1978. *Transformations: Growth and change in adult life.* NY: Simon & Schuster.

Hartman, W.E. & Fithian, M.A. 1979. The development of a treatment program for sexual dysfunction at the Center for Marital and Sexual Studies. In V.L. Bullough (Ed.). *The frontiers of sex research.* Buffalo, NY: Prometheus Books.

Hayflick, L. 1977. The cellular basis for biological aging. In C.E. Finch & L. Hayflick (Eds.). *Handbook of the biology of aging.* NY: Van Nostrand.

Hetherington, E.M., Cox, M., & Cox, R. 1982. Effects of divorce on parents and children. In M.E. Lamb (Ed.). *Nontraditional families.* Hillsdale, NJ: Erlbaum.

Holland, J.L. 1985. *Making vocational choices: A theory of vocational personalities and work environments* (2nd ed.). Englewood Cliffs, NJ: Prentice-Hall.

Horn, J.L. 1970. Organization of data on life-span development of human abilities. In L.R. Goulet & P.B. Baltes (Eds.). *Life-span developmental psychology: Theory and research.* NY: Academic Press.

Hyde, J.S. 1981. How large are cognitive gender differences? A meta-analysis using w^2 and d. *American Psychologist, 36,* 892–901.

Inlons-Peterson, M.J. & Reddel, M. 1984. What do people ask about a neonate? *Developmental Psychology, 20,* 358–359.

Jacques, J.M. & Chason, K.J. 1979. Cohabitation: Its impact on marital success. *The Family Coordinator, 28,* 35–39.

Jones, W.H., Chernovetz, M.E., & Hansson, R.O. 1978. The enigma of androgyny: Differential implications for males and females? *Journal of Consulting and Clinical Psychology, 46,* 298–313.

Jung, C.G. 1968. *The archetypes and the collective unconscious* (Bollingen Series XX; 2nd ed.). Princeton: Princeton University Press.

Kalish, R.A. 1981. *Death, grief, and caring relationships.* Monterey, CA: Brooks/Cole.

Kaplan, A. & Sedney, M.A. 1980. *Psychology and sex roles: An androgynous perspective.* Boston: Little, Brown.

Kaplan, H.S. 1974. *The new sex therapy.* NY: Brunner/Mazel.

Kaplan, H.S. 1979. *Disorders of sexual desire.* NY: Brunner/Mazel.

Kaplan, H.S. 1983. *The evaluation of sexual disorders.* NY: Brunner/Mazel.

Keniston, K. 1970. Youth: A "new" stage of life. *The American Scholar, 39,* 631–654.

Kimmel, D.C. 1974. *Adulthood and aging.* NY: Wiley.

Kolodny, R.C. 1981. Evaluating sex therapy: Process and outcome at the Masters & Johnson Institute. *Journal of Sex Research, 17,* 301–318.

Kolodny, R.C., Masters, W.H., & Johnson, V.E. 1979. *Textbook of sexual medicine.* Boston: Little, Brown.

Kübler-Ross, E. 1969. *On death and dying.* NY: Macmillan.

Kübler-Ross, E. 1974. *Questions and answers on death and dying.* NY: Macmillan.

Kübler-Ross, E. 1975. *Death: The final stage of growth.* Englewood Cliffs, NJ: Prentice-Hall.

Lee, I.S. & Cohen, B.L. 1979. A catalog of risks. *Health Physics, 36,* 707–722. Pergamon Press.

Lee, A.L. & Scheurer, V.L. 1983. Psychological androgyny and aspects of self-image in women and men. *Sex Roles, 9,* 289–306.

Levinson, D.J. 1978. *The season's of a man's life.* NY: Ballantine.

Maccoby, E.E. & Jacklin, C.N. 1974. *The psychology of sex differences.* Stanford, CA: Stanford University Press.

Maccoby, E.E. & Martin, J.A. 1983. Socialization in the context of the family: Parent-child interaction. In P.E. Mussen (Ed.). *Handbook of child psychology* (4th ed., Vol. 4). NY: Wiley.

Macklin, E. 1972. Heterosexual cohabitation among unmarried college students. *The Family Coordinator, 12,* 463–471.

Massad, C.M. 1981. Sex role identity and adjustment during adolescence. *Child Development, 52,* 1290–1294.

Masters, W.H., & Johnson, V.E. 1966. *Human sexual response.* Boston: Little, Brown.

Masters, W.H. & Johnson, V.E. 1970. *Human sexual inadequacy.* Boston: Little, Brown.

Masters, W.H., Johnson, V.E., & Kolodny, R.C. 1985. *Human sexuality* (2nd ed.). Boston: Little, Brown.

McCary, J.L. & McCary, S.P. 1982. *McCary's human sexuality* (4th ed.). Belmont, CA: Wadsworth.

Neal, J.H. 1983. Children's understanding of their parents' divorces. In L.A. Kurdek (Ed.). *Children and divorce. New directions for child development* (No. 19). San Francisco: Jossey-Bass.

Neugarten, B.L. 1967. The awareness of middle age. In R. Owen (Ed.). *Middle age.* London: BBC.

Neugarten, B.L. 1980 (February). Must everything be a mid-life crisis? *Prime Time,* 45–48.

Neugarten, B.L., Havighurst, R., & Tobin, S. 1968. Personality and patterns of aging. In B.L. Neugarten (Ed.). *Middle age and aging.* Chicago: University of Chicago Press.

Newcombe, N., Bandura, M.M., & Taylor, D.C. 1983. Sex differences in spatial ability and spatial activities. *Sex Roles, 9,* 377–386.

Nunes, J.S. & Bandeira, C.S. 1980. A sex therapy clinic in Portugal: Some results and a few questions. In R. Forleo & W. Pasini (Eds.). *Medical sexology.* Littleton, MA: PSG Publishing.

Olney, J. 1980. Biography, autobiography and the life course. In K.W. Back (Ed.). *Life course: Integrative theories and exemplary populations* (AAAS Selected Symposium 41). Boulder, CO: Westview Press for the American Association for the Advancement of Science.

Paffenbarger, R.S., Hyde, R.T., Wing, A.L., & Hsieh, C.C. 1986. Physical activity, all-cause mortality, and longevity of college alumni. *New England Journal of Medicine, 314,* 605–613.

Papalia, D.E. & Olds, S.W. 1986. *Human development* (3rd ed.). NY: McGraw-Hill.

Pleck, J. 1981. *Three conceptual issues in research on male roles* (Working paper No. 98). Wellesley College Center for Research on Women. Wellesley, MA.

Pogrebin, L.B. 1984. *Family politics: Love & power on an intimate frontier.* NY: McGraw-Hill.

Rogers, C. 1972. *Becoming partners: Marriage and its alternatives.* NY: Harper & Row.

Santrock, J.W. & Warshak, R.A. 1979. Father custody and social development in boys and girls. *Journal of Social Issues, 35,* 112–125.

Santrock, J.W., Warshak, R.A., Sitterle, K.A., Dozier, C., & Stephens, M. 1985. *The social development of children in stepfather and stepmother families.* Unpublished manuscript, University of Texas at Dallas, Richardson, TX. Cited in J.W. Santrock, *Life-span development* (2nd ed.). Dubuque, IA: Brown.

Sauber, M. & Corrigan, E.M. 1970. *The six year experience of unwed mothers as parents.* NY: Community Council of Greater New York.

Schaie, K.W. 1977. Toward a stage theory of adult cognitive development. *International Journal of Aging and Human Development, 8,* 129–138.

Schonfield, D. & Robertson, B.A. 1966. Memory storage and aging. *Canadian Journal of Psychology, 20,* 228–236.

Secunda, V. 1984. *By youth possessed: The denial of age in America.* NY: Bobbs-Merrill.

Spanier, G.G. & Castro, R. 1979. Adjustment to separation and divorce: An analysis of 50 case studies. *Journal of Divorce, 2,* 241–253.

Spence, J.T. 1984. Masculinity, femininity, and gender-related traits: A conceptual analysis and critique of current research. In B. Maher & W. Maher (Eds.). *Progress in Experimental Personality Research* (Vol. 13). Orlando, FL: Academic Press.

Spence, J.T. & Helmreich, R.L. 1978. *Masculinity & femininity: Their psychological dimensions, correlates, and antecedents.* Austin, TX: University of Texas Press.

Springer, K.J. 1981. Effectiveness of treatment of sexual dysfunction: Review and evaluation. *Journal of Sex Education and Therapy, 7,* 18–22.

Stein, P.J. 1976 (Sept.). Being single: Bucking the cultural imperative. Paper presented at the 71st annual meeting of the American Sociological Association.

Super, D.E. 1967. *The psychology of careers*. NY: Harper & Row.

Super, D.E. 1976. *Career education and the meanings of work*. Washington: U.S. Office of Education.

Taylor, M.C. & Hall, J.A. 1982. Psychological androgyny: Theories, methods and conclusions. *Psychological Bulletin, 92*, 347–366.

U.S. Bureau of the Census. 1984. *Marital status and living arrangements: March 1983*. Current Population Reports, Series P-20, No. 389.

U.S. Bureau of the Census. 1985. *Statistical abstract of the United States 1985*. Washington: U.S. Government Printing Office.

U.S. Bureau of Labor Statistics. 1986. Employment situation news release, April, 1986. Washington: U.S. Government Printing Office.

Upton, A.C. 1977. Pathology. In L.E. Finch & L. Hayflick (Eds.). *Handbook of the biology of aging*. NY: Van Nostrand Reinhold.

Vaillant, G.E. 1977. *Adaptation to life*. Boston: Little, Brown.

Veevers, J.E. 1980. *Childless by choice*. Toronto: Butterworth.

Wallerstein, J.S. 1983. Children of divorce: The psychological tasks of the child. *American Journal of Orthopsychiatry, 53*, 230–243.

Watson, R.E.L. 1983. Premarital cohabitation vs. traditional courtship: Their effects on subsequent marital adjustment. *Family Relations, 32*, 139–147.

Weinrach, S.G. 1984. Determinants of vocational choice: Holland's theory. In D. Brown & L. Brooks (Eds.). *Career choice and development. Applying contemporary theories to practice*. San Francisco: Jossey-Bass.

Chapter 18

Allport, G. 1954. *The nature of prejudice*. Reading, MA: Addison-Wesley.

Altman, I. & Taylor, D.S. 1973. *Social penetration: The development of interpersonal relationships*. NY: Holt, Rinehart & Winston.

Archer, R.L. & Berg, J.H. 1978. Disclosure reciprocity and its limits: A reactance analysis. *Journal of Experimental Social Psychology, 14*, 527–540.

Aronson, E. 1984. *The social animal*. San Francisco: Freeman.

Aronson, E. & Cope, V. 1968. My enemy's enemy is my friend. *Journal of Personality and Social Psychology, 8*, 8–12.

Aronson, E. & Linder, D. 1965. Gain and loss of esteem as determinants of interpersonal attractiveness. *Journal of Experimental Social Psychology, 1*, 156–171.

Aronson, E., Willerman, B. & Floyd, J. 1966. The effect of a pratfall on increasing interpersonal attractiveness. *Psychonomic Science, 4*, 157–158.

Asch, S.E. 1946. Forming impressions of personality. *Journal of Abnormal and Social Psychology, 41*, 258–290.

Backman, C.W. & Secord, P.F. 1959. The effect of perceived liking on interpersonal attraction. *Human Relations, 12*, 379–384.

Banuazizi, A. & Movahedi, S. 1975. Interpersonal dynamics in a simulated prison: A methodological analysis. *American Psychologist, 30*, 152–160.

Berscheid, E.S. & Walster, E. 1978. *Interpersonal attraction* (2nd ed.). Reading, MA: Addison-Wesley.

Brislin, R.W. & Lewis, S.A. 1968. Dating and physical attractiveness. *Psychological Reports, 22*, 976.

Byrne, D. & Clore, G.L. 1970. A reinforcement model of evaluative responses. *Personality: An International Journal*, 103–128.

Byrne, D. & Nelson, D. 1965. Attraction as a linear function of proportion of positive reinforcements. *Journal of Personality and Social Psychology, 1*, 659–663.

Bulman, R.J. & Wortman, C.B. 1977. Attributions of blame and coping in the "real world": Severe accident victims react to their lot. *Journal of Personality and Social Psychology, 35*, 351–363.

Caldwell, M. & Peplau, L.A. 1982. Sex differences in same sex friendships. *Sex Roles, 8*, 721–732.

Chaiken, A.L. & Derlega, V.J. 1974. *Self-disclosure*. Morristown, NJ: General Learning Press.

Clifford, M. & Walster, E. 1973. The effect of physical attractiveness on teacher expectation. *Sociology of Education, 46*, 248.

Cohen, C.E. 1977. Cognitive basis of stereotyping. Paper presented at American Psychological Association. Cited in Miller, A.G. (Ed.). 1982. In

the eye of the beholder: Contemporary issues in stereotyping. NY: Praeger Publishing.

Colman, A.M., Hargreaves, D.J., & Sluckin, W. 1981. Preferences for Christian names as a function of their experienced familiarity. *British Journal of Social Psychology, 20*, 3–5.

Darley, J.M. & Gross, P.H. 1983. A hypothesis confirming bias in labeling effects. *Journal of Personality and Social Psychology, 44*, 20–33.

Darley, J.M. & Berscheid, E. 1967. Increased liking as a result of the anticipation of personal contact. *Human Relations, 20*, 29–39.

Davis, K.E. 1985. Near and dear: Friendship and love compared. *Psychology Today, 19*, 22–30.

Dion, K.K. 1973. Young children's stereotyping of facial attractiveness. *Developmental Psychology, 9*, 183–188.

Dion, K.K., Berscheid, E., & Walster, E. 1972. What is beautiful is good. *Journal of Personality and Social Psychology, 24*, 285–290.

Dipboye, R.L., Fromkin, H.L. & Wiback, H. 1975. Relative importance of applicant sex, attractiveness, and scholastic standing in evaluation of job applicant resumes. *Journal of Applied Psychology, 60*, 39–43.

Drinnin, B. & Simons, J.A. 1981. *Who to fund: A values exploration. The facilitator's manual*. Ankeny, IA: Des Moines Area Community College.

Dunkling, L. & Gosling, W. 1983. *The New American dictionary of first names*. NY: New American Library.

Efran, M.G. 1974. The effect of physical appearance on the judgment of guilt, interpersonal attraction, and severity of recommended punishment in a simulated jury task. *Journal of Research on Personality, 8*, 45–54.

Ellis, A. & Beechley, R.M. 1954. Emotional disturbance in children with peculiar given names. *Journal of Genetic Psychology, 85*, 337–339.

Feldman, S. (Ed.). 1966. *Cognitive consistency: Motivational antecedents and behavioral consequents*. NY: Academic Press.

Festinger, L., Schachter, S., & Back, K. 1950. *Social pressures in informal groups: A study of human factors in housing*. Stanford, CA: Stanford University Press.

Fischer, C.S. 1982. *To dwell among friends*. Chicago: University of Chicago Press.

Freedman, T.L. 1975. *Crowding and behavior*. NY: Viking Press.

Fromm, E. 1956. *The art of loving*. NY: Harper & Row.

Gerbasi, K.C., Zuckerman, M., & Reis, H.T. 1977. Justice needs a new blindfold: A review of mock jury research. *Psychological Bulletin, 84*, 323–345.

Gerdes, E.P., Gehling, J.D., & Rapp, J.N. 1981. The effects of sex and sex-role concept on self-disclosure. *Sex Roles, 7*, 989–998.

Griffitt, W.B. & Veitch, R. 1971. Hot and crowded: Influences of population density and temperature on interpersonal affective behavior. *Journal of Personality and Social Psychology, 17*, 92–98.

Hamilton, D.L. 1980. Cognitive representations of persons. In E. Higgins et al. (Eds.). *Social cognition: The Ontario symposium on personality and social psychology*. Hillsdale, NJ: Erlbaum.

Hamilton, D.L. (Ed.). 1981. *Cognitive processes in stereotyping and intergroup behavior*. Hillsdale, NJ: Erlbaum.

Haney, C. & Zimbardo, P.G. 1977. The socialization into criminality: On becoming prisoner and a guard. In J.L. Tapp & F.L. Levine (Eds.). *Law, justice and the individual in society: Psychological and legal issues*. NY: Holt, Rinehart & Winston.

Hargreaves, D.J., Colman, A.M., & Sluckin, W. 1983. *Human Relations, 36*, 393–402.

Hartman, A.A., Nicolay, R.C., & Hurley, J. 1968. Unique personal names as a social adjustment factor. *Journal of Social Psychology, 75*, 107–110.

Heider, F. 1958. *The psychology of interpersonal relations*. NY: Wiley.

Johnson, D.F. & Pittenger, J.B. 1984. Attribution, the attractiveness stereotype, and the elderly. *Developmental Psychology, 20*, 1168–1172.

Johnson, M.P. & Leslie, L. 1982. Couple involvement and network structure. A test of the dyadic withdrawal hypothesis. *Social Psychology Quarterly, 4*, 34–43.

Jones, E.E. & Davis, K.E. 1965. From acts to dispositions: The attribution process in person perception. In L. Berkowitz (Ed.). *Advances in experimental social psychology, 2*, NY: Academic Press.

Jones, E.E. & Nisbett, R.E. 1972. The actor and the observer: Divergent perceptions of the causes of behavior. In E.E. Jones, D.E. Kanouse,

H.H. Kelley, R.E. Nisbett, S. Valins, & B. Weiner (Eds.). *Attribution: Perceiving the causes of behavior*, Morristown, NJ: General Learning Press.

Joubert, C.E. 1983. Unusual names and academic achievement. *Psychological Reports, 53*, 266.

Jourard, S.M. 1964. *The transparent self: Self-disclosure and well-being*. Princeton, NJ: Van Nostrand.

Jourard, S.M. 1971. *Self disclosure: An experimental analysis of the transparent self*. NY: Wiley.

Kelley, H.H. 1950. The warm-cold variable in first impressions of persons. *Journal of Personality, 18*, 431–439.

Kelley, H.H. et al. 1983. Close relationships. San Francisco: Freeman.

Kerckhoff, A.C. & Davis, K.E. 1962. Value consensus and need complementarity in mate selection. *American Sociological Review, 27*, 295–303.

Komarovsky, M. 1964. Cultural contradictions and sex roles. *American Journal of Sociology, 52*, 182–189.

Komarovsky, M. 1976. *Dilemmas of masculinity: A study of college youth*. NY: Norton.

Lerner, M.J. 1980. *The belief in a just world: A fundamental delusion*. NY: Plenum Press.

Levine, R.A. & Campbell, D.T. 1972. *Ethnocentrism: Theories of conflict, ethnic attitudes, and group behavior*. NY: Wiley.

Lott, A.J. & Lott, B.E. 1974. The role of reward in the formation of positive interpersonal attitudes. In T.L. Huston (Ed.). *Foundations of interpersonal attraction*. NY: Academic Press.

Lovibond, S.H., Adams, M., & Adams, W.G. 1979. The effects of three experimental prison environments on the behaviors of nonconvict volunteer subjects. *Australian Psychologist, 14*, 273–285.

MacDonald, A.P., Jr. 1972. More on the protestant ethic. *Journal of Consulting and Clinical Psychology, 39*, 116–122.

Maslow, A.H. 1962. *Toward a psychology of being*. Princeton, NJ: Van Nostrand.

McCary, J.L. 1978. *McCary's human sexuality* (3rd ed.). NY: Van Nostrand.

Mellon, S.L.W. 1981. *The evolution of love*. San Francisco: Freeman.

Milgram, S. 1970. The experience of living in the cities: A psychological analysis. *Science, 167*, 1461–1468.

Mills, J. & Clark, M.S. 1984. Exchange and communal relationships. In L. Wheeler (Ed.). *Review of Personality and Social Psychology* (Vol. 3). Beverly Hills, CA: Sage.

Nisbett, R.E., Borgida, E., Crandall, R., & Reed, H. 1976. Popular induction: Information is not necessarily informative. In J.S. Carroll & J.W. Payne (Eds.). *Cognition and social behavior*. Hillsdale, NJ: Erlbaum.

Nisbett, R.E. & Ross, L. 1981. *Human inference: Strategies and shortcomings of social judgment*. Englewood Cliffs, NJ: Prentice-Hall.

Norwood, R. 1985. *Women who love too much*. NY: St. Martin's Press.

Piaget, J. 1948. *The moral judgment of the child*. NY: Free Press.

Ross, L. 1977. The intuitive psychologist and his shortcomings: Distortions in the attribution process. In L. Berkowitz (Ed.). *Advances in experimental social psychology* (Vol. 10). NY: Academic Press.

Ross, L., Amabile, T., & Steinmetz, J. 1977. Social roles, social control and biases in the social perception process. *Journal of Personality and Social Psychology, 37*, 485–494.

Schonfield, D. 1982. Who is stereotyping whom and why? *Gerontologist, 22*, 267–272.

Sensenig, J., Jones, R.A., & Varney, L. 1973. Inspection of faces of own and other race as a function of students' prejudice. *Representative Research in Social Psychology, 4*, 85–92.

Sigall, H.F. 1984. Interpersonal attraction. In A.S. Kahn, M.V. Donnerstein, & E.I. Donnerstein. *Social Psychology*. Dubuque, IA: Brown.

Sigall, H., Page, R., & Brown, A.C. 1971. Effect of expenditure as a function of evaluation and evaluator attractiveness. *Representative Research in Social Psychology, 2*, 19–25.

Smith, R.J., Griffith, J.E., Griffith, H.K. & Steger, M.J. 1980. When is a stereotype a stereotype? *Psychological Reports, 46*, 643–651.

Stephan, C.W. & Langlois, J.H. 1984. Baby beautiful: Adult attributions of infant competence as a function of infant attractiveness. *Child Development, 55*, 576–585.

Stephan, W.G. & Rosenfield, D. 1982. Racial and ethnic stereotypes. In A.G. Miller (Ed.). *In the eye of the beholder: Contemporary issues in stereotyping*. NY: Praeger Publishing.

Stokols, D. & Schopler, J. 1973. Reactions to victims under conditions of situational detachment: The effects of responsibility, severity, and expected future interaction. *Journal of Personality and Social Psychology, 25*, 199–209.

Stroebe, M.S. & Stroebe, W. 1983. Who suffers more? Sex differences in health risks of the widowed. *Psychological Bulletin, 93*, 279–301.

Taylor, D.A., Altman, I., & Sorrentino, R. 1969. Interpersonal exchange as a function of rewards and costs and situational factors: Expectancy confirmation-disconfirmation. *Journal of Experimental Social Psychology, 5*, 324–339.

Thayer, S. & Saari, C. 1975. Demand characteristics are everywhere (anyway): A comment on the Stanford prison experiment. *American Psychologist, 30*, 1015–1016.

Thibaut, J.W. & Kelley, H.H. 1959. *The social psychology of groups*. NY: Wiley.

Udry, J.R. & Eckland, B.K. 1984. Benefits of being attractive: Differential payoffs for men and women. *Psychological Reports, 54*, 47–56.

Walster, E. 1966. The assignment of responsibility for an accident. *Journal of Personality and Social Psychology, 5*, 508–516.

Walster, E., Aronson, V., Abrahams, D., & Rottman, L. 1966. Importance of physical attractiveness in dating behavior. *Journal of Personality and Social Psychology, 5*, 508–516.

Walster, E. & Walster, G.W. 1978. *Love*. Reading, MA: Addison-Wesley.

Weiner, M.J. & Wright, F.E. 1973. Effects of undergoing arbitrary discrimination upon subsequent attitudes toward a minority group. *Journal of Applied Social Psychology, 3*, 94–102.

Weiss, R.S. 1976. The emotional impact of marital separation. *Journal of Social Issues, 32*, 135–145.

Willis, F.N., Willis, L.A., & Grier, J.A. 1982. Given names, social class, and professional achievement. *Psychological Reports, 51*, 543–549.

Yarkin, K.L., Toun, J.P., & Wallston, B.S. 1982. Blacks and women must try harder: Stimulus persons' race and sex attributions of causality. *Personality and Social Psychology Bulletin, 8*, 21–24.

Zimbardo, P.G. 1975. On transforming experimental research into advocacy for social change. In M. Deutsch & H. Hornstein (Eds.). *Applying social psychology: Implications for research, practice and training*. Hillsdale, NJ: Erlbaum.

Zweigenhaft, R.L. 1977. The other side of unusual first names. *Journal of Social Psychology, 103*, 291–302.

Chapter 19

Allport, F.M. 1920. The influence of the group upon association and thought. *Journal of Experimental Psychology, 3*, 159–182.

Andrews, K.H. & Kandel, D.B. 1979. Attitude and behavior: A specification of the contingent consistency hypothesis. *American Sociological Review, 44*, 298–310.

Asch, S.E. 1951. Effects of group pressure upon the modification and distortion of judgments. In H. Guetzkow (Ed.). *Groups, leadership, and men*. Pittsburgh: Carnegie Press.

Asch, S.E. 1955. Opinions and social pressure. *Scientific American, 193*, 31–35.

Asch, S.E. 1956. Studies of independence and conformity: A minority of one against a unanimous majority. *Psychological Monographs, 70* (9, Whole No. 416).

Atkin, C.K. 1976. *Political advertising effects on voters*. Paper presented at American Psychological Association meeting. Washington D.C.

Atkin, C.K. & Heald, G. 1976. Effects of political advertising. *Public Opinion Quarterly, 40*, 216–228.

Bales, R.F. 1958. Task roles and social roles in problem-solving groups. In E.E. Maccoby, T.M. Newcomb, & E.L. Hartley. *Readings in social psychology* (3rd ed.). NY: Holt, Rinehart & Winston.

Baran, S.J. & Blasko, V.J. 1984. Social perceptions and the by-products of advertising. *Journal of Communication, 34*, 12–20.

Bell, P.A. 1978. Affective state, attraction, and affiliation. *Personality and Social Psychology Bulletin, 4*, 616–619.

Benware, C. & Deci, E. 1975. Attitude change as a function of the inducement for exposing a proattitudinal communication. *Journal of Experimental Social Psychology, 11,* 271–278.

Berkowitz, L. 1954. Group standards, cohesiveness, and productivity. *Human Relations, 7,* 509–519.

Boggiano, A.K. & Ruble, D.N. 1979. Competence and the overjustification effect: A developmental study. *Journal of Personality and Social Psychology, 18,* 105–115.

Borgida, E. & Nisbett, R.E. 1977. The differential impact of abstract vs. concrete information on decisions. *Journal of Applied Social Psychology, 7,* 258–271.

Brehm, S. & Brehm, J.W. 1981. *Psychological reactance: A theory of freedom and control.* NY: Academic Press.

Bryan, J.H. & Test, M.A. 1967. Models and helping: Naturalistic studies in aiding behavior. *Journal of Personality and Social Psychology, 6,* 400–407.

Burger, J.M. & Petty, R.E. 1981. The low-ball technique: Task or person commitment? *Journal of Personality and Social Psychology, 40,* 492–500.

Caballero, M.J. & Solomon, P.J. 1984. Effects of model attractiveness on sales response. *Journal of Advertising, 13,* 17–23, 33.

Cann, A., Sherman, S.J., & Elkes, R. 1975. Effects of initial request size and timing of a second request on compliance: The foot-in-the-door technique and the door-in-the-face technique. *Journal of Personality and Social Psychology, 32,* 774–782.

Carnevale, P.J., Pruitt, D.G., & Carrington, P.I. 1982. Effects of future dependence, liking, and repeated requests for help on helping behavior. *Social Psychology Quarterly, 45,* 9–14.

Chafel, J.A. 1984. Social comparisons by young children in classroom contexts. *Early Child Development and Care, 14,* 109–124.

Chaiken, S. & Eagly, A.H. 1976. Communication modality as a determinant of message persuasiveness and message comprehensibility. *Journal of Personality and Social Psychology, 34,* 605–614.

Chen, S.C. 1937. Social modification of the activity of ants in nest-building. *Physiological Zoology, 10,* 420–436.

Clark, R.D., III & Word, L.E. 1972. Why don't bystanders help? Because of ambiguity? *Journal of Personality and Social Psychology, 24,* 392–400.

Cohen, S. 1980 (August). Training to understand TV advertising: Effects and some policy implications. Paper presented at the American Psychological Association convention in Montreal, Canada.

Crutchfield, R.A. 1955. Conformity and character. *American Psychologist, 10,* 191–198.

Cunningham, M.R. 1979. Weather, mood, and helping behavior: Quasi experiments with the sunshine Samaritan. *Journal of Personality and Social Psychology, 37,* 1947–1956.

Darley, J.M. & Latane, B. 1968. Bystander intervention in emergencies: Diffusion of responsibility. *Journal of Personality and Social Psychology, 8,* 377–383.

Davis, L.L. 1984. Judgment ambiguity, self-consciousness, and conformity in judgments. *Psychological Reports, 56,* 671–675.

Deci, E.L. 1975. *Intrinsic motivation.* NY: Plenum.

Deci, E.L. & Ryan, R.M. 1980. The empirical exploration of intrinsic motivational processes. In L. Berkowitz (Ed.). *Advances in experimental social psychology* (Vol. 13). NY: Academic Press.

Derlega, V.J. & Grezelak, J. 1982. *Cooperation and helping behavior: Theories and research.* NY: Academic Press.

Dershewitz, R.A. & Levin, G.S. 1984. The effect of the Tylenol scare on parent's use of over-the-counter drugs. *Clinical Pediatrics, 23,* 445–448.

Deutsch, M. & Gerard, H.B. 1955. A study of normative and informational social influence upon individual judgment. *Journal of Abnormal and Social Psychology, 51,* 629–636.

Diamond, E. & Bates, S. 1984. The political pitch. *Psychology Today, 18,* 22–32.

Diener, E. & Wallbom, M. 1976. Effects of self-awareness on antinormative behavior. *Journal of Research in Personality, 10,* 107–111.

Dion, K.K. & Stein, S. 1978. Physical attractiveness and interpersonal influence. *Journal of Experimental Social Psychology, 14,* 97–109.

Eagly, A.H. & Carli, L.L. 1981. Sex of researcher and sex-typed communications as determinants of sex differences in influenceability: A meta-analysis of social influence studies. *Psychological Bulletin, 90,* 1–20.

Evans, R.I., Rozelle, R.M., Maxwell, W.E., Raines, B.E., Dill, C.A., Guthrie, T.J., Henderson, A.H., & Hill, P.C. 1981. Social modeling films to deter smoking in adolescents: Results of a three year field investigation. *Journal of Applied Psychology, 66,* 399–414.

Eysenck, H.J. & Eysenck, M. 1983. *Mindwatchers: Why people behave the way they do.* Garden City, NY: Anchor Press/Doubleday.

Festinger, L. 1954. A theory of social comparison processes. *Human Relations, 7,* 117–140.

Festinger, L. & Carlsmith, J.M. 1959. Cognitive consequences of forced compliance. *Journal of Abnormal and Social Psychology, 58,* 203–210.

Fiedler, F.E. 1967. *A theory of leadership effectiveness.* NY: McGraw-Hill.

Fox, S. 1984. *The mirror makers.* NY: Morrow.

Franco, A.C. 1978. Altruism in children as a function of deservedness of reward, storytelling and vicarious reinforcement. *Phillipine Journal of Psychology, 11,* 3–14.

Freedman, J.L. & Fraser, S.C. 1966. Compliance without pressure: The foot-in-the-door technique. *Journal of Personality and Social Psychology, 4,* 195–202.

Galizio, M. & Hendrick, C. 1972. Effect of musical accompaniment on attitude: The guitar as a prop for persuasion. *Journal of Applied Social Psychology, 2,* 350–359.

Gerard, H.B., Wilhelmy, R.A., & Conolley, E.S. 1968. Conformity and group size. *Journal of Personality and Social Psychology, 8,* 79–82.

Gergen, K.J., Gergen, M.M., & Meter, K. 1972. Individual orientations to prosocial behavior. *Journal of Social Issues, 8,* 105–130.

Glynn, C.J. & McLeod, J.M. 1984. Public opinion du jour: An examination of the spiral of silence. *Public Opinion Quarterly, 48,* 731–740.

Goethals, G.R. & Nelson, E.R. 1973. Similarity in the influence process: The belief-value distinction. *Journal of Personality and Social Psychology, 25,* 117–122.

Gorn, G. 1982. The effects of music in advertising on choice behavior: A classical conditioning approach. *Journal of Marketing, 6,* 94–101.

Hall, J.A. 1980. Voice tone and persuasion. *Journal of Personality and Social Psychology, 38,* 924–934.

Himmelfarb, S. & Eagly, A.H. 1974. Orientations to the study of attitudes and their change. In S. Himmelfarb & A.H. Eagly (Eds.). *Readings in attitude change.* NY: Wiley.

Hoffman, M.L. 1981. Is altruism part of human nature? *Journal of Personality and Social Psychology, 40,* 121–137.

Holloway, S., Tucker, L., & Hornstein, H.A. 1977. The effects of social and nonsocial information on interpersonal behavior of males: The news makes news. *Journal of Personality and Social Psychology, 35,* 514–522.

Hovland, C.I., Lumsdaine, A.A., & Sheffield, F.D. 1949. *Experiments on mass communication. Studies in social psychology in World War II.* Princeton, NJ: Princeton University Press.

Hovland, C.I. & Mandell, W. 1952. An experimental comparison of conclusion-drawing by the communicator and by the audience. *Journal of Abnormal and Social Psychology, 47,* 581–588.

Hovland, C.I. & Weiss, W. 1951. The influence of source credibility on communication effectiveness. *Public Opinion Quarterly, 15,* 635–650.

Ingham, A.G., Levinger, G., Graves, J., & Peckham, V. 1974. The Ringelmann effect: Studies of group size and group performance. *Journal of Experimental Social Psychology, 10,* 371–384.

Jackson, J.M. & Williams, K.D. 1985. Social loafing on difficult tasks: Working collectively can improve performance. *Journal of Personality and Social Psychology, 49,* 937–942.

Jago, A.G. & Vroom, V.H. 1983. Sex differences in the incidence and evaluation of participative leader behavior. *Journal of Applied Psychology, 67,* 776–783.

Janis, I.L. 1972. *Victims of groupthink.* Boston: Houghton Mifflin.

Janis, I.L. 1982a. Counteracting the adverse effects of concurrence-seeking in policy-planning groups: Theory and research perspectives. In H. Brandstatter, J.H. Davis, & G. Stocker-Kreichgauer (Eds.). *Group decision making.* NY: Academic Press.

Janis, I.L. 1982b. *Groupthink: Psychological studies of policy decisions and fiascos* (2nd ed.). Boston: Houghton-Mifflin.

Janis, I.L. & Feshbach, S. 1953. Effects of fear-arousing communications. *Journal of Abnormal and Social Psychology, 48,* 79–92.

Janis, I.L., Kaye, D., & Kirschner, P. 1965. Facilitating effects of "eating-while-reading" on responsiveness to persuasive communications. *Journal of Personality and Social Psychology, 1,* 181–186.

Joslyn, R.A. 1981. The impact of campaign spot advertising on voting defections. *Human Communication Research, 7,* 347–360.

Kahle, L.R. & Berman, J. 1979. Attitudes cause behaviors: A cross-lagged panel analysis. *Journal of Personality and Social Psychology, 37,* 315–321.

Kahn, A.S. & Donnerstein, E. 1984. Social influence. In A.S. Kahn (Ed.). *Social Psychology.* Dubuque, IA: Brown.

Kahn, A.S. & Nelson, R.E. 1984. Women, men, and social behavior. In A.S. Kahn (Ed.). *Social Psychology.* Dubuque, IA: Brown.

Kiesler, C.A. 1971. *The psychology of commitment.* NY: Academic Press.

Kipnis, D. & Schmidt, S. 1985. The language of persuasion. *Psychology Today, 19,* 40–46.

Kohn, P.M. & Smart, R.G. 1984. The impact of television advertising on alcohol consumption: An experiment. *Journal of Studies on Alcohol, 45,* 295–301.

Krebs, D.L. 1970. Altruism: An examination of the concept and review of the literature. *Psychological Bulletin, 73,* 258–302.

Krech, D., Crutchfield, R.A., & Ballachey, E.I. 1962. *Individual in society.* NY: McGraw-Hill.

Lammers, H.B., Leibowitz,, L., Seymur, G.E., & Hennessey, J.E. 1983. Humor and cognitive responses to advertising stimuli: A trace consolidation approach. *Journal of Business Research, 11,* 173–185.

Langer, E.J. 1978. Rethinking the role of thought in social interaction. In J.H. Harvey, W.J. Ickes, & R.F. Kidd (Eds.). *New directions in attribution research, 2.* Hillsdale, NJ: Erlbaum.

Langer, E.J., Blank, A., & Chanowitz, B. 1978. The mindlessness of ostensibly thoughtful action: The role of "placebic" information in interpersonal interaction. *Journal of Personality and Social Psychology, 36,* 635–642.

LaPiere, R.T. 1934. Attitudes vs. action. *Social Forces, 13,* 230–237.

Latané, B. & Darley, J. 1970. *The unresponsive bystander: Why doesn't he help?* NY: Appleton-Century-Crofts.

Latané, B. & Rodin, J. 1969. A lady in distress: Inhibiting effects of friends on strangers on bystander intervention. *Journal of Experimental Social Psychology, 5,* 189–202.

Latané, B., Williams, K., & Harkis, S. 1979. Many hands make light the work: The causes and consequences of social loafing. *Journal of Personality and Social Psychology, 37,* 822–832.

Lefkowitz, M.M., Blake, R.R. & Mouton, J.S. 1955. Status factors in pedestrian violation of traffic signals. *Journal of Abnormal and Social Psychology, 51,* 704–706.

Lepper, M.R., Greene, D., & Nisbett, R.E. 1973. Undermining children's intrinsic interest with extrinsic rewards: A test of the overjustification hypothesis. *Journal of Personality and Social Psychology, 28,* 129–137.

Lerner, M.J. 1980. *The belief in a just world: A fundamental delusion.* NY: Plenum Press.

Lewin, I., Lippit, R., & White, R. 1939. Patterns of aggressive behavior in experimentally created "social climate". *Journal of Social Psychology, 10,* 271–299.

Lewis, S., Langan, C., & Hollander, E.P. 1972. Expectation of future interaction and the choice of less desirable alternatives in conformity. *Sociometry, 35,* 440–447.

Lichtenberg, J.W. 1984. Believing when the facts don't fit. *Journal of Counseling and Development, 63,* 10–11.

MacLachlan, J. 1979. What people really think of fast talkers. *Psychology Today, 13,* 113–117.

Maier, N.R. & Thurber, J.A. 1968. Accuracy at judgment of deception when an interview is watched, heard, and read. *Personal Psychology, 21,* 23–30.

McGuire, W.J. 1964. Inducing resistance to persuasion: Some contemporary approaches. In L. Berkowitz (Ed.). *Advances in experimental social psychology* (Vol. 1). NY: Academic Press.

Mendelsohn, H. & O'Keefe, G.J. 1976. *The people choose a president: Influences on voter decision making.* NY: Praeger.

Michaels, J.W., Blommel, J.M., Brocato, R.M., Linkous, R.A., & Rowe, J.S. 1982. Social facilitation and inhibition in a natural setting. *Replications in Social Psychology, 2,* 21–24.

Midlarsky, M. & Midlarsky, E. 1976. Status inconsistency, aggressive attitude, and helping behavior. *Journal of Personality, 44,* 371–391.

Milgram, S. 1974. *Obedience to authority: An experimental view.* NY: Harper & Row.

Milgram, S., Bickman, L., & Berkowitz, L. 1969. Note on the drawing power of crowds of different size. *Journal of Personality and Social Psychology, 13,* 79–82.

Miller, C.T. 1982. The role of performance-related similarity in social comparison of abilities: A test of the related attributes hypothesis. *Journal of Experimental Social Psychology, 18,* 513–523.

Miller, N. & Campbell, D.T. 1959. Recency and primacy in persuasion as a function of the timing of speeches and measurements. *Journal of Abnormal and Social Psychology, 59,* 1–9.

Miller, N., Maruyama, G., Beaber, R.J., & Valone, K. 1976. Speed of speech and persuasion. *Journal of Personality and Social Psychology, 34,* 615–624.

Morris, W.N. & Miller, R.S. 1975. The effects of consensus-breaking and consensus-preempting partners on reduction of conformity. *Journal of Experimental Social Psychology, 11,* 215–223.

Mullen, B., Atkins, J.L., Champion, D.S., Edwards, C., Hardy, D., Story, J.E., & Vanderklok, M. 1985. The false consensus effect: A meta-analysis of 115 hypothesis tests. *Journal of Experimental Social Psychology, 21,* 262–283.

Myers, D.G. 1983. *Social Psychology.* NY: McGraw-Hill.

Myers, D.G. & Lamm, H. 1975. The polarizing effect of group discussion. *American Scientist, 63,* 297–303.

Mynatt, C.R., Doherty, M.E., & Tweeny, R.D. 1977. Conformation bias in a simulated research environment: An experimental study of scientific inference. *Quarterly Journal of Experimental Psychology, 29,* 85–95.

Oskamp, S. 1984. *Applied social psychology.* Englewood Cliffs, NJ: Prentice-Hall.

Pallak, S.R., Pittman, T.S., & Pallak, M.S. 1984. Attitudes: Their nature, formation, and change. In A.S. Kahn (Ed.). *Social Psychology.* Dubuque, IA: Brown.

Parsons, M.A. 1984. Metropolitan school desegregation and parent and student attitudes: A longitudinal case study. *Urban Review, 16,* 102–115.

Perrin, S. & Spencer, C. 1980. The Asch effect—a child of its time? *Bulletin of the British Psychology Society, 3,* 405–406.

Pessin, J. 1933. The comparative effects of social and mechanical stimulation on memorizing. *American Journal of Psychology, 45,* 263–270.

Pessin, J. & Husband, R.W. 1933. Effects of social stimulation on human maze learning. *Journal of Abnormal and Social Psychology, 28,* 148–154.

Pittman, T.S., Pallack, S.R., & Pallak, M.S. 1984. Attitudes and behavior. In A.S. Kahn (Ed.). *Social Psychology.* Dubuque, IA: Brown.

Ray, J.J. 1984. Combining demographic and attitude variables to predict vote. *The Journal of Social Psychology, 122,* 145–146.

Robinson, J.P. 1972. Perceived media bias and the 1968 vote: Can the media affect behavior after all? *Journalism Quarterly, 49,* 239–246.

Rogers, R.W. & Mewborn, C.R. 1976. Fear appeals and attitude change: Effects of a threat's noxiousness, probability of occurrence, and the efficacy of coping responses. *Journal of Personality and Social Psychology, 34,* 54–61.

Rosenhan, D.L. 1970. The natural socialization of altruistic autonomy. In J. Macauley & L. Berkowitz (Eds.). *Altruism and helping behavior.* NY: Academic Press.

Rosenhan, D.L., Karylowski, J., Salovey, P., & Hargis, K. 1981. Emotion and altruism. In J.P. Rushton & R.M. Sorrention (Eds.). *Altruism and helping behavior.* Hillsdale, NJ: Erlbaum.

Ross, L., Greene, D., & House, P. 1977. The "false consensus effect": An egocentric bias in social perception and attribution processes. *Journal of Experimental Social Psychology, 13,* 279–301.

Rubin, R.B. 1981. Ideal traits and terms of address for male and female college professors. *Journal of Personality and Social Psychology, 41,* 966–974.

Santee, R.T. & Maslach, C. 1982. To agree or not to agree: Personal dissent amid social pressure to conform. *Journal of Personality and Social Psychology, 42,* 690–700.

Schachter, S. 1959. *The psychology of affiliation.* Stanford, CA: Stanford University Press.

Schwartz, S. & David, B.A. 1976. Responsibility and helping in an emergency: Effects of blame, ability and denial of responsibility. *Sociometry, 39,* 406–415.

Shaw, M.E. 1983. *Group dynamics: The psychology of small group behavior* (3rd ed.). NY: McGraw-Hill.

Shaw, M.E., Rothschild, G.H., & Strickland, J.F. 1957. Decision processes in communication nets. *Journal of Abnormal and Social Psychology, 54,* 323–330.

Sherif, M. 1935. A study of some social factors in perception. *Archives of Psychology, 27,* 60.

Sherif, M. 1936. *The psychology of social norms.* NY: Harper & Row.

Sherif, M. & Sherif, C.W. 1946. An *outline of social psychology* (rev. ed.). NY: Harper & Row.

Snyder, M. & DeBono, K.G. 1985. Appeals to image and claims about quality: Understanding the psychology of advertising. *Journal of Personality and Social Psychology, 49,* 586–597.

Sorrels, J.P. & Kelley, J. 1984. Conformity by omission. *Personality and Social Psychology Bulletin, 10,* 302–305.

Steininger, M. Newell, J.D., & Garcia, L.T. 1984. *Ethical issues in psychology.* Homewood, IL: Dorsey Press & Dow-Jones-Irwin Dorsey Professional Books.

Stitt, C. et al. 1983. Sex of leader, leader behavior, and subordinate satisfaction. *Sex Roles, 9,* 31–42.

Strohmer, D.C., Biggs, D.A. & McIntyre, W.F. 1984. Social comparison information and judgments about depression and seeking counseling. *Journal of Counseling Psychology, 31,* 592–595.

Strube, M.J. & Werner, C. 1984. Psychological reactance and relinquishment of control. *Personality and Social Psychology Bulletin, 10,* 225–234.

Swinyard, W.R. & Ray, M.L. 1979. Effects of praise and small requests on receptivity to direct-mail appeals. *Journal of Social Psychology, 108,* 177–184.

Toi, M. & Batson, C.D. 1982. More evidence that empathy is a source of altruistic motivation. *Journal of Personality and Social Psychology, 43,* 281–292.

Triplett, N. 1898. The dynamogenic factors in pacemaking and competition. *American Journal of Psychology, 9,* 507–533.

Walker, M., Harriman, S., & Costello, S. 1980. The influence of appearance on compliance with a request. *Journal of Social Psychology, 112,* 159–160.

Webb, E.J., Campbell, D.T., Schwartz, R.D., Sechrest, L., & Growve, J.B. 1981. *Nonreactive measures in the social sciences* (2nd ed.). Boston: Houghton Mifflin.

Wells, G.L. & Petty, R.W. 1980. The effects of overt head movements on persuasion: Compatibility and incompatibility of responses. *Basic and Applied Social Psychology, 1,* 219–230.

Weyant, K. 1978. Effects of mood states, cost and benefits on helping. *Journal of Personality and Social Psychology, 35,* 1169–1176.

Wheeler, L. & Koestner, R. 1984. Performance evaluation: On choosing to know the related attributes of others when we know their performance. *Journal of Experimental Social Psychology, 20,* 263–271.

Wilder, D.A. 1977. Perception of groups, size of opposition, and social influence. *Journal of Experimental Social Psychology, 13,* 253–268.

Williams, J.M. 1984. Assertiveness as a mediating variable in conformity to confederates of high and low status. *Psychological Reports, 55,* 415–418.

Williams, K.D. 1981. Identifiability as a deterrent to social loafing: two cheering studies. *Journal of Personality and Social Psychology, 40,* 303–311.

Williams, K.D. & Jackson, J.M. 1986. Social loafing: A review and theoretical integration of the literature. Paper presented at Midwest Psychological Association, Chicago.

Wood, W. & Eagly, A.H. 1981. Stages in the analysis of persuasive messages: The role of causal attributions and message comprehension. *Journal of Personality and Social Psychology, 40,* 246–259.

Zajonc, R.B. 1965. Social facilitation. *Science, 149,* 269–274.

Zajonc, R.B. 1968. Attitudinal effects of mere exposure. *Journal of Personality and Social Psychology Monograph Supplement, 9* (2, Pt. 2), 1–27.

Chapter 20

Aero, R. & Weiner, E. 1981. *The mind test.* NY: Morrow.

Anastasi, A. 1982. *Psychological testing* (5th ed.). NY: Macmillan.

Barth, J.T. & Macciochi, S.N. 1985. The Halstead-Reitan neuropsychological test battery. In C.S. Newmark (Ed.). *Major psychological assessment instruments.* Boston: Allyn & Bacon.

Bouchard, T.J., Jr., & McGue, M. 1981. Familial studies of intelligence: A review. *Science, 212,* 1055–1059.

Cattell, R.B. 1971. *Abilities: Their structure, growth, and action.* Boston: Houghton Mifflin.

Chi, M.T.H., Glaser, M., & Rees, E. 1982. Expertise in problem solving. In R.J. Sternberg (Ed.). *Advances in the psychology of human intelligence* (Vol. 1). Hillsdale, NJ: Erlbaum.

Cole, N.S. 1981. Bias in testing. *American Psychologist, 36,* 1067–1077.

Cunningham, W.R. & Owens, W.A. 1983. The Iowa State study of the adult development of intellectual abilities. In K.W. Schaie (Ed.). *Longitudinal studies of adult psychological development.* NY: Guilford.

Dana, R.H. 1985. Thematic apperception test (TAT). In C.S. Newmark (Ed.). *Major psychological assessment instruments.* Boston: Allyn & Bacon.

Erdberg, P. 1985. The Rorschach. In C.S. Newmark (Ed.). *Major psychological assessment instruments.* Boston: Allyn & Bacon.

Exner, J.E. 1974. *The Rorschach: A comprehensive system* (Vol. 1). NY: Wiley.

Exner, J.E. 1978. *The Rorschach: A comprehensive system* (Vol. 2). NY: Wiley.

Exner, J.E. & Weiner, I.B. 1982. *The Rorschach: A comprehensive system* (Vol. 3). NY: Wiley.

Eysenck, H.J. 1962. *Know your own IQ.* NY: Penguin.

Eysenck, H.J. 1981. *The intelligence controversy.* NY: Wiley.

Eysenck, H.J. & Kamin, L. 1981. *The intelligence controversy.* NY: Wiley.

Feldman, R.D. 1982. *Whatever happened to the quiz kids? Perils and profits of growing up gifted.* Chicago: Chicago Review Press.

Feuerstein, R. 1979. The dynamic assessment of retarded performers: The learning potential assessment device, theory, instruments, and techniques. Baltimore: University Park Press.

Feuerstein, R. 1980. *Instrumental enrichment: An intervention program for cognitive modifiability.* Baltimore: University Park Press.

Flynn, J.R. 1984. The mean IQ of Americans: Massive gains 1932 to 1978. *Psychological Bulletin, 95,* 29–51.

Forer, B.R. 1949. The fallacy of personal validation: A classroom demonstration of gullibility. *Journal of Abnormal and Social Psychology, 44,* 118–123.

Gardner, H. 1983. *Frames of mind: The theory of multiple intelligences.* NY: Basic Books.

Gould, S.J. 1981. *The mismeasure of man.* NY: Norton.

Guilford, J.P. 1982. Cognitive psychology's ambiguities: Some suggested remedies. *Psychological Review, 89,* 48–59.

Hall, E. 1986. Mining new gold from old research. *Psychology Today, 20,* 46–51.

Hathaway, S.R. & McKinley, J.C. 1940. A multiphasic personality schedule (Minnesota): Construction of the schedule. *Journal of Psychology, 10,* 249–254.

Horn, J.L. 1979. Trends in the measurement of intelligence. In R.J. Sternberg & D.K. Detterman (Ed.). *Human intelligence: Perspectives in its theory and measurement.* Norwood, NJ: Ablex.

House, A.E. & Lewis, M.L. 1985. Wechsler adult intelligence scale–revised. In C.S. Newmark (Ed.). *Major psychological assessment instruments.* Boston: Allyn & Bacon.

Jarvik, L.F. & Bank, L. 1983. Aging twins: Longitudinal psychometric data. In K.W. Schaie (Ed.). *Longitudinal studies of adult psychological development.* NY: Guilford.

Jensen, A.R. 1969. How much can we boost IQ and scholastic achievement? *Harvard Educational Review,* Reprint Series No. 2.

Jensen, A.R. 1980. *Bias in mental testing.* NY: Free Press.

Jensen, A.R. 1982. Reaction time and psychometric g. In H.J. Eysenck (Ed.). *A model for intelligence.* Berlin: Springer-Verlag.

Jensen, A.R. 1985. The nature of the black-white difference on various psychometric tests: Spearman's hypothesis. *The Behavioral and Brain Sciences, 8,* 193–219.

Keating, D.P. 1984. The Emperor's new clothes: The "new look" in intelligence research. In R.J. Sternberg (Ed.). *Advances in the psychology of human intelligence* (Vol. 5). Hillsdale, NJ: Erlbaum.

LaGrecia, A.M. & Stringer, S.A. 1985. The Wechsler intelligence scale for children–revised. In C.S. Newmark (Ed.). *Major psychological assessment instruments.* Boston: Allyn & Bacon.

Lefcourt, H.M. 1976. *Locus of control: Current trends in theory and research.* NJ: Erlbaum.

Lefcourt, H.M. 1981. *Research with the locus of control construct: Vol. 1.* NY: Academic Press.

Lefcourt, H.M. 1983. *Research with the locus of control construct: Vol. 2.* NY: Academic Press.

Lefcourt, H.M. et al. 1984. Locus of control and social support: Interactive moderators of stress. *Journal of Personality and Social Psychology, 47,* 378–389.

Lubin, B., Larsen, R.M., & Matarazzo, J.D. 1984. Patterns of psychological test usage in the United States: 1935–1982. *American Psychologist, 39,* 451–454.

Marks, D. & Kammann, R. 1980. *The psychology of the psychic.* Buffalo, NY: Prometheus.

McKean, K. 1985. Intelligence: New ways to measure the wisdom of man. *Discover, 6,* 25–41.

Miller, G.A. 1984. The test. *Science 84, 5,* 55–57.

Mohs, M. 1982. IQ. *Discover, 3,* 19–24.

Newmark, C.S. 1985. The MMPI. In C.S. Newmark (Ed.). *Major psychological assessment instruments.* Boston: Allyn & Bacon.

Parker, K. 1983. A meta-analysis of the reliability and validity of the Rorschach. *Journal of Personality Assessment, 47,* 227–231.

Piaget, J. 1950. *The psychology of intelligence.* London: Routledge & Kegan Paul.

Plomin, R. & DeFries, J.C. 1980. Genetics and intelligence: Recent data. *Intelligence, 4,* 15–24.

Redden, M.P. & Simons, J.A. 1986. *Manual for the Redden-Simons rap test.* Des Moines, IA: Drake University.

Scarr, S. 1981. Testing for children. *American Psychologist, 36,* 1159–1166.

Scarr, S. & Carter-Saltzman, L. 1982. Genetics and intelligence. In R.J. Sternberg (Ed.). *Handbook of human intelligence.* Cambridge, England: Cambridge University Press.

Scarr, S., Pakstis, A.J., Katz, S.H., & Barker, W.B. 1977. The absence of a relationship between degree of white ancestry and intellectual skills within a black population. *Human Genetics, 39,* 69–86.

Scarr, S. & Weinberg, R.A. 1976. IQ test performance of black children adopted by white families. *American Psychologist, 31,* 726–739.

Schaie, K.W. 1983a. The Seattle longitudinal study: A 21-year exploration of psychometric intelligence in adulthood. In K.W. Schaie (Ed.). *Longitudinal studies of adult psychological development.* NY: Guilford.

Schaie, K.W. 1983b. What can we learn from the longitudinal study of adult psychological development. In K.W. Schaie (Ed.). *Longitudinal studies of adult psychological development.* NY: Guilford.

Schulz, R. & Decker, S. 1985. Long-term adjustment to physical disability: The role of social support, perceived control & self-blame. *Journal of Personality & Social Psychology, 48,* 1162–1172.

Sherman, L.W. 1984. Development of children's perceptions of internal locus of control: A cross-sectional and longitudinal analysis. *Journal of Personality, 52,* 338–354.

Siegler, R.S. & Richards, D.D. 1982. The development of intelligence. In R.J. Steinberg (Ed.). *Handbook of human intelligence.* Cambridge: Cambridge University Press.

Spearman, C. 1927. *The abilities of man.* NY: Macmillan.

Squyres, E.M. & Craddick, R.A. 1982. A measure of time perspective with the TAT and some measures of reliability. *Journal of Personality Assessment, 46,* 257–259.

Sternberg, R.J. 1984. Toward a triarchic theory of human intelligence. *Behavioral & Brain Sciences, 7,* 269–315.

Sternberg, R.J. 1985. *Beyond IQ: A triarchic theory of human intelligence.* Cambridge: Cambridge University Press.

Sternberg, R.J. & Davidson, J.E. 1983. Insight in the gifted. *Educational Psychologist, 18,* 51–57.

Thurstone, L.L. 1938. *Primary mental abilities.* Chicago: University of Chicago Press.

Vernon, P.E. 1971. *The structure of human abilities.* London: Methuen.

Zajonc, R.B. 1986. The decline and rise of scholastic aptitude scores. *American Psychologist, 41,* 862–867.

Chapter 21

Agras, S. 1985. *Panic: Facing fears, phobias, and anxiety.* NY: Freeman.

Allison, R.B. 1984. Difficulties diagnosing the multiple personality syndrome in a death penalty case. *The International Journal of Clinical and Experimental Hypnosis, 32,* 102–117.

Altshuler, K.Z. & Weiner, M.F. 1985. Anorexia nervosa and depression: A dissenting view. *American Journal of Psychiatry, 142,* 328–331.

American Psychiatric Association. 1980. *Diagnostic and statistical manual of mental disorders (3rd ed.). (DSM III).* Washington: American Psychiatric Association.

Barlow, D.H. 1985. *Clinical handbook of psychological disorders.* NY: Guilford.

Bliss, E.L. 1980. Multiple personalities: A report of 14 cases with implications for schizophrenia and hysteria. *Archives of General Psychiatry, 37,* 1388–1397.

Bourne, P.G. 1970. *Men, stress and Vietnam.* Boston: Little, Brown.

Carr, D.B. & Sheehan, D.V. 1984. Panic anxiety: A new biological model. *Journal of Clinical Psychiatry, 45,* 323–330.

Confer, W.N. & Ables, B.S. 1983. *Multiple personality: Etiology, diagnosis, and treatment.* NY: Human Sciences Press.

Freedman, D.X. 1984. Psychiatric epidemiology counts. *Archive of General Psychiatry, 41,* 931–933.

Goodwin, J. 1980. The etiology of combat-related post-traumatic stress disorders. In T. Williams (Ed.). *Post-traumatic stress disorders of the Vietnam veteran.* Cincinnati: Disabled American Veterans.

Horstman, J. 1986. Don't panic: Help is on the way. *Des Moines Register,* July 1, 1T.

Keyes, D. 1981. *The minds of Billy Milligan.* NY: Random House.

Laing, R.D. 1985. *Wisdom, madness and folly.* NY: McGraw-Hill.

Langone, J. 1985. The war that has no ending. *Discover,* June, 44–54.

Leo, J. 1985. Are criminals born, not made? *Time,* October 21, 94.

Loeber, R. 1982. The stability of antisocial and delinquent child behavior: A review. *Child Development, 53,* 1431–1446.

Meltzer, H.Y. 1984. Schizoaffective disorder: Is news of its nonexistence premature? *Schizophrenia Bulletin, 10,* 11–13.

Myers, J.K., Weissman, M.M., Tischler, G.L., Holzer, C.E., Leaf, P.J., Orvaschel, H., Anthony, J.C., Boyd, J.H., Burke, J.D., Kramer, M., & Stoltzman, R. 1984. Six-month prevalence of psychiatric disorders in three communities. *Archives of General Psychiatry, 41,* 959–967.

Norton, G.R., Harrison, B., Hauch, J., & Rhodes, L. 1985. Characteristics of people with infrequent panic attacks. *Journal of Abnormal Psychology, 94,* 216–221.

Pines, M. 1984. When your body is afraid. *American Health,* June, 72–79.

Regier, D.A. 1984. Science news briefing: Introductory statement (press conference by National Institute of Mental Health—NIMH) October.

Regier, D.A., Myers, J.K., Kramer, M., Robins, L.N., Blazer, D.G., Hough, R.L., Eaton, W.W., & Locke, B.Z. 1984. The NIMH epidemiologic catchment area program. *Archives of General Psychiatry, 41,* 934–941.

Robins, L.N., Heizer, J.E., Weissman, M.M., Orvaschel, H., Gruenberg, E., Burke, J.D., & Regier, D.A. 1984. Lifetime prevalence of specific psychiatric disorders in three sites. *Archives of General Psychiatry, 41,* 949–958.

Rogers, C.R. 1961. *On becoming a person.* Boston: Houghton Mifflin.

Rogo, D.S. 1985. Multiple mix-ups. *Omni,* December, 94.

Schreiber, F.R. 1973. *Sybil.* Chicago: Regenery.

Seidenberg, R. & DeCrow, K. 1983. *Women who marry houses.* NY: McGraw-Hill.

Schumer, F. 1983. *Abnormal psychology.* Lexington, MA: Heath.

Szasz, T. 1977. *The theology of medicine: The political-philosophical foundations of medical ethics.* NY: Harper Colophon.

Thompson, A., Perret, D., & Leonard, M. (Eds.). 1985. *You can prevent child abuse and neglect!* (rev). Des Moines, IA: Commission on Children, Youth and Families.

Time. 1976. The secret life of Howard Hughes. *Time,* December 13, 22–41.

Uhde, T.W. et al. (NIMH Biological Psychiatry Branch, Unit on Anxiety and Affective Disorders, Bethesda, MD). 1984. The sleep of patients with panic disorder: A preliminary report. *Psychiatry Research, 12,* 251–259.

Walker, L.E. 1980. *The battered woman* NY: Harper & Row.

Watkins, J.G. 1984. The Bianchi (L.A. Hillside Strangler) case: Sociopath or multiple personality? *International Journal of Clinical and Experimental Hypnosis, 32*, 67–101.

Williams, T. 1980. A preferred model for development of interventions for psychological readjustment of Vietnam veterans: Group treatment. In T. Williams (Ed.). *Post-traumatic stress disorders of the Vietnam veteran.* Cincinnati: Disabled American Veterans.

Wilson, J.P. 1979. Identity, ideology and crisis: The Vietnam veteran in transition. *Forgotten warrior project.* Cleveland State University, 1978. (Reprinted by the Disabled American Veterans, Cincinnati, Ohio, 1979).

Wooden, W.S. 1985. The flames of youth. *Psychology Today, 19*, 22–28.

Chapter 22

Abrams, R. 1984. Genetic studies of the schizoaffective syndrome: A selective review. *Schizophrenia Bulletin, 10*, 26–29.

American Psychiatric Association. 1980. *Diagnostic and statistical manual of mental disorders* (3rd ed.). Washington, D.C.: American Psychiatric Association.

Baron, M., Gruen, R., Kane, J., & Asnis, L. 1985. Modern research criteria and the genetics of schizophrenia. *American Journal of Psychiatry, 142*, 697–701.

Berkowitz, R., Eberlein-Fries, R., Kuipers, L., & Leff, J. 1984. Educating relatives about schizophrenia. *Schizophrenia Bulletin, 10*, 418–429.

Bernheim, K.F. & Lewine, R.R.J. 1979. *Schizophrenia: Symptoms, causes, treatments.* NY: Norton.

Bernheim, K.F., Lewine, R.R.J., & Beales, C.T. 1982. *The caring family: Living with chronic mental illness.* NY: Random House.

Buchsbaum, M.S. 1984. The Genain Quadruplets. *Psychology Today, 18*, 46–51.

Consensus Development Panel on Mood disorders. 1985. Pharmacological prevention of recurrences. *American Journal of Psychiatry, 142*, 470–473.

Coryell, W. & Winokur, G. 1982. Course and outcome. In E.S. Paykel (Ed.). *Handbook of affective disorders.* NY: Guilford Press.

Falloon, I.R.H., McGill, C.W., & Boyd, J.L. 1984. *Family care of schizophrenia: A problem-solving approach to the treatment of mental illness.* NY: Guilford.

Hazelton, L. 1984. *The right to feel bad.* NY: Ballantine.

Jefferson, J.W. 1982. The use of lithium in childhood and adolescence: An overview. *Journal of Clinical Psychiatry, 43*, 174–177.

Kallman, F. 1938. *The genetics of schizophrenia.* NY: Augustin.

Klein, D.N., Depue, R.A., Slater, J.F. 1985. Cyclothymia in the adolescent offspring of parents with bipolar affective disorder. *Journal of Abnormal Psychology, 94*, 115–127.

Larson, J. 1984 (November). *Surviving schizophrenia: A survival skills workshop for families and a workshop for mental health professionals on psychoeducational approaches to families.* Ames, Ia.

Lester, G. & Lester, D. 1976. *Suicide: The gamble with death.* Englewood Cliffs, NJ: Prentice-Hall.

Lobel, B. & Hirschfeld, R.M.A. 1984. *Depression: What we know.* Rockville, Maryland: National Institute of Mental Health.

Lukoff, D., Snyder, K., Ventura, J., & Nuechterlein, K.H. 1984. Life events, familial stress, and coping in the developmental course of schizophrenia. *Schizophrenia Bulletin, 10*, 258.

McFarlane, W.R., Beels, C.C., & Rosenheck, S. 1983. New developments in the family treatment of the psychotic disorders. *Psychiatry Update* (Vol. II, part III, Chapter 17, 242–262). Washington: American Psychiatric Press.

McGrath, M.E. 1984. First person account: Where did I go? *Schizophrenia Bulletin, 10*, 638–640.

Mendel, W.M. 1976. *Schizophrenia: The experience and its treatment.* San Francisco: Jossey-Bass.

Myers, J.K., Weissman, M.M., Tischler, G.L., Holzer, C.E., Leaf, P.J., Orvaschel, H., Anthony, J.F., Boyd, J.H., Burke, J.D., Kramer, M., & Stoltzman, R. 1984. Six-month prevalence of psychiatric disorders in three communities. *Archives of General Psychiatry, 41*, 959–967.

Ornstein, R. 1985. *Psychology: The study of human experience.* NY: Harcourt Brace Jovanovich.

Perris, C. 1982. The distinction between bipolar and unipolar affective disorders. In E.S. Paykel (Ed.). *Handbook of affective disorders.* NY: Guilford.

Restak, R. 1984. *The brain.* NY: Bantam.

Sargent, M. & Swearingen, J. 1983. *Depressive disorders: Causes and treatment.* Rockville, Maryland: National Institute of Mental Health.

Talbott, J.A. (Ed.). 1978. *The chronic mental patient.* Washington, D.C.: American Psychiatric Association.

Torrey, E.F. 1983. *Surviving schizophrenia: A family manual.* NY: Harper & Row.

Tsuang, M. & Simpson, J.C. 1984. Schizoaffective disorder: Concept and reality. *Schizophrenia Bulletin, 10*, 14–24.

Vine, P. 1982. *Families in pain: Children, siblings, spouses and parents of the mentally ill speak out.* NY: Pantheon.

Wallace, C.J. 1984. Community and interpersonal functioning in the course of schizophrenic disorders. *Schizophrenia Bulletin, 10*, 233–253.

Wekstein, L. 1979. *Handbook of suicidology: Principles, problems, and practice.* NY: Brunner/Mazel.

Wetzel, J. 1984. *Clinical Handbook of Depression.* NY: Gardner.

Wilson, L. 1968. *This stranger, my son.* NY: Putman.

Zelt, D. 1981. First person account: The messiah quest. *Schizophrenia Bulletin, 7*, 527–532.

Chapter 23

Abeles, N. 1979. Psychodynamic theory. In H.M. Burks, Jr. & B. Steffire. *Theories of counseling* (3rd ed.). NY: McGraw-Hill.

Alter, J., Greenberg, N.F., & Doherty, S. 1985. The homeless: Out in the cold. *Newsweek*, December 16, 22–23.

Ansbacher, H.L. & Ansbacher, R.R. (Eds.). 1956. *The individual psychology of Alfred Adler: A systematic presentation in selections from his writings.* NY: Basic Books.

APA Monitor. 1982. "50% rule" triggers state suits. *APA Monitor, 13* (April), 2.

Bandura, A. 1969. *Principles of behavior modification.* NY: Holt, Rinehart & Winston.

Bassuk, E.L. 1984. The homelessness problem. *Scientific American, 251*, 40–45.

Consensus Development Conference on Electroconvulsive Therapy. 1985. Vol. 5, No. 11. Bethesda, MD: National Institute of Mental Health.

Consensus Development Panel on Mood disorders. 1985. Pharmacological prevention of recurrences. *American Journal of Psychiatry, 142*, 471–474.

Corey, G., Corey, M.S., & Callanan, P. 1984. *Issues and ethics for the helping professions.* Monterey, CA: Brooks/Cole.

Dinkmeyer, D., Pew, W.L., & Dinkmeyer, D.J. 1979. *Adlerian counseling and psychotherapy.* Monterey, CA: Wadsworth.

Dujovne, B.E. 1983. Sexual feeling, fantasies, and acting out in psychotherapy. *Psychotherapy: Theory, research, and practice, 20*, 243–250.

Farmer, F. 1972. *Will there really be a morning?* NY: Dell.

Farrell, M.H.J. 1985. Prescription drugs: The questions people ask most. *Good Housekeeping*, August, 183–185.

Fisher, K. 1984. Self-help authors' dark 'how-to' manual, *APA Monitor, 15*, 20–21.

Franklin, B. 1965. *The autobiography of Benjamin Franklin: A common wealth of a man.* NY: Airmont Publishing. (Originally published 1771).

Freeman, W. & Watts, J. 1950. *Psychosurgery.* Springfield, IL: Thomas.

Gaitskill, M. 1986. Love Hollywood Style. *Mother Jones, 11*, 8–10.

Goleman, D. & Speeth, K.R. (Eds.). 1982. *The essential psychotherapies.* NY: New American Library.

Holroyd, J.C. & Brodsky, A.M. 1977. Psychologists' attitudes and practices regarding erotic and nonerotic physical contact with patients. *American Psychologist, 32*, 843–849.

Jacobsen, E. 1929. *Progressive relaxation.* Chicago: University of Chicago Press.

Janicak, P.G., Davis, J.M., Gibbons, R.D., Ericksen, S., Chang, S., & Gallagher, P. 1985. Efficacy of ECT: A meta-analysis. *American Journal of Psychiatry, 142*, 297–299.

Kalinowsky, L. 1975. Psychosurgery. In A. Freedman, H. Kaplan, & B. Sadock (Eds.). *Comprehensive textbook of psychiatry/II.* Baltimore: Williams & Wilkins.

Kalinowsky, L. 1980. Convulsive therapies. In H. Kaplan, A. Freedman, & B. Sadock (Eds.). *Comprehensive textbook of psychiatry/III.* Baltimore: Williams & Wilkins.

Kazdin, A.E. & Wilcoxon, L.A. 1976. Systematic desensitization and nonspecific treatment effects: A methodological evaluation. *Psychological Bulletin, 83,* 729–758.

Kiesler, C.A. 1982a. Mental hospitals and alternative care: Noninstitutionalization as a potential public policy for mental patients. *American Psychologist, 37,* 349–360.

Kiesler, C.A. 1982b. Public and professional myths about mental hospitalization: An empirical assessment of policy-related beliefs. *American Psychologist, 37,* 1323–1339.

Knapp, S. 1980. A primer on malpractice for psychologists. *Professional Psychology, 11,* 606–612.

Mosak, H.H. & Dreikurs, R. 1973. Adlerian psychotherapy. In R. Corsini (Ed.). *Current psychotherapies.* Itasca, Il: Peacock.

Murray, J.B. 1985. Lithium therapy for mania and depression. *Journal of General Psychology, 112,* 5–33.

Price, R.H. & Lynn, S.J. 1986. *Abnormal psychology.* Chicago: Dorsey.

Rychlak, J.F. 1981. *Introduction to personality and psychotherapy: A theory-construction approach* (2nd ed.). Boston: Houghton Mifflin.

Sacks, O. 1985. *The man who mistook his wife for a hat and other clinical tales.* NY: Summitt Books.

Schumer, F. 1983. *Abnormal psychology.* Lexington, MA: Heath.

Shilling, L. 1984. *Perspectives on counseling theories.* Englewood Cliffs, NJ: Prentice-Hall.

Sporty, L.D. & Plon, L. 1984. Rapid, psychopharmacologically induced improvement can produce new psychological symptoms. *Canadian Journal of Psychiatry, 29,* 256–257.

Time. 1985. When liberty really means neglect. *Time,* December 2, 103.

Time. 1986. A hobo jungle with class. *Time,* March 31, 29.

Torrey, E.F. & Wolfe, S.M. 1986. *Care of the seriously mentally ill: A rating of state programs.* Washington: Public Citizen Health Research Group.

Valenstein, E.S. 1985. *Great and desperate cures: The rise and decline of psychosurgery and other radical treatments for mental illness.* NY: Basic Books.

Wander, P.H. & Klein, D.F. 1981. *Mind, mood, and medicine.* NY: Farrar Straus Girous.

Wolpe, J. 1958. *Psychotherapy by Reciprocal Inhibition.* Stanford: Stanford University Press.

Yates, A.J. 1975. *Theory and practice in behavior therapy.* NY: Wiley.

Zilbergeld, B. 1983. *The shrinking of America: Myths of psychological change.* Boston: Little, Brown.

Chapter 24

Beck, A. 1976. *Cognitive therapy and the emotional disorders.* NY: International Universities Press.

Berne, E. 1961. *Transactional analysis in psychotherapy.* NY: Grove Press.

Berne, E. 1964. *Games people play.* NY: Grove Press.

Berne, E. 1972. *What do you say after you say hello?* NY: Grove Press.

Corey, G. 1977. *Theory and practice of counseling and psychotherapy.* Belmont, CA: Wadsworth.

Dean, A. 1986. *Night light.* NY: Harper/Hazelden Books.

Elkin, I., Shea, T., Watkins, J. & Collins, J. 1985. NIMH treatment of depression collaborative research program: Comparative Treatment Outcome Findings. A summary of a presentation at the American Psychiatric Association annual meeting, May, 1986. Rockville, MD: NIMH.

Ellis, A. 1959. Requisite conditions for basic personality change. *Journal of Consulting Psychology, 23,* 538–549.

Ellis, A. 1962. *Reason and emotion in psychotherapy.* Secaucus, NJ: Citadel Press.

Ellis, A. 1973. Rational-emotive therapy. In R. Corsini (Ed.). *Current psychotherapies.* Itasca, IL: Peacock.

Ellis, A. 1974. Rational-emotive theory: Albert Ellis. In A. Burton (Ed.). *Operational theories of personality.* NY: Brunner/Mazel.

Ellis, A. 1977. The treatment of a psychopath with rational therapy. In S.J. Morse & R.I. Watson (Eds.). *Psychotherapies: A comparative casebook.* NY: Holt, Rinehart & Winston.

Ellis, A. & Harper, R. 1975. *A new guide to rational living* (rev. ed.). Hollywood: Wilshire Books.

Ellis, A. & Greiger, R. 1977. *A handbook of rational-emotive therapy.* NY: Springer.

Frankl, V.E. 1965. *The doctor and the soul: From psychotherapy to logotherapy.* NY: Bantam Books.

Frankl, V. 1962. *Man's search for meaning.* NY: Simon & Schuster.

Glasser, W. 1965. *Reality therapy: A new approach to psychiatry.* NY: Harper & Row.

Glasser, W. 1969. *Schools without failure.* NY: Harper & Row.

Glasser, W. & Zunin, L.M. 1973. Reality therapy. In R. Corsini (Ed.). *Current psychotherapies.* Itasca, IL: Peacock.

Glasser, W. 1984. *Control theory: A new explanation of how we control our lives.* NY: Harper & Row.

Harris, A.B. & Harris, T.A. 1985. *Staying OK.* NY: Harper & Row.

Kaplan, H. & Sadock, B. 1985. *Comprehensive textbook of psychiatry IV.* Baltimore, Md: Williams and Wilkins.

Kempler, W. 1973. Gestalt therapy. In R. Corsini (Ed.). *Current psychotherapies.* Itasca, IL: Peacock.

Lieberman, M., Yalom, I.D., & Miles, M.B. 1973. *Encounter groups: First facts.* NY: Basic Books.

Miller, R.C. & Berman, J.S. 1983. The efficacy of cognitive behavior therapies: A quantitative review of the research evidence. *Psychological Bulletin, 94,* 39–53.

Parloff, M. 1976. Shopping for the right therapy. *Saturday Review,* Feb. 21.

Patterson, C.H. 1986. *Theories of counseling and psychotherapy.* NY: Harper & Row.

Polster, E. & Polster, M. 1973. *Gestalt therapy integrated.* NY: Brunner/Mazel.

Perls, F.S. 1969. *In and out of the garbage pail.* Lafayette, CA: Real People Press.

Reynolds, D.K. 1984. *Playing ball on running water.* NY: Quill.

Rogers, C.R. 1957. The necessary and sufficient conditions of therapeutic personality change. *Journal of Consulting Psychology, 21,* 95–103.

Rogers, C.R. 1961a. *On becoming a person.* Boston: Houghton Mifflin.

Rogers, C.R. 1961b. The process equation of psychotherapy. *American Journal of Psychotherapy, 15,* 27–45.

Rogers, C.R. 1969. *Freedom to learn.* Columbus, OH: Merrill.

Rogers, C.R. 1970. *On encounter groups.* NY: Harper & Row.

Rogers, C.R. 1975. Empathic: An unappreciated way of being. *Counseling Psychologist, 5,* 2–10.

Shepherd, I. 1970. Limitations and cautions in the Gestalt approach. In J. Fagan & I. Shepherd (Eds.). *Gestalt therapy now.* NY: Harper Colophon.

Shilling, L.E. 1984. *Perspective on counseling theories.* Englewood Cliffs, NJ: Prentice-Hall.

Steiner, C.M. 1974. *Scripts people live: Transactional analysis of life scripts.* NY: Grove Press.

Epilogue

Barr, R. 1986. Alternative schools in an age of change. *Reaching out to help people: Alternative schools.* Des Moines, IA: 13th Annual Iowa Alternative Education Conference.

Fisher, J.D., Bell, P.A., & Baum, A. 1984. *Environmental psychology* (2nd ed.). NY: Holt, Rinehart & Winston.

Fromm, E. 1976. *To have or to be.* NY: Harper & Row.

Gardner, M. 1985. Slicing pi into millions. *Discover, 6,* 50–53.

Horowitz, I.A. & Willging, T.E. 1984. *The psychology of law.* Boston: Little, Brown.

Kozol, J. 1985. *Illiterate America.* Garden City, NY: Anchor Press/Doubleday.

Marks, J. 1979. *The search for the "Manchurian Candidate": The CIA and mind control.* NY: New York Times Book.

Appendix

Huff, D. 1954. *How to lie with statistics.* NY: Norton.

Kimble, G. 1978. *How to use (and mis-use) statistics.* Englewood Cliffs, NJ: Spectrum Books.

Knight-Ridder News Service. Crime rate plunges to 13-year low. *Knight-Ridder Newspapers,* October 3, 1986.

Pagano, R.L. 1981. *Understanding statistics in the behavioral sciences.* St. Paul, MN: West.

Shaughnessy, J.J. & Zechmeister, E.B. 1985. *Research methods in psychology.* NY: Knopf.

Name Index

Subject Index